W9-CXX-640

Applied UNIX Programming
Volume 2

Applied UNIX® Programming
Volume 2

Bharat Kurani

x/Open

For book and bookstore information

http://www.prenhall.com

Prentice Hall PTR
Upper Saddle River, New Jersey 07458

QA
76.76
.063
K86
1994
vol. 2

Acquisitions editor: *Michael E. Meehan*
Editorial assistant: *Kate Hargett*
Editorial/production supervision: *Mary Sudul*
Proofreader: *Karen Grossman*
Cover design: *Amy Rosen*
Cover design director: *Jerry Votta*
Manufacturing manager: *Alexis R. Heydt*

Text © 1997 by Prentice Hall PTR, Prentice-Hall, Inc.
Manual pages © 1997 by X/Open Company Limited
Diskette © 1997 by Antrix, Inc.

Published by Prentice Hall PTR
Prentice-Hall, Inc.
A Simon & Schuster Company
Upper Saddle River, New Jersey 07458

The publisher offers discounts on this book when ordered in bulk quantities.
For more information, contact Corporate Sales Department,
Prentice Hall PTR, One Lake Street, Upper Saddle River, NJ 07458.
Phone: 800-382-3419; Fax: 201-236-7141; E-mail: corpsales@prenhall.com

All product names mentioned herein are the trademarks of their respective owners.

All rights reserved. No part of this book may be
reproduced, in any form or by any means,
without permission in writing from the publisher.

Printed in the United States of America

10 9 8 7 6 5 4 3 2 1

ISBN 0-13-304346-0

Prentice-Hall International (UK) Limited, *London*
Prentice-Hall of Australia Pty. Limited, *Sydney*
Prentice-Hall Canada Inc., *Toronto*
Prentice-Hall Hispanoamericana, S.A., *Mexico*
Prentice-Hall of India Private Limited, *New Delhi*
Prentice-Hall of Japan, Inc., *Tokyo*
Simon & Schuster Asia Pte. Ltd., *Singapore*
Editora Prentice-Hall do Brasil, Ltda., *Rio de Janeiro*

Dedicated to my mother

Preface

Introduction

The implementation of Single UNIX Standards for the UNIX environment as described in the SINGLE UNIX® SPECIFICATION[1] and GO SOLO[2] by X/Open, has made it possible to have a common Application Programmer Interface (API) on the UNIX operating system running on different CPUs. This makes the tasks of software developing and porting easier. The software developer does not have to worry about which of the API library functions to use. Porting software is also easier, for a library function would work exactly in same way on any other system. The net gain is reduced software development and porting costs.

Currently, each UNIX operating system vendor has manual pages for the UNIX library functions in both electronic and hardcopy forms. Each vendor has library function implementations which are based on the UNIX operating system ported to the hardware platform.

The objective of APPLIED UNIX PROGRAMMING, Volume 2, is to provide examples for the UNIX library function along with the X/Open Single UNIX Specification manual pages in a single book. This book together with APPLIED UNIX PROGRAMMING, Volume 1, which describes the software development process, software internationalization, C and C++ programming languages will help anyone involved in software development significantly by eliminating the need to refer to many books and reference manuals to develop software.

This book covers UNIX operating systems C Library, Math Library, International Library, Transport Interface Library (TI), and Sockets Interface Library manual pages and examples for library function. Every X/Open Single UNIX Specification manual page description is followed by an example describing the implementation of library functions in software code.

This will help the software developer to simply "CUT" the program source code from the manual page and "PASTE" it into software code. The program source code also contains comments explaining the theory behind the implementation where necessary.

This book can also be used as a college text at the undergraduate level, as a practical reference in the UNIX programming courses. The book also provides a guide to writing good, bug-free software code.

---

2. The X/Open Single UNIX Specification consists of the following documentation:
   - X/Open CAE Specification, August 1994, System Interface Definitions, Issue 4, Version 2 (ISBN: 1-85912-036-9, C434)
   - X/Open CAE Specification, August 1994, System Interfaces and Headers, Issue 4, Version 2 (ISBN: 1-85912-037-7, C435)
   - X/Open CAE Specification, August 1994, Commands and Utilities, Issue 4, Version 2 (ISBN: 1-85912-034-2, C436)
   - X/Open CAE Specification, May 1996, X/Open Curses, Issue 4, Version 2 (ISBN: 1-85912-077-6, C437)
   - X/Open CAE Specification, August 1994, Networking Services, Issue 4 (ISBN: 1-85912-049-0, C438).

2. Go Solo — How to Implement and Go Solo with the Single UNIX Specification, March 1996, published by Prentice Hall (ISBN: 0-13-439381-3, X908P).

Benefits of Library Source Code

1. Software Development

   Reduces software development time by permitting the cutting and pasting of the example source code for a given library call, available on-line in the EXAMPLE section of a manual page.

2. Software Prototyping

   Reduces time to develop re-usable application-specific library calls for string manipulation, signal handling, memory management, i/o handling, etc.

3. Software Reliability and Performance

   Increases software reliability and performance due to fewer failures and proper de-allocation of data structures.

4. Software Testing

   Reduces testing and debugging time due to good error checking and recovery for each function call.

5. Introduction to Programming in UNIX

   Reduces UNIX learning time for a programmer or a student interested in learning UNIX.

Structure of the Book

This book contains descriptions of following libraries function:

System Interfaces contains the core of the operating system service Library, C Library, International Library, and Math Library interfaces manual pages followed by the C program source code.

Transport Interfaces (TI) contains an independent transport service interface, allowing multiple users to communicate at the OSI reference model transport layer manual pages, followed by the the C program source code.

Socket Interfaces (SI) contains network interfaces as defined by Berkeley Software Distribution manual pages followed by the C program source code.

IP Address Resolution Interface (IPARI) contains network address resolution interface used in conjunction with both Sockets and Transport interface when using the Internet Protocol (IP) manual pages followed by the C program source code.

Examples in the Book

This is an example oriented book. In every manual page, descriptions are followed by tested program source code. There are about 600 program source code listings. The program source code is also available on a floppy disk included with the book. This will allow the reader to easily understand the manual page description. All the source code was written by ANTRIX Inc.

Library function example source contents:

1. Include files needed to use a particular function

2. Function argument data type

3. Function usage

4. Return value of the function

5. Error checking and recovery

All the programs have been tested on the platforms listed below:

1. Sparc running Solaris 1.1

2. Sparc running Solaris 2.x

3. Intel X86/Pentium running Univel 2.x

4. Intel X86/Pentium running Solaris 2.5

5. MIPS running Silicon Graphics IRIS.

6. PRO RISC running Hewlett Packard HPUX.

7. PowerPC running Motorola UNIX SVR4.2 and IBM/AIX.

8. Motorola 88000RISC running UNIX SVR4.2

Programs using UNIX System V, Release 4 features will not work on UNIX System V, Release 3. The programs were also compiled and tested against GNU C and C++ release 2.5.x compiler.

Acknowledgements

First, I would like to thank my wife, Usha, my brother Hemant, his wife Deepa, my nephew Ravi and niece Shreena, and my uncles Dr. Deven Kurani and Hiren Kurani. Without their encouragement this book would not have been possible.

I would like to thank Michael Meehan, executive editor of Prentice Hall, for supporting this project and providing technical reviews to improve the contents of the book. During the course of project, we felt that it was not possible to complete this book but his perseverance made it possible to finish it.

Many thanks to technical reviewers for their invaluable for his input. Don Merusi, comments: "Bharat Kurani deserves an Oscar for his library source code examples. How frustrating it has been to do a man page on a UNIX function call, only to have to read through the drudgery of extreme, at times, excruciating academic explanations, with no examples". Jack Beidler (Computer Science Department, University of Scranton, PA); his comments: "As I took a careful look at this book, I realized that this could become very useful to experienced UNIX Programmers. I liked the manual pages layout with author enhancements. I felt the author's sample pieces of code are good ones, close to typical uses. Not the usual contrived illustrations that usually have nothing to do with reality, very nice."

I would like to thank X/Open Company Ltd. for granting permission to use the X/Open Single UNIX Specification manual pages which remain the copyright of X/Open Company Ltd. Special thanks to Dr. Phil Holmes and Grenville Edwards of X/Open for arranging this. Also, thanks to Cathy Hughes of X/Open for her help in building this book.

Thanks to Bernie O'Connor for suggestions and comments on the organization of the book.

Also sincere thanks to Brad Gilbertson of Abbott Laboratories for his advice and encouragement to complete this project.

Special thanks to DSOS group consisting of Gregg Hover, John Bean, Jim Charlton, Rosalie Eisen, Scott Gerken, and Tom Thompson at Abbott Diagnostics for their encouragement and help to complete this book.

I would also like to thank Marian Hirsch of Marian Hirsch Marketing Communications for her copy editing and proofreading work.

The author would like to sincerely thank the Usenet community for quick replies to technical issues. The author can be contacted for any comments, suggestions or inquires at bharat@antrix.com or bck@netcom.com.

Contents

Contents

Contents

Contents

Contents

Contents

Contents

Contents

List of Tables

Chapter 1

System Interfaces

This chapter describes the X/Open functions, macros and external variables to support application portability at the C-language source level.

NAME

a64l, l64a — convert between 32-bit integer and radix-64 ASCII string

SYNOPSIS

UX

```
#include <stdlib.h>

long a64l(const char *s);

char *l64a(long value);
```

DESCRIPTION

These functions are used to maintain numbers stored in radix-64 ASCII characters. This is a notation by which 32-bit integers can be represented by up to six characters; each character represents a digit in radix-64 notation. If the type **long** contains more than 32 bits, only the low-order 32 bits are used for these operations.

The characters used to represent 'digits' are `'.'` for 0, `'/'` for 1, `'0'` through `'9'` for 2–11, `'A'` through `'Z'` for 12-37, and `'a'` through `'z'` for 38-63.

The *a64l( )* function takes a pointer to a radix-64 representation, in which the first digit is the least significant, and returns a corresponding **long** value. If the string pointed to by *s* contains more than six characters, *a64l( )* uses the first six. If the first six characters of the string contain a null terminator, *a64l( )* uses only characters preceding the null terminator. The *a64l( )* function scans the character string from left to right with the least significant digit on the left, decoding each character as a 6-bit radix-64 number. If the type **long** contains more than 32 bits, the resulting value is sign-extended. The behaviour of *a64l( )* is unspecified if *s* is a null pointer or the string pointed to by *s* was not generated by a previous call to *l64a( )*.

The *l64a( )* function takes a **long** argument and returns a pointer to the corresponding radix-64 representation. The behaviour of *l64a( )* is unspecified if *value* is negative.

RETURN VALUE

On successful completion, *a64l( )* returns the **long** value resulting from conversion of the input string. If a string pointed to by *s* is an empty string, *a64l( )* returns 0L.

The *l64a( )* function returns a pointer to the radix-64 representation. If *value* is 0L, *l64a( )* returns a pointer to an empty string.

ERRORS

No errors are defined.

APPLICATION USAGE

The value returned by *l64a( )* may be a pointer into a static buffer. Subsequent calls to *l64a( )* may overwrite the buffer.

If the type **long** contains more than 32 bits, the result of *a64l(l64a(x))* is *x* in the low-order 32 bits.

SEE ALSO

strtoul( ), **<stdlib.h>**.

EXAMPLE

```
/*
 * Copyright (C) ANTRIX Inc.
 */

/* a64l.c
 * This program converts long string "123" to long integer
 * using function a64l.
 */

#include <stdio.h>
#include <stdlib.h>
#include <errno.h>

main()
{
  long       a64l_value;
  const char *str = "123L";

  fprintf (stdout,"convert string to long\n");
  a64l_value = a64l (str);
  if ( a64l_value != 0 ) {
      fprintf (stdout,"a64l() call successful\n");
      fprintf (stdout,"string %s converted to long is %ld\n",
                      str, a64l_value);
  }
  else
      fprintf (stderr,"ERROR: a64l() call failed\n");
}


/*
 * Copyright (C) ANTRIX Inc.
 */

/* l64a.c
 * This program converts long integer value 123 to base 64
 * representation using function l64a.
 */

#include <stdio.h>
#include <stdlib.h>
#include <errno.h>

main()
{
  char   *l64a_value;
  long   l = 123456;

  fprintf (stdout,"convert long to base 64 representation\n");
  l64a_value = (char *)l64a (l);
  if ( l64a_value != (char *)0 ) {
```

```
        fprintf (stdout,"l64a() call successful\n");
        fprintf (stdout,"long %ld converted to string is %s\n",
                        l, l64a_value);
   }
 else
        fprintf (stderr,"ERROR: l64a() call failed\n");
 }
```

NAME

abort — generate an abnormal process abort

SYNOPSIS

```
#include <stdlib.h>

void abort(void);
```

DESCRIPTION

The *abort( )* function causes abnormal process termination to occur, unless the signal SIGABRT is being caught and the signal handler does not return. The abnormal termination processing includes at least the effect of *fclose( )* on all open streams, and message catalogue descriptors, and the default actions defined for SIGABRT. The SIGABRT signal is sent to the calling process as if by means of *raise( )* with the argument SIGABRT.

The status made available to *wait( )* or *waitpid( )* by *abort( )* will be that of a process terminated by the SIGABRT signal. The *abort( )* function will override blocking or ignoring the SIGABRT signal.

RETURN VALUE

The *abort( )* function does not return.

ERRORS

No errors are defined.

APPLICATION USAGE

Catching the signal is intended to provide the application writer with a portable means to abort processing, free from possible interference from any implementation-provided library functions. If SIGABRT is neither caught nor ignored, and the current directory is writable, a core dump may be produced.

SEE ALSO

exit( ), *kill( )*, *raise( )*, *signal( )*, **<stdlib.h>**.

EXAMPLE

```
/*
 * Copyright (C) ANTRIX Inc.
 */

/* abort.c
 * This program generates an abnormal process abort signal
 * using function abort.
 */

#include <stdio.h>
#include <stdlib.h>
#include <unistd.h>
#include <sys/stat.h>
#include <signal.h>
#include <errno.h>

void handler(signal)
int signal;
{
  if (signal == SIGABRT)
     fprintf (stdout,"received signal SIGABRT\n");
  else
```

```
        fprintf (stderr,"ERROR: expected=%d, received=%d\n",
                           SIGABRT, signal);
}

main()
{
  int  access_value;

  fprintf (stdout,"register signal SIGABRT\n");
  signal (SIGABRT, handler);

  fprintf (stdout,"generate signal SIGABRT on ");
  fprintf (stdout,"process termination\n");
  access_value = access("none", W_OK);
  if ( access_value != 0) {
     fprintf(stderr, "Could not access file\n");
     abort ();
  }
  else
     fprintf(stdout, "Could access file\n");
}
```

NAME

abs — return integer absolute value

SYNOPSIS

```
#include <stdlib.h>

int abs(int i);
```

DESCRIPTION

The *abs*( ) function computes the absolute value of its integer operand, *i.* If the result cannot be represented, the behaviour is undefined.

RETURN VALUE

The *abs*( ) function returns the absolute value of its integer operand.

ERRORS

No errors are defined.

APPLICATION USAGE

In two's-complement representation, the absolute value of the negative integer with largest magnitude {INT_MIN} might not be representable.

SEE ALSO

fabs( ), *labs*( ), **<stdlib.h>**.

EXAMPLE

```
/*
 * Copyright (C) ANTRIX Inc.
 */

/* abs.c
 * This program returns absolute integer value of its
 * integer operand i using function abs.
 */

#include <stdio.h>
#include <stdlib.h>
#include <errno.h>

main()
{
  int  abs_value;
  int  i = -5;

  abs_value = abs (i);
  if ( abs_value == 5 )
     fprintf (stdout,"absolute value of %d is %d\n", i, abs_value);
  else
     fprintf (stderr,"ERROR: abs() call failed\n");
}
```

NAME

access — determine accessibility of a file

SYNOPSIS

```
#include <unistd.h>

int access(const char *path, int amode);
```

DESCRIPTION

The *access( )* function checks the file named by the pathname pointed to by the *path* argument for accessibility according to the bit pattern contained in *amode*, using the real user ID in place of the effective user ID and the real group ID in place of the effective group ID.

The value of *amode* is either the bitwise inclusive OR of the access permissions to be checked (R_OK, W_OK, X_OK) or the existence test, F_OK.

If any access permissions are to be checked, each will be checked individually, as described in the **XBD** specification, **Chapter 2**, **Definitions**. If the process has appropriate privileges, an implementation may indicate success for X_OK even if none of the execute file permission bits are set.

RETURN VALUE

If the requested access is permitted, *access( )* succeeds and returns 0. Otherwise, −1 is returned and *errno* is set to indicate the error.

ERRORS

The *access( )* function will fail if:

	[EACCES]	Permission bits of the file mode do not permit the requested access, or search permission is denied on a component of the path prefix.
UX	[ELOOP]	Too many symbolic links were encountered in resolving *path*.
	[ENAMETOOLONG]	
FIPS		The length of the *path* argument exceeds {PATH_MAX} or a pathname component is longer than {NAME_MAX}.
	[ENOENT]	A component of *path* does not name an existing file or *path* is an empty string.
	[ENOTDIR]	A component of the path prefix is not a directory.
	[EROFS]	Write access is requested for a file on a read-only file system.

The *access( )* function may fail if:

	[EINVAL]	The value of the *amode* argument is invalid.
UX	[ENAMETOOLONG]	
		Pathname resolution of a symbolic link produced an intermediate result whose length exceeds {PATH_MAX}.
EX	[ETXTBSY]	Write access is requested for a pure procedure (shared text) file that is being executed.

APPLICATION USAGE

Additional values of *amode* other than the set defined in the description may be valid, for example, if a system has extended access controls.

SEE ALSO

chmod( ), *stat( )*, **<unistd.h>**.

EXAMPLE

```c
/*
 * Copyright (C) ANTRIX Inc.
 */

/* access.c
 * This program checks the write accessibility of a file
 * using function access.
 */

#include <stdio.h>
#include <stdlib.h>
#include <unistd.h>
#include <sys/stat.h>
#include <errno.h>

#define  PERM_ALL    (S_IRWXU | S_IRWXG | S_IRWXO)

main()
{
  int         access_value;
  const char *path = "testfile";

  fprintf (stdout,"create testfile\n");
  creat (path, PERM_ALL);

  fprintf (stdout,"check testfile for write access permissions\n");
  access_value = access (path, W_OK);
  if ( access_value == 0 ) {
      fprintf (stdout,"access() call successful\n");
      fprintf (stdout,"testfile has write access\n");
  }
  else {
      fprintf (stderr,"ERROR: access() call failed\n");
      fprintf (stderr,"ERROR: %s\n", strerror(errno));
  }

  fprintf (stdout,"remove testfile\n");
  remove (path);
}
```

NAME

acos — arc cosine function

SYNOPSIS

```
#include <math.h>

double acos(double x);
```

DESCRIPTION

The *acos*( ) function computes the principal value of the arc cosine of *x*. The value of *x* should be in the range [−1,1].

RETURN VALUE

Upon successful completion, *acos*( ) returns the arc cosine of *x,* in the range [0, π] radians. If
EX the value of *x* is not in the range [−1,1], and is not ±Inf or NaN, either 0.0 or NaN is returned and *errno* is set to [EDOM].

EX If *x* is NaN, NaN is returned and *errno* may be set to [EDOM]. If *x* is ±Inf, either 0.0 is returned and *errno* is set to [EDOM], or NaN is returned and *errno* may be set to [EDOM].

ERRORS

The *acos*( ) function will fail if:

EX [EDOM]   The value *x* is not ±Inf or NaN and is not in the range [−1,1].

The *acos*( ) function may fail if:

EX [EDOM]   The value *x* is ±Inf or NaN.

EX No other errors will occur.

APPLICATION USAGE

An application wishing to check for error situations should set *errno* to 0 before calling *acos*( ). If *errno* is non-zero on return, or the value NaN is returned, an error has occurred.

SEE ALSO

cos( ), *isnan*( ), **<math.h>**.

EXAMPLE

```
/*
 * Copyright (C) ANTRIX Inc.
 */

/* acos.c
 * This program computes the principal value of the arc
 * cosine of 0.50 using function acos.
 */

#include <stdio.h>
#include <math.h>

main()
{
  double  acos_value;
  double  x = 0.50;
```

```
        acos_value = acos (x);
        fprintf (stdout,"acos of %f is %f\n", x, acos_value);
}
```

NAME

acosh, asinh, atanh — inverse hyperbolic functions

SYNOPSIS

UX

```
#include <math.h>
```

```
double acosh(double x);
```

```
double asinh(double x);
```

```
double atanh(double x);
```

DESCRIPTION

The *acosh*( ), *asinh*( ) and *atanh*( ) functions compute the inverse hyperbolic cosine, sine, and tangent of their argument, respectively.

RETURN VALUE

The *acosh*( ), *asinh*( ) and *atanh*( ) functions return the inverse hyperbolic cosine, sine, and tangent of their argument, respectively.

The *acosh*( ) function returns an implementation-dependent value (NaN or equivalent if available) and sets *errno* to [EDOM] when its argument is less than 1.0.

The *atanh*( ) function returns an implementation-dependent value (NaN or equivalent if available) and sets *errno* to [EDOM] when its argument has absolute value greater than 1.0.

If *x* is NaN, the *asinh*( ), *acosh*( ) and *atanh*( ) functions return NaN and may set *errno* to [EDOM].

ERRORS

The *acosh*( ) function will fail if:

[EDOM]   The *x* argument is less than 1.0.

The *atanh*( ) function will fail if:

[EDOM]   The *x* argument has an absolute value greater than 1.0.

The *atanh*( ) function will fail if:

[ERANGE]   The *x* argument has an absolute value equal to 1.0

The *asinh*( ), *acosh*( ) and *atanh*( ) functions may fail if:

[EDOM]   The value of *x* is NaN.

SEE ALSO

cosh( ), *sinh*( ), *tanh*( ), **<math.h>**.

EXAMPLE

```
/*
 * Copyright (C) ANTRIX Inc.
 */

/* acosh.c
 * This program computes the inverse hyperbolic cosine of x
 * using function acosh.
 */

#include <stdio.h>
#include <math.h>
```

```
main()
{
  double  acosh_value;
  double  x = 1.20;

  acosh_value = acosh (x);
  fprintf (stdout,"acosh of %f is %f\n", x, acosh_value);
}
```

NAME

advance — pattern match given a compiled regular expression (**TO BE WITHDRAWN**)

SYNOPSIS

EX
```
#include <regexp.h>

int advance(const char *string, const char *expbuf);
```

DESCRIPTION

Refer to *regexp*( ).

EXAMPLE

```
/*
 * Copyright (C) ANTRIX Inc.
 */

/* advance.c
 * This program pattern matches a given compiled regular
 * expression against a string using function advance.
 */

#include <stdio.h>
#include <stdlib.h>
#include <errno.h>

#define STRSIZE 100

char instring[STRSIZE];

#define     INIT        register char *sp = instring;
#define     GETC()      (*sp++)
#define     PEEKC()     (*sp)
#define     UNGETC(c)   (--sp)
#define     RETURN(c)   return((char *)0)
#define     ERROR(c)    comperr()
#include    <regexp.h>

extern char *loc1, *loc2, *locs;

main()
{
    int   advance_value;
    char string[10*STRSIZE];
    char expbuf[STRSIZE];

    strcpy(instring, "[A-Z]");
    strcpy(string, "Good bye");

    fprintf(stdout, "Produce compiled expression\n");
    compile(instring, expbuf, &expbuf[STRSIZE], ' ');

    fprintf(stdout, "Match upper case character G\n");
    advance_value = advance(string, expbuf);
    if (advance_value != 0) {
```

```
        fprintf(stdout, "advance call successful\n");
        fprintf(stdout, "advance_value=%d\n", advance_value);
    }
    else {
        fprintf(stderr, "ERROR: advance call failed\n");
        fprintf(stderr, "%d\n", advance_value);
    }
}

comperr()
{ }
```

NAME

alarm — schedule an alarm signal

SYNOPSIS

```
#include <unistd.h>

unsigned int alarm(unsigned int seconds);
```

DESCRIPTION

The *alarm*( ) function causes the system to send the calling process a SIGALRM signal after the number of real-time seconds specified by *seconds* have elapsed. Processor scheduling delays may prevent the process from handling the signal as soon as it is generated.

If *seconds* is 0, a pending alarm request, if any, is cancelled.

Alarm requests are not stacked; only one SIGALRM generation can be scheduled in this manner; if the SIGALRM signal has not yet been generated, the call will result in rescheduling the time at which the SIGALRM signal will be generated.

UX   Interactions between *alarm*( ) and any of *setitimer*( ), *ualarm*( ) or *usleep*( ) are unspecified.

RETURN VALUE

If there is a previous *alarm*( ) request with time remaining, *alarm*( ) returns a non-zero value that is the number of seconds until the previous request would have generated a SIGALRM signal. Otherwise, *alarm*( ) returns 0.

ERRORS

The *alarm*( ) function is always successful, and no return value is reserved to indicate an error.

APPLICATION USAGE

The *fork*( ) function clears pending alarms in the child process. A new process image created by one of the *exec* functions inherits the time left to an alarm signal in the old process' image.

SEE ALSO

exec, *fork*( ), *getitimer*( ), *pause*( ), *sigaction*( ), *ualarm*( ), *usleep*( ), **<signal.h>**, **<unistd.h>**.

EXAMPLE

```
/*
 * Copyright (C) ANTRIX Inc.
 */

/* alarm.c
 * This program schedules an alarm signal SIGALRM
 * of 2 seconds using function alarm.
 */

#include <stdio.h>
#include <stdlib.h>
#include <unistd.h>
#include <signal.h>
#include <errno.h>

void handler(signal)
int signal;
{
   if (signal == SIGALRM)
      fprintf (stdout,"received signal SIGALRM\n");
   else
```

```
        fprintf (stderr,"ERROR: expected=%d, received=%d\n",
                               SIGALRM, signal);
}

main()
{
  unsigned int   alarm_value;
  unsigned int   seconds = 2;

  signal (SIGALRM, handler);
  fprintf (stdout,"set alarm of 2 seconds\n");
  alarm_value = alarm (seconds);
  if ( alarm_value == 0 ) {
     fprintf (stdout,"alarm() call successful\n");
     fprintf (stdout,"alarm set to %d seconds\n", seconds);
  }
  else
     fprintf (stderr,"ERROR: alarm() call failed\n");

  fprintf (stdout,"try to sleep for 5 seconds\n");
  fprintf (stdout,"but wake up in 2 seconds\n");
  sleep (5);
}
```

NAME

asctime — convert date and time to string

SYNOPSIS

```
#include <time.h>

char *asctime(const struct tm *timeptr);
```

DESCRIPTION

The *asctime*( ) function converts the broken-down time in the structure pointed to by *timeptr* into a string in the form:

```
Sun Sep 16 01:03:52 1973\n\0
```

using the equivalent of the following algorithm:

```
char *asctime(const struct tm *timeptr)
{
        static char wday_name[7][3] = {
                "Sun", "Mon", "Tue", "Wed", "Thu", "Fri", "Sat"
        };
        static char mon_name[12][3] = {
                "Jan", "Feb", "Mar", "Apr", "May", "Jun",
                "Jul", "Aug", "Sep", "Oct", "Nov", "Dec"
        };
        static char result[26];

        sprintf(result, "%.3s %.3s%3d %.2d:%.2d:%.2d %d\n",
                wday_name[timeptr->tm_wday],
                mon_name[timeptr->tm_mon],
                timeptr->tm_mday, timeptr->tm_hour,
                timeptr->tm_min, timeptr->tm_sec,
                1900 + timeptr->tm_year);
        return result;
}
```

The **tm** structure is defined in the header **<time.h>**.

RETURN VALUE

Upon successful completion, *asctime*( ) returns a pointer to the string.

ERRORS

No errors are defined.

APPLICATION USAGE

The *asctime*( ), *ctime*( ), *gmtime*( ) and *localtime*( ) functions return values in one of two static objects: a broken-down time structure and an array of type **char**. Execution of any of the functions may overwrite the information returned in either of these objects by any of the other functions.

Values for the broken-down time structure can be obtained by calling *gmtime*( ) or *localtime*( ). This interface is included for compatibility with older implementations, and does not support localised date and time formats. Applications should use *strftime*( ) to achieve maximum portability.

SEE ALSO

clock( ), *ctime*( ), *difftime*( ), *gmtime*( ), *localtime*( ), *mktime*( ), *strftime*( ), *strptime*( ), *time*( ), *utime*( ), **<time.h>**.

EXAMPLE

```
/*
 * Copyright (C) ANTRIX Inc.
 */

/* asctime.c
 * This program converts known and current date and
 * time to a string using function asctime.
 */

#include <stdio.h>
#include <stdlib.h>
#include <time.h>
#include <errno.h>

main()
{
  char            *asctime_value;
  time_t          tloc;
  const struct tm *current_time;
  const struct tm  known_time = {
    /* sec, min, hour, mday, mon, year, wday, yday, isdst */
       40,  30,  2,    1,    8,   93,   0,    259,  0,
  };

  fprintf (stdout,"example 1\n");
  fprintf (stdout,"convert a known time, day, date and year to string\n");
  asctime_value = asctime (&known_time);
  if ( asctime_value != (char *)0 ) {
     fprintf (stdout,"asctime() call successful\n");
     fprintf (stdout,"asctime_value=%s\n", asctime_value);
  }
  else
     fprintf (stderr,"ERROR: asctime() call failed\n");

  fprintf (stdout,"example 2\n");
  fprintf (stdout,"convert current time, day, date and year to string\n");
  time (&tloc);
  current_time = localtime (&tloc);
  asctime_value = asctime (current_time);
  if ( asctime_value != (char *)0 ) {
     fprintf (stdout,"asctime() call successful\n");
     fprintf (stdout,"asctime_value=%s\n", asctime_value);
  }
  else
     fprintf (stderr,"ERROR: asctime() call failed\n");
}
```

NAME
asin — arc sine function

SYNOPSIS
```
#include <math.h>

double asin(double x);
```

DESCRIPTION
The *asin( )* function computes the principal value of the arc sine of *x*. The value of *x* should be in the range [−1,1].

RETURN VALUE
Upon successful completion, *asin( )* returns the arc sine of *x*, in the range [-π/2, π/2] radians. If
EX the value of *x* is not in the range [−1,1], and is not ±Inf or NaN, either 0.0 or NaN is returned and *errno* is set to [EDOM].

EX If *x* is NaN, NaN is returned and *errno* may be set to [EDOM].

EX If *x* is ±Inf, either 0.0 is returned and *errno* is set to [EDOM] or NaN is returned and *errno* may be set to [EDOM].

If the result underflows, 0.0 is returned and *errno* may be set to [ERANGE].

ERRORS
The *asin( )* function will fail if:

EX [EDOM]   The value *x* is not ±Inf or NaN and is not in the range [−1,1].

The *asin( )* function may fail if:

EX [EDOM]   The value of *x* is ±Inf or NaN.

[ERANGE]   The result underflows.

EX No other errors will occur.

APPLICATION USAGE
An application wishing to check for error situations should set *errno* to 0, then call *asin( )*. If *errno* is non-zero on return, or the return value is NaN, an error has occurred.

SEE ALSO
isnan( ), *sin( )*, **<math.h>**.

EXAMPLE
```
/*
 * Copyright (C) ANTRIX Inc.
 */


/* asin.c
 * This program computes the principal value of the arc
 * sine of 0.50 using function asin.
 */

#include <stdio.h>
#include <math.h>

main()
{
  double  asin_value;
```

```
        double   x = 0.50;

        asin_value = asin (x);
        fprintf (stdout,"asin of %f is %f\n", x, asin_value);
}
```

NAME

asinh — hyperbolic arc sine

SYNOPSIS

UX

```
#include <math.h>

double asinh(double x);
```

DESCRIPTION

Refer to *acosh*( ).

EXAMPLE

```
/*
 * Copyright (C) ANTRIX Inc.
 */

/* asinh.c
 * This program computes the inverse hyperbolic sine of x
 * using function asinh.
 */

#include <stdio.h>
#include <math.h>

main()
{
  double  asinh_value;
  double  x = 0.50;

  asinh_value = asinh (x);
  fprintf (stdout,"asinh of %f is %f\n", x, asinh_value);
}
```

NAME

assert — insert program diagnostics

SYNOPSIS

```
#include <assert.h>

void assert(int expression);
```

DESCRIPTION

The *assert*( ) macro inserts diagnostics into programs. When it is executed, if *expression* is false (that is, compares equal to 0), *assert*( ) writes information about the particular call that failed (including the text of the argument, the name of the source file and the source file line number — the latter are respectively the values of the preprocessing macros _ _FILE_ _ and _ _LINE_ _) on *stderr* and calls *abort*( ).

Forcing a definition of the name NDEBUG, either from the compiler command line or with the preprocessor control statement **#define NDEBUG** ahead of the **#include <assert.h>** statement, will stop assertions from being compiled into the program.

RETURN VALUE

The *assert*( ) macro returns no value.

ERRORS

No errors are defined.

SEE ALSO

abort( ), *stderr*( ), **<assert.h>**.

EXAMPLE

```
/*
 * Copyright (C) ANTRIX Inc.
 */

/* assert.c
 * This program inserts print diagnostics and aborts
 * the program using function assert.
 */

#include <stdio.h>
#include <math.h>
#include <sys/types.h>
#include <unistd.h>
#include <assert.h>
#include <errno.h>

main()
{
    double  acos_value;
    double  x = 0.50;

    fprintf(stdout, "Calculate acos value of 0.5\n");
    acos_value = acos(x);

    /* expression evaluates to 0 shall print out a message */
    /* on the standard error output of the form */
    /* assertion failed: expression, file xyz, line nnn */
```

```
        /* and abort the application */
        fprintf(stdout, "Check acos of %f value %f\n", x, acos_value);
        assert (acos_value > 2.1);

        fprintf (stderr,"ERROR: program did not print diagnostics ");
        fprintf (stderr,"and terminate\n");
}
```

NAME

atan — arc tangent function

SYNOPSIS

```
#include <math.h>

double atan(double x);
```

DESCRIPTION

The *atan*( ) function computes the principal value of the arc tangent of *x*.

RETURN VALUE

Upon successful completion, *atan*( ) returns the arc tangent of *x* in the range [-π/2, π/2] radians.

EX If *x* is NaN, NaN is returned and *errno* may be set to [EDOM].

If the result underflows, 0.0 is returned and *errno* may be set to [ERANGE].

ERRORS

The *atan*( ) function may fail if:

EX [EDOM]   The value of *x* is NaN.

[ERANGE]   The result underflows.

EX No other errors will occur.

APPLICATION USAGE

An application wishing to check for error situations should set *errno* to 0 before calling *atan*( ). If *errno* is non-zero on return, or the return value is NaN, an error has occurred.

SEE ALSO

atan2( ), *isnan*( ), *tan*( ), **<math.h>**.

EXAMPLE

```
/*
 * Copyright (C) ANTRIX Inc.
 */

/* atan.c
 * This program computes the principal value of the arc
 * tangent of 0.25 using function atan.
 */

#include <stdio.h>
#include <math.h>

main()
{
  double  atan_value;
  double  x = 0.25;

  atan_value = atan (x);
  fprintf (stdout,"atan of %f is %f\n", x, atan_value);
}
```

NAME

atan2 — arc tangent function

SYNOPSIS

```
#include <math.h>

double atan2(double y, double x);
```

DESCRIPTION

The *atan2( )* function computes the principal value of the arc tangent of *y/x*, using the signs of both arguments to determine the quadrant of the return value.

RETURN VALUE

Upon successful completion, *atan2( )* returns the arc tangent of *y/x* in the range $[-\pi, \pi]$ radians. If both arguments are 0.0, an implementation-dependent value is returned and *errno* may be set to [EDOM].

EX   If *x* or *y* is NaN, NaN is returned and *errno* may be set to [EDOM].

If the result underflows, 0.0 is returned and *errno* may be set to [ERANGE].

ERRORS

The *atan2( )* function may fail if:

EX   [EDOM]   Both arguments are 0.0 or one or more of the arguments is NaN.

[ERANGE]   The result underflows.

EX   No other errors will occur.

APPLICATION USAGE

An application wishing to check for error situations should set *errno* to 0 before calling *atan2( )*. If *errno* is non-zero on return, or the return value is NaN, an error has occurred.

SEE ALSO

atan( ), *isnan( )*, *tan( )*, **<math.h>**.

EXAMPLE

```
/*
 * Copyright (C) ANTRIX Inc.
 */

/* atan2.c
 * This program computes the principal value of the arc
 * tangent of 0.50/1.00 using function atan2.
 */

#include <stdio.h>
#include <math.h>

main()
{
  double  atan2_value;
  double  y = 0.50;
  double  x = 1.00;
```

```
    atan2_value = atan2 (y, x);
    fprintf (stdout,"atan2 of %f, %f is %f\n", y, x, atan2_value);
}
```

NAME

atanh — hyperbolic arc tangent

SYNOPSIS

UX
```
#include <math.h>

double atanh(double x);
```

DESCRIPTION

Refer to *acosh*( ).

EXAMPLE

```
/*
 * Copyright (C) ANTRIX Inc.
 */

/* atanh.c
 * This program computes the inverse hyperbolic tan of x
 * using function atanh.
 */

#include <stdio.h>
#include <math.h>

main()
{
  double  atanh_value;
  double  x = 0.75;

  atanh_value = atanh (x);
  fprintf (stdout,"atanh of %f is %f\n", x, atanh_value);
}
```

NAME

atexit — register function to run at process termination

SYNOPSIS

```
#include <stdlib.h>

int atexit(void (*func)(void));
```

DESCRIPTION

The *atexit*( ) function registers the function pointed to by *func* to be called without arguments. At normal process termination, functions registered by *atexit*( ) are called in the reverse order to that in which they were registered. Normal termination occurs either by a call to *exit*( ) or a return from *main*( ).

At least 32 functions can be registered with *atexit*( ).

After a successful call to any of the *exec* functions, any functions previously registered by *atexit*( ) are no longer registered.

RETURN VALUE

Upon successful completion, *atexit*( ) returns 0. Otherwise, it returns a non-zero value.

ERRORS

No errors are defined.

APPLICATION USAGE

The functions registered by a call to *atexit*( ) must return to ensure that all registered functions are called.

UX   The application should call *sysconf*( ) to obtain the value of {ATEXIT_MAX}, the number of functions that can be registered. There is no way for an application to tell how many functions have already been registered with *atexit*( ).

SEE ALSO

exit( ), *sysconf*( ), **<stdlib.h>**.

EXAMPLE

```
/*
 * Copyright (C) ANTRIX Inc.
 */

/* atexit.c
 * This program registers function func to run at process
 * termination using function atexit.
 */

#include <stdio.h>
#include <stdlib.h>
#include <errno.h>

void func()
{
  fprintf (stdout,"successfully invoked registered function\n");
  fprintf (stdout,"func() on exit() call\n");
}

main()
{
```

```
int   atexit_value;

fprintf (stdout,"register function func()\n");
fprintf (stdout,"to be invoked on exit() call\n");

atexit_value = atexit (func);
if ( atexit_value == 0 ) {
   fprintf (stdout,"atexit() call successful\n");
   fprintf (stdout,"registered function func()");
   fprintf (stdout, " to be invoked on exit()\n");
}
else
   fprintf (stderr,"ERROR: atexit() call failed\n");

fprintf (stdout,"invoke function func() on exit()\n");
exit (1);
}
```

NAME

atof — convert string to double-precision number

SYNOPSIS

```
#include <stdlib.h>

double atof(const char *str);
```

DESCRIPTION

The call *atof*(*str*) is equivalent to:

```
strtod(str,(char **)NULL),
```

except that the handling of errors may differ. If the value cannot be represented, the behaviour is undefined.

RETURN VALUE

The *atof*( ) function returns the converted value if the value can be represented.

ERRORS

No errors are defined.

APPLICATION USAGE

The *atof*( ) function is subsumed by *strtod*( ) but is retained because it is used extensively in existing code. If the number is not known to be in range, *strtod*( ) should be used because *atof*( ) is not required to perform any error checking.

SEE ALSO

strtod( ), **<stdlib.h>**.

EXAMPLE

```
/*
 * Copyright (C) ANTRIX Inc.
 */

/* atof.c
 * This program converts string "12.34" to double-precision
 * number using function atof.
 */

#include <stdio.h>
#include <stdlib.h>
#include <errno.h>

main()
{
    double      atof_value;
    const char *str = "12.34";

    fprintf (stdout,"convert string to double-precision\n");

    atof_value = atof (str);
    if ( atof_value == 12.34 ) {
        fprintf (stdout,"atof() call successful\n");
        fprintf (stdout,"string %s converted to\n"
                "double-precision number is %f\n", str, atof_value);
    }
```

```
    else
        fprintf (stderr,"ERROR: atof() call failed\n");
}
```

NAME

atoi — convert string to integer

SYNOPSIS

```
#include <stdlib.h>

int atoi(const char *str);
```

DESCRIPTION

The call *atoi*(*str*) is equivalent to:

```
(int) strtol(str, (char **)NULL, 10)
```

except that the handling of errors may differ. If the value cannot be represented, the behaviour is undefined.

RETURN VALUE

The *atoi*( ) function returns the converted value if the value can be represented.

ERRORS

No errors are defined.

APPLICATION USAGE

The *atoi*( ) function is subsumed by *strtol*( ) but is retained because it is used extensively in existing code. If the number is not known to be in range, *strtol*( ) should be used because *atoi*( ) is not required to perform any error checking.

SEE ALSO

strtol( ), **<stdlib.h>**.

EXAMPLE

```
/*
 * Copyright (C) ANTRIX Inc.
 */

/* atoi.c
 * This program converts string "123456" to integer
 * using function atoi.
 */

#include <stdio.h>
#include <stdlib.h>
#include <errno.h>

main()
{
   int       atoi_value;
   const char *str = "123456";

   fprintf (stdout,"convert string to integer\n");
   atoi_value = atoi (str);
   if ( atoi_value == 123456 ) {
      fprintf (stdout,"atoi() call successful\n");
      fprintf (stdout,"string %s converted to integer is %d\n",
                        str, atoi_value);
   }
   else
```

```
        fprintf (stderr,"ERROR: atoi() call failed\n");
}
```

NAME

atol — convert string to long integer

SYNOPSIS

```
#include <stdlib.h>

long int atol(const char *str);
```

DESCRIPTION

The call *atol(str)* is equivalent to:

```
strtol(str, (char **)NULL, 10)
```

except that the handling of errors may differ. If the value cannot be represented, the behaviour is undefined.

RETURN VALUE

The *atol( )* function returns the converted value if the value can be represented.

ERRORS

No errors are defined.

APPLICATION USAGE

The *atol( )* function is subsumed by *strtol( )* but is retained because it is used extensively in existing code. If the number is not known to be in range, *strtol( )* should be used because *atol( )* is not required to perform any error checking.

SEE ALSO

strtol( ), **<stdlib.h>**.

EXAMPLE

```
/*
 * Copyright (C) ANTRIX Inc.
 */

/* atol.c
 * This program converts long string "123" to long integer
 * using function atol.
 */

#include <stdio.h>
#include <stdlib.h>
#include <errno.h>

main()
{
  long       atol_value;
  const char *str = "123L";

  fprintf (stdout,"convert string to long\n");
  atol_value = atol (str);
  if ( atol_value == 123 ) {
     fprintf (stdout,"atol() call successful\n");
     fprintf (stdout,"string %s converted to long is %ld\n",
                     str, atol_value);
  }
  else
```

```
        fprintf (stderr,"ERROR: atol() call failed\n");
}
```

NAME

basename — return the last component of a pathname

SYNOPSIS

UX   `#include <libgen.h>`

`char *basename(char *path);`

DESCRIPTION

The *basename*( ) function takes the pathname pointed to by *path* and returns a pointer to the final component of the pathname, deleting any trailing '/' characters.

If the string consists entirely of the '/' character, *basename*( ) returns a pointer to the string "/" .

If *path* is a null pointer or points to an empty string, *basename*( ) returns a pointer to the string "."
.

RETURN VALUE

The *basename*( ) function returns a pointer to the final component of *path*.

EXAMPLES

Input String	Output String
"/usr/lib"	"lib"
"/usr/"	"usr"
"/"	"/"

APPLICATION USAGE

The *basename*( ) function may modify the string pointed to by *path*, and may return a pointer to static storage that may then be overwritten by a subsequent call to *basename*( ).

ERRORS

No errors are defined.

SEE ALSO

dirname( ), **<libgen.h>**.

EXAMPLE

```
/*
 * Copyright (C) ANTRIX Inc.
 */

/* basename.c
 * This program deletes any prefix ending in / and the suffix
 * from the string using function basename.
 */

#include <stdio.h>
#include <stdlib.h>
#include <libgen.h>
#include <errno.h>

main()
{
    char   *basename_value;
    char   *path = "/user/home/ANTRIX";
```

```
        fprintf (stdout,"delete the prefix from %s", path);
        basename_value = basename (path);
        if ( basename_value != (char *)0 ) {
            fprintf (stdout,"basename() call successful\n");
            fprintf (stdout,"basename_value = %s\n", basename_value);
        }
        else
            fprintf (stderr,"ERROR: basename() call failed\n");
    }
```

NAME

bcmp — memory operations

SYNOPSIS

UX   `#include <strings.h>`

`int bcmp(const void *s1, const void *s2, size_t n);`

DESCRIPTION

The *bcmp( )* function compares the first *n* bytes of the area pointed to by *s1* with the area pointed to by *s2*.

RETURN VALUE

The *bcmp( )* function returns 0 if *s1* and *s2* are identical, non-zero otherwise. Both areas are assumed to be *n* bytes long. If the value of *n* is 0, *bcmp( )* returns 0.

ERRORS

No errors are defined.

APPLICATION USAGE

For portability to implementations conforming to earlier versions of this document, *memcmp( )* is preferred over this function.

SEE ALSO

memcmp( ), **<strings.h>**.

EXAMPLE

```
/*
 * Copyright (C) ANTRIX Inc.
 */

/* bcmp.c
 * This program compares the first n bytes of the object pointed
 * by s1 to the first n bytes of the object pointed to by s2
 * using function bcmp.
 */

#include <stdio.h>
#include <stdlib.h>
#include <memory.h>
#include <errno.h>

main()
{
   int      bcmp_value;
   int      length;
   char     *str1 = "abc";
   char     *str2 = "abc";

   fprintf (stdout,"compare strings\n");
   length = strlen (str1);
   bcmp_value = bcmp (str1, str2, length);
   if ( bcmp_value == 0 )
       fprintf (stdout,"bcmp() call successful\n");
```

```
    else
        fprintf (stderr,"ERROR: bcmp() call failed\n");
}
```

NAME

bcopy — memory operations

SYNOPSIS

UX   `#include <strings.h>`

`void bcopy(const void *s1, void *s2, size_t n);`

DESCRIPTION

The *bcopy*( ) function copies *n* bytes from the area pointed to by *s1* to the area pointed to by *s2*.

RETURN VALUE

The *bcopy*( ) function returns no value.

ERRORS

No errors are defined.

APPLICATION USAGE

For portability to implementations conforming to earlier versions of this document, *memmove*( ) is preferred over this function.

The following are approximately equivalent (note the order of the arguments):

```
bcopy(s1,s2,n)  ~= memmove(s2,s1,n)
```

SEE ALSO

memmove( ), **<strings.h>**.

EXAMPLE

```
/*
 * Copyright (C) ANTRIX Inc.
 */

/* bcopy.c
 * This program copies n bytes from the object pointed to by s2
 * into the object pointed to by s1 using function bcopy.
 */

#include <stdio.h>
#include <stdlib.h>
#include <strings.h>
#include <errno.h>

main()
{
  char    *s1 = "hello world";
  char    *s2 ;

  fprintf (stdout,"copy strings\n");
  s2 = (char *)malloc(6);
  bzero (s2, 6);
  bcopy ((char *)s1, (char *)s2, 6);
  fprintf (stdout,"string in s2=%s\n", s2);
}
```

NAME

brk, sbrk — change space allocation

SYNOPSIS

UX

```
#include <unistd.h>
```

```
int brk(void *addr);
```

```
void *sbrk(int incr);
```

DESCRIPTION

The *brk*( ) and *sbrk*( ) functions are used to change the amount of space allocated for the calling process. The change is made by resetting the process' break value and allocating the appropriate amount of space. The amount of allocated space increases as the break value increases. The newly-allocated space is set to 0. However, if the application first decrements and then increments the break value, the contents of the reallocated space are unspecified.

The *brk*( ) function sets the break value to *addr* and changes the allocated space accordingly.

The *sbrk*( ) function adds *incr* bytes to the break value and changes the allocated space accordingly. If *incr* is negative, the amount of allocated space is decreased by *incr* bytes. The current value of the program break is returned by *sbrk*(0).

The behaviour of *brk*( ) and *sbrk*( ) is unspecified if an application also uses any other memory functions (such as *malloc*( ), *mmap*( ), *free*( )). Other functions may use these other memory functions silently.

RETURN VALUE

Upon successful completion, *brk*( ) returns 0. Otherwise, it returns −1 and sets *errno* to indicate the error.

Upon successful completion, *sbrk*( ) returns the prior break value. Otherwise, it returns (**void ***)−1 and sets *errno* to indicate the error.

ERRORS

The *brk*( ) and *sbrk*( ) functions will fail if:

[ENOMEM]   The requested change would allocate more space than allowed.

The *brk*( ) and *sbrk*( ) functions may fail if:

[EAGAIN]   The total amount of system memory available for allocation to this process is temporarily insufficient. This may occur even though the space requested was less than the maximum data segment size.

[ENOMEM]   The requested change would be impossible as there is insufficient swap space available, or would cause a memory allocation conflict.

APPLICATION USAGE

The *brk*( ) and *sbrk*( ) functions have been used in specialised cases where no other memory allocation function provided the same capability. The use of *mmap*( ) is now preferred because it can be used portably with all other memory allocation functions and with any function that uses other allocation functions.

It is unspecified whether the pointer returned by *sbrk*( ) is aligned suitably for any purpose.

SEE ALSO

exec, *malloc*( ), *mmap*( ), **<unistd.h>**.

EXAMPLE

```c
/*
 * Copyright (C) ANTRIX Inc.
 */

/* brk.c
 * This program sets the break value to endds and changes the
 * the allocated space accordingly using function brk.
 */

#include <stdio.h>
#include <stdlib.h>
#include <errno.h>

main()
{
   int   brk_value;
   int   endds = 50;

   fprintf (stdout,"set break value\n");
   brk_value = brk ((void *)&endds);
   if (brk_value == 0)
      fprintf(stdout, "brk call successful\n");
   else {
      fprintf (stderr,"ERROR: brk call failed\n");
      fprintf (stderr,"ERROR: %s\n", strerror(errno));
   }
}
/*
 * Copyright (C) ANTRIX Inc.
 */

/* sbrk.c
 * This program changes the amount of space allocated for
 * the calling process's data segment using function sbrk.
 */

#include <stdio.h>
#include <stdlib.h>
#include <errno.h>

main()
{
   char      *sbrk_value;

   fprintf (stdout,"get original break value\n");
   sbrk_value = (char *)sbrk (100);

   fprintf (stdout,"orignal sbrk_value=%d\n", sbrk_value );
   fprintf (stdout,"get previous break value set\n");
```

```
    sbrk_value = (char *)sbrk (200);
    fprintf (stdout,"new sbrk_value=%d\n", sbrk_value );
}
```

NAME

bsd_signal — simplified signal facilities

SYNOPSIS

UX   `#include <signal.h>`

`void (*bsd_signal(int sig, void (*func)(int)))(int);`

DESCRIPTION

The *bsd_signal*( ) function provides a partially compatible interface for programs written to historical system interfaces (see APPLICATION USAGE below).

The function call *bsd_signal*(*sig*, *func*) has an effect as if implemented as:

```
void (*bsd_signal(int sig, void (*func)(int)))(int)
{
        struct sigaction act, oact;

        act.sa_handler = func;
        act.sa_flags = SA_RESTART;
        sigemptyset(&act.sa_mask);
        sigaddset(&act.sa_mask, sig);
        if (sigaction(sig, &act, &oact) == -1)
               return(SIG_ERR);
        return(oact.sa_handler);
}
```

The handler function should be declared:

```
void handler(int sig);
```

where *sig* is the signal number. The behaviour is undefined if *func* is a function that takes more than one argument, or an argument of a different type.

RETURN VALUE

Upon successful completion, *bsd_signal*( ) returns the previous action for *sig*. Otherwise, SIG_ERR is returned and *errno* is set to indicate the error.

ERRORS

Refer to *sigaction*( ).

APPLICATION USAGE

This function is a direct replacement for the BSD *signal*( ) function for simple applications that are installing a single-argument signal handler function. If a BSD signal handler function is being installed that expects more than one argument, the application has to be modified to use *sigaction*( ). The *bsd_signal*( ) function differs from *signal*( ) in that the SA_RESTART flag is set and the SA_RESETHAND will be clear when *bsd_signal*( ) is used. The state of these flags is not specified for *signal*( ).

SEE ALSO

sigaction( ), *sigaddset*( ), *sigemptyset*( ), *signal*( ), **<signal.h>**.

NAME

bsearch — binary search a sorted table

SYNOPSIS

```
#include <stdlib.h>

void *bsearch(const void *key, const void *base, size_t nel,
              size_t width, int (*compar)(const void *, const void *));
```

DESCRIPTION

The *bsearch( )* function searches an array of *nel* objects, the initial element of which is pointed to by *base*, for an element that matches the object pointed to by *key*. The size of each element in the array is specified by *width*.

The comparison function pointed to by *compar* is called with two arguments that point to the *key* object and to an array element, in that order.

The function must return an integer less than, equal to, or greater than 0 if the *key* object is considered, respectively, to be less than, to match, or to be greater than the array element. The array must consist of: all the elements that compare less than, all the elements that compare equal to, and all the elements that compare greater than the *key* object, in that order.

RETURN VALUE

The *bsearch( )* function returns a pointer to a matching member of the array, or a null pointer if no match is found. If two or more members compare equal, which member is returned is unspecified.

ERRORS

No errors are defined.

EXAMPLES

The example below searches a table containing pointers to nodes consisting of a string and its length. The table is ordered alphabetically on the string in the node pointed to by each entry.

The code fragment below reads in strings and either finds the corresponding node and prints out the string and its length, or prints an error message.

```
#include <stdio.h>
#include <stdlib.h>
#include <string.h>

#define TABSIZE    1000

struct node {                      /* these are stored in the table */
    char *string;
    int length;
};
struct node table[TABSIZE];     /* table to be searched */
    .
    .
    .

{
    struct node *node_ptr, node;
    /* routine to compare 2 nodes */
    int node_compare(const void *, const void *);
    char str_space[20];            /* space to read string into */
    .
    .
```

```
        node.string = str_space;
        while (scanf("%s", node.string) != EOF) {
            node_ptr = (struct node *)bsearch((void *)(&node),
                    (void *)table, TABSIZE,
                    sizeof(struct node), node_compare);
            if (node_ptr != NULL) {
                (void)printf("string = %20s, length = %d\n",
                    node_ptr->string, node_ptr->length);
            } else {
                (void)printf("not found: %s\n", node.string);
            }
        }
}
/*
    This routine compares two nodes based on an
    alphabetical ordering of the string field.
*/
int
node_compare(const void *node1, const void *node2)
{
    return strcoll(((const struct node *)node1)->string,
        ((const struct node *)node2)->string);
}
```

APPLICATION USAGE

The pointers to the key and the element at the base of the table should be of type pointer-to-element.

The comparison function need not compare every byte, so arbitrary data may be contained in the elements in addition to the values being compared.

In practice, the array is usually sorted according to the comparison function.

SEE ALSO

hsearch( ), *lsearch*( ), *qsort*( ), *tsearch*( ), **<stdlib.h>**.

EXAMPLE

```
/*
 * Copyright (C) ANTRIX Inc.
 */

/* bsearch.c
 * This program does binary search for string "bbb"
 * from table using function bsearch.
 */

#include <stdio.h>
#include <stdlib.h>
#include <errno.h>

#define  TABLESIZE  5

struct node {
  char *string;
```

```
    int   length;
};

/* sorted table */
struct node table[TABLESIZE] = {
        { "aaa",  3 },
        { "bbb",  3 },
        { "ccc",  3 },
        { "ddd",  3 },
        { "eee",  3 },
};

int compare (node1, node2)
struct node *node1;
struct node *node2;
{
  return strcmp (node1->string, node2->string);
}

main()
{
  struct node find, *node_ptr;

  fprintf(stdout, "search for entry bbb\n");
  find.string = "bbb";

  fprintf (stdout,"search for string=%s\n", find.string);
  node_ptr = (struct node *)bsearch (
                                (const void *)(&find),
                                (const void *)&table[0],
                                TABLESIZE,
                                sizeof(struct node),
                                compare
                                );

  if ( node_ptr != (struct node *)0 ) {
     fprintf (stdout,"bsearch() call successful\n");
     fprintf (stdout,"found string=%s, length=%d\n",
              node_ptr->string, node_ptr->length);
  } else
     fprintf (stderr,"ERROR: bsearch() call failed\n");
}
```

NAME

bzero — memory operations

SYNOPSIS

UX `#include <strings.h>`

`void bzero(void *s, size_t n);`

DESCRIPTION

The *bzero*( ) function places *n* zero-valued bytes in the area pointed to by *s*.

RETURN VALUE

The *bzero*( ) function returns no value.

ERRORS

No errors are defined.

APPLICATION USAGE

For portability to implementations conforming to earlier versions of this document, *memset*( ) is preferred over this function.

SEE ALSO

memset( ), **<strings.h>**.

EXAMPLE

```
/*
 * Copyright (C) ANTRIX Inc.
 */

/* bzero.c
 * This program copies n 0 bytest in the string
 * using function bzero.
 */


#include <stdio.h>
#include <stdlib.h>
#include <sys/stat.h>
#include <strings.h>
#include <errno.h>

main()
{
    char        buf[4];
    char        *s;
    struct stat sbuf;
    struct stat *psbuf;

    s = (char *)malloc (12);

    fprintf (stdout,"initialize character array to null\n");
    bzero (buf, 4);
    bzero (s, 12);

    fprintf (stdout,"initialize structures to null\n");
    bzero ((char *)&sbuf, sizeof(sbuf));
```

```
        psbuf = (struct stat *)malloc(sizeof(stat));
        bzero ((char *)psbuf, sizeof(psbuf));
    }
```

NAME

calloc — memory allocator

SYNOPSIS

```
#include <stdlib.h>

void *calloc(size_t nelem, size_t elsize);
```

DESCRIPTION

The *calloc*( ) function allocates unused space for an array of *nelem* elements each of whose size in bytes is *elsize*. The space is initialised to all bits 0.

The order and contiguity of storage allocated by successive calls to *calloc*( ) is unspecified. The pointer returned if the allocation succeeds is suitably aligned so that it may be assigned to a pointer to any type of object and then used to access such an object or an array of such objects in the space allocated (until the space is explicitly freed or reallocated). Each such allocation will yield a pointer to an object disjoint from any other object. The pointer returned points to the start (lowest byte address) of the allocated space. If the space cannot be allocated, a null pointer is returned. If the size of the space requested is 0, the behaviour is implementation-dependent; the value returned will be either a null pointer or a unique pointer.

RETURN VALUE

Upon successful completion with both *nelem* and *elsize* non-zero, *calloc*( ) returns a pointer to the allocated space. If either *nelem* or *elsize* is 0, then either a null pointer or a unique pointer

EX value that can be successfully passed to *free*( ) is returned. Otherwise, it returns a null pointer and sets *errno* to indicate the error.

ERRORS

The *calloc*( ) function will fail if:

EX [ENOMEM]   Insufficient memory is available.

APPLICATION USAGE

There is now no requirement for the implementation to support the inclusion of **<malloc.h>**.

SEE ALSO

free( ), *malloc*( ), *realloc*( ), **<stdlib.h>**.

EXAMPLE

```
/*
 * Copyright (C) ANTRIX Inc.
 */

/* calloc.c
 * This program allocates unused memory space and initializes
 * to zero for a string using function calloc.
 */

#include <stdio.h>
#include <stdlib.h>
#include <malloc.h>
#include <errno.h>

main()
{
  char   *buf;
  int    i, nelem;
```

```
    size_t elsize;
    char   *string = "hello world";

    nelem = strlen (string);
    elsize = sizeof(char);

    fprintf (stdout,"allocate memory and initialize it to zero\n");
    buf = (char *)calloc (nelem, elsize);

    for ( i = 0; i < nelem; i++ ) {
        /* check array initialized to zero */
        if ( buf[i] != 0 ) {
            fprintf (stderr,"ERROR: expected c[%d]=0, received c[%d]=%d\n",
                                        i, i, buf[i] );
            fprintf (stderr,"ERROR: %s\n", strerror(errno));
        }
    }

    fprintf (stdout,"copy string in allocated area buf\n");
    strcpy (buf, string);
    fprintf (stdout,"calloc() allocated memory for string=%s\n", buf);
}
```

NAME

catclose — close a message catalogue descriptor

SYNOPSIS

EX
```
#include <nl_types.h>

int catclose(nl_catd catd);
```

DESCRIPTION

The *catclose*( ) function closes the message catalogue identified by *catd*. If a file descriptor is used to implement the type **nl_catd**, that file descriptor will be closed.

RETURN VALUE

Upon successful completion, *catclose*( ) returns 0. Otherwise –1 is returned, and *errno* is set to indicate the error.

ERRORS

The *catclose*( ) function may fail if:

[EBADF]   The catalogue descriptor is not valid.

[EINTR]   The *catclose*( ) function was interrupted by a signal.

SEE ALSO

catgets( ), *catopen*( ), **<nl_types.h>**.

EXAMPLE

```
/*
 * Copyright (C) ANTRIX Inc.
 */

/* catclose.c
 * This program closes a message catalogue descriptor catd
 * using function catclose.
 */

#include <stdio.h>
#include <stdlib.h>
#include <locale.h>
#include <limits.h>
#include <nl_types.h>
#include <errno.h>

#define CATALOG       "test.cat"
#define SETNUM        2
#define MSGNUM        3
#define MSGTEXT       "this is the third message in set #2.\n"
#define DEFAULT_STR   "this is default string\n"

#define PATH_LEN      255

main()
{
    nl_catd   catd;
    char      envbuf[PATH_LEN];
    char      buf[PATH_LEN];
    char      *string;
```

```
    setlocale (LC_ALL, "");
    fprintf (stdout,"initialize buffers\n");
    memset(envbuf, ' ', PATH_LEN);
    memset(buf, ' ', PATH_LEN);

    getcwd (buf, PATH_LEN);
    fprintf (stdout,"set NLSPATH variable\n");
    sprintf (envbuf, "NLSPATH=%s", buf);
    putenv (envbuf);

    fprintf (stdout,"open catalog file\n");
    catd = catopen (CATALOG, 0);
    if ( catd >= (nl_catd)0 ) {
        fprintf (stdout,"catalog () call successful\n");
        fprintf (stdout,"catalog file opened successfully\n");
        string = catgets(catd, SETNUM, MSGNUM, DEFAULT_STR);
        if ( strcmp (string, MSGTEXT) != 0)
            fprintf (stderr,"ERROR:\nexpected=%s\nreceived=%s",
                            MSGTEXT, string);
    }
    else
        fprintf (stderr,"ERROR: catopen() call failed\n");

    fprintf (stdout,"close catalog file\n");
    catclose (catd);
}


/* filename test.cat */
$ this is the test catalog for catgets
$delset 1
$set 1
1 This set contains only one message - we check for an error
    on message #2.\n
$delset 2
$set 2
1 this is the first message in set #2.\n
2 this is the second message in set #2.\n
3 this is the third message in set #2.\n
```

NAME

catgets — read a program message

SYNOPSIS

EX
```
#include <nl_types.h>

char *catgets(nl_catd catd, int set_id, int msg_id, const char *s);
```

DESCRIPTION

The *catgets*( ) function attempts to read message *msg_id*, in set *set_id*, from the message catalogue identified by *catd*. The *catd* argument is a message catalogue descriptor returned from an earlier call to *catopen*( ). The *s* argument points to a default message string which will be returned by *catgets*( ) if it cannot retrieve the identified message.

RETURN VALUE

If the identified message is retrieved successfully, *catgets*( ) returns a pointer to an internal buffer area containing the null-terminated message string. If the call is unsuccessful for any
UX reason, *s* is returned and *errno* may be set to indicate the error.

ERRORS

The *catgets*( ) function may fail if:

[EBADF]   The *catd* argument is not a valid message catalogue descriptor open for reading.

[EINTR]   The read operation was terminated due to the receipt of a signal, and no data was transferred.

UX [EINVAL]   The message catalog identified by *catd* is corrupted.

[ENOMSG]   The message identified by *set_id* and *msg_id* is not in the message catalog.

SEE ALSO

catclose( ), *catopen*( ), **<nl_types.h>**.

EXAMPLE

```
/*
 * Copyright (C) ANTRIX Inc.
 */

/* catgets.c
 * This program reads message from message catalogue identified
 * by catd using function catgets.
 */

#include <stdio.h>
#include <stdlib.h>
#include <locale.h>
#include <limits.h>
#include <nl_types.h>
#include <errno.h>

#define CATALOG      "test.cat"
#define SETNUM       2
#define MSGNUM       3
#define MSGTEXT      "this is the third message in set #2.\n"
#define DEFAULT_STR  "this is default string\n"
```

```
#define PATH_LEN      255

main()
{
  nl_catd      catd;
  char         envbuf[PATH_LEN];
  char         buf[PATH_LEN];
  char         *string;

  setlocale(LC_ALL, "");
  fprintf (stdout,"initialize buffers\n");
  memset (envbuf, ' ', PATH_LEN);
  memset (buf, ' ', PATH_LEN);

  getcwd (buf, PATH_LEN);
  fprintf (stdout,"set NLSPATH variable\n");
  sprintf (envbuf, "NLSPATH=%s", buf);
  putenv (envbuf);

  catd = catopen (CATALOG, 0);
  if ( catd >= (nl_catd)0 ) {
     fprintf (stdout,"catalog () call successful\n");
     fprintf (stdout,"catalog file opened successfully\n");
     string = catgets(catd, SETNUM, MSGNUM, DEFAULT_STR);
     if ( strcmp (string, MSGTEXT) != 0)
        fprintf (stderr,"ERROR:\nexpected=%s\nreceived=%s",
                       MSGTEXT, string);
  }
  else
     fprintf (stderr,"ERROR: catopen() call failed\n");

  fprintf (stdout,"close catalog file\n");
  catclose (catd);
}
/* filename test.cat */
$ this is the test catalog for catgets
$delset 1
$set 1
1 This set contains only one message - we check for an error
     on message #2.\n
$delset 2
$set 2
1 this is the first message in set #2.\n
2 this is the second message in set #2.\n
3 this is the third message in set #2.\n
```

NAME

catopen — open a message catalogue

SYNOPSIS

EX
```
#include <nl_types.h>

nl_catd catopen(const char *name, int oflag);
```

DESCRIPTION

The *catopen*( ) function opens a message catalogue and returns a message catalogue descriptor. The *name* argument specifies the name of the message catalogue to be opened. If *name* contains a "/", then *name* specifies a complete name for the message catalogue. Otherwise, the environment variable *NLSPATH* is used with *name* substituted for *%N* (see the **XBD** specification, **Chapter 6**, **Environment Variables**). If *NLSPATH* does not exist in the environment, or if a message catalogue cannot be found in any of the components specified by *NLSPATH*, then an implementation-dependent default path is used. This default may be affected by the setting of LC_MESSAGES if the value of *oflag* is NL_CAT_LOCALE, or the *LANG* environment variable if *oflag* is 0.

A message catalogue descriptor remains valid in a process until that process closes it, or a successful call to one of the *exec* functions. A change in the setting of the LC_MESSAGES category may invalidate existing open catalogues.

If a file descriptor is used to implement message catalogue descriptors, the FD_CLOEXEC flag will be set; see **<fcntl.h>**.

If the value of the *oflag* argument is 0, the *LANG* environment variable is used to locate the catalogue without regard to the LC_MESSAGES category. If the *oflag* argument is NL_CAT_LOCALE, the LC_MESSAGES category is used to locate the message catalogue (see the **XBD** specification, **Section 6.2**, **Internationalisation Variables**).

RETURN VALUE

Upon successful completion, *catopen*( ) returns a message catalogue descriptor for use on subsequent calls to *catgets*( ) and *catclose*( ). Otherwise *catopen*( ) returns (**nl_catd**) −1 and sets *errno* to indicate the error.

ERRORS

The *catopen*( ) function may fail if:

[EACCES]   Search permission is denied for the component of the path prefix of the message catalogue or read permission is denied for the message catalogue.

[EMFILE]   {OPEN_MAX} file descriptors are currently open in the calling process.

[ENAMETOOLONG]
                     The length of the pathname of the message catalogue exceeds {PATH_MAX}, or a pathname component is longer than {NAME_MAX}.

UX
[ENAMETOOLONG]
                     Pathname resolution of a symbolic link produced an intermediate result whose length exceeds {PATH_MAX}.

[ENFILE]   Too many files are currently open in the system.

[ENOENT]   The message catalogue does not exist or the *name* argument points to an empty string.

[ENOMEM]   Insufficient storage space is available.

[ENOTDIR]   A component of the path prefix of the message catalogue is not a directory.

APPLICATION USAGE

Some implementations of *catopen*( ) use *malloc*( ) to allocate space for internal buffer areas. The *catopen*( ) function may fail if there is insufficient storage space available to accommodate these buffers.

Portable applications must assume that message catalogue descriptors are not valid after a call to one of the *exec* functions.

Application writers should be aware that guidelines for the location of message catalogues have not yet been developed. Therefore they should take care to avoid conflicting with catalogues used by other applications and the standard utilities.

SEE ALSO

catclose( ), *catgets*( ), **<fcntl.h>**, **<nl_types.h>**.

EXAMPLE

```
/*
 * Copyright (C) ANTRIX Inc.
 */

/* catopen.c
 * This program opens a message catalogue and returns
 * a message catalogue descriptor.
 */

#include <stdio.h>
#include <stdlib.h>
#include <locale.h>
#include <limits.h>
#include <nl_types.h>
#include <errno.h>

#define CATALOG      "test.cat"
#define SETNUM       2
#define MSGNUM       3
#define MSGTEXT      "this is the third message in set #2.\n"
#define DEFAULT_STR  "this is default string\n"

#define PATH_LEN     255

main()
{
   nl_catd      catd;
   char         envbuf[PATH_LEN];
   char         buf[PATH_LEN];
   char         *string;

   setlocale (LC_ALL, "");
   fprintf (stdout,"initialize buffer\n");
   memset (envbuf, ' ', PATH_LEN);
   memset (buf, ' ', PATH_LEN);

   getcwd (buf, PATH_LEN);
```

```
      fprintf (stdout,"set NLSPATH variable\n");
      sprintf (envbuf, "NLSPATH=%s", buf);
      putenv (envbuf);

      fprintf (stdout,"open catalog file\n");
      catd = catopen (CATALOG, 0);
      if ( catd >= (nl_catd)0 ) {
         fprintf (stdout,"catalog () call successful\n");
         fprintf (stdout,"catalog file opened successfully\n");
         string = catgets(catd, SETNUM, MSGNUM, DEFAULT_STR);
         if ( strcmp (string, MSGTEXT) != 0)
            fprintf (stderr,"ERROR:\nexpected=%s\nreceived=%s",
                           MSGTEXT, string);
      }
      else
         fprintf (stderr,"ERROR: catopen() call failed\n");

      fprintf (stdout,"close catalog file\n");
      catclose (catd);
}
```

NAME

cbrt — cube root function

SYNOPSIS

UX   `#include <math.h>`

`double cbrt(double x);`

DESCRIPTION

The *cbrt*( ) function computes the cube root of *x*.

RETURN VALUE

On successful completion, *cbrt*( ) returns the cube root of *x*. If *x* is NaN, *cbrt*( ) returns NaN and *errno* may be set to [EDOM].

ERRORS

The *cbrt*( ) function may fail if:

[EDOM]   The value of *x* is NaN.

SEE ALSO

<math.h>.

EXAMPLE

```
/*
 * Copyright (C) ANTRIX Inc.
 */

/* cbrt.c
 * This program computes cube root of x
 * using function cbrt.
 */

#include <stdio.h>
#include <math.h>

main()
{
  double  cbrt_value;
  double  x = 8.00;

  cbrt_value = cbrt (x);
  fprintf (stdout,"cbrt of %f is %f\n", x, cbrt_value);
}
```

NAME

ceil — ceiling value function

SYNOPSIS

```
#include <math.h>

double ceil(double x);
```

DESCRIPTION

The *ceil*( ) function computes the smallest integral value not less than *x*.

RETURN VALUE

Upon successful completion, *ceil*( ) returns the smallest integral value not less than *x*, expressed as a type **double**.

EX   If *x* is NaN, NaN is returned and *errno* may be set to [EDOM].

EX   If the correct value would cause overflow, HUGE_VAL is returned and *errno* is set to [ERANGE]. If *x* is ±Inf or ±0, the value of *x* is returned.

ERRORS

The *ceil*( ) function will fail if:

[ERANGE]   The result overflows.

The *ceil*( ) function may fail if:

EX   [EDOM]   The value of *x* is NaN.

EX   No other errors will occur.

APPLICATION USAGE

The integral value returned by *ceil*( ) as a **double** may not be expressible as an **int** or **long int**. The return value should be tested before assigning it to an integer type to avoid the undefined results of an integer overflow.

An application wishing to check for error situations should set *errno* to 0 before calling *ceil*( ). If *errno* is non-zero on return, or the return value is NaN, an error has occurred.

The *ceil*( ) function can only overflow when the floating point representation has DBL_MANT_DIG > DBL_MAX_EXP.

SEE ALSO

floor( ), *isnan*( ), **<math.h>**.

EXAMPLE

```
/*
 * Copyright (C) ANTRIX Inc.
 */

/* ceil.c
 * This program computes the smallest integral value not
 * less than 0.25 using function ceil.
 */

#include <stdio.h>
#include <math.h>

main()
{
```

```
       double   ceil_value;
       double   x = 1.00/4.00 ;

       ceil_value = ceil (x);
       fprintf (stdout,"ceil of %f is %f\n", x, ceil_value);
}
```

NAME

cfgetispeed — get input baud rate

SYNOPSIS

```
#include <termios.h>

speed_t cfgetispeed(const struct termios *termios_p);
```

DESCRIPTION

The *cfgetispeed*( ) function extracts the input baud rate from the **termios** structure to which the *termios_p* argument points.

This function returns exactly the value in the **termios** data structure, without interpretation.

RETURN VALUE

Upon successful completion, *cfgetispeed*( ) returns a value of type **speed_t** representing the input baud rate.

ERRORS

No errors are defined.

SEE ALSO

cfgetospeed( ), *cfsetispeed*( ), *cfsetospeed*( ), *tcgetattr*( ), **<termios.h>**, the **XBD** specification, **Chapter 9**, **General Terminal Interface**.

EXAMPLE

```
/*
 * Copyright (C) ANTRIX Inc.
 */

/* cfgetispeed.c
 * This program gets the input baud rate from termios
 * structure using function cfgetispeed.
 */

#include <stdio.h>
#include <stdlib.h>
#include <unistd.h>
#include <termios.h>
#include <errno.h>

/* header file has definition #define B9600 13 for the
 * baud rate of 9600.
 */

main()
{
  speed_t cfgetispeed_value;
  struct  termios termios_p;

  fprintf (stdout,"get the input speed of stdin\n");
  ioctl (0, TCGETA, &termios_p);

  fprintf (stdout,"set the input speed of stdin\n");
  cfsetispeed (&termios_p, B9600);
```

```
        fprintf (stdout,"check the input speed of stdin\n");
        cfgetispeed_value = cfgetispeed (&termios_p);
        if ( cfgetispeed_value == B9600 ) {
            fprintf (stdout,"cfgetispeed() call successful\n");
            fprintf (stdout,"cfgetispeed_value=%d\n", cfgetispeed_value);
        }
        else {
            fprintf (stderr,"ERROR: cfgetispeed() call failed\n");
            fprintf (stderr,"ERROR: %s\n", strerror(errno));
        }
    }
```

NAME

cfgetospeed — get output baud rate

SYNOPSIS

```
#include <termios.h>

speed_t cfgetospeed(const struct termios *termios_p);
```

DESCRIPTION

The *cfgetospeed*( ) function extracts the output baud rate from the **termios** structure to which the *termios_p* argument points.

This function returns exactly the value in the **termios** data structure, without interpretation.

RETURN VALUE

Upon successful completion, *cfgetospeed*( ) returns a value of type **speed_t** representing the output baud rate.

ERRORS

No errors are defined.

SEE ALSO

cfgetispeed( ), *cfsetispeed*( ), *cfsetospeed*( ), *tcgetattr*( ), **<termios.h>**, the **XBD** specification, **Chapter 9**, **General Terminal Interface**.

EXAMPLE

```
/*
 * Copyright (C) ANTRIX Inc.
 */

/* cfgetospeed.c
 * This program gets the output baud rate from the termios
 * structure using function cfgetospeed.
 */

#include <stdio.h>
#include <stdlib.h>
#include <unistd.h>
#include <termios.h>
#include <errno.h>

/* header file has definition #define B9600 13 for the
 * baud rate of 9600.
 */

main()
{
  speed_t cfgetospeed_value;
  struct  termios termios_p;

  fprintf (stdout,"get the output speed of stdout\n");
  ioctl (1, TCGETA, &termios_p);

  fprintf (stdout,"set the output speed of stdout\n");
  cfsetospeed (&termios_p, B9600);
```

```
      fprintf (stdout,"check the output speed of stdout\n");
      cfgetospeed_value = cfgetospeed (&termios_p);
      if ( cfgetospeed_value == B9600 ) {
          fprintf (stdout,"cfgetospeed() call successful\n");
          fprintf (stdout,"cfgetospeed_value=%d\n", cfgetospeed_value);
      }
      else {
          fprintf (stderr,"ERROR: cfgetospeed() call failed\n");
          fprintf (stderr,"ERROR: %s\n", strerror(errno));
      }
  }
```

NAME

cfsetispeed — set input baud rate

SYNOPSIS

```
#include <termios.h>

int cfsetispeed(struct termios *termios_p, speed_t speed);
```

DESCRIPTION

The *cfsetispeed*( ) function sets the input baud rate stored in the structure pointed to by *termios_p* to *speed*.

There is no effect on the baud rates set in the hardware until a subsequent successful call to *tcsetattr*( ) on the same **termios** structure.

RETURN VALUE

EX   Upon successful completion, *cfsetispeed*( ) returns 0. Otherwise −1 is returned, and *errno* may be set to indicate the error.

ERRORS

The *cfsetispeed*( ) function may fail if:

EX   [EINVAL]   The *speed* value is not a valid baud rate.

UX   [EINVAL]   The value of *speed* is outside the range of possible speed values as specified in **<termios.h>**.

SEE ALSO

cfgetispeed( ), *cfgetospeed*( ), *cfsetospeed*( ), *tcsetattr*( ), **<termios.h>**, the **XBD** specification, **Chapter 9, General Terminal Interface**.

EXAMPLE

```
/*
 * Copyright (C) ANTRIX Inc.
 */

/* cfsetispeed.c
 * This program sets the input baud rate stored in the structure
 * pointed to by termios_p using function cfsetispeed.
 */

#include <stdio.h>
#include <unistd.h>
#include <termios.h>
#include <errno.h>

/* header file has definition #define B9600 13 for the
 * baud rate of 9600.
 */

main()
{
   int     cfsetispeed_value;
   struct  termios termios_p;
   speed_t cfgetispeed_value;

   fprintf (stdout,"get the input speed of stdin\n");
```

```
        ioctl (0, TCGETA, &termios_p);

        fprintf (stdout,"set the input speed of stdin\n");
        cfsetispeed_value = cfsetispeed (&termios_p, B9600);

        if ( cfsetispeed_value == 0) {
            fprintf (stdout,"cfsetispeed() call successful\n");
            cfgetispeed_value = cfgetispeed (&termios_p);
            fprintf (stdout,"cfgetispeed_value=%d\n", cfgetispeed_value );
        }
        else {
            fprintf (stderr,"ERROR: cfsetispeed() call failed\n");
            fprintf (stderr,"ERROR: %s\n", strerror(errno));
        }
    }
```

NAME

cfsetospeed — set output baud rate

SYNOPSIS

```
#include <termios.h>

int cfsetospeed(struct termios *termios_p, speed_t speed);
```

DESCRIPTION

The *cfsetospeed*( ) function sets the output baud rate stored in the structure pointed to by *termios_p* to *speed.*

There is no effect on the baud rates set in the hardware until a subsequent successful call to *tcsetattr*( ) on the same **termios** structure.

RETURN VALUE

EX   Upon successful completion, *cfsetospeed*( ) returns 0. Otherwise it returns −1 and *errno* may be set to indicate the error.

ERRORS

The *cfsetospeed*( ) function may fail if:

EX   [EINVAL]   The *speed* value is not a valid baud rate.

UX   [EINVAL]   The value of *speed* is outside the range of possible speed values as specified in **<termios.h>**.

SEE ALSO

cfgetispeed( ), *cfgetospeed*( ), *cfsetispeed*( ), *tcsetattr*( ), **<termios.h>**, the **XBD** specification, **Chapter 9**, **General Terminal Interface**.

EXAMPLE

```
/*
 * Copyright (C) ANTRIX Inc.
 */

/* cfsetospeed.c
 * This program sets the output baud rate stored in the structure
 * pointed to by termios_p using function cfsetospeed.
 */

#include <stdio.h>
#include <stdlib.h>
#include <unistd.h>
#include <termios.h>
#include <errno.h>

/* header file has definition #define B9600 13 for the
 * baud rate of 9600.
 */

main()
{
    int     cfsetospeed_value;
    struct  termios termios_p;
    speed_t cfgetospeed_value;
```

```
        fprintf (stdout,"get the output speed of stdout\n");
        ioctl (1, TCGETA, &termios_p);

        fprintf (stdout,"set the output speed of stdout\n");
        cfsetospeed_value = cfsetospeed (&termios_p, B9600);
        if ( cfsetospeed_value == 0 ) {
            fprintf (stdout,"cfsetospeed() call successful\n");
            cfgetospeed_value = cfgetospeed (&termios_p);
            fprintf (stdout,"cfgetospeed_value=%d\n", cfgetospeed_value);
        }
        else {
            fprintf (stderr,"ERROR: cfsetospeed() call failed\n");
            fprintf (stderr,"ERROR: %s\n", strerror(errno));
        }
    }
```

NAME

chdir — change working directory

SYNOPSIS

```
#include <unistd.h>

int chdir(const char *path);
```

DESCRIPTION

The *chdir*( ) function causes the directory named by the pathname pointed to by the *path* argument to become the current working directory; that is, the starting point for path searches for pathnames not beginning with /.

RETURN VALUE

Upon successful completion, 0 is returned. Otherwise, −1 is returned, the current working directory remains unchanged and *errno* is set to indicate the error.

ERRORS

The *chdir*( ) function will fail if:

[EACCES]　　　　Search permission is denied for any component of the pathname.

UX　[ELOOP]　　　　Too many symbolic links were encountered in resolving *path*.

[ENAMETOOLONG]

FIPS　　　　　　The *path* argument exceeds {PATH_MAX} in length or a pathname component is longer than {NAME_MAX}.

[ENOENT]　　　　A component of *path* does not name an existing directory or *path* is an empty string.

[ENOTDIR]　　　　A component of the pathname is not a directory.

The *chdir*( ) function may fail if:

UX　[ENAMETOOLONG]

　　　　　　Pathname resolution of a symbolic link produced an intermediate result whose length exceeds {PATH_MAX}.

SEE ALSO

chroot( ), *getcwd*( ), **<unistd.h>**.

EXAMPLE

```
/*
 * Copyright (C) ANTRIX Inc.
 */

/* chdir.c
 * This program changes the working directory named by path
 * to be the current working directory using function chdir.
 */

#include <stdio.h>
#include <stdlib.h>
#include <unistd.h>
#include <sys/stat.h>
#include <errno.h>

#define  PERM_ALL    (S_IRWXU | S_IRWXG | S_IRWXO)
```

```
main()
{
  int         chdir_value;
  char        curdir[255], newdir[255];
  const char *path = "testdir";

  fprintf (stdout,"get current working directory\n");
  getcwd (curdir, 255);

  fprintf (stdout,"make testdir directory\n");
  mkdir (path, PERM_ALL);

  fprintf (stdout,"change directory to testdir\n");
  chdir_value = chdir (path);
  if ( chdir_value == 0 ) {
      fprintf (stdout,"chdir() call successful\n");
      fprintf (stdout,"new directory is=%s\n", getcwd(newdir, 255) );
  }
  else {
      fprintf (stderr,"ERROR: chdir() call failed\n");
      fprintf (stderr,"ERROR: %s\n", strerror(errno));
  }

  fprintf (stdout,"change to original directory path\n");
  chdir (curdir);

  fprintf (stdout,"remove testdir directory\n");
  rmdir (path);
}
```

NAME

chmod — change mode of file

SYNOPSIS

OH
```
#include <sys/types.h>
#include <sys/stat.h>

int chmod(const char *path, mode_t mode);
```

DESCRIPTION

UX
The *chmod( )* function changes S_ISUID, S_ISGID, S_ISVTX and the file permission bits of the file named by the pathname pointed to by the *path* argument to the corresponding bits in the *mode* argument. The effective user ID of the process must match the owner of the file or the process must have appropriate privileges in order to do this.

S_ISUID, S_ISGID and the file permission bits are described in **<sys/stat.h>**.

UX
If a directory is writable and the mode bit S_ISVTX is set on the directory, a process may remove or rename files within that directory only if one or more of the following is true:

- The effective user ID of the process is the same as that of the owner ID of the file.

- The effective user ID of the process is the same as that of the owner ID of the directory.

- The process has appropriate privileges.

If the calling process does not have appropriate privileges, and if the group ID of the file does not match the effective group ID or one of the supplementary group IDs and if the file is a regular file, bit S_ISGID (set-group-ID on execution) in the file's mode will be cleared upon successful return from *chmod( )*.

Additional implementation-dependent restrictions may cause the S_ISUID and S_ISGID bits in *mode* to be ignored.

The effect on file descriptors for files open at the time of a call to *chmod( )* is implementation-dependent.

Upon successful completion, *chmod( )* will mark for update the *st_ctime* field of the file.

RETURN VALUE

Upon successful completion, 0 is returned. Otherwise, −1 is returned and *errno* is set to indicate the error. If −1 is returned, no change to the file mode will occur.

ERRORS

The *chmod( )* function will fail if:

[EACCES]   Search permission is denied on a component of the path prefix.

UX
[ELOOP]   Too many symbolic links were encountered in resolving *path*.

[ENAMETOOLONG]

FIPS
             The length of the *path* argument exceeds {PATH_MAX} or a pathname component is longer than {NAME_MAX}.

[ENOTDIR]   A component of the path prefix is not a directory.

[ENOENT]   A component of *path* does not name an existing file or *path* is an empty string.

[EPERM]   The effective user ID does not match the owner of the file and the process does not have appropriate privileges.

[EROFS]   The named file resides on a read-only file system.

The *chmod*( ) function may fail if:

UX   [EINTR]   A signal was caught during execution of the function.

EX   [EINVAL]   The value of the *mode* argument is invalid.

UX   [ENAMETOOLONG]
                         Pathname resolution of a symbolic link produced an intermediate result whose length exceeds {PATH_MAX}.

APPLICATION USAGE

In order to ensure that the S_ISUID and S_ISGID bits are set, an application requiring this should use *stat*( ) after a successful *chmod*( ) in order to verify this.

Any file descriptors currently open by any process on the file may become invalid if the mode of the file is changed to a value which would deny access to that process. One situation where this could occur is on a stateless file system.

SEE ALSO

chown( ), *mkdir*( ), *mkfifo*( ), *open*( ), *stat*( ), *statvfs*( ), **<sys/stat.h>**, **<sys/types.h>**.

EXAMPLE

```
/*
 * Copyright (C) ANTRIX Inc.
 */

/* chmod.c
 * This program changes the mode of file pointed to by path
 * from read, write and execute permissions for user, group
 * and other to read, write and execute permissions for user
 * and group only using function chmod.
 */

#include <stdio.h>
#include <stdlib.h>
#include <sys/types.h>
#include <sys/stat.h>
#include <errno.h>

#define   PERM_ALL    (S_IRWXU | S_IRWXG | S_IRWXO)
#define   PERM_SOME   (S_IRWXU | S_IRWXG )

main()
{
   int        chmod_value;
   const char *path = "testfile";
   struct stat orig_buf, new_buf;

   fprintf (stdout,"create testfile\n");
   creat (path, PERM_ALL);
   stat (path, &orig_buf);
   fprintf (stdout,"original permission mode=#0%o\n",
                   (S_IFREG ^ orig_buf.st_mode));

   fprintf (stdout,"change the permission of file\n");
   chmod_value = chmod (path, PERM_SOME);
```

```
        if ( chmod_value == 0 ) {
            fprintf (stdout,"chmod() call successful\n");
            stat (path, &new_buf);
            fprintf (stdout,"new permission mode=#0%o\n",
                     (S_IFREG ^ new_buf.st_mode));
        }
        else {
            fprintf (stderr,"ERROR: chmod() call failed\n");
            fprintf (stderr,"ERROR: %s\n", strerror(errno));
        }
        fprintf (stdout,"remove testfile\n");
        remove (path);
}
```

NAME

chown — change owner and group of a file

SYNOPSIS

OH
```
#include <sys/types.h>
#include <unistd.h>

int chown(const char *path, uid_t owner, gid_t group);
```

DESCRIPTION

The *path* argument points to a pathname naming a file. The user ID and group ID of the named file are set to the numeric values contained in *owner* and *group* respectively.

FIPS
On XSI-conformant systems {_POSIX_CHOWN_RESTRICTED} is always defined, therefore:

- Changing the user ID is restricted to processes with appropriate privileges.

- Changing the group ID is permitted to a process with an effective user ID equal to the user ID of the file, but without appropriate privileges, if and only if *owner* is equal to the file's user
EX
ID or (**uid_t**)–1 and *group* is equal either to the calling process' effective group ID or to one of its supplementary group IDs.

If the *path* argument refers to a regular file, the set-user-ID (S_ISUID) and set-group-ID (S_ISGID) bits of the file mode are cleared upon successful return from *chown*( ), unless the call is made by a process with appropriate privileges, in which case it is implementation-dependent whether these bits are altered. If *chown*( ) is successfully invoked on a file that is not a regular file, these bits may be cleared. These bits are defined in **<sys/stat.h>**.

EX
If *owner* or *group* is specified as (**uld_t**)–1 or (**gid_t**)–1 respectively, the corresponding ID of the file is unchanged.

Upon successful completion, *chown*( ) will mark for update the *st_ctime* field of the file.

RETURN VALUE

Upon successful completion, 0 is returned. Otherwise, –1 is returned and *errno* is set to indicate the error. If –1 is returned, no changes are made in the user ID and group ID of the file.

ERRORS

The *chown*( ) function will fail if:

[EACCES]   Search permission is denied on a component of the path prefix.

UX
[ELOOP]   Too many symbolic links were encountered in resolving *path*.

[ENAMETOOLONG]
FIPS
                  The length of the *path* argument exceeds {PATH_MAX} or a pathname component is longer than {NAME_MAX}.

[ENOTDIR]   A component of the path prefix is not a directory.

[ENOENT]   A component of *path* does not name an existing file or *path* is an empty string.

FIPS
[EPERM]   The effective user ID does not match the owner of the file, or the calling process does not have appropriate privileges.

[EROFS]   The named file resides on a read-only file system.

The *chown*( ) function may fail if:

UX
[EIO]   An I/O error occurred while reading or writing to the file system.

[EINTR]   The *chown*( ) function was interrupted by a signal which was caught.

[EINVAL]   The owner or group ID supplied is not a value supported by the
                 implementation.

UX   [ENAMETOOLONG]
                 Pathname resolution of a symbolic link produced an intermediate result whose
                 length exceeds {PATH_MAX}.

APPLICATION USAGE

Because {_POSIX_CHOWN_RESTRICTED} is always defined with a value other than −1 on
XSI-conformant systems, the error [EPERM] is always returned if the effective user ID does not
match the owner of the file, or the calling process does not have appropriate privileges.

SEE ALSO

chmod( ), **<sys/types.h>**, **<unistd.h>**.

EXAMPLE

```
/*
 * Copyright (C) ANTRIX Inc.
 */

/* chown.c: execute as root
 * This program changes the owner and group of a file
 * using function chown.
 */

#include <stdio.h>
#include <stdlib.h>
#include <unistd.h>
#include <sys/types.h>
#include <sys/stat.h>
#include <errno.h>

#define  PERM_ALL    (S_IRWXU | S_IRWXG | S_IRWXO)

main()
{
    int         chown_value;
    uid_t       owner = 2;
    gid_t       group = 2;
    const char  *path = "testfile";
    struct stat orig_buf, new_buf;

    fprintf (stdout,"create testfile\n");
    creat(path, PERM_ALL);
    stat (path, &orig_buf);

    fprintf (stdout,"original owner-id=%d, group-id=%d\n",
                    orig_buf.st_uid, orig_buf.st_gid);
    fprintf (stdout,"set owner-id and group-id to 2 which is bin\n");

    chown_value = chown (path, owner, group);
    if ( chown_value == 0 ) {
        fprintf (stdout,"chown() call successful\n");
        stat (path, &new_buf);
```

```
            fprintf (stdout,"new owner-id=%d, group-id=%d\n",
                    new_buf.st_uid, new_buf.st_gid );
   }
   else {
      fprintf (stderr,"ERROR: chown() call failed\n");
      fprintf (stderr,"ERROR: %s\n", strerror(errno));
   }

   fprintf (stdout,"remove testfile\n");
   remove (path);
}
```

NAME

chroot — change root directory (**TO BE WITHDRAWN**)

SYNOPSIS

EX
```
#include <unistd.h>
```

```
int chroot(const char *path);
```

DESCRIPTION

The *path* argument points to a pathname naming a directory. The *chroot*( ) function causes the named directory to become the root directory, that is the starting point for path searches for pathnames beginning with /. The process' working directory is unaffected by *chroot*( ).

The process must have appropriate privileges to change the root directory.

The dot-dot entry in the root directory is interpreted to mean the root directory itself. Thus, dot-dot cannot be used to access files outside the subtree rooted at the root directory.

RETURN VALUE

Upon successful completion, 0 is returned. Otherwise, –1 is returned and *errno* is set to indicate the error. If –1 is returned, no change is made in the root directory.

ERRORS

The *chroot*( ) function will fail if:

[EACCES]   Search permission is denied for a component of *path*.

UX   [ELOOP]   Too many symbolic links were encountered in resolving *path*.

[ENAMETOOLONG]
                    The length of the *path* argument exceeds {PATH_MAX} or a pathname component is longer than {NAME_MAX}.

[ENOENT]   A component of *path* does not name an existing directory or *path* is an empty string.

[ENOTDIR]   A component of the *path* name is not a directory.

[EPERM]   The effective user ID does not have appropriate privileges.

The *chroot*( ) function may fail if:

UX   [ENAMETOOLONG]
                    Pathname resolution of a symbolic link produced an intermediate result whose length exceeds {PATH_MAX}.

APPLICATION USAGE

There is no portable use that an application could make of this interface. It is therefore marked TO BE WITHDRAWN.

SEE ALSO

chdir( ), **<unistd.h>**.

EXAMPLE

```
/*
 * Copyright (C) ANTRIX Inc.
 */

/* chroot.c
 * This program causes the named directory to be the
 * current root directory using function chroot.
```

```
 */

#include <stdio.h>
#include <stdlib.h>
#include <limits.h>
#include <errno.h>

#define    PATH_LEN    255

main()
{
  int     chroot_value;
  char    path[PATH_LEN];
  char    newroot[PATH_LEN];

  memset(path, ' ', PATH_LEN);
  memset(newroot, ' ', PATH_LEN);

  fprintf(stdout, "get current directory\n");
  getcwd(path, PATH_LEN);

  fprintf (stdout,"change the root directory to current\n");
  fprintf (stdout,"working directory\n");
  chroot_value = chroot (path);
  if ( chroot_value != 0 ) {
     fprintf (stdout,"chroot() call successful\n");
     fprintf (stdout,"new root directory is=%s\n",
                     getcwd(newroot, PATH_LEN) );
  }
  else {
     fprintf (stderr,"ERROR: chroot() call failed\n");
     fprintf (stderr,"ERROR: %s\n", strerror(errno));
  }
}
```

NAME

clearerr — clear indicators on a stream

SYNOPSIS

```
#include <stdio.h>

void clearerr(FILE *stream);
```

DESCRIPTION

The *clearerr*( ) function clears the end-of-file and error indicators for the stream to which *stream* points.

RETURN VALUE

The *clearerr*( ) function returns no value.

ERRORS

No errors are defined.

SEE ALSO

<stdio.h>.

EXAMPLE

```
/*
 * Copyright (C) ANTRIX Inc.
 */

/* clearerr.c
 * This program clears error indicator eof for the stream
 * using function clearerr.
 */

#include <stdio.h>
#include <stdlib.h>
#include <string.h>
#include <errno.h>

main()
{
  int   i, err_value;
  char  *errmsg;
  char  *path = "testfile";
  FILE  *stream;

  fprintf (stdout,"set the regular file size limit\n");
  fprintf (stdout,"of the process to 2\n");
  ulimit (2, 2L);

  fprintf (stdout,"open a testfile\n");
  stream = fopen (path, "w");

  fprintf (stdout,"try and write 10000 characters\n");
  fprintf (stdout,"generate eof error\n");
  for ( i = 0; i < 10000; i++ )
      if ( fwrite("a", 1, 1, stream) != 1 )
          break;
```

```
        fprintf (stdout,"check error was generated\n");
        err_value = ferror (stream);
        errmsg = strerror (errno);
        fprintf (stderr,"ERROR: %s\n", errmsg );

        fprintf (stdout,"clear the error\n");
        clearerr (stream);

        err_value = ferror (stream);
        fprintf (stdout,"error is cleared err_value=%d\n", err_value);
        fprintf (stdout,"remove testfile\n");
        remove (path);
}
```

NAME

clock — report CPU time used

SYNOPSIS

```
#include <time.h>

clock_t clock(void);
```

DESCRIPTION

The *clock*( ) function returns the implementation's best approximation to the processor time used by the process since the beginning of an implementation-dependent time related only to the process invocation.

RETURN VALUE

EX

To determine the time in seconds, the value returned by *clock*( ) should be divided by the value of the macro CLOCKS_PER_SEC. CLOCKS_PER_SEC is defined to be one million in **<time.h>**. If the processor time used is not available or its value cannot be represented, the function returns the value (**clock_t**)–1.

ERRORS

No errors are defined.

SEE ALSO

asctime( ), *ctime*( ), *difftime*( ), *gmtime*( ), *localtime*( ), *mktime*( ), *strftime*( ), *strptime*( ), *time*( ), *utime*( ), **<time.h>**.

APPLICATION USAGE

In order to measure the time spent in a program, *clock*( ) should be called at the start of the program and its return value subtracted from the value returned by subsequent calls. The value returned by *clock*( ) is defined for compatibility across systems that have clocks with different resolutions. The resolution on any particular system may not be to microsecond accuracy.

The value returned by *clock*( ) may wrap around on some systems. For example, on a machine with 32-bit values for **clock_t**, it will wrap after 2147 seconds or 36 minutes.

EXAMPLE

```
/*
 * Copyright (C) ANTRIX Inc.
 */

/* clock.c
 * This program reports CPU time used using function clock.
 */

#include <stdio.h>
#include <stdlib.h>
#include <time.h>
#include <errno.h>

main()
{
  clock_t  clock_value;
  time_t   t;

  fprintf (stdout,"clock returns the amount of\n");
  fprintf (stdout,"CPU time (in microseconds)\n");
  fprintf (stdout,"used since the first call to clock\n");
```

```
        t = time ((clock_t *)0) + 10L;

    for ( clock_value = 0; t > time ((time_t *) 0) && !clock_value; )
        if ( (clock_value = clock()) < 0)
            fprintf (stdout, "ERROR: negative return value from clock");

    fprintf (stdout,"CPU time used in microseconds=%d\n", clock_value);
}
```

NAME

close — close a file descriptor

SYNOPSIS

```
#include <unistd.h>

int close(int fildes);
```

DESCRIPTION

The *close( )* function will deallocate the file descriptor indicated by *fildes*. To deallocate means to make the file descriptor available for return by subsequent calls to *open( )* or other functions that allocate file descriptors. All outstanding record locks owned by the process on the file associated with the file descriptor will be removed (that is, unlocked).

If *close( )* is interrupted by a signal that is to be caught, it will return –1 with *errno* set to [EINTR] and the state of *fildes* is unspecified.

When all file descriptors associated with a pipe or FIFO special file are closed, any data remaining in the pipe or FIFO will be discarded.

When all file descriptors associated with an open file description have been closed the open file description will be freed.

If the link count of the file is 0, when all file descriptors associated with the file are closed, the space occupied by the file will be freed and the file will no longer be accessible.

UX   If a STREAMS-based *fildes* is closed and the calling process was previously registered to receive a SIGPOLL signal for events associated with that STREAM, the calling process will be unregistered for events associated with the STREAM. The last *close( )* for a STREAM causes the STREAM associated with *fildes* to be dismantled. If O_NONBLOCK is not set and there have been no signals posted for the STREAM, and if there is data on the module's write queue, *close( )* waits for an unspecified time (for each module and driver) for any output to drain before dismantling the STREAM. The time delay can be changed via an I_SETCLTIME *ioctl( )* request. If the O_NONBLOCK flag is set, or if there are any pending signals, *close( )* does not wait for output to drain, and dismantles the STREAM immediately.

If the implementation supports STREAMS-based pipes, and *fildes* is associated with one end of a pipe, the last *close( )* causes a hangup to occur on the other end of the pipe. In addition, if the other end of the pipe has been named by *fattach( )*, then the last *close( )* forces the named end to be detached by *fdetach( )*. If the named end has no open file descriptors associated with it and gets detached, the STREAM associated with that end is also dismantled.

If *fildes* refers to the master side of a pseudo-terminal, a SIGHUP signal is sent to the process group, if any, for which the slave side of the pseudo-terminal is the controlling terminal. It is unspecified whether closing the master side of the pseudo-terminal flushes all queued input and output.

If *fildes* refers to the slave side of a STREAMS-based pseudo-terminal, a zero-length message may be sent to the master.

RETURN VALUE

Upon successful completion, 0 is returned. Otherwise, –1 is returned and *errno* is set to indicate the error.

ERRORS

The *close( )* function will fail if:

[EBADF]   The *fildes* argument is not a valid file descriptor.

[EINTR]   The *close*( ) function was interrupted by a signal.

UX   The *close*( ) function may fail if:

[EIO]   An I/O error occurred while reading from or writing to the file system.

APPLICATION USAGE

An application that had used the *stdio* routine *fopen*( ) to open a file should use the corresponding *fclose*( ) routine rather than *close*( ).

SEE ALSO

fattach( ), *fclose*( ), *fdetach*( ), *fopen*( ), *ioctl*( ), *open*( ), **<unistd.h>**, **XSH** specification, **Section 2.5**, **STREAMS**.

EXAMPLE

```
/*
 * Copyright (C) ANTRIX Inc.
 */

/* close.c
 * This program opens a file and then closes file in example 1
 * part of the program. In example 2 part of the program, it
 * reads data from an existing file and closes file using
 * function close.
 */

#include <stdio.h>
#include <stdlib.h>
#include <fcntl.h>
#include <sys/stat.h>
#include <errno.h>

#define  PERM_ALL   (S_IRWXU | S_IRWXG | S_IRWXO)

main()
{
    int   close_value;
    int   fildes, length, bytes;
    char  *buf;
    char  *path = "testfile";
    char  *string = "hello world";

    fprintf (stdout,"example 1\n");
    fprintf (stdout,"create a new file\n");
    fprintf (stdout,"and open for read, write and execute\n");
    fildes = open (path, O_CREAT, PERM_ALL);
    fprintf (stdout,"close testfile\n");
    close_value = close (fildes);
    if ( close_value == 0 ) {
        fprintf (stdout,"close() call successful\n");
        fprintf (stdout,"testfile closed successfully\n");
    }
    else {
        fprintf (stderr,"ERROR: close() call failed\n");
        fprintf (stderr,"ERROR: %s\n", strerror(errno));
```

```
    }
    fprintf (stdout,"remove testfile\n");
    remove (path);

    fprintf (stdout,"example 2\n");
    fprintf (stdout,"open an existing file for reading\n");

    length = strlen(string);
    fprintf (stdout,"create testfile\n");
    fildes = creat (path, PERM_ALL);
    fprintf (stdout,"write string\n");
    bytes = write (fildes, string, length);
    if (bytes != length)
        fprintf (stderr,"ERROR: unable to write in file\n");
    fprintf (stdout,"close testfile\n");
    close (fildes);

    fprintf (stdout,"open testfile for read only\n");
    fildes = open (path, O_RDONLY);
    buf = (char *)malloc (length);
    fprintf (stdout,"read string\n");
    bytes = read (fildes, buf, length );
    if (bytes == length)
        fprintf (stdout,"the string read is=%s\n", buf);
    else {
        fprintf (stderr,"ERROR: unable to read file\n");
        fprintf (stderr,"ERROR: %s\n", strerror(errno));
    }

    close (fildes);
    fprintf (stdout,"remove testfile\n");
    remove (path);
}
```

NAME

closedir — close a directory stream

SYNOPSIS

OH
```
#include <sys/types.h>
#include <dirent.h>

int closedir(DIR *dirp);
```

DESCRIPTION

The *closedir*( ) function closes the directory stream referred to by the argument *dirp*. Upon return, the value of *dirp* may no longer point to an accessible object of the type **DIR**. If a file descriptor is used to implement type **DIR**, that file descriptor will be closed.

RETURN VALUE

Upon successful completion, *closedir*( ) returns 0. Otherwise, −1 is returned and *errno* is set to indicate the error.

ERRORS

The *closedir*( ) function may fail if:

[EBADF]   The *dirp* argument does not refer to an open directory stream.

EX   [EINTR]   The *closedir*( ) function was interrupted by a signal.

SEE ALSO

opendir( ), **<dirent.h>**, **<sys/types.h>**.

EXAMPLE

```
/*
 * Copyright (C) ANTRIX Inc.
 */

/* closedir.c
 * This program closes a directory stream referred to by
 * the argument dirp using function closedir.
 */

#include <stdio.h>
#include <stdlib.h>
#include <sys/types.h>
#include <dirent.h>
#include <sys/stat.h>
#include <errno.h>

#define  PERM_ALL    (S_IRWXU | S_IRWXG | S_IRWXO)

main()
{
    int     i, closedir_value;
    char    *root  = "testdir";
    char    *leaf  = "testdir/subdir";
    struct  dirent *dirent_save;
    DIR     *dirp;

    fprintf (stdout,"make test directories\n");
    mkdir (root, PERM_ALL);
```

```
        mkdir (leaf, PERM_ALL);

        fprintf (stdout,"open testdir directory\n");
        dirp = opendir (root);

        fprintf (stdout,"directory names in testdir are:\n");
        for ( i = 0; i < 3; i++ ) {
            dirent_save = readdir (dirp);
            fprintf (stdout,"%s\n", dirent_save->d_name);
        }

        fprintf (stdout,"close directory\n");
        closedir_value = closedir (dirp);

        if ( closedir_value == 0 )
            fprintf (stdout,"closedir() call successful\n");
        else {
            fprintf (stderr,"ERROR: closedir() call failed\n");
            fprintf (stderr,"ERROR: %s\n", strerror(errno));
        }

        fprintf (stdout,"remove test directories\n");
        rmdir (leaf);
        rmdir (root);
}
```

NAME

closelog, openlog, setlogmask, syslog — control system log

SYNOPSIS

UX   `#include <syslog.h>`

`void closelog(void);`

`void openlog(const char *ident, int logopt, int facility);`

`int setlogmask(int maskpri);`

`void syslog(int priority, const char *message, ... /* arguments */);`

DESCRIPTION

The *syslog*( ) function sends a message to a logging facility, which logs it in an appropriate system log, writes it to the system console, forwards it to a list of users, or forwards it to the logging facility on another host over the network. The logged message includes a message header and a message body. The message header consists of a facility indicator, a severity level indicator, a timestamp, a tag string, and optionally the process ID.

The message body is generated from the *message* and following arguments in the same manner as if these were arguments to *printf*( ), except that occurrences of %m in the format string pointed to by the *message* argument are replaced by the error message string associated with the current value of *errno*. A trailing newline character is added if needed.

Values of the *priority* argument are formed by OR'ing together a severity level value and an optional facility value. If no facility value is specified, the current default facility value is used.

Possible values of severity level include:

LOG_EMERG   A panic condition. This is normally broadcast to each login.

LOG_ALERT   A condition that should be corrected immediately, such as a corrupted system database.

LOG_CRIT   Critical conditions, such as hard device errors.

LOG_ERR   Errors.

LOG_WARNING

                 Warning messages.

LOG_NOTICE   Conditions that are not error conditions, but that may require special handling.

LOG_INFO   Informational messages.

LOG_DEBUG   Messages that contain information normally of use only when debugging a program.

The facility indicates the application or system component generating the message. Possible facility values include:

LOG_USER   Messages generated by random processes. This is the default facility identifier if none is specified.

LOG_LOCAL0   Reserved for local use.

LOG_LOCAL1   Reserved for local use.

LOG_LOCAL2   Reserved for local use.

LOG_LOCAL3   Reserved for local use.

LOG_LOCAL4   Reserved for local use.

LOG_LOCAL5   Reserved for local use.

LOG_LOCAL6   Reserved for local use.

LOG_LOCAL7   Reserved for local use.

The *openlog( )* function sets process attributes that affect subsequent calls to *syslog( )*. The *ident* argument is a string that is prepended to every message. The *logopt* argument indicates logging options. Values for *logopt* are constructed by a bitwise-inclusive OP of zero or more of the following:

LOG_PID   Log the process ID with each message. This is useful for identifying specific processes.

LOG_CONS   Write messages to the system console if they cannot be sent to the logging facility. This option is safe to use in processes that have no controlling terminal, since *syslog( )* forks before opening the console.

LOG_NDELAY   Open the connection to the logging facility immediately. Normally the open is delayed until the first message is logged. This is useful for programs that need to manage the order in which file descriptors are allocated.

LOG_ODELAY   Delay open until *syslog( )* is called.

LOG_NOWAIT   Do not wait for child processes that have been forked to log messages onto the console. This option should be used by processes that enable notification of child termination using SIGCHLD, since *syslog( )* may otherwise block waiting for a child whose exit status has already been collected.

The *facility* argument encodes a default facility to be assigned to all messages that do not have an explicit facility already encoded. The initial default facility is LOG_USER.

The *openlog( )* and *syslog( )* functions may allocate a file descriptor. It is not necessary to call *openlog( )* prior to calling *syslog( )*.

The *closelog( )* function closes any open file descriptors allocated by previous calls to *openlog( )* or *syslog( )*.

The *setlogmask( )* function sets the log priority mask for the current process to *maskpri* and returns the previous mask. If the *maskpri* argument is 0, the current log mask is not modified. Calls by the current process to *syslog( )* with a priority not set in *maskpri* are rejected. The mask for an individual priority *pri* is calculated by the macro LOG_MASK(*pri*); the mask for all priorities up to and including *toppri* is given by the macro LOG_UPTO(*toppri*). The default log mask allows all priorities to be logged.

Symbolic constants for use as values of the *logopt*, *facility*, *priority*, and *maskpri* arguments are defined in the **<syslog.h>** header.

RETURN VALUE

The *setlogmask( )* function returns the previous log priority mask. The *closelog( )*, *openlog( )* and *syslog( )* functions return no value.

ERRORS

No errors are defined.

SEE ALSO

printf( ), **<syslog.h>**.

NAME

compile — produce compiled regular expression (**TO BE WITHDRAWN**)

SYNOPSIS

EX
```
#include <regexp.h>

char *compile(char *instring, char *expbuf, const char *endbuf, int eof);
```

DESCRIPTION

Refer to *regexp*( ).

EXAMPLE

```c
/*
 * Copyright (C) ANTRIX Inc.
 */

/* compile.c
 * This program takes an input a regular expression and
 * produces a compiled expression using function compile.
 */

#include <stdio.h>
#include <stdlib.h>
#include <errno.h>

#define STRSIZE 100

char instring[STRSIZE];
char *value = "True";

#define     INIT        register char *sp = instring;
#define     GETC()      (*sp++)
#define     PEEKC()     (*sp)
#define     UNGETC(c)   (--sp)
#define     RETURN(c)   return((char *)value)
#define     ERROR(c)    comperr()
#include    <regexp.h>

extern char *loc1, *loc2, *locs;

main()
{
    int    advance_value;
    char   *compile_value;
    char string[10*STRSIZE];
    char expbuf[STRSIZE];

    strcpy(instring, "^T");
    strcpy(string, "This is a test line");

    fprintf(stdout, "Produce compiled expression\n");
    compile_value = compile(instring, expbuf, &expbuf[STRSIZE], ' ');
    if (compile_value != (char *)0)
        fprintf(stdout, "compile_value=%s\n", compile_value);
```

```
    else {
        fprintf(stderr, "ERORR: compile call failed\n");
        fprintf(stderr, "ERORR: compile_value=%s\n", compile_value);
    }

    fprintf(stdout, "Match string beginning with T\n");
    advance_value = advance(string, expbuf);
    if (advance_value != 0) {
        fprintf(stdout, "advance call successful\n");
        fprintf(stdout, "advance_value=%d\n", advance_value);
    }
    else {
        fprintf(stderr, "ERROR: advance call failed\n");
        fprintf(stderr, "%d\n", advance_value);
    }
}

comperr()
{ }
```

NAME

confstr — get configurable variables

SYNOPSIS

```
#include <unistd.h>

size_t confstr(int name, char *buf, size_t len);
```

DESCRIPTION

The *confstr( )* function provides a method for applications to get configuration-defined string values. Its use and purpose are similar to *sysconf( )*, but it is used where string values rather than numeric values are returned.

The *name* argument represents the system variable to be queried. The implementation supports the *name* value of _CS_PATH, defined in **<unistd.h>**. It may support others.

If *len* is not 0, and if *name* has a configuration-defined value, *confstr( )* copies that value into the *len*-byte buffer pointed to by *buf*. If the string to be returned is longer than *len* bytes, including the terminating null, then *confstr( )* truncates the string to *len*–1 bytes and null-terminates the result. The application can detect that the string was truncated by comparing the value returned by *confstr( )* with *len*.

If *len* is 0 and *buf* is a null pointer, then *confstr( )* still returns the integer value as defined below, but does not return a string. If *len* is 0 but *buf* is not a null pointer, the result is unspecified.

RETURN VALUE

If *name* has a configuration-defined value, *confstr( )* returns the size of buffer that would be needed to hold the entire configuration-defined value. If this return value is greater than *len*, the string returned in *buf* is truncated.

If *name* is invalid, *confstr( )* returns 0 and sets *errno* to indicate the error.

If *name* does not have a configuration-defined value, *confstr( )* returns 0 and leaves *errno* unchanged.

ERRORS

The *confstr( )* function will fail if:

[EINVAL]   The value of the *name* argument is invalid.

APPLICATION USAGE

An application can distinguish between an invalid *name* parameter value and one that corresponds to a configurable variable that has no configuration-defined value by checking if *errno* is modified. This mirrors the behaviour of *sysconf( )*.

The original need for this function was to provide a way of finding the configuration-defined default value for the environment variable *PATH*. Since *PATH* can be modified by the user to include directories that could contain utilities replacing **XCU** specification standard utilities, applications need a way to determine the system-supplied *PATH* environment variable value that contains the correct search path for the standard utilities.

An application could use:

```
confstr(name, (char *)NULL, (size_t)0)
```

to find out how big a buffer is needed for the string value; use *malloc( )* to allocate a buffer to hold the string; and call *confstr( )* again to get the string. Alternately, it could allocate a fixed, static buffer that is big enough to hold most answers (perhaps 512 or 1024 bytes), but then use *malloc( )* to allocate a larger buffer if it finds that this is too small.

SEE ALSO

pathconf( ), *sysconf*( ), **<unistd.h>**, **<regexp.h>**, the **XCU** specification.

EXAMPLE

```
/*
 * Copyright (C) ANTRIX Inc.
 */

/* confstr.c
 * This program gets the configuration defined string
 * for _SC_ARG_MAX using function confstr.
 */

#include <stdio.h>
#include <stdlib.h>
#include <unistd.h>
#include <errno.h>

main()
{
   size_t  confstr_value;
   int     i;
   char    buf[512];

   fprintf (stdout,"get value of _CS_PATH\n");
   confstr_value = confstr (_CS_PATH, buf, 512);
   if ( confstr_value > 0 ) {
       fprintf (stdout,"confstr() call successful\n");
       fprintf (stdout,"confstr_value=%d\n", confstr_value );
       fprintf (stdout,"string is=%s\n", buf);
   }
   else {
       fprintf (stderr,"ERROR: confstr() call failed\n");
       fprintf (stderr,"ERROR: %s\n", strerror(errno));
   }
}
```

NAME

cos — cosine function

SYNOPSIS

```
#include <math.h>

double cos(double x);
```

DESCRIPTION

The *cos*( ) function computes the cosine of *x*, measured in radians.

RETURN VALUE

Upon successful completion, *cos*( ) returns the cosine of *x*.

EX   If *x* is NaN, NaN is returned and *errno* may be set to [EDOM].

EX   If *x* is ±Inf, either 0 is returned and *errno* is set to [EDOM], or NaN is returned and *errno* may be set to [EDOM].

If the result underflows, 0 is returned and *errno* may be set to [ERANGE].

ERRORS

The *cos*( ) function may fail if:

EX   [EDOM]   The value of *x* is NaN or *x* is ±Inf.

[ERANGE]   The result underflows.

EX   No other errors will occur.

APPLICATION USAGE

An application wishing to check for error situations should set *errno* to 0 before calling *cos*( ). If *errno* is non-zero on return, or the returned value is NaN, an error has occurred.

The *cos*( ) function may lose accuracy when its argument is far from 0.

SEE ALSO

acos( ), *isnan*( ), *sin*( ), *tan*( ), **<math.h>**.

EXAMPLE

```
/*
 * Copyright (C) ANTRIX Inc.
 */

/* cos.c
 * This program computes the cosine of 0.50, measured in
 * radians using function cos.
 */

#include <stdio.h>
#include <math.h>

main()
{
  double  cos_value;
  double  x   = 0.50;
```

```
    cos_value = cos (x);
    fprintf (stdout,"cos of %f is %f\n", x, cos_value);
}
```

NAME

cosh — hyperbolic cosine function

SYNOPSIS

```
#include <math.h>

double cosh(double x);
```

DESCRIPTION

The *cosh*( ) function computes the hyperbolic cosine of *x*.

RETURN VALUE

Upon successful completion, *cosh*( ) returns the hyperbolic cosine of *x*.

If the result would cause an overflow, HUGE_VAL is returned and *errno* is set to [ERANGE].

EX   If *x* is NaN, NaN is returned and *errno* may be set to [EDOM].

ERRORS

The *cosh*( ) function will fail if:

[ERANGE]   The result would cause an overflow.

The *cosh*( ) function may fail if:

EX   [EDOM]   The value of *x* is NaN.

EX   No other errors will occur.

APPLICATION USAGE

An application wishing to check for error situations should set *errno* to 0 before calling *cosh*( ). If *errno* is non-zero on return, or the returned value is NaN, an error has occurred.

SEE ALSO

acosh( ), *isnan*( ), *sinh*( ), *tanh*( ), **<math.h>**.

EXAMPLE

```
/*
 * Copyright (C) ANTRIX Inc.
 */

/* cosh.c
 * This program computes the hyperbolic cosine of 0.50
 * using function cosh.
 */

#include <stdio.h>
#include <math.h>

main()
{
  double  cosh_value;
  double  x = 0.50;

  cosh_value = cosh (x);
  fprintf (stdout,"cosh of %f is %f\n", x, cosh_value);
}
```

NAME

creat — create a new file or rewrite an existing one

SYNOPSIS

OH
```
#include <sys/types.h>
#include <sys/stat.h>
#include <fcntl.h>

int creat(const char *path, mode_t mode);
```

DESCRIPTION

The function call:

```
creat(path, mode)
```

is equivalent to:

```
open(path, O_WRONLY|O_CREAT|O_TRUNC, mode)
```

RETURN VALUE

Refer to *open*( ).

ERRORS

Refer to *open*( ).

SEE ALSO

open( ), **<fcntl.h>**, **<sys/stat.h>**, **<sys/types.h>**.

EXAMPLE

```
/*
 * Copyright (C) ANTRIX Inc.
 */

/* creat.c
 * This program creates a new file using function creat.
 */

#include <stdio.h>
#include <stdlib.h>
#include <unistd.h>
#include <fcntl.h>
#include <sys/stat.h>
#include <errno.h>

#define  PERM_ALL    (S_IRWXU | S_IRWXG | S_IRWXO)

main()
{
  int    fildes;
  int    bytes, length;
  char   *buf;
  const  char *path = "testfile";
  char   *string = "hello world";

  length = strlen(string);
  fprintf (stdout,"create testfile\n");
```

```
        fildes = creat (path, PERM_ALL);
        /* stdin is 0, stdout is 1, stderr is 2 */
        if ( fildes > 2 )
            fprintf (stdout,"creat() call created testfile\n");
        else {
            fprintf (stderr,"ERROR: creat() call failed\n");
            fprintf (stderr,"ERROR: %s\n", strerror(errno));
        }

        fprintf (stdout,"write string\n");
        write (fildes, string, length);
        fprintf (stdout,"close testfile\n");
        close (fildes);

        fprintf (stdout,"open testfile\n");
        fildes = open (path, O_RDONLY);
        buf = (char *)malloc (length);

        fprintf (stdout,"read string\n");
        bytes = read (fildes, buf, length);

        fprintf (stdout,"string in buf=%s\n", buf);
        fprintf (stdout,"number of bytes read=%d\n", bytes);
        fprintf (stdout,"remove testfile\n");
        remove (path);
    }
```

NAME

crypt — string encoding function

SYNOPSIS

EX   `#include <unistd.h>`

`char *crypt (const char *key, const char *salt);`

DESCRIPTION

The *crypt*( ) function is a string encoding function. The algorithm is implementation-dependent.

The *key* argument points to a string to be encoded. The *salt* argument is a string chosen from the set:

```
a b c d e f g h i j k l m n o p q r s t u v w x y z
A B C D E F G H I J K L M N O P Q R S T U V W X Y Z
0 1 2 3 4 5 6 7 8 9 . /
```

The first two characters of this string may be used to perturb the encoding algorithm.

RETURN VALUE

Upon successful completion, *crypt*( ) returns a pointer to the encoded string. The first two characters of the returned value are those of the *salt* argument.

Otherwise it returns a null pointer and sets *errno* to indicate the error.

ERRORS

The *crypt*( ) function will fail if:

[ENOSYS]   The functionality is not supported on this implementation.

APPLICATION USAGE

The return value of *crypt*( ) points to static data that is overwritten by each call.

The values returned by this function may not be portable among XSI-conformant systems.

SEE ALSO

encrypt( ), *setkey*( ), **<unistd.h>**.

EXAMPLE

```
/*
 * Copyright (C) ANTRIX Inc.
 */

/* crypt.c
 * This program encodes the string pointed to by key
 * function crypt.
 */

#include <stdio.h>
#include <stdlib.h>
#include <unistd.h>
#include <crypt.h>
#include <errno.h>

main()
{
   int     edflag;
   char    *new_key;
```

```
    const  char *key = "hello world";
    const  char *salt = "ho";

    fprintf (stdout,"previous key string=%s\n", key);
    new_key = crypt (key, salt);
    if (new_key != (char *)0)
        fprintf (stdout,"crypt() call successful\n");
    else
        fprintf (stdout,"ERROR: crypt() call failed\n");

    fprintf (stdout,"New key string after encryption=%s\n", new_key);
}
```

NAME

ctermid — generate pathname for controlling terminal

SYNOPSIS

```
#include <stdio.h>

char *ctermid(char *s);
```

DESCRIPTION

The *ctermid*( ) function generates a string that, when used as a pathname, refers to the current controlling terminal for the current process. If *ctermid*( ) returns a pathname, access to the file is not guaranteed.

RETURN VALUE

If *s* is a null pointer, the string is generated in an area that may be static (and therefore may be overwritten by each call), the address of which is returned. Otherwise *s* is assumed to point to a character array of at least {L_ctermid} bytes; the string is placed in this array and the value of *s* is returned. The symbolic constant {L_ctermid} is defined in **<stdio.h>**, and will have a value greater than 0.

The *ctermid*( ) function will return an empty string if the pathname that would refer to the controlling terminal cannot be determined, or if the function is unsuccessful.

ERRORS

No errors are defined.

APPLICATION USAGE

The difference between *ctermid*( ) and *ttyname*( ) is that *ttyname*( ) must be handed a file descriptor and returns a path of the terminal associated with that file descriptor, while *ctermid*( ) returns a string (such as */dev/tty*) that will refer to the current controlling terminal if used as a pathname.

SEE ALSO

ttyname( ), **<stdio.h>**.

EXAMPLE

```
/*
 * Copyright (C) ANTRIX Inc.
 */

/* ctermid.c
 * This program generates a string that, when used as a
 * pathname refers to current controlling terminal using
 * function ctermid.
 */

#include <stdio.h>
#include <stdlib.h>
#include <unistd.h>
#include <errno.h>

main()
{
  char   *ctermid_value;
  char   buf[L_ctermid];

  fprintf (stdout,"example 1\n");
```

```
    fprintf (stdout,"get the pathname of the controlling terminal\n");
    fprintf (stdout,"stored in internal static area\n");

    ctermid_value = ctermid ((char *)0);
    if ( ctermid_value != (char *)0 ) {
        fprintf (stdout,"ctermid() call successful\n");
        fprintf (stdout,"controlling terminal is %s\n", ctermid_value);
    }
    else
        fprintf (stderr,"ERROR: ctermid() call failed\n");

    fprintf (stdout,"example 2\n");
    fprintf (stdout,"get the pathname of the controlling terminal\n");
    fprintf (stdout,"stored in array buf\n");

    ctermid_value = ctermid (buf);
    if ( ctermid_value != (char *)0 ) {
        fprintf (stdout,"ctermid() call successful\n");
        fprintf (stdout,"controlling terminal is %s\n", ctermid_value);
        fprintf (stdout,"controlling terminal is buf=%s\n", buf);
    }
    else
        fprintf (stderr,"ERROR: ctermid() call failed\n");
}
```

NAME

ctime — convert time value to date and time string

SYNOPSIS

```
#include <time.h>

char *ctime(const time_t *clock);
```

DESCRIPTION

The *ctime*( ) function converts the time pointed to by *clock*, representing time in seconds since the Epoch, to local time in the form of a string. It is equivalent to:

```
asctime(localtime(clock))
```

RETURN VALUE

The *ctime*( ) function returns the pointer returned by *asctime*( ) with that broken-down time as an argument.

ERRORS

No errors are defined.

APPLICATION USAGE

The *asctime*( ), *ctime*( ), *gmtime*( ) and *localtime*( ) functions return values in one of two static objects: a broken-down time structure and an array of **char**. Execution of any of the functions may overwrite the information returned in either of these objects by any of the other functions.

Values for the broken-down time structure can be obtained by calling *gmtime*( ) or *localtime*( ). This interface is included for compatibility with older implementations, and does not support localised date and time formats. Applications should use the *strftime*( ) interface to achieve maximum portability.

SEE ALSO

asctime( ), *clock*( ), *difftime*( ), *gmtime*( ), *localtime*( ), *mktime*( ), *strftime*( ), *strptime*( ), *time*( ), *utime*( ), **<time.h>**.

EXAMPLE

```
/*
 * Copyright (C) ANTRIX Inc.
 */

/* ctime.c
 * This program converts time value pointed by clock in seconds
 * to date and string using function ctime.
 */

#include <stdio.h>
#include <stdlib.h>
#include <time.h>
#include <errno.h>

main()
{
  char    *ctime_value;
  time_t  tloc, clock;

  fprintf (stdout,"get current time\n");
  clock = time (&tloc);
```

```
fprintf (stdout,"convert date and time to string\n");
ctime_value = ctime (&clock);
if ( ctime_value != (char *)0 ) {
    fprintf (stdout,"ctime() call successful\n");
    fprintf (stdout,"current date and time is %s\n", ctime_value);
}
else {
    fprintf (stderr,"ERROR: ctime() call failed\n");
    fprintf (stderr,"ERROR: %s\n", strerror(errno));
}
}
```

NAME

cuserid — character login name of the user (**TO BE WITHDRAWN**)

SYNOPSIS

EX   `#include <stdio.h>`

`char *cuserid(char *s);`

DESCRIPTION

The *cuserid*( ) function generates a character representation of the name associated with the real or effective user ID of the process.

If *s* is a null pointer, this representation is generated in an area that may be static (and thus overwritten by subsequent calls to *cuserid*( )), the address of which is returned. If *s* is not a null pointer, *s* is assumed to point to an array of at least {L_cuserid} bytes; the representation is deposited in this array. The symbolic constant {L_cuserid} is defined in **<stdio.h>** and has a value greater than 0.

RETURN VALUE

If *s* is not a null pointer, *s* is returned. If *s* is not a null pointer and the login name cannot be found, the null byte '\0' will be placed at **s*. If *s* is a null pointer and the login name cannot be found, *cuserid*( ) returns a null pointer. If *s* is a null pointer and the login name can be found, the address of a buffer (possibly static) containing the login name is returned.

ERRORS

No errors are defined.

APPLICATION USAGE

The functionality of *cuserid*( ) defined in the POSIX.1-1988 standard (and Issue 3 of this document) differs from that of historical implementations (and Issue 2 of this document). In the ISO POSIX-1 standard, *cuserid*( ) is removed completely. In this document, therefore, both functionalities are allowed, but both are also marked TO BE WITHDRAWN.

The Issue 2 functionality can be obtained by using:

```
getpwuid(getuid())
```

The Issue 3 functionality can be obtained by using:

```
getpwuid(geteuid())
```

SEE ALSO

getlogin( ), *getpwnam*( ), *getpwuid*( ), *getuid*( ), *geteuid*( ), **<stdio.h>**.

EXAMPLE

```
/*
 * Copyright (C) ANTRIX Inc.
 */

/* cuserid.c
 * This program generates a character representation of the name
 * associated with the real or effective user ID of the process
 * using function cuserid.
 */

#include <stdio.h>
#include <stdlib.h>
#include <errno.h>
```

```
main()
{
  char   *cuserid_value;
  char   s[L_cuserid];

  fprintf (stdout,"example 1\n");
  fprintf (stdout,"null argument\n");
  fprintf (stdout,"generate character-string representation\n");
  fprintf (stdout,"of the login name\n");

  cuserid_value = cuserid ((char *)0);
  if ( cuserid_value != (char *)0 ) {
     fprintf (stdout,"cuserid() call successful\n");
     fprintf (stdout,"cuserid_value=%s\n", cuserid_value );
  }
  else
     fprintf (stderr,"ERROR: cuserid() call failed\n");

  fprintf (stdout,"example 2\n");
  fprintf (stdout,"array of s\n");
  fprintf (stdout,"generate character-string representation\n");
  fprintf (stdout,"of the login name\n");

  cuserid_value = cuserid (s);
  if ( cuserid_value != (char *)0 ) {
     fprintf (stdout,"cuserid() call successful\n");
     fprintf (stdout,"cuserid_value=%s\n", cuserid_value );
  }
  else
     fprintf (stderr,"ERROR: cuserid() call failed\n");
}
```

NAME

daylight — daylight savings time flag

SYNOPSIS

EX
```
#include <time.h>

extern int daylight;
```

DESCRIPTION

Refer to *tzset*( ).

EXAMPLE

```
/*
 * Copyright (C) ANTRIX Inc.
 */

/* daylight
 * This program prints the daylight savings time flag for
 * daylight integer variable.
 */

#include <stdio.h>
#include <stdlib.h>
#include <errno.h>

extern int daylight;
extern char *tzname[2];

main()
{
  char putenv1[]  = "TZ=one4two";

  fprintf (stdout,"tzname[0]=%s\n", tzname[0] );
  fprintf (stdout,"tzname[1]=%s\n", tzname[1] );
  fprintf (stdout,"daylight=%d\n", daylight);
  putenv (putenv1);

  tzset ();
  fprintf (stdout,"tzname[0]=%s\n", tzname[0] );
  fprintf (stdout,"tzname[1]=%s\n", tzname[1] );
  fprintf (stdout,"daylight=%d\n", daylight);
}
```

NAME

dbm_clearerr, dbm_close, dbm_delete, dbm_error, dbm_fetch, dbm_firstkey, dbm_nextkey, dbm_open, dbm_store — database functions

SYNOPSIS

UX
```
#include <ndbm.h>
```
```
int dbm_clearerr(DBM *db);
```
```
void dbm_close(DBM *db);
```
```
int dbm_delete(DBM *db, datum key);
```
```
int dbm_error(DBM *db);
```
```
datum dbm_fetch(DBM *db, datum key);
```
```
datum dbm_firstkey(DBM *db);
```
```
datum dbm_nextkey(DBM *db);
```
```
DBM *dbm_open(const char *file, int open_flags, mode_t file_mode);
```
```
int dbm_store(DBM *db, datum key, datum content, int store_mode);
```

DESCRIPTION

These functions create, access and modify a database.

A **datum** consists of at least two members, **dptr** and **dsize**. The **dptr** member points to an object that is **dsize** bytes in length. Arbitrary binary data, as well as character strings, may be stored in the object pointed to by **dptr**.

The database is stored in two files. One file is a directory containing a bit map of keys and has **.dir** as its suffix. The second file contains all data and has **.pag** as its suffix.

The *dbm_open( )* function opens a database. The *file* argument to the function is the pathname of the database. The function opens two files named *file*.**dir** and *file*.**pag.** The *open_flags* argument has the same meaning as the *flags* argument of *open( )* except that a database opened for write-only access opens the files for read and write access. The *file_mode* argument has the same meaning as the third argument of *open( )*.

The *dbm_close( )* function closes a database. The argument *db* must be a pointer to a **dbm** structure that has been returned from a call to *dbm_open( )*.

The *dbm_fetch( )* function reads a record from a database. The argument *db* is a pointer to a database structure that has been returned from a call to *dbm_open( )*. The argument *key* is a **datum** that has been initialised by the application program to the value of the key that matches the key of the record the program is fetching.

The *dbm_store( )* function writes a record to a database. The argument *db* is a pointer to a database structure that has been returned from a call to *dbm_open( )*. The argument *key* is a **datum** that has been initialised by the application program to the value of the key that identifies (for subsequent reading, writing or deleting) the record the program is writing. The argument *content* is a **datum** that has been initialised by the application program to the value of the record the program is writing. The argument *store_mode* controls whether *dbm_store( )* replaces any pre-existing record that has the same key that is specified by the *key* argument. The application program must set *store_mode* to either DBM_INSERT or DBM_REPLACE. If the database contains a record that matches the *key* argument and *store_mode* is DBM_REPLACE, the existing record is replaced with the new record. If the database contains a record that matches the *key* argument and *store_mode* is DBM_INSERT, the existing record is not replaced with the new record. If the database does not contain a record that matches the *key* argument and *store_mode* is either DBM_INSERT or DBM_REPLACE, the new record is inserted in the database.

The *dbm_delete*( ) function deletes a record and its key from the database. The argument *db* is a pointer to a database structure that has been returned from a call to *dbm_open*( ). The argument *key* is a **datum** that has been initialised by the application program to the value of the key that identifies the record the program is deleting.

The *dbm_firstkey*( ) function returns the first key in the database. The argument *db* is a pointer to a database structure that has been returned from a call to *dbm_open*( ).

The *dbm_nextkey*( ) function returns the next key in the database. The argument *db* is a pointer to a database structure that has been returned from a call to *dbm_open*( ). The *dbm_firstkey*( ) function must be called before calling *dbm_nextkey*( ). Subsequent calls to *dbm_nextkey*( ) return the next key until all of the keys in the database have been returned.

The *dbm_error*( ) function returns the error condition of the database. The argument *db* is a pointer to a database structure that has been returned from a call to *dbm_open*( ).

The *dbm_clearerr*( ) function clears the error condition of the database. The argument *db* is a pointer to a database structure that has been returned from a call to *dbm_open*( ).

These database functions support key/content pairs of at least 1024 bytes.

RETURN VALUE

The *dbm_store*( ) and *dbm_delete*( ) functions return 0 when they succeed and a negative value when they fail.

The *dbm_store*( ) function returns 1 if it is called with a *flags* value of DBM_INSERT and the function finds an existing record with the same key.

The *dbm_error*( ) function returns 0 if the error condition is not set and returns a non-zero value if the error condition is set.

The return value of *dbm_clearerr*( ) is unspecified .

The *dbm_firstkey*( ) and *dbm_nextkey*( ) functions return a key **datum**. When the end of the database is reached, the **dptr** member of the key is a null pointer. If an error is detected, the **dptr** member of the key is a null pointer and the error condition of the database is set.

The *dbm_fetch*( ) function returns a content **datum**. If no record in the database matches the key or if an error condition has been detected in the database, the **dptr** member of the content is a null pointer.

The *dbm_open*( ) function returns a pointer to a database structure. If an error is detected during the operation, *dbm_open*( ) returns a (**DBM ***)0.

ERRORS

No errors are defined.

APPLICATION USAGE

The following code can be used to traverse the database:

```
for(key = dbm_firstkey(db); key.dptr != NULL; key = dbm_nextkey(db))
```

The *dbm_* functions provided in this library should not be confused in any way with those of a general-purpose database management system. These functions do not provide for multiple search keys per entry, they do not protect against multi-user access (in other words they do not lock records or files), and they do not provide the many other useful database functions that are found in more robust database management systems. Creating and updating databases by use of these functions is relatively slow because of data copies that occur upon hash collisions.

These functions are useful for applications requiring fast lookup of relatively static information that is to be indexed by a single key.

The **dptr** pointers returned by these functions may point into static storage that may be changed by subsequent calls.

The *dbm_delete*( ) function does not physically reclaim file space, although it does make it available for reuse.

After calling *dbm_store*( ) or *dbm_delete*( ) during a pass through the keys by *dbm_firstkey*( ) and *dbm_nextkey*( ), the application should reset the database by calling *dbm_firstkey*( ) before again calling *dbm_nextkey*( ).

SEE ALSO

open( ), **<ndbm.h>**.

NAME

difftime — compute the difference between two calendar time values

SYNOPSIS

```
#include <time.h>

double difftime(time_t time1, time_t time0);
```

DESCRIPTION

The *difftime*( ) function computes the difference between two calendar times (as returned by *time*( )): *time1 – time0*.

RETURN VALUE

The *difftime*( ) function returns the difference expressed in seconds as a type **double**.

ERRORS

No errors are defined.

SEE ALSO

asctime( ), *clock*( ), *ctime*( ), *gmtime*( ), *localtime*( ), *mktime*( ), *strftime*( ), *strptime*( ), *time*( ), *utime*( ), **<time.h>**.

EXAMPLE

```
/*
 * Copyright (C) ANTRIX Inc.
 */

/* difftime.c
 * This program computes the difference between two calendar
 * value using function difftime.
 */

#include <stdio.h>
#include <stdlib.h>
#include <time.h>
#include <errno.h>

main()
{
  double  difftime_value;
  time_t  time0, time1;

  fprintf (stdout,"get current time\n");
  time0 = time ((time_t *)0);

  fprintf (stdout,"sleep for 2 seconds\n");
  sleep (2);
  fprintf (stdout,"get current time after 2 seconds\n");
  time1 = time ((time_t *)0);

  fprintf (stdout,"get the difference in time\n");
  difftime_value = difftime (time1, time0);
```

```
    fprintf(stdout, "difference in time should be 2 seconds\n");
    fprintf (stdout,"difference in calendar time is %f\n", difftime_value );
}
```

NAME

dirname — report the parent directory name of a file pathname

SYNOPSIS

UX
```
#include <libgen.h>

char *dirname(char *path);
```

DESCRIPTION

The *dirname( )* function takes a pointer to a character string that contains a pathname, and returns a pointer to a string that is a pathname of the parent directory of that file. Trailing '/' characters in the path are not counted as part of the path.

If *path* does not contain a '/', then *dirname( )* returns a pointer to the string "." . If *path* is a null pointer or points to an empty string, *dirname( )* returns a pointer to the string "." .

RETURN VALUE

The *dirname( )* function returns a pointer to a string that is the parent directory of *path*. If *path* is a null pointer or points to an empty string, a pointer to a string "." is returned.

ERRORS

No errors are defined.

EXAMPLES

Input String	Output String
"/usr/lib"	"/usr"
"/usr/"	"/"
"usr"	"."
"/"	"/"
"."	"."
".."	"."

The following code fragment reads a pathname, changes the current working directory to the parent directory, and opens the file.

```
char path[MAXPATHLEN], *pathcopy;
int fd;
fgets(path, MAXPATHLEN, stdin);
pathcopy = strdup(path);
chdir(dirname(pathcopy));
fd = open(basename(path), O_RDONLY);
```

APPLICATION USAGE

The *dirname( )* function may modify the string pointed to by *path*, and may return a pointer to static storage that may then be overwritten by subsequent calls to *dirname( )*.

The *dirname( )* and *basename( )* functions together yield a complete pathname. The expression *dirname(path)* obtains the pathname of the directory where *basename(path)* is found.

SEE ALSO

basename( ), **<libgen.h>**.

EXAMPLE

```
/*
 * Copyright (C) ANTRIX Inc.
 */

/* dirname.c
 * This program delivers all but the last level of the path name
 * from the string using function dirname.
 */

#include <stdio.h>
#include <stdlib.h>
#include <libgen.h>
#include <errno.h>

main()
{
  char   *dirname_value;
  char   *path = "/user/home/ANTRIX";

  fprintf (stdout,"delete the suffix from %s", path);
  dirname_value = dirname (path);
  if ( dirname_value != (char *)0 ) {
     fprintf (stdout,"dirname() call successful\n");
     fprintf (stdout,"dirname_value = %s\n", dirname_value);
  }
  else
     fprintf (stderr,"ERROR: dirname() call failed\n");
}
```

NAME

div — compute quotient and remainder of an integer division

SYNOPSIS

```
#include <stdlib.h>

div_t div(int numer, int denom);
```

DESCRIPTION

The *div*( ) function computes the quotient and remainder of the division of the numerator *numer* by the denominator *denom*. If the division is inexact, the resulting quotient is the integer of lesser magnitude that is the nearest to the algebraic quotient. If the result cannot be represented, the behaviour is undefined; otherwise, *quot * denom + rem* will equal *numer*.

RETURN VALUE

The *div*( ) function returns a structure of type **div_t**, comprising both the quotient and the remainder. The structure includes the following members, in any order:

```
int   quot;   /* quotient */
int   rem;    /* remainder */
```

ERRORS

No errors are defined.

SEE ALSO

ldiv( ), **<stdlib.h>**.

EXAMPLE

```
/*
 * Copyright (C) ANTRIX Inc.
 */

/* div.c
 * This program computes quotient and remainder of an integer
 * division 7/2 using function div.
 */

#include <stdio.h>
#include <stdlib.h>
#include <errno.h>

main()
{
  div_t   div_value;
  int     numer = 7;
  int     denom = 2;

  fprintf (stdout,"divide %d by %d\n", numer, denom);
  div_value = div (numer, denom);

  fprintf (stdout,"quotient of %d/%d is %d\n",
                  numer, denom, div_value.quot);
  fprintf (stdout,"remainder of %d/%d is %d\n",
                  numer, denom, div_value.rem);
}
```

NAME

drand48, erand48, jrand48, lcong48, lrand48, mrand48, nrand48, seed48, srand48 — generate uniformly distributed pseudo-random numbers

SYNOPSIS

EX
```
#include <stdlib.h>
```

```
double drand48(void);
```

```
double erand48(unsigned short int xsubi[3]);
```

```
long int jrand48(unsigned short int xsubi[3]);
```

```
void lcong48(unsigned short int param[7]);
```

```
long int lrand48(void);
```

```
long int mrand48(void);
```

```
long int nrand48(unsigned short int xsubi[3]);
```

```
unsigned short int *seed48(unsigned short int seed16v[3]);
```

```
void srand48(long int seedval);
```

DESCRIPTION

This family of functions generates pseudo-random numbers using a linear congruential algorithm and 48-bit integer arithmetic.

The *drand48( )* and *erand48( )* functions return non-negative, double-precision, floating-point values, uniformly distributed over the interval $[0.0, 1.0)$.

The *lrand48( )* and *nrand48( )* functions return non-negative, long integers, uniformly distributed over the interval $[0, 2^{31})$.

The *mrand48( )* and *jrand48( )* functions return signed long integers uniformly distributed over the interval $[-2^{31}, 2^{31})$.

The *srand48( )*, *seed48( )* and *lcong48( )* are initialisation entry points, one of which should be invoked before either *drand48( )*, *lrand48( )* or *mrand48( )* is called. (Although it is not recommended practice, constant default initialiser values will be supplied automatically if *drand48( )*, *lrand48( )* or *mrand48( )* is called without a prior call to an initialisation entry point.) The *erand48( )*, *nrand48( )* and *jrand48( )* functions do not require an initialisation entry point to be called first.

All the routines work by generating a sequence of 48-bit integer values, X_i, according to the linear congruential formula:

$$X_{n+1} = (aX_n + c)_{\bmod m} \qquad n \geq 0$$

The parameter $m = 2^{48}$; hence 48-bit integer arithmetic is performed. Unless *lcong48( )* is invoked, the multiplier value a and the addend value c are given by:

$$a = 5DEECE66D_{16} = 273673163155_8$$

$$c = B_{16} = 13_8$$

The value returned by any of the *drand48( )*, *erand48( )*, *jrand48( )*, *lrand48( )*, *mrand48( )* or *nrand48( )* functions is computed by first generating the next 48-bit X_i in the sequence. Then the appropriate number of bits, according to the type of data item to be returned, are copied from the high-order (leftmost) bits of X_i and transformed into the returned value.

The *drand48*( ), *lrand48*( ) and *mrand48*( ) functions store the last 48-bit X_i generated in an internal buffer; that is why they must be initialised prior to being invoked. The *erand48*( ), *nrand48*( ) and *jrand48*( ) functions require the calling program to provide storage for the successive X_i values in the array specified as an argument when the functions are invoked. That is why these routines do not have to be initialised; the calling program merely has to place the desired initial value of X_i into the array and pass it as an argument. By using different arguments, *erand48*( ), *nrand48*( ) and *jrand48*( ) allow separate modules of a large program to generate several *independent* streams of pseudo-random numbers, that is the sequence of numbers in each stream will *not* depend upon how many times the routines are called to generate numbers for the other streams.

The initialiser function *srand48*( ) sets the high-order 32 bits of X_i to the low-order 32 bits contained in its argument. The low-order 16 bits of X_i are set to the arbitrary value $330E_{16}$.

The initialiser function *seed48*( ) sets the value of X_i to the 48-bit value specified in the argument array. The low-order 16 bits of X_i are set to the low-order 16 bits of *seed16v[0]*. The mid-order 16 bits of X_i are set to the low-order 16 bits of *seed16v[1]*. The high-order 16 bits of X_i are set to the low-order 16 bits of *seed16v[2]*. In addition, the previous value of X_i is copied into a 48-bit internal buffer, used only by *seed48*( ), and a pointer to this buffer is the value returned by *seed48*( ). This returned pointer, which can just be ignored if not needed, is useful if a program is to be restarted from a given point at some future time — use the pointer to get at and store the last X_i value, and then use this value to reinitialise via *seed48*( ) when the program is restarted.

The initialiser function *lcong48*( ) allows the user to specify the initial X_i, the multiplier value *a*, and the addend value *c*. Argument array elements *param[0-2]* specify X_i, *param[3-5]* specify the multiplier *a*, and *param[6]* specifies the 16-bit addend *c*. After *lcong48*( ) is called, a subsequent call to either *srand48*( ) or *seed48*( ) will restore the "standard" multiplier and addend values, *a* and *c*, specified above.

RETURN VALUE

As described in the **DESCRIPTION** section above.

ERRORS

No errors are defined.

SEE ALSO

rand( ), **<stdlib.h>**.

EXAMPLE

```
/*
 * Copyright (C) ANTRIX Inc.
 */

/* drand48.c
 * This program generates non-negative, double precision, floating
 * point random values uniformly distributed over the interval
 * [0.0, 1.0) using function drand48.
 */

#include <stdio.h>
#include <stdlib.h>
#include <errno.h>

main()
{
```

```
int      i;
double   drand48_value;
long int seedval = 100;

srand48(100);
for ( i = 0; i < 5; i++ ) {
    drand48_value = drand48 ();
    fprintf (stdout,"random value in iteration %d is %f\n",
                    i, drand48_value);
}
}
```

NAME

dup, dup2 — duplicate an open file descriptor

SYNOPSIS

```
#include <unistd.h>

int dup(int fildes);

int dup2(int fildes, int fildes2);
```

DESCRIPTION

The *dup*( ) and *dup2*( ) functions provide an alternative interface to the service provided by *fcntl*( ) using the F_DUPFD command. The call:

```
fid = dup(fildes);
```

is equivalent to:

```
fid = fcntl(fildes, F_DUPFD, 0);
```

The call:

```
fid = dup2(fildes, fildes2);
```

is equivalent to:

```
close(fildes2);
fid = fcntl(fildes, F_DUPFD, fildes2);
```

except for the following:

- If *fildes2* is less than 0 or greater than or equal to {OPEN_MAX}, *dup2*( ) returns −1 with *errno* set to [EBADF].

- If *fildes* is a valid file descriptor and is equal to *fildes2*, *dup2*( ) returns *fildes2* without closing it.

- If *fildes* is not a valid file descriptor, *dup2*( ) returns −1 and does not close *fildes2*.

- The value returned is equal to the value of *fildes2* upon successful completion, or is −1 upon failure.

RETURN VALUE

Upon successful completion a non-negative integer, namely the file descriptor, is returned. Otherwise, −1 is returned and *errno* is set to indicate the error.

ERRORS

The *dup*( ) function will fail if:

[EBADF]   The *fildes* argument is not a valid open file descriptor.

[EMFILE]   The number of file descriptors in use by this process would exceed {OPEN_MAX}.

The *dup2*( ) function will fail if:

[EBADF]   The *fildes* argument is not a valid open file descriptor or the argument *fildes2* is negative or greater than or equal to {OPEN_MAX} .

[EINTR]   The *dup2*( ) function was interrupted by a signal.

SEE ALSO

close( ), *fcntl*( ), *open*( ), **<unistd.h>**.

EXAMPLE

```
/*
 * Copyright (C) ANTRIX Inc.
 */

/* dup.c
 * This program duplicates an open file descriptor using
 * function dup. File descriptor can also be duplicated
 * using function fcntl.
 */

#include <stdio.h>
#include <stdlib.h>
#include <unistd.h>
#include <sys/stat.h>
#include <errno.h>

#define  PERM_ALL    (S_IRWXU | S_IRWXG | S_IRWXO)

main()
{
  int    dup_value;
  int    fildes;
  char   *path = "testfile";

  fprintf (stdout,"create testfile\n");
  fildes = creat (path, PERM_ALL);

  fprintf (stdout,"duplicate file descriptor\n");
  dup_value = dup (fildes);
  if ( dup_value > 2 ) {
     fprintf (stdout,"dup() call successful\n");
     fprintf (stdout,"duplicated file descriptor is=%d\n", dup_value);
  }
  else {
     fprintf (stderr,"ERROR: dup() call failed\n");
     fprintf (stderr,"ERROR: %s\n", strerror(errno));
  }

  fprintf (stdout,"remove testfile\n");
  remove (path);
}

/*
 * Copyright (C) ANTRIX Inc.
 */
/* dup2.c
 * This program duplicates an open file descriptor using
 * function dup2. File descriptor can also be duplicated
 * using function fcntl.
 */
```

```
#include <stdio.h>
#include <stdlib.h>
#include <fcntl.h>
#include <unistd.h>
#include <sys/stat.h>
#include <errno.h>

#define  PERM_ALL   (S_IRWXU | S_IRWXG | S_IRWXO)

main()
{
  int  dup2_value;
  int  fildes, fildes2;
  char *path = "testfile";

  fprintf (stdout,"create testfile\n");
  fildes = creat (path, PERM_ALL);
  fildes2 = creat (path, PERM_ALL);

  fprintf (stdout,"dup2 causes fildes2 to refer\n");
  fprintf (stdout,"to the same file as fildes\n");
  dup2_value = dup2 (fildes, fildes2);
  if ( dup2_value == fildes2 ) {
      fprintf (stdout,"dup2() call successful\n");
      fprintf (stdout,"dup2 return value is %d\n", dup2_value);
      fprintf (stdout,"fildes2 value is %d\n", fildes2);
  }
  else {
      fprintf (stderr,"ERROR: dup2() call failed\n");
      fprintf (stderr,"ERROR: %s\n", strerror(errno));
  }

  remove(path);
}
```

NAME

ecvt, fcvt, gcvt — convert floating-point number to string

SYNOPSIS

UX

```
#include <stdlib.h>

char *ecvt(double value, int ndigit, int *decpt, int *sign);

char *fcvt(double value, int ndigit, int *decpt, int *sign);

char *gcvt(double value, int ndigit, char *buf);
```

DESCRIPTION

The *ecvt( )*, *fcvt( )* and *gcvt( )* functions convert floating-point numbers to null-terminated strings.

ecvt( )   Converts *value* to a null-terminated string of *ndigit* digits (where *ndigit* is reduced to an unspecified limit determined by the precision of a **double**) and returns a pointer to the string. The high-order digit is non-zero, unless the value is 0. The low-order digit is rounded. The position of the radix character relative to the beginning of the string is stored in the integer pointed to by *decpt* (negative means to the left of the returned digits). The radix character is not included in the returned string. If the sign of the result is negative, the integer pointed to by *sign* is non-zero, otherwise it is 0.

If the converted value is out of range or is not representable, the contents of the returned string are unspecified.

fcvt( )   Identical to *ecvt( )* except that *ndigit* specifies the number of digits desired after the radix point. The total number of digits in the result string is restricted to an unspecified limit as determined by the precision of a **double**.

gcvt( )   Converts *value* to a null-terminated string (similar to that of the %g format of *printf( )*) in the array pointed to by *buf* and returns *buf*. It produces *ndigit* significant digits (limited to an unspecified value determined by the precision of a **double**) in %f if possible, or %e (scientific notation) otherwise. A minus sign is included in the returned string if *value* is less than 0. A radix character is included in the returned string if *value* is not a whole number. Trailing zeros are suppressed where *value* is not a whole number. The radix character is determined by the current locale. If *setlocale( )* has not been called successfully, the default locale, "POSIX", is used. The default locale specifies a period (**.**) as the radix character. The LC_NUMERIC category determines the value of the radix character within the current locale.

RETURN VALUE

The *ecvt( )* and *fcvt( )* functions return a pointer to a null-terminated string of digits.

The *gcvt( )* function returns *buf*.

ERRORS

No errors are defined.

APPLICATION USAGE

The return values from *ecvt( )* and *fcvt( )* may point to static data which may be overwritten by subsequent calls to these functions.

For portability to implementations conforming to earlier versions of this document, *sprintf( )* is preferred over this function.

SEE ALSO

printf( ), *setlocale( )*, **<stdlib.h>**.

NAME

encrypt — encoding function

SYNOPSIS

EX　　`#include <unistd.h>`

`void encrypt (char block[64], int edflag);`

DESCRIPTION

The *encrypt*( ) function provides (rather primitive) access to an implementation-dependent encoding algorithm. The key generated by *setkey*( ) is used to encrypt the string *block* with *encrypt*( ).

The *block* argument to *encrypt*( ) is an array of length 64 bytes containing only the bytes with numerical value of 0 and 1. The array is modified in place to a similar array using the key set by *setkey*( ). If *edflag* is 0, the argument is encoded. If *edflag* is 1, the argument may be decoded (see the **APPLICATION USAGE** section below); if the argument is not decoded, *errno* will be set to [ENOSYS].

RETURN VALUE

The *encrypt*( ) function returns no value.

ERRORS

The *encrypt*( ) function will fail if:

[ENOSYS]　　　　The functionality is not supported on this implementation.

APPLICATION USAGE

In some environments, decoding may not be implemented. This is related to U.S. Government restrictions on encryption and decryption routines: the DES decryption algorithm cannot be exported outside the U.S.A. Historical practice has been to ship a different version of the encryption library without the decryption feature in the routines supplied. Thus the exported version of *encrypt*( ) does encoding but not decoding.

Because *encrypt*( ) does not return a value, applications wishing to check for errors should set *errno* to 0, call *encrypt*( ), then test *errno* and, if it is non-zero, assume an error has occurred.

SEE ALSO

crypt( ), *setkey*( ), **<unistd.h>**.

EXAMPLE

```
/*
 * Copyright (C) ANTRIX Inc.
 */

/* encrypt.c
 * This program provides access to an implementation dependent
 * encoding algorithm using function encrypt.
 */

#include <stdio.h>
#include <stdlib.h>
#include <crypt.h>
#include <errno.h>

main()
{
  int   edflag;
```

```
    char  block[64];

    memset(block, ' ', 64);
    strcpy(block, "10110101101");
    fprintf (stdout,"previous key value=%s\n", block);

    fprintf (stdout,"encrypt key value\n");
    encrypt (block, 0);
    fprintf (stdout,"encrypt() call successful\n");
    fprintf (stdout,"New key value after encryption=%s\n", block);
}
```

NAME

endgrent, getgrent, setgrent — group database entry functions

SYNOPSIS

UX

```
#include <grp.h>
```

```
void endgrent(void);
```

```
struct group *getgrent(void);
```

```
void setgrent(void);
```

DESCRIPTION

The *getgrent*( ) function returns a pointer to a structure containing the broken-out fields of an entry in the group database. When first called, *getgrent*( ) returns a pointer to a **group** structure containing the first entry in the group database. Thereafter, it returns a pointer to a **group** structure containing the next group structure in the group database, so successive calls may be used to search the entire database.

The *setgrent*( ) function effectively rewinds the group database to allow repeated searches.

The *endgrent*( ) function may be called to close the group database when processing is complete.

RETURN VALUE

When first called, *getgrent*( ) will return a pointer to the first group structure in the group database. Upon subsequent calls it returns the next group structure in the group database. The *getgrent*( ) function returns a null pointer on end-of-file or an error and *errno* may be set to indicate the error.

ERRORS

The *getgrent*( ) function may fail if:

[EINTR]   A signal was caught during the operation.

[EIO]   An I/O error has occurred.

[EMFILE]   {OPEN_MAX} file descriptors are currently open in the calling process.

[ENFILE]   The maximum allowable number of files is currently open in the system.

APPLICATION USAGE

The return value may point to a static area which is overwritten by a subsequent call to *getgrgid*( ), *getgrnam*( ) or *getgrent*( ).

These functions are provided due to their historical usage. Applications should avoid dependencies on fields in the group database, whether the database is a single file, or where in the filesystem namespace the database resides. Applications should use *getgrnam*( ) and *getgrgid*( ) whenever possible both because it avoids these dependencies and for greater portability with systems that conform to earlier versions of this document.

SEE ALSO

getgrgid( ), *getgrnam*( ), *getlogin*( ), *getpwent*( ), **<grp.h>**.

EXAMPLE

```
/*
 * Copyright (C) ANTRIX Inc.
 */

/* endgrent.c
 * This program informs that caller expects to do no further
 * group entry retrieval operations using function endgrent
 */

#include <stdio.h>
#include <stdlib.h>
#include <grp.h>
#include <errno.h>

main()
{
  struct    group *buf;

  fprintf (stdout,"get group file entries\n");
  do {
    buf = (struct group *)getgrent ();
    fprintf (stdout,"buf->gr_name=%s\n", buf->gr_name);
    fprintf (stdout,"buf->gr_gid=%d\n", buf->gr_gid);
    fprintf (stdout,"buf->gr_mem[0]=%s\n", buf->gr_mem[0]);
  } while (buf != (struct group *)0);

  fprintf (stdout,"close the group file\n");
  endgrent ();
}
```

NAME

endpwent, getpwent, setpwent — user database functions

SYNOPSIS

UX
```
#include <pwd.h>

void endpwent(void);

struct passwd *getpwent(void);

void setpwent(void);
```

DESCRIPTION

The *getpwent*( ) function returns a pointer to a structure containing the broken-out fields of an entry in the user database. Each entry in the user database contains a **passwd** structure. When first called, *getpwent*( ) returns a pointer to a **passwd** structure containing the first entry in the user database. Thereafter, it returns a pointer to a **passwd** structure containing the next entry in the user database. Successive calls can be used to search the entire user database.

If an end-of-file or an error is encountered on reading, *getpwent*( ) returns a null pointer.

The *setpwent*( ) function effectively rewinds the user database to allow repeated searches.

The *endpwent*( ) function may be called to close the user database when processing is complete.

RETURN VALUE

The *getpwent*( ) function returns a null pointer on end-of-file or error.

ERRORS

The *getpwent*( ), *setpwent*( ) and *endpwent*( ) functions may fail if:

[EIO]   An I/O error has occurred.

In addition, *getpwent*( ) and *setpwent*( ) may fail if:

[EMFILE]   {OPEN_MAX} file descriptors are currently open in the calling process.

[ENFILE]   The maximum allowable number of files is currently open in the system.

APPLICATION USAGE

The return value may point to a static area which is overwritten by a subsequent call to *getpwuid*( ), *getpwnam*( ) or *getpwent*( ).

These functions are provided due to their historical usage. Applications should avoid dependencies on fields in the password database, whether the database is a single file, or where in the filesystem namespace the database resides. Applications should use *getpwuid*( ) whenever possible both because it avoids these dependencies and for greater portability with systems that conform to earlier versions of this document.

SEE ALSO

endgrent( ), *getlogin*( ), *getpwnam*( ), *getpwuid*( ), **<pwd.h>**.

EXAMPLE

```
/*
 * Copyright (C) ANTRIX Inc.
 */

/* endpwent.c
 * This program informs that caller expects to do no further
 * password retrieval using function endpwent
 */

#include <stdio.h>
#include <stdlib.h>
#include <pwd.h>
#include <errno.h>

main()
{
  struct   passwd *buf;

  fprintf (stdout,"get passwd file entries\n");
  do {
    buf = (struct passwd *)getpwent ();
    fprintf (stdout,"buf_pw_name=%s\n", buf->pw_name);
    fprintf (stdout,"buf_pw_passwd=%s\n", buf->pw_passwd);
    fprintf (stdout,"buf_pw_uid=%d\n", buf->pw_uid);
    fprintf (stdout,"buf_pw_gid=%d\n", buf->pw_gid);
    fprintf (stdout,"buf_pw_dir=%s\n", buf->pw_dir);
    fprintf (stdout,"buf_pw_shell=%s\n", buf->pw_shell);
  } while (buf != (struct passwd *)0);

  fprintf (stdout,"close the passwd file\n");
  endpwent ();
}
```

NAME

endutxent, getutxent, getutxid, getutxline, pututxline, setutxent — user accounting database functions

SYNOPSIS

UX   `#include <utmpx.h>`

```
void endutxent(void);
```

```
struct utmpx *getutxent(void);
```

```
struct utmpx *getutxid(const struct utmpx *id);
```

```
struct utmpx *getutxline(const struct utmpx *line);
```

```
struct utmpx *pututxline(const struct utmpx *utmpx);
```

```
void setutxent(void);
```

DESCRIPTION

These functions provide access to the user accounting database.

The *getutxent*( ) function reads in the next entry from the user accounting database. If the database is not already open, it opens it. If it reaches the end of the database, it fails.

The *getutxid*( ) function searches forward from the current point in the database. If the **ut_type** value of the **utmpx** structure pointed to by *id* is BOOT_TIME, OLD_TIME or NEW_TIME, then it stops when it finds an entry with a matching **ut_type** value. If the **ut_type** value is INIT_PROCESS, LOGIN_PROCESS, USER_PROCESS, or DEAD_PROCESS, then it stops when it finds an entry whose type is one of these four and whose **ut_id** member matches the **ut_id** member of the **utmpx** structure pointed to by *id*. If the end of the database is reached without a match, *getutxid*( ) fails.

For all entries that match a request, the **ut_type** member indicates the type of the entry. Other members of the entry will contain meaningful data based on the value of the **ut_type** member as follows:

ut_type Member	Other Members with Meaningful Data
EMPTY	No others
BOOT_TIME	**ut_tv**
OLD_TIME	**ut_tv**
NEW_TIME	**ut_tv**
USER_PROCESS	**ut_id**, **ut_user** (login name of the user), **ut_line**, **ut_pid**, **ut_tv**
INIT_PROCESS	**ut_id**, **ut_pid**, **ut_tv**
LOGIN_PROCESS	**ut_id**, **ut_user** (implementation-specific name of the login process), **ut_pid**, **ut_tv**
DEAD_PROCESS	**ut_id**, **ut_pid**, **ut_tv**

The *getutxline*( ) function searches forward from the current point in the database until it finds an entry of the type LOGIN_PROCESS or USER_PROCESS which also has a **ut_line** value matching that in the **utmpx** structure pointed to by *line*. If the end of the database is reached without a match, *getutxline*( ) fails.

If the process has appropriate privileges, the *pututxline*( ) function writes out the structure into the user accounting database. It uses *getutxid*( ) to search for a record that satisfies the request. If this search succeeds, then the entry is replaced. Otherwise, a new entry is made at the end of the user accounting database.

The *setutxent*( ) function resets the input to the beginning of the database. This should be done before each search for a new entry if it is desired that the entire database be examined.

The *endutxent*( ) function closes the user accounting database.

RETURN VALUE

Upon successful completion, *getutxent*( ), *getutxid*( ) and *getutxline*( ) return a pointer to a **utmpx** structure containing a copy of the requested entry in the user accounting database. Otherwise a null pointer is returned.

Upon successful completion, *pututxline*( ) returns a pointer to a **utmpx** structure containing a copy of the entry added to the user accounting database. Otherwise a null pointer is returned.

The *endutxent*( ) and *setutxent*( ) functions return no value.

ERRORS

No errors are defined for the *endutxent*( ), *getutxent*( ), *getutxid*( ), *getutxline*( ) and *setutxent*( ) functions.

The *pututxline*( ) function may fail if:

[EPERM]   The process does not have appropriate privileges.

APPLICATION USAGE

The return value may point to a static area which is overwritten by a subsequent call to *getutxid*( ) or *getutxline*( ).

Implementations may cache the data written by *getutxid*( ) or *getutxline*( ). For this reason, to use *getutxline*( ) to search for multiple occurrences, it is necessary to zero out the static data after each success, or *getutxline*( ) could just return a pointer to the same **utmpx** structure over and over again.

There is one exception to the rule about removing the structure before further reads are done. The implicit read done by *pututxline*( ) (if it finds that it is not already at the correct place in the user accounting database) will not modify the static structure returned by *getutxent*( ), *getutxid*( ) or *getutxline*( ), if the application has just modified this structure and passed the pointer back to *pututxline*( ).

The sizes of the arrays in the structure can be found using the **sizeof** operator.

SEE ALSO

<utmpx.h>.

NAME

environ — array of character pointers to the environment strings

SYNOPSIS

```
extern char **environ;
```

DESCRIPTION

Refer to the **XBD** specification, **Chapter 6**, **Environment Variables** and *exec*.

APPLICATION USAGE

The *environ* array should not be accessed directly by the application.

NAME

    erand48 — generate uniformly distributed pseudo-random numbers

SYNOPSIS

EX   `#include <stdlib.h>`

    `double erand48(unsigned short int xsubi[3]);`

DESCRIPTION

    Refer to *drand48( )*.

EXAMPLE

```
/*
 * Copyright (C) ANTRIX Inc.
 */

/* erand48.c
 * This program generates non-negative, double precision, floating
 * point random values uniformly distributed over the interval
 * [0.0, 1.0) using function erand48.
 */

#include <stdio.h>
#include <stdlib.h>
#include <errno.h>

main()
{
  double          erand48_value;
  int             i;
  unsigned short  xsubi[3];

  xsubi[0] = 10;
  for ( i = 0; i < 5; i++ ) {
      erand48_value = erand48 (xsubi);
      fprintf (stdout,"random value in iteration %d is %f\n",
                      i, erand48_value);
  }
}
```

NAME

erf, erfc — error and complementary error functions

SYNOPSIS

EX

```
#include <math.h>

double erf(double x);

double erfc(double x);
```

DESCRIPTION

The *erf*( ) function computes the error function of *x*, defined as:

$$\frac{2}{\sqrt{\pi}} \int_0^x e^{-t^2}\, dt$$

The *erfc*( ) function computes 1.0 − *erf*(*x*).

RETURN VALUE

Upon successful completion, *erf*( ) and *erfc*( ) return the value of the error function and complementary error function, respectively.

If *x* is NaN, NaN is returned and *errno* may be set to [EDOM].

If the correct value would cause underflow, 0 is returned and *errno* may be set to [ERANGE].

ERRORS

The *erf*( ) and *erfc*( ) functions may fail if:

[EDOM]   The value of *x* is NaN.

[ERANGE]   The result underflows.

No other errors will occur.

APPLICATION USAGE

The *erfc*( ) function is provided because of the extreme loss of relative accuracy if *erf*(*x*) is called for large *x* and the result subtracted from 1.0.

An application wishing to check for error situations should set *errno* to 0 before calling *erf*( ). If *errno* is non-zero on return, or the return value is NaN, an error has occurred.

SEE ALSO

isnan( ), **<math.h>**.

EXAMPLE

```
/*
 * Copyright (C) ANTRIX Inc.
 */

/* erf.c
 * This program computes error function of 1.00 using
 * function erf.
 */

#include <stdio.h>
#include <math.h>

main()
{
  double  erf_value;
```

```
      double   x = 1.00;

      erf_value = erf (x);
      fprintf (stdout,"erf of %f is %f\n", x, erf_value);
}
/*
 * Copyright (C) ANTRIX Inc.
 */

/* erfc.c
 * This program computes the complementary error function
 * using function erfc.
 */

#include <stdio.h>
#include <math.h>

main()
{
   double   erfc_value;
   double   x = 0.40;

   erfc_value = erfc (x);
   fprintf (stdout,"erfc of %f is %f\n", x, erfc_value);
}
```

NAME

errno — XSI error return value

SYNOPSIS

```
#include <errno.h>
```

DESCRIPTION

The external variable or macro *errno* is used by many XSI functions to return error values. XSI-conformant systems may support the declaration:

```
extern int errno;
```

EX   Many functions provide an error number in *errno* which has type **int** and is defined in **<errno.h>**. The value of *errno* will be defined only after a call to a function for which it is explicitly stated to be set and until it is changed by the next function call. The value of *errno* should only be examined when it is indicated to be valid by a function's return value. Programs should obtain the definition of *errno* by the inclusion of **<errno.h>**. The practice of defining *errno* in a program as **extern int** *errno* is obsolescent. No function in this specification sets *errno* to 0 to indicate an error.

It is unspecified whether *errno* is a macro or an identifier declared with external linkage. If a macro definition is suppressed in order to access an actual object, or a program defines an identifier with the name **errno**, the behaviour is undefined.

The value of *errno* is 0 at program startup, but is never set to 0 by any XSI function. The symbolic values stored in *errno* are documented in the **ERRORS** sections on all relevant pages.

APPLICATION USAGE

Previously both POSIX and X/Open documents were more restrictive than the ISO C standard in that they required *errno* to be defined as an external variable, whereas the ISO C standard required only that *errno* be defined as a modifiable **lvalue** with type **int**.

This revision is aligned with the ISO C standard; future versions of the ISO POSIX-1 standard are likely to require this more flexible definition. The historical usage is obsolescent; some implementations may not support it.

A program that uses *errno* for error checking should set it to 0 before a function call, then inspect it before a subsequent function call.

SEE ALSO

<errno.h>, **XSH** specification, **Section 2.3**, **Error Numbers**.

EXAMPLE

```
/*
 * Copyright (C) ANTRIX Inc.
 */

/* errno.c
 * This program prints errno associated with a failure
 * for open function.
 */

#include <stdio.h>
#include <stdlib.h>
#include <string.h>
#include <errno.h>

/* errno is declared as "extern int errno" in errno.h */
```

```
 * header file
 */

main()
{
  int   err_value;
  char  *errmsg;
  char  *path = "testfile";
  FILE  *stream;

  fprintf (stdout,"open a testfile\n");
  stream = fopen (path, "r");

  fprintf (stdout,"check error was generated\n");
  fprintf (stderr,"errno value is: %d\n", errno );

  errmsg = strerror (errno);
  fprintf (stderr,"ERROR: %s\n", errmsg );
}
```

NAME

environ, execl, execv, execle, execve, execlp, execvp — execute a file

SYNOPSIS

```
#include <unistd.h>

extern char **environ;

int execl(const char *path, const char *arg0, ... /*, (char *)0 */);

int execv(const char *path, char *const argv[]);

int execle(const char *path,
           const char *arg0, ... /*, (char *)0, char *const envp[]*/);

int execve(const char *path, char *const argv[], char *const envp[]);

int execlp(const char *file, const char *arg0, ... /*, (char *)0 */);

int execvp(const char *file, char *const argv[]);
```

DESCRIPTION

The *exec* functions replace the current process image with a new process image. The new image is constructed from a regular, executable file called the *new process image file*. There is no return from a successful *exec*, because the calling process image is overlaid by the new process image.

When a C-language program is executed as a result of this call, it is entered as a C-language function call as follows:

```
int main (int argc, char *argv[]);
```

where *argc* is the argument count and *argv* is an array of character pointers to the arguments themselves. In addition, the following variable:

```
extern char **environ;
```

is initialised as a pointer to an array of character pointers to the environment strings. The *argv* and *environ* arrays are each terminated by a null pointer. The null pointer terminating the *argv* array is not counted in *argc*.

The arguments specified by a program with one of the *exec* functions are passed on to the new process image in the corresponding *main*( ) arguments.

The argument *path* points to a pathname that identifies the new process image file.

The argument *file* is used to construct a pathname that identifies the new process image file. If the *file* argument contains a slash character, the *file* argument is used as the pathname for this file. Otherwise, the path prefix for this file is obtained by a search of the directories passed as the environment variable *PATH* (see **XBD** specification, **Chapter 6**, **Environment Variables**). If this environment variable is not present, the results of the search are implementation-dependent.

EX   If the process image file is not a valid executable object, *execlp*( ) and *execvp*( ) use the contents of that file as standard input to a command interpreter conforming to *system*( ). In this case, the command interpreter becomes the new process image.

The arguments represented by *arg0, ...* are pointers to null-terminated character strings. These strings constitute the argument list available to the new process image. The list is terminated by a null pointer. The argument *arg0* should point to a filename that is associated with the process being started by one of the *exec* functions.

The argument *argv* is an array of character pointers to null-terminated strings. The last member of this array must be a null pointer. These strings constitute the argument list available to the new process image. The value in *argv*[0] should point to a filename that is associated with the process being started by one of the *exec* functions.

The argument *envp* is an array of character pointers to null-terminated strings. These strings constitute the environment for the new process image. The *envp* array is terminated by a null pointer.

For those forms not containing an *envp* pointer (*execl*( ), *execv*( ), *execlp*( ) and *execvp*( )), the environment for the new process image is taken from the external variable *environ* in the calling process.

The number of bytes available for the new process' combined argument and environment lists is {ARG_MAX}. It is implementation-dependent whether null terminators, pointers, and/or any alignment bytes are included in this total.

File descriptors open in the calling process image remain open in the new process image, except for those whose close-on-exec flag FD_CLOEXEC is set. For those file descriptors that remain open, all attributes of the open file description, including file locks remain unchanged.

Directory streams open in the calling process image are closed in the new process image.

EX The state of conversion descriptors and message catalogue descriptors in the new process image is undefined. For the new process, the equivalent of:

```
setlocale(LC_ALL, "C")
```

is executed at startup.

Signals set to the default action (SIG_DFL) in the calling process image are set to the default action in the new process image. Signals set to be ignored (SIG_IGN) by the calling process image are set to be ignored by the new process image. Signals set to be caught by the calling

UX process image are set to the default action in the new process image (see **<signal.h>**). After a successful call to any of the *exec* functions, alternate signal stacks are not preserved and the SA_ONSTACK flag is cleared for all signals.

After a successful call to any of the *exec* functions, any functions previously registered by *atexit*( ) are no longer registered.

UX If the ST_NOSUID bit is set for the file system containing the new process image file, then the effective user ID, effective group ID, saved set-user-ID and saved set-group-ID are unchanged in the new process image. Otherwise, if the set-user-ID mode bit of the new process image file is set, the effective user ID of the new process image is set to the user ID of the new process image file. Similarly, if the set-group-ID mode bit of the new process image file is set, the effective group ID of the new process image is set to the group ID of the new process image file. The real user ID, real group ID, and supplementary group IDs of the new process image remain

FIPS the same as those of the calling process image. The effective user ID and effective group ID of the new process image are saved (as the saved set-user-ID and the saved set-group-ID for use by *setuid*( ).

EX Any shared memory segments attached to the calling process image will not be attached to the new process image.

UX Any mappings established through *mmap*( ) are not preserved across an *exec*.

The new process also inherits at least the following attributes from the calling process image:

EX   nice value (see *nice*( ))
semadj values (see *semop*( ))
process ID
parent process ID
process group ID
session membership
real user ID
real group ID
supplementary group IDs
time left until an alarm clock signal (see *alarm*( ))
current working directory
root directory
file mode creation mask (see *umask*( ))

EX   file size limit (see *ulimit*( ))
process signal mask (see *sigprocmask*( ))
pending signal (see *sigpending*( ))
tms_utime, *tms_stime*, *tms_cutime*, and *tms_cstime* (see *times*( ))

UX   resource limits
controlling terminal
interval timers

All other process attributes defined in this document will be the same in the new and old process images. The inheritance of process attributes not defined by this document is implementation-dependent.

Upon successful completion, the *exec* functions mark for update the *st_atime* field of the file. If an *exec* function failed but was able to locate the *process image file*, whether the *st_atime* field is marked for update is unspecified. Should the *exec* function succeed, the process image file is considered to have been opened with *open*( ). The corresponding *close*( ) is considered to occur at a time after this open, but before process termination or successful completion of a subsequent call to one of the *exec* functions. The argv[ ] and envp[ ] arrays of pointers and the strings to which those arrays point will not be modified by a call to one of the *exec* functions, except as a consequence of replacing the process image.

RETURN VALUE

If one of the *exec* functions returns to the calling process image, an error has occurred; the return value is −1, and *errno* is set to indicate the error.

ERRORS

The *exec* functions will fail if:

[E2BIG]   The number of bytes used by the new process image's argument list and environment list is greater than the system-imposed limit of {ARG_MAX} bytes.

[EACCES]   Search permission is denied for a directory listed in the new process image file's path prefix, or the new process image file denies execution permission, or the new process image file is not a regular file and the implementation does not support execution of files of its type.

UX   [ELOOP]   Too many symbolic links were encountered in resolving *path*.

[ENAMETOOLONG]

FIPS   The length of the *path* or *file* arguments, or an element of the environment variable *PATH* prefixed to a file, exceeds {PATH_MAX}, or a pathname component is longer than {NAME_MAX}.

[ENOENT] A component of *path* or *file* does not name an existing file or *path* or *file* is an empty string.

[ENOTDIR] A component of the new process image file's path prefix is not a directory.

The *exec* functions, except for *execlp*( ) and *execvp*( ), will fail if:

[ENOEXEC] The new process image file has the appropriate access permission but is not in the proper format.

The *exec* functions may fail if:

UX [ENAMETOOLONG]
Pathname resolution of a symbolic link produced an intermediate result whose length exceeds {PATH_MAX}.

[ENOMEM] The new process image requires more memory than is allowed by the hardware or system-imposed memory management constraints.

EX [ETXTBSY] The new process image file is a pure procedure (shared text) file that is currently open for writing by some process.

APPLICATION USAGE

As the state of conversion descriptors and message catalogue descriptors in the new process image is undefined, portable applications should not rely on their use and should close them prior to calling one of the *exec* functions.

Applications that require other than the default POSIX locale should call *setlocale*( ) with the appropriate parameters to establish the locale of the new process.

SEE ALSO

alarm( ), *atexit*( ), *chmod*( ), *exit*( ), *fcntl*( ), *fork*( ), *fstatvfs*( ), *getenv*( ), *getitimer*( ), *getrlimit*( ), *mmap*( ), *nice*( ), *putenv*( ), *semop*( ), *setlocale*( ), *shmat*( ), *sigaction*( ), *sigaltstack*( ), *sigpending*( ), *sigprocmask*( ), *system*( ), *times*( ), *ulimit*( ), *umask*( ), **<unistd.h>**, **XBD** specification, **Chapter 9**, **General Terminal Interface**.

EXAMPLE

```
/*
 * Copyright (C) ANTRIX Inc.
 */


/* exec.c contains programs for different versions of exec
 * as execl, execv, execle, execve, execlp, execvp.
 * exec is used to execute a binary file.
 * To use any exec version, cut the .c and test file
 * associated with it.
 */

/* filename execl.c */


#include <stdio.h>
#include <stdlib.h>
#include <unistd.h>
#include <errno.h>
```

```
main()
{
  int      execl_value;

  fprintf (stdout,"execl execute\n");
  fprintf (stdout,"test1 hello world\n");
  execl_value = execl ("test1", "test1", "hello", "world", (char *)0);
  if ( execl_value == -1 ) {
     fprintf (stderr,"ERROR: execl() call failed\n");
     fprintf (stdout,"cannot find executable file test1\n");
     fprintf (stderr,"ERROR: %s\n", strerror(errno));
  }
}


/*  filename test1.c  */

#include <stdio.h>

main(argc, argv)
int argc ;
char *argv[] ;
{
    fprintf (stdout,"executing file test1\n") ;
    fprintf (stdout,"argument count argc=%d\n", argc) ;
    fprintf (stdout,"vector argv[0]=%s\n", argv[0]) ;
    fprintf (stdout,"vector argv[1]=%s\n", argv[1]) ;
    fprintf (stdout,"vector argv[2]=%s\n", argv[2]) ;
}


/* filename execv.c */

#include <stdio.h>
#include <stdlib.h>
#include <unistd.h>
#include <errno.h>

main()
{
  int      execv_value;
  char     *args[] = { "test2", "hello", "world", (char *)0 };

  fprintf (stdout,"execv execute\n");
  fprintf (stdout,"test2 args\n");
  execv_value = execv ("test2", args);
  if ( execv_value == -1 ) {
     fprintf (stderr,"ERROR: execv() call failed\n");
     fprintf (stdout,"cannot find executable file test2\n");
     fprintf (stderr,"ERROR: %s\n", strerror(errno));
  }
}
```

```
/*   filename test2.c  */

#include <stdio.h>

main(argc, argv)
int argc ;
char *argv[] ;
{
    fprintf (stdout,"executing file test2\n") ;
    fprintf (stdout,"argument count argc=%d\n", argc) ;
    fprintf (stdout,"vector argv[0]=%s\n", argv[0]) ;
    fprintf (stdout,"vector argv[1]=%s\n", argv[1]) ;
    fprintf (stdout,"vector argv[2]=%s\n", argv[2]) ;
}

/* filename execle.c */

#include <stdio.h>
#include <stdlib.h>
#include <unistd.h>
#include <errno.h>

main()
{
    int      execle_value;
    char     *evector[] = { "to", "everyone", (char*)0 };

    fprintf (stdout,"execle execute\n");
    fprintf (stdout,"test3 hello world evector\n");
    execle_value = execle ("test3", "test3", "hello", "world",
                                     (char *)0, evector);
    if ( execle_value = -1 ) {
        fprintf (stderr,"ERROR: execle() call failed\n");
        fprintf (stdout,"cannot find executable file test3\n");
        fprintf (stderr,"ERROR: %s\n", strerror(errno));
    }
}

/* filename test3.c */

#include <stdio.h>

main(argc, argv, envp)
int argc ;
char *argv[] ;
char *envp[] ;
{
    fprintf (stdout,"executing file test3\n") ;
    fprintf (stdout,"argument count argc=%d\n", argc) ;
    fprintf (stdout,"vector argv[0]=%s\n", argv[0] ) ;
    fprintf (stdout,"vector argv[1]=%s\n", argv[1] ) ;
    fprintf (stdout,"vector argv[2]=%s\n", argv[2] ) ;
```

```
      fprintf (stdout,"vector envp[0]=%s\n", envp[0] ) ;
      fprintf (stdout,"vector envp[1]=%s\n", envp[1] ) ;
}

/* filename execve.c */

#include <stdio.h>
#include <stdlib.h>
#include <unistd.h>
#include <errno.h>

main()
{
  int     execve_value;
  char    *args[] = { "test4", "hello", "world", (char *)0 };
  char    *evector[] = { "to", "all", (char *)0 };

  fprintf (stdout,"execute execve\n");
  fprintf (stdout,"test4, args, evector\n");
  execve_value = execve ("test4", args, evector);
  if ( execve_value = -1 ) {
     fprintf (stderr,"ERROR: execve() call failed\n");
     fprintf (stdout,"cannot find executable file test4\n");
     fprintf (stderr,"ERROR: %s\n", strerror(errno));
  }
}

/* filename test4.c */

#include <stdio.h>

main(argc, argv, envp)
int argc ;
char *argv[] ;
char *envp[] ;
{
   fprintf (stdout,"executing file test4\n") ;
   fprintf (stdout,"argument count argc=%d\n", argc) ;
   fprintf (stdout,"vector argv[0]=%s\n", argv[0] ) ;
   fprintf (stdout,"vector argv[1]=%s\n", argv[1] ) ;
   fprintf (stdout,"vector argv[2]=%s\n", argv[2] ) ;
   fprintf (stdout,"vector envp[0]=%s\n", envp[0] ) ;
   fprintf (stdout,"vector envp[1]=%s\n", envp[1] ) ;
}

/* filename execlp.c */

#include <stdio.h>
#include <stdlib.h>
#include <unistd.h>
#include <errno.h>
```

```
main()
{
  int     execlp_value;

  fprintf (stdout,"execlp exectue\n");
  fprintf (stdout,"test5 hello world\n");
  execlp_value = execlp ("test5", "test5", "hello", "world", (char *)0);
  if ( execlp_value == -1 ) {
     fprintf (stderr,"ERROR: execlp() call failed\n");
     fprintf (stdout,"cannot find executable file test5\n");
     fprintf (stderr,"ERROR: %s\n", strerror(errno));
  }
}

/*   filename test5.c   */

#include <stdio.h>

main(argc, argv)
int argc ;
char *argv[] ;
{
   fprintf (stdout,"cxecuting file test5\n") ;
   fprintf (stdout,"argument count argc=%d\n", argc) ;
   fprintf (stdout,"vector argv[0]=%s\n", argv[0]) ;
   fprintf (stdout,"vector argv[1]=%s\n", argv[1]) ;
   fprintf (stdout,"vector argv[2]=%s\n", argv[2]) ;
}

/* filename execvp.c */

#include <stdio.h>
#include <stdlib.h>
#include <unistd.h>
#include <errno.h>

main()
{
  int     execvp_value;
  char    *args[] = { "test6", "hello", "world", (char *)0 };

  fprintf (stdout,"execute execvp\n");
  fprintf (stdout,"test6 args\n");
  execvp_value = execvp ("test6", args);
  if ( execvp_value == -1 ) {
     fprintf (stderr,"ERROR: execvp() call failed\n");
     fprintf (stdout,"cannot find executable file test6\n");
     fprintf (stderr,"ERROR: %s\n", strerror(errno));
  }
}

/*   filename test6.c   */
```

```
#include <stdio.h>

main(argc, argv)
int argc ;
char *argv[] ;
{
    fprintf (stdout,"executing file test6\n") ;
    fprintf (stdout,"argument count argc=%d\n", argc) ;
    fprintf (stdout,"vector argv[0]=%s\n", argv[0]) ;
    fprintf (stdout,"vector argv[1]=%s\n", argv[1]) ;
    fprintf (stdout,"vector argv[2]=%s\n", argv[2]) ;
}
```

NAME

exit, _exit — terminate process

SYNOPSIS

```
#include <stdlib.h>

void exit(int status);

#include <unistd.h>

void _exit(int status);
```

DESCRIPTION

The *exit*( ) function first calls all functions registered by *atexit*( ), in the reverse order of their registration. Each function is called as many times as it was registered.

If a function registered by a call to *atexit*( ) fails to return, the remaining registered functions are not called and the rest of the *exit*( ) processing is not completed. If *exit*( ) is called more than once, the effects are undefined.

The *exit*( ) function then flushes all output streams, closes all open streams, and removes all files created by *tmpfile*( ).

The *_exit*( ) and *exit*( ) functions terminate the calling process with the following consequences:

EX
- All of the file descriptors, directory streams, conversion descriptors and message catalogue descriptors open in the calling process are closed.

UX
- If the parent process of the calling process is executing a *wait*( ), *wait3*( ), *waitid*( ) or *waitpid*( ),

UX
and has neither set its SA_NOCLDWAIT flag nor set SIGCHLD to SIG_IGN, it is notified of the calling process' termination and the low-order eight bits (that is, bits 0377) of *status* are made available to it. If the parent is not waiting, the child's status will be made available to it

UX
when the parent subsequently executes *wait*( ), *wait3*( ), *waitid*( ) or *waitpid*( ).

UX
- If the parent process of the calling process is not executing a *wait*( ), *wait3*( ), *waitid*( ) or

UX
waitpid( ), and has not set its SA_NOCLDWAIT flag, or set SIGCHLD to SIG_IGN, the calling process is transformed into a *zombie process*. A *zombie process* is an inactive process and

UX
it will be deleted at some later time when its parent process executes *wait*( ), *wait3*( ), *waitid*( ) or *waitpid*( ).

- Termination of a process does not directly terminate its children. The sending of a SIGHUP signal as described below indirectly terminates children in some circumstances.

- If the implementation supports the SIGCHLD signal, a SIGCHLD will be sent to the parent process.

- The parent process ID of all of the calling process' existing child processes and zombie processes is set to the process ID of an implementation-dependent system process. That is, these processes are inherited by a special system process.

UX
- Each mapped memory object is unmapped.

EX
- Each attached shared-memory segment is detached and the value of *shm_nattch* (see *shmget*( )) in the data structure associated with its shared memory ID is decremented by 1.

EX
- For each semaphore for which the calling process has set a *semadj* value, see *semop*( ), that value is added to the *semval* of the specified semaphore.

- If the process is a controlling process, the SIGHUP signal will be sent to each process in the foreground process group of the controlling terminal belonging to the calling process.

- If the process is a controlling process, the controlling terminal associated with the session is disassociated from the session, allowing it to be acquired by a new controlling process.

- If the exit of the process causes a process group to become orphaned, and if any member of the newly-orphaned process group is stopped, then a SIGHUP signal followed by a SIGCONT signal will be sent to each process in the newly-orphaned process group.

UX
- If the parent process has set its SA_NOCLDWAIT flag, or set SIGCHLD to SIG_IGN, the status will be discarded, and the lifetime of the calling process will end immediately.

RETURN VALUE

These functions do not return.

APPLICATION USAGE

Normally applications should use *exit*( ) rather than *_exit*( ).

ERRORS

No errors are defined.

SEE ALSO

atexit( ), *close*( ), *fclose*( ), *semop*( ), *shmget*( ), *sigaction*( ), *wait*( ), *wait3*( ), *waitid*( ), *waitpid*( ), **<stdlib.h>**, **<unistd.h>**.

EXAMPLE

```
/*
 * Copyright (C) ANTRIX Inc.
 */

/* exit.c
 * This program is terminated using function exit.
 */

#include <stdio.h>
#include <stdlib.h>
#include <stdlib.h>
#include <errno.h>

main()
{
  int  status;

  status = 1;
  fprintf (stdout,"hello world\n");
  fprintf (stdout,"exit from this program\n");
  exit (status);

  /* program will never execute statements below */
  fprintf (stderr,"ERROR: exit() call failed\n");
  fprintf (stdout,"exit() did not terminate program\n");
  fprintf (stderr,"ERROR: %s\n", strerror(errno));
}

/*
 * Copyright (C) ANTRIX Inc.
 */
```

```
/* _exit.c
 * This program is terminated using function _exit.
 */

#include <stdio.h>
#include <stdlib.h>
#include <unistd.h>
#include <errno.h>

main()
{
  int    status;

  status = 1;
  fprintf (stdout,"_exit terminates the current application\n");
  _exit (status);

  /* program will never execute statements below */
  fprintf (stderr,"ERROR: _exit() call failed\n");
  fprintf (stderr,"ERROR: %s\n", strerror(errno));
  fprintf (stdout,"_exit() did not terminate program\n");
}
```

NAME

exp — exponential function

SYNOPSIS

```
#include <math.h>

double exp(double x);
```

DESCRIPTION

The *exp( )* function computes the exponent of *x,* defined as e^x.

RETURN VALUE

Upon successful completion, *exp( )* returns the exponential value of *x.*

If the correct value would cause overflow, *exp( )* returns HUGE_VAL and sets *errno* to [ERANGE].

If the correct value would cause underflow, *exp( )* returns 0 and may set *errno* to [ERANGE].

EX   If *x* is NaN, NaN is returned and *errno* may be set to [EDOM].

ERRORS

The *exp( )* function will fail if:

[ERANGE]   The result overflows.

The *exp( )* function may fail if:

EX   [EDOM]   The value of *x* is NaN.

[ERANGE]   The result underflows.

EX   No other errors will occur.

APPLICATION USAGE

An application wishing to check for error situations should set *errno* to 0 before calling *exp( ).* If *errno* is non-zero on return, or the return value is NaN, an error has occurred.

SEE ALSO

isnan( ), *log( ),* **<math.h>**.

EXAMPLE

```
/*
 * Copyright (C) ANTRIX Inc.
 */

/* exp.c
 * This program computes the exponent of 1.00, defined as
 * e raise to 1 using function exp.
 */

#include <stdio.h>
#include <math.h>

main()
{
  double  exp_value;
  double  x = 1.00;

  exp_value = exp (x);
```

```
    fprintf (stdout,"exp of %f is %f\n", x, exp_value);
}
```

NAME

expm1 — computes exponential functions

SYNOPSIS

UX   `#include <math.h>`

`double expm1 (double x);`

DESCRIPTION

The *expm1( )* function computes e^x–1.0.

RETURN VALUE

If *x* is NaN, then the function returns NaN and *errno* may be set to EDOM.

If *x* is positive infinity, *expm1( )* returns positive infinity.

If *x* is negative infinity, *expm1( )* returns –1.0.

If the value overflows, *expm1( )* returns HUGE_VAL and may set *errno* to ERANGE.

ERRORS

The *expm1( )* function may fail if:

[EDOM]   The value of *x* is NaN.

[ERANGE]   The result overflows.

APPLICATION USAGE

The value of *expm1(x)* may be more accurate than *exp(x)*–1.0 for small values of *x*.

The *expm1( )* and *log1p( )* functions are useful for financial calculations of $((1+x)^n-1)/x$, namely:

expm1(*n* * log1p(*x*))/*x*

when *x* is very small (for example, when calculating small daily interest rates). These functions also simplify writing accurate inverse hyperbolic functions.

SEE ALSO

exp( ), *ilogb( )*, *log1p( )*, **<math.h>**.

EXAMPLE

```
/*
 * Copyright (C) ANTRIX Inc.
 */

/* expm1.c
 * This program computes the (e**x)-1 accurately even for tiny x
 * using function expm1.
 */

#include <stdio.h>
#include <math.h>

main()
{
  double  expm1_value;
  double  x = 1.00;

  expm1_value = expm1 (x);
```

```
       fprintf (stdout,"expm1 of %f is %f\n", x, expm1_value);
   }
```

NAME

fabs — absolute value function

SYNOPSIS

```
#include <math.h>

double fabs(double x);
```

DESCRIPTION

The *fabs*( ) function computes the absolute value of *x*, |x|.

RETURN VALUE

Upon successful completion, *fabs*( ) returns the absolute value of *x*.

EX   If *x* is NaN, NaN is returned and *errno* may be set to [EDOM].

If the result underflows, 0 is returned and *errno* may be set to [ERANGE].

ERRORS

The *fabs*( ) function may fail if:

EX   [EDOM]   The value of *x* is NaN.

[ERANGE]   The result underflows.

EX   No other errors will occur.

APPLICATION USAGE

An application wishing to check for error situations should set *errno* to 0 before calling *fabs*( ). If *errno* is non-zero on return, or the return value is NaN, an error has occurred.

SEE ALSO

isnan( ), **<math.h>**.

EXAMPLE

```
/*
 * Copyright (C) ANTRIX Inc.
 */

/* fabs.c
 * This program computes the absolute value of -1.2345
 * using function fabs.
 */

#include <stdio.h>
#include <math.h>

main()
{
  double  fabs_value;
  double  x = -1.2345;

  fabs_value = fabs (x);
  fprintf (stdout,"fabs of %f is %f\n", x, fabs_value);
}
```

NAME

fattach — attach a STREAMS-based file descriptor to a file in the file system name space

SYNOPSIS

UX
```
#include <stropts.h>
```

```
int fattach(int fildes, const char *path);
```

DESCRIPTION

The *fattach*( ) function attaches a STREAMS-based file descriptor to a file, effectively associating a pathname with *fildes*. The *fildes* argument must be a valid open file descriptor associated with a STREAMS file. The *path* argument points to a pathname of an existing file. The process must have appropriate privileges, or must be the owner of the file named by *path* and have write permission. A successful call to *fattach*( ) causes all pathnames that name the file named by *path* to name the STREAMS file associated with *fildes*, until the STREAMS file is detached from the file. A STREAMS file can be attached to more than one file and can have several pathnames associated with it.

The attributes of the named STREAMS file are initialised as follows: the permissions, user ID, group ID, and times are set to those of the file named by *path*, the number of links is set to 1, and the size and device identifier are set to those of the STREAMS file associated with *fildes*. If any attributes of the named STREAMS file are subsequently changed (for example, by *chmod*( )), neither the attributes of the underlying file nor the attributes of the STREAMS file to which *fildes* refers are affected.

File descriptors referring to the underlying file, opened prior to an *fattach*( ) call, continue to refer to the underlying file.

RETURN VALUE

Upon successful completion, *fattach*( ) returns 0. Otherwise, −1 is returned and *errno* is set to indicate the error.

ERRORS

The *fattach*( ) function will fail if:

[EACCES]   Search permission is denied for a component of the path prefix, or the process is the owner of *path* but does not have write permissions on the file named by *path*.

[EBADF]   The *fildes* argument is not a valid open file descriptor.

[ENOENT]   A component of *path* does not name an existing file or *path* is an empty string.

[ENOTDIR]   A component of the path prefix is not a directory.

[EPERM]   The effective user ID of the process is not the owner of the file named by *path* and the process does not have appropriate privilege.

[EBUSY]   The file named by *path* is currently a mount point or has a STREAMS file attached to it.

[ENAMETOOLONG]
                 The size of *path* exceeds {PATH_MAX}, or a component of *path* is longer than {NAME_MAX}.

[ELOOP]   Too many symbolic links were encountered in resolving *path*.

The *fattach*( ) function may fail if:

[EINVAL]   The *fildes* argument does not refer to a STREAMS file.

[ENAMETOOLONG]
>   Pathname resolution of a symbolic link produced an intermediate result whose
>   length exceeds {PATH_MAX}.

SEE ALSO
>   *fdetach*( ), *isastream*( ), **<stropts.h>**.

APPLICATION USAGE
>   The *fattach*( ) function behaves similarly to the traditional *mount*( ) function in the way a file is
>   temporarily replaced by the root directory of the mounted file system. In the case of *fattach*( ),
>   the replaced file need not be a directory and the replacing file is a STREAMS file.

EXAMPLE

```c
/*
 * Copyright (C) ANTRIX Inc.
 */

/* fattach.c
 * This program attaches a STREAM based file descriptor to an
 * object in the file system name space using function fattach.
 */

#include <stdio.h>
#include <stdlib.h>
#include <fcntl.h>
#include <sys/stat.h>
#include <errno.h>

#define  PERM_ALL   (S_IRWXU | S_IRWXG | S_IRWXO)

main()
{
  int     fattach_value;
  int     fildes, fd[2];
  int     length, compare;
  char    *buf;
  char    string[] = "hello world";
  char    *file = "testfile";

  memset(fd, 0, 2);
  length = strlen(string);

  fprintf (stdout,"create testfile\n");
  fildes = creat (file, PERM_ALL);

  fprintf (stdout,"close testfile\n");
  close (fildes);

  fprintf (stdout,"create pipe\n");
  pipe (fd);

  fprintf (stdout,"attach testfile to pipe\n");
  fprintf (stdout,"attach stream based descriptor to testfile\n");
  fattach_value = fattach (fd[0], file);
```

```
      if ( fattach_value == 0 )
         fprintf (stdout,"fattach() call successful\n");
      else {
         fprintf (stderr,"ERROR: fattach() call failed\n");
         fprintf (stderr,"ERROR: %s\n", strerror(errno));
      }

      fprintf (stdout,"open testfile\n");
      fildes = open (file, O_WRONLY);

      fprintf (stdout,"write string to testfile shall\n");
      fprintf (stdout,"operate on streams path\n");
      write (fildes, string, length);
      buf = (char *)malloc (length);

      fprintf (stdout,"read from the streams file\n");
      read (fd[1], buf, length);
      compare = strcmp(buf, string);
      if ( compare == 0 )
         fprintf (stdout,"string in buf=%s\n", buf);
      else
         fprintf (stderr,"ERROR: %s\n", strerror(errno));

      fprintf (stdout,"detach testfile\n");
      fdetach (file);

      close (fildes);
      fprintf (stdout,"remove testfile\n");
      remove (file);
   }
```

NAME

fchdir — change working directory

SYNOPSIS

UX   `#include <unistd.h>`

`int fchdir(int fildes);`

DESCRIPTION

The *fchdir( )* function has the same effect as *chdir( )* except that the directory that is to be the new current working directory is specified by the file descriptor *fildes*.

RETURN VALUE

Upon successful completion, *fchdir( )* returns 0. Otherwise, it returns −1 and sets *errno* to indicate the error. On failure the current working directory remains unchanged.

ERRORS

The *fchdir( )* function will fail if:

[EACCES]   Search permission is denied for the directory referenced by *fildes*.

[EBADF]   The *fildes* argument is not an open file descriptor.

[ENOTDIR]   The open file descriptor *fildes* does not refer to a directory.

The *fchdir( )* may fail if:

[EINTR]   A signal was caught during the execution of *fchdir( )*.

[EIO]   An I/O error occurred while reading from or writing to the file system.

SEE ALSO

chdir( ), *chroot( )*, **<unistd.h>**.

EXAMPLE

```
/*
 * Copyright (C) ANTRIX Inc.
 */

/* fchdir.c
 * This program changes the current working directory
 * using function fchdir.
 */

#include <stdio.h>
#include <stdlib.h>
#include <unistd.h>
#include <limits.h>
#include <fcntl.h>
#include <sys/stat.h>
#include <dirent.h>
#include <errno.h>

#define  PERM_ALL   (S_IRWXU | S_IRWXG | S_IRWXO)
#define  MAX_LEN    255

main()
{
    int     fchdir_value;
```

```
char    curdir[MAX_LEN];
char    newdir[MAX_LEN];
char    testdir[MAX_LEN];
DIR     *buf;

memset(curdir, ' ', MAX_LEN);
memset(newdir, ' ', MAX_LEN);
memset(testdir, ' ', MAX_LEN);

fprintf (stdout,"get current working directory\n");
getcwd (curdir, MAX_LEN);

fprintf (stdout,"current directory is=%s\n", curdir);
fprintf (stdout,"create test directories\n");
mkdir ("testpath", PERM_ALL);

strcpy (testdir, curdir);
strcat (testdir, "/testpath");

fprintf (stdout,"new directory=%s\n", testdir);
buf = opendir (testdir);
fprintf (stdout,"change directory\n");
fchdir_value = fchdir (buf->dd_fd);
if ( fchdir_value == 0 ) {
    fprintf (stdout,"fchdir() call successful\n");
    fprintf (stdout,"new directory is=%s\n", getcwd(newdir, MAX_LEN) );
}
else {
    fprintf (stderr,"ERROR: fchdir() call failed\n");
    fprintf (stderr,"ERROR: %s\n", strerror(errno));
}

fprintf (stdout,"restore original directory\n");
chdir (curdir);

fprintf (stdout,"close and remove directory\n");
closedir (buf);
rmdir ("testpath");
}
```

NAME

fchmod — change mode of file

SYNOPSIS

UX   `#include <sys/stat.h>`

`int fchmod(int fildes, mode_t mode);`

DESCRIPTION

The *fchmod*( ) function has the same effect as *chmod*( ) except that the file whose permissions are to be changed is specified by the file descriptor *fildes*.

RETURN VALUE

Upon successful completion, *fchmod*( ) returns 0. Otherwise, it returns −1 and sets *errno* to indicate the error.

ERRORS

The *fchmod*( ) function will fail if:

[EBADF]   The *fildes* argument is not an open file descriptor.

[EROFS]   The file referred to by *fildes* resides on a read-only file system.

[EPERM]   The effective user ID does not match the owner of the file and the process does not have appropriate privilege.

The *fchmod*( ) function may fail if:

[EINTR]   The *fchmod*( ) function was interrupted by a signal.

[EINVAL]   The value of the *mode* argument is invalid.

SEE ALSO

chmod( ), *chown*( ), *creat*( ), *fcntl*( ), *fstatvfs*( ), *mknod*( ), *open*( ), *read*( ), *stat*( ), *write*( ), **<sys/stat.h>**.

EXAMPLE

```
/*
 * Copyright (C) ANTRIX Inc.
 */

/* fchmod.c
 * This program changes access permission mode of file
 * using function fchmod.
 */

#include <stdio.h>
#include <stdlib.h>
#include <sys/types.h>
#include <sys/stat.h>
#include <fcntl.h>
#include <errno.h>

#define  PERM_ALL    (S_IRWXU | S_IRWXG | S_IRWXO)
#define  PERM_SOME   (S_IRWXU | S_IRWXG )

main()
{
    int     fchmod_value;
```

```
int     fildes;
struct  stat orig_buf, new_buf;
char    *file = "testfile";

fprintf (stdout,"create testfile\n");
fildes = creat (file, PERM_ALL);

stat (file, &orig_buf);
fprintf (stdout,"original permission mode=#0%o\n",
                (S_IFREG ^ orig_buf.st_mode));

fprintf (stdout,"change the permission of file\n");
fchmod_value = fchmod (fildes, PERM_SOME);

if ( fchmod_value  == 0 ) {
   fprintf (stdout,"fchmod() call successful\n");
   stat (file, &new_buf);
   fprintf (stdout,"new permission mode=#0%o\n",
                (S_IFREG ^ new_buf.st_mode));
}
else {
   fprintf (stderr,"ERROR: fchmod() call failed\n");
   fprintf (stderr,"ERROR: %s\n", strerror(errno));
}

fprintf (stdout,"remove testfile\n");
remove (file);
}
```

NAME

fchown — change owner and group of a file

SYNOPSIS

UX   `#include <unistd.h>`

`int fchown(int fildes, uid_t owner, gid_t group);`

DESCRIPTION

The *fchown*( ) function has the same effect as *chown*( ) except that the file whose owner and group are to be changed is specified by the file descriptor *fildes*.

RETURN VALUE

Upon successful completion, *fchown*( ) returns 0. Otherwise, it returns −1 and sets *errno* to indicate the error.

ERRORS

The *fchown*( ) function will fail if:

[EBADF]   The *fildes* argument is not an open file descriptor.

[EPERM]   The effective user ID does not match the owner of the file or the process does not have appropriate privilege.

[EROFS]   The file referred to by *fildes* resides on a read-only file system.

The *fchown*( ) function may fail if:

[EINVAL]   The owner or group ID is not a value supported by the implementation.

[EIO]   A physical I/O error has occurred.

[EINTR]   The *fchown*( ) function was interrupted by a signal which was caught.

SEE ALSO

chown( ), **<unistd.h>**.

EXAMPLE

```
/*
 * Copyright (C) ANTRIX Inc.
 */

/* fchown.c: run as root
 * This program changes the owner and group of a file
 * using function fchown.
 */

#include <stdio.h>
#include <stdlib.h>
#include <unistd.h>
#include <sys/types.h>
#include <sys/stat.h>
#include <errno.h>

#define  PERM_ALL    (S_IRWXU | S_IRWXG | S_IRWXO)

main()
{
  int      fchown_value;
```

```
int     fildes;
struct  stat orig_buf, new_buf;
char    *file = "testfile";

fprintf (stdout,"create testfile\n");
fildes = creat(file, PERM_ALL);

stat (file, &orig_buf);
fprintf (stdout,"original owner-id=%d, group-id=%d\n",
                  orig_buf.st_uid, orig_buf.st_gid );

fprintf (stdout,"set owner and group to 2 which is bin\n");
fchown_value = fchown (fildes, 2, 2);
if ( fchown_value == 0 ) {
   fprintf (stdout,"fchown() call successful\n");
   stat (file, &new_buf);
   fprintf (stdout,"new owner-id=%d, group-id=%d\n",
               new_buf.st_uid, new_buf.st_gid );
}
else {
   fprintf (stderr,"ERROR: fchown() call failed\n");
   fprintf (stderr,"ERROR: %s\n", strerror(errno));
}

fprintf (stdout,"remove testfile\n");
remove (file);
}
```

NAME

fclose — close a stream

SYNOPSIS

```
#include <stdio.h>

int fclose(FILE *stream);
```

DESCRIPTION

The *fclose( )* function causes the stream pointed to by *stream* to be flushed and the associated file to be closed. Any unwritten buffered data for the stream is written to the file; any unread buffered data is discarded. The stream is disassociated from the file. If the associated buffer was automatically allocated, it is deallocated. It marks for update the *st_ctime* and *st_mtime* fields of the underlying file, if the stream was writable, and if buffered data had not been written to the file yet. The *fclose( )* function will perform a *close( )* on the file descriptor that is associated with the stream pointed to by *stream*.

After the call to *fclose( )*, any use of *stream* causes undefined behaviour.

RETURN VALUE

Upon successful completion, *fclose( )* returns 0. Otherwise, it returns EOF and sets *errno* to indicate the error.

ERRORS

The *fclose( )* function will fail if:

[EAGAIN]	The O_NONBLOCK flag is set for the file descriptor underlying *stream* and the process would be delayed in the write operation.
[EBADF]	The file descriptor underlying stream is not valid.
EX [EFBIG]	An attempt was made to write a file that exceeds the maximum file size or the process' file size limit.
[EINTR]	The *fclose( )* function was interrupted by a signal.
[EIO]	The process is a member of a background process group attempting to write to its controlling terminal, TOSTOP is set, the process is neither ignoring nor blocking SIGTTOU and the process group of the process is orphaned. This error may also be returned under implementation-dependent conditions.
[ENOSPC]	There was no free space remaining on the device containing the file.
[EPIPE]	An attempt is made to write to a pipe or FIFO that is not open for reading by any process. A SIGPIPE signal will also be sent to the process.

The *fclose( )* function may fail if:

EX [ENXIO]	A request was made of a non-existent device, or the request was outside the device.

SEE ALSO

close( ), *fopen( )*, *getrlimit( )*, *ulimit( )*, **<stdio.h>**.

EXAMPLE

```
/*
 * Copyright (C) ANTRIX Inc.
 */

/* fclose.c
 * This program causes the stream to be flushed and the
```

```
 * associated file to be closed.
 */

#include <stdio.h>
#include <stdlib.h>
#include <sys/types.h>
#include <errno.h>

main()
{
  int    bytes, fclose_value;
  char   buf[12];
  char   *path = "testfile";
  char   string[] = "hello world";
  FILE   *stream;

  memset (buf, ' ', 12);
  bytes = strlen (string);

  fprintf (stdout,"open testfile\n");
  stream = fopen (path, "w+r");

  fprintf (stdout,"write a string to the file\n");
  fwrite (string, sizeof(char), bytes, stream);
  fflush (stream);

  fprintf (stdout,"seek to the beginning of the file\n");
  fseek (stream, 0, SEEK_SET);

  fprintf (stdout,"read the string file\n");
  fread (buf, sizeof(char), bytes, stream);
  fprintf (stdout,"string read in buf is %s\n", buf);

  fprintf (stdout,"close stream\n");
  fclose_value = fclose (stream);
  if (fclose_value == 0)
     printf("fclose() call successful\n");
  else {
     fprintf (stderr,"ERROR: fclose() call failed\n");
     fprintf (stderr,"ERROR: %s\n", strerror(errno));
  }

  fprintf (stdout,"remove testfile\n");
  remove (path);
}
```

NAME

fcntl — file control

SYNOPSIS

OH
```
#include <sys/types.h>
#include <unistd.h>
#include <fcntl.h>

int fcntl(int fildes, int cmd, ...);
```

DESCRIPTION

The *fcntl( )* function provides for control over open files. The *fildes* argument is a file descriptor.

The available values for *cmd* are defined in the header **<fcntl.h>**, which include:

F_DUPFD   Return a new file descriptor which is the lowest numbered available (that is, not already open) file descriptor greater than or equal to the third argument, *arg*, taken as an integer of type **int**. The new file descriptor refers to the same open file description as the original file descriptor, and shares any locks. The FD_CLOEXEC flag associated with the new file descriptor is cleared to keep the file open across calls to one of the *exec* functions.

F_GETFD   Get the file descriptor flags defined in **<fcntl.h>** that are associated with the file descriptor *fildes*. File descriptor flags are associated with a single file descriptor and do not affect other file descriptors that refer to the same file.

F_SETFD   Set the file descriptor flags defined in **<fcntl.h>**, that are associated with *fildes*, to the third argument, *arg*, taken as type **int**. If the FD_CLOEXEC flag in the third argument is 0, the file will remain open across the *exec* functions; otherwise the file will be closed upon successful execution of one of the *exec* functions.

F_GETFL   Get the file status flags and file access modes, defined in **<fcntl.h>**, for the file description associated with *fildes*. The file access modes can be extracted from the return value using the mask O_ACCMODE, which is defined in **<fcntl.h>**. File status flags and file access modes are associated with the file description and do not affect other file descriptors that refer to the same file with different open file descriptions.

F_SETFL   Set the file status flags, defined in **<fcntl.h>**, for the file description associated with *fildes* from the corresponding bits in the third argument, *arg*, taken as type **int**. Bits corresponding to the file access mode and the *oflag* values that are set in *arg* are ignored. If any bits in *arg* other than those mentioned here are changed by the application, the result is unspecified.

The following commands are available for advisory record locking. Record locking is supported for regular files, and may be supported for other files.

F_GETLK   Get the first lock which blocks the lock description pointed to by the third argument, *arg*, taken as a pointer to type **struct flock**, defined in **<fcntl.h>**. The information retrieved overwrites the information passed to *fcntl( )* in the structure **flock**. If no lock is found that would prevent this lock from being created, then the structure will be left unchanged except for the lock type which will be set to F_UNLCK.

F_SETLK   Set or clear a file segment lock according to the lock description pointed to by the third argument, *arg*, taken as a pointer to type **struct flock**, defined in **<fcntl.h>**. F_SETLK is used to establish shared (or read) locks (F_RDLCK) or exclusive (or write) locks (F_WRLCK), as well as to remove either type of lock (F_UNLCK). F_RDLCK, F_WRLCK and F_UNLCK are defined in **<fcntl.h>.** If a shared or exclusive lock cannot be set, *fcntl*( ) will return immediately with a return value of −1.

F_SETLKW   This command is the same as F_SETLK except that if a shared or exclusive lock is blocked by other locks, the process will wait until the request can be satisfied. If a signal that is to be caught is received while *fcntl*( ) is waiting for a region, *fcntl*( ) will be interrupted. Upon return from the process' signal handler, *fcntl*( ) will return −1 with *errno* set to [EINTR], and the lock operation will not be done.

Additional implementation-dependent commands may be defined in **<fcntl.h>**. Their names will start with F_.

When a shared lock is set on a segment of a file, other processes will be able to set shared locks on that segment or a portion of it. A shared lock prevents any other process from setting an exclusive lock on any portion of the protected area. A request for a shared lock will fail if the file descriptor was not opened with read access.

An exclusive lock will prevent any other process from setting a shared lock or an exclusive lock on any portion of the protected area. A request for an exclusive lock will fail if the file descriptor was not opened with write access.

The structure **flock** describes the type (**l_type**), starting offset (**l_whence**), relative offset (**l_start**), size (**l_len**) and process ID (**l_pid**) of the segment of the file to be affected.

The value of **l_whence** is SEEK_SET, SEEK_CUR or SEEK_END, to indicate that the relative offset **l_start** bytes will be measured from the start of the file, current position or end of the file, respectively. The value of **l_len** is the number of consecutive bytes to be locked. The value of

EX

l_len may be negative (where the definition of **off_t** permits negative values of **l_len**). The **l_pid** field is only used with F_GETLK to return the process ID of the process holding a blocking lock. After a successful F_GETLK request, that is, one in which a lock was found, the value of **l_whence** will be SEEK_SET.

EX

If **l_len** is positive, the area affected starts at **l_start** and ends at **l_start** + **l_len**−1. If **l_len** is negative, the area affected starts at **l_start** + **l_len** and ends at **l_start**−1. Locks may start and extend beyond the current end of a file, but must not be negative relative to the beginning of the file. A lock will be set to extend to the largest possible value of the file offset for that file by setting **l_len** to 0. If such a lock also has **l_start** set to 0 and **l_whence** is set to SEEK_SET, the whole file will be locked.

There will be at most one type of lock set for each byte in the file. Before a successful return from an F_SETLK or an F_SETLKW request when the calling process has previously existing locks on bytes in the region specified by the request, the previous lock type for each byte in the specified region will be replaced by the new lock type. As specified above under the descriptions of shared locks and exclusive locks, an F_SETLK or an F_SETLKW request will (respectively) fail or block when another process has existing locks on bytes in the specified region and the type of any of those locks conflicts with the type specified in the request.

All locks associated with a file for a given process are removed when a file descriptor for that file is closed by that process or the process holding that file descriptor terminates. Locks are not inherited by a child process created using *fork*( ).

A potential for deadlock occurs if a process controlling a locked region is put to sleep by attempting to lock another process' locked region. If the system detects that sleeping until a locked region is unlocked would cause a deadlock, *fcntl*( ) will fail with an [EDEADLK] error.

RETURN VALUE

Upon successful completion, the value returned depends on *cmd* as follows:

F_DUPFD	A new file descriptor.
F_GETFD	Value of flags defined in **<fcntl.h>**. The return value will not be negative.
F_SETFD	Value other than −1.
F_GETFL	Value of file status flags and access modes. The return value will not be negative.
F_SETFL	Value other than −1.
F_GETLK	Value other than −1.
F_SETLK	Value other than −1.
F_SETLKW	Value other than −1.

Otherwise, −1 is returned and *errno* is set to indicate the error.

ERRORS

The *fcntl*( ) function will fail if:

[EACCES] or [EAGAIN]

> The *cmd* argument is F_SETLK; the type of lock (**l_type**) is a shared (F_RDLCK) or exclusive (F_WRLCK) lock and the segment of a file to be locked is already exclusive-locked by another process, or the type is an exclusive lock and some portion of the segment of a file to be locked is already shared-locked or exclusive-locked by another process.

[EBADF]
> The *fildes* argument is not a valid open file descriptor, or the argument *cmd* is F_SETLK or F_SETLKW, the type of lock, **l_type**, is a shared lock (F_RDLCK), and *fildes* is not a valid file descriptor open for reading, or the type of lock **l_type**, is an exclusive lock (F_WRLCK), and *fildes* is not a valid file descriptor open for writing.

[EINTR]
> The *cmd* argument is F_SETLKW and the function was interrupted by a signal.

EX   [EINVAL]
> The *cmd* argument is invalid, or the *cmd* argument is F_DUPFD and *arg* is negative or greater than or equal to {OPEN_MAX}, or the *cmd* argument is F_GETLK, F_SETLK or F_SETLKW and the data pointed to by *arg* is not valid, or *fildes* refers to a file that does not support locking.

[EMFILE]
> The argument *cmd* is F_DUPFD and {OPEN_MAX} file descriptors are currently open in the calling process, or no file descriptors greater than or equal to *arg* are available.

[ENOLCK]
> The argument *cmd* is F_SETLK or F_SETLKW and satisfying the lock or unlock request would result in the number of locked regions in the system exceeding a system-imposed limit.

The *fcntl*( ) function may fail if:

[EDEADLK]   The *cmd* argument is F_SETLKW, the lock is blocked by some lock from
               another process and putting the calling process to sleep, waiting for that lock
               to become free would cause a deadlock.

SEE ALSO

close( ), *exec*, *open*( ), *sigaction*( ), **<fcntl.h>**, **<signal.h>**, **<sys/types.h>**, **<unistd.h>**.

EXAMPLE

```c
/*
 * Copyright (C) ANTRIX Inc.
 */

/* fcntl.c
 * This program provides control over open files using function
 * fcntl.
 */

#include <stdio.h>
#include <stdlib.h>
#include <fcntl.h>
#include <unistd.h>
#include <sys/stat.h>
#include <errno.h>

#define  PERM_ALL    (S_IRWXU | S_IRWXG | S_IRWXO)
#define  OFLAG       (O_RDWR | O_CREAT | O_APPEND)

main()
{
    int     fcntl_value;
    int     fd, length;
    char    *path = "testfile";
    char    *buf = "hello world";
    struct  flock lock;

    length = strlen (buf);
    fprintf (stdout,"create and open testfile\n");
    fd = open (path, OFLAG, PERM_ALL);

    fprintf (stdout,"write string\n");
    write (fd, buf, length);
    lock.l_type = F_WRLCK;
    lock.l_whence = SEEK_SET;
    lock.l_start = (off_t)0;
    lock.l_len = (off_t)length;

    fprintf (stdout,"set lock on file using fcntl\n");
    fcntl_value = fcntl (fd, F_SETLK, &lock);
    if ( fcntl_value != -1 ) {
        fprintf (stdout,"fcntl() call successful\n");
        fprintf (stdout,"duplicate a file descriptor using fcntl\n");
        fcntl_value = fcntl (fd, F_DUPFD, (fd + 1) );
```

```
            fprintf (stdout,"duplicate file descriptor value=%d\n", fcntl_value );
      }
      else {
            fprintf (stderr,"ERROR: fcntl() call failed\n");
            fprintf (stderr,"ERROR: could not set lock\n");
            fprintf (stderr,"ERROR: %s\n", strerror(errno));
      }

      fprintf (stdout,"remove testfile\n");
      remove (path);
}
```

NAME

fcvt — convert floating-point number to string

SYNOPSIS

UX
```
#include <stdlib.h>

char *fcvt(double value, int ndigit, int *decpt, int *sign);
```

DESCRIPTION

Refer to *ecvt( )*.

NAME

FD_CLR — macros for synchronous I/O multiplexing

SYNOPSIS

UX

```
#include <sys/time.h>
```

```
FD_CLR(int fd, fd_set *fdset);
```

```
FD_ISSET(int fd, fd_set *fdset);
```

```
FD_SET(int fd, fd_set *fdset);
```

```
FD_ZERO(fd_set *fdset);
```

DESCRIPTION

Refer to *select*( ).

EXAMPLE

```c
/*
 * Copyright (C) ANTRIX Inc.
 */

/* fd_clr.c
 * This program illustrates use of FD_CLR, FD_ISSET, FD_SET
 * and FD_ZERO i/o multiplexing macros.
 */

#include <stdio.h>
#include <stdlib.h>
#include <unistd.h>
#include <sys/select.h>
#include <errno.h>

main()
{
  int  set;
  fd_set perm_rfds, rfds;

  fprintf(stdout, "Zero out using FD_ZERO\n");
  FD_ZERO(&perm_rfds);
  set = FD_ISSET(10, &perm_rfds);
  fprintf(stdout, "FD_SET: set=%d\n", set);

  fprintf(stdout, "Set using FD_SET\n");
  FD_SET(10, &perm_rfds);
  fprintf(stdout, "FD_SET: perm_rfds=%d\n", perm_rfds);
  set = FD_ISSET(10, &perm_rfds);
  fprintf(stdout, "FD_SET: set=%d\n", set);

  fprintf(stdout, "Clear using FD_CLR\n");
  FD_CLR(0, &perm_rfds);
  fprintf(stdout, "FD_CLR: perm_rfds=%d\n", perm_rfds);
  set = FD_ISSET(10, &perm_rfds);
  fprintf(stdout, "FD_SET: set=%d\n", set);
}
```

NAME

fdetach — detach a name from a STREAMS-based file descriptor

SYNOPSIS

UX

```
#include <stropts.h>
```

```
int fdetach(const char *path);
```

DESCRIPTION

The *fdetach( )* function detaches a STREAMS-based file from the file to which it was attached by a previous call to *fattach( )*. The *path* argument points to the pathname of the attached STREAMS file. The process must have appropriate privileges or be the owner of the file. A successful call to *fdetach( )* causes all pathnames that named the attached STREAMS file to again name the file to which the STREAMS file was attached. All subsequent operations on *path* will operate on the underlying file and not on the STREAMS file.

All open file descriptions established while the STREAMS file was attached to the file referenced by *path*, will still refer to the STREAMS file after the *fdetach( )* has taken effect.

If there are no open file descriptors or other references to the STREAMS file, then a successful call to *fdetach( )* has the same effect as performing the last *close( )* on the attached file.

RETURN VALUE

Upon successful completion, *fdetach( )* returns 0. Otherwise, it returns −1 and sets *errno* to indicate the error.

ERRORS

The *fdetach( )* function will fail if:

[EACCES]   Search permission is denied on a component of the path prefix.

[EPERM]   The effective user ID is not the owner of *path* and the process does not have appropriate privileges.

[ENOTDIR]   A component of the path prefix is not a directory.

[ENOENT]   A component of *path* does not name an existing file or *path* is an empty string.

[EINVAL]   The *path* argument names a file that is not currently attached.

[ENAMETOOLONG]
                The size of a pathname exceeds {PATH_MAX}, or a pathname component is longer than {NAME_MAX}.

[ELOOP]   Too many symbolic links were encountered in resolving *path*.

The *fdetach( )* function may fail if:

[ENAMETOOLONG]
                Pathname resolution of a symbolic link produced an intermediate result whose length exceeds {PATH_MAX}.

SEE ALSO

fattach( ), **<stropts.h>**.

EXAMPLE

```
/*
 * Copyright (C) ANTRIX Inc.
 */

/* fdetach.c
 * This program detaches a name from a STREAMS based file
 * descriptor using function fdetach.
 */

#include <stdio.h>
#include <stdlib.h>
#include <fcntl.h>
#include <sys/stat.h>
#include <errno.h>

#define  PERM_ALL   (S_IRWXU | S_IRWXG | S_IRWXO)

main()
{
   int     fdetach_value;
   int     fildes, fd[2];
   int     length, compare;
   char    *buf;
   char    string[] = "hello world";
   char    *file = "testfile";

   memset(fd, 0, 2);
   length = strlen(string);

   fprintf (stdout,"create testfile\n");
   fildes = creat (file, PERM_ALL);

   fprintf (stdout,"close testfile\n");
   close (fildes);

   fprintf (stdout,"create pipe\n");
   pipe (fd);
   fprintf (stdout,"attach testfile to pipe\n");
   fprintf (stdout,"attach stream based descriptor to testfile\n");
   fattach (fd[0], file);

   fprintf (stdout,"open testfile for read only\n");
   fildes = open (file, O_WRONLY);

   fprintf (stdout,"write to testfile shall operate on streams path\n");
   write (fildes, string, length);
   buf = (char *)malloc (length);

   fprintf (stdout,"read from the streams file\n");
   read (fd[1], buf, length);
   compare = strcmp(buf, string);
```

```
    if ( compare == 0 )
       fprintf (stdout,"string in buf=%s\n", buf);
    else
       fprintf (stderr,"ERROR: expected=%s, received=%s\n", string, buf);

    fprintf (stdout,"detach testfile\n");
    fdetach_value = fdetach (file);
    if (fdetach_value == 0 )
       fprintf (stdout,"fdetach() call successful\n");
    else {
       fprintf (stderr,"ERROR: fdetach() call failed\n");
       fprintf (stderr,"ERROR: %s\n", strerror(errno));
    }

    fprintf (stdout,"close and remove testfile\n");
    close (fildes);
    remove (file);
}
```

NAME

fdopen — associate a stream with a file descriptor

SYNOPSIS

```
#include <stdio.h>

FILE *fdopen(int fildes, const char *mode);
```

DESCRIPTION

The *fdopen( )* function associates a stream with a file descriptor.

The *mode* argument is a character string having one of the following values:

EX	**r** or **rb**	open a file for reading
EX	**w** or **wb**	open a file for writing
EX	**a** or **ab**	open a file for writing at end of file
EX	**r+** or **rb+** or **r+b**	open a file for update (reading and writing)
EX	**w+** or **wb+** or **w+b**	open a file for update (reading and writing)
EX	**a+** or **ab+** or **a+b**	open a file for update (reading and writing) at end of file

The meaning of these flags is exactly as specified in *fopen( )*, except that modes beginning with **w** do not cause truncation of the file.

Additional values for the *mode* argument may be supported by an implementation.

The mode of the stream must be allowed by the file access mode of the open file. The file position indicator associated with the new stream is set to the position indicated by the file offset associated with the file descriptor.

EX   The error and end-of-file indicators for the stream are cleared. The *fdopen( )* function may cause the *st_atime* field of the underlying file to be marked for update.

RETURN VALUE

Upon successful completion, *fdopen( )* returns a pointer to a stream. Otherwise, a null pointer is returned and *errno* is set to indicate the error.

ERRORS

The *fdopen( )* function may fail if:

EX	[EBADF]	The *fildes* argument is not a valid file descriptor.
	[EINVAL]	The *mode* argument is not a valid mode.
	[EMFILE]	{FOPEN_MAX} streams are currently open in the calling process.
	[EMFILE]	{STREAM_MAX} streams are currently open in the calling process.
	[ENOMEM]	Insufficient space to allocate a buffer.

APPLICATION USAGE

{STREAM_MAX} is the number of streams that one process can have open at one time. If defined, it has the same value as {FOPEN_MAX}.

File descriptors are obtained from calls like *open( )*, *dup( )*, *creat( )* or *pipe( )*, which open files but do not return streams.

SEE ALSO

fclose( ), *fopen( )*, *open( )*, **<stdio.h>**, **XSH** specification, **Section 2.4.1**, **Interaction of File Descriptors and Standard I/O Streams**.

EXAMPLE

```
/*
 * Copyright (C) ANTRIX Inc.
 */

/* fdopen.c
 * This program associates a stream with a file descriptor
 * using function fdopen.
 */

#include <stdio.h>
#include <stdlib.h>
#include <fcntl.h>
#include <sys/types.h>
#include <sys/stat.h>
#include <errno.h>

#define  PERM_ALL    (S_IRWXU | S_IRWXG | S_IRWXO)

main()
{
  FILE  *stream;
  int   fildes, bytes;
  char  buf[12];
  char  *path = "testfile";
  char  string[] = "hello world";

  memset (buf, ' ', 12);
  bytes = strlen (string);
  fprintf (stdout,"create testfile\n");
  fildes = creat (path, PERM_ALL);

  fprintf (stdout,"write a string to testfile\n");
  write (fildes, string, bytes);

  fprintf (stdout,"close testfile\n");
  close (fildes);

  fprintf (stdout,"open testfile\n");
  fildes = open (path, O_RDONLY);

  fprintf (stdout,"get stream pointer from fildes\n");
  stream = fdopen (fildes, "r");
  if ( stream != (FILE *)0 )
     fprintf (stdout,"fdopen() call successful\n");
  else {
     fprintf (stderr,"ERROR: fdopen() call failed\n");
     fprintf (stderr,"ERROR: %s\n", strerror(errno));
  }

  fprintf (stdout,"read string from testfile\n");
  fread (buf, sizeof(char), bytes, stream);
```

```
        fprintf (stdout,"string read in buf is %s\n", buf);
        fclose (stream);

        fprintf (stdout,"remove testfile\n");
        remove (path);
}
```

NAME

feof — test end-of-file indicator on a stream

SYNOPSIS

```
#include <stdio.h>

int feof(FILE *stream);
```

DESCRIPTION

The *feof*( ) function tests the end-of-file indicator for the stream pointed to by *stream*.

RETURN VALUE

The *feof*( ) function returns non-zero if and only if the end-of-file indicator is set for *stream*.

ERRORS

No errors are defined.

SEE ALSO

clearerr( ), *ferror*( ), *fopen*( ), **<stdio.h>**.

EXAMPLE

```
/*
 * Copyright (C) ANTRIX Inc.
 */

/* feof.c
 * This program tests for end-of-file indicator on a stream
 * using function feof.
 */

#include <stdio.h>
#include <stdlib.h>
#include <errno.h>

main()
{
    int    i, err, feof_value;
    char   *path = "testfile";
    char   string[2], *errmsg;
    FILE   *stream;

    fprintf (stdout,"create and open testfile\n");
    stream = fopen (path, "w");
    fprintf (stdout,"write a character to testfile\n");
    fwrite ("a", 1, 1, stream);
    fprintf (stdout,"close testfile\n");
    fclose (stream );

    fprintf (stdout,"open testfile\n");
    stream = fopen (path, "r");
    fprintf (stdout,"read string from testfile\n");
    fread (string, sizeof(char), 2, stream );

    fprintf (stdout,"check EOF\n");
    feof_value = feof (stream);
    if ( feof_value != 0 ) {
```

```
        fprintf (stdout,"feof() call successful\n");
        fprintf (stdout,"feof_value=%d\n", feof_value );
    }
    else {
        fprintf (stderr,"ERROR: feof() call failed\n");
        fprintf (stderr,"ERROR: %s\n", strerror(errno));
    }

    fclose (stream);
    fprintf (stdout,"remove testfile\n");
    remove (path);
}
```

NAME

ferror — test error indicator on a stream

SYNOPSIS

```
#include <stdio.h>

int ferror(FILE *stream);
```

DESCRIPTION

The *ferror*( ) function tests the error indicator for the stream pointed to by *stream*.

RETURN VALUE

The *ferror*( ) function returns non-zero if and only if the error indicator is set for *stream*.

ERRORS

No errors are defined.

SEE ALSO

clearerr( ), *feof*( ), *fopen*( ), **<stdio.h>**.

EXAMPLE

```
/*
 * Copyright (C) ANTRIX Inc.
 */

/* ferror.c
 * This program tests for an error indicator on a stream
 * using function ferror.
 */

#include <stdio.h>
#include <stdlib.h>
#include <string.h>
#include <errno.h>

main()
{
    int    i, err, ferror_value;
    char   *errmsg;
    char   *path = "testfile";
    FILE   *stream;

    fprintf (stdout,"set the regular file size limit\n");
    fprintf (stdout,"of the process to 2\n");
    ulimit (2, 2L);
    fprintf (stdout,"create and open testfile\n");
    stream = fopen (path, "w");

    fprintf (stdout,"try and write 10000 characters\n");
    fprintf (stdout,"generate eof error\n");
    for ( i = 0; i < 10000; i++ )
      if (fwrite ("a", 1, 1, stream) != 1)
          break;

    fprintf (stdout,"check for I/O error\n");
    ferror_value = ferror (stream);
```

```
        if ( ferror_value != 0 ) {
            fprintf (stdout,"ferror() call successful\n");
            fprintf (stdout,"ferror_value=%d\n", ferror_value);
            errmsg = strerror (errno);
            fprintf (stderr,"ERROR: %s\n", errmsg );
        }
        else
            fprintf (stderr,"ERROR: ferror() call failed\n");

        fclose (stream);
        fprintf (stdout,"remove testfile\n");
        remove (path);
    }
```

NAME

fflush — flush a stream

SYNOPSIS

```
#include <stdio.h>

int fflush(FILE *stream);
```

DESCRIPTION

If *stream* points to an output stream or an update stream in which the most recent operation was not input, *fflush*( ) causes any unwritten data for that stream to be written to the file, and the *st_ctime* and *st_mtime* fields of the underlying file are marked for update.

If *stream* is a null pointer, *fflush*( ) performs this flushing action on all streams for which the behaviour is defined above.

RETURN VALUE

Upon successful completion, *fflush*( ) returns 0. Otherwise, it returns EOF and sets *errno* to indicate the error.

ERRORS

The *fflush*( ) function will fail if:

[EAGAIN]   The O_NONBLOCK flag is set for the file descriptor underlying *stream* and the process would be delayed in the write operation.

[EBADF]   The file descriptor underlying *stream* is not valid.

EX [EFBIG]   An attempt was made to write a file that exceeds the maximum file size or the process' file size limit.

[EINTR]   The *fflush*( ) function was interrupted by a signal.

[EIO]   The process is a member of a background process group attempting to write to its controlling terminal, TOSTOP is set, the process is neither ignoring nor blocking SIGTTOU and the process group of the process is orphaned. This error may also be returned under implementation-dependent conditions.

[ENOSPC]   There was no free space remaining on the device containing the file.

[EPIPE]   An attempt is made to write to a pipe or FIFO that is not open for reading by any process. A SIGPIPE signal will also be sent to the process.

The *fflush*( ) function may fail if:

EX [ENXIO]   A request was made of a non-existent device, or the request was outside the device.

SEE ALSO

getrlimit( ), *ulimit*( ), **<stdio.h>**.

EXAMPLE

```
/*
 * Copyright (C) ANTRIX Inc.
 */

/* fflush.c
 * This program causes any unwritten data for stream to
 * written to the file using function fflush.
 */
```

```
#include <stdio.h>
#include <stdlib.h>
#include <sys/types.h>
#include <errno.h>

main()
{
  int   fflush_value;
  FILE  *stream;
  int   fildes, bytes;
  char  buf[12];
  char  string[] = "hello world";
  char  *path = "testfile";

  memset (buf, ' ', 12);
  bytes = strlen (string);

  fprintf (stdout,"create and open testfile\n");
  stream = fopen (path, "w+r");

  fprintf (stdout,"write a string to testfile\n");
  fwrite (string, sizeof(char), bytes, stream);

  fprintf (stdout,"write the data in buffer to disk\n");
  fflush_value = fflush (stream);
  if (fflush_value == 0)
     printf("fflush() call successful\n");
  else {
     fprintf (stderr,"ERROR: fflush() call failed\n");
     fprintf (stderr,"ERROR: %s\n", strerror(errno));
  }

  fprintf (stdout,"seek to the beginning of testfile\n");
  fseek (stream, 0, SEEK_SET);
  fprintf (stdout,"read string from testfile\n");
  fread (buf, sizeof(char), bytes, stream);
  fprintf (stdout,"string read in buf is %s\n", buf);

  fclose (stream);
  fprintf (stdout,"remove testfile\n");
  remove (path);
}
```

NAME

ffs — find first set bit

SYNOPSIS

UX
```
#include <strings.h>
```

```
int ffs(int i);
```

DESCRIPTION

The *ffs( )* function finds the first bit set (beginning with the least significant bit) and returns the index of that bit. Bits are numbered starting at one (the least significant bit).

RETURN VALUE

The *ffs( )* function returns the index of the first bit set. If *i* is 0, then *ffs( )* returns 0.

ERRORS

No errors are defined.

SEE ALSO

<strings.h>.

EXAMPLE

```
/*
 * Copyright (C) ANTRIX Inc.
 */

/* ffs.c
 * This program finds the first bit set in the argument passed to it
 * and returns the index of that bit.
 */

#include <stdio.h>
#include <stdlib.h>
#include <unistd.h>
#include <errno.h>

main()
{
  int  ffs_value;
  int  i = 0070;

  fprintf(stdout, "find first bit set\n");
  ffs_value = ffs(i);
  fprintf(stdout, "ffs_value=%d\n");
}
```

NAME

fgetc — get a byte from a stream

SYNOPSIS

```
#include <stdio.h>

int fgetc(FILE *stream);
```

DESCRIPTION

The *fgetc( )* function obtains the next byte (if present) as an **unsigned char** converted to an **int**, from the input stream pointed to by *stream*, and advances the associated file position indicator for the stream (if defined).

The *fgetc( )* function may mark the *st_atime* field of the file associated with *stream* for update. The *st_atime* field will be marked for update by the first successful execution of *fgetc( )*, *fgets( )*, *fgetwc( )*, *fgetws( )*, *fread( )*, *fscanf( )*, *getc( )*, *getchar( )*, *gets( )* or *scanf( )* using *stream* that returns data not supplied by a prior call to *ungetc( )* or *ungetwc( )*.

RETURN VALUE

Upon successful completion, *fgetc( )* returns the next byte from the input stream pointed to by *stream*. If the stream is at end-of-file, the end-of-file indicator for the stream is set and *fgetc( )* returns EOF. If a read error occurs, the error indicator for the stream is set, *fgetc( )* returns EOF and sets *errno* to indicate the error.

ERRORS

The *fgetc( )* function will fail if data needs to be read and:

[EAGAIN]	The O_NONBLOCK flag is set for the file descriptor underlying *stream* and the process would be delayed in the *fgetc( )* operation.
[EBADF]	The file descriptor underlying *stream* is not a valid file descriptor open for reading.
[EINTR]	The read operation was terminated due to the receipt of a signal, and no data was transferred.

UX [EIO] A physical I/O error has occurred, or the process is in a background process group attempting to read from its controlling terminal, and either the process is ignoring or blocking the SIGTTIN signal or the process group is orphaned. This error may also be generated for implementation-dependent reasons.

The *fgetc( )* function may fail if:

EX [ENOMEM] Insufficient storage space is available.

EX [ENXIO] A request was made of a non-existent device, or the request was outside the capabilities of the device.

APPLICATION USAGE

If the integer value returned by *fgetc( )* is stored into a variable of type **char** and then compared against the integer constant EOF, the comparison may never succeed, because sign-extension of a variable of type **char** on widening to integer is implementation-dependent.

The *ferror( )* or *feof( )* functions must be used to distinguish between an error condition and an end-of-file condition.

SEE ALSO

feof( ), *ferror( )*, *fopen( )*, *getchar( )*, *getc( )*, **<stdio.h>**.

EXAMPLE

```
/*
 * Copyright (C) ANTRIX Inc.
 */

/* fgetc.c
 * This program obtains the next byte as an unsigned char
 * converted to an int from the input stream using function fgetc.
 */

#include <stdio.h>
#include <stdlib.h>
#include <sys/types.h>
#include <errno.h>

main()
{
  FILE   *stream;
  int    i, bytes;
  char   character, buf[12];
  char   string[] = "hello world";
  char   *path = "testfile";

  memset (buf, ' ', 12);
  bytes = strlen (string);
  fprintf (stdout,"create and open testfile\n");
  stream = fopen (path, "w+r");

  fprintf (stdout,"write string to testfile\n");
  fwrite (string, sizeof(char), bytes, stream);
  fflush (stream);
  fprintf (stdout,"seek to the beginning of testfile\n");
  fseek (stream, 0, SEEK_SET);

  fprintf (stdout,"get hello world string\n");
  fprintf (stdout,"one character at a time\n");
  for ( i = 0; i < 11; i++ ) {
      character = fgetc (stream);
      fprintf (stdout,"%c", character );
  }
  fprintf (stdout,"\n");
  fclose (stream);
  fprintf (stdout,"remove testfile\n");
  remove (path);
}
```

NAME

fgetpos — get current file position information

SYNOPSIS

```
#include <stdio.h>

int fgetpos(FILE *stream, fpos_t *pos);
```

DESCRIPTION

The *fgetpos()* function stores the current value of the file position indicator for the stream pointed to by *stream* in the object pointed to by *pos*. The value stored contains unspecified information usable by *fsetpos()* for repositioning the stream to its position at the time of the call to *fgetpos()*.

RETURN VALUE

Upon successful completion, *fgetpos()* returns 0. Otherwise, it returns a non-zero value and sets *errno* to indicate the error.

ERRORS

The *fgetpos()* function may fail if:

EX   [EBADF]   The file descriptor underlying *stream* is not valid.

[ESPIPE]   The file descriptor underlying *stream* is associated with a pipe or FIFO.

SEE ALSO

fopen(), *ftell()*, *rewind()*, *ungetc()*, **<stdio.h>**.

EXAMPLE

```
/*
 * Copyright (C) ANTRIX Inc.
 */

/* fgetpos.c
 * This program gets the current file position information using
 * function fgetpos.
 */

#include <stdio.h>
#include <stdlib.h>
#include <sys/types.h>
#include <errno.h>

main()
{
   fpos_t  fgetpos_value;
   int     bytes;
   fpos_t  set_pos = 6;
   fpos_t  new_pos;
   FILE    *stream;
   char    buf[12];
   char    string[] = "hello world";
   char    *path = "testfile";

   memset (buf, ' ', 12);
   bytes = strlen (string);
```

```
    fprintf (stdout,"create and open testfile\n");
    stream = fopen (path, "w+r");
    fprintf (stdout,"write string to testfile\n");
    fwrite (string, sizeof(char), bytes, stream);
    fflush (stream);

    fprintf (stdout,"seek to the beginning of file\n");
    fseek (stream, 0, SEEK_SET);
    fprintf (stdout,"reposition file pointer in a stream\n");
    fsetpos (stream, &set_pos);

    fprintf (stdout,"get file pointer in a stream\n");
    fgetpos_value = fgetpos (stream, &new_pos);
    if ( fgetpos_value == 0 ) {
        fprintf (stdout,"fgetpos() call successful\n");
        fread (buf, sizeof(char), strlen(string), stream);
        fprintf (stdout,"starting from postion %d string is %s\n", new_pos, buf
    }
    else {
        fprintf (stderr,"ERROR: fgetpos() call failed\n");
        fprintf (stderr,"ERROR: %s\n", strerror(errno));
    }

    fclose (stream);
    fprintf (stdout,"remove testfile\n");
    remove (path);
}
```

NAME

    fgets — get a string from a stream

SYNOPSIS

    `#include <stdio.h>`

    `char *fgets(char *s, int n, FILE *stream);`

DESCRIPTION

    The *fgets( )* function reads bytes from *stream* into the array pointed to by *s*, until *n*–1 bytes are read, or a newline character is read and transferred to *s*, or an end-of-file condition is encountered. The string is then terminated with a null byte.

    The *fgets( )* function may mark the *st_atime* field of the file associated with *stream* for update. The *st_atime* field will be marked for update by the first successful execution of *fgetc( )*, *fgets( )*, *fgetwc( )*, *fgetws( )*, *fread( )*, *fscanf( )*, *getc( )*, *getchar( )*, *gets( )* or *scanf( )* using *stream* that returns data not supplied by a prior call to *ungetc( )* or *ungetwc( )*.

RETURN VALUE

    Upon successful completion, *fgets( )* returns *s*. If the stream is at end-of-file, the end-of-file indicator for the stream is set and *fgets( )* returns a null pointer. If a read error occurs, the error indicator for the stream is set, *fgets( )* returns a null pointer and sets *errno* to indicate the error.

ERRORS

    Refer to *fgetc( )*.

SEE ALSO

    fopen( ), *fread( )*, *gets( )*, **<stdio.h>**.

EXAMPLE

```
/*
 * Copyright (C) ANTRIX Inc.
 */

/* fgets.c
 * This program gets a string from a stream using function
 * fgets.
 */

#include <stdio.h>
#include <stdlib.h>
#include <sys/types.h>
#include <errno.h>

main()
{
  char   *fgets_value;
  int    i, bytes;
  FILE   *stream;
  char   character, buf[12];
  char   string[] = "hello world";
  char   *path = "testfile";

  memset (buf, ' ', 12);
  bytes = strlen (string);
```

```
         fprintf (stdout,"create and open testfile\n");
         stream = fopen (path, "w+r");
         fprintf (stdout,"write string to testfile\n");
         fwrite (string, sizeof(char), bytes, stream);
         fflush (stream);

         fprintf (stdout,"seek to the beginning of testfile\n");
         fseek (stream, 0, SEEK_SET);

         fprintf (stdout,"get the string from testfile\n");
         fgets_value = fgets (buf, 12, stream);
         if (fgets_value != (char *)0) {
            fprintf (stdout,"fgets() call successful\n");
            fprintf (stdout,"fgets_value=%s\n", fgets_value );
            fprintf (stdout,"string read in buf is %s\n", buf);
         } else {
            fprintf (stdout,"fgets() call failed\n");
            fprintf (stderr,"ERROR: %s\n", strerror(errno));
         }

         fclose (stream);
         fprintf (stdout,"remove testfile\n");
         remove (path);
      }
```

NAME

fgetwc — get a wide-character code from a stream

SYNOPSIS

OH   `#include <stdio.h>`
WP   `#include <wchar.h>`

`wint_t fgetwc(FILE *stream);`

DESCRIPTION

The *fgetwc( )* function obtains the next character (if present) from the input stream pointed to by *stream*, converts that to the corresponding wide-character code and advances the associated file position indicator for the stream (if defined).

If an error occurs, the resulting value of the file position indicator for the stream is indeterminate.

The *fgetwc( )* function may mark the *st_atime* field of the file associated with *stream* for update. The *st_atime* field will be marked for update by the first successful execution of *fgetc( )*, *fgets( )*, *fgetwc( )*, *fgetws( )*, *fread( )*, *fscanf( )*, *getc( )*, *getchar( )*, *gets( )* or *scanf( )* using *stream* that returns data not supplied by a prior call to *ungetc( )* or *ungetwc( )*.

RETURN VALUE

Upon successful completion the *fgetwc( )* function returns the wide-character code of the character read from the input stream pointed to by *stream* converted to a type **wint_t**. If the stream is at end-of-file, the end-of-file indicator for the stream is set and *fgetwc( )* returns WEOF. If a read error occurs, the error indicator for the stream is set, *fgetwc( )* returns WEOF and sets *errno* to indicate the error.

ERRORS

The *fgetwc( )* function will fail if data needs to be read and:

[EAGAIN]   The O_NONBLOCK flag is set for the file descriptor underlying *stream* and the process would be delayed in the *fgetwc( )* operation.

[EBADF]   The file descriptor underlying *stream* is not a valid file descriptor open for reading.

[EINTR]   The read operation was terminated due to the receipt of a signal, and no data was transferred.

UX   [EIO]   A physical I/O error has occurred, or the process is in a background process group attempting to read from its controlling terminal, and either the process is ignoring or blocking the SIGTTIN signal or the process group is orphaned. This error may also be generated for implementation-dependent reasons.

The *fgetwc( )* function may fail if:

[ENOMEM]   Insufficient storage space is available.

[ENXIO]   A request was made of a non-existent device, or the request was outside the capabilities of the device.

[EILSEQ]   The data obtained from the input stream does not form a valid character.

APPLICATION USAGE

The *ferror( )* or *feof( )* functions must be used to distinguish between an error condition and an end-of-file condition.

SEE ALSO

feof( ), *ferror( )*, *fopen( )*, **<stdio.h>**, **<wchar.h>**.

EXAMPLE

```
/*
 * Copyright (C) ANTRIX Inc.
 */

/* fgetwc.c
 * This program gets a wide-character code from a stream
 * using function fgetwc.
 */

#include <stdio.h>
#include <stdlib.h>
#include <widec.h>
#include <sys/types.h>
#include <errno.h>

main()
{
  FILE      *stream;
  int       i, bytes;
  wchar_t   fgetwc_value, buf[12];
  wchar_t   *ws = L"hello world";
  char      *path = "testfile";

  memset (buf, ' ', 12);
  bytes = wcslen (ws);

  fprintf (stdout,"create and open testfile\n");
  stream = fopen (path, "w+r");

  fprintf (stdout,"write string to testfile\n");
  fputws(ws, stream);
  fflush (stream);
  fprintf (stdout,"seek to the beginning of testfile\n");
  fseek (stream, 0, SEEK_SET);

  fprintf (stdout,"get hello world\n");
  fprintf (stdout,"one wide character at a time\n");
  for ( i = 0; i < 11; i++ ) {
      fgetwc_value = fgetwc (stream);
      fprintf (stdout,"%wc", fgetwc_value);
  }
  fprintf (stdout,"\n");

  fclose (stream);
  fprintf (stdout,"remove testfile\n");
  remove (path);
}
```

NAME

fgetws — get a wide character string from a stream

SYNOPSIS

OH   `#include <stdio.h>`
WP   `#include <wchar.h>`

`wchar_t *fgetws(wchar_t *ws, int n, FILE *stream);`

DESCRIPTION

The *fgetws( )* function reads characters from the *stream*, converts these to the corresponding wide-character codes, places them in the **wchar_t** array pointed to by *ws*, until *n*−1 characters are read, or a newline character is read, converted and transferred to *ws*, or an end-of-file condition is encountered. The wide character string, *ws*, is then terminated with a null wide-character code.

If an error occurs, the resulting value of the file position indicator for the stream is indeterminate.

The *fgetws( )* function may mark the *st_atime* field of the file associated with *stream* for update. The *st_atime* field will be marked for update by the first successful execution of *fgetc( )*, *fgets( )*, *fgetwc( )*, *fgetws( )*, *fread( )*, *fscanf( )*, *getc( )*, *getchar( )*, *gets( )* or *scanf( )* using *stream* that returns data not supplied by a prior call to *ungetc( )* or *ungetwc( )*.

RETURN VALUE

Upon successful completion, *fgetws( )* returns *ws*. If the stream is at end-of-file, the end-of-file indicator for the stream is set and *fgetws( )* returns a null pointer. If a read error occurs, the error indicator for the stream is set, *fgetws( )* returns a null pointer and sets *errno* to indicate the error.

ERRORS

Refer to *fgetwc( )*.

SEE ALSO

fopen( ), *fread( )*, **<stdio.h>**, **<wchar.h>**.

EXAMPLE

```
/*
 * Copyright (C) ANTRIX Inc.
 */

/* fgetws.c
 * This program gets a wide character string from a stream
 * using function fgetws
 */

#include <stdio.h>
#include <stdlib.h>
#include <widec.h>
#include <sys/types.h>
#include <errno.h>

main()
{
    wchar_t   *fgetws_value;
    wchar_t   buf[12];
    wchar_t   *ws = L"hello world";
    int       i, bytes;
```

```
FILE       *stream;
char       *path = "testfile";

memset (buf, ' ', 12);
bytes = wcslen (ws);

fprintf (stdout,"create and open testfile\n");
stream = fopen (path, "w+r");
fprintf (stdout,"write wide string to testfile\n");
fputws(ws, stream);
fflush (stream);
fprintf (stdout,"seek to the beginning of testfile\n");
fseek (stream, 0, SEEK_SET);

fprintf (stdout,"get the string from testfile\n");
fgetws_value = fgetws (buf, 12, stream);
if (fgetws_value != (wchar_t *)0) {
   fprintf (stdout,"fgetws() call successful\n");
   fprintf (stdout,"fgetws_value=%ws\n", fgetws_value );
   fprintf (stdout,"string read in buf is %ws\n", buf);
} else {
   fprintf (stdout,"fgetws() call failed\n");
   fprintf (stderr,"ERROR: %s\n", strerror(errno));
}

fclose (stream);
fprintf (stdout,"remove testfile\n");
remove (path);
}
```

NAME

fileno — map stream pointer to file descriptor

SYNOPSIS

```
#include <stdio.h>

int fileno(FILE *stream);
```

DESCRIPTION

The *fileno( )* function returns the integer file descriptor associated with the stream pointed to by *stream*.

RETURN VALUE

Upon successful completion, *fileno( )* returns the integer value of the file descriptor associated with *stream*. Otherwise, the value –1 is returned and *errno* is set to indicate the error.

ERRORS

The *fileno( )* function may fail if:

EX   [EBADF]   The *stream* argument is not a valid stream.

SEE ALSO

fdopen( ), *fopen( )*, *stdin*, **<stdio.h>**, **XSH** specification, **Section 2.4.1**, **Interaction of File Descriptors and Standard I/O Streams**.

EXAMPLE

```
/*
 * Copyright (C) ANTRIX Inc.
 */

/* fileno.c
 * This program maps stream pointer to a file descriptor
 * using function fileno.
 */

#include <stdio.h>
#include <stdlib.h>
#include <errno.h>

main()
{
  int   fileno_value;
  FILE  *stream;
  char  *path = "testfile";

  fprintf (stdout,"create and open testfile\n");
  stream = fopen (path, "w");

  fprintf (stdout,"get file descriptor of testfile\n");
  fileno_value = fileno (stream);
  if (fileno_value > 2) {
     fprintf (stdout,"fileno() call successful\n");
     fprintf (stdout,"fileno_value=%d\n", fileno_value);
  }
  else {
     fprintf (stderr,"ERROR: fileno() call failed\n");
```

```
        fprintf (stderr,"ERROR: %s\n", strerror(errno));
    }

    fprintf (stdout,"remove testfile\n");
    remove (path);
}
```

NAME

floor — floor function

SYNOPSIS

```
#include <math.h>

double floor(double x);
```

DESCRIPTION

The *floor*( ) function computes the largest integral value not greater than *x*.

RETURN VALUE

Upon successful completion, *floor*( ) returns the largest integral value not greater than *x*, expressed as a **double**.

EX   If *x* is NaN, NaN is returned and *errno* may be set to [EDOM].

If the correct value would cause overflow, –HUGE_VAL is returned and *errno* is set to [ERANGE].

EX   If *x* is ±Inf or ±0, the value of *x* is returned.

ERRORS

The *floor*( ) function will fail if:

[ERANGE]   The result would cause an overflow.

The *floor*( ) function may fail if:

EX   [EDOM]   The value of *x* is NaN.

EX   No other errors will occur.

APPLICATION USAGE

The integral value returned by *floor*( ) as a **double** might not be expressible as an **int** or **long int**. The return value should be tested before assigning it to an integer type to avoid the undefined results of an integer overflow.

An application wishing to check for error situations should set *errno* to 0 before calling *floor*( ). If *errno* is non-zero on return, or the return value is NaN, an error has occurred.

The *floor*( ) function can only overflow when the floating point representation has DBL_MANT_DIG > DBL_MAX_EXP.

SEE ALSO

ceil( ), *isnan*( ), **<math.h>**.

EXAMPLE

```
/*
 * Copyright (C) ANTRIX Inc.
 */

/* floor.c
 * This program computes the largest integral value not
 * greater than -1.23 using function floor.
 */

#include <stdio.h>
#include <math.h>

main()
```

```
{
  double  floor_value;
  double  x = -1.23;

  floor_value = floor (x);
  fprintf (stdout,"floor of %f is %f\n", x, floor_value);
}
```

NAME

fmod — floating-point remainder value function

SYNOPSIS

```
#include <math.h>

double fmod(double x, double y);
```

DESCRIPTION

The *fmod*( ) function returns the floating-point remainder of the division of x by y.

RETURN VALUE

The *fmod*( ) function returns the value $x - i * y$, for some integer i such that, if y is non-zero, the result has the same sign as x and magnitude less than the magnitude of y.

EX If x or y is NaN, NaN is returned and *errno* may be set to [EDOM].

EX If y is 0, NaN is returned and *errno* is set to [EDOM], or 0 is returned and *errno* may be set to [EDOM].

EX If x is ±Inf, either 0 is returned and *errno* is set to [EDOM], or NaN is returned and *errno* may be set to [EDOM].

If y is non-zero, *fmod*(±0,y) returns the value of x. If x is not ±Inf, *fmod*(x,±Inf) returns the value of x.

If the result underflows, 0 is returned and *errno* may be set to [ERANGE].

ERRORS

The *fmod*( ) function may fail if:

EX [EDOM]   One or both of the arguments is NaN, or y is 0, or x is ±Inf.

[ERANGE]   The result underflows.

EX No other errors will occur.

APPLICATION USAGE

Portable applications should not call *fmod*( ) with y equal to 0, because the result is implementation-dependent. The application should verify y is non-zero before calling *fmod*( ).

An application wishing to check for error situations should set *errno* to 0 before calling *fmod*( ). If *errno* is non-zero on return, or the return value is NaN, an error has occurred.

SEE ALSO

isnan( ), **<math.h>**.

EXAMPLE

```
/*
 * Copyright (C) ANTRIX Inc.
 */

/* fmod.c
 * This program computes the floating-point remainder of
 * the division of 1.00 by 3.00 using function fmod.
 */

#include <stdio.h>
#include <math.h>

main()
```

```
    {
      double   fmod_value;
      double   x = 1.00;
      double   y = 3.00;

      fmod_value = fmod (x, y);
      fprintf (stdout,"fmod of %f, %f is %f\n", x, y, fmod_value);
    }
```

NAME

fmtmsg — display a message in the specified format on standard error and/or a system console

SYNOPSIS

UX

```
#include <fmtmsg.h>

int fmtmsg(long classification, const char *label, int severity,
        const char *text, const char *action, const char *tag);
```

DESCRIPTION

The *fmtmsg*( ) function can be used to display messages in a specified format instead of the traditional *printf*( ) function.

Based on a message's classification component, *fmtmsg*( ) writes a formatted message either to standard error, to the console, or to both.

A formatted message consists of up to five components as defined below. The component *classification* is not part of a message displayed to the user, but defines the source of the message and directs the display of the formatted message.

classification   Contains identifiers from the following groups of major classifications and subclassifications. Any one identifier from a subclass may be used in combination with a single identifier from a different subclass. Two or more identifiers from the same subclass should not be used together, with the exception of identifiers from the display subclass. (Both display subclass identifiers may be used so that messages can be displayed to both standard error and the system console).

Major Classifications

Identifies the source of the condition. Identifiers are: MM_HARD (hardware), MM_SOFT (software), and MM_FIRM (firmware).

Message Source Subclassifications

Identifies the type of software in which the problem is detected. Identifiers are: MM_APPL (application), MM_UTIL (utility), and MM_OPSYS (operating system).

Display Subclassifications

Indicates where the message is to be displayed. Identifiers are: MM_PRINT to display the message on the standard error stream, MM_CONSOLE to display the message on the system console. One or both identifiers may be used.

Status Subclassifications

Indicates whether the application will recover from the condition. Identifiers are: MM_RECOVER (recoverable) and MM_NRECOV (non-recoverable).

An additional identifier, MM_NULLMC, indicates that no classification component is supplied for the message.

label   Identifies the source of the message. The format is two fields separated by a colon. The first field is up to 10 bytes, the second is up to 14 bytes.

severity   Indicates the seriousness of the condition. Identifiers for the levels of *severity* are:

MM_HALT   Indicates that the application has encountered a severe fault and is halting. Produces the string "HALT".

MM_ERROR	Indicates that the application has detected a fault. Produces the string "ERROR".
MM_WARNING	Indicates a condition that is out of the ordinary, that might be a problem, and should be watched. Produces the string "WARNING".
MM_INFO	Provides information about a condition that is not in error. Produces the string "INFO".
MM_NOSEV	Indicates that no severity level is supplied for the message.

text Describes the error condition that produced the message. The character string is not limited to a specific size. If the character string is empty, then the text produced is unspecified.

action Describes the first step to be taken in the error-recovery process. The *fmtmsg( )* function precedes the action string with the prefix: "TO FIX:". The *action* string is not limited to a specific size.

tag An identifier that references on-line documentation for the message. Suggested usage is that *tag* includes the *label* and a unique identifying number. A sample *tag* is "XSI:cat:146".

The *MSGVERB* environment variable (for message verbosity) tells *fmtmsg( )* which message components it is to select when writing messages to standard error. The value of *MSGVERB* is a colon-separated list of optional keywords. Valid *keywords* are: `label`, `severity`, `text`, `action`, and `tag`. If *MSGVERB* contains a keyword for a component and the component's value is not the component's null value, *fmtmsg( )* includes that component in the message when writing the message to standard error. If *MSGVERB* does not include a keyword for a message component, that component is not included in the display of the message. The keywords may appear in any order. If *MSGVERB* is not defined, if its value is the null string, if its value is not of the correct format, or if it contains keywords other than the valid ones listed above, *fmtmsg( )* selects all components.

MSGVERB affects only which components are selected for display to standard error. All message components are included in console messages.

RETURN VALUE

The *fmtmsg( )* function returns one of the following values:

MM_OK	The function succeeded.
MM_NOTOK	The function failed completely.
MM_NOMSG	The function was unable to generate a message on standard error, but otherwise succeeded.
MM_NOCON	The function was unable to generate a console message, but otherwise succeeded.

APPLICATION USAGE

One or more message components may be systematically omitted from messages generated by an application by using the null value of the argument for that component.

EXAMPLES

Example 1:

The following example of *fmtmsg*( ):

```
fmtmsg(MM_PRINT, "XSI:cat", MM_ERROR, "illegal option",
"refer to cat in user's reference manual", "XSI:cat:001")
```

produces a complete message in the specified message format:

```
XSI:cat: ERROR: illegal option
TO FIX: refer to cat in user's reference manual XSI:cat:001
```

Example 2:

When the environment variable *MSGVERB* is set as follows:

```
MSGVERB=severity:text:action
```

and the Example 1 is used, *fmtmsg*( ) produces:

```
ERROR: illegal option
TO FIX: refer to cat in user's reference manual
```

SEE ALSO

printf( ), **<fmtmsg.h>**.

EXAMPLE

```
/*
 * Copyright (C) ANTRIX Inc.
 */

/* fmtmsg.c
 * This program displays a message on stderr or system
 * console using function fmtmsg.
 */

#include <stdio.h>
#include <stdlib.h>
#include <fmtmsg.h>
#include <errno.h>

char    *LABEL  = "fmtmsg";
char    *TEXT   = "Too many bugs\n";
char    *ACTION = "Check your source code";
char    *TAG    = "fmtmsg.tag:123";

main()
{
    int     fmtmsg_value;

    fprintf (stdout,"print user defined error message\n");
    fmtmsg_value = fmtmsg(MM_PRINT,LABEL,MM_ERROR,TEXT,ACTION,TAG);
    if ( fmtmsg_value == 0 )
        fprintf (stdout,"fmtmsg() call successful\n");
```

```
    else
       fprintf (stdout,"fmtmsg failed\n");
}
```

NAME

fnmatch — match filename or pathname

SYNOPSIS

```
#include <fnmatch.h>

int fnmatch(const char *pattern, const char *string, int flags);
```

DESCRIPTION

The *fnmatch*( ) function matches patterns as described in the **XCU** specification, **Section 2.13.1**, **Patterns Matching a Single Character**, and **Section 2.13.2**, **Patterns Matching Multiple Characters**. It checks the string specified by the *string* argument to see if it matches the pattern specified by the *pattern* argument.

The *flags* argument modifies the interpretation of *pattern* and *string*. It is the bitwise inclusive OR of zero or more of the flags defined in the header **<fnmatch.h>**. If the FNM_PATHNAME flag is set in *flags*, then a slash character in *string* will be explicitly matched by a slash in *pattern*; it will not be matched by either the asterisk or question-mark special characters, nor by a bracket expression. If the FNM_PATHNAME flag is not set, the slash character is treated as an ordinary character.

If FNM_NOESCAPE is not set in *flags*, a backslash character (\\) in *pattern* followed by any other character will match that second character in *string*. In particular, \\\\ will match a backslash in *string*. If FNM_NOESCAPE is set, a backslash character will be treated as an ordinary character.

If FNM_PERIOD is set in *flags*, then a leading period in *string* will match a period in *pattern*; as described by rule 2 in the **XCU** specification, **Section 2.13.3**, **Patterns Used for Filename Expansion** where the location of "leading" is indicated by the value of FNM_PATHNAME:

- If FNM_PATHNAME is set, a period is "leading" if it is the first character in *string* or if it immediately follows a slash.

- If FNM_PATHNAME is not set, a period is "leading" only if it is the first character of *string*.

If FNM_PERIOD is not set, then no special restrictions are placed on matching a period.

RETURN VALUE

If *string* matches the pattern specified by *pattern*, then *fnmatch*( ) returns 0. If there is no match, *fnmatch*( ) returns FNM_NOMATCH, which is defined in the header **<fnmatch.h>**. If an error occurs, *fnmatch*( ) returns another non-zero value.

ERRORS

No errors are defined.

APPLICATION USAGE

The *fnmatch*( ) function has two major uses. It could be used by an application or utility that needs to read a directory and apply a pattern against each entry. The *find* utility is an example of this. It can also be used by the *pax* utility to process its *pattern* operands, or by applications that need to match strings in a similar manner.

The name *fnmatch*( ) is intended to imply *filename* match, rather than *pathname* match. The default action of this function is to match filenames, rather than pathnames, since it gives no special significance to the slash character. With the FNM_PATHNAME flag, *fnmatch*( ) does match pathnames, but without tilde expansion, parameter expansion, or special treatment for period at the beginning of a filename.

SEE ALSO

glob( ), *wordexp*( ), **<fnmatch.h>**, the **XCU** specification.

EXAMPLE

```
/*
 * Copyright (C) ANTRIX Inc.
 */

/* fnmatch.c
 * This program checks for matches between the string and
 * pattern using function fnmatch.
 */

#include <stdio.h>
#include <stdlib.h>
#include <fnmatch.h>
#include <regexpr.h>
#include <errno.h>

main(argc, argv)
int argc;
char *argv[];
{
   int        fnmatch_value;
   const char string[] = "testfile";
   const char expbuf[] = "t.*";

   fprintf(stdout, "match string against the pattern\n");
   fnmatch_value = fnmatch(string, expbuf, (0|FNM_PATHNAME));
   if (fnmatch_value == 0)
      fprintf(stdout, "fnmatch call successful\n");
   else {
      fprintf(stdout, "ERROR: fnmatch call failed\n");
      fprintf(stdout, "%d\n", fnmatch_value);
   }
}
```

NAME

fopen — open a stream

SYNOPSIS

```
#include <stdio.h>

FILE *fopen(const char *filename, const char *mode);
```

DESCRIPTION

The *fopen( )* function opens the file whose pathname is the string pointed to by *filename*, and associates a stream with it.

The argument *mode* points to a string beginning with one of the following sequences:

r or **rb**	open file for reading
w or **wb**	truncate to zero length or create file for writing
a or **ab**	append; open or create file for writing at end-of-file
r+ or **rb+** or **r+b**	open file for update (reading and writing)
w+ or **wb+** or **w+b**	truncate to zero length or create file for update
a+ or **ab+** or **a+b**	append; open or create file for update, writing at end-of-file

The character b has no effect, but is allowed for ISO C standard conformance. Opening a file with read mode (r as the first character in the *mode* argument) fails if the file does not exist or cannot be read.

Opening a file with append mode (a as the first character in the *mode* argument) causes all subsequent writes to the file to be forced to the then current end-of-file, regardless of intervening calls to *fseek( )*.

When a file is opened with update mode (+ as the second or third character in the *mode* argument), both input and output may be performed on the associated stream. However, output must not be directly followed by input without an intervening call to *fflush( )* or to a file positioning function (*fseek( )*, *fsetpos( )* or *rewind( )*), and input must not be directly followed by output without an intervening call to a file positioning function, unless the input operation encounters end-of-file.

When opened, a stream is fully buffered if and only if it can be determined not to refer to an interactive device. The error and end-of-file indicators for the stream are cleared.

If *mode* is **w**, **a**, **w+** or **a+** and the file did not previously exist, upon successful completion, *fopen( )* function will mark for update the *st_atime*, *st_ctime* and *st_mtime* fields of the file and the *st_ctime* and *st_mtime* fields of the parent directory.

If *mode* is **w** or **w+** and the file did previously exist, upon successful completion, *fopen( )* will mark for update the *st_ctime* and *st_mtime* fields of the file. The *fopen( )* function will allocate a file descriptor as *open( )* does.

RETURN VALUE

Upon successful completion, *fopen( )* returns a pointer to the object controlling the stream. Otherwise, a null pointer is returned, and *errno* is set to indicate the error.

ERRORS

The *fopen( )* function will fail if:

[EACCES]   Search permission is denied on a component of the path prefix, or the file exists and the permissions specified by *mode* are denied, or the file does not exist and write permission is denied for the parent directory of the file to be created.

	[EINTR]	A signal was caught during *fopen*( ).
	[EISDIR]	The named file is a directory and *mode* requires write access.
UX	[ELOOP]	Too many symbolic links were encountered in resolving *path*.
	[EMFILE]	{OPEN_MAX} file descriptors are currently open in the calling process.
	[ENAMETOOLONG]	
FIPS		The length of the *filename* exceeds {PATH_MAX} or a pathname component is longer than {NAME_MAX}.
	[ENFILE]	The maximum allowable number of files is currently open in the system.
	[ENOENT]	A component of *filename* does not name an existing file or *filename* is an empty string.
	[ENOSPC]	The directory or file system that would contain the new file cannot be expanded, the file does not exist, and it was to be created.
	[ENOTDIR]	A component of the path prefix is not a directory.
	[ENXIO]	The named file is a character special or block special file, and the device associated with this special file does not exist.
	[EROFS]	The named file resides on a read-only file system and *mode* requires write access.

The *fopen*( ) function may fail if:

	[EINVAL]	The value of the *mode* argument is not valid.
EX	[EMFILE]	{FOPEN_MAX} streams are currently open in the calling process.
	[EMFILE]	{STREAM_MAX} streams are currently open in the calling process.
UX	[ENAMETOOLONG]	
		Pathname resolution of a symbolic link produced an intermediate result whose length exceeds {PATH_MAX}.
	[ENOMEM]	Insufficient storage space is available.
	[ETXTBSY]	The file is a pure procedure (shared text) file that is being executed and *mode* requires write access.

APPLICATION USAGE

{STREAM_MAX} is the number of streams that one process can have open at one time. If defined, it has the same value as {FOPEN_MAX}.

SEE ALSO

fclose( ), *fdopen*( ), *freopen*( ), **<stdio.h>**.

EXAMPLE

```
/*
 * Copyright (C) ANTRIX Inc.
 */

/* fopen.c
 * This program opens the file whose pathname is the string
 * pointed to by filename, and associates a stream with it
 * using function fopen.
 */
```

```
#include <stdio.h>
#include <stdlib.h>
#include <sys/types.h>
#include <errno.h>

main()
{
  FILE   *stream;
  int    bytes;
  char   buf[12];
  char   string[] = "hello world";
  char   *filename = "testfile";
  char   *mode = "w+r";

  memset (buf, ' ', 12);
  bytes = strlen(string);

  fprintf (stdout,"open and create testfile\n");
  stream = fopen (filename, "w+r");
  if ( stream != (FILE *)0 )
      fprintf (stdout,"fopen() call successful\n");
  else {
      fprintf (stderr,"ERROR: fopen() call failed\n");
      fprintf (stderr,"ERROR: %s\n", strerror(errno));
  }

  fprintf (stdout,"write string to testfile\n");
  fwrite (string, sizeof(char), bytes, stream);
  fflush (stream);

  fprintf (stdout,"seek to the beginning of the testfile\n");
  fseek (stream, 0, SEEK_SET);

  fprintf (stdout,"read the string\n");
  fread (buf, sizeof(char), bytes, stream);
  fprintf (stdout,"string read in buf is %s\n", buf);

  fclose (stream);
  fprintf (stdout,"remove testfile\n");
  remove (filename);
}
```

NAME

   fork — create a new process

SYNOPSIS

OH   `#include <sys/types.h>`
      `#include <unistd.h>`

      `pid_t fork(void);`

DESCRIPTION

   The *fork*( ) function creates a new process. The new process (child process) is an exact copy of the calling process (parent process) except as detailed below.

   - The child process has a unique process ID.

   - The child process ID also does not match any active process group ID.

   - The child process has a different parent process ID (that is, the process ID of the parent process).

   - The child process has its own copy of the parent's file descriptors. Each of the child's file descriptors refers to the same open file description with the corresponding file descriptor of the parent.

   - The child process has its own copy of the parent's open directory streams. Each open directory stream in the child process may share directory stream positioning with the corresponding directory stream of the parent.

EX - The child process may have its own copy of the parent's message catalogue descriptors.

   - The child process' values of *tms_utime*, *tms_stime*, *tms_cutime* and *tms_cstime* are set to 0.

   - The time left until an alarm clock signal is reset to 0.

EX - All *semadj* values are cleared.

   - File locks set by the parent process are not inherited by the child process.

   - The set of signals pending for the child process is initialised to the empty set.

UX - Interval timers are reset in the child process.

   The inheritance of process characteristics not defined by this document is implementation-dependent. After *fork*( ), both the parent and the child processes are capable of executing independently before either one terminates.

RETURN VALUE

   Upon successful completion, *fork*( ) returns 0 to the child process and returns the process ID of the child process to the parent process. Otherwise, −1 is returned to the parent process, no child process is created, and *errno* is set to indicate the error.

ERRORS

   The *fork*( ) function will fail if:

   [EAGAIN]   The system lacked the necessary resources to create another process, or the system-imposed limit on the total number of processes under execution system-wide or by a single user {CHILD_MAX} would be exceeded.

   The *fork*( ) function may fail if:

   [ENOMEM]   Insufficient storage space is available.

SEE ALSO

alarm( ), *exec*, *fcntl*( ), *semop*( ), *signal*( ), *times*( ), **<sys/types.h>**, **<unistd.h>**.

EXAMPLE

```
/*
 * Copyright (C) ANTRIX Inc.
 */

/* fork.c
 * This program creates a new process which is an exact copy
 * of the calling process using function fork.
 */

#include <stdio.h>
#include <stdlib.h>
#include <sys/types.h>
#include <sys/wait.h>
#include <errno.h>

main()
{
    int   fork_value;
    int   stat_loc;

    fprintf (stdout,"example 1\n");
    fprintf (stdout,"fork a child and parent, wait for child to exit\n");
    fprintf (stdout,"parent process-id=%d\n", getpid() );

    fork_value = fork ();
    if ( fork_value == 0 ) {
       fprintf (stdout,"child process-id=%d\n", getpid() );
      exit (10);
    } wait(&stat_loc);

    fprintf (stdout,"should be same as exit() argument 10\n");
    fprintf (stdout,"WEXITSTATUS(stat_loc)=%d\n", WEXITSTATUS(stat_loc) );

    fprintf (stdout,"example 2\n");
    fprintf (stdout,"fork a child and parent no wait\n");

    fork_value = fork();
    if ( fork_value == 0 )
       fprintf (stdout,"child process\n");
    else
       fprintf (stdout,"parent process\n");

    fprintf (stdout,"this statement executed by both parent and child\n");
}
```

[handwritten note: new process (child) will only execute codes that come after the call to fork()!]

fpathconf( )

NAME

fpathconf — get configurable pathname variables

SYNOPSIS

```
#include <unistd.h>

long int fpathconf(int fildes, int name);
```

DESCRIPTION

Refer to *pathconf*( ).

EXAMPLE

```
/*
 * Copyright (C) ANTRIX Inc.
 */

/* fpathconf.c
 * This program gets the configurable pathname variable
 * _PC_NAME_MAX value using function fpathconf.
 */

#include <stdio.h>
#include <stdlib.h>
#include <unistd.h>
#include <sys/stat.h>
#include <errno.h>

#define  PERM_ALL    (S_IRWXU | S_IRWXG | S_IRWXO)

main()
{
  long   fpathconf_value;
  int    fildes;
  char   *path = "testfile";

  fprintf (stdout,"create testfile\n");
  fildes = creat (path, PERM_ALL);

  fprintf (stdout,"get maximum name length\n");
  fpathconf_value = fpathconf (fildes, _PC_NAME_MAX);
  if ( fpathconf_value  >= 0 ) {
     fprintf (stdout,"fpathconf() successful\n");
     fprintf (stdout,"maximum file name length=%ld\n", fpathconf_value );
  }
  else {
     fprintf (stderr,"ERROR: fpathconf() call failed\n");
     fprintf (stderr,"ERROR: %s\n", strerror(errno));
  }

  fprintf (stdout,"remove testfile\n");
  remove (path);
}
```

NAME

fprintf, printf, sprintf — print formatted output

SYNOPSIS

```
#include <stdio.h>

int fprintf(FILE *stream, const char *format, ...);

int printf(const char *format, ...);

int sprintf(char *s, const char *format, ...);
```

DESCRIPTION

The *fprintf*( ) function places output on the named output *stream*. The *printf*( ) function places output on the standard output stream *stdout*. The *sprintf*( ) function places output followed by the null byte, '\0', in consecutive bytes starting at **s*; it is the user's responsibility to ensure that enough space is available.

Each of these functions converts, formats and prints its arguments under control of the *format*. The *format* is a character string, beginning and ending in its initial shift state, if any. The *format* is composed of zero or more directives: *ordinary characters*, which are simply copied to the output stream and *conversion specifications*, each of which results in the fetching of zero or more arguments. The results are undefined if there are insufficient arguments for the *format*. If the *format* is exhausted while arguments remain, the excess arguments are evaluated but are otherwise ignored.

EX   Conversions can be applied to the *n*th argument after the *format* in the argument list, rather than to the next unused argument. In this case, the conversion character % (see below) is replaced by the sequence %*n*$, where n is a decimal integer in the range [1, {NL_ARGMAX}], giving the position of the argument in the argument list. This feature provides for the definition of format strings that select arguments in an order appropriate to specific languages (see the **EXAMPLES** section).

In format strings containing the %*n*$ form of conversion specifications, numbered arguments in the argument list can be referenced from the format string as many times as required.

In format strings containing the % form of conversion specifications, each argument in the argument list is used exactly once.

All forms of the *fprintf*( ) functions allow for the insertion of a language-dependent radix character in the output string. The radix character is defined in the program's locale (category LC_NUMERIC). In the POSIX locale, or in a locale where the radix character is not defined, the radix character defaults to a period (.).

EX   Each conversion specification is introduced by the % character or by the character sequence %*n*$, after which the following appear in sequence:

- Zero or more *flags* (in any order), which modify the meaning of the conversion specification.

- An optional minimum *field width*. If the converted value has fewer bytes than the field width, it will be padded with spaces by default on the left; it will be padded on the right, if the left-adjustment flag (–), described below, is given to the field width. The field width takes the form of an asterisk (*), described below, or a decimal integer.

- An optional *precision* that gives the minimum number of digits to appear for the d, i, o, u, x and X conversions; the number of digits to appear after the radix character for the e, E and f conversions; the maximum number of significant digits for the g and G conversions; or the

EX   maximum number of bytes to be printed from a string in s and S conversions. The precision takes the form of a period (.) followed either by an asterisk (*), described below, or an optional decimal digit string, where a null digit string is treated as 0. If a precision appears with any other conversion character, the behaviour is undefined.

- An optional h specifying that a following d, i, o, u, x or X conversion character applies to a type **short int** or type **unsigned short int** argument (the argument will have been promoted according to the integral promotions, and its value will be converted to type **short int** or **unsigned short int** before printing); an optional h specifying that a following n conversion character applies to a pointer to a type **short int** argument; an optional l (ell) specifying that a following d, i, o, u, x or X conversion character applies to a type **long int** or **unsigned long int** argument; an optional l (ell) specifying that a following n conversion character applies to a pointer to a type **long int** argument; or an optional L specifying that a following e, E, f, g or G conversion character applies to a type **long double** argument. If an h, l or L appears with any other conversion character, the behaviour is undefined.

- A *conversion character* that indicates the type of conversion to be applied.

A field width, or precision, or both, may be indicated by an asterisk (*). In this case an argument of type **int** supplies the field width or precision. Arguments specifying field width, or precision, or both must appear in that order before the argument, if any, to be converted. A negative field width is taken as a – flag followed by a positive field width. A negative precision is taken as if EX the precision were omitted. In format strings containing the %*n*$ form of a conversion specification, a field width or precision may be indicated by the sequence **m$, where *m* is a decimal integer in the range [1, {NL_ARGMAX}] giving the position in the argument list (after the format argument) of an integer argument containing the field width or precision, for example:

EX
```
printf("%1$d:%2$.*3$d:%4$.*3$d\n", hour, min, precision, sec);
```

EX The *format* can contain either numbered argument specifications (that is, %*n*$ and **m$), or unnumbered argument specifications (that is, % and *), but normally not both. The only exception to this is that %% can be mixed with the %*n*$ form. The results of mixing numbered and unnumbered argument specifications in a *format* string are undefined. When numbered argument specifications are used, specifying the *N*th argument requires that all the leading arguments, from the first to the (*N–1*)th, are specified in the format string.

The flag characters and their meanings are:

EX '   The integer portion of the result of a decimal conversion (%i, %d, %u, %f, %g or %G) will be formatted with thousands' grouping characters. For other conversions the behaviour is undefined. The non-monetary grouping character is used.

–   The result of the conversion will be left-justified within the field. The conversion will be right-justified if this flag is not specified.

+   The result of a signed conversion will always begin with a sign (+ or –). The conversion will begin with a sign only when a negative value is converted if this flag is not specified.

space   If the first character of a signed conversion is not a sign or if a signed conversion results in no characters, a space will be prefixed to the result. This means that if the space and + flags both appear, the space flag will be ignored.

\#   This flag specifies that the value is to be converted to an alternative form. For o conversion, it increases the precision (if necessary) to force the first digit of the result to be 0. For x or X conversions, a non-zero result will have 0x (or 0X) prefixed to it. For e, E, f, g or G conversions, the result will always contain a radix character, even if no digits follow the radix character. Without this flag, a radix character appears in the result of these conversions only if a digit follows it. For g and G conversions, trailing zeros will *not* be removed from the result as they normally are. For other conversions, the behaviour is undefined.

0   For d, i, o, u, x, X, e, E, f, g and G conversions, leading zeros (following any indication of sign or base) are used to pad to the field width; no space padding is performed. If the 0 and − flags both appear, the 0 flag will be ignored. For d, i, o, u, x and X conversions, if a precision is specified, the 0 flag will be ignored. If the 0 and ' flags both appear, the grouping characters are inserted before zero padding. For other conversions, the behaviour is undefined.

The conversion characters and their meanings are:

d, i   The **int** argument is converted to a signed decimal in the style [−]*dddd*. The precision specifies the minimum number of digits to appear; if the value being converted can be represented in fewer digits, it will be expanded with leading zeros. The default precision is 1. The result of converting 0 with an explicit precision of 0 is no characters.

o   The **unsigned int** argument is converted to unsigned octal format in the style *dddd*. The precision specifies the minimum number of digits to appear; if the value being converted can be represented in fewer digits, it will be expanded with leading zeros. The default precision is 1. The result of converting 0 with an explicit precision of 0 is no characters.

u   The **unsigned int** argument is converted to unsigned decimal format in the style *dddd*. The precision specifies the minimum number of digits to appear; if the value being converted can be represented in fewer digits, it will be expanded with leading zeros. The default precision is 1. The result of converting 0 with an explicit precision of 0 is no characters.

x   The **unsigned int** argument is converted to unsigned hexadecimal format in the style *dddd*; the letters abcdef are used. The precision specifies the minimum number of digits to appear; if the value being converted can be represented in fewer digits, it will be expanded with leading zeros. The default precision is 1. The result of converting 0 with an explicit precision of 0 is no characters.

X   Behaves the same as the x conversion character except that letters ABCDEF are used instead of abcdef.

f   The **double** argument is converted to decimal notation in the style [−]*ddd.ddd*, where the number of digits after the radix character is equal to the precision specification. If the precision is missing, it is taken as 6; if the precision is explicitly 0 and no # flag is present, no radix character appears. If a radix character appears, at least one digit appears before it. The value is rounded to the appropriate number of digits.

EX   The *fprintf*( ) family of functions may make available character string representations for infinity and NaN.

e, E   The **double** argument is converted in the style [−]*d.ddd*e ± *dd*, where there is one digit before the radix character (which is non-zero if the argument is non-zero) and the number of digits after it is equal to the precision; if the precision is missing, it is taken as 6; if the precision is 0 and no # flag is present, no radix character appears. The value is rounded to the appropriate number of digits. The E conversion character will produce a number with E instead of e introducing the exponent. The exponent always contains at least two digits. If the value is 0, the exponent is 0.

EX   The *fprintf*( ) family of functions may make available character string representations for infinity and NaN.

g, G   The **double** argument is converted in the style f or e (or in the style E in the case of a G conversion character), with the precision specifying the number of significant digits. If an explicit precision is 0, it is taken as 1. The style used depends on the value converted; style e (or E) will be used only if the exponent resulting from such a conversion is less than –4 or greater than or equal to the precision. Trailing zeros are removed from the fractional portion of the result; a radix character appears only if it is followed by a digit.

EX   The *fprintf*( ) family of functions may make available character string representations for infinity and NaN.

c   The **int** argument is converted to an **unsigned char**, and the resulting byte is written.

s   The argument must be a pointer to an array of **char**. Bytes from the array are written up to (but not including) any terminating null byte. If the precision is specified, no more than that many bytes are written. If the precision is not specified or is greater than the size of the array, the array must contain a null byte.

p   The argument must be a pointer to **void**. The value of the pointer is converted to a sequence of printable characters, in an implementation-dependent manner.

n   The argument must be a pointer to an integer into which is written the number of bytes written to the output so far by this call to one of the *fprintf*( ) functions. No argument is converted.

EX   C   The **wchar_t** argument is converted to an array of bytes representing a character, and the resulting character is written. The conversion is the same as that expected from *wctomb*( ).

In a locale with state-dependent encoding the behaviour with regard to the stream's shift state is implementation-dependent.

EX   S   The argument must be a pointer an array of type **wchar_t**. Wide character codes from the array, up to but not including any terminating null wide-character code are converted to a sequence of bytes, and the resulting bytes are written. If the precision is specified no more than that many bytes are written and only complete characters are written. If the precision is not specified, or is greater than the size of the array of converted bytes, the array of wide characters must be terminated by a null wide character. The conversion is the same as that expected from *wcstombs*( ).

In a locale with state-dependent encoding the behaviour with regard to the stream's shift state is implementation-dependent.

%   Print a %; no argument is converted. The entire conversion specification must be %%.

If a conversion specification does not match one of the above forms, the behaviour is undefined.

In no case does a non-existent or small field width cause truncation of a field; if the result of a conversion is wider than the field width, the field is simply expanded to contain the conversion result. Characters generated by *fprintf*( ) and *printf*( ) are printed as if *fputc*( ) had been called.

The *st_ctime* and *st_mtime* fields of the file will be marked for update between the call to a successful execution of *fprintf*( ) or *printf*( ) and the next successful completion of a call to *fflush*( ) or *fclose*( ) on the same stream or a call to *exit*( ) or *abort*( ).

RETURN VALUE

Upon successful completion, these functions return the number of bytes transmitted excluding the terminating null in the case of *sprintf*( ) or a negative value if an output error was encountered.

ERRORS

For the conditions under which *fprintf*( ) and *printf*( ) will fail and may fail, refer to *fputc*( ) or *fputwc*( ).

In addition, all forms of *fprintf*( ) may fail if:

EX   [EILSEQ]   A wide-character code that does not correspond to a valid character has been detected.

EX   [EINVAL]   There are insufficient arguments.

UX   In addition, *printf*( ) and *fprintf*( ) may fail if:

      [ENOMEM]   Insufficient storage space is available.

EXAMPLES

To print the language-independent date and time format, the following statement could be used:

```
printf (format, weekday, month, day, hour, min);
```

For American usage, *format* could be a pointer to the string:

```
"%s, %s %d, %d:%.2d\n"
```

producing the message:

```
Sunday, July 3, 10:02
```

whereas for German usage, *format* could be a pointer to the string:

```
"%1$s, %3$d. %2$s, %4$d:%5$.2d\n"
```

producing the message:

```
Sonntag, 3. Juli, 10:02
```

APPLICATION USAGE

If the application calling *fprintf*( ) has any objects of type **wchar_t,** it must also include either **<sys/types.h>** or **<stddef.h>** to have **wchar_t** defined.

SEE ALSO

fputc( ), *fscanf*( ), *setlocale*( ), **<stdio.h>**, the **XBD** specification, **Chapter 5**, **Locale**.

EXAMPLE

```
/*
 * Copyright (C) ANTRIX Inc.
 */

/* fprintf.c
 * This program illustrates use of fprintf function.
 * Part 1 of this program prints different C type values using
 * function fprintf on stdout or terminal.
 * Part 2 of this program writes a string into a file using
 * function fprintf and then reads the string.
 */

#include <stdio.h>
#include <stdlib.h>
#include <unistd.h>
#include <errno.h>
```

```
main()
{

   int      bytes, fprintf_value;
   int      integer = 1;
   long     longer = 12L;
   float    floating = 1.2345;
   double   doubles = 1.234E10;
   char     character = 'a';
   char     string[] = "hello world";
   char     buf[12];
   char     *path = "testfile";
   FILE     *stream;

   fprintf (stdout,"part 1\n");
   fprintf (stdout,"write to stdout or terminal\n");
   fprintf (stdout, "integer=%d\n", integer);
   fprintf (stdout, "longer=%ld\n", longer);
   fprintf (stdout, "float=%f\n", floating);
   fprintf (stdout, "doubles=%f\n", doubles);
   fprintf (stdout, "character=%c\n", character);
   fprintf (stdout, "string=%s\n", string);

   fprintf (stdout,"part 2\n");
   fprintf (stdout,"write string to testfile\n");
   memset (buf, ' ', 12);
   bytes = strlen (string);

   stream = fopen (path, "w+r");
   fprintf_value = fprintf (stream, "%s", string);
   if (fprintf_value == bytes)
      fprintf (stdout,"fprintf() call successful\n");
   else {
      fprintf (stdout,"fprintf() call failed\n");
      fprintf (stderr,"ERROR: %s\n", strerror(errno));
   }
   fflush (stream);

   fprintf (stdout,"set file pointer to beginning of testfile\n");
   fseek (stream, 0, SEEK_SET);
   fprintf (stdout,"read string from testfile\n");
   fread (buf, sizeof(char), bytes, stream);
   fprintf (stdout,"string read in buf is %s\n", buf);

   fclose (stream);
   fprintf (stdout,"remove testfile\n");
   remove (path);
}
```

NAME

fputc — put byte on a stream

SYNOPSIS

```
#include <stdio.h>

int fputc(int c, FILE *stream);
```

DESCRIPTION

The *fputc( )* function writes the byte specified by *c* (converted to an **unsigned char**) to the output stream pointed to by *stream*, at the position indicated by the associated file-position indicator for the stream (if defined), and advances the indicator appropriately. If the file cannot support positioning requests, or if the stream was opened with append mode, the byte is appended to the output stream.

The *st_ctime* and *st_mtime* fields of the file will be marked for update between the successful execution of *fputc( )* and the next successful completion of a call to *fflush( )* or *fclose( )* on the same stream or a call to *exit( )* or *abort( )*.

RETURN VALUE

Upon successful completion, *fputc( )* returns the value it has written. Otherwise, it returns EOF, the error indicator for the stream is set, and *errno* is set to indicate the error.

ERRORS

The *fputc( )* function will fail if either the *stream* is unbuffered or the *stream*'s buffer needs to be flushed, and:

	[EAGAIN]	The O_NONBLOCK flag is set for the file descriptor underlying *stream* and the process would be delayed in the write operation.
	[EBADF]	The file descriptor underlying *stream* is not a valid file descriptor open for writing.
EX	[EFBIG]	An attempt was made to write to a file that exceeds the maximum file size or the process' file size limit.
	[EINTR]	The write operation was terminated due to the receipt of a signal, and no data was transferred.
UX	[EIO]	A physical I/O error has occurred, or the process is a member of a background process group attempting to write to its controlling terminal, TOSTOP is set, the process is neither ignoring nor blocking SIGTTOU and the process group of the process is orphaned. This error may also be returned under implementation-dependent conditions.
	[ENOSPC]	There was no free space remaining on the device containing the file.
	[EPIPE]	An attempt is made to write to a pipe or FIFO that is not open for reading by any process. A SIGPIPE signal will also be sent to the process.

The *fputc( )* function may fail if:

EX	[ENOMEM]	Insufficient storage space is available.
	[ENXIO]	A request was made of a non-existent device, or the request was outside the capabilities of the device.

SEE ALSO

ferror( ), *fopen( )*, *getrlimit( )*, *putc( )*, *puts( )*, *setbuf( )*, *ulimit( )*, **<stdio.h>**.

EXAMPLE

```c
/*
 * Copyright (C) ANTRIX Inc.
 */

/* fputc.c
 * This program writes the byte specified by c to output stream
 * using function fputc.
 */

#include <stdio.h>
#include <stdlib.h>
#include <sys/types.h>
#include <errno.h>

main()
{
  int   i, fputc_value;
  char  character;
  FILE  *stream;
  char  *path = "testfile";

  fprintf (stdout,"example 1\n");
  fprintf (stdout,"write character 'a' into file\n");
  stream = fopen (path, "w+r");

  fputc_value = fputc ('a', stream);
  if ( fputc_value == 'a' ) {
     fprintf (stdout,"fputc() call successful\n");
     fflush (stream);
     fseek (stream, 0, SEEK_SET);
     character = fgetc (stream);
     fprintf (stdout,"character read is '%c'\n", character );
  }
  else {
     fprintf (stderr,"ERROR: fputc() call failed\n");
     fprintf (stderr,"ERROR: %s\n", strerror(errno));
  }

  fclose (stream);
  fprintf (stdout,"remove testfile\n");
  remove (path);

  fprintf (stdout,"example 2\n");
  fprintf (stdout,"write all alphabet and numbers to stdout or terminal\n");
  for (i = '0'; i <= 'z'; i++)
      fputc (i, stdout);
  fputc ('\n', stdout);
}
```

NAME

fputs — put a string on a stream

SYNOPSIS

```
#include <stdio.h>

int fputs(const char *s, FILE *stream);
```

DESCRIPTION

The *fputs*( ) function writes the null-terminated string pointed to by *s* to the stream pointed to by *stream*. The terminating null byte is not written.

The *st_ctime* and *st_mtime* fields of the file will be marked for update between the successful execution of *fputs*( ) and the next successful completion of a call to *fflush*( ) or *fclose*( ) on the same stream or a call to *exit*( ) or *abort*( ).

RETURN VALUE

Upon successful completion, *fputs*( ) returns a non-negative number. Otherwise it returns EOF, sets an error indicator for the stream and *errno* is set to indicate the error.

ERRORS

Refer to *fputc*( ).

APPLICATION USAGE

The *puts*( ) function appends a newline character while *fputs*( ) does not.

SEE ALSO

fopen( ), *putc*( ), *puts*( ), **<stdio.h>**.

EXAMPLE

```
/*
 * Copyright (C) ANTRIX Inc.
 */

/* fputs.c
 * This program writes the null-terminated string pointed to
 * by s to the stream using function fputs.
 */

#include <stdio.h>
#include <stdlib.h>
#include <unistd.h>
#include <errno.h>

main()
{
  int    i, length, fputs_buf;
  char   *strptr, buf[12];
  char   s[] = "hello world";
  char   *path = "testfile";
  FILE   *stream;

  memset (buf, ' ', 12);
  length = strlen (s);

  fprintf (stdout,"create and open testfile\n");
  stream = fopen (path, "w+r");
```

```
        fprintf (stdout,"write string to testfile\n");
        fputs_buf = fputs (s, stream);
        fflush (stream);
        fprintf (stdout,"seek to the beginning of testfile\n");
        fseek (stream, 0, SEEK_SET);

        fprintf (stdout,"get string from testfile\n");
        strptr = fgets (buf, 12, stream);
        if ( strptr != (char *)0 ) {
            fprintf (stdout,"fgets() call successful\n");
            fprintf (stdout,"string in buf is %s\n", buf);
            fprintf (stdout,"string in strptr is %s\n", strptr);
        }
        else {
            fprintf (stderr,"ERROR: fgets() call failed\n");
            fprintf (stderr,"ERROR: %s\n", strerror(errno));
        }

        fclose (stream);
        fprintf (stdout,"remove testfile\n");
        remove (path);
}
```

NAME

fputwc — put wide-character code on a stream

SYNOPSIS

OH   `#include <stdio.h>`
WP   `#include <wchar.h>`

`wint_t fputwc(wint_t wc, FILE *stream);`

DESCRIPTION

The *fputwc( )* function writes the character corresponding to the wide-character code *wc* to the output stream pointed to by *stream*, at the position indicated by the associated file-position indicator for the stream (if defined), and advances the indicator appropriately. If the file cannot support positioning requests, or if the stream was opened with append mode, the character is appended to the output stream. If an error occurs whilst writing the character, the shift state of the output file is left in an undefined state.

The *st_ctime* and *st_mtime* fields of the file will be marked for update between the successful execution of *fputwc( )* and the next successful completion of a call to *fflush( )* or *fclose( )* on the same stream or a call to *exit( )* or *abort( )*.

RETURN VALUE

Upon successful completion, *fputwc( )* returns *wc*. Otherwise, it returns WEOF, the error indicator for the stream is set, and *errno* is set to indicate the error.

ERRORS

The *fputwc( )* function will fail if either the stream is unbuffered or data in the *stream*'s buffer needs to be written, and:

    [EAGAIN]   The O_NONBLOCK flag is set for the file descriptor underlying *stream* and the process would be delayed in the write operation.

    [EBADF]   The file descriptor underlying *stream* is not a valid file descriptor open for writing.

    [EFBIG]   An attempt was made to write to a file that exceeds the maximum file size or the process' file size limit.

    [EINTR]   The write operation was terminated due to the receipt of a signal, and no data was transferred.

UX   [EIO]   A physical I/O error has occurred, or the process is a member of a background process group attempting to write to its controlling terminal, TOSTOP is set, the process is neither ignoring nor blocking SIGTTOU and the process group of the process is orphaned. This error may also be returned under implementation-dependent conditions.

    [ENOSPC]   There was no free space remaining on the device containing the file.

    [EPIPE]   An attempt is made to write to a pipe or FIFO that is not open for reading by any process. A SIGPIPE signal will also be sent to the process.

The *fputwc*( ) function may fail if:

[ENOMEM]   Insufficient storage space is available.

[ENXIO]   A request was made of a non-existent device, or the request was outside the capabilities of the device.

[EILSEQ]   The wide-character code *wc* does not correspond to a valid character.

SEE ALSO

ferror( ), *fopen*( ), *setbuf*( ), *ulimit*( ), **<stdio.h>**, **<wchar.h>**.

EXAMPLE

```
/*
 * Copyright (C) ANTRIX Inc.
 */

/* fputwc.c
 * This program puts wide-character code on a stream
 * using function fputwc.
 */

#include <stdio.h>
#include <stdlib.h>
#include <widec.h>
#include <sys/types.h>
#include <errno.h>

main()
{
  wchar_t fputwc_value;
  wint_t  wc = 'a';
  int     i;
  char    *path = "testfile";
  FILE    *stream;

  fprintf (stdout,"example 1\n");
  fprintf (stdout,"write character 'a' into file\n");
  stream = fopen (path, "w+r");

  fputwc_value = fputwc (wc, stream);
  if ( fputwc_value == 'a' ) {
     fprintf (stdout,"fputwc() call successful\n");
     fflush (stream);
     fseek (stream, 0, SEEK_SET);
     wc = fgetwc (stream);
     fprintf (stdout,"character read is '%wc'\n", wc);
  }
  else {
     fprintf (stderr,"ERROR: fputwc() call failed\n");
     fprintf (stderr,"ERROR: %s\n", strerror(errno));
  }

  fclose (stream);
  fprintf (stdout,"remove testfile\n");
```

```
    remove (path);

    fprintf (stdout,"example 2\n");
    fprintf (stdout,"write all alphabet and numbers to stdout or terminal\n");
    for (i = '0'; i <= 'z'; i++)
        fputwc (i, stdout);
    fputwc ('\n', stdout);
}
```

NAME

fputws — put wide character string on a stream

SYNOPSIS

OH   `#include <stdio.h>`
WP   `#include <wchar.h>`

```
int fputws(const wchar_t *ws, FILE *stream);
```

DESCRIPTION

The *fputws*( ) function writes a character string corresponding to the (null-terminated) wide character string pointed to by *ws* to the stream pointed to by *stream*. No character corresponding to the terminating null wide-character code is written.

The *st_ctime* and *st_mtime* fields of the file will be marked for update between the successful execution of *fputws*( ) and the next successful completion of a call to *fflush*( ) or *fclose*( ) on the same stream or a call to *exit*( ) or *abort*( ).

RETURN VALUE

Upon successful completion, *fputws*( ) returns a non-negative number. Otherwise it returns −1, sets an error indicator for the stream and *errno* is set to indicate the error.

ERRORS

Refer to *fputwc*( ).

APPLICATION USAGE

The *fputws*( ) function does not append a newline character.

SEE ALSO

fopen( ), **<stdio.h>**, **<wchar.h>**.

EXAMPLE

```
/*
 * Copyright (C) ANTRIX Inc.
 */

/* fputws.c
 * This program puts a wide character string on a stream
 * using function fputws.
 */

#include <stdio.h>
#include <stdlib.h>
#include <widec.h>
#include <unistd.h>
#include <errno.h>

main()
{
    int     i, length, fputws_buf;
    wchar_t *strptr, buf[12];
    wchar_t *ws = L"hello world";
    FILE    *stream;
    char    *path = "testfile";

    memset (buf, ' ', 12);
    length = wcslen (ws);
```

```
fprintf (stdout,"create and open testfile\n");
stream = fopen (path, "w+r");
fprintf (stdout,"write wide string to testfile\n");
fputws_buf = fputws (ws, stream);
fflush (stream);

fprintf (stdout,"seek to the beginning of testfile\n");
fseek (stream, 0, SEEK_SET);

fprintf (stdout,"get string from testfile\n");
strptr = fgetws (buf, 12, stream);
if ( strptr != (wchar_t *)0 ) {
    fprintf (stdout,"fgetws() call successful\n");
    fprintf (stdout,"wide string in buf is %ws\n", buf);
    fprintf (stdout,"string in strptr is %ws\n", strptr);
}
else {
    fprintf (stderr,"ERROR: fgetws() call failed\n");
    fprintf (stderr,"ERROR: %s\n", strerror(errno));
}

fclose (stream);
fprintf (stdout,"remove testfile\n");
remove (path);
}
```

NAME

fread — binary input

SYNOPSIS

```
#include <stdio.h>

size_t fread(void *ptr, size_t size, size_t nitems, FILE *stream);
```

DESCRIPTION

The *fread( )* function reads, into the array pointed to by *ptr*, up to *nitems* members whose size is specified by *size* in bytes, from the stream pointed to by *stream*. The file position indicator for the stream (if defined) is advanced by the number of bytes successfully read. If an error occurs, the resulting value of the file position indicator for the stream is indeterminate. If a partial member is read, its value is indeterminate.

The *fread( )* function may mark the *st_atime* field of the file associated with *stream* for update. The *st_atime* field will be marked for update by the first successful execution of *fgetc( )*, *fgets( )*, *fgetwc( )*, *fgetws( )*, *fread( )*, *fscanf( )*, *getc( )*, *getchar( )*, *gets( )* or *scanf( )* using *stream* that returns data not supplied by a prior call to *ungetc( )* or *ungetwc( )*.

RETURN VALUE

Upon successful completion, *fread( )* returns the number of members successfully read which is less than *nitems* only if a read error or end-of-file is encountered. If *size* or *nitems* is 0, *fread( )* returns 0 and the contents of the array and the state of the stream remain unchanged. Otherwise, if a read error occurs, the error indicator for the stream is set and *errno* is set to indicate the error.

ERRORS

Refer to *fgetc( )*.

APPLICATION USAGE

The *ferror( )* or *feof( )* functions must be used to distinguish between an error condition and an end-of-file condition.

SEE ALSO

feof( ), *ferror( )*, *fopen( )*, *getc( )*, *gets( )*, *scanf( )*, **<stdio.h>**.

EXAMPLE

```
/*
 * Copyright (C) ANTRIX Inc.
 */

/* fread.c
 * This program reads, into the array pointed to by ptr, up to
 * nitems members whose size is specified by size in nitems using
 * function fread.
 */

#include <stdio.h>
#include <stdlib.h>
#include <sys/types.h>
#include <errno.h>

main()
{
    int     fread_value, nitems;
    char    ptr[12];
```

```
FILE  *stream;
char  string[] = "hello world";
char  *filename = "testfile";

memset (ptr, ' ', 12);
nitems = strlen (string);

fprintf (stdout,"create and open testfile\n");
stream = fopen (filename, "w+r");
fwrite (string, sizeof(char), nitems, stream);
fflush (stream);

fprintf (stdout,"seek to the beginning of testfile\n");
fseek (stream, 0, SEEK_SET);

fprintf (stdout,"read string from testfile\n");
fread_value = fread (ptr, sizeof(char), nitems, stream);
if ( fread_value == fread_value) {
   fprintf (stdout,"fread() call successful\n");
   fprintf (stdout,"string read in ptr is %s\n", ptr);
}
else {
   fprintf (stderr,"ERROR: fread() call failed\n");
   fprintf (stderr,"ERROR: %s\n", strerror(errno));
}

fclose (stream);
fprintf (stdout,"remove testfile\n");
remove (filename);
}
```

NAME

free — free allocated memory

SYNOPSIS

```
#include <stdlib.h>

void free(void *ptr);
```

DESCRIPTION

The *free( )* function causes the space pointed to by *ptr* to be deallocated; that is, made available for further allocation. If *ptr* is a null pointer, no action occurs. Otherwise, if the argument does not match a pointer earlier returned by the *calloc( )*, *malloc( )*, *realloc( )* or *valloc( )* function, or if the space is deallocated by a call to *free( )* or *realloc( )*, the behaviour is undefined.

UX

Any use of a pointer that refers to freed space causes undefined behaviour.

RETURN VALUE

The *free( )* function returns no value.

ERRORS

No errors are defined.

APPLICATION USAGE

There is now no requirement for the implementation to support the inclusion of **<malloc.h>**.

SEE ALSO

calloc( ), *malloc( )*, *realloc( )*, *valloc( )*, **<stdlib.h>**.

EXAMPLE

```
/*
 * Copyright (C) ANTRIX Inc.
 */

/* free.c
 * This program causes the space pointed to by ptr to be
 * deallocated using function free.
 */

#include <stdio.h>
#include <stdlib.h>
#include <malloc.h>
#include <errno.h>

main()
{
  char    *ptr;
  size_t  size;
  char    *string = "hello world";

  size = strlen (string);
  fprintf (stdout,"allocate memory\n");
  ptr = (char *)malloc (size);

  fprintf(stdout, "copy string in the space allocated\n");
  strcpy (ptr, string);

  fprintf(stdout, "string is %s\n", string);
```

```
    fprintf (stdout,"free allocated memory\n");
    free (ptr);
}
```

NAME

freopen — open a stream

SYNOPSIS

```
#include <stdio.h>

FILE *freopen(const char *filename, const char *mode, FILE *stream);
```

DESCRIPTION

The *freopen*( ) function first attempts to flush the stream and close any file descriptor associated with *stream*. Failure to flush or close the file successfully is ignored. The error and end-of-file indicators for the stream are cleared.

The *freopen*( ) function opens the file whose pathname is the string pointed to by *filename* and associates the stream pointed to by *stream* with it. The *mode* argument is used just as in *fopen*( ).

The original stream is closed regardless of whether the subsequent open succeeds.

RETURN VALUE

Upon successful completion, *freopen*( ) returns the value of *stream*. Otherwise a null pointer is returned and *errno* is set to indicate the error.

ERRORS

The *freopen*( ) function will fail if:

[EACCES]	Search permission is denied on a component of the path prefix, or the file exists and the permissions specified by *mode* are denied, or the file does not exist and write permission is denied for the parent directory of the file to be created.
[EINTR]	A signal was caught during *freopen*( ).
[EISDIR]	The named file is a directory and *mode* requires write access.
UX [ELOOP]	Too many symbolic links were encountered in resolving *path*.
[EMFILE]	{OPEN_MAX} file descriptors are currently open in the calling process.
[ENAMETOOLONG]	
FIPS	The length of the *filename* exceeds {PATH_MAX} or a pathname component is longer than {NAME_MAX}.
[ENFILE]	The maximum allowable number of files is currently open in the system.
[ENOENT]	A component of *filename* does not name an existing file or *filename* is an empty string.
[ENOSPC]	The directory or file system that would contain the new file cannot be expanded, the file does not exist, and it was to be created.
[ENOTDIR]	A component of the path prefix is not a directory.
[ENXIO]	The named file is a character special or block special file, and the device associated with this special file does not exist.
[EROFS]	The named file resides on a read-only file system and *mode* requires write access.

The *freopen*( ) function may fail if:

EX [EINVAL]	The value of the *mode* argument is not valid.

UX   **[ENAMETOOLONG]**
            Pathname resolution of a symbolic link produced an intermediate result whose length exceeds {PATH_MAX}.

[ENOMEM]   Insufficient storage space is available.

[ENXIO]   A request was made of a non-existent device, or the request was outside the capabilities of the device.

[ETXTBSY]   The file is a pure procedure (shared text) file that is being executed and *mode* requires write access.

APPLICATION USAGE

The *freopen( )* function is typically used to attach the preopened *streams* associated with *stdin*, *stdout* and *stderr* to other files.

SEE ALSO

fclose( ), *fopen( )*, *fdopen( )*, **<stdio.h>**.

EXAMPLE

```
/*
 * Copyright (C) ANTRIX Inc.
 */

/* freopen.c
 * This program opens the file whose pathname is the string
 * pointed to by filename and associates the stream with it
 * using function freopen.
 */

#include <stdio.h>
#include <stdlib.h>
#include <errno.h>

main()
{
    FILE    *stream1, *stream2;
    char     buf[12];
    char     string[] = "hello world";
    char    *filename = "testfile";

    memset (buf, ' ', 12);
    fprintf (stdout,"create and open testfile\n");
    stream1 = fopen (filename, "w");

    fprintf (stdout,"write string to testfile\n");
    fwrite (string, sizeof(char), strlen(string), stream1);

    fprintf (stdout,"close testfile\n");
    fclose (stream1);

    fprintf (stdout,"open testfile\n");
    stream1 = fopen (filename, "r");

    fprintf (stdout,"reopen testfile\n");
```

```
    fprintf (stdout,"and associate filename with stream2\n");
    stream2 = freopen (filename, "r", stream1);
    if ( stream2 != (FILE *)0 ) {
       fprintf (stdout,"freopen() call successful\n");
       fprintf (stdout,"string in buf is %s\n", buf);
    }
    else {
       fprintf (stderr,"ERROR: freopen() call failed\n");
       fprintf (stderr,"ERROR: %s\n", strerror(errno));
    }

    fprintf (stdout,"read testfile\n");
    fread (buf, sizeof(char), strlen(string), stream2);

    fprintf (stdout,"remove testfile\n");
    remove (filename);
}
```

NAME

frexp — extract mantissa and exponent from double precision number

SYNOPSIS

```
#include <math.h>

double frexp(double num, int *exp);
```

DESCRIPTION

The *frexp*( ) function breaks a floating-point number into a normalised fraction and an integral power of 2. It stores the integer exponent in the **int** object pointed to by *exp*.

RETURN VALUE

The *frexp*( ) function returns the value *x*, such that *x* is a **double** with magnitude in the interval [½, 1) or 0, and *num* equals *x* times 2 raised to the power *exp*.

If *num* is 0, both parts of the result are 0.

EX   If *num* is NaN, NaN is returned, *errno* may be set to [EDOM] and the value of *exp* is unspecified.

EX   If *num* is ±Inf, *num* is returned, *errno* may be set to [EDOM] and the value of *exp* is unspecified.

ERRORS

The *frexp*( ) function may fail if:

EX   [EDOM]   The value of *num* is NaN or ±Inf.

EX   No other errors will occur.

APPLICATION USAGE

An application wishing to check for error situations should set *errno* to 0 before calling *frexp*( ). If *errno* is non-zero on return, or the return value is NaN, an error has occurred.

SEE ALSO

isnan( ), *ldexp*( ), *modf*( ), **<math.h>**.

EXAMPLE

```
/*
 * Copyright (C) ANTRIX Inc.
 */

/* frexp.c
 * This program breaks a floating-point number into a normalized
 * fraction and an integral power of 2 using function frexp.
 */

#include <stdio.h>
#include <stdlib.h>
#include <math.h>
#include <errno.h>

main()
{
    double    frexp_value;
    double    num = 123.456;
    int       eptr;
```

```
            fprintf (stdout, "break %f number into a normalized\n", num);
            fprintf (stdout, "fraction and an integral power of 2\n");
            frexp_value = frexp (num, &eptr);

            fprintf (stdout,"fraction part is %f\n", frexp_value);
            fprintf (stdout,"exponent part is %d\n", eptr );
        }
```

NAME

fscanf, scanf, sscanf — convert formatted input

SYNOPSIS

```
#include <stdio.h>

int fscanf(FILE *stream, const char *format, ... );

int scanf(const char *format, ... );

int sscanf(const char *s, const char *format, ... );
```

DESCRIPTION

The *fscanf( )* function reads from the named input *stream*. The *scanf( )* function reads from the standard input stream *stdin*. The *sscanf( )* function reads from the string *s*. Each function reads bytes, interprets them according to a format, and stores the results in its arguments. Each expects, as arguments, a control string *format* described below, and a set of *pointer* arguments indicating where the converted input should be stored. The result is undefined if there are insufficient arguments for the format. If the format is exhausted while arguments remain, the excess arguments are evaluated but are otherwise ignored.

EX
Conversions can be applied to the *nth* argument after the *format* in the argument list, rather than to the next unused argument. In this case, the conversion character % (see below) is replaced by the sequence %*n*$, where *n* is a decimal integer in the range [1, {NL_ARGMAX}]. This feature provides for the definition of format strings that select arguments in an order appropriate to specific languages. In format strings containing the %*n*$ form of conversion specifications, it is unspecified whether numbered arguments in the argument list can be referenced from the format string more than once.

The *format* can contain either form of a conversion specification, that is, % or %*n*$, but the two forms cannot normally be mixed within a single *format* string. The only exception to this is that %% or %* can be mixed with the %*n*$ form.

The *fscanf( )* function in all its forms allows for detection of a language-dependent radix character in the input string. The radix character is defined in the program's locale (category LC_NUMERIC). In the POSIX locale, or in a locale where the radix character is not defined, the radix character defaults to a period (.).

The format is a character string, beginning and ending in its initial shift state, if any, composed of zero or more directives. Each directive is composed of one of the following: one or more white-space characters (space, tab, newline, vertical-tab or form-feed characters); an ordinary character (neither % nor a white-space character); or a conversion specification. Each

EX
conversion specification is introduced by the character % or the character sequence %*n*$ after which the following appear in sequence:

- An optional assignment-suppressing character *.

- An optional non-zero decimal integer that specifies the maximum field width.

- An optional size modifier h, l (ell) or L indicating the size of the receiving object. The conversion characters d, i and n must be preceded by h if the corresponding argument is a pointer to **short int** rather than a pointer to **int**, or by l (ell) if it is a pointer to **long int**. Similarly, the conversion characters o, u and x must be preceded by h if the corresponding argument is a pointer to **unsigned short int** rather than a pointer to **unsigned int**, or by l (ell) if it is a pointer to **unsigned long int**. Finally, the conversion characters e, f and g must be preceded by l (ell) if the corresponding argument is a pointer to **double** rather than a pointer to **float**, or by L if it is a pointer to **long double**. If an h, l (ell) or L appears with any other conversion character, the behaviour is undefined.

- A conversion character that specifies the type of conversion to be applied. The valid conversion characters are described below.

The *fscanf*( ) functions execute each directive of the format in turn. If a directive fails, as detailed below, the function returns. Failures are described as input failures (due to the unavailability of input bytes) or matching failures (due to inappropriate input).

A directive composed of one or more white-space characters is executed by reading input until no more valid input can be read, or up to the first byte which is not a white-space character which remains unread.

A directive that is an ordinary character is executed as follows. The next byte is read from the input and compared with the byte that comprises the directive; if the comparison shows that they are not equivalent, the directive fails, and the differing and subsequent bytes remain unread.

A directive that is a conversion specification defines a set of matching input sequences, as described below for each conversion character. A conversion specification is executed in the following steps:

Input white-space characters (as specified by *isspace*( )) are skipped, unless the conversion specification includes a [, c, C or n conversion character.

An item is read from the input, unless the conversion specification includes an n conversion character. An input item is defined as the longest sequence of input bytes (up to any specified maximum field width, which may be measured in characters or bytes dependent on the conversion character) which is an initial subsequence of a matching sequence. The first byte, if any, after the input item remains unread. If the length of the input item is 0, the execution of the conversion specification fails; this condition is a matching failure, unless an error prevented input, in which case it is an input failure.

Except in the case of a % conversion character, the input item (or, in the case of a %*n* conversion specification, the count of input bytes) is converted to a type appropriate to the conversion character. If the input item is not a matching sequence, the execution of the conversion specification fails; this condition is a matching failure. Unless assignment suppression was indicated by a *, the result of the conversion is placed in the object pointed to by the first argument following the *format* argument that has not already received a conversion

EX   result if the conversion specification is introduced by %, or in the *n*th argument if introduced by the character sequence %*n*$. If this object does not have an appropriate type, or if the result of the conversion cannot be represented in the space provided, the behaviour is undefined.

The following conversion characters are valid:

d   Matches an optionally signed decimal integer, whose format is the same as expected for the subject sequence of *strtol*( ) with the value 10 for the *base* argument. In the absence of a size modifier, the corresponding argument must be a pointer to **int**.

i   Matches an optionally signed integer, whose format is the same as expected for the subject sequence of *strtol*( ) with 0 for the *base* argument. In the absence of a size modifier, the corresponding argument must be a pointer to **int**.

o   Matches an optionally signed octal integer, whose format is the same as expected for the subject sequence of *strtoul*( ) with the value 8 for the *base* argument. In the absence of a size modifier, the corresponding argument must be a pointer to **unsigned int**.

u   Matches an optionally signed decimal integer, whose format is the same as expected for the subject sequence of *strtoul*( ) with the value 10 for the *base* argument. In the absence of a size modifier, the corresponding argument must be a pointer to **unsigned int**.

x   Matches an optionally signed hexadecimal integer, whose format is the same as expected for the subject sequence of *strtoul( )* with the value 16 for the *base* argument. In the absence of a size modifier, the corresponding argument must be a pointer to **unsigned int**.

e, f, g Matches an optionally signed floating-point number, whose format is the same as expected for the subject sequence of *strtod( )*. In the absence of a size modifier, the corresponding argument must be a pointer to **float**.

s   Matches a sequence of bytes that are not white-space characters. The corresponding argument must be a pointer to the initial byte of an array of **char**, **signed char** or **unsigned char** large enough to accept the sequence and a terminating null character code, which will be added automatically.

[Matches a non-empty sequence of bytes from a set of expected bytes (the *scanset*). The normal skip over white-space characters is suppressed in this case. The corresponding argument must be a pointer to the initial byte of an array of **char**, **signed char** or **unsigned char** large enough to accept the sequence and a terminating null byte, which will be added automatically. The conversion specification includes all subsequent bytes in the *format* string up to and including the matching right square bracket (]). The bytes between the square brackets (the *scanlist*) comprise the scanset, unless the byte after the left square bracket is a circumflex (^), in which case the scanset contains all bytes that do not appear in the scanlist between the circumflex and the right square bracket. If the conversion specification begins with [] or [^], the right square bracket is included in the scanlist and the next right square bracket is the matching right square bracket that ends the conversion specification; otherwise the first right square bracket is the one that ends the conversion specification. If a – is in the scanlist and is not the first character, nor the second where the first character is a ^, nor the last character, the behaviour is implementation-dependent.

c   Matches a sequence of bytes of the number specified by the field width (1 if no field width is present in the conversion specification). The corresponding argument must be a pointer to the initial byte of an array of **char**, **signed char** or **unsigned char** large enough to accept the sequence. No null byte is added. The normal skip over white-space characters is suppressed in this case.

p   Matches an implementation-dependent set of sequences, which must be the same as the set of sequences that is produced by the %p conversion of the corresponding *fprintf( )* functions. The corresponding argument must be a pointer to a pointer to **void**. The interpretation of the input item is implementation-dependent. If the input item is a value converted earlier during the same program execution, the pointer that results will compare equal to that value; otherwise the behaviour of the %p conversion is undefined.

n   No input is consumed. The corresponding argument must be a pointer to the integer into which is to be written the number of bytes read from the input so far by this call to the *fscanf( )* functions. Execution of a %n conversion specification does not increment the assignment count returned at the completion of execution of the function.

EX   C   Matches a sequence of characters of the number specified by the field width (1 if no field width is present in the directive). The sequence is converted to a sequence of wide-character codes in the same manner as *mbstowcs( )*. The corresponding argument must be a pointer to the initial wide-character code of an array of type

wchar_t large enough to accept the sequence which is the result of the conversion. No null wide-character code is added. If the matched sequence begins with the initial shift state, the conversion is the same as expected for *mbstowcs( )*; otherwise the behaviour of the conversion is undefined. The normal skip over white-space characters is suppressed in this case.

EX   S   Matches a sequence of characters that are not white space. The sequence is converted to a sequence of wide character codes in the same manner as *mbstowcs( )*. The corresponding argument must be a pointer to the initial wide-character code of an array of **wchar_t** large enough to accept the sequence and a terminating null wide-character code, which will be added automatically. If the field width is specified, it denotes the maximum number of characters to accept.

%   Matches a single %; no conversion or assignment occurs. The complete conversion specification must be %%.

If a conversion specification is invalid, the behaviour is undefined.

The conversion characters E, G and X are also valid and behave the same as, respectively, e, g and x.

If end-of-file is encountered during input, conversion is terminated. If end-of-file occurs before any bytes matching the current conversion specification (except for %n) have been read (other than leading white-space characters, where permitted), execution of the current conversion specification terminates with an input failure. Otherwise, unless execution of the current conversion specification is terminated with a matching failure, execution of the following conversion specification (if any) is terminated with an input failure.

Reaching the end of the string in *sscanf( )* is equivalent to encountering end-of-file for *fscanf( )*.

If conversion terminates on a conflicting input, the offending input is left unread in the input. Any trailing white space (including newline characters) is left unread unless matched by a conversion specification. The success of literal matches and suppressed assignments is only directly determinable via the %n conversion specification.

The *fscanf( )* and *scanf( )* functions may mark the *st_atime* field of the file associated with *stream* for update. The *st_atime* field will be marked for update by the first successful execution of *fgetc( )*, *fgets( )*, *fread( )*, *getc( )*, *getchar( )*, *gets( )*, *fscanf( )* or *fscanf( )* using *stream* that returns data not supplied by a prior call to *ungetc( )*.

RETURN VALUE

Upon successful completion, these functions return the number of successfully matched and assigned input items; this number can be 0 in the event of an early matching failure. If the input ends before the first matching failure or conversion, EOF is returned. If a read error occurs the error indicator for the stream is set, EOF is returned, and *errno* is set to indicate the error.

ERRORS

For the conditions under which the *fscanf( )* functions will fail and may fail, refer to *fgetc( )* or *fgetwc( )*.

In addition, *fscanf( )* may fail if:

EX   [EILSEQ]   Input byte sequence does not form a valid character.

EX   [EINVAL]   There are insufficient arguments.

EXAMPLES

The call:

```
int i, n; float x; char name[50];
n = scanf("%d%f%s", &i, &x, name);
```

with the input line:

```
25 54.32E-1 Hamster
```

will assign to *n* the value 3, to *i* the value 25, to *x* the value 5.432, and *name* will contain the string Hamster.

The call:

```
int i; float x; char name[50];
(void) scanf("%2d%f%*d %[0123456789]", &i, &x, name);
```

with input:

```
56789 0123 56a72
```

will assign 56 to *i*, 789.0 to *x*, skip 0123, and place the string 56\0 in *name*. The next call to *getchar*( ) will return the character a.

APPLICATION USAGE

If the application calling *fprintf*( ) has any objects of type **wchar_t,** it must also include either **<sys/types.h>** or **<stddef.h>** to have **wchar_t** defined.

The *fscanf*( ) function may recognise character string representations for infinity and NaN (a symbolic entity encoded in floating-point format) to support the ANSI/IEEE Std 754: 1985 standard.

In format strings containing the % form of conversion specifications, each argument in the argument list is used exactly once.

SEE ALSO

getc( ), *printf*( ), *setlocale*( ), *strtod*( ), *strtol*( ), *strtoul*( ), **<langinfo.h>**, **<stdio.h>**, the **XBD** specification, **Chapter 5**, **Locale**.

EXAMPLE

```
/*
 * Copyright (C) ANTRIX Inc.
 */

/* fscanf.c
 * This program reads from the named input stream according
 * to a format, and stores the results in its argument
 * using function fscanf.
 */

#include <stdio.h>
#include <stdlib.h>
#include <errno.h>

main()
{
    FILE    *stream;
    int     bytes;
```

```
        int     fscanf_value;
        char    str1[6], str2[6];
        char    string[] = "hello world";
        char    *filename = "testfile";

        memset (str1, ' ', 6);
        memset (str2, ' ', 6);
        bytes = strlen (string);

        fprintf (stdout,"create and open testfile\n");
        stream = fopen (filename, "w+r");

        fprintf (stdout,"write string to testfile\n");
        fwrite (string, sizeof(char), bytes, stream);
        fflush (stream);
        fprintf (stdout,"seek to the beginning of file\n");
        fseek (stream, 0, SEEK_SET);

        fprintf (stdout,"read strings in the buffer\n");
        fscanf_value = fscanf (stream, "%s %s", str1, str2);
        if ( fscanf_value == 2 ) {
           fprintf (stdout,"fscanf() call successful\n");
           fprintf (stdout,"string str1 is %s, string str2 is %s\n", str1, str2);
        }
        else {
           fprintf (stderr,"ERROR: fscanf() call failed\n");
           fprintf (stderr,"ERROR: %s\n", strerror(errno));
        }

        fprintf (stdout,"remove testfile\n");
        remove (filename);
}
```

NAME

fseek — reposition a file-position indicator in a stream

SYNOPSIS

```
#include <stdio.h>

int fseek(FILE *stream, long int offset, int whence);
```

DESCRIPTION

The *fseek( )* function sets the file-position indicator for the stream pointed to by *stream*.

The new position, measured in bytes from the beginning of the file, is obtained by adding *offset* to the position specified by *whence*. The specified point is the beginning of the file for SEEK_SET, the current value of the file-position indicator for SEEK_CUR, or end-of-file for SEEK_END.

WP — If the stream is to be used with wide character input/output functions, *offset* must either be 0 or a value returned by an earlier call to *ftell( )* on the same stream and *whence* must be SEEK_SET.

A successful call to *fseek( )* clears the end-of-file indicator for the stream and undoes any effects of *ungetc( )* and *ungetwc( )* on the same stream. After an *fseek( )* call, the next operation on an update stream may be either input or output.

If the most recent operation, other than *ftell( )*, on a given stream is *fflush( )*, the file offset in the underlying open file description will be adjusted to reflect the location specified by *fseek( )*.

The *fseek( )* function allows the file-position indicator to be set beyond the end of existing data in the file. If data is later written at this point, subsequent reads of data in the gap will return bytes with the value 0 until data is actually written into the gap.

The behaviour of *fseek( )* on devices which are incapable of seeking is implementation-dependent. The value of the file offset associated with such a device is undefined.

If the stream is writable and buffered data had not been written to the underlying file, *fseek( )* will cause the unwritten data to be written to the file and mark the *st_ctime* and *st_mtime* fields of the file for update.

RETURN VALUE

EX — The *fseek( )* function returns 0 if it succeeds; otherwise it returns –1 and sets *errno* to indicate the error.

ERRORS

The *fseek( )* function will fail if, either the *stream* is unbuffered or the *stream*'s buffer needed to be flushed, and the call to *fseek( )* causes an underlying *lseek( )* or *write( )* to be invoked:

[EAGAIN]	The O_NONBLOCK flag is set for the file descriptor and the process would be delayed in the write operation.
[EBADF]	The file descriptor underlying the stream file is not open for writing or the stream's buffer needed to be flushed and the file is not open.
EX [EFBIG]	An attempt was made to write a file that exceeds the maximum file size or the process' file size limit.
[EINTR]	The write operation was terminated due to the receipt of a signal, and no data was transferred.
[EINVAL]	The *whence* argument is invalid. The resulting file-position indicator would be set to a negative value.

UX	[EIO]	A physical I/O error has occurred, or the process is a member of a background process group attempting to perform a *write*( ) to its controlling terminal, TOSTOP is set, the process is neither ignoring nor blocking SIGTTOU and the process group of the process is orphaned. This error may also be returned under implementation-dependent conditions.
	[ENOSPC]	There was no free space remaining on the device containing the file.
	[EPIPE]	(a) The file descriptor underlying *stream* is associated with a pipe or FIFO.
		(b) An attempt was made to write to a pipe or FIFO that is not open for reading by any process; a SIGPIPE signal will also be sent to the process.
EX	[ENXIO]	A request was made of a non-existent device, or the request was outside the capabilities of the device.

APPLICATION USAGE

In a locale with state-dependent encoding, whether *fseek*( ) restores the stream's shift state is implementation-dependent.

SEE ALSO

fopen( ), *ftell*( ), *getrlimit*( ), *rewind*( ), *ulimit*( ), *ungetc*( ), **<stdio.h>**.

EXAMPLE

```
/*
 * Copyright (C) ANTRIX Inc.
 */

/* fseek.c
 * This program sets the file-position indicator to the
 * beginning of stream using function fseek.
 */

#include <stdio.h>
#include <stdlib.h>
#include <unistd.h>
#include <errno.h>

main()
{
    int     bytes, fseek_value;
    char    buf[12];
    char    string[] = "hello world";
    char    *filename = "testfile";
    FILE    *stream;

    memset (buf, ' ', 12);
    bytes = strlen (string);

    fprintf (stdout,"create and open testfile\n");
    stream - fopen (filename, "w+r");

    fprintf (stdout,"write string to testfile\n");
    fwrite (string, sizeof(char), bytes, stream);
    fflush (stream);
```

```
        fprintf (stdout,"seek to the beginning of testfile\n");
        fseek_value = fseek (stream, 0, SEEK_SET);
        if ( fseek_value == 0 )
           fprintf (stdout,"fseek() call successful\n");
        else {
           fprintf (stderr,"ERROR: fseek() call failed\n");
           fprintf (stderr,"ERROR: %s\n", strerror(errno));
        }

        fprintf (stdout,"read string\n");
        fread (buf, sizeof(char), bytes, stream);

        fprintf (stdout,"string read in buf is %s\n", buf);
        fclose (stream);
        fprintf (stdout,"remove testfile\n");
        remove (filename);
}
```

NAME

fsetpos — set current file position

SYNOPSIS

```
#include <stdio.h>

int fsetpos(FILE *stream, const fpos_t *pos);
```

DESCRIPTION

The *fsetpos( )* function sets the file position indicator for the stream pointed to by *stream* according to the value of the object pointed to by *pos*, which must be a value obtained from an earlier call to *fgetpos( )* on the same stream.

A successful call to *fsetpos( )* function clears the end-of-file indicator for the stream and undoes any effects of *ungetc( )* on the same stream. After an *fsetpos( )* call, the next operation on an update stream may be either input or output.

RETURN VALUE

The *fsetpos( )* function returns 0 if it succeeds; otherwise it returns a non-zero value and sets *errno* to indicate the error.

ERRORS

The *fsetpos( )* function may fail if:

EX   [EBADF]   The file descriptor underlying *stream* is not valid.

[ESPIPE]   The file descriptor underlying *stream* is associated with a pipe or FIFO.

SEE ALSO

fopen( ), *ftell( )*, *rewind( )*, *ungetc( )*, **<stdio.h>**.

EXAMPLE

```
/*
 * Copyright (C) ANTRIX Inc.
 */

/* fsetpos.c
 * This program sets the file position indicator for the stream
 * using function fsetpos.
 */

#include <stdio.h>
#include <stdlib.h>
#include <sys/types.h>
#include <errno.h>

main()
{
    fpos_t  fsetpos_value;
    fpos_t  set_pos = 6;
    fpos_t  new_pos;
    int     bytes;
    char    buf[12];
    char    string[] = "hello world";
    char    *filename = "testfile";
    FILE    *stream;
```

```
   memset (buf, ' ', 12);
   bytes = strlen (string);

   fprintf (stdout,"create and open testfile\n");
   stream = fopen (filename, "w+r");
   fprintf (stdout,"write string to testfile\n");
   fwrite (string, sizeof(char), bytes, stream);
   fflush (stream);

   fprintf (stdout,"seek to the beginning of testfile\n");
   fseek (stream, 0, SEEK_SET);

   fprintf (stdout,"reposition file pointer\n");
   fsetpos_value = fsetpos (stream, &set_pos);
   if ( fsetpos_value == 0 ) {
      fprintf (stdout,"fsetpos() call successful\n");
      fgetpos (stream, &new_pos);
      fread (buf, sizeof(char), strlen(string), stream);
      fprintf (stdout,"starting from postion %d string is %s\n",
                      new_pos, buf);
   }
   else {
      fprintf (stderr,"ERROR: fsetpos() call failed\n");
      fprintf (stderr,"ERROR: %s\n", strerror(errno));
   }

   fclose (stream);
   fprintf (stdout,"remove testfile\n");
   remove (filename);
}
```

NAME

fstat — get file status

SYNOPSIS

OH   `#include <sys/types.h>`
`#include <sys/stat.h>`

`int fstat(int `*fildes*`, struct stat *`*buf*`);`

DESCRIPTION

The *fstat*( ) function obtains information about an open file associated with the file descriptor *fildes*, and writes it to the area pointed to by *buf*.

The *buf* argument is a pointer to a **stat** structure, as defined in **<sys/stat.h>**, into which information is placed concerning the file.

The structure members **st_mode**, **st_ino**, **st_dev**, **st_uid**, **st_gid**, **st_atime**, **st_ctime** and **st_mtime** will have meaningful values for all file types defined in this document. The value of the member **st_nlink** will be set to the number of links to the file.

An implementation that provides additional or alternative file access control mechanisms may, under implementation-dependent conditions, cause *fstat*( ) to fail.

The *fstat*( ) function updates any time-related fields as described in **File Times Update** (see the **XBD** specification, **Chapter 4**, **Character Set**), before writing into the *stat* structure.

RETURN VALUE

Upon successful completion, 0 is returned. Otherwise, −1 is returned and *errno* is set to indicate the error.

ERRORS

The *fstat*( ) function will fail if:

[EBADF]   The *fildes* argument is not a valid file descriptor.

UX   [EIO]   An I/O error occurred while reading from the file system.

UX   The *fstat*( ) function may fail if:

[EOVERFLOW]   One of the values is too large to store into the structure pointed to by the *buf* argument.

SEE ALSO

lstat( ), *stat*( ), **<sys/stat.h>**, **<sys/types.h>**.

EXAMPLE

```
/*
 * Copyright (C) ANTRIX Inc.
 */

/* fstat.c
 * This program obtains information about an open file associated
 * with the file descriptor fildes, and writes it to the area
 * pointed to by buf using function fstat.
 */

#include <stdio.h>
#include <stdlib.h>
#include <sys/types.h>
#include <sys/stat.h>
```

```
#include <errno.h>

#define  PERM_ALL   (S_IRWXU | S_IRWXG | S_IRWXO)

main()
{
  int     fstat_value;
  int     fildes, length;
  char    *string = "hello world";
  char    *filename = "testfile";
  struct  stat buf;

  length = strlen(string);
  fprintf (stdout,"create testfile\n");
  fildes = creat (filename, PERM_ALL);

  fprintf (stdout,"write string\n");
  write (fildes, string, length);

  fprintf (stdout,"get status of testfile\n");
  fstat_value = fstat (fildes, &buf);
  if ( fstat_value == 0 ) {
     fprintf (stdout,"fstat() call successful\n");
     fprintf (stdout,"buf.st_mode=%o\n", (S_IFREG ^ buf.st_mode));
     fprintf (stdout,"buf.st_nlink=%d\n", buf.st_nlink );
     fprintf (stdout,"buf.st_uid=%d\n", buf.st_uid );
     fprintf (stdout,"buf.st_gid=%d\n", buf.st_gid );
     fprintf (stdout,"buf.st_size=%d\n", buf.st_size );
  }
  else {
     fprintf (stderr,"ERROR: fstat() call failed\n");
     fprintf (stderr,"ERROR: %s\n", strerror(errno));
  }

  fprintf (stdout,"remove testfile\n");
  remove (filename);
}
```

NAME

fstatvfs, statvfs — get file system information

SYNOPSIS

UX   `#include <sys/statvfs.h>`

`int fstatvfs(int fildes, struct statvfs *buf);`

`int statvfs(const char *path, struct statvfs *buf);`

DESCRIPTION

The *fstatvfs( )* function obtains information about the file system containing the file referenced by *fildes*.

The following flags can be returned in the **f_flag** member:

ST_RDONLY   read-only file system
ST_NOSUID   setuid/setgid bits ignored by exec

The *statvfs( )* function obtains descriptive information about the file system containing the file named by *path*.

For both functions, the *buf* argument is a pointer to a **statvfs** structure that will be filled. Read, write, or execute permission of the named file is not required, but all directories listed in the pathname leading to the file must be searchable.

RETURN VALUE

Upon successful completion, *statvfs( )* returns 0. Otherwise, it returns −1 and sets *errno* to indicate the error.

ERRORS

The *fstatvfs( )* and *statvfs( )* functions will fail if:

[EIO]   An I/O error occurred while reading the file system.

[EINTR]   A signal was caught during execution of the function.

The *fstatvfs( )* function will fail if:

[EBADF]   The *fildes* argument is not an open file descriptor.

The *statvfs( )* function will fail if:

[EACCES]   Search permission is denied on a component of the *path* prefix.

[ELOOP]   Too many symbolic links were encountered in resolving *path*.

[ENAMETOOLONG]
                 The length of a pathname exceeds {PATH_MAX}, or a pathname component is longer than {NAME_MAX}.

[ENOENT]   A component of *path* does not name an existing file or *path* is an empty string.

[ENOTDIR]   A component of the path prefix of *path* is not a directory.

The *statvfs( )* function may fail if:

[ENAMETOOLONG]
                 Pathname resolution of a symbolic link produced an intermediate result whose length exceeds {PATH_MAX}.

APPLICATION USAGE

It is unspecified whether all members of the **statvfs** structure have meaningful values on all file systems.

SEE ALSO

chmod( ), chown( ), creat( ), dup( ), exec, fcntl( ), link( ), mknod( ), open( ), pipe( ), read( ), time( ), unlink( ), ustat( ), utime( ), write( ), **<sys/statvfs.h>**.

EXAMPLE

```c
/*
 * Copyright (C) ANTRIX Inc.
 */

/* fstatvfs.c
 * This program gets the file system information
 * using function fstatvfs.
 */

#include <stdio.h>
#include <stdlib.h>
#include <fcntl.h>
#include <sys/types.h>
#include <sys/statvfs.h>
#include <errno.h>

main()
{
   int     fstatvfs_value;
   int     fildes;
   struct  statvfs  buf;

   fprintf (stdout,"open root file system\n");
   fildes = open("/", O_RDONLY);

   fprintf (stdout,"stat the root file system\n");
   fstatvfs_value = fstatvfs (fildes, &buf);
   if ( fstatvfs_value == 0 ) {
       fprintf (stdout,"fstatvfs() successful\n");
       fprintf (stdout,"buf.f_bsize=%d\n", buf.f_bsize);
       fprintf (stdout,"buf.f_blocks=%d\n", buf.f_blocks);
       fprintf (stdout,"buf.f_bfree=%d\n", buf.f_bfree);
       fprintf (stdout,"buf.f_bavail=%d\n", buf.f_bavail);
       fprintf (stdout,"buf.f_files=%d\n", buf.f_files);
   }
   else {
       fprintf (stderr,"ERROR: fstatvfs() call failed\n");
       fprintf (stderr,"ERROR: %s\n", strerror(errno));
   }

   fprintf (stdout,"close root file system\n");
   close (fildes);
}
```

NAME

fsync — synchronise changes to a file

SYNOPSIS

EX
```
#include <unistd.h>
```

```
int fsync(int fildes);
```

DESCRIPTION

The *fsync( )* function causes all modified data and attributes of the file referred to by *fildes* to be delivered to the underlying hardware.

RETURN VALUE

Upon successful completion, *fsync( )* returns 0. Otherwise, −1 is returned and *errno* is set to indicate the error.

ERRORS

The *fsync( )* function will fail if:

[EBADF]   The *fildes* argument is not a valid descriptor.

[EINTR]   The *fsync( )* function was interrupted by a signal.

[EINVAL]   The *fildes* argument does not refer to a file on which this operation is possible.

[EIO]   An I/O error occurred while reading from or writing to the file system.

APPLICATION USAGE

The *fsync( )* function should be used by programs which require modifications to a file to be completed before continuing; for example, a program which contains a simple transaction facility might use it to ensure that all modifications to a file or files caused by a transaction are recorded.

SEE ALSO

sync( ), **<unistd.h>**.

EXAMPLE

```
/*
 * Copyright (C) ANTRIX Inc.
 */

/* fsync.c
 * This program causes all modified data and attributes of the
 * file referred to by fildes to be delivered to the underlying
 * hardware using function fsync.
 */

#include <stdio.h>
#include <stdlib.h>
#include <unistd.h>
#include <sys/stat.h>
#include <fcntl.h>
#include <errno.h>

#define  PERM_ALL   (S_IRWXU | S_IRWXG | S_IRWXO)

main()
{
```

```
int    fsync_value;
int    fildes, bytes;
int    length;
char   *buf;
char   *string = "hello world";
char   *filename = "testfile";

length = strlen (string);
fprintf (stdout,"create testfile\n");
fildes = creat (filename, PERM_ALL);
fprintf (stdout,"write string\n");

write (fildes, string, length);
fprintf (stdout,"synchronize file's in-memory states\n");
fsync_value = fsync (fildes);
if ( fsync_value == 0 )
   fprintf (stdout,"fsync() call successful\n");
else {
   fprintf (stderr,"ERROR: fsync() call failed\n");
   fprintf (stderr,"ERROR: %s\n", strerror(errno));
}
fprintf (stdout,"close testfile\n");
close (fildes);

fprintf (stdout,"open testfile for read only\n");
fildes = open (filename, O_RDONLY);

buf = (char *)malloc (length);
fprintf (stdout,"read string\n");
bytes = read (fildes, buf, length );
fprintf (stdout,"string in buf=%s\n", buf);

fprintf (stdout,"close and remove testfile\n");
close (fildes);
remove (filename);
}
```

NAME

ftell — return a file offset in a stream

SYNOPSIS

```
#include <stdio.h>

long int ftell(FILE *stream);
```

DESCRIPTION

The *ftell*( ) function obtains the current value of the file-position indicator for the stream pointed to by *stream*.

RETURN VALUE

Upon successful completion, *ftell*( ) returns the current value of the file-position indicator for the stream measured in bytes from the beginning of the file.

Otherwise, *ftell*( ) returns –1L and sets *errno* to indicate the error.

ERRORS

The *ftell*( ) function will fail if:

[EBADF]　　　　　The file descriptor underlying *stream* is not an open file descriptor.

[ESPIPE]　　　　The file descriptor underlying *stream* is associated with a pipe or FIFO.

SEE ALSO

fopen( ), *fseek*( ), *lseek*( ), **<stdio.h>**.

EXAMPLE

```
/*
 * Copyright (C) ANTRIX Inc.
 */

/* ftell.c
 * This program obtains the current value of the file-position
 * indicator for the stream using function ftell.
 */

#include <stdio.h>
#include <stdlib.h>
#include <unistd.h>
#include <errno.h>

main()
{
  long  ftell_value;
  char  string[] = "hello world";
  char  *filename = "testfile";
  FILE  *stream;

  fprintf (stdout,"create and open testfile\n");
  stream = fopen (filename, "w");

  fprintf (stdout,"write string to testfile\n");
  fwrite (string, sizeof(char), strlen(string), stream);
  fflush (stream);
  fprintf (stdout,"change the position of file pointer\n");
```

```
    fseek(stream, 6, SEEK_SET);

    fprintf (stdout,"get current position of file pointer\n");
    ftell_value = ftell(stream);
    if ( ftell_value == 6 ) {
        fprintf (stdout,"ftell() call successful\n");
        fprintf (stdout,"ftell_value=%d\n", ftell_value );
    }
    else {
        fprintf (stderr,"ERROR: ftell() call failed\n");
        fprintf (stderr,"ERROR: %s\n", strerror(errno));
    }

    fprintf (stdout,"remove testfile\n");
    remove (filename);
}
```

NAME

ftime — get date and time

SYNOPSIS

UX

```
#include <sys/timeb.h>
```

```
int ftime(struct timeb *tp);
```

DESCRIPTION

The *ftime*( ) function sets the **time** and **millitm** members of the **timeb** structure pointed to by *tp* to contain the seconds and milliseconds portions, respectively, of the current time in seconds since 00:00:00 UTC (Coordinated Universal Time), January 1, 1970. The contents of the **timezone** and **dstflag** members of *tp* after a call to *ftime*( ) are unspecified.

RETURN VALUE

Upon successful completion, the *ftime*( ) function returns 0. Otherwise −1 is returned.

ERRORS

No errors are defined.

APPLICATION USAGE

For portability to implementations conforming to earlier versions of this document, *time*( ) is preferred over this function.

The millisecond value usually has a granularity greater than one due to the resolution of the system clock. Depending on any granularity (particularly a granularity of one) renders code non-portable.

SEE ALSO

ctime( ), *gettimeofday*( ), *time*( ), **<sys/timeb.h>**.

EXAMPLE

```
/*
 * Copyright (C) ANTRIX Inc.
 */

/* ftime.c
 * This program gets the date and time into a timeb structure
 * using function ftime
 */

#include <stdio.h>
#include <stdlib.h>
#include <sys/types.h>
#include <sys/timeb.h>
#include <errno.h>

main()
{
   int       ftime_value;
   struct    timeb  buf;

   fprintf (stdout,"get date and time\n");
   ftime_value = ftime (&buf);

   if ( ftime_value == 0 ) {
      fprintf (stdout,"ftime() call successful\n");
```

```
        fprintf (stdout,"buf.time=%d\n", buf.time);
        fprintf (stdout,"buf.millitm=%d\n", buf.millitm);
        fprintf (stdout,"buf.timezone=%d\n", buf.timezone);
        fprintf (stdout,"buf.dstflag=%d\n", buf.dstflag);
    }
  else
        fprintf (stderr,"ERROR: ftime() call failed\n");
}
```

NAME

ftok — generate an IPC key

SYNOPSIS

UX   `#include <sys/ipc.h>`

`key_t ftok(const char *path, int id);`

DESCRIPTION

The *ftok( )* function returns a key based on *path* and *id* that is usable in subsequent calls to *msgget( )*, *semget( )* and *shmget( )*. The *path* argument must be the pathname of an existing file that the process is able to *stat( )*.

The *ftok( )* function will return the same key value for all paths that name the same file, when called with the same *id* value, and will return different key values when called with different *id* values or with paths that name different files existing on the same file system at the same time. It is unspecified whether *ftok( )* returns the same key value when called again after the file named by *path* is removed and recreated with the same name.

Only the low order 8-bits of *id* are significant. The behaviour of *ftok( )* is unspecified if these bits are 0.

RETURN VALUE

Upon successful completion, *ftok( )* returns a key. Otherwise, *ftok( )* returns (**key_t**)–1 and sets *errno* to indicate the error.

ERRORS

The *ftok( )* function will fail if:

[EACCES]   Search permission is denied for a component of the path prefix.

[ELOOP]   Too many symbolic links were encountered in resolving *path*.

[ENAMETOOLONG]
                  The length of the *path* argument exceeds {PATH_MAX} or a pathname component is longer than {NAME_MAX}.

[ENOENT]   A component of *path* does not name an existing file or *path* is an empty string.

[ENOTDIR]   A component of the path prefix is not a directory.

The *ftok( )* function may fail if:

[ENAMETOOLONG]
                  Pathname resolution of a symbolic link produced an intermediate result whose length exceeds {PATH_MAX}.

APPLICATION USAGE

For maximum portability, *id* should be a single-byte character.

SEE ALSO

msgget( ), *semget( )*, *shmget( )*, **<sys/ipc.h>**.

EXAMPLE

```c
/*
 * Copyright (C) ANTRIX Inc.
 */

/* ftok.c
 * This program creates a standard interprocess key
 * using function ftok.
 */

#include <stdio.h>
#include <stdlib.h>
#include <sys/types.h>
#include <sys/ipc.h>
#include <sys/stat.h>
#include <errno.h>

#define  PERM_ALL   (S_IRWXU | S_IRWXG | S_IRWXO)

main()
{
  key_t  ftok_value;
  char   file = "testfile";

  fprintf (stdout,"create testfile\n");
  creat (file, PERM_ALL);

  fprintf (stdout,"get key for testfile\n");
  ftok_value = ftok (file, 'a');
  if ( ftok_value >= 0 ) {
     fprintf (stdout,"ftok() call successful\n");
     fprintf (stdout,"ftok_value=%d\n", ftok_value );
  }
  else {
     fprintf (stderr,"ERROR: ftok() call failed\n");
     fprintf (stderr,"ERROR: %s\n", strerror(errno));
  }

  fprintf (stdout,"remove testfile\n");
  remove (file);
}
```

NAME

ftruncate, truncate — truncate a file to a specified length

SYNOPSIS

UX
```
#include <unistd.h>

int ftruncate(int fildes, off_t length);

int truncate(const char *path, off_t length);
```

DESCRIPTION

The *ftruncate( )* function causes the regular file referenced by *fildes* to have a size of *length* bytes.

The *truncate( )* function causes the regular file named by *path* to have a size of *length* bytes.

The effect of *ftruncate( )* and *truncate( )* on other types of files is unspecified. If the file previously was larger than *length*, the extra data is lost. If it was previously shorter than *length*, bytes between the old and new lengths are read as zeroes. With *ftruncate( )*, the file must be open for writing; for *truncate( )*, the process must have write permission for the file.

If the request would cause the file size to exceed the soft file size limit for the process, the request will fail and the implementation will generate the SIGXFSZ signal for the process.

These functions do not modify the file offset for any open file descriptions associated with the file. On successful completion, if the file size is changed, these functions will mark for update the *st_ctime* and *st_mtime* fields of the file, and if the file is a regular file, the S_ISUID and S_ISGID bits of the file mode may be cleared.

RETURN VALUE

Upon successful completion, *ftruncate( )* and *truncate( )* returns 0. Otherwise a −1 is returned, and *errno* is set to indicate the error.

ERRORS

The *ftruncate( )* and *truncate( )* functions will fail if:

[EINTR]   A signal was caught during execution.

[EINVAL]   The *length* argument was less than 0.

[EFBIG] or [EINVAL]
               The *length* argument was greater than the maximum file size.

[EIO]   An I/O error occurred while reading from or writing to a file system.

The *ftruncate( )* function will fail if:

[EBADF] or [EINVAL]
               The *fildes* argument is not a file descriptor open for writing.

[EINVAL]   The *fildes* argument references a file that was opened without write permission.

The *truncate( )* function will fail if:

[EACCES]   A component of the path prefix denies search permission, or write permission is denied on the file.

[EISDIR]   The named file is a directory.

[ELOOP]   Too many symbolic links were encountered in resolving *path*.

[ENAMETOOLONG]
> The length of the specified pathname exceeds PATH_MAX bytes, or the length of a component of the pathname exceeds NAME_MAX bytes.

[ENOENT]   A component of *path* does not name an existing file or *path* is an empty string.

[ENOTDIR]   A component of the path prefix of *path* is not a directory.

[EROFS]   The named file resides on a read-only file system.

The *truncate*( ) function may fail if:

[ENAMETOOLONG]
> Pathname resolution of a symbolic link produced an intermediate result whose length exceeds {PATH_MAX}.

SEE ALSO
> *open*( ), **<unistd.h>**.

NAME

ftw — traverse (walk) a file tree

SYNOPSIS

EX   `#include <ftw.h>`

```
int ftw(const char *path,
        int (*fn)(const char *, const struct stat *ptr, int flag),
        int ndirs);
```

DESCRIPTION

The *ftw( )* function recursively descends the directory hierarchy rooted in *path*. For each object in the hierarchy, *ftw( )* calls the function pointed to by *fn*, passing it a pointer to a null-terminated character string containing the name of the object, a pointer to a **stat** structure containing information about the object, and an integer. Possible values of the integer, defined in the **<ftw.h>** header, are:

FTW_D   for a directory

FTW_DNR   for a directory that cannot be read

FTW_F   for a file

UX   FTW_SL   for a symbolic link (but see also FTW_NS below)

UX   FTW_NS   for an object other than a symbolic link on which *stat( )* could not successfully be
UX   executed. If the object is a symbolic link and *stat( )* failed, it is unspecified whether
                            ftw( ) passes FTW_SL or FTW_NS to the user-supplied function.

If the integer is FTW_DNR, descendants of that directory will not be processed. If the integer is FTW_NS, the **stat** structure will contain undefined values. An example of an object that would cause FTW_NS to be passed to the function pointed to by *fn* would be a file in a directory with read but without execute (search) permission.

The *ftw( )* function visits a directory before visiting any of its descendants.

UX   The *ftw( )* function uses at most one file descriptor for each level in the tree.

The argument *ndirs* should be in the range of 1 to {OPEN_MAX}.

The tree traversal continues until the tree is exhausted, an invocation of *fn* returns a non-zero value, or some error, other than [EACCES], is detected within *ftw( )*.

The *ndirs* argument specifies the maximum number of directory streams or file descriptors or both available for use by *ftw( )* while traversing the tree. When *ftw( )* returns it closes any directory streams and file descriptors it uses not counting any opened by the application-supplied *fn( )* function.

RETURN VALUE

If the tree is exhausted, *ftw( )* returns 0. If the function pointed to by *fn* returns a non-zero value, *ftw( )* stops its tree traversal and returns whatever value was returned by the function pointed to by *fn( )*. If *ftw( )* detects an error, it returns −1 and sets *errno* to indicate the error.

UX   If *ftw( )* encounters an error other than [EACCES] (see FTW_DNR and FTW_NS above), it returns −1 and *errno* is set to indicate the error. The external variable *errno* may contain any error value that is possible when a directory is opened or when one of the *stat* functions is executed on a directory or file.

ERRORS

The *ftw*( ) function will fail if:

[EACCES]   Search permission is denied for any component of *path* or read permission is denied for *path*.

[ELOOP]   Too many symbolic links were encountered.

[ENAMETOOLONG]
    The length of the *path* exceeds {PATH_MAX}, or a pathname component is longer than {NAME_MAX}.

[ENOENT]   A component of *path* does not name an existing file or *path* is an empty string.

[ENOTDIR]   A component of *path* is not a directory.

The *ftw*( ) function may fail if:

[EINVAL]   The value of the *ndirs* argument is invalid.

UX   [ENAMETOOLONG]
    Pathname resolution of a symbolic link produced an intermediate result whose length exceeds {PATH_MAX}.

In addition, if the function pointed to by *fn* encounters system errors, *errno* may be set accordingly.

APPLICATION USAGE

Because *ftw*( ) is recursive, it is possible for it to terminate with a memory fault when applied to very deep file structures.

The *ftw*( ) function uses *malloc*( ) to allocate dynamic storage during its operation. If *ftw*( ) is forcibly terminated, such as by *longjmp*( ) or *siglongjmp*( ) being executed by the function pointed to by *fn* or an interrupt routine, *ftw*( ) will not have a chance to free that storage, so it will remain permanently allocated. A safe way to handle interrupts is to store the fact that an interrupt has occurred, and arrange to have the function pointed to by *fn* return a non-zero value at its next invocation.

SEE ALSO

longjmp( ), *lstat*( ), *malloc*( ), *opendir*( ), *siglongjmp*( ), *stat*( ), **<ftw.h>**, **<sys/stat.h>**.

EXAMPLE

```
/*
 * Copyright (C) ANTRIX Inc.
 */

/* ftw.c
 * This program recursively descends the directory hierarchy
 * starting from root using function ftw.
 */

#include <stdio.h>
#include <sys/types.h>
#include <dirent.h>
#include <sys/stat.h>
#include <ftw.h>
#include <errno.h>

#define  PERM_ALL    (S_IRWXU | S_IRWXG | S_IRWXO)
```

```
int func (path, buf, integer, ftwbuf)
char *path;
struct stat *buf;
int integer;
struct FTW ftwbuf;
{
    /* print some information about the path */
    fprintf (stdout,"directory traversed=%s\n", path);
    fprintf (stdout,"buf->st_mode=%o\n", (S_IFDIR ^ buf->st_mode) );
    fprintf (stdout,"buf->st_uid=%d\n", buf->st_uid);
    fprintf (stdout,"buf->st_gid=%d\n", buf->st_gid);
    fprintf (stdout,"integer=%d\n", integer);

    return (0);
}

main()
{
    int     ftw_value;
    int     i, readdir_value;
    char    *root = "testdir";
    char    *leaf = "testdir/subdir";
    DIR     *dirp;
    struct  dirent *dirent_save;

    fprintf (stdout,"create test directory tree structure\n");
    mkdir (root, PERM_ALL);
    mkdir (leaf, PERM_ALL);

    ftw_value = ftw (root, func, 1);
    if ( ftw_value == 0 )
        fprintf (stdout,"ftw() call successful\n");
    else {
        fprintf (stderr,"ERROR: ftw() call failed\n");
        fprintf (stderr,"ERROR: %s\n", strerror(errno));
    }

    fprintf (stdout,"remove test directories\n");
    rmdir (leaf);
    rmdir (root);
}
```

NAME

fwrite — binary output

SYNOPSIS

```
#include <stdio.h>

size_t fwrite(const void *ptr, size_t size, size_t nitems,
          FILE *stream);
```

DESCRIPTION

The *fwrite( )* function writes, from the array pointed to by *ptr*, up to *nitems* members whose size is specified by *size*, to the stream pointed to by *stream*. The file-position indicator for the stream (if defined) is advanced by the number of bytes successfully written. If an error occurs, the resulting value of the file-position indicator for the stream is indeterminate.

The *st_ctime* and *st_mtime* fields of the file will be marked for update between the successful execution of *fwrite( )* and the next successful completion of a call to *fflush( )* or *fclose( )* on the same stream or a call to *exit( )* or *abort( )*.

RETURN VALUE

The *fwrite( )* function returns the number of members successfully written, which may be less than *nitems* if a write error is encountered. If *size* or *nitems* is 0, *fwrite( )* returns 0 and the state of the stream remains unchanged. Otherwise, if a write error occurs, the error indicator for the stream is set and *errno* is set to indicate the error.

ERRORS

Refer to *fputc( )*.

SEE ALSO

ferror( ), *fopen( )*, *printf( )*, *putc( )*, *puts( )*, *write( )*, **<stdio.h>**.

EXAMPLE

```
/*
 * Copyright (C) ANTRIX Inc.
 */

/* fwrite.c
 * This program writes form the array pointed to by ptr, up to
 * nitems members whose size is specified by size using
 * function fwrite.
 */

#include <stdio.h>
#include <stdlib.h>
#include <sys/types.h>
#include <errno.h>

main()
{
   int    length, nitems;
   char   buf[12];
   char   ptr[] = "hello world";
   char   *filename = "testfile";
   FILE   *stream;

   memset (buf, ' ', 12);
```

```
    length = strlen(ptr);

    fprintf (stdout,"create and open testfile\n");
    stream = fopen (filename, "w+r");

    fprintf (stdout,"write string to testfile\n");
    nitems = fwrite (ptr, sizeof(char), length, stream);
    if ( nitems == length ) {
        fprintf (stdout,"fwrite() call successful\n");
        fprintf (stdout,"number of nitems written is %d\n", nitems );
    }
    else {
        fprintf (stderr,"ERROR: fwrite() call failed\n");
        fprintf (stderr,"ERROR: %s\n", strerror(errno));
    }
    fflush (stream);

    fprintf (stdout,"seek to the beginning of testfile\n");
    fseek (stream, 0, SEEK_SET);

    fprintf (stdout,"read string from file\n");
    fread (buf, sizeof(char), length, stream);

    fclose (stream);
    fprintf (stdout,"remove testfile\n");
    remove (filename);
}
```

NAME

gamma, signgam — log gamma function (**TO BE WITHDRAWN**)

SYNOPSIS

EX
```
#include <math.h>

double gamma(double x);

extern int signgam;
```

DESCRIPTION

The *gamma*( ) function performs identically to *lgamma*( ), including the use of *signgam*.

APPLICATION USAGE

This interface is functionally equivalent to *lgamma*(.) and so it is marked to be withdrawn.

EXAMPLE

```c
/*
 * Copyright (C) ANTRIX Inc.
 */

/* gamma.c
 * This program computes logarithmic gamma of 1.23 using
 * function gamma.
 */

#include <stdio.h>
#include <math.h>

main()
{
    double  gamma_value;
    double  x = 1.23;

    gamma_value = gamma (x);
    fprintf (stdout,"gamma of %f is %f\n", x, gamma_value);
}
```

NAME

gcvt — convert floating-point number to string

SYNOPSIS

ux   `#include <stdlib.h>`

`char *gcvt(double value, int ndigit, char *buf);`

DESCRIPTION

Refer to *ecvt*( ).

NAME

getc — get byte from a stream

SYNOPSIS

```
#include <stdio.h>

int getc(FILE *stream);
```

DESCRIPTION

The *getc*( ) function is equivalent to *fgetc*( ), except that if it is implemented as a macro it may evaluate *stream* more than once, so the argument should never be an expression with side effects.

RETURN VALUE

Refer to *fgetc*( ).

ERRORS

Refer to *fgetc*( ).

APPLICATION USAGE

If the integer value returned by *getc*( ) is stored into a variable of type **char** and then compared against the integer constant EOF, the comparison may never succeed, because sign-extension of a variable of type **char** on widening to integer is implementation-dependent.

Because it may be implemented as a macro, *getc*( ) may treat incorrectly a *stream* argument with side effects. In particular, *getc*(*f++) may not work as expected. Therefore, use of this function is not recommended in such situations; *fgetc*( ) should be used instead.

SEE ALSO

fgetc( ), **<stdio.h>**.

EXAMPLE

```
/*
 * Copyright (C) ANTRIX Inc.
 */

/* getc.c
 * This program obtains the next byte as an unsigned char
 * converted to an int from the input stream using function
 * getc.
 */

#include <stdio.h>
#include <stdlib.h>
#include <sys/types.h>
#include <errno.h>

main()
{
    int    i, bytes;
    char   getc_value;
    char   buf[12];
    char   string[] = "hello world";
    char   *filename = "testfile";
    FILE   *stream;

    memset (buf, ' ', 12);
```

```
bytes = strlen(string);

fprintf (stdout,"create and open testfile\n");
stream = fopen (filename, "w+r");

fprintf (stdout,"write string to testfile\n");
fwrite (string, sizeof(char), bytes, stream);
fflush (stream);

fprintf (stdout,"seek to beginning of testfile\n");
fseek (stream, 0, SEEK_SET);

fprintf (stdout,"get string one character at a time\n");
for ( i = 0; i < 11; i++ ) {
    getc_value = getc (stream);
    fprintf (stdout,"%c", getc_value);
}

fprintf (stdout,"\n");
fprintf (stdout,"remove testfile\n");
remove (filename);
}
```

NAME

getchar — get byte from *stdin* stream

SYNOPSIS

```
#include <stdio.h>

int getchar(void);
```

DESCRIPTION

The *getchar*( ) function is equivalent to *getc(stdin)*.

RETURN VALUE

Refer to *fgetc*( ).

ERRORS

Refer to *fgetc*( ).

APPLICATION USAGE

If the integer value returned by *getchar*( ) is stored into a variable of type **char** and then compared against the integer constant EOF, the comparison may never succeed, because sign-extension of a variable of type **char** on widening to integer is implementation-dependent.

SEE ALSO

getc( ), **<stdio.h>**.

EXAMPLE

```
/*
 * Copyright (C) ANTRIX Inc.
 */

/* getchar.c
 * This program obtains the next byte as an unsigned char
 * converted to an int from the stdin input using function
 * getchar.
 */

#include <stdio.h>
#include <stdlib.h>
#include <errno.h>

main()
{
    int  getchar_value;

    fprintf (stdout,"Type a character and hit return key\n");
    getchar_value = getchar ();

    fprintf (stdout,"character typed is '%c'\n", getchar_value);
}
```

NAME

getcontext, setcontext — get and set current user context

SYNOPSIS

UX `#include <ucontext.h>`

`int getcontext(ucontext_t *ucp);`

`int setcontext(const ucontext_t *ucp);`

DESCRIPTION

The *getcontext*( ) function initialises the structure pointed to by *ucp* to the current user context of the calling process. The **ucontext_t** type that *ucp* points to defines the user context and includes the contents of the calling process' machine registers, the signal mask, and the current execution stack.

The *setcontext*( ) function restores the user context pointed to by *ucp*. A successful call to *setcontext*( ) does not return; program execution resumes at the point specified by the *ucp* argument passed to *setcontext*( ). The *ucp* argument should be created either by a prior call to *getcontext*( ), or by being passed as an argument to a signal handler. If the *ucp* argument was created with *getcontext*( ), program execution continues as if the corresponding call of *getcontext*( ) had just returned. If the *ucp* argument was created with *makecontext*( ), program execution continues with the function passed to *makecontext*( ). When that function returns, the process continues as if after a call to *setcontext*( ) with the *ucp* argument that was input to *makecontext*( ). If the *ucp* argument was passed to a signal handler, program execution continues with the program instruction following the instruction interrupted by the signal. If the **uc_link** member of the **ucontext_t** structure pointed to by the *ucp* argument is equal to 0, then this context is the main context, and the process will exit when this context returns. The effects of passing a *ucp* argument obtained from any other source are unspecified.

RETURN VALUE

On successful completion, *setcontext*( ) does not return and *getcontext*( ) returns 0. Otherwise, a value of −1 is returned.

ERRORS

No errors are defined.

APPLICATION USAGE

When a signal handler is executed, the current user context is saved and a new context is created. If the process leaves the signal handler via *longjmp*( ), then it is unspecified whether the context at the time of the corresponding *setjmp*( ) call is restored and thus whether future calls to *getcontext*( ) will provide an accurate representation of the current context, since the context restored by *longjmp*( ) may not contain all the information that *setcontext*( ) requires. Signal handlers should use *siglongjmp*( ) or *setcontext*( ) instead.

Portable applications should not modify or access the **uc_mcontext** member of **ucontext_t**. A portable application cannot assume that context includes any process-wide static data, possibly including *errno*. Users manipulating contexts should take care to handle these explicitly when required.

SEE ALSO

bsd_signal( ), *makecontext*( ), *setjmp*( ), *sigaction*( ), *sigaltstack*( ), *sigprocmask*( ), *sigsetjmp*( ), **<ucontext.h>**.

EXAMPLE

```
/*
 * Copyright (C) ANTRIX Inc.
 */
```

```
/* getcontext.c
 * This program gets the current user context
 * using function getcontext
 */

#include <stdio.h>
#include <stdlib.h>
#include <ucontext.h>
#include <signal.h>
#include <errno.h>

main()
{
  int        getcontext_value;
  ucontext_t ucp;
  sigset_t   mask;

  fprintf (stdout,"clear signal mask\n");
  sigemptyset (&mask);

  fprintf (stdout,"add signal SIGALRM to the mask\n");
  sigaddset (&mask, SIGALRM);

  fprintf (stdout,"set signal mask\n");
  sigprocmask (SIG_SETMASK, &mask, (sigset_t *)0);

  fprintf (stdout,"get user context\n");
  getcontext_value = getcontext (&ucp);
  if ( getcontext_value == 0 ) {
      fprintf (stdout,"getcontext() call successful\n");
      fprintf (stdout,"compare the signal masks\n");
      if ( memcmp(&mask, &ucp.uc_sigmask, sizeof(mask)) != 0)
          fprintf (stderr,"ERROR: saved signal mask are different\n");
  }
  else {
      fprintf (stderr,"ERROR: getcontext() call failed\n");
      fprintf (stderr,"ERROR: %s\n", strerror(errno));
  }
}
```

NAME

getcwd — get pathname of current working directory

SYNOPSIS

```
#include <unistd.h>

char *getcwd(char *buf, size_t size);
```

DESCRIPTION

The *getcwd*( ) function places an absolute pathname of the current working directory in the array pointed to by *buf*, and returns *buf*. The *size* argument is the size in bytes of the character array pointed to by the *buf* argument. If *buf* is a null pointer, the behaviour of *getcwd*( ) is undefined.

RETURN VALUE

Upon successful completion, *getcwd*( ) returns the *buf* argument. Otherwise, *getcwd*( ) returns a null pointer and sets *errno* to indicate the error. The contents of the array pointed to by *buf* is then undefined.

ERRORS

The *getcwd*( ) function will fail if:

[EINVAL]   The *size* argument is 0.

[ERANGE]   The size argument is greater than 0, but is smaller than the length of the pathname +1.

The *getcwd*( ) function may fail if:

[EACCES]   Read or search permission was denied for a component of the pathname.

EX   [ENOMEM]   Insufficient storage space is available.

APPLICATION USAGE

If *buf* is a null pointer, on some implementations, *getcwd*( ) will obtain *size* bytes of space using *malloc*( ). In this case, the pointer returned by *getcwd*( ) may be used as the argument in a subsequent call to *free*( ). Invoking *getcwd*( ) with *buf* as a null pointer is not recommended.

SEE ALSO

malloc( ), **<unistd.h>**.

EXAMPLE

```
/*
 * Copyright (C) ANTRIX Inc.
 */

/* getcwd.c
 * This program places an absolute pathname of the current working
 * directory in the array pointed to by buf, and returns buf using
 * function getcwd.
 */

#include <stdio.h>
#include <stdlib.h>
#include <unistd.h>
#include <limits.h>
#include <errno.h>

#define  PATH_LEN  255
```

```
main()
{
  char  *getcwd_value;
  char  buf[PATH_LEN];

  memset(buf, ' ', PATH_LEN);
  fprintf (stdout,"get current working directory\n");

  getcwd_value = getcwd (buf, PATH_LEN);
  if ( getcwd_value != (char *)0 ) {
      fprintf (stdout,"getcwd() call successful\n");
      fprintf (stdout,"current directory/buf=%s\n", buf);
      fprintf (stdout,"current directory/getcwd_value=%s\n", getcwd_value);
  }
  else {
      fprintf (stderr,"ERROR: getcwd() call failed\n");
      fprintf (stderr,"ERROR: %s\n", strerror(errno));
  }
}
```

NAME

getdate — convert user format date and time

SYNOPSIS

UX
```
#include <time.h>

struct tm *getdate(const char *string);

extern int getdate_err;
```

DESCRIPTION

The *getdate*( ) function converts a string representation of a date or time into a broken-down time.

Templates are used to parse and interpret the input string. The templates are contained in a text file identified by the environment variable *DATEMSK*. The *DATEMSK* variable should be set to indicate the full pathname of the file that contains the templates. The first line in the template that matches the input specification is used for interpretation and conversion into the internal time format.

The following field descriptors are supported:

%%   same as %

%a   abbreviated weekday name

%A   full weekday name

%b   abbreviated month name

%B   full month name

%c   locale's appropriate date and time representation

%d   day of month (01-31; the leading 0 is optional)

%D   date as %m/%d/%y

%e   same as %d

%h   abbreviated month name

%H   hour (00-23)

%I   hour (01-12)

%m   month number (01-12)

%M   minute (00-59)

%n   same as new line

%p   locale's equivalent of either AM or PM

%r   The locale's appropriate representation of time in AM and PM notation. In the POSIX locale, this is equivalent to %I:%M:%S %p

%R   The locale's appropriate representation of time. In the POSIX locale, this is equivalent to %H:%M

%S   seconds (00-61). Leap seconds are allowed but are not predictable through use of algorithms.

%t   same as tab

%T   time as %H:%M:%S

%w   weekday number (Sunday = 0 - 6)

%x   locale's appropriate date representation

%X   locale's appropriate time representation

%y   year within century (00-99)

%Y   year as ccyy (for example, 1994)

%Z   time zone name or no characters if no time zone exists. If the time zone supplied by %Z is not the time zone that *getdate*( ) expects, an invalid input specification error will result. The *getdate*( ) function calculates an expected time zone based on information supplied to the function (such as the hour, day, and month).

The match between the template and input specification performed by *getdate*( ) is case insensitive.

The month and weekday names can consist of any combination of upper and lower case letters. The process can request that the input date or time specification be in a specific language by setting the LC_TIME category (see *setlocale*( )).

Leading 0's are not necessary for the descriptors that allow leading 0's. However, at most two digits are allowed for those descriptors, including leading 0's. Extra whitespace in either the template file or in *string* is ignored.

The field descriptors %c, %x, and %X will not be supported if they include unsupported field descriptors.

The following rules apply for converting the input specification into the internal format:

- If %Z is being scanned, then *getdate*( ) initialises the broken-down time to be the current time in the scanned time zone. Otherwise it initialises the broken-down time based on the current local time as if *localtime*( ) had been called.

- If only the weekday is given, today is assumed if the given day is equal to the current day and next week if it is less,

- If only the month is given, the current month is assumed if the given month is equal to the current month and next year if it is less and no year is given (the first day of month is assumed if no day is given),

- If no hour, minute and second are given the current hour, minute and second are assumed,

- If no date is given, today is assumed if the given hour is greater than the current hour and tomorrow is assumed if it is less.

The external variable or macro *getdate_err* is used by *getdate*( ) to return error values.

RETURN VALUE

Upon successful completion, *getdate*( ) returns a pointer to a **struct tm**. Otherwise, it returns a null pointer and *getdate_err* is set to indicate the error.

ERRORS

The *getdate*( ) function will fail in the following cases, setting *getdate_err* to the value shown in the list below. Any changes to *errno* are unspecified.

1   The *DATEMSK* environment variable is null or undefined.

2   The template file cannot be opened for reading.

3   Failed to get file status information.

4   The template file is not a regular file.

5   An error is encountered while reading the template file.

6   Memory allocation failed (not enough memory available).

7   There is no line in the template that matches the input.

8   Invalid input specification. For example, February 31; or a time is specified that can not be represented in a **time_t** (representing the time in seconds since 00:00:00 UTC, January 1, 1970).

EXAMPLE

Example 1:

The following example shows the possible contents of a template:

```
%m
%A %B %d, %Y, %H:%M:%S
%A
%B
%m/%d/%y %I %p
%d,%m,%Y %H:%M
at %A the %dst of %B in %Y
run job at %I %p,%B %dnd
%A den %d. %B %Y %H.%M Uhr
```

Example 2:

The following are examples of valid input specifications for the template in Example 1:

```
getdate("10/1/87 4 PM");
getdate("Friday");
getdate("Friday September 18, 1987, 10:30:30");
getdate("24,9,1986 10:30");
getdate("at monday the 1st of december in 1986");
getdate("run job at 3 PM, december 2nd");
```

If the LC_TIME category is set to a German locale that includes `freitag` as a weekday name and `oktober` as a month name, the following would be valid:

```
getdate("freitag den 10. oktober 1986 10.30 Uhr");
```

Example 3:

The following examples shows how local date and time specification can be defined in the template.

Invocation	Line in Template
getdate("11/27/86")	%m/%d/%y
getdate("27.11.86")	%d.%m.%y
getdate("86-11-27")	%y-%m-%d
getdate("Friday 12:00:00")	%A %H:%M:%S

Example 4:

The following examples help to illustrate the above rules assuming that the current date is `Mon Sep 22 12:19:47 EDT 1986` and the LC_TIME category is set to the default `"C"` locale.

Input	Line in Template	Date
Mon	%a	Mon Sep 22 12:19:47 EDT 1986
Sun	%a	Sun Sep 28 12:19:47 EDT 1986
Fri	%a	Fri Sep 26 12:19:47 EDT 1986
September	%B	Mon Sep 1 12:19:47 EDT 1986
January	%B	Thu Jan 1 12:19:47 EST 1987
December	%B	Mon Dec 1 12:19:47 EST 1986
Sep Mon	%b %a	Mon Sep 1 12:19:47 EDT 1986
Jan Fri	%b %a	Fri Jan 2 12:19:47 EST 1987
Dec Mon	%b %a	Mon Dec 1 12:19:47 EST 1986
Jan Wed 1989	%b %a %Y	Wed Jan 4 12:19:47 EST 1989
Fri 9	%a %H	Fri Sep 26 09:00:00 EDT 1986
Feb 10:30	%b %H:%S	Sun Feb 1 10:00:30 EST 1987
10:30	%H:%M	Tue Sep 23 10:30:00 EDT 1986
13:30	%H:%M	Mon Sep 22 13:30:00 EDT 1986

APPLICATION USAGE

Although historical versions of *getdate*( ) did not require that **<time.h>** declare the external variable *getdate_err*, this document does require it. X/Open encourages applications to remove declarations of *getdate_err* and instead incorporate the declaration by including **<time.h>**.

SEE ALSO

ctime( ), *ctype*( ), *localtime*( ), *setlocale*( ), *strftime*( ), *times*( ), **<time.h>**.

EXAMPLE

```
/*
 * Copyright (C) ANTRIX Inc.
 */

/* getdate.c
 * This program converts the user-definable date and/or time
 * into a tm structure using function getdate
 */

#include <stdio.h>
#include <stdlib.h>
#include <time.h>
#include <errno.h>

extern int getdate_err;

main()
{
   struct    tm  *buf;
   char      *cur_time;

   fprintf (stdout,"get date\n");
   buf = getdate ("26,10,1994 10:30");
```

```
    if ( buf != (struct tm *)0 ) {
       fprintf (stdout,"getdate() call successful\n");
       cur_time = asctime (buf);
       fprintf (stdout,"cur_time=%s\n", cur_time);
    }
    else {
       fprintf (stderr,"ERROR: getdate() call failed\n");
       fprintf (stderr,"ERROR: %d\n", getdate_err);
    }
}
```

NAME

getdtablesize — get the file descriptor table size

SYNOPSIS

UX

```
#include <unistd.h>

int getdtablesize(void);
```

DESCRIPTION

The *getdtablesize*( ) function is equivalent to *getrlimit*( ) with the RLIMIT_NOFILE option.

RETURN VALUE

The *getdtablesize*( ) function returns the current soft limit as if obtained from a call to *getrlimit*( ) with the RLIMIT_NOFILE option.

ERRORS

No errors are defined.

APPLICATION USAGE

There is no direct relationship between the value returned by *getdtablesize*( ) and {OPEN_MAX} defined in **<limits.h>**.

SEE ALSO

close( ), *getrlimit*( ), *open*( ), *select*( ), *setrlimit*( ), **<limits.h>**, **<unistd.h>**.

EXAMPLE

```
/*
 * Copyright (C) ANTRIX Inc.
 */

/* getdtablesize.c
 * getdtablesize() function returns the current maximum size of
 * this table by calling the getrlimit() function
 */

#include <stdio.h>
#include <stdlib.h>
#include <unistd.h>
#include <errno.h>

main()
{
  int   getdtablesize_value;

  fprintf(stdout, "find maximum size\n");
  getdtablesize_value = getdtablesize();
  fprintf(stdout, "getdtablesize_value=%d\n", getdtablesize_value);
}
```

NAME

getegid — get effective group ID

SYNOPSIS

OH
```
#include <sys/types.h>
#include <unistd.h>

gid_t getegid(void);
```

DESCRIPTION

The *getegid*( ) function returns the effective group ID of the calling process.

RETURN VALUE

The *getegid*( ) function is always successful and no return value is reserved to indicate an error.

ERRORS

No errors are defined.

SEE ALSO

getgid( ), *setgid*( ), **<sys/types.h>**, **<unistd.h>**.

EXAMPLE

```c
/*
 * Copyright (C) ANTRIX Inc.
 */

/* getegid.c: run as root
 * This program returns the effective group ID of the calling
 * process using function getegid.
 */

#include <stdio.h>
#include <stdlib.h>
#include <unistd.h>
#include <sys/types.h>

main()
{
  gid_t   getegid_value;

  fprintf (stdout,"get effective group id\n");
  getegid_value = getegid ();
  fprintf (stdout,"getegid_value=%d\n", getegid_value);

  fprintf (stdout,"set group-id of 2 which is bin\n");
  setgid (2);
  getegid_value = getegid ();
  fprintf (stdout,"getegid_value=%d\n", getegid_value);
}
```

NAME

getenv — get value of environment variable

SYNOPSIS

```
#include <stdlib.h>

char *getenv(const char *name);
```

DESCRIPTION

The *getenv*( ) function searches the environment list for a string of the form "*name=value*", and returns a pointer to a string containing the *value* for the specified name. If the specified name cannot be found, a null pointer is returned. The string pointed to must not be modified by the application, but may be overwritten by a subsequent call to *getenv*( ) or *putenv*( ) but will not be overwritten by a call to any other function in this document.

EX

RETURN VALUE

Upon successful completion, *getenv*( ) returns a pointer to a string containing the *value* for the specified *name*. If the specified name cannot be found a null pointer is returned.

ERRORS

No errors are defined.

APPLICATION USAGE

The return value from *getenv*( ) may point to static data which may be overwritten by subsequent calls to *getenv*( ) or *putenv*( ).

SEE ALSO

exec, *putenv*( ), **<stdlib.h>**, the **XBD** specification, **Chapter 6**, **Environment Variables**.

EXAMPLE

```
/*
 * Copyright (C) ANTRIX Inc.
 */

/* getenv.c
 * This program gets the environment variable value of PATH
 * using function getenv.
 */

#include <stdio.h>
#include <stdlib.h>
#include <unistd.h>
#include <stdlib.h>
#include <errno.h>

main()
{
  char   *getenv_value;

  fprintf (stdout,"get environment value of env variable PATH\n");
  getenv_value = getenv ("PATH");
  if ( getenv_value != (char *)0 ) {
      fprintf (stdout,"getenv() call successful\n");
      fprintf (stdout,"environment variable PATH=%s\n", getenv_value);
  }
  else
```

```
        fprintf (stderr,"ERROR: getenv() call failed\n");
}
```

NAME
geteuid — get effective user ID

SYNOPSIS
OH   `#include <sys/types.h>`
`#include <unistd.h>`

`uid_t geteuid(void);`

DESCRIPTION
The *geteuid*( ) function returns the effective user ID of the calling process.

RETURN VALUE
The *geteuid*( ) function is always successful and no return value is reserved to indicate an error.

ERRORS
No errors are defined.

SEE ALSO
getuid( ), *setuid*( ), **<sys/types.h>**, **<unistd.h>**.

EXAMPLE
```
/*
 * Copyright (C) ANTRIX Inc.
 */

/* filename geteuid.c: run as root
 * This program returns the effective user ID of the calling process
 * using function geteuid.
 */

#include <stdio.h>
#include <stdlib.h>
#include <unistd.h>
#include <sys/types.h>

main()
{
  uid_t   geteuid_value;

  fprintf (stdout,"get effective user id\n");
  geteuid_value = geteuid ();
  fprintf (stdout,"geteuid_value=%d\n", geteuid_value);

  fprintf (stdout,"set user-id of 2 which is bin\n");
  setuid (2);
  geteuid_value = geteuid ();
}
```

NAME

　　getgid — get real group ID

SYNOPSIS

OH　　`#include <sys/types.h>`
　　`#include <unistd.h>`

　　`gid_t getgid(void);`

DESCRIPTION

　　The *getgid*( ) function returns the real group ID of the calling process.

RETURN VALUE

　　The *getgid*( ) function is always successful and no return value is reserved to indicate an error.

ERRORS

　　No errors are defined.

SEE ALSO

　　getuid( ), *setgid*( ), **<sys/types.h>**, **<unistd.h>**.

EXAMPLE

```
/*
 * Copyright (C) ANTRIX Inc.
 */

/* getgid.c
 * This program gets the real group ID of the calling process
 * using function getgid.
 */

#include <stdio.h>
#include <stdlib.h>
#include <sys/types.h>
#include <unistd.h>

main()
{
  gid_t   getgid_value;

  fprintf (stdout,"get group id\n");
  getgid_value = getgid ();
  fprintf (stdout,"getgid_value=%d\n", getgid_value) ;
}
```

NAME

getgrent — get group database entry

SYNOPSIS

UX   `#include <grp.h>`

`struct group *getgrent(void);`

DESCRIPTION

Refer to *endgrent*( ).

EXAMPLE

```
/*
 * Copyright (C) ANTRIX Inc.
 */

/* getgrent.c
 * This program gets the group entry
 * using function getgrent
 */

#include <stdio.h>
#include <stdlib.h>
#include <grp.h>
#include <errno.h>

main()
{
  struct  group *buf;

  fprintf (stdout,"get group file entries\n");
  do {
     buf = (struct group  *)getgrent ();
     fprintf (stdout,"buf->gr_name=%s\n", buf->gr_name);
     fprintf (stdout,"buf->gr_gid=%d\n", buf->gr_gid);
     fprintf (stdout,"buf->gr_mem[0]=%s\n", buf->gr_mem[0]);
  } while (buf != (struct group *)0);

  fprintf (stdout,"close the group file\n");
  endgrent ();
}
```

NAME

getgrgid — get group database entry for particular group ID

SYNOPSIS

OH
```
#include <sys/types.h>
#include <grp.h>

struct group *getgrgid(gid_t gid);
```

DESCRIPTION

The *getgrgid*( ) function searches the group database for an entry with a matching *gid*.

RETURN VALUE

Upon successful completion, *getgrgid*( ) returns a pointer to a **struct group** with the structure defined in **<grp.h>** with a matching entry if one is found. The *getgrgid*( ) function returns a null

EX pointer if either the requested entry was not found, or an error occurred. On error, *errno* will be set to indicate the error.

ERRORS

The *getgrgid*( ) function may fail if:

EX
[EIO]   An I/O error has occurred.

[EINTR]   A signal was caught during *getgrgid*( ).

[EMFILE]   {OPEN_MAX} file descriptors are currently open in the calling process.

[ENFILE]   The maximum allowable number of files is currently open in the system.

APPLICATION USAGE

The return value may point to a static area which is overwritten by a subsequent call to *getgrent*( ), *getgrgid*( ) or *getgrnam*( ).

Applications wishing to check for error situations should set *errno* to 0 before calling *getgrgid*( ). If *errno* is set on return, an error occurred.

SEE ALSO

endgrent( ), *getgrnam*( ), **<grp.h>**, **<limits.h>**, **<sys/types.h>**.

EXAMPLE

```
/*
 * Copyright (C) ANTRIX Inc.
 */

/* getgrgid.c
 * This program searches the group database for an entry
 * with a matching gid using function getgrgid.
 */

#include <stdio.h>
#include <stdlib.h>
#include <grp.h>
#include <errno.h>

main()
{
    gid_t        gid;
    struct group    *buf;
```

```
        fprintf (stdout,"get group id\n");
        gid = getgid ();

        fprintf (stdout,"get group file entry\n");
        buf = getgrgid (gid);
        if ( buf != (struct group *)0 ) {
            fprintf (stdout,"getgrgid() call was successful\n");
            fprintf (stdout,"buf->gr_name=%s\n", buf->gr_name);
            fprintf (stdout,"buf->gr_gid=%d\n", buf->gr_gid );
        }
        else {
            fprintf (stderr,"ERROR: getgrgid() call failed\n");
            fprintf (stderr,"ERROR: %s\n", strerror(errno));
        }
    }
```

NAME

getgrnam — search group database for particular name

SYNOPSIS

OH   `#include <sys/types.h>`
`#include <grp.h>`

`struct group *getgrnam(const char *name);`

DESCRIPTION

The *getgrnam*( ) function searches the group database for an entry with a matching *name*.

RETURN VALUE

The *getgrnam*( ) function returns a pointer to a **struct group** with the structure defined in **<grp.h>** with a matching entry if one is found. The *getgrnam*( ) function returns a null pointer if EX   either the requested entry was not found, or an error occurred. On error, *errno* will be set to indicate the error.

ERRORS

The *getgrnam*( ) function may fail if:

EX   [EIO]   An I/O error has occurred.

[EINTR]   A signal was caught during *getgrnam*( ).

[EMFILE]   {OPEN_MAX} file descriptors are currently open in the calling process.

[ENFILE]   The maximum allowable number of files is currently open in the system.

APPLICATION USAGE

The return value may point to a static area which is overwritten by a subsequent call to *getgrent*( ), *getgrgid*( ) or *getgrnam*( ).

Applications wishing to check for error situations should set *errno* to 0 before calling *getgrnam*( ). If *errno* is set on return, an error occurred.

SEE ALSO

endgrent( ), *getgrgid*( ), **<grp.h>**, **<limits.h>**, **<sys/types.h>**.

EXAMPLE

```
/*
 * Copyright (C) ANTRIX Inc.
 */

/* getgrnam.c
 * This program searches the group database for an entry
 * with matching name using function getgrnam.
 */

#include <stdio.h>
#include <stdlib.h>
#include <grp.h>
#include <errno.h>

main()
{
  char         *name = "bin";
  struct group *buf;
  gid_t        gid;
```

```
    fprintf (stdout,"get group name\n");
    buf = getgrnam (name);
    if ( buf != (struct group *)0 ) {
        fprintf (stdout,"getgrnam() call successful\n");
        fprintf (stdout,"buf->gr_name=%s\n", buf->gr_name);
        fprintf (stdout,"buf->gr_gid=%d\n", buf->gr_gid );
    }
    else {
        fprintf (stderr,"ERROR: getgrnam() call failed\n");
        fprintf (stderr,"ERROR: %s\n", strerror(errno));
    }
}
```

NAME

getgroups — get supplementary group IDs

SYNOPSIS

OH   `#include <sys/types.h>`
`#include <unistd.h>`

`int getgroups(int `*gidsetsize*`, gid_t `*grouplist*`[ ]);`

DESCRIPTION

The *getgroups*( ) function fills in the array *grouplist* with the current supplementary group IDs of the calling process.

The *gidsetsize* argument specifies the number of elements in the array *grouplist*. The actual number of supplementary group IDs stored in the array is returned. The values of array entries with indices greater than or equal to the value returned are undefined.

If *gidsetsize* is 0, *getgroups*( ) returns the number of supplementary group IDs associated with the calling process without modifying the array pointed to by *grouplist*.

RETURN VALUE

Upon successful completion, the number of supplementary group IDs is returned. A return value of −1 indicates failure and *errno* is set to indicate the error.

ERRORS

The *getgroups*( ) function will fail if:

[EINVAL]   The *gidsetsize* argument is non-zero and is less than the number of supplementary group IDs.

APPLICATION USAGE

It is unspecified whether the effective group ID of the calling process is included in, or omitted from, the returned list of supplementary group IDs.

SEE ALSO

getegid( ), *setgid*( ), **<sys/types.h>**, **<unistd.h>**.

EXAMPLE

```
/*
 * Copyright (C) ANTRIX Inc.
 */

/* getgroups.c: run as root
 * This program gets supplementary group IDs using function
 * gegroups.
 */

#include <stdio.h>
#include <stdlib.h>
#include <unistd.h>
#include <sys/types.h>
#include <errno.h>

main()
{
    int     setgroups_value;
    int     ngroups, gidsetsize;
    gid_t   *setglist;
```

```
        gid_t   *getglist;
        int     tgroups;

        setglist = (gid_t *)malloc (2*sizeof(gid_t));
        getglist = (gid_t *)malloc (2*sizeof(gid_t));
        ngroups = 2;
        setglist[0] = 2; /* bin */
        setglist[1] = 3; /* sys */

        fprintf (stdout,"set groups\n");
        setgroups (ngroups, setglist);
        gidsetsize = 2;

        fprintf (stdout,"get groups\n");
        tgroups = getgroups (gidsetsize, getglist);
        if ( tgroups = 2 ) {
           fprintf (stdout,"getgroups() call successful\n");
           fprintf (stdout,"total number of supplementary group-id=%d\n", tgroups);
           fprintf (stdout,"supplementary group-id[0]=%d\n", getglist[0]);
           fprintf (stdout,"supplementary group-id[1]=%d\n", getglist[1]);
        }
        else {
           fprintf (stderr,"ERROR: setgroups() call failed\n");
           fprintf (stderr,"ERROR: %s\n", strerror(errno));
        }
    }
```

NAME

gethostid — get an identifier for the current host

SYNOPSIS

UX   `#include <unistd.h>`

`long gethostid(void);`

DESCRIPTION

The *gethostid*( ) function retrieves a 32-bit identifier for the current host.

RETURN VALUE

Upon successful completion, *gethostid*( ) returns an identifier for the current host.

ERRORS

No errors are defined.

APPLICATION USAGE

X/Open does not define the domain in which the return value is unique.

SEE ALSO

random( ), **<unistd.h>**.

EXAMPLE

```
/*
 * Copyright (C) ANTRIX Inc.
 */

/* gethostid.c
 * This program gets the host id using function gethostid.
 */

#include <stdio.h>
#include <stdlib.h>
#include <unistd.h>
#include <errno.h>

main()
{
  long gethostid_value;

  fprintf (stdout,"get host id value\n");
  gethostid_value = gethostid ();
  fprintf (stdout,"host id=%d\n", gethostid_value);
}
```

NAME

getitimer, setitimer — get/set value of interval timer

SYNOPSIS

UX
```
#include <sys/time.h>

int getitimer(int which, struct itimerval *value);

int setitimer(int which, const struct itimerval *value,
        struct itimerval *ovalue);
```

DESCRIPTION

The *getitimer( )* function stores the current value of the timer specified by *which* into the structure pointed to by *value*. The *setitimer( )* function sets the timer specified by *which* to the value specified in the structure pointed to by *value*, and if *ovalue* is not a null pointer, stores the previous value of the timer in the structure pointed to by *ovalue*.

A timer value is defined by the **itimerval** structure. If *it_value* is non-zero, it indicates the time to the next timer expiration. If *it_interval* is non-zero, it specifies a value to be used in reloading *it_value* when the timer expires. Setting *it_value* to 0 disables a timer, regardless of the value of *it_interval*. Setting *it_interval* to 0 disables a timer after its next expiration (assuming *it_value* is non-zero).

Implementations may place limitations on the granularity of timer values. For each interval timer, if the requested timer value requires a finer granularity than the implementation supports, the actual timer value will be rounded up to the next supported value.

An XSI-conforming implementation provides each process with at least three interval timers, which are indicated by the *which* argument:

ITIMER_REAL

  Decrements in real time. A SIGALRM signal is delivered when this timer expires.

ITIMER_VIRTUAL

  Decrements in process virtual time. It runs only when the process is executing. A SIGVTALRM signal is delivered when it expires.

ITIMER_PROF

  Decrements both in process virtual time and when the system is running on behalf of the process. It is designed to be used by interpreters in statistically profiling the execution of interpreted programs. Each time the ITIMER_PROF timer expires, the SIGPROF signal is delivered.

The interaction between *setitimer( )* and any of *alarm( )*, *sleep( )* or *usleep( )* is unspecified.

RETURN VALUE

Upon successful completion, *getitimer( )* or *setitimer( )* returns 0. Otherwise, −1 is returned and *errno* is set to indicate the error.

ERRORS

The *setitimer( )* function will fail if:

[EINVAL]   The *value* argument is not in canonical form. (In canonical form, the number of microseconds is a non-negative integer less than 1,000,000 and the number of seconds is a non-negative integer.)

The *getitimer( )* and *setitimer( )* functions may fail if:

[EINVAL]   The *which* argument is not recognised.

SEE ALSO

alarm( ), *sleep*( ), *ualarm*( ), *usleep*( ), **<signal.h>**, **<sys/time.h>**.

EXAMPLE

```
/*
 * Copyright (C) ANTRIX Inc.
 */

/* getitimer.c
 * This program gets value of interval timer using function getitimer.
 */

#include <stdio.h>
#include <stdlib.h>
#include <time.h>
#include <sys/time.h>
#include <errno.h>

main()
{
  int      getitimer_value ;
  struct   itimerval value;
  struct   itimerval ovalue;
  struct   itimerval tp;

  value.it_interval.tv_sec = 1.0;
  value.it_interval.tv_usec= 1000;
  value.it_value.tv_sec = 2.0;
  value.it_value.tv_usec= 2000;

  fprintf (stdout,"set value of interval timer\n");
  setitimer (ITIMER_REALPROF, &value, &ovalue);

  fprintf (stdout,"get value of interval timer\n");
  getitimer_value = getitimer (ITIMER_REALPROF, &tp);
  if ( getitimer_value != -1 ) {
      fprintf (stdout,"getitimer() call successful\n");
      fprintf (stdout,"tp.it_interval.tv_sec=%d\n", tp.it_interval.tv_sec);
      fprintf (stdout,"tp.it_interval.tv_usec=%d\n", tp.it_interval.tv_usec);
      fprintf (stdout,"tp.it_value.tv_sec=%d\n", tp.it_value.tv_sec);
      fprintf (stdout,"tp.it_value.tv_usec=%d\n", tp.it_value.tv_usec);
  }
  else {
      fprintf (stderr,"ERROR: getitimer() call failed\n");
      fprintf (stderr,"ERROR: %s\n", strerror(errno));
  }
}
```

NAME

getlogin — get login name

SYNOPSIS

```
#include <unistd.h>

char *getlogin(void);
```

DESCRIPTION

The *getlogin*( ) function returns a pointer to a string giving a user name associated with the calling process, which is the login name associated with the calling process. If *getlogin*( ) returns a non-null pointer, then that pointer points to the name that the user logged in under, even if there are several login names with the same user ID.

RETURN VALUE

Upon successful completion, *getlogin*( ) returns a pointer to the login name or a null pointer if the user's login name cannot be found. Otherwise it returns a null pointer and sets *errno* to indicate the error.

EX

ERRORS

The *getlogin*( ) function may fail if:

EX

[EMFILE]   {OPEN_MAX} file descriptors are currently open in the calling process.

[ENFILE]   The maximum allowable number of files is currently open in the system.

[ENXIO]   The calling process has no controlling terminal.

APPLICATION USAGE

The return value may point to static data whose content is overwritten by each call.

Three names associated with the current process can be determined: *getpwuid*(*geteuid*( )) returns the name associated with the effective user ID of the process; *getlogin*( ) returns the name associated with the current login activity; and *getpwuid*(*getuid*( )) returns the name associated with the real user ID of the process.

SEE ALSO

getpwnam( ), *getpwuid*( ), *geteuid*( ), *getuid*( ), **<limits.h>**, **<unistd.h>**.

EXAMPLE

```
/*
 * Copyright (C) ANTRIX Inc.
 */

/* getlogin.c
 * This program gets the login name using function getlogin.
 */

#include <stdio.h>
#include <stdlib.h>
#include <errno.h>

main()
{
  char   *getlogin_value;

  fprintf (stdout,"get login name\n");
  getlogin_value = (char *)getlogin ();
```

```
    fprintf (stdout,"login name=%s\n", getlogin_value);
}
```

NAME

getmsg, getpmsg — receive next message from a STREAMS file

SYNOPSIS

UX

```
#include <stropts.h>
```

```
int getmsg(int fildes, struct strbuf *ctlptr, struct strbuf *dataptr,
        int *flagsp);
```

```
int getpmsg(int fildes, struct strbuf *ctlptr, struct strbuf *dataptr,
        int *bandp, int *flagsp);
```

DESCRIPTION

The *getmsg( )* function retrieves the contents of a message located at the head of the STREAM head read queue associated with a STREAMS file and places the contents into one or more buffers. The message contains either a data part, a control part, or both. The data and control parts of the message are placed into separate buffers, as described below. The semantics of each part is defined by the originator of the message.

The *getpmsg( )* function does the same thing as *getmsg( )*, but provides finer control over the priority of the messages received. Except where noted, all requirements on *getmsg( )* also pertain to *getpmsg( )*.

The *fildes* argument specifies a file descriptor referencing a STREAMS-based file.

The *ctlptr* and *dataptr* arguments each point to a **strbuf** structure, in which the **buf** member points to a buffer in which the data or control information is to be placed, and the **maxlen** member indicates the maximum number of bytes this buffer can hold. On return, the **len** member contains the number of bytes of data or control information actually received. The **len** member is set to 0 if there is a zero-length control or data part and **len** is set to −1 if no data or control information is present in the message.

When *getmsg( )* is called, *flagsp* should point to an integer that indicates the type of message the process is able to receive. This is described further below.

The *ctlptr* argument is used to hold the control part of the message, and *dataptr* is used to hold the data part of the message. If *ctlptr* (or *dataptr*) is a null pointer or the **maxlen** member is −1, the control (or data) part of the message is not processed and is left on the STREAM head read queue, and if the *ctlptr* (or *dataptr*) is not a null pointer, **len** is set to −1. If the **maxlen** member is set to 0 and there is a zero-length control (or data) part, that zero-length part is removed from the read queue and **len** is set to 0. If the **maxlen** member is set to 0 and there are more than 0 bytes of control (or data) information, that information is left on the read queue and **len** is set to 0. If the **maxlen** member in *ctlptr* (or *dataptr*) is less than the control (or data) part of the message, **maxlen** bytes are retrieved. In this case, the remainder of the message is left on the STREAM head read queue and a non-zero return value is provided.

By default, *getmsg( )* processes the first available message on the STREAM head read queue. However, a process may choose to retrieve only high-priority messages by setting the integer pointed to by *flagsp* to RS_HIPRI. In this case, *getmsg( )* will only process the next message if it is a high-priority message. When the integer pointed to by *flagsp* is 0, any message will be retrieved. In this case, on return, the integer pointed to by *flagsp* will be set to RS_HIPRI if a high-priority message was retrieved, or 0 otherwise.

For *getpmsg( )*, the flags are different. The *flagsp* argument points to a bitmask with the following mutually-exclusive flags defined: MSG_HIPRI, MSG_BAND, and MSG_ANY. Like *getmsg( )*, *getpmsg( )* processes the first available message on the STREAM head read queue. A process may choose to retrieve only high-priority messages by setting the integer pointed to by *flagsp* to MSG_HIPRI and the integer pointed to by *bandp* to 0. In this case, *getpmsg( )* will only process the next message if it is a high-priority message. In a similar manner, a process may choose to retrieve a message from a particular priority band by setting the integer pointed to by *flagsp* to MSG_BAND and the integer pointed to by *bandp* to the priority band of interest. In this case, *getpmsg*( ) will only process the next message if it is in a priority band equal to, or greater than, the integer pointed to by *bandp*, or if it is a high-priority message. If a process just wants to get the first message off the queue, the integer pointed to by *flagsp* should be set to MSG_ANY and the integer pointed to by *bandp* should be set to 0. On return, if the message retrieved was a high-priority message, the integer pointed to by *flagsp* will be set to MSG_HIPRI and the integer pointed to by *bandp* will be set to 0. Otherwise, the integer pointed to by *flagsp* will be set to MSG_BAND and the integer pointed to by *bandp* will be set to the priority band of the message.

If O_NONBLOCK is not set, *getmsg*( ) and *getpmsg*( ) will block until a message of the type specified by *flagsp* is available at the front of the STREAM head read queue. If O_NONBLOCK is set and a message of the specified type is not present at the front of the read queue, *getmsg*( ) and *getpmsg*( ) fail and set *errno* to [EAGAIN].

If a hangup occurs on the STREAM from which messages are to be retrieved, *getmsg*( ) and *getpmsg*( ) continue to operate normally, as described above, until the STREAM head read queue is empty. Thereafter, they return 0 in the *len* members of *ctlptr* and *dataptr*.

RETURN VALUE

Upon successful completion, *getmsg*( ) and *getpmsg*( ) return a non-negative value. A value of 0 indicates that a full message was read successfully. A return value of MORECTL indicates that more control information is waiting for retrieval. A return value of MOREDATA indicates that more data is waiting for retrieval. A return value of the bitwise logical OR of MORECTL and MOREDATA indicates that both types of information remain. Subsequent *getmsg*( ) and *getpmsg*( ) calls retrieve the remainder of the message. However, if a message of higher priority has come in on the STREAM head read queue, the next call to *getmsg*( ) or *getpmsg*( ) retrieves that higher-priority message before retrieving the remainder of the previous message.

Upon failure, *getmsg*( ) and *getpmsg*( ) return –1 and set *errno* to indicate the error.

ERRORS

The *getmsg*( ) and *getpmsg*( ) functions will fail if:

[EAGAIN]	The O_NONBLOCK flag is set and no messages are available.
[EBADF]	The *fildes* argument is not a valid file descriptor open for reading.
[EBADMSG]	The queued message to be read is not valid for *getmsg*( ) or *getpmsg*( ) or a pending file descriptor is at the STREAM head.
[EINTR]	A signal was caught during *getmsg*( ) or *getpmsg*( ).
[EINVAL]	An illegal value was specified by *flagsp*, or the STREAM or multiplexer referenced by *fildes* is linked (directly or indirectly) downstream from a multiplexer.
[ENOSTR]	A STREAM is not associated with *fildes*.

In addition, *getmsg*( ) and *getpmsg*( ) will fail if the STREAM head had processed an asynchronous error before the call. In this case, the value of *errno* does not reflect the result of *getmsg*( ) or *getpmsg*( ) but reflects the prior error.

SEE ALSO

poll( ), *putmsg*( ), *read*( ), *write*( ), **<stropts.h>**, XSH specification, **Section 2.5**, **STREAMS**.

EXAMPLE

```
/*
 * Copyright (C) ANTRIX Inc.
 */

/* getmsg.c
 * This program gets the next message off a stream
 * using function getmsg
 */

#include <stdio.h>
#include <stdlib.h>
#include <unistd.h>
#include <limits.h>
#include <stropts.h>
#include <fcntl.h>
#include <sys/stat.h>
#include <errno.h>

/* different text and length */
#define  MSGCTL1    "Control 1"
#define  MSGCTL2    "Control Two"
#define  MSGDAT1    "Data 1"
#define  MSGDAT2    "Data Two"
#define  MAX_MINPUT  255

char    buf1[MAX_MINPUT];
char    buf2[MAX_MINPUT];

#define SLAVE     "/dev/ptmx"

struct  strbuf ctrlbuf, databuf;

open_pty(m, s)
int  *m;
int  *s;
{
  char    *snm;
  fprintf (stdout,"open multiplexor and get slave device\n");
  *m = open (SLAVE, O_RDWR);
  grantpt (*m);
  unlockpt (*m);
  snm = (char *) ptsname (*m);
  *s = open (snm, O_RDWR);
}

close_pty(m, s)
    int m, s;
{
  fprintf (stdout,"close pty\n");
  close (m);
  close (s);
```

```
    }

main ()
{
    int   fdm, fds, flag;
    int   getmsg_value;

    open_pty (&fdm, &fds);

    fprintf (stdout,"write and send first message to stream\n");
    strcpy (buf1, MSGCTL1);
    ctrlbuf.maxlen = sizeof (buf1);
    ctrlbuf.len = strlen (buf1);
    ctrlbuf.buf = buf1;
    strcpy (buf2, MSGDAT1);
    databuf.maxlen = sizeof (buf2);
    databuf.len = strlen (buf2);
    databuf.buf = buf2;
    fprintf (stdout,"sending first message to stream\n");
    putmsg (fdm, &ctrlbuf, &databuf, 0);

    fprintf (stdout,"write and send second message to stream\n");
    strcpy (buf1, MSGCTL2);
    ctrlbuf.maxlen = sizeof (buf1);
    ctrlbuf.len = strlen (buf1);
    ctrlbuf.buf = buf1;
    strcpy (buf2, MSGDAT2);
    databuf.maxlen = sizeof (buf2);
    databuf.len = strlen (buf2);
    databuf.buf = buf2;

    fprintf (stdout,"sending second message to stream\n");
    putmsg (fdm, &ctrlbuf, &databuf, 0);

    fprintf (stdout,"receive message from a stream\n");
    ctrlbuf.maxlen = sizeof (buf1);
    ctrlbuf.len = 0;
    ctrlbuf.buf = buf1;
    memset (buf1, 0, sizeof(buf1));
    databuf.maxlen = sizeof (buf2);
    databuf.len = 0;
    databuf.buf = buf2;
    memset (buf2, 0, sizeof(buf2));
    flag = 0;

    getmsg_value = getmsg (fds, &ctrlbuf, &databuf, &flag);
    if (getmsg_value >= 0)
        fprintf (stdout,"getmsg() call successful\n");
    else
        fprintf (stderr,"ERROR: getmsg() call failed\n");

    fprintf (stdout,"check control and data parts of the message received\n");
```

```
    if ( strcmp(ctrlbuf.buf, MSGCTL1) == 0 )
        fprintf (stdout,"control message received=%s\n", ctrlbuf.buf);
    else
        fprintf (stderr,"ERROR: incorrect control message\n");

    if ( strcmp(databuf.buf, MSGDAT1) == 0 )
        fprintf (stdout,"data message received=%s\n", databuf.buf);
    else
        fprintf (stderr,"ERROR: incorrect data message\n");
    close_pty (fdm, fds);
}
```

NAME

getopt, optarg, optind, opterr, optopt — command option parsing

SYNOPSIS

```
#include <unistd.h>

int getopt(int argc, char * const argv[ ], const char *optstring);

extern char *optarg;
extern int optind, opterr, optopt;
```

DESCRIPTION

The *getopt( )* function is a command-line parser that can be used by applications that follow Utility Syntax Guidelines 3, 4, 5, 6, 7, 9 and 10 in the **XBD** specification, **Section 10.2, Utility Syntax Guidelines**. The remaining guidelines are not addressed by *getopt( )* and are the responsibility of the application.

The parameters *argc* and *argv* are the argument count and argument array as passed to *main( )* (see *exec*). The argument *optstring* is a string of recognised option characters; if a character is followed by a colon, the option takes an argument. All option characters allowed by Utility Syntax Guideline 3 are allowed in *optstring*. The implementation may accept other characters as an extension.

The variable *optind* is the index of the next element of the *argv[]* vector to be processed. It is initialised to 1 by the system, and *getopt( )* updates it when it finishes with each element of *argv[]*. When an element of *argv[]* contains multiple option characters, it is unspecified how *getopt( )* determines which options have already been processed.

The *getopt( )* function returns the next option character (if one is found) from *argv* that matches a character in *optstring*, if there is one that matches. If the option takes an argument, *getopt( )* sets the variable *optarg* to point to the option-argument as follows:

1. If the option was the last character in the string pointed to by an element of *argv*, then *optarg* contains the next element of *argv*, and *optind* is incremented by 2. If the resulting value of *optind* is not less than *argc*, this indicates a missing option-argument, and *getopt( )* returns an error indication.

2. Otherwise, *optarg* points to the string following the option character in that element of *argv*, and *optind* is incremented by 1.

If, when *getopt( )* is called:

`argv[optind]`	is a null pointer
`*argv[optind]`	is not the character −
`argv[optind]`	points to the string "−"

getopt( ) returns −1 without changing *optind*. If:

> `argv[optind]`   points to the string "−−"

getopt( ) returns −1 after incrementing *optind*.

If *getopt( )* encounters an option character that is not contained in *optstring*, it returns the question-mark (?) character. If it detects a missing option-argument, it returns the colon character (:) if the first character of *optstring* was a colon, or a question-mark character (?) otherwise. In either case, *getopt( )* will set the variable *optopt* to the option character that caused the error. If the application has not set the variable *opterr* to 0 and the first character of *optstring* is not a colon, *getopt( )* also prints a diagnostic message to *stderr* in the format specified for the *getopts* utility.

RETURN VALUE

The *getopt*( ) function returns the next option character specified on the command line.

A colon (:) is returned if *getopt*( ) detects a missing argument and the first character of *optstring* was a colon (:).

A question mark (?) is returned if *getopt*( ) encounters an option character not in *optstring* or detects a missing argument and the first character of *optstring* was not a colon (:).

Otherwise *getopt*( ) returns −1 when all command line options are parsed.

ERRORS

No errors are defined.

EXAMPLES

The following code fragment shows how one might process the arguments for a utility that can take the mutually exclusive options a and b and the options f and o, both of which require arguments:

```
#include <unistd.h>

int
main (int argc, char *argv[ ])
{
        int c;
        int bflg, aflg, errflg;
        char *ifile;
        char *ofile;
        extern char *optarg;
        extern int optind, optopt;
        . . .
        while ((c = getopt(argc, argv, ":abf:o:")) != -1) {
                switch (c) {
                case 'a':
                        if (bflg)
                                errflg++;
                        else
                                aflg++;
                        break;
                case 'b':
                        if (aflg)
                                errflg++;
                        else {
                                bflg++;
                                bproc( );
                        }
                        break;
                case 'f':
                        ifile = optarg;
                        break;
                case 'o':
                        ofile = optarg;
                        break;
                case ':':       /* -f or -o without operand */
                        fprintf(stderr,
                                "Option -%c requires an operand\n", optopt);
                        errflg++;
                        break;
                case '?':
                        fprintf(stderr,
```

```
                                "Unrecognised option: -%c\n", optopt);
                        errflg++;
                }
        }
        if (errflg) {
                fprintf(stderr, "usage: . . . ");
                exit(2);
        }
        for ( ; optind < argc; optind++) {
                if (access(argv[optind], R_OK)) {
        . . .
}
```

This code accepts any of the following as equivalent:

```
cmd -ao arg path path
cmd -a -o arg path path
cmd -o arg -a path path
cmd -a -o arg -- path path
cmd -a -oarg path path
cmd -aoarg path path
```

APPLICATION USAGE

The *getopt*( ) function is only required to support option characters included in Guideline 3. Many historical implementations of *getopt*( ) support other characters as options. This is an allowed extension, but applications that use extensions are not maximally portable. Note that support for multi-byte option characters is only possible when such characters can be represented as type **int**.

SEE ALSO

exec, *getopts*, **<unistd.h>**, the **XCU** specification.

EXAMPLE

```
/*
 * Copyright (C) ANTRIX Inc.
 */

/* getopt.c
 * This program parses the command line options using function
 * getopt.
 */

#include <stdio.h>
#include <stdlib.h>
#include <errno.h>

char *myopts[] = {
#define READ   0
           "read" ,
#define WRITE  1
           "write" ,
            0 ,
};

main(argc, argv)
int argc;
```

```
char *argv[];
{
  int     c, errflag;
  char    *options, *value;

  /* getopt [-a] [-b] [-c file] [-o read/write] */
  fprintf (stdout,"start processing options\n");
  while (( c = getopt (argc, argv, "abc:o:")) != -1) {
     switch (c) {
        case 'a':
                fprintf (stdout,"option typed is 'a'\n");
                break;
        case 'b':
                fprintf (stdout,"option typed is 'b'\n");
                break;
        case 'c':
                fprintf (stdout,"option typed is 'c' file\n");
                break;
        case '?':
                errflag++;
                break;
        case 'o':
                options = optarg;
                /* start processing suboptions */
                while (*options != ' ') {
                  switch (getsubopt (&options, myopts, &value)) {
                    case READ:
                        fprintf (stdout,"suboption typed is read\n");
                        break;
                    case WRITE:
                        fprintf (stdout,"suboption typed is write\n");
                        break;
                      default:
                        fprintf (stdout,"unknow token\n");
                        errflag++;
                        break;
                  } /* end switch */
                } /* end while processing suboptions */
                break;
    }   /* end options processing */
  } /* end getopt processing options */

  if (errflag)
     fprintf (stdout,"usage: getopt [-a] [-b] [-c file] [-o read/write]\n");
}
```

NAME

getpagesize — get the current page size

SYNOPSIS

UX   `#include <unistd.h>`

`int getpagesize(void);`

DESCRIPTION

The *getpagesize( )* function returns the current page size.

The *getpagesize( )* function is equivalent to *sysconf*(_SC_PAGE_SIZE) and *sysconf*(_SC_PAGESIZE).

RETURN VALUE

The *getpagesize( )* function returns the current page size.

ERRORS

No errors are defined.

APPLICATION USAGE

The value returned by *getpagesize( )* need not be the minimum value that *malloc( )* can allocate. Moreover, the application cannot assume that an object of this size can be allocated with *malloc( )*.

SEE ALSO

brk( ), *getrlimit( )*, *mmap( )*, *mprotect( )*, *munmap( )*, *msync( )*, *sysconf( )*, **<unistd.h>**.

EXAMPLE

```
/*
 * Copyright (C) ANTRIX Inc.
 */

/* getpagesize.c
 * This program gets system page size using function getpagesize.
 */

#include <stdio.h>
#include <stdlib.h>
#include <errno.h>

main()
{
  int getpagesize_value;

  fprintf (stdout,"get system page size\n");
  getpagesize_value = getpagesize ();
  fprintf (stdout,"page size=%d\n", getpagesize_value);
}
```

NAME

getpass — read a string of characters without echo (**TO BE WITHDRAWN**)

SYNOPSIS

EX
```
#include <unistd.h>
```
```
char *getpass(const char *prompt);
```

DESCRIPTION

The *getpass*( ) function opens the process' controlling terminal, writes to that device the null-terminated string *prompt,* disables echoing, reads a string of characters up to the next newline character or EOF, restores the terminal state and closes the terminal.

RETURN VALUE

Upon successful completion, *getpass*( ) returns a pointer to a null-terminated string of at most {PASS_MAX} bytes that were read from the terminal device. If an error is encountered, the terminal state is restored and a null pointer is returned.

ERRORS

The *getpass*( ) function may fail if:

[EINTR]　　　　The *getpass*( ) function was interrupted by a signal.

[EIO]　　　　The process is a member of a background process attempting to read from its controlling terminal, the process is ignoring or blocking the SIGTTIN signal or the process group is orphaned. This error may also be generated for implementation-dependent reasons.

[EMFILE]　　　　{OPEN_MAX} file descriptors are currently open in the calling process.

[ENFILE]　　　　The maximum allowable number of files is currently open in the system.

[ENXIO]　　　　The process does not have a controlling terminal.

APPLICATION USAGE

The return value points to static data whose content may be overwritten by each call.

This interface is marked TO BE WITHDRAWN because its name is misleading, and it provides no functionality which the user could not easily implement.

SEE ALSO

<limits.h>, **<unistd.h>**.

EXAMPLE

```
/*
 * Copyright (C) ANTRIX Inc.
 */

/* getpass.c
 * This program reads a string of characters without echo
 * using function getpass.
 */

#include <stdio.h>
#include <stdlib.h>
#include <errno.h>

main()
{
```

```
char        *getpass_value;
const char  *prompt = "passwd:";

getpass_value = (char *)getpass(prompt);
if ( getpass_value != (char *)0 ) {
    fprintf (stdout,"getpass() call successful\n");
    fprintf (stdout,"string typed is %s\n", getpass_value);
}
else
    fprintf (stderr,"ERROR: getpass() call failed\n");
}
```

NAME

getpgid — get process group ID

SYNOPSIS

UX

```
#include <unistd.h>

pid_t getpgid(pid_t pid);
```

DESCRIPTION

The *getpgid*( ) function returns the process group ID of the process whose process ID is equal to *pid*. If *pid* is equal to 0, *getpgid*( ) returns the process group ID of the calling process.

RETURN VALUE

Upon successful completion, *getpgid*( ) returns a process group ID. Otherwise, it returns (**pid_t**)–1 and sets *errno* to indicate the error.

ERRORS

The *getpgid*( ) function will fail if:

[EPERM]   The process whose process ID is equal to *pid* is not in the same session as the calling process, and the implementation does not allow access to the process group ID of that process from the calling process.

[ESRCH]   There is no process with a process ID equal to *pid*.

The *getpgid*( ) function may fail if:

[EINVAL]   The value of the *pid* argument is invalid.

SEE ALSO

exec, *fork*( ), *getpgrp*( ), *getpid*( ), *getsid*( ), *setpgid*( ), *setsid*( ), **<unistd.h>**.

EXAMPLE

```
/*
 * Copyright (C) ANTRIX Inc.
 */

/* getpgid.c
 * This program gets the process group ID of the process
 * using function getpgid
 */

#include <stdio.h>
#include <stdlib.h>
#include <sys/types.h>
#include <unistd.h>
#include <errno.h>

main()
{
   pid_t     getpgid_value;
   pid_t     pid;

   pid = getpid ();

   fprintf (stdout,"get process group id\n");
   getpgid_value = getpgid (pid);
   if ( getpgid_value != -1 ) {
```

```
        fprintf (stdout,"getpgid() call successful\n");
        fprintf (stdout,"process group-id=%d\n", getpgid_value);
    }
  else {
        fprintf (stderr,"ERROR: getpgid() call failed\n");
        fprintf (stderr,"ERROR: %s\n", strerror(errno));
    }
}
```

NAME

getpgrp — get process group ID

SYNOPSIS

OH
```
#include <sys/types.h>
#include <unistd.h>

pid_t getpgrp(void);
```

DESCRIPTION

The *getpgrp*( ) function returns the process group ID of the calling process.

RETURN VALUE

The *getpgrp*( ) function is always successful and no return value is reserved to indicate an error.

ERRORS

No errors are defined.

SEE ALSO

exec, *fork*( ), *getpgid*( ), *getpid*( ), *getppid*( ), *kill*( ), *setpgid*( ), *setsid*( ), **<sys/types.h>**, **<unistd.h>**.

EXAMPLE

```
/*
 * Copyright (C) ANTRIX Inc.
 */

/* getpgrp.c
 * This program returns the process group ID of the calling
 * process using function getpgrp.
 */

#include <stdio.h>
#include <stdlib.h>
#include <sys/types.h>
#include <errno.h>

main()
{
  pid_t  getpgrp_value;

  fprintf (stdout,"get process group\n");
  getpgrp_value = getpgrp ();
  if ( getpgrp_value != 0 ) {
      fprintf (stdout,"getpgrp() call successful\n");
      fprintf (stdout,"getpgrp_value=%d\n", getpgrp_value);
  }
  else {
      fprintf (stderr,"ERROR: getpgrp() call failed\n");
      fprintf (stderr,"ERROR: %s\n", strerror(errno));
  }
}
```

NAME

getpid — get process ID

SYNOPSIS

OH   `#include <sys/types.h>`
`#include <unistd.h>`

`pid_t getpid(void);`

DESCRIPTION

The *getpid*( ) function returns the process ID of the calling process.

RETURN VALUE

The *getpid*( ) function is always successful and no return value is reserved to indicate an error.

ERRORS

No errors are defined.

SEE ALSO

exec, *fork*( ), *getpgrp*( ), *getppid*( ), *kill*( ), *setpgid*( ), *setsid*( ), **<sys/types.h>**, **<unistd.h>**.

EXAMPLE

```
/*
 * Copyright (C) ANTRIX Inc.
 */

/* getpid.c
 * This program returns the process ID of the calling process
 * using function getpid.
 */

#include <stdio.h>
#include <stdlib.h>
#include <sys/types.h>
#include <errno.h>

main()
{
  pid_t   getpid_value;

  fprintf (stdout,"get process id\n");
  getpid_value = getpid ();
  fprintf (stdout,"getpid_value=%d\n", getpid_value);
}
```

NAME

getpmsg — get user database entry

SYNOPSIS

UX   `#include <pwd.h>`

```
int getpmsg(int fildes, struct strbuf *ctlptr, struct strbuf *dataptr,
       int *bandp, int *flagsp);
```

DESCRIPTION

Refer to *getmsg*( ).

EXAMPLE

```c
/*
 * Copyright (C) ANTRIX Inc.
 */

/* getpmsg.c
 * This program gets the next message off a stream
 * using function getpmsg
 */

#include <stdio.h>
#include <stdlib.h>
#include <unistd.h>
#include <limits.h>
#include <stropts.h>
#include <fcntl.h>
#include <sys/stat.h>
#include <errno.h>

/* different text and length */
#define  MSGCTL1    "Control 1"
#define  MSGCTL2    "Control Two"
#define  MSGDAT1    "Data 1"
#define  MSGDAT2    "Data Two"
#define  MAX_MINPUT  255

char    buf1[MAX_MINPUT];
char    buf2[MAX_MINPUT];

#define SLAVE     "/dev/ptmx"

struct  strbuf ctrlbuf, databuf;

open_pty(m, s)
int  *m;
int  *s;
{
   char    *snm;
   fprintf (stdout,"open multiplexor and get slave device\n");
   *m = open (SLAVE, O_RDWR);
   grantpt (*m);
   unlockpt (*m);
```

```
    snm = (char *) ptsname (*m);
    *s = open (snm, O_RDWR);
}

close_pty(m, s)
    int m, s;
{
  fprintf (stdout,"close pty\n");
  close (m);
  close (s);
}

main()
{
  int   fdm, fds, flag, band;
  int   getpmsg_value ;

  open_pty (&fdm, &fds);

  fprintf (stdout,"write and send first message to stream\n");
  strcpy (buf1, MSGCTL1);
  ctrlbuf.maxlen = sizeof (buf1);
  ctrlbuf.len = strlen (buf1);
  ctrlbuf.buf = buf1;
  strcpy (buf2, MSGDAT1);
  databuf.maxlen = sizeof (buf2);
  databuf.len = strlen (buf2);
  databuf.buf = buf2;
  fprintf (stdout,"sending first message to stream\n");
  putmsg (fdm, &ctrlbuf, &databuf, 0);

  fprintf (stdout,"write and send second message to stream\n");
  strcpy (buf1, MSGCTL2);
  ctrlbuf.maxlen = sizeof (buf1);
  ctrlbuf.len = strlen (buf1);
  ctrlbuf.buf = buf1;
  strcpy (buf2, MSGDAT2);
  databuf.maxlen = sizeof (buf2);
  databuf.len = strlen (buf2);
  databuf.buf = buf2;

  fprintf (stdout,"sending second message to stream\n");
  putmsg (fdm, &ctrlbuf, &databuf, 0);

  fprintf (stdout,"get message from stream\n");
  ctrlbuf.maxlen = sizeof (buf1);
  ctrlbuf.len = 0;
  ctrlbuf.buf = buf1;
  memset (buf1, 0, sizeof(buf1));
  databuf.maxlen = sizeof (buf2);
  databuf.len = 0;
  databuf.buf = buf2;
```

```
    memset (buf2, 0, sizeof(buf2));
    flag = MSG_ANY;
    band = 0;
    getpmsg_value = getpmsg (fds, &ctrlbuf, &databuf, &band, &flag);
    if (getpmsg_value >= 0)
        fprintf (stdout,"getpmsg() call successful\n");
    else
        fprintf (stderr,"ERROR: getpmsg() call failed\n");

    fprintf (stdout,"check control and data parts of the message received\n");
    if ( strcmp(ctrlbuf.buf, MSGCTL1) == 0 )
        fprintf (stdout,"control message received=%s\n", ctrlbuf.buf);
    else
        fprintf (stderr,"ERROR: incorrect control message\n");

    if ( strcmp(databuf.buf, MSGDAT1) == 0 )
        fprintf (stdout,"data message received=%s\n", databuf.buf);
    else
        fprintf (stderr,"ERROR: incorrect data message\n");
    close_pty (fdm, fds);
}
```

NAME
> getppid — get parent process ID

SYNOPSIS

OH
> ```
> #include <sys/types.h>
> #include <unistd.h>
>
> pid_t getppid(void);
> ```

DESCRIPTION
> The *getppid*( ) function returns the parent process ID of the calling process.

RETURN VALUE
> The *getppid*( ) function is always successful and no return value is reserved to indicate an error.

ERRORS
> No errors are defined.

SEE ALSO
> *exec*, *fork*( ), *getpgid*( ), *getpgrp*( ), *getpid*( ), *kill*( ), *setpgid*( ), *setsid*( ), **<sys/types.h>**, **<unistd.h>**.

EXAMPLE
> ```
> /*
>  * Copyright (C) ANTRIX Inc.
>  */
>
> /* getppid.c
>  * This program returns the parent process ID of the calling process
>  * using function getppid.
>  */
>
> #include <stdio.h>
> #include <stdlib.h>
> #include <sys/types.h>
> #include <errno.h>
>
> main()
> {
>   pid_t    getppid_value;
>
>   fprintf (stdout,"get parent process id\n");
>   getppid_value = getppid ();
>   fprintf (stdout,"getppid_value=%d\n", getppid_value);
> }
> ```

NAME

getpriority, setpriority — get or set process scheduling priority

SYNOPSIS

UX
```
#include <sys/resource.h>

int getpriority(int which, id_t who);

int setpriority(int which, id_t who, int priority);
```

DESCRIPTION

The *getpriority*( ) function obtains the current scheduling priority of a process, process group, or user. The *setpriority*( ) function sets the scheduling priority of a process, process group, or user.

Target processes are specified by the values of the *which* and *who* arguments. The *which* argument may be one of the following values: PRIO_PROCESS, PRIO_PGRP, or PRIO_USER, indicating that the *who* argument is to be interpreted as a process ID, a process group ID, or a user ID, respectively. A 0 value for the *who* argument specifies the current process, process group, or user.

If more than one process is specified, *getpriority*( ) returns the highest priority (lowest numerical value) pertaining to any of the specified processes, and *setpriority*( ) sets the priorities of all of the specified processes to the specified value.

The default *priority* is 0; negative priorities cause more favourable scheduling. While the range of valid priority values is [–20, 20], implementations may enforce more restrictive limits. If the value specified to *setpriority*( ) is less than the system's lowest supported priority value, the system's lowest supported value is used; if it is greater than the system's highest supported value, the system's highest supported value is used.

Only a process with appropriate privileges can raise its priority (ie. assign a lower numerical priority value).

RETURN VALUE

Upon successful completion, *getpriority*( ) returns an integer in the range from –20 to 20. Otherwise, –1 is returned and *errno* is set to indicate the error.

Upon successful completion, *setpriority*( ) returns 0. Otherwise, –1 is returned and *errno* is set to indicate the error.

ERRORS

The *getpriority*( ) and *setpriority*( ) functions will fail if:

[ESRCH]   No process could be located using the *which* and *who* argument values specified.

[EINVAL]   The value of the *which* argument was not recognised, or the value of the *who* argument is not a valid process ID, process group ID, or user ID.

In addition, *setpriority*( ) may fail if:

[EPERM]   A process was located, but neither the real nor effective user ID of the executing process match the effective user ID of the process whose priority is being changed.

[EACCES]   A request was made to change the priority to a lower numeric value (that is, to a higher priority) and the current process does not have appropriate privileges.

APPLICATION USAGE

The effect of changing the scheduling priority may vary depending on the process-scheduling algorithm in effect.

Because *getpriority*( ) can return the value –1 on successful completion, it is necessary to set *errno* to 0 prior to a call to *getpriority*( ). If *getpriority*( ) returns the value –1, then *errno* can be checked to see if an error occurred or if the value is a legitimate priority.

SEE ALSO

nice( ), **<sys/resource.h>**.

EXAMPLE

```
/*
 * Copyright (C) ANTRIX Inc.
 */

/* getpriority.c
 * This program gets the scheduling priority for the process
 * using function getpriority.
 */

#include <stdio.h>
#include <stdlib.h>
#include <sys/types.h>
#include <sys/time.h>
#include <sys/resource.h>
#include <errno.h>

main()
{
    int     getpriority_value;
    pid_t   who;

    fprintf (stdout,"get process id\n");
    who = getpid();

    fprintf (stdout, "get process current scheduling priority\n");
    getpriority_value = getpriority (PRIO_PROCESS, who);
    fprintf (stdout,"getpriority_value=%d\n", getpriority_value);
}
/*
 * Copyright (C) ANTRIX Inc.
 */

/* setpriority.c
 * This program sets the scheduling priority for the process
 * using function setpriority.
 */

#include <stdio.h>
#include <stdlib.h>
#include <sys/types.h>
#include <sys/time.h>
#include <sys/resource.h>
```

```
#include <errno.h>

main()
{
  int    setpriority_value;
  int    getpriority_value;
  pid_t  who;

  fprintf (stdout,"get process id\n");
  who = getpid();

  fprintf (stdout,"set priority to 2\n");
  who = setpriority(PRIO_PROCESS, who, 2);

  fprintf (stdout, "get process scheduling priority\n");
  getpriority_value = getpriority (PRIO_PROCESS, who);
  fprintf (stdout,"getpriority_value=%d\n", getpriority_value);
}
```

NAME

getpwent — get user database entry

SYNOPSIS

UX
```
#include <pwd.h>

struct passwd *getpwent(void);
```

DESCRIPTION

Refer to *endpwent*( ).

EXAMPLE

```c
/*
 * Copyright (C) ANTRIX Inc.
 */

/* getpwent.c
 * This program gets the password entry
 * using function getpwent
 */

#include <stdio.h>
#include <stdlib.h>
#include <pwd.h>
#include <errno.h>

main()
{
  struct  passwd *buf;

  fprintf (stdout,"open passwd file\n");
  fprintf (stdout,"get passwd entries\n");
  do {
     buf = (struct passwd *)getpwent ();
     fprintf (stdout,"buf_pw_name=%s\n", buf->pw_name);
     fprintf (stdout,"buf_pw_passwd=%s\n", buf->pw_passwd);
     fprintf (stdout,"buf_pw_uid=%d\n", buf->pw_uid);
     fprintf (stdout,"buf_pw_gid=%d\n", buf->pw_gid);
     fprintf (stdout,"buf_pw_dir=%s\n", buf->pw_dir);
     fprintf (stdout,"buf_pw_shell=%s\n", buf->pw_shell);
  }
  while ( buf != (struct passwd *)0 );

  fprintf (stdout,"close passwd file\n");
  endpwent ();
}
```

NAME

getpwnam — search user database for particular name

SYNOPSIS

OH `#include <sys/types.h>`
`#include <pwd.h>`

`struct passwd *getpwnam(const char *name);`

DESCRIPTION

The *getpwnam*( ) function searches the user database for an entry with a matching *name*.

RETURN VALUE

The *getpwnam*( ) function returns a pointer to a **struct passwd** with the structure as defined in **<pwd.h>** with a matching entry if found. A null pointer is returned if the requested entry is not
EX found, or an error occurs. On error, *errno* is set to indicate the error.

ERRORS

The *getpwnam*( ) function may fail if:

EX [EIO]   An I/O error has occurred.

[EINTR]   A signal was caught during *getpwnam*( ).

[EMFILE]   {OPEN_MAX} file descriptors are currently open in the calling process.

[ENFILE]   The maximum allowable number of files is currently open in the system.

APPLICATION USAGE

The return value may point to a static area which is overwritten by a subsequent call to *cuserid*( ), *getpwent*( ), *getpwnam*( ) or *getpwuid*( ).

Applications wishing to check for error situations should set *errno* to 0 before calling *getpwnam*( ). If *errno* is set to non-zero on return, an error occurred.

Three names associated with the current process can be determined: *getpwuid*(*geteuid*( )) returns the name associated with the effective user ID of the process; *getlogin*( ) returns the name associated with the current login activity; and *getpwuid*(*getuid*( )) returns the name associated with the real user ID of the process.

SEE ALSO

getpwuid( ), **<limits.h>**, **<pwd.h>**, **<sys/types.h>**.

EXAMPLE

```
/*
 * Copyright (C) ANTRIX Inc.
 */

/* getpwnam.c
 * This program searches the user database for an entry with a
 * matching name using function getpwnam.
 */

#include <stdio.h>
#include <stdlib.h>
#include <pwd.h>
#include <errno.h>

main()
```

```
{
  char            *login;
  struct passwd  *buf;

  fprintf (stdout,"get login name\n");
  /* can also use login = getlogin() */
  login = cuserid ((char *)0);

  fprintf (stdout,"get passwd entry determined by login name\n");
  buf = (struct passwd *)getpwnam (login);
  if ( buf != (struct passwd *)0 ) {
     fprintf (stdout,"getpwnam() call successful\n");
     fprintf (stdout,"buf->pw_name=%s\n", buf->pw_name);
     fprintf (stdout,"buf->pw_passwd=%s\n", buf->pw_passwd);
     fprintf (stdout,"buf->pw_uid=%d\n", buf->pw_uid);
     fprintf (stdout,"buf->pw_gid=%d\n", buf->pw_gid);
     fprintf (stdout,"buf->pw_dir=%s\n", buf->pw_dir);
     fprintf (stdout,"buf->pw_shell=%s\n", buf->pw_shell);
  }
  else
     fprintf (stderr,"ERROR: getpwnam() call failed\n");
}
```

NAME

getpwuid — search user database for particular user ID

SYNOPSIS

OH   `#include <sys/types.h>`
`#include <pwd.h>`

`struct passwd *getpwuid(uid_t uid);`

DESCRIPTION

The *getpwuid*( ) function searches the user database for an entry with a matching *uid*.

RETURN VALUE

The *getpwuid*( ) function returns a pointer to a **struct passwd** with the structure as defined in
<pwd.h> with a matching entry if found. A null pointer is returned if the requested entry is not
EX   found, or an error occurs. On error, *errno* is set to indicate the error.

ERRORS

The *getpwuid*( ) function may fail if:

EX   [EIO]   An I/O error has occurred.

[EINTR]   A signal was caught during *getpwuid*( ).

[EMFILE]   {OPEN_MAX} file descriptors are currently open in the calling process.

[ENFILE]   The maximum allowable number of files is currently open in the system.

APPLICATION USAGE

The return value may point to a static area which is overwritten by a subsequent call to
cuserid( ), *getpwent*( ), *getpwnam*( ) or *getpwuid*( ).

Applications wishing to check for error situations should set *errno* to 0 before calling *getpwuid*( ).
If *errno* is set to non-zero on return, an error occurred.

Three names associated with the current process can be determined: *getpwuid*(*geteuid*( ))
returns the name associated with the effective user ID of the process; *getlogin*( ) returns the
name associated with the current login activity; and *getpwuid*(*getuid*( )) returns the name
associated with the real user ID of the process.

SEE ALSO

cuserid( ), *getpwnam*( ), *geteuid*( ), *getuid*( ), *getlogin*( ), **<limits.h>**, **<pwd.h>**, **<sys/types.h>**.

EXAMPLE

```
/*
 * Copyright (C) ANTRIX Inc.
 */

/* getpwuid.c
 * This program searches the user database for an entry with
 * a matching uid using function getpwuid.
 */

#include <stdio.h>
#include <stdlib.h>
#include <pwd.h>
#include <errno.h>

main()
```

```
{
  uid_t            uid;
  struct passwd    *buf;

  fprintf (stdout,"get process user id\n");
  uid = getuid ();

  fprintf (stdout,"get passwd entry determined by user ID\n");
  buf = (struct passwd *) getpwuid (uid);
  if ( buf != (struct passwd *)0 ) {
     fprintf (stdout,"getpwuid() call successful\n");
     fprintf (stdout,"buf->pw_name=%s\n", buf->pw_name);
     fprintf (stdout,"buf->pw_passwd=%s\n", buf->pw_passwd);
     fprintf (stdout,"buf->pw_uid=%d\n", buf->pw_uid);
     fprintf (stdout,"buf->pw_gid=%d\n", buf->pw_gid);
     fprintf (stdout,"buf->pw_dir=%s\n", buf->pw_dir);
     fprintf (stdout,"buf->pw_shell=%s\n", buf->pw_shell);
  }
  else
     fprintf (stderr,"ERROR: getpwuid() call failed\n");
}
```

NAME

getrlimit, setrlimit — control maximum resource consumption

SYNOPSIS

UX   `#include <sys/resource.h>`

`int getrlimit(int` *resource*`, struct rlimit *`*rlp*`);`

`int setrlimit(int` *resource*`, const struct rlimit *`*rlp*`);`

DESCRIPTION

Limits on the consumption of a variety of resources by the calling process may be obtained with *getrlimit*( ) and set with *setrlimit*( ).

Each call to either *getrlimit*( ) or *setrlimit*( ) identifies a specific resource to be operated upon as well as a resource limit. A resource limit is represented by an **rlimit** structure. The **rlim_cur** member specifies the current or soft limit and the **rlim_max** member specifies the maximum or hard limit. Soft limits may be changed by a process to any value that is less than or equal to the hard limit. A process may (irreversibly) lower its hard limit to any value that is greater than or equal to the soft limit. Only a process with appropriate privileges can raise a hard limit. Both hard and soft limits can be changed in a single call to *setrlimit*( ) subject to the constraints described above.

The value RLIM_INFINITY, defined in **<sys/resource.h>**, is considered to be larger than any other limit value. If a call to *getrlimit*( ) returns RLIM_INFINITY for a resource, it means the implementation does not enforce limits on that resource. Specifying RLIM_INFINITY as any resource limit value on a successful call to *setrlimit*( ) inhibits enforcement of that resource limit.

The following resources are defined:

RLIMIT_CORE   This is the maximum size of a core file in bytes that may be created by a process. A limit of 0 will prevent the creation of a core file. If this limit is exceeded, the writing of a core file will terminate at this size.

RLIMIT_CPU   This is the maximum amount of CPU time in seconds used by a process. If this limit is exceeded, SIGXCPU is generated for the process. If the process is blocking, catching or ignoring SIGXCPU, the behaviour is unspecified.

RLIMIT_DATA   This is the maximum size of a process' data segment in bytes. If this limit is exceeded, the *brk*( ), *malloc*( ) and *sbrk*( ) functions will fail with *errno* set to [ENOMEM].

RLIMIT_FSIZE   This is the maximum size of a file in bytes that may be created by a process. A limit of 0 will prevent the creation of a file. If a write or truncate operation would cause this limit to be exceeded, SIGXFSZ is generated for the process. If the process is blocking, catching or ignoring SIGXFSZ, continued attempts to increase the size of a file from end-of-file to beyond the limit will fail with *errno* set to [EFBIG].

RLIMIT_NOFILE

This is a number one greater than the maximum value that the system may assign to a newly-created descriptor. If this limit is exceeded, functions that allocate new file descriptors may fail with errno set to [EMFILE]. This limit constrains the number of file descriptors that a process may allocate.

RLIMIT_STACK   This is the maximum size of a process' stack in bytes. The implementation will not automatically grow the stack beyond this limit. If this limit is exceeded, SIGSEGV is generated for the process. If the process is blocking or ignoring SIGSEGV, or is catching SIGSEGV and has not made arrangements to use

an alternate stack, the disposition of SIGSEGV will be set to SIG_DFL before
it is generated.

RLIMIT_AS   This is the maximum size of a process' total available memory, in bytes. If
                   this limit is exceeded, the *brk*( ), *malloc*( ), *mmap*( ) and *sbrk*( ) functions will
                   fail with *errno* set to [ENOMEM]. In addition, the automatic stack growth will
                   fail with the effects outlined above.

RETURN VALUE

Upon successful completion, *getrlimit*( ) and *setrlimit*( ) return 0. Otherwise, these functions
return −1 and set *errno* to indicate the error.

ERRORS

The *getrlimit*( ) and *setrlimit*( ) functions will fail if:

[EINVAL]   An invalid *resource* was specified; or in a *setrlimit*( ) call, the new **rlim_cur**
                   exceeds the new **rlim_max**.

[EPERM]   The limit specified to *setrlimit*( ) would have raised the maximum limit value,
                   and the calling process does not have appropriate privileges.

The *setrlimit*( ) function may fail if:

[EINVAL]   The limit specified cannot be lowered because current usage is already higher
                   than the limit.

SEE ALSO

brk( ), *exec*, *fork*( ), *getdtablesize*( ), *malloc*( ), *open*( ), *sigaltstack*( ), *sysconf*( ), *ulimit*( ),
<stropts.h>, **<sys/resource.h>**.

EXAMPLE

```
/*
 * Copyright (C) ANTRIX Inc.
 */

/* getrlimit.c
 * This program gets the maximum system resources consumption
 * using function getrlimit
 */

#include <stdio.h>
#include <stdlib.h>
#include <sys/time.h>
#include <sys/resource.h>
#include <errno.h>

main()
{
    int     getrlimit_value;
    struct  rlimit rlp;

    fprintf (stdout,"get system resource limits\n");
    getrlimit_value = getrlimit (RLIMIT_FSIZE, &rlp);
    if ( getrlimit_value == 0 ) {
        fprintf (stdout,"getrlimit() call successful\n");
        fprintf (stdout,"rlp.rlim_cur=%d\n", rlp.rlim_cur);
        fprintf (stdout,"rlp.rlim_max=%d\n", rlp.rlim_max);
```

```
      }
   else {
      fprintf (stderr,"ERROR: getrlimit() call failed\n");
      fprintf (stderr,"ERROR: %s\n", strerror(errno));
   }
}
```

NAME

getrusage — get information about resource utilisation

SYNOPSIS

UX   `#include <sys/resource.h>`

`int getrusage(int who, struct rusage *r_usage);`

DESCRIPTION

The *getrusage*( ) function provides measures of the resources used by the current process or its terminated and waited-for child processes. If the value of the *who* argument is RUSAGE_SELF, information is returned about resources used by the current process. If the value of the *who* argument is RUSAGE_CHILDREN, information is returned about resources used by the terminated and waited-for children of the current process. If the child is never waited for (for instance, if the parent has SA_NOCLDWAIT set or sets SIGCHLD to SIG_IGN), the resource information for the child process is discarded and not included in the resource information provided by *getrusage*( ).

The *r_usage* argument is a pointer to an object of type **struct rusage** in which the returned information is stored.

RETURN VALUE

Upon successful completion, *getrusage*( ) returns 0. Otherwise, −1 is returned, and *errno* is set to indicate the error.

ERRORS

The *getrusage*( ) function will fail if:

[EINVAL]   The value of the *who* argument is not valid.

SEE ALSO

exit( ), *sigaction*( ), *time*( ), *times*( ), *wait*( ), **<sys/resource.h>**.

EXAMPLE

```
/*
 * Copyright (C) ANTRIX Inc.
 */

/* getrusage.c
 * This program gets the scheduling priority for the process
 * using function getrusage.
 */

#include <stdio.h>
#include <stdlib.h>
#include <sys/types.h>
#include <time.h>
#include <sys/time.h>
#include <sys/resource.h>
#include <errno.h>

main()
{
    int     getrusage_value;
    pid_t   who;
    struct rusage ruse;
```

```
        fprintf (stdout,"get process id\n");
        who = getpid();

        fprintf (stdout, "get process current scheduling priority\n");
        sleep(2);
        getrusage_value = getrusage (who, &ruse);
        fprintf (stdout,"getrusage_value=%d\n", getrusage_value);
        fprintf (stdout,"user time used=%d\n", ruse.ru_utime.tv_sec);
        fprintf (stdout,"system time used=%d\n", ruse.ru_stime.tv_sec);
}
```

NAME

gets — get a string from *stdin* stream

SYNOPSIS

```
#include <stdio.h>

char *gets(char *s);
```

DESCRIPTION

The *gets*( ) function reads bytes from the standard input stream, *stdin,* into the array pointed to by *s*, until a newline is read or an end-of-file condition is encountered. Any newline is discarded and a null byte is placed immediately after the last byte read into the array.

The *gets*( ) function may mark the *st_atime* field of the file associated with *stream* for update. The *st_atime* field will be marked for update by the first successful execution of *fgetc*( ), *fgets*( ), *fread*( ), *getc*( ), *getchar*( ), *gets*( ), *fscanf*( ) or *scanf*( ) using *stream* that returns data not supplied by a prior call to *ungetc*( ).

RETURN VALUE

Upon successful completion, *gets*( ) returns *s*. If the stream is at end-of-file, the end-of-file indicator for the stream is set and *gets*( ) returns a null pointer. If a read error occurs, the error indicator for the stream is set, *gets*( ) returns a null pointer and sets *errno* to indicate the error.

ERRORS

Refer to *fgetc*( ).

APPLICATION USAGE

Reading a line that overflows the array pointed to by *s* causes undefined results. The use of *fgets*( ) is recommended.

SEE ALSO

feof( ), *ferror*( ), *fgets*( ), **<stdio.h>**.

EXAMPLE

```
/*
 * Copyright (C) ANTRIX Inc.
 */

/* gets.c
 * This program gets a string from stdin stream using function
 * gets.
 */

#include <stdio.h>
#include <stdlib.h>
#include <sys/types.h>
#include <errno.h>

main()
{
  char   *gets_value;
  char    string[12];

  memset(string,' ', 12);

  fprintf (stdout,"Type a string and hit return key\n");
  gets_value = gets (string);
```

```
    fprintf (stdout,"string typed is=%s\n", gets_value);
}
```

NAME

getsid — get process group ID of session leader

SYNOPSIS

UX
```
#include <unistd.h>

pid_t getsid(pid_t pid);
```

DESCRIPTION

The *getsid*( ) function obtains the process group ID of the process that is the session leader of the process specified by *pid*. If *pid* is (**pid_t**)0, it specifies the calling process.

RETURN VALUE

Upon successful completion, *getsid*( ) returns the process group ID of the session leader of the specified process. Otherwise, it returns (**pid_t**)–1 and sets *errno* to indicate the error.

ERRORS

The *getsid*( ) function will fail if:

[EPERM]   The process specified by *pid* is not in the same session as the calling process, and the implementation does not allow access to the process group ID of the session leader of that process from the calling process.

[ESRCH]   There is no process with a process ID equal to *pid*.

SEE ALSO

exec, *fork*( ), *getpid*( ), *getpgid*( ), *setpgid*( ), *setsid*( ), **<unistd.h>**.

EXAMPLE

```
/*
 * Copyright (C) ANTRIX Inc.
 */

/* getsid.c
 * This program gets the session ID of the process whose ID
 * is equal to pid using function getsid
 */

#include <stdio.h>
#include <stdlib.h>
#include <sys/types.h>
#include <errno.h>

main()
{
  int     getsid_value;
  int     setsid_value;
  int     stat_loc, pid;

  if ( fork() == 0 ) {
      fprintf (stdout,"current group-id=%d\n", getpgrp());
      pid = getpid ();
      getsid_value = getsid(pid);
      if ( getsid_value >= 0 ) {
          fprintf (stdout,"getsid() call successful\n");
          fprintf (stdout,"current session-id=%d\n", getsid_value);
          setsid_value = setsid ();
```

```
            fprintf (stdout,"setsid_value=%d\n", setsid_value);
            fprintf (stdout,"new group-id=%d\n", getpgrp());
            fprintf (stdout,"new session-id=%d\n", getsid(pid));
        }
        else {
            fprintf (stderr,"ERROR: getsid() call failed\n");
            fprintf (stderr,"ERROR: %s\n", strerror(errno));
        }
        exit (1);
    } wait(&stat_loc);
}
```

NAME

getsubopt — parse suboption arguments from a string

SYNOPSIS

UX

```
#include <stdlib.h>
```

```
int getsubopt(char **optionp, char * const *tokens, char **valuep);
```

DESCRIPTION

The *getsubopt( )* function parses suboption arguments in a flag argument that was initially parsed by *getopt( )*. These suboption arguments must be separated by commas and may consist of either a single token, or a token-value pair separated by an equal sign. Because commas delimit suboption arguments in the option string, they are not allowed to be part of the suboption arguments or the value of a suboption argument. Similarly, because the equal sign separates a token from its value, a token must not contain an equal sign.

The *getsubopt( )* function takes the address of a pointer to the option argument string, a vector of possible tokens, and the address of a value string pointer. If the option argument string at **optionp* contains only one suboption argument, *getsubopt( )* updates **optionp* to point to the null at the end of the string. Otherwise, it isolates the suboption argument by replacing the comma separator with a null, and updates **optionp* to point to the start of the next suboption argument. If the suboption argument has an associated value, *getsubopt( )* updates **valuep* to point to the value's first character. Otherwise it sets **valuep* to a null pointer.

The token vector is organised as a series of pointers to strings. The end of the token vector is identified by a null pointer.

When *getsubopt( )* returns, if **valuep* is not a null pointer then the suboption argument processed included a value. The calling program may use this information to determine if the presence or lack of a value for this suboption is an error.

Additionally, when *getsubopt( )* fails to match the suboption argument with the tokens in the *tokens* array, the calling program should decide if this is an error, or if the unrecognised option should be passed on to another program.

RETURN VALUE

The *getsubopt( )* function returns the index of the matched token string, or −1 if no token strings were matched.

ERRORS

No errors are defined.

SEE ALSO

getopt( ), **<stdlib.h>**.

EXAMPLE

```
/*
 * Copyright (C) ANTRIX Inc.
 */


/* getsubopt.c
 * This program parses the suboptions from a flag argument
 * using function getsubopt
 */

#include <stdio.h>
#include <stdlib.h>
#include <errno.h>
```

```
extern char *optarg;

char *myopts[] = {
#define READ    0
            "read" ,
#define WRITE   1
            "write" ,
             0
};

main(argc, argv)
int argc;
char *argv[];
{
  int      c, errflag;
  char     *options, *value;

  /* getopt [-a] [-b] [-c file] [-o read/write] */
  fprintf (stdout,"start processing options\n");
  while (( c = getopt (argc, argv, "abc:o:")) != -1) {
        switch (c) {
        case 'a':
                fprintf (stdout,"option typed is 'a'\n");
                break;
        case 'b':
                fprintf (stdout,"option typed is 'b'\n");
                break;
        case 'c':
                fprintf (stdout,"option typed is 'c' file\n");
                break;
        case '?':
                errflag++;
                break;
        case 'o':
                options = optarg;
                /* start processing suboptions */
                while (*options != ' ') {
                    switch (getsubopt (&options, myopts, &value)) {
                    case READ :
                        fprintf (stdout,"suboption typed is read\n");
                        break;
                    case WRITE :
                        fprintf (stdout,"suboption typed is write\n");
                        break;
                    default :
                        fprintf (stdout,"unknow token\n");
                        errflag++;
                        break;
                    }
                } /* end processing suboptions */
                break;
        }
```

```
    } /* end processing options */
    if (errflag)
        fprintf (stdout,"usage: getopt [-a] [-b] [-c file] [-o read/write]\n");
}

#if 0
/*
 * getsubopt - use this function if getsubopt is not defined
 *
 */
#ifdef __STDC__
        #pragma weak getsubopt = _getsubopt
#endif
#if 0
#include "synonyms.h"
#endif
#include <string.h>
#include <stdio.h>
#include <stdlib.h>

int
getsubopt(char **optionsp, char * const *tokens, char **valuep)
{
        register char *s = *optionsp, *p;
        register int i, optlen;

        *valuep = NULL;
        if (*s == ' ')
                return (-1);
        p = strchr(s, ',');          /* find next option */
        if (p == NULL) {
                p = s + strlen(s);
        } else {
                *p++ = ' ';          /* mark end and point to next */
        }
        *optionsp = p;                      /* point to next option */
        p = strchr(s, '=');          /* find value */
        if (p == NULL) {
                optlen = strlen(s);
                *valuep = NULL;
        } else {
                optlen = p - s;
                *valuep = ++p;
        }
        for (i = 0; tokens[i] != NULL; i++) {
                if ((optlen == strlen(tokens[i])) &&
                    (strncmp(s, tokens[i], optlen) == 0))
                        return (i);
        }
        /* no match, point value at option and return error */
        *valuep = s;
```

```
        return (-1);
}
#endif
```

NAME

gettimeofday — get the date and time

SYNOPSIS

UX   `#include <sys/time.h>`

`int gettimeofday(struct timeval *tp, void *tzp);`

DESCRIPTION

The *gettimeofday*( ) function obtains the current time, expressed as seconds and microseconds since 00:00 Coordinated Universal Time (UTC), January 1, 1970, and stores it in the **timeval** structure pointed to by *tp.* The resolution of the system clock is unspecified.

If *tzp* is not a null pointer, the behaviour is unspecified.

RETURN VALUE

The *gettimeofday*( ) function returns 0 and no value is reserved to indicate an error.

ERRORS

No errors are defined.

SEE ALSO

ctime( ), *ftime*( ), **<sys/time.h>**.

EXAMPLE

```
/*
 * Copyright (C) ANTRIX Inc.
 */

/* gettimeofday.c
 * This program gets date and time using function gettimeofday
 */

#include <stdio.h>
#include <stdlib.h>
#include <time.h>
#include <sys/time.h>
#include <errno.h>


main()
{
  int      gettimeofday_value ;
  struct   timeval tp;

  fprintf (stdout,"get time and date\n");
  gettimeofday_value = gettimeofday (&tp, (void *)0);
  if ( gettimeofday_value != -1 ) {
      fprintf (stdout,"gettimeofday() call successful\n");
      fprintf (stdout,"tp.tv_sec=%d\n", tp.tv_sec);
      fprintf (stdout,"tp.tv_usec=%d\n", tp.tv_usec);
  }
  else
      fprintf (stderr,"ERROR: gettimeofday() call failed\n");
}
```

NAME

getuid — get real user ID

SYNOPSIS

OH #include <sys/types.h>
#include <unistd.h>

uid_t getuid (void);

DESCRIPTION

The *getuid*( ) function returns the real user ID of the calling process.

RETURN VALUE

The *getuid*( ) function is always successful and no return value is reserved to indicate the error.

ERRORS

No errors are defined.

SEE ALSO

geteuid( ), *getgid*( ), *setuid*( ), **<sys/types.h>**, **<unistd.h>**.

EXAMPLE

```
/*
 * Copyright (C) ANTRIX Inc.
 */

/* getuid.c
 * This program returns real user ID of the calling process using
 * function getuid.
 */

#include <stdio.h>
#include <stdlib.h>
#include <sys/types.h>
#include <unistd.h>
#include <errno.h>

main()
{
  uid_t  getuid_value;

  fprintf (stdout,"get user id\n");
  getuid_value = getuid ();
  fprintf (stdout,"getuid_value=%d\n", getuid_value);
}
```

getutxent( )

NAME

getutxent, getutxid, getutxline — get user accounting database entries

SYNOPSIS

UX   `#include <utmpx.h>`

```
struct utmpx *getutxent(void);
```

```
struct utmpx *getutxid(const struct utmpx *id);
```

```
struct utmpx *getutxline(const struct utmpx *line);
```

DESCRIPTION

Refer to *endutxent( )*.

NAME

getw — get a word from a stream

SYNOPSIS

EX   `#include <stdio.h>`

`int getw(FILE *stream);`

DESCRIPTION

The *getw*( ) function reads the next word from the *stream*. The size of a word is the size of an **int** and may vary from machine to machine. The *getw*( ) function presumes no special alignment in the file.

The *getw*( ) function may mark the *st_atime* field of the file associated with *stream* for update. The *st_atime* field will be marked for update by the first successful execution of *fgetc*( ), *fgets*( ), *fread*( ), *getc*( ), *getchar*( ), *gets*( ), *fscanf*( ) or *scanf*( ) using *stream* that returns data not supplied by a prior call to *ungetc*( ).

RETURN VALUE

Upon successful completion, *getw*( ) returns the next word from the input stream pointed to by *stream*. If the stream is at end-of-file, the end-of-file indicator for the stream is set and *getw*( ) returns EOF. If a read error occurs, the error indicator for the stream is set, *getw*( ) returns EOF and sets *errno* to indicate the error.

ERRORS

Refer to *fgetc*( ).

APPLICATION USAGE

Because of possible differences in word length and byte ordering, files written using *putw*( ) are machine-dependent, and may not be read using *getw*( ) on a different processor.

Because the representation of EOF is a valid integer, applications wishing to check for errors should use *ferror*( ) and *feof*( ).

SEE ALSO

feof( ), *ferror*( ), *getc*( ), *putw*( ), **<stdio.h>**, **<utmpx.h>**.

EXAMPLE

```
/*
 * Copyright (C) ANTRIX Inc.
 */

/* getw.c
 * This program reads the next word from the stream using function
 * getw.
 */

#include <stdio.h>
#include <stdlib.h>
#include <fcntl.h>
#include <sys/stat.h>
#include <errno.h>

#define  PERM_ALL   (S_IRWXU | S_IRWXG | S_IRWXO)
#define  OFLAG      (O_CREAT | O_WRONLY | O_TRUNC)

main()
```

```
    {
        int    i, getw_value;
        int    fildes, length;
        char   buf[6];
        char   *filename = "testfile";
        FILE   *stream;

        memset (buf, ' ', 6);

        fprintf (stdout,"create and open testfile\n");
        fildes = open (filename, OFLAG, PERM_ALL);

        fprintf (stdout,"write string to testfile\n");
        for ( i = 0; i < 5; i++ )
            write (fildes, (char *)&i, sizeof (i));
        fprintf (stdout,"close testfile\n");
        close (fildes);

        fprintf (stdout,"open testfile\n");
        stream = fopen (filename, "r+");

        fprintf (stdout,"read word\n");
        for ( i = 0; i < 5; i++ ) {
            getw_value = getw (stream);
            fprintf (stdout,"%d\n", getw_value);
        }
        fclose (stream);
        fprintf (stdout,"remove testfile\n");
        remove ("testfile");
    }
```

NAME

getwc — get wide character from a stream

SYNOPSIS

OH   `#include <stdio.h>`
WP   `#include <wchar.h>`

```
wint_t getwc(FILE *stream);
```

DESCRIPTION

The *getwc( )* function is equivalent to *fgetwc( )*, except that if it is implemented as a macro it may evaluate *stream* more than once, so the argument should never be an expression with side effects.

RETURN VALUE

Refer to *fgetwc( )*.

ERRORS

Refer to *fgetwc( )*.

APPLICATION USAGE

This interface is provided in order to align with some current implementations, and with possible future ISO standards.

Because it may be implemented as a macro, *getwc( )* may treat incorrectly a *stream* argument with side effects. In particular, *getwc(*f++)* may not work as expected. Therefore, use of this function is not recommended; *fgetwc( )* should be used instead.

SEE ALSO

fgetwc( ), **<stdio.h>**, **<wchar.h>**.

EXAMPLE

```
/*
 * Copyright (C) ANTRIX Inc.
 */

/* getwc.c
 * This program gets wide character from a stream using function
 * getwc.
 */

#include <stdio.h>
#include <stdlib.h>
#include <wchar.h>
#include <sys/types.h>
#include <errno.h>

main()
{
    FILE     *stream;
    int      i, bytes;
    wint_t   getwc_value;
    wchar_t  buf[12];
    wchar_t  *ws = L"hello world";
    char     *filename = "testfile";

    memset (buf, ' ', 12);
```

```
        bytes = wcslen(ws);

        fprintf (stdout,"create and open testfile\n");
        stream = fopen (filename, "w+r");

        fprintf (stdout,"write string to testfile\n");
        fputws(ws, stream);
        fflush (stream);

        fprintf (stdout,"seek to beginning of testfile\n");
        fseek (stream, 0, SEEK_SET);

        fprintf (stdout,"get one wide character at a time\n");
        for ( i = 0; i < 11; i++ ) {
            getwc_value = getwc (stream);
            fprintf (stdout,"%wc", getwc_value);
        }
        fprintf (stdout,"\n");
        fprintf (stdout,"remove testfile\n");
        remove (filename);
}
```

NAME

getwchar — get wide character from *stdin* stream

SYNOPSIS

WP

```
#include <wchar.h>
```

```
wint_t getwchar(void);
```

DESCRIPTION

The *getwchar*( ) function is equivalent to *getwc*(*stdin*).

RETURN VALUE

Refer to *fgetwc*( ).

ERRORS

Refer to *fgetwc*( ).

APPLICATION USAGE

If the value returned by *getwchar*( ) is stored into a variable of type **wchar_t** and then compared against the **wint_t** macro WEOF, the comparison may never succeed.

SEE ALSO

fgetwc( ), *getwc*( ), **<wchar.h>**.

EXAMPLE

```
/*
 * Copyright (C) ANTRIX Inc.
 */

/* getwchar.c
 * This program gets wide character from stdin stream using
 * function getwchar.
 */

#include <stdio.h>
#include <stdlib.h>
#include <wchar.h>
#include <errno.h>

main()
{
    int   getwchar_value;

    fprintf (stdout,"Type a wide character and hit return key\n");
    getwchar_value = getwchar ();
    fprintf (stdout,"character typed is %wc\n", getwchar_value);
}
```

NAME

getwd — get the current working directory pathname

SYNOPSIS

UX
```
#include <unistd.h>

char *getwd(char *path_name);
```

DESCRIPTION

The *getwd*( ) function determines an absolute pathname of the current working directory of the calling process, and copies that pathname into the array pointed to by the *path_name* argument.

If the length of the pathname of the current working directory is greater than ({PATH_MAX} + 1) including the null byte, *getwd*( ) fails and returns a null pointer.

RETURN VALUE

Upon successful completion, a pointer to the string containing the absolute pathname of the current working directory is returned. Otherwise, *getwd*( ) returns a null pointer and the contents of the array pointed to by *path_name* are undefined.

ERRORS

No errors are defined.

APPLICATION USAGE

For portability to implementations conforming to earlier versions of this document, *getcwd*( ) is preferred over this function.

SEE ALSO

getcwd( ), **<unistd.h>**.

```
/*
 * Copyright (C) ANTRIX Inc.
 */

/* getwd.c
 * This program places an absolute pathname of the current working
 * directory in the array pointed to by buf, and returns buf using
 * function getwd.
 */

#include <stdio.h>
#include <stdlib.h>
#include <unistd.h>
#include <limits.h>
#include <errno.h>

#define  PATH_LEN   255

main()
{
  char   *getwd_value;
  char   buf[PATH_LEN];

  memset(buf, ' ', PATH_LEN);
  fprintf (stdout,"get current working directory\n");

  getwd_value = getwd (buf, PATH_LEN);
```

```
    if ( getwd_value != (char *)0 ) {
        fprintf (stdout,"getwd() call successful\n");
        fprintf (stdout,"current directory/buf=%s\n", buf);
        fprintf (stdout,"current directory/getwd_value=%s\n",
                        getwd_value);
    }
    else {
        fprintf (stderr,"ERROR: getwd() call failed\n");
        fprintf (stderr,"ERROR: %s\n", strerror(errno));
    }
}
```

NAME

glob, globfree — generate pathnames matching a pattern

SYNOPSIS

```
#include <glob.h>

int glob(const char *pattern, int flags,
        int(*errfunc)(const char *epath, int eerrno), glob_t *pglob);

void globfree(glob_t *pglob);
```

DESCRIPTION

The *glob*( ) function is a pathname generator that implements the rules defined in the **XCU** specification, **Section 2.13**, **Pattern Matching Notation**, with optional support for rule 3 in the **XCU** specification, **Section 2.13.3**, **Patterns Used for Filename Expansion**.

The structure type **glob_t** is defined in the header **<glob.h>** and includes at least the following members:

Member Type	Member Name	Description
size_t	gl_pathc	Count of paths matched by *pattern*.
char **	gl_pathv	Pointer to a list of matched pathnames.
size_t	gl_offs	Slots to reserve at the beginning of **gl_pathv**.

The argument *pattern* is a pointer to a pathname pattern to be expanded. The *glob*( ) function matches all accessible pathnames against this pattern and develops a list of all pathnames that match. In order to have access to a pathname, *glob*( ) requires search permission on every component of a path except the last, and read permission on each directory of any filename component of *pattern* that contains any of the following special characters:

          *   ?   [

The *glob*( ) function stores the number of matched pathnames into *pglob*–>**gl_pathc** and a pointer to a list of pointers to pathnames into *pglob*–>**gl_pathv**. The pathnames are in sort order as defined by the current setting of the LC_COLLATE category, see the **XBD** specification, **Section 5.3.2**, **LC_COLLATE** . The first pointer after the last pathname is a null pointer. If the pattern does not match any pathnames, the returned number of matched paths is set to 0, and the contents of *pglob*->**gl_pathv** are implementation-dependent.

It is the caller's responsibility to create the structure pointed to by *pglob*. The *glob*( ) function allocates other space as needed, including the memory pointed to by **gl_pathv**. The *globfree*( ) function frees any space associated with *pglob* from a previous call to *glob*( ).

The *flags* argument is used to control the behaviour of *glob*( ). The value of *flags* is a bitwise inclusive OR of zero or more of the following constants, which are defined in the header **<glob.h>**:

GLOB_APPEND   Append pathnames generated to the ones from a previous call to *glob*( ).

GLOB_DOOFFS   Make use of *pglob*–>**gl_offs**. If this flag is set, *pglob*–>**gl_offs** is used to specify how many null pointers to add to the beginning of *pglob*–>**gl_pathv**. In other words, *pglob*–>**gl_pathv** will point to *pglob*–>**gl_offs** null pointers, followed by *pglob*–>**gl_pathc** pathname pointers, followed by a null pointer.
he 2

GLOB_ERR   Causes *glob*( ) to return when it encounters a directory that it cannot open or read. Ordinarily, *glob*( ) continues to find matches.

GLOB_MARK   Each pathname that is a directory that matches *pattern* has a slash appended.

GLOB_NOCHECK   Support rule 3 in the **XCU** specification, **Section 2.13.3**, **Patterns Used for Filename Expansion**. If *pattern* does not match any pathname, then *glob*( ) returns a list consisting of only *pattern*, and the number of matched pathnames is 1.

GLOB_NOESCAPE   Disable backslash escaping.

GLOB_NOSORT   Ordinarily, *glob*( ) sorts the matching pathnames according to the current setting of the LC_COLLATE category, see the **XBD** specification, **Section 5.3.2**, **LC_COLLATE** . When this flag is used the order of pathnames returned is unspecified.

The GLOB_APPEND flag can be used to append a new set of pathnames to those found in a previous call to *glob*( ). The following rules apply when two or more calls to *glob*( ) are made with the same value of *pglob* and without intervening calls to *globfree*( ):

1. The first such call must not set GLOB_APPEND. All subsequent calls must set it.

2. All the calls must set GLOB_DOOFFS, or all must not set it.

3. After the second call, *pglob*–>**gl_pathv** points to a list containing the following:

    a. Zero or more null pointers, as specified by GLOB_DOOFFS and *pglob*–>**gl_offs**.

    b. Pointers to the pathnames that were in the *pglob*–>**gl_pathv** list before the call, in the same order as before.

    c. Pointers to the new pathnames generated by the second call, in the specified order.

4. The count returned in *pglob*–>**gl_pathc** will be the total number of pathnames from the two calls.

5. The application can change any of the fields after a call to *glob*( ). If it does, it must reset them to the original value before a subsequent call, using the same *pglob* value, to *globfree*( ) or *glob*( ) with the GLOB_APPEND flag.

If, during the search, a directory is encountered that cannot be opened or read and *errfunc* is not a null pointer, *glob*( ) calls (**errfunc*( )) with two arguments:

1. The *epath* argument is a pointer to the path that failed.

2. The *eerrno* argument is the value of *errno* from the failure, as set by *opendir*( ), *readdir*( ) or *stat*( ). (Other values may be used to report other errors not explicitly documented for those functions.)

The following constants are defined as error return values for *glob*( ):

GLOB_ABORTED   The scan was stopped because GLOB_ERR was set or (**errfunc*( )) returned non-zero.

GLOB_NOMATCH   The pattern does not match any existing pathname, and GLOB_NOCHECK was not set in flags.

GLOB_NOSPACE   An attempt to allocate memory failed.

If (**errfunc)*( ) is called and returns non-zero, or if the GLOB_ERR flag is set in *flags*, *glob*( ) stops the scan and returns GLOB_ABORTED after setting *gl_pathc* and *gl_pathv* in *pglob* to reflect the paths already scanned. If GLOB_ERR is not set and either *errfunc* is a null pointer or (**errfunc*( )) returns 0, the error is ignored.

RETURN VALUE

On successful completion, *glob*( ) returns 0. The argument *pglob*->**gl_pathc** returns the number of matched pathnames and the argument *pglob*->**gl_pathv** contains a pointer to a null-terminated list of matched and sorted pathnames. However, if *pglob*->**gl_pathc** is 0, the content of *pglob*->**gl_pathv** is undefined.

The *globfree*( ) function returns no value.

If *glob*( ) terminates due to an error, it returns one of the non-zero constants defined in **<glob.h>**. The arguments *pglob*->**gl_pathc** and *pglob*->**gl_pathv** are still set as defined above.

ERRORS

No errors are defined.

EXAMPLES

One use of the GLOB_DOOFFS flag is by applications that build an argument list for use with *execv*( ), *execve*( ) or *execvp*( ). Suppose, for example, that an application wants to do the equivalent of:

```
ls -l *.c
```

but for some reason:

```
system("ls -l *.c")
```

is not acceptable. The application could obtain approximately the same result using the sequence:

```
globbuf.gl_offs = 2;
glob ("*.c", GLOB_DOOFFS, NULL, &globbuf);
globbuf.gl_pathv[0] = "ls";
globbuf.gl_pathv[1] = "-l";
execvp ("ls", &globbuf.gl_pathv[0]);
```

Using the same example:

```
ls -l *.c *.h
```

could be approximately simulated using GLOB_APPEND as follows:

```
globbuf.gl_offs = 2;
glob ("*.c", GLOB_DOOFFS, NULL, &globbuf);
glob ("*.h", GLOB_DOOFFS|GLOB_APPEND, NULL, &globbuf);
   ...
```

APPLICATION USAGE

This function is not provided for the purpose of enabling utilities to perform pathname expansion on their arguments, as this operation is performed by the shell, and utilities are explicitly not expected to redo this. Instead, it is provided for applications that need to do pathname expansion on strings obtained from other sources, such as a pattern typed by a user or read from a file.

If a utility needs to see if a pathname matches a given pattern, it can use *fnmatch*( ).

Note that **gl_pathc** and **gl_pathv** have meaning even if *glob*( ) fails. This allows *glob*( ) to report partial results in the event of an error. However, if **gl_pathc** is 0, **gl_pathv** is unspecified even if *glob*( ) did not return an error.

The GLOB_NOCHECK option could be used when an application wants to expand a pathname if wildcards are specified, but wants to treat the pattern as just a string otherwise. The *sh* utility might use this for option-arguments, for example.

The new pathnames generated by a subsequent call with GLOB_APPEND are not sorted together with the previous pathnames. This mirrors the way that the shell handles pathname expansion when multiple expansions are done on a command line.

Applications that need tilde and parameter expansion should use *wordexp*( ).

SEE ALSO

execv( ), *fnmatch*( ), *opendir*( ), *readdir*( ), *stat*( ), *wordexp*( ), **<glob.h>**, the **XCU** specification.

EXAMPLE

```
/*
 * Copyright (C) ANTRIX Inc.
 */

/* glob.c
 * This program generates pathname matching a pattern
 * using function glob.
 */

#include <stdio.h>
#include <stdlib.h>
#include <glob.h>
#include <errno.h>

main()
{
    int     glob_value;
    int     flags;
    glob_t globbuf;

    globbuf.gl_offs = 2;
    glob_value = glob("*.c", GLOB_DOOFFS, NULL, &globbuf);
    if ( glob_value == 0 )
        fprintf (stdout,"glob() call successful\n");
    else {
        fprintf (stderr,"ERROR: glob() call failed\n");
        fprintf (stderr,"ERROR: %s\n", strerror(errno));
    }
    globbuf.gl_pathv[0] = "ls";
    globbuf.gl_pathv[1] = "-l";
    fprintf (stdout,"execute ls binary\n");
    execvp("ls", &globbuf.gl_pathv[0]);
    globfree();
}
```

NAME

gmtime — convert time value to broken-down UTC time

SYNOPSIS

```
#include <time.h>

struct tm *gmtime(const time_t *timer);
```

DESCRIPTION

The *gmtime*( ) function converts the time in seconds since the Epoch pointed to by *timer* into a broken-down time, expressed as Coordinated Universal Time (UTC).

RETURN VALUE

The *gmtime*( ) function returns a pointer to a **struct tm**.

ERRORS

No errors are defined.

APPLICATION USAGE

The *asctime*( ), *ctime*( ), *gmtime*( ) and *localtime*( ) functions return values in one of two static objects: a broken-down time structure and an array of **char**. Execution of any of the functions may overwrite the information returned in either of these objects by any of the other functions.

SEE ALSO

asctime( ), *clock*( ), *ctime*( ), *difftime*( ), *localtime*( ), *mktime*( ), *strftime*( ), *strptime*( ), *time*( ), *utime*( ), **<time.h>**.

EXAMPLE

```
/*
 * Copyright (C) ANTRIX Inc.
 */

/* gmtime.c
 * This program converts time value to broken-down time using
 * function gmtime.
 */

#include <stdio.h>
#include <stdlib.h>
#include <time.h>
#include <errno.h>

main()
{
   char    *current_time;
   time_t  tloc;
   time_t  clock;
   struct  tm  *buf;

   fprintf (stdout,"get current time\n");
   clock = time (&tloc);
   buf = gmtime (&clock);

   fprintf (stdout,"convert date and time to string\n");
   if ( buf != (struct tm *)0 ) {
       fprintf (stdout,"gmtime() call successful\n");
```

```
        current_time = asctime (buf);
        fprintf (stdout,"current time is %s\n", current_time);
    }
  else
      fprintf (stderr,"ERROR: gmtime() call failed\n");
  }
```

NAME

grantpt — grant access to the slave pseudo-terminal device

SYNOPSIS

UX

```
#include <stdlib.h>

int grantpt(int fildes);
```

DESCRIPTION

The *grantpt*( ) function changes the mode and ownership of the slave pseudo-terminal device associated with its master pseudo-terminal counter part. The *fildes* argument is a file descriptor that refers to a master pseudo-terminal device. The user ID of the slave is set to the real UID of the calling process and the group ID is set to an unspecified group ID. The permission mode of the slave pseudo-terminal is set to readable and writable by the owner, and writable by the group.

RETURN VALUE

Upon successful completion, *grantpt*( ) returns 0. Otherwise, it returns −1 and sets *errno* to indicate the error.

ERRORS

The *grantpt*( ) function may fail if:

[EBADF]   The *fildes* argument is not a valid open file descriptor.

[EINVAL]   The *fildes* argument is not associated with a master pseudo-terminal device.

[EACCES]   The corresponding slave pseudo-terminal device could not be accessed.

APPLICATION USAGE

The *grantpt*( ) function may also fail if the application has installed a signal handler to catch SIGCHLD signals.

SEE ALSO

open( ), *ptsname*( ), *unlockpt*( ), **<stdlib.h>**.

EXAMPLE

```
/*
 * Copyright (C) ANTRIX Inc.
 */

/* grantpt.c
 * This program grants access to the slave pseudo-terminal
 * device using function grantpt
 */

#include <stdio.h>
#include <stdlib.h>
#include <fcntl.h>
#include <errno.h>

/* name of the master pseudo-terminal device */
/* this name may be different in your machine */
#define MASTER        "/dev/ptmx"

main()
{
    int      grantpt_value;
```

```
int      fildes;
char     *ptsname_value;
char     *name;

fprintf (stdout,"open master terminal device\n");
fildes = open (MASTER, O_RDWR);

fprintf (stdout,"grant access to the slave pseudo-terminal device\n");
grantpt_value = grantpt (fildes);
if ( grantpt_value == 0 )
   fprintf (stdout,"grantpt() call successful\n");
else {
   fprintf (stderr,"ERROR: grantpt() call failed\n");
   fprintf (stderr,"ERROR: %s\n", strerror(errno));
}
fprintf (stdout,"unlock device\n");
unlockpt (fildes);

ptsname_value = (char *)ptsname (fildes);
fprintf (stdout,"name of the slave pseudo-terminal=%s\n", ptsname_value);
fprintf (stdout,"close device\n");
close (fildes);
}
```

NAME

hcreate — create hash search tables

SYNOPSIS

EX   `#include <search.h>`

`int hcreate(size_t nel);`

DESCRIPTION

Refer to *hsearch*( ).

EXAMPLE

```
/*
 * Copyright (C) ANTRIX Inc.
 */

/* hcreate.c
 * This program creates hash table searches using function hcreate.
 */

#include <stdio.h>
#include <stdlib.h>
#include <search.h>
#include <string.h>
#include <errno.h>

#define   TABLESIZE   5

main()
{
   int     i, hcreate_value;
   char    strkey[TABLESIZE][5];
   char    strdata[TABLESIZE][5];
   ENTRY   find, *buf, *found;
   ENTRY   item[TABLESIZE] ;

   fprintf (stdout,"create table\n");
   hcreate_value = hcreate (TABLESIZE);
   if ( hcreate_value != 0 )
      fprintf (stdout,"hcreate() call successful\n");
   else
      fprintf (stderr,"ERROR: hcreate() call failed\n");

   fprintf (stdout,"assign table with following value\n");
   for ( i = 0; i < 5; i++ ) {
       sprintf (strkey[i], "%d", (2*i));
       sprintf (strdata[i], "%d", (4*i));
       item[i].key = (char *)strkey[i];
       item[i].data = (void *)strdata[i];
       buf = hsearch (item[i], TABLESIZE);
       fprintf (stdout,"key=%s, data=%s\n", buf->key, buf->data);
   }

   fprintf (stdout,"search table for key=4 and data=8\n");
```

```
        find.key = (char *)"4";
        find.data = (char *)"8";

        found = hsearch (find, FIND);
        fprintf (stdout,"found->key=%s\n", found->key);
        fprintf (stdout,"found->data=%s\n", found->data);

        fprintf (stdout,"destroy table\n");
        hdestroy ();
}
```

NAME
hdestroy — destroy hash search tables

SYNOPSIS
EX   `#include <search.h>`

`void hdestroy(void);`

DESCRIPTION
Refer to *hsearch( )*.

EXAMPLE
```
/*
 * Copyright (C) ANTRIX Inc.
 */

/* hdestroy.c
 * This program destroys the hash search tables using function
 * hdestroy.
 */

#include <stdio.h>
#include <stdlib.h>
#include <search.h>
#include <string.h>
#include <errno.h>

#define   TABLESIZE   5

main()
{
  int      i;
  char     strkey[TABLESIZE][5];
  char     strdata[TABLESIZE][5];
  ENTRY    find, *buf, *found;
  ENTRY    item[TABLESIZE] ;

  fprintf (stdout,"create table\n");
  hcreate (TABLESIZE);

  fprintf (stdout,"assign table with following value\n");
  for ( i = 0; i < 5; i++ ) {
      sprintf (strkey[i], "%d", (2*i));
      sprintf (strdata[i], "%d", (4*i));
      item[i].key = (char *)strkey[i];
      item[i].data = (void *)strdata[i];
      buf = hsearch (item[i], TABLESIZE);
      fprintf (stdout,"key=%s, data=%s\n", buf->key, buf->data);
  }

  fprintf (stdout,"search table for key=4 and data=8\n");
  find.key = (char *)"4";
  find.data = (char *)"8";
```

```
        found = hsearch (find, FIND);
        fprintf (stdout,"found->key=%s\n", found->key);
        fprintf (stdout,"found->data=%s\n", found->data);

        fprintf (stdout,"destroy table\n");
        hdestroy ();
}
```

NAME

hsearch, hcreate, hdestroy — manage hash search tables

SYNOPSIS

EX
```
#include <search.h>
```

```
ENTRY *hsearch (ENTRY item, ACTION action);
```

```
int hcreate(size_t nel);
```

```
void hdestroy(void);
```

DESCRIPTION

The *hsearch*( ) function is a hash-table search routine. It returns a pointer into a hash table indicating the location at which an entry can be found. The *item* argument is a structure of type **ENTRY** (defined in the **<search.h>** header) containing two pointers: *item.key* points to the comparison key (a **char ***), and *item.data* (a **void ***) points to any other data to be associated with that key. The comparison function used by *hsearch*( ) is *strcmp*( ). The *action* argument is a member of an enumeration type **ACTION** indicating the disposition of the entry if it cannot be found in the table. ENTER indicates that the item should be inserted in the table at an appropriate point. FIND indicates that no entry should be made. Unsuccessful resolution is indicated by the return of a null pointer.

The *hcreate*( ) function allocates sufficient space for the table, and must be called before *hsearch*( ) is used. The *nel* argument is an estimate of the maximum number of entries that the table will contain. This number may be adjusted upward by the algorithm in order to obtain certain mathematically favourable circumstances.

The *hdestroy*( ) function disposes of the search table, and may be followed by another call to *hcreate*( ). After the call to *hdestroy*( ), the data can no longer be considered accessible.

RETURN VALUE

The *hsearch*( ) function returns a null pointer if either the action is FIND and the item could not be found or the action is ENTER and the table is full.

The *hcreate*( ) function returns 0 if it cannot allocate sufficient space for the table, and returns non-zero otherwise.

The *hdestroy*( ) function returns no value.

EXAMPLES

The following example will read in strings followed by two numbers and store them in a hash table, discarding duplicates. It will then read in strings and find the matching entry in the hash table and print it out.

```
#include <stdio.h>
#include <search.h>
#include <string.h>

struct info {              /* this is the info stored in the table */
    int age, room;         /* other than the key. */
};

#define NUM_EMPL   5000   /* # of elements in search table */
```

```
int main(void)
{
    char string_space[NUM_EMPL*20];     /* space to store strings */
    struct info info_space[NUM_EMPL];   /* space to store employee info*/
    char *str_ptr = string_space;       /* next space in string_space */
    struct info *info_ptr = info_space; /* next space in info_space */
    ENTRY item;
    ENTRY *found_item;                  /* name to look for in table */
    char name_to_find[30];

    int i = 0;

    /* create table; no error checking is performed */
    (void) hcreate(NUM_EMPL);
    while (scanf("%s%d%d", str_ptr, &info_ptr->age,
            &info_ptr->room) != EOF && i++ < NUM_EMPL) {

        /* put information in structure, and structure in item */
        item.key = str_ptr;
        item.data = info_ptr;
        str_ptr += strlen(str_ptr) + 1;
        info_ptr++;

        /* put item into table */
        (void) hsearch(item, ENTER);
    }

    /* access table */
    item.key = name_to_find;
    while (scanf("%s", item.key) != EOF) {
        if ((found_item = hsearch(item, FIND)) != NULL) {

            /* if item is in the table */
            (void)printf("found %s, age = %d, room = %d\n",
                found_item->key,
                ((struct info *)found_item->data)->age,
                ((struct info *)found_item->data)->room);
        } else
            (void)printf("no such employee %s\n", name_to_find);
    }
    return 0;
}
```

ERRORS

The *hsearch( )* and *hcreate( )* functions may fail if:

[ENOMEM]   Insufficient storage space is available.

APPLICATION USAGE

The *hsearch( )* and *hcreate( )* functions may use *malloc( )* to allocate space.

SEE ALSO

bsearch( ), *lsearch( )*, *malloc( )*, *strcmp( )*, *tsearch( )*, **<search.h>**.

EXAMPLE

```
/*
 * Copyright (C) ANTRIX Inc.
 */

/* hsearch.c
 * This program does a hash table search and returns a pointer
 * into hash table indicating the location at which an entry
 * can be found using function hsearch.
 */

#include <stdio.h>
#include <stdlib.h>
#include <search.h>
#include <string.h>
#include <errno.h>

#define   TABLESIZE   5

main()
{
  int      i;
  char     strkey[TABLESIZE][5];
  char     strdata[TABLESIZE][5];
  ENTRY    find, *buf, *found;
  ENTRY    item[TABLESIZE] ;

  fprintf (stdout,"create table\n");
  hcreate (TABLESIZE);

  fprintf (stdout,"assign table with following value\n");
  for ( i = 0; i < 5; i++ ) {
      sprintf (strkey[i], "%d", (2*i));
      sprintf (strdata[i], "%d", (4*i));
      item[i].key = (char *)strkey[i];
      item[i].data = (void *)strdata[i];
      buf = hsearch (item[i], TABLESIZE);
      fprintf (stdout,"key=%s, data=%s\n", buf->key, buf->data);
  }

  fprintf (stdout,"search table for key=4 and data=8\n");
  find.key = (char *)"4";
  find.data = (char *)"8";

  found = hsearch (find, FIND);
  if ( found != ( ENTRY *)0 ) {
      fprintf (stdout,"hsearch() call successful\n");
      fprintf (stdout,"found->key=%s\n", found->key);
      fprintf (stdout,"found->data=%s\n", found->data);
  }
  else
      fprintf (stderr,"ERROR: hsearch() call failed\n");
```

```
        fprintf (stdout,"destroy table\n");
        hdestroy ();
}
```

hypot( )

NAME

hypot — Euclidean distance function

SYNOPSIS

EX

```
#include <math.h>
```

```
double hypot(double x, double y);
```

DESCRIPTION

The *hypot*( ) function computes the length of the hypotenuse of a right-angled triangle:

$$\sqrt{x*x+y*y}$$

RETURN VALUE

Upon successful completion, *hypot*( ) returns the length of the hypotenuse of a right angled triangle with sides of length *x* and *y*.

If the result would cause overflow, HUGE_VAL is returned and *errno* may be set to [ERANGE].

If *x* or *y* is NaN, NaN is returned. and *errno* may be set to [EDOM].

If the correct result would cause underflow, 0 is returned and *errno* may be set to [ERANGE].

ERRORS

The *hypot*( ) function may fail if:

[EDOM]   The value of *x* or *y* is NaN.

[ERANGE]   The result overflows or underflows.

No other errors will occur.

APPLICATION USAGE

The *hypot*( ) function takes precautions against overflow during intermediate steps of the computation. If the calculated result would still overflow a double, then *hypot*( ) returns HUGE_VAL.

An application wishing to check for error situations should set *errno* to 0 before calling *hypot*( ). If *errno* is non-zero on return, or the return value is HUGE_VAL or NaN, an error has occurred.

SEE ALSO

isnan( ), *sqrt*( ), **<math.h>**.

EXAMPLE

```
/*
 * Copyright (C) ANTRIX Inc.
 */

/* hypot.c
 * This program computes the length of the hypotenuse of a
 * right-angled triangle using function hypot.
 */

#include <stdio.h>
#include <math.h>

main()
{
  double  hypot_value;
  double  x = 3.00;
```

```
        double  y = 4.00;

        hypot_value = hypot (x, y);
        fprintf (stdout,"hypot of %f, %f is %f\n", x, y, hypot_value);
}
```

NAME

iconv — code conversion function

SYNOPSIS

EX

```
#include <iconv.h>

size_t iconv(iconv_t cd, const char **inbuf, size_t *inbytesleft,
             char **outbuf, size_t *outbytesleft);
```

DESCRIPTION

The *iconv*( ) function converts the sequence of characters from one codeset, in the array specified by *inbuf*, into a sequence of corresponding characters in another codeset, in the array specified by *outbuf*. The codesets are those specified in the *iconv_open*( ) call that returned the conversion descriptor, *cd*. The *inbuf* argument points to a variable that points to the first character in the input buffer and *inbytesleft* indicates the number of bytes to the end of the buffer to be converted. The *outbuf* argument points to a variable that points to the first available byte in the output buffer and *outbytesleft* indicates the number of the available bytes to the end of the buffer.

For state-dependent encodings, the conversion descriptor *cd* is placed into its initial shift state by a call for which *inbuf* is a null pointer, or for which *inbuf* points to a null pointer. When *iconv*( ) is called in this way, and if *outbuf* is not a null pointer or a pointer to a null pointer, and *outbytesleft* points to a positive value, *iconv*( ) will place, into the output buffer, the byte sequence to change the output buffer to its initial shift state. If the output buffer is not large enough to hold the entire reset sequence, *iconv*( ) will fail and set *errno* to [E2BIG]. Subsequent calls with *inbuf* as other than a null pointer or a pointer to a null pointer cause the conversion to take place from the current state of the conversion descriptor.

If a sequence of input bytes does not form a valid character in the specified codeset, conversion stops after the previous successfully converted character. If the input buffer ends with an incomplete character or shift sequence, conversion stops after the previous successfully converted bytes. If the output buffer is not large enough to hold the entire converted input, conversion stops just prior to the input bytes that would cause the output buffer to overflow. The variable pointed to by *inbuf* is updated to point to the byte following the last byte successfully used in the conversion. The value pointed to by *inbytesleft* is decremented to reflect the number of bytes still not converted in the input buffer. The variable pointed to by *outbuf* is updated to point to the byte following the last byte of converted output data. The value pointed to by *outbytesleft* is decremented to reflect the number of bytes still available in the output buffer. For state-dependent encodings, the conversion descriptor is updated to reflect the shift state in effect at the end of the last successfully converted byte sequence.

If *iconv*( ) encounters a character in the input buffer that is valid, but for which an identical character does not exist in the target codeset, *iconv*( ) performs an implementation-dependent conversion on this character.

RETURN VALUE

The *iconv*( ) function updates the variables pointed to by the arguments to reflect the extent of the conversion and returns the number of non-identical conversions performed. If the entire string in the input buffer is converted, the value pointed to by *inbytesleft* will be 0. If the input conversion is stopped due to any conditions mentioned above, the value pointed to by *inbytesleft* will be non-zero and *errno* is set to indicate the condition. If an error occurs *iconv*( ) returns (**size_t**)–1 and sets *errno* to indicate the error.

ERRORS

The *iconv*( ) function will fail if:

[EILSEQ]   Input conversion stopped due to an input byte that does not belong to the input codeset.

[E2BIG]   Input conversion stopped due to lack of space in the output buffer.

[EINVAL]   Input conversion stopped due to an incomplete character or shift sequence at the end of the input buffer.

The *iconv*( ) function may fail if:

[EBADF]   The *cd* argument is not a valid open conversion descriptor.

APPLICATION USAGE

The *inbuf* argument indirectly points to the memory area which contains the conversion input data. The *outbuf* argument indirectly points to the memory area which is to contain the result of the conversion. The objects indirectly pointed to by *inbuf* and *outbuf* are not restricted to containing data that is directly representable in the ISO C language **char** data type. The type of *inbuf* and *outbuf*, **char ****, does not imply that the objects pointed to are interpreted as null-terminated C strings or arrays of characters. Any interpretation of a byte sequence that represents a character in a given character set encoding scheme is done internally within the code set converters. For example, the area pointed to indirectly by *inbuf* and/or *outbuf* can contain all zero octets that are not interpreted as string terminators but as coded character data according to the respective code set encoding scheme. The type of the data (**char**, **short int**, **long int**, and so on) read or stored in the objects is not specified, but may be inferred for both the input and output data by the converters determined by the *fromcode* and *tocode* arguments of *iconv_open*( ).

Regardless of the data type inferred by the converter, the size of the remaining space in both input and output objects (the *intbytesleft* and *outbytesleft* arguments) is always measured in bytes.

For implementations that support the conversion of state-dependent encodings, the conversion descriptor must be able to accurately reflect the shift-state in effect at the end of the last successful conversion. It is not required that the conversion descriptor itself be updated, which would require it to be a pointer type. Thus, implementations are free to implement the descriptor as a handle (other than a pointer type) by which the conversion information can be accessed and updated.

SEE ALSO

iconv_open( ), *iconv_close*( ), **<iconv.h>**.

EXAMPLE

```
/*
 * Copyright (C) ANTRIX Inc.
 */

/* iconv.c
 * This program converts the sequence of characters from codeset
 * 8859 to 646 using function iconv.
 */

#include <stdio.h>
#include <stdlib.h>
#include <iconv.h>
```

```
#include <sys/types.h>
#include <errno.h>

main()
{
  iconv_t  cd;
  size_t   iconv_value;
  size_t   outbytes;
  size_t   inbytes = 6;
  char     *fromcode = "8859";
  char     *tocode = "646";
  char     *inbuf = "ABCabc";
  char     buf[20];

  fprintf(stdout, "Get code conversion descriptor\n");
  cd = iconv_open (tocode, fromcode);

  fprintf(stdout, "convert sequence of characters\n");
  iconv_value = iconv(cd, &inbuf, &inbytes, &buf, &outbytes);
  if ( iconv_value != 0 )
     fprintf (stdout,"iconv() call successful\n");
  else {
     fprintf (stderr,"ERROR: iconv_conv() call failed\n");
     fprintf (stderr,"ERROR: %s\n", strerror(errno));
  }

  fprintf(stdout, "close the conversion file descriptor\n");
  iconv_close (cd);
}
```

NAME

iconv_close — code conversion deallocation function

SYNOPSIS

EX   `#include <iconv.h>`

`int iconv_close(iconv_t cd);`

DESCRIPTION

The *iconv_close*( ) function deallocates the conversion descriptor *cd* and all other associated resources allocated by *iconv_open*( ).

If a file descriptor is used to implement the type **iconv_t,** that file descriptor will be closed.

RETURN VALUE

Upon successful completion, 0 is returned. Otherwise, −1 is returned and *errno* is set to indicate the error.

ERRORS

The *iconv_close*( ) function may fail if:

[EBADF]   The conversion descriptor is invalid.

SEE ALSO

iconv( ), *iconv_open*( ), **<iconv.h>**.

EXAMPLE

```
/*
 * Copyright (C) ANTRIX Inc.
 */

/* iconv_close.c
 * This program deallocates the conversion descriptor cd
 * and associated resources using function iconv_close.
 */

#include <stdio.h>
#include <stdlib.h>
#include <iconv.h>
#include <sys/types.h>
#include <errno.h>

main()
{
  iconv_t  cd;
  size_t   outbytes;
  size_t   inbytes = 6;
  char     *fromcode = "8859";
  char     *tocode = "646fr";
  char     *inbuf = "ABCabc";
  char     buf[20];

  fprintf(stdout, "Get code conversion descriptor\n");
  cd = iconv_open (tocode, fromcode);

  fprintf(stdout, "convert sequence of characters\n");
  iconv(cd, &inbuf, &inbytes, &buf, &outbytes);
```

```
    fprintf(stdout, "close the conversion file descriptor\n");
    iconv_close (cd);
}
```

NAME

iconv_open — code conversion allocation function

SYNOPSIS

EX
```
#include <iconv.h>

iconv_t iconv_open(const char *tocode, const char *fromcode);
```

DESCRIPTION

The *iconv_open*( ) function returns a conversion descriptor that describes a conversion from the codeset specified by the string pointed to by the *fromcode* argument to the codeset specified by the string pointed to by the *tocode* argument. For state-dependent encodings, the conversion descriptor will be in a codeset-dependent initial shift state, ready for immediate use with *iconv*( ).

Settings of *fromcode* and *tocode* and their permitted combinations are implementation-dependent.

A conversion descriptor remains valid in a process until that process closes it.

If a file descriptor is used to implement conversion descriptors, the FD_CLOEXEC flag will be set; see **<fcntl.h>.**

RETURN VALUE

Upon successful completion, *iconv_open*( ) returns a conversion descriptor for use on subsequent calls to *iconv*( ). Otherwise *iconv_open*( ) returns (**iconv_t**)–1 and sets *errno* to indicate the error.

ERRORS

The *iconv_open*( ) function may fail if:

[EMFILE]   {OPEN_MAX} files descriptors are currently open in the calling process.

[ENFILE]   Too many files are currently open in the system.

[ENOMEM]   Insufficient storage space is available.

[EINVAL]   The conversion specified by *fromcode* and *tocode* is not supported by the implementation.

APPLICATION USAGE

Some implementations of *iconv_open*( ) use *malloc*( ) to allocate space for internal buffer areas. The *iconv_open*( ) function may fail if there is insufficient storage space to accommodate these buffers.

Portable applications must assume that conversion descriptors are not valid after a call to one of the *exec* functions.

SEE ALSO

iconv( ), *iconv_close*( ), **<iconv.h>.**

EXAMPLE

```
/*
 * Copyright (C) ANTRIX Inc.
 */

/* iconv_close.c
 * This program deallocates the conversion descriptor cd
 * and associated resources using function iconv_close.
 */
```

```c
#include <stdio.h>
#include <stdlib.h>
#include <iconv.h>
#include <sys/types.h>
#include <errno.h>

main()
{
  iconv_t   cd;
  size_t    outbytes;
  size_t    inbytes = 6;
  char      *fromcode = "8859";
  char      *tocode = "646fr";
  char      *inbuf = "ABCabc";
  char      buf[20];

  fprintf(stdout, "Get code conversion descriptor\n");
  cd = iconv_open (tocode, fromcode);

  fprintf(stdout, "convert sequence of characters\n");
  iconv(cd, &inbuf, &inbytes, &buf, &outbytes);

  fprintf(stdout, "close the conversion file descriptor\n");
  iconv_close (cd);
}
```

NAME

ilogb - returns an unbiased exponent

SYNOPSIS

UX
```
#include <math.h>

int ilogb (double x)
```

DESCRIPTION

The *ilogb*( ) function returns the exponent part of *x*. Formally, the return value is the integral part of $\log_r |x|$ as a signed integral value, for non-zero *x*, where *r* is the radix of the machine's floating point arithmetic.

The call *ilogb*(*x*) is equivalent to (**int**)*logb*(*x*).

RETURN VALUE

Upon successful completion, *ilogb*( ) returns the exponent part of *x*.

If *x* is 0 or NaN, then *ilogb*( ) returns INT_MIN. If *x* is ±Inf, then *ilogb*( ) returns INT_MAX.

ERRORS

No errors are defined.

SEE ALSO

logb( ), **<math.h>**.

EXAMPLE

```
/*
 * Copyright (C) ANTRIX Inc.
 */

/* ilogb.c
 * This program computes the unbiased exponent of its
 * floating-point value using function ilogb.
 */

#include <stdio.h>
#include <math.h>

main()
{
  double  ilogb_value;
  double  x = 2.00;

  ilogb_value = ilogb (x);
  fprintf (stdout,"ilogb of %f is %f\n", x, ilogb_value);
}
```

NAME

index — character string operations

SYNOPSIS

UX

```
#include <strings.h>
```

```
char *index(const char *s, int c);
```

DESCRIPTION

The *index( )* function is identical to *strchr( )*.

RETURN VALUE

See *strchr( )*.

ERRORS

See *strchr( )*.

APPLICATION USAGE

For portability to implementations conforming to earlier versions of this document, *strchr( )* is preferred over these functions.

SEE ALSO

strchr( ), **<strings.h>**.

EXAMPLE

```
/*
 * Copyright (C) ANTRIX Inc.
 */

/* index.c
 * This program locates the first occurrence of c in the
 * string pointed to by s using function index.
 */

#include <stdio.h>
#include <stdlib.h>
#include <strings.h>
#include <string.h>
#include <errno.h>

main()
{
  char    *index_value;
  int     c = 't';
  char    s[] = "one two three";

  fprintf (stdout,"return pointer to first occurrence of t\n");
  index_value = index(s, c);
  if ( index_value != (char *)0 ) {
     fprintf (stdout,"index() call successful\n");
     fprintf (stdout,"index_value=%s\n", index_value);
  }
  else
     fprintf (stderr,"ERROR: index() call failed\n");
}
```

NAME

initstate, random, setstate, srandom — pseudorandom number functions

SYNOPSIS

UX
```
#include <stdlib.h>

char *initstate(unsigned int seed, char *state, size_t size);

long random(void);

char *setstate(const char *state);

void srandom(unsigned int seed);
```

DESCRIPTION

The *random*( ) function uses a nonlinear additive feedback random-number generator employing a default state array size of 31 long integers to return successive pseudo-random numbers in the range from 0 to $2^{31}-1$. The period of this random-number generator is approximately 16 x $(2^{31}-1)$. The size of the state array determines the period of the random-number generator. Increasing the state array size increases the period.

With 256 bytes of state information, the period of the random-number generator is greater than 2^{69}.

Like *rand*( ), *random*( ) produces by default a sequence of numbers that can be duplicated by calling *srandom*( ) with 1 as the seed.

The *srandom*( ) function initialises the current state array using the value of *seed*.

The *initstate*( ) and *setstate*( ) functions handle restarting and changing random-number generators. The *initstate*( ) function allows a state array, pointed to by the *state* argument, to be initialised for future use. The *size* argument, which specifies the size in bytes of the state array, is used by *initstate*( ) to decide what type of random-number generator to use; the larger the state array, the more random the numbers. Values for the amount of state information are 8, 32, 64, 128, and 256 bytes. Other values greater than 8 bytes are rounded down to the nearest one of these values. For values smaller than 8, *random*( ) uses a simple linear congruential random number generator. The *seed* argument specifies a starting point for the random-number sequence and provides for restarting at the same point. The *initstate*( ) function returns a pointer to the previous state information array.

If *initstate*( ) has not been called, then *random*( ) behaves as though *initstate*( ) had been called with *seed* = 1 and *size* = 128.

If *initstate*( ) is called with *size* < 8, then *random*( ) uses a simple linear congruential random number generator.

Once a state has been initialised, *setstate*( ) allows switching between state arrays. The array defined by the *state* argument is used for further random-number generation until *initstate*( ) is called or *setstate*( ) is called again. The *setstate*( ) function returns a pointer to the previous state array.

RETURN VALUE

The *random*( ) function returns the generated pseudo-random number.

The *srandom*( ) function returns no value.

Upon successful completion, *initstate*( ) and *setstate*( ) return a pointer to the previous state array. Otherwise, a null pointer is returned.

ERRORS

No errors are defined.

APPLICATION USAGE

After initialisation, a state array can be restarted at a different point in one of two ways:

- The *initstate*( ) function can be used, with the desired seed, state array, and size of the array.

- The *setstate*( ) function, with the desired state, can be used, followed by *srandom*( ) with the desired seed. The advantage of using both of these functions is that the size of the state array does not have to be saved once it is initialised.

Although some implementations of *random*( ) have written messages to standard error, such implementations do not conform to this document.

SEE ALSO

drand48( ), *rand*( ), **<stdlib.h>**.

EXAMPLE

```
/*
 * Copyright (C) ANTRIX Inc.
 */

/* initstate.c
 * This program allows a state array, passed in as argument
 * to be initialized for future use by function random
 * using function initstate.
 */

#include <stdio.h>
#include <stdlib.h>
#include <errno.h>

static long state1[32] = {
    3,
    0x9a319039, 0x32d9c024, 0x9b663182, 0x5da1f342,
    0x7449e56b, 0xbeb1dbb0, 0xab5c5918, 0x946554fd,
    0x8c2e680f, 0xeb3d799f, 0xb11ee0b7, 0x2d436b86,
    0xda672e2a, 0x1588ca88, 0xe369735d, 0x904f35f7,
    0xd7158fd6, 0x6fa6f051, 0x616e6b96, 0xac94efdc,
    0xde3b81e0, 0xdf0a6fb5, 0xf103bc02, 0x48f340fb,
    0x36413f93, 0xc622c298, 0xf5a42ab8, 0x8a88d77b,
    0xf5ad9d0e, 0x8999220b, 0x27fb47b9
};

main()
{
    char *initstate_value;
    unsigned seed;
    int n;

    seed = 1;
    n = 128;
    fprintf(stdout, "initialize for future use\n");
    initstate_value = (char *)initstate(seed, state1, n);
```

```
        fprintf(stdout, "initstate_value =%s\n",initstate_value);

        fprintf(stdout, "switch the states\n");
        setstate(state1);
        fprintf(stdout, "%d\n",random());
        fprintf(stdout, "random value =%d\n",random());
}

/*
 * Copyright (C) ANTRIX Inc.
 */

/* random.c
 * This program computes a sequence of pseudo-randomom integers
 * using function random.
 */

#include <stdio.h>
#include <stdlib.h>
#include <errno.h>

main()
{
  long  i, random_value;

  for ( i = 0; i < 5; i++ ) {
      random_value = random ();
      fprintf (stdout,"randomom value in iteration %d is %d\n",
                      i, random_value);
  }
}

/*
 * Copyright (C) ANTRIX Inc.
 */

/* setstate.c
 * This program allows rapid switching between states
 * using function setstate.
 */

#include <stdio.h>
#include <stdlib.h>
#include <errno.h>

static long state1[32] = {
    3,
    0x9a319039, 0x32d9c024, 0x9b663182, 0x5da1f342,
    0x7449e56b, 0xbeb1dbb0, 0xab5c5918, 0x946554fd,
    0x8c2e680f, 0xeb3d799f, 0xb11ee0b7, 0x2d436b86,
    0xda672e2a, 0x1588ca88, 0xe369735d, 0x904f35f7,
    0xd7158fd6, 0x6fa6f051, 0x616e6b96, 0xac94efdc,
```

```
        0xde3b81e0, 0xdf0a6fb5, 0xf103bc02, 0x48f340fb,
        0x36413f93, 0xc622c298, 0xf5a42ab8, 0x8a88d77b,
        0xf5ad9d0e, 0x8999220b, 0x27fb47b9
};

main()
{
    char *setstate_value;
    unsigned seed;
    int n;

    seed = 1;
    n = 128;
    fprintf(stdout, "initialize for future use\n");
    initstate(seed, state1, n);

    fprintf(stdout, "switch the states\n");
    setstate_value = (char *)setstate(state1);
    fprintf(stdout, "random value =%d\n",random());
    fprintf(stdout, "setstate_value =%s\n",setstate_value);
}

/*
 * Copyright (C) ANTRIX Inc.
 */

/* srandom.c
 * This program initializes entry points for random number
 * generator srandom using function srandom.
 */

#include <stdio.h>
#include <stdlib.h>
#include <errno.h>

main()
{
    int          random_value;
    int          i;
    unsigned int seed = 100;

    srandom (100);
    for ( i = 0; i < 5; i++ ) {
        random_value = random ();
        fprintf (stdout,"random value in iteration %d is %d\n",
                        i, random_value);
    }
}
```

NAME

insque, remque — insert or remove an element in a queue

SYNOPSIS

UX
```
#include <search.h>
```
```
void insque(void *element, void *pred);
```
```
void remque(void *element);
```

DESCRIPTION

The *insque*( ) and *remque*( ) functions manipulate queues built from doubly-linked lists. The queue can be either circular or linear. An application using *insque*( ) or *remque*( ) must define a structure in which the first two members of the structure are pointers to the same type of structure, and any further members are application-specific. The first member of the structure is a forward pointer to the next entry in the queue. The second member is a backward pointer to the previous entry in the queue. If the queue is linear, the queue is terminated with null pointers. The names of the structure and of the pointer members are not subject to any special restriction.

The *insque*( ) function inserts the element pointed to by *element* into a queue immediately after the element pointed to by *pred*.

The *remque*( ) function removes the element pointed to by *element* from a queue.

If the queue is to be used as a linear list, invoking *insque*(&*element*, NULL), where *element* is the initial element of the queue, will initialise the forward and backward pointers of *element* to null pointers.

If the queue is to be used as a circular list, the application must initialise the forward pointer and the backward pointer of the initial element of the queue to the element's own address.

RETURN VALUE

The *insque*( ) and *remque*( ) functions do not return a value.

ERRORS

No errors are defined.

APPLICATION USAGE

The historical implementations of these functions described the arguments as being of type **struct qelem *** rather than as being of type **void *** as defined here. In those implementations, **struct qelem** was commonly defined in **<search.h>** as:

```
struct qelem {
    struct qelem    *q_forw;
    struct qelem    *q_back;
};
```

Applications using these functions, however, were never able to use this structure directly since it provided no room for the actual data contained in the elements. Most applications defined structures that contained the two pointers as the initial elements and also provided space for, or pointers to, the object's data. Applications that used these functions to update more than one type of table also had the problem of specifying two or more different structures with the same name, if they literally used **struct qelem** as specified.

As described here, the implementations were actually expecting a structure type where the first two members were forward and backward pointers to structures. With C compilers that didn't provide function prototypes, applications used structures as specified in the DESCRIPTION above and the compiler did what the application expected.

If this method had been carried forward with an ISO C compiler and the historical function prototype, most applications would have to be modified to cast pointers to the structures actually used to be pointers to **struct qelem** to avoid compilation warnings. By specifying **void *** as the argument type, applications won't need to change (unless they specifically referenced **struct qelem** and depended on it being defined in **<search.h>**).

SEE ALSO
> **<search.h>**.

EXAMPLE

```
/*
 * Copyright (C) ANTRIX Inc.
 */

/* insque.c
 * This program inserts an element from a queue
 * using function insque.
 */

#include   <stdio.h>
#include   <stdlib.h>
#include   <errno.h>

struct qelem {
  struct qelem *next;
  struct qelem *prev;
  char str[5];
};

static struct qelem *tail;

struct qelem *salloc()
{
  struct qelem *bytes;

  /* allocate memory for struct qelem */
  bytes = (struct qelem *)malloc(sizeof(struct qelem));
  return(bytes);
}

struct qelem *create_list(p, c)
struct qelem *p;
char c;
{
  if(p == NULL) {
    /* allocate memory and assign values */
    p = salloc();
    /* save decimal and ASCII value in the form of string */
    sprintf(p->str, "%c", c);
    p->next = NULL;
    p->prev = tail;
    tail = p;
  }
```

```
    else
      p->next = create_list(p->next, c);
    return(p);
}

print_next(p)
struct qelem *p;
{
  if(p != NULL) {
    printf("%s\n", p->str);
    print_next(p->next);
  }
}

print_prev(p)
struct qelem *p;
{
  if(p != NULL) {
    printf("%s\n", p->str);
    print_prev(p->prev);
  }
}

main()
{
  int i;
  struct qelem *head;
  struct qelem *add;

  head = tail = NULL;
  for(i = 'a'; i <= 'c'; i++)
      head = create_list(head, i);

  printf("forward traverse\n");
  print_next(head);

  printf("reverse traverse\n");
  print_prev(tail);

  printf("add an element and print elements\n");
  add = salloc();
  sprintf(add->str, "%c", 'd');
  tail->next = add;
  add->prev = tail;
  insque(add, tail);
  add->next = NULL;
  print_next(head);
}
```

NAME

ioctl — control device

SYNOPSIS

UX   `#include <stropts.h>`

`int ioctl(int `*`fildes`*`, int `*`request`*`, ... /* arg */);`

DESCRIPTION

The *ioctl*( ) function performs a variety of control functions on STREAMS devices. For non-STREAMS devices, the functions performed by this call are unspecified. The *request* argument and an optional third argument (with varying type) are passed to and interpreted by the appropriate part of the STREAM associated with *fildes*.

The *fildes* argument is an open file descriptor that refers to a device.

The *request* argument selects the control function to be performed and will depend on the STREAMS device being addressed.

The *arg* argument represents additional information that is needed by this specific STREAMS device to perform the requested function. The type of *arg* depends upon the particular control request, but it is either an integer or a pointer to a device-specific data structure.

The *ioctl*( ) commands applicable to STREAMS, their arguments, and error statuses that apply to each individual command are described below.

The following *ioctl*( ) commands, with error values indicated, are applicable to all STREAMS files:

I_PUSH   Pushes the module whose name is pointed to by *arg* onto the top of the current STREAM, just below the STREAM head. It then calls the *open*( ) function of the newly-pushed module.

The *ioctl*( ) function with the I_PUSH command will fail if:

[EINVAL]   Invalid module name.

[ENXIO]   Open function of new module failed.

[ENXIO]   Hangup received on *fildes*.

I_POP   Removes the module just below the STREAM head of the STREAM pointed to by *fildes*. The *arg* argument should be 0 in an I_POP request.

The *ioctl*( ) function with the I_POP command will fail if:

[EINVAL]   No module present in the STREAM.

[ENXIO]   Hangup received on *fildes*.

I_LOOK   Retrieves the name of the module just below the STREAM head of the STREAM pointed to by *fildes*, and places it in a character string pointed to by *arg*. The buffer pointed to by *arg* should be at least FMNAMESZ+1 bytes long, where FMNAMESZ is defined in **<stropts.h>**.

The *ioctl*( ) function with the I_LOOK command will fail if:

[EINVAL]   No module present in the STREAM.

I_FLUSH   This request flushes read and/or write queues, depending on the value of *arg*. Valid *arg* values are:

FLUSHR   Flush all read queues.

FLUSHW   Flush all write queues.

FLUSHRW   Flush all read and all write queues.

The *ioctl*( ) function with the I_FLUSH command will fail if:

[EINVAL]   Invalid *arg* value.

[EAGAIN] or [ENOSR]
                Unable to allocate buffers for flush message.

[ENXIO]   Hangup received on *fildes*.

I_FLUSHBAND   Flushes a particular band of messages. The *arg* argument points to a **bandinfo** structure. The **bi_flag** member may be one of FLUSHR, FLUSHW, or FLUSHRW as described above. The **bi_pri** member determines the priority band to be flushed.

I_SETSIG   Requests that the STREAMS implementation send the SIGPOLL signal to the calling process when a particular event has occurred on the STREAM associated with *fildes*. I_SETSIG supports an asynchronous processing capability in STREAMS. The value of *arg* is a bitmask that specifies the events for which the process should be signaled. It is the bitwise-OR of any combination of the following constants:

S_RDNORM   A normal (priority band set to 0) message has arrived at the head of a STREAM head read queue. A signal will be generated even if the message is of zero length.

S_RDBAND   A message with a non-zero priority band has arrived at the head of a STREAM head read queue. A signal will be generated even if the message is of zero length.

S_INPUT   A message, other than a high-priority message, has arrived at the head of a STREAM head read queue. A signal will be generated even if the message is of zero length.

S_HIPRI   A high-priority message is present on a STREAM head read queue. A signal will be generated even if the message is of zero length.

S_OUTPUT   The write queue for normal data (priority band 0) just below the STREAM head is no longer full. This notifies the process that there is room on the queue for sending (or writing) normal data downstream.

S_WRNORM   Same as S_OUTPUT.

S_WRBAND   The write queue for a non-zero priority band just below the STREAM head is no longer full. This notifies the process that there is room on the queue for sending (or writing) priority data downstream.

S_MSG   A STREAMS signal message that contains the SIGPOLL signal has reached the front of the STREAM head read queue.

S_ERROR   Notification of an error condition has reached the STREAM head.

S_HANGUP	Notification of a hangup has reached the STREAM head.
S_BANDURG	When used in conjunction with S_RDBAND, SIGURG is generated instead of SIGPOLL when a priority message reaches the front of the STREAM head read queue.

If *arg* is 0, the calling process will be unregistered and will not receive further SIGPOLL signals for the stream associated with *fildes*.

Processes that wish to receive SIGPOLL signals must explicitly register to receive them using I_SETSIG. If several processes register to receive this signal for the same event on the same STREAM, each process will be signaled when the event occurs.

The *ioctl( )* function with the I_SETSIG command will fail if:

[EINVAL]	The value of *arg* is invalid.
[EINVAL]	The value of *arg* is 0 and the calling process is not registered to receive the SIGPOLL signal.
[EAGAIN]	There were insufficient resources to store the signal request.

I_GETSIG   Returns the events for which the calling process is currently registered to be sent a SIGPOLL signal. The events are returned as a bitmask in an **int** pointed to by *arg*, where the events are those specified in the description of I_SETSIG above.

The *ioctl( )* function with the I_GETSIG command will fail if:

[EINVAL]	Process is not registered to receive the SIGPOLL signal.

I_FIND   This request compares the names of all modules currently present in the STREAM to the name pointed to by *arg*, and returns 1 if the named module is present in the STREAM, or returns 0 if the named module is not present.

The *ioctl( )* function with the I_FIND command will fail if:

[EINVAL]	*arg* does not contain a valid module name.

I_PEEK   This request allows a process to retrieve the information in the first message on the STREAM head read queue without taking the message off the queue. It is analogous to *getmsg( )* except that this command does not remove the message from the queue. The *arg* argument points to a **strpeek** structure.

The **maxlen** member in the **ctlbuf** and **databuf strbuf** structures must be set to the number of bytes of control information and/or data information, respectively, to retrieve. The **flags** member may be marked RS_HIPRI or 0, as described by *getmsg( )*. If the process sets **flags** to RS_HIPRI, for example, I_PEEK will only look for a high-priority message on the STREAM head read queue.

I_PEEK returns 1 if a message was retrieved, and returns 0 if no message was found on the STREAM head read queue, or if the RS_HIPRI flag was set in **flags** and a high-priority message was not present on the STREAM head read queue. It does not wait for a message to arrive. On return, **ctlbuf** specifies information in the control buffer, **databuf** specifies information in the data buffer, and **flags** contains the value RS_HIPRI or 0.

I_SRDOPT   Sets the read mode using the value of the argument *arg*. Read modes are described in *read*( ). Valid *arg* flags are:

RNORM   Byte-stream mode, the default.

RMSGD   Message-discard mode.

RMSGN   Message-nondiscard mode.

The bitwise inclusive OR of RMSGD and RMSGN will return [EINVAL]. The bitwise inclusive OR of RNORM and either RMSGD or RMSGN will result in the other flag overriding RNORM which is the default.

In addition, treatment of control messages by the STREAM head may be changed by setting any of the following flags in *arg*:

RPROTNORM   Fail *read*( ) with [EBADMSG] if a message containing a control part is at the front of the STREAM head read queue.

RPROTDAT   Deliver the control part of a message as data when a process issues a *read*( ).

RPROTDIS   Discard the control part of a message, delivering any data portion, when a process issues a *read*( ).

The *ioctl*( ) function with the I_SRDOPT command will fail if:

[EINVAL]   The *arg* argument is not valid.

I_GRDOPT   Returns the current read mode setting as, described above, in an **int** pointed to by the argument *arg*. Read modes are described in *read*( ).

I_NREAD   Counts the number of data bytes in the data part of the first message on the STREAM head read queue and places this value in the **int** pointed to by *arg*. The return value for the command is the number of messages on the STREAM head read queue. For example, if 0 is returned in *arg*, but the *ioctl*( ) return value is greater than 0, this indicates that a zero-length message is next on the queue.

I_FDINSERT Creates a message from specified buffer(s), adds information about another STREAM, and sends the message downstream. The message contains a control part and an optional data part. The data and control parts to be sent are distinguished by placement in separate buffers, as described below. The *arg* argument points to a **strfdinsert** structure.

The **len** member in the **ctlbuf strbuf** structure must be set to the size of a pointer plus the number of bytes of control information to be sent with the message. The **fildes** member specifies the file descriptor of the other STREAM, and the **offset** member, which must be suitably aligned for use as a pointer, specifies the offset from the start of the control buffer where I_FDINSERT will store a pointer whose interpretation is specific to the STREAM end. The **len** member in the **databuf strbuf** structure must be set to the number of bytes of data information to be sent with the message, or to 0 if no data part is to be sent.

The **flags** member specifies the type of message to be created. A normal message is created if **flags** is set to 0, and a high-priority message is created if **flags** is set to RS_HIPRI. For non-priority messages, I_FDINSERT will block if the STREAM write queue is full due to internal flow control conditions. For priority messages, I_FDINSERT does not block on this condition. For non-priority messages, I_FDINSERT does not block when the write queue is full and O_NONBLOCK is set. Instead, it fails and sets *errno* to [EAGAIN].

I_FDINSERT also blocks, unless prevented by lack of internal resources, waiting for the availability of message blocks in the STREAM, regardless of priority or whether O_NONBLOCK has been specified. No partial message is sent.

The *ioctl( )* function with the I_FDINSERT command will fail if:

[EAGAIN]   A non-priority message is specified, the O_NONBLOCK flag is set, and the STREAM write queue is full due to internal flow control conditions.

[EAGAIN] or [ENOSR]
                  Buffers can not be allocated for the message that is to be created.

[EINVAL]   One of the following:

                  • The *fd* member of the **strfdinsert** structure is not a valid, open STREAM file descriptor.

                  • The size of a pointer plus *offset* is greater than the *len* member for the buffer specified through *ctlptr*.

                  • The *offset* member does not specify a properly-aligned location in the data buffer.

                  • An undefined value is stored in **flags**.

[ENXIO]   Hangup received on *fd* or *fildes*.

[ERANGE]   The *len* member for the buffer specified through *databuf* does not fall within the range specified by the maximum and minimum packet sizes of the topmost STREAM module or the *len* member for the buffer specified through *databuf* is larger than the maximum configured size of the data part of a message; or the *len* member for the buffer specified through *ctlbuf* is larger than the maximum configured size of the control part of a message.

I_STR   Constructs an internal STREAMS *ioctl( )* message from the data pointed to by *arg*, and sends that message downstream.

This mechanism is provided to send *ioctl( )* requests to downstream modules and drivers. It allows information to be sent with *ioctl( )*, and returns to the process any information sent upstream by the downstream recipient. I_STR blocks until the system responds with either a positive or negative acknowledgement message, or until the request "times out" after some period of time. If the request times out, it fails with *errno* set to [ETIME].

At most, one I_STR can be active on a STREAM. Further I_STR calls will block until the active I_STR completes at the STREAM head. The default timeout interval for these requests is 15 seconds. The O_NONBLOCK flag has no effect on this call.

To send requests downstream, *arg* must point to a **strioctl** structure.

The **ic_cmd** member is the internal *ioctl( )* command intended for a downstream module or driver and **ic_timout** is the number of seconds (–1 = infinite, 0 = use implementation-dependent timeout interval, >0 = as specified) an I_STR request will wait for acknowledgement before timing out. **ic_len** is the number of bytes in the data argument, and **ic_dp** is a pointer to the data argument. The **ic_len** member has two uses: on input, it contains the length of the data argument passed in, and on return from the command, it contains the number of bytes being returned to the process (the buffer pointed to by **ic_dp** should be large enough to contain the maximum amount of data that any module or the driver in the STREAM can return).

The STREAM head will convert the information pointed to by the **strioctl** structure to an internal *ioctl( )* command message and send it downstream.

The *ioctl( )* function with the I_STR command will fail if:

[EAGAIN] or [ENOSR]
:   Unable to allocate buffers for the *ioctl( )* message.

[EINVAL]
:   The *ic_len* member is less than 0 or larger than the maximum configured size of the data part of a message, or *ic_timout* is less than –1.

[ENXIO]
:   Hangup received on *fildes*.

[ETIME]
:   A downstream *ioctl( )* timed out before acknowledgement was received.

An I_STR can also fail while waiting for an acknowledgement if a message indicating an error or a hangup is received at the STREAM head. In addition, an error code can be returned in the positive or negative acknowledgement message, in the event the *ioctl( )* command sent downstream fails. For these cases, I_STR fails with *errno* set to the value in the message.

I_SWROPT
:   Sets the write mode using the value of the argument *arg*. Valid bit settings for *arg* are:

    SNDZERO
    :   Send a zero-length message downstream when a *write( )* of 0 bytes occurs. To not send a zero-length message when a *write( )* of 0 bytes occurs, this bit must not be set in *arg* (for example, *arg* would be set to 0).

    The *ioctl( )* function with the I_SWROPT command will fail if:

    [EINVAL]
    :   *arg* is not the above value.

I_GWROPT
:   Returns the current write mode setting, as described above, in the **int** that is pointed to by the argument *arg*.

I_SENDFD
:   I_SENDFD creates a new reference to the open file description associated with the file descriptor *arg,* and writes a message on the STREAMS-based pipe *fildes* containing this reference, together with the user ID and group ID of the calling process.

    The *ioctl( )* function with the I_SENDFD command will fail if:

    [EAGAIN]
    :   The sending STREAM is unable to allocate a message block to contain the file pointer; or the read queue of the receiving STREAM head is full and cannot accept the message sent by I_SENDFD.

[EBADF]	The *arg* argument is not a valid, open file descriptor.
[EINVAL]	The *fildes* argument is not connected to a STREAM pipe.
[ENXIO]	Hangup received on *fildes*.

I_RECVFD Retrieves the reference to an open file description from a message written to a STREAMS-based pipe using the I_SENDFD command, and allocates a new file descriptor in the calling process that refers to this open file description. The *arg* argument is a pointer to an **strrecvfd** data structure as defined in **<stropts.h>**.

The **fd** member is a file descriptor. The **uid** and **gid** members are the effective user ID and effective group ID, respectively, of the sending process.

If O_NONBLOCK is not set I_RECVFD blocks until a message is present at the STREAM head. If O_NONBLOCK is set, I_RECVFD fails with *errno* set to [EAGAIN] if no message is present at the STREAM head.

If the message at the STREAM head is a message sent by an I_SENDFD, a new file descriptor is allocated for the open file descriptor referenced in the message. The new file descriptor is placed in the **fd** member of the **strrecvfd** structure pointed to by *arg*.

The *ioctl*( ) function with the I_RECVFD command will fail if:

[EAGAIN]	A message is not present at the STREAM head read queue and the O_NONBLOCK flag is set.
[EBADMSG]	The message at the STREAM head read queue is not a message containing a passed file descriptor.
[EMFILE]	The process has the maximum number of file descriptors currently open that it is allowed.
[ENXIO]	Hangup received on *fildes*.

I_LIST This request allows the process to list all the module names on the STREAM, up to and including the topmost driver name. If *arg* is a null pointer, the return value is the number of modules, including the driver, that are on the STREAM pointed to by *fildes*. This lets the process allocate enough space for the module names. Otherwise, it should point to an **str_list** structure.

The **sl_nmods** member indicates the number of entries the process has allocated in the array. Upon return, the **sl_modlist** member of the **str_list** structure contains the list of module names, and the number of entries that have been filled into the **sl_modlist** array is found in the **sl_nmods** member (the number includes the number of modules including the driver). The return value from *ioctl*( ) is 0. The entries are filled in starting at the top of the STREAM and continuing downstream until either the end of the STREAM is reached, or the number of requested modules (**sl_nmods**) is satisfied.

The *ioctl*( ) function with the I_LIST command will fail if:

| [EINVAL] | The **sl_nmods** member is less than 1. |

[EAGAIN] or [ENOSR]
        Unable to allocate buffers.

I_ATMARK This request allows the process to see if the message at the head of the STREAM head read queue is marked by some module downstream. The *arg* argument determines how the checking is done when there may be multiple marked messages on the STREAM head read queue. It may take on the following values:

ANYMARK   Check if the message is marked.

LASTMARK   Check if the message is the last one marked on the queue.

The bitwise inclusive OR of the flags ANYMARK and LASTMARK is permitted.

The return value is 1 if the mark condition is satisfied and 0 otherwise.

The *ioctl( )* function with the I_ATMARK command will fail if:

[EINVAL]   Invalid *arg* value.

I_CKBAND Check if the message of a given priority band exists on the STREAM head read queue. This returns 1 if a message of the given priority exists, 0 if no message exists, or –1 on error. *arg* should be of type **int**.

The *ioctl( )* function with the I_CKBAND command will fail if:

[EINVAL]   Invalid *arg* value.

I_GETBAND Return the priority band of the first message on the STREAM head read queue in the integer referenced by *arg*.

The *ioctl( )* function with the I_GETBAND command will fail if:

[ENODATA]   No message on the STREAM head read queue.

I_CANPUT Check if a certain band is writable. *arg* is set to the priority band in question. The return value is 0 if the band is flow-controlled, 1 if the band is writable, or –1 on error.

The *ioctl( )* function with the I_CANPUT command will fail if:

[EINVAL]   Invalid *arg* value.

I_SETCLTIME This request allows the process to set the time the STREAM head will delay when a STREAM is closing and there is data on the write queues. Before closing each module or driver, if there is data on its write queue, the STREAM head will delay for the specified amount of time to allow the data to drain. If, after the delay, data is still present, they will be flushed. The *arg* argument is a pointer to an integer specifying the number of milliseconds to delay, rounded up to the nearest valid value. If I_SETCLTIME is not performed on a STREAM, an implementation-dependent default timeout interval is used.

The *ioctl( )* function with the I_SETCLTIME command will fail if:

[EINVAL]   Invalid *arg* value.

I_GETCLTIME This request returns the close time delay in the integer pointed to by *arg*.

Multiplexed STREAMS Configurations

The following four commands are used for connecting and disconnecting multiplexed STREAMS configurations. These commands use an implementation-dependent default timeout interval.

I_LINK   Connects two STREAMs, where *fildes* is the file descriptor of the STREAM connected to the multiplexing driver, and *arg* is the file descriptor of the STREAM connected to another driver. The STREAM designated by *arg* gets connected below the multiplexing driver. I_LINK requires the multiplexing driver to send an acknowledgement message to the STREAM head regarding the connection. This call returns a multiplexer ID number (an identifier used to disconnect the multiplexer; see I_UNLINK) on success, and –1 on failure.

The *ioctl*( ) function with the I_LINK command will fail if:

[ENXIO]   Hangup received on *fildes*.

[ETIME]   Time out before acknowledgement message was received at STREAM head.

[EAGAIN] or [ENOSR]
           Unable to allocate STREAMS storage to perform the I_LINK.

[EBADF]   The *arg* argument is not a valid, open file descriptor.

[EINVAL]   The *fildes* argument does not support multiplexing; or *arg* is not a STREAM or is already connected downstream from a multiplexer; or the specified I_LINK operation would connect the STREAM head in more than one place in the multiplexed STREAM.

An I_LINK can also fail while waiting for the multiplexing driver to acknowledge the request, if a message indicating an error or a hangup is received at the STREAM head of *fildes*. In addition, an error code can be returned in the positive or negative acknowledgement message. For these cases, I_LINK fails with *errno* set to the value in the message.

I_UNLINK   Disconnects the two STREAMs specified by *fildes* and *arg*. *fildes* is the file descriptor of the STREAM connected to the multiplexing driver. The *arg* argument is the multiplexer ID number that was returned by the I_LINK *ioctl*( ) command when a STREAM was connected downstream from the multiplexing driver. If *arg* is MUXID_ALL, then all STREAMs that were connected to *fildes* are disconnected. As in I_LINK, this command requires acknowledgement.

The *ioctl*( ) function with the I_UNLINK command will fail if:

[ENXIO]   Hangup received on *fildes*.

[ETIME]   Time out before acknowledgement message was received at STREAM head.

[EAGAIN] or [ENOSR]
           Unable to allocate buffers for the acknowledgement message.

[EINVAL]   Invalid multiplexer ID number.

An I_UNLINK can also fail while waiting for the multiplexing driver to acknowledge the request if a message indicating an error or a hangup is received at the STREAM head of *fildes*. In addition, an error code can be returned in the positive or negative acknowledgement message. For these cases, I_UNLINK fails with *errno* set to the value in the message.

I_PLINK   Creates a *persistent connection* between two STREAMs, where *fildes* is the file descriptor of the STREAM connected to the multiplexing driver, and *arg* is the file descriptor of the STREAM connected to another driver. This call creates a persistent connection which can exist even if the file descriptor *fildes* associated with the upper STREAM to the multiplexing driver is closed. The STREAM designated by *arg* gets connected via a persistent connection below the multiplexing driver. I_PLINK requires the multiplexing driver to send an acknowledgement message to the STREAM head. This call returns a multiplexer ID number (an identifier that may be used to disconnect the multiplexer, see I_PUNLINK) on success, and −1 on failure.

The *ioctl*( ) function with the I_PLINK command will fail if:

[ENXIO]   Hangup received on *fildes*.

[ETIME]   Time out before acknowledgement message was received at STREAM head.

[EAGAIN] or [ENOSR]
              Unable to allocate STREAMS storage to perform the I_PLINK.

[EBADF]   The *arg* argument is not a valid, open file descriptor.

[EINVAL]   The *fildes* argument does not support multiplexing; or *arg* is not a STREAM or is already connected downstream from a multiplexer; or the specified I_PLINK operation would connect the STREAM head in more than one place in the multiplexed STREAM.

An I_PLINK can also fail while waiting for the multiplexing driver to acknowledge the request, if a message indicating an error or a hangup is received at the STREAM head of *fildes*. In addition, an error code can be returned in the positive or negative acknowledgement message. For these cases, I_PLINK fails with *errno* set to the value in the message.

I_PUNLINK   Disconnects the two STREAMs specified by *fildes* and *arg* from a persistent connection. The *fildes* argument is the file descriptor of the STREAM connected to the multiplexing driver. The *arg* argument is the multiplexer ID number that was returned by the I_PLINK *ioctl*( ) command when a STREAM was connected downstream from the multiplexing driver. If *arg* is MUXID_ALL then all STREAMs which are persistent connections to *fildes* are disconnected. As in I_PLINK, this command requires the multiplexing driver to acknowledge the request.

The *ioctl*( ) function with the I_PUNLINK command will fail if:

[ENXIO]   Hangup received on *fildes*.

[ETIME]   Time out before acknowledgement message was received at STREAM head.

[EAGAIN] or [ENOSR]
              Unable to allocate buffers for the acknowledgement message.

[EINVAL]   Invalid multiplexer ID number.

An I_PUNLINK can also fail while waiting for the multiplexing driver to acknowledge the request if a message indicating an error or a hangup is received at the STREAM head of *fildes*. In addition, an error code can be returned in the positive or negative acknowledgement message. For these cases, I_PUNLINK fails with *errno* set to the value in the message.

RETURN VALUE

Upon successful completion, *ioctl( )* returns a value other than –1 that depends upon the STREAMS device control function. Otherwise, it returns –1 and sets *errno* to indicate the error.

ERRORS

Under the following general conditions, *ioctl( )* will fail if:

[EBADF]   The *fildes* argument is not a valid open file descriptor.

[EINTR]   A signal was caught during the *ioctl( )* operation.

[EINVAL]   The STREAM or multiplexer referenced by *fildes* is linked (directly or indirectly) downstream from a multiplexer.

If an underlying device driver detects an error, then *ioctl( )* will fail if:

[EINVAL]   The *request* or *arg* argument is not valid for this device.

[EIO]   Some physical I/O error has occurred.

[ENOTTY]   The *fildes* argument is not associated with a STREAMS device that accepts control functions.

[ENXIO]   The *request* and *arg* arguments are valid for this device driver, but the service requested can not be performed on this particular sub-device.

[ENODEV]   The *fildes* argument refers to a valid STREAMS device, but the corresponding device driver does not support the *ioctl( )* function.

If a STREAM is connected downstream from a multiplexer, any *ioctl( )* command except I_UNLINK and I_PUNLINK will set *errno* to [EINVAL].

APPLICATION USAGE

The implementation-defined timeout interval for STREAMS has historically been 15 seconds.

SEE ALSO

close( ), *fcntl( )*, *getmsg( )*, *open( )*, *pipe( )*, *poll( )*, *putmsg( )*, *read( )*, *sigaction( )*, *write( )*, **<stropts.h>**, **XSH** specification, **Section 2.5**, **STREAMS**.

EXAMPLE

```
/*
 * Copyright (C) ANTRIX Inc.
 */

/* ioctl.c
 * This program gets the device attributes
 * using function ioctl
 */

#include <stdio.h>
#include <stdlib.h>
#include <unistd.h>
```

```
#include <sys/stat.h>
#include <fcntl.h>
#include <sys/types.h>
#include <sys/termio.h>
#include <errno.h>

main()
{
  int     ioctl_value;
  struct  termio tty_termio;

  fprintf (stdout,"get stdin attributes\n");
  ioctl_value = ioctl (0, TCGETA, &tty_termio);
  if ( ioctl_value != -1 ) {
     fprintf (stdout,"ioctl() call successful\n");
     fprintf (stdout,"ioctl_value = %d\n", ioctl_value);
     fprintf (stdout,"tty_termio.c_iflag=%d\n", tty_termio.c_iflag);
     fprintf (stdout,"tty_termio.c_oflag=%d\n", tty_termio.c_oflag);
     fprintf (stdout,"tty_termio.c_lflag=%d\n", tty_termio.c_lflag);
     fprintf (stdout,"tty_termio.c_cc[VINTR]=%d\n", tty_termio.c_cc[VINTR]);
     fprintf (stdout,"tty_termio.c_cc[VQUIT]=%d\n", tty_termio.c_cc[VQUIT]);
     fprintf (stdout,"tty_termio.c_cc[VERASE]=%d\n", tty_termio.c_cc[VERASE]);
     fprintf (stdout,"tty_termio.c_cc[VKILL]=%d\n", tty_termio.c_cc[VKILL]);
     fprintf (stdout,"tty_termio.c_cc[VEOF]=%d\n", tty_termio.c_cc[VEOF]);
  }
  else {
     fprintf (stderr,"ERROR: ioctl() call failed\n");
     fprintf (stderr,"ERROR: %s\n", strerror(errno));
  }
}
```

isalnum( )

NAME

isalnum — test for alphanumeric character

SYNOPSIS

```
#include <ctype.h>

int isalnum(int c);
```

DESCRIPTION

The *isalnum*( ) function tests whether *c* is a character of class **alpha** or **digit** in the program's current locale, see the **XBD** specification, **Chapter 5**, **Locale**.

In all cases *c* is an **int**, the value of which must be representable as an **unsigned char** or must equal the value of the macro EOF. If the argument has any other value, the behaviour is undefined.

RETURN VALUE

The *isalnum*( ) function returns non-zero if *c* is an alphanumeric character; otherwise it returns 0.

ERRORS

No errors are defined.

APPLICATION USAGE

To ensure application portability, especially across natural languages, only this function and those listed in the **SEE ALSO** section should be used for character classification.

SEE ALSO

isalpha( ), *iscntrl*( ), *isdigit*( ), *isgraph*( ), *islower*( ), *isprint*( ), *ispunct*( ), *isspace*( ), *isupper*( ), *isxdigit*( ), *setlocale*( ), **<ctype.h>**, **<stdio.h>**, the **XBD** specification, **Chapter 5**, **Locale**.

EXAMPLE

```
/*
 * Copyright (C) ANTRIX Inc.
 */

/* isalnum.c
 * This program tests whether c is a character of class alpha
 * or digit in the program's current locale using function isalnum.
 */

#include <stdio.h>
#include <stdlib.h>
#include <ctype.h>
#include <errno.h>

main()
{
  int   isalnum_value;
  int   c;

  c = '1';
  fprintf (stdout,"example 1\n");
  fprintf (stdout,"test if digit 1 is alphanumeric character\n");
  isalnum_value = isalnum (c);
  if ( isalnum_value != 0 ) {
     fprintf (stdout,"isalnum() call successful\n");
     fprintf (stdout,"isalnum_value=%d\n", isalnum_value);
```

```
    }
    else
        fprintf (stderr,"ERROR: isalnum() call failed\n");

    c = 'a';
    fprintf (stdout,"example 2\n");
    fprintf (stdout,"test if alphabet a is alphanumeric character\n");
    isalnum_value = isalnum (c);
    if ( isalnum_value != 0 ) {
        fprintf (stdout,"isalnum() call successful\n");
        fprintf (stdout,"isalnum_value=%d\n", isalnum_value);
    }
    else
        fprintf (stderr,"ERROR: isalnum() call failed\n");
}
```

NAME

isalpha — test for alphabetic character

SYNOPSIS

```
#include <ctype.h>

int isalpha(int c);
```

DESCRIPTION

The *isalpha( )* function tests whether *c* is a character of class **alpha** in the program's current locale, see the **XBD** specification, **Chapter 5**, **Locale**.

In all cases *c* is an **int**, the value of which must be representable as an **unsigned char** or must equal the value of the macro EOF. If the argument has any other value, the behaviour is undefined.

RETURN VALUE

The *isalpha( )* function returns non-zero if *c* is an alphabetic character; otherwise it returns 0.

ERRORS

No errors are defined.

APPLICATION USAGE

To ensure application portability, especially across natural languages, only this function and those listed in the **SEE ALSO** section should be used for character classification.

SEE ALSO

isalnum( ), *iscntrl( )*, *isdigit( )*, *isgraph( )*, *islower( )*, *isprint( )*, *ispunct( )*, *isspace( )*, *isupper( )*, *isxdigit( )*, *setlocale( )*, **<ctype.h>**, **<stdio.h>**, the **XBD** specification, **Chapter 5**, **Locale**.

EXAMPLE

```
/*
 * Copyright (C) ANTRIX Inc.
 */

/* isalpha.c
 * This program tests whether c is a character of class alpha
 * in the program's current locale using function isalpha.
 */

#include <stdio.h>
#include <stdlib.h>
#include <ctype.h>
#include <errno.h>

main()
{
  int   isalpha_value;
  int   c = 'a';

  fprintf (stdout,"test if character a is alphabet\n");
  isalpha_value = isalpha (c);
  if ( isalpha_value != 0 ) {
      fprintf (stdout,"isalpha() call successful\n");
      fprintf (stdout,"isalpha_value=%d\n", isalpha_value);
  }
  else
```

```
        fprintf (stderr,"ERROR: isalpha() call failed\n");
}
```

isascii( )

NAME

isascii — test for 7-bit US-ASCII character

SYNOPSIS

EX
```
#include <ctype.h>

int isascii(int c);
```

DESCRIPTION

The *isascii*( ) function tests whether *c* is a 7-bit US-ASCII character code.

The *isascii*( ) function is defined on all integer values.

RETURN VALUE

The *isascii*( ) function returns non-zero if *c* is a 7-bit US-ASCII character code between 0 and octal 0177 inclusive; otherwise it returns 0.

ERRORS

No errors are defined.

SEE ALSO

<ctype.h>.

EXAMPLE

```
/*
 * Copyright (C) ANTRIX Inc.
 */

/* isascii.c
 * This program tests whether c is a 7-bit US-ASCII character
 * code using function isascii.
 */

#include <stdio.h>
#include <stdlib.h>
#include <ctype.h>
#include <errno.h>

main()
{
  int  isascii_value;
  int  c = '*';

  fprintf (stdout,"test if * is an ascii character\n");
  isascii_value = isascii (c);
  if ( isascii_value != 0 ) {
     fprintf (stdout,"isascii() call successful\n");
     fprintf (stdout,"isascii_value=%d\n", isascii_value);
  }
  else
     fprintf (stderr,"ERROR: isascii() call failed\n");
}
```

NAME

isastream — test a file descriptor

SYNOPSIS

UX

```
#include <stropts.h>
```

```
int isastream(int fildes);
```

DESCRIPTION

The *isastream*( ) function tests whether *fildes*, an open file descriptor, is associated with a STREAMS-based file.

RETURN VALUE

Upon successful completion, *isastream*( ) returns 1 if *fildes* refers to a STREAMS-based file and 0 if not. Otherwise, *isastream*( ) returns –1 and sets *errno* to indicate the error.

ERRORS

The *isastream*( ) function will fail if:

[EBADF]   The *fildes* argument is not a valid open file descriptor.

SEE ALSO

<stropts.h>.

EXAMPLE

```
/*
 * Copyright (C) ANTRIX Inc.
 */

/* isastream.c
 * This program determines if a file descriptor represents a
 * a stream file using function isastream
 */

#include <stdio.h>
#include <stdlib.h>
#include <fcntl.h>
#include <sys/stat.h>
#include <errno.h>

#define  PERM_ALL   (S_IRWXU | S_IRWXG | S_IRWXO)

main()
{
  int     isastream_value;
  int     fildes;
  char    *file = "testfile";

  fprintf (stdout,"create testfile\n");
  fildes = creat (file, PERM_ALL);

  isastream_value = isastream (fildes);
  if ( isastream_value != -1 )
     fprintf (stdout,"isastream() call successful\n");
  else {
     fprintf (stderr,"ERROR: isastream() call failed\n");
```

```
        fprintf (stderr,"ERROR: %s\n", strerror(errno));
    }

    fprintf (stdout,"remove testfile\n");
    remove (file);
}
```

NAME

isatty — test for a terminal device

SYNOPSIS

```
#include <unistd.h>

int isatty(int fildes);
```

DESCRIPTION

The *isatty*( ) function tests whether *fildes*, an open file descriptor, is associated with a terminal device.

RETURN VALUE

The *isatty*( ) function returns 1 if *fildes* is associated with a terminal; otherwise it returns 0 and may set *errno* to indicate the error.

ERRORS

The *isatty*( ) function may fail if:

EX [EBADF]   The *fildes* argument is not a valid open file descriptor.

[ENOTTY]   The *fildes* argument is not associated with a terminal.

APPLICATION USAGE

The *isatty*( ) function does not necessarily indicate that a human being is available for interaction via *fildes*. It is quite possible that non-terminal devices are connected to the communications line.

SEE ALSO

<unistd.h>.

EXAMPLE

```
/*
 * Copyright (C) ANTRIX Inc.
 */

/* isatty.c
 * This program tests whether fildes, an open file descriptor
 * is associated with terminal device using function isatty.
 */

#include <stdio.h>
#include <stdlib.h>
#include <fcntl.h>
#include <errno.h>

main()
{
   int  isatty_value;
   int  fildes;
   char *ttyname_value;
   char  *filename = "testfile";

   fprintf (stdout,"get ttyname\n");
   ttyname_value = (char *)ttyname((int)0);
   fprintf (stdout,"ttyname is %s\n", ttyname_value);
```

```
        fprintf (stdout,"open tty\n");
        fildes = open (ttyname_value, O_RDONLY);

        fprintf (stdout,"test if fildes is associated with tty\n");
        isatty_value = isatty (fildes);
        if ( isatty_value == 1 )
            fprintf (stdout,"isatty() call successful\n");
        else
            fprintf (stderr,"ERROR: isatty() call failed\n");

        close (fildes);
}
```

NAME

iscntrl — test for control character

SYNOPSIS

```
#include <ctype.h>

int iscntrl(int c);
```

DESCRIPTION

The *iscntrl( )* function tests whether *c* is a character of class **cntrl** in the program's current locale, see the **XBD** specification, **Chapter 5**, **Locale**.

In all cases *c* is a type **int**, the value of which must be a character representable as an **unsigned char** or must equal the value of the macro EOF. If the argument has any other value, the behaviour is undefined.

RETURN VALUE

The *iscntrl( )* function returns non-zero if *c* is a control character; otherwise it returns 0.

ERRORS

No errors are defined.

APPLICATION USAGE

To ensure applications portability, especially across natural languages, only this function and those listed in the **SEE ALSO** section should be used for character classification.

SEE ALSO

isalnum( ), *isalpha( )*, *isdigit( )*, *isgraph( )*, *islower( )*, *isprint( )*, *ispunct( )*, *isspace( )*, *isupper( )*, *isxdigit( )*, *setlocale( )*, **<ctype.h>**, the **XBD** specification, **Chapter 5**, **Locale**.

EXAMPLE

```
/*
 * Copyright (C) ANTRIX Inc.
 */

/* iscntrl.c
 * This program tests whether c is a character of class cntrl
 * in the program's current locale using function iscntrl.
 */

#include <stdio.h>
#include <stdlib.h>
#include <ctype.h>
#include <errno.h>

main()
{
    int  iscntrl_value;
    int  c = ' 12';

    fprintf (stdout,"test if ascii equivalent of newline 012\n");
    fprintf (stdout,"is a control character\n");
    iscntrl_value = iscntrl (c);
    if ( iscntrl_value != 0 ) {
        fprintf (stdout,"iscntrl() call successful\n");
        fprintf (stdout,"iscntrl_value=%d\n", iscntrl_value);
    }
```

```
        else
            fprintf (stderr,"ERROR: iscntrl() call failed\n");
    }
```

NAME

isdigit — test for decimal digit

SYNOPSIS

```
#include <ctype.h>

int isdigit(int c);
```

DESCRIPTION

The *isdigit*( ) function tests whether *c* is a character of class **digit** in the program's current locale, see the **XBD** specification, **Chapter 5**, **Locale**.

In all cases *c* is an **int**, the value of which must be a character representable as an **unsigned char** or must equal the value of the macro EOF. If the argument has any other value, the behaviour is undefined.

RETURN VALUE

The *isdigit*( ) function returns non-zero if *c* is a decimal digit; otherwise it returns 0.

ERRORS

No errors are defined.

APPLICATION USAGE

To ensure applications portability, especially across natural languages, only this function and those listed in the **SEE ALSO** section should be used for character classification.

SEE ALSO

isalnum( ), *isalpha*( ), *iscntrl*( ), *isgraph*( ), *islower*( ), *isprint*( ), *ispunct*( ), *isspace*( ), *isupper*( ), *isxdigit*( ), **<ctype.h>**.

EXAMPLE

```
/*
 * Copyright (C) ANTRIX Inc.
 */

/* isdigit.c
 * This program tests whether c is a character of class digit
 * in the program's current locale using function isdigit.
 */

#include <stdio.h>
#include <stdlib.h>
#include <ctype.h>
#include <errno.h>

main()
{
    int  isdigit_value;
    int  c = '9';

    fprintf (stdout,"test if 9 is a digit\n");
    isdigit_value = isdigit (c);
    if ( isdigit_value != 0 ) {
        fprintf (stdout,"isdigit() call successful\n");
        fprintf (stdout,"isdigit_value=%d\n", isdigit_value);
    }
    else
```

```
        fprintf (stderr,"ERROR: isdigit() call failed\n");
    }
```

NAME

isgraph — test for visible character

SYNOPSIS

```
#include <ctype.h>

int isgraph(int c);
```

DESCRIPTION

The *isgraph*( ) function tests whether *c* is a character of class **graph** in the program's current locale, see the **XBD** specification, **Chapter 5**, **Locale**.

In all cases *c* is an **int**, the value of which must be a character representable as an **unsigned char** or must equal the value of the macro EOF. If the argument has any other value, the behaviour is undefined.

RETURN VALUE

The *isgraph*( ) function returns non-zero if *c* is a character with a visible representation; otherwise it returns 0.

ERRORS

No errors are defined.

APPLICATION USAGE

To ensure applications portability, especially across natural languages, only this function and those listed in the **SEE ALSO** section should be used for character classification.

SEE ALSO

isalnum( ), *isalpha*( ), *iscntrl*( ), *isdigit*( ), *islower*( ), *isprint*( ), *ispunct*( ), *isspace*( ), *isupper*( ), *isxdigit*( ), *setlocale*( ), **<ctype.h>**, the **XBD** specification, **Chapter 5**, **Locale**.

EXAMPLE

```
/*
 * Copyright (C) ANTRIX Inc.
 */

/* isgraph.c
 * This program tests whether c is a character of class graph
 * in the program's current locale using function c.
 */

#include <stdio.h>
#include <stdlib.h>
#include <ctype.h>
#include <errno.h>

main()
{
  int  isgraph_value;
  int  c = '*';

  fprintf (stdout,"test if * is a graph character\n");
  isgraph_value = isgraph (c);
  if ( isgraph_value != 0 )
      fprintf (stdout,"isgraph() call successful\n");
```

```
    else
        fprintf (stderr,"ERROR: isgraph() call failed\n");
}
```

NAME

islower — test for lower-case letter

SYNOPSIS

```
#include <ctype.h>

int islower(int c);
```

DESCRIPTION

The *islower*( ) function tests whether *c* is a character of class **lower** in the program's current locale, see the **XBD** specification, **Chapter 5**, **Locale**.

In all cases *c* is an **int**, the value of which must be a character representable as an **unsigned char** or must equal the value of the macro EOF. If the argument has any other value, the behaviour is undefined.

RETURN VALUE

The *islower*( ) function returns non-zero if *c* is a lower-case letter; otherwise it returns 0.

ERRORS

No errors are defined.

APPLICATION USAGE

To ensure applications portability, especially across natural languages, only this function and those listed in the **SEE ALSO** section should be used for character classification.

SEE ALSO

isalnum( ), *isalpha*( ), *iscntrl*( ), *isdigit*( ), *isgraph*( ), *isprint*( ), *ispunct*( ), *isspace*( ), *isupper*( ), *isxdigit*( ), *setlocale*( ), **<ctype.h>**, the **XBD** specification, **Chapter 5**, **Locale**.

```c
/*
 * Copyright (C) ANTRIX Inc.
 */


/* islower.c
 * This program tests whether c is a character of class lower
 * in the program's current locale using function islower.
 */

#include <stdio.h>
#include <stdlib.h>
#include <ctype.h>
#include <errno.h>

main()
{
    int  islower_value;
    int  c = 'a';

    fprintf (stdout,"test if a is lowercase character\n");
    islower_value = islower (c);
    if ( islower_value != 0 ) {
        fprintf (stdout,"islower() call successful\n");
        fprintf (stdout,"islower_value=%d\n", islower_value);
    }
```

```
    else
        fprintf (stderr,"ERROR: islower() call failed\n");
}
```

NAME

isnan — test for NaN

SYNOPSIS

EX   `#include <math.h>`

`int isnan(double x);`

DESCRIPTION

The *isnan*( ) function tests whether *x* is NaN.

RETURN VALUE

The *isnan*( ) function returns non-zero if *x* is NaN. Otherwise, 0 is returned.

ERRORS

No errors are defined.

APPLICATION USAGE

On systems not supporting NaN values, *isnan*( ) always returns 0.

SEE ALSO

<math.h>.

EXAMPLE

```
/*
 * Copyright (C) ANTRIX Inc.
 */

/* isnan.c
 * This program tests whether x is a NaN using function isnan.
 */

#include <stdio.h>
#include <stdlib.h>
#include <math.h>
#include <errno.h>

main()
{
   int     isnan_value;
   double  x = 0xFFFFFFFF;

   fprintf (stdout,"check 0xFFFFFFFF for nan\n");
   isnan_value = isnan (x);
   if ( isnan_value != 0 ) {
      fprintf (stdout,"isnan() call successful\n");
      fprintf (stdout,"number=#x%x is NaN\n", x);
   }
   else {
      fprintf (stderr,"ERROR: isnan() call failed\n");
      fprintf (stdout,"number=#x%x is not NaN\n", x);
   }
}
```

NAME

isprint — test for printing character

SYNOPSIS

```
#include <ctype.h>

int isprint(int c);
```

DESCRIPTION

The *isprint( )* function tests whether *c* is a character of class **print** in the program's current locale, see the **XBD** specification, **Chapter 5**, **Locale**.

In all cases *c* is an **int**, the value of which must be a character representable as an **unsigned char** or must equal the value of the macro EOF. If the argument has any other value, the behaviour is undefined.

RETURN VALUE

The *isprint( )* function returns non-zero if *c* is a printing character; otherwise it returns 0.

ERRORS

No errors are defined.

APPLICATION USAGE

To ensure applications portability, especially across natural languages, only this function and those listed in the **SEE ALSO** section should be used for character classification.

SEE ALSO

isalnum( ), *isalpha( )*, *iscntrl( )*, *isdigit( )*, *isgraph( )*, *islower( )*, *ispunct( )*, *isspace( )*, *isupper( )*, *isxdigit( )*, *setlocale( )*, **<ctype.h>**, the **XBD** specification, **Chapter 5**, **Locale**.

EXAMPLE

```
/*
 * Copyright (C) ANTRIX Inc.
 */

/* isprint.c
 * This program tests whether c is a character of class print
 * in the program's current locale using function isprint.
 */

#include <stdio.h>
#include <stdlib.h>
#include <ctype.h>
#include <errno.h>

main()
{
   int   isprint_value;
   int   c = '>';

   fprintf (stdout,"test if > is a printable character\n");
   isprint_value = isprint (c);
   if ( isprint_value != 0 ) {
      fprintf (stdout,"isprint() call successful\n");
      fprintf (stdout,"isprint_value=%d\n", isprint_value);
   }
   else
```

```
        fprintf (stderr,"ERROR: isprint() call failed\n");
}
```

NAME

ispunct — test for punctuation character

SYNOPSIS

```
#include <ctype.h>

int ispunct(int c);
```

DESCRIPTION

The *ispunct*( ) function tests whether *c* is a character of class **punct** in the program's current locale, see the **XBD** specification, **Chapter 5**, **Locale**.

In all cases *c* is an **int**, the value of which must be a character representable as an **unsigned char** or must equal the value of the macro EOF. If the argument has any other value, the behaviour is undefined.

RETURN VALUE

The *ispunct*( ) function returns non-zero if *c* is a punctuation character; otherwise it returns 0.

ERRORS

No errors are defined.

APPLICATION USAGE

To ensure applications portability, especially across natural languages, only this function and those listed in the **SEE ALSO** section should be used for character classification.

SEE ALSO

isalnum( ), *isalpha*( ), *iscntrl*( ), *isdigit*( ), *isgraph*( ), *islower*( ), *isprint*( ), *isspace*( ), *isupper*( ), *isxdigit*( ), *setlocale*( ), **<ctype.h>**, the **XBD** specification, **Chapter 5**, **Locale**.

EXAMPLE

```
/*
 * Copyright (C) ANTRIX Inc.
 */

/* ispunct.c
 * This program tests whether c is a character of class punct
 * in the program's current locale using function ispunct.
 */

#include <stdio.h>
#include <stdlib.h>
#include <ctype.h>
#include <errno.h>

main()
{
   int   ispunct_value;
   int   c = '!';

   fprintf (stdout,"test if ! is a punctuation character\n");
   ispunct_value = ispunct (c);
   if ( ispunct_value != 0 ) {
      fprintf (stdout,"ispunct() call successful\n");
      fprintf (stdout,"ispunct_value=%d\n", ispunct_value);
   }
   else {
```

```
            fprintf (stderr,"ERROR: ispunct() call failed\n");
            fprintf (stderr,"ERROR: %s\n", strerror(errno));
        }
    }
```

NAME

isspace — test for white-space character

SYNOPSIS

```
#include <ctype.h>

int isspace(int c);
```

DESCRIPTION

The *isspace*( ) function tests whether *c* is a character of class **space** in the program's current locale, see the **XBD** specification, **Chapter 5**, **Locale**.

In all cases *c* is an **int**, the value of which must be a character representable as an **unsigned char** or must equal the value of the macro EOF. If the argument has any other value, the behaviour is undefined.

RETURN VALUE

The *isspace*( ) function returns non-zero if *c* is a white-space character; otherwise it returns 0.

ERRORS

No errors are defined.

APPLICATION USAGE

To ensure applications portability, especially across natural languages, only this function and those listed in the **SEE ALSO** section should be used for character classification.

SEE ALSO

isalnum( ), *isalpha*( ), *iscntrl*( ), *isdigit*( ), *isgraph*( ), *islower*( ), *isprint*( ), *ispunct*( ), *isupper*( ), *isxdigit*( ), *setlocale*( ), **<ctype.h>**, the **XBD** specification, **Chapter 5**, **Locale**.

EXAMPLE

```
/*
 * Copyright (C) ANTRIX Inc.
 */

/* isspace.c
 * This program tests whether c is a character of class space
 * in the program's current locale using function isspace.
 */

#include <stdio.h>
#include <stdlib.h>
#include <ctype.h>
#include <errno.h>

main()
{
   int      isspace_value;
   int      c = '\n';

   fprintf (stdout,"test if '\n' is a space character\n");
   isspace_value = isspace (c);
   if ( isspace_value != 0 ) {
      fprintf (stdout,"isspace() call successful\n");
      fprintf (stdout,"isspace_value=%d\n", isspace_value);
   }
   else
```

```
        fprintf (stderr,"ERROR: isspace() call failed\n");
    }
```

NAME

isupper — test for upper-case letter

SYNOPSIS

```
#include <ctype.h>

int isupper(int c);
```

DESCRIPTION

The *isupper*( ) function tests whether *c* is a character of class **upper** in the program's current locale, see the **XBD** specification, **Chapter 5**, **Locale**.

In all cases *c* is an **int**, the value of which must be a character representable as an **unsigned char** or must equal the value of the macro EOF. If the argument has any other value, the behaviour is undefined.

RETURN VALUE

The *isupper*( ) function returns non-zero if *c* is an upper-case letter; otherwise it returns 0.

ERRORS

No errors are defined.

APPLICATION USAGE

To ensure applications portability, especially across natural languages, only this function and those listed in the **SEE ALSO** section should be used for character classification.

SEE ALSO

isalnum( ), *isalpha*( ), *iscntrl*( ), *isdigit*( ), *isgraph*( ), *islower*( ), *isprint*( ), *ispunct*( ), *isspace*( ), *isxdigit*( ), *setlocale*( ), **<ctype.h>**, the **XBD** specification, **Chapter 5**, **Locale**.

EXAMPLE

```c
/*
 * Copyright (C) ANTRIX Inc.
 */

/* isupper.c
 * This program tests whether c is a character of class upper
 * in the program's current locale using function isupper.
 */

#include <stdio.h>
#include <stdlib.h>
#include <ctype.h>
#include <errno.h>

main()
{
   int     isupper_value;
   int     c = 'A';

   fprintf (stdout,"test if A is an uppercase character\n");
   isupper_value = isupper (c);
   if ( isupper_value != 0 ) {
      fprintf (stdout,"isupper() call successful\n");
      fprintf (stdout,"isupper_value=%d\n", isupper_value);
   }
   else
```

```
        fprintf (stderr,"ERROR: isupper() call failed\n");
    }
```

NAME

iswalnum — test for an alphanumeric wide-character code

SYNOPSIS

WP

```
#include <wchar.h>
```

```
int iswalnum(wint_t wc);
```

DESCRIPTION

The *iswalnum*( ) function tests whether *wc* is a wide-character code representing a character of class **alpha** or **digit** in the program's current locale, see the **XBD** specification, **Chapter 5**, **Locale**.

In all cases *wc* is a **wint_t**, the value of which must be a wide-character code corresponding to a valid character in the current locale or must equal the value of the macro WEOF. If the argument has any other value, the behaviour is undefined.

RETURN VALUE

The *iswalnum*( ) function returns non-zero if *wc* is an alphanumeric wide-character code; otherwise it returns 0.

ERRORS

No errors are defined.

APPLICATION USAGE

To ensure applications portability, especially across natural languages, only this function and those listed in the **SEE ALSO** section should be used for classification of wide-character codes.

SEE ALSO

iswalpha( ), *iswcntrl*( ), *iswdigit*( ), *iswgraph*( ), *iswlower*( ), *iswprint*( ), *iswpunct*( ), *iswspace*( ), *iswupper*( ), *iswxdigit*( ), *setlocale*( ), **<wchar.h>**, **<stdio.h>**, the **XBD** specification, **Chapter 5**, **Locale**.

EXAMPLE

```
/*
 * Copyright (C) ANTRIX Inc.
 */

/* iswalnum.c
 * This program tests whether wc is wide-character code representing
 * a character of class alpha or digit in the program's current
 * locale using function iswalnum.
 */

#include <stdio.h>
#include <stdlib.h>
#include <wchar.h>
#include <ctype.h>
#include <errno.h>

main()
{
    int      iswalnum_value;
    wint_t   wc;

    wc = L'1';
    fprintf (stdout,"example 1\n");
```

```
    fprintf (stdout,"test if digit 1 is alphanumeric character\n");
    iswalnum_value = iswalnum (wc);
    if ( iswalnum_value != 0 ) {
        fprintf (stdout,"iswalnum() call successful\n");
        fprintf (stdout,"iswalnum_value=%d\n", iswalnum_value);
    }
    else
        fprintf (stderr,"ERROR: iswalnum() call failed\n");

    wc = L'a';
    fprintf (stdout,"example 2\n");
    fprintf (stdout,"test if alphabet a is alphanumeric character\n");
    iswalnum_value = iswalnum (wc);
    if ( iswalnum_value != 0 ) {
        fprintf (stdout,"iswalnum() call successful\n");
        fprintf (stdout,"iswalnum_value=%d\n", iswalnum_value);
    }
    else
        fprintf (stderr,"ERROR: iswalnum() call failed\n");
}
```

NAME

iswalpha — test for an alphabetic wide-character code

SYNOPSIS

WP   ```
#include <wchar.h>
```

```
int iswalpha(wint_t wc);
```

DESCRIPTION

The *iswalpha*( ) function tests whether *wc* is a wide-character code representing a character of class **alpha** in the program's current locale, see the **XBD** specification, **Chapter 5**, **Locale**.

In all cases *wc* is a **wint_t**, the value of which must be a wide-character code corresponding to a valid character in the current locale or must equal the value of the macro WEOF. If the argument has any other value, the behaviour is undefined.

RETURN VALUE

The *iswalpha*( ) function returns non-zero if *wc* is an alphabetic wide-character code; otherwise it returns 0.

ERRORS

No errors are defined.

APPLICATION USAGE

To ensure applications portability, especially across natural languages, only this function and those listed in the **SEE ALSO** section should be used for classification of wide-character codes.

SEE ALSO

iswalnum( ), *iswcntrl*( ), *iswdigit*( ), *iswgraph*( ), *iswlower*( ), *iswprint*( ), *iswpunct*( ), *iswspace*( ), *iswupper*( ), *iswxdigit*( ), *setlocale*( ), **<wchar.h>**, **<stdio.h>**, the **XBD** specification, **Chapter 5**, **Locale**.

EXAMPLE

```
/*
 * Copyright (C) ANTRIX Inc.
 */

/* iswalpha.c
 * This program tests whether wc is a wide-character code
 * representing a character of class alpha in the program's
 * current locale using function iswalpha.
 */

#include <stdio.h>
#include <stdlib.h>
#include <wchar.h>
#include <ctype.h>
#include <errno.h>

main()
{
  int      iswalpha_value;
  wint_t   wc = L'a';

  fprintf (stdout,"test if character a is alphabet\n");
  iswalpha_value = iswalpha (wc);
  if ( iswalpha_value != 0 ) {
```
```

```
        fprintf (stdout,"iswalpha() call successful\n");
        fprintf (stdout,"iswalpha_value=%d\n", iswalpha_value);
    }
    else
        fprintf (stderr,"ERROR: iswalpha() call failed\n");
}
```

NAME

iswcntrl — test for a control wide-character code

SYNOPSIS

WP

```
#include <wchar.h>
```

```
int iswcntrl(wint_t wc);
```

DESCRIPTION

The *iswcntrl( )* function tests whether *wc* is a wide-character code representing a character of class **control** in the program's current locale, see the **XBD** specification, **Chapter 5**, **Locale**.

In all cases *wc* is a **wint_t**, the value of which must be a wide-character code corresponding to a valid character in the current locale or must equal the value of the macro WEOF. If the argument has any other value, the behaviour is undefined.

RETURN VALUE

The *iswcntrl( )* function returns non-zero if *wc* is a control wide-character code; otherwise it returns 0.

ERRORS

No errors are defined.

APPLICATION USAGE

To ensure applications portability, especially across natural languages, only this function and those listed in the **SEE ALSO** section should be used for classification of wide-character codes.

SEE ALSO

iswalnum( ), *iswalpha( )*, *iswdigit( )*, *iswgraph( )*, *iswlower( )*, *iswprint( )*, *iswpunct( )*, *iswspace( )*, *iswupper( )*, *iswxdigit( )*, *setlocale( )*, **<wchar.h>**, the **XBD** specification, **Chapter 5**, **Locale**.

EXAMPLE

```
/*
 * Copyright (C) ANTRIX Inc.
 */

/* iswcntrl.c
 * This program tests whether wc is a wide-character code
 * representing a character of class control in the program's
 * current locale using function iswcntrl.
 */

#include <stdio.h>
#include <stdlib.h>
#include <wchar.h>
#include <ctype.h>
#include <errno.h>

main()
{
   int     iswcntrl_value;
   wint_t  wc = L' 12';

   fprintf (stdout,"test if ascii equivalent of newline 012\n");
   fprintf (stdout,"is a control character\n");
   iswcntrl_value = iswcntrl (wc);
   if ( iswcntrl_value != 0 ) {
```

```
          fprintf (stdout,"iswcntrl() call successful\n");
          fprintf (stdout,"iswcntrl_value=%d\n", iswcntrl_value);
     }
   else
        fprintf (stderr,"ERROR: iswcntrl() call failed\n");
   }
```

NAME

iswctype - test character for specified class

SYNOPSIS

WP   `#include <wchar.h>`

`int iswctype(wint_t wc, wctype_t charclass);`

DESCRIPTION

The *iswctype( )* function determines whether the wide-character code *wc* has the character class *charclass*, returning true or false. The *iswctype( )* function is defined on WEOF and wide-character codes corresponding to the valid character encodings in the current locale. If the *wc* argument is not in the domain of the function, the result is undefined. If the value of *charclass* is invalid (that is, not obtained by a call to *wctype( )* or *charclass* is invalidated by a subsequent call to *setlocale( )* that has affected category LC_CTYPE) the result is implementation-dependent.

RETURN VALUE

The *iswctype( )* function returns 0 for false and non-zero for true.

ERRORS

No errors are defined.

APPLICATION USAGE

The twelve strings — "alnum", "alpha", "blank" "cntrl", "digit", "graph", "lower", "print", "punct", "space", "upper" and "xdigit" — are reserved for the standard character classes. In the table below, the functions in the left column are equivalent to the functions in the right column.

```
iswalnum(wc)     iswctype(wc, wctype("alnum"))
iswalpha(wc)     iswctype(wc, wctype("alpha"))
iswcntrl(wc)     iswctype(wc, wctype("cntrl"))
iswdigit(wc)     iswctype(wc, wctype("digit"))
iswgraph(wc)     iswctype(wc, wctype("graph"))
iswlower(wc)     iswctype(wc, wctype("lower"))
iswprint(wc)     iswctype(wc, wctype("print"))
iswpunct(wc)     iswctype(wc, wctype("punct"))
iswspace(wc)     iswctype(wc, wctype("space"))
iswupper(wc)     iswctype(wc, wctype("upper"))
iswxdigit(wc)    iswctype(wc, wctype("xdigit"))
```

Note: The call:

```
iswctype(wc, wctype("blank"))
```

does not have an equivalent *isw*( )* function.

SEE ALSO

iswalnum( ), *iswalpha( )*, *iswcntrl( )*, *iswdigit( )*, *iswgraph( )*, *iswlower( )*, *iswprint( )*, *iswpunct( )*, *iswspace( )*, *iswupper( )*, *iswxdigit( )*, *wctype( )*, **<wchar.h>**.

EXAMPLE

```
/*
 * Copyright (C) ANTRIX Inc.
 */

/* iswctype.c
 * This program tests whether wc is a wide-character code of
```

```
 * character class corresponding to the valid character encodings
 * in the current locale using function iswctype.
 */

#include <stdio.h>
#include <stdlib.h>
#include <wchar.h>
#include <ctype.h>
#include <errno.h>

main()
{
  int    iswctype_value;
  wint_t wc = L' 12';

  fprintf (stdout,"test if ascii equivalent of newline 012\n");
  fprintf (stdout,"is a control character\n");
  iswctype_value = iswctype (wc, wctype("cntrl"));
  if ( iswctype_value != 0 ) {
     fprintf (stdout,"iswctype() call successful\n");
     fprintf (stdout,"iswctype_value=%d\n", iswctype_value);
  }
  else
     fprintf (stderr,"ERROR: iswctype() call failed\n");
}
```

NAME

iswdigit — test for a decimal digit wide-character code

SYNOPSIS

WP

```
#include <wchar.h>
```

```
int iswdigit(wint_t wc);
```

DESCRIPTION

The *iswdigit*( ) function tests whether *wc* is a wide-character code representing a character of class **digit** in the program's current locale, see the **XBD** specification, **Chapter 5**, **Locale**.

In all cases *wc* is a **wint_t**, the value of which must be a wide-character code corresponding to a valid character in the current locale or must equal the value of the macro WEOF. If the argument has any other value, the behaviour is undefined.

RETURN VALUE

The *iswdigit*( ) function returns non-zero if *wc* is a decimal digit wide-character code; otherwise it returns 0.

ERRORS

No errors are defined.

APPLICATION USAGE

To ensure applications portability, especially across natural languages, only this function and those listed in the **SEE ALSO** section should be used for classification of wide-character codes.

SEE ALSO

iswalnum( ), *iswalpha*( ), *iswcntrl*( ), *iswgraph*( ), *iswlower*( ), *iswprint*( ), *iswpunct*( ), *iswspace*( ), *iswupper*( ), *iswxdigit*( ), **<wchar.h>**.

EXAMPLE

```
/*
 * Copyright (C) ANTRIX Inc.
 */

/* iswdigit.c
 * This program tests whether wc is a wide-character code
 * representing a character of class digit in the program's
 * current locale.
 */

#include <stdio.h>
#include <stdlib.h>
#include <wchar.h>
#include <ctype.h>
#include <errno.h>

main()
{
   int     iswdigit_value;
   wint_t  wc = L'9';

   fprintf (stdout,"test if 9 is a digit\n");
   iswdigit_value = iswdigit (wc);
   if ( iswdigit_value != 0 ) {
      fprintf (stdout,"iswdigit() call successful\n");
```

```
        fprintf (stdout,"iswdigit_value=%d\n", iswdigit_value);
   }
  else
     fprintf (stderr,"ERROR: iswdigit() call failed\n");
}
```

iswgraph( )

NAME

iswgraph — test for a visible wide-character code

SYNOPSIS

WP
```
#include <wchar.h>
```
```
int iswgraph(wint_t wc);
```

DESCRIPTION

The *iswgraph*( ) function tests whether *wc* is a wide-character code representing a character of class **graph** in the program's current locale, see the **XBD** specification, **Chapter 5**, **Locale**.

In all cases *wc* is a **wint_t**, the value of which must be a wide-character code corresponding to a valid character in the current locale or must equal the value of the macro WEOF. If the argument has any other value, the behaviour is undefined.

RETURN VALUE

The *iswgraph*( ) function returns non-zero if *wc* is a wide-character code with a visible representation; otherwise it returns 0.

ERRORS

No errors are defined.

APPLICATION USAGE

To ensure applications portability, especially across natural languages, only this function and those listed in the **SEE ALSO** section should be used for classification of wide-character codes.

SEE ALSO

iswalnum( ), *iswalpha*( ), *iswcntrl*( ), *iswdigit*( ), *iswlower*( ), *iswprint*( ), *iswpunct*( ), *iswspace*( ), *iswupper*( ), *iswxdigit*( ), *setlocale*( ), **<wchar.h>**, the **XBD** specification, **Chapter 5**, **Locale**.

EXAMPLE

```
/*
 * Copyright (C) ANTRIX Inc.
 */

/* iswgraph.c
 * This program tests whether wc is a wide-character code
 * representing a character of class graph in the programmer's
 * current locale using function iswgraph.
 */

#include <stdio.h>
#include <stdlib.h>
#include <wchar.h>
#include <ctype.h>
#include <errno.h>

main()
{
  int     iswgraph_value;
  wint_t  wc = L'*';

  fprintf (stdout,"test if * is a graph character\n");
  iswgraph_value = iswgraph (wc);
  if ( iswgraph_value != 0 )
     fprintf (stdout,"iswgraph() call successful\n");
```

```
     else
        fprintf (stderr,"ERROR: iswgraph() call failed\n");
}
```

NAME

iswlower — test for a lower-case letter wide-character code

SYNOPSIS

WP
```
#include <wchar.h>

int iswlower(wint_t wc);
```

DESCRIPTION

The *iswlower*( ) function tests whether *wc* is a wide-character code representing a character of class **lower** in the program's current locale, see the **XBD** specification, **Chapter 5**, **Locale**.

In all cases *wc* is a **wint_t**, the value of which must be a wide-character code corresponding to a valid character in the current locale or must equal the value of the macro WEOF. If the argument has any other value, the behaviour is undefined.

RETURN VALUE

The *iswlower*( ) function returns non-zero if *wc* is a lower-case letter wide-character code; otherwise it returns 0.

ERRORS

No errors are defined.

APPLICATION USAGE

To ensure applications portability, especially across natural languages, only this function and those listed in the **SEE ALSO** section should be used for classification of wide-character codes.

SEE ALSO

iswalnum( ), *iswalpha*( ), *iswcntrl*( ), *iswdigit*( ), *iswgraph*( ), *iswprint*( ), *iswpunct*( ), *iswspace*( ), *iswupper*( ), *iswxdigit*( ), *setlocale*( ), **<wchar.h>**, the **XBD** specification, **Chapter 5**, **Locale**.

EXAMPLE

```
/*
 * Copyright (C) ANTRIX Inc.
 */

/* iswlower.c
 * This program tests whether wc is a wide-character code
 * representing a character of class lower in the program's
 * current locale using function iswlower.
 */

#include <stdio.h>
#include <stdlib.h>
#include <wchar.h>
#include <ctype.h>
#include <errno.h>

main()
{
    int     iswlower_value;
    wint_t  wc = L'a';

    fprintf (stdout,"test if a is lowercase character\n");
    iswlower_value = iswlower (wc);
    if ( iswlower_value != 0 ) {
        fprintf (stdout,"iswlower() call successful\n");
```

```
        fprintf (stdout,"iswlower_value=%d\n", iswlower_value);
    }
    else
        fprintf (stderr,"ERROR: iswlower() call failed\n");
}
```

NAME

iswprint — test for a printing wide-character code

SYNOPSIS

WP
```
#include <wchar.h>

int iswprint(wint_t wc);
```

DESCRIPTION

The *iswprint*( ) function tests whether *wc* is a wide-character code representing a character of class **print** in the program's current locale, see the **XBD** specification, **Chapter 5**, **Locale**.

In all cases *wc* is a **wint_t**, the value of which must be a wide-character code corresponding to a valid character in the current locale or must equal the value of the macro WEOF. If the argument has any other value, the behaviour is undefined.

RETURN VALUE

The *iswprint*( ) function returns non-zero if *wc* is a printing wide-character code; otherwise it returns 0.

ERRORS

No errors are defined.

APPLICATION USAGE

To ensure applications portability, especially across natural languages, only this function and those listed in the **SEE ALSO** section should be used for classification of wide-character codes.

SEE ALSO

iswalnum( ), *iswalpha*( ), *iswcntrl*( ), *iswdigit*( ), *iswgraph*( ), *iswlower*( ), *iswpunct*( ), *iswspace*( ), *iswupper*( ), *iswxdigit*( ), *setlocale*( ), **<wchar.h>**, the **XBD** specification, **Chapter 5**, **Locale**.

EXAMPLE

```
/*
 * Copyright (C) ANTRIX Inc.
 */

/* iswprint.c
 * This program tests whether wc is a wide-character code
 * representing a character of class print in the program's
 * current locale using function iswprint.
 */

#include <stdio.h>
#include <stdlib.h>
#include <wchar.h>
#include <ctype.h>
#include <errno.h>

main()
{
    int     iswprint_value;
    wint_t  wc = L'>';

    fprintf (stdout,"test if > is a printable character\n");
    iswprint_value = iswprint (wc);
    if ( iswprint_value != 0 ) {
        fprintf (stdout,"iswprint() call successful\n");
```

```
        fprintf (stdout,"iswprint_value=%d\n", iswprint_value);
    }
  else
      fprintf (stderr,"ERROR: iswprint() call failed\n");
}
```

NAME

iswpunct — test for a punctuation wide-character code

SYNOPSIS

WP
```
#include <wchar.h>
```

```
int iswpunct(wint_t wc);
```

DESCRIPTION

The *iswpunct( )* function tests whether *wc* is a wide-character code representing a character of class **punct** in the program's current locale, see the **XBD** specification, **Chapter 5**, **Locale**.

In all cases *wc* is a **wint_t**, the value of which must be a wide-character code corresponding to a valid character in the current locale or must equal the value of the macro WEOF. If the argument has any other value, the behaviour is undefined.

RETURN VALUE

The *iswpunct( )* function returns non-zero if *wc* is a punctuation wide-character code; otherwise it returns 0.

ERRORS

No errors are defined.

APPLICATION USAGE

To ensure applications portability, especially across natural languages, only this function and those listed in the **SEE ALSO** section should be used for classification of wide-character codes.

SEE ALSO

iswalnum( ), *iswalpha( )*, *iswcntrl( )*, *iswdigit( )*, *iswgraph( )*, *iswlower( )*, *iswprint( )*, *iswspace( )*, *iswupper( )*, *iswxdigit( )*, *setlocale( )*, **<wchar.h>**, the **XBD** specification, **Chapter 5**, **Locale**.

EXAMPLE

```
/*
 * Copyright (C) ANTRIX Inc.
 */

/* iswpunct.c
 * This program tests whether wc is a wide-character code
 * representing a character of class punct in the program's
 * current locale using function iswpunct.
 */

#include <stdio.h>
#include <stdlib.h>
#include <wchar.h>
#include <ctype.h>
#include <errno.h>

main()
{
    int     iswpunct_value;
    wint_t  wc = L'!';

    fprintf (stdout,"test if ! is a punctuation character\n");
    iswpunct_value = iswpunct (wc);
    if ( iswpunct_value != 0 ) {
        fprintf (stdout,"iswpunct() call successful\n");
```

```
        fprintf (stdout,"iswpunct_value=%d\n", iswpunct_value);
    }
    else {
        fprintf (stderr,"ERROR: iswpunct() call failed\n");
        fprintf (stderr,"ERROR: %s\n", strerror(errno));
    }
}
```

iswspace( )

NAME

iswspace — test for a white-space wide-character code

SYNOPSIS

WP   `#include <wchar.h>`

`int iswspace(wint_t wc);`

DESCRIPTION

The *iswspace*( ) function tests whether *wc* is a wide-character code representing a character of class **space** in the program's current locale, see the **XBD** specification, **Chapter 5**, **Locale**.

In all cases *wc* is a **wint_t**, the value of which must be a wide-character code corresponding to a valid character in the current locale or must equal the value of the macro WEOF. If the argument has any other value, the behaviour is undefined.

RETURN VALUE

The *iswspace*( ) function returns non-zero if *wc* is a white-space wide-character code; otherwise it returns 0.

ERRORS

No errors are defined.

APPLICATION USAGE

To ensure applications portability, especially across natural languages, only this function and those listed in the **SEE ALSO** section should be used for classification of wide-character codes.

SEE ALSO

iswalnum( ), *iswalpha*( ), *iswcntrl*( ), *iswdigit*( ), *iswgraph*( ), *iswlower*( ), *iswprint*( ), *iswpunct*( ), *iswupper*( ), *iswxdigit*( ), *setlocale*( ), **<wchar.h>**, the **XBD** specification, **Chapter 5**, **Locale**.

EXAMPLE

```
/*
 * Copyright (C) ANTRIX Inc.
 */

/* iswspace.c
 * This program tests whether wc is a wide-character code
 * representing a character of class space in the program's
 * current locale using function iswspace.
 */

#include <stdio.h>
#include <stdlib.h>
#include <wchar.h>
#include <ctype.h>
#include <errno.h>

main()
{
  int     iswspace_value;
  wint_t  wc = L'\n';

  fprintf (stdout,"test if '\n' is a space character\n");
  iswspace_value = iswspace (wc);
  if ( iswspace_value != 0 ) {
      fprintf (stdout,"iswspace() call successful\n");
```

```
        fprintf (stdout,"iswspace_value=%d\n", iswspace_value);
    }
  else
        fprintf (stderr,"ERROR: iswspace() call failed\n");
}
```

NAME

iswupper — test for an upper-case letter wide-character code

SYNOPSIS

WP
```
#include <wchar.h>
```

```
int iswupper(wint_t wc);
```

DESCRIPTION

The *iswupper*( ) function tests whether *wc* is a wide-character code representing a character of class **upper** in the program's current locale, see the **XBD** specification, **Chapter 5**, **Locale**.

In all cases *wc* is a **wint_t**, the value of which must be a wide-character code corresponding to a valid character in the current locale or must equal the value of the macro WEOF. If the argument has any other value, the behaviour is undefined.

RETURN VALUE

The *iswupper*( ) function returns non-zero if *wc* is an upper-case letter wide-character code; otherwise it returns 0.

ERRORS

No errors are defined.

APPLICATION USAGE

To ensure applications portability, especially across natural languages, only this function and those listed in the **SEE ALSO** section should be used for classification of wide-character codes.

SEE ALSO

iswalnum( ), *iswalpha*( ), *iswcntrl*( ), *iswdigit*( ), *iswgraph*( ), *iswlower*( ), *iswprint*( ), *iswpunct*( ), *iswspace*( ), *iswxdigit*( ), *setlocale*( ), **<wchar.h>**, the **XBD** specification, **Chapter 5**, **Locale**.

EXAMPLE

```
/*
 * Copyright (C) ANTRIX Inc.
 */

/* iswupper.c
 * This program tests whether wc is a wide-character code
 * representing a character of class upper in the program's
 * current locale using function iswupper.
 */

#include <stdio.h>
#include <stdlib.h>
#include <wchar.h>
#include <ctype.h>
#include <errno.h>

main()
{
  int     iswupper_value;
  wint_t  wc = L'A';

  fprintf (stdout,"test if A is an uppercase character\n");
  iswupper_value = iswupper (wc);
  if ( iswupper_value != 0 ) {
     fprintf (stdout,"iswupper() call successful\n");
```

```
        fprintf (stdout,"iswupper_value=%d\n", iswupper_value);
    }
  else
      fprintf (stderr,"ERROR: iswupper() call failed\n");
}
```

NAME

iswxdigit — test for a hexadecimal digit wide-character code

SYNOPSIS

WP
```
#include <wchar.h>
```
```
int iswxdigit(wint_t wc);
```

DESCRIPTION

The *iswxdigit*( ) function tests whether *wc* is a wide-character code representing a character of class **xdigit** in the program's current locale, see the **XBD** specification, **Chapter 5**, **Locale**.

In all cases *wc* is a **wint_t**, the value of which must be a wide-character code corresponding to a valid character in the current locale or must equal the value of the macro WEOF. If the argument has any other value, the behaviour is undefined.

RETURN VALUE

The *iswxdigit*( ) function returns non-zero if *wc* is a hexadecimal digit wide-character code; otherwise it returns 0.

ERRORS

No errors are defined.

APPLICATION USAGE

To ensure applications portability, especially across natural languages, only this function and those listed in the **SEE ALSO** section should be used for classification of wide-character codes.

SEE ALSO

iswalnum( ), *iswalpha*( ), *iswcntrl*( ), *iswdigit*( ), *iswgraph*( ), *iswlower*( ), *iswprint*( ), *iswpunct*( ), *iswspace*( ), *iswupper*( ), *setlocale*( ), **<wchar.h>**.

EXAMPLE

```
/*
 * Copyright (C) ANTRIX Inc.
 */

/* iswxdigit.c
 * This program tests whether wc is a wide-character code
 * representing a character of class xdigit in the program's
 * current locale using function iswxdigit.
 */

#include <stdio.h>
#include <stdlib.h>
#include <wchar.h>
#include <ctype.h>
#include <errno.h>

main()
{
   int     iswxdigit_value;
   wint_t  wc = L'F';

   fprintf (stdout,"test if F is a hexadecimal character\n");
   iswxdigit_value = iswxdigit (wc);
   if ( iswxdigit_value != 0 ) {
      fprintf (stdout,"iswxdigit() call successful\n");
```

```
      fprintf (stdout,"iswxdigit_value=%d\n", iswxdigit_value);
   }
   else
      fprintf (stderr,"ERROR: iswxdigit() call failed\n");
}
```

NAME

isxdigit — test for hexadecimal digit

SYNOPSIS

```
#include <ctype.h>

int isxdigit(int c);
```

DESCRIPTION

The *isxdigit*( ) function tests whether *c* is a character of class **xdigit** in the program's current locale, see the **XBD** specification, **Chapter 5**, **Locale**.

In all cases *c* is an **int**, the value of which must be a character representable as an **unsigned char** or must equal the value of the macro EOF. If the argument has any other value, the behaviour is undefined.

RETURN VALUE

The *isxdigit*( ) function returns non-zero if *c* is a hexadecimal digit; otherwise it returns 0.

ERRORS

No errors are defined.

APPLICATION USAGE

To ensure applications portability, especially across natural languages, only this function and those listed in the **SEE ALSO** section should be used for character classification.

SEE ALSO

isalnum( ), *isalpha*( ), *iscntrl*( ), *isdigit*( ), *isgraph*( ), *islower*( ), *isprint*( ), *ispunct*( ), *isspace*( ), *isupper*( ), **<ctype.h>**.

EXAMPLE

```
/*
 * Copyright (C) ANTRIX Inc.
 */

/* isxdigit.c
 * This program tests whether c is a character of class xdigit
 * in the program's current locale using function isxdigit.
 */

#include <stdio.h>
#include <stdlib.h>
#include <ctype.h>
#include <errno.h>

main()
{
    int     isxdigit_value;
    int     c = 'F';

    fprintf (stdout,"test if F is a hexadecimal character\n");
    isxdigit_value = isxdigit (c);
    if ( isxdigit_value != 0 ) {
        fprintf (stdout,"isxdigit() call successful\n");
        fprintf (stdout,"isxdigit_value=%d\n", isxdigit_value);
    }
    else
```

```
        fprintf (stderr,"ERROR: isxdigit() call failed\n");
    }
```

NAME

j0, j1, jn — Bessel functions of the first kind

SYNOPSIS

EX
```
#include <math.h>

double j0(double x);

double j1(double x);

double jn(int n, double x);
```

DESCRIPTION

The *j0*( ), *j1*( ) and *jn*( ) functions compute Bessel functions of *x* of the first kind of orders 0, 1 and *n* respectively.

RETURN VALUE

Upon successful completion, *j0*( ), *j1*( ) and *jn*( ) return the relevant Bessel value of *x* of the first kind.

If the *x* argument is too large in magnitude, 0 is returned and *errno* may be set to [ERANGE].

If *x* is NaN, NaN is returned and *errno* may be set to [EDOM].

If the correct result would cause underflow, 0 is returned and *errno* may be set to [ERANGE].

ERRORS

The *j0*( ), *j1*( ) and *jn*( ) functions may fail if:

[EDOM]   The value of *x* is NaN.

[ERANGE]   The value of *x* was too large in magnitude, or underflow occurred.

No other errors will occur.

APPLICATION USAGE

An application wishing to check for error situations should set *errno* to 0 before calling *j0*( ), *j1*( ) or *jn*( ). If *errno* is non-zero on return, or the return value is NaN, an error has occurred.

SEE ALSO

isnan( ), *y0*( ), **<math.h>**.

EXAMPLE

```
/*
 * Copyright (C) ANTRIX Inc.
 */

/* j0.c
 * This program computes Bessel functions of x of the first kind
 * of order 0 using function j0.
 */

#include <stdio.h>
#include <math.h>

main()
{
  double  j0_value;
  double  x = 10.00;
```

```
    j0_value = j0 (x);
    fprintf (stdout,"j0 of %f is %f\n", x, j0_value);
}

/*
 * Copyright (C) ANTRIX Inc.
 */

/* j1.c
 * This program computes Bessel functions of x of the first kind
 * of order 1 using function j1.
 */

#include <stdio.h>
#include <math.h>

main()
{
  double  j1_value;
  double  x = 10.00;

  j1_value = j1 (x);
  fprintf (stdout,"j1 of %f is %f\n", x, j1_value);
}

/*
 * Copyright (C) ANTRIX Inc.
 */

/* jn.c
 * This program computes Bessel functions of x of the first kind
 * of order n using function jn.
 */

#include <stdio.h>
#include <math.h>

main()
{
  double  jn_value;
  double  x = 1.00;
  int     n = 1;

  jn_value = jn (n, x);
  fprintf (stdout,"jn of %d, %f is %f\n", n, x, jn_value);
}
```

NAME

jrand48 — generate uniformly distributed pseudo-random long signed integers

SYNOPSIS

EX   `#include <stdlib.h>`

`long int jrand48(unsigned short int xsubi[3]);`

DESCRIPTION

Refer to *drand48*( ).

EXAMPLE

```
/*
 * Copyright (C) ANTRIX Inc.
 */

/* jrand48.c
 * This program generates signed long random integers uniformly
 * distributed over the interval [-2 raise 31, 2 raise 31]
 * using function jrand.
 */

#include <stdio.h>
#include <stdlib.h>
#include <errno.h>

main()
{
  double          jrand48_value;
  int             i;
  unsigned short  xsubi[3];

  xsubi[0] = 10;
  for ( i = 0; i < 5; i++ ) {
      jrand48_value = jrand48 (xsubi);
      fprintf (stdout,"random value in iteration %d is %d\n",
                      i, jrand48_value);
  }
}
```

NAME

kill — send a signal to a process or a group of processes

SYNOPSIS

OH
```
#include <sys/types.h>
#include <signal.h>

int kill(pid_t pid, int sig);
```

DESCRIPTION

The *kill*( ) function will send a signal to a process or a group of processes specified by *pid*. The signal to be sent is specified by *sig* and is either one from the list given in **<signal.h>** or 0. If *sig* is 0 (the null signal), error checking is performed but no signal is actually sent. The null signal can be used to check the validity of *pid*.

FIPS
{_POSIX_SAVED_IDS} will be defined on all XSI-conformant systems, and for a process to have permission to send a signal to a process designated by *pid*, the real or effective user ID of the sending process must match the real or saved set-user-ID of the receiving process, unless the sending process has appropriate privileges.

If *pid* is greater than 0, *sig* will be sent to the process whose process ID is equal to *pid*.

If *pid* is 0, *sig* will be sent to all processes (excluding an unspecified set of system processes) whose process group ID is equal to the process group ID of the sender, and for which the process has permission to send a signal.

EX
If *pid* is –1, *sig* will be sent to all processes (excluding an unspecified set of system processes) for which the process has permission to send that signal.

If *pid* is negative, but not –1, *sig* will be sent to all processes (excluding an unspecified set of system processes) whose process group ID is equal to the absolute value of *pid*, and for which the process has permission to send a signal.

If the value of *pid* causes *sig* to be generated for the sending process, and if *sig* is not blocked, either *sig* or at least one pending unblocked signal will be delivered to the sending process before *kill*( ) returns.

The user ID tests described above will not be applied when sending SIGCONT to a process that is a member of the same session as the sending process.

An implementation that provides extended security controls may impose further implementation-dependent restrictions on the sending of signals, including the null signal. In particular, the system may deny the existence of some or all of the processes specified by *pid*.

The *kill*( ) function is successful if the process has permission to send *sig* to any of the processes specified by *pid*. If *kill*( ) fails, no signal will be sent.

RETURN VALUE

Upon successful completion, 0 is returned. Otherwise, –1 is returned and *errno* is set to indicate the error.

ERRORS

The *kill*( ) function will fail if:

[EINVAL]	The value of the *sig* argument is an invalid or unsupported signal number.
[EPERM]	The process does not have permission to send the signal to any receiving process.
[ESRCH]	No process or process group can be found corresponding to that specified by *pid*.

kill( )

SEE ALSO

getpid( ), *raise*( ), *setsid*( ), *sigaction*( ), **<signal.h>**, **<sys/types.h>**.

EXAMPLE

```
/*
 * Copyright (C) ANTRIX Inc.
 */

/* kill.c
 * This program sends a SIGALRM and SIGPIPE to a process
 * using function kill.
 */

#include <stdio.h>
#include <stdlib.h>
#include <unistd.h>
#include <signal.h>
#include <sys/wait.h>
#include <errno.h>

void handler(signal)
int signal;
{
  if ( signal == SIGALRM )
      fprintf (stdout,"received signal SIGALRM\n");
  else
      fprintf (stderr,"ERROR: expected=%d, received=%d\n",
                       SIGALRM, signal);
}

void svc_child(signal)
int signal;
{
  if ( signal == SIGPIPE )
      fprintf (stdout,"received signal SIGPIPE\n");
  else
      fprintf (stderr,"ERROR: expected=%d, received=%d\n",
                       SIGPIPE, signal);
}

main()
{
  int     kill_value;
  int     stat_loc;
  pid_t   pid, child;

  fprintf (stdout,"example 1\n");
  fprintf (stdout,"get process id\n");
  pid = getpid ();
  fprintf (stdout,"set SIGALRM\n");
  signal (SIGALRM, handler);
  fprintf (stdout,"send signal SIGALRM\n");
  kill_value = kill (pid, SIGALRM);
```

```
    if ( kill_value == 0 )
       fprintf (stdout,"kill() call successful\n");
    else {
       fprintf (stderr,"ERROR: kill() call failed\n");
       fprintf (stderr,"ERROR: %s\n", strerror(errno));
    }

    fprintf (stdout,"example 2\n");
    fprintf (stdout,"send signal to child\n");
    child = fork();
    if ( child == 0 ) {
       fprintf (stdout,"This is child\n");
       fprintf (stdout,"setup svc_child handler for SIGPIPE\n");
       signal (SIGPIPE, svc_child);
       sleep (10);
       exit (1);
    }
    fprintf (stdout,"send SIGPIPE to child\n");
    kill_value = kill (child, SIGPIPE);
    if ( kill_value == 0 )
       fprintf (stdout,"kill() call successful\n");
    else {
       fprintf (stderr,"ERROR: kill() call failed\n");
       fprintf (stderr,"ERROR: %s\n", strerror(errno));
    }
    wait (&stat_loc);
    fprintf (stdout,"WEXITSTATUS(stat_loc)=%d\n", WEXITSTATUS(stat_loc) );
}
```

NAME

killpg — send a signal to a process group

SYNOPSIS

UX   ```
#include <signal.h>
```

```
int killpg(pid_t pgrp, int sig);
```

DESCRIPTION

The *killpg*( ) function sends the signal specified by *sig* to the process group specified by *pgrp*.

If *pgrp* is greater than 1, *killpg*(*pgrp*, *sig*) is equivalent to *kill*(–*pgrp*, *sig*). If *pgrp* is less than or equal to 1, the behaviour of *killpg*( ) is undefined.

RETURN VALUE

Refer to *kill*( ).

ERRORS

Refer to *kill*( ).

SEE ALSO

getpgid( ), *getpid*( ), *kill*( ), *raise*( ), **<signal.h>**.

EXAMPLE

```c
/*
 * Copyright (C) ANTRIX Inc.
 */

/* killpg.c
 * This program sends the signal sig to the process group pgrp
 * using function killpg.
 */

#include <stdio.h>
#include <stdlib.h>
#include <unistd.h>
#include <signal.h>
#include <sys/wait.h>
#include <errno.h>

void handler(signal)
int signal;
{
  if ( signal == SIGALRM )
     fprintf (stdout,"received signal SIGALRM\n");
  else
     fprintf (stderr,"ERROR: expected=%d, received=%d\n",
                     SIGALRM, signal);
}

main()
{
  int      killpg_value;
  int      stat_loc;
  pid_t    pid, child;
  pid_t    pgrp;
```
```

```
    fprintf (stdout,"get process group\n");
    pgrp = getpgrp();

    fprintf (stdout,"set SIGALRM\n");
    signal (SIGALRM, handler);

    fprintf (stdout,"send signal SIGALRM\n");
    killpg_value = killpg (pgrp, SIGALRM);
    if ( killpg_value == 0 )
        fprintf (stdout,"killpg() call successful\n");
    else {
        fprintf (stderr,"ERROR: killpg() call failed\n");
        fprintf (stderr,"ERROR: %s\n", strerror(errno));
    }
}
```

NAME

l64a — convert 32-bit integer to radix-64 ASCII string

SYNOPSIS

UX

```
#include <stdlib.h>

char *l64a(long value);
```

DESCRIPTION

Refer to *a64l( )*.

EXAMPLE

```
/*
 * Copyright (C) ANTRIX Inc.
 */

/* l64a.c
 * This program converts long integer value 123 to base 64
 * representation using function l64a.
 */

#include <stdio.h>
#include <stdlib.h>
#include <errno.h>

main()
{
  char  *l64a_value;
  long   l = 123456;

  fprintf (stdout,"convert long to base 64 representation\n");
  l64a_value = (char *)l64a (l);
  if ( l64a_value != (char *)0 ) {
     fprintf (stdout,"l64a() call successful\n");
     fprintf (stdout,"long %ld converted to string is %s\n",
                     l, l64a_value);
  }
  else
     fprintf (stderr,"ERROR: l64a() call failed\n");
}
```

NAME

labs — return long integer absolute value

SYNOPSIS

```
#include <stdlib.h>

long int labs(long int i);
```

DESCRIPTION

The *labs*( ) function computes the absolute value of its long integer operand, *i*. If the result cannot be represented, the behaviour is undefined.

RETURN VALUE

The *labs*( ) function returns the absolute value of its long integer operand.

ERRORS

No errors are defined.

SEE ALSO

abs( ), **<stdlib.h>**.

EXAMPLE

```
/*
 * Copyright (C) ANTRIX Inc.
 */

/* labs.c
 * This program computes the absolute value of its long integer
 * operand, i using function labs.
 */

#include <stdio.h>
#include <stdlib.h>
#include <errno.h>

main()
{
  long int  labs_value;
  long int  i = -5;

  labs_value = labs (i);
  if ( labs_value == 5 ) {
      fprintf (stdout,"labs() call successful\n");
      fprintf (stdout,"absolute value of %ld is %ld\n", i, labs_value);
  }
  else
      fprintf (stderr,"ERROR: labs() call failed\n");
}
```

NAME

lchown — change owner and group of a file

SYNOPSIS

UX

```
#include <unistd.h>
```

```
int lchown(const char *path, uid_t owner, gid_t group);
```

DESCRIPTION

The *lchown*( ) function has the same effect as *chown*( ) except in the case where the named file is a symbolic link. In this case *lchown*( ) changes the ownership of the symbolic link file itself, while *chown*( ) changes the ownership of the file or directory to which the symbolic link refers.

RETURN VALUE

Upon successful completion, *lchown*( ) returns 0. Otherwise, it returns −1 and sets *errno* to indicate an error.

ERRORS

The *lchown*( ) function will fail if:

[EACCES]　　　　Search permission is denied on a component of the path prefix of *path*.

[EINVAL]　　　　The owner or group id is not a value supported by the implementation.

[ENAMETOOLONG]

　　　　　　　　The length of a pathname exceeds {PATH_MAX}, or pathname component is longer than {NAME_MAX}.

[ENOENT]　　　　A component of *path* does not name an existing file or *path* is an empty string.

[ENOTDIR]　　　A component of the path prefix of *path* is not a directory.

[EOPNOTSUPP] The *path* argument names a symbolic link and the implementation does not support setting the owner or group of a symbolic link.

[ELOOP]　　　　Too many symbolic links were encountered in resolving *path*.

[EPERM]　　　　The effective user ID does not match the owner of the file and the process does not have appropriate privileges.

[EROFS]　　　　The file resides on a read-only file system.

The *lchown*( ) function may fail if:

[EIO]　　　　　An I/O error occurred while reading or writing to the file system.

[EINTR]　　　　A signal was caught during execution of the function.

[ENAMETOOLONG]

　　　　　　　　Pathname resolution of a symbolic link produced an intermediate result whose length exceeds {PATH_MAX}.

APPLICATION USAGE

On implementations which support symbolic links as directory entries rather than files, *lchown*( ) may fail.

SEE ALSO

chown( ), *symlink*( ), **<unistd.h>**.

EXAMPLE

```
/*
 * Copyright (C) ANTRIX Inc.
 */
```

```
/* lchown.c
 * This program changes the owner and group of a file
 * using function lchown
 */

#include <stdio.h>
#include <stdlib.h>
#include <unistd.h>
#include <sys/types.h>
#include <sys/stat.h>
#include <errno.h>

#define  PERM_ALL   (S_IRWXU | S_IRWXG | S_IRWXO)

main()
{
  int      lchown_value;
  struct   stat orig_buf, new_buf;
  char     *file1 = "testfile1";
  char     *file2 = "testfile2";

  fprintf (stdout,"create testfile1\n");
  creat (file1, PERM_ALL);

  fprintf (stdout,"create a link from testfile2 to testfile1\n");
  link (file1, file2);

  fprintf (stdout,"check link has been created\n");
  stat (file2, &orig_buf);
  fprintf (stdout,"original owner id=%d, group id=%d\n",
                    orig_buf.st_uid, orig_buf.st_gid );

  fprintf (stdout,"set owner and group to 2 which is bin\n");
  lchown_value = lchown (file2, 2, 2);
  if ( lchown_value == 0 ) {
     fprintf (stdout,"lchown() call successful\n");
     stat (file2, &new_buf);
     fprintf (stdout,"new owner id=%d, group id=%d\n",
                 new_buf.st_uid, new_buf.st_gid );
  }
  else {
     fprintf (stderr,"ERROR: lchown() call failed\n");
     fprintf (stderr,"ERROR: %s\n", strerror(errno));
  }

  fprintf (stdout,"remove testfiles\n");
  unlink (file2);
  remove (file1);
}
```

lcong48( )

NAME

lcong48 — seed uniformly distributed pseudo-random signed long integer generator

SYNOPSIS

EX   `#include <stdlib.h>`

`void lcong48(unsigned short int param[7]);`

DESCRIPTION

Refer to *drand48*( ).

EXAMPLE

```
/*
 * Copyright (C) ANTRIX Inc.
 */

/* lcong48.c
 * This program initializes entry points for random number
 * generator lrand48 using function lcong48.
 */

#include <stdio.h>
#include <stdlib.h>
#include <errno.h>

main()
{
  int     i;
  long    lrand48_value;
  unsigned short param[7] = { 2, 4, 6, 8, 10, 12, 14 };

  lcong48(param);
  for ( i = 0; i < 5; i++ ) {
      lrand48_value = lrand48 ();
      fprintf (stdout,"random value in iteration %d is %d\n",
                      i, lrand48_value);
  }
}
```

NAME

ldexp — load exponent of a floating point number

SYNOPSIS

```
#include <math.h>

double ldexp(double x, int exp);
```

DESCRIPTION

The *ldexp*( ) function computes the quantity $x * 2^{exp}$.

RETURN VALUE

Upon successful completion, *ldexp*( ) returns a **double** representing the value x multiplied by 2 raised to the power *exp*.

EX If the value of x is NaN, NaN is returned and *errno* may be set to [EDOM].

If *ldexp*( ) would cause overflow, ±HUGE_VAL is returned (according to the sign of x), and *errno* is set to [ERANGE].

If *ldexp*( ) would cause underflow, 0 is returned and *errno* may be set to [ERANGE].

ERRORS

The *ldexp*( ) function will fail if:

[ERANGE]   The value to be returned would have caused overflow.

The *ldexp*( ) function may fail if:

EX [EDOM]   The argument x is NaN.

[ERANGE]   The value to be returned would have caused underflow.

No other errors will occur.

APPLICATION USAGE

An application wishing to check for error situations should set *errno* to 0 before calling *ldexp*( ). If *errno* is non-zero on return, or the return value is NaN, an error has occurred.

SEE ALSO

frexp( ), *isnan*( ), **<math.h>**.

EXAMPLE

```
/*
 * Copyright (C) ANTRIX Inc.
 */

/* ldexp.c
 * This program computes the quantity x * 2 raise exp using
 * function ldexp.
 */

#include <stdio.h>
#include <stdlib.h>
#include <math.h>
#include <errno.h>

main()
{
  double   ldexp_value;
```

```
    double  x = 9;
    int     exp = 3;

    ldexp_value = ldexp (x, exp);
    fprintf (stdout,"%f * (2 power %d) is %f\n", x, exp, ldexp_value);
}
```

NAME

ldiv — compute quotient and remainder of a long division

SYNOPSIS

```
#include <stdlib.h>

ldiv_t ldiv(long int numer, long int denom);
```

DESCRIPTION

The *ldiv*( ) function computes the quotient and remainder of the division of the numerator *numer* by the denominator *denom*. If the division is inexact, the resulting quotient is the long integer of lesser magnitude that is the nearest to the algebraic quotient. If the result cannot be represented, the behaviour is undefined; otherwise, *quot * denom + rem* will equal *numer*.

RETURN VALUE

The *ldiv*( ) function returns a structure of type **ldiv_t**, comprising both the quotient and the remainder. The structure includes the following members, in any order:

```
long int   quot;    /* quotient */
long int   rem;     /* remainder */
```

ERRORS

No errors are defined.

SEE ALSO

div( ), **<stdlib.h>**.

EXAMPLE

```
/*
 * Copyright (C) ANTRIX Inc.
 */

/* ldiv.c
 * This program computes quotient and remainder of the division
 * of the numerator numer by the denominator denom using function
 * ldiv.
 */

#include <stdio.h>
#include <stdlib.h>
#include <errno.h>

main()
{
  ldiv_t     ldiv_value;
  long int   numer = 111;
  long int   denom = 2;

  fprintf (stdout,"long division of %ld by %ld\n", numer, denom);
  ldiv_value = ldiv (numer, denom);
  fprintf (stdout,"quotient of %ld/%ld is %ld\n",
                    numer, denom, ldiv_value.quot);
```

```
    fprintf (stdout,"remainder of %ld/%ld is %ld\n",
                numer, denom, ldiv_value.rem);
}
```

NAME

lfind — find entry in linear search table

SYNOPSIS

EX
```
#include <search.h>

void *lfind(const void *key, const void *base, size_t *nelp,
            size_t width, int (*compar)(const void *, const void *));
```

DESCRIPTION

Refer to *lsearch*( ).

EXAMPLE

```
/*
 * Copyright (C) ANTRIX Inc.
 */

/* lfind.c
 * This program does a linear search and returns a pointer
 * into a table indicating where entry may be found and if
 * entry is not found, it is added to the table using
 * function lfind.
 */

#include <stdio.h>
#include <stdlib.h>
#include <sys/types.h>
#include <search.h>
#include <errno.h>

#define  TABLESIZE    5

static  int   table[TABLESIZE];

/* compare () two functions for equality */
int compare (a, b)
const char  *a, *b;
{
  int    *i, *j;

  i = (int *) a;
  j = (int *) b;
  if ( *i == *j )
     return(0);
  else
     return(1);
}

main()
{
  int     i, size;
  int     *iptr;
  char    *found_item;
  size_t  nelp;
```

```
    fprintf (stdout,"create table of size 5\n");
    for ( i = 0; i < TABLESIZE; i++ )
    {
        table[i] = 2*i + 2;
        nelp = i;
        found_item = lsearch ((char *)&table[i], (char *)&table[0],
                             &nelp, sizeof(table[i]), compare);
        iptr = (int *) found_item;
        fprintf (stdout,"entered item in table[%d]=%d\n", i, *iptr);
        if ( *iptr != table[i] )
            fprintf (stderr,"ERROR: lsearch did not enter the item correctly");
    }

    fprintf (stdout,"find item at table[2]\n");
    nelp = TABLESIZE;
    found_item = lfind ((char *)&table[2], (char *)&table[0],
                             &nelp, sizeof(table[2]), compare);
    iptr = (int *) found_item;
    fprintf (stdout,"found item at table[2]=%d\n", *iptr);
    if ( *iptr != 6 )
        fprintf (stderr,"ERROR: lfind did not find item %d correctly",2);
}
```

NAME

lgamma — log gamma function

SYNOPSIS

EX   `#include <math.h>`

`double lgamma(double x);`

`extern int signgam;`

DESCRIPTION

The *lgamma*( ) function computes $\log_e|\Gamma(x)|$ where $\Gamma(x)$ is defined as $\int_0^\infty e^{-t}t^{x-1}\,dt$. The sign of $\Gamma(x)$ is returned in the external integer *signgam*. The argument x may not be a non-positive integer ($\Gamma(x)$ is defined over the reals, except the non-positive integers).

RETURN VALUE

Upon successful completion, *lgamma*( ) returns the logarithmic gamma of x.

If x is NaN, NaN is returned and *errno* may be set to [EDOM].

If x is a non-positive integer, either HUGE_VAL or NaN is returned and *errno* may be set to [EDOM].

If the correct value would cause overflow, *lgamma*( ) returns HUGE_VAL and may set *errno* to [ERANGE].

If the correct value would cause underflow, *lgamma*( ) returns 0 and may set *errno* to [ERANGE].

ERRORS

The *lgamma*( ) function may fail if:

[EDOM]   The value of x is a non-positive integer or NaN.

[ERANGE]   The value to be returned would have caused overflow or underflow.

No other errors will occur.

APPLICATION USAGE

An application wishing to check for error situations should set *errno* to 0 before calling *lgamma*( ). If *errno* is non-zero on return, or the return value is NaN, an error has occurred.

SEE ALSO

exp( ), *isnan*( ), **<math.h>**.

EXAMPLE

```
/*
 * Copyright (C) ANTRIX Inc.
 */

/* lgamma.c
 * This program computes logarithmic gamma of x using
 * function lgamma.
 */

#include <stdio.h>
#include <math.h>

main()
```

```
{
  double  lgamma_value;
  double  x = 1.40;

  lgamma_value = lgamma (x);
  fprintf (stdout,"lgamma of %f is %f\n", x, lgamma_value);
}
```

NAME

link — link to a file

SYNOPSIS

```
#include <unistd.h>

int link(const char *path1, const char *path2);
```

DESCRIPTION

The *link*( ) function creates a new link (directory entry) for the existing file, *path1*.

The *path1* argument points to a pathname naming an existing file. The *path2* argument points to a pathname naming the new directory entry to be created. The *link*( ) function will atomically create a new link for the existing file and the link count of the file is incremented by one.

If *path1* names a directory, *link*( ) will fail unless the process has appropriate privileges and the implementation supports using *link*( ) on directories.

Upon successful completion, *link*( ) will mark for update the *st_ctime* field of the file. Also, the *st_ctime* and *st_mtime* fields of the directory that contains the new entry are marked for update.

If *link*( ) fails, no link is created and the link count of the file will remain unchanged.

The implementation may require that the calling process has permission to access the existing file.

RETURN VALUE

Upon successful completion, 0 is returned. Otherwise, −1 is returned and *errno* is set to indicate the error.

ERRORS

The *link*( ) function will fail if:

[EACCES]	A component of either path prefix denies search permission, or the requested link requires writing in a directory with a mode that denies write permission, or the calling process does not have permission to access the existing file and this is required by the implementation.
[EEXIST]	The link named by *path2* exists.

UX   [ELOOP]   Too many symbolic links were encountered in resolving *path1* or *path2*.

[EMLINK]	The number of links to the file named by *path1* would exceed {LINK_MAX}.
[ENAMETOOLONG]	

FIPS   The length of *path1* or *path2* exceeds {PATH_MAX} or a pathname component is longer than {NAME_MAX}.

[ENOENT]	A component of either path prefix does not exist; the file named by *path1* does not exist; or *path1* or *path2* points to an empty string.
[ENOSPC]	The directory to contain the link cannot be extended.
[ENOTDIR]	A component of either path prefix is not a directory.
[EPERM]	The file named by *path1* is a directory and either the calling process does not have appropriate privileges or the implementation prohibits using *link*( ) on directories.
[EROFS]	The requested link requires writing in a directory on a read-only file system.

UX

[EXDEV]   The link named by *path2* and the file named by *path1* are on different file systems and the implementation does not support links between file systems, or *path1* refers to a named STREAM.

The *link*( ) function may fail if:

UX

[ENAMETOOLONG]

    Pathname resolution of a symbolic link produced an intermediate result whose length exceeds {PATH_MAX}.

APPLICATION USAGE

Some implementations do allow links between file systems.

SEE ALSO

symlink( ), *unlink*( ), **<unistd.h>**.

EXAMPLE

```
/*
 * Copyright (C) ANTRIX Inc.
 */

/* link.c
 * This program creates a new link for the existing file, path1
 * using function link.
 */

#include <stdio.h>
#include <stdlib.h>
#include <unistd.h>
#include <sys/stat.h>
#include <errno.h>

#define  PERM_ALL    (S_IRWXU | S_IRWXG | S_IRWXO)

main()
{
   int          link_value;
   const char   *path1 = "testfile1";
   const char   *path2 = "testfile2";
   struct stat orig_buf, new_buf;

   fprintf (stdout,"create testfile\n");
   creat (path1, PERM_ALL);

   fprintf (stdout,"get testfile1 status\n");
   stat (path1, &orig_buf);
   fprintf (stdout,"orig_buf.st_nlink=%d\n", orig_buf.st_nlink );

   fprintf (stdout,"create link from path1 to path2\n");
   link_value = link (path1, path2);
   if ( link_value == 0 ) {
      fprintf (stdout,"link() call successful\n");
      stat (path1, &new_buf);
      fprintf (stdout,"new_buf.st_nlink=%d\n", new_buf.st_nlink );
   }
```

```
        else {
            fprintf (stderr,"ERROR: link() call failed\n");
            fprintf (stderr,"ERROR: %s\n", strerror(errno));
        }

        fprintf (stdout,"remove testfile\n");
        unlink (path2);
        remove (path1);
}
```

NAME

loc1, loc2 — pointers to characters matched by regular expressions (**TO BE WITHDRAWN**)

SYNOPSIS

EX
```
#include <regexp.h>

extern char *loc1;
extern char *loc2;
```

DESCRIPTION

Refer to *regexp*( ).

APPLICATION USAGE

These variables are kept for historical reasons, but will be withdrawn in a future issue of this document.

New applications should use *fnmatch*( ), *glob*( ), *regcomp*( ) and *regexec*( ), which provide full internationalised regular expression functionality compatible with the ISO POSIX-2 standard, as described in the **XBD** specification, **Chapter 7**, **Regular Expressions**.

NAME

localeconv — determine program locale

SYNOPSIS

```
#include <locale.h>

struct lconv *localeconv(void);
```

DESCRIPTION

The *localeconv*( ) function sets the components of an object with the type **struct lconv** with the values appropriate for the formatting of numeric quantities (monetary and otherwise) according to the rules of the current locale.

The members of the structure with type **char *** are pointers to strings, any of which (except **decimal_point**) can point to "", to indicate that the value is not available in the current locale or is of zero length. The members with type **char** are non-negative numbers, any of which can be {CHAR_MAX} to indicate that the value is not available in the current locale.

The members include the following:

char *decimal_point
> The radix character used to format non-monetary quantities.

char *thousands_sep
> The character used to separate groups of digits before the decimal-point character in formatted non-monetary quantities.

char *grouping
> A string whose elements taken as one-byte integer values indicate the size of each group of digits in formatted non-monetary quantities.

char *int_curr_symbol
> The international currency symbol applicable to the current locale. The first three characters contain the alphabetic international currency symbol in accordance with those specified in the ISO 4217:1987 standard. The fourth character (immediately preceding the null byte) is the character used to separate the international currency symbol from the monetary quantity.

char *currency_symbol
> The local currency symbol applicable to the current locale.

char *mon_decimal_point
> The radix character used to format monetary quantities.

char *mon_thousands_sep
> The separator for groups of digits before the decimal-point in formatted monetary quantities.

char *mon_grouping
> A string whose elements taken as one-byte integer values indicate the size of each group of digits in formatted monetary quantities.

char *positive_sign
> The string used to indicate a non-negative valued formatted monetary quantity.

char *negative_sign
> The string used to indicate a negative valued formatted monetary quantity.

char int_frac_digits
> The number of fractional digits (those after the decimal-point) to be displayed in an internationally formatted monetary quantity.

char frac_digits
>   The number of fractional digits (those after the decimal-point) to be displayed in a formatted monetary quantity.

char p_cs_precedes

EX
>   Set to 1 if the **currency_symbol** or **int_curr_symbol** precedes the value for a non-negative formatted monetary quantity. Set to 0 if the symbol succeeds the value.

char p_sep_by_space

EX

EX
>   Set to 0 if no space separates the **currency_symbol** or **int_curr_symbol** from the value for a non-negative formatted monetary quantity. Set to 1 if a space separates the symbol from the value; and set to 2 if a space separates the symbol and the sign string, if adjacent.

char n_cs_precedes

EX
>   Set to 1 if the **currency_symbol** or **int_curr_symbol** precedes the value for a negative formatted monetary quantity. Set to 0 if the symbol succeeds the value.

char n_sep_by_space

EX

EX
>   Set to 0 if no space separates the **currency_symbol** or **int_curr_symbol** from the value for a negative formatted monetary quantity. Set to 1 if a space separates the symbol from the value; and set to 2 if a space separates the symbol and the sign string, if adjacent.

char p_sign_posn
>   Set to a value indicating the positioning of the **positive_sign** for a non-negative formatted monetary quantity.

char n_sign_posn
>   Set to a value indicating the positioning of the **negative_sign** for a negative formatted monetary quantity.

The elements of **grouping** and **mon_grouping** are interpreted according to the following:

{CHAR_MAX}   No further grouping is to be performed.

0   The previous element is to be repeatedly used for the remainder of the digits.

other   The integer value is the number of digits that comprise the current group. The next element is examined to determine the size of the next group of digits before the current group.

The values of **p_sign_posn** and **n_sign_posn** are interpreted according to the following:

EX   0   Parentheses surround the quantity and **currency_symbol** or **int_curr_symbol.**

EX   1   The sign string precedes the quantity and **currency_symbol** or **int_curr_symbol.**

EX   2   The sign string succeeds the quantity and **currency_symbol** or **int_curr_symbol.**

EX   3   The sign string immediately precedes the **currency_symbol** or **int_curr_symbol.**

EX   4   The sign string immediately succeeds the **currency_symbol** or **int_curr_symbol.**

The implementation will behave as if no function calls *localeconv*( ).

RETURN VALUE
>   The *localeconv*( ) function returns a pointer to the filled-in object. The structure pointed to by the return value must not be modified by the program, but may be overwritten by a subsequent call to *localeconv*( ). In addition, calls to *setlocale*( ) with the categories LC_ALL, LC_MONETARY, or LC_NUMERIC may overwrite the contents of the structure.

APPLICATION USAGE

The following table illustrates the rules which may be used by four countries to format monetary quantities.

Country	Positive format	Negative format	International format
Italy	L.1.230	–L.1.230	ITL.1.230
Netherlands	F 1.234,56	F –1.234,56	NLG 1.234,56
Norway	kr1.234,56	kr1.234,56–	NOK 1.234,56
Switzerland	SFrs.1,234.56	SFrs.1,234.56C	CHF 1,234.56

For these four countries, the respective values for the monetary members of the structure returned by *localeconv*( ) are:

	Italy	Netherlands	Norway	Switzerland
int_curr_symbol	"ITL."	"NLG "	"NOK "	"CHF "
currency_symbol	"L."	"F"	"kr"	"SFrs."
mon_decimal_point	""	","	","	"."
mon_thousands_sep	"."	"."	"."	","
mon_grouping	"\3"	"\3"	"\3"	"\3"
positive_sign	""	""	""	""
negative_sign	"-"	"-"	"-"	"C"
int_frac_digits	0	2	2	2
frac_digits	0	2	2	2
p_cs_precedes	1	1	1	1
p_sep_by_space	0	1	0	0
n_cs_precedes	1	1	1	1
n_sep_by_space	0	1	0	0
p_sign_posn	1	1	1	1
n_sign_posn	1	4	2	2

ERRORS

No errors are defined.

SEE ALSO

isalpha( ), *isascii*( ), *nl_langinfo*( ), *printf*( ), *scanf*( ), *setlocale*( ), *strcat*( ), *strchr*( ), *strcmp*( ), *strcoll*( ), *strcpy*( ), *strftime*( ), *strlen*( ), *strpbrk*( ), *strspn*( ), *strtok*( ), *strxrfm*( ), *strtod*( ), **<langinfo.h>**, **<locale.h>**.

EXAMPLE

```
/*
 * Copyright (C) ANTRIX Inc.
 */

/* localeconv.c
 * This program determines the program locale and sets the
 * components of an object with the type struct lconv with
 * values appropriate for the formatting of numeric quantities
 * using function localeconv.
 */

#include <stdio.h>
#include <stdlib.h>
```

```
#include <locale.h>
#include <errno.h>

main()
{
  struct lconv    *buf;

  fprintf (stdout,"set locale to C\n");
  setlocale (LC_ALL, "C");
  buf = (struct lconv *)malloc (sizeof(struct lconv) );

  fprintf (stdout,"get numeric formatting information\n");
  buf = localeconv ();
  /* print some members of the structures */
  if ( buf != (struct lconv *)0 ) {
     fprintf (stdout,"localeconv() call successful\n");
     fprintf (stdout,"buf->thousands_sep=%s\n", buf->thousands_sep );
     fprintf (stdout,"buf->grouping=%s\n", buf->grouping );
     fprintf (stdout,"buf->int_curr_symbol=%s\n", buf->int_curr_symbol);
     fprintf (stdout,"buf->currency_symbol=%s\n", buf->currency_symbol );
     fprintf (stdout,"buf->mon_decimal_point=%s\n", buf->mon_decimal_point);
     fprintf (stdout,"buf->mon_thousands_sep=%s\n", buf->mon_thousands_sep);
     fprintf (stdout,"buf->mon_grouping=%s\n", buf->mon_thousands_sep);
     fprintf (stdout,"buf->positive_sign=%s\n", buf->positive_sign);
     fprintf (stdout,"buf->negative_sign=%s\n", buf->negative_sign);
     fprintf (stdout,"buf->int_frac_digits=%d\n", buf->int_frac_digits);
     fprintf (stdout,"buf->frac_digits=%d\n", buf->frac_digits);
     fprintf (stdout,"buf->p_cs_precedes=%d\n", buf->p_cs_precedes);
  }
  else
     fprintf (stderr,"ERROR: localeconv() call failed\n");
}
```

NAME

localtime — convert time value to broken-down local time

SYNOPSIS

```
#include <time.h>

struct tm *localtime(const time_t *timer);
```

DESCRIPTION

The *localtime*( ) function converts the time in seconds since the Epoch pointed to by *timer* into a broken-down time, expressed as a local time. The function corrects for the timezone and any seasonal time adjustments. Local timezone information is used as though *localtime*( ) calls *tzset*( ).

RETURN VALUE

The *localtime*( ) function returns a pointer to the broken-down time structure.

ERRORS

No errors are defined.

APPLICATION USAGE

The *asctime*( ), *ctime*( ), *getdate*( ), *gettimeofday*( ), *gmtime*( ) and *localtime*( ) functions return values in one of two static objects: a broken-down time structure and an array of **char**. Execution of any of the functions may overwrite the information returned in either of these objects by any of the other functions.

SEE ALSO

asctime( ), *clock*( ), *ctime*( ), *difftime*( ), *getdate*( ), *gettimeofday*( ), *gmtime*( ), *mktime*( ), *strftime*( ), *strptime*( ), *time*( ), *utime*( ), **<time.h>**.

EXAMPLE

```
/*
 * Copyright (C) ANTRIX Inc.
 */

/* localtime.c
 * This program converts the time in seconds since the Epoch pointed
 * to by timer into a broken-down time, expressed as a local time.
 */

#include <stdio.h>
#include <stdlib.h>
#include <time.h>
#include <errno.h>

main()
{
    struct  tm   *buf;
    char        *current_time;
    time_t   tloc, clock;

    fprintf (stdout,"get current time\n");
    clock = time (&tloc);

    fprintf (stdout,"get local time after correction for time-zone\n");
    fprintf (stdout,"in struct buf of type tm\n");
```

```
    buf = localtime (&clock);

    fprintf (stdout,"convert date and time to string\n");
    current_time = asctime (buf);
    if ( buf != (struct tm *)0 ) {
        fprintf (stdout,"localtime() call successful\n");
        fprintf (stdout,"current time=%s\n", current_time);
    }
    else
        fprintf (stderr,"ERROR: localtime() call failed\n");
}
```

NAME

lockf — record locking on files

SYNOPSIS

UX

```
#include <unistd.h>

int lockf(int fildes, int function, off_t size);
```

DESCRIPTION

The *lockf*( ) function allows sections of a file to be locked with advisory-mode locks. Calls to *lockf*( ) from other processes which attempt to lock the locked file section will either return an error value or block until the section becomes unlocked. All the locks for a process are removed when the process terminates. Record locking with *lockf*( ) is supported for regular files and may be supported for other files.

The *fildes* argument is an open file descriptor. The file descriptor must have been opened with write-only permission (O_WRONLY) or with read/write permission (O_RDWR) to establish a lock with this function.

The *function* argument is a control value which specifies the action to be taken. The permissible values for *function* are defined in **<unistd.h>** as follows:

Function	Description
F_ULOCK	unlock locked sections
F_LOCK	lock a section for exclusive use
F_TLOCK	test and lock a section for exclusive use
F_TEST	test a section for locks by other processes

F_TEST detects if a lock by another process is present on the specified section; F_LOCK and F_TLOCK both lock a section of a file if the section is available; F_ULOCK removes locks from a section of the file.

The *size* argument is the number of contiguous bytes to be locked or unlocked. The section to be locked or unlocked starts at the current offset in the file and extends forward for a positive size or backward for a negative size (the preceding bytes up to but not including the current offset). If *size* is 0, the section from the current offset through the largest possible file offset is locked (that is, from the current offset through the present or any future end-of-file). An area need not be allocated to the file to be locked because locks may exist past the end-of-file.

The sections locked with F_LOCK or F_TLOCK may, in whole or in part, contain or be contained by a previously locked section for the same process. When this occurs, or if adjacent locked sections would occur, the sections are combined into a single locked section. If the request would cause the number of locks to exceed a system-imposed limit, the request will fail.

F_LOCK and F_TLOCK requests differ only by the action taken if the section is not available. F_LOCK blocks the calling process until the section is available. F_TLOCK makes the function fail if the section is already locked by another process.

File locks are released on first close by the locking process of any file descriptor for the file.

F_ULOCK requests may release (wholly or in part) one or more locked sections controlled by the process. Locked sections will be unlocked starting at the current file offset through *size* bytes or to the end of file if *size* is (**off_t**)0. When all of a locked section is not released (that is, when the beginning or end of the area to be unlocked falls within a locked section), the remaining portions of that section are still locked by the process. Releasing the center portion of a locked section will cause the remaining locked beginning and end portions to become two separate locked sections. If the request would cause the number of locks in the system to exceed a system-imposed limit, the request will fail.

A potential for deadlock occurs if a process controlling a locked section is blocked by accessing another process' locked section. If the system detects that deadlock would occur, *lockf( )* will fail with an [EDEADLK] error.

The interaction between *fcntl( )* and *lockf( )* locks is unspecified.

Blocking on a section is interrupted by any signal.

RETURN VALUE

Upon successful completion, *lockf( )* returns 0. Otherwise, it returns −1, sets *errno* to indicate an error, and existing locks are not changed.

ERRORS

The *lockf( )* function will fail if:

[EBADF]   The *fildes* argument is not a valid open file descriptor; or *function* is F_LOCK or F_TLOCK and *fildes* is not a valid file descriptor open for writing.

[EACCES] or [EAGAIN]
              The *function* argument is F_TLOCK or F_TEST and the section is already locked by another process.

[EDEADLK]   The *function* argument is F_LOCK and a deadlock is detected.

[EINTR]   A signal was caught during execution of the function.

The *lockf( )* function may fail if:

[EAGAIN]   The *function* argument is F_LOCK or F_TLOCK and the file is mapped with *mmap( )*.

[EDEADLK] or [ENOLCK]
              The *function* argument is F_LOCK, F_TLOCK, or F_ULOCK, and the request would cause the number of locks to exceed a system-imposed limit.

[EOPNOTSUPP] or [EINVAL]
              The implementation does not support the locking of files of the type indicated by the *fildes* argument.

[EINVAL]   The *function* argument is not one of F_LOCK, F_TLOCK, F_TEST or F_ULOCK; or *size* plus the current file offset is less than 0 or greater than the largest possible file offset.

APPLICATION USAGE

Record-locking should not be used in combination with the *fopen( )*, *fread( )*, *fwrite( )* and other *stdio* functions. Instead, the more primitive, non-buffered functions (such as *open( )*) should be used. Unexpected results may occur in processes that do buffering in the user address space. The process may later read/write data which is/was locked. The *stdio* functions are the most common source of unexpected buffering.

The *alarm( )* function may be used to provide a timeout facility in applications requiring it.

SEE ALSO

alarm( ), *chmod( )*, *close( )*, *creat( )*, *fcntl( )*, *mmap( )*, *open( )*, *read( )*, *write( )*, **<unistd.h>**.

EXAMPLE

```
/*
 * Copyright (C) ANTRIX Inc.
 */
```

```
/* lockf.c
 * This program performs record locking on file
 * using function lockf
 */

#include <stdio.h>
#include <stdlib.h>
#include <fcntl.h>
#include <unistd.h>
#include <sys/stat.h>
#include <errno.h>

#define   PERM_ALL    (S_IRWXU | S_IRWXG | S_IRWXO)
#define   OFLAG       (O_RDWR | O_CREAT | O_APPEND)

main()
{
  int     lockf_value;
  int     fildes, length;
  struct  flock lock;
  char    *string = "hello world";
  char    *file = "testfile";

  length = strlen (string);
  fprintf (stdout,"create and open testfile\n");

  fildes = open (file, OFLAG, PERM_ALL);
  fprintf (stdout,"write string to testfile\n");
  write (fildes, string, length);

  lock.l_type = F_WRLCK;
  lock.l_whence = SEEK_SET;
  lock.l_start = (off_t)0;
  lock.l_len = (off_t)length;

  fprintf (stdout,"set write lock on testfile\n");
  fcntl (fildes, F_SETLK, &lock);

  fprintf (stdout,"unlock testfile\n");
  lockf_value = lockf (fildes, F_ULOCK, length);
  if ( lockf_value == 0 )
     fprintf (stdout,"lockf() call successful\n");
  else {
     fprintf (stderr,"ERROR: lockf() call failed\n");
     fprintf (stderr,"ERROR: %s\n", strerror(errno));
  }
  close (fildes);

  fprintf (stdout,"remove testfile\n");
  remove (file);
}
```

NAME

locs — stop regular expression matching in a string (**TO BE WITHDRAWN**)

SYNOPSIS

EX
```
#include <regexp.h>
```
```
extern char *locs;
```

DESCRIPTION

Refer to *regexp( )*.

APPLICATION USAGE

This variable is kept for historical reasons, but will be withdrawn in a future issue of this document.

New applications should use *fnmatch( )*, *glob( )*, *regcomp( )* and *regexec( )*, which provide full internationalised regular expression functionality compatible with the ISO POSIX-2 standard, as described in the **XBD** specification, **Chapter 7**, **Regular Expressions**.

NAME

log — natural logarithm function

SYNOPSIS

```
#include <math.h>

double log(double x);
```

DESCRIPTION

The *log*( ) function computes the natural logarithm of *x*, $\log_e(x)$. The value of *x* must be positive.

RETURN VALUE

Upon successful completion, *log*( ) returns the natural logarithm of *x*.

EX If *x* is NaN, NaN is returned and *errno* may be set to [EDOM].

EX If *x* is less than 0, –HUGE_VAL or NaN is returned, and *errno* is set to [EDOM].

If *x* is 0, –HUGE_VAL is returned and *errno* may be set to [ERANGE].

ERRORS

The *log*( ) function will fail if:

[EDOM]   The value of *x* is negative.

The *log*( ) function may fail if:

EX [EDOM]   The value of *x* is NaN.

[ERANGE]   The value of *x* is 0.

EX No other errors will occur.

APPLICATION USAGE

An application wishing to check for error situations should set *errno* to 0 before calling *log*( ). If *errno* is non-zero on return, or the return value is NaN, an error has occurred.

SEE ALSO

exp( ), *isnan*( ), *log10*( ), *log1p*( ), **<math.h>**.

EXAMPLE

```
/*
 * Copyright (C) ANTRIX Inc.
 */

/* log.c
 * This program computes the natural logarithm of x using
 * function log.
 */

#include <stdio.h>
#include <math.h>

main()
{
  double  log_value;
  double  x = 2.00;

  log_value = log (x);
```

```
    fprintf (stdout,"log of %f is %f\n", x, log_value);
}
```

NAME

log10 — base 10 logarithm function

SYNOPSIS

```
#include <math.h>

double log10(double x);
```

DESCRIPTION

The *log10*( ) function computes the base 10 logarithm of *x*, $\log_{10}(x)$. The value of *x* must be positive.

RETURN VALUE

Upon successful completion, *log10*( ) returns the base 10 logarithm of *x*.

EX   If *x* is NaN, NaN is returned and *errno* may be set to [EDOM].

EX   If *x* is less than 0, –HUGE_VAL or NaN is returned, and *errno* is set to [EDOM].

If *x* is 0, –HUGE_VAL is returned and *errno* may be set to [ERANGE].

ERRORS

The *log10*( ) function will fail if:

[EDOM]   The value of *x* is negative.

The *log10*( ) function may fail if:

EX   [EDOM]   The value of *x* is NaN.

[ERANGE]   The value of *x* is 0.

EX   No other errors will occur.

APPLICATION USAGE

An application wishing to check for error situations should set *errno* to 0 before calling *log10*( ). If *errno* is non-zero on return, or the return value is NaN, an error has occurred.

SEE ALSO

isnan( ), *log*( ), *pow*( ), **<math.h>**.

EXAMPLE

```
/*
 * Copyright (C) ANTRIX Inc.
 */

/* log10.c
 * This program computes the base 10 logarithm of x
 * using function log10.
 */

#include <stdio.h>
#include <math.h>

main()
{
  double  log10_value;
  double  x = 10.00;

  log10_value = log10 (x);
```

```
    fprintf (stdout,"log10 of %f is %f\n", x, log10_value);
}
```

NAME

log1p — compute natural logarithm

SYNOPSIS

UX   `#include <math.h>`

`double log1p (double x);`

DESCRIPTION

The *log1p*( ) function computes $\log_e(1.0 + x)$. The value of *x* must be greater than −1.0.

RETURN VALUE

Upon successful completion, *log1p*( ) returns the natural logarithm of 1.0 + *x*.

If *x* is NaN, *log1p*( ) returns NaN and may set *errno* to [EDOM].

If *x* is less than −1.0, *log1p*( ) returns −HUGE_VAL or NaN and sets *errno* to [EDOM].

If *x* is −1.0, *log1p*( ) returns −HUGE_VAL and may set *errno* to [ERANGE].

ERRORS

The *log1p*( ) function will fail if:

[EDOM]   The value of *x* is less than −1.0.

The *log1p*( ) function may fail and set *errno* to:

[EDOM]   The value of *x* is NaN.

[ERANGE]   The value of *x* is −1.0.

No other errors will occur.

SEE ALSO

log( ), **<math.h>**.

EXAMPLE

```
/*
 * Copyright (C) ANTRIX Inc.
 */

/* log1p.c
 * This program computes the natural log1parithm of x+1 using
 * function log1p.
 */

#include <stdio.h>
#include <math.h>

main()
{
  double  log1p_value;
  double  x = 2.00;

  log1p_value = log1p (x);
  fprintf (stdout,"log1p of %f is %f\n", x, log1p_value);
}
```

logb( )

NAME

logb — radix-independent exponent

SYNOPSIS

UX   `#include <math.h>`

`double logb(double x);`

DESCRIPTION

The *logb*( ) function computes the exponent of *x*, which is the integral part of $\log_r |x|$, as a signed floating point value, for non-zero *x*, where *r* is the radix of the machine's floating-point arithmetic.

RETURN VALUE

Upon successful completion, *logb*( ) returns the exponent of *x*.

If *x* is 0.0, *logb*( ) returns –HUGE_VAL and sets *errno* to [EDOM].

If *x* is ±Inf, *logb*( ) returns +Inf.

If *x* is NaN, *logb*( ) returns NaN and may set *errno* to [EDOM].

ERRORS

The *logb*( ) function will fail if:

[EDOM]   The *x* argument is 0.0.

The *logb*( ) function may fail if:

[EDOM]   The *x* argument is NaN.

SEE ALSO

ilogb( ), **<math.h>**.

EXAMPLE

```
/*
 * Copyright (C) ANTRIX Inc.
 */

/* logb.c
 * This program computes the unbiased exponent of its
 * floating-point value using function logb.
 */

#include <stdio.h>
#include <math.h>

main()
{
  double  logb_value;
  double  x = 2.00;

  logb_value = logb (x);
  fprintf (stdout,"logb of %f is %f\n", x, logb_value);
}
```

NAME

_longjmp, _setjmp — non-local goto

SYNOPSIS

UX
```
#include <setjmp.h>
```
```
void _longjmp(jmp_buf env, int val);
```
```
int _setjmp(jmp_buf env);
```

DESCRIPTION

The *_longjmp( )* and *_setjmp( )* functions are identical to *longjmp( )* and *setjmp( )*, respectively, with the additional restriction that *_longjmp( )* and *_setjmp( )* do not manipulate the signal mask.

If *_longjmp( )* is called even though *env* was never initialised by a call to *_setjmp( )*, or when the last such call was in a function that has since returned, the results are undefined.

RETURN VALUE

Refer to *longjmp( )* and *setjmp( )*.

ERRORS

No errors are defined.

APPLICATION USAGE

If *_longjmp( )* is executed and the environment in which *_setjmp( )* was executed no longer exists, errors can occur. The conditions under which the environment of the *_setjmp( )* no longer exists include exiting the function that contains the *_setjmp( )* call, and exiting an inner block with temporary storage. This condition might not be detectable, in which case the *_longjmp( )* occurs and, if the environment no longer exists, the contents of the temporary storage of an inner block are unpredictable. This condition might also cause unexpected process termination. If the function has returned, the results are undefined.

Passing *longjmp( )* a pointer to a buffer not created by *setjmp( )*, passing *_longjmp( )* a pointer to a buffer not created by *_setjmp( )*, passing *siglongjmp( )* a pointer to a buffer not created by *sigsetjmp( )* or passing any of these three functions a buffer that has been modified by the user can cause all the problems listed above, and more.

The *_longjmp( )* and *_setjmp( )* functions are included to support programs written to historical system interfaces. New applications should use *siglongjmp( )* and *sigsetjmp( )* respectively.

SEE ALSO

longjmp( ), *setjmp( )*, *siglongjmp( )*, *sigsetjmp( )*, **<setjmp.h>**.

EXAMPLE

```
/*
 * Copyright (C) ANTRIX Inc.
 */

/* _longjmp.c
 * This program restores the environment saved by the most recent
 * invocation of the _setjmp() function in the same process, with
 * the corresponding jmp_buf argument using function _setjmp.
 */

#include <stdio.h>
#include <stdlib.h>
#include <signal.h>
#include <setjmp.h>
```

```
#include <errno.h>

main()
{
  int         val, _setjmp_value;
  static  int   save_int;
  static  long save_long;
  jmp_buf        buf;

  val = 5;
  fprintf (stdout,"save values\n");
  _setjmp_value = _setjmp (buf);
  if ( _setjmp_value == val ) {
      fprintf (stdout,"_setjmp_value=%d\n", _setjmp_value );
      fprintf (stdout,"save_int   = %d\n", save_int);
      fprintf (stdout,"save_long = %d\n", save_long);
      exit (0);
  }

  save_int =  1;
  save_long = 123456789;
  fprintf (stdout,"restore saved values\n");
  _longjmp (buf, val);
  fprintf (stderr,"ERROR: _longjmp() call failed\n");
}
```

NAME

longjmp — non-local goto

SYNOPSIS

```
#include <setjmp.h>

void longjmp(jmp_buf env, int val);
```

DESCRIPTION

The *longjmp( )* function restores the environment saved by the most recent invocation of *setjmp( )* in the same process, with the corresponding *jmp_buf* argument. If there is no such invocation, or if the function containing the invocation of *setjmp( )* has terminated execution in the interim, the behaviour is undefined. It is unspecified whether *longjmp( )* restores the signal mask, leaves the signal mask unchanged or restores it to its value at the time *setjmp( )* was called.

UX

All accessible objects have values as of the time *longjmp( )* was called, except that the values of objects of automatic storage duration are indeterminate if they meet all the following conditions:

- They are local to the function containing the corresponding *setjmp( )* invocation.

- They do not have volatile-qualified type.

- They are changed between the *setjmp( )* invocation and *longjmp( )* call.

As it bypasses the usual function call and return mechanisms, *longjmp( )* will execute correctly in contexts of interrupts, signals and any of their associated functions. However, if *longjmp( )* is invoked from a nested signal handler (that is, from a function invoked as a result of a signal raised during the handling of another signal), the behaviour is undefined.

RETURN VALUE

After *longjmp( )* is completed, program execution continues as if the corresponding invocation of *setjmp( )* had just returned the value specified by *val*. The *longjmp( )* function cannot cause *setjmp( )* to return 0; if *val* is 0, *setjmp( )* returns 1.

ERRORS

No errors are defined.

APPLICATION USAGE

Applications whose behaviour depends on the value of the signal mask should not use *longjmp( )* and *setjmp( )*, since their effect on the signal mask is unspecified, but should instead use the following alternatives:

- The *_longjmp( )* and *_setjmp( )* functions (which never modify the signal mask)

- The *siglongjmp( )* and *sigsetjmp( )* functions (which can save and restore the signal mask under application control).

SEE ALSO

setjmp( ), *sigaction( )*, *siglongjmp( )*, *sigsetjmp( )*, **<setjmp.h>**.

EXAMPLE

```
/*
 * Copyright (C) ANTRIX Inc.
 */

/* longjmp.c
 * This program restores the environment saved by the most recent
 * invocation of the setjmp() function in the same process, with
 * the corresponding jmp_buf argument using function setjmp.
```

```
   */

   #include <stdio.h>
   #include <stdlib.h>
   #include <signal.h>
   #include <setjmp.h>
   #include <errno.h>

   main()
   {
     int         val, setjmp_value;
     static  int  save_int;
     static  long save_long;
     jmp_buf      buf;

     val = 5;
     fprintf (stdout,"save values\n");
     setjmp_value = setjmp (buf);
     if ( setjmp_value == val ) {
         fprintf (stdout,"setjmp_value=%d\n", setjmp_value );
         fprintf (stdout,"save_int  = %d\n", save_int);
         fprintf (stdout,"save_long = %d\n", save_long);
         exit (0);
     }

     save_int =  1;
     save_long = 123456789;
     fprintf (stdout,"restore saved values\n");
     longjmp (buf, val);
     fprintf (stderr,"ERROR: longjmp() call failed\n");
   }
```

NAME

lrand48 — generate uniformly distributed pseudo-random non-negative long integers

SYNOPSIS

EX
```
#include <stdlib.h>

long int lrand48(void);
```

DESCRIPTION

Refer to *drand48*( ).

EXAMPLE

```c
/*
 * Copyright (C) ANTRIX Inc.
 */

/* lrand48.c
 * This program generates non-negative, long random integers,
 * uniformly distributed over the interval [0, 2 raise 31)
 * using function lrand48.
 */

#include <stdio.h>
#include <stdlib.h>
#include <errno.h>

main()
{
  int    i;
  int    seed_value = 100;
  long   lrand48_value;

  srand48(seed_value);
  for ( i = 0; i < 5; i++ ) {
      lrand48_value = lrand48 ();
      fprintf (stdout,"random value in iteration %d is %d\n",
                      i, lrand48_value);
  }
}
```

NAME

lsearch, lfind — linear search and update

SYNOPSIS

EX
```
#include <search.h>
```

```
void *lsearch(const void *key, void *base, size_t *nelp, size_t width,
              int (*compar)(const void *, const void *));
```

```
void *lfind(const void *key, const void *base, size_t *nelp,
            size_t width, int (*compar)(const void *, const void *));
```

DESCRIPTION

The *lsearch*( ) function is a linear search routine. It returns a pointer into a table indicating where an entry may be found. If the entry does not occur, it is added at the end of the table. The *key* argument points to the entry to be sought in the table. The *base* argument points to the first element in the table. The *width* argument is the size of an element in bytes. The *nelp* argument points to an integer containing the current number of elements in the table. The integer to which *nelp* points is incremented if the entry is added to the table. The *compar* argument points to a comparison function which the user must supply (*strcmp*( ), for example). It is called with two arguments that point to the elements being compared. The function must return 0 if the elements are equal and non-zero otherwise.

The *lfind*( ) function is the same as *lsearch*( ) except that if the entry is not found, it is not added to the table. Instead, a null pointer is returned.

RETURN VALUE

If the searched for entry is found, both *lsearch*( ) and *lfind*( ) return a pointer to it. Otherwise, *lfind*( ) returns a null pointer and *lsearch*( ) returns a pointer to the newly added element.

Both functions return a null pointer in case of error.

ERRORS

No errors are defined.

EXAMPLES

This fragment will read in less than or equal to TABSIZE strings of length less than or equal to ELSIZE and store them in a table, eliminating duplicates.

```
#include <stdio.h>
#include <string.h>
#include <search.h>

#define TABSIZE 50
#define ELSIZE 120

...
    char line[ELSIZE], tab[TABSIZE][ELSIZE];
    size_t nel = 0;
    ...
    while (fgets(line, ELSIZE, stdin) != NULL && nel < TABSIZE)
        (void) lsearch(line, tab, &nel,
            ELSIZE, (int (*)(const void *, const void *)) strcmp);
    ...
```

APPLICATION USAGE

The comparison function need not compare every byte, so arbitrary data may be contained in the elements in addition to the values being compared.

Undefined results can occur if there is not enough room in the table to add a new item.

SEE ALSO

bsearch( ), *hsearch*( ), *tsearch*( ), **<search.h>**.

EXAMPLE

```
/*
 * Copyright (C) ANTRIX Inc.
 */

/* lsearch.c
 * This program does a linear search and returns a pointer
 * into a table indicating where entry may be found using
 * function lsearch.
 */

#include <stdio.h>
#include <stdlib.h>
#include <sys/types.h>
#include <search.h>
#include <errno.h>

#define  TABLESIZE    5

static  int    table[TABLESIZE];

/* compare () two functions for equality */
int compare(a, b)
const char   *a, *b;
{
    int    *i, *j;

  i = (int *) a;
  j = (int *) b;
  if ( *i == *j )
     return(0);
  else
     return(1);
}

main()
{
   int     lsearch_value;
   int     i, size;
   int     *iptr;
   char    *found_item;
   size_t  nelp;

   fprintf (stdout,"create table of size 5\n");
   for ( i = 0; i < TABLESIZE; i++ )
```

```
    {
        table[i] = 2*i + 2;
        nelp = i;
        found_item = lsearch ((char *)&table[i], (char *)&table[0],
                              &nelp, sizeof(table[i]), compare);
        iptr = (int *) found_item;
        fprintf (stdout,"entered item in table[%d]=%d\n", i, *iptr);
        if ( *iptr != table[i] )
            fprintf (stderr,"ERROR: lsearch did not enter the item correctly");
    }

    fprintf (stdout,"find item in table[2]\n");
    nelp = TABLESIZE;
    found_item = lfind ((char *)&table[2], (char *)&table[0],
                        &nelp, sizeof(table[2]), compare);
    iptr = (int *) found_item;
    fprintf (stdout,"found item at table[2]=%d\n", *iptr);
    if ( *iptr != 6 )
        fprintf (stderr,"ERROR: lfind did not find item 2 correctly");
}
```

NAME

lseek — move read/write file offset

SYNOPSIS

OH
```
#include <sys/types.h>
#include <unistd.h>

off_t lseek(int fildes, off_t offset, int whence);
```

DESCRIPTION

The *lseek( )* function will set the file offset for the open file description associated with the file descriptor *fildes*, as follows:

- If *whence* is SEEK_SET the file offset is set to *offset* bytes.

- If *whence* is SEEK_CUR the file offset is set to its current location plus *offset*.

- If *whence* is SEEK_END the file offset is set to the size of the file plus *offset*.

The symbolic constants SEEK_SET, SEEK_CUR and SEEK_END are defined in the header **<unistd.h>**.

The behaviour of *lseek( )* on devices which are incapable of seeking is implementation-dependent. The value of the file offset associated with such a device is undefined.

The *lseek( )* function will allow the file offset to be set beyond the end of the existing data in the file. If data is later written at this point, subsequent reads of data in the gap will return bytes with the value 0 until data is actually written into the gap.

The *lseek( )* function will not, by itself, extend the size of a file.

RETURN VALUE

Upon successful completion, the resulting offset, as measured in bytes from the beginning of the file, is returned. Otherwise, (**off_t**)–1 is returned, *errno* is set to indicate the error and the file offset will remain unchanged.

ERRORS

The *lseek( )* function will fail if:

[EBADF]   The *fildes* argument is not an open file descriptor.

[EINVAL]   The *whence* argument is not a proper value, or the resulting file offset would be invalid.

[ESPIPE]   The *fildes* argument is associated with a pipe or FIFO.

SEE ALSO

open( ), **<sys/tyes.h>**, **<unistd.h>**.

EXAMPLE

```
/*
 * Copyright (C) ANTRIX Inc.
 */

/* lseek.c
 * This program sets the file offset for the open file descriptor
 * using function lseek.
 */

#include <stdio.h>
#include <stdlib.h>
```

```
#include <unistd.h>
#include <fcntl.h>
#include <sys/types.h>
#include <sys/stat.h>
#include <errno.h>

#define  PERM_ALL    (S_IRWXU | S_IRWXG | S_IRWXO)

main()
{
  off_t  lseek_value;
  int    fildes, length, offset;
  char   *buf;
  char   *string = "hello world";
  char   *filename = "testfile";

  length = strlen (string);
  offset = strlen ("hello");

  fprintf (stdout,"create testfile\n");
  fildes = creat (filename, PERM_ALL);
  fprintf (stdout,"write string\n");
  write (fildes, string, length);
  fprintf (stdout,"close testfile\n");
  close (fildes);

  fprintf (stdout,"open testfile for read only\n");
  fildes = open (filename, O_RDONLY);
  buf = (char *)malloc (length);

  fprintf (stdout,"seek to beginning of character w\n");
  lseek_value = lseek (fildes, offset, SEEK_SET);
  if ( lseek_value == offset ) {
     fprintf (stdout,"lseek() call successful\n");
     read (fildes, buf, length);
     fprintf (stdout,"string in buf=%s\n", buf);
  }
  else {
     fprintf (stderr,"ERROR: lseek() call failed\n");
     fprintf (stderr,"ERROR: %s\n", strerror(errno));
  }

  fprintf (stdout,"remove testfile\n");
  remove (filename);
}
```

NAME

lstat — get symbolic link status

SYNOPSIS

UX

```
#include <sys/stat.h>
```

```
int lstat(const char *path, struct stat *buf);
```

DESCRIPTION

The *lstat*( ) function has the same effect as *stat*( ), except when *path* refers to a symbolic link. In that case *lstat*( ) returns information about the link, while *stat*( ) returns information about the file the link references.

For symbolic links, the **st_mode** member will contain meaningful information when used with the file type macros, and the **st_size** member will contain the length of the pathname contained in the symbolic link. File mode bits and the contents of the remaining members of the stat structure are unspecified. The value returned in the **st_size** member is the length of the contents of the symbolic link, and does not count any trailing null.

RETURN VALUE

Upon successful completion, *lstat*( ) returns 0. Otherwise, it returns −1 and sets *errno* to indicate the error.

ERRORS

The *lstat*( ) function will fail if:

[EACCES]   A component of the path prefix denies search permission.

[EIO]   An error occurred while reading from the file system.

[ELOOP]   Too many symbolic links were encountered in resolving *path*.

[ENAMETOOLONG]
                  The length of a pathname exceeds {PATH_MAX}, or pathname component is longer than {NAME_MAX}.

[ENOTDIR]   A component of the path prefix is not a directory.

[ENOENT]   A component of *path* does not name an existing file or *path* is an empty string.

The *lstat*( ) function may fail if:

[ENAMETOOLONG]
                  Pathname resolution of a symbolic link produced an intermediate result whose length exceeds {PATH_MAX}.

[EOVERFLOW]   One of the members is too large to store into the structure pointed to by the *buf* argument.

SEE ALSO

fstat( ), *readlink*( ), *stat*( ), *symlink*( ), **<sys/stat.h>**.

EXAMPLE

```
/*
 * Copyright (C) ANTRIX Inc.
 */

/* lstat.c
 * This program obtains information about the named file and
 * writes it to the area pointed to by the buf argument using
 * function lstat
```

```
 */

#include <stdio.h>
#include <stdlib.h>
#include <sys/types.h>
#include <sys/stat.h>
#include <errno.h>

#define  PERM_ALL   (S_IRWXU | S_IRWXG | S_IRWXO)

main()
{
   int     lstat_value;
   int     fildes;
   char    *string = "hello world";
   char    *file1 = "testfile1";
   char    *file2 = "testfile2";
   struct  stat buf;

   fprintf (stdout,"create testfile\n");
   fildes = creat (file1, PERM_ALL);

   fprintf (stdout,"write string\n");
   write (fildes, string, strlen(string));

   fprintf (stdout,"create link from testfile2 to testfile1\n");
   link (file1, file2);

   fprintf (stdout,"get testfile1 status\n");
   lstat_value = lstat (file1, &buf);
   if ( lstat_value == 0 ) {
      fprintf (stdout,"lstat() call successful\n");
      fprintf (stdout,"buf.st_nlink=%d\n", buf.st_nlink );
      fprintf (stdout,"buf.st_uid=%d\n", buf.st_uid );
      fprintf (stdout,"buf.st_gid=%d\n", buf.st_gid );
      fprintf (stdout,"buf.st_size=%d\n", buf.st_size );
   }
   else {
      fprintf (stderr,"ERROR: lstat failed\n");
      fprintf (stderr,"ERROR: %s\n", strerror(errno));
   }

   fprintf (stdout,"remove testfiles\n");
   unlink (file2);
   remove (file1);
}
```

NAME

makecontext, swapcontext — manipulate user contexts

SYNOPSIS

UX `#include <ucontext.h>`

`void makecontext(ucontext_t *ucp, (void *func)(), int argc, ...);`

`int swapcontext(ucontext_t *oucp, const ucontext_t *ucp);`

DESCRIPTION

The *makecontext( )* function modifies the context specified by *ucp*, which has been initialised using *getcontext( )*. When this context is resumed using *swapcontext( )* or *setcontext( )*, program execution continues by calling *func( )*, passing it the arguments that follow *argc* in the *makecontext( )* call.

Before a call is made to *makecontext( )*, the context being modified should have a stack allocated for it. The value of *argc* must match the number of integer arguments passed to *func( )*, otherwise the behaviour is undefined.

The *uc_link* member is used to determine the context that will be resumed when the context being modified by *makecontext( )* returns. The *uc_link* member should be initialised prior to the call to *makecontext( )*.

The *swapcontext( )* function saves the current context in the context structure pointed to by *oucp* and sets the context to the context structure pointed to by *ucp*.

RETURN VALUE

On successful completion, *swapcontext( )* returns 0. Otherwise, −1 is returned and *errno* is set to indicate the error.

ERRORS

The *makecontext( )* and *swapcontext( )* functions will fail if:

[ENOMEM]   The *ucp* argument does not have enough stack left to complete the operation.

SEE ALSO

exit( ), *getcontext( )*, *sigaction( )*, *sigprocmask( )*, **<ucontext.h>**.

NAME

malloc — memory allocator

SYNOPSIS

```
#include <stdlib.h>

void *malloc(size_t size);
```

DESCRIPTION

The *malloc*( ) function allocates unused space for an object whose size in bytes is specified by *size* and whose value is indeterminate.

The order and contiguity of storage allocated by successive calls to *malloc*( ) is unspecified. The pointer returned if the allocation succeeds is suitably aligned so that it may be assigned to a pointer to any type of object and then used to access such an object in the space allocated (until the space is explicitly freed or reallocated). Each such allocation will yield a pointer to an object disjoint from any other object. The pointer returned points to the start (lowest byte address) of the allocated space. If the space cannot be allocated, a null pointer is returned. If the size of the space requested is 0, the behaviour is implementation-dependent; the value returned will be either a null pointer or a unique pointer.

RETURN VALUE

Upon successful completion with *size* not equal to 0, *malloc*( ) returns a pointer to the allocated space. If *size* is 0, either a null pointer or a unique pointer that can be successfully passed to
EX *free*( ) will be returned. Otherwise, it returns a null pointer and sets *errno* to indicate the error.

ERRORS

The *malloc*( ) function will fail if:

EX [ENOMEM]   Insufficient storage space is available.

APPLICATION USAGE

There is now no requirement for the implementation to support the inclusion of **<malloc.h>**.

SEE ALSO

calloc( ), *free*( ), *realloc*( ), **<stdlib.h>**.

EXAMPLE

```
/*
 * Copyright (C) ANTRIX Inc.
 */

/* malloc.c
 * This program allocates unused space for an object of size
 * byte using function malloc.
 */

#include <stdio.h>
#include <stdlib.h>
#include <malloc.h>
#include <errno.h>

main()
{
    char    *buf;
    char    *string = "hello world";
    size_t  size;
```

```
    size = strlen (string);

    fprintf (stdout,"allocate memory\n");
    buf = (char *)malloc (size);
    strcpy (buf, string);
    if ( buf != (char *)0 ) {
        fprintf (stdout,"malloc() call successful\n");
        fprintf (stdout,"allocated string=%s\n", buf );
    }
    else
        fprintf (stderr,"ERROR: malloc() call failed\n");

    fprintf (stdout,"free memory\n");
    free (buf);
}
```

NAME

mblen — get number of bytes in a character

SYNOPSIS

```
#include <stdlib.h>

int mblen(const char *s, size_t n);
```

DESCRIPTION

If *s* is not a null pointer, *mblen*( ) determines the number of bytes constituting the character pointed to by *s*. Except that the shift state of *mbtowc*( ) is not affected, it is equivalent to:

```
mbtowc((wchar_t *)0, s, n);
```

The implementation will behave as if no function defined in this document calls *mblen*( ).

The behaviour of this function is affected by the LC_CTYPE category of the current locale. For a state-dependent encoding, this function is placed into its initial state by a call for which its character pointer argument, *s*, is a null pointer. Subsequent calls with *s* as other than a null pointer cause the internal state of the function to be altered as necessary. A call with *s* as a null pointer causes this function to return a non-zero value if encodings have state dependency, and 0 otherwise. If the implementation employs special bytes to change the shift state, these bytes do not produce separate wide-character codes, but are grouped with an adjacent character. Changing the LC_CTYPE category causes the shift state of this function to be indeterminate.

RETURN VALUE

If *s* is a null pointer, *mblen*( ) returns a non-zero or 0 value, if character encodings, respectively, do or do not have state-dependent encodings. If *s* is not a null pointer, *mblen*( ) either returns 0 (if *s* points to the null byte), or returns the number of bytes that constitute the character (if the next *n* or fewer bytes form a valid character), or returns −1 (if they do not form a valid character) and may set *errno* to indicate the error. In no case will the value returned be greater than *n* or the value of the MB_CUR_MAX macro.

ERRORS

The *mblen*( ) function may fail if:

EX   [EILSEQ]   Invalid character sequence is detected.

SEE ALSO

mbtowc( ), *mbstowcs*( ), *wctomb*( ), *wcstombs*( ), **<stdlib.h>**.

EXAMPLE

```
/*
 * Copyright (C) ANTRIX Inc.
 */

/* mblen.c
 * This program determines the number of bytes constituting
 * the character pointed to by s using function mblen.
 */

#include <stdio.h>
#include <stdlib.h>
#include <locale.h>
#include <errno.h>

main()
{
```

```
    int    mblen_value;
    char   s[2];

    memset (s, ' ', 2);
    setlocale (LC_ALL, "C");
    s[0] = 'a';

    fprintf (stdout,"get number of bytes comprising character a\n");
    mblen_value = mblen (s, 1);
    fprintf (stdout,"mblen_value=%d\n", mblen_value);
}
```

NAME

mbstowcs — convert a character string to a wide character string

SYNOPSIS

```
#include <stdlib.h>

size_t mbstowcs(wchar_t *pwcs, const char *s, size_t n);
```

DESCRIPTION

The *mbstowcs*( ) function converts a sequence of characters that begins in the initial shift state from the array pointed to by *s* into a sequence of corresponding wide-character codes and stores not more than *n* wide-character codes into the array pointed to by *pwcs*. No characters that follow a null byte (which is converted into a wide-character code with value 0) will be examined or converted. Each character is converted as if by a call to *mbtowc*( ), except that the shift state of *mbtowc*( ) is not affected.

No more than *n* elements will be modified in the array pointed to by *pwcs*. If copying takes place between objects that overlap, the behaviour is undefined.

EX   The behaviour of this function is affected by the LC_CTYPE category of the current locale. If *pwcs* is a null pointer, *mbstowcs*( ) returns the length required to convert the entire array regardless of the value of *n*, but no values are stored.

RETURN VALUE

If an invalid character is encountered, *mbstowcs*( ) returns (**size_t**)–1 and may set *errno* to indicate the error. Otherwise, *mbstowcs*( ) returns the number of the array elements modified (or required if *pwcs* is null), not including a terminating 0 code, if any. The array will not be zero-terminated if the value returned is *n*.

ERRORS

The *mbstowcs*( ) function may fail if:

EX   [EILSEQ]   Invalid byte sequence is detected.

SEE ALSO

mblen( ), *mbtowc*( ), *wctomb*( ), *wcstombs*( ), **<stdlib.h>**.

EXAMPLE

```
/*
 * Copyright (C) ANTRIX Inc.
 */

/* mbstowcs.c
 * This program converts a character string to a wide character
 * string using function mbstowcs.
 */

#include <stdio.h>
#include <stdlib.h>
#include <locale.h>
#include <errno.h>

main()
{
   int     i, mbstowcs_value;
   wchar_t wide[50];
   char    string[] = "hello world";
```

```
        setlocale (LC_ALL, "C");
        memset ((char *)&wide, 0, sizeof(wide));

        fprintf (stdout,"convert multibyte string to wide string\n");
        mbstowcs_value = mbstowcs (wide, string, sizeof(string));
        fprintf (stdout,"mbstowcs_value=%d\n", mbstowcs_value);

        for ( i = 0; i < sizeof(string); i++)
            fprintf (stdout,"%wc", wide[i]);

        fprintf (stdout,"\n");
}
```

NAME

mbtowc — convert a character to a wide-character code

SYNOPSIS

```
#include <stdlib.h>

int mbtowc(wchar_t *pwc, const char *s, size_t n);
```

DESCRIPTION

If *s* is not a null pointer, *mbtowc*( ) determines the number of the bytes that constitute the character pointed to by *s*. It then determines the wide-character code for the value of type **wchar_t** that corresponds to that character. (The value of the wide-character code corresponding to the null byte is 0.) If the character is valid and *pwc* is not a null pointer, *mbtowc*( ) stores the wide-character code in the object pointed to by *pwc*.

The behaviour of this function is affected by the LC_CTYPE category of the current locale. For a state-dependent encoding, this function is placed into its initial state by a call for which its character pointer argument, *s*, is a null pointer. Subsequent calls with *s* as other than a null pointer cause the internal state of the function to be altered as necessary. A call with *s* as a null pointer causes this function to return a non-zero value if encodings have state dependency, and 0 otherwise. If the implementation employs special bytes to change the shift state, these bytes do not produce separate wide-character codes, but are grouped with an adjacent character. Changing the LC_CTYPE category causes the shift state of this function to be indeterminate. At most *n* bytes of the array pointed to by *s* will be examined.

The implementation will behave as if no function defined in this document calls *mbtowc*( ).

RETURN VALUE

If *s* is a null pointer, *mbtowc*( ) returns a non-zero or 0 value, if character encodings, respectively, do or do not have state-dependent encodings. If *s* is not a null pointer, *mbtowc*( ) either returns 0 (if *s* points to the null byte), or returns the number of bytes that constitute the converted character (if the next *n* or fewer bytes form a valid character), or returns −1 and may set *errno* to indicate the error (if they do not form a valid character).

In no case will the value returned be greater than *n* or the value of the MB_CUR_MAX macro.

ERRORS

The *mbtowc*( ) function may fail if:

EX   **[EILSEQ]**   Invalid character sequence is detected.

SEE ALSO

mblen( ), *mbstowcs*( ), *wctomb*( ), *wcstombs*( ), **<stdlib.h>**.

EXAMPLE

```
/*
 * Copyright (C) ANTRIX Inc.
 */

/* mbtowc.c
 * This program converts a character to a wide character code
 * using function mbtowc.
 */

#include <stdio.h>
#include <stdlib.h>
#include <wchar.h>
#include <locale.h>
```

```
main()
{
   int     mbtowc_value;
   char    c[2];
   wchar_t pwc[10];

   memset (c, ' ', 2);
   setlocale (LC_ALL, "C");
   c[0] = 'a';

   fprintf (stdout,"convert multibyte to wide character\n");
   mbtowc_value = mbtowc (pwc, c, sizeof(c));
   fprintf (stdout,"mbtowc_value=%d\n", mbtowc_value);
   fprintf (stdout,"pwc=%ws\n", pwc);
}
```

NAME

memccpy — copy bytes in memory

SYNOPSIS

EX
```
#include <string.h>

void *memccpy(void *s1, const void *s2, int c, size_t n);
```

DESCRIPTION

The *memccpy*( ) function copies bytes from memory area *s2* into *s1*, stopping after the first occurrence of byte *c* (converted to an **unsigned char**) is copied, or after *n* bytes are copied, whichever comes first. If copying takes place between objects that overlap, the behaviour is undefined.

RETURN VALUE

The *memccpy*( ) function returns a pointer to the byte after the copy of *c* in *s1*, or a null pointer if *c* was not found in the first *n* bytes of *s2*.

ERRORS

No errors are defined.

APPLICATION USAGE

The *memccpy*( ) function does not check for the overflow of the receiving memory area.

SEE ALSO

<string.h>.

EXAMPLE

```
/*
 * Copyright (C) ANTRIX Inc.
 */

/* memccpy.c
 * This program copies bytes from memory area s2 into s1 stopping
 * after the first occurrence of byte c is copied or after n bytes
 * are copied whichever comes first using function memccpy.
 */

#include <stdio.h>
#include <stdlib.h>
#include <memory.h>
#include <errno.h>

main()
{
  char   s1[12];
  char   *s2 = "hello world";

  memset (s1, ' ', 12);

  fprintf (stdout,"copy string in s1\n");
  memccpy (s1, s2, 'o', 12);
  fprintf (stdout,"string in s1=%s\n", s1);
}
```

NAME
memchr — find byte in memory

SYNOPSIS
```
#include <string.h>

void *memchr(const void *s, int c, size_t n);
```

DESCRIPTION
The *memchr*( ) function locates the first occurrence of *c* (converted to an **unsigned char**) in the initial *n* bytes (each interpreted as **unsigned char**) of the object pointed to by *s*.

RETURN VALUE
The *memchr*( ) function returns a pointer to the located byte, or a null pointer if the byte does not occur in the object.

ERRORS
No errors are defined.

SEE ALSO
<string.h>.

EXAMPLE
```
/*
 * Copyright (C) ANTRIX Inc.
 */

/* memchr.c
 * This program locates the first occurrence of c in the initial
 * n bytes of the object pointed to by s using function memchr.
 */

#include <stdio.h>
#include <stdlib.h>
#include <memory.h>
#include <errno.h>

main()
{
   int        c = 'w';
   char       *buf;
   const char *s = "hello world";

   fprintf (stdout,"return pointer to first occurrence of w\n");
   buf = (char *)memchr (s, c, 12);
   if ( buf != (char *)0 ) {
       fprintf (stdout,"memchr() call successful\n");
       fprintf (stdout,"string in buf=%s\n", buf);
   }
   else
       fprintf (stderr,"ERROR: memchr() call failed\n");
}
```

memcmp( )

NAME

memcmp — compare bytes in memory

SYNOPSIS

```
#include <string.h>

int memcmp(const void *s1, const void *s2, size_t n);
```

DESCRIPTION

The *memcmp*( ) function compares the first *n* bytes (each interpreted as **unsigned char**) of the object pointed to by *s1* to the first *n* bytes of the object pointed to by *s2*.

The sign of a non-zero return value is determined by the sign of the difference between the values of the first pair of bytes (both interpreted as type **unsigned char**) that differ in the objects being compared.

RETURN VALUE

The *memcmp*( ) function returns an integer greater than, equal to or less than 0, if the object pointed to by *s1* is greater than, equal to or less than the object pointed to by *s2* respectively.

ERRORS

No errors are defined.

SEE ALSO

<string.h>.

EXAMPLE

```
/*
 * Copyright (C) ANTRIX Inc.
 */

/* memcmp.c
 * This program compares the first n bytes of the object pointed
 * by s1 to the first n bytes of the object pointed to by s2
 * using function memcmp.
 */

#include <stdio.h>
#include <stdlib.h>
#include <memory.h>
#include <errno.h>

main()
{
    int     memcmp_value;
    int     length;
    char    *str1 = "abc";
    char    *str2 = "abc";
    typedef struct {
            int a;
            char c;
    } svalues;

    svalues s1 = { 2, 'z' };
    svalues s2 = { 2, 'z' };
```

514   Applied UNIX Programming, Volume 2

```
        fprintf (stdout,"example 1\n");
        fprintf (stdout,"compare strings\n");
        length = strlen (str1);
        memcmp_value = memcmp (str1, str2, length);
        if ( memcmp_value == 0 )
            fprintf (stdout,"memcmp() call successful\n");
        else
            fprintf (stderr,"ERROR: memcmp() call failed\n");

        fprintf (stdout,"example 2\n");
        fprintf (stdout,"compare structures\n");
        memcmp_value = memcmp ((svalues *)&s1, (svalues *)&s2, sizeof(svalues));
        if ( memcmp_value == 0 )
            fprintf (stdout,"memcmp() call successful\n");
        else
            fprintf (stderr,"ERROR: memcmp() call failed\n");
}
```

NAME

memcpy — copy bytes in memory

SYNOPSIS

```
#include <string.h>

void *memcpy(void *s1, const void *s2, size_t n);
```

DESCRIPTION

The *memcpy*( ) function copies *n* bytes from the object pointed to by *s2* into the object pointed to by *s1*. If copying takes place between objects that overlap, the behaviour is undefined.

RETURN VALUE

The *memcpy*( ) function returns *s1*; no return value is reserved to indicate an error.

ERRORS

No errors are defined.

APPLICATION USAGE

The *memcpy*( ) function does not check for the overflowing of the receiving memory area.

SEE ALSO

<string.h>.

EXAMPLE

```
/*
 * Copyright (C) ANTRIX Inc.
 */

/* memcpy.c
 * This program copies n bytes from the object pointed to by s2
 * into the object pointed to by s1 using function memcpy.
 */

#include <stdio.h>
#include <stdlib.h>
#include <memory.h>
#include <errno.h>

main()
{
   char     str1[6];
   char     *str2 = "hello world";
   typedef struct {
              int a;
              int b;
   } svalues;

   svalues s1 ;
   svalues s2 = { 2, 4 };

   fprintf (stdout,"example 1\n");
   fprintf (stdout,"copy strings\n");
   memset (str1, ' ', 6);
   memcpy (str1, str2, 5);
   fprintf (stdout,"string in str1=%s\n", str1);
```

```
        fprintf (stdout,"example 2\n");
        fprintf (stdout,"copy structures\n");
        memcpy ((svalues *)&s1, (svalues *)&s2, sizeof(svalues));
        fprintf (stdout,"s1.a=%d s1.b=%d\n", s1.a, s1.b );
        fprintf (stdout,"s2.a=%d s2.b=%d\n", s2.a, s2.b );
    }
```

NAME

memmove — copy bytes in memory with overlapping areas

SYNOPSIS

```
#include <string.h>

void *memmove(void *s1, const void *s2, size_t n);
```

DESCRIPTION

The *memmove*( ) function copies *n* bytes from the object pointed to by *s2* into the object pointed to by *s1*. Copying takes place as if the *n* bytes from the object pointed to by *s2* are first copied into a temporary array of *n* bytes that does not overlap the objects pointed to by *s1* and *s2*, and then the *n* bytes from the temporary array are copied into the object pointed to by *s1*.

RETURN VALUE

The *memmove*( ) function returns *s1*; no return value is reserved to indicate an error.

ERRORS

No errors are defined.

SEE ALSO

<string.h>.

EXAMPLE

```
/*
 * Copyright (C) ANTRIX Inc.
 */

/* memmove.c
 * This program copies first n bytes from the string pointed
 * to by s2 into the object pointed to by s1 using function
 * memmove.
 */

#include <stdio.h>
#include <stdlib.h>
#include <memory.h>
#include <errno.h>

main()
{
  char   s1[12];
  char   *s2 = "hello world";

  memset (s1, ' ', 12);

  fprintf (stdout,"copy n bytes from area s2 to s1\n");
  memmove (s1, s2, 12);

  fprintf (stdout,"string in s1=%s\n", s1);
  fprintf (stdout,"string in s2=%s\n", s2);
}
```

NAME

memset — set bytes in memory

SYNOPSIS

```
#include <string.h>

void *memset(void *s, int c, size_t n);
```

DESCRIPTION

The *memset*( ) function copies *c* (converted to an **unsigned char**) into each of the first *n* bytes of the object pointed to by *s*.

RETURN VALUE

The *memset*( ) function returns *s*; no return value is reserved to indicate an error.

ERRORS

No errors are defined.

SEE ALSO

<string.h>.

EXAMPLE

```
/*
 * Copyright (C) ANTRIX Inc.
 */

/* memset.c
 * This program copies c into each of the first n bytes of
 * the object pointed to by s using function memset.
 */


#include <stdio.h>
#include <stdlib.h>
#include <sys/stat.h>
#include <memory.h>
#include <errno.h>

main()
{
    char        buf[4];
    char        *s;
    struct stat sbuf;
    struct stat *psbuf;

    memset (buf, ' ', 4);
    memset (buf, 'z', 4);
    buf[4] = ' ';
    fprintf (stdout,"%s\n", buf);

    s = (char *)malloc (12);

    fprintf (stdout,"initialize character array to null\n");
    memset (s, ' ', 12);
    fprintf (stdout,"set character array to a\n");
    memset (s, 'a', 12);
```

```
        fprintf (stdout,"string=%s\n", s);

        fprintf (stdout,"initialize structures to null\n");
        memset ((char *)&sbuf, ' ', sizeof(sbuf));
        psbuf = (struct stat *)malloc(sizeof(stat));
        memset ((char *)psbuf, ' ', sizeof(psbuf));
}
```

NAME

mkdir — make a directory

SYNOPSIS

OH   `#include <sys/types.h>`
`#include <sys/stat.h>`

`int mkdir(const char *path, mode_t mode);`

DESCRIPTION

The *mkdir*( ) function creates a new directory with name *path*. The file permission bits of the new directory are initialised from *mode*. These file permission bits of the *mode* argument are modified by the process' file creation mask.

When bits in *mode* other than the file permission bits are set, the meaning of these additional bits is implementation-dependent.

The directory's user ID is set to the process' effective user ID. The directory's group ID is set to the group ID of the parent directory or to the effective group ID of the process.

The newly created directory will be an empty directory.

Upon successful completion, *mkdir*( ) will mark for update the *st_atime*, *st_ctime* and *st_mtime* fields of the directory. Also, the *st_ctime* and *st_mtime* fields of the directory that contains the new entry are marked for update.

RETURN VALUE

Upon successful completion, *mkdir*( ) returns 0. Otherwise, −1 is returned, no directory is created and *errno* is set to indicate the error.

ERRORS

The *mkdir*( ) function will fail if:

[EACCES]   Search permission is denied on a component of the path prefix, or write permission is denied on the parent directory of the directory to be created.

[EEXIST]   The named file exists.

UX   [ELOOP]   Too many symbolic links were encountered in resolving *path*.

[EMLINK]   The link count of the parent directory would exceed {LINK_MAX}.

[ENAMETOOLONG]

FIPS   The length of the *path* argument exceeds {PATH_MAX} or a pathname component is longer than {NAME_MAX}.

[ENOENT]   A component of the path prefix specified by *path* does not name an existing directory or *path* is an empty string.

[ENOSPC]   The file system does not contain enough space to hold the contents of the new directory or to extend the parent directory of the new directory.

[ENOTDIR]   A component of the path prefix is not a directory.

[EROFS]   The parent directory resides on a read-only file system.

The *mkdir*( ) function may fail if:

UX   [ENAMETOOLONG]
             Pathname resolution of a symbolic link produced an intermediate result whose length exceeds {PATH_MAX}.

mkdir( )

SEE ALSO

 umask( ), **\<sys/stat.h\>**, **\<sys/types.h\>**.

EXAMPLE

```
/*
 * Copyright (C) ANTRIX Inc.
 */

/* mkdir.c
 * This program creates a new directory with name path. The file
 * permission bits of the new directory are initialized from mode
 * using function mkdir.
 */

#include <stdio.h>
#include <stdlib.h>
#include <sys/types.h>
#include <sys/stat.h>
#include <errno.h>

#define  PERM_ALL    (S_IRWXU | S_IRWXG | S_IRWXO)

main()
{
  int           mkdir_value;
  char          *path = "testdir";
  struct stat   buf;

  fprintf (stdout,"create testdir directory\n");
  mkdir_value = mkdir (path, PERM_ALL);
  if ( mkdir_value == 0 ) {
     fprintf (stdout,"mkdir() call successful\n");
     stat ("testfile", &buf);
     fprintf (stdout,"buf.st_mode=%o\n", buf.st_mode );
  }
  else {
     fprintf (stderr,"ERROR: mkdir() call failed\n");
     fprintf (stderr,"ERROR: %s\n", strerror(errno));
  }

  fprintf (stdout,"remove directory\n");
  rmdir (path);
}
```

NAME

mkfifo — make a FIFO special file

SYNOPSIS

OH
```
#include <sys/types.h>
#include <sys/stat.h>

int mkfifo(const char *path, mode_t mode);
```

DESCRIPTION

The *mkfifo*( ) function creates a new FIFO special file named by the pathname pointed to by *path*. The file permission bits of the new FIFO are initialised from *mode*. The file permission bits of the *mode* argument are modified by the process' file creation mask.

When bits in *mode* other than the file permission bits are set, the effect is implementation-dependent.

The FIFO's user ID will be set to the process' effective user ID. The FIFO's group ID will be set to the group ID of the parent directory or to the effective group ID of the process.

Upon successful completion, *mkfifo*( ) will mark for update the *st_atime*, *st_ctime* and *st_mtime* fields of the file. Also, the *st_ctime* and *st_mtime* fields of the directory that contains the new entry are marked for update.

RETURN VALUE

Upon successful completion, 0 is returned. Otherwise, −1 is returned, no FIFO is created and *errno* is set to indicate the error.

ERRORS

The *mkfifo*( ) function will fail if:

[EACCES]   A component of the path prefix denies search permission, or write permission is denied on the parent directory of the FIFO to be created.

[EEXIST]   The named file already exists.

UX   [ELOOP]   Too many symbolic links were encountered in resolving *path*.

[ENAMETOOLONG]

FIPS   The length of the *path* argument exceeds {PATH_MAX} or a pathname component is longer than {NAME_MAX}.

[ENOENT]   A component of the path prefix specified by *path* does not name an existing directory or *path* is an empty string.

[ENOSPC]   The directory that would contain the new file cannot be extended or the file system is out of file-allocation resources.

[ENOTDIR]   A component of the path prefix is not a directory.

[EROFS]   The named file resides on a read-only file system.

The *mkfifo*( ) function may fail if:

UX   [ENAMETOOLONG]

             Pathname resolution of a symbolic link produced an intermediate result whose length exceeds {PATH_MAX}.

SEE ALSO

umask( ), **<sys/stat.h>**, **<sys/types.h>**.

EXAMPLE

```
/*
 * Copyright (C) ANTRIX Inc.
 */

/* mkfifo.c
 * This program creates a FIFO special file named by the pathname
 * pointed to by path. The file permission bits are initialised
 * from mode using function mkfifo.
 */

#include <stdio.h>
#include <stdlib.h>
#include <sys/types.h>
#include <sys/stat.h>
#include <errno.h>

#define  PERM_ALL    (S_IRWXU | S_IRWXG | S_IRWXO)

main()
{
  int         mkfifo_value;
  const char  *path = "testfile";
  struct stat  buf;

  fprintf (stdout,"create FIFO testfile\n");
  mkfifo_value = mkfifo (path, PERM_ALL);

  fprintf (stdout,"check file created is FIFO testfile\n");
  if ( mkfifo_value == 0 ) {
     fprintf (stdout,"mkfifo() call successful\n");
     stat ("testfile", &buf);
     fprintf (stdout,"buf.st_mode=%o\n", (S_IFIFO ^ buf.st_mode) );
     fprintf (stdout,"buf.st_nlink=%d\n", buf.st_nlink );
     fprintf (stdout,"buf.st_uid=%d\n", buf.st_uid );
     fprintf (stdout,"buf.st_gid=%d\n", buf.st_gid );
  }
  else {
     fprintf (stderr,"ERROR: mkfifo() call failed\n");
     fprintf (stderr,"ERROR: %s\n", strerror(errno));
  }

  fprintf (stdout,"remove testfile\n");
  remove (path);
}
```

NAME

mknod — make a directory, a special or regular file

SYNOPSIS

UX `#include <sys/stat.h>`

`int mknod(const char *path, mode_t mode, dev_t dev);`

DESCRIPTION

The *mknod( )* function creates a new file named by the pathname to which the argument *path* points.

The file type for *path* is OR-ed into the *mode* argument, and must be selected from one of the following symbolic constants:

Name	Description
S_IFIFO	FIFO-special
S_IFCHR	Character-special (non-portable)
S_IFDIR	Directory (non-portable)
S_IFBLK	Block-special (non-portable)
S_IFREG	Regular (non-portable)

The only portable use of *mknod( )* is to create a FIFO-special file. If *mode* is not S_IFIFO or *dev* is not 0, the behaviour of *mknod( )* is unspecified.

The permissions for the new file are OR-ed into the *mode* argument, and may be selected from any combination of the following symbolic constants:

Name	Description
S_ISUID	Set user ID on execution.
S_ISGID	Set group ID on execution.
S_IRWXU	Read, write or execute (search) by owner.
S_IRUSR	Read by owner.
S_IWUSR	Write by owner.
S_IXUSR	Execute (search) by owner.
S_IRWXG	Read, write or execute (search) by group.
S_IRGRP	Read by group.
S_IWGRP	Write by group.
S_IXGRP	Execute (search) by group.
S_IRWXO	Read, write or execute (search) by others.
S_IROTH	Read by others.
S_IWOTH	Write by others.
S_IXOTH	Execute (search) by others.
S_ISVTX	On directories, restricted deletion flag.

The user ID of the file is initialised to the effective user ID of the process. The group ID of the file is initialised to either the effective group ID of the process or the group ID of the parent directory.

The owner, group, and other permission bits of *mode* are modified by the file mode creation mask of the process. The *mknod( )* function clears each bit whose corresponding bit in the file mode creation mask of the process is set.

Upon successful completion, *mknod( )* marks for update the *st_atime*, *st_ctime* and *st_mtime* fields of the file. Also, the *st_ctime* and *st_mtime* fields of the directory that contains the new entry are marked for update.

Only a process with appropriate privileges may invoke *mknod*( ) for file types other than FIFO-special.

RETURN VALUE

Upon successful completion, *mknod*( ) returns 0. Otherwise, it returns −1, the new file is not created, and *errno* is set to indicate the error.

ERRORS

The *mknod*( ) function will fail if:

[EPERM]	The invoking process does not have appropriate privileges and the file type is not FIFO-special.
[ENOTDIR]	A component of the path prefix is not a directory.
[ENOENT]	A component of the path prefix specified by *path* does not name an existing directory or *path* is an empty string.
[EACCES]	A component of the path prefix denies search permission, or write permission is denied on the parent directory.
[EROFS]	The directory in which the file is to be created is located on a read-only file system.
[EEXIST]	The named file exists.
[EIO]	An I/O error occurred while accessing the file system.
[EINVAL]	An invalid argument exists.
[ENOSPC]	The directory that would contain the new file cannot be extended or the file system is out of file allocation resources.
[ELOOP]	Too many symbolic links were encountered in resolving *path*.
[ENAMETOOLONG]	
	The length of a pathname exceeds {PATH_MAX}, or pathname component is longer than {NAME_MAX}.

The *mknod*( ) function may fail if:

[ENAMETOOLONG]	
	Pathname resolution of a symbolic link produced an intermediate result whose length exceeds {PATH_MAX}.

APPLICATION USAGE

For portability to implementations conforming to earlier versions of this document, *mkfifo*( ) is preferred over this function for making FIFO special files.

SEE ALSO

chmod( ), *creat*( ), *exec*, *mkdir*( ), *mkfifo*( ), *open*( ), *stat*( ), *umask*( ), **<sys/stat.h>**.

EXAMPLE

```
/*
 * Copyright (C) ANTRIX Inc.
 */

/* mknod.c
 * This program makes a special file
 * using function mknod
```

```
 */

#include <stdio.h>
#include <stdlib.h>
#include <sys/types.h>
#include <sys/stat.h>
#include <fcntl.h>
#include <errno.h>

#define  PERM_ALL   (S_IRWXU | S_IRWXG | S_IRWXO)

main()
{
  int   mknod_value;
  char  *file = "testfile";

  fprintf (stdout,"make testfile node\n");
  mknod_value = mknod (file, (S_IFIFO | PERM_ALL), 0);
  if ( mknod_value == 0 )
     fprintf (stdout,"mknod() call successful\n");
  else {
     fprintf (stderr,"ERROR: mknod() call failed\n");
     fprintf (stderr,"ERROR: %s\n", strerror(errno));
  }

  fprintf (stdout,"remove testfile\n");
  remove (file);
}
```

NAME

mkstemp — make a unique file name

SYNOPSIS

UX
```
#include <stdlib.h>
```

```
int mkstemp(char *template);
```

DESCRIPTION

The *mkstemp*( ) function replaces the contents of the string pointed to by *template* by a unique file name, and returns a file descriptor for the file open for reading and writing. The function thus prevents any possible race condition between testing whether the file exists and opening it for use. The string in *template* should look like a file name with six trailing 'X's; *mkstemp*( ) replaces each 'X' with a character from the portable file name character set. The characters are chosen such that the resulting name does not duplicate the name of an existing file.

RETURN VALUE

Upon successful completion, *mkstemp*( ) returns an open file descriptor. Otherwise −1 is returned if no suitable file could be created.

ERRORS

No errors are defined.

APPLICATION USAGE

It is possible to run out of letters.

The *mkstemp*( ) function does not check to determine whether the file name part of *template* exceeds the maximum allowable file name length.

For portability with previous versions of this document, *tmpfile*( ) is preferred over this function.

SEE ALSO

getpid( ), *open*( ), *tmpfile*( ), *tmpnam*( ), **<stdlib.h>**.

EXAMPLE

```
/*
 * Copyright (C) ANTRIX Inc.
 */

/* mkstemp.c
 * This program replaces the contents of the template string
 * with a unique file name using function mkstemp
 */

#include <stdio.h>
#include <stdlib.h>
#include <errno.h>

main()
{
  char    template[255] = "fileXXXXXX";

  fprintf (stdout,"create a temporary file\n");
  mkstemp (template);

  fprintf (stdout,"check file was created\n");
```

```
     fprintf (stdout,"temporary file name is %s\n", template);
}
```

NAME

mktemp — make a unique filename

SYNOPSIS

UX
```
#include <stdlib.h>
```
```
char *mktemp(char *template);
```

DESCRIPTION

The *mktemp*( ) function replaces the contents of the string pointed to by *template* by a unique filename and returns *template*. The application must initialise *template* to be a filename with six trailing 'X's; *mktemp*( ) replaces each 'X' with a single byte character from the portable filename character set.

RETURN VALUE

The *mktemp*( ) function returns the pointer *template*. If a unique name cannot be created, *template* points to a null string.

ERRORS

No errors are defined.

APPLICATION USAGE

Between the time a pathname is created and the file opened, it is possible for some other process to create a file with the same name. The *mkstemp*( ) function avoids this problem.

For portability with previous versions of this document, *tmpnam*( ) is preferred over this function.

SEE ALSO

mkstemp( ), *tmpfile*( ), *tmpnam*( ), **<stdlib.h>**.

EXAMPLE

```
/*
 * Copyright (C) ANTRIX Inc.
 */

/* mktemp.c
 * This program replaces the contents of the string
 * with a unique file name using function mktemp
 */

#include <stdio.h>
#include <stdlib.h>
#include <errno.h>

main()
{
  char    *mktemp_value;

    fprintf (stdout,"create a temporary file\n");
    mktemp_value = mktemp ("fileXXXXXXXX");

    fprintf (stdout,"check file was created\n");
    if ( mktemp_value != (char *)0 ) {
       fprintf (stdout,"mktemp() call successful\n");
       fprintf (stdout,"temporary file name is %s\n", mktemp_value);
    }
    else {
```

```
            fprintf (stderr,"ERROR: mktemp() call failed\n");
            fprintf (stderr,"ERROR: %s\n", strerror(errno));
        }
    }
```

NAME

mktime — convert broken-down time into time since the Epoch

SYNOPSIS

```
#include <time.h>

time_t mktime(struct tm *timeptr);
```

DESCRIPTION

The *mktime( )* function converts the broken-down time, expressed as local time, in the structure pointed to by *timeptr*, into a time since the Epoch value with the same encoding as that of the values returned by *time( )*. The original values of the *tm_wday* and *tm_yday* components of the structure are ignored, and the original values of the other components are not restricted to the ranges described in the **<time.h>** entry.

A positive or 0 value for *tm_isdst* causes *mktime( )* to presume initially that Daylight Savings Time, respectively, is or is not in effect for the specified time. A negative value for *tm_isdst* causes *mktime( )* to attempt to determine whether Daylight Saving Time is in effect for the specified time.

Local timezone information is set as though *mktime( )* called *tzset( )*.

Upon successful completion, the values of the *tm_wday* and *tm_yday* components of the structure are set appropriately, and the other components are set to represent the specified time since the Epoch, but with their values forced to the ranges indicated in the **<time.h>** entry; the final value of *tm_mday* is not set until *tm_mon* and *tm_year* are determined.

RETURN VALUE

The *mktime( )* function returns the specified time since the Epoch encoded as a value of type **time_t**. If the time since the Epoch cannot be represented, the function returns the value **(time_t)**−1.

ERRORS

No errors are defined.

EXAMPLES

What day of the week is July 4, 2001?

```
#include <stdio.h>
#include <time.h>

struct tm time_str;

char daybuf[20];

int main(void)
{
        time_str.tm_year = 2001 - 1900;
        time_str.tm_mon = 7 - 1;
        time_str.tm_mday = 4;
        time_str.tm_hour = 0;
        time_str.tm_min = 0;
        time_str.tm_sec = 1;
        time_str.tm_isdst = -1;
        if (mktime(&time_str) == -1)
                (void)puts("-unknown-");
        else {
                (void)strftime(daybuf, sizeof(daybuf), "%A", &time_str);
                (void)puts(daybuf);
        }
        return 0;
}
```

SEE ALSO

asctime( ), *clock*( ), *ctime*( ), *difftime*( ), *gmtime*( ), *localtime*( ), *strftime*( ), *strptime*( ), *time*( ), *utime*( ), **<time.h>**.

EXAMPLE

```
/*
 * Copyright (C) ANTRIX Inc.
 */

/* mktime.c
 * This program converts the broken-down time, expressed as local
 * time, in the structure pointed to by timeptr, into a time
 * since the Epoch value with the same encoding as that of the
 * values returned by the time() function using mktime function.
 */

#include <stdio.h>
#include <stdlib.h>
#include <time.h>
#include <errno.h>

main()
{
   time_t    tloc, mktime_value;
   struct    tm *current_time;
   struct    tm known_time = {
      /* sec, min, hour, mday, mon, year, wday, yday, isdst */
```

```
      40,  30,  2,   1,   8,  93,  0,   259, 0,
   };

   fprintf (stdout,"example  1\n");
   fprintf (stdout,"get current time\n");
   time (&tloc);
   fprintf (stdout,"get local time after correction for time-zone\n");
   fprintf (stdout,"in struct buf of type tm\n");
   current_time = localtime (&tloc);
   fprintf (stdout," convert tm structure to a calendar time\n");
   mktime_value = mktime (current_time);
   if ( mktime_value != (time_t)0 ) {
       fprintf (stdout,"mktime() call successful\n");
       fprintf (stdout,"mktime_value=%d\n", mktime_value);
       fprintf (stdout,"tloc=%d\n", tloc);
   }
   else
       fprintf (stderr,"ERROR: mktime() call failed\n");

   fprintf (stdout,"example 2\n");
   fprintf (stdout,"convert known time structure to a calendar time\n");
   mktime_value = mktime (&known_time);
   if ( mktime_value != (time_t)0 ) {
       fprintf (stdout,"mktime() call successful\n");
       fprintf (stdout,"mktime_value=%d\n", mktime_value);
   }
   else
       fprintf (stderr,"ERROR: mktime() call failed\n");
}
```

NAME

mmap — map pages of memory

SYNOPSIS

UX   `#include <sys/mman.h>`

```
void *mmap(void *addr, size_t len, int prot, int flags,
     int fildes, off_t off);
```

DESCRIPTION

The *mmap( )* function establishes a mapping between a process' address space and a file. The format of the call is as follows:

```
pa=mmap(addr, len, prot, flags, fildes, off);
```

The *mmap( )* function establishes a mapping between the process' address space at an address *pa* for *len* bytes and the file associated with the file descriptor *fildes* at offset *off* for *len* bytes. The value of *pa* is an unspecified function of the argument *addr* and values of *flags*, further described below. A successful *mmap( )* call returns *pa* as its result. The address ranges covered by [*pa, pa + len*) and [*off, off + len*) must be legitimate for the possible (not necessarily current) address space of a process and the file, respectively.

If the size of the mapped file changes after the call to *mmap( )*, the effect of references to portions of the mapped region that correspond to added or removed portions of the file is unspecified.

The *mmap( )* function is supported for regular files. Support for any other type of file is unspecified.

The *prot* argument determines whether read, write, execute, or some combination of accesses are permitted to the pages being mapped. The protection options are defined in **<sys/mman.h>**:

PROT_READ   Page can be read.

PROT_WRITE   Page can be written.

PROT_EXEC   Page can be executed.

PROT_NONE   Page cannot be accessed.

Implementations need not enforce all combinations of access permissions. However, writes shall only be permitted when PROT_WRITE has been set.

The *flags* argument provides other information about the handling of the mapped pages. The options are defined in **<sys/mman.h>**:

MAP_SHARED   Share changes.

MAP_PRIVATE   Changes are private.

MAP_FIXED   Interpret addr exactly.

The MAP_PRIVATE and MAP_SHARED flags control the visibility of write references to the memory region. Exactly one of these flags must be specified. The mapping type is retained across a *fork( )*.

If MAP_SHARED is set in *flags*, write references to the memory region by the calling process may change the file and are visible in all MAP_SHARED mappings of the same portion of the file by any process.

If MAP_PRIVATE is set in *flags*, write references to the memory region by the calling process do not change the file and are not visible to any process in other mappings of the same portion of the file.

It is unspecified whether write references by processes that have mapped the memory region using MAP_SHARED are visible to processes that have mapped the same portion of the file using MAP_PRIVATE.

It is also unspecified whether write references to a memory region mapped with MAP_SHARED are visible to processes reading the file and whether writes to a file are visible to processes that have mapped the modified portion of that file, except for the effect of *msync*( ).

When MAP_FIXED is set in the *flags* argument, the implementation is informed that the value of *pa* must be *addr*, exactly. If MAP_FIXED is set, *mmap*( ) may return (**void ***)–1 and set errno to [EINVAL]. If a MAP_FIXED request is successful, the mapping established by *mmap*( ) replaces any previous mappings for the process' pages in the range [*pa, pa + len*).

When MAP_FIXED is not set, the implementation uses *addr* in an unspecified manner to arrive at *pa*. The *pa* so chosen will be an area of the address space which the implementation deems suitable for a mapping of *len* bytes to the file. All implementations interpret an *addr* value of 0 as granting the implementation complete freedom in selecting *pa*, subject to constraints described below. A non-zero value of *addr* is taken to be a suggestion of a process address near which the mapping should be placed. When the implementation selects a value for *pa*, it never places a mapping at address 0, nor does it replace any extant mapping, nor map into dynamic memory allocation areas.

The *off* argument is constrained to be aligned and sized according to the value returned by *sysconf*( ) when passed _SC_PAGESIZE or _SC_PAGE_SIZE. When MAP_FIXED is specified, the argument *addr* must also meet these constraints. The implementation performs mapping operations over whole pages. Thus, while the argument *len* need not meet a size or alignment constraint, the implementation will include, in any mapping operation, any partial page specified by the range [*pa, pa + len*).

The implementation always zero-fills any partial page at the end of a memory region. Further, the implementation never writes out any modified portions of the last page of a file that are beyond the end of the mapped portion of the file. If the mapping established by *mmap*( ) extends into pages beyond the page containing the last byte of the file, an application reference to any of the pages in the mapping that are beyond the last page results in the delivery of a SIGBUS or SIGSEGV signal.

The *mmap*( ) function adds an extra reference to the file associated with the file descriptor *fildes* which is not removed by a subsequent *close*( ) on that file descriptor. This reference is removed when there are no more mappings to the file.

The **st_atime** field of the mapped file may be marked for update at any time between the *mmap*( ) call and the corresponding *munmap*( ) call. The initial read or write reference to a mapped region will cause the file's **st_atime** field to be marked for update if it has not already been marked for update.

The **st_ctime** and **st_mtime** fields of a file that is mapped with MAP_SHARED and PROT_WRITE, will be marked for update at some point in the interval between a write reference to the mapped region and the next call to *msync*( ) with MS_ASYNC or MS_SYNC for that portion of the file by any process. If there is no such call, these fields may be marked for update at any time after a write reference if the underlying file is modified as a result.

There may be implementation-dependent limits on the number of memory regions that can be mapped (per process or per system). If such a limit is imposed, whether the number of memory regions that can be mapped by a process is decreased by the use of *shmat*( ) is implementation-dependent.

RETURN VALUE

Upon successful completion, *mmap*( ) returns the address at which the mapping was placed (*pa*). Otherwise, it returns a value of –1 and sets *errno* to indicate the error.

ERRORS

The *mmap*( ) function will fail if:

[EBADF]	The *fildes* argument is not a valid open file descriptor.
[EACCES]	The *fildes* argument is not open for read, regardless of the protection specified, or *fildes* is not open for write and PROT_WRITE was specified for a MAP_SHARED type mapping.
[ENXIO]	Addresses in the range [*off, off + len*) are invalid for *fildes*.
[EINVAL]	The *addr* argument (if MAP_FIXED was specified) or *off* is not a multiple of the page size as returned by *sysconf*( ), or are considered invalid by the implementation.
[EINVAL]	The value of *flags* is invalid (neither MAP_PRIVATE nor MAP_SHARED is set).
[EMFILE]	The number of mapped regions would exceed an implementation-dependent limit (per process or per system).
[ENODEV]	The *fildes* argument refers to a file whose type is not supported by *mmap*( ).
[ENOMEM]	MAP_FIXED was specified, and the range [*addr, addr + len*) exceeds that allowed for the address space of a process; or if MAP_FIXED was not specified and there is insufficient room in the address space to effect the mapping.

APPLICATION USAGE

Use of *mmap*( ) may reduce the amount of memory available to other memory allocation functions.

Use of MAP_FIXED may result in unspecified behaviour in further use of *brk*( ), *sbrk*( ), *malloc*( ) and *shmat*( ). The use of MAP_FIXED is discouraged, as it may prevent an implementation from making the most effective use of resources.

The application must ensure correct synchronisation when using *mmap*( ) in conjunction with any other file access method, such as *read*( ) and *write*( ), standard input/output, and shmat .

The *mmap*( ) function allows access to resources via address space manipulations, instead of *read*( )/*write*( ). Once a file is mapped, all a process has to do to access it is use the data at the address to which the file was mapped. So, using pseudo-code to illustrate the way in which an existing program might be changed to use *mmap*( ), the following:

```
fildes = open(...)
lseek(fildes, some_offset)
read(fildes, buf, len)
/* use data in buf */
```

becomes:

```
fildes = open(...)
address = mmap(0, len, PROT_READ, MAP_PRIVATE, fildes, some_offset)
/* use data at address */
```

SEE ALSO

> *exec*, *fcntl*( ), *fork*( ), *lockf*( ), *msync*( ), *munmap*( ), *mprotect*( ), *shmat*( ), *sysconf*( ), **<sys/mman.h>**.

EXAMPLE

```
/*
 * Copyright (C) ANTRIX Inc.
 */

/* mmap.c : run as root
 * This program establishes a mapping between a process
 * address space and a virtual memory object using function mmap
 */

#include <stdio.h>
#include <stdlib.h>
#include <unistd.h>
#include <fcntl.h>
#include <sys/stat.h>
#include <sys/mman.h>
#include <errno.h>

#define  OFLAG      (O_RDWR | O_CREAT | O_TRUNC)
#define  PERM_ALL    (PROT_READ | PROT_WRITE | PROT_EXEC)

main()
{
    int     fd, pagesize;
    int     buf[1024], i, j;
    int     *addr;
    int     size;

    memset(buf, 0, 1024);

    fprintf (stdout,"get page size\n");
    pagesize = sysconf (_SC_PAGESIZE);
    size = pagesize/sizeof(int);

    fprintf (stdout,"create and write to file\n");
    fd = open("testfile", OFLAG, PERM_ALL);
    for ( j = 0; j < pagesize; j += sizeof (buf) ) {
        for ( i = 0; i < sizeof (buf)/sizeof (buf[0]); i++)
            buf[i] = i + j;
            write (fd, (void *)buf, sizeof (buf));
    }
    fprintf (stdout,"close testfile\n");
    close (fd);

    fprintf (stdout,"open testfile\n");
    fd = open ("testfile", O_RDWR, PERM_ALL);

    fprintf (stdout,"map page of memory\n");
    addr = (int *)mmap (0, pagesize, PROT_READ, MAP_SHARED, fd, 0);
```

```
    if ( addr != (int *)-1 ) {
        fprintf (stdout,"mmap() call successful\n");
        fprintf (stdout,"read mapped pages\n");
        for ( j = 0; j < size; j++ ) {
            i = addr[j];
            if ( i != j ) {
                fprintf (stderr,"ERROR: offset %d.\nexpected %x\nactual %x",
                                    j, j, i);
                break;
            }
        }
        fprintf (stdout,"unmap pages\n");
        munmap (addr, pagesize);
    }
    else {
        fprintf (stderr,"ERROR: mmap() call failed\n");
        fprintf (stderr,"ERROR: %s\n", strerror(errno));
    }
    close (fd);

    fprintf (stdout,"remove testfile\n");
    remove ("testfile");
}
```

modf( )

NAME
modf — decompose floating-point number

SYNOPSIS
```
#include <math.h>

double modf(double x, double *iptr);
```

DESCRIPTION
The *modf*( ) function breaks the argument x into integral and fractional parts, each of which has the same sign as the argument. It stores the integral part as a double in the object pointed to by *iptr*.

RETURN VALUE
Upon successful completion, *modf*( ) returns the signed fractional part of *x*.

EX   If *x* is NaN, NaN is returned, *errno* may be set to [EDOM] and *iptr* is set to NaN.

If the correct value would cause underflow, 0 is returned and *errno* may be set to [ERANGE].

ERRORS
The *modf*( ) function may fail if:

EX   [EDOM]   The value of *x* is NaN.

[ERANGE]   The result underflows.

EX   No other errors will occur.

APPLICATION USAGE
An application wishing to check for error situations should set *errno* to 0 before calling *modf*( ). If *errno* is non-zero on return, or the return value is NaN, an error has occurred.

SEE ALSO
frexp( ), *isnan*( ), *ldexp*( ), **<math.h>**.

EXAMPLE
```
/*
 * Copyright (C) ANTRIX Inc.
 */

/* modf.c
 * This program breaks the argument 10.12 into integral and
 * fraction part using function modf.
 */

#include <stdio.h>
#include <stdlib.h>
#include <math.h>
#include <errno.h>

main()
{
  double  modf_value;
  double  ipart;
  double  x = 10.12;

  modf_value = modf (x, &ipart);
  fprintf (stdout,"integral part %f is %f\n", x, ipart);
```

```
    fprintf (stdout,"fractional part of %f is %f\n", x, modf_value);
}
```

NAME

mprotect — set protection of memory mapping

SYNOPSIS

UX   `#include <sys/mman.h>`

```
int mprotect(void *addr, size_t len, int prot);
```

DESCRIPTION

The *mprotect*( ) function changes the access protections on the mappings specified by the range [*addr, addr + len*), rounding *len* up to the next multiple of the page size as returned by *sysconf*( ), to be that specified by *prot*. Legitimate values for *prot* are the same as those permitted for *mmap*( ) and are defined in **<sys/mman.h>**:

PROT_READ   Page can be read.

PROT_WRITE   Page can be written.

PROT_EXEC   Page can be executed.

PROT_NONE   Page cannot be accessed.

When *mprotect*( ) fails for reasons other than [EINVAL], the protections on some of the pages in the range [*addr, addr + len*) may have been changed.

RETURN VALUE

Upon successful completion, *mprotect*( ) returns 0. Otherwise, it returns −1 and sets *errno* to indicate the error.

ERRORS

The *mprotect*( ) function will fail if:

[EACCES]   The *prot* argument specifies a protection that violates the access permission the process has to the underlying memory object.

[EINVAL]   The *addr* argument is not a multiple of the page size as returned by *sysconf*( ).

[ENOMEM]   Addresses in the range [*addr, addr + len*) are invalid for the address space of a process, or specify one or more pages which are not mapped.

The *mprotect*( ) function may fail if:

[EAGAIN]   The *prot* argument specifies PROT_WRITE over a MAP_PRIVATE mapping and there are insufficient memory resources to reserve for locking the private page.

SEE ALSO

mmap( ), *sysconf*( ), **<sys/mman.h>**.

NAME

mrand48 — generate uniformly distributed pseudo-random signed long integers

SYNOPSIS

EX
```
#include <stdlib.h>

long int mrand48(void);
```

DESCRIPTION

Refer to *drand48*( ).

EXAMPLE

```
/*
 * Copyright (C) ANTRIX Inc.
 */

/* mrand48.c
 * This program generates signed long random integers uniformly
 * distributed over the interval [-2 raise 31, 2 raise 31).
 * using function mrand48.
 */

#include <stdio.h>
#include <stdlib.h>
#include <errno.h>

main()
{
   int    i;
   int    seed_value = 100;
   long   mrand48_value;

   srand48(seed_value);
   for ( i = 0; i < 5; i++ ) {
       mrand48_value = mrand48 ();
       fprintf (stdout,"random value in iteration %d is %d\n",
                      i, mrand48_value);
   }
}
```

NAME

msgctl — message control operations

SYNOPSIS

EX

```
#include <sys/msg.h>
```

```
int msgctl(int msqid, int cmd, struct msqid_ds *buf);
```

DESCRIPTION

The *msgctl*( ) function provides message control operations as specified by *cmd*. The following values for *cmd*, and the message control operations they specify, are:

IPC_STAT   Place the current value of each member of the **msqid_ds** data structure associated with *msqid* into the structure pointed to by *buf*. The contents of this structure are defined in **<sys/msg.h>**.

IPC_SET   Set the value of the following members of the **msqid_ds** data structure associated with *msqid* to the corresponding value found in the structure pointed to by *buf*:

```
msg_perm.uid
msg_perm.gid
msg_perm.mode
msg_qbytes
```

IPC_SET can only be executed by a process with appropriate privileges or that has an effective user ID equal to the value of **msg_perm.cuid** or **msg_perm.uid** in the **msqid_ds** data structure associated with *msqid*. Only a process with appropriate privileges can raise the value of *msg_qbytes*.

IPC_RMID   Remove the message queue identifier specified by *msqid* from the system and destroy the message queue and **msqid_ds** data structure associated with it. IPC_RMD can only be executed by a process with appropriate privileges or one that has an effective user ID equal to the value of **msg_perm.cuid** or **msg_perm.uid** in the **msqid_ds** data structure associated with *msqid*.

RETURN VALUE

Upon successful completion, *msgctl*( ) returns 0. Otherwise, it returns −1 and *errno* will be set to indicate the error.

ERRORS

The *msgctl*( ) function will fail if:

[EACCES]   The argument *cmd* is IPC_STAT and the calling process does not have read permission, see the **XSH** specification, **Section 2.6**, **Interprocess Communication**.

[EINVAL]   The value of *msqid* is not a valid message queue identifier; or the value of *cmd* is not a valid command.

[EPERM]   The argument *cmd* is IPC_RMID or IPC_SET and the effective user ID of the calling process is not equal to that of a process with appropriate privileges and it is not equal to the value of **msg_perm.cuid** or **msg_perm.uid** in the data structure associated with *msqid*.

[EPERM]   The argument *cmd* is IPC_SET, an attempt is being made to increase to the value of *msg_qbytes*, and the effective user ID of the calling process does not have appropriate privileges.

FUTURE DIRECTIONS

The IEEE 1003.4 Standards Committee is developing alternative interfaces for interprocess Communication. Application developers who need to use IPC should design their applications so that modules using the routines described in this document can be easily modified to use alternative methods at a later date.

SEE ALSO

msgget( ), *msgrcv*( ), *msgsnd*( ), **<sys/msg.h>**, **XSH** specification, **Section 2.6**, **Interprocess Communication**.

EXAMPLE

```
/*
 * Copyright (C) ANTRIX Inc.
 */

/* msgctl.c
 * This program provides message control operations as specified
 * by the cmd IPC_STAT using function msgctl.
 */

#include <stdio.h>
#include <stdlib.h>
#include <unistd.h>
#include <fcntl.h>
#include <sys/stat.h>
#include <sys/ipc.h>
#include <sys/msg.h>
#include <errno.h>

#define   PERM_ALL    (S_IRWXU | S_IRWXG | S_IRWXO)

main()
{
  int     msgctl_value;
  int     msqid;
  struct  msqid_ds  buf;

  fprintf (stdout,"get message id\n");
  msqid = msgget (IPC_PRIVATE, IPC_CREAT | PERM_ALL);

  fprintf (stdout,"get message id status\n");
  msgctl_value = msgctl (msqid, IPC_STAT, &buf);
  if ( msgctl_value == 0 ) {
      fprintf (stdout,"msgctl() call successful\n");
      fprintf (stdout,"buf.msg_perm.cuid=%d\n", buf.msg_perm.cuid );
      fprintf (stdout,"buf.msg_perm.uid=%d\n", buf.msg_perm.uid );
      fprintf (stdout,"buf.msg_perm.cgid=%d\n", buf.msg_perm.cgid );
      fprintf (stdout,"buf.msg_perm.gid=%d\n", buf.msg_perm.gid );
      fprintf (stdout,"buf.msg_perm.mode=%d\n", buf.msg_perm.mode );
      fprintf (stdout,"buf.msg_qnum=%d\n", buf.msg_qnum );
      fprintf (stdout,"buf.msg_lspid=%d\n", buf.msg_lspid );
      fprintf (stdout,"buf.msg_lrpid=%d\n", buf.msg_lrpid );
      fprintf (stdout,"buf.msg_stime=%d\n", buf.msg_stime );
```

```
        fprintf (stdout,"buf.msg_rtime=%d\n", buf.msg_rtime );
        fprintf (stdout,"buf.msg_qbytes=%d\n", buf.msg_qbytes );
    }
    else {
        fprintf (stderr,"ERROR: msgctl() call failed\n");
        fprintf (stderr,"ERROR: %s\n", strerror(errno));
    }

    fprintf (stdout,"remove message id\n");
    msgctl (msqid, IPC_RMID, (void *)0 );
}
```

NAME

msgget — get message queue

SYNOPSIS

EX   `#include <sys/msg.h>`

`int msgget(key_t key, int msgflg);`

DESCRIPTION

The *msgget*( ) function returns the message queue identifier associated with the argument *key*.

A message queue identifier, associated message queue and data structure, see **<sys/msg.h>**, are created for the argument *key* if one of the following is true:

- The argument *key* is equal to IPC_PRIVATE.

- The argument *key* does not already have a message queue identifier associated with it, and (*msgflg* & IPC_CREAT) is non-zero.

Upon creation, the data structure associated with the new message queue identifier is initialised as follows:

- **msg_perm.cuid**, **msg_perm.uid**, **msg_perm.cgid** and **msg_perm.gid** are set equal to the effective user ID and effective group ID, respectively, of the calling process.

- The low-order 9 bits of **msg_perm.mode** are set equal to the low-order 9 bits of *msgflg*.

- **msg_qnum**, **msg_lspid**, **msg_lrpid**, **msg_stime** and **msg_rtime** are set equal to 0.

- **msg_ctime** is set equal to the current time.

- **msg_qbytes** is set equal to the system limit.

RETURN VALUE

Upon successful completion, *msgget*( ) returns a non-negative integer, namely a message queue identifier. Otherwise, it returns −1 and *errno* is set to indicate the error.

ERRORS

The *msgget*( ) function will fail if:

[EACCES]   A message queue identifier exists for the argument *key*, but operation permission as specified by the low-order 9 bits of *msgflg* would not be granted, see the **XSH** specification, **Section 2.6**, **Interprocess Communication**.

[EEXIST]   A message queue identifier exists for the argument *key* but ((*msgflg* & IPC_CREAT) && (*msgflg* & IPC_EXCL)) is non-zero.

[ENOENT]   A message queue identifier does not exist for the argument *key* and (*msgflg* & IPC_CREAT) is 0.

[ENOSPC]   A message queue identifier is to be created but the system-imposed limit on the maximum number of allowed message queue identifiers system-wide would be exceeded.

FUTURE DIRECTIONS

The IEEE 1003.4 Standards Committee is developing alternative interfaces for interprocess communication. Application developers who need to use IPC should design their applications so that modules using the routines described in this document can be easily modified to use alternative methods at a later date.

SEE ALSO

msgctl( ), *msgrcv*( ), *msgsnd*( ), **<sys/msg.h>**, **XSH** specification, **Section 2.6, Interprocess Communication**.

EXAMPLE

```c
/*
 * Copyright (C) ANTRIX Inc.
 */

/* msgget.c
 * This program returns the message queue identifier associated
 * with the argument key IPC_PRIVATE using function msgget.
 */

#include <stdio.h>
#include <stdlib.h>
#include <unistd.h>
#include <fcntl.h>
#include <sys/stat.h>
#include <sys/ipc.h>
#include <sys/msg.h>
#include <errno.h>

#define  PERM_ALL   (S_IRWXU | S_IRWXG | S_IRWXO)

main()
{
  int    msqid;
  struct msqid_ds  buf;

  fprintf (stdout,"get message id\n");
  msqid = msgget (IPC_PRIVATE, IPC_CREAT | PERM_ALL);
  if ( msqid >= 0 ) {
     fprintf (stdout,"msgget() call successful\n");
     fprintf (stdout,"get message id status\n");
     msgctl (msqid, IPC_STAT, &buf);
     fprintf (stdout,"buf.msg_perm.cuid=%d\n", buf.msg_perm.cuid );
     fprintf (stdout,"buf.msg_perm.uid=%d\n", buf.msg_perm.uid );
     fprintf (stdout,"buf.msg_perm.cgid=%d\n", buf.msg_perm.cgid );
     fprintf (stdout,"buf.msg_perm.gid=%d\n", buf.msg_perm.gid );
     fprintf (stdout,"buf.msg_perm.mode=%d\n", buf.msg_perm.mode );
     fprintf (stdout,"buf.msg_qnum=%d\n", buf.msg_qnum );
     fprintf (stdout,"buf.msg_qbytes=%d\n", buf.msg_qbytes );
  }
  else {
     fprintf (stderr,"ERROR: msgget() call failed\n");
     fprintf (stderr,"ERROR: %s\n", strerror(errno));
  }

  fprintf (stdout,"remove message id\n");
  msgctl (msqid, IPC_RMID, (void *)0 );
}
```

NAME

msgrcv — message receive operation

SYNOPSIS

EX   `#include <sys/msg.h>`

```
int msgrcv(int msqid, void *msgp, size_t msgsz, long int msgtyp,
           int msgflg);
```

DESCRIPTION

The *msgrcv*( ) function reads a message from the queue associated with the message queue identifier specified by *msqid* and places it in the user-defined buffer pointed to by *msgp*.

The argument *msgp* points to a user-defined buffer that must contain first a field of type **long int** that will specify the type of the message, and then a data portion that will hold the data bytes of the message. The structure below is an example of what this user-defined buffer might look like:

```
struct mymsg {
        long int    mtype;      /* message type */
        char        mtext[1];   /* message text */
}
```

The structure member **mtype** is the received message's type as specified by the sending process.

The structure member **mtext** is the text of the message.

The argument *msgsz* specifies the size in bytes of **mtext**. The received message is truncated to *msgsz* bytes if it is larger than *msgsz* and (*msgflg* & MSG_NOERROR) is non-zero. The truncated part of the message is lost and no indication of the truncation is given to the calling process.

The argument *msgtyp* specifies the type of message requested as follows:

- If *msgtyp* is 0, the first message on the queue is received.

- If *msgtyp* is greater than 0, the first message of type *msgtyp* is received.

- If *msgtyp* is less than 0, the first message of the lowest type that is less than or equal to the absolute value of *msgtyp* is received.

The argument *msgflg* specifies the action to be taken if a message of the desired type is not on the queue. These are as follows:

- If (*msgflg* & IPC_NOWAIT) is non-zero, the calling process will return immediately with a return value of −1 and *errno* set to [ENOMSG].

- If (*msgflg* & IPC_NOWAIT) is 0, the calling process will suspend execution until one of the following occurs:

  — A message of the desired type is placed on the queue.

  — The message queue identifier *msqid* is removed from the system; when this occurs, *errno* is set equal to [EIDRM] and −1 is returned.

  — The calling process receives a signal that is to be caught; in this case a message is not received and the calling process resumes execution in the manner prescribed in *sigaction*( ).

Upon successful completion, the following actions are taken with respect to the data structure associated with *msqid*:

- **msg_qnum** is decremented by 1.
- **msg_lrpid** is set equal to the process ID of the calling process.
- **msg_rtime** is set equal to the current time.

RETURN VALUE

Upon successful completion, *msgrcv( )* returns a value equal to the number of bytes actually placed into the buffer *mtext*. Otherwise, no message will be received, *msgrcv( )* will return −1 and *errno* will be set to indicate the error.

ERRORS

The *msgrcv( )* function will fail if:

[E2BIG]   The value of **mtext** is greater than *msgsz* and (*msgflg* & MSG_NOERROR) is 0.

[EACCES]   Operation permission is denied to the calling process. See the **XSH** specification, **Section 2.6**, **Interprocess Communication**.

[EIDRM]   The message queue identifier *msqid* is removed from the system.

[EINTR]   The *msgrcv( )* function was interrupted by a signal.

[EINVAL]   *msqid* is not a valid message queue identifier; or the value of *msgsz* is less than 0.

[ENOMSG]   The queue does not contain a message of the desired type and (*msgflg* & IPC_NOWAIT) is non-zero.

APPLICATION USAGE

The value passed as the *msgp* argument should be converted to type **void ***.

FUTURE DIRECTIONS

The IEEE 1003.4 Standards Committee is developing alternative interfaces for interprocess communication. Application developers who need to use IPC should design their applications so that modules using the routines described in this document can be easily modified to use alternative methods at a later date.

SEE ALSO

msgctl( ), *msgget( )*, *msgsnd( )*, *sigaction( )*, **<sys/msg.h>**, **XSH** specification, **Section 2.6**, **Interprocess Communication**.

EXAMPLE

```
/*
 * Copyright (C) ANTRIX Inc.
 */

/* msgrcv.c
 * This program reads a message from the queue associated with
 * the message queue identifier specified by msqid and places
 * it in the user-defined buffer pointed to by msgp using function
 * msgrcv.
 */

#include <stdio.h>
#include <stdlib.h>
```

```
#include <sys/types.h>
#include <sys/stat.h>
#include <sys/ipc.h>
#include <sys/msg.h>
#include <errno.h>

#define  PERM_ALL    (S_IRWXU | S_IRWXG | S_IRWXO)

struct msgbuf1 {
   long mtype;
   char mtext[512];
} sndbuf, rcvbuf, *msgp;

main()
{
  int    msgsnd_value;
  int    msgrcv_value;
  int    i, c;
  int    option, msqid, msgsz, msgflg;
  long   mtype, msgtyp;
  struct msqid_ds msqid_ds, *buf;

  buf = &msqid_ds;

  fprintf (stdout,"Enter code to send or receive\n");
  fprintf (stdout,"send = 1\n");
  fprintf (stdout,"receive = 99\n");
  scanf("%d", &option);

  if (option == 1) {

    msgp = &sndbuf;

    /* get msgid */
    msqid = msgget (IPC_PRIVATE, IPC_CREAT | PERM_ALL);
#ifdef MSGID
    fprintf (stdout,"Enter the msqid of the message\n");
    scanf("%d", &msqid);
#endif
    fprintf (stdout,"msqid is %d\n", msqid);

    fprintf (stdout,"Enter message type for the message\n");
    scanf("%ld", &msgtyp);
    msgp->mtype = msgtyp;

    fprintf (stdout,"Enter message to send\n");
    for (i = 0; ((c = getchar()) != EOF); i++)
        sndbuf.mtext[i] = c;

    /* save the message size */
    msgsz = i;
```

```
        fprintf (stdout,"Echo message to be send\n");
        for (i = 0; i < msgsz; i++)
            putchar(sndbuf.mtext[i]);

        /* IPC_NOWAIT flag set */
        msgflg = IPC_NOWAIT;

        printf("Send message\n");
        msgsnd_value = msgsnd(msqid, (const void*)msgp, msgsz, msgflg);

        if (msgsnd_value == -1) {
            fprintf (stderr,"ERROR: msgsnd() call failed\n");
            fprintf (stderr,"ERROR: %s\n", strerror(errno));
        }
        else {
            fprintf (stdout,"get message queue status\n");
            msgctl (msqid, IPC_STAT, buf);
            fprintf (stdout,"buf->msg_qnum=%d\n", buf->msg_qnum );
            fprintf (stdout,"buf->msg_lspid=%d\n", buf->msg_lspid );
            fprintf (stdout,"buf->msg_stime=%d\n", buf->msg_stime );
            fprintf (stdout,"buf->msg_qbytes=%d\n", buf->msg_qbytes );
        }
    }

    if (option == 99) {

        /* initialize the message pointer to receive buffer */
        msgp = &rcvbuf;

        /* get msgid */
        msqid = msgget (IPC_PRIVATE, IPC_CREAT | PERM_ALL);
#ifdef MSGID
        fprintf (stdout,"Enter the msqid of the message\n");
        scanf("%d", &msqid);
#endif

        fprintf (stdout,"Enter message type for the message\n");
        scanf("%ld", &msgtyp);
        msgp->mtype = msgtyp;
        msgflg = IPC_NOWAIT;

        fprintf (stdout,"Enter number of bytes to receive\n");
        scanf ("%d", &msgsz);

        fprintf (stdout,"Receive the message\n");
        msgrcv_value = msgrcv(msqid, (void *)msgp, msgsz, msgtyp, msgflg);

        if (msgrcv_value == -1) {
            fprintf (stderr,"ERROR: msgrcv() call failed\n");
            fprintf (stderr,"ERROR: %s\n", strerror(errno));
        }
        else {
```

```
        for (i = 0; i < msgrcv_value ; i++)
            putchar(rcvbuf.mtext[i]);
    }
    fprintf (stdout,"get message queue status\n");
    msgctl (msqid, IPC_STAT, buf);
    fprintf (stdout,"buf->msg_qnum=%d\n", buf->msg_qnum );
    fprintf (stdout,"buf->msg_lspid=%d\n", buf->msg_lspid );
    fprintf (stdout,"buf->msg_lrpid=%d\n", buf->msg_lrpid );
    fprintf (stdout,"buf->msg_qbytes=%d\n", buf->msg_qbytes );
  }
}
```

NAME

    msgsnd — message send operation

SYNOPSIS

EX   `#include <sys/msg.h>`

    `int msgsnd(int msqid, const void *msgp, size_t msgsz, int msgflg);`

DESCRIPTION

The *msgsnd*( ) function is used to send a message to the queue associated with the message queue identifier specified by *msqid*.

The argument *msgp* points to a user-defined buffer that must contain first a field of type **long int** that will specify the type of the message, and then a data portion that will hold the data bytes of the message. The structure below is an example of what this user-defined buffer might look like:

```
struct mymsg {
        long int     mtype;        /* message type */
        char         mtext[1];     /* message text */
}
```

The structure member **mtype** is a non-zero positive type **long int** that can be used by the receiving process for message selection.

The structure member **mtext** is any text of length *msgsz* bytes. The argument *msgsz* can range from 0 to a system-imposed maximum.

The argument *msgflg* specifies the action to be taken if one or more of the following are true:

- The number of bytes already on the queue is equal to **msg_qbytes**, see **<sys/msg.h>**.
- The total number of messages on all queues system-wide is equal to the system-imposed limit.

These actions are as follows:

- If (*msgflg* & IPC_NOWAIT) is non-zero, the message will not be sent and the calling process will return immediately.
- If (*msgflg* & IPC_NOWAIT) is 0, the calling process will suspend execution until one of the following occurs:

    — The condition responsible for the suspension no longer exists, in which case the message is sent.

    — The message queue identifier *msqid* is removed from the system; when this occurs, *errno* is set equal to [EIDRM] and −1 is returned.

    — The calling process receives a signal that is to be caught; in this case the message is not sent and the calling process resumes execution in the manner prescribed in *sigaction*( ).

Upon successful completion, the following actions are taken with respect to the data structure associated with *msqid*, see **<sys/msg.h>**:

- **msg_qnum** is incremented by 1.
- **msg_lspid** is set equal to the process ID of the calling process.
- **msg_stime** is set equal to the current time.

RETURN VALUE

Upon successful completion, *msgsnd*( ) returns 0. Otherwise, no message will be sent, *msgsnd*( ) will return −1 and *errno* will be set to indicate the error.

ERRORS

The *msgsnd*( ) function will fail if:

[EACCES]	Operation permission is denied to the calling process. See the **XSH** specification, **Section 2.6**, **Interprocess Communication**.
[EAGAIN]	The message cannot be sent for one of the reasons cited above and (*msgflg* & IPC_NOWAIT) is non-zero.
[EIDRM]	The message queue identifier *msgid* is removed from the system.
[EINTR]	The *msgsnd*( ) function was interrupted by a signal.
[EINVAL]	The value of *msqid* is not a valid message queue identifier, or the value of **mtype** is less than 1; or the value of *msgsz* is less than 0 or greater than the system-imposed limit.

APPLICATION USAGE

The value passed as the *msgp* argument should be converted to type **void ***.

FUTURE DIRECTIONS

The IEEE 1003.4 Standards Committee is developing alternative interfaces for interprocess communication. Application developers who need to use IPC should design their applications so that modules using the routines described in this document can be easily modified to use alternative methods at a later date.

SEE ALSO

msgctl( ), *msgget*( ), *msgrcv*( ), *sigaction*( ), **<sys/msg.h>**, **XSH** specification, **Section 2.6**, **Interprocess Communication**.

EXAMPLE

```
/*
 * Copyright (C) ANTRIX Inc.
 */

/* msgsnd.c
 * This program is used to send a message to the queue associated
 * with the message queue identifier specified by msqid using
 * function msgsnd.
 */

#include <stdio.h>
#include <stdlib.h>
#include <sys/types.h>
#include <sys/stat.h>
#include <sys/ipc.h>
#include <sys/msg.h>
#include <errno.h>

#define  PERM_ALL    (S_IRWXU | S_IRWXG | S_IRWXO)

struct msgbuf1 {
    long mtype;
```

```
      char mtext[512];
} sndbuf, rcvbuf, *msgp;

main()
{
  int msgsnd_value;
  int msgrcv_value;
  int i, c;
  int option, msqid, msgsz, msgflg;
  long mtype, msgtyp;
  struct msqid_ds msqid_ds, *buf;

  buf = &msqid_ds;

  fprintf (stdout,"Enter code to send or receive\n");
  fprintf (stdout,"send = 1\n");
  fprintf (stdout,"receive = 99\n");
  scanf("%d", &option);

  if (option == 1) {

    msgp = &sndbuf;

    /* get msgid */
    msqid = msgget (IPC_PRIVATE, IPC_CREAT | PERM_ALL);
#ifdef MSGID
    fprintf (stdout,"Enter the msqid of the message\n");
    scanf("%d", &msqid);
#endif
    fprintf (stdout,"msqid is %d\n", msqid);

    fprintf (stdout,"Enter message type for the message\n");
    scanf("%ld", &msgtyp);
    msgp->mtype = msgtyp;

    fprintf (stdout,"Enter message to send\n");
    for (i = 0; ((c = getchar()) != EOF); i++)
        sndbuf.mtext[i] = c;

    /* save the message size */
    msgsz = i;

    fprintf (stdout,"Echo message to be send\n");
    for (i = 0; i < msgsz; i++)
        putchar(sndbuf.mtext[i]);

    /* IPC_NOWAIT flag set */
    msgflg = IPC_NOWAIT;

    printf("Send message\n");
    msgsnd_value = msgsnd(msqid, (const void*)msgp, msgsz, msgflg);
```

```
        if (msgsnd_value == -1) {
            fprintf (stderr,"ERROR: msgsnd() call failed\n");
            fprintf (stderr,"ERROR: %s\n", strerror(errno));
        }
        else {
            fprintf (stdout,"get message queue status\n");
            msgctl (msqid, IPC_STAT, buf);
            fprintf (stdout,"buf->msg_qnum=%d\n", buf->msg_qnum );
            fprintf (stdout,"buf->msg_lspid=%d\n", buf->msg_lspid );
            fprintf (stdout,"buf->msg_stime=%d\n", buf->msg_stime );
            fprintf (stdout,"buf->msg_qbytes=%d\n", buf->msg_qbytes );
        }
    }

    if (option == 99) {

        /* initialize the message pointer to receive buffer */
        msgp = &rcvbuf;

        /* get msgid */
        msqid = msgget (IPC_PRIVATE, IPC_CREAT | PERM_ALL);
#ifdef MSGID
        fprintf (stdout,"Enter the msqid of the message\n");
        scanf("%d", &msqid);
#endif

        fprintf (stdout,"Enter message type for the message\n");
        scanf("%ld", &msgtyp);
        msgp->mtype = msgtyp;
        msgflg = IPC_NOWAIT;

        fprintf (stdout,"Enter number of bytes to receive\n");
        scanf ("%d", &msgsz);

        fprintf (stdout,"Receive the message\n");
        msgrcv_value = msgrcv(msqid, (void *)msgp, msgsz, msgtyp, msgflg);

        if (msgrcv_value == -1) {
            fprintf (stderr,"ERROR: msgrcv() call failed\n");
            fprintf (stderr,"ERROR: %s\n", strerror(errno));
        }
        else {
            for (i = 0; i < msgrcv_value ; i++)
                putchar(rcvbuf.mtext[i]);
        }
        fprintf (stdout,"get message queue status\n");
        msgctl (msqid, IPC_STAT, buf);
        fprintf (stdout,"buf->msg_qnum=%d\n", buf->msg_qnum );
        fprintf (stdout,"buf->msg_lspid=%d\n", buf->msg_lspid );
        fprintf (stdout,"buf->msg_lrpid=%d\n", buf->msg_lrpid );
```

```
        fprintf (stdout,"buf->msg_qbytes=%d\n", buf->msg_qbytes );
    }
}
```

NAME

msync — synchronise memory with physical storage

SYNOPSIS

UX

```
#include <sys/mman.h>
```

```
int msync(void *addr, size_t len, int flags);
```

DESCRIPTION

The *msync( )* function writes all modified copies of pages over the range [*addr, addr + len*) to the underlying hardware, or invalidates any copies so that further references to the pages will be obtained by the system from their permanent storage locations.

The *flags* argument is one of the following:

MS_ASYNC   perform asynchronous writes

MS_SYNC   perform synchronous writes

MS_INVALIDATE   invalidate mappings

If *flags* is MS_ASYNC or MS_SYNC, the function synchronises the file contents to match the current contents of the memory region.

- All write references to the memory region made prior to the call are visible by subsequent read operations on the file.

- It is unspecified whether writes to the same portion of the file prior to the call are visible by read references to the memory region.

- It is unspecified whether unmodified pages in the specified range are also written to the underlying hardware.

If *flags* is MS_ASYNC, the function may return immediately once all write operations are scheduled; if *flags* is MS_SYNC, the function does not return until all write operations are completed.

If *flags* is MS_INVALIDATE, the function synchronises the contents of the memory region to match the current file contents.

- All writes to the mapped portion of the file made prior to the call are visible by subsequent read references to the mapped memory region.

- It is unspecified whether write references prior to the call, by any process, to memory regions mapped to the same portion of the file using MAP_SHARED, are visible by read references to the region.

If *msync( )* causes any write to the file, then the file's **st_ctime** and **st_mtime** fields are marked for update.

RETURN VALUE

Upon successful completion, *msync( )* returns 0. Otherwise, it returns –1 and sets *errno* to indicate the error.

ERRORS

The *msync( )* function will fail if:

[EINVAL]   The *addr* argument is not a multiple of the page size as returned by *sysconf( )*.

[EIO]   An I/O error occurred while reading from or writing to the file system.

[ENOMEM] Some or all the addresses in the range [*addr*, *addr* + *len*) are invalid for the address space of the process or pages not mapped are specified.

APPLICATION USAGE

The *msync*( ) function should be used by programs that require a memory object to be in a known state, for example in building transaction facilities.

Normal system activity can cause pages to be written to disk. Therefore, there are no guarantees that *msync*( ) is the only control over when pages are or are not written to disk.

SEE ALSO

mmap( ), *sysconf*( ), **<sys/mman.h>**.

EXAMPLE

```
/*
 * Copyright (C) ANTRIX Inc.
 */

/* msync.c : run as root
 * This program synchronizes memory with physical storage
 * using function msync
 */

#include <stdio.h>
#include <stdlib.h>
#include <unistd.h>
#include <fcntl.h>
#include <sys/stat.h>
#include <sys/mman.h>
#include <errno.h>

#define  OFLAG     (O_RDWR | O_CREAT | O_TRUNC)
#define  PERM_ALL   (PROT_READ | PROT_WRITE | PROT_EXEC)

main()
{
   int     msync_value;
   int     fd, pagesize;
   int     buf[1024], i, j;
   int     *addr;
   int     size;
   char    *file = "testfile";

   fprintf (stdout,"get page size\n");
   memset(buf, 0, 1024);

   pagesize = sysconf (_SC_PAGESIZE);
   size = pagesize/sizeof(int);

   fprintf (stdout,"create and write to file\n");
   fd = open(file, OFLAG, PERM_ALL);
   for ( j = 0; j < pagesize; j += sizeof (buf) ) {
      for ( i = 0; i < sizeof (buf)/sizeof (buf[0]); i++)
         buf[i] = i + j;
```

```
        write (fd, (void *)buf, sizeof (buf));
    }

    fprintf (stdout,"close testfile\n");
    close (fd);

    fprintf (stdout,"open testfile\n");
    fd = open (file, O_RDWR, PERM_ALL);
    fprintf (stdout,"map page of memory\n");
    addr = (int *)mmap (0, pagesize, PROT_READ, MAP_SHARED, fd, 0);
    msync_value = (addr+pagesize, pagesize, MS_SYNC);
    if (msync_value == 0) {
        fprintf (stdout,"msync() call successful\n");
        /* read mapped pages */
        for ( j = 0; j < size; j++ ) {
            i = addr[j];
            if ( i != j ) {
                fprintf (stderr,"ERROR: offset %d.\nexpected %x\nactual %x",
                            j, j, i);
                break;
            } /* end if */
        } /* end for */
        fprintf (stdout,"unmap pages\n");
        munmap (addr, pagesize);
    }
    else {
        fprintf (stderr,"ERROR: msync() call failed\n");
        fprintf (stderr,"ERROR: %s\n", strerror(errno));
    }
    close (fd);

    fprintf (stdout,"remove testfile\n");
    remove (file);
}
```

NAME

munmap — unmap pages of memory

SYNOPSIS

UX   `#include <sys/mman.h>`

`int munmap(void *addr, size_t len);`

DESCRIPTION

The *munmap*( ) function removes the mappings for pages in the range [*addr, addr + len*), rounding the *len* argument up to the next multiple of the page size as returned by *sysconf*( ). If *addr* is not the address of a mapping established by a prior call to *mmap*( ), the behaviour is undefined. After a successful call to *munmap*( ) and before any subsequent mapping of the unmapped pages, further references to these pages will result in the delivery of a SIGBUS or SIGSEGV signal to the process.

RETURN VALUE

Upon successful completion, *munmap*( ) returns 0. Otherwise, it returns −1 and sets *errno* to indicate the error.

ERRORS

The *munmap*( ) function will fail if:

[EINVAL]   The *addr* argument is not a multiple of the page size as returned by *sysconf*( ).

[EINVAL]   Addresses in the range [*addr, addr + len*) are outside the valid range for the address space of a process.

[EINVAL]   The *len* argument is 0.

SEE ALSO

mmap( ), *sysconf*( ), **<signal.h>**, **<sys/mman.h>**.

EXAMPLE

```
/*
 * Copyright (C) ANTRIX Inc.
 */

/* munmap.c: run as root
 * This program unmaps pages of memory
 * using function munmap
 */

#include <stdio.h>
#include <stdlib.h>
#include <unistd.h>
#include <fcntl.h>
#include <sys/stat.h>
#include <sys/mman.h>
#include <errno.h>

#define  OFLAG      (O_RDWR | O_CREAT | O_TRUNC)
#define  PERM_ALL    (PROT_READ | PROT_WRITE | PROT_EXEC)

main()
{
```

```c
int     munmap_value;
int     fd, pagesize;
int     i, j, buf[1024];
int     *addr;
int     size;
char    *file = "testfile";

printf("get page size\n");
memset(buf, 0, 1024);

pagesize = sysconf (_SC_PAGESIZE);
size = pagesize/sizeof(int);

fprintf (stdout,"create and write to file\n");
fd = open (file, OFLAG, PERM_ALL);
for ( j = 0; j < pagesize; j += sizeof (buf) ) {
  for ( i = 0; i < sizeof (buf)/sizeof (buf[0]); i++)
     buf[i] = i + j;
     write (fd, (void *)buf, sizeof (buf));
}

fprintf (stdout,"close testfile\n");
close (fd);

fprintf (stdout,"open testfile\n");
fd = open (file, O_RDWR, PERM_ALL);

fprintf (stdout,"map page of memory\n");
addr = (int *)mmap (0, pagesize, PROT_READ, MAP_SHARED, fd, 0);

fprintf (stdout,"read mapped pages\n");
for ( j = 0; j < size; j++) {
    i = addr[j];
    if ( i != j ) {
    fprintf (stderr,"ERROR: offset %d.\nexpected %x\nactual %x",
                    j, j, i);
    break;
    }
}
fprintf (stdout,"unmap pages\n");
munmap_value = munmap (addr, pagesize);
if ( munmap_value == 0 )
   fprintf (stdout,"munmap() call successful\n");
else {
   fprintf (stderr,"ERROR: munmap() call failed\n");
   fprintf (stderr,"ERROR: %s\n", strerror(errno));
}
close (fd);
```

```
        fprintf (stdout,"remove testfile\n");
        remove (file);
}
```

NAME

nextafter — next representable double-precision floating-point number

SYNOPSIS

UX   `#include <math.h>`

`double nextafter(double x, double y);`

DESCRIPTION

The *nextafter( )* function computes the next representable double-precision floating-point value following *x* in the direction of *y*. Thus, if *y* is less than *x*, *nextafter( )* returns the largest representable floating-point number less than *x*.

RETURN VALUE

The *nextafter( )* function returns the next representable double-precision floating-point value following *x* in the direction of *y*.

If *x* or *y* is NaN, then *nextafter( )* returns NaN and may set *errno* to [EDOM].

If *x* is finite and the correct function value would overflow, HUGE_VAL is returned and *errno* is set to [ERANGE].

ERRORS

The *nextafter( )* function will fail if:

[ERANGE]   The correct value would overflow.

The *nextafter( )* function may fail if:

[EDOM]   The *x* or *y* argument is NaN.

SEE ALSO

<math.h>.

EXAMPLE

```
/*
 * Copyright (C) ANTRIX Inc.
 */

/* nextafter.c
 * This program returns the next representable double-precision
 * floating point value using function nextafter
 */

#include <stdio.h>
#include <stdlib.h>
#include <math.h>
#include <errno.h>

main()
{
  double  retval;
  double  x = 2.123;
  double  y = 3.00;

  retval = nextafter (x, y);
```

```
    fprintf (stdout,"next representable neighbor of (2.123, 3)
        is %f\n", retval);
}
```

NAME

nftw — walk a file tree

SYNOPSIS

UX `#include <ftw.h>`

```
int nftw(const char *path,
   int (*fn)(const char *, const struct stat *, int, struct FTW *),
   int depth, int flags);
```

DESCRIPTION

The *nftw( )* function recursively descends the directory hierarchy rooted in *path*. The *nftw( )* function has a similar effect to *ftw( )* except that it takes an additional argument *flags*, which is a bitwise inclusive-OR of zero or more of the following flags:

FTW_CHDIR If set, *nftw( )* will change the current working directory to each directory as it reports files in that directory. If clear, *nftw( )* will not change the current working directory.

FTW_DEPTH If set, *nftw( )* will report all files in a directory before reporting the directory itself. If clear, *nftw( )* will report any directory before reporting the files in that directory.

FTW_MOUNT If set, *nftw( )* will only report files in the same file system as *path*. If clear, *nftw( )* will report all files encountered during the walk.

FTW_PHYS If set, *nftw( )* performs a physical walk and does not follow symbolic links. If clear, *nftw( )* will follow links instead of reporting them, and will not report the same file twice.

At each file it encounters, *nftw( )* calls the user-supplied function *fn( )* with four arguments:

- The first argument is the pathname of the object.

- The second argument is a pointer to the **stat** buffer containing information on the object.

- The third argument is an integer giving additional information. Its value is one of the following:

    FTW_F The object is a file.

    FTW_D The object is a directory.

    FTW_DP The object is a directory and subdirectories have been visited. (This condition will only occur if the FTW_DEPTH flag is included in *flags*.)

    FTW_SL The object is a symbolic link. (This condition will only occur if the FTW_PHYS flag is included in *flags*.)

    FTW_SLN The object is a symbolic link that does not name an existing file. (This condition will only occur if the FTW_PHYS flag is not included in *flags*.)

    FTW_DNR The object is a directory that cannot be read. The *fn( )* function will not be called for any of its descendants.

    FTW_NS The *stat( )* function failed on the object because of lack of appropriate permission. The **stat** buffer passed to *fn( )* is undefined. Failure of *stat( )* for any other reason is considered an error and *nftw( )* returns –1.

- The fourth argument is a pointer to an **FTW** structure. The value of **base** is the offset of the object's filename in the pathname passed as the first argument to *fn( )*. The value of **level** indicates depth relative to the root of of the walk, where the root level is 0.

The argument *depth* limits the directory depth for the search. At most one file descriptor will be used for each directory level.

RETURN VALUE

The *nftw*( ) function continues until the first of the following conditions occurs:

- An invocation of *fn*( ) returns a non-zero value, in which case *nftw*( ) returns that value.
- The *nftw*( ) function detects an error other than [EACCES] (see FTW_DNR and FTW_NS above), in which case *nftw*( ) returns –1 and sets *errno* to indicate the error.
- The tree is exhausted, in which case *nftw*( ) returns 0.

ERRORS

The *nftw*( ) function will fail if:

[EACCES]   Search permission is denied for any component of *path* or read permission is denied for *path*, or *fn*( ) returns –1 and does not reset *errno*.

[ENAMETOOLONG]
                    The length of the *path* string exceeds {PATH_MAX}, or a pathname component is longer than {NAME_MAX}.

[ENOENT]   A component of *path* does not name an existing file or *path* is an empty string.

[ENOTDIR]   A component of *path* is not a directory.

The *nftw*( ) function may fail if:

[ELOOP]   Too many symbolic links were encountered in resolving *path*.

[EMFILE]   {OPEN_MAX} file descriptors are currently open in the calling process.

[ENAMETOOLONG]
                    Pathname resolution of a symbolic link produced an intermediate result whose length exceeds {PATH_MAX}.

[ENFILE]   Too many files are currently open in the system.

In addition, *errno* may be set if the function pointed by *fn*( ) causes *errno* to be set.

SEE ALSO

lstat( ), *opendir*( ), *readdir*( ), *stat*( ), **<ftw.h>**.

EXAMPLE

```
/*
 * Copyright (C) ANTRIX Inc.
 */

/* nftw.c
 * This program recursively descends the directory hierarchy
 * using function nftw
 */

#include <stdio.h>
#include <sys/types.h>
#include <dirent.h>
#include <sys/stat.h>
#include <ftw.h>
#include <errno.h>
```

```
#define  PERM_ALL    (S_IRWXU | S_IRWXG | S_IRWXO)

int func (path, buf, integer, ftwbuf)
char *path;
struct stat *buf;
int integer;
struct FTW ftwbuf;
{
   /* print some information about the path */
   fprintf (stdout,"directory traversed=%s\n", path);
   fprintf (stdout,"buf->st_mode=%o\n", (S_IFDIR ^ buf->st_mode) );
   fprintf (stdout,"buf->st_uid=%d\n", buf->st_uid);
   fprintf (stdout,"buf->st_gid=%d\n", buf->st_gid);
   fprintf (stdout,"integer=%d\n", integer);

   return (0);
}

main()
{
  int     nftw_value;
  int     i, readdir_value;
  DIR     *dirp;
  struct  dirent *dirent_save;
  char    *root = "testdir";
  char    *leaf = "testdir/subdir";

  fprintf (stdout,"create test directory tree structure\n");
  mkdir (root, PERM_ALL);
  mkdir (leaf, PERM_ALL);

  nftw_value = nftw (root, func, 1, FTW_PHYS);
  if ( nftw_value == 0 )
     fprintf (stdout,"nftw() call successful\n");
  else {
     fprintf (stderr,"ERROR: nftw() call failed\n");
     fprintf (stderr,"ERROR: %s\n", strerror(errno));
  }

  fprintf (stdout,"remove test directories\n");
  rmdir (leaf);
  rmdir (root);
}
```

NAME

nice — change priority of a process

SYNOPSIS

EX   `#include <unistd.h>`

`int nice(int incr);`

DESCRIPTION

The *nice*( ) function adds the value of *incr* to the nice value of the calling process. A process' nice value is a non-negative number for which a more positive value results in lower CPU priority.

A maximum nice value of 2 * {NZERO} −1 and a minimum nice value of 0 are imposed by the system. Requests for values above or below these limits result in the nice value being set to the corresponding limit. Only a process with appropriate privileges can lower the nice value.

RETURN VALUE

Upon successful completion, *nice*( ) returns the new nice value minus {NZERO}. Otherwise, −1 is returned, the process' *nice* value is not changed, and *errno* is set to indicate the error.

UX

ERRORS

The *nice*( ) function will fail if:

[EPERM]   The *incr* argument is negative and the calling process does not have appropriate privileges.

APPLICATION USAGE

As −1 is a permissible return value in a successful situation, an application wishing to check for error situations should set *errno* to 0, then call *nice*( ), and if it returns −1, check to see if *errno* is non-zero.

SEE ALSO

<limits.h>, <unistd.h>.

EXAMPLE

```
/*
 * Copyright (C) ANTRIX Inc.
 */

/* nice.c
 * This program changes priority of a process and results in
 * lower CPU priority using function nice.
 */

#include <stdio.h>
#include <stdlib.h>
#include <unistd.h>
#include <limits.h>
#include <errno.h>

#define   MAXNICE   (2*NZERO - 1)

main()
{
   int   nice_value;
```

```
        fprintf (stdout,"change priority of a time sharing process\n");
        nice_value = nice (NZERO);
        if ( nice_value != (MAXNICE - NZERO + 1) ) {
            fprintf (stdout,"nice() call successful\n");
            fprintf (stdout,"new nice value is=%d\n", nice_value);
        }
        else {
            fprintf (stderr,"ERROR: nice() call failed\n");
            fprintf (stderr,"ERROR: %s\n", strerror(errno));
        }
    }
```

NAME

nl_langinfo — language information

SYNOPSIS

EX
```
#include <langinfo.h>

char *nl_langinfo(nl_item item);
```

DESCRIPTION

The *nl_langinfo*( ) function returns a pointer to a string containing information relevant to the particular language or cultural area defined in the program's locale (see **<langinfo.h>**). The manifest constant names and values of *item* are defined in **<langinfo.h>**. For example:

```
nl_langinfo (ABDAY_1)
```

would return a pointer to the string "Dom" if the identified language was Portuguese, and "Sun" if the identified language was English.

RETURN VALUE

In a locale where *langinfo* data is not defined, *nl_langinfo*( ) returns a pointer to the corresponding string in the POSIX locale. In all locales, *nl_langinfo*( ) returns a pointer to an empty string if *item* contains an invalid setting.

ERRORS

No errors are defined.

APPLICATION USAGE

The array pointed to by the return value should not be modified by the program, but may be modified by further calls to *nl_langinfo*( ). In addition, calls to *setlocale*( ) with a category corresponding to the category of *item* (see **<langinfo.h>**), or to the category LC_ALL, may overwrite the array.

SEE ALSO

setlocale( ), **<langinfo.h>**, **<nl_types.h>**, the **XBD** specification, **Chapter 5**, **Locale**.

EXAMPLE

```
/*
 * Copyright (C) ANTRIX Inc.
 */

/* nl_langinfo.c
 * This program provides language information relevant to the
 * particular language or cultural area defined in the program's
 * locale using function nl_langinfo.
 */

#include <stdio.h>
#include <stdlib.h>
#include <nl_types.h>
#include <langinfo.h>
#include <locale.h>
#include <errno.h>

main()
{
    char    *string;
    int     i;
```

```
    nl_item   item;

    fprintf (stdout,"set locale\n");
    setlocale (LC_ALL, "C");

    for ( i = DAY_1; i < DAY_7; i++ ) {
      string = nl_langinfo (i);
      if ( string != (char *)0 )
         fprintf (stdout,"%s\n",  string);
      else
         fprintf (stderr,"ERROR: nl_langinfo() call failed\n");
    }
}
```

NAME

nrand48 — generate uniformly distributed pseudo-random non-negative long integers

SYNOPSIS

EX
```
#include <stdlib.h>
```

```
long int nrand48(unsigned short int xsubi[3]);
```

DESCRIPTION

Refer to *drand48*( ).

EXAMPLE

```
/*
 * Copyright (C) ANTRIX Inc.
 */

/* nrand48.c
 * This program generates non-negative, long integers, uniformly
 * distributed over the interval [0, 2 raise 31) using function
 * nrand48.
 */

#include <stdio.h>
#include <stdlib.h>
#include <errno.h>

main()
{
  int                  i;
  unsigned short int xsubi[3];
  double               nrand48_value;

  xsubi[0] = 1;
  xsubi[1] = 2;
  xsubi[2] = 4;
  for ( i = 0; i < 5; i++ ) {
      nrand48_value = nrand48 (xsubi);
      fprintf (stdout,"random value in iteration %d is %d\n",
                    i, nrand48_value);
  }
}
```

NAME

open — open a file

SYNOPSIS

OH
```
#include <sys/types.h>
#include <sys/stat.h>
#include <fcntl.h>

int open(const char *path, int oflag , ... );
```

DESCRIPTION

The *open*( ) function establishes the connection between a file and a file descriptor. It creates an open file description that refers to a file and a file descriptor that refers to that open file description. The file descriptor is used by other I/O functions to refer to that file. The *path* argument points to a pathname naming the file.

The *open*( ) function will return a file descriptor for the named file that is the lowest file descriptor not currently open for that process. The open file description is new, and therefore the file descriptor does not share it with any other process in the system. The FD_CLOEXEC file descriptor flag associated with the new file descriptor will be cleared.

The file offset used to mark the current position within the file is set to the beginning of the file.

The file status flags and file access modes of the open file description will be set according to the value of *oflag*.

Values for *oflag* are constructed by a bitwise-inclusive-OR of flags from the following list, defined in **<fcntl.h>**. Applications must specify exactly one of the first three values (file access modes) below in the value of *oflag*:

O_RDONLY　　　Open for reading only.

O_WRONLY　　　Open for writing only.

O_RDWR　　　　Open for reading and writing. The result is undefined if this flag is applied to a FIFO.

Any combination of the following may be used:

O_APPEND　　　If set, the file offset will be set to the end of the file prior to each write.

O_CREAT　　　　If the file exists, this flag has no effect except as noted under O_EXCL below. Otherwise, the file is created; the user ID of the file is set to the effective user

FIPS　　　　　　ID of the process; the group ID of the file is set to the group ID of the file's parent directory or to the effective group ID of the process; and the access permission bits (see **<sys/stat.h>**) of the file mode are set to the value of the third argument taken as type **mode_t** modified as follows: a bitwise-AND is performed on the file-mode bits and the corresponding bits in the complement of the process' file mode creation mask. Thus, all bits in the file mode whose corresponding bit in the file mode creation mask is set are cleared. When bits other than the file permission bits are set, the effect is unspecified. The third argument does not affect whether the file is open for reading, writing or for both.

O_EXCL　　　　　If O_CREAT and O_EXCL are set, *open*( ) will fail if the file exists. The check for the existence of the file and the creation of the file if it does not exist will be atomic with respect to other processes executing *open*( ) naming the same filename in the same directory with O_EXCL and O_CREAT set. If O_CREAT is not set, the effect is undefined.

O_NOCTTY　　If set and *path* identifies a terminal device, *open*( ) will not cause the terminal device to become the controlling terminal for the process.

O_NONBLOCK　When opening a FIFO with O_RDONLY or O_WRONLY set:

If O_NONBLOCK is set:
> An *open*( ) for reading only will return without delay. An *open*( ) for writing only will return an error if no process currently has the file open for reading.

If O_NONBLOCK is clear:
> An *open*( ) for reading only will block until a process opens the file for writing. An *open*( ) for writing only will block until a process opens the file for reading.

When opening a block special or character special file that supports non-blocking opens:

If O_NONBLOCK is set:
> The *open*( ) function will return without blocking for the device to be ready or available. Subsequent behaviour of the device is device-specific.

If O_NONBLOCK is clear:
> The *open*( ) function will block until the device is ready or available before returning.

Otherwise, the behaviour of O_NONBLOCK is unspecified.

EX　　O_SYNC　　If O_SYNC is set on a regular file, writes to that file will cause the process to block until the data is delivered to the underlying hardware.

O_TRUNC　　If the file exists and is a regular file, and the file is successfully opened O_RDWR or O_WRONLY, its length is truncated to 0 and the mode and owner are unchanged. It will have no effect on FIFO special files or terminal device files. Its effect on other file types is implementation-dependent. The result of using O_TRUNC with O_RDONLY is undefined.

If O_CREAT is set and the file did not previously exist, upon successful completion, *open*( ) will mark for update the *st_atime, st_ctime* and *st_mtime* fields of the file and the *st_ctime* and *st_mtime* fields of the parent directory.

If O_TRUNC is set and the file did previously exist, upon successful completion, *open*( ) will mark for update the *st_ctime* and *st_mtime* fields of the file.

UX　If *path* refers to a STREAMS file, *oflag* may be constructed from O_NONBLOCK OR-ed with either O_RDONLY, O_WRONLY, or O_RDWR. Other flag values are not applicable to STREAMS devices and have no effect on them. The value O_NONBLOCK affects the operation of STREAMS drivers and certain functions applied to file descriptors associated with STREAMS files. For STREAMS drivers, the implementation of O_NONBLOCK is device-specific.

If *path* names the master side of a pseudo-terminal device, then it is unspecified whether *open*( ) locks the slave side so that it cannot be opened. Portable applications must call *unlockpt*( ) before opening the slave side.

RETURN VALUE

Upon successful completion, the function will open the file and return a non-negative integer representing the lowest numbered unused file descriptor. Otherwise, −1 is returned and *errno* is set to indicate the error. No files will be created or modified if the function returns −1.

ERRORS

The *open*( ) function will fail if:

	[EACCES]	Search permission is denied on a component of the path prefix, or the file exists and the permissions specified by *oflag* are denied, or the file does not exist and write permission is denied for the parent directory of the file to be created, or O_TRUNC is specified and write permission is denied.
	[EEXIST]	O_CREAT and O_EXCL are set, and the named file exists.
	[EINTR]	A signal was caught during *open*( ).
UX	[EIO]	The *path* argument names a STREAMS file and a hangup or error occurred during the *open*( ).
	[EISDIR]	The named file is a directory and *oflag* includes O_WRONLY or O_RDWR.
UX	[ELOOP]	Too many symbolic links were encountered in resolving *path*.
	[EMFILE]	{OPEN_MAX} file descriptors are currently open in the calling process.

[ENAMETOOLONG]

FIPS   The length of the *path* argument exceeds {PATH_MAX} or a pathname component is longer than {NAME_MAX}.

	[ENFILE]	The maximum allowable number of files is currently open in the system.
	[ENOENT]	O_CREAT is not set and the named file does not exist; or O_CREAT is set and either the path prefix does not exist or the *path* argument points to an empty string.
UX	[ENOSR]	The *path* argument names a STREAMS-based file and the system is unable to allocate a STREAM.
	[ENOSPC]	The directory or file system that would contain the new file cannot be expanded, the file does not exist, and O_CREAT is specified.
	[ENOTDIR]	A component of the path prefix is not a directory.
	[ENXIO]	O_NONBLOCK is set, the named file is a FIFO, O_WRONLY is set and no process has the file open for reading.
EX	[ENXIO]	The named file is a character special or block special file, and the device associated with this special file does not exist.
	[EROFS]	The named file resides on a read-only file system and either O_WRONLY, O_RDWR, O_CREAT (if file does not exist) or O_TRUNC is set in the *oflag* argument.

The *open*( ) function may fail if:

UX	[EAGAIN]	The *path* argument names the slave side of a pseudo-terminal device that is locked.
EX	[EINVAL]	The value of the *oflag* argument is not valid.
UX	[ENAMETOOLONG]	

UX   Pathname resolution of a symbolic link produced an intermediate result whose length exceeds {PATH_MAX}.

UX	[ENOMEM]	The *path* argument names a STREAMS file and the system is unable to allocate resources.

EX
[ETXTBSY]   The file is a pure procedure (shared text) file that is being executed and *oflag* is O_WRONLY or O_RDWR.

SEE ALSO

chmod( ), *close*( ), *creat*( ), *dup*( ), *fcntl*( ), *lseek*( ), *read*( ), *umask*( ), *unlockpt*( ), *write*( ), **<fcntl.h>**, **<sys/stat.h>**, **<sys/types.h>**.

EXAMPLE

```c
/*
 * Copyright (C) ANTRIX Inc.
 */

/* open.c
 * This program establishes the connection between a file
 * and a file descriptor i.e it opens a file using function
 * open.
 */

#include <stdio.h>
#include <stdlib.h>
#include <fcntl.h>
#include <sys/stat.h>
#include <errno.h>

#define  PERM_ALL    (S_IRWXU | S_IRWXG | S_IRWXO)

main()
{
   int    fildes;
   int    length, bytes;
   char   *buf;
   char   *string = "hello world";
   char   *path = "testfile";

   fprintf (stdout,"example 1\n");

   fprintf (stdout,"create a new file and open for read,");
   fprintf (stdout, "write and execute\n");
   fildes = open (path, O_CREAT, PERM_ALL);
   if ( fildes > 2 )
      fprintf (stdout,"open() call successful\n");
   else {
      fprintf (stderr,"ERROR: open() call failed\n");
      fprintf (stderr,"ERROR: %s\n", strerror(errno));
   }

   close (fildes);
   fprintf (stdout,"remove testfile\n");
   remove (path);

   fprintf (stdout,"example 2\n");

   fprintf (stdout,"open an existing file for reading\n");
```

```
        length = strlen (string);
        fildes = creat (path, PERM_ALL);
        bytes = write (fildes, string, length);
        if (bytes != length)
            fprintf (stderr,"ERROR: unable to write in file\n");
        fprintf (stdout,"close testfile\n");
        close (fildes);

        fprintf (stdout,"open testfile for read only\n");
        fildes = open (path, O_RDONLY);
        if ( fildes > 2 )
            fprintf (stdout,"open() call successful\n");
        else {
            fprintf (stderr,"ERROR: open() call failed\n");
            fprintf (stderr,"ERROR: %s\n", strerror(errno));
        }

        buf = (char *)malloc (length);
        read (fildes, buf, length );
        fprintf (stdout,"the string read is=%s\n", buf);

        close (fildes);
        fprintf (stdout,"remove testfile\n");
        remove (path);
}
```

NAME

opendir — open directory

SYNOPSIS

OH   `#include <sys/types.h>`
`#include <dirent.h>`

`DIR *opendir(const char *dirname);`

DESCRIPTION

The *opendir( )* function opens a directory stream corresponding to the directory named by the *dirname* argument. The directory stream is positioned at the first entry. If the type **DIR**, is implemented using a file descriptor, applications will only be able to open up to a total of {OPEN_MAX} files and directories. A successful call to any of the *exec* functions will close any directory streams that are open in the calling process.

RETURN VALUE

Upon successful completion, *opendir( )* returns a pointer to an object of type **DIR**. Otherwise, a null pointer is returned and *errno* is set to indicate the error.

ERRORS

The *opendir( )* function will fail if:

[EACCES]   Search permission is denied for the component of the path prefix of *dirname* or read permission is denied for *dirname.*

UX   [ELOOP]   Too many symbolic links were encountered in resolving *path.*

[ENAMETOOLONG]
FIPS   The length of the *dirname* argument exceeds {PATH_MAX}, or a pathname component is longer than {NAME_MAX}.

[ENOENT]   A component of *dirname* does not name an existing directory or *dirname* is an empty string.

[ENOTDIR]   A component of *dirname* is not a directory.

The *opendir( )* function may fail if:

[EMFILE]   {OPEN_MAX} file descriptors are currently open in the calling process.

UX   [ENAMETOOLONG]
Pathname resolution of a symbolic link produced an intermediate result whose length exceeds {PATH_MAX}.

[ENFILE]   Too many files are currently open in the system.

APPLICATION USAGE

The *opendir( )* function should be used in conjunction with *readdir( )*, *closedir( )* and *rewinddir( )* to examine the contents of the directory (see the **EXAMPLES** section in *readdir( )*). This method is recommended for portability.

SEE ALSO

closedir( ), *lstat( )*, *readdir( )*, *rewinddir( )*, *symlink( )*, **<dirent.h>**, **<limits.h>**, **<sys/types.h>**.

EXAMPLE

```
/*
 * Copyright (C) ANTRIX Inc.
 */

/* opendir.c
 * This program opens a directory stream corresponding to the
 * directory named by the dirname argument using function opendir.
 */

#include <stdio.h>
#include <stdlib.h>
#include <sys/types.h>
#include <dirent.h>
#include <sys/stat.h>
#include <errno.h>

#define  PERM_ALL    (S_IRWXU | S_IRWXG | S_IRWXO)

main()
{
  DIR     *buf;
  int     i;
  struct  dirent *dirent_save;
  const   char *dirname = "testdir";
  const   char *subdir = "testdir/subdir";

  fprintf (stdout,"create test directories\n");
  mkdir (dirname, PERM_ALL);
  mkdir (subdir, PERM_ALL);

  fprintf (stdout,"open testdir directory\n");
  buf = opendir (dirname);
  if ( buf != (DIR *)0 ) {
     fprintf (stdout,"opendir() call was successful\n");
     fprintf (stdout,"buf->dd_fd=%d\n", buf->dd_fd );
     fprintf (stdout,"buf->dd_loc=%d\n", buf->dd_loc );
     fprintf (stdout,"buf->dd_size=%d\n", buf->dd_size );
     fprintf (stdout,"buf->dd_buf=%s\n", buf->dd_buf );
     fprintf (stdout,"directory names in testdir are:\n");
     for (i = 0; i < 3; i++ ) {
         dirent_save = readdir (buf);
         fprintf (stdout,"%s\n", dirent_save->d_name);
     }
  }
  else {
     fprintf (stderr,"ERROR: opendir() call failed\n");
     fprintf (stderr,"ERROR: %s\n", strerror(errno));
  }

  closedir (buf);
  fprintf (stdout,"remove directories\n");
```

```
        rmdir (subdir);
        rmdir (dirname);
    }
```

NAME

openlog — open a connection to the logging facility

SYNOPSIS

UX
```
#include <syslog.h>
```

```
void openlog(const char *ident, int logopt, int facility);
```

DESCRIPTION

Refer to *closelog*( ).

NAME

optarg, opterr, optind, optopt — options parsing variables

SYNOPSIS

```
#include <stdio.h>

extern char *optarg;

extern int opterr, optind, optopt;
```

DESCRIPTION

Refer to *getopt( )*.

NAME

fpathconf, pathconf — get configurable pathname variables

SYNOPSIS

```
#include <unistd.h>

long int fpathconf(int fildes, int name);

long int pathconf(const char *path, int name);
```

DESCRIPTION

The *fpathconf( )* and *pathconf( )* functions provide a method for the application to determine the current value of a configurable limit or option (*variable*) that is associated with a file or directory.

For *pathconf( )*, the *path* argument points to the pathname of a file or directory.

For *fpathconf( )*, the *fildes* argument is an open file descriptor.

The *name* argument represents the variable to be queried relative to that file or directory. Implementations will support all of the variables listed in the following table and may support others. The variables in the following table come from **<limits.h>** or **<unistd.h>** and the symbolic constants, defined in **<unistd.h>**, are the corresponding values used for *name:*

Variable	Value of *name*	Notes
LINK_MAX	_PC_LINK_MAX	1
MAX_CANON	_PC_MAX_CANON	2
MAX_INPUT	_PC_MAX_INPUT	2
NAME_MAX	_PC_NAME_MAX	3, 4
PATH_MAX	_PC_PATH_MAX	4, 5
PIPE_BUF	_PC_PIPE_BUF	6
_POSIX_CHOWN_RESTRICTED	_PC_CHOWN_RESTRICTED	7
_POSIX_NO_TRUNC	_PC_NO_TRUNC	3, 4
_POSIX_VDISABLE	_PC_VDISABLE	2

Notes:

1. If *path* or *fildes* refers to a directory, the value returned applies to the directory itself.

2. If *path* or *fildes* does not refer to a terminal file, it is unspecified whether an implementation supports an association of the variable name with the specified file.

3. If *path* or *fildes* refers to a directory, the value returned applies to filenames within the directory.

4. If *path* or *fildes* does not refer to a directory, it is unspecified whether an implementation supports an association of the variable name with the specified file.

5. If *path* or *fildes* refers to a directory, the value returned is the maximum length of a relative pathname when the specified directory is the working directory.

6. If *path* refers to a FIFO, or *fildes* refers to a pipe or FIFO, the value returned applies to the referenced object. If *path* or *fildes* refers to a directory, the value returned applies to any FIFO that exists or can be created within the directory. If *path* or *fildes* refers to any other type of file, it is unspecified whether an implementation supports an association of the variable name with the specified file.

7. If *path* or *fildes* refers to a directory, the value returned applies to any files, other than directories, that exist or can be created within the directory.

RETURN VALUE

If *name* is an invalid value, both *pathconf( )* and *fpathconf( )* return −1 and *errno* is set to indicate the error.

If the variable corresponding to *name* has no limit for the *path* or file descriptor, both *pathconf( )* and *fpathconf( )* return −1 without changing *errno*. If the implementation needs to use *path* to determine the value of *name* and the implementation does not support the association of *name* with the file specified by *path*, or if the process did not have appropriate privileges to query the file specified by *path*, or *path* does not exist, *pathconf( )* returns −1 and *errno* is set to indicate the error.

If the implementation needs to use *fildes* to determine the value of *name* and the implementation does not support the association of *name* with the file specified by *fildes*, or if *fildes* is an invalid file descriptor, *fpathconf( )* will return −1 and *errno* is set to indicate the error.

Otherwise *pathconf( )* or *fpathconf( )* returns the current variable value for the file or directory without changing *errno*. The value returned will not be more restrictive than the corresponding value available to the application when it was compiled with the implementation's **<limits.h>** or **<unistd.h>**.

ERRORS

The *pathconf( )* function will fail if:

[EINVAL]   The value of *name* is not valid.

UX   [ELOOP]   Too many symbolic links were encountered in resolving *path*.

The *pathconf( )* function may fail if:

[EACCES]   Search permission is denied for a component of the path prefix.

[EINVAL]   The implementation does not support an association of the variable *name* with the specified file.

[ENAMETOOLONG]

FIPS   The length of the *path* argument exceeds {PATH_MAX} or a pathname component is longer than {NAME_MAX}.

UX   [ENAMETOOLONG]

                  Pathname resolution of a symbolic link produced an intermediate result whose length exceeds {PATH_MAX}.

[ENOENT]   A component of *path* does not name an existing file or *path* is an empty string.

[ENOTDIR]   A component of the path prefix is not a directory.

The *fpathconf( )* function will fail if:

[EINVAL]   The value of *name* is not valid.

The *fpathconf( )* function may fail if:

[EBADF]   The *fildes* argument is not a valid file descriptor.

[EINVAL]   The implementation does not support an association of the variable *name* with the specified file.

SEE ALSO

sysconf( ), **<limits.h>**, **<unistd.h>**.

EXAMPLE

```
/*
 * Copyright (C) ANTRIX Inc.
 */

/* pathconf.c
 * This program gets the configurable pathname variable
 * _PC_NAME_MAX value using function pathconf.
 */

#include <stdio.h>
#include <stdlib.h>
#include <unistd.h>
#include <sys/stat.h>
#include <errno.h>

#define  PERM_ALL    (S_IRWXU | S_IRWXG | S_IRWXO)

main()
{
  long  pathconf_value;
  int   fildes;
  char  *path = "testfile";

  fprintf (stdout,"create testfile\n");
  fildes = creat (path, PERM_ALL);

  fprintf (stdout,"get _PC_NAME_MAX allowable limit for testfile\n");
  pathconf_value = pathconf (path, _PC_NAME_MAX);
  if ( pathconf_value >= 0 ) {
     fprintf (stdout,"pathconf() call successful\n");
     fprintf (stdout,"maximum file name length=%ld\n", pathconf_value );
  }
  else {
     fprintf (stderr,"ERROR: pathconf() call failed\n");
     fprintf (stderr,"ERROR: %s\n", strerror(errno));
  }

  fprintf (stdout,"remove testfile\n");
  remove (path);
}
```

NAME

pause — suspend process until signal is received

SYNOPSIS

```
#include <unistd.h>

int pause(void);
```

DESCRIPTION

The *pause*( ) function suspends the calling process until delivery of a signal whose action is either to execute a signal-catching function or to terminate the process.

If the action is to terminate the process, *pause*( ) will not return.

If the action is to execute a signal-catching function, *pause*( ) will return after the signal-catching function returns.

RETURN VALUE

Since *pause*( ) suspends process execution indefinitely unless interrupted by a signal, there is no successful completion return value. A value of −1 is returned and *errno* is set to indicate the error.

ERRORS

The *pause*( ) function will fail if:

[EINTR]   A signal is caught by the calling process and control is returned from the signal-catching function.

SEE ALSO

sigsuspend( ), **<unistd.h>**.

EXAMPLE

```
/*
 * Copyright (C) ANTRIX Inc.
 */

/* pause.c
 * This program suspends the calling process until delivery of
 * a signal SIGALRM using function pause.
 */

#include <stdio.h>
#include <stdlib.h>
#include <unistd.h>
#include <signal.h>
#include <errno.h>

void handler(signal)
int signal;
{
  if ( signal == SIGALRM )
     fprintf (stdout,"received signal SIGALRM\n");
  else
     fprintf (stderr,"ERROR: expected=%d, received=%d\n",
                     SIGALRM, signal);
  exit (1);
}
```

```
main()
{
  int      pause_value;

  fprintf (stdout,"set signal SIGALRM\n");
  signal (SIGALRM, handler);

  fprintf (stdout,"set an alarm for 2 seconds\n");
  alarm (2);

  fprintf (stdout,"suspend process\n");
  pause_value = pause ();
  if (pause_value == -1) {
      fprintf (stderr,"ERROR: pause() call failed\n");
      fprintf (stderr,"ERROR: %s\n", strerror(errno));
  }
}
```

NAME

pclose — close a pipe stream to or from a process

SYNOPSIS

```
#include <stdio.h>

int pclose(FILE *stream);
```

DESCRIPTION

The *pclose*( ) function closes a stream that was opened by *popen*( ), waits for the command to terminate, and returns the termination status of the process that was running the command language interpreter. However, if a call caused the termination status to be unavailable to *pclose*( ), then *pclose*( ) returns −1 with *errno* set to [ECHILD] to report this situation; this can happen if the application calls one of the following functions:

- *wait*( )

- *waitpid*( ) with a *pid* argument less than or equal to 0 or equal to the process ID of the command line interpreter

- any other function not defined in this document that could do one of the above.

In any case, *pclose*( ) will not return before the child process created by *popen*( ) has terminated.

If the command language interpreter cannot be executed, the child termination status returned by *pclose*( ) will be as if the command language interpreter terminated using *exit*(127) or *_exit*(127).

The *pclose*( ) function will not affect the termination status of any child of the calling process other than the one created by *popen*( ) for the associated stream.

If the argument *stream* to *pclose*( ) is not a pointer to a stream created by *popen*( ), the result of *pclose*( ) is undefined.

RETURN VALUE

Upon successful return, *pclose*( ) returns the termination status of the command language interpreter. Otherwise, *pclose*( ) returns −1 and sets *errno* to indicate the error.

ERRORS

The *pclose*( ) function will fail if:

[ECHILD]   The status of the child process could not be obtained, as described above.

SEE ALSO

fork( ), *popen*( ), *waitpid*( ), **<stdio.h>**.

EXAMPLE

```
/*
 * Copyright (C) ANTRIX Inc.
 */

/* pclose.c
 * This program closes a stream that was open by popen, waits
 * for the command to terminate, and returns the termination
 * status of the process that was running the command using
 * function pclose.
 */

#include <stdio.h>
```

```
#include <stdlib.h>
#include <limits.h>
#include <errno.h>

#define  PATH_LEN   255

main()
{
   int    pclose_value;
   char   command[PATH_LEN];
   char   buf[PATH_LEN];
   FILE   *stream;

   memset (command, ' ', PATH_LEN);
   memset (buf, ' ', PATH_LEN);

   fprintf (stdout,"create command to be executed\n");
   strcpy (command, "./ptest1");
   strcat (command, " ");
   strcat (command, "testfile");

   fprintf (stdout,"write string to pipe and\n");
   fprintf (stdout, "wait for while to read\n");
   stream = (FILE *)popen (command, "w");
   fputs ("hello world\n", stream);
   fflush (stream);
   sleep (4);

   pclose_value = pclose (stream);
   if ( pclose_value != -1 ) {
      fprintf (stdout,"pclose() call successful\n");
      /* read string from file */
      stream = fopen ("testfile", "r");
      fgets (buf, sizeof(buf), stream);
      fprintf (stdout,"string read is buf=%s\n", buf);
   }
   else {
      fprintf (stderr,"ERROR: pclose() call failed\n");
      fprintf (stderr,"ERROR: %s\n", strerror(errno));
   }
   fclose (stream);
   remove ("testfile");
}

/* ptest1.c
 * Compile this program separately
 */

#include <stdio.h>
#include <stdlib.h>
#include <errno.h>
```

```
main(argc, argv)
int argc;
char *argv[];
{
    char    buf[BUFSIZ];
    FILE    *fp;

    memset (buf, ' ', BUFSIZ);
    argc--; argv++;
    fp = fopen(*argv, "w+");
    fgets (buf, sizeof(buf), stdin);
            fputs (buf, fp);
    fflush (fp);
    fclose (fp);
    exit (1);
}
```

NAME

perror — write error messages to standard error

SYNOPSIS

```
#include <stdio.h>

void perror(const char *s);
```

DESCRIPTION

The *perror*( ) function maps the error number in the external variable *errno* to a language-dependent error message, which is written to the standard error stream as follows: first (if *s* is not a null pointer and the character pointed to by *s* is not the null byte), the string pointed to by *s* followed by a colon and a space character; then an error message string followed by a newline character. The contents of the error message strings are the same as those returned by *strerror*( ) with argument *errno*.

The *perror*( ) function will mark the file associated with the standard error stream as having been written (*st_ctime*, *st_mtime* marked for update) at some time between its successful completion and *exit*( ), *abort*( ), or the completion of *fflush*( ) or *fclose*( ) on *stderr*.

RETURN VALUE

The *perror*( ) function returns no value.

ERRORS

No errors are defined.

SEE ALSO

strerror( ), **<stdio.h>**.

EXAMPLE

```
/*
 * Copyright (C) ANTRIX Inc.
 */

/* perror.c
 * This program writes error messages to standard error
 * using function perror.
 */

#include <stdio.h>
#include <stdlib.h>
#include <errno.h>

main()
{
  int    remove_value;
  char   *string = "ERROR testfile";
  char   *path = "testfile";

  fprintf (stdout,"try removing file which does not exist\n");
  remove_value = remove (path);

  fprintf (stdout,"write message to standard error\n");
```

```
    if ( remove_value == -1 )
       perror (string);
 }
```

NAME
pipe — create an interprocess channel

SYNOPSIS
```
#include <unistd.h>

int pipe(int fildes[2]);
```

DESCRIPTION
The *pipe*( ) function will create a pipe and place two file descriptors, one each into the arguments *fildes*[0] and *fildes*[1], that refer to the open file descriptions for the read and write ends of the pipe. Their integer values will be the two lowest available at the time of the *pipe*( ) call. (The *fcntl*( ) function can be used to set both these flags.)

Data can be written to the file descriptor *fildes*[1] and read from file descriptor *fildes*[0]. A read on the file descriptor *fildes*[0] will access data written to file descriptor *fildes*[1] on a first-in-first-out basis. It is unspecified whether *fildes*[0] is also open for writing and whether *fildes*[1] is also open for reading.

UX

A process has the pipe open for reading (correspondingly writing) if it has a file descriptor open that refers to the read end, *fildes*[0] (write end, *fildes*[1]).

Upon successful completion, *pipe*( ) will mark for update the *st_atime*, *st_ctime* and *st_mtime* fields of the pipe.

RETURN VALUE
Upon successful completion, 0 is returned. Otherwise, −1 is returned and *errno* is set to indicate the error.

ERRORS
The *pipe*( ) function will fail if:

[EMFILE]   More than {OPEN_MAX} minus two file descriptors are already in use by this process.

[ENFILE]   The number of simultaneously open files in the system would exceed a system-imposed limit.

SEE ALSO
fcntl( ), *read*( ), *write*( ), **<fcntl.h>**, **<unistd.h>**.

EXAMPLE
```
/*
 * Copyright (C) ANTRIX Inc.
 */

/* pipe.c
 * This program creates a pipe and places two file descriptors
 * one each into the arguments fildes[0] and fildes[1], that refer
 * to the open file descriptions for the read and write ends of
 * the pipe using function pipe.
 */

#include <stdio.h>
#include <stdlib.h>
#include <unistd.h>
#include <errno.h>
```

```
main()
{
  int    pipe_value;
  int    fildes[2], length;
  char   *buf;
  char   *string = "hello world";

  memset(fildes, 0, 2);
  length = strlen (string);

  fprintf (stdout,"create pipe\n");
  pipe_value = pipe (fildes);
  if ( pipe_value == 0 ) {
     fprintf (stdout,"pipe() call successful\n");
     fprintf (stdout,"write string at the opening fildes[1] of pipe\n");
     write (fildes[1], string, length);
     buf = (char *)malloc (length);
     fprintf (stdout,"read string at the end fildes[0] of pipe\n");
     read (fildes[0], buf, length);
     fprintf (stdout,"string in buf=%s\n", buf);
  }
  else {
     fprintf (stderr,"ERROR: pipe() call failed\n");
     fprintf (stderr,"ERROR: %s\n", strerror(errno));
  }
}
```

NAME

poll — input/output multiplexing

SYNOPSIS

UX   `#include <poll.h>`

`int poll(struct pollfd fds[], nfds_t nfds, int timeout);`

DESCRIPTION

The *poll*( ) function provides applications with a mechanism for multiplexing input/output over a set of file descriptors. For each member of the array pointed to by *fds*, *poll*( ) examines the given file descriptor for the event(s) specified in *events*. The number of **pollfd** structures in the *fds* array is specified by *nfds*. The *poll*( ) function identifies those file descriptors on which an application can read or write data, or on which certain events have occurred.

The *fds* argument specifies the file descriptors to be examined and the events of interest for each file descriptor. It is a pointer to an array with one member for each open file descriptor of interest. The array's members are **pollfd** structures within which **fd** specifies an open file descriptor and **events** and **revents** are bitmasks constructed by OR-ing a combination of the following event flags:

POLLIN   Data other than high-priority data may be read without blocking. For STREAMS, this flag is set in **revents** even if the message is of zero length.

POLLRDNORM   Normal data (priority band equals 0) may be read without blocking. For STREAMS, this flag is set in **revents** even if the message is of zero length.

POLLRDBAND   Data from a non-zero priority band may be read without blocking. For STREAMS, this flag is set in **revents** even if the message is of zero length.

POLLPRI   High-priority data may be received without blocking. For STREAMS, this flag is set in **revents** even if the message is of zero length.

POLLOUT   Normal data (priority band equals 0) may be written without blocking.

POLLWRNORM   Same as POLLOUT.

POLLWRBAND   Priority data (priority band greater than 0) may be written.

POLLERR   An error has occurred on the device or stream. This flag is only valid in the **revents** bitmask; it is ignored in the **events** member.

POLLHUP   The device has been disconnected. This event and POLLOUT are mutually exclusive; a stream can never be writable if a hangup has occurred. However, this event and POLLIN, POLLRDNORM, POLLRDBAND or POLLPRI are not mutually exclusive. This flag is only valid in the **revents** bitmask; it is ignored in the **events** member.

POLLNVAL   The specified **fd** value is invalid. This flag is only valid in the **revents** member; it is ignored in the **events** member.

If the value of **fd** is less than 0, **events** is ignored and **revents** is set to 0 in that entry on return from *poll*( ).

In each **pollfd** structure, *poll*( ) clears the **revents** member except that where the application requested a report on a condition by setting one of the bits of **events** listed above, *poll*( ) sets the corresponding bit in **revents** if the requested condition is true. In addition, *poll*( ) sets the POLLHUP, POLLERR, and POLLNVAL flag in **revents** if the condition is true, even if the application did not set the corresponding bit in **events**.

If none of the defined events have occurred on any selected file descriptor, *poll*( ) waits at least *timeout* milliseconds for an event to occur on any of the selected file descriptors. If the value of *timeout* is 0, *poll*( ) returns immediately. If the value of *timeout* is −1, *poll*( ) blocks until a requested event occurs or until the call is interrupted.

Implementations may place limitations on the granularity of timeout intervals. If the requested timeout interval requires a finer granularity than the implementation supports, the actual timeout interval will be rounded up to the next supported value.

The *poll*( ) function is not affected by the O_NONBLOCK flag.

The *poll*( ) function supports regular files, terminal and pseudo-terminal devices, STREAMS-based files, FIFOs and pipes. The behaviour of *poll*( ) on elements of *fds* that refer to other types of file is unspecified.

Regular files always poll TRUE for reading and writing.

RETURN VALUE

Upon successful completion, *poll*( ) returns a non-negative value. A positive value indicates the total number of file descriptors that have been selected (that is, file descriptors for which the **revents** member is non-zero). A value of 0 indicates that the call timed out and no file descriptors have been selected. Upon failure, *poll*( ) returns −1 and sets *errno* to indicate the error.

ERRORS

The *poll*( ) function will fail if:

[EAGAIN]   The allocation of internal data structures failed but a subsequent request may succeed.

[EINTR]   A signal was caught during *poll*( ).

[EINVAL]   The *nfds* argument is greater than {OPEN_MAX}, or one of the **fd** members refers to a STREAM or multiplexer that is linked (directly or indirectly) downstream from a multiplexer.

SEE ALSO

getmsg( ), *putmsg*( ), *read*( ), *select*( ), *write*( ), **<poll.h>**, **<stropts.h>**, **XSH** specification, **Section 2.5**, **STREAMS**.

EXAMPLE

```
/*
 * Copyright (C) ANTRIX Inc.
 */

/* poll.c
 * This program provides users with a mechanism for multiplexing
 * input/output  over  a set of file descriptors that reference
 * open files using function poll
 */

#include <unistd.h>
#include <limits.h>
#include <stdio.h>
#include <stdlib.h>
#include <poll.h>
#include <stropts.h>
#include <fcntl.h>
```

```
#include <sys/stat.h>
#include <errno.h>

char      *string = "hello world\n";
#define  CLONE      "/dev/ptmx"
#define  BUFLEN     (sizeof(string)-1)

open_pty (m, s)
int  *m;
int  *s;
{
  int     arg;
  char    *snm;

  fprintf (stdout,"open multiplexor and get slave device\n");
  *m = open (CLONE, O_RDWR);
  grantpt (*m);
  unlockpt (*m);
  snm = (char *)ptsname (*m);
  *s = open (snm, O_RDWR);

  fprintf (stdout,"set up to toss resources on close\n");
  arg = 0;
  ioctl (*m, I_SETCLTIME, &arg);
  ioctl (*s, I_SETCLTIME, &arg);
}

main()
{
  int       fdm, fds, band, flag;
  int       poll_value;
  char      inbuf[BUFLEN];
  struct    pollfd fdsp[1];
  struct    strbuf ctlbuf, datbuf;

  memset(inbuf, ' ', BUFLEN);
  open_pty (&fdm, &fds);

  fprintf (stdout,"write band 1 data, hi-pri, then band 0 data\n");
  ctlbuf.maxlen = 0;
  ctlbuf.len    = 0;
  ctlbuf.buf    = string;
  datbuf.maxlen = BUFLEN;
  datbuf.len    = BUFLEN;
  datbuf.buf    = string;
  putpmsg (fdm, (struct strbuf *)NULL, &datbuf, 1, MSG_BAND);
  putpmsg (fdm, &ctlbuf, &datbuf, 0, MSG_HIPRI);

  write (fdm, string, BUFLEN);
  sleep (2);
  fprintf (stdout,"ensure POLLPRI set at stream head\n");
  memset ((char *)&fdsp[0], 0, sizeof(struct pollfd));
```

```
        fdsp[0].fd = fds;
        fdsp[0].events = POLLIN | POLLRDNORM | POLLRDBAND | POLLPRI;
        poll (fdsp, 1, 0);

        fprintf (stdout,"now read the first hi-pri record\n");
        ctlbuf.maxlen = BUFLEN;
        ctlbuf.len    = 0;
        ctlbuf.buf    = inbuf;
        datbuf.maxlen = BUFLEN;
        datbuf.len    = 0;
        datbuf.buf    = inbuf;
        flag = MSG_ANY;
        band = 0;
        getpmsg (fds, &ctlbuf, &datbuf, &band, &flag);

        fprintf (stdout,"ensure POLLRDBAND at stream head.\n");
        memset ((char *)&fdsp[0], 0, sizeof(struct pollfd));
        fdsp[0].fd = fds;
        fdsp[0].events = POLLIN | POLLRDNORM | POLLRDBAND | POLLPRI;
        poll (fdsp, 1, 0);
        fprintf (stdout,"read band 1 msg.\n");
        ctlbuf.maxlen = BUFLEN;
        ctlbuf.len    = 0;
        ctlbuf.buf    = inbuf;
        datbuf.maxlen = BUFLEN;
        datbuf.len    = 0;
        datbuf.buf    = inbuf;
        flag = MSG_ANY;
        band = 0;
        getpmsg (fds, &ctlbuf, &datbuf, &band, &flag);

        fprintf (stdout,"ensure POLLIN and POLLRDNORM is set\n");
        memset ((char *)&fdsp[0], 0, sizeof(struct pollfd));
        fdsp[0].fd = fds;
        fdsp[0].events = POLLIN | POLLRDNORM | POLLRDBAND | POLLPRI;
        poll_value = poll (fdsp, 1, 0);
        if (poll_value >= 0)
           fprintf (stdout,"poll() call successful\n");
        else {
           fprintf (stderr,"ERROR: poll() call failed\n");
           fprintf (stderr,"ERROR: %s\n", strerror(errno));
        }
        flag = read (fds, inbuf, BUFLEN);
        if (flag == -1) {
           printf("ERROR: read() failed\n");
           fprintf (stderr,"ERROR: %s\n", strerror(errno));
        }
        close (fdm);
        close (fds);
}
```

NAME

popen — initiate pipe streams to or from a process

SYNOPSIS

```
#include <stdio.h>

FILE *popen(const char *command, const char *mode);
```

DESCRIPTION

The *popen*( ) function executes the command specified by the string *command*. It creates a pipe between the calling program and the executed command, and returns a pointer to a stream that can be used to either read from or write to the pipe.

If the implementation supports the referenced **XCU** specification, the environment of the executed command will be as if a child process were created within the *popen*( ) call using *fork*( ), and the child invoked the *sh* utility using the call:

```
execl(shell path, "sh", "-c", command, (char *)0);
```

where *shell path* is an unspecified pathname for the *sh* utility.

The *popen*( ) function ensures that any streams from previous *popen*( ) calls that remain open in the parent process are closed in the new child process.

The *mode* argument to *popen*( ) is a string that specifies I/O mode:

1. If *mode* is **r**, when the child process is started its file descriptor STDOUT_FILENO will be the writable end of the pipe, and the file descriptor *fileno*(*stream*) in the calling process, where *stream* is the stream pointer returned by *popen*( ), will be the readable end of the pipe.

2. If *mode* is **w**, when the child process is started its file descriptor STDIN_FILENO will be the readable end of the pipe, and the file descriptor *fileno*(*stream*) in the calling process, where *stream* is the stream pointer returned by *popen*( ), will be the writable end of the pipe.

3. If *mode* is any other value, the result is undefined.

After *popen*( ), both the parent and the child process will be capable of executing independently before either terminates.

RETURN VALUE

On successful completion, *popen*( ) returns a pointer to an open stream that can be used to read or write to the pipe. Otherwise, it returns a null pointer and may set *errno* to indicate the error.

ERRORS

The *popen*( ) function may fail if:

EX   [EMFILE]   {FOPEN_MAX} streams are currently open in the calling process.

EX   [EMFILE]   {STREAM_MAX} streams are currently open in the calling process.

[EINVAL]   The *mode* argument is invalid.

The *popen*( ) function may also set *errno* values as described by *fork*( ) or *pipe*( ).

APPLICATION USAGE

Because open files are shared, a mode **r** command can be used as an input filter and a mode **w** command as an output filter.

Buffered reading before opening an input filter may leave the standard input of that filter mispositioned. Similar problems with an output filter may be prevented by careful buffer flushing, for example, with *fflush( )*.

A stream opened by *popen( )* should be closed by *pclose( )*.

The behaviour of *popen( )* is specified for values of *mode* of **r** and **w**. Other modes such as **rb** and **wb** might be supported by specific implementations, but these would not be portable features. Note that historical implementations of *popen( )* only check to see if the first character of *mode* is r. Thus, a *mode* of **robert the robot** would be treated as *mode* **r**, and a *mode* of **anything else** would be treated as *mode* **w**.

If the application calls *waitpid( )* with a *pid* argument greater than 0, and it still has a stream that was called with *popen( )* open, it must ensure that *pid* does not refer to the process started by *popen( )*.

To determine whether or not the **XCU** specification environment is present, use the function call:

```
sysconf(_SC_2_VERSION)
```

(see *sysconf( )*).

SEE ALSO

sh, *pclose( )*, *pipe( )*, *sysconf( )*, *system( )*, **<stdio.h>**.

EXAMPLE

```
/*
 * Copyright (C) ANTRIX Inc.
 */

/* popen.c
 * This program executes the command specified by the string
 * command. It creates a pipe between the calling program
 * and the executed command using function popen.
 */

#include <stdio.h>
#include <stdlib.h>
#include <limits.h>
#include <errno.h>

#define PATH_LEN   255

main()
{
  char   command[PATH_LEN];
  char   buf[PATH_LEN];
  FILE   *stream;

  memset (command, ' ', PATH_LEN);
  memset (buf, ' ', PATH_LEN);

  strcpy (command, "./ptest1");
```

```
        strcat (command, " ");
        strcat (command, "testfile");
        fprintf (stdout,"execute ./ptest1 testfile\n");
        stream = (FILE *)popen (command, "w");
        if ( stream != (FILE *)0 ) {
            fprintf (stdout,"popen() call successful\n");
            fprintf (stdout,"write string to pipe and\n");
            fprintf (stdout,"wait for while to read\n");
            fputs ("hello world\n", stream);
            fflush (stream);
            sleep (4);
            pclose (stream);
            fprintf (stdout,"read string from testfile\n");
            stream = fopen ("testfile", "r");
            fgets (buf, sizeof(buf), stream);
            fprintf (stdout,"string read is buf=%s\n", buf);
            fclose (stream);
            fprintf (stdout,"remove testfile\n");
            remove ("testfile");
        }
        else {
            fprintf (stderr,"ERROR: popen() failed\n");
            fprintf (stderr,"ERROR: %s\n", strerror(errno));
        }
}

/* ptest1.c
 * Compile this program separately
 */

#include <stdio.h>
#include <stdlib.h>
#include <errno.h>

main(argc, argv)
int argc;
char *argv[];
{
    char    buf[BUFSIZ];
    FILE    *fp;

    memset (buf, ' ', BUFSIZ);
    argc--; argv++;
    fp = fopen(*argv, "w+");
    fgets (buf, sizeof(buf), stdin);
            fputs (buf, fp);
    fflush (fp);
    fclose (fp);
    exit (1);
}
```

NAME

pow — power function

SYNOPSIS

```
#include <math.h>

double pow(double x, double y);
```

DESCRIPTION

The *pow*( ) function computes the value of *x* raised to the power *y*, x^y. If *x* is negative, *y* must be an integer value.

RETURN VALUE

Upon successful completion, *pow*( ) returns the value of *x* raised to the power *y*.

If *x* is 0 and *y* is 0, 1.0 is returned.

EX If *y* is NaN, or *y* is non-zero and *x* is NaN, NaN is returned and *errno* may be set to [EDOM]. If *y* is 0.0 and *x* is NaN, either 1.0 is returned, or NaN is returned and *errno* may be set to [EDOM].

EX If *x* is 0.0 and *y* is negative, −HUGE_VAL is returned and *errno* may be set to [EDOM] or [ERANGE].

If the correct value would cause overflow, ±HUGE_VAL is returned, and *errno* is set to [ERANGE].

If the correct value would cause underflow, 0 is returned and *errno* may be set to [ERANGE].

ERRORS

The *pow*( ) function will fail if:

[EDOM]   The value of *x* is negative and *y* is non-integral.

[ERANGE]   The value to be returned would have caused overflow.

The *pow*( ) function may fail if:

EX [EDOM]   The value of *x* is 0.0 and *y* is negative, or *y* is NaN.

[ERANGE]   The correct value would cause underflow.

EX No other errors will occur.

APPLICATION USAGE

An application wishing to check for error situations should set *errno* to 0 before calling *pow*( ). If *errno* is non-zero on return, or the return value is NaN, an error has occurred.

SEE ALSO

exp( ), *isnan*( ), **<math.h>**.

EXAMPLE

```
/*
 * Copyright (C) ANTRIX Inc.
 */

/* pow.c
 * This program computes the value of 2.00 raised to the
 * power 5.00 using function pow.
 */

#include <stdio.h>
```

```
#include <math.h>

main()
{
  double  pow_value;
  double  x = 2.00;
  double  y = 5.00;

  pow_value = pow (x, y);
  fprintf (stdout,"pow of %f, %f is %f\n", x, y, pow_value);
}
```

NAME

printf — print formatted output

SYNOPSIS

```
#include <stdio.h>

int printf(const char *format, ...);
```

DESCRIPTION

Refer to *fprintf*( ).

EXAMPLE

```
/*
 * Copyright (C) ANTRIX Inc.
 */

/* printf.c
 * This program prints the formatted output on the standard
 * output stream stdout using function printf.
 */

#include <stdio.h>
#include <stdlib.h>
#include <errno.h>

main()
{

    int    integer = 1;
    long   longer = 12L;
    float  floating = 1.2345;
    double doubles = 1.234E10;
    char   character = 'a';
    char   *string = "hello world";

    printf ("integer=%d\n", integer);
    printf ("longer=%ld\n", longer);
    printf ("float=%f\n", floating);
    printf ("doubles=%f\n", doubles);
    printf ("character=%c\n", character);
    printf ("string=%s\n", string);
}
```

NAME

ptsname — get name of the slave pseudo-terminal device

SYNOPSIS

UX   `#include <stdlib.h>`

`char *ptsname(int `*`fildes`*`);`

DESCRIPTION

The *ptsname*( ) function returns the name of the slave pseudo-terminal device associated with a master pseudo-terminal device. The *fildes* argument is a file descriptor that refers to the master device. The *ptsname*( ) function returns a pointer to a string containing the pathname of the corresponding slave device.

RETURN VALUE

Upon successful completion, *ptsname*( ) returns a pointer to a string which is the name of the pseudo-terminal slave device. Upon failure, *ptsname*( ) returns a null pointer. This could occur if *fildes* is an invalid file descriptor or if the slave device name does not exist in the file system.

ERRORS

No errors are defined.

APPLICATION USAGE

The value returned may point to a static data area that is overwritten by each call to *ptsname*( ).

SEE ALSO

grantpt( ), *open*( ), *ttyname*( ), *unlockpt*( ), **<stdlib.h>**.

EXAMPLE

```
/*
 * Copyright (C) ANTRIX Inc.
 */

/* ptsname.c
 * This program returns the name of the slave pseudo-terminal
 * device associated with a master pseudo-terminal device
 * using function ptsname
 */

#include <stdio.h>
#include <stdlib.h>
#include <fcntl.h>
#include <errno.h>

/* name of the master pseudo-terminal device */
/* this name may be different in your machine */
#define MASTER      "/dev/ptmx"

main()
{
  char    *ptsname_value;
  int     fildes;
  char    *name;

  fprintf (stdout,"open master terminal device\n");
  fildes = open (MASTER, O_RDWR);
```

```
    fprintf (stdout,"grant access to the slave pseud-terminal device\n");
    grantpt (fildes);

    fprintf (stdout,"unlock device\n");
    unlockpt (fildes);
    ptsname_value = (char *)ptsname (fildes);
    if ( ptsname_value != (char *)0 ) {
        fprintf (stdout,"ptsname() call successful\n");
        fprintf (stdout,"name of the slave pseudo-terminal=%s\n",
                         ptsname_value);
    }
    else {
        fprintf (stderr,"ERROR: ptsname() call failed\n");
        fprintf (stderr,"ERROR: %s\n", strerror(errno));
    }
    fprintf (stdout,"close device\n");
    close (fildes);
}
```

NAME

putc — put byte on a stream

SYNOPSIS

```
#include <stdio.h>

int putc(int c, FILE *stream);
```

DESCRIPTION

The *putc*( ) function is equivalent to *fputc*( ), except that if it is implemented as a macro it may evaluate *stream* more than once, so the argument should never be an expression with side-effects.

RETURN VALUE

Refer to *fputc*( ).

ERRORS

Refer to *fputc*( ).

APPLICATION USAGE

Because it may be implemented as a macro, *putc*( ) may treat a *stream* argument with side-effects incorrectly. In particular, *putc*(*c*, *f*++) may not work correctly. Therefore, use of this function is not recommended in such situations; *fputc*( ) should be used instead.

SEE ALSO

fputc( ), **<stdio.h>**.

EXAMPLE

```
/*
 * Copyright (C) ANTRIX Inc.
 */

/* putc.c
 * This program writes the byte specified by c to output stream
 * pointed to by stream using function putc.
 */

#include <stdio.h>
#include <stdlib.h>
#include <errno.h>

main()
{
   int    i, putc_value;
   char   character;
   FILE   *stream;
   char   *path = "testfile";

   fprintf (stdout,"example 1\n");

   fprintf (stdout,"write character 'a' into file\n");
   stream = fopen (path, "w+r");

   putc_value = putc ('a', stream);
   if ( putc_value == 'a' ) {
       fprintf (stdout,"putc() call successful\n");
```

```
        fflush (stream);
        fseek (stream, 0, SEEK_SET);
        character = fgetc (stream);
        fprintf (stdout,"character read is '%c'\n", character );
    }
    else {
        fprintf (stderr,"ERROR: putc() call failed\n");
        fprintf (stderr,"ERROR: %s\n", strerror(errno));
    }

    fclose (stream);
    fprintf (stdout,"remove testfile\n");
    remove (path);

    fprintf (stdout,"example 2\n");
    fprintf (stdout,"write all alphabet and numbers to stdout\n");
    for ( i = '0'; i <= 'z'; i++ )
        putc (i, stdout);
    putc('\n', stdout);
}
```

NAME

putchar — put byte on *stdout* stream

SYNOPSIS

```
#include <stdio.h>

int putchar(int c);
```

DESCRIPTION

The function call *putchar(c)* is equivalent to *putc(c, stdout)*.

RETURN VALUE

Refer to *fputc( )*.

SEE ALSO

putc( ), **<stdio.h>**.

EXAMPLE

```c
/*
 * Copyright (C) ANTRIX Inc.
 */

/* putchar.c
 * This program puts a byte on stdout stream using function
 * putchar.
 */

#include <stdio.h>
#include <stdlib.h>
#include <errno.h>

main()
{
  int  putchar_value;
  int  c = 'a';

  fprintf (stdout,"write a character to terminal\n");
  putchar_value = putchar (c);
  if ( putchar_value == c ) {
     fprintf (stdout,"\nputchar() call successful\n");
     fprintf (stdout,"character written is '%c'\n", putchar_value);
  }
  else
     fprintf (stderr,"ERROR: putchar() call failed\n");
}
```

NAME

putenv — change or add value to environment

SYNOPSIS

EX   `#include <stdlib.h>`

`int putenv(const char *string);`

DESCRIPTION

The *putenv*( ) function uses the *string* argument to set environment variable values. The *string* argument should point to a string of the form "*name=value*". The *putenv*( ) function makes the value of the environment variable *name* equal to *value* by altering an existing variable or creating a new one. In either case, the string pointed to by *string* becomes part of the environment, so altering the string will change the environment. The space used by *string* is no longer used once a new string-defining *name* is passed to *putenv*( ).

RETURN VALUE

Upon successful completion, *putenv*( ) returns 0. Otherwise, it returns a non-zero value and sets *errno* to indicate the error.

ERRORS

The *putenv*( ) function may fail if:

[ENOMEM]   Insufficient memory was available.

APPLICATION USAGE

The *putenv*( ) function manipulates the environment pointed to by *environ*, and can be used in conjunction with *getenv*( ).

This routine may use *malloc*( ) to enlarge the environment.

A potential error is to call *putenv*( ) with an automatic variable as the argument, then return from the calling function while *string* is still part of the environment.

Although *string* is currently defined as **const char ***, using a constant string as the argument is not recommended. The environment pointed to by *environ* has historically been classified as modifiable storage.

FUTURE DIRECTIONS

In a future revision of this document, the type of *string* will be changed to **char ***.

SEE ALSO

exec, *getenv*( ), *malloc*( ), **<stdlib.h>**.

EXAMPLE

```
/*
 * Copyright (C) ANTRIX Inc.
 */

/* putenv.c
 * This program sets environment variable CURDIR using function
 * putenv.
 */

#include <stdio.h>
#include <stdlib.h>
#include <limits.h>
#include <unistd.h>
```

```
#include <errno.h>

#define PATH_LEN 255

main()
{
  int   putenv_value;
  char  curdir[PATH_LEN];
  char  string[PATH_LEN];
  char  *getenv_value;
  char  *getcwd_value;

  memset (curdir, ' ', PATH_LEN);
  memset (string, ' ', PATH_LEN);

  strcpy (string, "CURDIR=");
  getcwd_value = getcwd (curdir, PATH_LEN);
  strcat (string, getcwd_value);

  fprintf (stdout,"set environment variable\n");
  fprintf (stdout,"%s\n", string );
  putenv_value = putenv (string);
  if ( putenv_value == 0 )
      fprintf (stdout,"putenv() call successful\n");
  else
      fprintf (stderr,"ERROR: putenv() call failed\n");
  fprintf (stdout,"get the value of environment variable\n");

  getenv_value = getenv ("CURDIR");
  fprintf (stdout,"getenv_value=%s\n", getenv_value);
}
```

NAME

putmsg, putpmsg — send a message on a STREAM

SYNOPSIS

UX   `#include <stropts.h>`

```
int putmsg(int fildes, const struct strbuf *ctlptr,
      const struct strbuf *dataptr, int flags);
```

```
int putpmsg(int fildes, const struct strbuf *ctlptr,
      const struct strbuf *dataptr, int band, int flags);
```

DESCRIPTION

The *putmsg( )* function creates a message from a process buffer(s) and sends the message to a STREAMS file. The message may contain either a data part, a control part, or both. The data and control parts are distinguished by placement in separate buffers, as described below. The semantics of each part is defined by the STREAMS module that receives the message.

The *putpmsg( )* function does the same thing as *putmsg( )*, but the process can send messages in different priority bands. Except where noted, all requirements on *putmsg( )* also pertain to *putpmsg( )*.

The *fildes* argument specifies a file descriptor referencing an open STREAM. The *ctlptr* and *dataptr* arguments each point to a **strbuf** structure.

The *ctlptr* argument points to the structure describing the control part, if any, to be included in the message. The *buf* member in the **strbuf** structure points to the buffer where the control information resides, and the *len* member indicates the number of bytes to be sent. The *maxlen* member is not used by *putmsg( )*. In a similar manner, the argument *dataptr* specifies the data, if any, to be included in the message. The *flags* argument indicates what type of message should be sent and is described further below.

To send the data part of a message, *dataptr* must not be a null pointer and the *len* member of *dataptr* must be 0 or greater. To send the control part of a message, the corresponding values must be set for *ctlptr*. No data (control) part will be sent if either *dataptr* (*ctlptr*) is a null pointer or the *len* member of *dataptr* (*ctlptr*) is set to −1.

For *putmsg( )*, if a control part is specified and *flags* is set to RS_HIPRI, a high priority message is sent. If no control part is specified, and *flags* is set to RS_HIPRI, *putmsg( )* fails and sets *errno* to [EINVAL]. If *flags* is set to 0, a normal message (priority band equal to 0) is sent. If a control part and data part are not specified and *flags* is set to 0, no message is sent and 0 is returned.

The STREAM head guarantees that the control part of a message generated by *putmsg( )* is at least 64 bytes in length.

For *putpmsg( )*, the flags are different. The *flags* argument is a bitmask with the following mutually-exclusive flags defined: MSG_HIPRI and MSG_BAND. If *flags* is set to 0, *putpmsg( )* fails and sets *errno* to [EINVAL]. If a control part is specified and *flags* is set to MSG_HIPRI and *band* is set to 0, a high-priority message is sent. If *flags* is set to MSG_HIPRI and either no control part is specified or *band* is set to a non-zero value, *putpmsg( )* fails and sets *errno* to [EINVAL]. If *flags* is set to MSG_BAND, then a message is sent in the priority band specified by *band*. If a control part and data part are not specified and *flags* is set to MSG_BAND, no message is sent and 0 is returned.

The *putmsg( )* function blocks if the STREAM write queue is full due to internal flow control conditions, with the following exceptions:

- For high-priority messages, *putmsg*( ) does not block on this condition and continues processing the message.

- For other messages, *putmsg*( ) does not block but fails when the write queue is full and O_NONBLOCK is set.

The *putmsg*( ) function also blocks, unless prevented by lack of internal resources, while waiting for the availability of message blocks in the STREAM, regardless of priority or whether O_NONBLOCK has been specified. No partial message is sent.

RETURN VALUE

Upon successful completion, *putmsg*( ) and *putpmsg*( ) return 0. Otherwise, they return −1 and set *errno* to indicate the error.

ERRORS

The *putmsg*( ) and *putpmsg*( ) functions will fail if:

[EAGAIN]   A non-priority message was specified, the O_NONBLOCK flag is set, and the STREAM write queue is full due to internal flow control conditions; or buffers could not be allocated for the message that was to be created.

[EBADF]   *fildes* is not a valid file descriptor open for writing.

[EINTR]   A signal was caught during *putmsg*( ).

[EINVAL]   An undefined value is specified in *flags*, or *flags* is set to RS_HIPRI or MSG_HIPRI and no control part is supplied, or the STREAM or multiplexer referenced by *fildes* is linked (directly or indirectly) downstream from a multiplexer, or *flags* is set to MSG_HIPRI and *band* is non-zero (for *putpmsg*( ) only).

[ENOSR]   Buffers could not be allocated for the message that was to be created due to insufficient STREAMS memory resources.

[ENOSTR]   A STREAM is not associated with *fildes*.

[ENXIO]   A hangup condition was generated downstream for the specified STREAM.

[EPIPE] or [EIO] The *fildes* argument refers to a STREAMS-based pipe and the other end of the pipe is closed. A SIGPIPE signal is generated for the calling process.

[ERANGE]   The size of the data part of the message does not fall within the range specified by the maximum and minimum packet sizes of the topmost STREAM module. This value is also returned if the control part of the message is larger than the maximum configured size of the control part of a message, or if the data part of a message is larger than the maximum configured size of the data part of a message.

In addition, *putmsg*( ) and *putpmsg*( ) will fail if the STREAM head had processed an asynchronous error before the call. In this case, the value of *errno* does not reflect the result of *putmsg*( ) or *putpmsg*( ) but reflects the prior error.

SEE ALSO

getmsg( ), *poll*( ), *read*( ), *write*( ), **<stropts.h>**, **XSH** specification, **Section 2.5**, **STREAMS**.

EXAMPLE

```
/*
 * Copyright (C) ANTRIX Inc.
 */
```

```c
/* putmsg.c
 * This program sends a message on a stream
 * using function putmsg
 */

#include <stdio.h>
#include <stdlib.h>
#include <unistd.h>
#include <limits.h>
#include <stropts.h>
#include <fcntl.h>
#include <sys/stat.h>
#include <errno.h>

/* different text and length */
#define   MSGCTL1    "Control 1"
#define   MSGCTL2    "Control Two"
#define   MSGDAT1    "Data 1"
#define   MSGDAT2    "Data Two"
#define   MAX_MINPUT  255

char    buf1[MAX_MINPUT];
char    buf2[MAX_MINPUT];

#define SLAVE     "/dev/ptmx"

struct   strbuf ctrlbuf, databuf;

open_pty(m, s)
int   *m;
int   *s;
{
  char    *snm;
  fprintf (stdout,"open multiplexor and get slave device\n");
  *m = open (SLAVE, O_RDWR);
  grantpt (*m);
  unlockpt (*m);
  snm = (char *) ptsname (*m);
  *s = open (snm, O_RDWR);
}

close_pty(m, s)
   int m, s;
{
  fprintf (stdout,"close pty\n");
  close (m);
  close (s);
}

main()
{
  int   fdm, fds, flag;
```

```
open_pty (&fdm, &fds);

fprintf (stdout,"write first message to stream\n");
strcpy (buf1, MSGCTL1);
ctrlbuf.maxlen = sizeof (buf1);
ctrlbuf.len = strlen (buf1);
ctrlbuf.buf = buf1;
strcpy (buf2, MSGDAT1);
databuf.maxlen = sizeof (buf2);
databuf.len = strlen (buf2);
databuf.buf = buf2;
fprintf (stdout,"sending first message on a stream\n");
putmsg (fdm, &ctrlbuf, &databuf, 0);

fprintf (stdout,"send second message to stream\n");
strcpy (buf1, MSGCTL2);
ctrlbuf.maxlen = sizeof (buf1);
ctrlbuf.len = strlen (buf1);
ctrlbuf.buf = buf1;
strcpy (buf2, MSGDAT2);
databuf.maxlen = sizeof (buf2);
databuf.len = strlen (buf2);
databuf.buf = buf2;

fprintf (stdout,"send second message to stream\n");
putmsg (fdm, &ctrlbuf, &databuf, 0);

fprintf (stdout,"get message from stream\n");
ctrlbuf.maxlen = sizeof (buf1);
ctrlbuf.len = 0;
ctrlbuf.buf = buf1;
memset (buf1, 0, sizeof(buf1));
databuf.maxlen = sizeof (buf2);
databuf.len = 0;
databuf.buf = buf2;
memset (buf2, 0, sizeof(buf2));
flag = 0;
getmsg (fds, &ctrlbuf, &databuf, &flag);

fprintf (stdout,"check control and data parts of the message received\n");
if ( strcmp(ctrlbuf.buf, MSGCTL1) == 0 )
    fprintf (stdout,"control message received=%s\n", ctrlbuf.buf);
else
    fprintf (stderr,"ERROR: incorrect control message\n");

if ( strcmp(databuf.buf, MSGDAT1) == 0 )
    fprintf (stdout,"data message received=%s\n", databuf.buf);
else {
    fprintf (stderr,"ERROR: incorrect data message\n");
    fprintf (stderr,"ERROR: %s\n", strerror(errno));
}
```

```
     close_pty (fdm, fds);
}
```

NAME

puts — put a string on standard output

SYNOPSIS

```
#include <stdio.h>

int puts(const char *s);
```

DESCRIPTION

The *puts*( ) function writes the string pointed to by *s*, followed by a newline character, to the standard output stream *stdout*. The terminating null byte is not written.

The *st_ctime* and *st_mtime* fields of the file will be marked for update between the successful execution of *puts*( ) and the next successful completion of a call to *fflush*( ) or *fclose*( ) on the same stream or a call to *exit*( ) or *abort*( ).

RETURN VALUE

Upon successful completion, *puts*( ) returns a non-negative number. Otherwise it returns EOF, sets an error indicator for the stream and *errno* is set to indicate the error.

ERRORS

Refer to *fputc*( ).

APPLICATION USAGE

The *puts*( ) function appends a newline character, while *fputs*( ) does not.

SEE ALSO

fputs( ), *fopen*( ), *putc*( ), *stdio*( ), **<stdio.h>**.

EXAMPLE

```
/*
 * Copyright (C) ANTRIX Inc.
 */

/* puts.c
 * This program writes the string pointed to by s, followed by
 * a newline character, to the standard output stream stdout
 * using function puts.
 */

#include <stdio.h>
#include <stdlib.h>
#include <errno.h>

main()
{
   int    puts_value;
   int    length;
   char   *s = "hello world";

   /* add one byte to length for null terminated string */
   length = strlen (s) + 1;

   fprintf (stdout,"write string to stdout or terminal\n");
   puts_value = puts (s);
   if ( puts_value == length ) {
       fprintf (stdout,"puts() call successful\n");
```

```
        fprintf (stdout,"string length returned is %d\n", puts_value );
    }
    else
        fprintf (stderr,"ERROR: puts() call failed\n");

    puts ("\n");
}
```

NAME

pututxline — put entry into user accounting database

SYNOPSIS

UX `#include <utmpx.h>`

`struct utmpx *pututxline(const struct utmpx *utmpx);`

DESCRIPTION

Refer to *endutxent*( ).

NAME

putw — put a word on a stream

SYNOPSIS

EX
```
#include <stdio.h>
```

```
int putw(int w, FILE *stream);
```

DESCRIPTION

The *putw*( ) function writes the word (that is, type **int**) *w* to the output *stream* (at the position at which the file offset, if defined, is pointing). The size of a word is the size of a type **int** and varies from machine to machine. The *putw*( ) function neither assumes nor causes special alignment in the file.

The *st_ctime* and *st_mtime* fields of the file will be marked for update between the successful execution of *putw*( ) and the next successful completion of a call to *fflush*( ) or *fclose*( ) on the same stream or a call to *exit*( ) or *abort*( ).

RETURN VALUE

Upon successful completion, *putw*( ) returns 0. Otherwise, a non-zero value is returned, the error indicators for the stream are set, and *errno* is set to indicate the error.

ERRORS

Refer to *fputc*( ).

APPLICATION USAGE

Because of possible differences in word length and byte ordering, files written using *putw*( ) are machine-dependent, and may not be readable using *getw*( ) on a different processor.

SEE ALSO

fopen( ), *fwrite*( ), *getw*( ), **<stdio.h>**.

EXAMPLE

```
/*
 * Copyright (C) ANTRIX Inc.
 */

/* putw.c
 * This program writes the word on a stream using function
 * putw.
 */

#include <stdio.h>
#include <fcntl.h>
#include <sys/stat.h>
#include <errno.h>

#define  PERM_ALL   (S_IRWXU | S_IRWXG | S_IRWXO)
#define  OFLAG      (O_CREAT | O_WRONLY | O_TRUNC)

main()
{
  int   putw_value;
  int   i, getw_value;
  int   fildes, length;
  FILE  *stream;
  char  buf[12];
```

```
char  *path = "testfile";

memset (buf, ' ', 12);

fprintf (stdout,"create and open testfile\n");
stream = fopen (path, "w+");

fprintf (stdout,"write to testfile\n");
for ( i = 0; i < 5; i++ ) {
    putw_value = putw (i, stream);
    if ( putw_value != 0 )
        fprintf (stderr,"ERROR: putw() call failed\n");
}
fclose (stream);

fprintf (stdout,"read from testfile\n");
stream = fopen (path, "r");
for ( i = 0; i < 5; i++ ) {
    getw_value = getw (stream);
    fprintf (stdout,"%d\n", getw_value);
}
fclose (stream);
fprintf (stdout,"remove testfile\n");
remove (path);
}
```

NAME

putwc — put wide character on a stream

SYNOPSIS

OH   `#include <stdio.h>`
WP   `#include <wchar.h>`

```
wint_t putwc(wint_t wc, FILE *stream);
```

DESCRIPTION

The *putwc( )* function is equivalent to *fputwc( )*, except that if it is implemented as a macro it may evaluate *stream* more than once, so the argument should never be an expression with side-effects.

RETURN VALUE

Refer to *fputwc( )*.

ERRORS

Refer to *fputwc( )*.

APPLICATION USAGE

This interface is provided in order to align with some current implementations, and with possible future ISO standards.

Because it may be implemented as a macro, *putwc( )* may treat a *stream* argument with side-effects incorrectly. In particular, *putwc (wc, *f++)* may not work correctly. Therefore, use of this function is not recommended; *fputwc( )* should be used instead.

SEE ALSO

fputwc( ), **<stdio.h>**, **<wchar.h>**.

EXAMPLE

```
/*
 * Copyright (C) ANTRIX Inc.
 */

/* putwc.c
 * This program writes wide character on a stream using function
 * putwc.
 */

#include <stdio.h>
#include <stdlib.h>
#include <wchar.h>
#include <errno.h>

main()
{
    int     i;
    wint_t  putwc_value;
    wint_t  wc = L'a';
    wint_t  character;
    char    *path = "testfile";
    FILE    *stream;

    fprintf (stdout,"example 1\n");
    fprintf (stdout,"write character 'a' into file\n");
```

```
stream = fopen (path, "w+r");
putwc_value = putwc (wc, stream);
if ( putwc_value == wc ) {
    fprintf (stdout,"putwc() call successful\n");
    fflush (stream);
    fseek (stream, 0, SEEK_SET);
    character = fgetwc (stream);
    fprintf (stdout,"character read is %wc\n", character );
}
else {
    fprintf (stderr,"ERROR: putwc() call failed\n");
    fprintf (stderr,"ERROR: %s\n", strerror(errno));
}

fclose (stream);
fprintf (stdout,"remove testfile\n");
remove (path);

fprintf (stdout,"example 2\n");
fprintf (stdout,"write all alphabet and numbers to stdout\n");

for ( i = '0'; i <= 'z'; i++ )
    putwc (i, stdout);

putwc('\n', stdout);
}
```

NAME

putwchar — put wide character on *stdout* stream

SYNOPSIS

WP   `#include <wchar.h>`

`wint_t putwchar(wint_t wc);`

DESCRIPTION

The function call *putwchar(wc)* is equivalent to *putwc(wc, stdout)*.

RETURN VALUE

Refer to *fputwc( )*.

SEE ALSO

fputwc( ), *putwc( )*, **<wchar.h>**.

EXAMPLE

```
/*
 * Copyright (C) ANTRIX Inc.
 */

/* putwchar.c
 * This program puts wide character on stdout stream using
 * function putwchar.
 */

#include <stdio.h>
#include <stdlib.h>
#include <wchar.h>
#include <errno.h>

main()
{
  wint_t   putwchar_value;
  wint_t   wc = L'a';

  fprintf (stdout,"write a character to terminal\n");
  putwchar_value = putwchar (wc);
  if ( putwchar_value == wc ) {
     fprintf (stdout,"\nputwchar() call successful\n");
     fprintf (stdout,"character written is %wc\n", putwchar_value);
  }
  else
     fprintf (stderr,"ERROR: putwchar() call failed\n");
}
```

NAME

qsort — sort a table of data

SYNOPSIS

```
#include <stdlib.h>

void qsort(void *base, size_t nel, size_t width
        int (*compar)(const void *, const void *));
```

DESCRIPTION

The *qsort*( ) function sorts an array of *nel* objects, the initial element of which is pointed to by *base*. The size of each object, in bytes, is specified by the *width* argument.

The contents of the array are sorted in ascending order according to a comparison function. The *compar* argument is a pointer to the comparison function, which is called with two arguments that point to the elements being compared. The function must return an integer less than, equal to, or greater than 0, if the first argument is considered respectively less than, equal to, or greater than the second. If two members compare as equal, their order in the sorted array is unspecified.

RETURN VALUE

The *qsort*( ) function returns no value.

ERRORS

No errors are defined.

APPLICATION USAGE

The comparison function need not compare every byte, so arbitrary data may be contained in the elements in addition to the values being compared.

SEE ALSO

<stdlib.h>.

EXAMPLE

```
/*
 * Copyright (C) ANTRIX Inc.
 */

/* qsort.c
 * This program sorts table of data in ascending order according
 * to a comparison function using qsort function.
 */

#include <stdio.h>
#include <stdlib.h>
#include <errno.h>

#define   TABLESIZE    5

int table[TABLESIZE] = { 2, 3, 1, 5, 4 };

int compare (i, j)
int *i;
int *j;
{
  if ( *i == *j )
     return (0);
```

```
    if ( *i > *j )
        return (1);
    return (-1);
}

main()
{
    int  i;

    fprintf (stdout,"unsorted table is:\n");
    for ( i = 0; i < 5; i++ )
        fprintf (stdout,"table[%d]=%d\n", i, table[i]);
    qsort ((void *)&table[0], TABLESIZE, sizeof(int), compare);

    fprintf (stdout,"sorted table is:\n");
    for ( i = 0; i < 5; i++ )
        fprintf (stdout,"table[%d]=%d\n", i, table[i]);

}
```

NAME

raise — send a signal to the executing process

SYNOPSIS

```
#include <signal.h>

int raise(int sig);
```

DESCRIPTION

The *raise*( ) function sends the signal *sig* to the executing process.

RETURN VALUE

EX Upon successful completion, 0 is returned. Otherwise, a non-zero value is returned and *errno* is set to indicate the error.

ERRORS

The *raise*( ) function will fail if:

EX [EINVAL] The value of the *sig* argument is an invalid signal number.

SEE ALSO

kill( ), *sigaction*( ), **<signal.h>**, **<sys/types.h>**.

EXAMPLE

```
/*
 * Copyright (C) ANTRIX Inc.
 */

/* raise.c
 * This program sends signal SIGALRM to the executing process
 * using function raise.
 */

#include <stdio.h>
#include <stdlib.h>
#include <signal.h>
#include <errno.h>

void handler(signal)
int signal;
{
  if ( signal == SIGALRM )
     fprintf (stdout,"received signal SIGALRM\n");
  else
     fprintf (stderr,"ERROR: expected=%d, received=%d\n",
                     SIGALRM, signal);
}

main()
{
  int   raise_value;

  signal (SIGALRM, handler);

  fprintf (stdout,"send signal SIGALRM to program\n");
  raise_value = raise (SIGALRM);
```

```
    if ( raise_value == 0 )
        fprintf (stdout,"raise() call successful\n");
    else {
        fprintf (stderr,"ERROR: raise() call failed\n");
        fprintf (stderr,"ERROR: %s\n", strerror(errno));
    }
}
```

NAME

rand — pseudo-random number generator

SYNOPSIS

```
#include <stdlib.h>

int rand (void);

void srand(unsigned int seed);
```

DESCRIPTION

EX

The *rand*( ) function computes a sequence of pseudo-random integers in the range 0 to {RAND_MAX} with a period of at least 2^{32}.

The *srand*( ) function uses the argument as a seed for a new sequence of pseudo-random numbers to be returned by subsequent calls to *rand*( ). If *srand*( ) is then called with the same seed value, the sequence of pseudo-random numbers will be repeated. If *rand*( ) is called before any calls to *srand*( ) are made, the same sequence will be generated as when *srand*( ) is first called with a seed value of 1.

The implementation will behave as if no function defined in this document calls *rand*( ) or *srand*.

RETURN VALUE

The *rand*( ) function returns the next pseudo-random number in the sequence. The *srand*( ) function returns no value.

ERRORS

No errors are defined.

APPLICATION USAGE

The *drand48*( ) function provides a much more elaborate random number generator.

The following code defines a pair of functions which could be incorporated into applications wishing to ensure that the same sequence of numbers is generated across different machines:

```
static unsigned long int next = 1;
int myrand(void)     /* RAND_MAX assumed to be 32767 */
{
        next = next * 1103515245 + 12345;
        return ((unsigned int) (next/65536) % 32768);
}

void mysrand(unsigned int seed)
{
        next = seed;
}
```

SEE ALSO

drand48( ), *srand*( ), **<stdlib.h>**.

EXAMPLE

```
/*
 * Copyright (C) ANTRIX Inc.
 */

/* rand.c
 * This program computes a sequence of pseudo-random integers
 * using function rand.
 */
```

```
#include <stdio.h>
#include <stdlib.h>
#include <errno.h>

main()
{
  int  i, rand_value;

  for ( i = 0; i < 5; i++ ) {
      rand_value = rand ();
      fprintf (stdout,"random value in iteration %d is %d\n",
                    i, rand_value);
  }
}
```

NAME

random — generate pseudorandom number

SYNOPSIS

UX

```
#include <stdlib.h>

long random(void);
```

DESCRIPTION

Refer to *initstate*( ).

EXAMPLE

```c
/*
 * Copyright (C) ANTRIX Inc.
 */

/* random.c
 * This program computes a sequence of pseudo-randomom integers
 * using function random.
 */

#include <stdio.h>
#include <stdlib.h>
#include <errno.h>

main()
{
  long  i, random_value;

  for ( i = 0; i < 5; i++ ) {
      random_value = random ();
      fprintf (stdout,"randomom value in iteration %d is %d\n",
                      i, random_value);
  }
}
```

NAME

read, readv — read from file

SYNOPSIS

```
#include <unistd.h>

ssize_t read(int fildes, void *buf, size_t nbyte);
```

UX
```
#include <sys/uio.h>

ssize_t readv(int fildes, const struct iovec *iov, int iovcnt);
```

DESCRIPTION

The *read*( ) function attempts to read *nbyte* bytes from the file associated with the open file descriptor, *fildes*, into the buffer pointed to by *buf*.

If *nbyte* is 0, *read*( ) will return 0 and have no other results.

On files that support seeking (for example, a regular file), the *read*( ) starts at a position in the file given by the file offset associated with *fildes*. The file offset is incremented by the number of bytes actually read.

Files that do not support seeking, for example, terminals, always read from the current position. The value of a file offset associated with such a file is undefined.

No data transfer will occur past the current end-of-file. If the starting position is at or after the end-of-file, 0 will be returned. If the file refers to a device special file, the result of subsequent *read*( ) requests is implementation-dependent.

If the value of *nbyte* is greater than {SSIZE_MAX}, the result is implementation-dependent.

When attempting to read from an empty pipe or FIFO:

- If no process has the pipe open for writing, *read*( ) will return 0 to indicate end-of-file.

- If some process has the pipe open for writing and O_NONBLOCK is set, *read*( ) will return –1 and set *errno* to [EAGAIN].

- If some process has the pipe open for writing and O_NONBLOCK is clear, *read*( ) will block until some data is written or the pipe is closed by all processes that had the pipe open for writing.

When attempting to read a file (other than a pipe or FIFO) that supports non-blocking reads and has no data currently available:

- If O_NONBLOCK is set, *read*( ) will return a –1 and set *errno* to [EAGAIN].

- If O_NONBLOCK is clear, *read*( ) will block until some data becomes available.

- The use of the O_NONBLOCK flag has no effect if there is some data available.

The *read*( ) function reads data previously written to a file. If any portion of a regular file prior to the end-of-file has not been written, *read*( ) returns bytes with value 0. For example, *lseek*( ) allows the file offset to be set beyond the end of existing data in the file. If data is later written at this point, subsequent reads in the gap between the previous end of data and the newly written data will return bytes with value 0 until data is written into the gap.

Upon successful completion, where *nbyte* is greater than 0, *read*( ) will mark for update the *st_atime* field of the file, and return the number of bytes read. This number will never be greater than *nbyte*. The value returned may be less than *nbyte* if the number of bytes left in the file is less than *nbyte*, if the *read*( ) request was interrupted by a signal, or if the file is a pipe or FIFO or special file and has fewer than *nbyte* bytes immediately available for reading. For example, a *read*( ) from a file associated with a terminal may return one typed line of data.

If a *read*( ) is interrupted by a signal before it reads any data, it will return −1 with *errno* set to [EINTR].

FIPS   If a *read*( ) is interrupted by a signal after it has successfully read some data, it will return the number of bytes read.

UX   A *read*( ) from a STREAMS file can read data in three different modes: byte-stream mode, message-nondiscard mode, and message-discard mode. The default is byte-stream mode. This can be changed using the I_SRDOPT *ioctl*( ) request, and can be tested with the I_GRDOPT *ioctl*( ). In byte-stream mode, *read*( ) retrieves data from the STREAM until as many bytes as were requested are transferred, or until there is no more data to be retrieved. Byte-stream mode ignores message boundaries.

In STREAMS message-nondiscard mode, *read*( ) retrieves data until as many bytes as were requested are transferred, or until a message boundary is reached. If *read*( ) does not retrieve all the data in a message, the remaining data is left on the STREAM, and can be retrieved by the next *read*( ) call. Message-discard mode also retrieves data until as many bytes as were requested are transferred, or a message boundary is reached. However, unread data remaining in a message after the *read*( ) returns is discarded, and is not available for a subsequent *read*( ), *readv*( ) or *getmsg*( ) call.

How *read*( ) handles zero-byte STREAMS messages is determined by the current read mode setting. In byte-stream mode, *read*( ) accepts data until it has read *nbyte* bytes, or until there is no more data to read, or until a zero-byte message block is encountered. The *read*( ) function then returns the number of bytes read, and places the zero-byte message back on the STREAM to be retrieved by the next *read*( ), *readv*( ) or *getmsg*( ). In message-nondiscard mode or message-discard mode, a zero-byte message returns 0 and the message is removed from the STREAM. When a zero-byte message is read as the first message on a STREAM, the message is removed from the STREAM and 0 is returned, regardless of the read mode.

A *read*( ) from a STREAMS file returns the data in the message at the front of the STREAM head read queue, regardless of the priority band of the message.

By default, STREAMs are in control-normal mode, in which a *read*( ) from a STREAMS file can only process messages that contain a data part but do not contain a control part. The *read*( ) fails if a message containing a control part is encountered at the STREAM head. This default action can be changed by placing the STREAM in either control-data mode or control-discard mode with the I_SRDOPT *ioctl*( ) command. In control-data mode, *read*( ) converts any control part to data and passes it to the application before passing any data part originally present in the same message. In control-discard mode, *read*( ) discards message control parts but returns to the process any data part in the message.

In addition, *read*( ) and *readv*( ) will fail if the STREAM head had processed an asynchronous error before the call. In this case, the value of *errno* does not reflect the result of *read*( ) or *readv*( ) but reflects the prior error. If a hangup occurs on the STREAM being read, *read*( ) continues to operate normally until the STREAM head read queue is empty. Thereafter, it returns 0.

UX   The *readv*( ) function is equivalent to *read*( ), but places the input data into the *iovcnt* buffers specified by the members of the *iov* array: *iov*[0], *iov*[1], ..., *iov*[*iovcnt*−1]. The *iovcnt* argument is valid if greater than 0 and less than or equal to {IOV_MAX}.

Each *iovec* entry specifies the base address and length of an area in memory where data should be placed. The *readv*( ) function always fills an area completely before proceeding to the next.

Upon successful completion, *readv*( ) marks for update the *st_atime* field of the file.

RETURN VALUE

UX   Upon successful completion, *read*( ) and *readv*( ) return a non-negative integer indicating the number of bytes actually read. Otherwise, the functions return −1 and set *errno* to indicate the error.

ERRORS

UX   The *read*( ) and *readv*( ) functions will fail if:

[EAGAIN]	The O_NONBLOCK flag is set for the file descriptor and the process would be
UX	delayed in *read*( ) or *readv*( ).
[EBADF]	The *fildes* argument is not a valid file descriptor open for reading.

UX   [EBADMSG]   The file is a STREAM file that is set to control-normal mode and the message waiting to be read includes a control part.

    [EINTR]   The read operation was terminated due to the receipt of a signal, and no data was transferred.

UX   [EINVAL]   The STREAM or multiplexer referenced by *fildes* is linked (directly or indirectly) downstream from a multiplexer.

    [EIO]   A physical I/O error has occurred.

    [EIO]   The process is a member of a background process attempting to read from its controlling terminal, the process is ignoring or blocking the SIGTTIN signal or the process group is orphaned. This error may also be generated for implementation-dependent reasons.

UX   [EISDIR]   The *fildes* argument refers to a directory and the implementation does not allow the directory to be read using *read*( ) or *readv*( ). The *readdir*( ) function should be used instead.

The *readv*( ) function will fail if:

    [EINVAL]   The sum of the *iov_len* values in the *iov* array overflowed an **ssize_t**.

UX   The *read*( ) and *readv*( ) functions may fail if:

EX   [ENXIO]   A request was made of a non-existent device, or the request was outside the capabilities of the device.

UX   The *readv*( ) function may fail if:

    [EINVAL]   The *iovcnt* argument was less than or equal to 0, or greater than {IOV_MAX}.

SEE ALSO

fcntl( ), *ioctl*( ), *lseek*( ), *open*( ), *pipe*( ), **<stropts.h>**, **<sys/uio.h>**, **<unistd.h>**, **XBD** specification, **Chapter 9**, **General Terminal Interface**.

EXAMPLE

```
/*
 * Copyright (C) ANTRIX Inc.
 */
```

```
/* read.c
 * This program attempts to read nbyte bytes from the file
 * associated with open file descriptor fildes, into buffer
 * pointed to by buf using function read.
 */

#include <stdio.h>
#include <stdlib.h>
#include <unistd.h>
#include <fcntl.h>
#include <sys/types.h>
#include <sys/stat.h>
#include <errno.h>

#define  PERM_ALL    (S_IRWXU | S_IRWXG | S_IRWXO)

main()
{
  int    bytes;
  int    fildes, length;
  char   *buf;
  char   *string = "hello world";
  char   *path = "testfile";

  length = strlen (string);

  fprintf (stdout,"create testfile\n");
  fildes = creat (path, PERM_ALL);
  fprintf (stdout,"write string\n");
  write (fildes, string, length);
  fprintf (stdout,"close testfile\n");
  close (fildes);

  fprintf (stdout,"open testfile for read\n");
  fildes = open (path, O_RDONLY);

  buf = (char *)malloc (length);
  fprintf (stdout,"read string\n");
  bytes = read (fildes, buf, length );
  if ( bytes == length ) {
     fprintf (stdout,"string in buf=%s\n", buf);
     fprintf (stdout,"number of bytes read=%d\n", bytes);
  }

  close(fildes);
  fprintf (stdout,"remove testfile\n");
  remove (path);
}

/*
 * Copyright (C) ANTRIX Inc.
 */
```

```
/* readv.c
 * This program reads data from a file
 * using function readv
 */

#include <stdio.h>
#include <stdlib.h>
#include <fcntl.h>
#include <unistd.h>
#include <sys/types.h>
#include <sys/uio.h>
#include <sys/stat.h>
#include <errno.h>

#define  PERM_ALL    (S_IRWXU | S_IRWXG | S_IRWXO)

main()
{
  int     i, bytes, fildes;
  int     len1, len2, compare;
  char    *str1 = "hello";
  char    *str2 = "world";
  struct  iovec iov_write[2], iov_read[2];
  char    *file = "testfile";

  len1 = strlen (str1);
  len2 = strlen (str2);
  fprintf (stdout,"create testfile\n");
  fildes = creat (file, PERM_ALL);

  iov_write[0].iov_base = (char *)malloc (len1);
  iov_write[0].iov_len = len1;
  iov_write[0].iov_base = "hello";
  iov_write[1].iov_base = (char *)malloc (len2);
  iov_write[1].iov_len = len2;
  iov_write[1].iov_base = "world";

  fprintf (stdout,"write strings\n");
  writev (fildes, iov_write, 2);

  fprintf (stdout,"close testfile\n");
  close (fildes);

  iov_read[0].iov_base = (char *)malloc (len1);
  iov_read[0].iov_len = len1;
  iov_read[1].iov_base = (char *)malloc (len2);
  iov_read[1].iov_len = len2;

  fprintf (stdout,"open testfile for read only\n");
  fildes = open (file, O_RDONLY);

  fprintf (stdout,"read strings\n");
```

```
        bytes = readv (fildes, iov_read, 2);
        if ( bytes > 0 )
            fprintf (stdout,"readv() call successful\n");
        else {
            fprintf (stderr,"ERROR: readv() call failed\n");
            fprintf (stderr,"ERROR: %s\n", strerror(errno));
        }
        for ( i = 0; i < 2; i++ ) {
            compare = memcmp (iov_read[i].iov_base, iov_write[i].iov_base,
                              iov_write[i].iov_len);
            if (compare == 0)
                fprintf (stdout,"iov_read[i].iov_base=%s\n", iov_read[i].iov_base);
        }

        fprintf (stdout,"remove testfile\n");
        remove (file);
}
```

NAME

readdir — read directory

SYNOPSIS

OH   `#include <sys/types.h>`
`#include <dirent.h>`

`struct dirent *readdir(DIR *dirp);`

DESCRIPTION

The type **DIR**, which is defined in the header **<dirent.h>**, represents a *directory stream*, which is an ordered sequence of all the directory entries in a particular directory. Directory entries represent files; files may be removed from a directory or added to a directory asynchronously to the operation of *readdir*( ).

The *readdir*( ) function returns a pointer to a structure representing the directory entry at the current position in the directory stream specified by the argument *dirp*, and positions the directory stream at the next entry. It returns a null pointer upon reaching the end of the directory stream. The structure *dirent* defined by the **<dirent.h>** header describes a directory entry.

EX   If entries for dot or dot-dot exist, one entry will be returned for dot and one entry will be returned for dot-dot; otherwise they will not be returned.

The pointer returned by *readdir*( ) points to data which may be overwritten by another call to *readdir*( ) on the same directory stream. This data is not overwritten by another call to *readdir*( ) on a different directory stream.

If a file is removed from or added to the directory after the most recent call to *opendir*( ) or *rewinddir*( ), whether a subsequent call to *readdir*( ) returns an entry for that file is unspecified.

The *readdir*( ) function may buffer several directory entries per actual read operation; *readdir*( ) marks for update the *st_atime* field of the directory each time the directory is actually read.

EX   After a call to *fork*( ), either the parent or child (but not both) may continue processing the directory stream using *readdir*( ), *rewinddir*( ) or *seekdir*( ). If both the parent and child processes use these functions, the result is undefined.

UX   If the entry names a symbolic link, the value of the **d_ino** member is unspecified.

RETURN VALUE

Upon successful completion, *readdir*( ) returns a pointer to an object of type **struct dirent**. When an error is encountered, a null pointer is returned and *errno* is set to indicate the error. When the end of the directory is encountered, a null pointer is returned and *errno* is not changed.

ERRORS

The *readdir*( ) function may fail if:

[EBADF]   The *dirp* argument does not refer to an open directory stream.

UX   [ENOENT]   The current position of the directory stream is invalid.

EXAMPLES

The following sample code will search the current directory for the entry *name*:

```
dirp = opendir(".");
while ((dp = readdir(dirp)) != NULL)
        if (strcmp(dp->d_name, name) == 0) {
                closedir(dirp);
                return FOUND;
        }
closedir(dirp);
return NOT_FOUND;
```

APPLICATION USAGE

The *readdir( )* function should be used in conjunction with *opendir( )*, *closedir( )* and *rewinddir( )* to examine the contents of the directory. As *readdir( )* returns a null pointer both at the end of the directory and on error, an application wishing to check for error situations should set *errno* to 0, then call *readdir( )*, then check *errno* and if it is non-zero, assume an error has occurred.

SEE ALSO

closedir( ), *lstat( )*, *opendir( )*, *rewinddir( )*, *symlink( )*, **<dirent.h>**, **<sys/types.h>**.

EXAMPLE

```
/*
 * Copyright (C) ANTRIX Inc.
 */

/* readdir.c
 * This program reads directory entries in a particular directory
 * using function readdir.
 */

#include <stdio.h>
#include <stdlib.h>
#include <sys/types.h>
#include <dirent.h>
#include <sys/stat.h>
#include <errno.h>

#define  PERM_ALL    (S_IRWXU | S_IRWXG | S_IRWXO)

main()
{
  int     readdir_value;
  int     i, compare;
  long    location;
  DIR     *dirp;
  struct  dirent *buf1, *buf2;
  struct  dirent *dirent_save;
  char    *root = "testdir";
  char    *leaf = "testdir/subdir";

  fprintf (stdout,"make test directories\n");
  mkdir (root, PERM_ALL);
  mkdir (leaf, PERM_ALL);
```

```
        fprintf (stdout,"open testdir directory\n");
        dirp = opendir (root);

        fprintf (stdout,"directory names in testdir are:\n");
        for ( i = 0; i < 3; i++ ) {
            location = telldir (dirp);
            dirent_save = readdir (dirp);
            fprintf (stdout,"%s\n", dirent_save->d_name);
        }

        fprintf (stdout,"close and remove directories\n");
        closedir (dirp);
        rmdir (leaf);
        rmdir (root);
    }
```

NAME

readlink — read the contents of a symbolic link

SYNOPSIS

UX
```
#include <unistd.h>
```

```
int readlink(const char *path, char *buf, size_t bufsiz);
```

DESCRIPTION

The *readlink( )* function places the contents of the symbolic link referred to by *path* in the buffer *buf* which has size *bufsiz*. If the number of bytes in the symbolic link is less than *bufsiz*, the contents of the remainder of *buf* are unspecified.

RETURN VALUE

Upon successful completion, *readlink( )* returns the count of bytes placed in the buffer. Otherwise, it returns a value of −1, leaves the buffer unchanged, and sets *errno* to indicate the error.

ERRORS

The *readlink( )* function will fail if:

[EACCES]   Search permission is denied for a component of the path prefix of *path*.

[EINVAL]   The *path* argument names a file that is not a symbolic link.

[EIO]   An I/O error occurred while reading from the file system.

[ENOENT]   A component of *path* does not name an existing file or *path* is an empty string.

[ELOOP]   Too many symbolic links were encountered in resolving *path*.

[ENAMETOOLONG]
              The length of *path* exceeds {PATH_MAX}, or a pathname component is longer than {NAME_MAX}.

[ENOTDIR]   A component of the path prefix is not a directory.

The *readlink( )* function may fail if:

[EACCES]   Read permission is denied for the directory.

[ENAMETOOLONG]
              Pathname resolution of a symbolic link produced an intermediate result whose length exceeds {PATH_MAX}.

APPLICATION USAGE

Portable applications should not assume that the returned contents of the symbolic link are null-terminated.

SEE ALSO

stat( ), *symlink( )*, **<unistd.h>**.

EXAMPLE

```
/*
 * Copyright (C) ANTRIX Inc.
 */

/* readlink.c
 * This program reads the value of a symbolic link
 * using function readlink
 */
```

```
#include <stdio.h>
#include <stdlib.h>
#include <unistd.h>
#include <fcntl.h>
#include <sys/stat.h>
#include <errno.h>

#define  PERM_ALL   (S_IRWXU | S_IRWXG | S_IRWXO)

main()
{
  int     bytes;
  int     fildes, length;
  char    buf[12];
  char    *string = "hello world";
  char    *file1 = "testfile1";
  char    *file2 = "testfile2";

  fprintf (stdout,"create testfile1\n");
  fildes = creat (file1, PERM_ALL);

  fprintf (stdout,"write string\n");
  write (fildes, string, strlen(string));

  fprintf (stdout,"close testfile1\n");
  close (fildes);

  fprintf (stdout,"create symbolic link testfile2\n");
  symlink (file1, file2);

  memset (buf, ' ', sizeof(buf));
  length = strlen (file1);

  fprintf (stdout,"read link name in testfile2\n");
  bytes = readlink (file2, buf, length);
  if ( bytes == length ) {
     fprintf (stdout,"readlink() call successful\n");
     fprintf (stdout,"filename in buf=%s\n", buf);
     fprintf (stdout,"number of bytes read=%d\n", bytes);
  }
  else {
     fprintf (stderr,"ERROR: readlink() call failed\n");
     fprintf (stderr,"ERROR: %s\n", strerror(errno));
  }
  fprintf (stdout,"remove testfiles\n");
  unlink (file2);
  remove (file1);
}
```

NAME

readv — vectored read from file

SYNOPSIS

UX

```
#include <sys/uio.h>

ssize_t readv(int fildes, const struct iovec *iov, int iovcnt);
```

DESCRIPTION

Refer to *read*( ).

EXAMPLE

```
/*
 * Copyright (C) ANTRIX Inc.
 */

/* readv.c
 * This program reads data from a file
 * using function readv
 */

#include <stdio.h>
#include <stdlib.h>
#include <fcntl.h>
#include <unistd.h>
#include <sys/types.h>
#include <sys/uio.h>
#include <sys/stat.h>
#include <errno.h>

#define  PERM_ALL   (S_IRWXU | S_IRWXG | S_IRWXO)

main()
{
  int     i, bytes, fildes;
  int     len1, len2, compare;
  char    *str1 = "hello";
  char    *str2 = "world";
  struct  iovec iov_write[2], iov_read[2];
  char    *file = "testfile";

  len1 = strlen (str1);
  len2 = strlen (str2);
  fprintf (stdout,"create testfile\n");
  fildes = creat (file, PERM_ALL);

  iov_write[0].iov_base = (char *)malloc (len1);
  iov_write[0].iov_len = len1;
  iov_write[0].iov_base = "hello";
  iov_write[1].iov_base = (char *)malloc (len2);
  iov_write[1].iov_len = len2;
  iov_write[1].iov_base = "world";

  fprintf (stdout,"write strings\n");
```

```
writev (fildes, iov_write, 2);

fprintf (stdout,"close testfile\n");
close (fildes);

iov_read[0].iov_base = (char *)malloc (len1);
iov_read[0].iov_len = len1;
iov_read[1].iov_base = (char *)malloc (len2);
iov_read[1].iov_len = len2;

fprintf (stdout,"open testfile for read only\n");
fildes = open (file, O_RDONLY);

fprintf (stdout,"read strings\n");
bytes = readv (fildes, iov_read, 2);
if ( bytes > 0 )
    fprintf (stdout,"readv() call successful\n");
else {
    fprintf (stderr,"ERROR: readv() call failed\n");
    fprintf (stderr,"ERROR: %s\n", strerror(errno));
}
for ( i = 0; i < 2; i++ ) {
    compare = memcmp (iov_read[i].iov_base, iov_write[i].iov_base,
                      iov_write[i].iov_len);
    if (compare == 0)
        fprintf (stdout,"iov_read[i].iov_base=%s\n", iov_read[i].iov_base);
}

fprintf (stdout,"remove testfile\n");
remove (file);
}
```

NAME

realloc — memory reallocator

SYNOPSIS

```
#include <stdlib.h>

void *realloc(void *ptr, size_t size);
```

DESCRIPTION

The *realloc( )* function changes the size of the memory object pointed to by *ptr* to the size specified by *size*. The contents of the object will remain unchanged up to the lesser of the new and old sizes. If the new size of the memory object would require movement of the object, the space for the previous instantiation of the object is freed. If the new size is larger, the contents of the newly allocated portion of the object are unspecified. If *size* is 0 and *ptr* is not a null pointer, the object pointed to is freed. If the space cannot be allocated, the object remains unchanged.

If *ptr* is a null pointer, *realloc( )* behaves like *malloc( )* for the specified size.

If *ptr* does not match a pointer returned earlier by *calloc( )*, *malloc( )* or *realloc( )* or if the space has previously been deallocated by a call to *free( )* or *realloc( )*, the behaviour is undefined.

The order and contiguity of storage allocated by successive calls to *realloc( )* is unspecified. The pointer returned if the allocation succeeds is suitably aligned so that it may be assigned to a pointer to any type of object and then used to access such an object in the space allocated (until the space is explicitly freed or reallocated). Each such allocation will yield a pointer to an object disjoint from any other object. The pointer returned points to the start (lowest byte address) of the allocated space. If the space cannot be allocated, a null pointer is returned.

RETURN VALUE

Upon successful completion with a size not equal to 0, *realloc( )* returns a pointer to the (possibly moved) allocated space. If *size* is 0, either a null pointer or a unique pointer that can be successfully passed to *free( )* is returned. If there is not enough available memory, *realloc( )*

EX returns a null pointer and sets *errno* to [ENOMEM].

ERRORS

The *realloc( )* function will fail if:

EX [ENOMEM] Insufficient memory is available.

SEE ALSO

calloc( ), *free( )*, *malloc( )*, **<stdlib.h>**.

EXAMPLE

```
/*
 * Copyright (C) ANTRIX Inc.
 */

/* realloc.c
 * This program changes the size of the memory object pointed
 * to by ptr to the size using function realloc.
 */

#include <stdio.h>
#include <stdlib.h>
#include <malloc.h>
#include <errno.h>
```

```
main()
{
  char   *realloc_value;
  char   *ptr;
  char   *str1 = "Hello";
  char   *str2 = "World";
  int    strlen1, strlen2;

  strlen1 = strlen (str1);
  fprintf (stdout,"allocate memory\n");
  ptr = (char *)malloc (strlen1);
  strcpy (ptr, str1);
  fprintf (stdout,"allocated string=%s\n", ptr);

  strlen2 = strlen (str2);
  fprintf (stdout,"reallocate memory\n");
  realloc_value = (char *)realloc (ptr, strlen2);
  strcpy (ptr+strlen1, str2);
  if ( realloc_value != (char *)0 ) {
      fprintf (stdout,"realloc() call successful\n");
      fprintf (stdout,"re-allocated string=%s\n", ptr);
  }
  else {
      fprintf (stderr,"ERROR: realloc() call failed\n");
      fprintf (stderr,"ERROR: %s\n", strerror(errno));
  }
}
```

NAME

realpath — resolve pathname

SYNOPSIS

UX
```
#include <stdlib.h>

char *realpath(const char *file_name, char *resolved_name);
```

DESCRIPTION

The *realpath*( ) function derives, from the pathname pointed to by *file_name*, an absolute pathname that names the same file, whose resolution does not involve ".", "..", or symbolic links. The generated pathname is stored, up to a maximum of {PATH_MAX} bytes, in the buffer pointed to by *resolved_name*.

RETURN VALUE

On successful completion, *realpath*( ) returns a pointer to the resolved name. Otherwise, *realpath*( ) returns a null pointer and sets *errno* to indicate the error, and the contents of the buffer pointed to by *resolved_name* are undefined.

ERRORS

The *realpath*( ) function will fail if:

[EACCES]   Read or search permission was denied for a component of *file_name*.

[EINVAL]   Either the *file_name* or *resolved_name* argument is a null pointer.

[EIO]   An error occurred while reading from the file system.

[ELOOP]   Too many symbolic links were encountered in resolving *path*.

[ENAMETOOLONG]
                 The *file_name* argument is longer than {PATH_MAX} or a pathname component is longer than {NAME_MAX}.

[ENOENT]   A component of *file_name* does not name an existing file or *file_name* points to an empty string.

[ENOTDIR]   A component of the path prefix is not a directory.

The *realpath*( ) function may fail if:

[ENAMETOOLONG]
                 Pathname resolution of a symbolic link produced an intermediate result whose length exceeds {PATH_MAX}.

[ENOMEM]   Insufficient storage space is available.

SEE ALSO

getcwd( ), *sysconf*( ), **<stdlib.h>**.

EXAMPLE

```
/*
 * Copyright (C) ANTRIX Inc.
 */

/* realpath.c
 * This program resolves all links an references to . and .. in filename
 * using function realpath.
 */

#include <stdio.h>
```

```
#include <stdlib.h>
#include <unistd.h>
#include <fcntl.h>
#include <sys/stat.h>
#include <limits.h>
#include <errno.h>

#define  PATH_LEN  255
#define  PERM_ALL  (S_IRWXU | S_IRWXG | S_IRWXO)

main()
{
  int   fildes;
  char  *realpath_value;
  char  *file = "./testfile";
  char  resolved_name[PATH_LEN];

  memset(resolved_name, ' ', PATH_LEN);

  fprintf (stdout,"create testfile\n");
  fildes = creat (file, PERM_ALL);

  fprintf (stdout,"get resolved path name\n");
  realpath_value = realpath (file, resolved_name);
  if ( realpath_value != (char *)0 ) {
     fprintf (stdout,"realpath() call successful\n");
     fprintf (stdout,"realpath_value = %s\n", realpath_value);
     fprintf (stdout,"resolved_name = %s\n", resolved_name);
  }
  else {
     fprintf (stderr,"ERROR: realpath() call failed\n");
     fprintf (stderr,"ERROR: %s\n", strerror(errno));
  }

  close(fildes);
  fprintf (stdout,"remove testfile\n");
  remove (file);
}
```

NAME

re_comp, re_exec — compile and execute regular expressions (**TO BE WITHDRAWN**)

SYNOPSIS

UX   `#include <re_comp.h>`

`char *re_comp(const char *string);`

`int re_exec(const char *string);`

DESCRIPTION

The *re_comp*( ) function converts a regular expression string (RE) into an internal form suitable for pattern matching. The *re_exec*( ) function compares the string pointed to by the *string* argument with the last regular expression passed to *re_comp*( ).

If *re_comp*( ) is called with a null pointer argument, the current regular expression remains unchanged.

Strings passed to both *re_comp*( ) and *re_exec*( ) must be terminated by a null byte, and may include newline characters.

The *re_comp*( ) and *re_exec*( ) functions support *simple regular expressions*, which are defined below.

The following one-character REs match a single character:

1.1 An ordinary character (not one of those discussed in 1.2 below) is a one-character RE that matches itself.

1.2 A backslash (\) followed by any special character is a one-character RE that matches the special character itself. The special characters are:

    a. **.**, *****, **[**, and **** (period, asterisk, left square bracket, and backslash, respectively), which are always special, except when they appear within square brackets (**[]**; see 1.4 below).

    b. **^** (caret or circumflex), which is special at the beginning of an entire RE (see 3.1 and 3.2 below), or when it immediately follows the left of a pair of square brackets (**[]**) (see 1.4 below).

    c. **$** (dollar symbol), which is special at the end of an entire RE (see 3.2 below).

    d. The character used to bound (delimit) an entire RE, which is special for that RE.

1.3 A period (**.**) is a one-character RE that matches any character except new-line.

1.4 A non-empty string of characters enclosed in square brackets (**[]**) is a one-character RE that matches any one character in that string. If, however, the first character of the string is a circumflex (**^**), the one-character RE matches any character except new-line and the remaining characters in the string. The **^** has this special meaning only if it occurs first in the string. The minus (**-**) may be used to indicate a range of consecutive ASCII characters; for example, **[0-9]** is equivalent to **[0123456789]**. The **-** loses this special meaning if it occurs first (after an initial **^**, if any) or last in the string. The right square bracket (**]**) does not terminate such a string when it is the first character within it (after an initial **^**, if any); for example, **[]a-f]** matches either a right square bracket (**]**) or one of the letters **a** through **f** inclusive. The four characters listed in 1.2.a above stand for themselves within such a string of characters.

The following rules may be used to construct REs from one-character REs:

2.1 A one-character RE is a RE that matches whatever the one-character RE matches.

2.2 A one-character RE followed by an asterisk (*) is a RE that matches zero or more occurrences of the one-character RE. If there is any choice, the longest leftmost string that permits a match is chosen.

2.3 A one-character RE followed by \{*m*\}, \{*m*,\}, or \{*m,n*\} is a RE that matches a range of occurrences of the one-character RE. The values of *m* and *n* must be non-negative integers less than 256; \{*m*\} matches exactly *m* occurrences; \{*m*,\} matches at least *m* occurrences; \{*m,n*\} matches any number of occurrences between *m* and *n* inclusive. Whenever a choice exists, the RE matches as many occurrences as possible.

2.4 The concatenation of REs is a RE that matches the concatenation of the strings matched by each component of the RE.

2.5 A RE enclosed between the character sequences \(and \) is a RE that matches whatever the unadorned RE matches.

2.6 The expression \n matches the same string of characters as was matched by an expression enclosed between \(and \) earlier in the same RE. Here *n* is a digit; the sub-expression specified is that beginning with the *n*-th occurrence of \(counting from the left. For example, the expression ^\(.*\)\1$ matches a line consisting of two repeated appearances of the same string.

Finally, an entire RE may be constrained to match only an initial segment or final segment of a line (or both).

3.1 A circumflex (^) at the beginning of an entire RE constrains that RE to match an initial segment of a line.

3.2 A dollar symbol ($) at the end of an entire RE constrains that RE to match a final segment of a line. The construction ^*entire RE*$ constrains the entire RE to match the entire line.

The null RE (that is, //) is equivalent to the last RE encountered.

The behaviour of *re_comp*( ) and *re_exec*( ) in locales other than the POSIX locale is unspecified.

RETURN VALUE

The *re_comp*( ) function returns a null pointer when the string pointed to by the *string* argument is successfully converted. Otherwise, a pointer to an unspecified error message string is returned.

Upon successful completion, *re_exec*( ) returns 1 if *string* matches the last compiled regular expression. Otherwise, *re_exec*( ) returns 0 if *string* fails to match the last compiled regular expression, and −1 if the compiled regular expression is invalid (indicating an internal error).

ERRORS

No errors are defined.

APPLICATION USAGE

For portability to implementations conforming to earlier versions of this document, *regcomp*( ) and *regexec*( ) are preferred to these functions.

SEE ALSO

regcomp( ), **<re_comp.h>**.

EXAMPLE

```
/*
 * Copyright (C) ANTRIX Inc.
 */

/* re_comp.c
 * This program takes an input a regular expression and
 * produces a compiled expression using function re_comp.
 */

#include <stdio.h>
#include <stdlib.h>
#include <errno.h>

#define STRSIZE 100

char instring[STRSIZE];

main()
{
  char  *re_comp_value;
  int   re_exec_value;
  char string[10*STRSIZE];
  char expbuf[STRSIZE];

  strcpy(instring, "^T");
  strcpy(string, "This is a test line");

  fprintf(stdout, "Produce compiled expression\n");
  re_comp_value = re_comp(instring);
  if (re_comp_value == (char *)0)
      fprintf(stdout, "re_comp_value=%s\n", re_comp_value);
  else {
      fprintf(stderr, "ERORR: re_comp call failed\n");
      fprintf(stderr, "ERORR: re_comp_value=%s\n", re_comp_value);
  }

  fprintf(stdout, "Match string beginning with T\n");
  re_exec_value = re_exec(string);
  fprintf(stdout, "re_exec_value=%d\n", re_exec_value);
}


/*
 * Copyright (C) ANTRIX Inc.
 */

/* re_exec.c
 * This program matches a compiled expressing using
 * function re_comp.
 */
```

```
#include <stdio.h>
#include <stdlib.h>
#include <errno.h>

#define STRSIZE 100

char instring[STRSIZE];

main()
{
  char  *re_comp_value;
  int    re_exec_value;
  char string[10*STRSIZE];
  char expbuf[STRSIZE];

  strcpy(instring, "^T");
  strcpy(string, "This is a test line");

  fprintf(stdout, "Produce compiled expression\n");
  re_comp_value = re_comp(instring);
  if (re_comp_value == (char *)0)
      fprintf(stdout, "re_comp_value=%s\n", re_comp_value);
  else {
      fprintf(stderr, "ERORR: re_comp call failed\n");
      fprintf(stderr, "ERORR: re_comp_value=%s\n", re_comp_value);
  }

  fprintf(stdout, "Match string beginning with T\n");
  re_exec_value = re_exec(string);
  if (re_exec_value == 1) {
      fprintf(stdout, "re_exec call successful\n");
      fprintf(stdout, "re_exec_value=%d\n", re_exec_value);
  }
  else {
      fprintf(stderr, "ERROR: re_exec call failed\n");
      fprintf(stderr, "%d\n", re_exec_value);
  }
}
```

NAME

regcmp, regex — compile and execute regular expression (**TO BE WITHDRAWN**)

SYNOPSIS

UX
```
#include <libgen.h>

char *regcmp (const char *string1 , ... /*, (char *)0 */);

char *regex (const char *re, const char *subject , ... );

extern char *__loc1;
```

DESCRIPTION

The *regcmp*( ) function compiles a regular expression consisting of the concatenated arguments and returns a pointer to the compiled form. The end of arguments is indicated by a null pointer. The *malloc*( ) function is used to create space for the compiled form. It is the process' responsibility to free unneeded space so allocated. A null pointer returned from *regcmp*( ) indicates an invalid argument.

The *regex*( ) function executes a compiled pattern against the *subject* string. Additional arguments of type **char** * must be passed to receive matched subexpressions back. If an insufficient number of arguments is passed to accept all the values that the regular expression returns, the behaviour is undefined. A global character pointer _ _**loc1** points to the first matched character in the *subject* string. Both *regcmp*( ) and *regex*( ) were largely borrowed from the editor, and are defined in *re_comp*( ), but the syntax and semantics have been changed slightly. The following are the valid symbols and their associated meanings:

[]*.^ These symbols retain their meaning as defined in *re_comp*().

$ Matches the end of the string; \n matches a new-line.

- Used within brackets, the hyphen signifies an ASCII character range. For example, [a-z] is equivalent to [abcd ... xyz] . The - can represent itself only if used as the first or last character. For example, the character class expression []-] matches the characters] and -.

+ A regular expression followed by + means one or more times. For example, [0-9]+ is equivalent to [0-9][0-9]* .

{*m*} {*m*,} {*m*,*u*}
Integer values enclosed in { } indicate the number of times the preceding regular expression can be applied. The value *m* is the minimum number and *u* is a number, less than 256, which is the maximum. If the value of either *m* or *u* is 256 or greater, the behaviour is undefined. The syntax **{*m*}** indicates the exact number of times the regular expression can be applied. The syntax **{*m*,}** is analogous to **{*m*,infinity}**. The plus (+) and asterisk (*) operations are equivalent to **{1,}** and **{0,}** respectively.

(...)$*n* The value of the enclosed regular expression is returned. The value is stored in the (*n*+1)th argument following the *subject* argument. A maximum of ten enclosed regular expressions are allowed. The *regex*( ) function makes its assignments unconditionally.

(...) Parentheses are used for grouping. An operator, such as *, **+**, or { }, can work on a single character or a regular expression enclosed in parentheses. For example, (a*(cb+)*)$0 .

Since all of the above defined symbols are special characters, they must be escaped to be used as themselves.

The behaviour of *regcmp*( ) and *regex*( ) in locales other than the POSIX locale is unspecified.

RETURN VALUE

Upon successful completion, *regcmp*( ) returns a pointer to the compiled regular expression. Otherwise, a null pointer is returned and *errno* may be set to indicate the error.

Upon successful completion, *regex*( ) returns a pointer to the next unmatched character in the subject string. Otherwise, a null pointer is returned.

The *regex*( ) function returns a null pointer on failure, or a pointer to the next unmatched character on success.

ERRORS

The *regcmp*( ) function may fail if:

[ENOMEM]   Insufficient storage space was available.

No errors are defined for *regex*( ).

APPLICATION USAGE

For portability to implementations conforming to earlier versions of this document, *regcomp*( ) is preferred over this function.

User programs that use *regcmp*( ) may run out of memory if *regcmp*( ) is called iteratively without freeing compiled regular expression strings that are no longer required.

SEE ALSO

malloc( ), *regcomp*( ), **<libgen.h>**.

NAME

regcomp, regexec, regerror, regfree — regular expression matching

SYNOPSIS

OH
```
#include <sys/types.h>
#include <regex.h>

int regcomp(regex_t *preg, const char *pattern, int cflags);

int regexec(const regex_t *preg, const char *string,
            size_t nmatch, regmatch_t pmatch[], int eflags);

size_t regerror(int errcode, const regex_t *preg,
                char *errbuf, size_t errbuf_size);

void regfree(regex_t *preg);
```

DESCRIPTION

These functions interpret *basic* and *extended* regular expressions as described in the **XBD** specification, **Chapter 7**, **Regular Expressions**.

The structure type **regex_t** contains at least the following member:

Member Type	Member Name	Description
size_t	re_nsub	Number of parenthesised subexpressions.

The structure type **regmatch_t** contains at least the following members:

Member Type	Member Name	Description
regoff_t	rm_so	Byte offset from start of *string* to start of substring.
regoff_t	rm_eo	Byte offset from start of *string* of the first character after the end of substring.

The *regcomp( )* function will compile the regular expression contained in the string pointed to by the *pattern* argument and place the results in the structure pointed to by *preg*. The *cflags* argument is the bitwise inclusive OR of zero or more of the following flags, which are defined in the header **<regex.h>**:

REG_EXTENDED   Use Extended Regular Expressions.

REG_ICASE   Ignore case in match. (See the **XBD** specification, **Chapter 7**, **Regular Expressions**.)

REG_NOSUB   Report only success/fail in *regexec( )*.

REG_NEWLINE   Change the handling of newline characters, as described in the text.

The default regular expression type for *pattern* is a Basic Regular Expression. The application can specify Extended Regular Expressions using the REG_EXTENDED *cflags* flag.

On successful completion, it returns 0; otherwise it returns non-zero, and the content of *preg* is undefined.

If the REG_NOSUB flag was not set in *cflags*, then *regcomp( )* will set *re_nsub* to the number of parenthesised subexpressions (delimited by \(\) in basic regular expressions or ( ) in extended regular expressions) found in *pattern*.

The *regexec*( ) function compares the null-terminated string specified by *string* with the compiled regular expression *preg* initialised by a previous call to *regcomp*( ). If it finds a match, *regexec*( ) returns 0; otherwise it returns non-zero indicating either no match or an error. The *eflags* argument is the bitwise inclusive OR of zero or more of the following flags, which are defined in the header **<regex.h>**:

REG_NOTBOL   The first character of the string pointed to by *string* is not the beginning of the line. Therefore, the circumflex character (^), when taken as a special character, will not match the beginning of *string*.

REG_NOTEOL   The last character of the string pointed to by *string* is not the end of the line. Therefore, the dollar sign ($), when taken as a special character, will not match the end of *string*.

If *nmatch* is 0 or REG_NOSUB was set in the *cflags* argument to *regcomp*( ), then *regexec*( ) will ignore the *pmatch* argument. Otherwise, the *pmatch* argument must point to an array with at least *nmatch* elements, and *regexec*( ) will fill in the elements of that array with offsets of the substrings of *string* that correspond to the parenthesised subexpressions of *pattern*: *pmatch*[*i*].*rm_so* will be the byte offset of the beginning and *pmatch*[*i*].*rm_eo* will be one greater than the byte offset of the end of substring *i*. (Subexpression *i* begins at the *i*th matched open parenthesis, counting from 1.) Offsets in *pmatch*[0] identify the substring that corresponds to the entire regular expression. Unused elements of *pmatch* up to *pmatch*[*nmatch*–1] will be filled with –1. If there are more than *nmatch* subexpressions in *pattern* (*pattern* itself counts as a subexpression), then *regexec*( ) will still do the match, but will record only the first *nmatch* substrings.

When matching a basic or extended regular expression, any given parenthesised subexpression of *pattern* might participate in the match of several different substrings of *string*, or it might not match any substring even though the pattern as a whole did match. The following rules are used to determine which substrings to report in *pmatch* when matching regular expressions:

1. If subexpression *i* in a regular expression is not contained within another subexpression, and it participated in the match several times, then the byte offsets in *pmatch*[*i*] will delimit the last such match.

2. If subexpression *i* is not contained within another subexpression, and it did not participate in an otherwise successful match, the byte offsets in *pmatch*[*i*] will be –1. A subexpression does not participate in the match when:

    * or \{ \} appears immediately after the subexpression in a basic regular expression, or *, ?, or { } appears immediately after the subexpression in an extended regular expression, and the subexpression did not match (matched 0 times)

    or:

    | is used in an extended regular expression to select this subexpression or another, and the other subexpression matched.

3. If subexpression *i* is contained within another subexpression *j*, and *i* is not contained within any other subexpression that is contained within *j*, and a match of subexpression *j* is reported in *pmatch*[*j*], then the match or non-match of subexpression *i* reported in *pmatch*[*i*] will be as described in 1. and 2. above, but within the substring reported in *pmatch*[*j*] rather than the whole string.

4. If subexpression *i* is contained in subexpression *j*, and the byte offsets in *pmatch*[*j*] are –1, then the pointers in *pmatch*[*i*] also will be –1.

5. If subexpression *i* matched a zero-length string, then both byte offsets in *pmatch*[*i*] will be the byte offset of the character or null terminator immediately following the zero-length string.

If, when *regexec*( ) is called, the locale is different from when the regular expression was compiled, the result is undefined.

If REG_NEWLINE is not set in *cflags*, then a newline character in *pattern* or *string* will be treated as an ordinary character. If REG_NEWLINE is set, then newline will be treated as an ordinary character except as follows:

1. A newline character in *string* will not be matched by a period outside a bracket expression or by any form of a non-matching list (see the **XBD** specification, **Chapter 7**, **Regular Expressions**).

2. A circumflex (ˆ) in *pattern*, when used to specify expression anchoring (see the **XBD** specification, **Section 7.3.8**, **BRE Expression Anchoring**), will match the zero-length string immediately after a newline in *string*, regardless of the setting of REG_NOTBOL.

3. A dollar-sign ($) in *pattern*, when used to specify expression anchoring, will match the zero-length string immediately before a newline in *string*, regardless of the setting of REG_NOTEOL.

The *regfree*( ) function frees any memory allocated by *regcomp*( ) associated with *preg*.

The following constants are defined as error return values:

REG_NOMATCH	*regexec*( ) failed to match.
REG_BADPAT	Invalid regular expression.
REG_ECOLLATE	Invalid collating element referenced.
REG_ECTYPE	Invalid character class type referenced.
REG_EESCAPE	Trailing \ in pattern.
REG_ESUBREG	Number in *digit* invalid or in error.
REG_EBRACK	[ ] imbalance.
REG_ENOSYS	The function is not supported.
REG_EPAREN	\(\) or ( ) imbalance.
REG_EBRACE	\{ \} imbalance.
REG_BADBR	Content of \{ \} invalid: not a number, number too large, more than two numbers, first larger than second.
REG_ERANGE	Invalid endpoint in range expression.
REG_ESPACE	Out of memory.
REG_BADRPT	?, * or + not preceded by valid regular expression.

The *regerror*( ) function provides a mapping from error codes returned by *regcomp*( ) and *regexec*( ) to unspecified printable strings. It generates a string corresponding to the value of the *errcode* argument, which must be the last non-zero value returned by *regcomp*( ) or *regexec*( ) with the given value of *preg*. If *errcode* is not such a value, the content of the generated string is unspecified.

If *preg* is a null pointer, but *errcode* is a value returned by a previous call to *regexec*( ) or *regcomp*( ), the *regerror*( ) still generates an error string corresponding to the value of *errcode*, but it might not be as detailed under some implementations.

If the *errbuf_size* argument is not 0, *regerror( )* will place the generated string into the buffer of size *errbuf_size* bytes pointed to by *errbuf*. If the string (including the terminating null) cannot fit in the buffer, *regerror( )* will truncate the string and null-terminate the result.

If *errbuf_size* is 0, *regerror( )* ignores the *errbuf* argument, and returns the size of the buffer needed to hold the generated string.

If the *preg* argument to *regexec( )* or *regfree( )* is not a compiled regular expression returned by *regcomp( )*, the result is undefined. A *preg* is no longer treated as a compiled regular expression after it is given to *regfree( )*.

RETURN VALUE

On successful completion, the *regcomp( )* function returns 0. Otherwise, it returns an integer value indicating an error as described in **<regex.h>**, and the content of *preg* is undefined.

On successful completion, the *regexec( )* function returns 0. Otherwise it returns REG_NOMATCH to indicate no match, or REG_ENOSYS to indicate that the function is not supported.

Upon successful completion, the *regerror( )* function returns the number of bytes needed to hold the entire generated string. Otherwise, it returns 0 to indicate that the function is not implemented.

The *regfree( )* function returns no value.

ERRORS

No errors are defined.

EXAMPLES

```
#include <regex.h>

/*
 * Match string against the extended regular expression in
 * pattern, treating errors as no match.
 *
 * return 1 for match, 0 for no match
 */

int
match(const char *string, char *pattern)
{
        int     status;
        regex_t         re;

        if (regcomp(&re, pattern, REG_EXTENDED | REG_NOSUB) != 0) {
                return(0);      /* report error */
        }
        status = regexec(&re, string, (size_t) 0, NULL, 0);
        regfree(&re);
        if (status != 0) {
                return(0);      /* report error */
        }
        return(1);
}
```

The following demonstrates how the REG_NOTBOL flag could be used with *regexec*( ) to find all substrings in a line that match a pattern supplied by a user. (For simplicity of the example, very little error checking is done.)

```
(void) regcomp (&re, pattern, 0);
/* this call to regexec() finds the first match on the line */
error = regexec (&re, &buffer[0], 1, &pm, 0);
while (error == 0) {/* while matches found */
        /* substring found between pm.rm_so and pm.rm_eo */
        /* This call to regexec() finds the next match */
        error = regexec (&re, buffer + pm.rm_eo, 1, &pm, REG_NOTBOL);
}
```

APPLICATION USAGE

An application could use:

```
regerror(code,preg,(char *)NULL,(size_t)0)
```

to find out how big a buffer is needed for the generated string, *malloc*( ) a buffer to hold the string, and then call *regerror*( ) again to get the string. Alternately, it could allocate a fixed, static buffer that is big enough to hold most strings, and then use *malloc*( ) to allocate a larger buffer if it finds that this is too small.

To match a pattern as described in the **XCU** specification, **Section 2.13**, **Pattern Matching Notation** use the *fnmatch*( ) function.

SEE ALSO

fnmatch( ), *glob*( ), **<regex.h>**, **<sys/types.h>**.

EXAMPLE

```
/*
 * Copyright (C) ANTRIX Inc.
 */

/* regcomp.c
 * This program compiles the regular expression contained in the
 * string pointed to by the pattern argument and place the result
 * in the structure pointed to by preg using function regcomp.
 */

#include <stdio.h>
#include <stdlib.h>
#include <sys/types.h>
#include <regex.h>
#include <errno.h>

#define STRSIZE 100

main()
{
  int  regcomp_value;
  regex_t preg;
  char pattern[STRSIZE];

  fprintf(stdout, "compile the expression in the string\n");
  regcomp_value = regcomp(&preg, "^Good.*",(REG_EXTENDED|REG_NOSUB));
```

```
    if ( regcomp_value == 0 )
       fprintf (stdout,"regcomp() call successful\n");
    else {
       fprintf (stderr,"ERROR: regcomp() call failed\n");
       fprintf (stderr,"ERROR: %s\n", strerror(errno));
    }

    strcpy(pattern, "Good Day");

    fprintf(stdout, "compare string with compiled expression\n");
    regexec(&preg, pattern, (size_t)0, NULL, 0);

    fprintf(stdout, "free compile regular expression\n");
    regfree(&preg);
}

/*
 * Copyright (C) ANTRIX Inc.
 */

/* regexec.c
 * This program compiles the regular expression and matches the
 * string pointed to by the pattern argument using function
 * regexec.
 */

#include <stdio.h>
#include <stdlib.h>
#include <sys/types.h>
#include <regex.h>
#include <errno.h>

#define STRSIZE 100

main()
{
  int   regexec_value;
  int   regcomp_value;
  regex_t preg;
  char pattern[STRSIZE];

  fprintf(stdout, "compile the expression in the string\n");
  regcomp_value = regcomp(&preg, "^Check", (REG_EXTENDED|REG_NOSUB));

  strcpy(pattern, "Check regexec");

  fprintf(stdout, "compare string with compiled expression\n");
  regexec_value = regexec(&preg, pattern, (size_t)0, NULL, 0);
  if ( regexec_value == 0 )
     fprintf (stdout,"regexec() call successful\n");
  else {
     fprintf (stderr,"ERROR: regexec() call failed\n");
```

```
            fprintf (stderr,"ERROR: %s\n", strerror(errno));
      }

      fprintf(stdout, "free compile regular expression\n");
      regfree(&preg);
}


/*
 * Copyright (C) ANTRIX Inc.
 */

/* regerror.c
 * This program prints string and mapping of error codes returned
 * by the regcomp and regexec using function regerror.
 */

#include <stdio.h>
#include <stdlib.h>
#include <sys/types.h>
#include <regex.h>
#include <errno.h>

#define STRSIZE 100

main()
{
      int   regcomp_value;
      int   regexec_value;
      regex_t preg;
      char pattern[STRSIZE];
      char errbuf[STRSIZE];

      fprintf(stdout, "compile the expression in the string\n");
      regcomp_value = regcomp(&preg,"<>",(REG_EXTENDED|REG_NOSUB));

      fprintf(stdout, "check for error\n");
      regerror(regcomp_value, &preg, errbuf, STRSIZE);
      if ( regcomp_value == 0 )
          fprintf (stdout,"regcomp() call successful\n");
      else {
          fprintf (stderr,"ERROR: regexec() call failed\n");
          fprintf (stderr,"ERROR: %s\n", strerror(errno));
          fprintf (stderr,"ERROR: %s\n", errbuf);
      }

      fprintf(stdout, "free compile regular expression\n");
      regfree(&preg);
}
```

NAME

regex — execute regular expression (**TO BE WITHDRAWN**)

SYNOPSIS

UX ```
#include <libgen.h>
```

```
char *regex (const char *re, const char *subject , ... );
```

DESCRIPTION

Refer to *regcmp*( ).
```

NAME

advance, compile, step, loc1, loc2, locs — compile and match regular expressions (**TO BE WITHDRAWN**)

SYNOPSIS

EX
```
#define INIT declarations
#define GETC() getc code
#define PEEK() peek code
#define UNGETC() ungetc code
#define RETURN(ptr) return code
#define ERROR(val) error code
```

```
#include <regexp.h>
```

```
char *compile(char *instring, char *expbuf,
              const char *endbuf, int eof);
```

```
int step(const char *string, const char *expbuf);
```

```
int advance(const char *string, const char *expbuf);
```

```
extern char *loc1, *loc2, *locs;
```

DESCRIPTION

These are general-purpose, regular expression-matching functions to be used in programs that perform regular expression matching, using the Regular Expressions described in **Simple Regular Expressions (Historical Version)** on page 667. These functions are defined by the **<regexp.h>** header.

Implementations may also accept internationalised simple regular expressions as input.

Programs must have the following five macros declared before the **#include <regexp.h>** statement. These macros are used by *compile()*. The macros GETC(), PEEKC() and UNGETC() operate on the regular expression given as input to *compile()*.

GETC()   This macro returns the value of the next character (byte) in the regular expression pattern. Successive calls to GETC() should return successive characters of the regular expression.

PEEKC()   This macro returns the next character (byte) in the regular expression. Immediately successive calls to PEEKC() should return the same byte, which should also be the next character returned by GETC().

UNGETC(*c*)   This macro causes the argument *c* to be returned by the next call to GETC() and PEEKC(). No more than one character of pushback is ever needed and this character is guaranteed to be the last character read by GETC(). The value of the macro UNGETC(*c*) is always ignored.

RETURN(*ptr*)   This macro is used on normal exit of the *compile()* function. The value of the argument *ptr* is a pointer to the character after the last character of the compiled regular expression. This is useful to programs that have memory allocation to manage.

ERROR(*val*)   This macro is the abnormal return from *compile()*. The argument *val* is an error number (see the **ERRORS** section below for meanings). This call should never return.

The *step()* and *advance()* functions do pattern matching given a character string and a compiled regular expression as input.

The *compile*( ) function takes as input a simple regular expression (see **Simple Regular Expressions (Historical Version)** on page 667) and produces a compiled expression that can be used with *step*( ) and *advance*( ).

The first parameter *instring* is never used explicitly by *compile*( ) but is useful for programs that pass down different pointers to input characters. It is sometimes used in the INIT declaration (see below). Programs which invoke functions to input characters or have characters in an external array can pass down (**char ***) 0 for this parameter.

The next parameter *expbuf* is a character pointer. It points to the place where the compiled regular expression will be placed.

The parameter *endbuf* is one more than the highest address where the compiled regular expression may be placed. If the compiled expression cannot fit in (*endbuf–expbuf*) bytes, a call to ERROR(50) is made.

The parameter *eof* is the character which marks the end of the regular expression.

Each program that includes the **<regexp.h>** header must have a **#define** statement for INIT. It is used for dependent declarations and initialisations. Most often it is used to set a register variable to point to the beginning of the regular expression so that this register variable can be used in the declarations for GETC( ), PEEKC( ) and UNGETC( ). Otherwise it can be used to declare external variables that might be used by GETC( ), PEEKC( ) and UNGETC( ). See the **EXAMPLES** section below.

The first parameter to *step*( ) is a pointer to a string of characters to be checked for a match. This string should be null-terminated.

The second parameter, *expbuf*, is the compiled regular expression which was obtained by a call to *compile*.

The *step*( ) function returns non-zero if some substring of *string* matches the regular expression in *expbuf*, and 0, if there is no match. If there is a match, two external character pointers are set as a side effect to the call to *step*( ). The variable *loc1* points to the first character that matched the regular expression; the variable *loc2* points to the character after the last character that matches the regular expression. Thus if the regular expression matches the entire input string, *loc1* will point to the first character of *string* and *loc2* will point to the null at the end of *string*.

The *advance*( ) function returns non-zero if the initial substring of *string* matches the regular expression in *expbuf*. If there is a match an external character pointer, *loc2*, is set as a side effect. The variable *loc2* points to the next character in *string* after the last character that matched.

When *advance*( ) encounters a * or \{ \} sequence in the regular expression, it will advance its pointer to the string to be matched as far as possible and will recursively call itself trying to match the rest of the string to the rest of the regular expression. As long as there is no match, *advance*( ) will back up along the string until it finds a match or reaches the point in the string that initially matched the * or \{ \}. It is sometimes desirable to stop this backing up before the initial point in the string is reached. If the external character pointer *locs* is equal to the point in the string at some time during the backing up process, *advance*( ) will break out of the loop that backs up and will return 0.

The external variables *circf*, *sed* and *nbra* are reserved.

Simple Regular Expressions (Historical Version)

A Simple Regular Expression (SRE) specifies a set of character strings. A member of this set of strings is said to be *matched* by the SRE.

A *pattern* is constructed from one or more SREs. An SRE consists of *ordinary characters* or *metacharacters*.

Within a pattern, all alphanumeric characters that are not part of a bracket expression, back-reference or duplication match themselves, that is to say, the SRE pattern *abc*, when applied to a set of strings, will match only those strings containing the character sequence *abc* anywhere in them.

Most other characters also match themselves. However, a small set of characters, known as the *metacharacters*, have special meanings when encountered in patterns. They are described below.

Simple Regular Expression Construction

SREs are constructed as follows:

Expression   Meaning

c　　　　　The character *c*, where *c* is not a special character.

c　　　　The character *c*, where *c* is any character with special meaning, see below.

^　　　　　The beginning of the string being compared.

$　　　　　The end of the string being compared.

.　　　　　Any character.

[*s*]　　　　Any character in the non-empty set *s*, where *s* is a sequence of characters. Ranges may be specified as *c*–*c*. The character] may be included in the set by placing it first in the set. The character – may be included in the set by placing it first or last in the set. The character ^ may be included in the set by placing it anywhere other than first in the set, see below. Ranges in Simple Regular Expressions are only valid if the *LC_COLLATE* category is set to the C locale. Otherwise, the effect of using the range notation is unspecified.

[^*s*]　　　Any character not in the set *s*, where *s* is defined as above.

r*　　　　Zero or more successive occurrences of the regular expression *r*. The longest leftmost match is chosen.

rx　　　　The occurrence of regular expression *r* followed by the occurrence of regular expression *x*. (Concatenation.)

r\\{*m,n*\\}　Any number of *m* through *n* successive occurrences of the regular expression *r*. The regular expression *r*\\{*m*\\} matches exactly *m* occurrences, *r*\\{*m*,\\} matches at least *m* occurrences. The maximum number of occurrences is matched.

\\(*r*\\)　　　The regular expression *r*. The \\(and \\) sequences are ignored.

n　　　　When *n* (where *n* is a number in the range 1 to 9) appears in a concatenated regular expression, it stands for the regular expression *x*, where *x* is the *n*th regular expression enclosed in \\(and \\) sequences that appeared earlier in the concatenated regular expression. For example, in the pattern \\(*r*\\)*x*\\(*y* the \2 matches the regular expression *y*, giving *rxyzy*.

Characters that have special meaning except where they appear within square brackets, [ ] , or are preceded by \ are: . , * , [, \. Other special characters, such as $ have special meaning in more restricted contexts.

The character ˆ at the beginning of an expression permits a successful match only immediately after a newline or at the beginning of each of the strings to which the match is applied, and the character **$** at the end of an expression requires a trailing newline.

Two characters have special meaning only when used within square brackets. The character – denotes a range, [*c–c*], unless it is just after the left square bracket or before the right square bracket, [–*c*] or [*c*–], in which case it has no special meaning. The character ˆ has the meaning *complement of* if it immediately follows the left square bracket, [ˆ*c*]. Elsewhere between brackets, [*c*ˆ], it stands for the ordinary character ˆ. The right square bracket (]) loses its special meaning and represents itself in a bracket expression if it occurs first in the list after any initial circumflex (ˆ) character.

The special meaning of the \ operator can be escaped *only* by preceding it with another \, that is, \\.

SRE Operator Precedence

The precedence of the operators is as shown below:

[. . .]   high precedence
*
concatenation   low precedence

Internationalised SREs

Character expressions within square brackets are constructed as follows:

Expression Meaning

c   The single character *c* where *c* is not a special character.

[[:*class*:]]   A character class expression. Any character of type *class*, as defined by category LC_CTYPE in the program's locale (see the **XBD** specification, **Chapter 5, Locale**). For *class*, one of the following should be substituted:

alpha	a letter
upper	an upper-case letter
lower	a lower-case letter
digit	a decimal digit
xdigit	a hexadecimal digit
alnum	an alphanumeric (letter or digit)
space	a character producing white space in displayed text
punct	a punctuation character
print	a printing character
graph	a character with a visible representation
cntrl	a control character

[[=*c*=]]   An equivalence class. Any collation element defined as having the same relative order in the current collation sequence as *c*. As an example, if **A** and **a** belong to the same equivalence class, then both [[=*A*=]*b*] and [[=*a*=]*b*] are equivalent to [*Aab*].

[[.*cc.*]]   A collating symbol. Multi-character collating elements must be represented as collating symbols to distinguish them from single-character collating elements. As an example, if the string *ch* is a valid collating element, then [[.*ch.*]] will be treated as an element matching the same string of characters, while *ch* will be treated as a simple list of *c* and *h*. If the string is not a valid collating element in the current collating sequence definition, the symbol will be treated as an invalid expression.

[*c–c*]   Any collation element in the character expression range *c–c*, where *c* can identify a collating symbol or an equivalence class. If the character – appears immediately after an opening square bracket, for example, [*–c*], or immediately prior to a closing square bracket, for example, [*c–*], it has no special meaning.

^   Immediately following an opening square bracket, means the complement of, for example, [^*c*]. Otherwise, it has no special meaning.

Within square brackets, a **.** that is not part of a [[.*cc.*]] sequence, or a **:** that is not part of a [[:*class*:]] sequence, or an **=** that is not part of a [[=*c*=]] sequence, matches itself.

SRE Examples

Below are examples of regular expressions:

Pattern	Meaning
ab.d	ab *any character* d
ab.*d	ab *any sequence of characters (including none)* d
ab[xyz]d	ab *one of* x y *or* z d
ab[^c]d	ab *anything except* c d
^abcd$	*a line containing only* abcd
[a-d]	*any one of* a b c *or* d

RETURN VALUE

The *compile*( ) function uses the macro RETURN( ) on success and the macro ERROR( ) on failure, see above. The *step*( ) and *advance*( ) functions return non-zero on a successful match and 0 if there is no match.

ERRORS

11	Range endpoint too large.
16	Bad number.
25	*digit* out of range.
36	Illegal or missing delimiter.
41	No remembered search string.
42	\\(\\) imbalance.
43	Too many \\(.
44	More than two numbers given in \\{ \\} .
45	} expected after \\ .
46	First number exceeds second in \\{ \\} .
49	[ ] imbalance.
50	Regular expression overflow.

EXAMPLES

The following is an example of how the regular expression macros and calls might be defined by an application program:

```
#define INIT          char *sp = instring;
#define GETC()        (*sp++)
#define PEEKC()       (*sp)
#define UNGETC(c)     (--sp)
#define RETURN(c)     return;
#define ERROR(c)      regerr()

#include <regexp.h>
. . .
        (void) compile(*argv, expbuf, &expbuf[ESIZE], '\0');
. . .
        if (step(linebuf, expbuf) )
                    succeed();
```

APPLICATION USAGE

These functions are kept for historical reasons, but will be withdrawn in a future issue of this document.

New applications should use the new functions *fnmatch*( ), *glob*( ), *regcomp*( ) and *regexec*( ), which provide full internationalised regular expression functionality compatible with the ISO POSIX-2 standard, as described in the **XBD** specification, **Chapter 7**, **Regular Expressions**.

SEE ALSO

fnmatch( ), *glob*( ), *regcomp*( ), *regexec*( ), *setlocale*( ), **<regex.h>**, **<regexp.h>**, the **XBD** specification, **Chapter 7**, **Regular Expressions**.

EXAMPLE

```
/*
 * Copyright (C) ANTRIX Inc.
 */

/* compile.c
 * This program takes an input a regular expression and
 * produces a compiled expression using function compile.
 */

#include <stdio.h>
#include <stdlib.h>
#include <errno.h>

#define STRSIZE 100

char instring[STRSIZE];
char *value = "True";

#define         INIT            register char *sp = instring;
#define         GETC()          (*sp++)
#define         PEEKC()         (*sp)
#define         UNGETC(c)       (--sp)
#define         RETURN(c)       return((char *)value)
#define         ERROR(c)        comperr()
```

```
    #include        <regexp.h>

    extern char *loc1, *loc2, *locs;

    main()
    {
      int    advance_value;
      char   *compile_value;
      char string[10*STRSIZE];
      char expbuf[STRSIZE];

      strcpy(instring, "^T");
      strcpy(string, "This is a test line");

      fprintf(stdout, "Produce compiled expression\n");
      compile_value = compile(instring, expbuf, &expbuf[STRSIZE], ' ');
      if (compile_value != (char *)0)
         fprintf(stdout, "compile_value=%s\n", compile_value);
      else {
         fprintf(stderr, "ERORR: compile call failed\n");
         fprintf(stderr, "ERORR: compile_value=%s\n", compile_value);
      }

      fprintf(stdout, "Match string beginning with T\n");
      advance_value = advance(string, expbuf);
      if (advance_value != 0) {
         fprintf(stdout, "advance call successful\n");
         fprintf(stdout, "advance_value=%d\n", advance_value);
      }
      else {
         fprintf(stderr, "ERROR: advance call failed\n");
         fprintf(stderr, "%d\n", advance_value);
      }
    }

    comperr()
    { }

    /*
     * Copyright (C) ANTRIX Inc.
     */

    /* step.c
     * This program matches the substring of string with the
     * regular expression in expbuf using function step.
     */

    #include <stdio.h>
    #include <stdlib.h>
    #include <errno.h>

    #define STRSIZE 100
```

```
        char instring[STRSIZE];
        char *value = "True";

        #define       INIT           register char *sp = instring;
        #define       GETC()         (*sp++)
        #define       PEEKC()        (*sp)
        #define       UNGETC(c)      (--sp)
        #define       RETURN(c)      return((char *)value)
        #define       ERROR(c)       comperr()
        #include      <regexp.h>

        extern char *loc1, *loc2, *locs;

        main()
        {
          int   step_value;
          char *compile_value;
          char string[10*STRSIZE];
          char expbuf[STRSIZE];

          strcpy(instring, "[a-d]");
          strcpy(string, "efgcxyz");

          fprintf(stdout, "Produce compiled expression\n");
          compile_value = compile(instring, expbuf, &expbuf[STRSIZE], ' ');

          fprintf(stdout, "Match character c\n");
          step_value = step(string, expbuf);
          if (step_value != 0) {
             fprintf(stdout, "step call successful\n");
             fprintf(stdout, "step_value=%d\n", step_value);
          }
          else {
             fprintf(stderr, "ERROR: step call failed\n");
             fprintf(stderr, "%d\n", step_value);
          }
        }

        comperr()
        { }

        /*
         * Copyright (C) ANTRIX Inc.
         */

        /* advance.c
         * This program pattern matches a given compiled regular
         * expression against a string using function advance.
         */

        #include <stdio.h>
        #include <stdlib.h>
```

```
#include <errno.h>

#define STRSIZE 100

char instring[STRSIZE];

#define        INIT         register char *sp = instring;
#define        GETC()       (*sp++)
#define        PEEKC()      (*sp)
#define        UNGETC(c)    (--sp)
#define        RETURN(c)    return((char *)0)
#define        ERROR(c)     comperr()
#include        <regexp.h>

extern char *loc1, *loc2, *locs;

main()
{
  int   advance_value;
  char string[10*STRSIZE];
  char expbuf[STRSIZE];

  strcpy(instring, "[A-Z]");
  strcpy(string, "Good bye");

  fprintf(stdout, "Produce compiled expression\n");
  compile(instring, expbuf, &expbuf[STRSIZE], ' ');

  fprintf(stdout, "Match upper case character G\n");
  advance_value = advance(string, expbuf);
  if (advance_value != 0) {
     fprintf(stdout, "advance call successful\n");
     fprintf(stdout, "advance_value=%d\n", advance_value);
  }
  else {
     fprintf(stderr, "ERROR: advance call failed\n");
     fprintf(stderr, "%d\n", advance_value);
  }
}

comperr()
{ }
```

NAME

remainder — remainder function

SYNOPSIS

UX
```
#include <math.h>

double remainder(double x, double y);
```

DESCRIPTION

The *remainder*( ) function returns the floating point remainder $r = x - ny$ when y is non-zero. The value n is the integral value nearest the exact value x/y. When $| n - x/y | = \frac{1}{2}$, the value n is chosen to be even.

The behaviour of *remainder*( ) is independent of the rounding mode.

RETURN VALUE

The *remainder*( ) function returns the floating point remainder $r = x - ny$ when y is non-zero.

When y is 0, *remainder*( ) returns (NaN or equivalent if available) and sets *errno* to [EDOM].

If the value of x is ±Inf, *remainder*( ) returns NaN and sets *errno* to [EDOM].

If x or y is NaN, then the function returns NaN and *errno* may be set to [EDOM].

ERRORS

The *remainder*( ) function will fail if:

[EDOM]   The y argument is 0 or the x argument is positive or negative infinity.

The *remainder*( ) function may fail if:

[EDOM]   The x or y argument is NaN.

SEE ALSO

abs( ), **<math.h>**.

EXAMPLE

```
/*
 * Copyright (C) ANTRIX Inc.
 */

/* remainder.c
 * This program returns a remainder of x with respect to y
 * using function remainder
 */

#include <stdio.h>
#include <math.h>

main()
{
  double  remainder_value;
  double  x = -120.40;
  double  y = -40.40;

  remainder_value = remainder (x,y);
  fprintf (stdout,"remainder of -120.40, -40.40 is %f\n", remainder_value);
}
```

NAME

remove — remove files

SYNOPSIS

```
#include <stdio.h>

int remove(const char *path);
```

DESCRIPTION

The *remove( )* function causes the file named by the pathname pointed attempt to open that file using that name will fail, unless it is created anew.

EX   If *path* does not name a directory, *remove(path)* is equivalent to *unlink(path)*.

If *path* names a directory, *remove (path)* is equivalent to *rmdir (path)*.

RETURN VALUE

EX   Refer to *rmdir( )* or *unlink( )*.

ERRORS

EX   Refer to *rmdir( )* or *unlink( )*.

SEE ALSO

rmdir( ), *unlink( )*, **<stdio.h>**.

EXAMPLE

```
/*
 * Copyright (C) ANTRIX Inc.
 */

/* remove.c
 * This program removes file using function remove.
 */

#include <stdio.h>
#include <stdlib.h>
#include <sys/stat.h>
#include <errno.h>

#define  PERM_ALL    (S_IRWXU | S_IRWXG | S_IRWXO)

main()
{
  int    remove_value;
  char   *filename = "testfile";

  fprintf (stdout,"create testfile\n");
  creat (filename, PERM_ALL);

  fprintf (stdout,"remove testfile\n");
  remove_value = remove (filename);
  if ( remove_value == 0 )
      fprintf (stdout,"remove() call successful\n");
  else {
      fprintf (stderr,"ERROR: remove() call failed\n");
```

```
        fprintf (stderr,"ERROR: %s\n", strerror(errno));
    }
}
```

NAME

remque — remove an element from a queue

SYNOPSIS

UX

```
#include <search.h>

void remque(void *element);
```

DESCRIPTION

Refer to *insque*( ).

EXAMPLE

```c
/*
 * Copyright (C) ANTRIX Inc.
 */

/* remque.c
 * This program removes an element from a queue
 * using function remque.
 */

#include   <stdio.h>
#include   <stdlib.h>
#include   <errno.h>

struct qelem {
  struct qelem *next;
  struct qelem *prev;
  char str[5];
};

static struct qelem *tail;

struct qelem *salloc()
{
  struct qelem *bytes;

  /* allocate memory for struct qelem */
  bytes = (struct qelem *)malloc(sizeof(struct qelem));
  return(bytes);
}

struct qelem *create_list(p, c)
struct qelem *p;
char c;
{
  if(p == NULL) {
    /* allocate memory and assign values */
    p = salloc();
    /* save decimal and ASCII value in the form of string */
    sprintf(p->str, "%c", c);
    p->next = NULL;
    p->prev = tail;
    tail = p;
```

```
        }
        else
          p->next = create_list(p->next, c);
        return(p);
    }

    print_next(p)
    struct qelem *p;
    {
        if(p != NULL) {
            printf("%s\n", p->str);
            print_next(p->next);
        }
    }

    print_prev(p)
    struct qelem *p;
    {
        if(p != NULL) {
            printf("%s\n", p->str);
            print_prev(p->prev);
        }
    }

    main()
    {
        int i;
        struct qelem *head;
        struct qelem *add;

        head = tail = NULL;
        for(i = 'a'; i <= 'c'; i++)
            head = create_list(head, i);

        printf("forward traverse\n");
        print_next(head);

        printf("reverse traverse\n");
        print_prev(tail);

        printf("add an element and print list\n");
        add = salloc();
        sprintf(add->str, "%c", 'd');
        tail->next = add;
        add->prev = tail;
        insque(add, tail);
        add->next = NULL;
        print_next(head);

        printf("remove an element and print list\n");
        remque(add);
        tail->next = NULL;
```

```
        add->prev = NULL;
        print_next(head);
}
```

NAME

rename — rename a file

SYNOPSIS

```
#include <stdio.h>

int rename(const char *old, const char *new);
```

DESCRIPTION

The *rename()* function changes the name of a file. The *old* argument points to the pathname of the file to be renamed. The *new* argument points to the new pathname of the file.

If the *old* argument and the *new* argument both refer to, and both link to the same existing file, *rename()* returns successfully and performs no other action.

If the *old* argument points to the pathname of a file that is not a directory, the *new* argument must not point to the pathname of a directory. If the link named by the *new* argument exists, it is removed and *old* renamed to *new*. In this case, a link named *new* will remain visible to other processes throughout the renaming operation and will refer either to the file referred to by *new* or *old* before the operation began. Write access permission is required for both the directory containing *old* and the directory containing *new*.

If the *old* argument points to the pathname of a directory, the *new* argument must not point to the pathname of a file that is not a directory. If the directory named by the *new* argument exists, it will be removed and *old* renamed to *new*. In this case, a link named *new* will exist throughout the renaming operation and will refer either to the file referred to by *new* or *old* before the operation began. Thus, if *new* names an existing directory, it must be an empty directory.

UX   If *old* points to a pathname that names a symbolic link, the symbolic link is renamed. If *new* points to a pathname that names a symbolic link, the symbolic link is removed.

The *new* pathname must not contain a path prefix that names *old*. Write access permission is required for the directory containing *old* and the directory containing *new*. If the *old* argument points to the pathname of a directory, write access permission may be required for the directory named by *old*, and, if it exists, the directory named by *new*.

If the link named by the *new* argument exists and the file's link count becomes 0 when it is removed and no process has the file open, the space occupied by the file will be freed and the file will no longer be accessible. If one or more processes have the file open when the last link is removed, the link will be removed before *rename()* returns, but the removal of the file contents will be postponed until all references to the file are closed.

Upon successful completion, *rename()* will mark for update the *st_ctime* and *st_mtime* fields of the parent directory of each file.

RETURN VALUE

Upon successful completion, *rename()* returns 0. Otherwise, −1 is returned, *errno* is set to indicate the error, and neither the file named by *old* nor the file named by *new* will be changed or created.

ERRORS

The *rename( )* function will fail if:

[EACCES]	A component of either path prefix denies search permission; or one of the directories containing *old* or *new* denies write permissions; or, write permission is required and is denied for a directory pointed to by the *old* or *new* arguments.

UX
[EBUSY]	The directory named by *old* or *new* is currently in use by the system or another process, and the implementation considers this an error, or the file named by *old* or *new* is a named STREAM.

[EEXIST] or [ENOTEMPTY]
The link named by *new* is a directory that is not an empty directory.

[EINVAL]   The *new* directory pathname contains a path prefix that names the *old* directory.

UX [EIO]   A physical I/O error has occurred.

[EISDIR]   The *new* argument points to a directory and the *old* argument points to a file that is not a directory.

UX [ELOOP]   Too many symbolic links were encountered in resolving either pathname.

[EMLINK]   The file named by *old* is a directory, and the link count of the parent directory of *new* would exceed {LINK_MAX}.

[ENAMETOOLONG]
FIPS
The length of the *old* or *new* argument exceeds {PATH_MAX} or a pathname component is longer than {NAME_MAX}.

[ENOENT]   The link named by *old* does not name an existing file, or either *old* or *new* points to an empty string.

[ENOSPC]   The directory that would contain *new* cannot be extended.

[ENOTDIR]   A component of either path prefix is not a directory; or the *old* argument names a directory and *new* argument names a non-directory file.

UX [EPERM] or [EACCES]
The S_ISVTX flag is set on the directory containing the file referred to by *old* and the caller is not the file owner, nor is the caller the directory owner, nor does the caller have appropriate privileges; or *new* refers to an existing file, the S_ISVTX flag is set on the directory containing this file and the caller is not the file owner, nor is the caller the directory owner, nor does the caller have appropriate privileges.

[EROFS]   The requested operation requires writing in a directory on a read-only file system.

[EXDEV]   The links named by *new* and *old* are on different file systems and the implementation does not support links between file systems.

The *rename( )* function may fail if:

UX [ENAMETOOLONG]
Pathname resolution of a symbolic link produced an intermediate result whose length exceeds {PATH_MAX}.

EX [ETXTBSY] The file to be renamed is a pure procedure (shared text) file that is being executed.

SEE ALSO

link( ), *rmdir*( ), *symlink*( ), *unlink*( ), **<stdio.h>**.

EXAMPLE

```c
/*
 * Copyright (C) ANTRIX Inc.
 */

/* rename.c
 * This program changes the name of a file using function
 * rename.
 */

#include <stdio.h>
#include <stdlib.h>
#include <sys/stat.h>
#include <errno.h>

#define  PERM_ALL   (S_IRWXU | S_IRWXG | S_IRWXO)

main()
{
  int    rename_value;
  char  *filename1 = "testfile1";
  char  *filename2 = "testfile2";

  fprintf (stdout,"create testfile1\n");
  creat (filename1, PERM_ALL);

  fprintf (stdout,"rename it to testfile2\n");
  rename_value = rename (filename1, filename2);
  if ( rename_value == 0 )
     fprintf (stdout,"rename() call successful\n");
  else {
     fprintf (stderr,"ERROR: rename() call failed\n");
     fprintf (stderr,"ERROR: %s\n", strerror(errno));
  }
  fprintf (stdout,"remove testfile2\n");
  remove (filename2);
}
```

NAME

rewind — reset file position indicator in a stream

SYNOPSIS

```
#include <stdio.h>

void rewind(FILE *stream);
```

DESCRIPTION

The call:

```
rewind(stream)
```

is equivalent to:

```
(void) fseek(stream, 0L, SEEK_SET)
```

except that *rewind*( ) also clears the error indicator.

RETURN VALUE

The *rewind*( ) function returns no value.

ERRORS

Refer to *fseek*( ) with the exception of EINVAL which does not apply.

APPLICATION USAGE

Because *rewind*( ) does not return a value, an application wishing to detect errors should clear *errno*, then call *rewind*( ), and if *errno* is non-zero, assume an error has occurred.

SEE ALSO

fseek( ), **<stdio.h>**.

EXAMPLE

```
/*
 * Copyright (C) ANTRIX Inc.
 */

/* rewind.c
 * This program resets file position indicator in a stream using
 * function rewind.
 */

#include <stdio.h>
#include <stdlib.h>
#include <unistd.h>
#include <errno.h>

main()
{
    int   rewind_value;
    int   orig_pos, new_pos;
    FILE  *stream;
    char  string[] = "hello world";
    char  *filename = "testfile";

    fprintf (stdout,"create and open testfile\n");
    stream = fopen (filename, "w");
```

```
        fprintf (stdout,"write string to testfile\n");
        fwrite (string, sizeof(char), strlen(string), stream);
        fflush (stream);

        fprintf (stdout,"reposition file pointer\n");
        fseek (stream, 6, SEEK_SET);
        orig_pos = ftell (stream);
        fprintf (stdout,"original position of stream %d\n", orig_pos);

        fprintf (stdout,"seek file pointer to the beginning\n");
        rewind (stream);

        new_pos = ftell (stream);
        fprintf (stdout,"new position of stream after rewind %d\n", new_pos);

        fclose (stream);
        fprintf (stdout,"remove testfile\n");
        remove (filename);
}
```

NAME

rewinddir — reset position of directory stream to the beginning of a directory

SYNOPSIS

OH
```
#include <sys/types.h>
#include <dirent.h>

void rewinddir(DIR *dirp);
```

DESCRIPTION

The *rewinddir*( ) function resets the position of the directory stream to which *dirp* refers to the beginning of the directory. It also causes the directory stream to refer to the current state of the corresponding directory, as a call to *opendir*( ) would have done. If *dirp* does not refer to a directory stream, the effect is undefined.

EX
After a call to the *fork*( ) function, either the parent or child (but not both) may continue processing the directory stream using *readdir*( ), *rewinddir*( ) or *seekdir*( ). If both the parent and child processes use these functions, the result is undefined.

RETURN VALUE

The *rewinddir*( ) function does not return a value.

ERRORS

No errors are defined.

APPLICATION USAGE

The *rewinddir*( ) function should be used in conjunction with *opendir*( ), *readdir*( ) and *closedir*( ) to examine the contents of the directory. This method is recommended for portability.

SEE ALSO

closedir( ), *opendir*( ), *readdir*( ), **<dirent.h>**, **<sys/types.h>**.

EXAMPLE

```
/*
 * Copyright (C) ANTRIX Inc.
 */

/* rewinddir.c
 * This program resets position of directory stream to the
 * beginning of a directory using function rewinddir.
 */

#include <stdio.h>
#include <stdlib.h>
#include <sys/types.h>
#include <dirent.h>
#include <sys/stat.h>
#include <errno.h>

#define  PERM_ALL    (S_IRWXU | S_IRWXG | S_IRWXO)

main()
{
   int     i, readdir_value;
   DIR     *dirp;
   struct  dirent *dirent_save;
   char    *root = "testdir";
```

```
char    *leaf = "testdir/subdir";

fprintf (stdout,"create test directories\n");
mkdir (root, PERM_ALL);
mkdir (leaf, PERM_ALL);

fprintf (stdout,"open testdir directory\n");
dirp = opendir (root);

fprintf (stdout,"determine location of 2nd directory entry\n");
fprintf (stdout,"directory names in testdir are:\n");
for ( i = 0; i < 3; i++ ) {
    dirent_save = readdir (dirp);
    fprintf (stdout,"%s\n", dirent_save->d_name);

}

fprintf (stdout,"reset the position of the directory pointer to\n");
fprintf (stdout,"the beginning\n");
rewinddir (dirp);

fprintf (stdout,"determine location of 2nd directory entry\n");
fprintf (stdout,"directory names in testdir after rewinddir are:\n");
for ( i = 0; i < 3; i++ ) {
    dirent_save = readdir (dirp);
    fprintf (stdout,"%s\n", dirent_save->d_name);
}

fprintf (stdout,"close and remove test directories\n");
closedir (dirp);
rmdir (leaf);
rmdir (root);
}
```

NAME

rindex — character string operations

SYNOPSIS

UX   `#include <strings.h>`

`char *rindex(const char *s, int c);`

DESCRIPTION

The *rindex*( ) function is identical to *strrchr*( ).

RETURN VALUE

See *strrchr*( ).

ERRORS

See *strrchr*( ).

APPLICATION USAGE

For portability to implementations conforming to earlier versions of this document, *strrchr*( ) is preferred over these functions.

SEE ALSO

strrchr( ), **<strings.h>**.

EXAMPLE

```
/*
 * Copyright (C) ANTRIX Inc.
 */

/* rindex.c
 * This program locates the last occurrence of c in the string
 * pointed to by s using function rindex.
 */

#include <stdio.h>
#include <stdlib.h>
#include <strings.h>
#include <string.h>
#include <errno.h>

main()
{
  char    *rindex_value;
  const  char s[] = "one two three";
  int    c = 't';

  fprintf (stdout,"return to last occurrence of character t\n");
  rindex_value = rindex (s, c);
  if ( rindex_value != (char *)0 ) {
     fprintf (stdout,"rindex() call successful\n");
     fprintf (stdout,"rindex_value=%s\n", rindex_value);
  }
  else
     fprintf (stderr,"ERROR: rindex() call failed\n");
}
```

NAME

rint — round-to-nearest integral value

SYNOPSIS

UX

```
#include <math.h>
```

```
double rint(double x);
```

DESCRIPTION

The *rint*( ) function returns the integral value (represented as a **double**) nearest *x* in the direction of the current rounding mode. The current rounding mode is implementation dependent.

If the current rounding mode rounds toward negative infinity, then *rint*( ) is identical to *floor*( ). If the current rounding mode rounds toward positive infinity, then *rint*( ) is identical to *ceil*( ).

RETURN VALUE

Upon successful completion, the *rint*( ) function returns the integer (represented as a double precision number) nearest *x* in the direction of the current rounding mode.

When *x* is ±Inf, *rint*( ) returns *x*.

If the value of *x* is NaN, NaN is returned and *errno* may be set to EDOM.

ERRORS

The *rint*( ) function may fail if:

[EDOM]   The *x* argument is NaN.

SEE ALSO

abs( ), *isnan*( ), **<math.h>**.

EXAMPLE

```
/*
 * Copyright (C) ANTRIX Inc.
 */

/* rint.c
 * This program computes the integral value
 * according to IEEE754 using function rint.
 */

#include <stdio.h>
#include <math.h>

main()
{
  double  rint_value;
  double  x = 4.25;

  rint_value = rint (x);
  fprintf (stdout,"rint of %f is %f\n", x, rint_value);
}
```

NAME

rmdir — remove a directory

SYNOPSIS

```
#include <unistd.h>

int rmdir(const char *path);
```

DESCRIPTION

The *rmdir*( ) function removes a directory whose name is given by *path*. The directory is removed only if it is an empty directory.

If the directory is the root directory or the current working directory of any process, it is unspecified whether the function succeeds, or whether it fails and sets *errno* to [EBUSY].

UX If *path* names a symbolic link, then *rmdir*( ) fails and sets *errno* to [ENOTDIR].

If the directory's link count becomes 0 and no process has the directory open, the space occupied by the directory will be freed and the directory will no longer be accessible. If one or more processes have the directory open when the last link is removed, the dot and dot-dot entries, if present, are removed before *rmdir*( ) returns and no new entries may be created in the directory, but the directory is not removed until all references to the directory are closed.

Upon successful completion, the *rmdir*( ) function marks for update the *st_ctime* and *st_mtime* fields of the parent directory.

RETURN VALUE

Upon successful completion, the function *rmdir*( ) returns 0. Otherwise, −1 is returned, and *errno* is set to indicate the error. If −1 is returned, the named directory is not changed.

ERRORS

The *rmdir*( ) function will fail if:

[EACCES]   Search permission is denied on a component of the path prefix, or write permission is denied on the parent directory of the directory to be removed.

[EBUSY]   The directory to be removed is currently in use by the system or another process and the implementation considers this to be an error.

[EEXIST] or [ENOTEMPTY]
The *path* argument names a directory that is not an empty directory.

UX [EIO]   A physical I/O error has occurred.

UX [ELOOP]   Too many symbolic links were encountered in resolving *path*.

[ENAMETOOLONG]

FIPS   The length of the *path* argument exceeds {PATH_MAX} or a pathname component is longer than {NAME_MAX}.

[ENOENT]   A component of *path* does not name an existing file, or the *path* argument names a non-existent directory or points to an empty string.

[ENOTDIR]   A component of the path is not a directory.

[EPERM] or [EACCES]

UX   The S_ISVTX flag is set on the parent directory of the directory to be removed and the caller is not the owner of the directory to be removed, nor is the caller the owner of the parent directory, nor does the caller have the appropriate privileges.

[EROFS]   The directory entry to be removed resides on a read-only file system.

The *rmdir*( ) function may fail if:

UX   [ENAMETOOLONG]
                Pathname resolution of a symbolic link produced an intermediate result whose
                length exceeds {PATH_MAX}.

SEE ALSO
mkdir( ), *remove*( ), *unlink*( ), **<unistd.h>**.

EXAMPLE

```c
/*
 * Copyright (C) ANTRIX Inc.
 */

/* rmdir.c
 * This program removes a directory using function rmdir.
 */

#include <stdio.h>
#include <stdlib.h>
#include <sys/stat.h>
#include <errno.h>

#define  PERM_ALL   (S_IRWXU | S_IRWXG | S_IRWXO)

main()
{
   int   rmdir_value;
   char  *dir = "testdir";

   fprintf (stdout,"create testdir directory\n");
   mkdir (dir, PERM_ALL);

   fprintf (stdout,"remove testdir directory\n");
   rmdir_value = rmdir (dir);
   if ( rmdir_value == 0 )
      fprintf (stdout,"rmdir() call successful\n");
   else {
      fprintf (stderr,"ERROR: rmdir() call failed\n");
      fprintf (stderr,"ERROR: %s\n", strerror(errno));
   }
}
```

NAME

sbrk — change space allocation

SYNOPSIS

UX   `#include <unistd.h>`

`void *sbrk(int incr);`

DESCRIPTION

Refer to *brk*( ).

EXAMPLE

```
/*
 * Copyright (C) ANTRIX Inc.
 */

/* sbrk.c
 * This program changes the amount of space allocated for
 * the calling process's data segment using function sbrk.
 */

#include <stdio.h>
#include <stdlib.h>
#include <errno.h>

main()
{
  char     *sbrk_value;

  fprintf (stdout,"get original break value\n");
  sbrk_value = (char *)sbrk (100);

  fprintf (stdout,"orignal sbrk_value=%d\n", sbrk_value );
  fprintf (stdout,"get previous break value set\n");

  sbrk_value = (char *)sbrk (200);
  fprintf (stdout,"new sbrk_value=%d\n", sbrk_value );
}
```

NAME

scalb — load exponent of a radix-independent floating-point number

SYNOPSIS

UX   `#include <math.h>`

`double scalb(double x, double n);`

DESCRIPTION

The *scalb*( ) function computes $x * r^n$, where r is the radix of the machine's floating point arithmetic. When r is 2, *scalb*( ) is equivalent to *ldexp*( ).

RETURN VALUE

Upon successful completion, the *scalb*( ) function returns $x * r^n$.

If the correct value would overflow, *scalb*( ) returns ±HUGE_VAL (according to the sign of x) and sets *errno* to [ERANGE].

If the correct value would underflow, *scalb*( ) returns 0 and sets *errno* to [ERANGE].

The *scalb*( ) function returns x when x is ±Inf.

If x or n is NaN, then *scalb*( ) returns NaN and may set *errno* to [EDOM].

ERRORS

The *scalb*( ) function will fail if:

[ERANGE]   The correct value would overflow or underflow.

The *scalb*( ) function may fail if:

[EDOM]   The x or n argument is NaN.

APPLICATION USAGE

An application wishing to check for error situations should set *errno* to 0 before calling *scalb*( ). If *errno* is non-zero on return, or the return value is NaN, an error has occurred.

SEE ALSO

ldexp( ), **<math.h>**.

EXAMPLE

```
/*
 * Copyright (C) ANTRIX Inc.
 */

/* scalb.c
 * This program computes the quantity value * 2 exp
 * using function scalb.
 */

#include <stdio.h>
#include <math.h>
#include <stdlib.h>
#include <errno.h>

main()
{
  double  scalb_value;
  double  x = 8.00;
  double  y = 2.00;
```

```
        scalb_value = scalb (x,y);
        fprintf (stdout,"scalb of (8, 2) is %f\n", scalb_value);
}
```

NAME
scanf — convert formatted input

SYNOPSIS
```
#include <stdio.h>

int scanf(const char *format, ... );
```

DESCRIPTION
Refer to *fscanf( )*.

EXAMPLE
```c
/*
 * Copyright (C) ANTRIX Inc.
 */

/* scanf.c
 * This program reads from the stdin according to a format
 * and stores the results in its argument using function
 * scanf.
 */

#include <stdio.h>
#include <stdlib.h>
#include <errno.h>

main()
{
   int    scanf_value;
   int    value;
   char   str1[6], str2[6];

   memset (str1, ' ', 6);
   memset (str2, ' ', 6);

   fprintf (stdout,"Please type in string: Good Bye 99\n" );

   scanf_value = scanf ("%s %s %d", str1, str2, &value);
   if ( scanf_value == 3 ) {
      fprintf (stdout,"scanf() call successful\n");
      fprintf (stdout,"string str1 is %s\n", str1 );
      fprintf (stdout,"string str2 is %s\n", str2 );
      fprintf (stdout,"value=%d\n", value);
   }
   else
      fprintf (stderr,"ERROR: scanf() call failed\n");
}
```

NAME

seed48 — seed uniformly distributed pseudo-random non-negative long integer generator

SYNOPSIS

EX   `#include <stdlib.h>`

`unsigned short int *seed48(unsigned short int seed16v[3]);`

DESCRIPTION

Refer to *drand48*( ).

EXAMPLE

```
/*
 * Copyright (C) ANTRIX Inc.
 */

/* filename seed48.c
 * This program initializes entry points for random number
 * generator drand48 using function seed48.
 */

#include <stdio.h>
#include <stdlib.h>
#include <errno.h>

main()
{
    int                i;
    unsigned short int *seed_value;
    unsigned short int org_value;
    unsigned short int seed16v[3];
    double             drand48_value;

    seed16v[0] = 15;
    seed_value = seed48(seed16v);
    for ( i = 0; i < 5; i++ ) {
        drand48_value = drand48 ();
        fprintf (stdout,"random value in iteration %d is %f\n",
                        i, drand48_value);
    }

    seed48(seed_value);
    for ( i = 0; i < 5; i++ ) {
        drand48_value = drand48 ();
        fprintf (stdout,"random value in iteration %d is %f\n",
                        i, drand48_value);
    }
}
```

NAME

seekdir — set position of directory stream

SYNOPSIS

EX OH `#include <sys/types.h>`

EX `#include <dirent.h>`

`void seekdir(DIR *dirp, long int loc);`

DESCRIPTION

The *seekdir( )* function sets the position of the next *readdir( )* operation on the directory stream specified by *dirp* to the position specified by *loc*. The value of *loc* should have been returned from an earlier call to *telldir( )*. The new position reverts to the one associated with the directory stream when *telldir( )* was performed.

UX If the value of *loc* was not obtained from an earlier call to *telldir( )* or if a call to *rewinddir( )* occurred between the call to *telldir( )* and the call to *seekdir( )*, the results of subsequent calls to *readdir( )* are unspecified.

RETURN VALUE

The *seekdir( )* function returns no value.

ERRORS

No errors are defined.

SEE ALSO

opendir( ), *readdir( )*, *telldir( )*, **<dirent.h> <stdio.h>**, **<sys/types.h>**.

EXAMPLE

```
/*
 * Copyright (C) ANTRIX Inc.
 */

/* seekdir.c
 * This program sets position of directory stream using function
 * seekdir.
 */

#include <stdio.h>
#include <stdlib.h>
#include <sys/types.h>
#include <dirent.h>
#include <sys/stat.h>

#define  PERM_ALL   (S_IRWXU | S_IRWXG | S_IRWXO)

main()
{
    int     readdir_value;
    int     i, compare;
    long    location;
    DIR     *dirp;
    struct  dirent *buf1, *buf2;
    struct  dirent *dirent_save;
```

```
char    *root = "testdir";
char    *leaf = "testdir/subdir";

fprintf (stdout,"create test directories\n");
mkdir (root, PERM_ALL);
mkdir (leaf, PERM_ALL);

dirp = opendir (root);
dirent_save = (struct dirent *)malloc (sizeof(struct dirent));
buf1 = (struct dirent *)malloc (sizeof(struct dirent));
buf2 = (struct dirent *)malloc (sizeof(struct dirent));

fprintf (stdout,"determine location of 2nd directory entry\n");
for ( i = 0; i < 3; i++ ) {
    location = telldir (dirp);
    dirent_save = readdir (dirp);
}

fprintf (stdout,"save directory entry for subdir\n");
memcpy ((void *)buf1, (void *)dirent_save, sizeof (struct dirent));
closedir (dirp);

fprintf (stdout,"open directory entry\n");
dirp = opendir ("testdir");

fprintf (stdout,"seek to the directory subdir\n");
seekdir (dirp, location);
buf2 = readdir (dirp);

compare = memcmp ((void *)buf1,(void *)buf2,sizeof(struct dirent));
if ( compare == 0 ) {
    fprintf (stdout,"directory name in buf1->d_name=%s\n", buf1->d_name);
    fprintf (stdout,"directory name in buf2->d_name=%s\n", buf2->d_name);
}
else
    fprintf (stderr,"ERROR: the directory entry names are different\n");

fprintf (stdout,"close and remove test directories\n");
closedir (dirp);
rmdir (leaf);
rmdir (root);
}
```

NAME

select — synchronous I/O multiplexing

SYNOPSIS

UX   `#include <sys/time.h>`

```
int select(int nfds, fd_set *readfds, fd_set *writefds,
        fd_set *errorfds, struct timeval *timeout);
```

```
void FD_CLR(int fd, fd_set *fdset);
```

```
int FD_ISSET(int fd, fd_set *fdset);
```

```
void FD_SET(int fd, fd_set *fdset);
```

```
void FD_ZERO(fd_set *fdset);
```

DESCRIPTION

The *select*( ) function indicates which of the specified file descriptors is ready for reading, ready for writing, or has an error condition pending. If the specified condition is false for all of the specified file descriptors, *select*( ) blocks, up to the specified timeout interval, until the specified condition is true for at least one of the specified file descriptors.

The *select*( ) function supports regular files, terminal and pseudo-terminal devices, STREAMS-based files, FIFOs and pipes. The behaviour of *select*( ) on file descriptors that refer to other types of file is unspecified.

The *nfds* argument specifies the range of file descriptors to be tested. The *select*( ) function tests file descriptors in the range of 0 to *nfds*–1.

If the *readfs* argument is not a null pointer, it points to an object of type **fd_set** that on input specifies the file descriptors to be checked for being ready to read, and on output indicates which file descriptors are ready to read.

If the *writefs* argument is not a null pointer, it points to an object of type **fd_set** that on input specifies the file descriptors to be checked for being ready to write, and on output indicates which file descriptors are ready to write.

If the *errorfds* argument is not a null pointer, it points to an object of type **fd_set** that on input specifies the file descriptors to be checked for error conditions pending, and on output indicates which file descriptors have error conditions pending.

On successful completion, the objects pointed to by the *readfs*, *writefs*, and *errorfds* arguments are modified to indicate which file descriptors are ready for reading, ready for writing, or have an error condition pending, respectively. For each file descriptor less than *nfds*, the corresponding bit will be set on successful completion if it was set on input and the associated condition is true for that file descriptor.

If the *timeout* argument is not a null pointer, it points to an object of type **struct timeval** that specifies a maximum interval to wait for the selection to complete. If the *timeout* argument points to an object of type **struct timeval** whose members are 0, *select*( ) does not block. If the *timeout* argument is a null pointer, *select*( ) blocks until an event causes one of the masks to be returned with a valid (non-zero) value. If the time limit expires before any event occurs that would cause one of the masks to be set to a non-zero value, *select*( ) completes successfully and returns 0.

Implementations may place limitations on the maximum timeout interval supported. On all implementations, the maximum timeout interval supported will be at least 31 days. If the *timeout* argument specifies a timeout interval greater than the implementation-dependent maximum value, the maximum value will be used as the actual timeout value. Implementations may also place limitations on the granularity of timeout intervals. If the requested timeout interval requires a finer granularity than the implementation supports, the actual timeout interval will be rounded up to the next supported value.

If the *readfs*, *writefs*, and *errorfds* arguments are all null pointers and the *timeout* argument is not a null pointer, *select*( ) blocks for the time specified, or until interrupted by a signal. If the *readfs*, *writefs*, and *errorfds* arguments are all null pointers and the *timeout* argument is a null pointer, *select*( ) blocks until interrupted by a signal.

File descriptors associated with regular files always select true for ready to read, ready to write, and error conditions.

On failure, the objects pointed to by the *readfs*, *writefs*, and *errorfds* arguments are not modified. If the timeout interval expires without the specified condition being true for any of the specified file descriptors, the objects pointed to by the *readfs*, *writefs*, and *errorfds* arguments have all bits set to 0.

File descriptor masks of type **fd_set** can be initialised and tested with FD_CLR( ), FD_ISSET( ), FD_SET( ), and FD_ZERO( ). It is unspecified whether each of these is a macro or a function. If a macro definition is suppressed in order to access an actual function, or a program defines an external identifier with any of these names, the behaviour is undefined.

FD_CLR(*fd*, &*fdset*) Clears the bit for the file descriptor *fd* in the file descriptor set *fdset*.

FD_ISSET(*fd*, &*fdset*) Returns a non-zero value if the bit for the file descriptor *fd* is set in the file descriptor set pointed to by *fdset*, and 0 otherwise.

FD_SET(*fd*, &*fdset*) Sets the bit for the file descriptor *fd* in the file descriptor set *fdset*.

FD_ZERO(&*fdset*) Initialises the file descriptor set *fdset* to have zero bits for all file descriptors.

The behaviour of these macros is undefined if the *fd* argument is less than 0 or greater than or equal to FD_SETSIZE.

RETURN VALUE

FD_CLR( ), FD_SET( ) and FD_ZERO( ) return no value. FD_ISSET( ) a non-zero value if the bit for the file descriptor *fd* is set in the file descriptor set pointed to by *fdset*, and 0 otherwise.

On successful completion, *select*( ) returns the total number of bits set in the bit masks. Otherwise, −1 is returned, and *errno* is set to indicate the error.

ERRORS

Under the following conditions, *select*( ) fails and sets *errno* to:

[EBADF] One or more of the file descriptor sets specified a file descriptor that is not a valid open file descriptor.

[EINTR] The *select*( ) function was interrupted before any of the selected events occurred and before the timeout interval expired.

  If SA_RESTART has been set for the interrupting signal, it is implementation-dependent whether *select*( ) restarts or returns with [EINTR].

[EINVAL] An invalid timeout interval was specified.

[EINVAL] The *nfds* argument is less than 0, or greater than or equal to FD_SETSIZE.

[EINVAL] One of the specified file descriptors refers to a STREAM or multiplexer that is linked (directly or indirectly) downstream from a multiplexer.

APPLICATION USAGE

The use of a timeout does not affect any pending timers set up by *alarm*( ), *ualarm*( ) or *settimer*( ).

On successful completion, the object pointed to by the *timeout* argument may be modified.

SEE ALSO

fcntl( ), *poll*( ), *read*( ), *write*( ), **<sys/time.h>**.

NAME

semctl — semaphore control operations

SYNOPSIS

EX
```
#include <sys/sem.h>

int semctl(int semid, int semnum, int cmd, ...);
```

DESCRIPTION

The *semctl*( ) function provides a variety of semaphore control operations as specified by *cmd*. The fourth argument is optional and depends upon the operation requested. If required, it is of type **union semun**, which the application program must explicitly declare:

```
union semun {
        int val;
        struct semid_ds *buf;
        unsigned short *array;
} arg;
```

The following semaphore control operations as specified by *cmd* are executed with respect to the semaphore specified by *semid* and *semnum*. The level of permission required for each operation is shown with each command, see the **XSH** specification, **Section 2.6, Interprocess Communication**. The symbolic names for the values of *cmd* are defined by the **<sys/sem.h>** header:

GETVAL   Return the value of *semval*, see **<sys/sem.h>**. Requires read permission.

SETVAL   Set the value of *semval* to *arg.val*, where *arg* is the value of the fourth argument to *semctl*( ). When this command is successfully executed, the *semadj* value corresponding to the specified semaphore in all processes is cleared. Requires alter permission, see the **XSH** specification, **Section 2.6, Interprocess Communication**.

GETPID   Return the value of *sempid*. Requires read permission.

GETNCNT   Return the value of *semncnt*. Requires read permission.

GETZCNT   Return the value of *semzcnt*. Requires read permission.

The following values of *cmd* operate on each *semval* in the set of semaphores:

GETALL   Return the value of *semval* for each semaphore in the semaphore set and place into the array pointed to by *arg.array*, where *arg* is the fourth argument to *semctl*( ). Requires read permission.

SETALL   Set the value of *semval* for each semaphore in the semaphore set according to the array pointed to by *arg.array*, where *arg* is the fourth argument to *semctl*( ). When this command is successfully executed, the *semadj* values corresponding to each specified semaphore in all processes are cleared. Requires alter permission.

The following values of *cmd* are also available:

IPC_STAT   Place the current value of each member of the **semid_ds** data structure associated with *semid* into the structure pointed to by *arg.buf*, where *arg* is the fourth argument to *semctl*( ). The contents of this structure are defined in **<sys/sem.h>**. Requires read permission.

IPC_SET   Set the value of the following members of the **semid_ds** data structure associated with *semid* to the corresponding value found in the structure pointed to by *arg.buf*, where *arg* is the fourth argument to *semctl( )*:

```
sem_perm.uid
sem_perm.gid
sem_perm.mode
```

The mode bits specified in the **XSH** specification, **Section 2.6.1**, **IPC General Description** are copied into the corresponding bits of the **sem_perm.mode** associated with *semid*. The stored values of any other bits are unspecified.

This command can only be executed by a process that has an effective user ID equal to either that of a process with appropriate privileges or to the value of **sem_perm.cuid** or **sem_perm.uid** in the **semid_ds** data structure associated with *semid*.

IPC_RMID   Remove the semaphore-identifier specified by *semid* from the system and destroy the set of semaphores and **semid_ds** data structure associated with it. This command can only be executed by a process that has an effective user ID equal to either that of a process with appropriate privileges or to the value of **sem_perm.cuid** or **sem_perm.uid** in the **semid_ds** data structure associated with *semid*.

RETURN VALUE

If successful, the value returned by *semctl( )* depends on *cmd* as follows:

GETVAL   The value of *semval*.

GETPID   The value of *sempid*.

GETNCNT   The value of *semncnt*.

GETZCNT   The value of *semzcnt*.

All others   0.

Otherwise, *semctl( )* returns −1 and *errno* indicates the error.

ERRORS

The *semctl( )* function will fail if:

[EACCES]   Operation permission is denied to the calling process, see the **XSH** specification, **Section 2.6**, **Interprocess Communication**.

[EINVAL]   The value of *semid* is not a valid semaphore identifier, or the value of *semnum* is less than 0 or greater than or equal to *sem_nsems*, or the value of *cmd* is not a valid command.

[EPERM]   The argument *cmd* is equal to IPC_RMID or IPC_SET and the effective user ID of the calling process is not equal to that of a process with appropriate privileges and it is not equal to the value of **sem_perm.cuid** or **sem_perm.uid** in the data structure associated with *semid*.

[ERANGE]   The argument *cmd* is equal to SETVAL or SETALL and the value to which *semval* is to be set is greater than the system-imposed maximum.

APPLICATION USAGE

The fourth parameter in the **SYNOPSIS** section is now specified as ... in order to avoid a clash with the ISO C standard when referring to the union *semun* (as defined in XPG3) and for backward compatibility.

FUTURE DIRECTIONS

The IEEE 1003.4 standards committee is developing alternative interfaces for interprocess communication. Application developers who need to use IPC should design their applications so that modules using the routines described in this document can be easily modified to use alternative methods at a later date.

SEE ALSO

semget( ), *semop*( ), **<sys/sem.h>**, **XSH** specification, **Section 2.6**, **Interprocess Communication**.

EXAMPLE

See sockets library examples.

```c
/*
 * Copyright (C) ANTRIX Inc.
 */

/* semctl.c
 * This program provides status of semaphore id using function
 * semctl.
 */

#include <stdio.h>
#include <stdlib.h>
#include <unistd.h>
#include <fcntl.h>
#include <sys/stat.h>
#include <sys/ipc.h>
#include <sys/sem.h>
#include <errno.h>

#define   PERM_ALL   (S_IRWXU | S_IRWXG | S_IRWXO)
#define   NSEMS   8

main()
{
    int     semctl_value;
    int     shmid;
    struct  semid_ds  sem_ds;
    union semun {
        int    val;
        struct semid_ds *buf;
        unsigned short  *array;
    } arg;

    arg.buf = &sem_ds;

    printf("get semaphore id\n");
    shmid = semget (IPC_PRIVATE, NSEMS, PERM_ALL);

    memset ((void *)&sem_ds, 0, sizeof(sem_ds));
    printf("find the status of semaphore id\n");
    semctl_value = semctl (shmid, 0, IPC_STAT, arg);
```

```
    if ( semctl_value == 0 ) {
        fprintf (stdout,"semctl() call successful\n");
        fprintf (stdout,"sem_ds.sem_perm.uid=%d\n", sem_ds.sem_perm.uid);
        fprintf (stdout,"sem_ds.sem_perm.gid=%d\n", sem_ds.sem_perm.gid);
        fprintf (stdout,"sem_ds.sem_perm.mode=%o\n",
                        (sem_ds.sem_perm.mode & 0777) );
        fprintf (stdout,"sem_ds.sem_perm.cuid=%d\n", sem_ds.sem_perm.cuid);
        fprintf (stdout,"sem_ds.sem_perm.cgid=%d\n", sem_ds.sem_perm.cgid);
        fprintf (stdout,"sem_ds.sem_nsems=%d\n", sem_ds.sem_nsems);
        fprintf (stdout,"sem_ds.sem_otime=%d\n", sem_ds.sem_otime);
    }
    else {
        fprintf (stderr,"ERROR: semctl() call failed\n");
        fprintf (stderr,"ERROR: %s\n", strerror(errno));
    }

    fprintf (stdout,"remove shmid\n");
    semctl (shmid, 0, IPC_RMID, arg);
}
```

NAME

semget — get set of semaphores

SYNOPSIS

EX
```
#include <sys/sem.h>
```

```
int semget(key_t key, int nsems, int semflg);
```

DESCRIPTION

The *semget*( ) function returns the semaphore identifier associated with *key*.

A semaphore identifier with its associated **semid_ds** data structure and its associated set of *nsems* semaphores, see **<sys/sem.h>**, are created for *key* if one of the following is true:

- The argument *key* is equal to IPC_PRIVATE .

- The argument *key* does not already have a semaphore identifier associated with it and (*semflg* & IPC_CREAT) is non-zero.

Upon creation, the **semid_ds** data structure associated with the new semaphore identifier is initialised as follows:

- In the operation permissions structure *sem_perm.cuid*, *sem_perm.uid*, *sem_perm.cgid* and *sem_perm.gid* are set equal to the effective user ID and effective group ID, respectively, of the calling process.

- The low-order 9 bits of *sem_perm.mode* are set equal to the low-order 9 bits of *semflg*.

- The variable *sem_nsems* is set equal to the value of *nsems*.

- The variable *sem_otime* is set equal to 0 and *sem_ctime* is set equal to the current time.

- The data structure associated with each semaphore in the set is not initialised. The *semctl*( ) function with the command SETVAL or SETALL can be used to initialise each semaphore.

RETURN VALUE

Upon successful completion, *semget*( ) returns a non-negative integer, namely a semaphore identifier; otherwise, it returns −1 and *errno* will be set to indicate the error.

ERRORS

The *semget*( ) function will fail if:

[EACCES]	A semaphore identifier exists for *key*, but operation permission as specified by the low-order 9 bits of *semflg* would not be granted. See the **XSH** specification, **Section 2.6**, **Interprocess Communication**.
[EEXIST]	A semaphore identifier exists for the argument *key* but ((*semflg* & IPC_CREAT) && (*semflg* & IPC_EXCL)) is non-zero.
[EINVAL]	The value of *nsems* is either less than or equal to 0 or greater than the system-imposed limit, or a semaphore identifier exists for the argument *key*, but the number of semaphores in the set associated with it is less than *nsems* and *nsems* is not equal to 0.
[ENOENT]	A semaphore identifier does not exist for the argument *key* and (*semflg* & IPC_CREAT) is equal to 0.
[ENOSPC]	A semaphore identifier is to be created but the system-imposed limit on the maximum number of allowed semaphores system-wide would be exceeded.

FUTURE DIRECTIONS

The IEEE 1003.4 standards committee is developing alternative interfaces for interprocess communication. Application developers who need to use IPC should design their applications so that modules using the routines described in this document can be easily modified to use alternative methods at a later date.

SEE ALSO

semctl( ), *semop*( ), **<sys/sem.h>**, **XSH** specification, **Section 2.6**, **Interprocess Communication**.

EXAMPLE

```
/*
 * Copyright (C) ANTRIX Inc.
 */

/* semget.c
 * This programs gets semaphore identifier using function semget.
 */

#include <stdio.h>
#include <stdlib.h>
#include <unistd.h>
#include <fcntl.h>
#include <sys/stat.h>
#include <sys/ipc.h>
#include <sys/sem.h>
#include <errno.h>

#define  PERM_ALL    (S_IRWXU | S_IRWXG | S_IRWXO)
#define  NSEMS    8

main()
{
   int     shmid;
   struct  semid_ds sem_ds;
   union semun {
      int     val;
      struct semid_ds *buf;
      unsigned short  *array;
   } arg;

   arg.buf = &sem_ds;

   fprintf (stdout,"get semaphore id\n");
   shmid = semget (IPC_PRIVATE, NSEMS, PERM_ALL);
   if ( shmid >= 0 ) {
      fprintf (stdout,"semget() call successful\n");
      memset ((void *)&sem_ds, 0, sizeof(sem_ds));
      fprintf (stdout,"stat semaphore id\n");
      semctl (shmid, 0, IPC_STAT, arg);
      fprintf (stdout,"sem_ds.sem_perm.uid=%d\n", sem_ds.sem_perm.uid);
      fprintf (stdout,"sem_ds.sem_perm.gid=%d\n", sem_ds.sem_perm.gid);
      fprintf (stdout,"sem_ds.sem_perm.mode=%o\n",
```

```
                             (sem_ds.sem_perm.mode & 0777) );
        fprintf (stdout,"sem_ds.sem_perm.cuid=%d\n", sem_ds.sem_perm.cuid);
        fprintf (stdout,"sem_ds.sem_perm.cgid=%d\n", sem_ds.sem_perm.cgid);
        fprintf (stdout,"sem_ds.sem_nsems=%d\n", sem_ds.sem_nsems);
        fprintf (stdout,"sem_ds.sem_otime=%d\n", sem_ds.sem_otime);
    }
    else {
        fprintf (stderr,"ERROR: semget() call failed\n");
        fprintf (stderr,"ERROR: %s\n", strerror(errno));
    }

    fprintf (stdout,"remove shmid\n");
    semctl (shmid, 0, IPC_RMID, arg);
}
```

NAME

semop — semaphore operations

SYNOPSIS

EX

```
#include <sys/sem.h>
```

```
int semop(int semid, struct sembuf *sops, size_t nsops);
```

DESCRIPTION

The *semop*( ) function is used to perform atomically a user-defined array of semaphore operations on the set of semaphores associated with the semaphore identifier specified by the argument *semid*.

The argument *sops* is a pointer to a user-defined array of semaphore operation structures. The implementation will not modify elements of this array unless the application uses implementation-dependent extensions.

The argument *nsops* is the number of such structures in the array.

Each structure, **sembuf**, includes the following members:

Member Type	Member Name	Description
short	sem_num	semaphore number
short	sem_op	semaphore operation
short	sem_flg	operation flags

Each semaphore operation specified by *sem_op* is performed on the corresponding semaphore specified by *semid* and *sem_num*.

The variable *sem_op* specifies one of three semaphore operations:

1. If *sem_op* is a negative integer and the calling process has alter permission, one of the following will occur:

   - If *semval*, see **<sys/sem.h>**, is greater than or equal to the absolute value of *sem_op*, the absolute value of *sem_op* is subtracted from *semval*. Also, if (*sem_flg* & SEM_UNDO) is non-zero, the absolute value of *sem_op* is added to the calling process' *semadj* value for the specified semaphore.

   - If *semval* is less than the absolute value of *sem_op* and (*sem_flg* & IPC_NOWAIT) is non-zero, *semop*( ) will return immediately.

   - If *semval* is less than the absolute value of *sem_op* and (*sem_flg* & IPC_NOWAIT) is 0, *semop*( ) will increment the *semncnt* associated with the specified semaphore and suspend execution of the calling process until one of the following conditions occurs:

     — The value of *semval* becomes greater than or equal to the absolute value of *sem_op*. When this occurs, the value of *semncnt* associated with the specified semaphore is decremented, the absolute value of *sem_op* is subtracted from *semval* and, if (*sem_flg* & SEM_UNDO) is non-zero, the absolute value of *sem_op* is added to the calling process' *semadj* value for the specified semaphore.

     — The *semid* for which the calling process is awaiting action is removed from the system. When this occurs, *errno* is set equal to [EIDRM] and −1 is returned.

     — The calling process receives a signal that is to be caught. When this occurs, the value of *semncnt* associated with the specified semaphore is decremented, and the calling process resumes execution in the manner prescribed in *sigaction*( ).

2. If *sem_op* is a positive integer and the calling process has alter permission, the value of *sem_op* is added to *semval* and, if (*sem_flg* & SEM_UNDO) is non-zero, the value of *sem_op* is subtracted from the calling process' *semadj* value for the specified semaphore.

3. If *sem_op* is 0 and the calling process has read permission, one of the following will occur:

   - If *semval* is 0, *semop( )* will return immediately.

   - If *semval* is non-zero and (*sem_flg* & IPC_NOWAIT) is non-zero, *semop( )* will return immediately.

   - If *semval* is non-zero and (*sem_flg* & IPC_NOWAIT) is 0, *semop( )* will increment the *semzcnt* associated with the specified semaphore and suspend execution of the calling process until one of the following occurs:

     — The value of *semval* becomes 0, at which time the value of *semzcnt* associated with the specified semaphore is decremented.

     — The *semid* for which the calling process is awaiting action is removed from the system. When this occurs, *errno* is set equal to [EIDRM] and −1 is returned.

     — The calling process receives a signal that is to be caught. When this occurs, the value of *semzcnt* associated with the specified semaphore is decremented, and the calling process resumes execution in the manner prescribed in *sigaction( )*.

Upon successful completion, the value of *sempid* for each semaphore specified in the array pointed to by *sops* is set equal to the process ID of the calling process.

RETURN VALUE

Upon successful completion, *semop( )* returns 0. Otherwise, it returns −1 and *errno* will be set to indicate the error.

ERRORS

The *semop( )* function will fail if:

[E2BIG]   The value of *nsops* is greater than the system-imposed maximum.

[EACCES]   Operation permission is denied to the calling process, see the **XSH** specification, **Section 2.6**, **Interprocess Communication**.

[EAGAIN]   The operation would result in suspension of the calling process but (*sem_flg* & IPC_NOWAIT) is non-zero.

[EFBIG]   The value of *sem_num* is less than 0 or greater than or equal to the number of semaphores in the set associated with *semid*.

[EIDRM]   The semaphore identifier *semid* is removed from the system.

[EINTR]   The *semop( )* function was interrupted by a signal.

[EINVAL]   The value of *semid* is not a valid semaphore identifier, or the number of individual semaphores for which the calling process requests a SEM_UNDO would exceed the system-imposed limit.

[ENOSPC]   The limit on the number of individual processes requesting a SEM_UNDO would be exceeded.

[ERANGE]   An operation would cause a *semval* to overflow the system-imposed limit, or an operation would cause a *semadj* value to overflow the system-imposed limit.

FUTURE DIRECTIONS

The IEEE 1003.4 Standards Committee is developing alternative interfaces for interprocess communication. Application developers who need to use IPC should design their applications so that modules using the routines described in this document can be easily modified to use alternative methods at a later date.

SEE ALSO

exec, *exit*( ), *fork*( ), *semctl*( ), *semget*( ), **<sys/ipc.h>**, **<sys/sem.h>**, **<sys/types.h>**, XSH specification, **Section 2.6**, **Interprocess Communication**.

EXAMPLE

```
/*
 * Copyright (C) ANTRIX Inc.
 */

/* semop.c
 * This program performs semaphore operations on the set of
 * semaphores associated with the semaphore identifier using
 * function semop.
 */

#include <stdio.h>
#include <stdlib.h>
#include <unistd.h>
#include <fcntl.h>
#include <sys/stat.h>
#include <sys/ipc.h>
#include <sys/sem.h>
#include <errno.h>

#define   KEYVAL     ((key_t) 1234)
#define   PERM_ALL  (S_IRWXU | S_IRWXG | S_IRWXO)
#define   NSEMS      1

main()
{
  int      semop_value;
  int      semid, newval;
  struct   semid_ds  sem_ds;
  struct   sembuf  semoper;
  union semun {
     int      val;
     struct   semid_ds *buf;
     unsigned short  *array;
  } arg;

  arg.buf = &sem_ds;

  fprintf (stdout,"get semaphore id\n");
  semid = semget (100, NSEMS, IPC_CREAT|IPC_EXCL|PERM_ALL);
  memset ((void *)&sem_ds, 0, sizeof(sem_ds));
  arg.val = 8;
```

```
      fprintf (stdout,"set value\n");
      semctl (semid, 0, SETVAL, arg);
      semoper.sem_num =  0;
      semoper.sem_op  = -5;
      semoper.sem_flg =  0;

      fprintf (stdout,"perform operation\n");
      semop_value = semop (semid, &semoper, (unsigned int)1);
      if ( semop_value == 0 ) {
         fprintf (stdout,"semop() call successful\n");
         /* newval = (8 - 5) i.e 3 */
         newval = semctl (semid, 0, GETVAL, arg);
         if ( newval == 3 )
            fprintf (stdout,"newval after semaphore operation=%d\n", newval);
         else
            fprintf (stderr,"ERROR: semaphore operation failed\n");
      }
      else {
         fprintf (stdout,"fail: semop() call failed\n");
         fprintf (stderr,"ERROR: %s\n", strerror(errno));
      }

      fprintf (stdout,"remove semid\n");
      semctl (semid, 0, IPC_RMID, arg);
}
```

NAME

setbuf — assign buffering to a stream

SYNOPSIS

```
#include <stdio.h>

void setbuf(FILE *stream, char *buf);
```

DESCRIPTION

Except that it returns no value, the function call:

```
setbuf(stream, buf)
```

is equivalent to:

```
setvbuf(stream, buf, _IOFBF, BUFSIZ)
```

if *buf* is not a null pointer, or to:

```
setvbuf(stream, buf, _IONBF, BUFSIZ)
```

if *buf* is a null pointer.

RETURN VALUE

The *setbuf*( ) function returns no value.

ERRORS

No errors are defined.

APPLICATION USAGE

A common source of error is allocating buffer space as an "automatic" variable in a code block, and then failing to close the stream in the same block.

With *setbuf*( ), allocating a buffer of *size* bytes does not necessarily imply that all of *size* bytes are used for the buffer area.

SEE ALSO

fopen( ), *setvbuf*( ), **<stdio.h>**.

EXAMPLE

```
/*
 * Copyright (C) ANTRIX Inc.
 */

/* setbuf.c
 * This program assigns buffering to a stream using function
 * setbuf.
 */

#include <stdio.h>
#include <fcntl.h>
#include <sys/stat.h>
#include <errno.h>

#define  PERM_ALL    (S_IRWXU | S_IRWXG | S_IRWXO)

main()
{
  int    fildes, length;
  FILE   *stream;
```

```
    char   character, *ptr;
    char   buf[BUFSIZ];
    char   string[] = "hello world";
    char   *filename = "testfile";

    length = strlen (string);
    fprintf (stdout,"initialize buffer to zero\n");
    memset (buf, 0, (size_t)sizeof(buf));

    fildes = creat (filename, PERM_ALL);
    fprintf (stdout,"write string\n");
    write (fildes, string, length);
    close (fildes);

    fprintf (stdout,"open a stream\n");
    stream = fopen (filename, "r");
    fprintf (stdout,"assign buffering to a stream\n");
    setbuf (stream, buf);
    character = fgetc (stream);

    fprintf (stdout,"use buffer to retrieve data\n");
    for (ptr = buf; ptr != (char *)0; ) {
       ptr = (char *)memchr (ptr, string[0], (sizeof(buf) - (ptr - buf)));
       fprintf (stdout,"string is=%s\n", ptr);
       if (ptr && memcmp(ptr, string, sizeof(string)-1) == 0)
          break;
    }

    fprintf (stdout,"subsequent reads gets that data\n");
    if (ptr) {
       *(ptr+1) = 'z';
       character = fgetc (stream);
       fprintf (stdout,"character=%c\n", character);
    }

    close (stream);
    fprintf (stdout,"remove testfile\n");
    remove (filename);
}
```

NAME

setcontext — set current user context

SYNOPSIS

UX

```
#include <ucontext.h>

int setcontext(const ucontext_t *ucp);
```

DESCRIPTION

Refer to *getcontext*( ).

EXAMPLE

```c
/*
 * Copyright (C) ANTRIX Inc.
 */

/* setcontext.c
 * This program sets the current user context
 * using function setcontext.
 */

#include <stdio.h>
#include <stdlib.h>
#include <signal.h>
#include <ucontext.h>
#include <errno.h>

int flag = 0;
int first_time = 0;

main()
{
   int          i;
   ucontext_t   ucp1, ucp2;

   fprintf (stdout,"initial getcontext call -- shouldn't return here\n");
   i = getcontext (&ucp1);
   if ( i != 0 )
      fprintf (stderr,"ERROR: expected 0, returned %d\n", i);

   flag++;

   fprintf (stdout,"setcontext returns to getcontext point\n");
   i = getcontext (&ucp2);
   if (i != 0)
      fprintf (stderr,"ERROR: expected 0, returned %d\n", i);
   if ( first_time == 0 ) {
      first_time++;
      flag++;
      setcontext (&ucp2);
      flag++;
   }

   if (flag == 2)
```

```
        fprintf (stdout,"setcontext() call successful\n");
    else
        fprintf (stdout,"expected flag value of 2, actual %d\n");
}
```

NAME

setgid — set-group-ID

SYNOPSIS

OH
```
#include <sys/types.h>
#include <unistd.h>

int setgid(gid_t gid);
```

DESCRIPTION

FIPS
If the process has appropriate privileges, *setgid*( ) sets the real group ID, effective group ID and the saved set-group-ID to *gid*.

FIPS
FIPS
If the process does not have appropriate privileges, but *gid* is equal to the real group ID or the saved set-group-ID, *setgid*( ) function sets the effective group ID to *gid*; the real group ID and saved set-group-ID remain unchanged.

Any supplementary group IDs of the calling process remain unchanged.

RETURN VALUE

Upon successful completion, 0 is returned. Otherwise, −1 is returned and *errno* is set to indicate the error.

ERRORS

The *setgid*( ) function will fail if:

[EINVAL]   The value of the *gid* argument is invalid and is not supported by the implementation.

[EPERM]   The process does not have appropriate privileges and *gid* does not match the
FIPS   real group ID or the saved set-group-ID.

SEE ALSO

exec, *getgid*( ), *setuid*( ), **<sys/types.h>**, **<unistd.h>**.

EXAMPLE

```
/*
 * Copyright (C) ANTRIX Inc.
 */

/* setgid.c: run as root
 * This program sets the real group ID, effective group ID and
 * the saved set-group-ID to gid if the process has appropriate
 * privileges using function setgid.
 */

#include <stdio.h>
#include <stdlib.h>
#include <unistd.h>
#include <sys/types.h>
#include <errno.h>

main()
{
    int     setgid_value;
    int     getgid_value;
    gid_t   gid = 2;
```

```
        fprintf (stdout,"set group id to bin\n");
        setgid_value = setgid (gid);
        if ( setgid_value == 0 ) {
            fprintf (stdout,"setgid() call successful\n");
            getgid_value = getgid();
            fprintf (stdout,"getgid_value=%d\n", getgid_value);
        }
        else {
            fprintf (stderr,"ERROR: setgid() call failed\n");
            fprintf (stderr,"ERROR: %s\n", strerror(errno));
        }
}
```

NAME

setgrent — reset group database to first entry

SYNOPSIS

UX   `#include <grp.h>`

`void setgrent(void);`

DESCRIPTION

Refer to *endgrent*( ).

EXAMPLE

```
/*
 * Copyright (C) ANTRIX Inc.
 */

/* setgrent.c
 * This program sets the group entry
 * using function setgrent.
 */

#include <stdio.h>
#include <stdlib.h>
#include <grp.h>
#include <errno.h>

main()
{
    struct      group *buf;
    int         i;

    fprintf (stdout,"go to the end of group file\n");
    for ( i = 0; i < 2; i++ ) {
        buf = (struct group  *)getgrent ();
        fprintf (stdout,"read entry number=%d\n", i);
        fprintf (stdout,"buf->gr_name=%s\n", buf->gr_name);
        fprintf (stdout,"buf->gr_gid=%d\n\n", buf->gr_gid);
    }

    fprintf (stdout,"rewind the group file\n");
    setgrent ();

    fprintf (stdout,"getgrent prints first entry\n");
    buf = (struct group  *)getgrent ();
    fprintf (stdout,"buf->gr_name=%s\n", buf->gr_name);
    fprintf (stdout,"buf->gr_gid=%d\n", buf->gr_gid);

    endgrent ();
}
```

NAME

setitimer — set value of interval timer

SYNOPSIS

UX   `#include <sys/time.h>`

```
int setitimer(int which, const struct itimerval *value,
      struct itimerval *ovalue);
```

DESCRIPTION

Refer to *getitimer*( ).

EXAMPLE

```
/*
 * Copyright (C) ANTRIX Inc.
 */

/* setitimer.c
 * This program sets value of interval timer using function setitimer
 */

#include <stdio.h>
#include <stdlib.h>
#include <time.h>
#include <sys/time.h>
#include <errno.h>

main()
{
   int      getitimer_value ;
   int      setitimer_value ;
   struct   itimerval value;
   struct   itimerval ovalue;
   struct   itimerval tp;

   value.it_interval.tv_sec = 1.0;
   value.it_interval.tv_usec= 1000;
   value.it_value.tv_sec = 2.0;
   value.it_value.tv_usec= 2000;

   fprintf (stdout,"set value of interval timer\n");
   setitimer_value = setitimer (ITIMER_REALPROF, &value, &ovalue);

   fprintf (stdout,"set value of interval timer again\n");
   fprintf (stdout,"and retreive original\n");
   setitimer_value = setitimer (ITIMER_REALPROF, &value, &ovalue);
   if ( setitimer_value != -1 ) {
       fprintf (stdout,"setitimer() call successful\n");
       fprintf (stdout,"ovalue.it_interval.tv_sec=%d\n",
                       ovalue.it_interval.tv_sec);
       fprintf (stdout,"ovalue.it_interval.tv_usec=%d\n",
                       ovalue.it_interval.tv_usec);
       fprintf (stdout,"ovalue.it_value.tv_sec=%d\n",
                       ovalue.it_value.tv_sec);
```

```
            fprintf (stdout,"ovalue.it_value.tv_usec=%d\n",
                        ovalue.it_value.tv_usec);
    }
    else {
        fprintf (stderr,"ERROR: setitimer() call failed\n");
        fprintf (stderr,"ERROR: %s\n", strerror(errno));
    }

    fprintf (stdout,"get value of interval timer\n");
    getitimer_value = getitimer (ITIMER_REALPROF, &tp);
    fprintf (stdout,"tp.it_interval.tv_sec=%d\n", tp.it_interval.tv_sec);
    fprintf (stdout,"tp.it_interval.tv_usec=%d\n", tp.it_interval.tv_usec);
    fprintf (stdout,"tp.it_value.tv_sec=%d\n", tp.it_value.tv_sec);
    fprintf (stdout,"tp.it_value.tv_usec=%d\n", tp.it_value.tv_usec);
}
```

NAME

_setjmp — set jump point for a non-local goto

SYNOPSIS

UX   `#include <setjmp.h>`

`int _setjmp(jmp_buf env);`

DESCRIPTION

Refer to *_longjmp*( ).

EXAMPLE

```
/*
 * Copyright (C) ANTRIX Inc.
 */

/* _setjmp.c
 * This program saves the calling environment in its env argument
 * using function _setjmp for later use by the _longjmp function.
 */

#include <stdio.h>
#include <signal.h>
#include <setjmp.h>
#include <errno.h>

main()
{
  int    _setjmp_value;
  int    val;
  jmp_buf env;
  static int  save_int;
  static long save_long;

  val = 5;

  fprintf (stdout,"save values\n");
  _setjmp_value = _setjmp (env);
  if ( _setjmp_value == val ) {
     fprintf (stdout,"_setjmp_value=%d\n", _setjmp_value );
     fprintf (stdout,"save_int  = %d\n", save_int);
     fprintf (stdout,"save_long = %d\n", save_long);
     exit (0);
  }
  save_int =  1;
  save_long = 123456789;

  fprintf (stdout,"restore values\n");
  _longjmp (env, val);
  fprintf (stderr,"ERROR: _longjmp() call failed\n");
}
```

setjmp( )

NAME

setjmp — set jump point for a non-local goto

SYNOPSIS

```
#include <setjmp.h>

int setjmp(jmp_buf env);
```

DESCRIPTION

A call to *setjmp( )*, saves the calling environment in its *env* argument for later use by *longjmp( )*.

It is unspecified whether *setjmp( )* is a macro or a function. If a macro definition is suppressed in order to access an actual function, or a program defines an external identifier with the name *setjmp* the behaviour is undefined.

All accessible objects have values as of the time *longjmp( )* was called, except that the values of objects of automatic storage duration which are local to the function containing the invocation of the corresponding *setjmp( )* which do not have volatile-qualified type and which are changed between the *setjmp( )* invocation and *longjmp( )* call are indeterminate.

An invocation of *setjmp( )* must appear in one of the following contexts only:

- the entire controlling expression of a selection or iteration statement

- one operand of a relational or equality operator with the other operand an integral constant expression, with the resulting expression being the entire controlling expression of a selection or iteration statement

- the operand of a unary "!" operator with the resulting expression being the entire controlling expression of a selection or iteration

- the entire expression of an expression statement (possibly cast to **void**).

RETURN VALUE

If the return is from a direct invocation, *setjmp( )* returns 0. If the return is from a call to *longjmp( )*, *setjmp( )* returns a non-zero value.

ERRORS

No errors are defined.

APPLICATION USAGE

In general, *sigsetjmp( )* is more useful in dealing with errors and interrupts encountered in a low-level subroutine of a program.

SEE ALSO

longjmp( ), *sigsetjmp( )*, **<setjmp.h>**. First released in Issue 1.

Derived from Issue 1 of the SVID.

Issue 4

The following changes are incorporated in this issue:

- This issue states that *setjmp( )* is a macro or a function; previous issues stated that it was a macro. Warnings have also been added about the suppression of a *setjmp( )* macro definition.

- Text describing the accessibility of objects after a *longjmp( )* call is added to the **DESCRIPTION** section. This text is imported from the entry for *longjmp( )*.

- Text describing the contexts in which calls to *setjmp*( ) are valid is moved to the **DESCRIPTION** section from the APPLICATION USAGE section.

- The **APPLICATION USAGE** section is changed to refer to *sigsetjmp*( ).

EXAMPLE

```
/*
 * Copyright (C) ANTRIX Inc.
 */

/* setjmp.c
 * This program saves the calling environment in its env argument
 * using function setjmp for later use by the longjmp function.
 */

#include <stdio.h>
#include <signal.h>
#include <setjmp.h>
#include <errno.h>

main()
{
   int     setjmp_value;
   int     val;
   jmp_buf env;
   static  int  save_int;
   static  long save_long;

   val = 5;

   fprintf (stdout,"save values\n");
   setjmp_value = setjmp (env);
   if ( setjmp_value == val ) {
      fprintf (stdout,"setjmp_value=%d\n", setjmp_value );
      fprintf (stdout,"save_int  = %d\n", save_int);
      fprintf (stdout,"save_long = %d\n", save_long);
      exit (0);
   }

   save_int =  1;
   save_long = 123456789;

   fprintf (stdout,"restore values\n");
   longjmp (env, val);
   fprintf (stderr,"ERROR: longjmp() call failed\n");
}
```

NAME

setkey — set encoding key (**OPTIONAL FUNCTIONALITY**)

SYNOPSIS

EX
```
#include <stdlib.h>
```

```
void setkey(const char *key);
```

DESCRIPTION

The *setkey()* function provides (rather primitive) access to an implementation-dependent encoding algorithm. The argument of *setkey()* is an array of length 64 bytes containing only the bytes with numerical value of 0 and 1. If this string is divided into groups of 8, the low-order bit in each group is ignored; this gives a 56-bit key which is used by the algorithm. This is the key that will be used with the algorithm to encode a string *block* passed to *encrypt()*.

RETURN VALUE

No values are returned.

ERRORS

The *setkey()* function will fail if:

[ENOSYS]   The functionality is not supported on this implementation.

APPLICATION USAGE

In some environments, decoding may not be implemented. This is related to U.S. Government restrictions on encryption and decryption routines: the DES decryption algorithm cannot be exported outside the U.S.A. Historical practice has been to ship a different version of the encryption library without the decryption feature in the routines supplied. Thus the exported version of *encrypt()* does encoding but not decoding.

Because *setkey()* does not return a value, applications wishing to check for errors should set *errno* to 0, call *setkey()*, then test *errno* and, if it is non-zero, assume an error has occurred.

SEE ALSO

crypt(), *encrypt()*, **<stdlib.h>**.

EXAMPLE

```
/*
 * Copyright (C) ANTRIX Inc.
 */

/* setkey.c
 * This program provides access to an implementation-dependent
 * encoding algorithm using function setkey.
 */

#include <stdio.h>
#include <stdlib.h>
#include <crypt.h>
#include <errno.h>

main()
{
    int    i, edflag;
    char   block[64];

    memset(block, ' ', 64);
```

```
    for (i = 0; i < 64; i++)
        block[i] = '1';
    fprintf (stdout,"previous key value=%s\n", block);

    fprintf (stdout,"set encoding key\n");
    setkey(block);

    fprintf (stdout,"encrypt key value\n");
    encrypt (block, 0);
    fprintf (stdout,"encrypt() call successful\n");
    fprintf (stdout,"New key value after encryption=%s\n", block);
}
```

NAME

setlocale — set program locale

SYNOPSIS

```
#include <locale.h>

char *setlocale(int category, const char *locale);
```

DESCRIPTION

The *setlocale*( ) function selects the appropriate piece of the program's locale, as specified by the *category* and *locale* arguments, and may be used to change or query the program's entire locale or portions thereof. The value LC_ALL for *category* names the program's entire locale; other values for *category* name only a part of the program's locale:

LC_COLLATE   Affects the behaviour of regular expressions and the collation functions.

LC_CTYPE   Affects the behaviour of regular expressions, character classification, character conversion functions, and wide character functions.

LC_MESSAGES Affects what strings are expected by commands and utilities as affirmative or negative responses, what strings are given by commands and utilities as affirmative or negative responses, and the content of messages.

LC_MONETARY Affects the behaviour of functions that handle monetary values.

LC_NUMERIC   Affects the radix character for the formatted input/output functions and the string conversion functions.

LC_TIME   Affects the behaviour of the time conversion functions.

The *locale* argument is a pointer to a character string containing the required setting of *category*. The contents of this string are implementation-dependent. In addition, the following preset values of *locale* are defined for all settings of *category*:

"POSIX"   Specifies the minimal environment for C-language translation called POSIX locale. If *setlocale*( ) is not invoked, the POSIX locale is the default.

"C"   Same as POSIX.

" "   Specifies an implementation-dependent native environment. For XSI-conformant systems, this corresponds to the value of the associated environment variables, *LC_** and *LANG*; see the **XBD** specification, **Chapter 5**, **Locale** and the **XBD** specification, **Chapter 6**, **Environment Variables**.

A null pointer

    Used to direct *setlocale*( ) to query the current internationalised environment and return the name of the *locale*( ).

RETURN VALUE

Upon successful completion, *setlocale*( ) returns the string associated with the specified category for the new locale. Otherwise, *setlocale*( ) returns a null pointer and the program's locale is not changed.

A null pointer for *locale* causes *setlocale*( ) to return a pointer to the string associated with the *category* for the program's current locale. The program's locale is not changed.

The string returned by *setlocale*( ) is such that a subsequent call with that string and its associated *category* will restore that part of the program's locale. The string returned must not be modified by the program, but may be overwritten by a subsequent call to *setlocale*( ).

APPLICATION USAGE

The following code illustrates how a program can initialise the international environment for one language, while selectively modifying the program's locale such that regular expressions and string operations can be applied to text recorded in a different language:

```
setlocale(LC_ALL, "De");
setlocale(LC_COLLATE, "Fr@dict");
```

Internationalised programs must call *setlocale*( ) to initiate a specific language operation. This can be done by calling *setlocale*( ) as follows:

```
setlocale(LC_ALL, "");
```

Changing the setting of LC_MESSAGES has no effect on catalogues that are already opened by calls to *catopen*( ).

ERRORS

No errors are defined.

SEE ALSO

exec, *isalnum*( ), *isalpha*( ), *iscntrl*( ), *isgraph*( ), *islower*( ), *isprint*( ), *ispunct*( ), *isspace*( ), *isupper*( ), *iswalnum*( ), *iswalpha*( ), *iswcntrl*( ), *iswgraph*( ), *iswlower*( ), *iswprint*( ), *iswpunct*( ), *iswspace*( ), *iswupper*( ), *localeconv*( ), *mblen*( ), *mbstowcs*( ), *mbtowc*( ), *nl_langinfo*( ), *printf*( ), *scanf*( ), *setlocale*( ), *strcoll*( ), *strerror*( ), *strfmon*( ), *strtod*( ), *strxfrm*( ), *tolower*( ), *toupper*( ), *towlower*( ), *towupper*( ), *wcscoll*( ), *wcstod*( ), *wcstombs*( ), *wcsxfrm*( ), *wctomb*( ), **<langinfo.h>**, **<locale.h>**.

EXAMPLE

```
/*
 * Copyright (C) ANTRIX Inc.
 */

/* setlocale.c
 * This program sets the program locale to english using
 * function setlocale.
 */

#include <stdio.h>
#include <stdlib.h>
#include <locale.h>
#include <errno.h>

main()
{
  char  *setlocale_value;

  fprintf (stdout,"set locale value\n");
  setlocale_value = setlocale (LC_ALL, "C");
  fprintf (stdout,"setlocale_value=%s\n", setlocale_value);
}
```

NAME

setlogmask — set log priority mask

SYNOPSIS

UX   `#include <syslog.h>`

`int setlogmask(int maskpri);`

DESCRIPTION

Refer to *closelog*( ).

NAME

setpgid — set process group ID for job control

SYNOPSIS

OH
```
#include <sys/types.h>
#include <unistd.h>

int setpgid(pid_t pid, pid_t pgid);
```

DESCRIPTION

The *setpgid*( ) function is used either to join an existing process group or create a new process group within the session of the calling process. The process group ID of a session leader will not change. Upon successful completion, the process group ID of the process with a process ID that matches *pid* will be set to *pgid*. As a special case, if *pid* is 0, the process ID of the calling process will be used. Also, if *pgid* is 0, the process group ID of the indicated process will be used.

RETURN VALUE

Upon successful completion, *setpgid*( ) returns 0. Otherwise −1 is returned and *errno* is set to indicate the error.

ERRORS

The *setpgid*( ) function will fail if:

[EACCES]   The value of the *pid* argument matches the process ID of a child process of the calling process and the child process has successfully executed one of the *exec* functions.

[EINVAL]   The value of the *pgid* argument is less than 0, or is not a value supported by the implementation.

[EPERM]   The process indicated by the *pid* argument is a session leader.

The value of the *pid* argument matches the process ID of a child process of the calling process and the child process is not in the same session as the calling process.

The value of the *pgid* argument is valid but does not match the process ID of the process indicated by the *pid* argument and there is no process with a process group ID that matches the value of the *pgid* argument in the same session as the calling process.

[ESRCH]   The value of the *pid* argument does not match the process ID of the calling process or of a child process of the calling process.

SEE ALSO

exec, *getpgrp*( ), *setsid*( ), *tcsetpgrp*( ), **<sys/types.h>**, **<unistd.h>**.

EXAMPLE

```
/*
 * Copyright (C) ANTRIX Inc.
 */

/* setpgid.c
 * This program sets process group ID for job control using
 * function setpgid.
 */

#include <stdio.h>
```

```
#include <stdlib.h>
#include <unistd.h>
#include <sys/types.h>
#include <errno.h>

main()
{
   int     setpgid_value;
   pid_t   child_pgid, parent_pgid;
   pid_t   child, parent;
   int     stat_loc;

   if (fork() == 0)   {
      child = getpid ();
      child_pgid = getpgid (child);
      fprintf (stdout,"original child_pgid=%d\n", child_pgid);
      setpgid_value = setpgid (child, 0);
      child_pgid = getpgid (child);
      fprintf (stdout,"new child_pgid=%d\n", child_pgid);
      if ( setpgid_value == 0 )
         fprintf (stdout,"setpgid() call successful\n");
      else {
         fprintf (stderr,"ERROR: setpgid() call failed\n");
         fprintf (stderr,"ERROR: %s\n", strerror(errno));
      }
      exit (1);
   } wait (&stat_loc);

   parent = getpid ();
   parent_pgid = getpgid (parent);
   fprintf (stdout,"parent_pgid=%d\n", parent_pgid);
}
```

NAME

setpgrp — set process group ID

SYNOPSIS

UX

```
#include <unistd.h>
```

```
pid_t setpgrp(void);
```

DESCRIPTION

If the calling process is not already a session leader, *setpgrp*( ) sets the process group ID of the calling process to the process ID of the calling process. If *setpgrp*( ) creates a new session, then the new session has no controlling terminal.

The *setpgrp*( ) function has no effect when the calling process is a session leader.

RETURN VALUE

Upon successful completion, *setpgrp*( ) returns the new process group ID.

ERRORS

No errors are defined.

SEE ALSO

exec, *fork*( ), *getpid*( ), *getsid*( ), *kill*( ), *setsid*( ), **<unistd.h>**.

EXAMPLE

```c
/*
 * Copyright (C) ANTRIX Inc.
 */

/* setpgrp.c
 * This program sets the process group ID
 * using function setpgrp.
 */

#include <stdio.h>
#include <stdlib.h>
#include <sys/types.h>
#include <errno.h>

main()
{
  int      setpgrp_value;
  int      setsid_value;
  int      stat_loc, pid;

  if ( fork() == 0 ) {
    pid = getpid ();
    fprintf (stdout,"current group-id=%d\n", getpgrp());
    fprintf (stdout,"current session-id=%d\n", getsid(pid));
    setpgrp_value = setpgrp ();
    if ( setpgrp_value >= 0 ) {
      fprintf (stdout,"setpgrp() call successful\n");
      fprintf (stdout,"new group-id=%d\n", getpgrp());
      fprintf (stdout,"new session-id=%d\n", getsid(pid));
    }
    else {
```

```
            fprintf (stderr,"ERROR: setpgrp() call failed\n");
            fprintf (stderr,"ERROR: %s\n", strerror(errno));
        }
        exit (1);
    } wait(&stat_loc);
}
```

NAME

setpriority — set process scheduling priority

SYNOPSIS

UX
```
#include <sys/resource.h>
```
```
int setpriority(int which, id_t who, int priority);
```

DESCRIPTION

Refer to *getpriority*( ).

EXAMPLE

```
/*
 * Copyright (C) ANTRIX Inc.
 */

/* setpriority.c
 * This program sets the scheduling priority for the process
 * using function setpriority.
 */

#include <stdio.h>
#include <stdlib.h>
#include <sys/types.h>
#include <sys/time.h>
#include <sys/resource.h>
#include <errno.h>

main()
{
  int    setpriority_value;
  int    getpriority_value;
  pid_t  who;

  fprintf (stdout,"get process id\n");
  who = getpid();

  fprintf (stdout,"set priority to 2\n");
  who = setpriority(PRIO_PROCESS, who, 2);

  fprintf (stdout, "get process scheduling priority\n");
  getpriority_value = getpriority (PRIO_PROCESS, who);
  fprintf (stdout,"getpriority_value=%d\n", getpriority_value);
}
```

NAME

setregid — set real and effective group IDs

SYNOPSIS

UX
```
#include <unistd.h>
```
```
int setregid(gid_t rgid, gid_t egid);
```

DESCRIPTION

The *setregid*( ) function is used to set the real and effective group IDs of the calling process. If *rgid* is −1, the real group ID is not changed; if *egid* is −1, the effective group ID is not changed. The real and effective group IDs may be set to different values in the same call.

Only a process with appropriate privileges can set the real group ID and the effective group ID to any valid value.

A non-privileged process can set either the real group ID to the saved set-group-ID from *execv*( ), or the effective group ID to the saved set-group-ID or the real group ID.

Any supplementary group IDs of the calling process remain unchanged.

RETURN VALUE

Upon successful completion, 0 is returned. Otherwise, −1 is returned and *errno* is set to indicate the error and neither of the group IDs will be changed.

ERRORS

The *setregid*( ) function will fail if:

[EINVAL]   The value of the *rgid* or *egid* argument is invalid or out-of-range.

[EPERM]   The process does not have appropriate privileges and a change other than changing the real group ID to the saved set-group-ID, or changing the effective group ID to the real group ID or the saved group ID, was requested.

APPLICATION USAGE

If a set-group-ID process sets its effective group ID to its real group ID, it can still set its effective group ID back to the saved set-group-ID.

SEE ALSO

exec, *getuid*( ), *setreuid*( ), *setuid*( ), **<unistd.h>**.

EXAMPLE

```
/*
 * Copyright (C) ANTRIX Inc.
 */

/* setregid.c: run as root
 * This program sets the real group ID, effective group ID and
 * the saved set-group-ID to gid if the process has appropriate
 * privileges using function setregid.
 */

#include <stdio.h>
#include <stdlib.h>
#include <unistd.h>
#include <sys/types.h>
#include <errno.h>

main()
```

```
{
    int     setregid_value;
    int     getgid_value;
    int     getegid_value;
    gid_t   gid = 2;

    fprintf (stdout,"set group id to bin\n");
    setregid_value = setregid (gid, gid);
    if ( setregid_value == 0 ) {
        fprintf (stdout,"setregid() call successful\n");
        getgid_value = getgid();
        fprintf (stdout,"getgid_value=%d\n", getgid_value);
        getegid_value = getegid();
        fprintf (stdout,"getegid_value=%d\n", getegid_value);
    }
    else {
        fprintf (stderr,"ERROR: setregid() call failed\n");
        fprintf (stderr,"ERROR: %s\n", strerror(errno));
    }
}
```

NAME

setreuid — set real and effective user IDs

SYNOPSIS

UX
```
#include <unistd.h>
```

```
int setreuid(uid_t ruid, uid_t euid);
```

DESCRIPTION

The *setreuid*( ) function sets the real and effective user IDs of the current process to the values specified by the *ruid* and *euid* arguments. If *ruid* or *euid* is −1, the corresponding effective or real user ID of the current process is left unchanged.

A process with appropriate privileges can set either ID to any value. An unprivileged process can only set the effective user ID if the *euid* argument is equal to either the real, effective, or saved user ID of the process.

It is unspecified whether a process without appropriate privileges is permitted to change the real user ID to match the current real, effective or saved user ID of the process.

RETURN VALUE

Upon successful completion, 0 is returned. Otherwise, −1 is returned and *errno* is set to indicate the error.

ERRORS

The *setreuid*( ) function will fail if:

[EINVAL]   The value of the *ruid* or *euid* argument is invalid or out-of-range.

[EPERM]   The current process does not have appropriate privileges, and either an attempt was made to change the effective user ID to a value other than the real user ID or the saved set-user-ID or an an attempt was made to change the real user ID to a value not permitted by the implementation.

SEE ALSO

getuid( ), *setuid*( ), **<unistd.h>**.

EXAMPLE

```
/*
 * Copyright (C) ANTRIX Inc.
 */

/* setreuid.c: run as root
 * This program sets the real user ID, effective user ID, and
 * the saved set-user-ID to uid, if the process had appropriate
 * privileges using function setreuid.
 */

#include <stdio.h>
#include <stdlib.h>
#include <sys/types.h>
#include <errno.h>

main()
{
    int      setreuid_value;
    uid_t    getuid_value;
    uid_t    geteuid_value;
```

```
        uid_t   uid = 2;

        fprintf (stdout,"set user id\n");
        setreuid_value = setreuid (uid, uid);
        if ( setreuid_value == 0 ) {
            fprintf (stdout,"setreuid() call successful\n");
            getuid_value = getuid ();
            fprintf (stdout,"getuid_value=%d\n", getuid_value);
            geteuid_value = geteuid ();
            fprintf (stdout,"geteuid_value=%d\n", geteuid_value);
        }
        else {
            fprintf (stderr,"ERROR: setreuid() call failed\n");
            fprintf (stderr,"ERROR: %s\n", strerror(errno));
        }
    }
```

NAME

setrlimit — control maximum resource consumption

SYNOPSIS

UX   `#include <sys/resource.h>`

`int setrlimit(int resource, const struct rlimit *rlp);`

DESCRIPTION

Refer to *getrlimit*( ).

EXAMPLE

```
/*
 * Copyright (C) ANTRIX Inc.
 */

/* setrlimit.c
 * This program sets the maximum system resource consumption
 * using function setrlimit.
 */

#include <stdio.h>
#include <stdlib.h>
#include <sys/time.h>
#include <sys/resource.h>
#include <errno.h>

main()
{
   int     setrlimit_value;
   struct  rlimit rlp, new_rlp;

   fprintf (stdout,"get the current limit\n");
   getrlimit (RLIMIT_FSIZE, &rlp);
   rlp.rlim_cur = rlp.rlim_cur - 10;

   fprintf (stdout,"set new limit\n");
   setrlimit_value = setrlimit (RLIMIT_FSIZE, &rlp);
   if ( setrlimit_value == 0 ) {
      fprintf (stdout,"setrlimit() call successful\n");
      getrlimit (RLIMIT_FSIZE, &new_rlp);
      fprintf (stdout,"new_rlp.rlim_cur=%d\n", new_rlp.rlim_cur);
      fprintf (stdout,"new_rlp.rlim_max=%d\n", new_rlp.rlim_max);
   }
   else {
      fprintf (stderr,"ERROR: setrlimit() call failed\n");
      fprintf (stderr,"ERROR: %s\n", strerror(errno));
   }
}
```

NAME

setsid — create session and set process group ID

SYNOPSIS

OH `#include <sys/types.h>`
`#include <unistd.h>`

`pid_t setsid(void);`

DESCRIPTION

The *setsid*( ) function creates a new session, if the calling process is not a process group leader. Upon return the calling process will be the session leader of this new session, will be the process group leader of a new process group, and will have no controlling terminal. The process group ID of the calling process will be set equal to the process ID of the calling process. The calling process will be the only process in the new process group and the only process in the new session.

RETURN VALUE

Upon successful completion, *setsid*( ) returns the value of the process group ID of the calling process. Otherwise it returns (**pid_t**)–1 and sets *errno* to indicate the error.

ERRORS

The *setsid*( ) function will fail if:

[EPERM]   The calling process is already a process group leader, or the process group ID of a process other than the calling process matches the process ID of the calling process.

SEE ALSO

getsid( ), *setpgid*( ), *setpgrp*( ), **<sys/types.h>**, **<unistd.h>**.

EXAMPLE

```
/*
 * Copyright (C) ANTRIX Inc.
 */

/* setsid.c
 * This program creates session and sets process group ID using
 * function setsid.
 */

#include <stdio.h>
#include <stdlib.h>
#include <sys/types.h>
#include <errno.h>

main()
{
   int  setsid_value;
   int  stat_loc, pid;

   if ( fork() == 0 ) {
      pid = getpid ();
      fprintf (stdout,"current group-id=%d\n", getpgrp());
      fprintf (stdout,"current session-id=%d\n", getsid(pid));
      setsid_value = setsid ();
```

```
        if ( setsid_value >= 0 ) {
            fprintf (stdout,"setsid() call successful\n");
            fprintf (stdout,"setsid_value=%d\n", setsid_value);
            fprintf (stdout,"new group-id=%d\n", getpgrp());
            fprintf (stdout,"new session-id=%d\n", getsid(pid));
        }
        else {
            fprintf (stderr,"ERROR: setsid() call failed\n");
            fprintf (stderr,"ERROR: %s\n", strerror(errno));
        }
        exit (1);
    } wait(&stat_loc);
}
```

NAME

setstate — switch pseudorandom number generator state arrays

SYNOPSIS

UX
```
#include <stdlib.h>

char *setstate(const char *state);
```

DESCRIPTION

Refer to *initstate*( ).

EXAMPLE

```c
/*
 * Copyright (C) ANTRIX Inc.
 */

/* setstate.c
 * This program allows rapid switching between states
 * using function setstate.
 */

#include <stdio.h>
#include <stdlib.h>
#include <errno.h>

static long state1[32] = {
    3,
    0x9a319039, 0x32d9c024, 0x9b663182, 0x5da1f342,
    0x7449e56b, 0xbeb1dbb0, 0xab5c5918, 0x946554fd,
    0x8c2e680f, 0xeb3d799f, 0xb11ee0b7, 0x2d436b86,
    0xda672e2a, 0x1588ca88, 0xe369735d, 0x904f35f7,
    0xd7158fd6, 0x6fa6f051, 0x616e6b96, 0xac94efdc,
    0xde3b81e0, 0xdf0a6fb5, 0xf103bc02, 0x48f340fb,
    0x36413f93, 0xc622c298, 0xf5a42ab8, 0x8a88d77b,
    0xf5ad9d0e, 0x8999220b, 0x27fb47b9
};

main()
{
    char *setstate_value;
    unsigned seed;
    int n;

    seed = 1;
    n = 128;
    fprintf(stdout, "initialize for future use\n");
    initstate(seed, state1, n);

    fprintf(stdout, "switch the states\n");
    setstate_value = setstate(state1);
    fprintf(stdout, "%d\n",random());
}
```

NAME

setuid — set-user-ID

SYNOPSIS

OH
```
#include <sys/types.h>
#include <unistd.h>

int setuid(uid_t uid);
```

DESCRIPTION

FIPS   If the process has appropriate privileges, *setuid*( ) sets the real user ID, effective user ID, and the saved set-user-ID to *uid*.

FIPS   If the process does not have appropriate privileges, but *uid* is equal to the real user ID or the
FIPS   saved set-user-ID, *setuid*( ) sets the effective user ID to *uid*; the real user ID and saved set-user-ID remain unchanged.

RETURN VALUE

Upon successful completion, 0 is returned. Otherwise, −1 is returned and *errno* is set to indicate the error.

ERRORS

The *setuid*( ) function will fail and return −1 and set *errno* to the corresponding value if one or more of the following are true:

[EINVAL]   The value of the *uid* argument is invalid and not supported by the implementation.

[EPERM]   The process does not have appropriate privileges and *uid* does not match the
FIPS   real user ID or the saved set-user-ID.

SEE ALSO

exec, *geteuid*( ), *getuid*( ), *setgid*( ), **<sys/types.h>**, **<unistd.h>**.

EXAMPLE

```
/*
 * Copyright (C) ANTRIX Inc.
 */

/* setuid.c: run as root
 * This program stes the real user ID, effective user ID, and
 * the saved set-user-ID to uid, if the process had appropriate
 * privileges using function setuid.
 */

#include <stdio.h>
#include <stdlib.h>
#include <sys/types.h>
#include <errno.h>

main()
{
   int     setuid_value;
   uid_t   getuid_value;
   uid_t   uid - 2;

   fprintf (stdout,"set user id\n");
```

```
        setuid_value = setuid (uid);
        if ( setuid_value == 0 ) {
            fprintf (stdout,"setuid() call successful\n");
            getuid_value = getuid ();
            fprintf (stdout,"getuid_value=%d\n", getuid_value);
        }
        else {
            fprintf (stderr,"ERROR: setuid() call failed\n");
            fprintf (stderr,"ERROR: %s\n", strerror(errno));
        }
    }
```

NAME

    setutxent — reset user accounting database to first entry

SYNOPSIS

UX   `#include <utmpx.h>`

       `void setutxent(void);`

DESCRIPTION

    Refer to *endutxent( )*.

NAME

setvbuf — assign buffering to a stream

SYNOPSIS

```
#include <stdio.h>

int setvbuf(FILE *stream, char *buf, int type, size_t size);
```

DESCRIPTION

The *setvbuf*( ) function may be used after the stream pointed to by *stream* is associated with an open file but before any other operation is performed on the stream. The argument *type* determines how *stream* will be buffered, as follows: _IOFBF causes input/output to be fully buffered; _IOLBF causes input/output to be line buffered; _IONBF causes input/output to be unbuffered. If *buf* is not a null pointer, the array it points to may be used instead of a buffer allocated by *setvbuf*( ). The argument *size* specifies the size of the array. The contents of the array at any time are indeterminate.

For information about streams, see the **XSH** specification, **Section 2.4**, **Standard I/O Streams**.

RETURN VALUE

Upon successful completion, *setvbuf*( ) returns 0. Otherwise, it returns a non-zero value if an invalid value is given for *type* or if the request cannot be honoured.

ERRORS

The *setvbuf*( ) function may fail if:

EX   [EBADF]   The file descriptor underlying *stream* is not valid.

APPLICATION USAGE

A common source of error is allocating buffer space as an "automatic" variable in a code block, and then failing to close the stream in the same block.

With *setvbuf*( ), allocating a buffer of *size* bytes does not necessarily imply that all of *size* bytes are used for the buffer area.

Applications should note that many implementations only provide line buffering on input from terminal devices.

SEE ALSO

fopen( ), *setbuf*( ), **<stdio.h>**.

EXAMPLE

```
/*
 * Copyright (C) ANTRIX Inc.
 */

/* setvbuf.c
 * This program assigns buffering to a stream using function
 * setvbuf.
 */

#include <stdio.h>
#include <stdlib.h>
#include <fcntl.h>
#include <sys/stat.h>
#include <errno.h>

#define  PERM_ALL    (S_IRWXU | S_IRWXG | S_IRWXO)
```

```
main()
{
  int    setvbuf_value;
  int    fildes, length;
  FILE   *stream;
  char   character, *ptr;
  char   buf[BUFSIZ];
  char   string[] = "hello world";
  char   *filename = "testfile";

  length = strlen (string);
  fprintf (stdout,"initialize buffer to zero\n");
  memset (buf, 0, (size_t) sizeof(buf));

  fprintf (stdout,"create testfile\n");
  fildes = creat (filename, PERM_ALL);

  fprintf (stdout,"write string\n");
  write (fildes, string, length);

  fprintf (stdout,"close testfile\n");
  close (fildes);

  fprintf (stdout,"open testfile for read\n");
  stream = fopen (filename, "r");

  fprintf (stdout,"assigning buffering to a stream\n");
  setvbuf_value = setvbuf (stream, buf, _IOFBF, sizeof(buf));
  if ( setvbuf_value == 0 )
     fprintf (stdout,"setvbuf() call successful\n");
  else
     fprintf (stderr,"ERROR: setvbuf() call failed\n");

  character = fgetc(stream);
  fprintf (stdout,"use buffer to retrieve data\n");
  for (ptr = buf; ptr != (char *)0; ) {
    ptr = (char *)memchr (ptr, string[0], (sizeof(buf) - (ptr - buf)));
    fprintf (stdout,"string is=%s\n", ptr);
    if (ptr && memcmp(ptr, string, sizeof(string)-1) == 0)
       break;
  }

  fprintf (stdout,"subsequent reads gets that data\n");
  if (ptr) {
     *(ptr+1) = 'z';
     character = fgetc (stream);
     fprintf (stdout,"character=%c\n", character);
  }
  close (stream);
```

```
        fprintf (stdout,"remove testfile\n");
        remove (filename);
}
```

NAME

shmat — shared memory attach operation

SYNOPSIS

EX
```
#include <sys/shm.h>
```
```
void *shmat(int shmid, const void *shmaddr, int shmflg);
```

DESCRIPTION

The *shmat*( ) function attaches the shared memory segment associated with the shared memory identifier specified by *shmid* to the address space of the calling process. The segment is attached at the address specified by one of the following criteria:

- If *shmaddr* is a null pointer, the segment is attached at the first available address as selected by the system.

- If *shmaddr* is not a null pointer and (*shmflg* & SHM_RND) is non-zero, the segment is attached at the address given by (*shmaddr* − ((*ptrdiff_t*)*shmaddr* % SHMLBA)) The character % is the C-language remainder operator.

- If *shmaddr* is not a null pointer and (*shmflg* & SHM_RND) is 0, the segment is attached at the address given by *shmaddr*.

- The segment is attached for reading if (*shmflg* & SHM_RDONLY) is non-zero and the calling process has read permission; otherwise, if it is 0 and the calling process has read and write permission, the segment is attached for reading and writing.

RETURN VALUE

Upon successful completion, *shmat*( ) increments the value of *shm_nattach* in the data structure associated with the shared memory ID of the attached shared memory segment and returns the segment's start address.

Otherwise, the shared memory segment is not attached, *shmat*( ) returns −1 and *errno* is set to indicate the error.

ERRORS

The *shmat*( ) function will fail if:

[EACCES]	Operation permission is denied to the calling process, see the **XSH** specification, **Section 2.6**, **Interprocess Communication**.
[EINVAL]	The value of *shmid* is not a valid shared memory identifier; the *shmaddr* is not a null pointer and the value of (*shmaddr* − ((*ptrdiff_t*)*shmaddr* % SHMLBA)) is an illegal address for attaching shared memory; or the *shmaddr* is not a null pointer, (*shmflg* & SHM_RND) is 0 and the value of *shmaddr* is an illegal address for attaching shared memory.
[EMFILE]	The number of shared memory segments attached to the calling process would exceed the system-imposed limit.
[ENOMEM]	The available data space is not large enough to accommodate the shared memory segment.
[ENOSYS]	The function is not implemented.

FUTURE DIRECTIONS

The IEEE 1003.4 standards committee is developing alternative interfaces for interprocess communication. Application developers who need to use IPC should design their applications so that modules using the routines described in this document can be easily modified to use alternative methods at a later date.

SEE ALSO

exec, *exit*( ), *fork*( ), *shmctl*( ), *shmdt*( ), *shmget*( ), **<sys/shm.h>**, **XSH** specification, **Section 2.6**, **Interprocess Communication**.

EXAMPLE

```c
/*
 * Copyright (C) ANTRIX Inc.
 */

/* shmat.c
 * This program attaches the shared memory segment associated
 * with the shared memory identifier by shmid using function
 * shmat.
 */

#include <stdio.h>
#include <stdlib.h>
#include <sys/types.h>
#include <sys/ipc.h>
#include <sys/shm.h>
#include <sys/stat.h>
#include <sys/wait.h>
#include <errno.h>

#define SHM_PERM    (S_IRWXU | S_IRWXG | S_IRWXO)

main()
{
  int    *shmat_value;
  int    shmid, i, stat_loc;
  int    shmarr[10];
  pid_t  pid;

  fprintf (stdout,"get shmid\n");
  shmid = shmget (IPC_PRIVATE, sizeof(shmarr), IPC_CREAT | SHM_PERM);
  shmat_value = (int *)shmat (shmid, 0, 0);

  printf("child and parent sharing the same memory locations\n");
  pid = fork ();
  if (pid == 0) {
    fprintf (stdout,"child writes to memory locations\n");
    for (i = 0; i < 10; i++) {
      shmat_value[i] = 2*i;
      fprintf (stdout,"child sets shmat_value[%d]=%d\n",
                        i, shmat_value[i]);
    }
    exit (1);
  }
  wait (&stat_loc);

  fprintf (stdout,"parent to read memory locations\n");
  for (i = 0; i < 10; i++)
    fprintf (stdout,"parent reads shmat_value[%d]=%d\n",
```

```
                        i, shmat_value[i]);
    shmdt ((void *)shmat_value);
}
```

NAME

shmctl — shared memory control operations

SYNOPSIS

EX
```
#include <sys/shm.h>
```

```
int shmctl(int shmid, int cmd, struct shmid_ds *buf);
```

DESCRIPTION

The *shmctl( )* function provides a variety of shared memory control operations as specified by *cmd*. The following values for *cmd* are available:

IPC_STAT
Place the current value of each member of the **shmid_ds** data structure associated with *shmid* into the structure pointed to by *buf*. The contents of the structure are defined in **<sys/shm.h>**.

IPC_SET
Set the value of the following members of the **shmid_ds** data structure associated with *shmid* to the corresponding value found in the structure pointed to by *buf*:

```
shm_perm.uid
shm_perm.gid
shm_perm.mode        low-order nine bits
```

IPC_SET can only be executed by a process that has an effective user ID equal to either that of a process with appropriate privileges or to the value of **shm_perm.cuid** or **shm_perm.uid** in the **shmid_ds** data structure associated with *shmid*.

IPC_RMID
Remove the shared memory identifier specified by *shmid* from the system and destroy the shared memory segment and **shmid_ds** data structure associated with it. IPC_RMID can only be executed by a process that has an effective user ID equal to either that of a process with appropriate privileges or to the value of *shm_perm.cuid* or *shm_perm.uid* in the **shmid_ds** data structure associated with *shmid*.

RETURN VALUE

Upon successful completion, *shmctl( )* returns 0. Otherwise, it returns −1 and *errno* will be set to indicate the error.

ERRORS

The *shmctl( )* function will fail if:

[EACCES]
The argument *cmd* is equal to IPC_STAT and the calling process does not have read permission, see the **XSH** specification, **Section 2.6**, **Interprocess Communication**.

[EINVAL]
The value of *shmid* is not a valid shared memory identifier, or the value of *cmd* is not a valid command.

[ENOSYS]
The function is not implemented.

[EPERM]
The argument *cmd* is equal to IPC_RMID or IPC_SET and the effective user ID of the calling process is not equal to that of a process with appropriate privileges and it is not equal to the value of **shm_perm.cuid** or **shm_perm.uid** in the data structure associated with *shmid*.

The *shmctl( )* function may fail if:

UX   [EOVERFLOW]   The *cmd* argument is IPC_STAT and the **gid** or **uid** value is too large to be
         stored in the structure pointed to by the *buf* argument.

FUTURE DIRECTIONS

The IEEE 1003.4 standards committee is developing alternative interfaces for interprocess
communication. Application developers who need to use IPC should design their applications
so that modules using the routines described in this document can be easily modified to use
alternative methods at a later date.

SEE ALSO

shmat( ), *shmdt*( ), *shmget*( ), **<sys/shm.h>**, **XSH** specification, **Section 2.6**, **Interprocess
Communication**.

EXAMPLE

```
/*
 * Copyright (C) ANTRIX Inc.
 */

/* shmctl.c
 * This program illustrates shared memory control operations
 * as specified by IPC_STAT using function shmctl.
 */

#include <stdio.h>
#include <stdlib.h>
#include <sys/types.h>
#include <sys/ipc.h>
#include <sys/shm.h>
#include <sys/stat.h>
#include <sys/wait.h>
#include <errno.h>

#define SHM_PERM     (S_IRWXU | S_IRWXG | S_IRWXO)

main()
{
  int     shmctl_value;
  int     *shmat_value;
  int     shmid, i;
  int     shmarr[10];
  struct  shmid_ds buf;

  fprintf (stdout,"get shmid\n");
  shmid = shmget (IPC_PRIVATE, sizeof(shmarr), IPC_CREAT | SHM_PERM);

  fprintf (stdout,"attach shared memory\n");
  shmat_value = (int *)shmat (shmid, 0, 0);
  for (i = 0; i < 10; i++)
     shmat_value[i] = i;

  fprintf (stdout,"get shmid status\n");
  shmctl_value = shmctl ( shmid, IPC_STAT, &buf );
  if (shmctl_value == 0) {
     fprintf (stdout,"shmctl() call successful\n");
```

```
            fprintf (stdout,"buf.shm_cpid=%d\n", buf.shm_cpid);
            fprintf (stdout,"buf.shm_lpid=%d\n", buf.shm_lpid);
    }
    else {
        fprintf (stdout,"error: shmctl() call failed\n");
        fprintf (stderr,"ERROR: %s\n", strerror(errno));
    }

    fprintf (stdout,"detach shared memory\n");
    shmdt ((void *)shmat_value);
}
```

NAME

shmdt — shared memory detach operation

SYNOPSIS

EX
```
#include <sys/shm.h>
```

```
int shmdt(const void *shmaddr);
```

DESCRIPTION

The *shmdt*( ) function detaches from the calling process' address space the shared memory segment located at the address specified by *shmaddr*.

RETURN VALUE

Upon successful completion, *shmdt*( ) will decrement the value of *shm_nattach* in the data structure associated with the shared memory ID of the attached shared memory segment and return 0.

Otherwise, the shared memory segment will not be detached, *shmdt*( ) will return −1 and *errno* will be set to indicate the error.

ERRORS

The *shmdt*( ) function will fail if:

[EINVAL]   The value of *shmaddr* is not the data segment start address of a shared memory segment.

[ENOSYS]   The function is not implemented.

FUTURE DIRECTIONS

The IEEE 1003.4 Standards Committee is developing alternative interfaces for interprocess communication. Application developers who need to use IPC should design their Applications so that modules using the routines described in this document can be easily modified to use alternative methods at a later date.

SEE ALSO

exec, *exit*( ), *fork*( ), *shmat*( ), *shmctl*( ), *shmget*( ), **<sys/shm.h>**, **XSH** specification, **Section 2.6**, **Interprocess Communication**.

EXAMPLE

```
/*
 * Copyright (C) ANTRIX Inc.
 */

/* shmdt.c
 * This program detaches from the calling process address space
 * the shared memory segment using function shmdt.
 */

#include <stdio.h>
#include <stdlib.h>
#include <sys/types.h>
#include <sys/ipc.h>
#include <sys/shm.h>
#include <sys/stat.h>
#include <sys/wait.h>
#include <errno.h>

#define SHM_PERM    (S_IRWXU | S_IRWXG | S_IRWXO)
```

```
main()
{
   int      shmdt_value;
   int      *shmat_value;
   int      i, shmid, stat_loc;
   int      shmarr[10];
   pid_t    pid;

   fprintf (stdout,"get shmid\n");
   shmid = shmget (IPC_PRIVATE, sizeof(shmarr), IPC_CREAT | SHM_PERM);

   fprintf (stdout,"attach shared memory\n");
   shmat_value = (int *)shmat (shmid, 0, 0);

   fprintf (stdout,"child and parent sharing the same memory locations\n");
   pid = fork ();
   if ( pid == 0 ) {
      fprintf (stdout,"child writes to memory locations\n");
      for ( i = 0; i < 10; i++ ) {
          shmat_value[i] = 2*i;
          fprintf (stdout,"shmat_value[i]=%d\n", shmat_value[i]);
      }
      exit (1);
   }
   wait (&stat_loc);

   fprintf (stdout,"parent to read memory locations\n");
   for ( i = 0; i < 10; i++ )
       fprintf (stdout,"shmat_value[i] = %d\n", shmat_value[i]);

   fprintf (stdout,"detach shared memory\n");
   shmdt_value = shmdt ((void *)shmat_value);
   if ( shmdt_value == 0 )
      fprintf (stdout,"shmdt() call successful\n");
   else {
      fprintf (stderr,"ERROR: shmdt() call failed\n");
      fprintf (stderr,"ERROR: %s\n", strerror(errno));
   }
}
```

NAME

shmget — get shared memory segment

SYNOPSIS

EX   `#include <sys/shm.h>`

`int shmget(key_t key, size_t size, int shmflg);`

DESCRIPTION

The *shmget*( ) function returns the shared memory identifier associated with *key*.

A shared memory identifier, associated data structure and shared memory segment of at least *size* bytes, see **<sys/shm.h>**, are created for *key* if one of the following is true:

- The argument *key* is equal to IPC_PRIVATE.

- The argument *key* does not already have a shared memory identifier associated with it and (*shmflg* & IPC_CREAT) is non-zero.

Upon creation, the data structure associated with the new shared memory identifier is initialised as follows:

- The value of **shm_perm.cuid**, **shm_perm.uid**, **shm_perm.cgid** and **shm_perm.gid** are set equal to the effective user ID and effective group ID, respectively, of the calling process.

- The low-order nine bits of **shm_perm.mode** are set equal to the low-order nine bits of *shmflg*. The value of **shm_segsz** is set equal to the value of *size*.

- The values of **shm_lpid**, **shm_nattch**, **shm_atime** and **shm_dtime** are set equal to 0.

- The value of **shm_ctime** is set equal to the current time.

RETURN VALUE

Upon successful completion, *shmget*( ) returns a non-negative integer, namely a shared memory identifier; otherwise, it returns –1 and *errno* will be set to indicate the error.

ERRORS

The *shmget*( ) function will fail if:

[EACCES]   A shared memory identifier exists for *key* but operation permission as specified by the low-order nine bits of *shmflg* would not be granted. See the **XSH** specification, **Section 2.6**, **Interprocess Communication**.

[EEXIST]   A shared memory identifier exists for the argument *key* but (*shmflg* & IPC_CREAT) && (*shmflg* & IPC_EXCL) is non-zero.

[EINVAL]   The value of *size* is less than the system-imposed minimum or greater than the system-imposed maximum, or a shared memory identifier exists for the argument *key* but the size of the segment associated with it is less than *size* and *size* is not 0.

[ENOENT]   A shared memory identifier does not exist for the argument *key* and (*shmflg* & IPC_CREAT) is 0.

[ENOMEM]   A shared memory identifier and associated shared memory segment are to be created but the amount of available physical memory is not sufficient to fill the request.

[ENOSPC]   A shared memory identifier is to be created but the system-imposed limit on the maximum number of allowed shared memory identifiers system-wide would be exceeded.

[ENOSYS]   The function is not implemented.

FUTURE DIRECTIONS

The IEEE 1003.4 standards committee is developing alternative interfaces for interprocess communication. Application developers who need to use IPC should design their applications so that modules using the routines described in this document can be easily modified to use alternative methods at a later date.

SEE ALSO

shmat( ), *shmctl( )*, *shmdt( )*, **<sys/shm.h>**, **XSH** specification, **Section 2.6**, **Interprocess Communication**.

EXAMPLE

```
/*
 * Copyright (C) ANTRIX Inc.
 */

/* shmget.c
 * This program returns the shared memory identifier associated
 * key IPC_PRIVATE using function shmget.
 */

#include <stdio.h>
#include <stdlib.h>
#include <sys/types.h>
#include <sys/ipc.h>
#include <sys/shm.h>
#include <sys/stat.h>
#include <sys/wait.h>
#include <errno.h>

#define SHM_PERM     (S_IRWXU | S_IRWXG | S_IRWXO)

main()
{
  int     *shmat_value;
  int     shmid, i, stat_loc;
  int     shmarr[10];
  pid_t   pid;

  fprintf (stdout,"get shmid\n");
  shmid = shmget (IPC_PRIVATE, sizeof(shmarr), IPC_CREAT | SHM_PERM);
  if ( shmid > 0 )
     fprintf (stdout,"shmget() call successful\n");
  else {
     fprintf (stderr,"ERROR: shmget() call failed\n");
     fprintf (stderr,"ERROR: %s\n", strerror(errno));
  }

  fprintf (stdout,"attach shared memory\n");
  shmat_value = (int *)shmat (shmid, 0, 0);
  pid = fork ();
  if ( pid == 0 ) {
     fprintf (stdout,"child writes to memory locations\n");
```

```
        for ( i = 0; i < 10; i++ ) {
            shmat_value[i] = 2*i;
            fprintf (stdout,"shmat_value[i]=%d\n", shmat_value[i]);
        }
        exit (1);
    }
    wait (&stat_loc);

    fprintf (stdout,"parent to read memory locations\n");
    for ( i = 0; i < 10; i++ )
        fprintf (stdout,"shmat_value[i] = %d\n", shmat_value[i]);
    fprintf (stdout,"detach shared memory\n");
    shmdt ((void *)shmat_value);
}
```

NAME

sigaction — examine and change signal action

SYNOPSIS

```
#include <signal.h>

int sigaction(int sig, const struct sigaction *act,
          struct sigaction *oact);
```

DESCRIPTION

The *sigaction*( ) function allows the calling process to examine and/or specify the action to be associated with a specific signal. The argument *sig* specifies the signal; acceptable values are defined in **<signal.h>**.

The structure **sigaction**, used to describe an action to be taken, is defined in the header **<signal.h>** to include at least the following members:

Member Type	Member Name	Description
`void(*) (int)`	`sa_handler`	SIG_DFL, SIG_IGN or pointer to a function.
`sigset_t`	`sa_mask`	Additional set of signals to be blocked during execution of signal-catching function.
`int`	`sa_flags`	Special flags to affect behaviour of signal.
`void(*) (int, siginfo_t *, void *)`	`sa_sigaction`	Signal-catching function.

UX

If the argument *act* is not a null pointer, it points to a structure specifying the action to be associated with the specified signal. If the argument *oact* is not a null pointer, the action previously associated with the signal is stored in the location pointed to by the argument *oact*. If the argument *act* is a null pointer, signal handling is unchanged; thus, the call can be used to enquire about the current handling of a given signal. The *sa_handler* field of the **sigaction** structure identifies the action to be associated with the specified signal. If the *sa_handler* field specifies a signal-catching function, the *sa_mask* field identifies a set of signals that will be added to the process' signal mask before the signal-catching function is invoked. The SIGKILL and SIGSTOP signals will not be added to the signal mask using this mechanism; this restriction will be enforced by the system without causing an error to be indicated.

The *sa_flags* field can be used to modify the behaviour of the specified signal.

The following flags, defined in the header **<signal.h>**, can be set in *sa_flags*:

SA_NOCLDSTOP   Do not generate SIGCHLD when children stop.

UX   SA_ONSTACK   If set and an alternate signal stack has been declared with *sigaltstack*( ) or *sigstack*( ), the signal will be delivered to the calling process on that stack. Otherwise, the signal will be delivered on the current stack.

SA_RESETHAND   If set, the disposition of the signal will be reset to SIG_DFL and the SA_SIGINFO flag will be cleared on entry to the signal handler (Note: SIGILL and SIGTRAP cannot be automatically reset when delivered; the system silently enforces this restriction). Otherwise, the disposition of the signal will not be modified on entry to the signal handler.

In addition, if this flag is set, *sigaction*( ) behaves as if the SA_NODEFER flag were also set.

SA_RESTART   This flag affects the behaviour of interruptible functions; that is, those specified to fail with *errno* set to [EINTR]. If set, and a function specified as interruptible is interrupted by this signal, the function will restart and will not fail with [EINTR] unless otherwise specified. If the flag is not set, interruptible functions interrupted by this signal will fail with *errno* set to [EINTR].

SA_SIGINFO

If cleared and the signal is caught, the signal-catching function will be entered as:

```
void func(int signo);
```

where *signo* is the only argument to the signal catching function. In this case the **sa_handler** member must be used to describe the signal catching function and the application must not modify the **sa_sigaction** member.

If SA_SIGINFO is set and the signal is caught, the signal-catching function will be entered as:

```
void func(int signo, siginfo_t *info, void *context);
```

where two additional arguments are passed to the signal catching function. If the second argument is not a null pointer, it will point to an object of type **siginfo_t** explaining the reason why the signal was generated; the third argument can be cast to a pointer to an object of type **ucontext_t** to refer to the receiving process' context that was interrupted when the signal was delivered. In this case the **sa_sigaction** member must be used to describe the signal catching function and the application must not modify the **sa_handler** member.

The **si_signo** member contains the system-generated signal number.

The **si_errno** member may contain implementation-dependent additional error information; if non-zero, it contains an error number identifying the condition that caused the signal to be generated.

The **si_code** member contains a code identifying the cause of the signal. If the value of **si_code** is less than or equal to 0, then the signal was generated by a process and **si_pid** and **si_uid** respectively indicate the process ID and the real user ID of the sender. The values of **si_pid** and **si_uid** are otherwise meaningless.

SA_NOCLDWAIT

If set, and *sig* equals SIGCHLD, child processes of the calling processes will not be transformed into zombie processes when they terminate. If the calling process subsequently waits for its children, and the process has no unwaited for children that were transformed into zombie processes, it will block until all of its children terminate, and *wait()*, *wait3()*, *waitid()* and *waitpid()* will fail and set *errno* to [ECHILD]. Otherwise, terminating child processes will be transformed into zombie processes, unless SIGCHLD is set to SIG_IGN.

SA_NODEFER

If set and *sig* is caught, *sig* will not be added to the process' signal mask on entry to the signal handler unless it is included in **sa_mask**. Otherwise, *sig* will always be added to the process' signal mask on entry to the signal handler.

If *sig* is SIGCHLD and the SA_NOCLDSTOP flag is not set in *sa_flags*, and the implementation supports the SIGCHLD signal, then a SIGCHLD signal will be generated for the calling process whenever any of its child processes stop. If *sig* is SIGCHLD and the SA_NOCLDSTOP flag is set in *sa_flags*, then the implementation will not generate a SIGCHLD signal in this way.

When a signal is caught by a signal-catching function installed by *sigaction*( ), a new signal mask is calculated and installed for the duration of the signal-catching function (or until a call to either *sigprocmask*( ) or *sigsuspend*( ) is made). This mask is formed by taking the union of the
UX   current signal mask and the value of the *sa_mask* for the signal being delivered unless SA_NODEFER or SA_RESETHAND is set, and then including the signal being delivered. If and when the user's signal handler returns normally, the original signal mask is restored.

Once an action is installed for a specific signal, it remains installed until another action is
UX   explicitly requested (by another call to *sigaction*( )), until the SA_RESETHAND flag causes resetting of the handler, or until one of the *exec* functions is called.

If the previous action for *sig* had been established by *signal*( ), the values of the fields returned in the structure pointed to by *oact* are unspecified, and in particular *oact->sa_handler* is not necessarily the same value passed to *signal*( ). However, if a pointer to the same structure or a copy thereof is passed to a subsequent call to *sigaction*( ) via the *act* argument, handling of the signal will be as if the original call to *signal*( ) were repeated.

If *sigaction*( ) fails, no new signal handler is installed.

It is unspecified whether an attempt to set the action for a signal that cannot be caught or ignored to SIG_DFL is ignored or causes an error to be returned with *errno* set to [EINVAL].

A signal is said to be *generated* for (or sent to) a process when the event that causes the signal first occurs. Examples of such events include detection of hardware faults, timer expiration and terminal activity, as well as the invocation of *kill*( ). In some circumstances, the same event generates signals for multiple processes.

Each process has an action to be taken in response to each signal defined by the system (see **Signal Actions** on page 762). A signal is said to be *delivered* to a process when the appropriate action for the process and signal is taken.

During the time between the generation of a signal and its delivery, the signal is said to be *pending*. Ordinarily, this interval cannot be detected by an application. However, a signal can be *blocked* from delivery to a process. If the action associated with a blocked signal is anything other than to ignore the signal, and if that signal is generated for the process, the signal will remain pending until either it is unblocked or the action associated with it is set to ignore the signal. If the action associated with a blocked signal is to ignore the signal and if that signal is generated for the process, it is unspecified whether the signal is discarded immediately upon generation or remains pending.

Each process has a *signal mask* that defines the set of signals currently blocked from delivery to it. The signal mask for a process is initialised from that of its parent. The *sigaction*( ), *sigprocmask*( ) and *sigsuspend*( ) functions control the manipulation of the signal mask.

The determination of which action is taken in response to a signal is made at the time the signal is delivered, allowing for any changes since the time of generation. This determination is independent of the means by which the signal was originally generated. If a subsequent occurrence of a pending signal is generated, it is implementation-dependent as to whether the signal is delivered more than once. The order in which multiple, simultaneously pending signals are delivered to a process is unspecified.

When any stop signal (SIGSTOP, SIGTSTP, SIGTTIN, SIGTTOU) is generated for a process, any pending SIGCONT signals for that process will be discarded. Conversely, when SIGCONT is generated for a process, all pending stop signals for that process will be discarded. When SIGCONT is generated for a process that is stopped, the process will be continued, even if the SIGCONT signal is blocked or ignored. If SIGCONT is blocked and not ignored, it will remain pending until it is either unblocked or a stop signal is generated for the process.

An implementation will document any condition not specified by this document under which the implementation generates signals.

Signal Actions

There are three types of action that can be associated with a signal: SIG_DFL, SIG_IGN or a *pointer to a function*. Initially, all signals will be set to SIG_DFL or SIG_IGN prior to entry of the *main*( ) routine (see the *exec* functions). The actions prescribed by these values are as follows:

SIG_DFL — signal-specific default action

- The default actions for the signals defined in this document are specified under **<signal.h>** .

- If the default action is to stop the process, the execution of that process is temporarily suspended. When a process stops, a SIGCHLD signal will be generated for its parent process, unless the parent process has set the SA_NOCLDSTOP flag. While a process is stopped, any additional signals that are sent to the process will not be delivered until the process is continued, except SIGKILL which always terminates the receiving process. A process that is a member of an orphaned process group will not be allowed to stop in response to the SIGTSTP, SIGTTIN or SIGTTOU signals. In cases where delivery of one of these signals would stop such a process, the signal will be discarded.

- Setting a signal action to SIG_DFL for a signal that is pending, and whose default action is to ignore the signal (for example, SIGCHLD), will cause the pending signal to be discarded, whether or not it is blocked.

SIG_IGN — ignore signal

- Delivery of the signal will have no effect on the process. The behaviour of a process is undefined after it ignores a SIGFPE, SIGILL or SIGSEGV signal that was not generated by *kill*( ) or *raise*( ).

- The system will not allow the action for the signals SIGKILL or SIGSTOP to be set to SIG_IGN.

- Setting a signal action to SIG_IGN for a signal that is pending will cause the pending signal to be discarded, whether or not it is blocked.

UX
- If a process sets the action for the SIGCHLD signal to SIG_IGN, the behaviour is unspecified, except as specified below.

If the action for the SIGCHLD signal is set to SIG_IGN, child processes of the calling processes will not be transformed into zombie processes when they terminate. If the calling process subsequently waits for its children, and the process has no unwaited for children that were transformed into zombie processes, it will block until all of its children terminate, and *wait*( ), *wait3*( ), *waitid*( ) and *waitpid*( ) will fail and set *errno* to [ECHILD].

pointer to a function — catch signal

- On delivery of the signal, the receiving process is to execute the signal-catching function at the specified address. After returning from the signal-catching function, the receiving process will resume execution at the point at which it was interrupted.

UX

- If SA_SIGINFO is cleared, the signal-catching function will be entered as:

```
void func(int signo);
```

where *func* is the specified signal-catching function and *signo* is the signal number of the signal being delivered.

UX

- If SA_SIGINFO is set, the signal-catching function will be entered as:

```
void func(int signo, siginfo_t *siginfo, void *ucontextptr);
```

where *func* is the specified signal-catching function, *signo* is the signal number of the signal being delivered, *siginfo* points to an object of type **siginfo_t** associated with the signal being delivered, and *ucontextptr* points to a **ucontext_t**.

UX

- The behaviour of a process is undefined after it returns normally from a signal-catching function for a SIGBUS, SIGFPE, SIGILL or SIGSEGV signal that was not generated by *kill*( ) or *raise*( ).

- The system will not allow a process to catch the signals SIGKILL and SIGSTOP.

- If a process establishes a signal-catching function for the SIGCHLD signal while it has a terminated child process for which it has not waited, it is unspecified whether a SIGCHLD signal is generated to indicate that child process.

- When signal-catching functions are invoked asynchronously with process execution, the behaviour of some of the functions defined by this document is unspecified if they are called from a signal-catching function.

  The following table defines a set of functions that are either reentrant or not interruptible by signals. Therefore applications may invoke them, without restriction, from signal-catching functions:

access( )	*fstat*( )	*read*( )	*sysconf*( )
alarm( )	*getegid*( )	*rename*( )	*tcdrain*( )
cfgetispeed( )	*geteuid*( )	*rmdir*( )	*tcflow*( )
cfgetospeed( )	*getgid*( )	*setgid*( )	*tcflush*( )
cfsetispeed( )	*getgroups*( )	*setpgid*( )	*tcgetattr*( )
cfsetospeed( )	*getpgrp*( )	*setsid*( )	*tcgetpgrp*( )
chdir( )	*getpid*( )	*setuid*( )	*tcsendbreak*( )
chmod( )	*getppid*( )	*sigaction*( )	*tcsetattr*( )
chown( )	*getuid*( )	*sigaddset*( )	*tcsetpgrp*( )
close( )	*kill*( )	*sigdelset*( )	*time*( )
creat( )	*link*( )	*sigemptyset*( )	*times*( )
dup2( )	*lseek*( )	*sigfillset*( )	*umask*( )
dup( )	*mkdir*( )	*sigismember*( )	*uname*( )
execle( )	*mkfifo*( )	*signal*( )	*unlink*( )
execve( )	*open*( )	*sigpending*( )	*utime*( )
_exit( )	*pathconf*( )	*sigprocmask*( )	*wait*( )
fcntl( )	*pause*( )	*sigsuspend*( )	*waitpid*( )
fork( )	*pipe*( )	*sleep*( )	*write*( )
fpathconf( )	*raise*( )	*stat*( )	

EX

All functions not in the above table are considered to be unsafe with respect to signals. In the presence of signals, all functions defined by this document will behave as defined when called from or interrupted by a signal-catching function, with a single exception: when a signal interrupts an unsafe function and the signal-catching function calls an unsafe function, the behaviour is undefined.

Signal Effects on Other Functions

Signals affect the behaviour of certain functions defined by this document if delivered to a process while it is executing such a function. If the action of the signal is to terminate the process, the process will be terminated and the function will not return. If the action of the signal is to stop the process, the process will stop until continued or terminated. Generation of a SIGCONT signal for the process causes the process to be continued, and the original function will continue at the point the process was stopped. If the action of the signal is to invoke a signal-catching function, the signal-catching function will be invoked; in this case the original function is said to be *interrupted* by the signal. If the signal-catching function executes a **return** statement, the behaviour of the interrupted function will be as described individually for that function. Signals that are ignored will not affect the behaviour of any function; signals that are blocked will not affect the behaviour of any function until they are unblocked and then delivered.

RETURN VALUE

Upon successful completion, *sigaction*( ) returns 0. Otherwise −1 is returned, *errno* is set to indicate the error and no new signal-catching function will be installed.

ERRORS

The *sigaction*( ) function will fail if:

[EINVAL]   The *sig* argument is not a valid signal number or an attempt is made to catch a signal that cannot be caught or ignore a signal that cannot be ignored.

The *sigaction*( ) function may fail if:

[EINVAL]   An attempt was made to set the action to SIG_DFL for a signal that cannot be caught or ignored (or both).

APPLICATION USAGE

The *sigaction*( ) function supersedes the *signal*( ) interface, and should be used in preference. In particular, *sigaction*( ) and *signal*( ) should not be used in the same process to control the same signal. The behaviour of reentrant functions, as defined in the description, is as specified by this document, regardless of invocation from a signal-catching function. This is the only intended meaning of the statement that reentrant functions may be used in signal-catching functions without restrictions. Applications must still consider all effects of such functions on such things as data structures, files and process state. In particular, application writers need to consider the restrictions on interactions when interrupting *sleep*( ) and interactions among multiple handles for a file description. The fact that any specific function is listed as reentrant does not necessarily mean that invocation of that function from a signal-catching function is recommended.

In order to prevent errors arising from interrupting non-reentrant function calls, applications should protect calls to these functions either by blocking the appropriate signals or through the use of some programmatic semaphore. This document does not address the more general problem of synchronising access to shared data structures. Note in particular that even the "safe" functions may modify the global variable *errno*; the signal-catching function may want to save and restore its value. Naturally, the same principles apply to the reentrancy of application routines and asynchronous data access. Note that *longjmp*( ) and *siglongjmp*( ) are not in the list of reentrant functions. This is because the code executing after *longjmp*( ) and *siglongjmp*( ) can call any unsafe functions with the same danger as calling those unsafe functions directly from the signal handler. Applications that use *longjmp*( ) and *siglongjmp*( ) from within signal handlers require rigorous protection in order to be portable. Many of the other functions that are excluded from the list are traditionally implemented using either *malloc*( ) or *free*( ) functions or the standard I/O library, both of which traditionally use data structures in a non-reentrant manner. Because any combination of different functions using a common data structure can cause reentrancy problems, this document does not define the behaviour when any unsafe function is called in a signal handler that interrupts an unsafe function.

If the signal occurs other than as the result of calling *abort*( ), *kill*( ) or *raise*( ), the behaviour is undefined if the signal handler calls any function in the standard library other than one of the functions listed in the table above or refers to any object with static storage duration other than by assigning a value to a static storage duration variable of type **volatile sig_atomic_t**. Furthermore, if such a call fails, the value of *errno* is indeterminate.

UX Usually, the signal is executed on the stack that was in effect before the signal was delivered. An alternate stack may be specified to receive a subset of the signals being caught.

When the signal handler returns, the receiving process will resume execution at the point it was interrupted unless the signal handler makes other arrangements. If *longjmp*( ) or *_longjmp*( ) is used to leave the signal handler, then the signal mask must be explicitly restored by the process.

POSIX.4-1993 defines the third argument of a signal handling function when SA_SIGINFO is set as a **void** * instead of a **ucontext_t** *, but without requiring type checking. New applications should explicitly cast the third argument of the signal handling function to **uncontext_t** *.

The BSD optional four argument signal handling function is not supported by this specification. The BSD declaration would be

```
void handler(int sig, int code, struct sigcontext *scp,
        char *addr);
```

where *sig* is the signal number, *code* is additional information on certain signals, *scp* is a pointer to the sigcontext structure, and *addr* is additional address information. Much the same information is available in the objects pointed to by the second argument of the signal handler specified when SA_SIGINFO is set.

FUTURE DIRECTIONS

The *fpathconf*( ) function is marked as an extension in the list of safe functions because it is not included in the corresponding list in the ISO POSIX-1 standard, but it is expected to be added in a future revision of that standard.

SEE ALSO

bsd_signal( ), *kill*( ), *_longjmp*( ), *longjmp*( ), *raise*( ), *sigaddset*( ), *sigaltstack*( ), *sigdelset*( ), *sigemptyset*( ), *sigfillset*( ), *sigismember*( ), *signal*( ), *sigprocmask*( ), *sigsuspend*( ), *wait*( ), *wait3*( ), *waitid*( ), *waitpid*( ), **<signal.h>**, **<ucontext.h>**.

EXAMPLE

```
/*
 * Copyright (C) ANTRIX Inc.
 */

/* sigaction.c
 * This program allows the calling process to specify and examine
 * the action associated with signal using function sigaction.
 */

#include <stdio.h>
#include <stdlib.h>
#include <signal.h>
```

```
void handler(signal)
int signal;
{
  if ( signal == SIGALRM )
     fprintf (stdout,"received signal SIGALRM\n");
  else
     fprintf (stderr,"ERROR: expected=%d, received=%d\n",
                          SIGALRM, signal);
}

main()
{
  int      sigaction_value;
  struct   sigaction  act, oact;

  fprintf (stdout,"example 1\n");
  fprintf (stdout,"set the signal\n");
  sigemptyset (&act.sa_mask);
  sigemptyset (&oact.sa_mask);
  sigaddset (&act.sa_mask, SIGALRM);
  act.sa_handler = handler;
  act.sa_flags =  SA_ONSTACK;
  sigaction_value = sigaction (SIGALRM, &act, &oact);
  if ( sigaction_value == 0 ) {
     fprintf (stdout,"sigaction() call successful\n");
     kill(getpid(), SIGALRM);
  }
  else
     fprintf (stderr,"ERROR: sigaction() call failed\n");

  fprintf (stdout,"example 2\n");
  fprintf (stdout,"examine the signal\n");
  sigemptyset (&act.sa_mask);
  sigemptyset (&oact.sa_mask);
  sigaddset (&act.sa_mask, SIGALRM);
  act.sa_handler = handler;
  act.sa_flags =  SA_ONSTACK;
  sigaction_value = sigaction (SIGALRM, &act, &oact);
  if ( sigaction_value == 0 ) {
    fprintf (stdout,"sigaction() call successful\n");
    sigaction (SIGALRM, &act, &oact);
    if ( sigismember(&oact.sa_mask, SIGALRM) == 1 )
      fprintf (stdout,"previous signal set was SIGALRM\n");
    else
      fprintf (stderr,"ERROR: did not reterive previous signal SIGALRM\n");
    if ( oact.sa_handler == handler )
      fprintf (stdout,"previous signal function set was handler\n");
    else
      fprintf (stderr,"ERROR: did not reterive previous signal handler\n");
  }
```

```
    else
        fprintf (stdout,"error: sigaction() call failed\n") ;
}
```

NAME

sigaddset — add a signal to a signal set

SYNOPSIS

```
#include <signal.h>

int sigaddset(sigset_t *set, int signo);
```

DESCRIPTION

The *sigaddset*( ) function adds the individual signal specified by the *signo* to the signal set pointed to by *set*.

RETURN VALUE

Upon successful completion, *sigaddset*( ) returns 0. Otherwise, it returns −1 and sets *errno* to indicate the error.

ERRORS

The *sigaddset*( ) function may fail if:

[EINVAL]   The value of the *signo* argument is an invalid or unsupported signal number.

APPLICATION USAGE

Applications should call either *sigemptyset*( ) or *sigfillset*( ) at least once for each object of type **sigset_t** prior to any other use of that object. If such an object is not initialised in this way, but is nonetheless supplied as an argument to any of *sigaction*( ), *sigaddset*( ), *sigdelset*( ), *sigismember*( ), *sigpending*( ) or *sigprocmask*( ), the results are undefined.

SEE ALSO

sigaction( ), *sigdelset*( ), *sigemptyset*( ), *sigfillset*( ), *sigismember*( ), *sigpending*( ), *sigprocmask*( ), *sigsuspend*( ), **<signal.h>**.

EXAMPLE

```
/*
 * Copyright (C) ANTRIX Inc.
 */

/* sigaddset.c
 * This program adds the individual signal SIGALRM to the
 * signal set specified by set using function sigaddset.
 */

#include <stdio.h>
#include <stdlib.h>
#include <signal.h>
#include <errno.h>

main()
{
  int       sigaddset_value;
  int       sigismember_value;
  sigset_t set;

  fprintf (stdout,"empty signal set\n");
  sigemptyset (&set);

  fprintf (stdout,"add signal to set\n");
  sigaddset_value = sigaddset (&set, SIGALRM);
```

```
        if ( sigaddset_value == 0 )
            fprintf (stdout,"sigaddset() call successful\n");
        else
            fprintf (stderr,"ERROR: sigaddset() call failed\n");
        fprintf (stdout,"check SIGALRM is member of set\n");

        sigismember_value = sigismember (&set, SIGALRM);
        if ( sigismember_value != 1 )
            fprintf (stderr,"ERROR: SIGALRM is not a member of set\n");
}
```

NAME

sigaltstack - set and/or get signal alternate stack context.

SYNOPSIS

UX
```
#include <signal.h>
```
```
int sigaltstack(const stack_t *ss, stack_t *oss);
```

DESCRIPTION

The *sigaltstack*( ) function allows a process to define and examine the state of an alternate stack for signal handlers. Signals that have been explicitly declared to execute on the alternate stack will be delivered on the alternate stack.

If *ss* is not a null pointer, it points to a **stack_t** structure that specifies the alternate signal stack that will take effect upon return from *sigaltstack*( ). The **ss_flags** member specifies the new stack state. If it is set to SS_DISABLE, the stack is disabled and **ss_sp** and **ss_size** are ignored. Otherwise the stack will be enabled, and the **ss_sp** and **ss_size** members specify the new address and size of the stack.

The range of addresses starting at **ss_sp**, up to but not including **ss_sp** + **ss_size**, is available to the implementation for use as the stack. This interface makes no assumptions regarding which end is the stack base and in which direction the stack grows as items are pushed.

If *oss* is not a null pointer, on successful completion it will point to a **stack_t** structure that specifies the alternate signal stack that was in effect prior to the call to *sigaltstack*( ). The **ss_sp** and **ss_size** members specify the address and size of that stack. The **ss_flags** member specifies the stack's state, and may contain one of the following values:

SS_ONSTACK   The process is currently executing on the alternate signal stack. Attempts to modify the alternate signal stack while the process is executing on it fails. This flag must not be modified by processes.

SS_DISABLE   The alternate signal stack is currently disabled.

The value SIGSTKSZ is a system default specifying the number of bytes that would be used to cover the usual case when manually allocating an alternate stack area. The value MINSIGSTKSZ is defined to be the minimum stack size for a signal handler. In computing an alternate stack size, a program should add that amount to its stack requirements to allow for the system implementation overhead. The constants SS_ONSTACK, SS_DISABLE, SIGSTKSZ, and MINSIGSTKSZ are defined in **<signal.h>**.

After a successful call to one of the *exec* functions, there are no alternate signal stacks in the new process image.

RETURN VALUE

Upon successful completion, *sigaltstack*( ) returns 0. Otherwise, it returns −1 and sets *errno* to indicate the error.

ERRORS

The *sigaltstack*( ) function will fail if:

[EINVAL]   The *ss* argument is not a null pointer, and the **ss_flags** member pointed to by *ss* contains flags other than SS_DISABLE.

[ENOMEM]   The size of the alternate stack area is less than MINSIGSTKSZ.

[EPERM]   An attempt was made to modify an active stack.

APPLICATION USAGE

The following code fragment illustrates a method for allocating memory for an alternate stack:

```
      if ((sigstk.ss_sp = malloc(SIGSTKSZ)) == NULL)
          /* error return */
      sigstk.ss_size = SIGSTKSZ;
      sigstk.ss_flags = 0;
      if (sigaltstack(&sigstk,(stack_t *)0) < 0)
          perror("sigaltstack");
```

In some implementations, a signal (whether or not indicated to execute on the alternate stack) will always execute on the alternate stack if it is delivered while another signal is being caught using the alternate stack.

On some implementations, stack space is automatically extended as needed. On those implementations, automatic extension is typically not available for an alternate stack. If the stack overflows, the behaviour is undefined.

SEE ALSO

sigaction( ), *sigsetjmp*( ), **<signal.h>**.

EXAMPLE

```
/*
 * Copyright (C) ANTRIX Inc.
 */

/* sigaltstack.c
 * This program sets the alternate stack context
 * using function sigaltstack.
 */

#include <stdio.h>
#include <stdlib.h>
#include <signal.h>
#include <sys/wait.h>
#include <errno.h>

static char *Top;                   /* Top of Stack */
static char *End;                   /* End of Stack */
int     sig_rcvd;

onstack()
{
    char    character;

    if (&character < End || Top < &character)
        printf("%s\n%s%#x\n%s%#x\n%s%#x\n",
           "auto declaration was outside boundaries of declared stack.",
           "top of stack = ", Top,
           "end of stack = ", End,
           "received auto address = ", &character);
}


void
altstack()
{
```

```
        stack_t oss;
        onstack ();

        sigaltstack ( (stack_t *)0, &oss);
        if (oss.ss_flags != SS_ONSTACK)
          fprintf (stdout,"oss.ss_flags != SS_ONSTACK, ss_flags=%#x\n",
                        oss.ss_flags);

        if ((char *)oss.ss_sp != End)
          fprintf (stdout,"oss.ss_sp != Eos, ss_sp=%#x, End=%#x\n",
                        oss.ss_sp, End);

        if (oss.ss_size != (Top - End))
          fprintf (stdout,"oss.ss_size != Tos-End, ss_size=%#x, Top-End=%#x\n",
                        oss.ss_size, Top-End);
        sig_rcvd++;
}

offstack()
{
    char    character;

    if (End < &character && &character < Top)
      fprintf (stdout,"%s\n%s%#x\n%s%#x\n%s%#x\n",
         "auto declaration is on the alternate stack and shouldn't be.",
         "top of stack = ", Top,
         "end of stack = ", End,
         "received Auto Address = ", &character);
}

main()
{
  int     sigaltstack_value;
  int     stat_loc;
  pid_t   child ;
  struct  sigaction act;
  stack_t ss;


  fprintf (stdout,"fork a child\n");
  child = fork();
  if (child == 0) {
     ss.ss_sp = (int *)malloc (SIGSTKSZ);
     ss.ss_size = SIGSTKSZ;
     ss.ss_flags = 0;
     Top = (char *)ss.ss_sp + ss.ss_size;
     End = (char *)ss.ss_sp;
     fprintf (stdout,"establish stack\n");
     sigaltstack_value = sigaltstack (&ss, &ss);
     if ( sigaltstack_value == 0 ) {
         fprintf (stdout,"sigaltstack() call successful\n");
         sigemptyset (&act.sa_mask);
```

```
            act.sa_handler = altstack;
            act.sa_flags = SA_ONSTACK;
            sigaction (SIGALRM, &act, (struct sigaction *)0);
            kill (getpid(), SIGALRM);
            sigaltstack ((stack_t *)0, &ss);
            offstack ();
        }
        else
            fprintf (stderr,"ERROR: sigaltstack() call failed\n");
        sigemptyset (&act.sa_mask);
        exit (10);
    } wait (&stat_loc );

    fprintf (stdout,"should be same as exit() argument 10\n");
    fprintf (stdout,"WEXITSTATUS(stat_loc)=%d\n", WEXITSTATUS(stat_loc));
}
```

NAME

sigdelset — delete a signal from a signal set

SYNOPSIS

```
#include <signal.h>

int sigdelset(sigset_t *set, int signo);
```

DESCRIPTION

The *sigdelset*( ) function deletes the individual signal specified by *signo* from the signal set pointed to by *set*.

RETURN VALUE

Upon successful completion, *sigdelset*( ) returns 0. Otherwise, it returns −1 and sets *errno* to indicate the error.

ERRORS

The *sigdelset*( ) function may fail if:

[EINVAL]   The *signo* argument is not a valid signal number, or is an unsupported signal number.

APPLICATION USAGE

Applications should call either *sigemptyset*( ) or *sigfillset*( ) at least once for each object of type **sigset_t** prior to any other use of that object. If such an object is not initialised in this way, but is nonetheless supplied as an argument to any of *sigaction*( ), *sigaddset*( ), *sigdelset*( ), *sigismember*( ), *sigpending*( ) or *sigprocmask*( ), the results are undefined.

SEE ALSO

sigaction( ),   *sigaddset*( ),   *sigemptyset*( ),   *sigfillset*( ),   *sigismember*( ),   *sigpending*( ), *sigprocmask*( ), *sigsuspend*( ), **<signal.h>**.

EXAMPLE

```
/*
 * Copyright (C) ANTRIX Inc.
 */

/* sigdelset.c
 * This program deletes the individual signal SIGALRM from
 * the signal set using function sigdelset.
 */

#include <stdio.h>
#include <stdlib.h>
#include <signal.h>
#include <errno.h>

main()
{
  int       sigdelset_value;
  int       sigismember_value;
  sigset_t set;

  fprintf (stdout,"empty signal set\n");
  sigemptyset (&set);
```

```
        fprintf (stdout,"add signal SIGALRM to the set\n");
        sigaddset (&set, SIGALRM);

        fprintf (stdout,"delete signal SIGALRM\n");
        sigdelset_value = sigdelset (&set, SIGALRM);
        if ( sigdelset_value == 0 )
           fprintf (stdout,"sigdelset() call successful\n");
        else
           fprintf (stderr,"ERROR: sigdelset() call failed\n");

        fprintf (stdout,"check SIGALRM is deleted from the set\n");
        sigismember_value = sigismember (&set, SIGALRM);
        if ( sigismember_value != 0 )
           fprintf (stderr,"ERROR: SIGALRM was not deleted from the set\n");
    }
```

NAME

sigemptyset — initialise and empty a signal set

SYNOPSIS

```
#include <signal.h>

int sigemptyset(sigset_t *set);
```

DESCRIPTION

The *sigemptyset*( ) function initialises the signal set pointed to by *set*, such that all signals defined in this document are excluded.

RETURN VALUE

Upon successful completion, *sigemptyset*( ) returns 0. Otherwise, it returns −1 and sets *errno* to indicate the error.

ERRORS

No errors are defined.

APPLICATION USAGE

Applications should call *sigemptyset*( ) or *sigfillset*( ) at least once for each object of type **sigset_t** before any other use of that object.

SEE ALSO

sigaction( ), *sigaddset*( ), *sigdelset*( ), *sigfillset*( ), *sigismember*( ), *sigpending*( ), *sigprocmask*( ), *sigsuspend*( ), **<signal.h>**.

EXAMPLE

```
/*
 * Copyright (C) ANTRIX Inc.
 */

/* sigemptyset.c
 * This program initialises the signal set such that all signals
 * are excluded from the set using function sigemptyset.
 */

#include <stdio.h>
#include <stdlib.h>
#include <signal.h>
#include <errno.h>

main()
{
   int      sigismember_value;
   int      sigemptyset_value;
   sigset_t set;

   fprintf (stdout,"fill signal set\n");
   sigfillset (&set);

   fprintf (stdout,"empty signal set\n");
   sigemptyset value = sigemptyset (&set);
   if ( sigemptyset_value == 0 )
      fprintf (stdout,"sigemptyset() call successful\n");
   else
```

```
        fprintf (stderr,"ERROR: sigemptyset() call failed\n");
    sigismember_value = sigismember (&set, SIGALRM);

    if ( sigismember_value != 0 )
        fprintf (stderr,"ERROR: signal set is not empty\n");
}
```

NAME

sigfillset — initialise and fill a signal set

SYNOPSIS

```
#include <signal.h>

int sigfillset(sigset_t *set);
```

DESCRIPTION

The *sigfillset( )* function initialises the signal set pointed to by *set*, such that all signals defined in this document are included.

RETURN VALUE

Upon successful completion, *sigfillset( )* returns 0. Otherwise, it returns −1 and sets *errno* to indicate the error.

ERRORS

No errors are defined.

APPLICATION USAGE

Applications should call *sigemptyset( )* or *sigfillset( )* at least once for each object of type **sigset_t** before any other use of that object.

SEE ALSO

sigaction( ),   *sigaddset( )*,   *sigdelset( )*,   *sigemptyset( )*,   *sigismember( )*,   *sigpending( )*,
sigprocmask( ), *sigsuspend( )*, **<signal.h>**.

EXAMPLE

```
/*
 * Copyright (C) ANTRIX Inc.
 */

/* sigfillset.c
 * This program initialises the signal set, such that all
 * the signals defined are included from the set using
 * function sigfillset.
 */

#include <stdio.h>
#include <stdlib.h>
#include <signal.h>
#include <errno.h>

main()
{
   int      sigfillset_value;
   int      sigismember_value;
   sigset_t set;

   fprintf (stdout,"fill signal set\n");
   sigfillset_value = sigfillset (&set);
   if (sigfillset_value == 0)
      fprintf (stdout,"sigfillset() call successful\n");
   else
      fprintf (stderr,"ERROR: sigfillset() call failed\n");
```

```
        fprintf (stdout,"check SIGALRM is member of the set\n");
        sigismember_value = sigismember (&set, SIGALRM);
        if (sigismember_value != 1)
            fprintf (stderr,"ERROR: SIGALRM is not in the set\n");
    }
```

NAME

sighold, sigignore — add a signal to the signal mask or set a signal disposition to be ignored

SYNOPSIS

```
#include <signal.h>

int sighold(int sig);

int sigignore(int sig);
```

DESCRIPTION

Refer to *signal*( ).

EXAMPLE

```
/*
 * Copyright (C) ANTRIX Inc.
 */

/* sighold.c
 * This program holds signal to the calling process's signal mask
 * using function sighold.
 */

#include <stdio.h>
#include <stdlib.h>
#include <unistd.h>
#include <signal.h>

void handler(signal)
int signal;
{
   if ( signal == SIGALRM )
      fprintf (stdout,"received signal SIGALRM\n");
   else
      fprintf (stderr,"ERROR: expected=%d, received=%d\n",
                        SIGALRM, signal);
}

main()
{
   int      sighold_value;
   pid_t    pid;

   pid = getpid ();
   fprintf (stdout,"register signal handler\n");
   signal (SIGALRM, handler);

   fprintf (stdout,"sighold holds the signal SIGALRM in que\n");
   sighold_value = sighold (SIGALRM);
   if ( sighold_value == 0 )
      fprintf (stdout,"sighold() call successful\n");
   else
      fprintf (stderr,"ERROR: sighold() call failed\n");

   kill (pid, SIGALRM );
```

```
    fprintf (stdout,"sigrelse releases the signal SIGALRM in que\n");
}
```

NAME

siginterrupt — allow signals to interrupt functions

SYNOPSIS

UX　　#include <signal.h>

int siginterrupt(int *sig*, int *flag*);

DESCRIPTION

The *siginterrupt*( ) function is used to change the restart behaviour when a function is interrupted by the specified signal. The function *siginterrupt*(*sig*, *flag*) has an effect as if implemented as:

```
siginterrupt(int sig, int flag) {
    int ret;
    struct sigaction act;

    (void) sigaction(sig, NULL, &act);
    if (flag)
        act.sa_flags &= ~SA_RESTART;
    else
        act.sa_flags |= SA_RESTART;
    ret = sigaction(sig, &act, NULL);
    return ret;
}
```

RETURN VALUE

Upon successful completion, *siginterrupt*( ) returns 0. Otherwise −1 is returned and *errno* is set to indicate the error.

ERRORS

The *siginterrupt*( ) function will fail if:

[EINVAL]　　　　　The *sig* argument is not a valid signal number.

APPLICATION USAGE

The *siginterrupt*( ) function supports programs written to historical system interfaces. A portable application, when being written or rewritten, should use *sigaction*( ) with the SA_RESTART flag instead of *siginterrupt*( ).

SEE ALSO

sigaction( ), **<signal.h>**.

NAME

sigismember — test for a signal in a signal set

SYNOPSIS

```
#include <signal.h>

int sigismember(const sigset_t *set, int signo);
```

DESCRIPTION

The *sigismember( )* function tests whether the signal specified by *signo* is a member of the set pointed to by *set*.

RETURN VALUE

Upon successful completion, *sigismember( )* returns 1 if the specified signal is a member of the specified set, or 0 if it is not. Otherwise, it returns –1 and sets *errno* to indicate the error.

ERRORS

The *sigismember( )* function may fail if:

[EINVAL]   The *signo* argument is not a valid signal number, or is an unsupported signal number.

APPLICATION USAGE

Applications should call either *sigemptyset( )* or *sigfillset( )* at least once for each object of type **sigset_t** prior to any other use of that object. If such an object is not initialised in this way, but is nonetheless supplied as an argument to any of *sigaction( )*, *sigaddset( )*, *sigdelset( )*, *sigismember( )*, *sigpending( )* or *sigprocmask( )*, the results are undefined.

SEE ALSO

sigaction( ), *sigaddset( )*, *sigdelset( )*, *sigfillset( )*, *sigemptyset( )*, *sigpending( )*, *sigprocmask( )*, *sigsuspend( )*, **<signal.h>**.

EXAMPLE

```
/*
 * Copyright (C) ANTRIX Inc.
 */

/* sigismember.c
 * This program test for signal SIGALRM in the signal set
 * using function sigismember.
 */

#include <stdio.h>
#include <stdlib.h>
#include <signal.h>

main()
{
   int      sigismember_value;
   sigset_t set;

   fprintf (stdout,"empty signal set\n");
   sigemptyset (&set);

   fprintf (stdout,"add signal SIGALRM to the set\n");
   sigaddset (&set, SIGALRM);
```

```
    fprintf (stdout,"check SIGALRM is member of the set\n");
    sigismember_value = sigismember (&set, SIGALRM);
    if ( sigismember_value == 1 )
        fprintf (stdout,"sigismember() call successful\n");
    else
        fprintf (stdout,"error: sigismember() call failed\n") ;
}
```

NAME

siglongjmp — non-local goto with signal handling

SYNOPSIS

```
#include <setjmp.h>

void siglongjmp(sigjmp_buf env, int val);
```

DESCRIPTION

The *siglongjmp( )* function restores the environment saved by the most recent invocation of *sigsetjmp( )* in the same process, with the corresponding *sigjmp_buf* argument. If there is no such invocation, or if the function containing the invocation of *sigsetjmp( )* has terminated execution in the interim, the behaviour is undefined.

All accessible objects have values as of the time *siglongjmp( )* was called, except that the values of objects of automatic storage duration which are local to the function containing the invocation of the corresponding *sigsetjmp( )* which do not have volatile-qualified type and which are changed between the *sigsetjmp( )* invocation and *siglongjmp( )* call are indeterminate.

As it bypasses the usual function call and return mechanisms, *siglongjmp( )* will execute correctly in contexts of interrupts, signals and any of their associated functions. However, if *siglongjmp( )* is invoked from a nested signal handler (that is, from a function invoked as a result of a signal raised during the handling of another signal), the behaviour is undefined.

The *siglongjmp( )* function will restore the saved signal mask if and only if the *env* argument was initialised by a call to *sigsetjmp( )* with a non-zero *savemask* argument.

RETURN VALUE

After *siglongjmp( )* is completed, program execution continues as if the corresponding invocation of *sigsetjmp( )* had just returned the value specified by *val*. The *siglongjmp( )* function cannot cause *sigsetjmp( )* to return 0; if *val* is 0, *sigsetjmp( )* returns the value 1.

ERRORS

No errors are defined.

APPLICATION USAGE

The distinction between *setjmp( )* or *longjmp( )* and *sigsetjmp( )* or *siglongjmp( )* is only significant for programs which use *sigaction( )*, *sigprocmask( )* or *sigsuspend( )*.

SEE ALSO

longjmp( ), *setjmp( )*, *sigprocmask( )*, *sigsetjmp( )*, *sigsuspend( )*, **<setjmp.h>**.

EXAMPLE

```
/*
 * Copyright (C) ANTRIX Inc.
 */

/* siglongjmp.c
 * This program restores the environment saved by the most
 * recent invocation of the sigsetjmp in the same process
 * using function siglongjmp.
 */

#include <stdio.h>
#include <stdlib.h>
#include <signal.h>
#include <setjmp.h>
```

```
#define SIGSET 0

main()
{
  int       sigsetjmp_value;
  int       val;
  sigjmp_buf  env;
  static int  save_int;
  static long save_long;
  static  sigset_t sigmask1;
  static  sigset_t sig_fill, sigcurr, sigemp;

  val = 5;
  sigfillset (&sig_fill);
  sigemptyset (&sigemp);
  sigsetjmp_value = sigsetjmp (env, 1);
  fprintf (stdout,"save values\n");
  if ( sigsetjmp_value == val ) {
      fprintf (stdout,"sigsetjmp_value=%d\n", sigsetjmp_value );
      fprintf (stdout,"save_int=%d\n", save_int);
      fprintf (stdout,"save_long=%d\n", save_long);
      sigprocmask (0, (sigset_t *)0, &sigcurr);
      if (memcmp (&sigcurr, &sigmask1, sizeof(sigcurr)) ) {
          fprintf (stderr,"ERROR: signal not correct after sigsetjmp\n");
#if SIGSET
          /* comment out statements below */
          /* if sigset member name is different */
          fprintf (stdout,"expected=#x%o, received=#x%o\n",
                   sigmask1.s[0], sigcurr.s[0] );
          fprintf (stdout,"expected=#x%o, received=#x%o\n",
                   sigmask1.s[1], sigcurr.s[1] );
#endif
      }
      exit (0);
  }
  save_int =  1;
  save_long = 123456789;
  sigprocmask (SIG_SETMASK, &sig_fill, &sigmask1);
  fprintf (stdout,"restore values\n");
  siglongjmp (env, val);
  fprintf (stdout,"error: siglongjmp() call failed\n") ;
}
```

NAME

signal, sigset, sighold, sigrelse, sigignore, sigpause — signal management

SYNOPSIS

```
#include <signal.h>

void (*signal(int sig, void (*func)(int)))(int);
```

UX
```
int sighold(int sig);
```

```
int sigignore(int sig);
```

```
int sigpause(int sig);
```

```
int sigrelse(int sig);
```

```
void (*sigset(int sig, void (*disp)(int)))(int);
```

DESCRIPTION

The *signal*( ) function chooses one of three ways in which receipt of the signal number *sig* is to be subsequently handled. If the value of *func* is SIG_DFL, default handling for that signal will occur. If the value of *func* is SIG_IGN, the signal will be ignored. Otherwise, *func* must point to a function to be called when that signal occurs. Such a function is called a *signal handler*.

When a signal occurs, if *func* points to a function, first the equivalent of a:

```
signal(sig, SIG_DFL);
```

is executed or an implementation-dependent blocking of the signal is performed. (If the value of *sig* is SIGILL, whether the reset to SIG_DFL occurs is implementation-dependent.) Next the equivalent of:

```
(*func)(sig);
```

is executed. The *func* function may terminate by executing a **return** statement or by calling *abort*( ), *exit*( ), or *longjmp*( ). If *func*( ) executes a **return** statement and the value of *sig* was SIGFPE or any other implementation-dependent value corresponding to a computational exception, the behaviour is undefined. Otherwise, the program will resume execution at the point it was interrupted.

If the signal occurs other than as the result of calling *abort*( ), *kill*( ) or *raise*( ), the behaviour is undefined if the signal handler calls any function in the standard library other than one of the functions listed on the *sigaction*( ) page or refers to any object with static storage duration other than by assigning a value to a static storage duration variable of type **volatile sig_atomic_t**. Furthermore, if such a call fails, the value of *errno* is indeterminate.

At program startup, the equivalent of:

```
signal(sig, SIG_IGN);
```

is executed for some signals, and the equivalent of:

```
signal(sig, SIG_DFL);
```

is executed for all other signals (see *exec*).

UX
The *sigset*( ), *sighold*( ), *sigignore*( ), *sigpause*( ) and *segrelse*( ) functions provide simplified signal management.

The *sigset*( ) function is used to modify signal dispositions. The *sig* argument specifies the signal, which may be any signal except SIGKILL and SIGSTOP. The *disp* argument specifies the signal's disposition, which may be SIG_DFL, SIG_IGN or the address of a signal handler. If *sigset*( ) is used, and *disp* is the address of a signal handler, the system will add *sig* to the calling process' signal mask before executing the signal handler; when the signal handler returns, the system will restore the calling process' signal mask to its state prior the delivery of the signal. In addition, if *sigset*( ) is used, and *disp* is equal to SIG_HOLD, *sig* will be added to the calling process' signal mask and *sig*'s disposition will remain unchanged. If *sigset*( ) is used, and disp is not equal to SIG_HOLD, sig will be removed from the calling process' signal mask.

The *sighold*( ) function adds *sig* to the calling process' signal mask.

The *sigrelse*( ) function removes *sig* from the calling process' signal mask.

The *sigignore*( ) function sets the disposition of *sig* to SIG_IGN.

The *sigpause*( ) function removes *sig* from the calling process' signal mask and suspends the calling process until a signal is received.

If the action for the SIGCHLD signal is set to SIG_IGN, child processes of the calling processes will not be transformed into zombie processes when they terminate. If the calling process subsequently waits for its children, and the process has no unwaited for children that were transformed into zombie processes, it will block until all of its children terminate, and *wait*( ), *wait3*( ), *waitid*( ) and *waitpid*( ) will fail and set *errno* to [ECHILD].

RETURN VALUE

If the request can be honoured, *signal*( ) returns the value of *func*( ) for the most recent call to *signal*( ) for the specified signal *sig*. Otherwise, SIG_ERR is returned and a positive value is stored in *errno*.

UX   Upon successful completion, *sigset*( ) returns SIG_HOLD if the signal had been blocked and the signal's previous disposition if it had not been blocked. Otherwise, SIG_ERR is returned and *errno* is set to indicate the error.

For all other functions, upon successful completion, 0 is returned. Otherwise, –1 is returned and *errno* is set to indicate the error.

ERRORS

The *signal*( ) function will fail if:

[EINVAL]   The *sig* argument is not a valid signal number or an attempt is made to catch a signal that cannot be caught or ignore a signal that cannot be ignored.

The *signal*( ) function may fail if:

[EINVAL]   An attempt was made to set the action to SIG_DFL for a signal that cannot be caught or ignored (or both).

UX   The *sigset*( ), *sighold*( ), *sigrelse*( ), *sigignore*( ) and *sigpause*( ) functions will fail if:

[EINVAL]   The *sig* argument is an illegal signal number.

The *sigset*( ), and *sigignore*( ) functions will fail if:

[EINVAL]   An attempt is made to catch a signal that cannot be caught, or to ignore a signal that cannot be ignored.

APPLICATION USAGE

The *sigaction*( ) function provides a more comprehensive and reliable mechanism for controlling signals; new applications should use *sigaction*( ) rather than *signal*( ).

UX   The *sighold*( ) function, in conjunction with *sigrelse*( ) or *sigpause*( ), may be used to establish critical regions of code that require the delivery of a signal to be temporarily deferred.

The *sigsuspend*( ) function should be used in preference to *sigpause*( ) for broader portability.

SEE ALSO

exec, *pause*( ), *sigaction*( ), *waitid*( ), **<signal.h>**.

EXAMPLE

```c
/*
 * Copyright (C) ANTRIX Inc.
 */

/* signal.c
 * This program specifies what signal handler procedure to
 * be called on receipt of SIGALRM using function signal.
 */

#include <stdio.h>
#include <stdlib.h>
#include <unistd.h>
#include <signal.h>
#include <errno.h>

void handler(signal)
int signal;
{
  if ( signal == SIGALRM )
     fprintf (stdout,"received signal SIGALRM\n");
  else
     fprintf (stderr,"ERROR: expected=%d, received=%d\n",
                     SIGALRM, signal);
}

main()
{
  pid_t   pid;

  fprintf (stdout,"get process id\n");
  pid = getpid ();

  fprintf (stdout,"register signal handler\n");
  signal (SIGALRM, handler);

  fprintf (stdout,"send signal SIGALRM to current process\n");
  kill (pid, SIGALRM);
}
```

NAME

signgam — storage for sign of *lgamma*( )

SYNOPSIS

EX   `#include <math.h>`

`extern int signgam;`

DESCRIPTION

Refer to *lgamma*( ).

EXAMPLE

```
/*
 * Copyright (C) ANTRIX Inc.
 */

/* signgam.c
 * This program the sign of gamma(x) in the external integer
 * signgam using function lgamma.
 */

#include <stdio.h>
#include <math.h>

extern int signgam;

main()
{
  double  lgamma_value;
  double  x = 1.40;

  fprintf (stdout,"signgam %d\n", signgam);
  lgamma_value = lgamma (x);

  fprintf (stdout,"lgamma of %f is %f\n", x, lgamma_value);
  fprintf (stdout,"signgam %d\n", signgam);
}
```

NAME

sigpause — remove a signal from the signal mask and suspend the process

SYNOPSIS

```
#include <signal.h>

int sigpause(int sig);
```

DESCRIPTION

Refer to *signal*( ).

EXAMPLE

```
/*
 * Copyright (C) ANTRIX Inc.
 */

/* sigpause.c
 * This program removes signal from the calling process's signal
 * mask and suspends the calling process until a signal is
 * received using function sigpause.
 */

#include <stdio.h>
#include <stdlib.h>
#include <unistd.h>
#include <signal.h>
#include <sys/wait.h>
#include <errno.h>

main()
{
  int       stat_loc;
  pid_t     child;

  fprintf (stdout,"fork a child\n");
  child = fork ();
  if ( child == 0 ) {
     sigset (SIGPIPE, SIG_DFL);
     fprintf (stdout,"sigpause to suspend child process\n");
     sigpause (SIGPIPE);
     fprintf (stderr,"ERROR: sigpause did not suspend child\n");
  }

  fprintf (stdout,"parent sleeps for 2 seconds while child in suspension\n");
  sleep (2);

  fprintf (stdout,"wake up child by sending signal SIGALRM\n");
  kill (child, SIGALRM);
  waitpid (child, &stat_loc, WUNTRACED);
}
```

NAME

sigpending — examine pending signals

SYNOPSIS

```
#include <signal.h>

int sigpending(sigset_t *set);
```

DESCRIPTION

The *sigpending*( ) function stores the set of signals that are blocked from delivery and pending to the calling process, in the object pointed to by *set*.

RETURN VALUE

Upon successful completion, *sigpending*( ) returns 0. Otherwise –1 is returned and *errno* is set to indicate the error.

ERRORS

No errors are defined.

SEE ALSO

sigaddset( ), *sigdelset*( ), *sigemptyset*( ), *sigfillset*( ), *sigismember*( ), *sigprocmask*( ), **<signal.h>**.

EXAMPLE

```
/*
 * Copyright (C) ANTRIX Inc.
 */

/* sigpending.c
 * This program examines the set of pending signals using function
 * sigpending.
 */

#include <stdio.h>
#include <stdlib.h>
#include <signal.h>
#include <errno.h>

void handler(signal)
int signal;
{
  if ( signal == SIGALRM )
     fprintf (stdout,"received signal SIGALRM\n");
  else
     fprintf (stderr,"ERROR: expected=%d, received=%d\n",
                     SIGALRM, signal);
}

main()
{
  int      sigpending_value;
  int      member;
  sigset_t set;
  pid_t    pid;

  fprintf (stdout,"get process id\n");
  pid = getpid ();
```

```
      fprintf (stdout,"register signal handler\n");
      signal (SIGALRM, handler);

      fprintf (stdout,"sighold shall hold SIGALRM in queue\n");
      sighold (SIGALRM);
      kill (pid, SIGALRM);
      sigpending_value = sigpending (&set);
      if ( sigpending_value == 0 ) {
          fprintf (stdout,"sigpending() call successful\n");
          member = sigismember (&set, SIGALRM);
          if ( member == 1 )
              fprintf (stdout,"signal SIGALRM is pending\n");
          else
              fprintf (stderr,"ERROR: SIGALRM is not pending\n");
      }
      else
          fprintf (stderr,"ERROR: sigpending() call failed\n");

      fprintf (stdout,"release the signal SIGALRM in queue\n");
      sigrelse (SIGALRM );
}
```

sigprocmask( )

System Interfaces

NAME

sigprocmask — examine and change blocked signals

SYNOPSIS

```
#include <signal.h>

int sigprocmask(int how, const sigset_t *set, sigset_t *oset);
```

DESCRIPTION

The *sigprocmask*( ) function allows the calling process to examine and/or change its signal mask.

If the argument *set* is not a null pointer, it points to a set of signals to be used to change the currently blocked set.

The argument *how* indicates the way in which the set is changed, and consists of one of the following values:

SIG_BLOCK   The resulting set will be the union of the current set and the signal set pointed to by *set*.

SIG_SETMASK   The resulting set will be the signal set pointed to by *set*.

SIG_UNBLOCK   The resulting set will be the intersection of the current set and the complement of the signal set pointed to by *set*. The resulting set will be the signal set pointed to by *set*.

If the argument *oset* is not a null pointer, the previous mask is stored in the location pointed to by *oset*. If *set* is a null pointer, the value of the argument *how* is not significant and the process' signal mask is unchanged; thus the call can be used to enquire about currently blocked signals.

If there are any pending unblocked signals after the call to *sigprocmask*( ), at least one of those signals will be delivered before the call to *sigprocmask*( ) returns.

It is not possible to block those signals which cannot be ignored. This is enforced by the system without causing an error to be indicated.

If any of the SIGFPE, SIGILL or SIGSEGV signals are generated while they are blocked, the result is undefined, unless the signal was generated by a call to *kill*( ) or *raise*( ).

If *sigprocmask*( ) fails, the process' signal mask is not changed.

RETURN VALUE

Upon successful completion, *sigprocmask*( ) returns 0. Otherwise −1 is returned, *errno* is set to indicate the error and the process' signal mask will be unchanged.

ERRORS

The *sigprocmask*( ) function will fail if:

[EINVAL]   The value of the *how* argument is not equal to one of the defined values.

SEE ALSO

sigaction( ), *sigaddset*( ), *sigdelset*( ), *sigemptyset*( ), *sigfillset*( ), *sigismember*( ), *sigpending*( ), *sigsuspend*( ), **<signal.h>**.

EXAMPLE

```
/*
 * Copyright (C) ANTRIX Inc.
 */

/* sigprocmask.c
```

```
 * This program changes and examines the signal mask using
 * function sigprocmask.
 */

#include <stdio.h>
#include <stdlib.h>
#include <signal.h>
#include <errno.h>

main()
{
  int       sigprocmask_value;
  sigset_t set, oset;

  sigemptyset (&set);
  sigaddset (&set, SIGALRM);

  fprintf (stdout,"change and examine signal mask\n");
  sigprocmask_value = sigprocmask (SIG_SETMASK, &set, &oset);
  if ( sigprocmask_value == 0 ) {
     fprintf (stdout,"sigprocmask() call successful\n");
     sigprocmask (SIG_SETMASK, &set, &oset);
     if ( sigismember (&oset, SIGALRM) != 1 )
        fprintf (stderr,"ERROR: SIGALRM is not a member of set\n");
  }
  else
     fprintf (stderr,"ERROR: sigprocmask() call failed\n");
}
```

NAME

sigrelse, sigset — remove a signal from signal mask or modify signal disposition

SYNOPSIS

```
#include <signal.h>

int sigrelse(int sig);

void (*sigset(int sig, void (*disp)(int)))(int);
```

DESCRIPTION

Refer to *signal*( ).

EXAMPLE

```
/*
 * Copyright (C) ANTRIX Inc.
 */

/* sigrelse.c
 * This program removes signal from the calling process's signal mask
 * using function sigrelse.
 */

#include <stdio.h>
#include <stdlib.h>
#include <unistd.h>
#include <signal.h>
#include <errno.h>

void handler(signal)
int signal;
{
  if ( signal == SIGALRM )
     fprintf (stdout,"received signal SIGALRM\n");
  else
     fprintf (stderr,"ERROR: expected=%d, received=%d\n", SIGALRM, signal);
}

main()
{
  int     sigrelse_value;
  pid_t   pid;

  fprintf (stdout,"get process id\n");
  pid = getpid ();

  fprintf (stdout,"register signal handler\n");
  signal (SIGALRM, handler);

  fprintf (stdout,"sighold holds the signal SIGALRM in queue\n");
  sighold (SIGALRM);
  kill (pid, SIGALRM );

  fprintf (stdout,"sigrelse releases the signal SIGALRM in queue\n");
  sigrelse_value = sigrelse (SIGALRM );
```

```
    if ( sigrelse_value == 0 )
        fprintf (stdout,"sigrelse() call successful\n");
    else
        fprintf (stderr,"ERROR: sigrelse() call failed\n");
}
```

NAME

sigsetjmp — set jump point for a non-local goto

SYNOPSIS

```
#include <setjmp.h>

int sigsetjmp(sigjmp_buf env, int savemask);
```

DESCRIPTION

A call to *sigsetjmp*( ) saves the calling environment in its *env* argument for later use by *siglongjmp*( ). It is unspecified whether *sigsetjmp*( ) is a macro or a function. If a macro definition is suppressed in order to access an actual function, or a program defines an external identifier with the name *sigsetjmp* the behaviour is undefined.

If the value of the *savemask* argument is not 0, *sigsetjmp*( ) will also save the process' current signal mask as part of the calling environment.

All accessible objects have values as of the time *siglongjmp*( ) was called, except that the values of objects of automatic storage duration which are local to the function containing the invocation of the corresponding *sigsetjmp*( ) which do not have volatile-qualified type and which are changed between the *sigsetjmp*( ) invocation and *siglongjmp*( ) call are indeterminate.

An invocation of *sigsetjmp*( ) must appear in one of the following contexts only:

- the entire controlling expression of a selection or iteration statement

- one operand of a relational or equality operator with the other operand an integral constant expression, with the resulting expression being the entire controlling expression of a selection or iteration statement

- the operand of a unary (!) operator with the resulting expression being the entire controlling expression of a selection or iteration

- the entire expression of an expression statement (possibly cast to **void**).

RETURN VALUE

If the return is from a successful direct invocation, *sigsetjmp*( ) returns 0. If the return is from a call to *siglongjmp*( ), *sigsetjmp*( ) returns a non-zero value.

ERRORS

No errors are defined.

APPLICATION USAGE

The distinction between *setjmp*( )/*longjmp*( ) and *sigsetjmp*( )/*siglongjmp*( ) is only significant for programs which use *sigaction*( ), *sigprocmask*( ) or *sigsuspend*( ).

SEE ALSO

siglongjmp( ), *signal*( ), *sigprocmask*( ), *sigsuspend*( ), **<setjmp.h>**.

EXAMPLE

```
/*
 * Copyright (C) ANTRIX Inc.
 */

/* sigsetjmp.c
 * This program saves the calling environment in its env argument
 * using function sigsetjmp for later use by the siglongjmp function.
 */

#include <stdio.h>
```

```
#include <stdlib.h>
#include <signal.h>
#include <setjmp.h>
#include <errno.h>

#define  SIGSET  0

main()
{
  int     sigsetjmp_value;
  int     val;
  sigjmp_buf  buf;
  static int  save_int;
  static long save_long;
  static  sigset_t sigmask1;
  static  sigset_t sig_fill, sigcurr, sigemp;

  val = 5;
  sigfillset (&sig_fill);
  sigemptyset (&sigemp);
  sigsetjmp_value = sigsetjmp (buf, 1);
  fprintf (stdout,"save values\n");
  if ( sigsetjmp_value == val ) {
      fprintf (stdout,"sigsetjmp_value=%d\n", sigsetjmp_value );
      fprintf (stdout,"save_int  = %d\n", save_int);
      fprintf (stdout,"save_long = %d\n", save_long);
      sigprocmask (0, (sigset_t *)0, &sigcurr);
      if (memcmp (&sigcurr, &sigmask1, sizeof(sigcurr)) ) {
          fprintf (stderr,"ERROR: signal not correct after sigsetjmp\n" );
#if SIGSET
          /* comment out statements below */
          /* if sigset member name is different */
          fprintf (stdout,"expected=#x%o, received=#x%o\n",
                  sigmask1.s[0], sigcurr.s[0] );
          fprintf (stdout,"expected=#x%o, received=#x%o\n",
                  sigmask1.s[1], sigcurr.s[1] );
#endif
      }
      exit (0);
  }
  save_int = 1;
  save_long = 123456789;
  sigprocmask (SIG_SETMASK, &sig_fill, &sigmask1);
  siglongjmp (buf, val);
  fprintf (stderr,"ERROR: siglongjmp() call failed\n");
}
```

NAME

sigstack — set and/or get alternate signal stack context (**TO BE WITHDRAWN**)

SYNOPSIS

UX   `#include <signal.h>`

`int sigstack(struct sigstack *ss, struct sigstack *oss);`

DESCRIPTION

The *sigstack*( ) function allows the calling process to indicate to the system an area of its address space to be used for processing signals received by the process.

If the *ss* argument is not a null pointer, it must point to a **sigstack** structure. The length of the application-supplied stack must be at least SIGSTKSZ bytes. If the alternate signal stack overflows, the resulting behaviour is undefined. (See **APPLICATION USAGE** below.)

- The value of the **ss_onstack** member indicates whether the process wants the system to use an alternate signal stack when delivering signals.

- The value of the **ss_sp** member indicates the desired location of the alternate signal stack area in the process' address space.

- If the *ss* argument is a null pointer, the current alternate signal stack context is not changed.

If the *oss* argument is not a null pointer, it points to a **sigstack** structure in which the current alternate signal stack context is placed. The value stored in the **ss_onstack** member of *oss* will be non-zero if the process is currently executing on the alternate signal stack. If the *oss* argument is a null pointer, the current alternate signal stack context is not returned.

When a signal's action indicates its handler should execute on the alternate signal stack (specified by calling *sigaction*( )), the implementation checks to see if the process is currently executing on that stack. If the process is not currently executing on the alternate signal stack, the system arranges a switch to the alternate signal stack for the duration of the signal handler's execution.

After a successful call to one of the *exec* functions, there are no alternate signal stacks in the new process image.

RETURN VALUE

Upon successful completion, *sigstack*( ) returns 0. Otherwise, it returns −1 and sets *errno* to indicate the error.

ERRORS

The *sigstack*( ) function will fail if:

[EPERM]   An attempt was made to modify an active stack.

APPLICATION USAGE

A portable application, when being written or rewritten, should use *sigaltstack*( ) instead of *sigstack*( ).

On some implementations, stack space is automatically extended as needed. On those implementations, automatic extension is typically not available for an alternate stack. If a signal stack overflows, the resulting behaviour of the process is undefined.

The direction of stack growth is not indicated in the historical definition of **struct sigstack**. The only way to portably establish a stack pointer is for the application to determine stack growth direction, or to allocate a block of storage and set the stack pointer to the middle. The implementation may assume that the size of the signal stack is SIGSTKSZ as found in **<signal.h>**. An implementation that would like to specify a signal stack size other than

SIGSTKSZ should use *sigaltstack*( ).

Programs should not use *longjmp*( ) to leave a signal handler that is running on a stack established with *sigstack*( ). Doing so may disable future use of the signal stack. For abnormal exit from a signal handler, *siglongjmp*( ), *setcontext*( ), or *swapcontext*( ) may be used. These functions fully support switching from one stack to another.

The *sigstack*( ) function requires the application to have knowledge of the underlying system's stack architecture. For this reason, *sigaltstack*( ) is recommended over this function.

SEE ALSO

exec, *fork*( ), *_longjmp*( ), *longjmp*( ), *setjmp*( ), *sigaltstack*( ), *siglongjmp*( ), *sigsetjmp*( ), **<signal.h>**.

sigsuspend( )

NAME

sigsuspend — wait for a signal

SYNOPSIS

```
#include <signal.h>

int sigsuspend(const sigset_t *sigmask);
```

DESCRIPTION

The *sigsuspend*( ) function replaces the process' current signal mask with the set of signals pointed to by *sigmask* and then suspends the process until delivery of a signal whose action is either to execute a signal-catching function or to terminate the process.

If the action is to terminate the process then *sigsuspend*( ) will never return. If the action is to execute a signal-catching function, then *sigsuspend*( ) will return after the signal-catching function returns, with the signal mask restored to the set that existed prior to the *sigsuspend*( ) call.

It is not possible to block signals that cannot be ignored. This is enforced by the system without causing an error to be indicated.

RETURN VALUE

Since *sigsuspend*( ) suspends process execution indefinitely, there is no successful completion return value. If a return occurs, −1 is returned and *errno* is set to indicate the error.

ERRORS

The *sigsuspend*( ) function will fail if:

[EINTR]   A signal is caught by the calling process and control is returned from the signal-catching function.

SEE ALSO

pause( ), *sigaction*( ), *sigaddset*( ), *sigdelset*( ), *sigemptyset*( ), *sigfillset*( ), **<signal.h>**.

EXAMPLE

```
/*
 * Copyright (C) ANTRIX Inc.
 */

/* sigsuspend.c
 * This program replaces the process current signal mask with
 * set of signals pointed to by set using function sigsuspend
 */

#include <stdio.h>
#include <stdlib.h>
#include <signal.h>
#include <errno.h>

void handler(signal)
int signal;
{
  if ( signal == SIGALRM )
     fprintf (stdout,"received signal SIGALRM\n");
  else
     fprintf (stderr,"ERROR: expected=%d, received=%d\n",
                 SIGALRM, signal);
```

```
      exit (1);
}

main()
{
  int      sigsuspend_value;
  sigset_t set;

  fprintf (stdout,"empty signal set\n");
  sigemptyset (&set);

  fprintf (stdout,"add SIGALRM to signal set\n");
  sigaddset (&set, SIGALRM);
  sigprocmask (SIG_SETMASK, &set, (sigset_t *)0);
  sigfillset (&set);

  fprintf (stdout,"remove SIGALRM signal from set\n");
  sigdelset (&set, SIGALRM);

  fprintf (stdout,"setup signal handler for SIGALRM\n");
  signal (SIGALRM, handler);
  alarm (2);
  sigsuspend_value = sigsuspend (&set);
  if ( sigsuspend_value == -1 )
      fprintf (stderr,"ERROR: sigsuspend() call failed\n");
}
```

NAME

sin — sine function

SYNOPSIS

```
#include <math.h>

double sin(double x);
```

DESCRIPTION

The *sin( )* function computes the sine of its argument *x*, measured in radians.

RETURN VALUE

Upon successful completion, *sin( )* returns the sine of *x*.

EX   If *x* is NaN, NaN is returned and *errno* may be set to [EDOM].

EX   If *x* is ±Inf, either 0.0 is returned and *errno* is set to [EDOM], or NaN is returned and *errno* may be set to [EDOM].

If the correct result would cause underflow, 0.0 is returned and *errno* may be set to [ERANGE].

ERRORS

The *sin( )* function may fail if:

EX   [EDOM]   The value of *x* is NaN, or *x* is ±Inf.

[ERANGE]   The result underflows.

EX   No other errors will occur.

APPLICATION USAGE

An application wishing to check for error situations should set *errno* to 0 before calling *sin( )*. If *errno* is non-zero on return, or the return value is NaN, an error has occurred.

The *sin( )* function may lose accuracy when its argument is far from 0.0 .

SEE ALSO

asin( ), *isnan( )*, **<math.h>**.

EXAMPLE

```
/*
 * Copyright (C) ANTRIX Inc.
 */

/* sin.c
 * This program computes the sine of its argument x, measured
 * in radians using function sin.
 */

#include <stdio.h>
#include <math.h>

main()
{
  double  sin_value;
  double  x = 0.50;

  sin_value = sin (x);
```

```
        fprintf (stdout,"sin of %f is %f\n", x, sin_value);
    }
```

NAME

sinh — hyperbolic sine function

SYNOPSIS

```
#include <math.h>

double sinh(double x);
```

DESCRIPTION

The *sinh( )* function computes the hyperbolic sine of *x*.

RETURN VALUE

Upon successful completion, *sinh( )* returns the hyperbolic sine of *x*.

If the result would cause an overflow, ±HUGE_VAL is returned and *errno* is set to [ERANGE].

If the result would cause underflow, 0.0 is returned and *errno* may be set to [ERANGE].

EX   If *x* is NaN, NaN is returned and *errno* may be set to [EDOM].

ERRORS

The *sinh( )* function will fail if:

[ERANGE]   The result would cause overflow.

The *sinh( )* function may fail if:

EX   [EDOM]   The value of *x* is NaN.

[ERANGE]   The result would cause underflow.

EX   No other errors will occur.

APPLICATION USAGE

An application wishing to check for error situations should set *errno* to 0 before calling *sinh( )*. If *errno* is non-zero on return, or the return value is NaN, an error has occurred.

SEE ALSO

asinh( ), *cosh( )*, *isnan( )*, *tanh( )*, **<math.h>**.

EXAMPLE

```
/*
 * Copyright (C) ANTRIX Inc.
 */

/* sinh.c
 * This program computes the hyperbolic sine of x using
 * function sinh.
 */

#include <stdio.h>
#include <math.h>

main()
{
  double  sinh_value;
  double  x = 0.50;

  sinh_value = sinh (x);
```

```
    fprintf (stdout,"sinh of %f is %f\n", x, sinh_value);
}
```

NAME

sleep — suspend execution for an interval of time

SYNOPSIS

```
#include <unistd.h>

unsigned int sleep(unsigned int seconds);
```

DESCRIPTION

The *sleep( )* function will cause the current process to be suspended from execution until either the number of real-time seconds specified by the argument *seconds* has elapsed or a signal is delivered to the calling process and its action is to invoke a signal-catching function or to terminate the process. The suspension time may be longer than requested due to the scheduling of other activity by the system.

If a SIGALRM signal is generated for the calling process during execution of *sleep( )* and if the SIGALRM signal is being ignored or blocked from delivery, it is unspecified whether *sleep( )* returns when the SIGALRM signal is scheduled. If the signal is being blocked, it is also unspecified whether it remains pending after *sleep( )* returns or it is discarded.

If a SIGALRM signal is generated for the calling process during execution of *sleep( )*, except as a result of a prior call to *alarm( )*, and if the SIGALRM signal is not being ignored or blocked from delivery, it is unspecified whether that signal has any effect other than causing *sleep( )* to return.

If a signal-catching function interrupts *sleep( )* and examines or changes either the time a SIGALRM is scheduled to be generated, the action associated with the SIGALRM signal, or whether the SIGALRM signal is blocked from delivery, the results are unspecified.

If a signal-catching function interrupts *sleep( )* and calls *siglongjmp( )* or *longjmp( )* to restore an environment saved prior to the *sleep( )* call, the action associated with the SIGALRM signal and the time at which a SIGALRM signal is scheduled to be generated are unspecified. It is also unspecified whether the SIGALRM signal is blocked, unless the process' signal mask is restored as part of the environment.

UX   Interactions between *sleep( )* and any of *setitimer( )*, *ualarm( )* or *usleep( )* are unspecified.

RETURN VALUE

If *sleep( )* returns because the requested time has elapsed, the value returned will be 0. If *sleep( )* returns because of premature arousal due to delivery of a signal, the return value will be the "unslept" amount (the requested time minus the time actually slept) in seconds.

ERRORS

No errors are defined.

SEE ALSO

alarm( ), *getitimer( )*, *pause( )*, *sigaction( )*, *sigsetjmp( )*, *ualarm( )*, *usleep( )*, **<unistd.h>**.

EXAMPLE

```
/*
 * Copyright (C) ANTRIX Inc.
 */

/* sleep.c
 * This program suspends execution for an interval of time
 * using function sleep.
 */

#include <stdio.h>
```

```
#include <stdlib.h>
#include <time.h>
#include <errno.h>

main()
{
  char     *ctime_value;
  char     *current_time;
  time_t   clock, tloc;
  struct   tm  *buf;

  clock = time (&tloc);
  fprintf (stdout,"current clock ticks is %d\n", clock);

  ctime_value = ctime (&clock);
  buf = localtime (&clock);
  current_time = asctime (buf);
  fprintf (stdout,"current time is %s\n", current_time);

  fprintf (stdout,"sleep for 5 seconds\n");
  sleep (5);
  clock = time (&tloc);

  fprintf (stdout,"current clock ticks after 5 seconds is %d\n", clock);
  ctime_value = ctime (&clock);
  buf = localtime (&clock);
  current_time = asctime (buf);

  fprintf (stdout,"current time after 5 seconds is %s\n", current_time);
}
```

NAME

sprintf — print formatted output

SYNOPSIS

```
#include <stdio.h>

int sprintf(char *s, const char *format, ...);
```

DESCRIPTION

Refer to *fprintf( )*.

EXAMPLE

```c
/*
 * Copyright (C) ANTRIX Inc.
 */

/* sprintf.c
 * This program places formatted output followed by the null
 * byte ' ' in consecutive bytes in string using function
 * sprintf.
 */

#include <stdio.h>
#include <stdlib.h>
#include <limits.h>
#include <errno.h>

main()
{
  int    sprintf_value;
  char   string[255];

  fprintf(stdout, "write formatted output in string\n");
  sprintf_value = sprintf (string, "%s %s", "hello", "99");
  if ( sprintf_value == 8 ) {
      fprintf (stdout,"sprintf() call successful\n");
      fprintf (stdout,"string=%s\n", string);
      fprintf (stdout,"sprintf_value=%d\n", sprintf_value);
  }
  else
      fprintf (stderr,"ERROR: sprintf() call failed\n");
}
```

NAME

sqrt — square root function

SYNOPSIS

```
#include <math.h>

double sqrt(double x);
```

DESCRIPTION

The *sqrt*( ) function computes the square root of *x*, $\sqrt{x}$.

RETURN VALUE

Upon successful completion, *sqrt*( ) returns the square root of *x*.

EX   If *x* is NaN, NaN is returned and *errno* may be set to [EDOM].

EX   If *x* is negative, 0.0 or NaN is returned and *errno* is set to [EDOM].

ERRORS

The *sqrt*( ) function will fail if:

[EDOM]   The value of *x* is negative.

The *sqrt*( ) function may fail if:

EX   [EDOM]   The value of *x* is NaN.

EX   No other errors will occur.

APPLICATION USAGE

An application wishing to check for error situations should set *errno* to 0 before calling *sqrt*( ). If *errno* is non-zero on return, or the return value is NaN, an error has occurred.

SEE ALSO

isnan( ), **<math.h>**, **<stdio.h>**.

EXAMPLE

```
/*
 * Copyright (C) ANTRIX Inc.
 */

/* sqrt.c
 * This program computes the square root of x using
 * function sqrt.
 */

#include <stdio.h>
#include <math.h>

main()
{
  double  sqrt_value;
  double  x = 625.00;

  sqrt_value = sqrt (x);
  fprintf (stdout,"sqrt of %f is %f\n", x, sqrt_value);
}
```

NAME

srand — seed simple pseudo-random number generator

SYNOPSIS

```
#include <stdlib.h>

void srand(unsigned int seed);
```

DESCRIPTION

Refer to *rand*( ).

EXAMPLE

```
/*
 * Copyright (C) ANTRIX Inc.
 */

/* srand.c
 * This program initializes entry points for random number
 * generator rand using function srand.
 */

#include <stdio.h>
#include <stdlib.h>
#include <errno.h>

main()
{
   int          rand_value;
   int          i;
   unsigned int seed = 100;

   srand (100);
   for ( i = 0; i < 5; i++ ) {
       rand_value = rand ();
       fprintf (stdout,"random value in iteration %d is %d\n",
                       i, rand_value);
   }
}
```

NAME

srand48 — seed uniformly distributed double-precision pseudo-random number generator

SYNOPSIS

EX
```
#include <stdlib.h>

void srand48(long int seedval);
```

DESCRIPTION

Refer to *drand48*( ).

EXAMPLE

```
/*
 * Copyright (C) ANTRIX Inc.
 */

/* srand48.c
 * This program initializes entry points for random number
 * generator rand using function srand48.
 */

#include <stdio.h>
#include <stdlib.h>
#include <errno.h>

main()
{
  int          lrand48_value;
  int          i;
  unsigned int seed = 100;

  srand48 (100);
  for ( i = 0; i < 5; i++ ) {
      lrand48_value = lrand48 ();
      fprintf (stdout,"random value in iteration %d is %d\n",
                      i, lrand48_value);
  }
}
```

NAME

srandom — seed pseudorandom number generator

SYNOPSIS

UX

```
#include <stdlib.h>

void srandom(unsigned int seed);
```

DESCRIPTION

Refer to *initstate*( ).

EXAMPLE

```
/*
 * Copyright (C) ANTRIX Inc.
 */

/* srandom.c
 * This program initializes entry points for random number
 * generator srandom using function srandom.
 */

#include <stdio.h>
#include <stdlib.h>
#include <errno.h>

main()
{
  int           random_value;
  int           i;
  unsigned int seed = 100;

  srandom (100);
  for ( i = 0; i < 5; i++ ) {
      random_value = random ();
      fprintf (stdout,"random value in iteration %d is %d\n",
                      i, random_value);
  }
}
```

NAME

sscanf — convert formatted input

SYNOPSIS

```
#include <stdio.h>

int sscanf(const char *s, const char *format, ...);
```

DESCRIPTION

Refer to *fscanf( )*.

EXAMPLE

```
/*
 * Copyright (C) ANTRIX Inc.
 */

/* sscanf.c
 * This program reads from the named input from string according
 * to a format, and stores the results in its argument
 * using function sscanf.
 */

#include <stdio.h>
#include <stdlib.h>
#include <errno.h>

main()
{
  int    sscanf_value;
  int    value;
  char   str1[6];
  char   string[] = "hello 9";

  sscanf_value = sscanf (string, "%s %d", str1, &value);
  if ( sscanf_value == 2 ) {
     fprintf (stdout,"sscanf() call successful\n");
     fprintf (stdout,"string str1 is %s\n", str1);
     fprintf (stdout,"value is %d\n", value);
  }
  else
     fprintf (stderr,"ERROR: sscanf() call failed\n");
}
```

NAME

stat — get file status

SYNOPSIS

OH
```
#include <sys/types.h>
#include <sys/stat.h>

int stat(const char *path, struct stat *buf);
```

DESCRIPTION

The *stat*( ) function obtains information about the named file and writes it to the area pointed to by the *buf* argument. The *path* argument points to a pathname naming a file. Read, write or execute permission of the named file is not required, but all directories listed in the pathname leading to the file must be searchable. An implementation that provides additional or alternate file access control mechanisms may, under implementation-dependent conditions, cause *stat*( ) to fail. In particular, the system may deny the existence of the file specified by *path*.

The *buf* argument is a pointer to a *stat* structure, as defined in the header **<sys/stat.h>**, into which information is placed concerning the file.

The *stat*( ) function updates any time-related fields (as described in the definition of **File Times Update** in the **XBD** specification), before writing into the **stat** structure.

The structure members *st_mode*, *st_ino*, *st_dev*, *st_uid*, *st_gid*, *st_atime*, *st_ctime* and *st_mtime* will have meaningful values for all file types defined in this document. The value of the member *st_nlink* will be set to the number of links to the file.

RETURN VALUE

Upon successful completion, 0 is returned. Otherwise, −1 is returned and *errno* is set to indicate the error.

ERRORS

The *stat*( ) function will fail if:

[EACCES]	Search permission is denied for a component of the path prefix.

UX
[EIO]	An error occurred while reading from the file system.

UX
[ELOOP]	Too many symbolic links were encountered in resolving *path*.

[ENAMETOOLONG]

FIPS
The length of the *path* argument exceeds {PATH_MAX} or a pathname component is longer than {NAME_MAX}.

[ENOENT]	A component of *path* does not name an existing file or *path* is an empty string.
[ENOTDIR]	A component of the path prefix is not a directory.

UX   The *stat*( ) function may fail if:

UX   [ENAMETOOLONG]

Pathname resolution of a symbolic link produced an intermediate result whose length exceeds {PATH_MAX}.

[EOVERFLOW]   A value to be stored would overflow one of the members of the **stat** structure.

SEE ALSO

fstat( ), *lstat*( ), **<sys/stat.h>**, **<sys/types.h>**.

EXAMPLE

```
/*
 * Copyright (C) ANTRIX Inc.
```

```
 */

/* stat.c
 * This program obtains information about the named file and
 * writes it to the area pointed to by the buf argument using
 * function stat.
 */

#include <stdio.h>
#include <stdlib.h>
#include <sys/types.h>
#include <sys/stat.h>
#include <errno.h>

#define  PERM_ALL    (S_IRWXU | S_IRWXG | S_IRWXO)

main()
{
  int     stat_value;
  int     fildes;
  struct  stat buf;
  char    *string = "hello world";
  char    *path = "testfile";

  fprintf (stdout,"create testfile\n");
  fildes = creat (path, PERM_ALL);

  fprintf (stdout,"write string to testfile\n");
  write (fildes, string, strlen(string));

  fprintf (stdout,"get status of testfile\n");
  stat_value = stat (path, &buf);
  if ( stat_value == 0 ) {
      fprintf (stdout,"stat() call successful\n");
      fprintf (stdout,"buf.st_mode=%o\n", (S_IFREG ^ buf.st_mode) );
      fprintf (stdout,"buf.st_nlink=%d\n", buf.st_nlink );
      fprintf (stdout,"buf.st_uid=%d\n", buf.st_uid );
      fprintf (stdout,"buf.st_gid=%d\n", buf.st_gid );
      fprintf (stdout,"buf.st_size=%d\n", buf.st_size );
  }
  else {
      fprintf (stderr,"ERROR: stat() call failed\n");
      fprintf (stderr,"ERROR: %s\n", strerror(errno));
  }

  fprintf (stdout,"remove testfile\n");
  remove (path);
}
```

NAME

statvfs — get file system information

SYNOPSIS

UX   `#include <sys/statvfs.h>`

`int statvfs(const char *path, struct statvfs *buf);`

DESCRIPTION

Refer to *fstatvfs*( ).

EXAMPLE

```
/*
 * Copyright (C) ANTRIX Inc.
 */

/* statvfs.c
 * This program gets the file system information
 * using function statvfs.
 */

#include <stdio.h>
#include <stdlib.h>
#include <sys/types.h>
#include <sys/statvfs.h>
#include <errno.h>

main()
{
   int      statvfs_value;
   struct   statvfs  buf;

   fprintf (stdout,"stat the root file system\n");
   statvfs_value = statvfs("/", &buf);
   if ( statvfs_value == 0 ) {
      fprintf (stdout,"statvfs successful\n");
      fprintf (stdout,"buf.f_bsize=%d\n", buf.f_bsize);
      fprintf (stdout,"buf.f_blocks=%d\n", buf.f_blocks);
      fprintf (stdout,"buf.f_bfree=%d\n", buf.f_bfree);
      fprintf (stdout,"buf.f_bavail=%d\n", buf.f_bavail);
      fprintf (stdout,"buf.f_files=%d\n", buf.f_files);
   }
   else {
      fprintf (stdout,"statvfs failed\n");
      fprintf (stderr,"ERROR: %s\n", strerror(errno));
   }
}
```

NAME

stderr, stdin, stdout — standard I/O streams

SYNOPSIS

```
#include <stdio.h>

extern FILE *stderr, *stdin, *stdout;
```

DESCRIPTION

A file with associated buffering is called a *stream* and is declared to be a pointer to a defined type **FILE**. The *fopen( )* function creates certain descriptive data for a stream and returns a pointer to designate the stream in all further transactions. Normally, there are three open streams with constant pointers declared in the **<stdio.h>** header and associated with the standard open files.

At program startup, three streams are predefined and need not be opened explicitly: *standard input* (for reading conventional input), *standard output* (for writing conventional output) and *standard error* (for writing diagnostic output). When opened, the standard error stream is not fully buffered; the standard input and standard output streams are fully buffered if and only if the stream can be determined not to refer to an interactive device.

The following symbolic values in **<unistd.h>** define the file descriptors that will be associated with the C-language *stdin*, *stdout* and *stderr* when the application is started:

STDIN_FILENO   Standard input value, *stdin*. Its value is 0.

STDOUT_FILENO   Standard output value, *stdout*. Its value is 1.

STDERR_FILENO   Standard error value, *stderr*. Its value is 2.

SEE ALSO

fclose( ), *feof( )*, *ferror( )*, *fileno( )*, *fopen( )*, *fread( )*, *fseek( )*, *getc( )*, *gets( )*, *popen( )*, *printf( )*, *putc( )*, *puts( )*, *read( )*, *scanf( )*, *setbuf( )*, *setvbuf( )*, *tmpfile( )*, *ungetc( )*, *vprintf( )*, **<stdio.h>**, **<unistd.h>**.

EXAMPLE

```
/*
 * Copyright (C) ANTRIX Inc.
 */

/* stdin.c
 * This program illustrates use of stdin, stdout and stderr
 * streams. The file descriptor associated with stdin (0),
 * stdout (1) and stderr(2) and can be used by read, write
 * calls.
 */

#include <stdio.h>
#include <stdlib.h>
#include <unistd.h>
#include <errno.h>

main()
{

    int     bytes, fprintf_value;
    int     integer = 1;
```

```
long     longer = 12L;
float    floating = 1.2345;
double   doubles = 1.234E10;
char     character = 'a';
char     string[] = "hello world";
char     buf[255];
char     errmsg[] = "ERROR: invalid value\n";

memset(buf,' ', 255);

fprintf (stdout,"write to stdout or terminal\n");
fprintf (stdout, "integer=%d\n", integer);
fprintf (stdout, "longer=%ld\n", longer);
fprintf (stdout, "float=%f\n", floating);
fprintf (stdout, "doubles=%f\n", doubles);
fprintf (stdout, "character=%c\n", character);
fprintf (stdout, "string=%s\n", string);

fprintf (stdout,"fgets: Type a string and hit return key\n");
fgets (buf, 255, stdin);
fprintf (stdout,"string typed is=%s\n", buf);

memset(buf,' ', 255);
fprintf (stdout,"read: Type a string and hit return key\n");
read(0, buf, 255);

fprintf (stdout,"Write error to stderr\n");
if (integer != 2) {
  fprintf (stderr, "ERROR: Expected=2, Actual=%d\n", integer);
  write (2, errmsg, strlen(errmsg));
}

}
```

NAME

step — pattern match with regular expressions (**TO BE WITHDRAWN**)

SYNOPSIS

EX
```
#include <regexp.h>
```

```
int step(const char *string, const char *expbuf);
```

DESCRIPTION

Refer to *regexp*( ).

EXAMPLE

```
/*
 * Copyright (C) ANTRIX Inc.
 */

/* step.c
 * This program matches the substring of string with the
 * regular expression in expbuf using function step.
 */

#include <stdio.h>
#include <stdlib.h>
#include <errno.h>

#define STRSIZE 100

char instring[STRSIZE];
char *value = "True";

#define        INIT            register char *sp = instring;
#define        GETC()          (*sp++)
#define        PEEKC()         (*sp)
#define        UNGETC(c)       (--sp)
#define        RETURN(c)       return((char *)value)
#define        ERROR(c)        comperr()
#include        <regexp.h>

extern char *loc1, *loc2, *locs;

main()
{
    int  step_value;
    char *compile_value;
    char string[10*STRSIZE];
    char expbuf[STRSIZE];

    strcpy(instring, "[a-d]");
    strcpy(string, "efgcxyz");

    fprintf(stdout, "Produce compiled expression\n");
    compile_value = compile(instring, expbuf, &expbuf[STRSIZE], ' ');

    fprintf(stdout, "Match character c\n");
```

```
        step_value = step(string, expbuf);
        if (step_value != 0) {
           fprintf(stdout, "step call successful\n");
           fprintf(stdout, "step_value=%d\n", step_value);
        }
        else {
           fprintf(stderr, "ERROR: step call failed\n");
           fprintf(stderr, "%d\n", step_value);
        }
    }

    comperr()
    { }
```

NAME

strcasecmp, strncasecmp — case-insensitive string comparisons

SYNOPSIS

UX   `#include <strings.h>`

`int strcasecmp(const char *s1, const char *s2);`

`int strncasecmp(const char *s1, const char *s2, size_t n);`

DESCRIPTION

The *strcasecmp( )* function compares, while ignoring differences in case, the string pointed to by *s1* to the string pointed to by *s2*. The *strncasecmp( )* function compares, while ignoring differences in case, not more than *n* bytes from the string pointed to by *s1* to the string pointed to by *s2*.

These functions assume the ASCII character set when equating lower and upper case characters. In the POSIX locale, *strcasecmp( )* and *strncasecmp( )* do upper to lower conversions, then a byte comparison. The results are unspecified in other locales.

RETURN VALUE

Upon completion, *strcasecmp( )* returns an integer greater than, equal to or less than 0, if the string pointed to by *s1* is, ignoring case, greater than, equal to or less than the string pointed to by *s2* respectively.

Upon successful completion, *strncasecmp( )* returns an integer greater than, equal to or less than 0, if the possibly null-terminated array pointed to by *s1* is, ignoring case, greater than, equal to or less than the possibly null-terminated array pointed to by *s2* respectively.

ERRORS

No errors are defined.

SEE ALSO

<strings.h>.

EXAMPLE

```
/*
 * Copyright (C) ANTRIX Inc.
 */

/* strcasecmp.c
 * This program compares the string pointed to by s1
 * to the string pointed to by s2 ignoring cases
 * using function strcasecmp.
 */

#include <stdio.h>
#include <stdlib.h>
#include <string.h>
#include <errno.h>

main()
{
    int         strcasecmp_value;
    const char  s1[] = "hello world";
    const char  s2[] = "Hello World";
```

```
        fprintf (stdout,"compare strings\n");
        strcasecmp_value = strcasecmp(s1, s2);
        if ( strcasecmp_value == 0 )
            fprintf (stdout,"strcasecmp() call successful\n");
        else
            fprintf (stderr,"ERROR: strcasecmp() call failed\n");
}


/*
 * Copyright (C) ANTRIX Inc.
 */

/* strncasecmp.c
 * This program compares n bytes of string s1 and s2
 * ignoring cases using function strncasecmp.
 */

#include <stdio.h>
#include <stdlib.h>
#include <string.h>
#include <errno.h>


main()
{
  int        strncasecmp_value;
  size_t     n = 5;
  const char s1[] = "hello world";
  const char s2[] = "HelLO all";

  fprintf (stdout,"compare first 5 bytes\n");
  strncasecmp_value = strncasecmp (s1, s2, n);
  if ( strncasecmp_value == 0 )
     fprintf (stdout,"strncasecmp() call successful\n");
  else
     fprintf (stderr,"ERROR: strncasecmp() call failed\n");
}
```

NAME

strcat — concatenate two strings

SYNOPSIS

```
#include <string.h>

char *strcat(char *s1, const char *s2);
```

DESCRIPTION

The *strcat*( ) function appends a copy of the string pointed to by *s2* (including the terminating null byte) to the end of the string pointed to by *s1*. The initial byte of *s2* overwrites the null byte at the end of *s1*. If copying takes place between objects that overlap, the behaviour is undefined.

RETURN VALUE

The *strcat*( ) function returns *s1*; no return value is reserved to indicate an error.

ERRORS

No errors are defined.

APPLICATION USAGE

This issue is aligned with the ANSI C standard; this does not affect compatibility with XPG3 applications. Reliable error detection by this function was never guaranteed.

SEE ALSO

strncat( ), **<string.h>**.

EXAMPLE

```
/*
 * Copyright (C) ANTRIX Inc.
 */

/* strcat.c
 * This program appends a copy of string pointed to by s2
 * to the end of the string pointed to by s1 using function
 * strcat.
 */

#include <stdio.h>
#include <stdlib.h>
#include <string.h>
#include <errno.h>

main()
{
  char    *strcat_value;
  char    s2[12] = "hello ";
  char    s1[6] = "world";

  fprintf (stdout,"concatenate strings\n");
  strcat_value = strcat (s2, s1);
  if ( strcat_value != (char *)0 ) {
     fprintf (stdout,"strcat() call successful\n");
     fprintf (stdout,"s2=%s\n", s2);
     fprintf (stdout,"strcat_value=%s\n", strcat_value);
  }
  else
```

```
        fprintf (stderr,"ERROR: strcat() call failed\n");
}
```

NAME

strchr — string scanning operation

SYNOPSIS

```
#include <string.h>

char *strchr(const char *s, int c);
```

DESCRIPTION

The *strchr*( ) function locates the first occurrence of *c* (converted to an **unsigned char**) in the string pointed to by *s*. The terminating null byte is considered to be part of the string.

RETURN VALUE

Upon completion, *strchr*( ) returns a pointer to the byte, or a null pointer if the byte was not found.

ERRORS

No errors are defined.

SEE ALSO

strrchr( ), **<string.h>**.

EXAMPLE

```
/*
 * Copyright (C) ANTRIX Inc.
 */

/* strchr.c
 * This program locates the first occurrence of c in the
 * string pointed to by s using function strchr.
 */

#include <stdio.h>
#include <stdlib.h>
#include <string.h>
#include <errno.h>

main()
{
  char    *strchr_value;
  int     c = 't';
  char    s[] = "one two three";

  fprintf (stdout,"return pointer to first occurrence of t\n");
  strchr_value = strchr(s, c);
  if ( strchr_value != (char *)0 ) {
      fprintf (stdout,"strchr() call successful\n");
      fprintf (stdout,"strchr_value=%s\n", strchr_value);
  }
  else
      fprintf (stderr,"ERROR: strchr() call failed\n");
}
```

NAME

strcmp — compare two strings

SYNOPSIS

```
#include <string.h>

int strcmp(const char *s1, const char *s2);
```

DESCRIPTION

The *strcmp*( ) function compares the string pointed to by *s1* to the string pointed to by *s2*.

The sign of a non-zero return value is determined by the sign of the difference between the values of the first pair of bytes (both interpreted as type **unsigned char**) that differ in the strings being compared.

RETURN VALUE

Upon completion, *strcmp*( ) returns an integer greater than, equal to or less than 0, if the string pointed to by *s1* is greater than, equal to or less than the string pointed to by *s2* respectively.

ERRORS

No errors are defined.

SEE ALSO

strncmp( ), **<string.h>**.

EXAMPLE

```
/*
 * Copyright (C) ANTRIX Inc.
 */

/* strcmp.c
 * This program compares the string pointed to by s1
 * to the string pointed to by s2 using function strcmp.
 */

#include <stdio.h>
#include <stdlib.h>
#include <string.h>
#include <errno.h>

main()
{
  int        strcmp_value;
  const char s1[] = "hello world";
  const char s2[] = "hello world";

  fprintf (stdout,"compare strings\n");
  strcmp_value = strcmp(s1, s2);
  if ( strcmp_value == 0 )
     fprintf (stdout,"strcmp() call successful\n");
  else
     fprintf (stderr,"ERROR: strcmp() call failed\n");
}
```

NAME

strcoll — string comparison using collating information

SYNOPSIS

```
#include <string.h>

int strcoll(const char *s1, const char *s2);
```

DESCRIPTION

The *strcoll*( ) function compares the string pointed to by *s1* to the string pointed to by *s2*, both interpreted as appropriate to the LC_COLLATE category of the current locale.

RETURN VALUE

Upon successful completion, *strcoll*( ) returns an integer greater than, equal to or less than 0, according to whether the string pointed to by *s1* is greater than, equal to or less than the string pointed to by *s2* when both are interpreted as appropriate to the current locale. On error, *strcoll*( ) may set *errno*, but no return value is reserved to indicate an error.

ERRORS

The *strcoll*( ) function may fail if:

EX [EINVAL]   The *s1* or *s2* arguments contain characters outside the domain of the collating sequence.

APPLICATION USAGE

Because no return value is reserved to indicate an error, an application wishing to check for error situations should set *errno* to 0, then call *strcoll*( ), then check *errno* and if it is non-zero, assume an error has occurred.

This issue is aligned with the ANSI C standard; this does not affect compatibility with XPG3 applications. Reliable error detection by this function was never guaranteed.

The *strxfrm*( ) and *strcmp*( ) functions should be used for sorting large lists.

SEE ALSO

strcmp( ), *strxfrm*( ), **<string.h>**.

EXAMPLE

```
/*
 * Copyright (C) ANTRIX Inc.
 */

/* strcoll.c
 * This program compares the string pointed to by s1 to the
 * string pointed to by s2, both interpreted as appropriate to
 * the LC_COLLATE category of the current locale.
 */

#include <stdio.h>
#include <stdlib.h>
#include <string.h>
#include <locale.h>
#include <errno.h>

main()
{
    int    strcoll_value;
    char   s1[] = "AAA";
```

```
        char   s2[] = "aaa";

        setlocale (LC_ALL, "C");
        fprintf (stdout,"compare two strings\n");
        strcoll_value = strcoll (s1, s2);
        if ( strcoll_value < 0 ) {
            fprintf (stdout,"strcoll() call successful\n");
            fprintf (stdout,"strcoll_value=%d\n", strcoll_value);
        }
        else
            fprintf (stderr,"ERROR: strcoll() call failed\n");
}
```

NAME

strcpy — copy a string

SYNOPSIS

```
#include <string.h>

char *strcpy(char *s1, const char *s2);
```

DESCRIPTION

The *strcpy*( ) function copies the string pointed to by *s2* (including the terminating null byte) into the array pointed to by *s1*. If copying takes place between objects that overlap, the behaviour is undefined.

RETURN VALUE

The *strcpy*( ) function returns *s1*; no return value is reserved to indicate an error.

ERRORS

No errors are defined.

APPLICATION USAGE

Character movement is performed differently in different implementations. Thus overlapping moves may yield surprises.

This issue is aligned with the ANSI C standard; this does not affect compatibility with XPG3 applications. Reliable error detection by this function was never guaranteed.

SEE ALSO

strncpy( ), **<string.h>**.

EXAMPLE

```
/*
 * Copyright (C) ANTRIX Inc.
 */

/* strcpy.c
 * This program copies the string pointed to by s2 into the
 * array pointed to by s1 using function strcpy.
 */

#include <stdio.h>
#include <stdlib.h>
#include <string.h>
#include <errno.h>

main()
{
    char        *strcpy_value;
    char        s1[12];
    const char  *s2 = "hello world";

    memset (s1, ' ', 12);

    fprintf (stdout,"copy string in buffer\n");
    strcpy_value = strcpy (s1, s2);
    if ( strcpy_value != (char *)0 ) {
        fprintf (stdout,"strcpy() call successful\n");
        fprintf (stdout,"strcpy_value=%s\n", strcpy_value );
```

```
        fprintf (stdout,"s1=%s\n", s1);
    }
  else
      fprintf (stderr,"ERROR: strcpy() failed\n");
  }
```

NAME

strcspn — get length of complementary substring

SYNOPSIS

```
#include <string.h>

size_t strcspn(const char *s1, const char *s2);
```

DESCRIPTION

The *strcspn*( ) function computes the length of the maximum initial segment of the string pointed to by *s1* which consists entirely of bytes *not* from the string pointed to by *s2*.

RETURN VALUE

The *strcspn*( ) function returns *s1*; no return value is reserved to indicate an error.

ERRORS

No errors are defined.

SEE ALSO

strspn( ), **<string.h>**.

EXAMPLE

```
/*
 * Copyright (C) ANTRIX Inc.
 */

/* strcspn.c
 * This program computes the length of the maximum initial
 * segment of the string pointed to by s1 which consists entirely
 * of bytes not from the string pointed to by s2 using function
 * strcspn.
 */

#include <stdio.h>
#include <stdlib.h>
#include <string.h>
#include <errno.h>

main()
{
  size_t      strcspn_value;
  const char  s1[] = "abcdefgh";
  const char  s2[] = "ef";

  fprintf (stdout,"return the length of the initial segment\n");
  fprintf (stdout,"of first string not from string second string\n");
  strcspn_value = strcspn (s1, s2);
  if ( strcspn_value != 0 ) {
     fprintf (stdout,"strcspn() call successful\n");
     fprintf (stdout,"strcspn_value=%d\n", strcspn_value );
  }
  else
     fprintf (stderr,"ERROR: strcspn() call failed\n");
}
```

strdup( )

NAME

strdup — duplicate a string

SYNOPSIS

UX

```
#include <string.h>

char *strdup(const char *s1);
```

DESCRIPTION

The *strdup*( ) function returns a pointer to a new string, which is a duplicate of the string pointed to by *s1*. The returned pointer can be passed to *free*( ). A null pointer is returned if the new string cannot be created.

RETURN VALUE

The *strdup*( ) function returns a pointer to a new string on success. Otherwise it returns a null pointer and sets *errno* to indicate the error.

ERRORS

The *strdup*( ) function may fail if:

[ENOMEM]   Storage space available is insufficient.

SEE ALSO

malloc( ), *free*( ), **<string.h>**.

EXAMPLE

```
/*
 * Copyright (C) ANTRIX Inc.
 */

/* strdup.c
 * This program returns a pointer to a new string that is a
 * duplicate of the string using function strdup.
 */

#include <stdio.h>
#include <stdlib.h>
#include <string.h>
#include <errno.h>

main()
{
  char    *strdup_value;
  char    *string = "hello world";

  strdup_value = (char *)malloc (string);

  fprintf (stdout,"duplicate string\n");
  strdup_value = strdup (string);
  if ( strdup_value != (char *)0 ) {
     fprintf (stdout,"strdup() call successful\n");
     fprintf (stdout,"strdup_value=%s\n", strdup_value);
  }
  else
```

```
        fprintf (stderr,"ERROR: strdup() call failed\n");
}
```

NAME
strerror — get error message string

SYNOPSIS
```
#include <string.h>

char *strerror(int errnum);
```

DESCRIPTION
The *strerror( )* function maps the error number in *errnum* to a locale-dependent error message string and returns a pointer thereto. The string pointed to must not be modified by the program, but may be overwritten by a subsequent call to *strerror( )* or *popen( )*.

EX   The contents of the error message strings returned by *strerror( )* should be determined by the setting of the LC_MESSAGES category in the current locale.

The implementation will behave as if no function defined in this document calls *strerror( )*.

RETURN VALUE
EX   Upon successful completion, *strerror( )* returns a pointer to the generated message string. On error *errno* may be set, but no return value is reserved to indicate an error.

ERRORS
The *strerror( )* function may fail if:

EX   [EINVAL]   The value of *errnum* is not a valid error message number.

APPLICATION USAGE
Because no return value is reserved to indicate an error, an application wishing to check for error situations should set *errno* to 0, then call *strerror( )*, then check *errno* and if it is non-zero, assume an error has occurred.

SEE ALSO
<string.h>.

EXAMPLE
```
/*
 * Copyright (C) ANTRIX Inc.
 */

/* strerror.c
 * This program maps the error number in errnum to a locale
 * dependent error message string and returns a pointer thereto
 * using function strerror.
 */

#include <stdio.h>
#include <stdlib.h>
#include <errno.h>
#include <string.h>

extern int   errno;
extern int   sys_nerr;
extern char *sys_errlist[];

main()
{
    char   *strerror_value;
```

```
int    i;
char  *filename = "testfile";

fprintf (stdout,"example 1\n");
fprintf (stdout,"try to delete a non-existing file should\n");
fprintf (stdout,"generate error\n");

remove (filename);
strerror_value = strerror (errno);
if ( strerror_value != (char *)0 ) {
    fprintf (stdout,"strerror() call successful\n");
    fprintf (stdout,"print the error\n");
    fprintf (stdout,"error was:=%s\n" , strerror_value);
}
else
    fprintf (stderr,"ERROR: strerror() call failed\n");

fprintf (stdout,"example 2\n");
fprintf (stdout,"print all the errors from the database\n");
for (i = 1; i <= sys_nerr; i++ ) {
    strerror_value = strerror (i);
    fprintf (stderr,"ERROR: %s\n" , strerror_value);
}

fprintf (stdout,"example 3\n");
fprintf (stdout,"print all the errors from the array sys_errlist[]\n");
for (i = 1; i < sys_nerr; i++ )
    fprintf (stdout,"error: %s\n" , sys_errlist[i]);
}
```

NAME

strfmon — convert monetary value to string

SYNOPSIS

EI EX `#include <monetary.h>`

`ssize_t strfmon(char *s, size_t maxsize, const char *format, ...);`

DESCRIPTION

The *strfmon*( ) function places characters into the array pointed to by *s* as controlled by the string pointed to by *format*. No more than *maxsize* bytes are placed into the array.

The format is a character string that contains two types of objects: plain characters, which are simply copied to the output stream, and conversion specifications, each of which results in the fetching of zero or more arguments which are converted and formatted. The results are undefined if there are insufficient arguments for the format. If the format is exhausted while arguments remain, the excess arguments are simply ignored.

A conversion specification consists of the following sequence:

- a % character
- optional flags
- optional field width
- optional left precision
- optional right precision
- a required conversion character that determines the conversion to be performed.

Flags

One or more of the following optional flags can be specified to control the conversion:

=*f*   An = followed by a single character *f* which is used as the numeric fill character. The fill character must be representable in a single byte in order to work with precision and width counts. The default numeric fill character is the space character. This flag does not affect field width filling which always uses the space character. This flag is ignored unless a left precision (see below) is specified.

^   Do not format the currency amount with grouping characters. The default is to insert the grouping characters if defined for the current locale.

+ or (Specify the style of representing positive and negative currency amounts. Only one of + or (may be specified. If + is specified, the locale's equivalent of + and − are used (for example, in the U.S.A.: the empty string if positive and − if negative). If (is specified, negative amounts are enclosed within parentheses. If neither flag is specified, the + style is used.

!   Suppress the currency symbol from the output conversion.

−   Specify the alignment. If this flag is present all fields are left-justified (padded to the right) rather than right-justified.

Field Width

w   A decimal digit string *w* specifying a minimum field width in bytes in which the result of the conversion is right-justified (or left-justified if the flag – is specified). The default is 0.

Left Precision

#n   A # followed by a decimal digit string *n* specifying a maximum number of digits expected to be formatted to the left of the radix character. This option can be used to keep the formatted output from multiple calls to the *strfmon( )* aligned in the same columns. It can also be used to fill unused positions with a special character as in `$***123.45`. This option causes an amount to be formatted as if it has the number of digits specified by *n*. If more than *n* digit positions are required, this conversion specification is ignored. Digit positions in excess of those actually required are filled with the numeric fill character (see the *=f* flag above).

If grouping has not been suppressed with the ^ flag, and it is defined for the current locale, grouping separators are inserted before the fill characters (if any) are added. Grouping separators are not applied to fill characters even if the fill character is a digit.

To ensure alignment, any characters appearing before or after the number in the formatted output such as currency or sign symbols are padded as necessary with space characters to make their positive and negative formats an equal length.

Right Precision

.p   A period followed by a decimal digit string *p* specifying the number of digits after the radix character. If the value of the right precision *p* is 0, no radix character appears. If a right precision is not included, a default specified by the current locale is used. The amount being formatted is rounded to the specified number of digits prior to formatting.

Conversion Characters

The conversion characters and their meanings are:

i   The **double** argument is formatted according to the locale's international currency format (for example, in the U.S.A.: `USD 1,234.56`).

n   The **double** argument is formatted according to the locale's national currency format (for example, in the U.S.A.: `$1,234.56`).

%   Convert to a %; no argument is converted. The entire conversion specification must be %%.

Locale Information

The LC_MONETARY category of the program's locale affects the behaviour of this function including the monetary radix character (which may be different from the numeric radix character affected by the LC_NUMERIC category), the grouping separator, the currency symbols and formats. The international currency symbol should be conformant with the ISO 4217:1987 standard.

RETURN VALUE

If the total number of resulting bytes including the terminating null byte is not more than *maxsize*, *strfmon*( ) returns the number of bytes placed into the array pointed to by *s*, not including the terminating null byte. Otherwise, −1 is returned, the contents of the array are indeterminate, and *errno* is set to indicate the error.

ERRORS

The *strfmon*( ) function will fail if:

[ENOSYS]   The function is not supported.

[E2BIG]   Conversion stopped due to lack of space in the buffer.

EXAMPLES

Given a locale for the U.S.A. and the values 123.45, −123.45 and 3456.781:

Conversion Specification	Output	Comments

`%n`	`$123.45`
	`-$123.45`
	`$3,456.78`
		default formatting

`%11n`	`$123.45`
	`-$123.45`
	`$3,456.78`
		right align within an 11 character field

`%#5n`	`$   123.45`
	`-$   123.45`
	`$ 3,456.78`
		aligned columns for values up to 99,999

`%=*#5n`	`$***123.45`
	`-$***123.45`
	`$*3,456.78`
		specify a fill character

`%=0#5n`	`$000123.45`
	`-$000123.45`
	`$03,456.78`
		fill characters do not use grouping even if the fill character is a digit

`%^#5n`	`$   123.45`
	`-$   123.45`
	`$ 3456.78`
		disable the grouping separator

`%^#5.0n`	`$   123`
	`-$   123`
	`$ 3457`
		round off to whole units

`%^#5.4n`	`$   123.4500`
	`-$   123.4500`
	`$ 3456.7810`
		increase the precision

`%(#5n`	`   123.45`
	`($   123.45)`
	`$ 3,456.78`
		use an alternative pos/neg style

`%!(#5n`	`   123.45`
	`(   123.45)`
	`3,456.78`
		disable the currency symbol

FUTURE DIRECTIONS

This interface is expected to be mandatory in a future issue of this document.

Lower-case conversion characters are reserved for future use and upper-case for implementation-dependent use.

SEE ALSO

localeconv( ), **<monetary.h>**.

EXAMPLE

```
/*
 * Copyright (C) ANTRIX Inc.
 */

/* strfmon.c
 * This program converts the monetary value to string using
 * function strfmon.
 */

#include <stdio.h>
#include <stdlib.h>
#include <monetary.h>
#include <errno.h>

main()
{
  size_t      strfmon_value;
  char s[255];
  const char *format;
  int         value;

  fprintf (stdout,"convert known currency value to string\n");
  strfmon_value = strfmon (s, sizeof(s), "%^#5.4n", 123.45);
  fprintf (stdout,"Monetary Value: %s\n", s);
  if ( strfmon_value != -1 ) {
      fprintf (stdout,"strfmon() call successful\n");
      fprintf (stdout,"Monetary Value: %d\n", strfmon_value);
  }
  else {
      fprintf (stderr,"ERROR: strfmon() call failed\n");
      fprintf (stderr,"ERROR: %s\n", strerror(errno));
  }
}
```

NAME

strftime — convert date and time to string

SYNOPSIS

```
#include <time.h>

size_t strftime(char *s, size_t maxsize, const char *format,
                const struct tm *timptr);
```

DESCRIPTION

The *strftime*( ) function places bytes into the array pointed to by *s* as controlled by the string pointed to by *format*. The *format* string consists of zero or more conversion specifications and ordinary characters. A conversion specification consists of a % character and a terminating conversion character that determines the conversion specification's behaviour. All ordinary characters (including the terminating null byte) are copied unchanged into the array. If copying takes place between objects that overlap, the behaviour is undefined. No more than *maxsize* bytes are placed into the array. Each conversion specification is replaced by appropriate characters as described in the following list. The appropriate characters are determined by the program's locale and by the values contained in the structure pointed to by *timptr*.

Local timezone information is used as though *strftime*( ) called *tzset*( ).

	%a	is replaced by the locale's abbreviated weekday name.
	%A	is replaced by the locale's full weekday name.
	%b	is replaced by the locale's abbreviated month name.
	%B	is replaced by the locale's full month name.
	%c	is replaced by the locale's appropriate date and time representation.
EX	%C	is replaced by the century number (the year divided by 100 and truncated to an integer) as a decimal number [00-99].
	%d	is replaced by the day of the month as a decimal number [01,31].
EX	%D	same as %m/%d/%y.
	%e	is replaced by the day of the month as a decimal number [1,31]; a single digit is preceded by a space.
	%h	same as %b.
	%H	is replaced by the hour (24-hour clock) as a decimal number [00,23].
	%I	is replaced by the hour (12-hour clock) as a decimal number [01,12].
	%j	is replaced by the day of the year as a decimal number [001,366].
	%m	is replaced by the month as a decimal number [01,12].
	%M	is replaced by the minute as a decimal number [00,59].
EX	%n	is replaced by a newline character.
	%p	is replaced by the locale's equivalent of either a.m. or p.m.
EX	%r	is replaced by the time in a.m. and p.m. notation; in the POSIX locale this is equivalent to %I:%M:%S %p.
EX	%R	is replaced by the time in 24 hour notation (%H:%M).
	%S	is replaced by the second as a decimal number [00,61].
EX	%t	is replaced by a tab character.
	%T	is replaced by the time (%H:%M:%S).
	%u	is replaced by the weekday as a decimal number [1,7], with 1 representing Monday.
	%U	is replaced by the week number of the year (Sunday as the first day of the week) as a decimal number [00,53].
	%V	is replaced by the week number of the year (Monday as the first day of the week) as a decimal number [01,53]. If the week containing 1 January has four or more days in the new year, then it is considered week 1. Otherwise, it is week 53 of the previous year, and the next week is week 1.
	%w	is replaced by the weekday as a decimal number [0,6], with 0 representing Sunday.

%W   is replaced by the week number of the year (Monday as the first day of the week) as a decimal number [00,53]. All days in a new year preceding the first Monday are considered to be in week 0.

%x   is replaced by the locale's appropriate date representation.

%X   is replaced by the locale's appropriate time representation.

%y   is replaced by the year without century as a decimal number [00,99].

%Y   is replaced by the year with century as a decimal number.

%Z   is replaced by the timezone name or abbreviation, or by no bytes if no timezone information exists.

%%   is replaced by %.

If a conversion specification does not correspond to any of the above, the behaviour is undefined.

Modified Conversion Specifiers

EX   Some conversion specifiers can be modified by the E or O modifier characters to indicate that an alternative format or specification should be used rather than the one normally used by the unmodified conversion specifier. If the alternative format or specification does not exist for the current locale, (see ERA in the **XBD** specification, **Section 5.3.5**) the behaviour will be as if the unmodified conversion specification were used.

%Ec   is replaced by the locale's alternative appropriate date and time representation.

%EC   is replaced by the name of the base year (period) in the locale's alternative representation.

%Ex   is replaced by the locale's alternative date representation.

%EX   is replaced by the locale' alternative time representation.

%Ey   is replaced by the offset from %EC (year only) in the locale's alternative representation.

%EY   is replaced by the full alternative year representation.

%Od   is replaced by the day of the month, using the locale's alternative numeric symbols, filled as needed with leading zeros if there is any alternative symbol for zero, otherwise with leading spaces.

%Oe   is replaced by the day of month, using the locale's alternative numeric symbols, filled as needed with leading spaces.

%OH   is replaced by the hour (24-hour clock) using the locale's alternative numeric symbols.

%OI   is replaced by the hour (12-hour clock) using the locale's alternative numeric symbols.

%Om   is replaced by the month using the locale's alternative numeric symbols.

%OM   is replaced by the minutes using the locale's alternative numeric symbols.

%OS   is replaced by the seconds using the locale's alternative numeric symbols.

%Ou   is replaced by the weekday as a number in the locale's alternative representation (Monday=1).

%OU   is replaced by the week number of the year (Sunday as the first day of the week, rules corresponding to %U) using the locale's alternative numeric symbols.

%OV   is replaced by the week number of the year (Sunday as the first day of the week, rules corresponding to %V) using the locale's alternative numeric symbols.

%Ow   is replaced by the number of the weekday (Sunday=0) using the locale's alternative numeric symbols.

%OW   is replaced by the week number of the year (Monday as the first day of the week) using the locale's alternative numeric symbols.

%Oy   is replaced by the year (offset from %C) in the locale's alternative representation and using the locale's alternative symbols.

RETURN VALUE

If the total number of resulting bytes including the terminating null byte is not more than *maxsize*, *strftime*( ) returns the number of bytes placed into the array pointed to by *s*, not including the terminating null byte. Otherwise, 0 is returned and the contents of the array are indeterminate.

ERRORS

No errors are defined.

APPLICATION USAGE

The range of values for %S is [00,61] rather than [00,59] to allow for the occasional leap second and even more occasional double leap second.

Some of the conversion specifications marked EX are duplicates of others. They are included for compatibility with *nl_cxtime*( ) and *nl_ascxtime*( ), which were published in Issue 2.

SEE ALSO

asctime( ), *clock*( ), *ctime*( ), *difftime*( ), *gmtime*( ), *localtime*( ), *mktime*( ), *strptime*( ), *time*( ), *utime*( ), **<time.h>**.

```
/*
 * Copyright (C) ANTRIX Inc.
 */

/* strftime.c
 * This program converts date and time to string using
 * function strftime.
 */

#include <stdio.h>
#include <stdlib.h>
#include <time.h>
#include <errno.h>

main()
{
    size_t      strftime_value;
    struct tm *timeptr;
    struct tm *gmtime();
    char s[256];
    time_t curtime;

    fprintf (stdout,"print current date and time\n");
    curtime = time ((long *)0);
    timeptr = localtime (&curtime);
    strftime_value = strftime (s, sizeof(s),
                    "%a %b %m/%d/%y Time: %H:%M%p", timeptr);

    if ( strftime_value >= 0 ) {
        fprintf (stdout,"strftime() call successful\n");
        fprintf (stdout,"Date: %s\n", s);
    }
    else {
        fprintf (stderr,"ERROR: strftime() call failed\n");
```

```
        fprintf (stderr,"ERROR: %s\n", strerror(errno));
    }
}
```

NAME

strlen — get string length

SYNOPSIS

```
#include <string.h>

size_t strlen(const char *s);
```

DESCRIPTION

The *strlen*( ) function computes the number of bytes in the string to which *s* points, not including the terminating null byte.

RETURN VALUE

The *strlen*( ) function returns *s*; no return value is reserved to indicate an error.

ERRORS

No errors are defined.

SEE ALSO

<string.h>.

EXAMPLE

```
/*
 * Copyright (C) ANTRIX Inc.
 */

/* strlen.c
 * This program computes the number of bytes in the string
 * to which s points not including the null terminating byte
 * using function strlen.
 */

#include <stdio.h>
#include <stdlib.h>
#include <string.h>
#include <errno.h>

main()
{
  int    strlen_value;
  char   *s = "hello world";

  fprintf (stdout,"get the length of string\n");
  strlen_value = strlen (s);
  if ( strlen_value == 11 ) {
      fprintf (stdout,"strlen() call successful\n");
      fprintf (stdout,"length of the %s is %d\n", s, strlen_value);
  }
  else
      fprintf (stderr,"ERROR: strlen() call failed\n");
}
```

NAME

strncasecmp — case-insensitive string comparison

SYNOPSIS

UX   `#include <strings.h>`

`int strncasecmp(const char *s1, const char *s2, size_t n);`

DESCRIPTION

Refer to *strcasecmp*( ).

EXAMPLE

```
/*
 * Copyright (C) ANTRIX Inc.
 */

/* strncasecmp.c
 * This program compares n bytes of string s1 and s2
 * ignoring cases using function strncasecmp.
 */

#include <stdio.h>
#include <stdlib.h>
#include <string.h>
#include <errno.h>


main()
{
  int        strncasecmp_value;
  size_t     n = 5;
  const char s1[] = "hello world";
  const char s2[] = "HelLO all";

  fprintf (stdout,"compare first 5 bytes\n");
  strncasecmp_value = strncasecmp (s1, s2, n);
  if ( strncasecmp_value == 0 )
     fprintf (stdout,"strncasecmp() call successful\n");
  else
     fprintf (stderr,"ERROR: strncasecmp() call failed\n");
}
```

NAME

strncat — concatenate part of two strings

SYNOPSIS

```
#include <string.h>

char *strncat(char *s1, const char *s2, size_t n);
```

DESCRIPTION

The *strncat*( ) function appends not more than *n* bytes (a null byte and bytes that follow it are not appended) from the array pointed to by *s2* to the end of the string pointed to by *s1*. The initial byte of *s2* overwrites the null byte at the end of *s1*. A terminating null byte is always appended to the result. If copying takes place between objects that overlap, the behaviour is undefined.

RETURN VALUE

The *strncat*( ) function returns *s1*; no return value is reserved to indicate an error.

ERRORS

No errors are defined.

SEE ALSO

strcat( ), **<string.h>**.

EXAMPLE

```
/*
 * Copyright (C) ANTRIX Inc.
 */

/* strncat.c
 * This program concatenates part of two strings using function
 * strncat.
 */

#include <stdio.h>
#include <stdlib.h>
#include <string.h>
#include <errno.h>

main()
{
   char        *strncat_value;
   char        s1[12] ;
   const char s2[] = "hello world";

   memset (s1, ' ', 12);
   fprintf (stdout,"copy first 5 characters only\n");
   strncat_value = strncat(s1, s2, 5);
   if ( strncat_value != (char *)0 ) {
       fprintf (stdout,"strncat() call successful\n");
       fprintf (stdout,"strncat_value=%s\n", strncat_value);
   }
   else
       fprintf (stderr,"ERROR: strncat() call failed\n");
}
```

NAME

strncmp — compare part of two strings

SYNOPSIS

```
#include <string.h>

int strncmp(const char *s1, const char *s2, size_t n);
```

DESCRIPTION

The *strncmp*( ) function compares not more than *n* bytes (bytes that follow a null byte are not compared) from the array pointed to by *s1* to the array pointed to by *s2*.

The sign of a non-zero return value is determined by the sign of the difference between the values of the first pair of bytes (both interpreted as type **unsigned char**) that differ in the strings being compared.

RETURN VALUE

Upon successful completion, *strncmp*( ) returns an integer greater than, equal to or less than 0, if the possibly null-terminated array pointed to by *s1* is greater than, equal to or less than the possibly null-terminated array pointed to by *s2* respectively.

ERRORS

No errors are defined.

SEE ALSO

strcmp( ), **<string.h>**.

EXAMPLE

```
/*
 * Copyright (C) ANTRIX Inc.
 */

/* strncmp.c
 * This program compares n bytes of string s1 and s2 using
 * function strncmp.
 */

#include <stdio.h>
#include <stdlib.h>
#include <string.h>
#include <errno.h>


main()
{
   int        strncmp_value;
   size_t     n = 5;
   const char s1[] = "hello world";
   const char s2[] = "hello all";

   fprintf (stdout,"compare first 5 bytes\n");
   strncmp_value = strncmp (s1, s2, n);
   if ( strncmp_value == 0 )
      fprintf (stdout,"strncmp() call successful\n");
   else
```

```
        fprintf (stderr,"ERROR: strncmp() call failed\n");
}
```

NAME

strncpy — copy part of a string

SYNOPSIS

```
#include <string.h>

char *strncpy(char *s1, const char *s2, size_t n);
```

DESCRIPTION

The *strncpy*( ) function copies not more than *n* bytes (bytes that follow a null byte are not copied) from the array pointed to by *s2* to the array pointed to by *s1*. If copying takes place between objects that overlap, the behaviour is undefined.

If the array pointed to by *s2* is a string that is shorter than *n* bytes, null bytes are appended to the copy in the array pointed to by *s1*, until *n* bytes in all are written.

RETURN VALUE

The *strncpy*( ) function returns *s1*; no return value is reserved to indicate an error.

ERRORS

No errors are defined.

APPLICATION USAGE

Character movement is performed differently in different implementations. Thus overlapping moves may yield surprises.

If there is no null byte in the first *n* bytes of the array pointed to by *s2*, the result will not be null-terminated.

SEE ALSO

strcpy( ), **<string.h>**.

EXAMPLE

```
/*
 * Copyright (C) ANTRIX Inc.
 */

/* strncpy.c
 * This program copies not more than n bytes from the array
 * pointed to by s2 to the array pointed to by s1 using function
 * strncpy.
 */

#include <stdio.h>
#include <stdlib.h>
#include <string.h>
#include <errno.h>

main()
{
    char        *strncpy_value;
    size_t      n = 5;
    char        s1[12] ;
    const char  s2[] = "hello world";

    memset (s1, ' ', 12);
```

```
        fprintf (stdout,"copy first 5 bytes\n");
        strncpy_value = strncpy (s1, s2, n);
        if ( strncpy_value != (char *)0 ) {
           fprintf (stdout,"strncpy() call successful\n");
           fprintf (stdout,"strncpy_value=%s\n", strncpy_value );
           fprintf (stdout,"s1=%s\n", s1 );
        }
        else
           fprintf (stderr,"ERROR: strncpy() call failed\n");
}
```

NAME

strpbrk — scan string for byte

SYNOPSIS

```
#include <string.h>

char *strpbrk(const char *s1, const char *s2);
```

DESCRIPTION

The *strpbrk*( ) function locates the first occurrence in the string pointed to by *s1* of any byte from the string pointed to by *s2*.

RETURN VALUE

Upon successful completion, *strpbrk*( ) returns a pointer to the byte or a null pointer if no byte from *s2* occurs in *s1*.

ERRORS

No errors are defined.

SEE ALSO

strchr( ), *strrchr*( ), **<string.h>**.

EXAMPLE

```
/*
 * Copyright (C) ANTRIX Inc.
 */

/* strpbrk.c
 * This program locates the first occurrence in the string
 * pointed to by s1 of any byte from the string pointed to
 * by s2 using function strpbrk.
 */

#include <stdio.h>
#include <stdlib.h>
#include <string.h>
#include <errno.h>

main()
{
  char              *strpbrk_value;
  const char s1[] = "one two three";
  const char s2[] = "t";

  fprintf (stdout,"return pointer to first occurrence of string t\n");
  strpbrk_value = strpbrk (s1, s2);
  if ( strpbrk_value != (char *)0 ) {
     fprintf (stdout,"strpbrk() call successful\n");
     fprintf (stdout,"strpbrk_value=%s\n", strpbrk_value);
  }
  else
     fprintf (stderr,"ERROR: strpbrk() call failed\n");
}
```

NAME

strptime — date and time conversion

SYNOPSIS

EI EX   `#include <time.h>`

`char *strptime(const char *buf, const char *format, struct tm *tm);`

DESCRIPTION

The *strptime*( ) function converts the character string pointed to by *buf* to values which are stored in the **tm** structure pointed to by *tm*, using the format specified by *format*.

The *format* is composed of zero or more directives. Each directive is composed of one of the following: one or more white-space characters (as specified by *isspace*( )); an ordinary character (neither % nor a white-space character); or a conversion specification. Each conversion specification is composed of a % character followed by a conversion character which specifies the replacement required. There must be white-space or other non-alphanumeric characters between any two conversion specifications. The following conversion specifications are supported:

%a	is the day of week, using the locale's weekday names; either the abbreviated or full name may be specified.
%A	is the same as %a.
%b	is the month, using the locale's month names; either the abbreviated or full name may be specified.
%B	is the same as %b.
%c	is replaced by the locale's appropriate date and time representation.
%C	is the century number [0,99]; leading zeros are permitted but not required.
%d	is the day of month [1,31]; leading zeros are permitted but not required.
%D	is the date as %m/%d/%y.
%e	is the same as %d.
%h	is the same as %b.
%H	is the hour (24-hour clock) [0,23]; leading zeros are permitted but not required.
%I	is the hour (12-hour clock) [1,12]; leading zeros are permitted but not required.
%j	is the day number of the year [1,366]; leading zeros are permitted but not required.
%m	is the month number [1,12]; leading zeros are permitted but not required.
%M	is the minute [0-59]; leading zeros are permitted but not required.
%n	is any white space.
%p	is the locale's equivalent of a.m or p.m.
%r	is the time as %I:%M:%S %p.
%R	is the time as %H:%M.
%S	is the seconds [0,61]; leading zeros are permitted but not required.
%t	is any white space.
%T	is the time as %H:%M:%S.
%U	is the week number of the year (Sunday as the first day of the week) as a decimal number [00,53]; leading zeros are permitted but not required.
%w	is the weekday as a decimal number [0,6], with 0 representing Sunday; leading zeros are permitted but not required.
%W	is the the week number of the year (Monday as the first day of the week) as a decimal number [00,53]; leading zeros are permitted but not required.
%x	is the date, using the locale's date format.
%X	is the time, using the locale's time format.

NAME

strrchr — string scanning operation

SYNOPSIS

```
#include <string.h>

char *strrchr(const char *s, int c);
```

DESCRIPTION

The *strrchr*( ) function locates the last occurrence [...]
to by *s*. The terminating null byte is considered to [...]

RETURN VALUE

Upon successful completion, *strrchr*( ) returns a p[...]
occur in the string.

ERRORS

No errors are defined.

SEE ALSO

strchr( ), **<string.h>**.

EXAMPLE

```
/*
 * Copyright (C) ANTRIX Inc.
 */

/* strrchr.c
 * This program locates the last occu[...]
 * pointed to by s using function str[...]
 */

#include <stdio.h>
#include <stdlib.h>
#include <string.h>
#include <errno.h>

main()
{
  char   *strrchr_value;
  const  char s[] = "one two three";
  int    c = 't';

  fprintf (stdout,"return to last occ[...]
  strrchr_value = strrchr (s, c);
  if ( strrchr_value != (char *)0 ) {
     fprintf (stdout,"strrchr() call [...]
     fprintf (stdout,"strrchr_value=%[...]
  }
  else
     fprintf (stderr,"ERROR: strrchr()[...]
}
```

%y   is the year within the century [0,99]; leading zeros are permitted but not required
%Y   is the year, including the century (for example, 1988).
%%   is replaced by %.

Modified Directives

Some directives can be modified by the E and O modifier characters to indicate that an alternative format or specification should be used rather than the one normally used by the unmodified directive. If the alternative format or specification does not exist in the current locale, the behaviour will be as if the unmodified directive were used.

%Ec   is the locale's alternative appropriate date and time representation.
%EC   is the name of the base year (period) in the locale's alternative representation.
%Ex   is the locale's alternative date representation.
%EX   is the locale's alternative time representation.
%Ey   is the offset from %EC (year only) in the locale's alternative representation.
%EY   is the full alternative year representation.
%Od   is the day of the month using the locale's alternative numeric symbols; leading zeros are permitted but not required.
%Oe   is the same as %Od.
%OH   is the hour (24-hour clock) using the locale's alternative numeric symbols.
%OI   is the hour (12-hour clock) using the locale's alternative numeric symbols.
%Om   is the month using the locale's alternative numeric symbols.
%OM   is the minutes using the locale's alternative numeric symbols.
%OS   is the seconds using the locale's alternative numeric symbols.
%OU   is the week number of the year (Sunday as the first day of the week) using the locale's alternative numeric symbols.
%Ow   is the number of the weekday (Sunday=0) using the locale's alternative numeric symbols.
%OW   is the week number of the year (Monday as the first day of the week) using the locale's alternative numeric symbols.
%Oy   is the year (offset from %C) in the locale's alternative representation and using the locale's alternative numeric symbols.

A directive composed of white-space characters is executed by scanning input up to the first character that is not white space (which remains unscanned), or until no more characters can be scanned.

A directive that is an ordinary character is executed by scanning the next character from the buffer. If the character scanned from the buffer differs from the one comprising the directive, the directive fails, and the differing and subsequent characters remain unscanned.

A series of directives composed of %n, %t, white-space characters or any combination is executed by scanning up to the first character that is not white space (which remains unscanned), or until no more characters can be scanned.

Any other conversion specification is executed by scanning characters until a character matching the next directive is scanned, or until no more characters can be scanned. These characters, except the one matching the next directive, are then compared to the locale values associated with the conversion specifier. If a match is found, values for the appropriate **tm** structure members are set to values corresponding to the locale information. Case is ignored when matching items in *buf* such as month or weekday names. If no match is found, *strptime*( ) fails and no more characters are scanned.

strptime( )

RETURN VALUE

Upon successful completion, strptime( ) re[...]
character parsed. Otherwise, a null pointer i[...]

ERRORS

The strptime( ) function will fail if:

[ENOSYS]   The functionality is not sup[...]

APPLICATION USAGE

Several "same as" formats, and the special [...]
in order to ease the use of identical format st[...]

FUTURE DIRECTIONS

This function is expected to be mandatory in [...]

SEE ALSO

scanf( ), strftime( ), time( ), **<time.h>**.

EXAMPLE

```
/*
 * Copyright (C) ANTRIX Inc.
 */


/* strptime.c
 * This program converts the char
 * buf to values which are stored
 * function strptime.
 */

#include <stdio.h>
#include <stdlib.h>
#include <time.h>
#include <errno.h>

main()
{
  char   *strptime_value;
  size_t strftime_value;
  struct tm *timeptr, *time_base(
  char s[256] = "24 27 0 20 1 96

  fprintf (stdout,"initialize the
  strptime_value = strptime (s, "!

  fprintf (stdout,"convert date a
  strftime_value = strftime(s,siz
  fprintf (stdout,"Date: %s\n", s
}
```

strspn( )

NAME

strspn — get length of substring

SYNOPSIS

```
#include <string.h>

size_t strspn(const char *s1, const char *s2);
```

DESCRIPTION

The strspn( ) function computes the length of the maximum initial segment of the string pointed to by s1 which consists entirely of bytes from the string pointed to by s2.

RETURN VALUE

The strspn( ) function returns s1; no return value is reserved to indicate an error.

ERRORS

No errors are defined.

SEE ALSO

strcspn( ), **<string.h>**.

EXAMPLE

```
/*
 * Copyright (C) ANTRIX Inc.
 */


/* strspn.c
 * This program computes the length of the maximum initial
 * segment of the string pointed to by s1 which consists
 * entirely of bytes from the string pointed to by s2.
 */

#include <stdio.h>
#include <stdlib.h>
#include <string.h>
#include <errno.h>

main()
{
  const char s1[] = "abcdefgh";
  const char s2[] = "abcxyz";
  size_t     strspn_value;

  fprintf (stdout,"length of initial segment of string s1\n");
  fprintf (stdout,"consisting entirely of characters from string s2\n");
  strspn_value = strspn (s1, s2);
  if ( strspn_value != 0 ) {
     fprintf (stdout,"strspn() call successful\n");
     fprintf (stdout,"strspn_value=%d\n", strspn_value );
  }
  else
     fprintf (stderr,"ERROR: strspn() call failed\n");
}
```

NAME

strstr — find substring

SYNOPSIS

```
#include <string.h>

char *strstr(const char *s1, const char *s2);
```

DESCRIPTION

The *strstr*( ) function locates the first occurrence in the string pointed to by *s1* of the sequence of bytes (excluding the terminating null byte) in the string pointed to by *s2*.

RETURN VALUE

Upon successful completion, *strstr*( ) returns a pointer to the located string or a null pointer if the string is not found.

If *s2* points to a string with zero length, the function returns *s1*.

ERRORS

No errors are defined.

SEE ALSO

strchr( ), **<string.h>**.

EXAMPLE

```
/*
 * Copyright (C) ANTRIX Inc.
 */

/* strstr.c
 * This program locates the first occurrence in the string pointed
 * to by s1 of the sequence of bytes excluding the terminating
 * null byte in the string pointed to by s2 using function strstr.
 */

#include <stdio.h>
#include <stdlib.h>
#include <string.h>
#include <errno.h>

main()
{
  const  char s1[] = "one two three two three";
  const  char s2[] = "two";
  char              *strstr_value;

  fprintf (stdout,"locate the first occurrence in string s1 of the\n");
  fprintf (stdout,"sequence of characters in string s2\n");
  strstr_value = (char *)strstr (s1, s2);
  if ( strstr_value != (char *)0 ) {
      fprintf (stdout,"strstr() call successful\n");
      fprintf (stdout,"strstr_value=%s\n", strstr_value );
  }
  else
```

```
        fprintf (stderr,"ERROR: strstr() call failed\n");
    }
```

NAME

strtod — convert string to double-precision number

SYNOPSIS

```
#include <stdlib.h>

double strtod(const char *str, char **endptr);
```

DESCRIPTION

The *strtod*( ) function converts the initial portion of the string pointed to by *str* to type **double** representation. First it decomposes the input string into three parts: an initial, possibly empty, sequence of white-space characters (as specified by *isspace*( )); a subject sequence interpreted as a floating-point constant; and a final string of one or more unrecognised characters, including the terminating null byte of the input string. Then it attempts to convert the subject sequence to a floating-point number, and returns the result.

The expected form of the subject sequence is an optional + or – sign, then a non-empty sequence of digits optionally containing a radix character, then an optional exponent part. An exponent part consists of e or E, followed by an optional sign, followed by one or more decimal digits. The subject sequence is defined as the longest initial subsequence of the input string, starting with the first non-white-space character, that is of the expected form. The subject sequence is empty if the input string is empty or consists entirely of white-space characters, or if the first character that is not white space is other than a sign, a digit or a radix character.

If the subject sequence has the expected form, the sequence starting with the first digit or the radix character (whichever occurs first) is interpreted as a floating constant of the C language, except that the radix character is used in place of a period, and that if neither an exponent part nor a radix character appears, a radix character is assumed to follow the last digit in the string. If the subject sequence begins with a minus sign, the value resulting from the conversion is negated. A pointer to the final string is stored in the object pointed to by *endptr*, provided that *endptr* is not a null pointer.

The radix character is defined in the program's locale (category LC_NUMERIC). In the POSIX locale, or in a locale where the radix character is not defined, the radix character defaults to a period (.).

In other than the POSIX locale, other implementation-dependent subject sequence forms may be accepted.

If the subject sequence is empty or does not have the expected form, no conversion is performed; the value of *str* is stored in the object pointed to by *endptr*, provided that *endptr* is not a null pointer.

RETURN VALUE

EX

Upon successful completion, *strtod*( ) returns the converted value. If no conversion could be performed, 0 is returned, and *errno* may be set to [EINVAL].

If the correct value is outside the range of representable values, ±HUGE_VAL is returned (according to the sign of the value), and *errno* is set to [ERANGE].

If the correct value would cause an underflow, 0 is returned and *errno* is set to [ERANGE].

ERRORS

The *strtod*( ) function will fail if:

[ERANGE]   The value to be returned would cause overflow or underflow.

The *strtod*( ) function may fail if:

EX   [EINVAL]   No conversion could be performed.

APPLICATION USAGE

Because 0 is returned on error and is also a valid return on success, an application wishing to
check for error situations should set *errno* to 0, then call *strtod*( ), then check *errno* and if it is
non-zero, assume an error has occurred.

SEE ALSO

isspace( ), *localeconv*( ), *scanf*( ), *setlocale*( ), *strtol*( ), **<stdlib.h>**, the **XBD** specification,
Chapter 5, **Locale**.

EXAMPLE

```
/*
 * Copyright (C) ANTRIX Inc.
 */

/* strtod.c
 * This program converts string to double-precision number using
 * function strtod.
 */

#include <stdio.h>
#include <stdlib.h>
#include <string.h>
#include <errno.h>

main()
{
    double      strtod_value;
    char        *endptr;
    const char  *str = " -123E1";

    /* leading space and negative number */
    fprintf (stdout,"convert string to double precision number\n");
    strtod_value = strtod (str, &endptr);
    if ( strtod_value != (double)0 ) {
        fprintf (stdout,"strtod() call successful\n");
        fprintf (stdout,"strtod_value=%f\n", strtod_value);
        fprintf (stdout,"original pointer value %d\n", str);
        /* should be string address + 7 */
        fprintf (stdout,"final pointer value %d\n", endptr);
    }
    else
        fprintf (stderr,"ERROR: strtod() call failed\n");
}
```

NAME

strtok — split string into tokens

SYNOPSIS

```
#include <string.h>

char *strtok(char *s1, const char *s2);
```

DESCRIPTION

A sequence of calls to *strtok*( ) breaks the string pointed to by *s1* into a sequence of tokens, each of which is delimited by a byte from the string pointed to by *s2*. The first call in the sequence has *s1* as its first argument, and is followed by calls with a null pointer as their first argument. The separator string pointed to by *s2* may be different from call to call.

The first call in the sequence searches the string pointed to by *s1* for the first byte that is *not* contained in the current separator string pointed to by *s2*. If no such byte is found, then there are no tokens in the string pointed to by *s1* and *strtok*( ) returns a null pointer. If such a byte is found, it is the start of the first token.

The *strtok*( ) function then searches from there for a byte that *is* contained in the current separator string. If no such byte is found, the current token extends to the end of the string pointed to by *s1*, and subsequent searches for a token will return a null pointer. If such a byte is found, it is overwritten by a null byte, which terminates the current token. The *strtok*( ) function saves a pointer to the following byte, from which the next search for a token will start.

Each subsequent call, with a null pointer as the value of the first argument, starts searching from the saved pointer and behaves as described above.

The implementation will behave as if no function defined in this document calls *strtok*( ).

RETURN VALUE

Upon successful completion, *strtok*( ) returns a pointer to the first byte of a token. Otherwise, if there is no token, *strtok*( ) returns a null pointer.

ERRORS

No errors are defined.

SEE ALSO

<string.h>.

EXAMPLE

```
/*
 * Copyright (C) ANTRIX Inc.
 */

/* strtok.c
 * This program breaks the string pointed to by s1 into a
 * sequence of tokens, each of which is delimited by a byte
 * from the string pointed to by s2 using function strtok.
 */

#include <stdio.h>
#include <stdlib.h>
#include <string.h>
#include <errno.h>

main()
{
```

```
char        *strtok_value;
char        s1[] = "abc-*def";
const  char s2[] = "$#&*-";

fprintf (stdout,"return pointer to the first character of\n");
fprintf (stdout,"the first token\n");
strtok_value = strtok (s1, s2);
if ( strtok_value != (char *)0 ) {
    fprintf (stdout,"strtok() call successful\n");
    fprintf (stdout,"strtok_value=%s\n", strtok_value);
}
else
    fprintf (stderr,"ERROR: strtok() call failed\n");
}
```

NAME

strtol — convert string to long integer

SYNOPSIS

```
#include <stdlib.h>

long int strtol(const char *str, char **endptr, int base);
```

DESCRIPTION

The *strtol*( ) function converts the initial portion of the string pointed to by *str* to a type **long int** representation. First it decomposes the input string into three parts: an initial, possibly empty, sequence of white-space characters (as specified by *isspace*( )); a subject sequence interpreted as an integer represented in some radix determined by the value of *base*; and a final string of one or more unrecognised characters, including the terminating null byte of the input string. Then it attempts to convert the subject sequence to an integer, and returns the result.

If the value of *base* is 0, the expected form of the subject sequence is that of a decimal constant, octal constant or hexadecimal constant, any of which may be preceded by a + or − sign. A decimal constant begins with a non-zero digit, and consists of a sequence of decimal digits. An octal constant consists of the prefix 0 optionally followed by a sequence of the digits 0 to 7 only. A hexadecimal constant consists of the prefix 0x or 0X followed by a sequence of the decimal digits and letters a (or A) to f (or F) with values 10 to 15 respectively.

If the value of *base* is between 2 and 36, the expected form of the subject sequence is a sequence of letters and digits representing an integer with the radix specified by *base*, optionally preceded by a + or − sign. The letters from a (or A) to z (or Z) inclusive are ascribed the values 10 to 35; only letters whose ascribed values are less than that of *base* are permitted. If the value of *base* is 16, the characters 0x or 0X may optionally precede the sequence of letters and digits, following the sign if present.

The subject sequence is defined as the longest initial subsequence of the input string, starting with the first non-white-space character, that is of the expected form. The subject sequence contains no characters if the input string is empty or consists entirely of white-space characters, or if the first non-white-space character is other than a sign or a permissible letter or digit.

If the subject sequence has the expected form and the value of *base* is 0, the sequence of characters starting with the first digit is interpreted as an integer constant. If the subject sequence has the expected form and the value of *base* is between 2 and 36, it is used as the base for conversion, ascribing to each letter its value as given above. If the subject sequence begins with a minus sign, the value resulting from the conversion is negated. A pointer to the final string is stored in the object pointed to by *endptr*, provided that *endptr* is not a null pointer.

In other than the POSIX locale, additional implementation-dependent subject sequence forms may be accepted.

If the subject sequence is empty or does not have the expected form, no conversion is performed; the value of *str* is stored in the object pointed to by *endptr*, provided that *endptr* is not a null pointer.

RETURN VALUE

EX

Upon successful completion *strtol*( ) returns the converted value, if any. If no conversion could be performed, 0 is returned and *errno* may be set to [EINVAL].

If the correct value is outside the range of representable values, LONG_MAX or LONG_MIN is returned (according to the sign of the value), and *errno* is set to [ERANGE].

ERRORS

The *strtol*( ) function will fail if:

[ERANGE]   The value to be returned is not representable.

The *strtol*( ) function may fail if:

EX   [EINVAL]   The value of *base* is not supported.

APPLICATION USAGE

Because 0, LONG_MIN and LONG_MAX are returned on error and are also valid returns on success, an application wishing to check for error situations should set *errno* to 0, then call *strtol*( ), then check *errno* and if it is non-zero, assume an error has occurred.

SEE ALSO

isalpha( ), *scanf*( ), *strtod*( ), **<stdlib.h>**.

EXAMPLE

```
/*
 * Copyright (C) ANTRIX Inc.
 */

/* strtol.c
 * This program converts the initial portion of the string
 * pointed to by str to a type long int representation using
 * function strtol.
 */

#include <stdio.h>
#include <stdlib.h>
#include <errno.h>

main()
{
  long        strtol_value;
  char        *endptr;
  const char  str[] - "123";

  fprintf (stdout,"convert string to decimal\n");
  strtol_value = strtol (str, &endptr, 10);
  if ( strtol_value == (long )123 ) {
     fprintf (stdout,"strtol() call successful\n");
     fprintf (stdout,"strtol_value=%ld\n", strtol_value );
     fprintf (stdout,"original pointer value %d\n", str);
     /* should be string address + 3 */
     fprintf (stdout,"final pointer value %d\n", endptr);
  }
  else
     fprintf (stderr,"ERROR: strtol() call failed\n");
}
```

NAME

strtoul — convert string to unsigned long

SYNOPSIS

```
#include <stdlib.h>

unsigned long int strtoul(const char *str, char **endptr, int base);
```

DESCRIPTION

The *strtoul*( ) function converts the initial portion of the string pointed to by *str* to a type **unsigned long int** representation. First it decomposes the input string into three parts: an initial, possibly empty, sequence of white-space characters (as specified by *isspace*( )); a subject sequence interpreted as an integer represented in some radix determined by the value of *base*; and a final string of one or more unrecognised characters, including the terminating null byte of the input string. Then it attempts to convert the subject sequence to an unsigned integer, and returns the result.

If the value of *base* is 0, the expected form of the subject sequence is that of a decimal constant, octal constant or hexadecimal constant, any of which may be preceded by a + or − sign. A decimal constant begins with a non-zero digit, and consists of a sequence of decimal digits. An octal constant consists of the prefix 0 optionally followed by a sequence of the digits 0 to 7 only. A hexadecimal constant consists of the prefix 0x or 0X followed by a sequence of the decimal digits and letters a (or A) to f (or F) with values 10 to 15 respectively.

If the value of *base* is between 2 and 36, the expected form of the subject sequence is a sequence of letters and digits representing an integer with the radix specified by *base*, optionally preceded by a + or − sign. The letters from a (or A) to z (or Z) inclusive are ascribed the values 10 to 35; only letters whose ascribed values are less than that of *base* are permitted. If the value of *base* is 16, the characters 0x or 0X may optionally precede the sequence of letters and digits, following the sign if present.

The subject sequence is defined as the longest initial subsequence of the input string, starting with the first non-white-space character, that is of the expected form. The subject sequence contains no characters if the input string is empty or consists entirely of white-space characters, or if the first non-white-space character is other than a sign or a permissible letter or digit.

If the subject sequence has the expected form and the value of *base* is 0, the sequence of characters starting with the first digit is interpreted as an integer constant. If the subject sequence has the expected form and the value of *base* is between 2 and 36, it is used as the base for conversion, ascribing to each letter its value as given above. If the subject sequence begins with a minus sign, the value resulting from the conversion is negated. A pointer to the final string is stored in the object pointed to by *endptr*, provided that *endptr* is not a null pointer.

In other than the POSIX locale, additional implementation-dependent subject sequence forms may be accepted.

If the subject sequence is empty or does not have the expected form, no conversion is performed; the value of *str* is stored in the object pointed to by *endptr*, provided that *endptr* is not a null pointer.

RETURN VALUE

Upon successful completion *strtoul*( ) returns the converted value, if any. If no conversion could
EX be performed, 0 is returned and *errno* may be set to [EINVAL]. If the correct value is outside the range of representable values, {ULONG_MAX} is returned and *errno* is set to [ERANGE].

ERRORS

The *strtoul*( ) function will fail if:

EX   [EINVAL]   The value of *base* is not supported.

          [ERANGE]   The value to be returned is not representable.

The *strtoul*( ) function may fail if:

EX   [EINVAL]   No conversion could be performed.

APPLICATION USAGE

Because 0 and {ULONG_MAX} are returned on error and are also valid returns on success, an application wishing to check for error situations should set *errno* to 0, then call *strtoul*( ), then check *errno* and if it is non-zero, assume an error has occurred.

Unlike *strtod*( ) and *strtol*( ), *strtoul*( ) must always return a non-negative number; so, using the return value of *strtoul*( ) for out-of-range numbers with *strtoul*( ) could cause more severe problems than just loss of precision if those numbers can ever be negative.

SEE ALSO

isalpha( ), *scanf*( ), *strtod*( ), *strtol*( ), **<stdlib.h>**.

EXAMPLE

```
/*
 * Copyright (C) ANTRIX Inc.
 */

/* strtoul.c
 * This program converts the initial portion of the string
 * pointed to by str to a type unsigned long int representation
 * using function strtoul.
 */

#include <stdio.h>
#include <stdlib.h>
#include <errno.h>

main()
{
  unsigned long  strtoul_value;
  char           *endptr;
  const char     str[] = "123";

  fprintf (stdout,"convert string to decimal\n");
  strtoul_value = strtoul (str, &endptr, 10);
  if ( strtoul_value == (unsigned long)123 ) {
     fprintf (stdout,"strtoul() call successful\n");
     fprintf (stdout,"strtoul_value=%ld\n", strtoul_value );
     fprintf (stdout,"original pointer value %d\n", str);
     /* should be string address + 3 */
     fprintf (stdout,"final pointer value %d\n", endptr);
  }
  else
```

```
        fprintf (stderr,"ERROR: strtoul() call failed\n");
}
```

NAME

strxfrm — string transformation

SYNOPSIS

```
#include <string.h>

size_t strxfrm(char *s1, const char *s2, size_t n);
```

DESCRIPTION

The *strxfrm*( ) function transforms the string pointed to by *s2* and places the resulting string into the array pointed to by *s1*. The transformation is such that if *strcmp*( ) is applied to two transformed strings, it returns a value greater than, equal to or less than 0, corresponding to the result of *strcoll*( ) applied to the same two original strings. No more than *n* bytes are placed into the resulting array pointed to by *s1*, including the terminating null byte. If *n* is 0, *s1* is permitted to be a null pointer. If copying takes place between objects that overlap, the behaviour is undefined.

RETURN VALUE

Upon successful completion, *strxfrm*( ) returns the length of the transformed string (not including the terminating null byte). If the value returned is *n* or more, the contents of the array pointed to by *s1* are indeterminate.

EX   On error *strxfrm*( ) may set *errno* but no return value is reserved to indicate an error.

ERRORS

The *strxfrm*( ) function may fail if:

EX   [EINVAL]   The string pointed to by the *s2* argument contains characters outside the domain of the collating sequence.

APPLICATION USAGE

The transformation function is such that two transformed strings can be ordered by *strcmp*( ) as appropriate to collating sequence information in the program's locale (category LC_COLLATE).

The fact that when *n* is 0, *s1* is permitted to be a null pointer, is useful to determine the size of the *s1* array prior to making the transformation.

Because no return value is reserved to indicate an error, an application wishing to check for error situations should set *errno* to 0, then call *strcoll*( ), then check *errno* and if it is non-zero, assume an error has occurred.

This issue is aligned with the ANSI C standard; this does not affect compatibility with XPG3 applications. Reliable error detection by this function was never guaranteed.

SEE ALSO

strcmp( ), *strcoll*( ), **<string.h>**.

EXAMPLE

```
/*
 * Copyright (C) ANTRIX Inc.
 */

/* strxfrm.c
 * This program transforms the string pointed to by s2 and places
 * the resulting string into the array pointed to by s1 using
 * function strxfrm.
 */

#include <stdio.h>
```

```
#include <stdlib.h>
#include <string.h>
#include <locale.h>
#include <ctype.h>
#include <errno.h>

main()
{

    int     ret_cmp;
    size_t len1, len2;
    char    *trans1;
    char    *trans2;

    char s1[] = "jfg";
    char s2[] = "efg";

    /* set LC_COLLATE to french locale */
    fprintf (stdout,"set locale to french\n");
    setlocale (LC_COLLATE, "fr") ;

    len1 = strxfrm(NULL, s1, 0) + 1 ;
    len2 = strxfrm(NULL, s2, 0) + 1 ;

    trans1 = (char *) malloc(len1) ;
    trans2 = (char *) malloc(len2) ;
    strxfrm(trans1, s1, len1) ;
    strxfrm(trans2, s2, len2) ;

    ret_cmp = strcmp(trans1, trans2) ;
    fprintf (stdout,"string comparison value on transformed\n");
    fprintf (stdout,"string using strcmp=%d\n", ret_cmp) ;
    free (trans1) ;
    free (trans2) ;

    ret_cmp = strcoll(s1, s2);
    fprintf (stdout,"string comparison value on original\n");
    fprintf (stdout,"string using strcoll=%d\n", ret_cmp) ;
}
```

NAME

swab — swap bytes

SYNOPSIS

EX
```
#include <unistd.h>
```

```
void swab(const void *src, void *dest, ssize_t nbytes);
```

DESCRIPTION

The *swab*( ) function copies *nbytes* bytes, which are pointed to by *src*, to the object pointed to by *dest*, exchanging adjacent bytes. The *nbytes* argument should be even. If *nbytes* is odd *swab*( ) copies and exchanges *nbytes*–1 bytes and the disposition of the last byte is unspecified. If copying takes place between objects that overlap, the behaviour is undefined. If *nbytes* is negative, *swab*( ) does nothing.

ERRORS

No errors are defined.

SEE ALSO

<unistd.h>.

EXAMPLE

```
/*
 * Copyright (C) ANTRIX Inc.
 */

/* swab.c
 * This program swaps bytest exchanging adjacent bytes using
 * function swab.
 */

#include <stdio.h>
#include <stdlib.h>
#include <errno.h>

main()
{
  int   bytes;
  char  tobuf1[7];
  char  tobuf2[6];
  char  even[7] = { 'a' , 'b', 'c', 'd', 'e', 'f', ' '};
  char  odd[6]  = { 'a' , 'b', 'c', 'd', 'e', ' '};

  memset (tobuf1, ' ', 6);
  memset (tobuf2, ' ', 5);

  fprintf (stdout,"example 1\n");
  fprintf (stdout,"even characters\n");
  bytes = strlen (even);
  swab (even, tobuf1, bytes);
  fprintf (stdout,"even=%s\n", even);
  fprintf (stdout,"tobuf1=%s\n", tobuf1);

  fprintf (stdout,"example 2\n");
  fprintf (stdout,"odd characters\n");
```

```
        bytes = strlen (odd);
        swab (odd, tobuf2, bytes);
        fprintf (stdout,"odd=%s\n", odd);
        fprintf (stdout,"tobuf2=%s\n", tobuf2);
    }
```

NAME

swapcontext — swap user context

SYNOPSIS

UX   `#include <ucontext.h>`

`int swapcontext(ucontext_t *oucp, const ucontext_t *ucp);`

DESCRIPTION

Refer to *makecontext( )*.

NAME

symlink — make symbolic link to a file

SYNOPSIS

UX
```
#include <unistd.h>
```
```
int symlink(const char *path1, const char *path2);
```

DESCRIPTION

The *symlink*( ) function creates a symbolic link. Its name is the pathname pointed to by *path2*, which must be a pathname that does not name an existing file or symbolic link. The contents of the symbolic link are the string pointed to by *path1*.

RETURN VALUE

Upon successful completion, *symlink*( ) returns 0. Otherwise, it returns –1 and sets *errno* to indicate the error.

ERRORS

The *symlink*( ) function will fail if:

[EACCES]　　　Write permission is denied in the directory where the symbolic link is being created, or search permission is denied for a component of the path prefix of *path2*.

[EEXIST]　　　The *path2* argument names an existing file or symbolic link.

[EIO]　　　　　An I/O error occurs while reading from or writing to the file system.

[ELOOP]　　　Too many symbolic links were encountered in resolving *path2*.

[ENAMETOOLONG]

The length of the *path2* argument exceeds {PATH_MAX}, or a pathname component is longer than {NAME_MAX}.

[ENOENT]　　　A component of *path2* does not name an existing file or *path2* is an empty string.

[ENOSPC]　　　The directory in which the entry for the new symbolic link is being placed cannot be extended because no space is left on the file system containing the directory, or the new symbolic link cannot be created because no space is left on the file system which will contain the link, or the file system is out of file-allocation resources.

[ENOTDIR]　　　A component of the path prefix of *path2* is not a directory.

[EROFS]　　　　The new symbolic link would reside on a read-only file system.

The *symlink*( ) function may fail if:

[ENAMETOOLONG]

Pathname resolution of a symbolic link produced an intermediate result whose length exceeds {PATH_MAX}.

APPLICATION USAGE

Like a hard link, a symbolic link allows a file to have multiple logical names. The presence of a hard link guarantees the existence of a file, even after the original name has been removed. A symbolic link provides no such assurance; in fact, the file named by the *path1* argument need not exist when the link is created. A symbolic link can cross file system boundaries.

Normal permission checks are made on each component of the symbolic link pathname during its resolution.

SEE ALSO

lchown( ), *link*( ), *lstat*( ), *open*( ), *readlink*( ), **<unistd.h>**.

EXAMPLE

```c
/*
 * Copyright (C) ANTRIX Inc.
 */

/* symlink.c
 * This program makes a symbolic link to a file
 * using function symlink
 */

#include <stdio.h>
#include <stdlib.h>
#include <unistd.h>
#include <sys/stat.h>
#include <errno.h>

#define  PERM_ALL   (S_IRWXU | S_IRWXG | S_IRWXO)

main()
{
   int     symlink_value;
   char    *file1 = "testfile1";
   char    *file2 = "testfile2";

   fprintf (stdout,"create testfile1\n");
   creat (file1, PERM_ALL);

   fprintf (stdout,"make a symbolic link\n");
   symlink_value = symlink (file1, file2);
   if (symlink_value == 0)
      fprintf (stdout,"symlink() call successful\n");
   else {
      fprintf (stderr,"ERROR: symlink() call failed\n");
      fprintf (stderr,"ERROR: %s\n", strerror(errno));
   }

   fprintf (stdout,"remove testfiles\n");
   unlink (file2);
   remove (file1);
}
```

NAME

sync — schedule filesystem updates

SYNOPSIS

UX   `#include <unistd.h>`

`void sync(void);`

DESCRIPTION

The *sync*( ) function causes all information in memory that updates file systems to be scheduled for writing out to all file systems.

The writing, although scheduled, is not necessarily complete upon return from *sync*( ).

RETURN VALUE

The *sync*( ) function returns no value.

ERRORS

No errors are defined.

SEE ALSO

fsync( ), **<unistd.h>**.

EXAMPLE

```
/*
 * Copyright (C) ANTRIX Inc.
 */

/* sync.c
 * This program updates super block and causes all information
 * in memory to be written out to disk using function sync
 */

#include <stdio.h>
#include <stdlib.h>

main()
{
   fprintf (stdout,"update the super block\n");
   sync();
}
```

NAME

sysconf — get configurable system variables

SYNOPSIS

```
#include <unistd.h>

long int sysconf(int name);
```

DESCRIPTION

The *sysconf*( ) function provides a method for the application to determine the current value of a configurable system limit or option *(variable)*.

The *name* argument represents the system variable to be queried. The following table lists the minimal set of system variables from **<limits.h>**, **<unistd.h>** or **<time.h>** (for CLK_TCK) that can be returned by *sysconf*( ), and the symbolic constants, defined in **<unistd.h>** that are the corresponding values used for *name*.

Variable	Value of name
ARG_MAX	_SC_ARG_MAX
BC_BASE_MAX	_SC_BC_BASE_MAX
BC_DIM_MAX	_SC_BC_DIM_MAX
BC_SCALE_MAX	_SC_BC_SCALE_MAX
BC_STRING_MAX	_SC_BC_STRING_MAX
CHILD_MAX	_SC_CHILD_MAX
CLK_TCK	_SC_CLK_TCK
COLL_WEIGHTS_MAX	_SC_COLL_WEIGHTS_MAX
EXPR_NEST_MAX	_SC_EXPR_NEST_MAX
LINE_MAX	_SC_LINE_MAX
NGROUPS_MAX	_SC_NGROUPS_MAX
OPEN_MAX	_SC_OPEN_MAX
PASS_MAX	_SC_PASS_MAX (**TO BE WITHDRAWN**)
_POSIX2_C_BIND	_SC_2_C_BIND
_POSIX2_C_DEV	_SC_2_C_DEV
_POSIX2_C_VERSION	_SC_2_C_VERSION
_POSIX2_CHAR_TERM	_SC_2_CHAR_TERM
_POSIX2_FORT_DEV	_SC_2_FORT_DEV
_POSIX2_FORT_RUN	_SC_2_FORT_RUN
_POSIX2_LOCALEDEF	_SC_2_LOCALEDEF
_POSIX2_SW_DEV	_SC_2_SW_DEV
_POSIX2_UPE	_SC_2_UPE
_POSIX2_VERSION	_SC_2_VERSION
_POSIX_JOB_CONTROL	_SC_JOB_CONTROL
_POSIX_SAVED_IDS	_SC_SAVED_IDS
_POSIX_VERSION	_SC_VERSION
RE_DUP_MAX	_SC_RE_DUP_MAX
STREAM_MAX	_SC_STREAM_MAX
TZNAME_MAX	_SC_TZNAME_MAX

EX

	Variable	Value of name
EX	_XOPEN_CRYPT	_SC_XOPEN_CRYPT
	_XOPEN_ENH_I18N	_SC_XOPEN_ENH_I18N
	_XOPEN_SHM	_SC_XOPEN_SHM
	_XOPEN_VERSION	_SC_XOPEN_VERSION
	_XOPEN_XCU_VERSION	_SC_XOPEN_XCU_VERSION
UX	ATEXIT_MAX	_SC_ATEXIT_MAX
	IOV_MAX	_SC_IOV_MAX
	PAGESIZE	_SC_PAGESIZE
	PAGESIZE	_SC_PAGE_SIZE
	_XOPEN_UNIX	_SC_XOPEN_UNIX

RETURN VALUE

If *name* is an invalid value, *sysconf*( ) returns −1 and sets *errno* to indicate the error. If the variable corresponding to *name* is associated with functionality that is not supported by the system, *sysconf*( ) returns −1 without changing the value of *errno*.

Otherwise, *sysconf*( ) returns the current variable value on the system. The value returned will not be more restrictive than the corresponding value described to the application when it was compiled with the implementation's **<limits.h>**, **<unistd.h>** or **<time.h>**. The value will not change during the lifetime of the calling process.

ERRORS

The *sysconf*( ) function will fail if:

[EINVAL] The value of the *name* argument is invalid.

APPLICATION USAGE

As −1 is a permissible return value in a successful situation, an application wishing to check for error situations should set *errno* to 0, then call *sysconf*( ), and, if it returns −1, check to see if *errno* is non-zero.

If the value of:

```
sysconf(_SC_2_VERSION)
```

is not equal to the value of the {_POSIX2_VERSION} symbolic constant, the utilities available via *system*( ) or *popen*( ) might not behave as described in the **XCU** specification. This would mean that the application is not running in an environment that conforms to the **XCU** specification. Some applications might be able to deal with this, others might not. However, the interfaces defined in this document will continue to operate as specified, even if:

```
sysconf(_SC_2_VERSION)
```

reports that the utilities no longer perform as specified.

SEE ALSO

pathconf( ), **<limits.h>**, **<time.h>**, **<unistd.h>**.

EXAMPLE

```
/*
 * Copyright (C) ANTRIX Inc.
 */

/* sysconf.c
 * This program gets the configurable system variable _SC_ARG_MAX
```

```
 * using function sysconf.
 */

#include <stdio.h>
#include <stdlib.h>
#include <unistd.h>
#include <errno.h>

main()
{
  int  sysconf_value;

  fprintf (stdout,"get value of _SC_ARG_MAX\n");
  sysconf_value = sysconf (_SC_ARG_MAX);
  if ( sysconf_value > 0 ) {
     fprintf (stdout,"sysconf() call successful\n");
     fprintf (stdout,"sysconf_value=%d\n", sysconf_value );
  }
  else
     fprintf (stderr,"ERROR: sysconf() call failed\n");
}
```

NAME

syslog — log a message

SYNOPSIS

UX   `#include <syslog.h>`

`void syslog(int priority, const char *message, ... /* argument */);`

DESCRIPTION

Refer to *closelog*( ).

NAME

system — issue a command

SYNOPSIS

```
#include <stdlib.h>

int system(const char *command);
```

DESCRIPTION

The *system*( ) function passes the string pointed to by *command* to the host environment to be executed by a command processor in an implementation-dependent manner. If the implementation supports the **XCU** specification commands, the environment of the executed command will be as if a child process were created using *fork*( ), and the child process invoked the *sh* utility (see *sh* in the **XCU** specification) using *execl*( ) as follows:

```
execl(<shell path>, "sh", "-c", command, (char *)0);
```

where *<shell path>* is an unspecified pathname for the *sh* utility.

The *system*( ) function ignores the SIGINT and SIGQUIT signals, and blocks the SIGCHLD signal, while waiting for the command to terminate. If this might cause the application to miss a signal that would have killed it, then the application should examine the return value from *system*( ) and take whatever action is appropriate to the application if the command terminated due to receipt of a signal.

The *system*( ) function will not affect the termination status of any child of the calling processes other than the process or processes it itself creates.

The *system*( ) function will not return until the child process has terminated.

RETURN VALUE

If *command* is a null pointer, *system*( ) returns non-zero only if a command processor is available.

If *command* is not a null pointer, *system*( ) returns the termination status of the command language interpreter in the format specified by *waitpid*( ). The termination status of the command language interpreter is as specified for the *sh* utility, except that if some error prevents the command language interpreter from executing after the child process is created, the return value from *system*( ) will be as if the command language interpreter had terminated using *exit*(127) or *_exit*(127). If a child process cannot be created, or if the termination status for the command language interpreter cannot be obtained, *system*( ) returns −1 and sets *errno* to indicate the error.

ERRORS

The *system*( ) function may set *errno* values as described by *fork*( ).

In addition, *system*( ) may fail if:

[ECHILD]   The status of the child process created by *system*( ) is no longer available.

APPLICATION USAGE

If the return value of *system*( ) is not −1, its value can be decoded through the use of the macros described in **<sys/wait.h>**. For convenience, these macros are also provided in **<stdlib.h>**.

To determine whether or not the **XCU** specification's environment is present, use:

```
sysconf(_SC_2_VERSION)
```

The *sh* may not be available after a call to *chroot*( ).

Note that, while *system*( ) must ignore SIGINT and SIGQUIT and block SIGCHLD while waiting for the child to terminate, the handling of signals in the executed command is as specified by *fork*( ) and *exec*. For example, if SIGINT is being caught or is set to SIG_DFL when *system*( ) is called, then the child will be started with SIGINT handling set to SIG_DFL.

Ignoring SIGINT and SIGQUIT in the parent process prevents coordination problems (two processes reading from the same terminal, for example) when the executed command ignores or catches one of the signals. It is also usually the correct action when the user has given a command to the application to be executed synchronously (as in the "!" command in many interactive applications). In either case, the signal should be delivered only to the child process, not to the application itself. There is one situation where ignoring the signals might have less than the desired effect. This is when the application uses *system*( ) to perform some task invisible to the user. If the user typed the interrupt character (^C, for example) while *system*( ) is being used in this way, one would expect the application to be killed, but only the executed command will be killed. Applications that use *system*( ) in this way should carefully check the return status from *system*( ) to see if the executed command was successful, and should take appropriate action when the command fails.

Blocking SIGCHLD while waiting for the child to terminate prevents the application from catching the signal and obtaining status from *system*( )'s child process before *system*( ) can get the status itself.

The context in which the utility is ultimately executed may differ from that in which *system*( ) was called. For example, file descriptors that have the FD_CLOEXEC flag set will be closed, and the process ID and parent process ID will be different. Also, if the executed utility changes its environment variables or its current working directory, that change will not be reflected in the caller's context.

There is no defined way for an application to find the specific path for the shell. However, *confstr*( ) can provide a value for *PATH* that is guaranteed to find the *sh* utility.

SEE ALSO

exec, *pipe*( ), *waitpid*( ), **<limits.h>**, **<signal.h>**, **<stdlib.h>**, the **XCU** specification.

EXAMPLE

```
/*
 * Copyright (C) ANTRIX Inc.
 */

/* system.c
 * This program passed the string pointed to by command to the
 * host environment to by executed by a command process using
 * function system.
 */

#include <stdio.h>
#include <stdlib.h>
#include <errno.h>

main()
{
    int         system_value;
    const char *command = "echo Hello World";

    fprintf (stdout,"execute echo binary\n");
```

```
        system_value = system (command);
        if ( system_value == 0 )
            fprintf (stdout,"system() call successful\n");
        else {
            fprintf (stderr,"ERROR: system() call failed\n");
            fprintf (stderr,"ERROR: %s\n", strerror(errno));
        }
    }
```

NAME

tan — tangent function

SYNOPSIS

```
#include <math.h>

double tan(double x);
```

DESCRIPTION

The *tan*( ) function computes the tangent of its argument *x*, measured in radians.

RETURN VALUE

Upon successful completion, *tan*( ) returns the tangent of *x*.

EX   If *x* is NaN, NaN is returned and *errno* may be set to [EDOM].

EX   If *x* is ±Inf, either 0.0 is returned and *errno* is set to [EDOM], or NaN is returned and *errno* may be set to [EDOM].

If the correct value would cause overflow, ±HUGE_VAL is returned and *errno* is set to [ERANGE].

If the correct value would cause underflow, 0.0 is returned and *errno* may be set to [ERANGE].

ERRORS

The *tan*( ) function will fail if:

[ERANGE]   The value to be returned would cause overflow.

The *tan*( ) function may fail if:

EX   [EDOM]   The value *x* is NaN or ±Inf.

[ERANGE]   The value to be returned would cause underflow.

EX   No other errors will occur.

APPLICATION USAGE

An application wishing to check for error situations should set *errno* to 0 before calling *tan*( ). If *errno* is non-zero on return, or the return value is NaN, an error has occurred.

The *tan*( ) function may lose accuracy when its argument is far from 0.0 .

SEE ALSO

atan( ), *isnan*( ), **<math.h>**.

EXAMPLE

```
/*
 * Copyright (C) ANTRIX Inc.
 */

/* tan.c
 * This program computes the tangent of its argument x, measured
 * in radians using function tan.
 */

#include <stdio.h>
#include <math.h>

main()
{
```

```
    double  tan_value;
    double  x = 45.00;

    tan_value = tan (x);
    fprintf (stdout,"tan of %f is %f\n", x, tan_value);
}
```

NAME

tanh — hyperbolic tangent function

SYNOPSIS

```
#include <math.h>

double tanh(double x);
```

DESCRIPTION

The *tanh( )* function computes the hyperbolic tangent of *x*.

RETURN VALUE

Upon successful completion, *tanh( )* returns the hyperbolic tangent of *x*.

EX   If *x* is NaN, NaN is returned and *errno* may be set to [EDOM].

If the correct value would cause underflow, 0.0 is returned and *errno* may be set to [ERANGE].

ERRORS

The *tanh( )* function may fail if:

EX   [EDOM]   The value of *x* is NaN.

[ERANGE]   The correct result would cause underflow.

EX   No other errors will occur.

APPLICATION USAGE

An application wishing to check for error situations should set *errno* to 0 before calling *tanh( )*. If *errno* is non-zero on return, or the return value is NaN, an error has occurred.

SEE ALSO

atanh( ), *isnan( )*, *tan( )*, **<math.h>**.

EXAMPLE

```
/*
 * Copyright (C) ANTRIX Inc.
 */

/* tanh.c
 * This program computes the hyperbolic tangent of x using function
 * tanh.
 */

#include <stdio.h>
#include <math.h>

main()
{
  double  tanh_value;
  double  x = 0.22;

  tanh_value = tanh (x);
  fprintf (stdout,"tanh of %f is %f\n", x, tanh_value);
}
```

NAME

 tcdrain — wait for transmission of output

SYNOPSIS

 `#include <termios.h>`

 `int tcdrain(int fildes);`

DESCRIPTION

 The *tcdrain*( ) function waits until all output written to the object referred to by *fildes* is transmitted. The *fildes* argument is an open file descriptor associated with a terminal.

 Any attempts to use *tcdrain*( ) from a process which is a member of a background process group on a *fildes* associated with its controlling terminal, will cause the process group to be sent a SIGTTOU signal. If the calling process is blocking or ignoring SIGTTOU signals, the process is allowed to perform the operation, and no signal is sent.

RETURN VALUE

 Upon successful completion, 0 is returned. Otherwise, −1 is returned and *errno* is set to indicate the error.

ERRORS

 The *tcdrain*( ) function will fail if:

 [EBADF] The *fildes* argument is not a valid file descriptor.

 [EINTR] A signal interrupted *tcdrain*( ).

 [ENOTTY] The file associated with *fildes* is not a terminal.

 The *tcdrain*( ) function may fail if:

 [EIO] The process group of the writing process is orphaned, and the writing process is not ignoring or blocking SIGTTOU.

FUTURE DIRECTIONS

 In the ISO POSIX-1 standard, the possibility of an [EIO] error occurring is described in Section 7.1.1.4, Terminal Access Control, but it is not mentioned in the *tcdrain*( ) interface definition. It has become clear that this omission was unintended, so it is likely that the [EIO] error will be reclassified as a "will fail" when the POSIX standard is next updated.

SEE ALSO

 tcflush( ), **<termios.h>**, **<unistd.h>**, the **XBD** specification, **Chapter 9**, **General Terminal Interface**.

EXAMPLE

```
/*
 * Copyright (C) ANTRIX Inc.
 */

/* tcdrain.c
 * This program waits until all output written to the object
 * referred to by fildes is transmitted using function tcdrain.
 */

#include <stdio.h>
#include <unistd.h>
#include <termios.h>
#include <errno.h>
```

```
main()
{
    int     tcdrain_value;
    struct  termios termios_p;
    int     stat_loc;
    int     fildes = 1;

    if (fork() == 0) {
        fprintf (stdout,"get the output speed of stdout\n");
        ioctl (fildes, TCGETA, &termios_p);
        cfsetospeed (&termios_p, B300);
        termios_p.c_lflag &= ~ICANON;
        tcsetattr(fildes, TCSANOW, &termios_p);
        write(fildes, "hello world\n", 13);

        fprintf (stdout,"wait until all output is written\n");
        tcdrain_value = tcdrain (fildes);
        if ( tcdrain_value == 0 )
            fprintf (stdout,"tcdrain() call successful\n");
        else {
            fprintf (stderr,"ERROR: tcdrain() call failed\n");
            fprintf (stderr,"ERROR: %s\n", strerror(errno));
        }
        exit (1);
    } wait(&stat_loc);
}
```

NAME

tcflow — suspend or restart the transmission or reception of data

SYNOPSIS

```
#include <termios.h>

int tcflow(int fildes, int action);
```

DESCRIPTION

The *tcflow*( ) function suspends transmission or reception of data on the object referred to by *fildes*, depending on the value of *action*. The *fildes* argument is an open file descriptor associated with a terminal.

- If *action* is TCOOFF, output is suspended.

- If *action* is TCOON, suspended output is restarted.

- If *action* is TCIOFF, the system transmits a STOP character, which is intended to cause the terminal device to stop transmitting data to the system.

- If *action* is TCION, the system transmits a START character, which is intended to cause the terminal device to start transmitting data to the system.

The default on the opening of a terminal file is that neither its input nor its output are suspended.

Attempts to use *tcflow*( ) from a process which is a member of a background process group on a *fildes* associated with its controlling terminal, will cause the process group to be sent a SIGTTOU signal. If the calling process is blocking or ignoring SIGTTOU signals, the process is allowed to perform the operation, and no signal is sent.

RETURN VALUE

Upon successful completion, 0 is returned. Otherwise, −1 is returned and *errno* is set to indicate the error.

ERRORS

The *tcflow*( ) function will fail if:

[EBADF]   The *fildes* argument is not a valid file descriptor.

[EINVAL]   The *action* argument is not a supported value.

[ENOTTY]   The file associated with *fildes* is not a terminal.

The *tcflow*( ) function may fail if:

[EIO]   The process group of the writing process is orphaned, and the writing process is not ignoring or blocking SIGTTOU.

FUTURE DIRECTIONS

In the ISO POSIX-1 standard, the possibility of an [EIO] error occurring is described in Section 7.1.1.4, Terminal Access Control, but it is not mentioned in the *tcflow*( ) interface definition. It has become clear that this omission was unintended, so it is likely that the [EIO] error will be re-classified as a "will fail" when the POSIX standard is next updated.

SEE ALSO

tcsendbreak( ), **<termios.h>**, **<unistd.h>**, the **XBD** specification, **Chapter 9**, **General Terminal Interface**.

EXAMPLE

```
/*
 * Copyright (C) ANTRIX Inc.
 */

/* tcflow.c
 * This program suspends transmission or reception of data on
 * the object referred to by fildes using function tcflow.
 */

#include <stdio.h>
#include <stdlib.h>
#include <unistd.h>
#include <termios.h>
#include <errno.h>

main()
{
  int     tcflow_value;
  char    buf[] = "hello world\n";
  int     stat_loc;
  int     fildes = 0;

  if (fork() == 0) {
    fprintf (stdout,"suspend transmission or reception of data\n");
    tcflow_value = tcflow (fildes, TCOOFF);
    if ( tcflow_value == 0 )
       fprintf (stdout,"tcflow() call successful\n");
    else {
       fprintf (stderr,"ERROR: tcflow() call failed\n");
       fprintf (stderr,"ERROR: %s\n", strerror(errno));
    }

    fprintf (stdout,"write string to stdin\n");
    write(fildes, buf, sizeof(buf));
    fprintf (stdout,"no output\n");
    sleep(2);
    fprintf (stdout,"restart the output\n");
    tcflow (fildes, TCOON);
    exit (1);
  } wait( &stat_loc);
}
```

NAME

tcflush — flush non-transmitted output data, non-read input data or both

SYNOPSIS

```
#include <termios.h>

int tcflush(int fildes, int queue_selector);
```

DESCRIPTION

Upon successful completion, *tcflush*( ) discards data written to the object referred to by *fildes* (an open file descriptor associated with a terminal) but not transmitted, or data received but not read, depending on the value of *queue_selector*:

- If *queue_selector* is TCIFLUSH it flushes data received but not read.

- If *queue_selector* is TCOFLUSH it flushes data written but not transmitted.

- If *queue_selector* is TCIOFLUSH it flushes both data received but not read and data written but not transmitted.

FIPS   Attempts to use *tcflush*( ) from a process which is a member of a background process group on a *fildes* associated with its controlling terminal, will cause the process group to be sent a SIGTTOU signal. If the calling process is blocking or ignoring SIGTTOU signals, the process is allowed to perform the operation, and no signal is sent.

RETURN VALUE

Upon successful completion, 0 is returned. Otherwise, −1 is returned and *errno* is set to indicate the error.

ERRORS

The *tcflush*( ) function will fail if:

[EBADF]   The *fildes* argument is not a valid file descriptor.

[EINVAL]   The *queue_selector* argument is not a supported value.

[ENOTTY]   The file associated with *fildes* is not a terminal.

The *tcflow*( ) function may fail if:

[EIO]   The process group of the writing process is orphaned, and the writing process is not ignoring or blocking SIGTTOU.

FUTURE DIRECTIONS

In the ISO POSIX-1 standard, the possibility of an [EIO] error occurring is described in Section 7.1.1.4, Terminal Access Control, but it is not mentioned in the *tcflow*( ) interface definition. It has become clear that this omission was unintended, so it is likely that the [EIO] error will be reclassified as a "will fail" when the POSIX standard is next updated.

SEE ALSO

tcdrain( ), **<termios.h>**, **<unistd.h>**, the **XBD** specification, **Chapter 9, General Terminal Interface**.

EXAMPLE

```
/*
 * Copyright (C) ANTRIX Inc.
 */

/* tcflush.c
 * This program discards data written to the object referred to
 * by fildes, an open file descriptor associated with a terminal,
```

```
 * but not transmitted, or data received but not read using function
 * tcflush.
 */


#include <stdio.h>
#include <stdlib.h>
#include <unistd.h>
#include <termios.h>
#include <errno.h>

main()
{
  int     tcflush_value;
  int     stat_loc;
  int     fildes = 1;
  char    buf[] = "hello world\n";

  if (fork() == 0) {

    fprintf (stdout,"suspend transmission or reception of data\n");
    tcflow (fildes, TCOOFF);
    fprintf (stdout,"write string to stdout\n");
    write(fildes, buf, sizeof(buf));

    fprintf (stdout,"flush the stdin and discard the output\n");
    tcflush_value = tcflush (fildes, TCIOFLUSH);
    if ( tcflush_value == 0 )
      fprintf (stdout,"tcflush() call successful\n");
    else {
      fprintf (stderr,"ERROR: tcflush() call failed\n");
      fprintf (stderr,"ERROR: %s\n", strerror(errno));
    }

    fprintf (stdout,"no output yet\n");
    sleep(4);

    fprintf (stdout,"restart the output\n");
    tcflow (fildes, TCOON);
    exit (1);
  } wait( &stat_loc);
}
```

NAME

tcgetattr — get the parameters associated with the terminal

SYNOPSIS

```
#include <termios.h>

int tcgetattr(int fildes, struct termios *termios_p);
```

DESCRIPTION

The *tcgetattr*( ) function gets the parameters associated with the terminal referred to by *fildes* and stores them in the **termios** structure referenced by *termios_p*. The *fildes* argument is an open file descriptor associated with a terminal.

The *termios_p* argument is a pointer to a **termios** structure.

The *tcgetattr*( ) operation is allowed from any process.

If the terminal device supports different input and output baud rates, the baud rates stored in the **termios** structure returned by *tcgetattr*( ) reflect the actual baud rates, even if they are equal. If differing baud rates are not supported, the rate returned as the output baud rate is the actual baud rate. If the terminal device does not support split baud rates, the input baud rate stored in the **termios** structure will be 0.

EX

RETURN VALUE

Upon successful completion, 0 is returned. Otherwise, −1 is returned and *errno* is set to indicate the error.

ERRORS

The *tcgetattr*( ) function will fail if:

[EBADF]   The *fildes* argument is not a valid file descriptor.

[ENOTTY]   The file associated with *fildes* is not a terminal.

FUTURE DIRECTIONS

In a future issue of this document, implementations which do not support differing baud rates will be prohibited from returning 0 as the input baud rate.

SEE ALSO

tcsetattr( ), **<termios.h>**, the **XBD** specification, **Chapter 9**, **General Terminal Interface**.

EXAMPLE

```
/*
 * Copyright (C) ANTRIX Inc.
 */

/* tcgetattr.c
 * This program gets terminal attributes
 * using function tcgetattr
 */

#include <stdio.h>
#include <stdlib.h>
#include <termios.h>
#include <unistd.h>
#include <fcntl.h>
#include <errno.h>

main()
```

```
{
    int     tcgetattr_value;
    int     fildes;
    struct  termios termios_p;
    char    *name;

    name = (char *)ttyname ((int)0);
    fildes = open (name, O_RDWR);

    fprintf (stdout,"get tty attributes\n");
    tcgetattr_value = tcgetattr (fildes, &termios_p );
    if ( tcgetattr_value == 0 ) {
        fprintf (stdout,"tcgetattr() call successful\n");
        fprintf (stdout,"termios_p.c_iflag=%d\n", termios_p.c_iflag);
        fprintf (stdout,"termios_p.c_oflag=%d\n", termios_p.c_oflag);
        fprintf (stdout,"termios_p.c_lflag=%d\n", termios_p.c_lflag);
        fprintf (stdout,"termios_p.c_cc[VINTR]=%d\n", termios_p.c_cc[VINTR]);
        fprintf (stdout,"termios_p.c_cc[VQUIT]=%d\n", termios_p.c_cc[VQUIT]);
        fprintf (stdout,"termios_p.c_cc[VERASE]=%d\n", termios_p.c_cc[VERASE]);
        fprintf (stdout,"termios_p.c_cc[VKILL]=%d\n", termios_p.c_cc[VKILL] );
        fprintf (stdout,"termios_p.c_cc[VEOF]=%d\n", termios_p.c_cc[VEOF]);
    }
    else {
        fprintf (stderr,"ERROR: tcgetattr() call failed\n");
        fprintf (stderr,"ERROR: %s\n", strerror(errno));
    }

    close (fildes);
}
```

NAME

tcgetpgrp — get foreground process group ID

SYNOPSIS

OH
```
#include <sys/types.h>
#include <unistd.h>

pid_t tcgetpgrp(int fildes);
```

DESCRIPTION

FIPS
The *tcgetpgrp*( ) function will return the value of the process group ID of the foreground process group associated with the terminal.

If there is no foreground process group, *tcgetpgrp*( ) returns a value greater than 1 that does not match the process group ID of any existing process group.

The *tcgetpgrp*( ) function is allowed from a process that is a member of a background process group; however, the information may be subsequently changed by a process that is a member of a foreground process group.

RETURN VALUE

Upon successful completion, *tcgetpgrp*( ) returns the value of the process group ID of the foreground process associated with the terminal. Otherwise, −1 is returned and *errno* is set to indicate the error.

ERRORS

The *tcgetpgrp*( ) function will fail if:

[EBADF]   The *fildes* argument is not a valid file descriptor.

[ENOTTY]   The calling process does not have a controlling terminal, or the file is not the controlling terminal.

SEE ALSO

setsid( ), *setpgid*( ), *tcsetpgrp*( ), **<sys/types.h>**, **<unistd.h>**.

EXAMPLE

```
/*
 * Copyright (C) ANTRIX Inc.
 */

/* tcgetpgrp.c
 * This program gets foreground process group ID associated
 * with the terminal using function tcgetpgrp.
 */

#include <stdio.h>
#include <stdlib.h>
#include <errno.h>

main()
{
    int     tcgetpgrp_value;

    fprintf (stdout,"get process group id of stdin\n");
    tcgetpgrp_value = tcgetpgrp (0);
    if ( tcgetpgrp_value > 0 ) {
        fprintf (stdout,"tcgetpgrp() call successful\n");
```

```
        fprintf (stdout,"process group id=%d\n", tcgetpgrp_value);
    }
    else {
        fprintf (stderr,"ERROR: tcgetpgrp() call failed\n");
        fprintf (stderr,"ERROR: %s\n", strerror(errno));
    }
}
```

NAME

tcgetsid — get process group ID for session leader for controlling terminal

SYNOPSIS

UX   `#include <termios.h>`

`pid_t tcgetsid(int fildes);`

DESCRIPTION

The *tcgetsid*( ) function obtains the process group ID of the session for which the terminal specified by *fildes* is the controlling terminal.

RETURN VALUE

Upon successful completion, *tcgetsid*( ) returns the process group ID associated with the terminal. Otherwise, a value of (**pid_t**)−1 is returned and *errno* is set to indicate the error.

ERRORS

The *tcgetsid*( ) function will fail if:

[EACCES]   The *fildes* argument is not associated with a controlling terminal.

[EBADF]   The *fildes* argument is not a valid file descriptor.

[ENOTTY]   The file associated with *fildes* is not a terminal.

SEE ALSO

<termios.h>.

EXAMPLE

```
/*
 * Copyright (C) ANTRIX Inc.
 */

/* getsid.c
 * This program gets the session ID of the process whose ID
 * is equal to pid using function getsid
 */

#include <stdio.h>
#include <stdlib.h>
#include <sys/types.h>
#include <errno.h>

main()
{
   int     getsid_value;
   int     setsid_value;
   int     stat_loc, pid;

   if ( fork() == 0 ) {
      fprintf (stdout,"current group-id=%d\n", getpgrp());
      pid = getpid ();
      getsid_value = getsid(pid);
      if ( getsid_value >= 0 ) {
         fprintf (stdout,"getsid() call successful\n");
         fprintf (stdout,"current session-id=%d\n", getsid_value);
         setsid_value = setsid ();
```

```
            fprintf (stdout,"setsid_value=%d\n", setsid_value);
            fprintf (stdout,"new group-id=%d\n", getpgrp());
            fprintf (stdout,"new session-id=%d\n", getsid(pid));
        }
        else {
            fprintf (stderr,"ERROR: getsid() call failed\n");
            fprintf (stderr,"ERROR: %s\n", strerror(errno));
        }
        exit (1);
    } wait(&stat_loc);
}
```

NAME

tcsendbreak — send a "break" for a specific duration

SYNOPSIS

```
#include <termios.h>

int tcsendbreak(int fildes, int duration);
```

DESCRIPTION

The *fildes* argument is an open file descriptor associated with a terminal.

If the terminal is using asynchronous serial data transmission, *tcsendbreak*( ) will cause transmission of a continuous stream of zero-valued bits for a specific duration. If *duration* is 0, it will cause transmission of zero-valued bits for at least 0.25 seconds, and not more than 0.5 seconds. If *duration* is not 0, it will send zero-valued bits for an implementation-dependent period of time.

If the terminal is not using asynchronous serial data transmission, it is implementation-dependent whether *tcsendbreak*( ) sends data to generate a break condition or returns without taking any action.

FIPS   Attempts to use *tcsendbreak*( ) from a process which is a member of a background process group on a *fildes* associated with its controlling terminal, will cause the process group to be sent a SIGTTOU signal. If the calling process is blocking or ignoring SIGTTOU signals, the process is allowed to perform the operation, and no signal is sent.

RETURN VALUE

Upon successful completion, 0 is returned. Otherwise, −1 is returned and *errno* is set to indicate the error.

ERRORS

The *tcsendbreak*( ) function will fail if:

[EBADF]   The *fildes* argument is not a valid file descriptor.

[ENOTTY]   The file associated with *fildes* is not a terminal.

The *tcsendbreak*( ) function may fail if:

[EIO]   The process group of the writing process Is orphaned, and the writing process is not ignoring or blocking SIGTTOU.

FUTURE DIRECTIONS

In the ISO POSIX-1 standard, the possibility of an [EIO] error occurring is described in Section 7.1.1.4, Terminal Access Control, but it is not mentioned in the *tcsendbreak*( ) interface definition. It has become clear that this omission was unintended, so it is likely that the [EIO] error will be reclassified as a "will fail" when the POSIX standard is next updated.

SEE ALSO

<termios.h>, <unistd.h>, the **XBD** specification, **Chapter 9**, **General Terminal Interface**.

EXAMPLE

```
/*
 * Copyright (C) ANTRIX Inc.
 */

/* tcsendbreak.c
 * This program send a "break" for a specific duration to an
 * open file descriptor associated with a terminal using function
 * tcsendbreak.
```

```
 */

#include <stdio.h>
#include <stdlib.h>
#include <errno.h>

main()
{
   int     tcsendbreak_value;
   int     fildes = 1;
   int     duration = 0;

   fprintf (stdout,"transmit zero bits for .25 sec to stdout\n");
   tcsendbreak_value = tcsendbreak (fildes, duration);
   if ( tcsendbreak_value == 0 )
      fprintf (stdout,"tcsendbreak() call successful\n");
   else {
      fprintf (stderr,"ERROR: tcsendbreak() call failed\n");
      fprintf (stderr,"ERROR: %s\n", strerror(errno));
   }
}
```

NAME

tcsetattr — set the parameters associated with the terminal

SYNOPSIS

```
#include <termios.h>

int tcsetattr(int fildes, int optional_actions,
              const struct termios *termios_p);
```

DESCRIPTION

The *tcsetattr*( ) function sets the parameters associated with the terminal referred to by the open file descriptor *fildes* (an open file descriptor associated with a terminal) from the **termios** structure referenced by *termios_p* as follows:

- If *optional_actions* is TCSANOW, the change will occur immediately.

- If *optional_actions* is TCSADRAIN, the change will occur after all output written to *fildes* is transmitted. This function should be used when changing parameters that affect output.

- If *optional_actions* is TCSAFLUSH, the change will occur after all output written to *fildes* is transmitted, and all input so far received but not read will be discarded before the change is made.

If the output baud rate stored in the **termios** structure pointed to by *termios_p* is the zero baud rate, B0, the modem control lines will no longer be asserted. Normally, this will disconnect the line.

If the input baud rate stored in the **termios** structure pointed to by *termios_p* is 0, the input baud rate given to the hardware will be the same as the output baud rate stored in the **termios** structure.

The *tcsetattr*( ) function will return successfully if it was able to perform any of the requested actions, even if some of the requested actions could not be performed. It will set all the attributes that implementation supports as requested and leave all the attributes not supported by the implementation unchanged. If no part of the request can be honoured, it will return −1 and set *errno* to [EINVAL]. If the input and output baud rates differ and are a combination that is not supported, neither baud rate is changed. A subsequent call to *tcgetattr*( ) will return the actual state of the terminal device (reflecting both the changes made and not made in the previous *tcsetattr*( ) call). The *tcsetattr*( ) function will not change the values in the **termios** structure whether or not it actually accepts them.

The effect of *tcsetattr*( ) is undefined if the value of the **termios** structure pointed to by *termios_p* was not derived from the result of a call to *tcgetattr*( ) on *fildes*; an application should modify only fields and flags defined by this document between the call to *tcgetattr*( ) and *tcsetattr*( ), leaving all other fields and flags unmodified.

No actions defined by this document, other than a call to *tcsetattr*( ) or a close of the last file descriptor in the system associated with this terminal device, will cause any of the terminal attributes defined by this document to change.

FIPS   Attempts to use *tcsetattr*( ) from a process which is a member of a background process group on a *fildes* associated with its controlling terminal, will cause the process group to be sent a SIGTTOU signal. If the calling process is blocking or ignoring SIGTTOU signals, the process is allowed to perform the operation, and no signal is sent.

RETURN VALUE

Upon successful completion, 0 is returned. Otherwise, −1 is returned and *errno* is set to indicate the error.

ERRORS

The *tcsetattr*( ) function will fail if:

[EBADF]   The *fildes* argument is not a valid file descriptor.

[EINTR]   A signal interrupted *tcsetattr*( ).

[EINVAL]   The *optional_actions* argument is not a supported value, or an attempt was
                made to change an attribute represented in the **termios** structure to an
                unsupported value.

[ENOTTY]   The file associated with *fildes* is not a terminal.

The *tcsetattr*( ) function may fail if:

[EIO]   The process group of the writing process is orphaned, and the writing process
                is not ignoring or blocking SIGTTOU.

APPLICATION USAGE

If trying to change baud rates, applications should call *tcsetattr*( ) then call *tcgetattr*( ) in order to
determine what baud rates were actually selected.

FUTURE DIRECTIONS

Using an input baud rate of 0 to set the input rate equal to the output rate may not be supported
in a future issue of this document.

In the ISO POSIX-1 standard, the possibility of an [EIO] error occurring is described in Section
7.1.1.4, Terminal Access Control, but it is not mentioned in the *tcsetattr*( ) interface definition. It
has become clear that this omission was unintended, so it is likely that the [EIO] error will be
reclassified as a "will fail" when the POSIX standard is next updated.

SEE ALSO

cfgetispeed( ), *tcgetattr*( ), **<termios.h>**, **<unistd.h>**, the **XBD** specification, **Chapter 9**, **General
Terminal Interface**.

EXAMPLE

```
/*
 * Copyright (C) ANTRIX Inc.
 */

/* tcsetattr.c
 * This program sets the parameters associated with the
 * terminal referred to by the open file descriptor fildes
 * using function tcsetattr.
 */

#include <stdio.h>
#include <stdlib.h>
#include <termios.h>
#include <unistd.h>
#include <fcntl.h>
#include <errno.h>

main()
{
    int     tcsetattr_value;
    int     fildes, origval;
    struct  termios origbuf;
```

```
            struct  termios newbuf;
            char    *name;

            fprintf (stdout,"get stdin terminal name\n");
            name = (char *)ttyname ((int)0);
            fildes = open (name, O_RDWR);

            fprintf (stdout,"get the terminal attribute values\n");
            tcgetattr (fildes, &origbuf );
            origval = origbuf.c_cc[VERASE];
            origbuf.c_cc[VERASE]= 'Z';

            fprintf (stdout,"change some attribute values\n");
            tcsetattr_value = tcsetattr (fildes, TCSANOW, &origbuf);
            if ( tcsetattr_value == 0 ) {
               fprintf (stdout,"tcsetattr() call successful\n");
               fprintf (stdout,"get new attributes\n");
               tcgetattr (fildes, &newbuf);
               fprintf (stdout,"newbuf.c_cc[VERASE]=%c\n", newbuf.c_cc[VERASE] );
            }
            else {
               fprintf (stderr,"ERROR: tcsetattr() call failed\n");
               fprintf (stderr,"ERROR: %s\n", strerror(errno));
            }

            fprintf (stdout,"restore original value\n");
            origbuf.c_cc[VERASE] = origval;
            tcsetattr (fildes, TCSANOW, &origbuf );
            close (fildes);
        }
```

NAME

tcsetpgrp — set foreground process group ID

SYNOPSIS

OH   `#include <sys/types.h>`
`#include <unistd.h>`

`int tcsetpgrp(int `*`fildes`*`, pid_t `*`pgid_id`*`);`

DESCRIPTION

FIPS   If the process has a controlling terminal, *tcsetpgrp*( ) will set the foreground process group ID associated with the terminal to *pgid_id*. The file associated with *fildes* must be the controlling terminal of the calling process and the controlling terminal must be currently associated with the session of the calling process. The value of *pgid_id* must match a process group ID of a process in the same session as the calling process.

RETURN VALUE

Upon successful completion, 0 is returned. Otherwise, −1 is returned and *errno* is set to indicate the error.

ERRORS

The *tcsetpgrp*( ) function will fail if:

[EBADF]   The *fildes* argument is not a valid file descriptor.

[EINVAL]   This implementation does not support the value in the *pgid_id* argument.

[ENOTTY]   The calling process does not have a controlling terminal, or the file is not the controlling terminal, or the controlling terminal is no longer associated with the session of the calling process.

FIPS   [EPERM]   The value of *pgid_id* does not match the process group ID of a process in the same session as the calling process.

SEE ALSO

tcgetpgrp( ), **<sys/types.h>**, **<unistd.h>**.

EXAMPLE

```
/*
 * Copyright (C) ANTRIX Inc.
 */

/* tcsetpgrp.c
 * This program sets foreground process group ID associated with
 * terminal using tcsetpgrp.
 */

#include <stdio.h>
#include <stdlib.h>
#include <sys/types.h>
#include <unistd.h>
#include <sys/stat.h>
#include <fcntl.h>
#include <errno.h>

main()
{
    int     tcsetpgrp_value;
```

```
int     stat_loc, pgroupid;
int     fildes;
pid_t   child, grandchild;
char    *name;

fprintf (stdout,"get stdin terminal name\n");
name = (char *)ttyname ((int)1);
fildes = open (name, O_WRONLY);

fprintf (stdout,"fork a child\n");
child = fork ();
if ( child == 0 ) {
   pgroupid = tcgetpgrp (fildes);
   fprintf (stdout,"current process group-id=%d\n", pgroupid);
   setsid ();
   tcsetpgrp_value = tcsetpgrp (fildes, pgroupid);
   fprintf (stdout,"new process group-id=%d\n", tcgetpgrp(fildes) );
   exit (1);
} wait(&stat_loc);
}
```

NAME

tdelete — delete node from binary search tree

SYNOPSIS

EX
```
#include <search.h>
```

```
void *tdelete(const void *key, void **rootp,
              int (*compar)(const void *, const void *));
```

DESCRIPTION

Refer to *tsearch( )*.

EXAMPLE

```c
/*
 * Copyright (C) ANTRIX Inc.
 */

/* tdelete.c
 * This program deletes node from binary search tree using
 * function tdelete.
 */

#include <stdio.h>
#include <stdlib.h>
#include <search.h>
#include <errno.h>

#define  TREESIZE        5

char          key[TREESIZE];
char          *rootp;

compare(const void *ptr1, const void *ptr2)
{
    char    *p1 = (char *) ptr1;
    char    *p2 = (char *) ptr2;

    if (*p1 > *p2)
       return(1);
    if (*p1 == *p2)
       return(0);
    return(-1);
}

main()
{
    char    *found_item;
    char    *delete_item;
    char    i, item;

    fprintf (stdout,"create binary tree\n");
    for (i = 0; i < TREESIZE; i++ ) {
        key[i] = 2*i + 2;
        found_item = tsearch (&key[i], (void **)&rootp, compare);
```

```
        item = **((char **)found_item);
        if ( item == key[i] )
            fprintf (stdout,"item=%d, key[%d]=%d\n", item, i, key[i]);
        else {
            fprintf (stderr,"ERROR: unable to create binary tree\n");
            break;
        }
    }

    fprintf (stdout,"delete an item\n");
    delete_item = tdelete (&key[1],(void **)&rootp,compare);
    if (delete_item == (char *)0)
        fprintf (stderr,"ERROR: unable to delete item %d\n", key[1]);

    fprintf (stdout,"find all the elements of binary tree\n");
    for ( i = 0; i < TREESIZE; i++) {
        found_item = tfind (&key[i], (void **)&rootp, compare);
        item = **((char **)found_item);
        if ( item == key[i] )
            fprintf (stdout,"item=%d, key[%d]=%d\n", item, i, key[i]);
        else
            fprintf (stdout,"deleted item for key[%d]=%d\n", i, key[i]);
    }
}
```

NAME

    telldir — current location of a named directory stream

SYNOPSIS

EX   `#include <dirent.h>`

       `long int telldir(DIR *dirp);`

DESCRIPTION

    The *telldir*( ) function obtains the current location associated with the directory stream specified by *dirp*.

UX   If the most recent operation on the directory stream was a *seekdir*( ), the directory position returned from the *telldir*( ) is the same as that supplied as a *loc* argument for *seekdir*( ).

RETURN VALUE

    Upon successful completion, *telldir*( ) returns the current location of the specified directory stream.

ERRORS

    No errors are defined.

SEE ALSO

    opendir( ), *readdir*( ), *seekdir*( ), **<dirent.h>**.

EXAMPLE

```
/*
 * Copyright (C) ANTRIX Inc.
 */

/* telldir.c
 * This program returns the current location of a named directory
 * stream using function telldir.
 */

#include <stdio.h>
#include <stdlib.h>
#include <sys/types.h>
#include <dirent.h>
#include <sys/stat.h>
#include <errno.h>

#define  PERM_ALL   (S_IRWXU | S_IRWXG | S_IRWXO)

main()
{
   long    telldir_value;
   DIR     *dirp;
   int     i;
   struct  dirent *dirent_save;
   char    *root = "testdir";
   char    *leaf = "testdir/subdir";

   fprintf (stdout,"create test directories\n");
   mkdir (root, PERM_ALL);
   mkdir (leaf, PERM_ALL);
```

```
        fprintf (stdout,"open testdir directory\n");
        dirp = opendir (root);
        for (i = 0; i < 3; i++) {
          telldir_value = telldir (dirp);
          dirent_save = readdir (dirp);
          fprintf (stdout,"directory name=%s current location=%d\n",
                          dirent_save->d_name, telldir_value);

        }

        fprintf (stdout,"close and remove test directories\n");
        closedir (dirp);
        rmdir (leaf);
        rmdir (root);
      }
```

NAME

tempnam — create a name for a temporary file

SYNOPSIS

EX
```
#include <stdio.h>

char *tempnam(const char *dir, const char *pfx);
```

DESCRIPTION

The *tempnam*( ) function generates a pathname that may be used for a temporary file.

The *tempnam*( ) function allows the user to control the choice of a directory. The *dir* argument points to the name of the directory in which the file is to be created. If *dir* is a null pointer or points to a string which is not a name for an appropriate directory, the path prefix defined as {P_tmpdir} in the **<stdio.h>** header is used. If that directory is not accessible, an implementation-dependent directory may be used.

Many applications prefer their temporary files to have certain initial letter sequences in their names. The *pfx* argument should be used for this. This argument may be a null pointer or point to a string of up to five bytes to be used as the beginning of the filename.

RETURN VALUE

Upon successful completion, *tempnam*( ) allocates space for a string, puts the generated pathname in that space and returns a pointer to it. The pointer is suitable for use in a subsequent call to *free*( ). Otherwise it returns a null pointer and sets *errno* to indicate the error.

ERRORS

The *tempnam*( ) function will fail if:

[ENOMEM]   Insufficient storage space is available.

APPLICATION USAGE

This function only creates pathnames. It is the application's responsibility to create and remove the files. Between the time a pathname is created and the file is opened, it is possible for some other process to create a file with the same name. Applications may find *tmpfile*( ) more useful.

Some implementations of *tempnam*( ) may use *tmpnam*( ) internally. On such implementations, if called more than {TMP_MAX} times in a single process, the behaviour is implementation-dependent.

SEE ALSO

fopen( ), *free*( ), *open*( ), *tmpfile*( ), *tmpnam*( ), *unlink*( ), **<stdio.h>**.

EXAMPLE

```
/*
 * Copyright (C) ANTRIX Inc.
 */

/* tempnam.c
 * This program creates a pathname that can by used for a
 * temporary file using function tempnam.
 */

#include <stdio.h>
#include <stdlib.h>
#include <errno.h>

main()
```

```
{
    char     *tempnam_value;
    const  char *dir = "/tmp";

    fprintf (stdout,"example 1\n");
    fprintf (stdout,"create temporary file in current directory\n");
    tempnam_value = tempnam ((char *)0, "file");
    if ( tempnam_value != (char *)0 ) {
        fprintf (stdout,"tempnam() call successful\n");
        fprintf (stdout,"tempnam_value=%s\n", tempnam_value);
    }
    else
        fprintf (stderr,"ERROR: tempnam() call failed\n");

    fprintf (stdout,"example 2\n");
    fprintf (stdout,"create temporary file in /tmp directory\n");
    tempnam_value = tempnam (dir, "file");
    if ( tempnam_value != (char *)0 ) {
        fprintf (stdout,"tempnam() call successful\n");
        fprintf (stdout,"tempnam_value=%s\n", tempnam_value);
    }
    else
        fprintf (stderr,"ERROR: tempnam() call failed\n");
}
```

NAME

tfind — search binary search tree

SYNOPSIS

EX
```
#include <search.h>

void *tfind(const void *key, void *const *rootp,
            int (*compar)(const void *, const void *));
```

DESCRIPTION

Refer to *tsearch( )*.

EXAMPLE

```c
/*
 * Copyright (C) ANTRIX Inc.
 */

/* tfind.c
 * This program performs binary search using function tfind.
 */

#include <stdio.h>
#include <stdlib.h>
#include <search.h>
#include <errno.h>

#define   TREESIZE       5

char         key[TREESIZE];
char         *rootp;

compare(const void *ptr1, const void *ptr2)
{
  char     *p1 = (char *) ptr1;
  char     *p2 = (char *) ptr2;

  if (*p1 > *p2)
     return(1);
  if (*p1 == *p2)
     return(0);
  return(-1);
}

main()
{
  char     *found_item;
  char     i, item;

  fprintf (stdout,"create binary tree\n");
  for (i = 0; i < TREESIZE; i++ ) {
      key[i] = 2*i + 2;
      found_item = tsearch (&key[i], (void **)&rootp, compare);
      item = **((char **)found_item);
      if ( item == key[i] )
```

```
                    fprintf (stdout,"item=%d, key[%d]=%d\n", item, i, key[i]);
            else {
                fprintf (stderr,"ERROR: unable to create binary tree\n");
                break;
            }
    }

    fprintf (stdout,"find all elements of binary tree\n");
    for ( i = 0; i < TREESIZE; i++ ) {
        found_item = tfind (&key[i], (void **)&rootp, compare);
        item = **((char **)found_item);
        if ( item == key[i] )
            fprintf (stdout,"item=%d, key[%d]=%d\n", item, i, key[i]);
        else {
            fprintf (stderr,"ERROR: unable to find key[%d]=%d\n", i, key[i] );
            break;
        }
    }
}
```

NAME

time — get time

SYNOPSIS

```
#include <time.h>

time_t time(time_t *tloc);
```

DESCRIPTION

The *time*( ) function returns the value of time in seconds since the Epoch.

The *tloc* argument points to an area where the return value is also stored. If *tloc* is a null pointer, no value is stored.

RETURN VALUE

Upon successful completion, *time*( ) returns the value of time. Otherwise, (**time_t**)–1 is returned.

ERRORS

No errors are defined.

SEE ALSO

asctime( ), *clock*( ), *ctime*( ), *difftime*( ), *gmtime*( ), *localtime*( ), *mktime*( ), *strftime*( ), *strptime*( ), *utime*( ), **<time.h>**.

EXAMPLE

```
/*
 * Copyright (C) ANTRIX Inc.
 */

/* time.c
 * This program gets the value of time in seconds since the Epoch
 * using function time.
 */

#include <stdio.h>
#include <stdlib.h>
#include <sys/types.h>
#include <time.h>
#include <errno.h>

main()
{
  time_t    time_value;
  time_t    tloc;
  char      s[256];
  struct    tm *timeptr;

  fprintf (stdout,"get clock ticks\n");
  time_value = time (&tloc);
  fprintf (stdout,"time_value=%d\n", time_value);
  fprintf (stdout,"tloc=%d\n", tloc);

  fprintf (stdout,"convert to string\n");
  timeptr = localtime (&time_value);
  strftime (s, sizeof(s), "%a %b %m/%d/%y Time: %H:%M%p",
```

```
                          timeptr);
    fprintf (stdout,"Date: %s\n", s);
}
```

NAME

times — get process and waited-for child process times

SYNOPSIS

```
#include <sys/times.h>

clock_t times(struct tms *buffer);
```

DESCRIPTION

The *times*( ) function fills the **tms** structure pointed to by *buffer* with time-accounting information. The structure **tms** is defined in **<sys/times.h>**.

All times are measured in terms of the number of clock ticks used.

The times of a terminated child process are included in the **tms_cutime** and **tms_cstime** elements of the parent when *wait*( ) or *waitpid*( ) returns the process ID of this terminated child. If a child process has not waited for its children, their times will not be included in its times.

- The **tms_utime** structure member is the CPU time charged for the execution of user instructions of the calling process.

- The **tms_stime** structure member is the CPU time charged for execution by the system on behalf of the calling process.

- The **tms_cutime** structure member is the sum of the **tms_utime** and **tms_cutime** times of the child processes.

- The **tms_cstime** structure member is the sum of the **tms_stime** and **tms_cstime** times of the child processes.

RETURN VALUE

Upon successful completion, *times*( ) returns the elapsed real time, in clock ticks, since an arbitrary point in the past (for example, system start-up time). This point does not change from one invocation of *times*( ) within the process to another. The return value may overflow the possible range of type **clock_t**. If *times*( ) fails, (**clock_t**)–1 is returned and *errno* is set to indicate the error.

ERRORS

No errors are defined.

APPLICATION USAGE

Applications should use *sysconf*(_SC_CLK_TCK) to determine the number of clock ticks per second as it may vary from system to system.

SEE ALSO

exec, *fork*( ), *sysconf*( ), *time*( ), *wait*( ), **<sys/times.h>**.

EXAMPLE

```
/*
 * Copyright (C) ANTRIX Inc.
 */

/* times.c
 * This program fills the tms structure pointed to by buffer
 * with time accounting information and returns the elapsed
 * real time, in clock ticks, since an arbitrary point in the
 * past using function times.
 */
```

```
#include <stdio.h>
#include <stdlib.h>
#include <sys/types.h>
#include <sys/times.h>
#include <errno.h>

main()
{
  clock_t    times_value;
  clock_t    times_later;
  clock_t    delta;
  struct     tms buffer;

  fprintf (stdout,"get process times\n");
  times_value = times (&buffer);
  if ( times_value > (long)0 ) {
     fprintf (stdout,"times() call successful\n");
     fprintf (stdout,"times_value=%d\n", times_value);
     fprintf (stdout,"buffer.tms_utime=%d\n", buffer.tms_utime);
     fprintf (stdout,"buffer.tms_stime=%d\n", buffer.tms_stime);
     fprintf (stdout,"buffer.tms_cutime=%d\n", buffer.tms_cutime);
     fprintf (stdout,"buffer.tms_cstime=%d\n", buffer.tms_cstime);
     sleep (5);
     times_later = times (&buffer);
     delta = times_later - times_value;
     if ( delta < 0 )
        fprintf (stderr,"ERROR: invalid times return\n");
  }
  else {
     fprintf (stderr,"ERROR: times() call failed\n");
     fprintf (stderr,"ERROR: %s\n", strerror(errno));
  }
}
```

NAME

timezone — difference from UTC and local standard time

SYNOPSIS

EX

```
#include <time.h>

extern long int timezone;
```

DESCRIPTION

Refer to *tzset*( ).

NAME

tmpfile — create a temporary file

SYNOPSIS

```
#include <stdio.h>

FILE *tmpfile(void);
```

DESCRIPTION

The *tmpfile*( ) function creates a temporary file and opens a corresponding stream. The file will automatically be deleted when all references to the file are closed. The file is opened as in *fopen*( ) for update (w+).

RETURN VALUE

Upon successful completion, *tmpfile*( ) returns a pointer to the stream of the file that is created. Otherwise, it returns a null pointer and sets *errno* to indicate the error.

ERRORS

The *tmpfile*( ) function will fail if:

[EINTR]   A signal was caught during *tmpfile*( ).

[EMFILE]   {OPEN_MAX} file descriptors are currently open in the calling process.

[ENFILE]   The maximum allowable number of files is currently open in the system.

[ENOSPC]   The directory or file system which would contain the new file cannot be expanded.

The *tmpfile*( ) function may fail if:

EX   [EMFILE]   {FOPEN_MAX} streams are currently open in the calling process.

[ENOMEM]   Insufficient storage space is available.

APPLICATION USAGE

The stream refers to a file which is unlinked. If the process is killed in the period between file creation and unlinking, a permanent file may be left behind.

On some implementations, an error message may be printed if the stream cannot be opened.

SEE ALSO

fopen( ), *tmpnam*( ), *unlink*( ), **<stdio.h>**.

EXAMPLE

```
/*
 * Copyright (C) ANTRIX Inc.
 */

/* tmpfile.c
 * This program creates a temporary file and opens a corresponding
 * stream using function tmpfile.
 */

#include <stdio.h>
#include <stdlib.h>
#include <errno.h>

main()
{
```

```
FILE      *stream;
int       length;
char      buf[12];
char      string[] = "hello world";

memset (buf, ' ', 12);
length = strlen (string);

fprintf (stdout,"create a temporary file\n");
stream = tmpfile ();
if ( stream != (FILE *)0 )
    fprintf (stdout,"tmpfile() call successful\n");
else
    fprintf (stderr,"ERROR: tmpfile() call failed\n");

fprintf (stdout,"write string to temporary file\n");
fwrite (string, sizeof(char), length, stream);
fseek (stream, 0, SEEK_SET);
fflush (stream);
fread (buf, sizeof(char), strlen(string), stream);

fprintf (stdout,"string in buf is %s\n", buf);
fclose (stream);
}
```

NAME

tmpnam — create a name for a temporary file

SYNOPSIS

```
#include <stdio.h>

char *tmpnam(char *s);
```

DESCRIPTION

The *tmpnam*( ) function generates a string that is a valid filename and that is not the same as the name of an existing file.

The *tmpnam*( ) function generates a different string each time it is called from the same process, up to {TMP_MAX} times. If it is called more than {TMP_MAX} times, the behaviour is implementation-dependent.

The implementation will behave as if no function defined in this document calls *tmpnam*( ).

RETURN VALUE

Upon successful completion, *tmpnam*( ) returns a pointer to a string.

If the argument *s* is a null pointer, *tmpnam*( ) leaves its result in an internal static object and returns a pointer to that object. Subsequent calls to *tmpnam*( ) may modify the same object. If the argument *s* is not a null pointer, it is presumed to point to an array of at least {L_tmpnam} **char**s; *tmpnam*( ) writes its result in that array and returns the argument as its value.

ERRORS

No errors are defined.

APPLICATION USAGE

This function only creates filenames. It is the application's responsibility to create and remove the files.

Between the time a pathname is created and the file is opened, it is possible for some other process to create a file with the same name. Applications may find *tmpfile*( ) more useful.

SEE ALSO

fopen( ), *open*( ), *tempnam*( ), *tmpfile*( ), *unlink*( ), **<stdio.h>**.

EXAMPLE

```
/*
 * Copyright (C) ANTRIX Inc.
 */

/* tmpnam.c
 * This program creates a name for a temporary file using function
 * tmpnam.
 */

#include <stdio.h>
#include <stdlib.h>
#include <errno.h>

main()
{
   char    *tmpnam_value;
   char    s[] =  "testfile";
```

```
      fprintf (stdout,"example 1\n");
      fprintf (stdout,"create temporary file\n");
      tmpnam_value = tmpnam ((char *)0);
      if ( tmpnam_value != (char *)0 ) {
          fprintf (stdout,"tmpnam() call successful\n");
          fprintf (stdout,"tmpnam_value=%s\n", tmpnam_value);
      }
      else
          fprintf (stderr,"ERROR: tmpnam() call failed\n");

      fprintf (stdout,"example 2\n");
      fprintf (stdout,"create temporary file using path prefix\n");
      tmpnam_value = tmpnam (s);
      if ( tmpnam_value != (char *)0 ) {
          fprintf (stdout,"tmpnam() call successful\n");
          fprintf (stdout,"tmpnam_value=%s\n", tmpnam_value);
      }
      else
          fprintf (stderr,"ERROR: tmpnam() call failed\n");
  }
```

NAME

toascii — translate integer to a 7-bit ASCII character

SYNOPSIS

EX
```
#include <ctype.h>

int toascii(int c);
```

DESCRIPTION

The *toascii*( ) function converts its argument into a 7-bit ASCII character.

RETURN VALUE

The *toascii*( ) function returns the value (*c* & 0x7f).

ERRORS

No errors are returned.

SEE ALSO

isascii( ), **<ctype.h>**.

EXAMPLE

```
/*
 * Copyright (C) ANTRIX Inc.
 */

/* toascii.c
 * This program translates an integer to a 7-bit ASCII
 * character using function toascii.
 */

#include <stdio.h>
#include <stdlib.h>
#include <errno.h>

main()
{
  int     toascii_value;
  int     i, ret_val;

  fprintf (stdout,"turn off all bits that are not part\n");
  fprintf (stdout,"of a standard ASCII character\n");
  for (i=0; i < 255; i++) {
    if (isalpha(i)) {
      ret_val = toascii (i);
      fprintf (stdout,"%c", ret_val );
    }
  }
  fprintf (stdout,"\n");

  ret_val = toascii(1234);
  fprintf (stdout,"%c\n", ret_val);
}
```

NAME

_tolower — transliterate upper-case characters to lower-case

SYNOPSIS

EX
```
#include <ctype.h>

int _tolower(int c);
```

DESCRIPTION

The _tolower( ) macro is equivalent to tolower(c) except that the argument c must be an upper-case letter.

RETURN VALUE

On successful completion, _tolower( ) returns the lower-case letter corresponding to the argument passed.

ERRORS

No errors are defined.

SEE ALSO

tolower( ), isupper( ), **<ctype.h>**, the **XBD** specification, **Chapter 5**, **Locale**.

EXAMPLE

```
/*
 * Copyright (C) ANTRIX Inc.
 */

/* _tolower.c
 * This program transliterates upper-case characters to lower
 * case using function _tolower.
 */

#include <stdio.h>
#include <stdlib.h>
#include <locale.h>
#include <ctype.h>
#include <errno.h>

main()
{
  int   _tolower_value;
  int   c = 'A';

  _tolower_value = _tolower (c);
  if ( _tolower_value == 'a' )
      fprintf (stdout,"lowercase of 'A' is '%c'\n", _tolower_value);
  else
      fprintf (stderr,"ERROR: _tolower() call failed\n");
}
```

NAME

tolower — transliterate upper-case characters to lower-case

SYNOPSIS

```
#include <ctype.h>

int tolower(int c);
```

DESCRIPTION

The *tolower*( ) function has as a domain a type **int**, the value of which is representable as an **unsigned char** or the value of EOF. If the argument has any other value, the behaviour is undefined. If the argument of *tolower*( ) represents an upper-case letter, and there exists a corresponding lower-case letter (as defined by character type information in the program locale category LC_CTYPE), the result is the corresponding lower-case letter. All other arguments in the domain are returned unchanged.

RETURN VALUE

On successful completion, *tolower*( ) returns the lower-case letter corresponding to the argument passed; otherwise it returns the argument unchanged.

ERRORS

No errors are defined.

SEE ALSO

setlocale( ), **<ctype.h>**, the **XBD** specification, **Chapter 5**, **Locale**.

EXAMPLE

```
/*
 * Copyright (C) ANTRIX Inc.
 */

/* tolower.c
 * This program transliterates upper-case characters to lower
 * case using function tolower.
 */

#include <stdio.h>
#include <stdlib.h>
#include <locale.h>
#include <ctype.h>
#include <errno.h>

main()
{
  int    tolower_value;
  int    c = 'A';

  tolower_value = tolower (c);
  if ( tolower_value == 'a' )
     fprintf (stdout,"lowercase of 'A' is '%c'\n", tolower_value);
  else
     fprintf (stderr,"ERROR: tolower() call failed\n");
}
```

NAME

_toupper — transliterate lower-case characters to upper-case

SYNOPSIS

EX
```
#include <ctype.h>
```
```
int _toupper(int c);
```

DESCRIPTION

The *_toupper*( ) macro is equivalent to *toupper*( ) except that the argument *c* must be a lower-case letter.

RETURN VALUE

On successful completion, *_toupper*( ) returns the upper-case letter corresponding to the argument passed.

ERRORS

No errors are defined.

SEE ALSO

islower( ), *toupper*( ), **<ctype.h>**, the **XBD** specification, **Chapter 5**, **Locale**.

EXAMPLE

```
/*
 * Copyright (C) ANTRIX Inc.
 */

/* _tolower.c
 * This program transliterates upper-case characters to lower
 * case using function _tolower.
 */

#include <stdio.h>
#include <stdlib.h>
#include <locale.h>
#include <ctype.h>
#include <errno.h>

main()
{
  int   _tolower_value;
  int   c = 'A';

  _tolower_value = _tolower (c);
  if ( _tolower_value == 'a' )
      fprintf (stdout,"lowercase of 'A' is '%c'\n", _tolower_value);
  else
      fprintf (stderr,"ERROR: _tolower() call failed\n");
}
```

NAME

toupper — transliterate lower-case characters to upper-case

SYNOPSIS

```
#include <ctype.h>

int toupper(int c);
```

DESCRIPTION

The *toupper*( ) function has as a domain a type **int**, the value of which is representable as an **unsigned char** or the value of EOF. If the argument has any other value, the behaviour is undefined. If the argument of *toupper*( ) represents a lower-case letter, and there exists a corresponding upper-case letter (as defined by character type information in the program locale category LC_CTYPE), the result is the corresponding upper-case letter. All other arguments in the domain are returned unchanged.

RETURN VALUE

On successful completion, *toupper*( ) returns the upper-case letter corresponding to the argument passed.

ERRORS

No errors are defined.

SEE ALSO

setlocale( ), **<ctype.h>**, the **XBD** specification, **Chapter 5**, **Locale**.

EXAMPLE

```
/*
 * Copyright (C) ANTRIX Inc.
 */

/* toupper.c
 * This program transliterates lower-case characters to upper-case
 * using function toupper.
 */

#include <stdio.h>
#include <stdlib.h>
#include <locale.h>
#include <ctype.h>
#include <errno.h>

main()
{
  int     toupper_value;
  int     c = 'a';

  toupper_value = toupper (c);
  if ( toupper_value == 'A' )
     fprintf (stdout,"uppercase of 'a' is '%c'\n", toupper_value);
  else
     fprintf (stderr,"ERROR: toupper() call failed\n");
}
```

NAME

towlower — transliterate upper-case wide-character code to lower-case

SYNOPSIS

WP
```
#include <wchar.h>
```

```
wint_t towlower(wint_t wc);
```

DESCRIPTION

The *towlower*( ) function has as a domain a type **wint_t**, the value of which must be a character representable as a **wchar_t**, and must be a wide-character code corresponding to a valid character in the current locale or the value of WEOF. If the argument has any other value, the behaviour is undefined. If the argument of *towlower*( ) represents an upper-case wide-character code, and there exists a corresponding lower-case wide-character code (as defined by character type information in the program locale category LC_CTYPE), the result is the corresponding lower-case wide-character code. All other arguments in the domain are returned unchanged.

RETURN VALUE

On successful completion, *towlower*( ) returns the lower-case letter corresponding to the argument passed; otherwise it returns the argument unchanged.

ERRORS

No errors are defined.

SEE ALSO

setlocale( ), **<wchar.h>**, the **XBD** specification, **Chapter 5**, **Locale**.

EXAMPLE

```
/*
 * Copyright (C) ANTRIX Inc.
 */

/* towlower.c
 * This program transliterates upper-case wide character code to
 * lower-case using function towlower
 */

#include <stdio.h>
#include <stdlib.h>
#include <locale.h>
#include <wchar.h>
#include <wctype.h>
#include <errno.h>

main()
{
  wint_t     towlower_value;
  wint_t     wc = L'A';

  towlower_value = towlower (wc);
  if ( towlower_value == L'a' ) {
     fprintf (stdout,"towlower() call successful\n");
     fprintf (stdout,"lowercase of 'A' is %wc\n", towlower_value);
  }
  else
```

```
        fprintf (stderr,"ERROR: towlower() call failed\n");
}
```

NAME

towupper — transliterate lower-case wide-character code to upper-case

SYNOPSIS

WP
```
#include <wchar.h>

wint_t towupper(wint_t wc);
```

DESCRIPTION

The *towupper( )* function has as a domain a type **wint_t**, the value of which must be a character representable as a **wchar_t**, and must be a wide-character code corresponding to a valid character in the current locale or the value of WEOF. If the argument has any other value, the behaviour is undefined. If the argument of *towupper( )* represents a lower-case wide-character code, and there exists a corresponding upper-case wide-character code (as defined by character type information in the program locale category LC_CTYPE), the result is the corresponding upper-case wide-character code. All other arguments in the domain are returned unchanged.

RETURN VALUE

Upon successful completion, *towupper( )* returns the upper-case letter corresponding to the argument passed. Otherwise it returns the argument unchanged.

ERRORS

No errors are defined.

SEE ALSO

setlocale( ), **<wchar.h>**, the **XBD** specification, **Chapter 5**, **Locale**.

EXAMPLE

```
/*
 * Copyright (C) ANTRIX Inc.
 */

/* towupper.c
 * This program transliterates lower-case wide-character code
 * to upper-case using function towupper.
 */

#include <stdio.h>
#include <stdlib.h>
#include <locale.h>
#include <wchar.h>
#include <wctype.h>
#include <errno.h>

main()
{
  wint_t      towupper_value;
  wint_t      wc = L'a';

  towupper_value = towupper (wc);
  if ( towupper_value == L'A' ) {
      fprintf (stdout,"towupper() call successful\n");
      fprintf (stdout,"uppercase of 'a' is %wc\n", towupper_value);
  }
  else
```

```
        fprintf (stderr,"ERROR: towupper() call failed\n");
}
```

NAME

truncate — truncate a file to a specified length

SYNOPSIS

UX `#include <unistd.h>`

`int truncate(const char *path, off_t length);`

DESCRIPTION

Refer to *ftruncate*( ).

EXAMPLE

```
/*
 * Copyright (C) ANTRIX Inc.
 */

/* truncate.c
 * This program sets a file to a specified length
 * from the string using function truncate.
 */

#include <stdio.h>
#include <stdlib.h>
#include <unistd.h>
#include <fcntl.h>
#include <sys/stat.h>
#include <libgen.h>
#include <errno.h>

#define  PERM_ALL   (S_IRWXU | S_IRWXG | S_IRWXO)

main()
{
  int    truncate_value;
  int    fildes ;
  char   *path = "filename123456789";

  fprintf (stdout,"create testfile\n");
  fildes = creat (path, PERM_ALL);

  fprintf (stdout,"truncate %s to 8 characters\n", path);
  truncate_value = truncate (path, 8);
  if ( truncate_value == 0 ) {
     fprintf (stdout,"truncate() call successful\n");
     fprintf (stdout,"truncate_value = %d\n", truncate_value);
  }
  else {
     fprintf (stderr,"ERROR: truncate() call failed\n");
     fprintf (stderr,"ERROR: %s\n", strerror(errno));
  }

  fprintf (stdout,"remove testfile\n");
```

```
        remove (path);
        remove ("filename");
    }
```

NAME

tdelete, tfind, tsearch, twalk — manage binary search tree

SYNOPSIS

EX
```
#include <search.h>
```

```
void *tsearch(const void *key, void **rootp,
    int (*compar)(const void *, const void *));
```

```
void *tfind(const void *key, void *const *rootp,
    int(*compar)(const void *, const void *));
```

```
void *tdelete(const void *key, void **rootp,
    int(*compar)(const void *, const void *));
```

```
void twalk(const void *root,
    void (*action)(const void *, VISIT, int));
```

DESCRIPTION

The *tsearch*( ), *tfind*( ), *tdelete*( ) and *twalk*( ) functions manipulate binary search trees. Comparisons are made with a user-supplied routine, the address of which is passed as the *compar* argument. This routine is called with two arguments, the pointers to the elements being compared. The user-supplied routine must return an integer less than, equal to or greater than 0, according to whether the first argument is to be considered less than, equal to or greater than the second argument. The comparison function need not compare every byte, so arbitrary data may be contained in the elements in addition to the values being compared.

The *tsearch*( ) function is used to build and access the tree. The *key* argument is a pointer to an element to be accessed or stored. If there is a node in the tree whose element is equal to the value pointed to by *key*, a pointer to this found node is returned. Otherwise, the value pointed to by *key* is inserted (that is, a new node is created and the value of *key* is copied to this node), and a pointer to this node returned. Only pointers are copied, so the calling routine must store the data. The *rootp* argument points to a variable that points to the root node of the tree. A null pointer value for the variable pointed to by *rootp* denotes an empty tree; in this case, the variable will be set to point to the node which will be at the root of the new tree.

Like *tsearch*( ), *tfind*( ) will search for a node in the tree, returning a pointer to it if found. However, if it is not found, *tfind*( ) will return a null pointer. The arguments for *tfind*( ) are the same as for *tsearch*( ).

The *tdelete*( ) function deletes a node from a binary search tree. The arguments are the same as for *tsearch*( ). The variable pointed to by *rootp* will be changed if the deleted node was the root of the tree. The *tdelete*( ) function returns a pointer to the parent of the deleted node, or a null pointer if the node is not found.

The *twalk*( ) function traverses a binary search tree. The *root* argument is a pointer to the root node of the tree to be traversed. (Any node in a tree may be used as the root for a walk below that node.) The argument *action* is the name of a routine to be invoked at each node. This routine is, in turn, called with three arguments. The first argument is the address of the node being visited. The structure pointed to by this argument is unspecified and must not be modified by the application, but it is guaranteed that a pointer-to-node can be converted to pointer-to-pointer-to-element to access the element stored in the node. The second argument is a value from an enumeration data type:

```
typedef enum { preorder, postorder, endorder, leaf } VISIT;
```

(defined in **<search.h>**), depending on whether this is the first, second or third time that the node is visited (during a depth-first, left-to-right traversal of the tree), or whether the node is a leaf. The third argument is the level of the node in the tree, with the root being level 0.

RETURN VALUE

If the node is found, both *tsearch*( ) and *tfind*( ) return a pointer to it. If not, *tfind*( ) returns a null pointer, and *tsearch*( ) returns a pointer to the inserted item.

A null pointer is returned by *tsearch*( ) if there is not enough space available to create a new node.

A null pointer is returned by *tsearch*( ), *tfind*( ) and *tdelete*( ) if *rootp* is a null pointer on entry.

The *tdelete*( ) function returns a pointer to the parent of the deleted node, or a null pointer if the node is not found.

The *twalk*( ) function returns no value.

ERRORS

No errors are defined.

EXAMPLES

The following code reads in strings and stores structures containing a pointer to each string and a count of its length. It then walks the tree, printing out the stored strings and their lengths in alphabetical order.

```
#include <search.h>
#include <string.h>
#include <stdio.h>

#define STRSZ      10000
#define NODSZ 500

struct node {         /* pointers to these are stored in the tree */
      char    *string;
      int     length;
};

char    string_space[STRSZ]; /* space to store strings */
struct node nodes[NODSZ];   /* nodes to store */
void *root = NULL;          /* this points to the root */

int main(int argc, char *argv[])
{
      char          *strptr = string_space;
      struct node   *nodeptr = nodes;
      void          print_node(const void *, VISIT, int);
      int           i = 0, node_compare(const void *, const void *);

      while (gets(strptr) != NULL && i++ < NODSZ)   {
            /* set node */
            nodeptr->string = strptr;
            nodeptr->length = strlen(strptr);
            /* put node into the tree */
            (void) tsearch((void *)nodeptr, (void **)&root,
                    node_compare);
            /* adjust pointers, so we do not overwrite tree */
            strptr += nodeptr->length + 1;
            nodeptr++;
      }
      twalk(root, print_node);
```

```
        return 0;
}
/*
 *      This routine compares two nodes, based on an
 *      alphabetical ordering of the string field.
 */
int
node_compare(const void *node1, const void *node2)
{
        return strcmp(((const struct node *) node1)->string,
                ((const struct node *) node2)->string);
}
/*
 *      This routine prints out a node, the second time
 *      twalk encounters it or if it is a leaf.
 */
void
print_node(const void *ptr, VISIT order, int level)
{
        const struct node *p = *(const struct node **) ptr;

        if (order == postorder || order == leaf)  {
                (void) printf("string = %s,  length = %d\n",
                        p->string, p->length);
        }
}
```

APPLICATION USAGE

The *root* argument to *twalk*( ) is one level of indirection less than the *rootp* arguments to *tsearch*( ) and *tdelete*( ).

There are two nomenclatures used to refer to the order in which tree nodes are visited. The *tsearch*( ) function uses **preorder**, **postorder** and **endorder** to refer respectively to visiting a node before any of its children, after its left child and before its right, and after both its children. The alternative nomenclature uses **preorder**, **inorder** and **postorder** to refer to the same visits, which could result in some confusion over the meaning of **postorder**.

If the calling function alters the pointer to the root, the result is undefined.

SEE ALSO

bsearch( ), *hsearch*( ), *lsearch*( ), **<search.h>**.

EXAMPLE

```
/*
 * Copyright (C) ANTRIX Inc.
 */

/* tsearch.c
 * This program is used to build and access the tree and search
 * for a node in the tree using function tsearch.
 */

#include <stdio.h>
#include <stdlib.h>
```

```
#include <search.h>
#include <errno.h>

#define   TREESIZE        5

char          key[TREESIZE];
char          *rootp;

compare(const void *ptr1, const void *ptr2)
{
  char     *p1 = (char *) ptr1;
  char     *p2 = (char *) ptr2;

  if (*p1 > *p2)
     return(1);
  if (*p1 == *p2)
     return(0);
  return(-1);
}

main()
{
  char     *found_item;
  char     i, item;

  fprintf (stdout,"create binary tree\n");
  for (i = 0; i < TREESIZE; i++ ) {
    key[i] = 2*i + 2;
    found_item = tsearch (&key[i], (void **)&rootp, compare);
    item = **((char **)found_item);
    if ( item == key[i] )
       fprintf (stdout,"item=%d, key[%d]=%d\n", item, i, key[i]);
    else {
       fprintf (stderr,"ERROR: unable to create binary tree\n");
       break;
    }
  }

  fprintf (stdout,"find all the elements of binary tree\n");
  for (i = 0; i < TREESIZE; i++ ) {
    found_item = tfind (&key[i], (void **)&rootp, compare);
    item = **((char **)found_item);
    if ( item == key[i] )
       fprintf (stdout,"item=%d, key[%d]=%d\n", item, i, key[i]);
    else {
       fprintf (stderr,"ERROR: unable to find key[%d]=%d\n", i, key[i]);
       break;
    }
  }
}
```

NAME

ttyname — find pathname of a terminal

SYNOPSIS

```
#include <unistd.h>

char *ttyname(int fildes);
```

DESCRIPTION

The *ttyname*( ) function returns a pointer to a string containing a null-terminated pathname of the terminal associated with file descriptor *fildes*. The return value may point to static data whose content is overwritten by each call.

RETURN VALUE

Upon successful completion, *ttyname*( ) returns a pointer to a string. Otherwise, a null pointer is
EX   returned and *errno* is set to indicate the error.

ERRORS

The *ttyname*( ) function may fail if:

EX   [EBADF]   The *fildes* argument is not a valid file descriptor.

EX   [ENOTTY]   The *fildes* argument does not refer to a terminal device.

SEE ALSO

<unistd.h>.

EXAMPLE

```
/*
 * Copyright (C) ANTRIX Inc.
 */

/* ttyname.c
 * This program is used find pathname of a terminal using function
 * ttyname.
 */

#include <stdio.h>
#include <stdlib.h>
#include <unistd.h>
#include <errno.h>

main()
{
  char      *ttyname_value;
  int        fildes = 0;

  fprintf (stdout,"get ttyname\n");
  ttyname_value = ttyname(fildes);
  fprintf (stdout,"ttyname_value=%s\n", ttyname_value );
}
```

UX

NAME

ttyslot — find the slot of the current user in the user accounting database

SYNOPSIS

```
#include <stdlib.h>
```

```
int ttyslot(void);  (TO BE WITHDRAWN)
```

DESCRIPTION

The *ttyslot*( ) function returns the index of the current user's entry in the user accounting database. The current user's entry is an entry for which the **utline** member matches the name of a terminal device associated with any of the process' file descriptors 0, 1 or 2. The index is an ordinal number representing the record number in the database of the current user's entry. The first entry in the database is represented by the return value 0.

RETURN VALUE

Upon successful completion, *ttyslot*( ) returns the index of the current user's entry in the user accounting database. The *ttyslot*( ) function returns −1 if an error was encountered while searching the database or if none of file descriptors 0, 1, or 2 is associated with a terminal device.

ERRORS

No errors are defined.

SEE ALSO

endutxent( ), *ttyname*( ), **<stdlib.h>**.

EXAMPLE

```
/*
 * Copyright (C) ANTRIX Inc.
 */

/* ttyslot.c
 * This program finds the slot in the utmp file of the
 * current user using function ttyslot.
 */

#include <stdio.h>
#include <stdlib.h>
#include <errno.h>

main()
{
  int  ttyslot_value;

  fprintf (stdout,"get ttyslot index\n");
  ttyslot_value = ttyslot ();
  fprintf (stdout,"index value=%d\n", ttyslot_value);
}
```

NAME

twalk — traverse binary search tree

SYNOPSIS

EX   `#include <search.h>`

```
void twalk(const void *root,
           void (*action)(const void *, VISIT, int ));
```

DESCRIPTION

Refer to *tsearch*( ).

EXAMPLE

```
/*
 * Copyright (C) ANTRIX Inc.
 */

/* twalk.c
 * This program traverses a binary search tree using function
 * twalk.
 */

#include <stdio.h>
#include <stdlib.h>
#include <search.h>
#include <errno.h>

#define  TABLESIZE  5

struct node {
      char *string;
      int  length;
};

/* sorted table */
struct node table[TABLESIZE] = {
      { "aaa", 3 },
      { "bbb", 3 },
      { "ccc", 3 },
      { "ddd", 3 },
      { "eee", 3 },
};

int compare (node1, node2)
struct node *node1;
struct node *node2;
{
   return strcmp (node1->string, node2->string);
}

void print_node(node, order, level)
void **node;
VISIT order;
int level;
```

```
{
    if (order == preorder || order == leaf)
        fprintf (stdout,"length=%d, string=%s\n",
                (*(struct node **)node)->length,
                (*(struct node **)node)->string);
}

main()
{
    int i ;
    void *root = 0;
    struct node *nodeptr = table;

    for ( i = 0; i < 5; i++ ) {
        tsearch((void *)nodeptr, &root, compare);
        nodeptr++;
    }
    twalk (root, print_node);
}
```

NAME

   tzname — timezone strings

SYNOPSIS

```
#include <time.h>

extern char *tzname[];
```

DESCRIPTION

   Refer to *tzset( )*.

EXAMPLE

```
/*
 * Copyright (C) ANTRIX Inc.
 */

/* tzname.c
 * This program is uses the value of the environment variable
 * TZ to set time conversion information used by localtime,
 * ctime, strftime, mktime using function tzset and also prints
 * value of tzname.
 */

#include <stdio.h>
#include <stdlib.h>
#include <errno.h>

extern char *tzname[2];

main()
{
  char putenv1[]  = "TZ=one4two";

  fprintf (stdout,"tzname[0]=%s\n", tzname[0] );
  fprintf (stdout,"tzname[1]=%s\n", tzname[1] );
  putenv (putenv1);
  tzset ();
  fprintf (stdout,"tzname[0]=%s\n", tzname[0] );
  fprintf (stdout,"tzname[1]=%s\n", tzname[1] );
}
```

tzset( )

System Interfaces

tzset( )

tzset( )

```
 * ctime, strftime, mktime using function tzset.
 */

#include <stdio.h>
#include <stdlib.h>
#include <errno.h>

extern char *tzname[2];

main()
{
  char putenv1[]  = "TZ=one4two";

  fprintf (stdout,"tzname[0]=%s\n", tzname[0] );
  fprintf (stdout,"tzname[1]=%s\n", tzname[1] );
  putenv (putenv1);
  tzset ();
  fprintf (stdout,"tzname[0]=%s\n", tzname[0] );
  fprintf (stdout,"tzname[1]=%s\n", tzname[1] );
}
```

NAME

ualarm — set the interval timer

SYNOPSIS

UX
```
#include <unistd.h>

useconds_t ualarm(useconds_t useconds, useconds_t interval);
```

DESCRIPTION

The *ualarm( )* function causes the SIGALRM signal to be generated for the calling process after
the number of real-time microseconds specified by the *useconds* argument has elapsed. When
the *interval* argument is non-zero, repeated timeout notification occurs with a period in
microseconds specified by the *interval* argument. If the notification signal, SIGALRM, is not
caught or ignored, the calling process is terminated.

Implementations may place limitations on the granularity of timer values. For each interval
timer, if the requested timer value requires a finer granularity than the implementation supports,
the actual timer value will be rounded up to the next supported value.

Interactions between *ualarm( )* and either *alarm( )* or *sleep( )* are unspecified.

RETURN VALUE

The *ualarm( )* function returns the number of microseconds remaining from the previous
ualarm( ) call. If no timeouts are pending or if *ualarm( )* has not previously been called, *ualarm( )*
returns 0.

ERRORS

No errors are defined.

APPLICATION USAGE

The *ualarm( )* function is a simplified interface to *setitimer( )*, and uses the ITIMER_REAL
interval timer.

SEE ALSO

alarm( ), *setitimer( )*, *sleep( )*, **<unistd.h>**.

EXAMPLE

```
/*
 * Copyright (C) ANTRIX Inc.
 */

/* ualarm.c
 * This program schedules an alarm signal SIGALRM
 * after 2000000 microseconds using function ualarm.
 */

#include <stdio.h>
#include <stdlib.h>
#include <unistd.h>
#include <signal.h>
#include <errno.h>

void handler(signal)
int signal;
{
  if (signal == SIGALRM)
     fprintf (stdout,"received signal SIGALRM\n");
```

```
        else
            fprintf (stderr,"ERROR: expected=%d, received=%d\n",
                                    SIGALRM, signal);
    }

    main()
    {
      unsigned int   ualarm_value;
      unsigned int   usecs = 2000000;
      unsigned int   interval = 1;

      signal (SIGALRM, handler);
      fprintf (stdout,"set alarm of 2000000 micro seconds\n");
      ualarm_value = ualarm (usecs, interval);
      if ( ualarm_value == 0 ) {
          fprintf (stdout,"ualarm() call successful\n");
          fprintf (stdout,"ualarm set to %d micro seconds\n", usecs);
      }
      else
          fprintf (stderr,"ERROR: ualarm() call failed\n");

      fprintf (stdout,"try to sleep for 5 seconds\n");
      fprintf (stdout,"but wake up in 2 seconds\n");
      sleep (5);
    }
```

NAME

ulimit — get and set process limits

SYNOPSIS

EX
```
#include <ulimit.h>
```

```
long int ulimit(int cmd, ...);
```

DESCRIPTION

The *ulimit*( ) function provides for control over process limits. The *cmd* values, defined in **<ulimit.h>** include:

UX UL_GETFSIZE   Return the soft file size limit of the process. The limit is in units of 512-byte
UX   blocks and is inherited by child processes. Files of any size can be read. The
                      return value is the integer part of the soft file size limit divided by 512. If the
                      result cannot be represented as a **long int**, the result is unspecified.

UX UL_SETFSIZE   Set the hard and soft file size limits for output operations of the process to the
                      value of the second argument, taken as a **long int**. Any process may
UX   decrease its own hard limit, but only a process with appropriate privileges may
UX   increase the limit. The new file size limit is returned. The hard and soft file
                      size limits are set to the specified value multiplied by 512. If the result would
                      overflow an **rlimit_t**, the actual value set is unspecified.

RETURN VALUE

Upon successful completion, *ulimit*( ) returns the value of the requested limit. Otherwise −1 is returned and *errno* is set to indicate the error.

ERRORS

The *ulimit*( ) function will fail and the limit will be unchanged if:

[EINVAL]   The *cmd* argument is not valid.

[EPERM]   A process not having appropriate privileges attempts to increase its file size limit.

APPLICATION USAGE

As all return values are permissible in a successful situation, an application wishing to check for error situations should set *errno* to 0, then call *ulimit*( ), and, if it returns −1, check to see if *errno* is non-zero.

SEE ALSO

getrlimit( ), *setrlimit*( ), *write*( ), **<ulimit.h>**.

EXAMPLE

```
/*
 * Copyright (C) ANTRIX Inc.
 */

/* ulimit.c
 * This program gets and sets process limits using function
 * ulimit.
 */

#include <stdio.h>
#include <stdlib.h>
#include <sys/ulimit.h>
#include <errno.h>
```

```
main()
{
  long  ulimit_value;

  fprintf (stdout,"get current file size\n");
  ulimit_value = ulimit (UL_GETFSIZE);
  fprintf (stdout,"current file size, ulimit=%d\n", ulimit_value);

  fprintf (stdout,"decrease the file size to 20\n");
  ulimit_value = ulimit (UL_SETFSIZE, 20);
  if ( ulimit_value == 20 ) {
      fprintf (stdout,"ulimit() call successful\n");
      fprintf (stdout,"ulimit=%d\n", ulimit_value);
  }
  else {
      fprintf (stdout,"errno: ulimit() call failed\n");
      fprintf (stderr,"ERROR: %s\n", strerror(errno));
  }
}
```

NAME

umask — set and get file mode creation mask

SYNOPSIS

OH
```
#include <sys/types.h>
#include <sys/stat.h>

mode_t umask(mode_t cmask);
```

DESCRIPTION

The *umask*( ) function sets the process' file mode creation mask to *cmask* and returns the previous value of the mask. Only the file permission bits of *cmask* (see **<sys/stat.h>**) are used; the meaning of the other bits is implementation-dependent.

The process' file mode creation mask is used during *open*( ), *creat*( ), *mkdir*( ) and *mkfifo*( ) to turn off permission bits in the *mode* argument supplied. Bit positions that are set in *cmask* are cleared in the mode of the created file.

RETURN VALUE

The file permission bits in the value returned by *umask*( ) will be the previous value of the file mode creation mask. The state of any other bits in that value is unspecified, except that a subsequent call to *umask*( ) with the returned value as *cmask* will leave the state of the mask the same as its state before the first call, including any unspecified use of those bits.

ERRORS

No errors are defined.

SEE ALSO

creat( ), *mkdir*( ), *mkfifo*( ), *open*( ), **<sys/stat.h>**, **<sys/types.h>**.

EXAMPLE

```
/*
 * Copyright (C) ANTRIX Inc.
 */

/* umask.c
 * This program sets and and gets file mode creation mask using
 * function umask.
 */

#include <stdio.h>
#include <stdlib.h>
#include <sys/types.h>
#include <sys/stat.h>
#include <errno.h>

#define  PERM_ALL    (S_IRWXU | S_IRWXG | S_IRWXO)
#define  PERM_FEW    (S_IRWXU)

main()
{
   mode_t  umask_value;

   fprintf (stdout,"change umask value\n");
   umask_value = umask (PERM_ALL);
```

```
        fprintf (stdout,"umask_value=%o\n", umask_value);
        umask_value = umask (PERM_FEW);
        if ( umask_value == PERM_ALL ) {
            fprintf (stdout,"umask() call successful\n");
            fprintf (stdout,"umask_value=%o\n", umask_value);
        }
        else {
            fprintf (stderr,"ERROR: umask() call failed\n");
            fprintf (stderr,"ERROR: %s\n", strerror(errno));
        }
    }
```

NAME

uname — get name of current system

SYNOPSIS

```
#include <sys/utsname.h>

int uname(struct utsname *name);
```

DESCRIPTION

The *uname*( ) function stores information identifying the current system in the structure pointed to by *name*.

The *uname*( ) function uses the *utsname* structure defined in **<sys/utsname.h>**.

The *uname*( ) function returns a string naming the current system in the character array *sysname*. Similarly, *nodename* contains the name that the system is known by on a communications network. The arrays *release* and *version* further identify the operating system. The array *machine* contains a name that identifies the hardware that the system is running on.

The format of each member is implementation-dependent.

RETURN VALUE

Upon successful completion, a non-negative value is returned. Otherwise, −1 is returned and *errno* is set to indicate the error.

ERRORS

No errors are defined.

APPLICATION USAGE

The inclusion of the *nodename* member in this structure does not imply that it is sufficient information for interfacing to communications networks.

SEE ALSO

<sys/utsname.h>.

EXAMPLE

```
/*
 * Copyright (C) ANTRIX Inc.
 */

/* uname.c
 * This program gets name of current system in the structure
 * pointed to by name using function uname.
 */

#include <stdio.h>
#include <stdlib.h>
#include <sys/utsname.h>
#include <errno.h>

main()
{
    struct  utsname *uname_value;
    struct  utsname name, zero;

    fprintf (stdout,"get system information\n");
    uname_value = (struct utsname *)uname (&name);
    if (uname_value != (struct utsname *)0 ) {
```

```
        fprintf (stdout,"uname() call successful\n");
        fprintf (stdout,"name.sysname=%s\n", name.sysname);
        fprintf (stdout,"name.nodename=%s\n", name.nodename);
        fprintf (stdout,"name.release=%s\n", name.release);
        fprintf (stdout,"name.version=%s\n", name.version);
        fprintf (stdout,"name.machine=%s\n", name.machine);
    }
    else {
        fprintf (stderr,"ERROR: uname() call failed\n");
        fprintf (stderr,"ERROR: %s\n", strerror(errno));
    }
}
```

ungetc( )

NAME

ungetc — push byte back into input stream

SYNOPSIS

```
#include <stdio.h>

int ungetc(int c, FILE *stream);
```

DESCRIPTION

The *ungetc*( ) function pushes the byte specified by *c* (converted to an **unsigned char**) back onto the input stream pointed to by *stream*. The pushed-back bytes will be returned by subsequent reads on that stream in the reverse order of their pushing. A successful intervening call (with the stream pointed to by *stream*) to a file-positioning function (*fseek*( ), *fsetpos*( ) or *rewind*( )) discards any pushed-back bytes for the stream. The external storage corresponding to the stream is unchanged.

One byte of push-back is guaranteed. If *ungetc*( ) is called too many times on the same stream without an intervening read or file-positioning operation on that stream, the operation may fail.

If the value of *c* equals that of the macro EOF, the operation fails and the input stream is unchanged.

A successful call to *ungetc*( ) clears the end-of-file indicator for the stream. The value of the file-position indicator for the stream after reading or discarding all pushed-back bytes will be the same as it was before the bytes were pushed back. The file-position indicator is decremented by each successful call to *ungetc*( ); if its value was 0 before a call, its value is indeterminate after the call.

RETURN VALUE

Upon successful completion, *ungetc*( ) returns the byte pushed back after conversion. Otherwise it returns EOF.

ERRORS

No errors are defined.

SEE ALSO

fseek( ), *getc*( ), *fsetpos*( ), *read*( ), *rewind*( ), *setbuf*( ), **<stdio.h>**.

EXAMPLE

```
/*
 * Copyright (C) ANTRIX Inc.
 */

/* ungetc.c
 * This program pushes the byte specified by c back onto the
 * input stream using function ungetc.
 */

#include <stdio.h>
#include <sys/types.h>
#include <sys/stat.h>
#include <errno.h>

main()
{
  int    ungetc_value;
  int    i, fildes, bytes;
```

```
char    c;
char    buf[12];
char    string[] = "hello world";
char    *filename = "testfile";
FILE    *stream;

bytes = strlen(string);

fprintf (stdout,"create and open testfile\n");
stream = fopen (filename, "w+r");

fprintf (stdout,"write string to testfile\n");
fwrite (string, sizeof(char), bytes, stream);
fflush (stream);

fseek (stream, 0, SEEK_SET);
fprintf (stdout,"read characters\n");
for (i = 0; i < 11; i++ ) {
    c = fgetc (stream);
    fprintf (stdout,"%c", c);
}
fprintf (stdout,"\n");

fprintf (stdout,"unget character\n");
ungetc_value = ungetc (c, stream);

fprintf (stdout,"character placed back is '%c'\n", ungetc_value);
fclose (stream);
fprintf (stdout,"remove testfile\n");
remove (filename);
}
```

NAME

ungetwc — push wide-character code back into input stream

SYNOPSIS

OH   `#include <stdio.h>`

WP   `#include <wchar.h>`

```
wint_t ungetwc(wint_t wc, FILE *stream);
```

DESCRIPTION

The *ungetwc( )* function pushes the character corresponding to the wide character code specified by *wc* back onto the input stream pointed to by *stream*. The pushed-back characters will be returned by subsequent reads on that stream in the reverse order of their pushing. A successful intervening call (with the stream pointed to by *stream*) to a file-positioning function (*fseek( )*, *fsetpos( )* or *rewind( )*) discards any pushed-back characters for the stream. The external storage corresponding to the stream is unchanged.

One character of push-back is guaranteed. If *ungetwc( )* is called too many times on the same stream without an intervening read or file-positioning operation on that stream, the operation may fail.

If the value of *wc* equals that of the macro WEOF, the operation fails and the input stream is unchanged.

A successful call to *ungetwc( )* clears the end-of-file indicator for the stream. The value of the file-position indicator for the stream after reading or discarding all pushed-back characters will be the same as it was before the characters were pushed back. The file-position indicator is decremented (by one or more) by each successful call to *ungetwc( )*; if its value was 0 before a call, its value is indeterminate after the call.

RETURN VALUE

Upon successful completion, *ungetwc( )* returns the wide-character code corresponding to the pushed-back character. Otherwise it returns WEOF.

ERRORS

The *ungetwc( )* function may fail if:

[EILSEQ]   An invalid character sequence is detected, or a wide-character code does not correspond to a valid character.

SEE ALSO

fseek( ), *fsetpos( )*, *read( )*, *rewind( )*, *setbuf( )*, **<stdio.h>**, **<wchar.h>**.

EXAMPLE

```
/*
 * Copyright (C) ANTRIX Inc.
 */

/* ungetwc.c
 * This program pushes wide-character code back into input
 * stream using function ungetwc.
 */

#include <stdio.h>
#include <wchar.h>
#include <sys/types.h>
#include <sys/stat.h>
#include <errno.h>
```

```
main()
{
   int     ungetwc_value;
   int     i, fildes, bytes;
   wint_t  wc;
   wchar_t buf[12];
   wchar_t *ws = L"hello world";
   char    *filename = "testfile";
   FILE    *stream;

   bytes = wcslen(ws);

   fprintf (stdout,"create and open testfile\n");
   stream = fopen (filename, "w+r");

   fprintf (stdout,"write string to testfile\n");
   fputws(ws, stream);
   fflush (stream);

   fseek (stream, 0, SEEK_SET);
   fprintf (stdout,"read characters\n");
   for (i = 0; i < 11; i++ ) {
       wc = fgetwc (stream);
       fprintf (stdout,"%wc", wc );
   }
   fprintf (stdout,"\n");

   fprintf (stdout,"unget wide character\n");
   ungetwc_value = ungetc (wc, stream);

   fprintf (stdout,"character placed back is %wc\n", ungetwc_value );
   fclose (stream);

   fprintf (stdout,"remove testfile\n");
   remove (filename);
}
```

NAME

unlink — remove directory entry

SYNOPSIS

```
#include <unistd.h>

int unlink(const char *path);
```

DESCRIPTION

UX   The *unlink*( ) function removes a link to a file. If *path* names a symbolic link, *unlink*( ) removes the symbolic link named by *path* and does not affect any file or directory named by the contents of the symbolic link. Otherwise, *unlink*( ) removes the link named by the pathname pointed to by *path* and decrements the link count of the file referenced by the link.

When the file's link count becomes 0 and no process has the file open, the space occupied by the file will be freed and the file will no longer be accessible. If one or more processes have the file open when the last link is removed, the link will be removed before *unlink*( ) returns, but the removal of the file contents will be postponed until all references to the file are closed.

The *path* argument must not name a directory unless the process has appropriate privileges and the implementation supports using *unlink*( ) on directories.

Upon successful completion, *unlink*( ) will mark for update the *st_ctime* and *st_mtime* fields of the parent directory. Also, if the file's link count is not 0, the *st_ctime* field of the file will be marked for update.

RETURN VALUE

Upon successful completion, 0 is returned. Otherwise, −1 is returned and *errno* is set to indicate the error. If −1 is returned, the named file will not be changed.

ERRORS

The *unlink*( ) function will fail and not unlink the file if:

[EACCES]   Search permission is denied for a component of the path prefix, or write permission is denied on the directory containing the directory entry to be removed.

[EBUSY]   The file named by the *path* argument cannot be unlinked because it is being used by the system or another process and the implementation considers this
UX   an error, or the file named by *path* is a named STREAM.

[ELOOP]   Too many symbolic links were encountered in resolving *path*.

[ENAMETOOLONG]
FIPS   The length of the *path* argument exceeds {PATH_MAX} or a pathname component is longer than {NAME_MAX}.

[ENOENT]   A component of *path* does not name an existing file or *path* is an empty string.

[ENOTDIR]   A component of the path prefix is not a directory.

[EPERM]   The file named by *path* is a directory, and either the calling process does not have appropriate privileges, or the implementation prohibits using *unlink*( ) on directories.

UX   [EPERM] or [EACCES]
                The S_ISVTX flag is set on the directory containing the file referred to by the *path* argument and the caller is not the file owner, nor is the caller the directory owner, nor does the caller have appropriate privileges.

[EROFS]   The directory entry to be unlinked is part of a read-only file system.

The *unlink( )* function may fail and not unlink the file if:

UX   [ENAMETOOLONG]
               Pathname resolution of a symbolic link produced an intermediate result whose
               length exceeds {PATH_MAX}.

EX   [ETXTBSY]   The entry to be unlinked is the last directory entry to a pure procedure (shared
               text) file that is being executed.

APPLICATION USAGE

Applications should use *rmdir( )* to remove a directory.

SEE ALSO

close( ), *link( )*, *remove( )*, *rmdir( )*, **<unistd.h>**.

EXAMPLE

```
/*
 * Copyright (C) ANTRIX Inc.
 */

/* unlink.c
 * This program removes the link named by the pathname pointed
 * to by path and decrements the link count of the file
 * referenced by the link using function unlink.
 */

#include <stdio.h>
#include <stdlib.h>
#include <sys/stat.h>
#include <errno.h>

#define  PERM_ALL    (S_IRWXU | S_IRWXG | S_IRWXO)

main()
{
  int    unlink_value;
  char   *path = "testfile";

  fprintf (stdout,"creat testfile\n");
  creat (path, PERM_ALL);

  fprintf (stdout,"unlink testfile\n");
  unlink_value = unlink (path);
  if ( unlink_value == 0 )
     fprintf (stdout,"unlink() call successful\n");
  else {
     fprintf (stderr,"ERROR: unlink() call failed\n");
     fprintf (stderr,"ERROR: %s\n", strerror(errno));
  }
}
```

NAME

unlockpt — unlock a pseudo-terminal master/slave pair

SYNOPSIS

UX
```
#include <stdlib.h>

int unlockpt(int fildes);
```

DESCRIPTION

The *unlockpt*( ) function unlocks the slave pseudo-terminal device associated with the master to which *fildes* refers.

Portable applications must call *unlockpt*( ) before opening the slave side of a pseudo-terminal device.

RETURN VALUE

Upon successful completion, *unlockpt*( ) returns 0. Otherwise, it returns −1 and sets *errno* to indicate the error.

ERRORS

The *unlockpt*( ) function may fail if:

[EBADF]   The *fildes* argument is not a file descriptor open for writing.

[EINVAL]   The *fildes* argument is not associated with a master pseudo-terminal device.

SEE ALSO

grantpt( ), *open*( ), *ptsname*( ), **<stdlib.h>**.

EXAMPLE

```
/*
 * Copyright (C) ANTRIX Inc.
 */

/* unlockpt.c
 * This program clears a lock flag associated with the
 * slave pseudo-terminal using function unlockpt
 */

#include <stdio.h>
#include <stdlib.h>
#include <fcntl.h>
#include <errno.h>

/* name of the master pseudo-terminal device */
/* this name may be different in your machine */
#define MASTER      "/dev/ptmx"

main()
{
    int     unlockpt_value;
    int     fildes;
    char    *ptsname_value;
    char    *name;

    fprintf (stdout,"open master device\n");
    fildes = open (MASTER, O_RDWR);
```

```
    fprintf (stdout,"grant access to the slave pseudo-terminal device\n");
    grantpt (fildes);

    fprintf (stdout,"unlock device\n");
    unlockpt_value = unlockpt (fildes);
    if ( unlockpt_value == 0 )
        fprintf (stdout,"unlockpt() call successful\n");
    else {
        fprintf (stderr,"ERROR: unlockpt() call failed\n");
        fprintf (stderr,"ERROR: %s\n", strerror(errno));
    }
    ptsname_value = (char *)ptsname (fildes);

    fprintf (stdout,"name of the slave pseudo-terminal=%s\n",
                    ptsname_value);

    fprintf (stdout,"close device\n");
    close (fildes);
}
```

NAME

usleep — suspend execution for an interval

SYNOPSIS

UX   `#include <unistd.h>`

`int usleep(useconds_t useconds);`

DESCRIPTION

The *usleep( )* function suspends the current process from execution for the number of microseconds specified by the *useconds* argument. Because of other activity, or because of the time spent in processing the call, the actual suspension time may be longer than the amount of time specified.

The *useconds* argument must be less than 1,000,000. If the value of *useconds* is 0, then the call has no effect.

The *usleep( )* function uses the process' real-time interval timer to indicate to the system when the process should be woken up.

There is one real-time interval timer for each process. The *usleep( )* function will not interfere with a previous setting of this timer. If the process has set this timer prior to calling *usleep( )*, and if the time specified by *useconds* equals or exceeds the interval timer's prior setting, the process will be woken up shortly before the timer was set to expire.

Implementations may place limitations on the granularity of timer values. For each interval timer, if the requested timer value requires a finer granularity than the implementation supports, the actual timer value will be rounded up to the next supported value.

Interactions between *usleep( )* and either *alarm( )* or *sleep( )* are unspecified.

RETURN VALUE

On successful completion, *usleep( )* returns 0. Otherwise, it returns −1 and sets *errno* to indicate the error.

ERRORS

The *usleep( )* function may fail if:

[EINVAL]   The time interval specified 1,000,000 or more microseconds.

APPLICATION USAGE

The *usleep( )* function is included for its historical usage. The *setitimer( )* function is preferred over this function.

SEE ALSO

alarm( ), *getitimer( )*, *sigaction( )*, *sleep( )*, **<unistd.h>**.

EXAMPLE

```
/*
 * Copyright (C) ANTRIX Inc.
 */

/* usleep.c
 * This program suspends execution for an interval of time
 * in micro seconds using function usleep.
 */

#include <stdio.h>
#include <stdlib.h>
```

```
#include <time.h>
#include <errno.h>

main()
{
  char     *ctime_value;
  char     *current_time;
  time_t   clock, tloc;
  struct   tm  *buf;
  unsigned int useconds = 5000000;

  clock = time (&tloc);
  fprintf (stdout,"current clock ticks is %d\n", clock);

  ctime_value = ctime (&clock);
  buf = localtime (&clock);
  current_time = asctime (buf);
  fprintf (stdout,"current time is %s\n", current_time);

  fprintf (stdout,"sleep for 5 seconds\n");
  usleep (useconds);
  clock = time (&tloc);

  fprintf (stdout,"current clock ticks after 5 seconds is %d\n", clock);
  ctime_value = ctime (&clock);
  buf = localtime (&clock);
  current_time = asctime (buf);

  fprintf (stdout,"current time after 5 seconds is %s\n", current_time);
}
```

NAME

utime — set file access and modification times

SYNOPSIS

OH
```
#include <sys/types.h>
#include <utime.h>

int utime(const char *path, const struct utimbuf *times);
```

DESCRIPTION

The *utime*( ) function sets the access and modification times of the file named by the *path* argument.

If *times* is a null pointer, the access and modification times of the file are set to the current time. The effective user ID of the process must match the owner of the file, or the process must have write permission to the file or have appropriate privileges, to use *utime*( ) in this manner.

If *times* is not a null pointer, *times* is interpreted as a pointer to a **utimbuf** structure and the access and modification times are set to the values contained in the designated structure. Only a process with effective user ID equal to the user ID of the file or a process with appropriate privileges may use *utime*( ) this way.

The **utimbuf** structure is defined by the header **<utime.h>**. The times in the structure **utimbuf** are measured in seconds since the Epoch.

Upon successful completion, *utime*( ) will mark the time of the last file status change, **st_ctime**, to be updated, see **<sys/stat.h>**.

RETURN VALUE

Upon successful completion, 0 is returned. Otherwise, −1 is returned and *errno* is set to indicate the error, and the file times will not be affected.

ERRORS

The *utime*( ) function will fail if:

[EACCES]	Search permission is denied by a component of the path prefix; or the *times* argument is a null pointer and the effective user ID of the process does not match the owner of the file and write access is denied.

UX
[ELOOP]	Too many symbolic links were encountered in resolving *path*.

[ENAMETOOLONG]

FIPS
The length of the *path* argument exceeds {PATH_MAX} or a pathname component is longer than {NAME_MAX}.

[ENOENT]	A component of *path* does not name an existing file or *path* is an empty string.
[ENOTDIR]	A component of the path prefix is not a directory.
[EPERM]	The *times* argument is not a null pointer and the calling process' effective user ID has write access to the file but does not match the owner of the file and the calling process does not have the appropriate privileges.
[EROFS]	The file system containing the file is read-only.

The *utime*( ) function may fail if:

UX
[ENAMETOOLONG]

Pathname resolution of a symbolic link produced an intermediate result whose length exceeds {PATH_MAX}.

SEE ALSO

    <sys/types.h>, **<utime.h>**.

EXAMPLE

```
/*
 * Copyright (C) ANTRIX Inc.
 */

/* utime.c
 * This program sets file access and modification times using
 * function utime.
 */

#include <stdio.h>
#include <stdlib.h>
#include <sys/types.h>
#include <utime.h>
#include <sys/stat.h>
#include <fcntl.h>
#include <errno.h>

#define   PERM_ALL   (S_IRWXU | S_IRWXG | S_IRWXO)

main()
{
  int      utime_value;
  struct   stat buf;
  char     *path = "testfile";

  fprintf (stdout,"create testfile\n");
  creat (path, PERM_ALL);

  fprintf (stdout,"print the access and modification time\n");
  stat (path, &buf);
  fprintf (stdout,"buf.st_atime=%d\n", buf.st_atime);
  fprintf (stdout,"buf.st_mtime=%d\n", buf.st_mtime);

  fprintf (stdout,"sleep for 5 seconds\n");
  sleep (5);
  utime_value = utime (path, (struct utimbuf *)0 );
  if ( utime_value == 0 ) {
     fprintf (stdout,"utime() call successful\n");
     fprintf (stdout,"print new access and modification time\n");
     stat ("testfile", &buf);
     fprintf (stdout,"new values\n");
     fprintf (stdout,"buf.st_atime=%d\n", buf.st_atime);
     fprintf (stdout,"buf.st_mtime=%d\n", buf.st_mtime);
  }
  else {
     fprintf (stderr,"ERROR: utime() call failed\n");
     fprintf (stderr,"ERROR: %s\n", strerror(errno));
  }
```

```
        fprintf (stdout,"remove testfile\n");
        remove (path);
}
```

NAME

utimes — set file access and modification times

SYNOPSIS

UX
```
#include <sys/time.h>

int utimes(const char *path, const struct timeval times[2]);
```

DESCRIPTION

The *utimes*( ) function sets the access and modification times of the file pointed to by the *path* argument to the value of the *times* argument. The *utimes*( ) function allows time specifications accurate to the microsecond.

For *utimes*( ), the *times* argument is an array of **timeval** structures. The first array member represents the date and time of last access, and the second member represents the date and time of last modification. The times in the **timeval** structure are measured in seconds and microseconds since the Epoch, although rounding toward the nearest second may occur.

If the *times* argument is a null pointer, the access and modification times of the file are set to the current time. The effective user ID of the process must be the same as the owner of the file, or must have write access to the file or appropriate privileges to use this call in this manner. Upon completion, *utimes*( ) will mark the time of the last file status change, *st_ctime*, for update.

RETURN VALUE

Upon successful completion, 0 is returned. Otherwise, −1 is returned and *errno* is set to indicate the error, and the file times will not be affected.

ERRORS

The *utimes*( ) function will fail if:

[EACCES]   Search permission is denied by a component of the path prefix; or the *times* argument is a null pointer and the effective user ID of the process does not match the owner of the file and write access is denied.

[ELOOP]   Too many symbolic links were encountered in resolving *path*.

[ENAMETOOLONG]

The length of the *path* argument exceeds {PATH_MAX} or a pathname component is longer than {NAME_MAX}.

[ENOENT]   A component of *path* does not name an existing file or *path* is an empty string.

[ENOTDIR]   A component of the path prefix is not a directory.

[EPERM]   The *times* argument is not a null pointer and the calling process' effective user ID has write access to the file but does not match the owner of the file and the calling process does not have the appropriate privileges.

[EROFS]   The file system containing the file is read-only.

The *utimes*( ) function may fail if:

[ENAMETOOLONG]

Pathname resolution of a symbolic link produced an intermediate result whose length exceeds {PATH_MAX}.

SEE ALSO

<sys/time.h>.

EXAMPLE

```
/*
 * Copyright (C) ANTRIX Inc.
```

```
 */

/* utimes.c
 * This program sets the file access and modification times
 * using function utimes.
 */

#include <stdio.h>
#include <stdlib.h>
#include <fcntl.h>
#include <unistd.h>
#include <sys/stat.h>
#include <sys/types.h>
#include <time.h>
#include <errno.h>

#define PERM_ALL    (S_IRWXU | S_IRWXG | S_IRWXO)

main()
{
  int   utimes_value;
  int   fildes;
  char *filename = "testfile";

  fprintf (stdout,"create testfile\n");
  fildes = creat (filename, PERM_ALL);

  fprintf (stdout,"set access and modification times to current\n");
  utimes_value = utimes (filename, (struct utimbuf *)0);
  if ( utimes_value == 0 )
     fprintf (stdout,"utimes() call successful\n");
  else {
     fprintf (stderr,"ERROR: utimes() call failed\n");
     fprintf (stderr,"ERROR: %s\n", strerror(errno));
  }

  fprintf (stdout,"close and remove testfile\n");
  close (fildes);
  remove (filename);
}
```

NAME

valloc — page-aligned memory allocator (**TO BE WITHDRAWN**)

SYNOPSIS

UX   `#include <stdlib.h>`

`void *valloc(size_t size);`

DESCRIPTION

The *valloc*( ) function has the same effect as *malloc*( ), except that the allocated memory will be aligned to a multiple of the value returned by *sysconf*(_SC_PAGESIZE).

RETURN VALUE

Upon successful completion, *valloc*( ) returns a pointer to the allocated memory. Otherwise, *valloc*( ) returns a null pointer and sets *errno* to indicate the error.

If *size* is 0, the behaviour is implementation-dependent; the value returned will be either a null pointer or a unique pointer. When *size* is 0 and *valloc*( ) returns a null pointer, *errno* is not modified.

ERRORS

The *valloc*( ) function will fail if:

[ENOMEM]   Storage space available is insufficient.

APPLICATION USAGE

Applications should avoid using *valloc*( ) but should use *malloc*( ) or *mmap*( ) instead. On systems with a large page size, the number of successful *valloc*( ) operations may be zero.

SEE ALSO

malloc( ), *sysconf*( ), **<stdlib.h>**.

EXAMPLE

```
/*
 * Copyright (C) ANTRIX Inc.
 */

/* valloc.c
 * This program allocates unused space for an object of size
 * byte using function valloc.
 */

#include <stdio.h>
#include <stdlib.h>
#include <malloc.h>
#include <errno.h>

main()
{
  char    *buf;
  char    *string = "hello world";
  size_t  size;

  size = strlen (string);

  fprintf (stdout,"allocate memory\n");
  buf = (char *)valloc (size);
```

```
        strcpy (buf, string);
        if ( buf != (char *)0 ) {
            fprintf (stdout,"valloc() call successful\n");
            fprintf (stdout,"allocated string=%s\n", buf );
        }
        else
            fprintf (stderr,"ERROR: valloc() call failed\n");

        fprintf (stdout,"free memory\n");
        free (buf);
    }
```

NAME

vfork — create new process; share virtual memory

SYNOPSIS

UX
```
#include <unistd.h>

pid_t vfork(void);
```

DESCRIPTION

The *vfork( )* function has the same effect as *fork( )*, except that the behaviour is undefined if the process created by *vfork( )* either modifies any data other than a variable of type **pid_t** used to store the return value from *vfork( )*, or returns from the function in which *vfork( )* was called, or calls any other function before successfully calling *_exit( )* or one of the *exec* family of functions.

RETURN VALUE

Upon successful completion, *vfork( )* returns 0 to the child process and returns the process ID of the child process to the parent process. Otherwise, −1 is returned to the parent, no child process is created, and *errno* is set to indicate the error.

ERRORS

The *vfork( )* function will fail if:

[EAGAIN]   The system-wide limit on the total number of processes under execution would be exceeded, or the system-imposed limit on the total number of processes under execution by a single user would be exceeded.

[ENOMEM]   There is insufficient swap space for the new process.

APPLICATION USAGE

On some systems, *vfork( )* is the same as *fork( )*.

The *vfork( )* function differs from *fork( )* only in that the child process can share code and data with the calling process (parent process). This speeds cloning activity significantly at a risk to the integrity of the parent process if *vfork( )* is misused.

The use of *vfork( )* for any purpose except as a prelude to an immediate call to a function from the *exec* family, or to *_exit( )*, is not advised.

The *vfork( )* function can be used to create new processes without fully copying the address space of the old process. If a forked process is simply going to call *exec*, the data space copied from the parent to the child by *fork( )* is not used. This is particularly inefficient in a paged environment, making *vfork( )* particularly useful. Depending upon the size of the parent's data space, *vfork( )* can give a significant performance improvement over *fork( )*.

The *vfork( )* function can normally be used just like *fork( )*. It does not work, however, to return while running in the child's context from the caller of *vfork( )* since the eventual return from *vfork( )* would then return to a no longer existent stack frame. Be careful, also, to call *_exit( )* rather than *exit( )* if you cannot *exec*, since *exit( )* flushes and closes standard I/O channels, thereby damaging the parent process' standard I/O data structures. (Even with *fork( )*, it is wrong to call *exit( )*, since buffered data would then be flushed twice.)

If signal handlers are invoked in the child process after *vfork( )*, they must follow the same rules as other code in the child process.

The [*vfork*, *exec*] window begins at the *vfork( )* call and ends when the child completes its *exec* call.

vfork( )

SEE ALSO

> *exec*, *exit*( ), *fork*( ), *wait*( ), **<unistd.h>**.

EXAMPLE

```
/*
 * Copyright (C) ANTRIX Inc.
 */

/* vfork.c
 * This program creates a new process which is an exact copy
 * of the calling process in a virtual memory efficient way
 * using function vfork.
 */

#include <stdio.h>
#include <stdlib.h>
#include <unistd.h>
#include <sys/types.h>
#include <sys/wait.h>
#include <errno.h>

main()
{
  int  vfork_value;
  int  stat_loc;

  fprintf (stdout,"vfork a child and parent, wait for child to exit\n");
  fprintf (stdout,"parent process-id=%d\n", getpid() );

  vfork_value = vfork ();
  if ( vfork_value == 0 ) {
    fprintf (stdout,"child process-id=%d\n", getpid() );
    sleep(5);
    exit (10);
  } wait(&stat_loc);

  fprintf (stdout,"should be same as exit() argument 10\n");
  fprintf (stdout,"WEXITSTATUS(stat_loc)=%d\n", WEXITSTATUS(stat_loc) );
}
```

NAME

vfprintf, vprintf, vsprintf — format output of a stdarg argument list

SYNOPSIS

```
#include <stdarg.h>
#include <stdio.h>

int vprintf(const char *format, va_list ap);

int vfprintf(FILE *stream, const char *format, va_list ap);

int vsprintf(char *s, const char *format, va_list ap);
```

DESCRIPTION

The *vprintf( )*, *vfprintf( )* and *vsprintf( )* functions are the same as *printf( )*, *fprintf( )* and *sprintf( )* respectively, except that instead of being called with a variable number of arguments, they are called with an argument list as defined by **<stdarg.h>**.

These functions do not invoke the *va_end* macro. As these functions invoke the *va_arg* macro, the value of *ap* after the return is indeterminate.

APPLICATION USAGE

Applications using these functions should call *va_end*(*ap*) afterwards to clean up.

RETURN VALUE

Refer to *printf( )*.

ERRORS

Refer to *printf( )*.

SEE ALSO

printf( ), **<stdarg.h>**, **<stdio.h>**.

EXAMPLE

```
/*
 * Copyright (C) ANTRIX Inc.
 */

/* vprintf.c
 * This program formats output of a stdarg argument list
 * using function vprintf.
 */

#include <varargs.h>
#include <stdio.h>
#include <stdlib.h>
#include <errno.h>

#define STYLE 0

#if STYLE1

do_vprintf1(values, format)
char *values;
char *format;
{
    va_list ap;
```

```
    va_start (ap, format);
    fprintf (stdout,"printing %s:\n", values);
    va_arg (ap, char *);
    vprintf (format, ap);
    va_end (ap);
}

#else

do_vprintf2(va_alist)
va_dcl
{
  char *format;
  va_list ap;

  va_start(ap);
  fprintf (stdout,"printing values\n");
  format = va_arg(ap, char*);
  vprintf(format,ap);
  va_end(ap);
}

#endif

main()
{
  int   i = 1;
  float f = 1.2345;
  char  c = 'a';
  char  *s = "hello world";
  char  *formats = "i=%d, f=%f, c=%c, s=%s\n";

#if STYLE
  do_vprintf1("all values", formats, i, f, c, s);
#else
  do_vprintf2(formats, i, f, c, s);
#endif
}

/*
 * Copyright (C) ANTRIX Inc.
 */

/* vfprintf.c
 * This program formats output of a stdarg argument list
 * using function vfprintf.
 */

#include <varargs.h>
#include <stdio.h>
#include <stdlib.h>
#include <errno.h>
```

```
#define STYLE 0

#if STYLE

do_vfprintf1(values, format)
char *values;
char *format;
{
  va_list ap;

  va_start (ap, format);
  fprintf (stdout, "printing %s:\n", values);
  va_arg (ap, char *);
  vfprintf (stdout, format, ap);
  va_end (ap);
}

#else

do_vfprintf2(va_alist)
va_dcl
{
  char *format;
  FILE *fp;
  va_list ap;

  va_start(ap);
  fprintf (stdout,"printing values\n");
  format = va_arg(ap, char*);
  fp = va_arg(ap, FILE*);
  vfprintf(fp, format,ap);
  va_end(ap);
}

#endif

main()
{
  int    i = 1;
  float  f = 1.2345;
  char   c = 'a';
  char   *s = "hello world";
  char   *formats = "i=%d, f=%f, c=%c, s=%s\n";

#if STYLE
  do_vfprintf1("all values", formats, i, f, c, s);
#else
  do_vfprintf2(stdout, formats, i, f, c, s);
#endif
}

/*
```

```
 * Copyright (C) ANTRIX Inc.
 */

/* vsprintf.c
 * This program formats output of a stdarg argument list
 * using function vsprintf.
 */

#include <varargs.h>
#include <stdio.h>
#include <stdlib.h>
#include <errno.h>

#define STYLE 0

#if STYLE

do_vsprintf1(values, format)
char *values;
char *format;
{
  va_list ap;
  char   result[255];

  va_start (ap, format);
  fprintf (stdout, "printing %s:\n", values);
  va_arg (ap, char *);
  vsprintf (result, format, ap);
  va_end (ap);
  fprintf (stdout,"result=%s\n", result);
}

#else

do_vsprintf2(va_alist)
va_dcl
{
  char *format;
  char *buffer;
  va_list ap;

  va_start(ap);
  fprintf (stdout,"printing values\n");
  format = va_arg(ap, char*);
  buffer = va_arg(ap, char*);
  vsprintf(buffer, format,ap);
  va_end(ap);
}

#endif

main()
```

```
{
  int   i = 1;
  float f = 1.2345;
  char  c = 'a';
  char  *s = "hello world";
  char  *formats = "i=%d, f=%f, c=%c, s=%s\n";

#if STYLE
  do_vsprintf1("all values", formats, i, f, c, s);
#else
  do_vsprintf2(formats, i, f, c, s);
#endif
}
```

NAME

wait, waitpid — wait for child process to stop or terminate

SYNOPSIS

OH
```
#include <sys/types.h>
#include <sys/wait.h>

pid_t wait(int *stat_loc);

pid_t waitpid(pid_t pid, int *stat_loc, int options);
```

DESCRIPTION

The *wait*( ) and *waitpid*( ) functions allow the calling process to obtain status information pertaining to one of its child processes. Various options permit status information to be obtained for child processes that have terminated or stopped. If status information is available for two or more child processes, the order in which their status is reported is unspecified.

The *wait*( ) function will suspend execution of the calling process until status information for one of its terminated child processes is available, or until delivery of a signal whose action is either to execute a signal-catching function or to terminate the process. If status information is available prior to the call to *wait*( ), return will be immediate.

The *waitpid*( ) function will behave identically to *wait*( ), if the *pid* argument is (**pid_t**)–1 and the *options* argument is 0. Otherwise, its behaviour will be modified by the values of the *pid* and *options* arguments.

The *pid* argument specifies a set of child processes for which status is requested. The *waitpid*( ) function will only return the status of a child process from this set:

- If *pid* is equal to (**pid_t**)–1, status is requested for any child process. In this respect, *waitpid*( ) is then equivalent to *wait*( ).

- If *pid* is greater than 0, it specifies the process ID of a single child process for which status is requested.

- If *pid* is 0, status is requested for any child process whose process group ID is equal to that of the calling process.

- If *pid* is less than (**pid_t**)–1, status is requested for any child process whose process group ID is equal to the absolute value of *pid*.

The *options* argument is constructed from the bitwise-inclusive OR of zero or more of the following flags, defined in the header **<sys/wait.h>**.

UX
WCONTINUED The *waitpid*( ) function will report the status of any continued child process specified by *pid* whose status has not been reported since it continued from a job control stop.

WNOHANG The *waitpid*( ) function will not suspend execution of the calling process if status is not immediately available for one of the child processes specified by *pid*.

WUNTRACED The status of any child processes specified by *pid* that are stopped, and whose status has not yet been reported since they stopped, will also be reported to the requesting process.

UX
If the calling process has SA_NOCLDWAIT set or has SIGCHLD set to SIG_IGN, and the process has no unwaited for children that were transformed into zombie processes, it will block until all of its children terminate, and *wait*( ) and *waitpid*( ) will fail and set *errno* to [ECHILD].

If *wait*( ) or *waitpid*( ) return because the status of a child process is available, these functions will return a value equal to the process ID of the child process. In this case, if the value of the argument *stat_loc* is not a null pointer, information will be stored in the location pointed to by *stat_loc*. If and only if the status returned is from a terminated child process that returned 0 from *main*( ) or passed 0 as the *status* argument to *_exit*( ) or *exit*( ), the value stored at the location pointed to by *stat_loc* will be 0. Regardless of its value, this information may be interpreted using the following macros, which are defined in **<sys/wait.h>** and evaluate to integral expressions; the *stat_val* argument is the integer value pointed to by *stat_loc*.

WIFEXITED(*stat_val*) Evaluates to a non-zero value if status was returned for a child process that terminated normally.

WEXITSTATUS(*stat_val*) If the value of WIFEXITED(*stat_val*) is non-zero, this macro evaluates to the low-order 8 bits of the *status* argument that the child process passed to *_exit*( ) or *exit*( ), or the value the child process returned from *main*( ).

WIFSIGNALED(*stat_val*) Evaluates to non-zero value if status was returned for a child process that terminated due to the receipt of a signal that was not caught (see **<signal.h>**).

WTERMSIG(*stat_val*) If the value of WIFSIGNALED(*stat_val*) is non-zero, this macro evaluates to the number of the signal that caused the termination of the child process.

WIFSTOPPED(*stat_val*) Evaluates to a non-zero value if status was returned for a child process that is currently stopped.

WSTOPSIG(*stat_val*) If the value of WIFSTOPPED(*stat_val*) is non-zero, this macro evaluates to the number of the signal that caused the child process to stop.

UX   WIFCONTINUED(*stat_val*)

Evaluates to a non-zero value if status was returned for a child process that has continued from a job control stop.

UX If the information pointed to by *stat_loc* was stored by a call to *waitpid*( ) that specified the WUNTRACED flag and did not specify the WCONTINUED flag, exactly one of the macros WIFEXITED(**stat_loc*), WIFSIGNALED(**stat_loc*), and WIFSTOPPED(**stat_loc*), will evaluate to a non-zero value.

UX If the information pointed to by *stat_loc* was stored by a call to *waitpid*( ) that specified the WUNTRACED and WCONTINUED flags, exactly one of the macros WIFEXITED(**stat_loc*),
UX WIFSIGNALED(**stat_loc*), WIFSTOPPED(**stat_loc*), and WIFCONTINUED(**stat_loc*), will evaluate to a non-zero value.

UX If the information pointed to by *stat_loc* was stored by a call to *waitpid*( ) that did not specify the WUNTRACED or WCONTINUED flags, or by a call to the *wait*() function, exactly one of the macros WIFEXITED(**stat_loc*) and WIFSIGNALED(**stat_loc*) will evaluate to a non-zero value.

UX If the information pointed to by *stat_loc* was stored by a call to *waitpid*( ) that did not specify the WUNTRACED flag and specified the WCONTINUED flag, or by a call to the *wait*() function,
UX exactly one of the macros WIFEXITED(**stat_loc*), WIFSIGNALED(**stat_loc*), and WIFCONTINUED(**stat_loc*), will evaluate to a non-zero value.

There may be additional implementation-dependent circumstances under which *wait*( ) or *waitpid*( ) report status. This will not occur unless the calling process or one of its child processes explicitly makes use of a non-standard extension. In these cases the interpretation of the reported status is implementation-dependent.

If a parent process terminates without waiting for all of its child processes to terminate, the remaining child processes will be assigned a new parent process ID corresponding to an implementation-dependent system process.

RETURN VALUE

If *wait*( ) or *waitpid*( ) returns because the status of a child process is available, these functions will return a value equal to the process ID of the child process for which status is reported. If *wait*( ) or *waitpid*( ) returns due to the delivery of a signal to the calling process, −1 will be returned and *errno* will be set to [EINTR]. If *waitpid*( ) was invoked with WNOHANG set in *options*, it has at least one child process specified by *pid* for which status is not available, and status is not available for any process specified by *pid*, 0 will be returned. Otherwise, (**pid_t**)−1 will be returned, and *errno* will be set to indicate the error.

ERRORS

The *wait*( ) function will fail if:

[ECHILD]   The calling process has no existing unwaited-for child processes.

[EINTR]   The function was interrupted by a signal. The value of the location pointed to by *stat_loc* is undefined.

The *waitpid*( ) function will fail if:

[ECHILD]   The process or process group specified by *pid* does not exist or is not a child of the calling process.

[EINTR]   The function was interrupted by a signal. The value of the location pointed to by *stat_loc* is undefined.

[EINVAL]   The *options* argument is not valid.

SEE ALSO

exec, *exit*( ), *fork*( ), *wait3*( ), *waitid*( ), **<sys/types.h>**, **<sys/wait.h>**.

EXAMPLE

```
/*
 * Copyright (C) ANTRIX Inc.
 */

/* wait.c
 * This program suspends execution of the calling process and
 * obtains status information pertaining to one of its child
 * process that have terminated or stopped using function wait.
 */

#include <stdio.h>
#include <stdlib.h>
#include <sys/types.h>
#include <sys/wait.h>
#include <errno.h>

main()
{
    int   wait_value;
    int   fork_value;
    int   stat_loc;
```

```
        fprintf (stdout,"fork a child and parent\n");
        fprintf (stdout,"wait for child to exit\n");

        fork_value = fork ();
        if ( fork_value == 0 ) {
           fprintf (stdout,"child process id=%d\n", getpid());
           exit (10);
        }
        wait_value = wait (&stat_loc);

        fprintf (stdout,"wait_value=%d\n", wait_value );
        fprintf (stdout,"should be same as exit() argument 10\n");
        fprintf (stdout,"WEXITSTATUS(stat_loc)=%d\n", WEXITSTATUS(stat_loc) );
}

/*
 * Copyright (C) ANTRIX Inc.
 */

/* waitpid.c
 * This program suspends execution of the calling process and
 * obtains status information pertaining to one of its child
 * process that have terminated or stopped using function waitpid.
 */


#include <stdio.h>
#include <stdlib.h>
#include <sys/types.h>
#include <sys/wait.h>
#include <errno.h>

main()
{
  pid_t   waitpid_value;
  int     fork_value;
  int     stat_loc;

  fprintf (stdout,"fork a child and parent\n");
  fprintf (stdout,"wait for child to exit\n");
  fork_value = fork ();
  if ( fork_value == 0 ) {
     fprintf (stdout,"child process id=%d\n", getpid());
     exit (10);
  }
  waitpid_value = waitpid (fork_value, &stat_loc, WUNTRACED);
  fprintf (stdout,"should be same as exit() argument 10\n");
  fprintf (stdout,"waitpid_value=%d\n", waitpid_value );
  fprintf (stdout,"WEXITSTATUS(stat_loc)=%d\n", WEXITSTATUS(stat_loc) );
}
```

NAME

wait3 — wait for child process to change state

SYNOPSIS

UX   `#include <sys/wait.h>`

`pid_t wait3 (int *stat_loc, int options, struct rusage *resource_usage);`

DESCRIPTION

The *wait3*( ) function allows the calling process to obtain status information for specified child processes.

The following call:

```
wait3(stat_loc, options, resource_usage);
```

is equivalent to the call:

```
waitpid((pid_t)-1, stat_loc, options);
```

except that on successful completion, if the *resource_usage* argument to *wait3*( ) is not a null pointer, the rusage structure that the third argument points to is filled in for the child process identified by the return value.

RETURN VALUE

See *waitpid*( ).

ERRORS

In addition to the error conditions specified on *waitpid*( ), under the following conditions, *wait3*( ) may fail and set *errno* to:

[ECHILD]   The calling process has no existing unwaited-for child processes, or if the set of processes specified by the argument *pid* can never be in the states specified by the argument *options*.

SEE ALSO

exec, *exit*( ), *fork*( ), *pause*( ), **<sys/wait.h>**.

EXAMPLE

```
/*
 * Copyright (C) ANTRIX Inc.
 */

/* wait3.c
 * This program suspends execution of the calling process and
 * obtains status information pertaining to one of its child
 * process that have terminated or stopped using function wait3.
 */


#include <stdio.h>
#include <stdlib.h>
#include <sys/types.h>
#include <sys/wait.h>
#include <time.h>
#include <sys/time.h>
#include <sys/resource.h>
#include <errno.h>
```

```
main()
{
  pid_t  wait3_value;
  int    fork_value;
  int    stat_loc;
  struct rusage res;

  fprintf (stdout,"fork a child and parent\n");
  fprintf (stdout,"wait for child to exit\n");
  fork_value = fork ();
  if ( fork_value == 0 ) {
      fprintf (stdout,"child process id=%d\n", getpid());
      exit (10);
  }
  wait3_value = wait3 (&stat_loc, WUNTRACED, &res);
  fprintf (stdout,"should be same as exit() argument 10\n");
  fprintf (stdout,"wait3_value=%d\n", wait3_value );
  fprintf (stdout,"WEXITSTATUS(stat_loc)=%d\n", WEXITSTATUS(stat_loc) );
}
```

NAME

waitid — wait for child process to change state

SYNOPSIS

UX

```
#include <sys/wait.h>

int waitid(idtype_t idtype, id_t id, siginfo_t *infop, int options);
```

DESCRIPTION

The *waitid*( ) function suspends the calling process until one of its children changes state. It records the current state of a child in the structure pointed to by *infop*. If a child process changed state prior to the call to *waitid*( ), *waitid*( ) returns immediately.

The *idtype* and *id* arguments are used to specify which children *waitid*( ) will wait for.

If *idtype* is P_PID, *waitid*( ) will wait for the child with a process ID equal to (**pid_t**)*pid*.

If *idtype* is P_PGID, *waitid*( ) will wait for any child with a process group ID equal to (**pid_t**)*pid*.

If *idtype* is P_ALL, *waitid*( ) will wait for any children and *id* is ignored.

The *options* argument is used to specify which state changes *waitid*( ) will wait for. It is formed by OR-ing together one or more of the following flags:

WEXITED   Wait for processes that have exited.

WSTOPPED   Status will be returned for any child that has stopped upon receipt of a signal.

WCONTINUED   Status will be returned for any child that was stopped and has been continued.

WNOHANG   Return immediately if there are no children to wait for.

WNOWAIT   Keep the process whose status is returned in *infop* in a waitable state. This will not affect the state of the process; the process may be waited for again after this call completes.

The *infop* argument must point to a **siginfo_t** structure. If *waitid*( ) returns because a child process was found that satisfied the conditions indicated by the arguments *idtype* and *options*, then the structure pointed to by *infop* will be filled in by the system with the status of the process. The **si_signo** member will always be equal to SIGCHLD.

RETURN VALUE

If *waitid*( ) returns due to the change of state of one of its children, 0 is returned. Otherwise, –1 is returned and *errno* is set to indicate the error.

ERRORS

The *waitid*( ) function will fail if:

[ECHILD]   The calling process has no existing unwaited-for child processes.

[EINTR]   The *waitid*( ) function was interrupted due to the receipt of a signal by the calling process.

[EINVAL]   An invalid value was specified for *options*, or *idtype* and *id* specify an invalid set of processes.

SEE ALSO

    exec, *exit*( ), *wait*( ), **<sys/wait.h>**.

EXAMPLE

```
/*
 * Copyright (C) ANTRIX Inc.
 */

/* waitid.c
 * This program waits for child process to change state
 * using function waitid
 */

#include <stdio.h>
#include <stdlib.h>
#include <sys/types.h>
#include <wait.h>
#include <errno.h>

main()
{
   int       waitid_value;
   int       pid;
   siginfo_t infop;

   fprintf (stdout,"fork a child and parent\n");
   fprintf (stdout,"wait for child to exit\n");
   pid = fork ();
   if ( pid == 0 ) {
      fprintf (stdout,"child process id=%d\n", getpid());
      exit (10);
   }
   waitid_value = waitid(P_PID, pid, &infop, WEXITED);

   if ( waitid_value == 0 ) {
      fprintf (stdout,"waitid() call successful\n");
      fprintf (stdout,"infop.si_signo=%d\n", infop.si_signo);
      fprintf (stdout,"infop.si_status=%d\n", infop.si_status);
      fprintf (stdout,"infop.si_pid=%d\n", infop.si_pid);
   }
   else {
      fprintf (stderr,"ERROR: waitid() call failed\n");
      fprintf (stderr,"ERROR: %s\n", strerror(errno));
   }
}
```

NAME

waitpid — wait for child process to stop or terminate

SYNOPSIS

OH
```
#include <sys/types.h>
#include <sys/wait.h>

pid_t waitpid(pid_t pid, int *stat_loc, int options);
```

DESCRIPTION

Refer to *wait*( ).

EXAMPLE

```c
/*
 * Copyright (C) ANTRIX Inc.
 */

/* waitpid.c
 * This program suspends execution of the calling process and
 * obtains status information pertaining to one of its child
 * process that have terminated or stopped using function waitpid.
 */

#include <stdio.h>
#include <stdlib.h>
#include <sys/types.h>
#include <sys/wait.h>
#include <errno.h>

main()
{
  pid_t   waitpid_value;
  int     fork_value;
  int     stat_loc;

  fprintf (stdout,"fork a child and parent\n");
  fprintf (stdout,"wait for child to exit\n");
  fork_value = fork ();
  if ( fork_value == 0 ) {
     fprintf (stdout,"child process id=%d\n", getpid());
     exit (10);
  }
  waitpid_value = waitpid (fork_value, &stat_loc, WUNTRACED);
  fprintf (stdout,"should be same as exit() argument 10\n");
  fprintf (stdout,"waitpid_value=%d\n", waitpid_value );
  fprintf (stdout,"WEXITSTATUS(stat_loc)=%d\n", WEXITSTATUS(stat_loc));
}
```

NAME

wcscat — concatenate two wide character strings

SYNOPSIS

WP   `#include <wchar.h>`

`wchar_t *wcscat(wchar_t *ws1, const wchar_t *ws2);`

DESCRIPTION

The *wcscat*( ) function appends a copy of the wide character string pointed to by *ws2* (including the terminating null wide-character code) to the end of the wide character string pointed to by *ws1*. The initial wide-character code of *ws2* overwrites the null wide-character code at the end of *ws1*. If copying takes place between objects that overlap, the behaviour is undefined.

RETURN VALUE

The *wcscat*( ) function returns *s1*; no return value is reserved to indicate an error.

ERRORS

No errors are defined.

SEE ALSO

wcsncat( ), **<wchar.h>**.

EXAMPLE

```
/*
 * Copyright (C) ANTRIX Inc.
 */

/* wcscat.c
 * This program appends a copy of the wide character string
 * pointed to by ws2 using function wcscat.
 */

#include <stdio.h>
#include <stdlib.h>
#include <wchar.h>
#include <errno.h>

main()
{
  wchar_t  *wcscat_value;
  wchar_t  ws1[12];
  wchar_t  ws2[] = L"world";

  wcscpy (ws1, L"hello ");

  fprintf (stdout,"concatenate strings\n");
  wcscat_value = wcscat (ws1, ws2);
  if ( wcscat_value != (wchar_t *)0 ) {
     fprintf (stdout,"wcscat() call successful\n");
     fprintf (stdout,"ws1=%ws\n", ws1);
     fprintf (stdout,"wcscat_value=%ws\n", wcscat_value);
  }
  else
```

```
        fprintf (stderr,"ERROR: wcscat() call failed\n");
    }
```

NAME

wcschr — wide character string scanning operation

SYNOPSIS

WP   `#include <wchar.h>`

`wchar_t *wcschr(const wchar_t *ws, wchar_t wc);`

DESCRIPTION

The *wcschr*( ) function locates the first occurrence of *wc* in the wide character string pointed to by *ws*. The value of *wc* must be a character representable as a type **wchar_t** and must be a wide-character code corresponding to a valid character in the current locale. The terminating null wide-character code is considered to be part of the wide character string.

RETURN VALUE

Upon completion, *wcschr*( ) returns a pointer to the wide-character code, or a null pointer if the wide-character code is not found.

ERRORS

No errors are defined.

SEE ALSO

wcsrchr( ), **<wchar.h>**.

EXAMPLE

```
/*
 * Copyright (C) ANTRIX Inc.
 */

/* wcschr.c
 * This program locates the first occurrence of wc in the wide
 * character string pointed to by ws using function wcschr.
 */

#include <stdio.h>
#include <stdlib.h>
#include <wchar.h>
#include <errno.h>

main()
{
  wchar_t   *wcschr_value;
  wchar_t   *ws = L"one two three";
  wint_t     wc = L't';

  fprintf (stdout,"return pointer to first occurrence of t\n");
  wcschr_value = wcschr(ws, wc);
  if ( wcschr_value != (wchar_t *)0 ) {
      fprintf (stdout,"wcschr() call successful\n");
      fprintf (stdout,"wcschr_value=%ws\n", wcschr_value);
  }
  else
      fprintf (stderr,"ERROR: wcschr() call failed\n");
}
```

NAME

wcscmp — compare two wide character strings

SYNOPSIS

WP
```
#include <wchar.h>
```

```
int wcscmp(const wchar_t *ws1, const wchar_t *ws2);
```

DESCRIPTION

The *wcscmp*( ) function compares the wide character string pointed to by *ws1* to the wide character string pointed to by *ws2*.

The sign of a non-zero return value is determined by the sign of the difference between the values of the first pair of wide-character codes that differ in the objects being compared.

RETURN VALUE

Upon completion, *wcscmp*( ) returns an integer greater than, equal to or less than 0, if the wide character string pointed to by *ws1* is greater than, equal to or less than the wide character string pointed to by *ws2* respectively.

ERRORS

No errors are defined.

SEE ALSO

wcsncmp( ), **<wchar.h>**.

EXAMPLE

```
/*
 * Copyright (C) ANTRIX Inc.
 */

/* wcscmp.c
 * This program compares the wide character string pointed to
 * by ws1 to wide character string pointed to by ws2 using
 * function wcscmp.
 */

#include <stdio.h>
#include <stdlib.h>
#include <wchar.h>
#include <errno.h>

main()
{
    int     wcscmp_value;
    wchar_t ws1[] = L"hello world";
    wchar_t ws2[] = L"hello world";

    fprintf (stdout,"compare wide character strings\n");
    wcscmp_value = wcscmp(ws1, ws2);
    if ( wcscmp_value == 0 )
        fprintf (stdout,"wcscmp() call successful\n");
    else
        fprintf (stderr,"ERROR: wcscmp() call failed\n");
}
```

NAME

wcscoll — wide character string comparison using collating information

SYNOPSIS

EI WP
```
#include <wchar.h>

int wcscoll(const wchar_t *ws1, const wchar_t *ws2);
```

DESCRIPTION

The *wcscoll*( ) function compares the wide character string pointed to by *ws1* to the wide character string pointed to by *ws2*, both interpreted as appropriate to the LC_COLLATE category of the current locale.

RETURN VALUE

Upon successful completion, *wcscoll*( ) returns an integer greater than, equal to or less than 0, according to whether the wide character string pointed to by *ws1* is greater than, equal to or less than the wide character string pointed to by *ws2*, when both are interpreted as appropriate to the current locale. On error, *wcscoll*( ) may set *errno*, but no return value is reserved to indicate an error.

ERRORS

The *wcscoll*( ) function may fail if:

[EINVAL]   The *ws1* or *ws2* arguments contain wide character codes outside the domain of the collating sequence.

[ENOSYS]   The function is not supported.

APPLICATION USAGE

Because no return value is reserved to indicate an error, an application wishing to check for error situations should set *errno* to 0, then call *wcscoll*( ), then check *errno* and if it is non-zero, assume an error has occurred.

The *wcsxfrm*( ) and *wcscmp*( ) functions should be used for sorting large lists.

SEE ALSO

wcscmp( ), *wcsxfrm*( ), **<wchar.h>**.

EXAMPLE

```
/*
 * Copyright (C) ANTRIX Inc.
 */

/* wcscoll.c
 * This program compares the wide character string pointed to by ws1
 * to the wide character string pointed to by ws2, both interpreted
 * as appropriate to the LC_COLLATE category of the current locale
 * using function wcscoll.
 */

#include <stdio.h>
#include <stdlib.h>
#include <string.h>
#include <wchar.h>
#include <locale.h>
#include <errno.h>

main()
```

```
{
  wint_t      wcscoll_value;
  wchar_t     ws1[] = L"AAA";
  wchar_t     ws2[] = L"aaa";

  /* setting LC_ALL includes LC_COLLATE */
  setlocale (LC_ALL, "C");

  fprintf (stdout,"compare two strings\n");
  wcscoll_value = wcscoll (ws1, ws2);
  if ( wcscoll_value < 0 ) {
     fprintf (stdout,"wcscoll() call successful\n");
     fprintf (stdout,"wcscoll_value=%d\n", wcscoll_value);
  }
  else
     fprintf (stderr,"ERROR: wcscoll() call failed\n");
}
```

NAME

wcscpy — copy a wide character string

SYNOPSIS

WP   `#include <wchar.h>`

`wchar_t *wcscpy(wchar_t *ws1, const wchar_t *ws2);`

DESCRIPTION

The *wcscpy*( ) function copies the wide character string pointed to by *ws2* (including the terminating null wide-character code) into the array pointed to by *ws1*. If copying takes place between objects that overlap, the behaviour is undefined.

RETURN VALUE

The *wcscpy*( ) function returns *ws1*; no return value is reserved to indicate an error.

ERRORS

No errors are defined.

APPLICATION USAGE

Wide character code movement is performed differently in different implementations. Thus overlapping moves may yield surprises.

SEE ALSO

wcsncpy( ), **<wchar.h>**.

EXAMPLE

```
/*
 * Copyright (C) ANTRIX Inc.
 */

/* wcscpy.c
 * This program copies a wide character string pointed to by
 * ws2 into the array pointed to by ws1 using function wcscpy.
 */

#include <stdio.h>
#include <stdlib.h>
#include <wchar.h>
#include <errno.h>

main()
{
  wchar_t  *wcscpy_value;
  wchar_t  ws1[12];
  wchar_t  ws2[] = L"hello world";

  memset (ws1, ' ', 12);

  fprintf (stdout,"copy wide character string in buffer\n");
  wcscpy_value = wcscpy (ws1, ws2);
  if ( wcscpy_value != (wchar_t *)0 ) {
      fprintf (stdout,"wcscpy() call successful\n");
      fprintf (stdout,"wcscpy_value=%ws\n", wcscpy_value );
      fprintf (stdout,"wide string ws1=%ws\n", ws1);
  }
```

```
    else
       fprintf (stderr,"ERROR: wcscpy() failed\n");
}
```

NAME

wcscspn — get length of complementary wide substring

SYNOPSIS

WP   `#include <wchar.h>`

`size_t wcscspn(const wchar_t *ws1, const wchar_t *ws2);`

DESCRIPTION

The *wcscspn*( ) function computes the length of the maximum initial segment of the wide character string pointed to by *ws1* which consists entirely of wide-character codes *not* from the wide character string pointed to by *ws2*.

RETURN VALUE

The *wcscspn*( ) function returns *ws1*; no return value is reserved to indicate an error.

ERRORS

No errors are defined.

SEE ALSO

wcsspn( ), **<wchar.h>**.

EXAMPLE

```
/*
 * Copyright (C) ANTRIX Inc.
 */

/* wcscspn.c
 * This program computes the length of the maximum initial segment
 * of the wide character string pointed to by ws1 using function
 * wcscspn.
 */

#include <stdio.h>
#include <stdlib.h>
#include <wchar.h>
#include <errno.h>

main()
{
  size_t    wcscspn_value;
  wchar_t   ws1[] = L"abcdefgh" ;
  wchar_t   ws2[] = L"ef";

  fprintf (stdout,"return the length of the initial segment\n");
  fprintf (stdout,"of first string not from string second string\n");
  wcscspn_value = wcscspn (ws1, ws2);
  if ( wcscspn_value != 0 ) {
      fprintf (stdout,"wcscspn() call successful\n");
      fprintf (stdout,"wcscspn_value=%d\n", wcscspn_value );
  }
  else
      fprintf (stderr,"ERROR: wcscspn() call failed\n");
}
```

NAME

wcsftime — convert date and time to wide character string

SYNOPSIS

EI WP   `#include <wchar.h>`

```
size_t wcsftime(wchar_t *wcs, size_t maxsize, const char *format,
                const struct tm *timptr);
```

DESCRIPTION

The *wcsftime*( ) function places wide-character codes into the array pointed to by *wcs* as controlled by the string pointed to by *format*.

This function behaves as if the character string generated by *strftime*( ) is passed to *mbstowcs*( ) as the character string argument, and *mbstowcs*( ) places the result in the wide character string argument of *wcsftime*( ) up to a limit of *maxsize* wide-character codes.

If copying takes place between objects that overlap, the behaviour is undefined.

RETURN VALUE

If the total number of resulting wide character codes including the terminating null wide-character code is no more than *maxsize*, *wcsftime*( ) returns the number of wide-character codes placed into the array pointed to by *wcs*, not including the terminating null wide-character code. Otherwise 0 is returned and the contents of the array are indeterminate. If the function is not implemented, *errno* will be set to indicate the error.

ERRORS

The *wcsftime*( ) function will fail if:

[ENOSYS]   The function is not implemented.

SEE ALSO

strftime( ), *mbstowcs*( ), **<wchar.h>**.

EXAMPLE

```
/*
 * Copyright (C) ANTRIX Inc.
 */

/* wcsftime.c
 * This program converts date and time to wide string using
 * function wcsftime.
 */

#include <stdio.h>
#include <stdlib.h>
#include <wchar.h>
#include <time.h>
#include <errno.h>

main()
{
    size_t  wcsftime_value;
    struct  tm *timeptr;
    struct  tm *gmtime();
    wchar_t wcs[256];
    time_t  curtime;
```

```
        fprintf (stdout,"print current date and time\n");
        curtime = time ((long *)0);
        timeptr = localtime (&curtime);
        wcsftime_value = wcsftime (wcs, sizeof(wcs),
                        "%a %b %m/%d/%y Time: %H:%M%p", timeptr);

        if ( wcsftime_value >= 0 ) {
            fprintf (stdout,"wcsftime() call successful\n");
            fprintf (stdout,"Date: %ws\n", wcs);
        }
        else {
            fprintf (stderr,"ERROR: wcsftime() call failed\n");
            fprintf (stderr,"ERROR: %s\n", strerror(errno));
        }
}
```

NAME

wcslen — get wide character string length

SYNOPSIS

WP   `#include <wchar.h>`

`size_t wcslen(const wchar_t *ws);`

DESCRIPTION

The *wcslen*( ) function computes the number of wide-character codes in the wide character string to which *ws* points, not including the terminating null wide-character code.

RETURN VALUE

The *wcslen*( ) function returns *ws*; no return value is reserved to indicate an error.

ERRORS

No errors are defined.

SEE ALSO

<wchar.h>.

EXAMPLE

```
/*
 * Copyright (C) ANTRIX Inc.
 */

/* wcslen.c
 * This program computes the number of wide-character codes
 * in the wide character string to which ws points.
 */

#include <stdio.h>
#include <stdlib.h>
#include <wchar.h>
#include <errno.h>

main()
{
    int     wcslen_value;
    wchar_t *ws = L"hello world";

    fprintf (stdout,"get the length of string\n");
    wcslen_value = wcslen (ws);
    if ( wcslen_value == 11 ) {
        fprintf (stdout,"wcslen() call successful\n");
        fprintf (stdout,"length of the %ws is %d\n", ws, wcslen_value);
    }
    else
        fprintf (stderr,"ERROR: wcslen() call failed\n");
}
```

NAME

wcsncat — concatenate part of two wide character strings

SYNOPSIS

WP
```
#include <wchar.h>
```

```
wchar_t *wcsncat(wchar_t *ws1, const wchar_t *ws2, size_t n);
```

DESCRIPTION

The *wcsncat*( ) function appends not more than *n* wide-character codes (a null wide-character code and wide character codes that follow it are not appended) from the array pointed to by *ws2* to the end of the wide character string pointed to by *ws1*. The initial wide-character code of *ws2* overwrites the null wide-character code at the end of *ws1*. A terminating null wide-character code is always appended to the result. If copying takes place between objects that overlap, the behaviour is undefined.

RETURN VALUE

The *wcsncat*( ) function returns *ws1*; no return value is reserved to indicate an error.

ERRORS

No errors are defined.

SEE ALSO

wcscat( ), **<wchar.h>**.

EXAMPLE

```
/*
 * Copyright (C) ANTRIX Inc.
 */

/* wcsncat.c
 * This program appends not more than n wide-character codes
 * from the array pointed to by ws2 to the end of the wide
 * character string pointed to by ws1 using function wcsncat.
 */

#include <stdio.h>
#include <stdlib.h>
#include <wchar.h>
#include <errno.h>

#define STRING   hello

main()
{
  wchar_t   *wcsncat_value;
  wchar_t    ws1[12];
  wchar_t   *ws2 = L"hello world";

  memset (ws1, ' ', 12);

  fprintf (stdout,"copy first 5 characters only\n");
  wcsncat_value = wcsncat((wchar_t *)ws1, ws2, 5);
  if ( wcsncat_value != (wchar_t *)0 ) {
      fprintf (stdout,"wcsncat() call successful\n");
      fprintf (stdout,"wcsncat_value=%ws\n", wcsncat_value);
```

```
    }
  else
     fprintf (stderr,"ERROR: wcsncat() call failed\n");
  }
```

NAME

wcsncmp — compare part of two wide character strings

SYNOPSIS

WP `#include <wchar.h>`

`int wcsncmp(const wchar_t *ws1, const wchar_t *ws2, size_t n);`

DESCRIPTION

The *wcsncmp*( ) function compares not more than *n* wide-character codes (wide-character codes that follow a null wide character code are not compared) from the array pointed to by *ws1* to the array pointed to by *ws2*.

The sign of a non-zero return value is determined by the sign of the difference between the values of the first pair of wide-character codes that differ in the objects being compared.

RETURN VALUE

Upon successful completion, *wcsncmp*( ) returns an integer greater than, equal to or less than 0, if the possibly null-terminated array pointed to by *ws1* is greater than, equal to or less than the possibly null-terminated array pointed to by *ws2* respectively.

ERRORS

No errors are defined.

SEE ALSO

wcscmp( ), **<wchar.h>**.

EXAMPLE

```
/*
 * Copyright (C) ANTRIX Inc.
 */

/* wcsncmp.c
 * This program compares n wide character codes from the array
 * pointed to by ws1 to the array pointed to by ws2 using
 * function wcsncmp.
 */

#include <stdio.h>
#include <stdlib.h>
#include <wchar.h>
#include <string.h>
#include <errno.h>


main()
{
    int         wcsncmp_value;
    size_t      n = 5;
    const wchar_t *ws1 = L"hello world";
    const wchar_t *ws2 = L"hello all";

    fprintf (stdout,"compare first 5 bytes\n");
    wcsncmp_value = wcsncmp (ws1, ws2, n);
    if ( wcsncmp_value == 0 )
        fprintf (stdout,"wcsncmp() call successful\n");
```

```
    else
       fprintf (stderr,"ERROR: wcsncmp() call failed\n");
}
```

NAME

wcsncpy — copy part of a wide character string

SYNOPSIS

WP
```
#include <wchar.h>

wchar_t *wcsncpy(wchar_t *ws1, const wchar_t *ws2, size_t n);
```

DESCRIPTION

The *wcsncpy*( ) function copies not more than *n* wide-character codes (wide-character codes that follow a null wide character code are not copied) from the array pointed to by *ws2* to the array pointed to by *ws1*. If copying takes place between objects that overlap, the behaviour is undefined.

If the array pointed to by *ws2* is a wide character string that is shorter than *n* wide-character codes, null wide-character codes are appended to the copy in the array pointed to by *ws1*, until *n* wide-character codes in all are written.

RETURN VALUE

The *wcsncpy*( ) function returns *ws1*; no return value is reserved to indicate an error.

ERRORS

No errors are defined.

APPLICATION USAGE

Wide character code movement is performed differently in different implementations. Thus overlapping moves may yield surprises.

If there is no null wide-character code in the first *n* wide-character codes of the array pointed to by *ws2*, the result will not be null-terminated.

SEE ALSO

wcscpy( ), **<wchar.h>**.

EXAMPLE

```
/*
 * Copyright (C) ANTRIX Inc.
 */

/* wcsncpy.c
 * This program copies not more than n wide-character codes
 * from the array pointed to by ws2 to the array pointed to
 * by array ws1 using function wcsncpy.
 */

#include <stdio.h>
#include <stdlib.h>
#include <wchar.h>
#include <errno.h>

main()
{
  wchar_t *wcsncpy_value;
  wchar_t  ws1[12] ;
  wchar_t *ws2 = L"hello world";

  memset (ws1, ' ', 12);
```

```
        fprintf (stdout,"copy first 5 bytes\n");
        wcsncpy_value = wcsncpy (ws1, ws2, 5);
        if ( wcsncpy_value != (wchar_t *)0 ) {
            fprintf (stdout,"wcsncpy() call successful\n");
            fprintf (stdout,"wcsncpy_value=%ws\n", wcsncpy_value);
            fprintf (stdout,"ws1=%ws\n", ws1);
        }
        else
            fprintf (stderr,"ERROR: wcsncpy() call failed\n");
    }
```

NAME

wcspbrk — scan wide character string for wide-character code

SYNOPSIS

WP   `#include <wchar.h>`

`wchar_t *wcspbrk(const wchar_t *ws1, const wchar_t *ws2);`

DESCRIPTION

The *wcspbrk*( ) function locates the first occurrence in the wide character string pointed to by *ws1* of any wide-character code from the wide character string pointed to by *ws2*.

RETURN VALUE

Upon successful completion, *wcspbrk*( ) returns a pointer to the wide-character code or a null pointer if no wide-character code from *ws2* occurs in *ws1*.

ERRORS

No errors are defined.

SEE ALSO

wcschr( ), *wcsrchr*( ), **<wchar.h>**.

EXAMPLE

```
/*
 * Copyright (C) ANTRIX Inc.
 */

/* wcspbrk.c
 * This program locates the first occurrence in the wide character
 * string pointed to by ws1 of any wide-character code from the
 * wide character string pointed to by ws2 using function wcspbrk.
 */

#include <stdio.h>
#include <stdlib.h>
#include <wchar.h>
#include <errno.h>

main()
{
  wchar_t   *wcspbrk_value;
  wchar_t   *ws1 = L"one two three" ;
  wchar_t   *ws2 = L"t" ;

  fprintf (stdout,"return pointer to first occurrence of string t\n");
  wcspbrk_value = wcspbrk (ws1, ws2);
  if ( wcspbrk_value != (wchar_t *)0 ) {
     fprintf (stdout,"wcspbrk() call successful\n");
     fprintf (stdout,"wcspbrk_value=%ws\n", wcspbrk_value);
  }
  else
     fprintf (stderr,"ERROR: wcspbrk() call failed\n");
}
```

NAME

wcsrchr — wide character string scanning operation

SYNOPSIS

WP
```
#include <wchar.h>
```

```
wchar_t *wcsrchr(const wchar_t *ws, wchar_t wc);
```

DESCRIPTION

The *wcsrchr*( ) function locates the last occurrence of *wc* in the wide character string pointed to by *ws*. The value of *wc* must be a character representable as a type **wchar_t** and must be a wide-character code corresponding to a valid character in the current locale. The terminating null wide-character code is considered to be part of the wide character string.

RETURN VALUE

Upon successful completion, *wcsrchr*( ) returns a pointer to the wide-character code or a null pointer if *wc* does not occur in the wide character string.

ERRORS

No errors are defined.

SEE ALSO

wcschr( ), **<wchar.h>**.

EXAMPLE

```
/*
 * Copyright (C) ANTRIX Inc.
 */

/* wcsrchr.c
 * This program locates the last occurrence of wc in the wide
 * character string pointed to by ws using function wcsrchr.
 */

#include <stdio.h>
#include <stdlib.h>
#include <wchar.h>
#include <errno.h>

main()
{
  wchar_t  *wcsrchr_value;
  wchar_t  *ws = L"one two three";
  wint_t   wc = L't';

  fprintf (stdout,"return to last occurrence of character t\n");
  wcsrchr_value = wcsrchr (ws, wc);
  if ( wcsrchr_value != (wchar_t *)0 ) {
      fprintf (stdout,"wcsrchr() call successful\n");
      fprintf (stdout,"wcsrchr_value=%ws\n", wcsrchr_value);
  }
  else
      fprintf (stderr,"ERROR: wcsrchr() call failed\n");
}
```

NAME

wcsspn — get length of wide substring

SYNOPSIS

WP `#include <wchar.h>`

`size_t wcsspn(const wchar_t *ws1, const wchar_t *ws2);`

DESCRIPTION

The *wcsspn*( ) function computes the length of the maximum initial segment of the wide character string pointed to by *ws1* which consists entirely of wide-character codes from the wide string pointed to by *ws2*.

RETURN VALUE

The *wcsspn*( ) function returns *ws1*; no return value is reserved to indicate an error.

ERRORS

No errors are defined.

SEE ALSO

wcscspn( ), **<wchar.h>**.

EXAMPLE

```
/*
 * Copyright (C) ANTRIX Inc.
 */

/* wcsspn.c
 * This program computes the length of the maximum initial segment
 * of the wide character string pointed to by ws1 which consists
 * entirely of wide-character codes from the wide string pointed
 * to by ws2 using function wcsspn.
 */

#include <stdio.h>
#include <stdlib.h>
#include <wchar.h>
#include <errno.h>

main()
{
  size_t   wcsspn_value;
  wchar_t  *ws1 = L"abcdefgh";
  wchar_t  *ws2 = L"abcxyz";

  fprintf (stdout,"length of initial segment of string ws1\n");
  fprintf (stdout,"consisting entirely of characters from string ws2\n");
  wcsspn_value = wcsspn (ws1, ws2);
  if ( wcsspn_value != 0 ) {
      fprintf (stdout,"wcsspn() call successful\n");
      fprintf (stdout,"wcsspn_value=%d\n", wcsspn_value );
  }
  else
      fprintf (stderr,"ERROR: wcsspn() call failed\n");
}
```

NAME

wcstod — convert wide character string to double-precision number

SYNOPSIS

WP

```
#include <wchar.h>
```

```
double wcstod(const wchar_t *nptr, wchar_t **endptr);
```

DESCRIPTION

The *wcstod*( ) function converts the initial portion of the wide character string pointed to by *nptr* to **double** representation. First it decomposes the input wide character string into three parts: an initial, possibly empty, sequence of white-space wide character codes (as specified by *iswspace*( )); a subject sequence interpreted as a floating-point constant; and a final wide-character string of one or more unrecognised wide-character codes, including the terminating null wide character code of the input wide character string. Then it attempts to convert the subject sequence to a floating-point number, and returns the result.

The expected form of the subject sequence is an optional + or − sign, then a non-empty sequence of digits optionally containing a radix, then an optional exponent part. An exponent part consists of e or E , followed by an optional sign, followed by one or more decimal digits. The subject sequence is defined as the longest initial subsequence of the input wide character string, starting with the first non-white-space wide-character code, that is of the expected form. The subject sequence contains no wide-character codes if the input wide character string is empty or consists entirely of white-space wide-character codes, or if the first wide-character code that is not white space other than a sign, a digit or a radix.

If the subject sequence has the expected form, the sequence of wide-character codes starting with the first digit or the radix (whichever occurs first) is interpreted as a floating constant as defined in the C language, except that the radix is used in place of a period, and that if neither an exponent part nor a radix appears, a radix is assumed to follow the last digit in the wide character string. If the subject sequence begins with a minus sign, the value resulting from the conversion is negated. A pointer to the final wide character string is stored in the object pointed to by *endptr*, provided that *endptr* is not a null pointer.

The radix is defined in the program's locale (category LC_NUMERIC). In the POSIX locale, or in a locale where the radix is not defined, the radix defaults to a period (.).

In other than the POSIX locale, other implementation-dependent subject sequence forms may be accepted.

If the subject sequence is empty or does not have the expected form, no conversion is performed; the value of *nptr* is stored in the object pointed to by *endptr,* provided that *endptr* is not a null pointer.

RETURN VALUE

The *wcstod*( ) function returns the converted value, if any. If no conversion could be performed,

EX

0 is returned and *errno* may be set to [EINVAL].

If the correct value is outside the range of representable values, ±HUGE_VAL is returned (according to the sign of the value), and *errno* is set to [ERANGE] .

If the correct value would cause underflow, 0 is returned and *errno* is set to [ERANGE] .

ERRORS

The *wcstod*( ) function will fail if:

[ERANGE]   The value to be returned would cause overflow or underflow.

The *wcstod*( ) function may fail if:

EX   [EINVAL]   No conversion could be performed.

APPLICATION USAGE

Because 0 is returned on error and is also a valid return on success, an application wishing to check for error situations should set *errno* to 0, then call *wcstod*( ), then check *errno* and if it is non-zero, assume an error has occurred.

SEE ALSO

iswspace( ), *localeconv*( ), *scanf*( ), *setlocale*( ), *wcstol*( ), **<wchar.h>**, the **XBD** specification, **Chapter 5**, **Locale**.

EXAMPLE

```
/*
 * Copyright (C) ANTRIX Inc.
 */

/* wcstod.c
 * This program converts the initial portion of the wide-character
 * string pointed to by nptr to double representation using function
 * wcstod.
 */

#include <stdio.h>
#include <stdlib.h>
#include <wchar.h>
#include <errno.h>

main()
{
    double    wcstod_value;
    wchar_t   *endptr;
    wchar_t   *nptr = L" -123E1";

    /* leading space and negative number */
    fprintf (stdout,"convert string to double precision number\n");
    wcstod_value = wcstod (nptr, &endptr);
    if ( wcstod_value != (double)0 ) {
        fprintf (stdout,"wcstod() call successful\n");
        fprintf (stdout,"wcstod_value=%f\n", wcstod_value);
        fprintf (stdout,"original pointer value %d\n", nptr);
        /* should be string address + 7 */
        fprintf (stdout,"final pointer value %d\n", endptr);
    }
    else
        fprintf (stderr,"ERROR: wcstod() call failed\n");
}
```

NAME

wcstok — split wide character string into tokens

SYNOPSIS

WP

```
#include <wchar.h>

wchar_t *wcstok(wchar_t *ws1, const wchar_t *ws2);
```

DESCRIPTION

A sequence of calls to *wcstok*( ) breaks the wide character string pointed to by *ws1* into a sequence of tokens, each of which is delimited by a wide-character code from the wide character string pointed to by *ws2*. The first call in the sequence has *ws1* as its first argument, and is followed by calls with a null pointer as their first argument. The separator string pointed to by *ws2* may be different from call to call.

The first call in the sequence searches the wide character string pointed to by *ws1* for the first wide-character code that is *not* contained in the current separator string pointed to by *ws2*. If no such wide-character code is found, then there are no tokens in the wide character string pointed to by *ws1* and *wcstok*( ) returns a null pointer. If such a wide-character code is found, it is the start of the first token.

The *wcstok*( ) function then searches from there for a wide-character code that *is* contained in the current separator string. If no such wide-character code is found, the current token extends to the end of the wide character string pointed to by *ws1*, and subsequent searches for a token will return a null pointer. If such a wide-character code is found, it is overwritten by a null wide character, which terminates the current token. The *wcstok*( ) function saves a pointer to the following wide-character code, from which the next search for a token will start.

Each subsequent call, with a null pointer as the value of the first argument, starts searching from the saved pointer and behaves as described above.

The implementation will behave as if no function calls *wcstok*( ).

RETURN VALUE

Upon successful completion, the *wcstok*( ) function returns a pointer to the first wide-character code of a token. Otherwise, if there is no token, *wcstok*( ) returns a null pointer.

ERRORS

No errors are defined.

SEE ALSO

<wchar.h>.

EXAMPLE

```
/*
 * Copyright (C) ANTRIX Inc.
 */

/* wcstok.c
 * This program breaks the wide character string pointed to by
 * ws1 into a sequence of tokens using function wcstok.
 */

#include <stdio.h>
#include <stdlib.h>
#include <wchar.h>
#include <errno.h>
```

```
main()
{
  wchar_t   *wcstok_value;
  wchar_t   ws1[] = L"abc-*def";
  wchar_t   ws2[] = L"$#&*-";

  fprintf (stdout,"return pointer to the first character of\n");
  fprintf (stdout,"the first token\n");
  wcstok_value = wcstok (ws1, ws2);
  if ( wcstok_value != (wchar_t *)0 ) {
      fprintf (stdout,"wcstok() call successful\n");
      fprintf (stdout,"wcstok_value=%ws\n", wcstok_value);
  }
  else
      fprintf (stderr,"ERROR: wcstok() call failed\n");
}
```

NAME

wcstol — convert wide character string to long integer

SYNOPSIS

WP
```
#include <wchar.h>
```

```
long int wcstol(const wchar_t *nptr, wchar_t **endptr, int base);
```

DESCRIPTION

The *wcstol*( ) function converts the initial portion of the wide character string pointed to by *nptr* to **long int** representation. First it decomposes the input wide character string into three parts: an initial, possibly empty, sequence of white-space wide-character codes (as specified by *iswspace*( )), a subject sequence interpreted as an integer represented in some radix determined by the value of *base*; and a final wide character string of one or more unrecognised wide character codes, including the terminating null wide-character code of the input wide character string. Then it attempts to convert the subject sequence to an integer, and returns the result.

If *base* is 0, the expected form of the subject sequence is that of a decimal constant, octal constant or hexadecimal constant, any of which may be preceded by a + or – sign. A decimal constant begins with a non-zero digit, and consists of a sequence of decimal digits. An octal constant consists of the prefix 0 optionally followed by a sequence of the digits 0 to 7 only. A hexadecimal constant consists of the prefix 0x or 0X followed by a sequence of the decimal digits and letters a (or A) to f (or F) with values 10 to 15 respectively.

If the value of *base* is between 2 and 36, the expected form of the subject sequence is a sequence of letters and digits representing an integer with the radix specified by *base*, optionally preceded by a + or – sign, but not including an integer suffix. The letters from a (or A) to z (or Z) inclusive are ascribed the values 10 to 35; only letters whose ascribed values are less than that of *base* are permitted. If the value of *base* is 16, the wide-character code representations of 0x or 0X may optionally precede the sequence of letters and digits, following the sign if present.

The subject sequence is defined as the longest initial subsequence of the input wide character string, starting with the first non-white-space wide-character code, that is of the expected form. The subject sequence contains no wide-character codes if the input wide character string is empty or consists entirely of white-space wide-character code, or if the first non-white-space wide-character code is other than a sign or a permissible letter or digit.

If the subject sequence has the expected form and *base* is 0, the sequence of wide-character codes starting with the first digit is interpreted as an integer constant. If the subject sequence has the expected form and the value of *base* is between 2 and 36, it is used as the base for conversion, ascribing to each letter its value as given above. If the subject sequence begins with a minus sign, the value resulting from the conversion is negated. A pointer to the final wide character string is stored in the object pointed to by *endptr*, provided that *endptr* is not a null pointer.

In other than the POSIX locale, additional implementation-dependent subject sequence forms may be accepted.

If the subject sequence is empty or does not have the expected form, no conversion is performed; the value of *nptr* is stored in the object pointed to by *endptr*, provided that *endptr* is not a null pointer.

RETURN VALUE

Upon successful completion, *wcstol*( ) returns the converted value, if any. If no conversion could be performed, 0 is returned and *errno* may be set to indicate the error. If the correct value is outside the range of representable values, {LONG_MAX} or {LONG_MIN} is returned (according to the sign of the value), and *errno* is set to [ERANGE] .

ERRORS

The *wcstol*( ) function will fail if:

[EINVAL]   The value of *base* is not supported.

[ERANGE]   The value to be returned is not representable.

The *wcstol*( ) function may fail if:

[EINVAL]   No conversion could be performed.

APPLICATION USAGE

Because 0, {LONG_MIN} and {LONG_MAX} are returned on error and are also valid returns on success, an application wishing to check for error situations should set *errno* to 0, then call *wcstol*( ), then check *errno* and if it is 0, assume an error has occurred.

SEE ALSO

iswalpha( ), *scanf*( ), *wcstod*( ), **<wchar.h>**.

EXAMPLE

```
/*
 * Copyright (C) ANTRIX Inc.
 */

/* wcstol.c
 * This program converts the initial portion of the wide character
 * string pointed to by nptr to long int representation using
 * function wcstol.
 */

#include <stdio.h>
#include <stdlib.h>
#include <wchar.h>
#include <errno.h>

main()
{
  long     wcstol_value;
  wchar_t  *endptr;
  wchar_t  *nptr = L"123";

  fprintf (stdout,"convert string to decimal\n");
  wcstol_value = wcstol (nptr, &endptr, 10);
  if ( wcstol_value == (long )123 ) {
      fprintf (stdout,"wcstol() call successful\n");
      fprintf (stdout,"wcstol_value=%ld\n", wcstol_value );
      fprintf (stdout,"original pointer value %d\n", nptr);
      /* should be string address + 3 */
      fprintf (stdout,"final pointer value %d\n", endptr);
  }
```

```
    else
        fprintf (stderr,"ERROR: wcstol() call failed\n");
}
```

NAME

wcstombs — convert a wide character string to a character string

SYNOPSIS

```
#include <stdlib.h>

size_t wcstombs(char *s, const wchar_t *pwcs, size_t n);
```

DESCRIPTION

The *wcstombs*( ) function converts the sequence of wide-character codes that are in the array pointed to by *pwcs* into a sequence of characters that begins in the initial shift state and stores these characters into the array pointed to by *s*, stopping if a character would exceed the limit of *n* total bytes or if a null byte is stored. Each wide-character code is converted as if by a call to *wctomb*( ), except that the shift state of *wctomb*( ) is not affected.

The behaviour of this function is affected by the LC_CTYPE category of the current locale.

EX
No more than *n* bytes will be modified in the array pointed to by *s*. If copying takes place between objects that overlap, the behaviour is undefined. If *s* is a null pointer, *wcstombs*( ) returns the length required to convert the entire array regardless of the value of *n*, but no values are stored. function returns the number of bytes required for the character array.

RETURN VALUE

If a wide-character code is encountered that does not correspond to a valid character (of one or more bytes each), *wcstombs*( ) returns (**size_t**)–1. Otherwise, *wcstombs*( ) returns the number of bytes stored in the character array, not including any terminating null byte. The array will not be null-terminated if the value returned is *n*.

ERRORS

The *wcstombs*( ) function may fail if:

EX
[EILSEQ]   A wide-character code does not correspond to a valid character.

SEE ALSO

mblen( ), *mbtowc*( ), *mbstowcs*( ), *wctomb*( ), **<stdlib.h>**.

EXAMPLE

```
/*
 * Copyright (C) ANTRIX Inc.
 */

/* wcstombs.c
 * This program converts the sequence of pwcs-character codes
 * that are in the array pointed to by pwcs into a sequence
 * of characters that begins in the initial shift state and
 * stores characters into the array pointed to by s using
 * function wcstombs.
 */

#include <stdio.h>
#include <stdlib.h>
#include <wchar.h>
#include <locale.h>
#include <errno.h>

#define NWCHAR  26
```

```
main()
{
  int      i, wcstombs_value;
  wchar_t pwcs[NWCHAR];
  char     s[NWCHAR] ;

  fprintf (stdout,"set locale\n");
  setlocalc (LC_ALL, "C");
  for (i = 0; i < NWCHAR; i++)
      pwcs[i] = 0x61 + i;

  fprintf (stdout,"convert pwcs string to multibyte string\n");
  wcstombs_value = wcstombs (s, pwcs, NWCHAR);
  fprintf (stdout,"wcstombs_value=%d\n", wcstombs_value);
  for ( i = 0; i < NWCHAR; i++ )
      fprintf (stdout,"%wc", s[i]);
  fprintf (stdout,"\n");
}
```

NAME

wcstoul — convert wide character string to unsigned long

SYNOPSIS

WP

```
#include <wchar.h>

unsigned long int wcstoul(const wchar_t *nptr, wchar_t **endptr,
                          int base);
```

DESCRIPTION

The *wcstoul*( ) function converts the initial portion of the wide character string pointed to by *nptr* to **unsigned long int** representation. First it decomposes the input wide-character string into three parts: an initial, possibly empty, sequence of white-space wide-character codes (as specified by *iswspace*( )); a subject sequence interpreted as an integer represented in some radix determined by the value of *base*; and a final wide-character string of one or more unrecognised wide character codes, including the terminating null wide-character code of the input wide character string. Then it attempts to convert the subject sequence to an unsigned integer, and returns the result.

If *base* is 0, the expected form of the subject sequence is that of a decimal constant, octal constant or hexadecimal constant, any of which may be preceded by a + or − sign. A decimal constant begins with a non-zero digit, and consists of a sequence of decimal digits. An octal constant consists of the prefix 0 optionally followed by a sequence of the digits 0 to 7 only. A hexadecimal constant consists of the prefix 0x or 0X followed by a sequence of the decimal digits and letters a (or A) to f (or F) with values 10 to 15 respectively.

If the value of *base* is between 2 and 36, the expected form of the subject sequence is a sequence of letters and digits representing an integer with the radix specified by *base*, optionally preceded by a + or − sign, but not including an integer suffix. The letters from a (or A) to z (or Z) inclusive are ascribed the values 10 to 35; only letters whose ascribed values are less than that of *base* are permitted. If the value of *base* is 16, the wide-character codes 0x or 0X may optionally precede the sequence of letters and digits, following the sign if present.

The subject sequence is defined as the longest initial subsequence of the input wide-character string, starting with the first wide-character code that is not white space and is of the expected form. The subject sequence contains no wide-character codes if the input wide-character string is empty or consists entirely of white-space wide-character codes, or if the first wide-character code that is not white space is other than a sign or a permissible letter or digit.

If the subject sequence has the expected form and *base* is 0, the sequence of wide-character codes starting with the first digit is interpreted as an integer constant. If the subject sequence has the expected form and the value of *base* is between 2 and 36, it is used as the base for conversion, ascribing to each letter its value as given above. If the subject sequence begins with a minus sign, the value resulting from the conversion is negated. A pointer to the final wide character string is stored in the object pointed to by *endptr*, provided that *endptr* is not a null pointer.

In other than the POSIX locale, additional implementation-dependent subject sequence forms may be accepted.

If the subject sequence is empty or does not have the expected form, no conversion is performed; the value of *nptr* is stored in the object pointed to by *endptr*, provided that *endptr* is not a null pointer.

RETURN VALUE

Upon successful completion, *wcstoul*( ) returns the converted value, if any. If no conversion could be performed, 0 is returned and *errno* may be set to indicate the error. If the correct value is outside the range of representable values, {ULONG_MAX} is returned and *errno* is set to [ERANGE] .

ERRORS

The *wcstoul*( ) function will fail if:

[EINVAL]   The value of *base* is not supported.

[ERANGE]   The value to be returned is not representable.

The *wcstoul*( ) function may fail if:

[EINVAL]   No conversion could be performed.

APPLICATION USAGE

Because 0 and {ULONG_MAX} are returned on error and 0 is also a valid return on success, an application wishing to check for error situations should set *errno* to 0, then call *wcstoul*( ), then check *errno* and if it is non-zero, assume an error has occurred.

Unlike *wcstod*( ) and *wcstol*( ), *wcstoul*( ) must always return a non-negative number; so, using the return value of *wcstoul*( ) for out-of-range numbers with *wcstoul*( ) could cause more severe problems than just loss of precision if those numbers can ever be negative.

SEE ALSO

iswalpha( ), *scanf*( ), *wcstod*( ), *wcstol*( ), **<wchar.h>**.

EXAMPLE

```
/*
 * Copyright (C) ANTRIX Inc.
 */


/* wcstoul.c
 * This program converts the initial portion of the wide
 * character string pointed to by nptr to unsigned long int
 * representation using function wcstoul.
 */


#include <stdio.h>
#include <stdlib.h>
#include <wchar.h>
#include <errno.h>

main()
{
    unsigned  long  int wcstoul_value;
    wchar_t    *endptr;
    wchar_t    *nptr = L"123";

    fprintf (stdout,"convert wide nptr to decimal\n");
    wcstoul_value = wcstoul (nptr, &endptr, 10);
    if ( wcstoul_value == (unsigned long int)123 ) {
        fprintf (stdout,"wcstoul() call successful\n");
        fprintf (stdout,"wcstoul_value=%ld\n", wcstoul_value );
        fprintf (stdout,"original pointer value %d\n", nptr);
```

```
                /* should be nptr address + 3 */
                fprintf (stdout,"final pointer value %d\n", endptr);
        }
     else
            fprintf (stderr,"ERROR: wcstoul() call failed\n");
     }
```

NAME

wcswcs — find wide substring

SYNOPSIS

WP `#include <wchar.h>`

`wchar_t *wcswcs(const wchar_t *ws1, const wchar_t *ws2);`

DESCRIPTION

The *wcswcs*( ) function locates the first occurrence in the wide character string pointed to by *ws1* of the sequence of wide-character codes (excluding the terminating null wide-character code) in the wide character string pointed to by *ws2*.

RETURN VALUE

Upon successful completion, *wcswcs*( ) returns a pointer to the located wide character string or a null pointer if the wide character string is not found.

If *ws2* points to a wide character string with zero length, the function returns *ws1*.

ERRORS

No errors are defined.

SEE ALSO

wcschr( ), **<wchar.h>**.

EXAMPLE

```
/*
 * Copyright (C) ANTRIX Inc.
 */

/* wcswcs.c
 * This function locates the first occurrence in the wide character
 * string pointed to by ws1 of the sequence of wide-character codes
 * in the wide character string pointed to by ws2 using function
 * wcswcs.
 */

#include <stdio.h>
#include <stdlib.h>
#include <wchar.h>
#include <string.h>
#include <errno.h>

main()
{
  wchar_t   *wcswcs_value;
  wchar_t   ws1[] = L"one two three two three";
  wchar_t   ws2[] = L"two";

  fprintf (stdout,"locate the first occurrence in string ws1 of the\n");
  fprintf (stdout,"sequence of characters in string ws2\n");
  wcswcs_value = wcswcs (ws1, ws2);
  if ( wcswcs_value != (wchar_t *)0 ) {
     fprintf (stdout,"wcswcs() call successful\n");
     fprintf (stdout,"wcswcs_value=%ws\n", wcswcs_value );
  }
```

```
    else
        fprintf (stderr,"ERROR: wcswcs() call failed\n");
}
```

NAME

wcswidth — number of column positions of a wide character string

SYNOPSIS

WP
```
#include <wchar.h>

int wcswidth(const wchar_t *pwcs, size_t n);
```

DESCRIPTION

The *wcswidth*( ) function determines the number of column positions required for *n* wide-character codes (or fewer than *n* wide-character codes if a null wide-character code is encountered before *n* wide-character codes are exhausted) in the string pointed to by *pwcs*.

RETURN VALUE

The *wcswidth*( ) function either returns 0 (if *pwcs* points to a null wide-character code), or returns the number of column positions to be occupied by the wide character string pointed to by *pwcs*, or returns −1 (if any of the first *n* wide-character codes in the wide character string pointed to by *pwcs* is not a printing wide-character code).

ERRORS

No errors are defined.

SEE ALSO

wcwidth( ), **<wchar.h>**, the definition of **Column Position** in the **XBD** specification, **Chapter 2**, **Glossary**.

EXAMPLE

```
/*
 * Copyright (C) ANTRIX Inc.
 */

/* wcswidth.c
 * This program determines the number of column positions
 * required for n wide character codes in the pwcs pointed
 * to by pwcs using function wcswidth.
 */

#include <stdio.h>
#include <stdlib.h>
#include <wchar.h>
#include <errno.h>

main()
{
   int     wcswidth_value;
   wchar_t *pwcs = L"hello world";
   size_t  n = 5;

   fprintf (stdout,"get number of column position\n");
   wcswidth_value = wcswidth(pwcs, n);
   if ( wcswidth_value != 0 ) {
      fprintf (stdout,"wcswidth() call successful\n");
      fprintf (stdout,"wcswidth_value=%d\n", wcswidth_value);
   }
   else
```

```
        fprintf (stderr,"ERROR: wcswidth() call failed\n");
}
```

NAME

wcsxfrm — wide character string transformation

SYNOPSIS

EI WP   `#include <wchar.h>`

`size_t wcsxfrm(wchar_t *ws1, const wchar_t *ws2, size_t n);`

DESCRIPTION

The *wcsxfrm( )* function transforms the wide character string pointed to by *ws2* and places the resulting wide character string into the array pointed to by *ws1*. The transformation is such that if *wcscmp( )* is applied to two transformed wide strings, it returns a value greater than, equal to or less than 0, corresponding to the result of *wcscoll( )* applied to the same two original wide character strings. No more than *n* wide-character codes are placed into the resulting array pointed to by *ws1*, including the terminating null wide-character code. If *n* is 0, *ws1* is permitted to be a null pointer. If copying takes place between objects that overlap, the behaviour is undefined.

RETURN VALUE

The *wcsxfrm( )* function returns the length of the transformed wide character string (not including the terminating null wide-character code). If the value returned is *n* or more, the contents of the array pointed to by *ws1* are indeterminate.

On error, the *wcsxfrm( )* function returns (**size_t**)–1, and sets *errno* to indicate the error.

ERRORS

The *wcsxfrm( )* function may fail if:

[EINVAL]   The wide character string pointed to by *ws2* contains wide-character codes outside the domain of the collating sequence.

[ENOSYS]   The function is not supported.

APPLICATION USAGE

The transformation function is such that two transformed wide character strings can be ordered by *wcscmp( )* as appropriate to collating sequence information in the program's locale (category LC_COLLATE).

The fact that when *n* is 0, *ws1* is permitted to be a null pointer, is useful to determine the size of the *ws1* array prior to making the transformation.

Because no return value is reserved to indicate an error, an application wishing to check for error situations should set *errno* to 0, then call *wcscoll( )*, then check *errno* and if it is non-zero, assume an error has occurred.

SEE ALSO

wcscmp( ), *wcscoll( )*, **<wchar.h>**.

EXAMPLE

```
/*
 * Copyright (C) ANTRIX Inc.
 */

/* wcsxfrm.c
 * This program transforms the wide character string pointed
 * to by ws2 and places the resulting wide character string
 * into the array pointed to by ws1 using function wcsxfrm.
 */
```

```
#include <stdio.h>
#include <stdlib.h>
#include <wchar.h>
#include <string.h>
#include <locale.h>
#include <ctype.h>
#include <errno.h>

main()
{
    int    ret_cmp;
    size_t len1, len2;
    wchar_t *trans1;
    wchar_t *trans2;

    wchar_t ws1[] = L"jfg" ;
    wchar_t ws2[] = L"efg" ;

    fprintf(stdout, "set LC_COLLATE to french locale\n");
    setlocale (LC_COLLATE, "fr") ;

    len1 = wcsxfrm(NULL, ws1, 0) + 1 ;
    len2 = wcsxfrm(NULL, ws2, 0) + 1 ;

    trans1 = (wchar_t *) malloc(len1) ;
    trans2 = (wchar_t *) malloc(len2) ;
    wcsxfrm(trans1, ws1, len1) ;
    wcsxfrm(trans2, ws2, len2) ;

    ret_cmp = wcscmp(trans1, trans2) ;
    fprintf (stdout,"string comparison value on transformed\n");
    fprintf (stdout,"string using wcscmp=%d\n", ret_cmp) ;
    free (trans1) ;
    free (trans2) ;

    ret_cmp = wcscoll(ws1, ws2);
    fprintf (stdout,"string comparison value on original\n");
    fprintf (stdout,"string using wcscoll=%d\n", ret_cmp) ;
}
```

NAME

wctomb — convert a wide-character code to a character

SYNOPSIS

```
#include <stdlib.h>

int wctomb(char *s, wchar_t wchar);
```

DESCRIPTION

The *wctomb*( ) function determines the number of bytes needed to represent the character corresponding to the wide-character code whose value is *wchar* (including any change in the shift state). It stores the character representation (possibly multiple bytes and any special bytes to change shift state) in the array object pointed to by *s* (if *s* is not a null pointer). At most {MB_CUR_MAX} bytes are stored. If *wchar* is 0, *wctomb*( ) is left in the initial shift state.

The behaviour of this function is affected by the LC_CTYPE category of the current locale. For a state-dependent encoding, this function is placed into its initial state by a call for which its character pointer argument, *s*, is a null pointer. Subsequent calls with *s* as other than a null pointer cause the internal state of the function to be altered as necessary. A call with *s* as a null pointer causes this function to return a non-zero value if encodings have state dependency, and 0 otherwise. Changing the LC_CTYPE category causes the shift state of this function to be indeterminate.

The implementation will behave as if no function defined in this document calls *wctomb*( ).

RETURN VALUE

If *s* is a null pointer, *wctomb*( ) returns a non-zero or 0 value, if character encodings, respectively, do or do not have state-dependent encodings. If *s* is not a null pointer, *wctomb*( ) returns –1 if the value of *wchar* does not correspond to a valid character, or returns the number of bytes that constitute the character corresponding to the value of *wchar*.

In no case will the value returned be greater than the value of the MB_CUR_MAX macro.

ERRORS

No errors are defined.

SEE ALSO

mblen( ), *mbtowc*( ), *mbstowcs*( ), *wcstombs*( ), **<stdlib.h>**.

EXAMPLE

```
/*
 * Copyright (C) ANTRIX Inc.
 */

/* wctomb.c
 * This program converts a wide-character code to a character
 * using function wctomb.
 */

#include <stdio.h>
#include <stdlib.h>
#include <locale.h>
#include <errno.h>

main()
{
    int      wctomb_value;
```

```
      char    s[2];
      wchar_t  c = L'Z';

      fprintf (stdout,"set locale\n");
      setlocale (LC_ALL, "C");

      fprintf (stdout,"convert wide character to multibyte character\n");
      wctomb_value = wctomb (s, 'Z');
      fprintf (stdout,"wctomb_value=%d\n", wctomb_value);
      fprintf (stdout,"s[0]=%c\n", s[0]);
}
```

NAME

wctype - define character class

SYNOPSIS

WP   `#include <wchar.h>`

`wctype_t wctype(const char *charclass);`

DESCRIPTION

The *wctype( )* function is defined for valid character class names as defined in the current locale. The *charclass* is a string identifying a generic character class for which codeset-specific type information is required. The following character class names are defined in all locales — "alnum", "alpha", "blank" "cntrl", "digit", "graph", "lower", "print", "punct", "space", "upper" and "xdigit".

Additional character class names defined in the locale definition file (category LC_CTYPE) can also be specified.

The function returns a value of type **wctype_t**, which can be used as the second argument to subsequent calls of *iswctype( )*. The *wctype( )* function determines values of **wctype_t** according to the rules of the coded character set defined by character type information in the program's locale (category LC_CTYPE). The values returned by *wctype( )* are valid until a call to *setlocale( )* that modifies the category LC_CTYPE.

RETURN VALUE

The *wctype( )* function returns 0 if the given character class name is not valid for the current locale (category LC_CTYPE), otherwise it returns an object of type **wctype_t** that can be used in calls to *iswctype( )*.

ERRORS

No errors are defined.

SEE ALSO

iswctype( ), **<wchar.h>**.

EXAMPLE

```
/*
 * Copyright (C) ANTRIX Inc.
 */

/* wctype.c
 * This program tests whether wc is a wide-character code of
 * character class corresponding to the valid character encodings
 * in the current locale using function wctype.
 */

#include <stdio.h>
#include <stdlib.h>
#include <wchar.h>
#include <ctype.h>
#include <errno.h>

main()
{
  wctype_t wctype_value;
  int      iswctype_value;
  wint_t   wc = L' 12';
```

```
    fprintf (stdout,"test if ascii equivalent of newline 012\n");
    fprintf (stdout,"is a control character\n");
    wctype_value = wctype("cntrl");
    if ( wctype_value != 0) {
        fprintf (stdout,"wctype() call successful\n");
        fprintf (stdout,"wctype_value=%d\n", wctype_value);
    }
    else
        fprintf (stderr,"ERROR: wctype() call failed\n");

    iswctype_value = iswctype (wc, wctype_value);
    if ( iswctype_value != 0 ) {
        fprintf (stdout,"iswctype() call successful\n");
        fprintf (stdout,"iswctype_value=%d\n", iswctype_value);
    }
    else
        fprintf (stderr,"ERROR: iswctype() call failed\n");
}
```

NAME

wcwidth — number of column positions of a wide-character code

SYNOPSIS

WP

```
#include <wchar.h>
```

```
int wcwidth(wchar_t wc);
```

DESCRIPTION

The *wcwidth*( ) function determines the number of column positions required for the wide character *wc*. The value of *wc* must be a character representable as a **wchar_t**, and must be a wide-character code corresponding to a valid character in the current locale.

RETURN VALUE

The *wcwidth*( ) function either returns 0 (if *wc* is a null wide-character code), or returns the number of column positions to be occupied by the wide-character code *wc*, or returns −1 (if *wc* does not correspond to a printing wide-character code).

ERRORS

No errors are defined.

SEE ALSO

wcswidth( ), **<wchar.h>**.

EXAMPLE

```
/*
 * Copyright (C) ANTRIX Inc.
 */

/* wcwidth.c
 * This program determines the number of column positions required
 * for the wide character wc using function wcwidth.
 */

#include <stdio.h>
#include <stdlib.h>
#include <wchar.h>
#include <errno.h>

main()
{
   int        wcwidth_value;
   wint_t wc = L't';

   fprintf (stdout,"get number of column position\n");
   wcwidth_value = wcwidth(wc);
   if ( wcwidth_value != 0 ) {
       fprintf (stdout,"wcwidth() call successful\n");
       fprintf (stdout,"wcwidth_value=%d\n", wcwidth_value);
   }
   else
       fprintf (stderr,"ERROR: wcwidth() call failed\n");
}
```

NAME

wordexp, wordfree — perform word expansions

SYNOPSIS

```
#include <wordexp.h>

int wordexp(const char *words, wordexp_t *pwordexp, int flags);

void wordfree(wordexp_t *pwordexp);
```

DESCRIPTION

The *wordexp*( ) function performs word expansions as described in the **XCU** specification, **Section 2.6**, **Word Expansions**, subject to quoting as in the **XCU** specification, **Section 2.2**, **Quoting**, and places the list of expanded words into the structure pointed to by *pwordexp*.

The *words* argument is a pointer to a string containing one or more words to be expanded. The expansions will be the same as would be performed by the shell if *words* were the part of a command line representing the arguments to a utility. Therefore, *words* must not contain an unquoted newline or any of the unquoted shell special characters:

| &   ;   <   >

except in the context of command substitution as specified in the **XCU** specification, **Section 2.6.3**, **Command Substitution**. It also must not contain unquoted parentheses or braces, except in the context of command or variable substitution. If the argument *words* contains an unquoted comment character (number sign) that is the beginning of a token, *wordexp*( ) may treat the comment character as a regular character, or may interpret it as a comment indicator and ignore the remainder of *words*.

The structure type **wordexp_t** is defined in the header **<wordexp.h>** and includes at least the following members:

Member Type	Member Name	Description
size_t	we_wordc	Count of words matched by *words*.
char **	we_wordv	Pointer to list of expanded words.
size_t	we_offs	Slots to reserve at the beginning of *pwordexp*->**we_wordv**.

The *wordexp*( ) function stores the number of generated words into *pwordexp*–>**we_wordc** and a pointer to a list of pointers to words in *pwordexp*–>**we_wordv**. Each individual field created during field splitting (see the **XCU** specification, **Section 2.6.5**, **Field Splitting**) or pathname expansion (see the **XCU** specification, **Section 2.6.6**, **Pathname Expansion**) is a separate word in the *pwordexp*–>**we_wordv** list. The words are in order as described in the **XCU** specification, **Section 2.6**, **Word Expansions**. The first pointer after the last word pointer will be a null pointer. The expansion of special parameters described in the **XCU** specification, **Section 2.5.2**, **Special Parameters** is unspecified.

It is the caller's responsibility to allocate the storage pointed to by *pwordexp*. The *wordexp*( ) function allocates other space as needed, including memory pointed to by *pwordexp*–>**we_wordv**. The *wordfree*( ) function frees any memory associated with *pwordexp* from a previous call to *wordexp*( ).

The *flags* argument is used to control the behaviour of *wordexp*( ). The value of *flags* is the bitwise inclusive OR of zero or more of the following constants, which are defined in **<wordexp.h>**:

WRDE_APPEND   Append words generated to the ones from a previous call to *wordexp*( ).

WRDE_DOOFFS   Make use of *pwordexp*–>**we_offs**. If this flag is set, *pwordexp*–>**we_offs** is used to specify how many null pointers to add to the beginning of *pwordexp*–>**we_wordv**. In other words, *pwordexp*–>**we_wordv** will point to *pwordexp*–>**we_offs** null pointers, followed by *pwordexp*–>**we_wordc** word pointers, followed by a null pointer.

WRDE_NOCMD   Fail if command substitution, as specified in the **XCU** specification, **Section 2.6.3**, **Command Substitution**, is requested.

WRDE_REUSE   The *pwordexp* argument was passed to a previous successful call to *wordexp*( ), and has not been passed to *wordfree*( ). The result will be the same as if the application had called *wordfree*( ) and then called *wordexp*( ) without WRDE_REUSE.

WRDE_SHOWERR   Do not redirect *stderr* to **/dev/null**.

WRDE_UNDEF   Report error on an attempt to expand an undefined shell variable.

The WRDE_APPEND flag can be used to append a new set of words to those generated by a previous call to *wordexp*( ). The following rules apply when two or more calls to *wordexp*( ) are made with the same value of *pwordexp* and without intervening calls to *wordfree*( ):

1. The first such call must not set WRDE_APPEND. All subsequent calls must set it.

2. All of the calls must set WRDE_DOOFFS, or all must not set it.

3. After the second and each subsequent call, *pwordexp*–>**we_wordv** will point to a list containing the following:

    a. zero or more null pointers, as specified by WRDE_DOOFFS and *pwordexp*–>**we_offs**

    b. pointers to the words that were in the *pwordexp*–>**we_wordv** list before the call, in the same order as before

    c. pointers to the new words generated by the latest call, in the specified order

4. The count returned in *pwordexp*–>**we_wordc** will be the total number of words from all of the calls.

5. The application can change any of the fields after a call to *wordexp*( ), but if it does it must reset them to the original value before a subsequent call, using the same *pwordexp* value, to *wordfree*( ) or *wordexp*( ) with the WRDE_APPEND or WRDE_REUSE flag.

If *words* contains an unquoted:

    <newline> | & ; < > ( ) { }

in an inappropriate context, *wordexp*( ) will fail, and the number of expanded words will be 0.

Unless WRDE_SHOWERR is set in *flags*, *wordexp*( ) will redirect *stderr* to **/dev/null** for any utilities executed as a result of command substitution while expanding *words*. If WRDE_SHOWERR is set, *wordexp*( ) may write messages to *stderr* if syntax errors are detected while expanding *words*.

If WRDE_DOOFFS is set, then *pwordexp*–>**we_offs** must have the same value for each *wordexp*( ) call and *wordfree*( ) call using a given *pwordexp*.

The following constants are defined as error return values:

WRDE_BADCHAR   One of the unquoted characters:

<newline> | & ; < > ( ) { }

appears in *words* in an inappropriate context.

WRDE_BADVAL   Reference to undefined shell variable when WRDE_UNDEF is set in *flags*.

WRDE_CMDSUB   Command substitution requested when WRDE_NOCMD was set in flags.

WRDE_NOSPACE   Attempt to allocate memory failed.

WRDE_SYNTAX   Shell syntax error, such as unbalanced parentheses or unterminated string.

RETURN VALUE

On successful completion, *wordexp*( ) returns 0.

Otherwise, a non-zero value as described in **<wordexp.h>** is returned to indicate an error. If *wordexp*( ) returns the value WRDE_NOSPACE, then *pwordexp*–>**we_wordc** and *pwordexp*–>**we_wordv** will be updated to reflect any words that were successfully expanded. In other cases, they will not be modified.

The *wordfree*( ) function returns no value.

ERRORS

No errors are defined.

APPLICATION USAGE

This function is intended to be used by an application that wants to do all of the shell's expansions on a word or words obtained from a user. For example, if the application prompts for a filename (or list of filenames) and then uses *wordexp*( ) to process the input, the user could respond with anything that would be valid as input to the shell.

The WRDE_NOCMD flag is provided for applications that, for security or other reasons, want to prevent a user from executing shell commands. Disallowing unquoted shell special characters also prevents unwanted side effects such as executing a command or writing a file.

SEE ALSO

fnmatch( ), *glob*( ), **<wordexp.h>**, the **XCU** specification.

NAME

write, writev — write on a file

SYNOPSIS

```
#include <unistd.h>

ssize_t write(int fildes, const void *buf, size_t nbyte);

#include <sys/uio.h>

ssize_t writev(int fildes, const struct iovec *iov, int iovcnt);
```

UX *(marks the `#include <sys/uio.h>` and `writev` lines)*

DESCRIPTION

The *write( )* function attempts to write *nbyte* bytes from the buffer pointed to by *buf* to the file associated with the open file descriptor, *fildes*.

If *nbyte* is 0, *write( )* will return 0 and have no other results if the file is a regular file; otherwise, the results are unspecified.

On a regular file or other file capable of seeking, the actual writing of data proceeds from the position in the file indicated by the file offset associated with *fildes*. Before successful return from *write( )*, the file offset is incremented by the number of bytes actually written. On a regular file, if this incremented file offset is greater than the length of the file, the length of the file will be set to this file offset.

EX   If the O_SYNC flag of the file status flags is set and *fildes* refers to a regular file, a successful *write( )* does not return until the data is delivered to the underlying hardware.

On a file not capable of seeking, writing always takes place starting at the current position. The value of a file offset associated with such a device is undefined.

If the O_APPEND flag of the file status flags is set, the file offset will be set to the end of the file prior to each write and no intervening file modification operation will occur between changing the file offset and the write operation.

EX   If a *write( )* requests that more bytes be written than there is room for (for example, the *ulimit* or the physical end of a medium), only as many bytes as there is room for will be written. For example, suppose there is space for 20 bytes more in a file before reaching a limit. A write of 512 bytes will return 20. The next write of a non-zero number of bytes will give a failure return

UX   (except as noted below) and the implementation will generate a SIGXFSZ signal for the process.

If *write( )* is interrupted by a signal before it writes any data, it will return −1 with *errno* set to [EINTR].

FIPS   If *write( )* is interrupted by a signal after it successfully writes some data, it will return the number of bytes written.

If the value of *nbyte* is greater than {SSIZE_MAX}, the result is implementation-dependent.

After a *write( )* to a regular file has successfully returned:

- Any successful *read( )* from each byte position in the file that was modified by that write will return the data specified by the *write( )* for that position until such byte positions are again modified.

- Any subsequent successful *write( )* to the same byte position in the file will overwrite that file data.

Write requests to a pipe or FIFO will be handled the same as a regular file with the following exceptions:

- There is no file offset associated with a pipe, hence each write request will append to the end of the pipe.

- Write requests of {PIPE_BUF} bytes or less will not be interleaved with data from other processes doing writes on the same pipe. Writes of greater than {PIPE_BUF} bytes may have data interleaved, on arbitrary boundaries, with writes by other processes, whether or not the O_NONBLOCK flag of the file status flags is set.

- If the O_NONBLOCK flag is clear, a write request may cause the process to block, but on normal completion it will return *nbyte*.

- If the O_NONBLOCK flag is set, *write( )* requests will be handled differently, in the following ways:

    — The *write( )* function will not block the process.

    — A write request for {PIPE_BUF} or fewer bytes will have the following effect: If there is sufficient space available in the pipe, *write( )* will transfer all the data and return the number of bytes requested. Otherwise, *write( )* will transfer no data and return −1 with *errno* set to [EAGAIN].

    — A write request for more than {PIPE_BUF} bytes will case one of the following:

        a. When at least one byte can be written, transfer what it can and return the number of bytes written. When all data previously written to the pipe is read, it will transfer at least {PIPE_BUF} bytes.

        b. When no data can be written, transfer no data and return −1 with *errno* set to [EAGAIN].

When attempting to write to a file descriptor (other than a pipe or FIFO) that supports non-blocking writes and cannot accept the data immediately:

- If the O_NONBLOCK flag is clear, *write( )* will block until the data can be accepted.

- If the O_NONBLOCK flag is set, *write( )* will not block the process. If some data can be written without blocking the process, *write( )* will write what it can and return the number of bytes written. Otherwise, it will return −1 and *errno* will be set to [EAGAIN].

Upon successful completion, where *nbyte* is greater than 0, *write( )* will mark for update the *st_ctime* and *st_mtime* fields of the file, and if the file is a regular file, the S_ISUID and S_ISGID bits of the file mode may be cleared.

UX   If *fildes* refers to a STREAM, the operation of *write( )* is determined by the values of the minimum and maximum *nbyte* range ("packet size") accepted by the STREAM. These values are determined by the topmost STREAM module. If *nbyte* falls within the packet size range, *nbyte* bytes will be written. If *nbyte* does not fall within the range and the minimum packet size value is 0, *write( )* will break the buffer into maximum packet size segments prior to sending the data downstream (the last segment may contain less than the maximum packet size). If *nbyte* does not fall within the range and the minimum value is non-zero, *write( )* will fail with *errno* set to [ERANGE]. Writing a zero-length buffer (*nbyte* is 0) to a STREAMS device sends 0 bytes with 0 returned. However, writing a zero-length buffer to a STREAMS-based pipe or FIFO sends no message and 0 is returned. The process may issue I_SWROPT *ioctl( )* to enable zero-length messages to be sent across the pipe or FIFO.

When writing to a STREAM, data messages are created with a priority band of 0. When writing to a STREAM that is not a pipe or FIFO:

- If O_NONBLOCK is clear, and the STREAM cannot accept data (the STREAM write queue is full due to internal flow control conditions), *write( )* will block until data can be accepted.

- If O_NONBLOCK is set and the STREAM cannot accept data, *write*( ) will return −1 and set *errno* to [EAGAIN].

- If O_NONBLOCK is set and part of the buffer has been written while a condition in which the STREAM cannot accept additional data occurs, *write*( ) will terminate and return the number of bytes written.

In addition, *write*( ) and *writev*( ) will fail if the STREAM head had processed an asynchronous error before the call. In this case, the value of *errno* does not reflect the result of *write*( ) or *writev*( ) but reflects the prior error.

The *writev*( ) function is equivalent to *write*( ), but gathers the output data from the *iovcnt* buffers specified by the members of the *iov* array: *iov*[0], *iov*[1], ..., *iov*[*iovcnt*-1]. *iovcnt* is valid if greater than 0 and less than or equal to {IOV_MAX}, defined in **<limits.h>**.

Each **iovec** entry specifies the base address and length of an area in memory from which data should be written. The *writev*( ) function will always write a complete area before proceeding to the next.

If *fildes* refers to a regular file and all of the **iov_len** members in the array pointed to by *iov* are 0, *writev*( ) will return 0 and have no other effect. For other file types, the behaviour is unspecified.

If the sum of the **iov_len** values is greater than SSIZE_MAX, the operation fails and no data is transferred.

RETURN VALUE

Upon successful completion, *write*( ) will return the number of bytes actually written to the file associated with *fildes*. This number will never be greater than *nbyte*. Otherwise, −1 is returned and *errno* is set to indicate the error.

UX Upon successful completion, *writev*( ) returns the number of bytes actually written. Otherwise, it returns a value of −1, the file-pointer remains unchanged, and *errno* is set to indicate an error.

ERRORS

UX The *write*( ) and *writev*( ) functions will fail if:

[EAGAIN]	The O_NONBLOCK flag is set for the file descriptor and the process would be delayed in the *write*( ) operation.
[EBADF]	The *fildes* argument is not a valid file descriptor open for writing.
[EFBIG]	An attempt was made to write a file that exceeds the implementation-dependent maximum file size or the process' file size limit.
[EINTR]	The write operation was terminated due to the receipt of a signal, and no data was transferred.
[EIO]	A physical I/O error has occurred.
[EIO]	The process is a member of a background process group attempting to write to its controlling terminal, TOSTOP is set, the process is neither ignoring nor blocking SIGTTOU and the process group of the process is orphaned. This error may also be returned under implementation-dependent conditions.
[ENOSPC]	There was no free space remaining on the device containing the file.
[EPIPE]	An attempt is made to write to a pipe or FIFO that is not open for reading by any process, or that only has one end open. A SIGPIPE signal will also be sent to the process.

EX (to the left of the [EFBIG] row)

UX (to the left of the first [EIO] row)

UX (to the left of the [EPIPE] row)

UX   [ERANGE]   The transfer request size was outside the range supported by the STREAMS file associated with *fildes*.

The *writev( )* function will fail if:

[EINVAL]   The sum of the **iov_len** values in the *iov* array would overflow an **ssize_t**.

UX   The *write( )* and *writev( )* functions may fail if:

UX   [EINVAL]   The STREAM or multiplexer referenced by *fildes* is linked (directly or indirectly) downstream from a multiplexer.

EX   [ENXIO]   A request was made of a non-existent device, or the request was outside the capabilities of the device.

UX   [ENXIO]   A hangup occurred on the STREAM being written to.

UX   A write to a STREAMS file may fail if an error message has been received at the STREAM head. In this case, *errno* is set to the value included in the error message.

The *writev( )* function may fail and set *errno* to:

[EINVAL]   The *iovcnt* argument was less than or equal to 0, or greater than {IOV_MAX}.

SEE ALSO

    chmod( ), *creat( )*, *dup( )*, *fcntl( )*, *getrlimit( )*, *lseek( )*, *open( )*, *pipe( )*, *ulimit( )*, **<limits.h>**, **<stropts.h>**, **<sys/uio.h>**, **<unistd.h>**.

EXAMPLE

```
/*
 * Copyright (C) ANTRIX Inc.
 */

/* write.c
 * This program writes nbytes from the buffer pointed to by
 * buf to the file associated with the open file descriptor
 * fildes using function write.
 */

#include <stdio.h>
#include <stdlib.h>
#include <fcntl.h>
#include <unistd.h>
#include <sys/types.h>
#include <sys/stat.h>
#include <errno.h>

#define  PERM_ALL    (S_IRWXU | S_IRWXG | S_IRWXO)

main()
{
  int   write_value;
  int   fildes, nbytes, length;
  char  *string;
  char  *buf = "hello world";
  char  *filename = "testfile";

  nbytes = strlen (buf);
```

```
    fprintf (stdout,"create testfile\n");
    fildes = creat (filename, PERM_ALL);

    fprintf (stdout,"write string\n");
    write_value = write (fildes, buf, nbytes);
    if ( write_value == nbytes ) {
        fprintf (stdout,"write() call successful\n");
        fprintf (stdout,"write_value=%d\n", write_value);
    }
    else
        fprintf (stderr,"ERROR: write() call failed\n");

    fprintf (stdout,"close testfile\n");
    close (fildes);

    fprintf (stdout,"open testfile for read only\n");
    fildes = open (filename, O_RDONLY);
    string = (char *)malloc (nbytes);

    fprintf (stdout,"read string\n");
    length = read (fildes, string, nbytes );
    if ( length == nbytes ) {
        fprintf (stdout,"read() call successful\n");
        fprintf (stdout,"string read is=%s\n", string);
        fprintf (stdout,"number of length read=%d\n", length);
    }
    else {
        fprintf (stderr,"ERROR: read() call failed\n");
        fprintf (stderr,"ERROR: %s\n", strerror(errno));
    }

    fprintf (stdout,"close and remove testfile\n");
    close (fildes);
    remove (filename);
}


/*
 * Copyright (C) ANTRIX Inc.
 */

/* writev.c
 * This program writes data on to a file
 * using function writev.
 */

#include <stdio.h>
#include <stdlib.h>
#include <fcntl.h>
#include <unistd.h>
#include <sys/types.h>
#include <sys/uio.h>
```

```
#include <sys/stat.h>
#include <errno.h>

#define  PERM_ALL   (S_IRWXU | S_IRWXG | S_IRWXO)

main()
{
  int     i, bytes, fildes;
  int     len1, len2, compare;
  char    *str1 = "hello";
  char    *str2 = "world";
  struct  iovec iov_write[2], iov_read[2];
  char    *file = "testfile";

  len1 = strlen (str1);
  len2 = strlen (str2);

  fprintf (stdout,"open testfile\n");
  fildes = creat (file, PERM_ALL);
  iov_write[0].iov_base = (char *)malloc (len1);
  iov_write[0].iov_len = len1;
  iov_write[0].iov_base = "hello";
  iov_write[1].iov_base = (char *)malloc (len2);
  iov_write[1].iov_len = len2;
  iov_write[1].iov_base = "world";

  fprintf (stdout,"write strings\n");
  bytes = writev(fildes, iov_write, 2);
  if ( bytes == (len1 + len2) ) {
     fprintf (stdout,"writev() call successful\n");
     fprintf (stdout,"bytes=%d\n", bytes);
  }
  else {
     fprintf (stderr,"ERROR: writev() call failed\n");
     fprintf (stderr,"ERROR: %s\n", strerror(errno));
  }

  fprintf (stdout,"close testfile\n");
  close(fildes);
  iov_read[0].iov_base = (char *)malloc (len1);
  iov_read[0].iov_len = len1;
  iov_read[1].iov_base = (char *)malloc (len2);
  iov_read[1].iov_len = len2;

  fprintf (stdout,"open testfile for read only\n");
  fildes = open (file, O_RDONLY);
  readv (fildes, iov_read, 2);
  for ( i = 0; i < 2; i++ ) {
    compare = memcmp (iov_read[i].iov_base, iov_write[i].iov_base,
                      iov_write[i].iov_len);
    if (compare == 0)
      fprintf (stdout,"iov_read[i].iov_base=%s\n", iov_read[i].iov_base);
```

```
    }

    fprintf (stdout,"remove testfile\n");
    remove (file);
}
```

NAME

y0, y1, yn — Bessel functions of the second kind

SYNOPSIS

EX

```
#include <math.h>

double y0(double x);

double y1 (double x);

double yn (int n, double x);
```

DESCRIPTION

The *y0( )*, *y1( )* and *yn( )* functions compute Bessel functions of *x* of the second kind of orders 0, 1 and *n* respectively. The value of *x* must be positive.

RETURN VALUE

Upon successful completion, *y0( )*, *y1( )* and *yn( )* will return the relevant Bessel value of *x* of the second kind.

If *x* is NaN, NaN is returned and *errno* may be set to [EDOM].

If the *x* argument to *y0( )*, *y1( )* or *yn( )* is negative, –HUGE_VAL or NaN is returned, and *errno* may be set to [EDOM].

If *x* is 0.0, –HUGE_VAL is returned and *errno* may be set to [ERANGE] or [EDOM].

If the correct result would cause underflow, 0.0 is returned and *errno* may be set to [ERANGE].

If the correct result would cause overflow, –HUGE_VAL or 0.0 is returned and *errno* may be set to [ERANGE].

ERRORS

The *y0( )*, *y1( )* and *yn( )* functions may fail if:

[EDOM]   The value of *x* is negative or NaN.

[ERANGE]   The value of *x* is too large in magnitude, or *x* is 0.0, or the correct result would cause overflow or underflow.

No other errors will occur.

APPLICATION USAGE

An application wishing to check for error situations should set *errno* to 0 before calling *y0( )*, *y1( )* or *yn( )*. If *errno* is non-zero on return, or the return value is NaN, an error has occurred.

SEE ALSO

isnan( ), *j0( )*, **<math.h>**.

EXAMPLE

```
/*
 * Copyright (C) ANTRIX Inc.
 */

/* y0.c
 * This program computes Bessel function of x of the second
 * kind of the order 0 using function y0.
 */

#include <stdio.h>
#include <math.h>
```

```
main()
{
  double  y0_value;
  double  x = 10.00;

  y0_value = y0 (x);
  fprintf (stdout,"y0 of %f is %f\n", x, y0_value);
}



/*
 * Copyright (C) ANTRIX Inc.
 */

/* y1.c
 * This program computes Bessel function of x of the second
 * kind of the order 1 using function y1.
 */

#include <stdio.h>
#include <math.h>

main()
{
  double  y1_value;
  double  x = 10.00;

  y1_value = y1 (x);
  fprintf (stdout,"y1 of %f is %f\n", x, y1_value);
}



/*
 * Copyright (C) ANTRIX Inc.
 */

/* yn.c
 * This program computes Bessel function of x of the second
 * kind of the order n using function yn.
 */

#include <stdio.h>
#include <math.h>

main()
{
  double  yn_value;
  double  x = 10.00;
  int     n = 1;

  yn_value = yn (n, x);
```

```
    fprintf (stdout,"yn of %d, %f is %f\n", n, x, yn_value);
}
```

Chapter 2

Sockets Interfaces

This chapter gives an overview of the Sockets interfaces and includes functions, macros and external variables to support portability at the C-language source level.

2.1   Sockets Overview

All network protocols are associated with a specific protocol family. A protocol family provides basic services to the protocol implementation to allow it to function within a specific network environment. These services can include packet fragmentation and reassembly, routing, addressing, and basic transport. A protocol family can support multiple methods of addressing, though the current protocol implementations do not. A protocol family normally comprises a number of protocols, one per socket type. It is not required that a protocol family support all socket types. A protocol family can contain multiple protocols supporting the same socket abstraction.

A protocol supports one of the socket abstractions detailed in the manual page for the *socket*( ) function. A specific protocol can be accessed either by creating a socket of the appropriate type and protocol family, or by requesting the protocol explicitly when creating a socket. Protocols normally accept only one type of address format, usually determined by the addressing structure inherent in the design of the protocol family and network architecture. Certain semantics of the basic socket abstractions are protocol specific. All protocols are expected to support the basic model for their particular socket type, but can, in addition, provide nonstandard facilities or extensions to a mechanism. For example, a protocol supporting the SOCK_STREAM abstraction can allow more than one byte of out-of-band data to be transmitted per out-of-band message.

This specification covers local UNIX connections and Internet protocols.

Addressing

Associated with each address family is an address format. All network addresses adhere to a general structure, called a **sockaddr**. The length of the structure varies according to the address family.

Routing

Sockets provides packet routing facilities. A routing information database is maintained, which is used in selecting the appropriate network interface when transmitting packets.

Interfaces

Each network interface in a system corresponds to a path through which messages can be sent and received. A network interface usually has a hardware device associated with it, though certain interfaces such as the loopback interface do not.

NAME

accept — accept a new connection on a socket

SYNOPSIS

UX

```
#include <sys/socket.h>

int accept (int socket, struct sockaddr *address, size_t *address_len);
```

DESCRIPTION

The *accept( )* function extracts the first connection on the queue of pending connections, creates a new socket with the same socket type protocol and address family as the specified socket, and allocates a new file descriptor for that socket.

The function takes the following arguments:

socket	Specifies a socket that was created with *socket( )*, has been bound to an address with *bind( )*, and has issued a successful call to *listen( )*.
address	Either a null pointer, or a pointer to a **sockaddr** structure where the address of the connecting socket will be returned.
address_len	Points to a **size_t** which on input specifies the length of the supplied **sockaddr** structure, and on output specifies the length of the stored address.

If *address* is not a null pointer, the address of the peer for the accepted connection is stored in the **sockaddr** structure pointed to by *address*, and the length of this address is stored in the object pointed to by *address_len*.

If the actual length of the address is greater than the length of the supplied **sockaddr** structure, the stored address will be truncated.

If the protocol permits connections by unbound clients, and the peer is not bound, then the value stored in the object pointed to by *address* is unspecified.

If the listen queue is empty of connection requests and O_NONBLOCK is not set on the file descriptor for the socket, *accept( )* will block until a connection is present. If the *listen( )* queue is empty of connection requests and O_NONBLOCK is set on the file descriptor for the socket, *accept( )* will fail and set *errno* to [EWOULDBLOCK] or [EAGAIN].

The accepted socket cannot itself accept more connections. The original socket remains open and can accept more connections.

RETURN VALUE

Upon successful completion, *accept( )* returns the nonnegative file descriptor of the accepted socket. Otherwise, −1 is returned and *errno* is set to indicate the error.

ERRORS

The *accept( )* function will fail if:

[EBADF]	The *socket* argument is not a valid file descriptor.
[ECONNABORTED]	A connection has been aborted.
[ENOTSOCK]	The *socket* argument does not refer to a socket.
[EOPNOTSUPP]	The socket type of the specified socket does not support accepting connections.

[EAGAIN] or [EWOULDBLOCK]

O_NONBLOCK is set for the socket file descriptor and no connections are present to be accepted.

[EINTR]	The *accept*( ) function was interrupted by a signal that was caught before a valid connection arrived.
[EINVAL]	The *socket* is not accepting connections.
[EMFILE]	{OPEN_MAX} file descriptors are currently open in the calling process.
[ENFILE]	The maximum number of file descriptors in the system are already open.

The *accept*( ) function may fail if:

[ENOMEM]	There was insufficient memory available to complete the operation.
[ENOBUFS]	No buffer space is available.
[ENOSR]	There was insufficient STREAMS resources available to complete the operation.
[EPROTO]	A protocol error has occurred; for example, the STREAMS protocol stack has not been initialised.

APPLICATION USAGE

When a connection is available, *select*( ) will indicate that the file descriptor for the socket is ready for reading.

SEE ALSO

bind( ), *connect*( ), *listen*( ), *socket*( ), **<sys/socket>**.

EXAMPLE

See examples at the end of chapter.

NAME

bind — bind a name to a socket

SYNOPSIS

UX
```
#include <sys/socket.h>
```

```
int bind(int socket, const struct sockaddr *address,
    size_t address_len);
```

DESCRIPTION

The *bind*( ) function assigns an *address* to an unnamed socket. Sockets created with *socket*( ) function are initially unnamed; they are identified only by their address family.

The function takes the following arguments:

socket   Specifies the file descriptor of the socket to be bound.

address   Points to a **sockaddr** structure containing the address to be bound to the socket. The length and format of the address depend on the address family of the socket.

address_len   Specifies the length of the **sockaddr** structure pointed to by the *address* argument.

RETURN VALUE

Upon successful completion, *bind*( ) returns 0. Otherwise, −1 is returned and *errno* is set to indicate the error.

ERRORS

The *bind*( ) function will fail if:

[EBADF]   The *socket* argument is not a valid file descriptor.

[ENOTSOCK]   The *socket* argument does not refer to a socket.

[EADDRNOTAVAIL] The specified address is not available from the local machine.

[EADDRINUSE] The specified address is already in use.

[EINVAL]   The socket is already bound to an address, and the protocol does not support binding to a new address; or the socket has been shut down.

[EACCES]   The specified address is protected and the current user does not have permission to bind to it.

[EAFNOSUPPORT] The specified address is not a valid address for the address family of the specified socket.

[EOPNOTSUPP] The socket type of the specified socket does not support binding to an address.

If the address family of the socket is AF_UNIX, then *bind*( ) will fail if:

[EDESTADDRREQ] or [EISDIR]
       The *address* argument is a null pointer.

[EACCES]   A component of the path prefix denies search permission, or the requested name requires writing in a directory with a mode that denies write permission.

[ENOTDIR]   A component of the path prefix of the pathname in *address* is not a directory.

[ENAMETOOLONG]	A component of a pathname exceeded {NAME_MAX} characters, or an entire pathname exceeded {PATH_MAX} characters.
[ENOENT]	A component of the pathname does not name an existing file or the pathname is an empty string.
[ELOOP]	Too many symbolic links were encountered in translating the pathname in *address*.
[EIO]	An I/O error occurred.
[EROFS]	The name would reside on a read-only filesystem.

The *bind*( ) function may fail if:

[EINVAL]	The *address_len* argument is not a valid length for the address family.
[EISCONN]	The socket is already connected.
[ENAMETOOLONG]	Pathname resolution of a symbolic link produced an intermediate result whose length exceeds {PATH_MAX}.
[ENOBUFS]	Insufficient resources were available to complete the call.
[ENOSR]	There were insufficient STREAMS resources for the operation to complete.

APPLICATION USAGE

An application program can retrieve the assigned socket name with the *getsockname*( ) function.

SEE ALSO

connect( ), *getsockname*( ), *listen*( ), *socket*( ), **<sys/socket>**.

EXAMPLE

See examples at the end of chapter.

NAME

close — close a file descriptor

Note: The **XSH** specification contains the basic definition of this interface. The following additional information pertains to Sockets.

DESCRIPTION

UX If *fildes* refers to a socket, *close*( ) causes the socket to be destroyed. If the socket is connection-oriented, and the SOCK_LINGER option is set for the socket, and the socket has untransmitted data, then *close*( ) will block for up to the current linger interval until all data is transmitted.

EXAMPLE

See examples at the end of chapter.

NAME

connect — connect a socket

SYNOPSIS

UX   `#include <sys/socket.h>`

```
int connect(int socket, const struct sockaddr *address,
    size_t address_len);
```

DESCRIPTION

The *connect*( ) function requests a connection to be made on a socket. The function takes the following arguments:

socket   Specifies the file descriptor associated with the socket.

address   Points to a **sockaddr** structure containing the peer address. The length and format of the address depend on the address family of the socket.

address_len   Specifies the length of the **sockaddr** structure pointed to by the *address* argument.

If the initiating socket is not connection-oriented, then *connect*( ) sets the socket's peer address, but no connection is made. For SOCK_DGRAM sockets, the peer address identifies where all datagrams are sent on subsequent *send*( ) calls, and limits the remote sender for subsequent *recv*( ) calls. If *address* is a null address for the protocol, the socket's peer address will be reset.

If the initiating socket is connection-oriented, then *connect*( ) attempts to establish a connection to the address specified by the *address* argument.

If the connection cannot be established immediately and O_NONBLOCK is not set for the file descriptor for the socket, *connect*( ) will block for up to an unspecified timeout interval until the connection is established. If the timeout interval expires before the connection is established, *connect*( ) will fail and the connection attempt will be aborted. If *connect*( ) is interrupted by a signal that is caught while blocked waiting to establish a connection, *connect*( ) will fail and set *errno* to [EINTR], but the connection request will not be aborted, and the connection will be established asynchronously.

If the connection cannot be established immediately and O_NONBLOCK is set for the file descriptor for the socket, *connect*( ) will fail and set *errno* to [EINPROGRESS], but the connection request will not be aborted, and the connection will be established asynchronously. Subsequent calls to *connect*( ) for the same socket, before the connection is established, will fail and set *errno* to [EALREADY].

When the connection has been established asynchronously, *select*( ) and *poll*( ) will indicate that the file descriptor for the socket is ready for writing.

RETURN VALUE

Upon successful completion, *connect*( ) returns 0. Otherwise, −1 is returned and *errno* is set to indicate the error.

ERRORS

The *connect*( ) function will fail if:

[EADDRNOTAVAIL]   The specified address is not available from the local machine.

[EAFNOSUPPORT]   The specified address is not a valid address for the address family of the specified socket.

[EALREADY]   A connection request is already in progress for the specified socket.

[EBADF]	The *socket* argument is not a valid file descriptor.
[ECONNREFUSED]	The target address was not listening for connections or refused the connection request.
[EINPROGRESS]	O_NONBLOCK is set for the file descriptor for the socket and the connection cannot be immediately established; the connection will be established asynchronously.
[EINTR]	The attempt to establish a connection was interrupted by delivery of a signal that was caught; the connection will be established asynchronously.
[EISCONN]	The specified socket is connection-oriented and is already connected.
[ENETUNREACH]	No route to the network is present.
[ENOTSOCK]	The *socket* argument does not refer to a socket.
[EPROTOTYPE]	The specified address has a different type than the socket bound to the specified peer address.
[ETIMEDOUT]	The attempt to connect timed out before a connection was made.

If the address family of the socket is AF_UNIX, then *connect( )* will fail if:

[ENOTDIR]	A component of the path prefix of the pathname in *address* is not a directory.
[ENAMETOOLONG]	A component of a pathname exceeded {NAME_MAX} characters, or an entire pathname exceeded {PATH_MAX} characters.
[EACCES]	Search permission is denied for a component of the path prefix; or write access to the named socket is denied.
[EIO]	An I/O error occurred while reading from or writing to the file system.
[ELOOP]	Too many symbolic links were encountered in translating the pathname in *address*.
[ENOENT]	A component of the pathname does not name an existing file or the pathname is an empty string.

The *connect( )* function may fail if:

[EADDRINUSE]	Attempt to establish a connection that uses addresses that are already in use.
[ECONNRESET]	Remote host reset the connection request.
[EHOSTUNREACH]	The destination host cannot be reached (probably because the host is down or a remote router cannot reach it).
[EINVAL]	The *address_len* argument is not a valid length for the address family; or invalid address family in sockaddr structure.
[ENAMETOOLONG]	Pathname resolution of a symbolic link produced an intermediate result whose length exceeds {PATH_MAX}.
[ENETDOWN]	The local interface used to reach the destination is down.
[ENOBUFS]	No buffer space is available.

[ENOSR]	There were insufficient STREAMS resources available to complete the operation.
[EOPNOTSUPP]	The socket is listening and can not be connected.

APPLICATION USAGE

If *connect*( ) fails, the state of the socket is unspecified. Portable applications should close the file descriptor and create a new socket before attempting to reconnect.

SEE ALSO

accept( ), *bind*( ), *close*( ), *getsockname*( ), *poll*( ), *select*( ), *send*( ), *shutdown*( ), *socket*( ), **<sys/socket.h>**.

EXAMPLE

See examples at the end of chapter.

NAME

fcntl — file control

Note: The **XSH** specification contains the basic definition of this interface. The following additional information pertains to Sockets.

DESCRIPTION

UX   The following additional values for *cmd* are defined in **<fcntl.h>**:

F_GETOWN   If *fildes* refers to a socket, get the process or process group ID specified to receive SIGURG signals when out-of-band data is available. Positive values indicate a process ID; negative values, other than –1, indicate a process group ID. If *fildes* does not refer to a socket, the results are unspecified.

F_SETOWN   If *fildes* refers to a socket, set the process or process group ID specified to receive SIGURG signals when out-of-band data is available, using the value of the third argument, *arg*, taken as type **int**. Positive values indicate a process ID; negative values, other than –1, indicate a process group ID. If *fildes* does not refer to a socket, the results are unspecified.

RETURN VALUE

UX   Upon successful completion, the value returned depends on *cmd* as follows:

F_GETOWN   Value of the socket owner process or process group; this will not be –1.

F_SETOWN   Value other than –1.

EXAMPLE

See examples at the end of chapter.

NAME

fgetpos — get current file position information

Note: The **XSH** specification contains the basic definition of this interface. The following additional information pertains to Sockets.

ERRORS

UX   The *fgetpos( )* function may fail if:

[ESPIPE]   The file descriptor underlying *stream* is associated with a socket.

EXAMPLE

See examples at the end of chapter.

NAME

fsetpos — set current file position

Note: The **XSH** specification contains the basic definition of this interface. The following additional information pertains to Sockets.

ERRORS

UX   The *fsetpos*( ) function may fail if:

[ESPIPE]   The file descriptor underlying *stream* is associated with a socket.

EXAMPLE

See examples at the end of chapter.

NAME

ftell — return a file offset in a stream

Note: The **XSH** specification contains the basic definition of this interface. The following additional information pertains to Sockets.

ERRORS

UX The *ftell*( ) function may fail if:

[ESPIPE] The file descriptor underlying *stream* is associated with a socket.

EXAMPLE

See examples at the end of chapter.

NAME

getpeername — get the name of the peer socket

SYNOPSIS

UX
```
#include <sys/socket.h>

int getpeername(int socket, struct sockaddr *address,
                size_t *address_len);
```

DESCRIPTION

The *getpeername*( ) function retrieves the peer address of the specified socket, stores this address in the **sockaddr** structure pointed to by the *address* argument, and stores the length of this address in the object pointed to by the *address_len* argument.

If the actual length of the address is greater than the length of the supplied **sockaddr** structure, the stored address will be truncated.

If the protocol permits connections by unbound clients, and the peer is not bound, then the value stored in the object pointed to by *address* is unspecified.

RETURN VALUE

Upon successful completion, 0 is returned. Otherwise, −1 is returned and *errno* is set to indicate the error.

ERRORS

The *getpeername*( ) function will fail if:

[EBADF]   The *socket* argument is not a valid file descriptor.

[ENOTSOCK]   The *socket* argument does not refer to a socket.

[ENOTCONN]   The socket is not connected or otherwise has not had the peer prespecified.

[EINVAL]   The socket has been shut down.

[EOPNOTSUPP]   The operation is not supported for the socket protocol.

The *getpeername*( ) function may fail if:

[ENOBUFS]   Insufficient resources were available in the system to complete the call.

[ENOSR]   There were insufficient STREAMS resources available for the operation to complete.

SEE ALSO

accept( ), *bind*( ), *getsockname*( ), *socket*( ), **<sys/socket.h>**.

EXAMPLE

See examples at the end of chapter.

NAME

getsockname — get the socket name

SYNOPSIS

UX   `#include <sys/socket.h>`

```
int getsockname(int socket, struct sockaddr *address,
                size_t *address_len);
```

DESCRIPTION

The *getsockname*( ) function retrieves the locally-bound name of the specified socket, stores this address in the **sockaddr** structure pointed to by the *address* argument, and stores the length of this address in the object pointed to by the *address_len* argument.

If the actual length of the address is greater than the length of the supplied **sockaddr** structure, the stored address will be truncated.

If the socket has not been bound to a local name, the value stored in the object pointed to by *address* is unspecified.

RETURN VALUE

Upon successful completion, 0 is returned, the *address* argument points to the address of the socket, and the *address_len* argument points to the length of the address. Otherwise, −1 is returned and *errno* is set to indicate the error.

ERRORS

The *getsockname*( ) function will fail:

[EBADF]   The *socket* argument is not a valid file descriptor.

[ENOTSOCK]   The *socket* argument does not refer to a socket.

[EOPNOTSUPP]   The operation is not supported for this socket's protocol.

The *getsockname*( ) function may fail if:

[EINVAL]   The socket has been shut down.

[ENOBUFS]   Insufficient resources were available in the system to complete the call.

[ENOSR]   There were insufficient STREAMS resources available for the operation to complete.

SEE ALSO

accept( ), *bind*( ), *getpeername*( ), *socket*( ), **<sys/socket.h>**.

EXAMPLE

See examples at the end of chapter.

NAME

getsockopt — get the socket options

SYNOPSIS

UX

```
#include <sys/socket.h>

int getsockopt(int socket, int level, int option_name, void *option_value,
    size_t *option_len);
```

DESCRIPTION

The *getsockopt*( ) function retrieves the value for the option specified by the *option_name* argument for the socket specified by the *socket* argument. If the size of the option value is greater than *option_len*, the value stored in the object pointed to by the *option_value* argument will be silently truncated. Otherwise, the object pointed to by the *option_len* argument will be modified to indicate the actual length of the value.

The *level* argument specifies the protocol level at which the option resides. To retrieve options at the socket level, specify the *level* argument as SOL_SOCKET. To retrieve options at other levels, supply the appropriate protocol number for the protocol controlling the option. For example, to indicate that an option will be interpreted by the TCP (Transport Control Protocol), set *level* to the protocol number of TCP, as defined in the **<netinet/in.h>** header, or as determined by using *getprotobyname*( ) function.

The *option_name* argument specifies a single option to be retrieved. It can be one of the following values defined in **<sys/socket.h>**:

SO_DEBUG   Reports whether debugging information is being recorded. This option stores an **int** value.

SO_ACCEPTCONN   Reports whether socket listening is enabled. This option stores an **int** value.

SO_BROADCAST   Reports whether transmission of broadcast messages is supported, if this is supported by the protocol. This option stores an **int** value.

SO_REUSEADDR   Reports whether the rules used in validating addresses supplied to *bind*( ) should allow reuse of local addresses, if this is supported by the protocol. This option stores an **int** value.

SO_KEEPALIVE   Reports whether connections are kept active with periodic transmission of messages, if this is supported by the protocol.

                If the connected socket fails to respond to these messages, the connection is broken and processes writing to that socket are notified with a SIGPIPE signal. This option stores an **int** value.

SO_LINGER   Reports whether the socket lingers on *close*( ) if data is present. If SO_LINGER is set, the system blocks the process during *close*( ) until it can transmit the data or until the end of the interval indicated by the **l_linger** member, whichever comes first. If SO_LINGER is not specified, and *close*( ) is issued, the system handles the call in a way that allows the process to continue as quickly as possible. This option stores a **linger** structure.

SO_OOBINLINE   Reports whether the socket leaves received out-of-band data (data marked urgent) in line. This option stores an **int** value.

SO_SNDBUF   Reports send buffer size information. This option stores an **int** value.

SO_RCVBUF	Reports receive buffer size information. This option stores an **int** value.
SO_ERROR	Reports information about error status and clears it. This option stores an **int** value.
SO_TYPE	Reports the socket type. This option stores an **int** value.

For boolean options, 0 indicates that the option is disabled and 1 indicates that the option is enabled.

Options at other protocol levels vary in format and name.

RETURN VALUE

Upon successful completion, *getsockopt*( ) returns 0. Otherwise, −1 is returned and *errno* is set to indicate the error.

ERRORS

The *getsockopt*( ) function will fail if:

[EBADF]	The *socket* argument is not a valid file descriptor.
[ENOPROTOOPT]	The option is not supported by the protocol.
[ENOTSOCK]	The *socket* argument does not refer to a socket.
[EINVAL]	The specified option is invalid at the specified socket level.
[EOPNOTSUPP]	The operation is not supported by the socket protocol.

The *getsockopt*( ) function may fail if:

[EINVAL]	The socket has been shut down.
[ENOBUFS]	Insufficient resources are available in the system to complete the call.
[ENOSR]	There were insufficient STREAMS resources available for the operation to complete.

SEE ALSO

bind( ), *close*( ), *endprotoent*( ), *setsockopt*( ), *socket*( ), **<sys/socket.h>**.

EXAMPLE

See examples at the end of chapter.

NAME

listen — listen for socket connections and limit the queue of incoming connections

SYNOPSIS

UX
```
#include <sys/socket.h>

int listen(int socket, int backlog);
```

DESCRIPTION

The *listen( )* function marks a connection-oriented socket, specified by the *socket* argument, as accepting connections, and limits the number of outstanding connections in the socket's listen queue to the value specified by the *backlog* argument.

If *listen( )* is called with a *backlog* argument value that is less than 0, the function sets the length of the socket's listen queue to 0.

Implementations may limit the length of the socket's listen queue. If *backlog* exceeds the implementation-dependent maximum queue length, the length of the socket's listen queue will be set to the maximum supported value.

RETURN VALUE

Upon successful completions, *listen( )* returns 0. Otherwise, −1 is returned and *errno* is set to indicate the error.

ERRORS

The *listen( )* function will fail if:

[EBADF]   The *socket* argument is not a valid file descriptor.

[ENOTSOCK]   The *socket* argument does not refer to a socket.

[EOPNOTSUPP]   The socket protocol does not support *listen( )*.

[EINVAL]   The *socket* is already connected.

[EDESTADDRREQ]   The socket is not bound to a local address, and the protocol does not support listening on an unbound socket.

The *listen( )* function may fail if:

[EINVAL]   The *socket* has been shut down.

[ENOBUFS]   Insufficient resources are available in the system to complete the call.

SEE ALSO

accept( ), *connect( )*, *socket( )*, **<sys/socket.h>**.

EXAMPLE

See examples at the end of chapter.

NAME

lseek — move read/write file offset

Note: The **XSH** specification contains the basic definition of this interface. The following additional information pertains to Sockets.

ERRORS

UX   The *lseek*( ) function will fail if:

[ESPIPE]   The file descriptor underlying *stream* is associated with a socket.

EXAMPLE

See examples at the end of chapter.

NAME

poll — input/output multiplexing

Note: The **XSH** specification contains the basic definition of this interface. The following additional information pertains to Sockets.

DESCRIPTION

ux The *poll( )* function supports sockets.

A file descriptor for a socket that is listening for connections will indicate that it is ready for reading, once connections are available. A file descriptor for a socket that is connecting asynchronously will indicate that it is ready for writing, once a connection has been established.

EXAMPLE

See examples at the end of chapter.

NAME

read, readv — read from file

Note: The **XSH** specification contains the basic definition of this interface. The following additional information pertains to Sockets.

DESCRIPTION

UX   If *fildes* refers to a socket, *read*( ) is equivalent to *recv*( ) with no flags set.

EXAMPLE

See examples at the end of chapter.

NAME

recv — receive a message from a connected socket

SYNOPSIS

UX

```
#include <sys/socket.h>
```

```
ssize_t recv(int socket, void *buffer, size_t length, int flags);
```

DESCRIPTION

The *recv*( ) function receives messages from a connected socket. The function takes the following arguments:

socket	Specifies the socket file descriptor.
buffer	Points to a buffer where the message should be stored.
length	Specifies the length in bytes of the buffer pointed to by the *buffer* argument.
flags	Specifies the type of message reception. Values of this argument are formed by logically OR'ing zero or more of the following values:

MSG_PEEK	Peeks at an incoming message. The data is treated as unread and the next *recv*( ) or similar function will still return this data.
MSG_OOB	Requests out-of-band data. The significance and semantics of out-of-band data are protocol-specific.
MSG_WAITALL	Requests that the function block until the full amount of data requested can be returned. The function may return a smaller amount of data if a signal is caught, the connection is terminated, or an error is pending for the socket.

The *recv*( ) function returns the length of the message written to the buffer pointed to by the *buffer* argument. For message-based sockets such as SOCK_DGRAM and SOCK_SEQPACKET, the entire message must be read in a single operation. If a message is too long to fit in the supplied buffer, and MSG_PEEK is not set in the *flags* argument, the excess bytes are discarded. For stream-based sockets such as SOCK_STREAM, message boundaries are ignored. In this case, data is returned to the user as soon as it becomes available, and no data is discarded.

If the MSG_WAITALL flag is not set, data will be returned only up to the end of the first message.

If no messages are available at the socket and O_NONBLOCK is not set on the socket's file descriptor, *recv*( ) blocks until a message arrives. If no messages are available at the socket and O_NONBLOCK is set on the socket's file descriptor, *recv*( ) fails and sets *errno* to [EWOULDBLOCK] or [EAGAIN].

RETURN VALUE

Upon successful completion, *recv*( ) returns the length of the message in bytes. If no messages are available to be received and the peer has performed an orderly shutdown, *recv*( ) returns 0. Otherwise, −1 is returned and *errno* is set to indicate the error.

ERRORS

The *recv*( ) function will fail if:

[EBADF]	The *socket* argument is not a valid file descriptor.
[ECONNRESET]	A connection was forcibly closed by a peer.
[EINTR]	The *recv*( ) function was interrupted by a signal that was caught, before any data was available.
[EINVAL]	The MSG_OOB flag is set and no out-of-band data is available.
[ENOTCONN]	A receive is attempted on a connection-oriented socket that is not connected.
[ENOTSOCK]	The *socket* argument does not refer to a socket.
[EOPNOTSUPP]	The specified flags are not supported for this socket type or protocol.
[ETIMEDOUT]	The connection timed out during connection establishment, or due to a transmission timeout on active connection.
[EWOULDBLOCK] or [EAGAIN]	The socket's file descriptor is marked O_NONBLOCK and no data is waiting to be received; or MSG_OOB is set and no out-of-band data is available and either the socket's file descriptor is marked O_NONBLOCK or the socket does not support blocking to await out-of-band data.

The *recv*( ) function may fail if:

[EIO]	An I/O error occurred while reading from or writing to the file system.
[ENOBUFS]	Insufficient resources were available in the system to perform the operation.
[ENOMEM]	Insufficient memory was available to fulfill the request.
[ENOSR]	There were insufficient STREAMS resources available for the operation to complete.

APPLICATION USAGE

The *recv*( ) function is identical to *recvfrom*( ) with a zero *address_len* argument, and to *read*( ) if no flags are used.

The *select*( ) and *poll*( ) functions can be used to determine when data is available to be received.

SEE ALSO

poll( ), *read*( ), *recvmsg*( ), *recvfrom*( ), *select*( ), *send*( ), *sendmsg*( ), *sendto*( ), *shutdown*( ), *socket*( ), *write*( ), **<sys/socket.h>**.

EXAMPLE

See examples at the end of chapter.

NAME

recvfrom — receive a message from a socket

SYNOPSIS

UX

```
#include <sys/socket.h>

ssize_t recvfrom(int socket, void *buffer, size_t length, int flags,
        struct sockaddr *address, size_t *address_len);
```

DESCRIPTION

The *recvfrom*( ) function receives a message from a connection-oriented or connectionless socket. It is normally used with connectionless sockets because it permits the application to retrieve the source address of received data.

The function takes the following arguments:

socket	Specifies the socket file descriptor.
buffer	Points to the buffer where the message should be stored.
length	Specifies the length in bytes of the buffer pointed to by the *buffer* argument.
flags	Specifies the type of message reception. Values of this argument are formed by logically OR'ing zero or more of the following values:

	MSG_PEEK	Peeks at an incoming message. The data is treated as unread and the next *recvfrom*( ) or similar function will still return this data.
	MSG_OOB	Requests out-of-band data. The significance and semantics of out-of-band data are protocol-specific.
	MSG_WAITALL	Requests that the function block until the full amount of data requested can be returned. The function may return a smaller amount of data if a signal is caught, the connection is terminated, or an error is pending for the socket.

address	A null pointer, or points to a **sockaddr** structure in which the sending address is to be stored. The length and format of the address depend on the address family of the socket.
address_len	Specifies the length of the **sockaddr** structure pointed to by the *address* argument.

The *recvfrom*( ) function returns the length of the message written to the buffer pointed to by the *buffer* argument. For message-based sockets such as SOCK_DGRAM and SOCK_SEQPACKET, the entire message must be read in a single operation. If a message is too long to fit in the supplied buffer, and MSG_PEEK is not set in the *flags* argument, the excess bytes are discarded. For stream-based sockets such as SOCK_STREAM, message boundaries are ignored. In this case, data is returned to the user as soon as it becomes available, and no data is discarded.

If the MSG_WAITALL flag is not set, data will be returned only up to the end of the first message.

Not all protocols provide the source address for messages. If the *address* argument is not a null pointer and the protocol provides the source address of messages, the source address of the received message is stored in the **sockaddr** structure pointed to by the *address* argument, and the length of this address is stored in the object pointed to by the *address_len* argument.

If the actual length of the address is greater than the length of the supplied **sockaddr** structure, the stored address will be truncated.

If the *address* argument is not a null pointer and the protocol does not provide the source address of messages, the the value stored in the object pointed to by *address* is unspecified.

If no messages are available at the socket and O_NONBLOCK is not set on the socket's file descriptor, *recvfrom( )* blocks until a message arrives. If no messages are available at the socket and O_NONBLOCK is set on the socket's file descriptor, *recvfrom( )* fails and sets *errno* to [EWOULDBLOCK] or [EAGAIN].

RETURN VALUE

Upon successful completion, *recvfrom( )* returns the length of the message in bytes. If no messages are available to be received and the peer has performed an orderly shutdown, *recvfrom( )* returns 0. Otherwise the function returns –1 and sets *errno* to indicate the error.

ERRORS

The *recvfrom( )* function will fail if:

[EBADF]	The *socket* argument is not a valid file descriptor.
[ECONNRESET]	A connection was forcibly closed by a peer.
[EINTR]	A signal interrupted *recvfrom( )* before any data was available.
[EINVAL]	The MSG_OOB flag is set and no out-of-band data is available.
[ENOTCONN]	A receive is attempted on a connection-oriented socket that is not connected.
[ENOTSOCK]	The *socket* argument does not refer to a socket.
[EOPNOTSUPP]	The specified flags are not supported for this socket type.
[ETIMEDOUT]	The connection timed out during connection establishment, or due to a transmission timeout on active connection.
[EWOULDBLOCK] or [EAGAIN]	The socket's file descriptor is marked O_NONBLOCK and no data is waiting to be received; or MSG_OOB is set and no out-of-band data is available and either the socket's file descriptor is marked O_NONBLOCK or the socket does not support blocking to await out-of-band data.

The *recvfrom( )* function may fail if:

[EIO]	An I/O error occurred while reading from or writing to the file system.
[ENOBUFS]	Insufficient resources were available in the system to perform the operation.
[ENOMEM]	Insufficient memory was available to fulfill the request.
[ENOSR]	There were insufficient STREAMS resources available for the operation to complete.

APPLICATION USAGE

The *select( )* and *poll( )* functions can be used to determine when data is available to be received.

SEE ALSO

poll( ), *read*( ), *recv*( ), *recvmsg*( ), *select*( ) *send*( ), *sendmsg*( ), *sendto*( ), *shutdown*( ), *socket*( ), *write*( ), **<sys/socket.h>**.

EXAMPLE

See examples at the end of chapter.

NAME

recvmsg — receive a message from a socket

SYNOPSIS

UX   `#include <sys/socket.h>`

`ssize_t recvmsg(int socket, struct msghdr *message, int flags);`

DESCRIPTION

The *recvmsg( )* function receives a message from a connection-oriented or connectionless socket. It is normally used with connectionless sockets because it permits the application to retrieve the source address of received data.

The function takes the following arguments:

socket   Specifies the socket file descriptor.

message   Points to a **msghdr** structure, containing both the buffer to store the source address and the buffers for the incoming message. The length and format of the address depend on the address family of the socket. The **msg_flags** member is ignored on input, but may contain meaningful values on output.

flags   Specifies the type of message reception. Values of this argument are formed by logically OR'ing zero or more of the following values:

MSG_OOB	Requests out-of-band data. The significance and semantics of out-of-band data are protocol-specific.
MSG_PEEK	Peeks at the incoming message.
MSG_WAITALL	Requests that the function block until the full amount of data requested can be returned. The function may return a smaller amount of data if a signal is caught, the connection is terminated, or an error is pending for the socket.

The *recvmsg( )* function receives messages from unconnected or connected sockets and returns the length of the message.

The *recvmsg( )* function returns the total length of the message. For message-based sockets such as SOCK_DGRAM and SOCK_SEQPACKET, the entire message must be read in a single operation. If a message is too long to fit in the supplied buffers, and MSG_PEEK is not set in the *flags* argument, the excess bytes are discarded, and MSG_TRUNC is set in the **msg_flags** member of the **msghdr** structure. For stream-based sockets such as SOCK_STREAM, message boundaries are ignored. In this case, data is returned to the user as soon as it becomes available, and no data is discarded.

If the MSG_WAITALL flag is not set, data will be returned only up to the end of the first message.

If no messages are available at the socket and O_NONBLOCK is not set on the socket's file descriptor, *recvfrom( )* blocks until a message arrives. If no messages are available at the socket and O_NONBLOCK is set on the socket's file descriptor, *recvfrom( )* function fails and sets *errno* to [EWOULDBLOCK] or [EAGAIN].

In the **msghdr** structure, the **msg_name** and **msg_namelen** members specify the source address if the socket is unconnected. If the socket is connected, the **msg_name** and **msg_namelen** members are ignored. The **msg_name** member may be a null pointer if no names are desired or required. The **msg_iov** and **msg_iovlen** members describe the scatter/gather locations.

On successful completion, the **msg_flags** member of the message header is the bitwise-inclusive OR of all of the following flags that indicate conditions detected for the received message:.

MSG_EOR   End of record was received (if supported by the protocol).

MSG_OOB   Out-of-band data was received.

MSG_TRUNC   Normal data was truncated.

MSG_CTRUNC   Control data was truncated.

RETURN VALUE

Upon successful completion, *recvmsg*( ) returns the length of the message in bytes. If no messages are available to be received and the peer has performed an orderly shutdown, *recvmsg*( ) returns 0. Otherwise, −1 is returned and *errno* is set to indicate the error.

ERRORS

The *recvmsg*( ) function will fail if:

[EBADF]   The *socket* argument is not a valid open file descriptor.

[ENOTSOCK]   The *socket* argument does not refer to a socket.

[EINVAL]   The sum of the **iov_len** values overflows an **ssize_t**.

[EWOULDBLOCK] or [EAGAIN]
                    The socket's file descriptor is marked O_NONBLOCK and no data is waiting to be received; or MSG_OOB is set and no out-of-band data is available and either the socket's file descriptor is marked O_NONBLOCK or the socket does not support blocking to await out-of-band data.

[EINTR]   This function was interrupted by a signal before any data was available.

[EOPNOTSUPP]   The specified flags are not supported for this socket type.

[ENOTCONN]   A receive is attempted on a connection-oriented socket that is not connected.

[ETIMEDOUT]   The connection timed out during connection establishment, or due to a transmission timeout on active connection.

[EINVAL]   The MSG_OOB flag is set and no out-of-band data is available.

[ECONNRESET]   A connection was forcibly closed by a peer.

The *recvmsg*( ) function may fail if:

[EINVAL]   The **msg_iovlen** member of the **msghdr** structure pointed to by *msg* is less than or equal to 0, or is greater than {IOV_MAX}.

[EIO]   An IO error occurred while reading from or writing to the file system.

[ENOBUFS]   Insufficient resources were available in the system to perform the operation.

[ENOMEM]   Insufficient memory was available to fulfill the request.

[ENOSR]   There were insufficient STREAMS resources available for the operation to complete.

APPLICATION USAGE

The *select*( ) and *poll*( ) functions can be used to determine when data is available to be received.

SEE ALSO

poll( ), *recv*( ), *recvfrom*( ), *select*( ), *send*( ), *sendmsg*( ), *sendto*( ), *shutdown*( ), *socket*( ), **<sys/socket.h>**.

EXAMPLE

See examples at the end of chapter.

NAME

select — synchronous I/O multiplexing

Note: The **XSH** specification contains the basic definition of this interface. The following additional information pertains to Sockets.

DESCRIPTION

UX A file descriptor for a socket that is listening for connections will indicate that it is ready for reading, when connections are available. A file descriptor for a socket that is connecting asynchronously will indicate that it is ready for writing, when a connection has been established.

EXAMPLE

See examples at the end of chapter.

NAME

send — send a message on a socket

SYNOPSIS

UX   `#include <sys/socket.h>`

     `ssize_t send(int socket, const void *buffer, size_t length, int flags);`

DESCRIPTION

socket	Specifies the socket file descriptor.
buffer	Points to the buffer containing the message to send.
length	Specifies the length of the message in bytes.
flags	Specifies the type of message transmission. Values of this argument are formed by logically OR'ing zero or more of the following flags:

	MSG_EOR	Terminates a record (if supported by the protocol)
	MSG_OOB	Sends out-of-band data on sockets that support out-of-band communications. The significance and semantics of out-of-band data are protocol-specific.

The *send*( ) function initiates transmission of a message from the specified socket to its peer. The *send*( ) function sends a message only when the socket is connected.

The length of the message to be sent is specified by the *length* argument. If the message is too long to pass through the underlying protocol, *send*( ) fails and no data is transmitted.

Successful completion of a call to *send*( ) does not guarantee delivery of the message. A return value of −1 indicates only locally-detected errors.

If space is not available at the sending socket to hold the message to be transmitted and the socket file descriptor does not have O_NONBLOCK set, *send*( ) blocks until space is available. If space is not available at the sending socket to hold the message to be transmitted and the socket file descriptor does have O_NONBLOCK set, *send*( ) will fail. The *select*( ) and *poll*( ) functions can be used to determine when it is possible to send more data.

RETURN VALUE

Upon successful completion, *send*( ) returns the number of bytes sent. Otherwise, −1 is returned and *errno* is set to indicate the error.

APPLICATION USAGE

The *send*( ) function is identical to *sendto*( ) with a null pointer *dest_len* argument, and to *write*( ) if no flags are used.

ERRORS

The *send*( ) function will fail if:

[EBADF]	The *socket* argument is not a valid file descriptor.
[ECONNRESET]	A connection was forcibly closed by a peer.
[EDESTADDRREQ]	The socket is not connection-oriented and no peer address is set.
[EINTR]	A signal interrupted *send*( ) before any data was transmitted.
[EMSGSIZE]	The message is too large be sent all at once, as the socket requires.

[ENOTCONN]	The socket is not connected or otherwise has not had the peer prespecified.
[ENOTSOCK]	The *socket* argument does not refer to a socket.
[EOPNOTSUPP]	The *socket* argument is associated with a socket that does not support one or more of the values set in *flags*.
[EPIPE]	The socket is shut down for writing, or the socket is connection-oriented and the peer is closed or shut down for reading. In the latter case, and if the socket is of type SOCK_STREAM, the SIGPIPE signal is generated to the calling process.
[EWOULDBLOCK] or [EAGAIN]	The socket's file descriptor is marked O_NONBLOCK and the requested operation would block.

The *send*( ) function may fail if:

[ENETDOWN]	The local interface used to reach the destination is down.
[ENETUNREACH]	No route to the network is present.
[ENOBUFS]	Insufficient resources were available in the system to perform the operation.
[ENOSR]	There were insufficient STREAMS resources available for the operation to complete.
[EIO]	An I/O error occurred while reading from or writing to the file system.

SEE ALSO

connect( ), *getsockopt*( ), *poll*( ), *recv*( ), *recvfrom*( ), *recvmsg*( ), *select*( ), *sendmsg*( ), *sendto*( ), *setsockopt*( ), *shutdown*( ), *socket*( ), **<sys/socket.h>**.

EXAMPLE

See examples at the end of chapter.

NAME

sendmsg — send a message on a socket using a message structure

SYNOPSIS

UX

```
#include <sys/socket.h>

ssize_t sendmsg (int socket, const struct msghdr *message, int flags);
```

DESCRIPTION

The *sendmsg( )* function sends a message through a connection-oriented or connectionless socket. If the socket is connectionless, the message will be sent to the address specified by *msghdr*. If the socket is connection-oriented, the destination address in *msghdr* is ignored.

The function takes the following arguments:

socket   Specifies the socket file descriptor.

message   Points to a **msghdr** structure, containing both the destination address and the buffers for the outgoing message. The length and format of the address depend on the address family of the socket. The **msg_flags** member is ignored.

flags   Specifies the type of message transmission. The application may specify 0 or the following flag:

                        MSG_EOR   Terminates a record (if supported by the protocol)

                        MSG_OOB   Sends out-of-band data on sockets that support out-of-bound data. The significance and semantics of out-of-band data are protocol-specific.

Successful completion of a call to *sendmsg( )* does not guarantee delivery of the message. A return value of −1 indicates only locally-detected errors.

If space is not available at the sending socket to hold the message to be transmitted and the socket file descriptor does not have O_NONBLOCK set, *sendmsg( )* function blocks until space is available. If space is not available at the sending socket to hold the message to be transmitted and the socket file descriptor does have O_NONBLOCK set, *sendmsg( )* function will fail.

If the socket protocol supports broadcast and the specified address is a broadcast address for the socket protocol, *sendmsg( )* will fail if the SO_BROADCAST option is not set for the socket.

RETURN VALUE

Upon successful completion, *sendmsg( )* function returns the number of bytes sent. Otherwise, −1 is returned and *errno* is set to indicate the error.

ERRORS

The *sendmsg( )* function will fail if:

[EAFNOSUPPORT]   Addresses in the specified address family cannot be used with this socket.

[EBADF]   The *socket* argument is not a valid file descriptor.

[ECONNRESET]   A connection was forcibly closed by a peer.

[EINTR]   A signal interrupted *sendmsg( )* before any data was transmitted.

[EINVAL]   The sum of the **iov_len** values overflows an **ssize_t**.

[EMSGSIZE]	The message is too large to be sent all at once, as the socket requires.
[ENOTCONN]	The socket is connection-oriented but is not connected.
[ENOTSOCK]	The *socket* argument does not refer a socket.
[EOPNOTSUPP]	The *socket* argument is associated with a socket that does not support one or more of the values set in *flags*.
[EPIPE]	The socket is shut down for writing, or the socket is connection-oriented and the peer is closed or shut down for reading. In the latter case, and if the socket is of type SOCK_STREAM, the SIGPIPE signal is generated to the calling process.

[EWOULDBLOCK] or [EAGAIN]
> The socket's file descriptor is marked O_NONBLOCK and the requested operation would block.

If the address family of the socket is AF_UNIX, then *sendmsg( )* will fail if:

[EACCES]	Search permission is denied for a component of the path prefix; or write access to the named socket is denied.
[EIO]	An I/O error occurred while reading from or writing to the file system.
[ELOOP]	Too many symbolic links were encountered in translating the pathname in the socket address.
[ENAMETOOLONG]	A component of a pathname exceeded {NAME_MAX} characters, or an entire pathname exceeded {PATH_MAX} characters.
[ENOENT]	A component of the pathname does not name an existing file or the pathname is an empty string.
[ENOTDIR]	A component of the path prefix of the pathname in the socket address is not a directory.

The *sendmsg( )* function may fail if:

[EDESTADDRREQ]	The socket is not connection-oriented and does not have its peer address set, and no destination address was specified.
[EHOSTUNREACH]	The destination host cannot be reached (probably because the host is down or a remote router cannot reach it).
[EINVAL]	The **msg_iovlen** member of the **msghdr** structure pointed to by *msg* is less than or equal to 0, or is greater than {IOV_MAX}.
[EIO]	An I/O error occurred while reading from or writing to the file system.
[EISCONN]	A destination address was specified and the socket is connection-oriented and is already connected.
[ENETDOWN]	The local interface used to reach the destination is down.
[ENETUNREACH]	No route to the network is present.
[ENOBUFS]	Insufficient resources were available in the system to perform the operation.
[ENOMEM]	Insufficient memory was available to fulfill the request.
[ENOSR]	There were insufficient STREAMS resources available for the operation to complete.

If the address family of the socket is AF_UNIX, then *sendmsg*( ) may fail if:

[ENAMETOOLONG] Pathname resolution of a symbolic link produced an intermediate result whose length exceeds {PATH_MAX}.

APPLICATION USAGE

The *select*( ) and *poll*( ) functions can be used to determine when it is possible to send more data.

SEE ALSO

getsockopt( ), *poll*( ) *recv*( ), *recvfrom*( ), *recvmsg*( ), *select*( ), *send*( ), *sendto*( ), *setsockopt*( ), *shutdown*( ), *socket*( ), **<sys/socket.h>**.

EXAMPLE

See examples at the end of chapter.

NAME

sendto — send a message on a socket

SYNOPSIS

UX `#include <sys/socket.h>`

```
ssize_t sendto(int socket, const void *message, size_t length, int flags,
      const struct sockaddr *dest_addr, size_t dest_len);
```

DESCRIPTION

The *sendto*( ) function sends a message through a connection-oriented or connectionless socket. If the socket is connectionless, the message will be sent to the address specified by *dest_addr*. If the socket is connection-oriented, *dest_addr* is ignored.

The function takes the following arguments:

socket	Specifies the socket file descriptor.
message	Points to a buffer containing the message to be sent.
length	Specifies the size of the message in bytes.
flags	Specifies the type of message transmission. Values of this argument are formed by logically OR'ing zero or more of the following flags:

	MSG_EOR	Terminates a record (if supported by the protocol)
	MSG_OOB	Sends out-of-band data on sockets that support out-of-band data. The significance and semantics of out-of-band data are protocol-specific.

dest_addr	Points to a **sockaddr** structure containing the destination address. The length and format of the address depend on the address family of the socket.
dest_len	Specifies the length of the **sockaddr** structure pointed to by the *dest_addr* argument.

If the socket protocol supports broadcast and the specified address is a broadcast address for the socket protocol, *sendto*( ) will fail if the SO_BROADCAST option is not set for the socket.

The *dest_addr* argument specifies the address of the target. The *length* argument specifies the length of the message.

Successful completion of a call to *sendto*( ) does not guarantee delivery of the message. A return value of −1 indicates only locally-detected errors.

If space is not available at the sending socket to hold the message to be transmitted and the socket file descriptor does not have O_NONBLOCK set, *sendto*( ) blocks until space is available. If space is not available at the sending socket to hold the message to be transmitted and the socket file descriptor does have O_NONBLOCK set, *sendto*( ) will fail.

RETURN VALUE

Upon successful completion, *sendto*( ) returns the number of bytes sent. Otherwise, −1 is returned and *errno* is set to indicate the error.

ERRORS

The *sendto*( ) function will fail if:

[EAFNOSUPPORT]	Addresses in the specified address family cannot be used with this socket.

[EBADF]	The *socket* argument is not a valid file descriptor.
[ECONNRESET]	A connection was forcibly closed by a peer.
[EINTR]	A signal interrupted *sendto*( ) before any data was transmitted.
[EMSGSIZE]	The message is too large to be sent all at once, as the socket requires.
[ENOTCONN]	The socket is connection-oriented but is not connected.
[ENOTSOCK]	The *socket* argument does not refer to a socket.
[EOPNOTSUPP]	The *socket* argument is associated with a socket that does not support one or more of the values set in *flags*.
[EPIPE]	The socket is shut down for writing, or the socket is connection-oriented and the peer is closed or shut down for reading. In the latter case, and if the socket is of type SOCK_STREAM, the SIGPIPE signal is generated to the calling process.
[EWOULDBLOCK] or [EAGAIN]	The socket's file descriptor is marked O_NONBLOCK and the requested operation would block.

If the address family of the socket is AF_UNIX, then *sendto*( ) will fail if:

[EACCES]	Search permission is denied for a component of the path prefix; or write access to the named socket is denied.
[EIO]	An I/O error occurred while reading from or writing to the file system.
[ELOOP]	Too many symbolic links were encountered in translating the pathname in the socket address.
[ENAMETOOLONG]	A component of a pathname exceeded {NAME_MAX} characters, or an entire pathname exceeded {PATH_MAX} characters.
[ENOENT]	A component of the pathname does not name an existing file or the pathname is an empty string.
[ENOTDIR]	A component of the path prefix of the pathname in the socket address is not a directory.

The *sendto*( ) function may fail if:

[EDESTADDRREQ]	The socket is not connection-oriented and does not have its peer address set, and no destination address was specified.
[EHOSTUNREACH]	The destination host cannot be reached (probably because the host is down or a remote router cannot reach it).
[EINVAL]	The *dest_len* argument is not a valid length for the address family.
[EIO]	An I/O error occurred while reading from or writing to the file system.
[EISCONN]	A destination address was specified and the socket is connection-oriented and is already connected.
[ENETDOWN]	The local interface used to reach the destination is down.
[ENETUNREACH]	No route to the network is present.
[ENOBUFS]	Insufficient resources were available in the system to perform the operation.

| [ENOMEM] | Insufficient memory was available to fulfill the request. |
| [ENOSR] | There were insufficient STREAMS resources available for the operation to complete. |

If the address family of the socket is AF_UNIX, then *sendto*( ) may fail if:

| [ENAMETOOLONG] | Pathname resolution of a symbolic link produced an intermediate result whose length exceeds {PATH_MAX}. |

APPLICATION USAGE

The *select*( ) and *poll*( ) functions can be used to determine when it is possible to send more data.

SEE ALSO

getsockopt( ), *poll*( ), *recv*( ), *recvfrom*( ), *recvmsg*( ), *select*( ), *send*( ), *sendmsg*( ), *setsockopt*( ), *shutdown*( ), *socket*( ), **<sys/socket.h>**.

EXAMPLE

See examples at the end of chapter.

NAME

setsockopt — set the socket options

SYNOPSIS

UX
```
#include <sys/socket.h>

int setsockopt(int socket, int level, int option_name, const void
                  *option_value, size_t option_len);
```

DESCRIPTION

The *setsockopt*( ) function sets the option specified by the *option_name* argument, at the protocol level specified by the *level* argument, to the value pointed to by the *option_value* argument for the socket associated with the file descriptor specified by the *socket* argument.

The *level* argument specifies the protocol level at which the option resides. To set options at the socket level, specify the *level* argument as SOL_SOCKET. To set options at other levels, supply the appropriate protocol number for the protocol controlling the option. For example, to indicate that an option will be interpreted by the TCP (Transport Control Protocol), set *level* to the protocol number of TCP, as defined in the **<netinet/in.h>** header, or as determined by using *getprotobyname*( ).

The *option_name* argument specifies a single option to set. The *option_name* argument and any specified options are passed uninterpreted to the appropriate protocol module for interpretations. The **<sys/socket.h>** header defines the socket level options. The socket level options can be enabled or disabled. The options are as follows:

SO_DEBUG
Turns on recording of debugging information. This option enables or disables debugging in the underlying protocol modules. This option takes an **int** value.

SO_BROADCAST
Permits sending of broadcast messages, if this is supported by the protocol. This option takes an **int** value.

SO_REUSEADDR
Specifies that the rules used in validating addresses supplied to *bind*( ) should allow reuse of local addresses, if this is supported by the protocol. This option takes an **int** value.

SO_KEEPALIVE
Keeps connections active by enabling the periodic transmission of messages, if this is supported by the protocol. This option takes an **int** value.

If the connected socket fails to respond to these messages, the connection is broken and processes writing to that socket are notified with a SIGPIPE signal.

SO_LINGER
Lingers on a *close*( ) if data is present. This option controls the action taken when unsent messages queue on a socket and *close*( ) is performed. If SO_LINGER is set, the system blocks the process during *close*( ) until it can transmit the data or until the time expires. If SO_LINGER is not specified, and *close*( ) is issued, the system handles the call in a way that allows the process to continue as quickly as possible. This option takes a **linger** structure, as defined in the **<sys/socket.h>** header, to specify the state of the option and linger interval.

SO_OOBINLINE
Leaves received out-of-band data (data marked urgent) in line. This option takes an **int** value.

SO_SNDBUF	Sets send buffer size. This option takes an **int** value.
SO_RCVBUF	Sets receive buffer size. This option takes an **int** value.

For boolean options, 0 indicates that the option is disabled and 1 indicates that the option is enabled.

Options at other protocol levels vary in format and name.

RETURN VALUE

Upon successful completion, *setsockopt*( ) returns 0. Otherwise, −1 is returned and *errno* is set to indicate the error.

ERRORS

The *setsockopt*( ) function will fail if:

[EBADF]	The *socket* argument is not a valid file descriptor.
[EINVAL]	The specified option is invalid at the specified socket level or the socket has been shut down.
[ENOPROTOOPT]	The option is not supported by the protocol.
[ENOTSOCK]	The *socket* argument does not refer to a socket.

The *setsockopt*( ) function may fail if:

[ENOMEM]	There was insufficient memory available for the operation to complete.
[ENOBUFS]	Insufficient resources are available in the system to complete the call.
[ENOSR]	There were insufficient STREAMS resources available for the operation to complete.

APPLICATION USAGE

The *setsockopt*( ) function provides an application program with the means to control socket behaviour. An application program can use *setsockopt*( ) to allocate buffer space, control timeouts, or permit socket data broadcasts. The **<sys/socket.h>** header defines the socket-level options available to *setsockopt*( ).

Options may exist at multiple protocol levels. The SO_ options are always present at the uppermost socket level.

SEE ALSO

bind( ), *endprotoent*( ), *getsockopt*( ), *socket*( ), **<sys/socket.h>**.

EXAMPLE

See examples at the end of chapter.

NAME

shutdown — shut down socket send and receive operations

SYNOPSIS

UX `#include <sys/socket.h>`

`int shutdown(int socket, int how);`

DESCRIPTION

socket   Specifies the file descriptor of the socket.

how   Specifies the type of shutdown. The values are as follows:

SHUT_RD   Disables further receive operations.

SHUT_WR   Disables further send operations.

SHUT_RDWR   Disables further send and receive operations.

The *shutdown*( ) function disables subsequent send and/or receive operations on a socket, depending on the value of the *how* argument.

RETURN VALUE

Upon successful completion, *shutdown*( ) returns 0. Otherwise, −1 is returned and *errno* is set to indicate the error.

ERRORS

The *shutdown*( ) function will fail if:

[EBADF]   The *socket* argument is not a valid file descriptor.

[ENOTCONN]   The socket is not connected.

[ENOTSOCK]   The *socket* argument does not refer to a socket.

[EINVAL]   The *how* argument is invalid.

The *shutdown*( ) function may fail if:

[ENOBUFS]   Insufficient resources were available in the system to perform the operation.

[ENOSR]   There were insufficient STREAMS resources available for the operation to complete.

SEE ALSO

getsockopt( ), *read*( ), *recv*( ), *recvfrom*( ), *recvmsg*( ), *select*( ), *send*( ), *sendto*( ), *setsockopt*( ), *socket*( ), *write*( ), **<sys/socket.h>**.

EXAMPLE

See examples at the end of chapter.

NAME

socket — create an endpoint for communication

SYNOPSIS

UX
```
#include <sys/socket.h>
```

```
int socket(int domain, int type, int protocol);
```

DESCRIPTION

The *socket*( ) function creates an unbound socket in a communications domain, and returns a file descriptor that can be used in later function calls that operate on sockets.

The function takes the following arguments:

domain   Specifies the communications domain in which a socket is to be created.

type   Specifies the type of socket to be created.

protocol   Specifies a particular protocol to be used with the socket. Specifying a *protocol* of 0 causes *socket*( ) to use an unspecified default protocol appropriate for the requested socket type.

The *domain* argument specifies the address family used in the communications domain. The address families supported by the system are implementation-dependent.

The **<sys/socket.h>** header defines at least the following values for the *domain* argument:

AF_UNIX   File system pathnames.

AF_INET   Internet address.

The *type* argument specifies the socket type, which determines the semantics of communication over the socket. The socket types supported by the system are implementation-dependent. Possible socket types include:

SOCK_STREAM   Provides sequenced, reliable, bidirectional, connection-oriented byte streams, and may provide a transmission mechanism for out-of-band data.

SOCK_DGRAM   Provides datagrams, which are connectionless, unreliable messages of fixed maximum length.

SOCK_SEQPACKET Provides sequenced, reliable, bidirectional, connection-oriented transmission path for records. A record can be sent using one or more output operations and received using one or more input operations, but a single operation never transfers part of more than one record. Record boundaries are visible to the receiver via the MSG_EOR flag.

If the *protocol* argument is non-zero, it must specify a protocol that is supported by the address family. The protocols supported by the system are implementation-dependent.

RETURN VALUE

Upon successful completion, *socket*( ) returns a nonnegative integer, the socket file descriptor. Otherwise a value of –1 is returned and *errno* is set to indicate the error.

ERRORS

The *socket*( ) function will fail if:

[EACCES]   The process does not have appropriate privileges.

[EAFNOSUPPORT]   The implementation does not support the specified address family.

[EMFILE]   No more file descriptors are available for this process.

[ENFILE]   No more file descriptors are available for the system.

[EPROTONOSUPPORT]
          The protocol is not supported by the address family, or the protocol is not supported by the implementation.

[EPROTOTYPE]   The socket type is not supported by the protocol.

The *socket( )* function may fail if:

[ENOBUFS]   Insufficient resources were available in the system to perform the operation.

[ENOMEM]   Insufficient memory was available to fulfill the request.

[ENOSR]   There were insufficient STREAMS resources available for the operation to complete.

APPLICATION USAGE

The documentation for specific address families specify which protocols each address family supports. The documentation for specific protocols specify which socket types each protocol supports.

The application can determine if an address family is supported by trying to create a socket with *domain* set to the protocol in question.

SEE ALSO

accept( ), *bind( )*, *connect( )*, *getsockname( )*, *getsockopt( )*, *listen( )*, *recv( )*, *recvfrom( )*, *recvmsg( )*, *send( )*, *sendmsg( )*, *setsockopt( )*, *shutdown( )*, *socketpair( )*, **<netinet/in.h>**, **<sys/socket.h>**.

EXAMPLE

See examples at the end of chapter.

NAME

socketpair — create a pair of connected sockets

SYNOPSIS

UX
```
#include <sys/socket.h>

int socketpair(int domain, int type, int protocol,
               int socket_vector[2]);
```

DESCRIPTION

The *socketpair*( ) function creates an unbound pair of connected sockets in a specified *domain*, of a specified *type*, under the protocol optionally specified by the *protocol* argument. The two sockets are identical. The file descriptors used in referencing the created sockets are returned in *socket_vector*[0] and *socket_vector*[1].

domain　　　　　Specifies the communications domain in which the sockets are to be created.

type　　　　　Specifies the type of sockets to be created.

protocol　　　　　Specifies a particular protocol to be used with the sockets. Specifying a *protocol* of 0 causes *socketpair*( ) to use an unspecified default protocol appropriate for the requested socket type.

socket_vector　　　　　Specifies a 2-integer array to hold the file descriptors of the created socket pair.

The *type* argument specifies the socket type, which determines the semantics of communications over the socket. The socket types supported by the system are implementation-dependent. Possible socket types include:

SOCK_STREAM　　　　　Provides sequenced, reliable, bidirectional, connection-oriented byte streams, and may provide a transmission mechanism for out-of-band data.

SOCK_DGRAM　　　　　Provides datagrams, which are connectionless, unreliable messages of fixed maximum length.

SOCK_SEQPACKET　Provides sequenced, reliable, bidirectional, connection-oriented transmission path for records. A record can be sent using one or more output operations and received using one or more input operations, but a single operation never transfers part of more than one record. Record boundaries are visible to the receiver via the MSG_EOR flag.

If the *protocol* argument is non-zero, it must specify a protocol that is supported by the address family. The protocols supported by the system are implementation-dependent.

RETURN VALUE

Upon successful completion, this function returns 0. Otherwise, −1 is returned and *errno* is set to indicate the error.

ERRORS

The *socketpair*( ) function will fail if:

[EAFNOSUPPORT]　　　The implementation does not support the specified address family.

[EMFILE]　　　　　No more file descriptors are available for this process.

[ENFILE]　　　　　No more file descriptors are available for the system.

[EOPNOTSUPP]   The specified protocol does not permit creation of socket pairs.

[EPROTONOSUPPORT]
                      The protocol is not supported by the address family, or the protocol is not
                      supported by the implementation.

[EPROTOTYPE]   The socket type is not supported by the protocol.

The *socketpair*( ) function may fail if:

[EACCES]   The process does not have appropriate privileges.

[ENOMEM]   Insufficient memory was available to fulfill the request.

[ENOBUFS]   Insufficient resources were available in the system to perform the
                      operation.

[ENOSR]   There were insufficient STREAMS resources available for the operation
                      to complete.

APPLICATION USAGE

The documentation for specific address families specifies which protocols each address family
supports. The documentation for specific protocols specifies which socket types each protocol
supports.

The *socketpair*( ) function is used primarily with UNIX domain sockets and need not be
supported for other domains.

SEE ALSO

socket( ), **<sys/socket.h>**.

EXAMPLE

See examples at the end of chapter.

NAME

write, writev — write on a file

Note: The **XSH** specification contains the basic definition of this interface. The following additional information pertains to Sockets.

DESCRIPTION

UX If *fildes* refers to a socket, *write*( ) is equivalent to *send*( ) with no flags set.

EXAMPLE 1

```
/*
 * Copyright (C) ANTRIX Inc.
 */

/* cltsvr.c
 *
 * Description: A socketpair program that mimics a client server pair
 *
 * Protocol:    The client sends a NAME (such as Bill) followed by a new
 *              line. The server reads the name up to and including the
 *              newline and replies "Hello NAME, nice to see you today"
 *              followed by newline.
 *
 * Request:     client sends a name followed by newline.
 * Reply:       server reads name and prints to standard output the reply
 *              "Hello NAME, nice to see you today"
 */

#include <stdio.h>
#include <sys/types.h>
#include <sys/socket.h>
#include <errno.h>

int client(fd1, name)
int fd1;
char *name;
{
    char c;
    char buf[BUFSIZ];
    int byte;

    /* send request to server including newline */
    fprintf(stdout, "client sending request: %s\n", name);
    write(fd1, name, strlen(name));
    write(fd1, "\n", 1);

    /* now wait for reply from server */
    /* and write the reply to stdout */
    while(1)
    {
        bzero(buf, sizeof(buf));
        byte = read(fd1, buf, BUFSIZ);
        if(!strcmp(buf, "\n"))
        {
            fflush(stdout);
            break;
        }
        if(byte >= 1)
            fprintf(stdout, "client received reply: %s\n", buf);
        else
            exit(1);
```

```
    } /* end while */
  }

  int server(fd0)
  int fd0;
  {
    char c;
    int i, byte;
    char reply[BUFSIZ];
    char request[BUFSIZ];
    char *msg1 = "Hello ";
    char *msg2 = ", nice to see you today";

    i = 0;

    bzero(reply, sizeof(reply));
    bzero(request, sizeof(request));

    /* read the request from client */
    while(1)
    {
      byte = read(fd0, &c, 1);
      if(byte != 1) {
          fprintf(stderr, "ERROR: server unable to read request\n");
          exit(-1);
      } /* end if */
      if( c == '\n')
        break;
      request[i++] = c;
    } /* end while */

    /* write the reply to client */
    fprintf(stdout, "server received request: %s\n", request);
    strcpy(reply, msg1);
    strcat(reply, request);
    strcat(reply, msg2);

    fprintf(stdout, "server sending reply: %s\n",reply);
    write(fd0, reply, sizeof(reply));
    write(fd0, "\n", 1);
  }

  main(argc, argv)
  int argc;
  char *argv[];
  {
    int i;
    int byte, cpid, socks[2];

    /* check usage */
    if(argc < 2) {
        fprintf(stderr, "usage: %s <NAME>\n", argv[0]);
```

```
      exit(-1);
   }

   /* create a local pair of connected sockets */
   byte = socketpair(AF_UNIX, SOCK_STREAM, 0, socks);
   if(byte < 0) {
      perror("socketpair");
      exit(-1);
   }
   /* make two processes to talk to each other */
   cpid = fork();
   if(cpid == 0) {
      /* make child process client */
      close(socks[0] );
      /* client to send request */
      byte = client(socks[1], argv[1]);
   }
   else {
      /* make parent process server */
      close(socks[1]);
      /* server to read the request */
      byte = server(socks[0]);
   }
}
```

EXAMPLE 2

```c
/*
 * Copyright (C) ANTRIX Inc.
 */

/* client1.c
 *
 * Description: A client & server pair that establishes a socket the client
 *              sends a request and the server sends a reply using TCP.
 *
 * Protocol:    The client sends a NAME (such as Bill) followed by a
 *              newline on port #10203 using TCP. The server provides
 *              greeting service on port #10203 using TCP. The server
 *              reads the name up to and including the newline and replies
 *              "Hello NAME, nice to see you today" followed by newline.
 *
 * Request:     client sends a name followed by newline.
 * Reply:       server reads name and prints to standard output the reply
 *              "Hello NAME, nice to see you today"
 *
 * Usage:       run the server in the background as server1 &
 *              run the client as client1 Bill &
 *              Transmission Control Protocol (TCP) Properties
 *              connection oriented, byte stream, fragmentation, sequenced
 *              reliable, flow control.
 *
 * Sequence:
 *
 *              SERVER                          CLIENT
 *
 *              socket()                        socket()
 *                 |                               |
 *              bind()                             |
 *                 |                               |
 *              listen()                           |
 *                 |                               |
 *              accept()                           |
 *                 |                               |
 *                 |<----------------------->connect()
 *                 |                               |
 *              recv() or read()<--request-- send() or write()
 *                 |                               |
 *              send() or write()---reply--->recv() or read()
 */

#include <stdio.h>
#include <sys/types.h>
#include <sys/socket.h>
#include <netinet/in.h>
#include <netdb.h>
#include <errno.h>
```

```
#define MAXHOSTNAME 32
#define PORT_NUM    10203

main(argc, argv)
int argc;
char *argv[];
{
  int socketfd, byte;           /* sockets file descriptor */
  int len, flags;
  int err, on = 1;
  struct sockaddr_in sa;        /* socket addr structs */
  struct hostent *hp;           /* result of host name lookup */
  struct servent *sp;           /* result of service lookup */
  struct sockaddr name;
  int    namelen = 10;
  char buf[BUFSIZ];             /* data buffer */
  char localhost[MAXHOSTNAME+1]; /* local host name */

  /* check usage */
  if(argc < 2)
  {
      fprintf(stderr, "usage: %s <NAME>\n", argv[0]);
      exit(-1);
  }
  /* initialize structures and buffer */
  bzero(&sa, sizeof(sa));
  bzero(buf, sizeof(buf));

  /* get host information */
  gethostname(localhost, MAXHOSTNAME);
  if((hp = gethostbyname(localhost)) ==(struct hostent *)0)
  {
      fprintf(stderr, "ERROR: %s cannot get host info?\n", argv[0]);
      exit(-1);
  }

  /* load host address and address type into socket struct */
  bcopy((char *)hp->h_addr,(char *)&sa.sin_addr, hp->h_length);
  sa.sin_family = hp->h_addrtype;
  /* should be unreserved port number greater than 1024 */
  sa.sin_port = htons(PORT_NUM);

  /* look up the socket number for the whois service */
  /* in /etc/services file */
  if(( sp = getservbyname("whois", "tcp") ) == NULL)
  {
      fprintf(stderr, "ERROR: %s no whois service on this host\n", argv[0]);
      exit(-1);
  }

  /* allocate an open socket with tcp */
  if((socketfd = socket(hp->h_addrtype, SOCK_STREAM, 0)) < 0 )
```

```
    {
        fprintf(stderr, "ERROR: %s socket call failed\n", argv[0]);
        exit(-1);
    }

    /* get socket name */
    if (getsockname(socketfd, &name, &namelen) == -1)
    {
        fprintf(stderr, "ERROR: getsockname call failed\n");
        exit(-1);
    }

    /* get peer name */
    if (getpeername(socketfd, &name, &namelen) == -1)
    {
        fprintf(stderr, "ERROR: getpeername call failed\n");
        exit(-1);
    }

    /* get socket options */
    if (getsockopt(socketfd, SOL_SOCKET, SO_ERROR,
                   (char *)&err, &namelen) == -1)
    {
        fprintf(stderr, "ERROR: getsockopt call failed\n");
        exit(-1);
    }

    /* set socket option */
    if (setsockopt(socketfd, SOL_SOCKET, SO_DONTROUTE,
                   (char *)&on, sizeof(on)) == -1)
    {
        fprintf(stderr, "ERROR: setsockopt call failed\n");
        exit(-1);
    }

    /* connect to the remote server */
    if(connect(socketfd, &sa, sizeof(sa)) < 0)
    {
        fprintf(stderr, "ERROR: %s connect call failed\n", argv[0]);
        exit(-1);
    }

    /* send request to server including newline */
    fprintf(stdout, "client sending request: %s\n", argv[1]);
#ifdef DEBUG
    byte = write(socketfd, argv[1], strlen(argv[1]));
#else
    byte = send(socketfd, argv[1], strlen(argv[1]), 0);
#endif
    if(byte != strlen(argv[1]) )
    {
        fprintf(stderr, "ERROR: %s write error\n", argv[0]);
```

```
      exit(-1);
   }
#ifdef DEBUG
   write(socketfd, "\n", 1);
#else
   send(socketfd, "\n", 1, 0);
#endif

   /* read the reply and output to display */
   fflush(stdout);
   do
   {
      bzero(buf, sizeof(buf));
#ifdef DEBUG
      len = read(socketfd, buf, BUFSIZ);
#else
      len = recv(socketfd, buf, BUFSIZ, flags);
#endif
      if(!strcmp(buf, "\n"))
         break;
      fprintf(stdout, "client received reply: %s\n", buf);
   } while (len > 0);

   close(socketfd);
   exit(0);
}
/*
 * Copyright (C) ANTRIX Inc.
 */

/* server1.c
 *
 * Description: A client & server pair that establishes a socket the client
 *              sends a request and the server sends a reply using TCP.
 *
 * Protocol:    The client sends a NAME (such as Bill) followed by a newline
 *              on port #10203 using TCP. The server provides greeting
 *              service on port #10203 using TCP. The server reads the name
 *              up to and including the newline and replies
 *              "Hello NAME, nice to see you today" followed by newline.
 *
 * Request:     client sends a name followed by newline.
 * Reply:       server reads name and prints to standard output the reply
 *              "Hello NAME, nice to see you today"
 *
 * Usage:       run the server in the background as server1 &
 *              run the client as client1 Bill &
 *              Transmission Control Protocol (TCP) Properties
 *              connection oriented, byte stream, fragmentation, sequenced
 *              reliable, flow control.
 *
 * Sequence:
```

```
 *
 *                   SERVER                     CLIENT
 *
 *                   socket()                   socket()
 *                      |                          |
 *                   bind()                        |
 *                      |                          |
 *                   listen()                      |
 *                      |                          |
 *                   accept()                      |
 *                      |                          |
 *                      |<----------------------->connect()
 *                      |                          |
 *                   recv() or read()<--request-- send() or write()
 *                      |                          |
 *                   send() or write()---reply--->recv() or read()
 */

#include <stdio.h>
#include <sys/types.h>
#include <sys/socket.h>
#include <netinet/in.h>
#include <arpa/inet.h>
#include <netdb.h>
#include <errno.h>

#define BACKLOG      5
#define MAXHOSTNAME  32
#define PORT_NUM     10203

void service(sock)
int sock;
{
  char c;
  int i, byte, flags;
  char buf[BUFSIZ];
  char reply[BUFSIZ];
  char request[BUFSIZ];
  char *msg1 = "Hello ";
  char *msg2 = ", nice to see you today";

  i = 0;
  bzero((char *)reply, sizeof(reply));
  bzero((char *)request, sizeof(request));

  /* read the request from client */
#ifdef DEBUG
  while(1)
  {
    byte = read(sock, &c, 1);
    if(byte != 1)
    {
```

```
          fprintf(stderr, "ERROR: server unable to read request\n");
          exit(-1);
        } /* end if */
        if( c == '\n')
            break;
        request[i++] = c;
      } /* end while */
#else
   while (1)
     {
       bzero((char *)buf, sizeof(buf));
       byte = recv(sock, buf, BUFSIZ, flags);
       if (!strcmp(buf, "\n"))
           break;
       strcpy(request, buf);
     }
#endif

   fprintf(stdout, "server received request: %s\n", request);
   /* write the reply to client */
#ifdef DEBUG
   fprintf(stdout, "responding to a request...\n");
#endif
   strcpy(reply, msg1);
   strcat(reply, request);
   strcat(reply, msg2);

   fprintf(stdout, "server sending reply: %s\n", reply);
#ifdef DEBUG
   write(sock, reply, sizeof(reply));
   write(sock, "\n", 1);
#else
   send(sock, reply, sizeof(reply),0);
   send(sock, "\n", 1, 0);
#endif
}

main(argc, argv)
int argc;
char *argv[];
{
  int i;
  int sockfd, newsockfd;        /* sockets file descriptor */
  char *inetaddr;               /* internet address String */
  struct sockaddr_in sa, isa;   /* socket addr structs */
  struct hostent *hp;           /* result of host name lookup */
  struct servent *sp;           /* result of service lookup */
  char localhost[MAXHOSTNAME+1]; /* local host name */

  /* initialize structures and buffers */
  bzero(&sa, sizeof(sa));
  bzero(&isa, sizeof(isa));
```

```
    /* get our own host information */
    gethostname(localhost, MAXHOSTNAME);
    if((hp = gethostbyname(localhost)) == NULL)
    {
        fprintf(stderr, "ERROR %s cannot get host info?\n", argv[0]);
        exit(-1);
    }

#ifdef DEBUG
    fprintf(stdout, "Name of the machine %s\n", localhost);
#endif

    /* look up the 'whois' service entry */
    /* in /etc/services file */
    if(( sp = getservbyname("whois", "tcp") ) == NULL)
    {
        fprintf(stderr, "ERROR %s no whois service on this host\n", argv[0]);
        exit(-1);
    }

    /* load host address and address type into socket struct */
    bcopy(hp->h_addr_list[0],(char *)&sa.sin_addr, hp->h_length);
    sa.sin_family = hp->h_addrtype;
    /* should be unreserved port number greater than 1024 */
    sa.sin_port = htons(PORT_NUM);

#ifdef DEBUG
    fprintf(stdout, "using inet address %s\n", inet_ntoa(sa.sin_addr));
#endif

    /* allocate an open socket for incoming connections */
    /* using tcp stream */
    if((sockfd = socket(hp->h_addrtype, SOCK_STREAM, 0)) < 0 )
    {
        fprintf(stderr, "ERROR: %s socket call failed\n", argv[0]);
        exit(-1);
    }

    /* bind the socket to the service port to hear incomings */
    if(bind(sockfd, &sa, sizeof(sa)) < 0)
    {
        fprintf(stderr, "ERROR: %s bind call failed\n", argv[0]);
        exit(-1);
    }

#ifdef DEBUG
    fprintf(stdout, "ready to serve request\n");
#endif

    /* set max# of connections we will fall behind */
    listen(sockfd, BACKLOG);
```

```
/* go to an infinite loop waiting for new connections */
for(;;)
{
    i = sizeof(isa);
    if(( newsockfd = accept(sockfd, &isa, &i)) < 0 )
    {
        fprintf(stderr, "ERROR: %s accept failed\n", argv[0]);
    }
    service(newsockfd);
    close(newsockfd);
} /* end for */
}
```

EXAMPLE 3

```
/*
 * Copyright (C) ANTRIX Inc.
 */

/* client2.c
 *
 * Description: A client & server pair that establishes a socket the client
 *              sends a request and the server sends a reply using UDP.
 *
 * Protocol:    The client sends a NAME (such as Bill) followed by a newline
 *              on port #11012 using UDP. The server provides greeting
 *              service on port #11012 using UDP. The server reads the name
 *              up to and including the newline and replies
 *              "Hello NAME, nice to see you today" followed by newline.
 *
 * Request:     client sends a name followed by newline.
 * Reply:       server reads name and prints to standard output the reply
 *              "Hello NAME, nice to see you today"
 *
 * Usage:       run the server in the background as server2 &
 *              run the client as client2 Bill &
 *              User Datagram Protocol (UDP) Properties
 *              connectionless, packet type, unsequenced, unreliable,
 *              no flow control.
 *
 * Sequence:
 *
 *              SERVER                          CLIENT
 *
 *              socket()                        socket()
 *                 |                               |
 *              bind()                             |
 *                 |                               |
 *                 |                               |
 *              recvfrom()                         |
 *                 |                               |
 *                 |<---------request---------sendto()
 *                 |                               |
 *              sendto()-----reply---------->recvfrom()
 */

#include <stdio.h>
#include <sys/types.h>
#include <sys/socket.h>
#include <netinet/in.h>
#include <netdb.h>
#include <errno.h>

#define MAXHOSTNAME 32
#define PORT_NUM    11012
```

```
main(argc, argv)
int argc;
char *argv[];
{
    int socketfd, byte, addr_len;   /* sockets file descriptor */
    struct sockaddr_in sa, isa;     /* socket addr structs */
    struct hostent *hp;             /* result of host name lookup */
    struct servent *sp;             /* result of service lookup */
    char buf[BUFSIZ];               /* data buffer */
    char localhost[MAXHOSTNAME+1];  /* local host name */

    /* check usage */
    if(argc < 2)
    {
        fprintf(stderr, "usage: %s <NAME>\n", argv[0]);
        exit(-1);
    }
    /* initialize structures and buffer */
    bzero(&sa, sizeof(sa));
    bzero(buf, sizeof(buf));

    /* get host information */
    gethostname(localhost, MAXHOSTNAME);
    if((hp = gethostbyname(localhost)) ==(struct hostent *)0)
    {
        fprintf(stderr, "ERROR: %s cannot get host info?\n", argv[0]);
        exit(-1);
    }

    /* load host address and address type into socket struct */
    bcopy((char *)hp->h_addr,(char *)&sa.sin_addr, hp->h_length);
    sa.sin_family = hp->h_addrtype;
    /* put the socket number into the socket port */
    /* should be unreserved port number greater than 1024 */
    sa.sin_port = htons(PORT_NUM);

    /* look up the socket number for the time service */
    /* in /etc/services file */
    if(( sp = getservbyname("time", "udp") ) == NULL)
    {
        fprintf(stderr, "ERROR: %s no time service on this host\n", argv[0]);
        exit(-1);
    }

    /* allocate an open socket of type udp */
    if((socketfd = socket(hp->h_addrtype, SOCK_DGRAM, 0)) < 0 )
    {
        fprintf(stderr, "ERROR: %s socket call failed\n", argv[0]);
        exit(-1);
    }

    /* send request to server including newline */
```

```
     fprintf(stdout, "client sending request: %s\n", argv[1]);
     byte = sendto(socketfd, argv[1], strlen(argv[1]), 0, &sa, sizeof(sa));
     if(byte != strlen(argv[1]))
     {
        fprintf(stderr, "ERROR: %s unable to send request\n", argv[0]);
        exit(-1);
     }

     /* read the reply and output to display */
     fflush(stdout);
     fflush(stderr);
     byte = read(socketfd, buf, BUFSIZ);
#ifdef DEBUG
     byte = recvfrom(socketfd, buf, BUFSIZ, 0, &isa, &addr_len);
#endif
     fprintf(stdout, "client received reply: %s", buf);
     fflush(stdout);

     close(socketfd);
     exit(0);
}
/*
 * Copyright (C) ANTRIX Inc.
 */


/* server2.c
 *
 * Description: A client & server pair that establishes a socket the client
 *              sends a request and the server sends a reply using UDP.
 *
 * Protocol:    The client sends a NAME (such as Bill) followed by a newline
 *              on port #11012 using UDP. The server provides greeting
 *              service on port #11012 using UDP. The server reads the name
 *              up to and including the newline and replies
 *              "Hello NAME, nice to see you today" followed by newline.
 *
 * Request:     client sends a name followed by newline.
 * Reply:       server reads name and prints to standard output the reply
 *              "Hello NAME, nice to see you today"
 *
 * Usage:       run the server in the background as server2 &
 *              run the client as client2 Bill &
 *              User Datagram Protocol (UDP) Properties
 *              connectionless, packet type, unsequenced, unreliable,
 *              no flow control.
 *
 * Sequence:
 *
 *              SERVER                          CLIENT
 *
 *              socket()                        socket()
 *                 |                               |
```

```
*                bind()                          |
*                  |                             |
*                  |                             |
*                recvfrom()                      |
*                  |                             |
*                  |<---------request---------sendto()
*                  |                             |
*                sendto()-----reply---------->recvfrom()
*/

#include <stdio.h>
#include <sys/types.h>
#include <sys/socket.h>
#include <netinet/in.h>
#include <arpa/inet.h>
#include <netdb.h>
#include <errno.h>

#define BACKLOG      5
#define MAXHOSTNAME  32
#define PORT_NUM     11012

void service(sock)
int sock;
{
   char c;
   int i, byte, client_len;
   char reply[BUFSIZ];
   char request[BUFSIZ];
   char *msg1 = "Hello ";
   char *msg2 = ", nice to see you today\n";
   struct sockaddr_in client_addr;

   i = 0;
   bzero((char *)reply, sizeof(reply));
   bzero((char *)request, sizeof(request));

   client_len = sizeof(client_addr);

   /* read the request from client */
   byte = recvfrom(sock, request, sizeof(request), 0, &client_addr, &client_le
   if(byte == -1)
      fprintf(stderr, "ERROR: unable to receive request\n");

   request[byte] = ' ';
   fprintf(stdout, "server received request: %s\n", request);

#ifdef DEBUG
   fprintf(stdout, "responding to a request...\n");
#endif
   strcpy(reply, msg1);
   strcat(reply, request);
```

```
        strcat(reply, msg2);

     /* write the reply to client */
     fprintf(stdout, "server sending reply: %s", reply);
     fflush(stdout);

     byte = sendto(sock, reply, strlen(reply), 0, &client_addr, client_len);
     if(byte == -1)
         fprintf(stderr, "ERROR: unable to send reply\n");
}

main(argc, argv)
int argc;
char *argv[];
{
  int i;
  int sockfd, newsockfd;        /* sockets file descriptor */
  char *inetaddr;               /* internet address String */
  struct sockaddr_in sa, isa;   /* socket addr structs */
  struct hostent *hp;           /* result of host name lookup */
  struct servent *sp;           /* result of service lookup */
  char localhost[MAXHOSTNAME+1]; /* local host name */

  /* initialize structures and buffers */
  bzero(&sa, sizeof(sa));
  bzero(&isa, sizeof(isa));

  /* get our own host information */
  gethostname(localhost, MAXHOSTNAME);
  if((hp = gethostbyname(localhost)) == NULL)
  {
      fprintf(stderr, "ERROR %s cannot get host info?\n", argv[0]);
      exit(-1);
  }

#ifdef DEBUG
  fprintf(stdout, "Name of the machine %s\n", localhost);
#endif

  /* look up the 'time' service entry */
  /* in /etc/services file */
  if(( sp = getservbyname("time", "udp") ) == NULL)
  {
      fprintf(stderr, "ERROR %s no time service on this host\n", argv[0]);
      exit(-1);
  }

  /* load host address and address type into socket struct */
  bcopy(hp->h_addr_list[0],(char *)&sa.sin_addr, hp->h_length);
  sa.sin_family = hp->h_addrtype;
  /* should be unreserved port number greater than 1024 */
  sa.sin_port = htons(PORT_NUM);
```

```
#ifdef DEBUG
   fprintf(stdout, "using inet address %s\n", inet_ntoa(sa.sin_addr));
#endif

   /* allocate an open socket for incoming connections */
   /* using udp stream */
   if((sockfd = socket(hp->h_addrtype, SOCK_DGRAM, 0)) < 0 )
   {
      fprintf(stderr, "ERROR: %s socket call failed\n", argv[0]);
      exit(-1);
   }

   /* bind the socket to the service port to hear incomings */
   if(bind(sockfd, &sa, sizeof(sa)) < 0)
   {
      fprintf(stderr, "ERROR: %s bind call failed\n", argv[0]);
      exit(-1);
   }

#ifdef DEBUG
   fprintf(stdout, "ready to serve request\n");
#endif
   /* go to an infinite loop waiting for new connections */
   for(;;)
   {
      service(sockfd);
   }
}
```

EXAMPLE 4

```
/*
 * Copyright (C) ANTRIX Inc.
 */

/* client3.c
 *
 * Description: A client & server pair that establishes a socket the
 *              client sends a request and the concurrent server sends
 *              a reply using TCP
 *
 * Protocol:    The client sends a NAME (such as Bill) followed by a
 *              newline on port #12045 using TCP. The server provides
 *              greeting service on port #12045 using TCP. The server
 *              reads the name up to and including the newline and replies
 *              "Hello NAME, nice to see you today" followed by newline.
 *              Send the same client request 2 times
 *              Allow for 5 second delay between requests
 *              Allow for multiply connections
 *              Allow for multiple requests on a given connection
 *              Close connection on special character . (period)
 *
 * Request:     client sends a name followed by newline.
 * Reply:       server reads name and prints to standard output the reply
 *              "Hello NAME, nice to see you today"
 *
 * Usage:       run the server in the background as server3 &
 *              run the client as client3 Bill &
 *              Transmission Control Protocol (TCP) Properties
 *              connection oriented, byte stream, fragmentation, sequenced
 *              reliable, flow control.
 *
 * Sequence:
 *
 *              SERVER                          CLIENT
 *
 *              socket()                        socket()
 *                 |                               |
 *              bind()                             |
 *                 |                               |
 *              listen()                           |
 *                 |                               |
 *              select()                           |
 *                 |                               |
 *              accept()                           |
 *                 |                               |
 *                 |<---------------------->connect()
 *                 |                               |
 *              recv() or read()<--request-- send() or write()
 *                 |                               |
 *              send() or write()---reply--->recv() or read()
 */
```

```
#include <stdio.h>
#include <sys/types.h>
#include <sys/socket.h>
#include <netinet/in.h>
#include <netdb.h>
#include <errno.h>

#define MAXHOSTNAME 32
#define PORT_NUM    12045

main(argc, argv)
int argc ;
char *argv[] ;
{
  int i, number = 0 ;
  char c;
  int socketfd, byte, len;      /* sockets file descriptor */
  struct sockaddr_in sa;        /* socket addr structs */
  struct hostent *hp;           /* result of host name lookup */
  struct servent *sp;           /* result of service lookup */
  char buf[BUFSIZ];             /* data buffer */
  char localhost[MAXHOSTNAME+1]; /* local host name */

  /* check usage */
  if(argc < 2)
  {
     fprintf(stderr, "usage: %s <NAME>\n", argv[0]);
     exit(-1);
  }
  /* initialize structures and buffer */
  bzero(&sa, sizeof(sa));
  bzero(buf, sizeof(buf));

  /* get host information */
  gethostname(localhost, MAXHOSTNAME);
  if((hp = gethostbyname(localhost)) ==(struct hostent *)0)
  {
     fprintf(stderr, "ERROR: %s cannot get host info?\n", argv[0]);
     exit(-1);
  }

  /* load host address and address type into socket struct */
  bcopy((char *)hp->h_addr,(char *)&sa.sin_addr, hp->h_length);
  sa.sin_family = hp->h_addrtype;
  /* put the echo socket number into the socket port */
  /* should be unreserved port number greater than 1024 */
  sa.sin_port = htons(PORT_NUM);

  /* look up the socket number for the echo service */
  /* in /etc/services file */
  if(( sp = getservbyname("echo", "tcp") ) == NULL)
  {
```

```
            fprintf(stderr, "ERROR: %s no echo service on this host\n", argv[0]);
            exit(-1);
        }

        /* allocate an open socket with tcp */
        if((socketfd = socket(hp->h_addrtype, SOCK_STREAM, 0)) < 0 )
        {
            fprintf(stderr, "ERROR: %s socket call failed\n", argv[0]);
            exit(-1);
        }

        /* connect to the remote server */
        if(connect(socketfd, &sa, sizeof(sa)) < 0)
        {
            fprintf(stderr, "ERROR: %s connect call failed\n", argv[0]);
            exit(-1);
        }

        /* send request to server including newline */
        fprintf(stdout, "client sending request: %s\n", argv[1]);
        for (i = 0 ; i < 2 ; i++ )
        {
          byte = write(socketfd, argv[1], strlen(argv[1]));
          if(byte != strlen(argv[1]) )
          {
              fprintf(stderr, "ERROR: %s write error\n", argv[0]);
              exit(-1);
          }
          write(socketfd, "\n", 1);
          /*sleep for 5 seconds for server to build up the request */
          sleep(5);
        }

        /* inform server we have sent all the request */
        /* and close connection */
        write(socketfd, ".", 1) ;
        fflush(stdout);

        /* read the reply and output to display */
        i = 0;
        do
        {
          len = read(socketfd, &c, 1);
          if( c == '\n') {
            if(strlen(buf))
              fprintf(stdout, "client received reply: %s\n", buf);
            i = 0;
            bzero(buf, sizeof(buf));
          }
          else
            buf[i++] = c;
        } while (len > 0);
```

```
   close(socketfd);
   exit(0);
}
/*
 * Copyright (C) ANTRIX Inc.
 */

/* server3.c
 *
 * Description: A client & server pair that establishes a socket the client
 *              sends a request and the concurrent server sends a reply
 *              using TCP
 *
 * Protocol:    The client sends a NAME (such as Bill) followed by a newline
 *              on port #12045 using TCP. The server provides greeting
 *              service on port #12045 using TCP. The server reads the name
 *              up to and including the newline and replies
 *              "Hello NAME, nice to see you today" followed by newline.
 *              Send the same client request 2 times
 *              Allow for 5 second delay between requests
 *              Allow for multiply connections
 *              Allow for multiple requests on a given connection
 *              Close connection on special character . (period)
 *
 * Request:     client sends a name followed by newline.
 * Reply:       server reads name and prints to standard output the reply
 *              "Hello NAME, nice to see you today"
 *
 * Usage:       run the server in the background as server3 &
 *              run the client as client3 Bill &
 *              Transmission Control Protocol (TCP) Properties
 *              connection oriented, byte stream, fragmentation, sequenced
 *              reliable, flow control.
 *
 * Sequence:
 *
 *              SERVER                        CLIENT
 *
 *              socket()                      socket()
 *                 |                             |
 *              bind()                           |
 *                 |                             |
 *              listen()                         |
 *                 |                             |
 *              select()                         |
 *                 |                             |
 *              accept()                         |
 *                 |                             |
 *                 |<------------------------>connect()
 *                 |                             |
 *              recv() or read()<--request-- send() or write()
 *                 |                             |
```

```
 *                     send() or write()---reply--->recv() or read()
 */


#include <stdio.h>
#include <sys/types.h>
#include <sys/socket.h>
#include <sys/time.h>
#include <sys/sysmacros.h>
#include <netinet/in.h>
#include <arpa/inet.h>
#include <netdb.h>
#include <errno.h>

#define BACKLOG      5
#define MAXHOSTNAME 32
#define PORT_NUM    12045

int service(sock)
int sock;
{
  int i, result;
  char c;
  char request[BUFSIZ];
  char reply[BUFSIZ];

  /* initialize requestfers */
  i = 0;
  bzero(request, sizeof(request));
  bzero(reply, sizeof(reply));

  while(1)
  {
    result = read(sock, &c, 1);
    /* nothing to read */
    if(result != 1)
    {
      fprintf(stderr, "ERROR: nothing to read?\n");
      exit(-1);
    } /* end if */

    if(c == '.')
      return(0);

    /* if newline end of request */
    if( c == '\n')
    {
      request[i++] = ' ';
#ifdef DEBUG
      fprintf(stdout, "responding to a request...\n");
#endif
      /* lookup the requested user and format rsp */
```

```
            sprintf(reply, "%s %s, %s", "Hello", request, "nice to see you today");
            fprintf(stdout, "server servicing request on channel=%d\n", sock);
            fprintf(stdout, "server sending reply: %s\n", reply);
            fflush(stdout);
            write(sock, reply, strlen(reply));
            write(sock, "\n", 1);
            i = 0;
            bzero((char *)request, sizeof(request));
            return(1);
        } else
            request[i++] = c;
    } /* end while(1) */
}

int get_max(max_fd, fd_array)
int max_fd;
fd_set fd_array;
{
    int i, new_max = 0;

    for(i = 0; i < max_fd + 1; i++)
    {
        if(FD_ISSET(i, &fd_array))
            new_max = i;
    }
    fprintf(stdout, "current max file descriptor=%d\n", new_max);
    return(new_max);
}

main(argc, argv)
int argc;
char *argv[];
{
    int i, j, count;                 /* integer variables */
    fd_set perm_rfds, rfds;          /* bit mask for file descriptor */
    int max_fd;                      /* temporary file descriptor */
    int found;                       /* select return value */
    int sockfd, newsockfd;           /* sockets file descriptor */
    char *inetaddr;                  /* internet address String */
    struct sockaddr_in sa, isa;      /* socket addr structs */
    struct hostent *hp;              /* result of host name lookup */
    struct servent *sp;              /* result of service lookup */
    char localhost[MAXHOSTNAME+1];   /* local host name */

    /* initialize structures and buffers */
    bzero(&sa, sizeof(sa));
    bzero(&isa, sizeof(isa));

    /* get our own host information */
    gethostname(localhost, MAXHOSTNAME);
    if((hp = gethostbyname(localhost)) == NULL)
    {
```

```
      fprintf(stderr, "ERROR %s cannot get host info?\n", argv[0]);
      exit(-1);
   }

#ifdef DEBUG
   fprintf(stdout, "name of the machine %s\n", localhost);
#endif

   /* look up the 'echo' service entry */
   /* in /etc/services file */
   if(( sp = getservbyname("echo", "tcp") ) == NULL)
   {
      fprintf(stderr, "ERROR %s no echo service on this host\n", argv[0]);
      exit(-1);
   }

   /* load host address and address type into socket struct */
   bcopy(hp->h_addr_list[0],(char *)&sa.sin_addr, hp->h_length);
   sa.sin_family = hp->h_addrtype;
   /* should be unreserved port number greater than 1024 */
   sa.sin_port = htons(PORT_NUM);

#ifdef DEBUG
   fprintf(stdout, "using inet address %s\n", inet_ntoa(sa.sin_addr));
#endif

   /* allocate an open socket for incoming connections */
   /* using tcp stream */
   if((sockfd = socket(hp->h_addrtype, SOCK_STREAM, 0)) < 0 )
   {
      fprintf(stderr, "ERROR: %s socket call failed\n", argv[0]);
      exit(-1);
   }

   /* bind the socket to the port to service incoming */
   /* request */
   if(bind(sockfd, &sa, sizeof(sa)) < 0)
   {
      fprintf(stderr, "ERROR: %s bind call failed\n", argv[0]);
      exit(-1);
   }

#ifdef DEBUG
   fprintf(stdout, "ready to serve request\n");
#endif

   /* set max# of connections we will fall behind */
   listen(sockfd, BACKLOG);

   /* initialize the file descriptors */
   FD_ZERO(&perm_rfds);
   FD_SET(sockfd, &perm_rfds);
```

```
    max_fd = sockfd;

    /* go to an infinite loop waiting for new connections */
    for(;;)
    {
#ifdef DEBUG
    fprintf(stdout, "before select() call\n");
    fprintf(stdout, "service incoming request\n" );
#endif
    bcopy(&perm_rfds, &rfds, sizeof(fd_set));
    found = select(max_fd + 1,(fd_set *)&rfds,(fd_set *)0,
                        (fd_set *)0, (struct timeval *)0);
#ifdef DEBUG
    fprintf(stdout, "after select() call client connected\n" );
    fflush(stdout);
#endif
    if(found < 0)
      if(errno == EINTR)
      {
         fprintf(stdout, "just an interrupt\n");
         continue;
      }
      else {
         perror("select call failed\n");
         exit(-1);
      } /*end else */

    for(i = 0; i < max_fd + 1; i++)
    {
      if(FD_ISSET(i, &rfds) == 0)
        continue;
      if(i == sockfd) {
        j = sizeof(isa);
        if(( newsockfd = accept(sockfd, &isa, &j)) < 0 )
        {
           perror("accept failed");
           exit(-1);
        }
        fprintf(stdout,"server accepting connection on channel=%d\n",newsockf
        fflush(stdout);
        FD_SET(newsockfd, &perm_rfds);
        max_fd = MAX(max_fd, newsockfd);
      } /* end if i == sockfd */
      else {
        fprintf(stdout, "server reading request on channel=%d\n", i);
        count = service(i);
          if(count == 0)
          {
            fprintf(stdout, "server closing connection on channel=%d\n", i);
            fflush(stdout);
            close(i);
            FD_CLR(i, &perm_rfds);
```

```
                max_fd = get_max(max_fd, perm_rfds);
            } /* if count == 0 */
        } /* else */
    } /* for loop */
  } /* infinite loop */
}
```

Transport Interfaces

3.1 How to Prepare XTI Applications

In a software development environment, a program, for example that uses XTI functions must be compiled with the XTI Library. This can be done using the following command (for example, for normal library):

```
cc file.c -lxti
```

The syntax for shared libraries is implementation-dependent.

3.2 Key for Parameter Arrays

For each XTI function description, a table is given which summarises the contents of the input and output parameter. The key is given below:

x   The parameter value is meaningful. (Input parameter must be set before the call and output parameter may be read after the call.)

(x)   The content of the object pointed to by the x pointer is meaningful.

?   The parameter value is meaningful but the parameter is optional.

(?)   The content of the object pointed to by the ? pointer is optional.

/   The parameter value is meaningless.

=   The parameter after the call keeps the same value as before the call.

3.3 Return of TLOOK Error

Many of the XTI functions contained in this chapter return a [TLOOK] error to report the occurrence of an asynchronous event. For these functions a complete list describing the function and the events is provided in the **Networking Services, Issue 4** specification, **Section 5.6**, **Events and TLOOK Error Indication**.

NAME

t_accept - accept a connect request

SYNOPSIS

```
#include <xti.h>

int t_accept(int fd, int resfd, struct t_call *call);
```

DESCRIPTION

Parameters	Before call	After call
fd	x	/
resfd	x	/
call->addr.maxlen	/	/
call->addr.len	x	/
call->addr.buf	? (?)	/
call->opt.maxlen	/	/
call->opt.len	x	/
call->opt.buf	? (?)	/
call->udata.maxlen	/	/
call->udata.len	x	/
call->udata.buf	? (?)	/
call->sequence	x	/

This function is issued by a transport user to accept a connect request. The parameter *fd* identifies the local transport endpoint where the connect indication arrived; *resfd* specifies the local transport endpoint where the connection is to be established, and *call* contains information required by the transport provider to complete the connection. The parameter *call* points to a **t_call** structure which contains the following members:

```
struct netbuf addr;
struct netbuf opt;
struct netbuf udata;
int sequence;
```

In *call*, *addr* is the protocol address of the calling transport user, *opt* indicates any options associated with the connection, *udata* points to any user data to be returned to the caller, and *sequence* is the value returned by *t_listen*( ) that uniquely associates the response with a previously received connect indication. The address of the caller, *addr* may be null (length zero). Where *addr* is not null then it may optionally be checked by XTI.

A transport user may accept a connection on either the same, or on a different, local transport endpoint than the one on which the connect indication arrived. Before the connection can be accepted on the same endpoint (*resfd==fd*), the user must have responded to any previous connect indications received on that transport endpoint (via *t_accept*( ) or *t_snddis*( )). Otherwise, *t_accept*( ) will fail and set *t_errno* to [TINDOUT].

If a different transport endpoint is specified (*resfd!=fd*), then the user may or may not choose to bind the endpoint before the *t_accept*( ) is issued. If the endpoint is not bound prior to the *t_accept*( ), then the transport provider will automatically bind it to the same protocol address *fd* is bound to. If the transport user chooses to bind the endpoint it must be bound to a protocol address with a *qlen* of zero and must be in the T_IDLE state before the *t_accept*( ) is issued.

The call to *t_accept*( ) will fail with *t_errno* set to [TLOOK] if there are indications (for example, connect or disconnect) waiting to be received on the endpoint *fd*.

The *udata* argument enables the called transport user to send user data to the caller and the amount of user data must not exceed the limits supported by the transport provider as returned in the *connect* field of the *info* argument of *t_open*( ) or *t_getinfo*( ). If the *len* field of *udata* is zero, no data will be sent to the caller. All the *maxlen* fields are meaningless.

When the user does not indicate any option (call->opt.len = 0) it is assumed that the connection is to be accepted unconditionally. The transport provider may choose options other than the defaults to ensure that the connection is accepted successfully.

CAVEATS

There may be transport provider-specific restrictions on address binding. See the **Networking Services, Issue 4** specification, **Appendix A**, **ISO Transport Protocol Information** and the **Networking Services, Issue 4** specification, **Appendix B**, **Internet Protocol-specific Information**.

Some transport providers do not differentiate between a connect indication and the connection itself. If the connection has already been established after a successful return of *t_listen*( ), *t_accept*( ) will assign the existing connection to the transport endpoint specified by *resfd* (see the **Networking Services, Issue 4** specification, **Appendix B**, **Internet Protocol-specific Information**).

VALID STATES

fd: T_INCON resfd (fd!=resfd): T_IDLE

ERRORS

On failure, *t_errno* is set to one of the following:

[TBADF]	The file descriptor *fd* or *resfd* does not refer to a transport endpoint.
[TOUTSTATE]	The function was called in the wrong sequence on the transport endpoint referenced by *fd*, or the transport endpoint referred to by *resfd* is not in the appropriate state.
[TACCES]	The user does not have permission to accept a connection on the responding transport endpoint or to use the specified options.
[TBADOPT]	The specified options were in an incorrect format or contained illegal information.
[TBADDATA]	The amount of user data specified was not within the bounds allowed by the transport provider.
[TBADADDR]	The specified protocol address was in an incorrect format or contained illegal information.
[TBADSEQ]	An invalid sequence number was specified.
[TLOOK]	An asynchronous event has occurred on the transport endpoint referenced by *fd* and requires immediate attention.
[TNOTSUPPORT]	This function is not supported by the underlying transport provider.
[TSYSERR]	A system error has occurred during execution of this function.
[TINDOUT]	The function was called with *fd==resfd* but there are outstanding connection indications on the endpoint. Those other connection indications must be handled either by rejecting them via *t_snddis*(3) or accepting them on a different endpoint via *t_accept*(3).
[TPRIVMISMATCH]	The file descriptors *fd* and *resfd* do not refer to the same transport provider.

[TRESQLEN]	The endpoint referenced by *resfd* (where *resfd* != *fd*) was bound to a protocol address with a *qlen* that is greater than zero.
[TPROTO]	This error indicates that a communication problem has been detected between XTI and the transport provider for which there is no other suitable XTI *(t_errno)*.
[TRESADDR]	This transport provider requires both *fd* and *resfd* to be bound to the same address. This error results if they are not.

RETURN VALUE

Upon successful completion, a value of 0 is returned. Otherwise, a value of −1 is returned and *t_errno* is set to indicate an error.

SEE ALSO

t_connect( ), *t_getstate*( ), *t_listen*( ), *t_open*( ), *t_optmgmt*( ), *t_rcvconnect*( ).

EXAMPLE

See examples at the end of chapter.

NAME

t_alloc - allocate a library structure

SYNOPSIS

```
#include <xti.h>

char *t_alloc(int fd, int struct_type, int fields);
```

DESCRIPTION

Parameters	Before call	After call
fd	x	/
struct_type	x	/
fields	x	/

The *t_alloc( )* function dynamically allocates memory for the various transport function argument structures as specified below. This function will allocate memory for the specified structure, and will also allocate memory for buffers referenced by the structure.

The structure to allocate is specified by *struct_type* and must be one of the following:

```
T_BIND        struct     t_bind
T_CALL        struct     t_call
T_OPTMGMT     struct     t_optmgmt
T_DIS         struct     t_discon
T_UNITDATA    struct     t_unitdata
T_UDERROR     struct     t_uderr
T_INFO        struct     t_info
```

where each of these structures may subsequently be used as an argument to one or more transport functions.

Each of the above structures, except T_INFO, contains at least one field of type **struct netbuf**. For each field of this type, the user may specify that the buffer for that field should be allocated as well. The length of the buffer allocated will be equal to or greater than the appropriate size as returned in the *info* argument of *t_open( )* or *t_getinfo( )*. The relevant fields of the *info* argument are described in the following list. The *fields* argument specifies which buffers to allocate, where the argument is the bitwise-or of any of the following:

T_ADDR   The *addr* field of the **t_bind**, **t_call**, **t_unitdata** or **t_uderr** structures.

T_OPT   The *opt* field of the **t_optmgmt**, **t_call**, **t_unitdata** or **t_uderr** structures.

T_UDATA   The *udata* field of the **t_call**, **t_discon** or **t_unitdata** structures.

T_ALL   All relevant fields of the given structure. Fields which are not supported by the transport provider specified by *fd* will not be allocated.

For each relevant field specified in *fields*, *t_alloc( )* will allocate memory for the buffer associated with the field, and initialise the *len* field to zero and the *buf* pointer and *maxlen* field accordingly. Irrelevant or unknown values passed in fields are ignored. Since the length of the buffer allocated will be based on the same size information that is returned to the user on a call to *t_open( )* and *t_getinfo( )*, *fd* must refer to the transport endpoint through which the newly allocated structure will be passed. In this way the appropriate size information can be accessed. If the size value associated with any specified field is −1 or −2 (see *t_open( )* or *t_getinfo( )*), *t_alloc( )* will be unable to determine the size of the buffer to allocate and will fail, setting *t_errno* to [TSYSERR] and *errno* to [EINVAL]. For any field not specified in *fields*, *buf* will be set to the null pointer and *len* and *maxlen* will be set to zero.

Use of *t_alloc*( ) to allocate structures will help ensure the compatibility of user programs with future releases of the transport interface functions.

VALID STATES

ALL - apart from T_UNINIT

ERRORS

On failure, *t_errno* is set to one of the following:

[TBADF]   The specified file descriptor does not refer to a transport endpoint.

[TSYSERR]   A system error has occurred during execution of this function.

[TNOSTRUCTYPE]   Unsupported *struct_type* requested. This can include a request for a structure type which is inconsistent with the transport provider type specified, that is, connection-oriented or connectionless.

[TPROTO]   This error indicates that a communication problem has been detected between XTI and the transport provider for which there is no other suitable XTI *(t_errno)*.

RETURN VALUE

On successful completion, *t_alloc*( ) returns a pointer to the newly allocated structure. On failure, a null pointer is returned.

SEE ALSO

t_free( ), *t_getinfo*( ), *t_open*( ).

EXAMPLE

See examples at the end of chapter.

NAME

t_bind - bind an address to a transport endpoint

SYNOPSIS

```
#include <xti.h>

int t_bind(int fd, struct t_bind *req, struct t_bind *ret);
```

DESCRIPTION

Parameters	Before call	After call
fd	x	/
req->addr.maxlen	/	/
req->addr.len	x>=0	/
req->addr.buf	x (x)	/
req->qlen	x >=0	/
ret->addr.maxlen	x	/
ret->addr.len	/	x
ret->addr.buf	?	(?)
ret->qlen	/	x >=0

This function associates a protocol address with the transport endpoint specified by *fd* and activates that transport endpoint. In connection mode, the transport provider may begin enqueuing incoming connect indications, or servicing a connection request on the transport endpoint. In connectionless mode, the transport user may send or receive data units through the transport endpoint.

The *req* and *ret* arguments point to a **t_bind** structure containing the following members:

```
struct netbuf addr;
unsigned qlen;
```

The *addr* field of the **t_bind** structure specifies a protocol address, and the *qlen* field is used to indicate the maximum number of outstanding connect indications.

The parameter *req* is used to request that an address, represented by the **netbuf** structure, be bound to the given transport endpoint. The parameter *len* specifies the number of bytes in the address, and *buf* points to the address buffer. The parameter *maxlen* has no meaning for the *req* argument. On return, *ret* contains the address that the transport provider actually bound to the transport endpoint; this is the same as the address specified by the user in *req*. In *ret*, the user specifies *maxlen,* which is the maximum size of the address buffer, and *buf* which points to the buffer where the address is to be placed. On return, *len* specifies the number of bytes in the bound address, and *buf* points to the bound address. If *maxlen* is not large enough to hold the returned address, an error will result.

If the requested address is not available, *t_bind*( ) will return −1 with *t_errno* set as appropriate. If no address is specified in *req* (the *len* field of *addr* in *req* is zero or *req* is NULL), the transport provider will assign an appropriate address to be bound, and will return that address in the *addr* field of *ret*. If the transport provider could not allocate an address, *t_bind*( ) will fail with *t_errno* set to [TNOADDR].

The parameter *req* may be a null pointer if the user does not wish to specify an address to be bound. Here, the value of *qlen* is assumed to be zero, and the transport provider will assign an address to the transport endpoint. Similarly, *ret* may be a null pointer if the user does not care what address was bound by the provider and is not interested in the negotiated value of *qlen*. It is valid to set *req* and *ret* to the null pointer for the same call, in which case the provider chooses the address to bind to the transport endpoint and does not return that information to the user.

The *qlen* field has meaning only when initialising a connection-mode service. It specifies the number of outstanding connect indications that the transport provider should support for the given transport endpoint. An outstanding connect indication is one that has been passed to the transport user by the transport provider but which has not been accepted or rejected. A value of *qlen* greater than zero is only meaningful when issued by a passive transport user that expects other users to call it. The value of *qlen* will be negotiated by the transport provider and may be changed if the transport provider cannot support the specified number of outstanding connect indications. However, this value of *qlen* will never be negotiated from a requested value greater than zero to zero. This is a requirement on transport providers; see **CAVEATS** below. On return, the *qlen* field in *ret* will contain the negotiated value.

If *fd* refers to a connection-mode service, this function allows more than one transport endpoint to be bound to the same protocol address (however, the transport provider must also support this capability), but it is not possible to bind more than one protocol address to the same transport endpoint. If a user binds more than one transport endpoint to the same protocol address, only one endpoint can be used to listen for connect indications associated with that protocol address. In other words, only one *t_bind*( ) for a given protocol address may specify a value of *qlen* greater than zero. In this way, the transport provider can identify which transport endpoint should be notified of an incoming connect indication. If a user attempts to bind a protocol address to a second transport endpoint with a value of *qlen* greater than zero, *t_bind*( ) will return −1 and set *t_errno* to [TADDRBUSY]. When a user accepts a connection on the transport endpoint that is being used as the listening endpoint, the bound protocol address will be found to be busy for the duration of the connection, until a *t_unbind*( ) or *t_close*( ) call has been issued. No other transport endpoints may be bound for listening on that same protocol address while that initial listening endpoint is active (in the data transfer phase or in the T_IDLE state). This will prevent more than one transport endpoint bound to the same protocol address from accepting connect indications.

If *fd* refers to a connectionless-mode service, only one endpoint may be associated with a protocol address. If a user attempts to bind a second transport endpoint to an already bound protocol address, *t_bind*( ) will return −1 and set *t_errno* to [TADDRBUSY].

VALID STATES

T_UNBND

ERRORS

On failure, *t_errno* is set to one of the following:

[TBADF]	The specified file descriptor does not refer to a transport endpoint.
[TOUTSTATE]	The function was issued in the wrong sequence.
[TBADADDR]	The specified protocol address was in an incorrect format or contained illegal information.
[TNOADDR]	The transport provider could not allocate an address.
[TACCES]	The user does not have permission to use the specified address.
[TBUFOVFLW]	The number of bytes allowed for an incoming argument *(maxlen)* is greater than 0 but not sufficient to store the value of that argument. The provider's state will change to T_IDLE and the information to be returned in *ret* will be discarded.
[TSYSERR]	A system error has occurred during execution of this function.
[TADDRBUSY]	The requested address is in use.

[TPROTO]   This error indicates that a communication problem has been detected between XTI and the transport provider for which there is no other suitable XTI *(t_errno)*.

RETURN VALUE

Upon successful completion, a value of 0 is returned. Otherwise, a value of −1 is returned and *t_errno* is set to indicate an error.

SEE ALSO

t_alloc( ), *t_close( )*, *t_open( )*, *t_optmgmt( )*, *t_unbind( )*.

CAVEATS

The requirement that the value of *qlen* never be negotiated from a requested value greater than zero to zero implies that transport providers, rather than the XTI implementation itself, accept this restriction.

A transport provider may not allow an explicit binding of more than one transport endpoint to the same protocol address, although it allows more than one connection to be accepted for the same protocol address. To ensure portability, it is, therefore, recommended not to bind transport endpoints that are used as responding endpoints *(resfd)* in a call to *t_accept( )*, if the responding address is to be the same as the called address.

EXAMPLE

See examples at the end of chapter.

NAME

t_close - close a transport endpoint

SYNOPSIS

```
#include <xti.h>

int t_close(int fd);
```

DESCRIPTION

Parameters	Before call	After call
fd	x	/

The *t_close()* function informs the transport provider that the user is finished with the transport endpoint specified by *fd*, and frees any local library resources associated with the endpoint. In addition, *t_close()* closes the file associated with the transport endpoint.

The function *t_close()* should be called from the T_UNBND state (see *t_getstate()*). However, this function does not check state information, so it may be called from any state to close a transport endpoint. If this occurs, the local library resources associated with the endpoint will be freed automatically. In addition, *close()* will be issued for that file descriptor; the *close()* will be abortive if there are no other descriptors in this, or in another process which references the transport endpoint, and in this case will break any transport connection that may be associated with that endpoint.

A *t_close()* issued on a connection endpoint may cause data previously sent, or data not yet received, to be lost. It is the responsibility of the transport user to ensure that data is received by the remote peer.

VALID STATES

ALL - apart from T_UNINIT

ERRORS

On failure, *t_errno* is set to the following:

[TBADF]   The specified file descriptor does not refer to a transport endpoint.

[TPROTO]   This error indicates that a communication problem has been detected between XTI and the transport provider for which there is no other suitable XTI *(t_errno)*.

RETURN VALUE

Upon successful completion, a value of 0 is returned. Otherwise, a value of −1 is returned and *t_errno* is set to indicate an error.

SEE ALSO

t_getstate(), *t_open()*, *t_unbind()*.

EXAMPLE

See examples at the end of chapter.

NAME

t_connect - establish a connection with another transport user

SYNOPSIS

```
#include <xti.h>

int t_connect(int fd, struct t_call *sndcall, struct t_call *rcvcall);
```

DESCRIPTION

Parameters	Before call	After call
fd	x	/
sndcall->addr.maxlen	/	/
sndcall->addr.len	x	/
sndcall->addr.buf	x (x)	/
sndcall->opt.maxlen	/	/
sndcall->opt.len	x	/
sndcall->opt.buf	x (x)	/
sndcall->udata.maxlen	/	/
sndcall->udata.len	x	/
sndcall->udata.buf	? (?)	/
sndcall->sequence	/	/
rcvcall->addr.maxlen	x	/
rcvcall->addr.len	/	x
rcvcall->addr.buf	?	(?)
rcvcall->opt.maxlen	x	/
rcvcall->opt.len	/	x
rcvcall->opt.buf	?	(?)
rcvcall->udata.maxlen	x	/
rcvcall->udata.len	/	x
rcvcall->udata.buf	?	(?)
rcvcall->sequence	/	/

This function enables a transport user to request a connection to the specified destination transport user. This function can only be issued in the T_IDLE state. The parameter *fd* identifies the local transport endpoint where communication will be established, while *sndcall* and *rcvcall* point to a **t_call** structure which contains the following members:

```
struct netbuf addr;
struct netbuf opt;
struct netbuf udata;
int sequence;
```

The parameter *sndcall* specifies information needed by the transport provider to establish a connection and *rcvcall* specifies information that is associated with the newly established connection.

In *sndcall*, *addr* specifies the protocol address of the destination transport user, *opt* presents any protocol-specific information that might be needed by the transport provider, *udata* points to optional user data that may be passed to the destination transport user during connection establishment, and *sequence* has no meaning for this function.

On return, in *rcvcall*, *addr* contains the protocol address associated with the responding transport endpoint, *opt* represents any protocol-specific information associated with the connection, *udata* points to optional user data that may be returned by the destination transport user during connection establishment, and *sequence* has no meaning for this function.

The *opt* argument permits users to define the options that may be passed to the transport provider. These options are specific to the underlying protocol of the transport provider and are described for ISO and TCP protocols in the **Networking Services, Issue 4** specification, **Appendix A**, **ISO Transport Protocol Information**, the **Networking Services, Issue 4** specification, **Appendix B**, **Internet Protocol-specific Information** and the **Networking Services, Issue 4** specification, **Appendix F**, **Headers and Definitions for XTI**. The user may choose not to negotiate protocol options by setting the *len* field of *opt* to zero. In this case, the provider may use default options.

If used, *sndcall->opt.buf* must point to a buffer with the corresponding options; the *maxlen* and *buf* fields of the **netbuf** structure pointed by *rcvcall->addr* and *rcvcall->opt* must be set before the call.

The *udata* argument enables the caller to pass user data to the destination transport user and receive user data from the destination user during connection establishment. However, the amount of user data must not exceed the limits supported by the transport provider as returned in the *connect* field of the *info* argument of *t_open( )* or *t_getinfo( )*. If the *len* of *udata* is zero in *sndcall*, no data will be sent to the destination transport user.

On return, the *addr*, *opt* and *udata* fields of *rcvcall* will be updated to reflect values associated with the connection. Thus, the *maxlen* field of each argument must be set before issuing this function to indicate the maximum size of the buffer for each. However, *rcvcall* may be a null pointer, in which case no information is given to the user on return from *t_connect( )*.

By default, *t_connect( )* executes in synchronous mode, and will wait for the destination user's response before returning control to the local user. A successful return (that is, return value of zero) indicates that the requested connection has been established. However, if O_NONBLOCK is set (via *t_open( )* or *fcntl( )*), *t_connect( )* executes in asynchronous mode. In this case, the call will not wait for the remote user's response, but will return control immediately to the local user and return −1 with *t_errno* set to [TNODATA] to indicate that the connection has not yet been established. In this way, the function simply initiates the connection establishment procedure by sending a connect request to the destination transport user. The *t_rcvconnect( )* function is used in conjunction with *t_connect( )* to determine the status of the requested connection.

When a synchronous *t_connect( )* call is interrupted by the arrival of a signal, the state of the corresponding transport endpoint is T_OUTCON, allowing a further call to either *t_rcvconnect( )*, *t_rcvdis( )* or *t_snddis( )*.

VALID STATES
T_IDLE

ERRORS
On failure, *t_errno* is set to one of the following:

[TBADF]	The specified file descriptor does not refer to a transport endpoint.
[TOUTSTATE]	The function was issued in the wrong sequence.
[TNODATA]	O_NONBLOCK was set, so the function successfully initiated the connection establishment procedure, but did not wait for a response from the remote user.
[TBADADDR]	The specified protocol address was in an incorrect format or contained illegal information.
[TBADOPT]	The specified protocol options were in an incorrect format or contained illegal information.

[TBADDATA]	The amount of user data specified was not within the bounds allowed by the transport provider.
[TACCES]	The user does not have permission to use the specified address or options.
[TBUFOVFLW]	The number of bytes allocated for an incoming argument *(maxlen)* is greater than 0 but not sufficient to store the value of that argument. If executed in synchronous mode, the provider's state, as seen by the user, changes to T_DATAXFER, and the information to be returned in *rcvcall* is discarded.
[TLOOK]	An asynchronous event has occurred on this transport endpoint and requires immediate attention.
[TNOTSUPPORT]	This function is not supported by the underlying transport provider.
[TSYSERR]	A system error has occurred during execution of this function.
[TADDRBUSY]	This transport provider does not support multiple connections with the same local and remote addresses. This error indicates that a connection already exists.
[TPROTO]	This error indicates that a communication problem has been detected between XTI and the transport provider for which there is no other suitable XTI *(t_errno)*.

RETURN VALUE

Upon successful completion, a value of 0 is returned. Otherwise, a value of –1 is returned and *t_errno* is set to indicate an error.

SEE ALSO

t_accept( ), *t_alloc*( ), *t_getinfo*( ), *t_listen*( ), *t_open*( ), *t_optmgmt*( ), *t_rcvconnect*( ).

EXAMPLE

See examples at the end of chapter.

NAME
t_error - produce error message

SYNOPSIS
```
#include <xti.h>

int t_error(char *errmsg);
```

DESCRIPTION

Parameters	Before call	After call
errmsg	x	/

The *t_error( )* function produces a language-dependent message on the standard error output which describes the last error encountered during a call to a transport function. The argument string *errmsg* is a user-supplied error message that gives context to the error.

The error message is written as follows: first (if *errmsg* is not a null pointer and the character pointed to be *errmsg* is not the null character) the string pointed to by *errmsg* followed by a colon and a space; then a standard error message string for the current error defined in *t_errno*. If *t_errno* has a value different from [TSYSERR], the standard error message string is followed by a newline character. If, however, *t_errno* is equal to [TSYSERR], the *t_errno* string is followed by the standard error message string for the current error defined in *errno* followed by a newline.

The language for error message strings written by *t_error()* is implementation-defined. If it is in English, the error message string describing the value in *t_errno* is identical to the comments following the *t_errno* codes defined in **xti.h**. The contents of the error message strings describing the value in *errno* are the same as those returned by the *strerror(3C)* function with an argument of *errno*.

The error number, *t_errno*, is only set when an error occurs and it is not cleared on successful calls.

EXAMPLE
If a *t_connect( )* function fails on transport endpoint *fd2* because a bad address was given, the following call might follow the failure:

```
t_error("t_connect failed on fd2");
```

The diagnostic message to be printed would look like:

```
t_connect failed on fd2: incorrect addr format
```

where *incorrect addr format* identifies the specific error that occurred, and *t_connect failed on fd2* tells the user which function failed on which transport endpoint.

VALID STATES
All - apart from T_UNINIT

ERRORS
No errors are defined for the *t_error( )* function.

RETURN VALUE
Upon completion, a value of 0 is returned.

EXAMPLE
See examples at the end of chapter.

NAME

t_free - free a library structure

SYNOPSIS

```
#include <xti.h>

int t_free(char *ptr, int struct_type);
```

DESCRIPTION

Parameters	Before call	After call
ptr	x	/
struct_type	x	/

The *t_free( )* function frees memory previously allocated by *t_alloc( )*. This function will free memory for the specified structure, and will also free memory for buffers referenced by the structure.

The argument *ptr* points to one of the seven structure types described for *t_alloc( )*, and *struct_type* identifies the type of that structure which must be one of the following:

```
T_BIND          struct      t_bind
T_CALL          struct      t_call
T_OPTMGMT       struct      t_optmgmt
T_DIS           struct      t_discon
T_UNITDATA      struct      t_unitdata
T_UDERROR       struct      t_uderr
T_INFO          struct      t_info
```

where each of these structures is used as an argument to one or more transport functions.

The function *t_free( )* will check the *addr*, *opt* and *udata* fields of the given structure (as appropriate) and free the buffers pointed to by the *buf* field of the **netbuf** structure. If *buf* is a null pointer, *t_free( )* will not attempt to free memory. After all buffers are freed, *t_free( )* will free the memory associated with the structure pointed to by *ptr*.

Undefined results will occur if *ptr* or any of the *buf* pointers points to a block of memory that was not previously allocated by *t_alloc( )*.

VALID STATES

ALL - apart from T_UNINIT

ERRORS

On failure, *t_errno* is set to the following:

[TSYSERR]   A system error has occurred during execution of this function.

[TNOSTRUCTYPE] Unsupported *struct_type* requested.

[TPROTO]   This error indicates that a communication problem has been detected between XTI and the transport provider for which there is no other suitable XTI *(t_errno)*.

RETURN VALUE

Upon successful completion, a value of 0 is returned. Otherwise, a value of −1 is returned and *t_errno* is set to indicate an error.

SEE ALSO

t_alloc( ).

EXAMPLE

See examples at the end of chapter.

NAME

t_getinfo - get protocol-specific service information

SYNOPSIS

```
#include <xti.h>

int t_getinfo(int fd, struct t_info *info);
```

DESCRIPTION

Parameters	Before call	After call
fd	x	/
info->addr	/	x
info->options	/	x
info->tsdu	/	x
info->etsdu	/	x
info->connect	/	x
info->discon	/	x
info->servtype	/	x
info->flags	/	x

This function returns the current characteristics of the underlying transport protocol and/or transport connection associated with file descriptor *fd*. The *info* pointer is used to return the same information returned by *t_open*( ), although not necessarily precisely the same values. This function enables a transport user to access this information during any phase of communication.

This argument points to a **t_info** structure which contains the following members:

```
long addr;      /* max size of the transport protocol address     */
long options;   /* max number of bytes of protocol-specific options */
long tsdu;      /* max size of a transport service data unit (TSDU) */
long etsdu;     /* max size of an expedited transport service      */
                /* data unit (ETSDU)                               */
long connect;   /* max amount of data allowed on connection        */
                /* establishment functions                         */
long discon;    /* max amount of data allowed on t_snddis()        */
                /* and t_rcvdis() functions                        */
long servtype;  /* service type supported by the transport provider */
long flags;     /* other info about the transport provider         */
```

The values of the fields have the following meanings:

addr   A value greater than zero indicates the maximum size of a transport protocol address and a value of –2 specifies that the transport provider does not provide user access to transport protocol addresses.

options   A value greater than zero indicates the maximum number of bytes of protocol-specific options supported by the provider, and a value of –2 specifies that the transport provider does not support user-settable options.

tsdu   A value greater than zero specifies the maximum size of a transport service data unit (TSDU); a value of zero specifies that the transport provider does not support the concept of TSDU, although it does support the sending of a datastream with no logical boundaries preserved across a connection; a value of –1 specifies that there is no limit on the size of a TSDU; and a value of –2 specifies that the transfer of normal data is not supported by the transport provider.

etsdu   A value greater than zero specifies the maximum size of an expedited transport service data unit (ETSDU); a value of zero specifies that the transport provider does not support the concept of ETSDU, although it does support the sending of an expedited data stream with no logical boundaries preserved across a connection; a value of –1 specifies that there is no limit on the size of an ETSDU; and a value of –2 specifies that the transfer of expedited data is not supported by the transport provider. Note that the semantics of expedited data may be quite different for different transport providers (see the **Networking Services, Issue 4** specification, **Appendix A**, **ISO Transport Protocol Information** and the **Networking Services, Issue 4** specification, **Appendix B**, **Internet Protocol-specific Information**).

connect   A value greater than zero specifies the maximum amount of data that may be associated with connection establishment functions and a value of –2 specifies that the transport provider does not allow data to be sent with connection establishment functions.

discon   A value greater than zero specifies the maximum amount of data that may be associated with the *t_snddis*( ) and *t_rcvdis*( ) functions and a value of –2 specifies that the transport provider does not allow data to be sent with the abortive release functions.

servtype   This field specifies the service type supported by the transport provider, as described below.

flags   This is a bit field used to specify other information about the transport provider. If the T_SENDZERO bit is set in flags, this indicates that the underlying transport provider supports the sending of zero-length TSDUs. See the **Networking Services, Issue 4** specification, **Appendix A**, **ISO Transport Protocol Information** for a discussion of the separate issue of zero-length fragments within a TSDU.

If a transport user is concerned with protocol independence, the above sizes may be accessed to determine how large the buffers must be to hold each piece of information. Alternatively, the *t_alloc*( ) function may be used to allocate these buffers. An error will result if a transport user exceeds the allowed data size on any function. The value of each field may change as a result of protocol option negotiation during connection establishment (the *t_optmgmt*( ) call has no affect on the values returned by *t_getinfo*( )). These values will only change from the values presented to *t_open*( ) after the endpoint enters the T_DATAXFER state.

The *servtype* field of *info* specifies one of the following values on return:

T_COTS   The transport provider supports a connection-mode service but does not support the optional orderly release facility.

T_COTS_ORD   The transport provider supports a connection-mode service with the optional orderly release facility.

T_CLTS   The transport provider supports a connectionless-mode service. For this service type, *t_open*( ) will return –2 for *etsdu*, *connect* and *discon*.

VALID STATES
ALL - apart from T_UNINIT

ERRORS
On failure, *t_errno* is set to one of the following:

[TBADF]	The specified file descriptor does not refer to a transport endpoint.
[TSYSERR]	A system error has occurred during execution of this function.
[TPROTO]	This error indicates that a communication problem has been detected between XTI and the transport provider for which there is no other suitable XTI *(t_errno)*.

RETURN VALUE

Upon successful completion, a value of 0 is returned. Otherwise, a value of −1 is returned and *t_errno* is set to indicate an error.

SEE ALSO

t_alloc( ), *t_open*( ).

EXAMPLE

See examples at the end of chapter.

NAME

t_getprotaddr - get the protocol addresses

SYNOPSIS

```
#include <xti.h>

int t_getprotaddr(int fd, struct t_bind *boundaddr, struct t_bind *peeraddr);
```

DESCRIPTION

Parameters	Before call	After call
fd	x	/
boundaddr->maxlen	x	/
boundaddr->addr.len	/	x
boundaddr->addr.buf	?	(?)
boundaddr->qlen	/	/
peeraddr->maxlen	x	/
peeraddr->addr.len	/	x
peeraddr->addr.buf	?	(?)
peeraddr->qlen	/	/

The *t_getprotaddr*( ) function returns local and remote protocol addresses currently associated with the transport endpoint specified by *fd*. In *boundaddr* and *peeraddr* the user specifies *maxlen,* which is the maximum size of the address buffer, and *buf* which points to the buffer where the address is to be placed. On return, the *buf* field of *boundaddr* points to the address, if any, currently bound to *fd*, and the *len* field specifies the length of the address. If the transport endpoint is in the T_UNBND state, zero is returned in the *len* field of *boundaddr*. The *buf* field of *peeraddr* points to the address, if any, currently connected to *fd*, and the *len* field specifies the length of the address. If the transport endpoint is not in the T_DATAXFER state, zero is returned in the *len* field of *peeraddr*.

VALID STATES

ALL - apart from T_UNINIT

ERRORS

On failure, *t_errno* is set to one of the following:

[TBADF]	The specified file descriptor does not refer to a transport endpoint.
[TBUFOVFLW]	The number of bytes allocated for an incoming argument (*maxlen)* is greater than 0 but not sufficient to store the value of that argument.
[TSYSERR]	A system error has occurred during execution of this function.
[TPROTO]	This error indicates that a communication problem has been detected between XTI and the transport provider for which there is no other suitable XTI *(t_errno).*

RETURN VALUE

Upon successful completion, a value of zero is returned. Otherwise, a value of −1 is returned and *t_errno* is set to indicate the error.

SEE ALSO

t_bind( ).

EXAMPLE

See examples at the end of chapter.

NAME

t_getstate - get the current state

SYNOPSIS

```
#include <xti.h>

int t_getstate(int fd);
```

DESCRIPTION

Parameters	Before call	After call
fd	x	/

The *t_getstate*( ) function returns the current state of the provider associated with the transport endpoint specified by *fd*.

VALID STATES

ALL - apart from T_UNINIT

ERRORS

On failure, *t_errno* is set to one of the following:

[TBADF]   The specified file descriptor does not refer to a transport endpoint.

[TSTATECHNG]   The transport provider is undergoing a transient state change.

[TSYSERR]   A system error has occurred during execution of this function.

[TPROTO]   This error indicates that a communication problem has been detected between XTI and the transport provider for which there is no other suitable XTI *(t_errno)*.

RETURN VALUE

State is returned upon successful completion. Otherwise, a value of −1 is returned and *t_errno* is set to indicate an error. The current state is one of the following:

T_UNBND   Unbound.

T_IDLE   Idle.

T_OUTCON   Outgoing connection pending.

T_INCON   Incoming connection pending.

T_DATAXFER   Data transfer.

T_OUTREL   Outgoing orderly release (waiting for an orderly release indication).

T_INREL   Incoming orderly release (waiting to send an orderly release request).

If the provider is undergoing a state transition when *t_getstate*( ) is called, the function will fail.

SEE ALSO

t_open( ).

EXAMPLE

See examples at the end of chapter.

NAME

t_listen - listen for a connect indication

SYNOPSIS

```
#include <xti.h>

int t_listen(int fd, struct t_call *call);
```

DESCRIPTION

Parameters	Before call	After call
fd	x	/
call->addr.maxlen	x	/
call->addr.len	/	x
call->addr.buf	?	(?)
call->opt.maxlen	x	/
call->opt.len	/	x
call->opt.buf	?	(?)
call->udata.maxlen	x	/
call->udata.len	/	x
call->udata.buf	?	(?)
call->sequence	/	x

This function listens for a connect request from a calling transport user. The argument *fd* identifies the local transport endpoint where connect indications arrive, and on return, *call* contains information describing the connect indication. The parameter *call* points to a **t_call** structure which contains the following members:

```
struct netbuf addr;
struct netbuf opt;
struct netbuf udata;
int sequence;
```

In *call*, *addr* returns the protocol address of the calling transport user. This address is in a format usable in future calls to *t_connect*( ). Note, however that *t_connect*( ) may fail for other reasons, for example [TADDRBUSY]. *opt* returns options associated with the connect request, *udata* returns any user data sent by the caller on the connect request, and *sequence* is a number that uniquely identifies the returned connect indication. The value of *sequence* enables the user to listen for multiple connect indications before responding to any of them.

Since this function returns values for the *addr*, *opt* and *udata* fields of *call*, the *maxlen* field of each must be set before issuing the *t_listen*( ) to indicate the maximum size of the buffer for each.

By default, *t_listen*( ) executes in synchronous mode and waits for a connect indication to arrive before returning to the user. However, if O_NONBLOCK is set via *t_open*( ) or *fcntl*( ), *t_listen*( ) executes asynchronously, reducing to a poll for existing connect indications. If none are available, it returns −1 and sets *t_errno* to [TNODATA].

VALID STATES

T_IDLE, T_INCON

ERRORS

On failure, *t_errno* is set to one of the following:

[TBADF]   The specified file descriptor does not refer to a transport endpoint.

[TBADQLEN]	The argument *qlen* of the endpoint referenced by *fd* is zero.
[TBUFOVFLW]	The number of bytes allocated for an incoming argument *(maxlen)* is greater than 0 but not sufficient to store the value of that argument. The provider's state, as seen by the user, changes to T_INCON, and the connect indication information to be returned in *call* is discarded. The value of *sequence* returned can be used to do a *t_snddis( )*.
[TNODATA]	O_NONBLOCK was set, but no connect indications had been queued.
[TLOOK]	An asynchronous event has occurred on this transport endpoint and requires immediate attention.
[TNOTSUPPORT]	This function is not supported by the underlying transport provider.
[TOUTSTATE]	The function was issued in the wrong sequence on the transport endpoint referenced by *fd*.
[TSYSERR]	A system error has occurred during execution of this function.
[TQFULL]	The maximum number of outstanding indications has been reached for the endpoint referenced by *fd*.
[TPROTO]	This error indicates that a communication problem has been detected between XTI and the transport provider for which there is no other suitable XTI *(t_errno)*.

CAVEATS

Some transport providers do not differentiate between a connect indication and the connection itself. If this is the case, a successful return of *t_listen( )* indicates an existing connection (see the **Networking Services, Issue 4** specification, **Appendix B**, **Internet Protocol-specific Information**).

RETURN VALUE

Upon successful completion, a value of 0 is returned. Otherwise, a value of −1 is returned and *t_errno* is set to indicate an error.

SEE ALSO

fcntl( ), *t_accept( )*, *t_alloc( )*, *t_bind( )*, *t_connect( )*, *t_open( )*, *t_optmgmt( )*, *t_rcvconnect( )*.

EXAMPLE

See examples at the end of chapter.

NAME

t_look - look at the current event on a transport endpoint

SYNOPSIS

```
#include <xti.h>

int t_look(int fd);
```

DESCRIPTION

Parameters	Before call	After call
fd	x	/

This function returns the current event on the transport endpoint specified by *fd*. This function enables a transport provider to notify a transport user of an asynchronous event when the user is calling functions in synchronous mode. Certain events require immediate notification of the user and are indicated by a specific error, [TLOOK], on the current or next function to be executed. Details on events which cause functions to fail [TLOOK] may be found in the **Networking Services, Issue 4** specification, **Section 5.6**, **Events and TLOOK Error Indication**.

This function also enables a transport user to poll a transport endpoint periodically for asynchronous events.

VALID STATES

ALL - apart from T_UNINIT

ERRORS

On failure, *t_errno* is set to one of the following:

[TBADF]   The specified file descriptor does not refer to a transport endpoint.

[TSYSERR]   A system error has occurred during execution of this function.

[TPROTO]   This error indicates that a communication problem has been detected between XTI and the transport provider for which there is no other suitable XTI *(t_errno)*.

RETURN VALUE

Upon success, *t_look*( ) returns a value that indicates which of the allowable events has occurred, or returns zero if no event exists. One of the following events is returned:

T_LISTEN   Connection indication received.

T_CONNECT   Connect confirmation received.

T_DATA   Normal data received.

T_EXDATA   Expedited data received.

T_DISCONNECT   Disconnect received.

T_UDERR   Datagram error indication.

T_ORDREL   Orderly release indication.

T_GODATA   Flow control restrictions on normal data flow that led to a [TFLOW] error have been lifted. Normal data may be sent again.

T_GOEXDATA   Flow control restrictions on expedited data flow that led to a [TFLOW] error have been lifted. Expedited data may be sent again.

On failure, −1 is returned and *t_errno* is set to indicate the error.

SEE ALSO

t_open( ), *t_snd*( ), *t_sndudata*( ).

APPLICATION USAGE

Additional functionality is provided through the Event Management (EM) interface.

EXAMPLE

See examples at the end of chapter.

NAME

t_open - establish a transport endpoint

SYNOPSIS

```
#include <xti.h>
#include <fcntl.h>

int t_open(char *name, int oflag, struct t_info *info);
```

DESCRIPTION

Parameters	Before call	After call
name	x	/
oflag	x	/
info->addr	/	x
info->options	/	x
info->tsdu	/	x
info->etsdu	/	x
info->connect	/	x
info->discon	/	x
info->servtype	/	x
info->flags	/	x

The *t_open( )* function must be called as the first step in the initialisation of a transport endpoint. This function establishes a transport endpoint by supplying a transport provider identifier that indicates a particular transport provider (that is, transport protocol) and returning a file descriptor that identifies that endpoint.

The argument *name* points to a transport provider identifier and *oflag* identifies any open flags (as in *open( )*). The argument *oflag* is constructed from O_RDWR optionally bitwise inclusive-OR'ed with O_NONBLOCK. These flags are defined by the header **<fcntl.h>**. The file descriptor returned by *t_open( )* will be used by all subsequent functions to identify the particular local transport endpoint.

This function also returns various default characteristics of the underlying transport protocol by setting fields in the **t_info** structure. This argument points to a **t_info** which contains the following members:

```
long addr;      /* max size of the transport protocol address  */
long options;   /* max number of bytes of                      */
                /* protocol-specific options                   */
long tsdu;      /* max size of a transport service data        */
                /* unit (TSDU)                                 */
long etsdu;     /* max size of an expedited transport          */
                /* service data unit (ETSDU)                   */
long connect;   /* max amount of data allowed on               */
                /* connection establishment functions          */
long discon;    /* max amount of data allowed on               */
                /* t_snddis() and t_rcvdis() functions         */
long servtype;  /* service type supported by the               */
                /* transport provider                          */
long flags;     /* other info about the transport provider     */
```

The values of the fields have the following meanings:

addr
A value greater than zero indicates the maximum size of a transport protocol address and a value of –2 specifies that the transport provider does not provide user access to transport protocol addresses.

options
A value greater than zero indicates the maximum number of bytes of protocol-specific options supported by the provider and a value of –2 specifies that the transport provider does not support user-settable options.

tsdu
A value greater than zero specifies the maximum size of a transport service data unit (TSDU); a value of zero specifies that the transport provider does not support the concept of TSDU, although it does support the sending of a data stream with no logical boundaries preserved across a connection; a value of –1 specifies that there is no limit to the size of a TSDU; and a value of –2 specifies that the transfer of normal data is not supported by the transport provider.

etsdu
A value greater than zero specifies the maximum size of an expedited transport service data unit (ETSDU); a value of zero specifies that the transport provider does not support the concept of ETSDU, although it does support the sending of an expedited data stream with no logical boundaries preserved across a connection; a value of –1 specifies that there is no limit on the size of an ETSDU; and a value of –2 specifies that the transfer of expedited data is not supported by the transport provider. Note that the semantics of expedited data may be quite different for different transport providers (see the **Networking Services, Issue 4** specification, **Appendix A**, **ISO Transport Protocol Information** and the **Networking Services, Issue 4** specification, **Appendix B**, **Internet Protocol-specific Information**).

connect
A value greater than zero specifies the maximum amount of data that may be associated with connection establishment functions and a value of –2 specifies that the transport provider does not allow data to be sent with connection establishment functions.

discon
A value greater than zero specifies the maximum amount of data that may be associated with the *t_snddis( )* and *t_rcvdis( )* functions and a value of –2 specifies that the transport provider does not allow data to be sent with the abortive release functions.

servtype
This field specifies the service type supported by the transport provider, as described below.

flags
This is a bit field used to specify other information about the transport provider. If the T_SENDZERO bit is set in flags, this indicates the underlying transport provider supports the sending of zero-length TSDUs. See the **Networking Services, Issue 4** specification, **Appendix A**, **ISO Transport Protocol Information** for a discussion of the separate issue of zero-length fragments within a TSDU.

If a transport user is concerned with protocol independence, the above sizes may be accessed to determine how large the buffers must be to hold each piece of information. Alternatively, the *t_alloc( )* function may be used to allocate these buffers. An error will result if a transport user exceeds the allowed data size on any function.

The *servtype* field of *info* specifies one of the following values on return:

T_COTS   The transport provider supports a connection-mode service but does not support the optional orderly release facility.

T_COTS_ORD   The transport provider supports a connection-mode service with the optional orderly release facility.

T_CLTS   The transport provider supports a connectionless-mode service. For this service type, *t_open*( ) will return −2 for *etsdu*, *connect* and *discon*.

A single transport endpoint may support only one of the above services at one time.

If *info* is set to a null pointer by the transport user, no protocol information is returned by *t_open*( ).

VALID STATES
T_UNINIT

ERRORS
On failure, *t_errno* is set to the following:

[TBADFLAG]   An invalid flag is specified.

[TBADNAME]   Invalid transport provider name.

[TSYSERR]   A system error has occurred during execution of this function.

[TPROTO]   This error indicates that a communication problem has been detected between XTI and the transport provider for which there is no other suitable XTI *(t_errno)*.

RETURN VALUES
A valid file descriptor is returned upon successful completion. Otherwise, a value of −1 is returned and *t_errno* is set to indicate an error.

SEE ALSO
open( ).

EXAMPLE
See examples at the end of chapter.

NAME

t_optmgmt - manage options for a transport endpoint

SYNOPSIS

```
#include <xti.h>

int t_optmgmt(int fd, struct t_optmgmt *req, struct t_optmgmt *ret);
```

DESCRIPTION

Parameters	Before call	After call
fd	x	/
req->opt.maxlen	/	/
req->opt.len	x	/
req->opt.buf	x (x)	/
req->flags	x	/
ret->opt.maxlen	x	/
ret->opt.len	/	x
ret->opt.buf	?	(?)
ret->flags	/	x

The *t_optmgmt*( ) function enables a transport user to retrieve, verify or negotiate protocol options with the transport provider. The argument *fd* identifies a transport endpoint.

The *req* and *ret* arguments point to a **t_optmgmt** structure containing the following members:

```
struct netbuf opt;
long flags;
```

The *opt* field identifies protocol options and the *flags* field is used to specify the action to take with those options.

The options are represented by a **netbuf** structure in a manner similar to the address in *t_bind*( ). The argument *req* is used to request a specific action of the provider and to send options to the provider. The argument *len* specifies the number of bytes in the options, *buf* points to the options buffer, and *maxlen* has no meaning for the *req* argument. The transport provider may return options and flag values to the user through *ret*. For *ret*, *maxlen* specifies the maximum size of the options buffer and *buf* points to the buffer where the options are to be placed. On return, *len* specifies the number of bytes of options returned. The value in *maxlen* has no meaning for the *req* argument, but must be set in the *ret* argument to specify the maximum number of bytes the options buffer can hold.

Each option in the options buffer is of the form **struct t_opthdr** possibly followed by an option value.

The *level* field of **struct t_opthdr** identifies the XTI level or a protocol of the transport provider. The *name* field identifies the option within the level, and *len* contains its total length; that is, the length of the option header **t_opthdr** plus the length of the option value. If *t_optmgmt*( ) is called with the action T_NEGOTIATE set, the *status* field of the returned options contains information about the success or failure of a negotiation.

Each option in the input or output option buffer must start at a long-word boundary. The macro **OPT_NEXTHDR(pbuf, buflen, poption)** can be used for that purpose. The parameter *pbuf* denotes a pointer to an option buffer *opt.buf*, and *buflen* is its length. The parameter *poption* points to the current option in the option buffer. **OPT_NEXTHDR** returns a pointer to the position of the next option or returns a null pointer if the option buffer is exhausted. The macro is helpful for writing and reading. See **<xti.h>** in the **Networking Services, Issue 4** specification, **Appendix F**, **Headers and Definitions for XTI** for the exact definition.

If the transport user specifies several options on input, all options must address the same level.

If any option in the options buffer does not indicate the same level as the first option, or the level specified is unsupported, then the *t_optmgmt*( ) request will fail with [TBADOPT]. If the error is detected, some options have possibly been successfully negotiated. The transport user can check the current status by calling *t_optmgmt*( ) with the T_CURRENT flag set.

The **Networking Services, Issue 4** specification, **Chapter 6**, **The Use of Options in XTI** contains a detailed description about the use of options and should be read before using this function.

The *flags* field of *req* must specify one of the following actions:

T_NEGOTIATE   This action enables the transport user to negotiate option values.

The user specifies the options of interest and their values in the buffer specified by *req->opt.buf* and *req->opt.len*. The negotiated option values are returned in the buffer pointed to by *ret->opt.buf*. The *status* field of each returned option is set to indicate the result of the negotiation. The value is T_SUCCESS if the proposed value was negotiated, T_PARTSUCCESS if a degraded value was negotiated, T_FAILURE if the negotiation failed (according to the negotiation rules), T_NOTSUPPORT if the transport provider does not support this option or illegally requests negotiation of a privileged option, and T_READONLY if modification of a read-only option was requested. If the status is T_SUCCESS, T_FAILURE, T_NOTSUPPORT or T_READONLY, the returned option value is the same as the one requested on input.

The overall result of the negotiation is returned in *ret->flags*.

This field contains the worst single result, whereby the rating is done according to the order T_NOTSUPPORT, T_READONLY, T_FAILURE, T_PARTSUCCESS, T_SUCCESS. The value T_NOTSUPPORT is the worst result and T_SUCCESS is the best.

For each level, the option T_ALLOPT (see below) can be requested on input. No value is given with this option; only the **t_opthdr** part is specified. This input requests to negotiate all supported options of this level to their default values. The result is returned option by option in *ret->opt.buf*. (Note that depending on the state of the transport endpoint, not all requests to negotiate the default value may be successful.)

T_CHECK   This action enables the user to verify whether the options specified in *req* are supported by the transport provider.

If an option is specified with no option value (it consists only of a **t_opthdr** structure), the option is returned with its *status* field set to T_SUCCESS if it is supported, T_NOTSUPPORT if it is not or needs additional user privileges, and T_READONLY if it is read-only (in the current XTI state). No option value is returned.

If an option is specified with an option value, the *status* field of the returned option has the same value, as if the user had tried to negotiate this value with T_NEGOTIATE. If the status is T_SUCCESS, T_FAILURE, T_NOTSUPPORT or T_READONLY, the returned option value is the same as the one requested on input.

The overall result of the option checks is returned in *ret->flags*. This field contains the worst single result of the option checks, whereby the rating is the same as for T_NEGOTIATE.

Note that no negotiation takes place. All currently effective option values remain unchanged.

T_DEFAULT This action enables the transport user to retrieve the default option values. The user specifies the options of interest in *req->opt.buf*. The option values are irrelevant and will be ignored; it is sufficient to specify the **t_opthdr** part of an option only. The default values are then returned in *ret->opt.buf*.

The *status* field returned is T_NOTSUPPORT if the protocol level does not support this option or the transport user illegally requested a privileged option, T_READONLY if the option is read-only, and set to T_SUCCESS in all other cases. The overall result of the request is returned in *ret->flags*. This field contains the worst single result, whereby the rating is the same as for T_NEGOTIATE.

For each level, the option T_ALLOPT (see below) can be requested on input. All supported options of this level with their default values are then returned. In this case, *ret->opt.maxlen* must be given at least the value *info->options* (see *t_getinfo( )*, *t_open( )*) before the call.

T_CURRENT This action enables the transport user to retrieve the currently effective option values. The user specifies the options of interest in *req->opt.buf*. The option values are irrelevant and will be ignored; it is sufficient to specify the **t_opthdr** part of an option only. The currently effective values are then returned in *ret->opt.buf*.

The *status* field returned is T_NOTSUPPORT if the protocol level does not support this option or the transport user illegally requested a privileged option, T_READONLY if the option is read-only, and set to T_SUCCESS in all other cases. The overall result of the request is returned in *ret->flags*. This field contains the worst single result, whereby the rating is the same as for T_NEGOTIATE.

For each level, the option T_ALLOPT (see below) can be requested on input. All supported options of this level with their currently effective values are then returned.

The option T_ALLOPT can only be used with *t_optmgmt( )* and the actions T_NEGOTIATE, T_DEFAULT and T_CURRENT. It can be used with any supported level and addresses all supported options of this level. The option has no value; it consists of a **t_opthdr** only. Since in a *t_optmgmt( )* call only options of one level may be addressed, this option should not be requested together with other options. The function returns as soon as this option has been processed.

Options are independently processed in the order they appear in the input option buffer. If an option is multiply input, it depends on the implementation whether it is multiply output or whether it is returned only once.

Transport providers may not be able to provide an interface capable of supporting T_NEGOTIATE and/or T_CHECK functionalities. When this is the case, the error [TNOTSUPPORT] is returned.

The function *t_optmgmt*( ) may block under various circumstances and depending on the implementation. The function will block, for instance, if the protocol addressed by the call resides on a separate controller. It may also block due to flow control constraints; that is, if data sent previously across this transport endpoint has not yet been fully processed. If the function is interrupted by a signal, the option negotiations that have been done so far may remain valid. The behaviour of the function is not changed if O_NONBLOCK is set.

XTI-LEVEL OPTIONS

XTI-level options are not specific for a particular transport provider. An XTI implementation supports none, all or any subset of the options defined below. An implementation may restrict the use of any of these options by offering them only in the privileged or read-only mode, or if *fd* relates to specific transport providers.

The subsequent options are not association-related (see **Chapter 5**, **The Use of Options**). They may be negotiated in all XTI states except T_UNINIT.

The protocol level is XTI_GENERIC. For this level, the following options are defined:

option name	type of option value	legal option value	meaning
XTI_DEBUG	array of unsigned longs	see text	enable debugging
XTI_LINGER	struct linger	see text	linger on close if data is present
XTI_RCVBUF	unsigned long	size in octets	receive buffer size
XTI_RCVLOWAT	unsigned long	size in octets	receive low-water mark
XTI_SNDBUF	unsigned long	size in octets	send buffer size
XTI_SNDLOWAT	unsigned long	size in octets	send low-water mark

Table 3-1 XTI-level Options

A request for XTI_DEBUG is an absolute requirement. A request to activate XTI_LINGER is an absolute requirement; the timeout value to this option is not. XTI_RCVBUF, XTI_RCVLOWAT, XTI_SNDBUF and XTI_SNDLOWAT are not absolute requirements.

XTI_DEBUG   This option enables debugging. The values of this option are implementation-defined. Debugging is disabled if the option is specified with "no value"; that is, with an option header only.

The system supplies utilities to process the traces. Note that an implementation may also provide other means for debugging.

XTI_LINGER   This option is used to linger the execution of a *t_close*( ) or *close*( ) if send data is still queued in the send buffer. The option value specifies the linger period. If a *close*( ) or *t_close*( ) is issued and the send buffer is not empty, the system attempts to send the pending data within the linger period before closing the endpoint. Data still pending after the linger period has elapsed is discarded.

Depending on the implementation, *t_close*( ) or *close*( ) either block for at maximum the linger period, or immediately return, whereupon the system holds the connection in existence for at most the linger period.

The option value consists of a structure **t_linger** declared as:

```
struct t_linger {
    long l_onoff;     /* switch option on/off    */
    long l_linger;    /* linger period in seconds */
}
```

Legal values for the field *l_onoff* are:

T_NO   switch option off
T_YES activate option

The value *l_onoff* is an absolute requirement.

The field *l_linger* determines the linger period in seconds. The transport user can request the default value by setting the field to T_UNSPEC. The default timeout value depends on the underlying transport provider (it is often T_INFINITE). Legal values for this field are T_UNSPEC, T_INFINITE and all non-negative numbers.

The *l_linger* value is not an absolute requirement. The implementation may place upper and lower limits to this value. Requests that fall short of the lower limit are negotiated to the lower limit.

Note that this option does not linger the execution of *t_snddis( )*.

XTI_RCVBUF   This option is used to adjust the internal buffer size allocated for the receive buffer. The buffer size may be increased for high-volume connections, or decreased to limit the possible backlog of incoming data.

This request is not an absolute requirement. The implementation may place upper and lower limits on the option value. Requests that fall short of the lower limit are negotiated to the lower limit.

Legal values are all positive numbers.

XTI_RCVLOWAT   This option is used to set a low-water mark in the receive buffer. The option value gives the minimal number of bytes that must have accumulated in the receive buffer before they become visible to the transport user. If and when the amount of accumulated receive data exceeds the low-water mark, a T_DATA event is created, an event mechanism (for example, *poll( )* or *select( )*) indicates the data, and the data can be read by *t_rcv( )* or *t_rcvudata( )*.

This request is not an absolute requirement. The implementation may place upper and lower limits on the option value. Requests that fall short of the lower limit are negotiated to the lower limit.

Legal values are all positive numbers.

XTI_SNDBUF   This option is used to adjust the internal buffer size allocated for the send buffer.

This request is not an absolute requirement. The implementation may place upper and lower limits on the option value. Requests that fall short of the lower limit are negotiated to the lower limit.

Legal values are all positive numbers.

XTI_SNDLOWAT   This option is used to set a low-water mark in the send buffer. The option value gives the minimal number of bytes that must have accumulated in the send buffer before they are sent.

This request is not an absolute requirement. The implementation may place upper and lower limits on the option value. Requests that fall short of the lower limit are negotiated to the lower limit.

Legal values are all positive numbers.

VALID STATES
ALL - apart from T_UNINIT

ERRORS
On failure, *t_errno* is set to one of the following:

[TBADF]	The specified file descriptor does not refer to a transport endpoint.
[TOUTSTATE]	The function was issued in the wrong sequence.
[TACCES]	The user does not have permission to negotiate the specified options.
[TBADOPT]	The specified options were in an incorrect format or contained illegal information.
[TBADFLAG]	An invalid flag was specified.
[TBUFOVFLW]	The number of bytes allowed for an incoming argument *(maxlen)* is greater than 0 but not sufficient to store the value of that argument. The information to be returned in *ret* will be discarded.
[TSYSERR]	A system error has occurred during execution of this function.
[TPROTO]	This error indicates that a communication problem has been detected between XTI and the transport provider for which there is no other suitable XTI *(t_errno)*.
[TNOTSUPPORT]	This action is not supported by the transport provider.

RETURN VALUE
Upon successful completion, a value of 0 is returned. Otherwise, a value of −1 is returned and *t_errno* is set to indicate an error.

SEE ALSO
t_accept( ), *t_alloc*( ), *t_connect*( ), *t_getinfo*( ), *t_listen*( ), *t_open*( ), *t_rcvconnect*( ), **Networking Services, Issue 4** specification, **Chapter 6**, **The Use of Options in XTI**.

EXAMPLE
See examples at the end of chapter.

t_rcv( )

NAME

t_rcv - receive data or expedited data sent over a connection

SYNOPSIS

```
#include <xti.h>

int t_rcv(int fd, char *buf, unsigned int nbytes, int *flags);
```

DESCRIPTION

Parameters	Before call	After call
fd	x	/
buf	x	(x)
nbytes	x	/
flags	/	x

This function receives either normal or expedited data. The argument *fd* identifies the local transport endpoint through which data will arrive, *buf* points to a receive buffer where user data will be placed, and *nbytes* specifies the size of the receive buffer. The argument *flags* may be set on return from *t_rcv( )* and specifies optional flags as described below.

By default, *t_rcv( )* operates in synchronous mode and will wait for data to arrive if none is currently available. However, if O_NONBLOCK is set (via *t_open( )* or *fcntl( )*), *t_rcv( )* will execute in asynchronous mode and will fail if no data is available. (See [TNODATA] below.)

On return from the call, if T_MORE is set in *flags*, this indicates that there is more data, and the current transport service data unit (TSDU) or expedited transport service data unit (ETSDU) must be received in multiple *t_rcv( )* calls. In the asynchronous mode, the T_MORE flag may be set on return from the *t_rcv( )* call even when the number of bytes received is less than the size of the receive buffer specified. Each *t_rcv( )* with the T_MORE flag set indicates that another *t_rcv( )* must follow to get more data for the current TSDU. The end of the TSDU is identified by the return of a *t_rcv( )* call with the T_MORE flag not set. If the transport provider does not support the concept of a TSDU as indicated in the *info* argument on return from *t_open( )* or *t_getinfo( )*, the T_MORE flag is not meaningful and should be ignored. If *nbytes* is greater than zero on the call to *t_rcv( )*, *t_rcv( )* will return 0 only if the end of a TSDU is being returned to the user.

On return, the data returned is expedited data if T_EXPEDITED is set in *flags*. If the number of bytes of expedited data exceeds *nbytes*, *t_rcv( )* will set T_EXPEDITED and T_MORE on return from the initial call. Subsequent calls to retrieve the remaining ETSDU will have T_EXPEDITED set on return. The end of the ETSDU is identified by the return of a *t_rcv( )* call with the T_MORE flag not set.

In synchronous mode, the only way for the user to be notified of the arrival of normal or expedited data is to issue this function or check for the T_DATA or T_EXDATA events using the *t_look( )* function. Additionally, the process can arrange to be notified via the EM interface.

VALID STATES

T_DATAXFER, T_OUTREL

ERRORS

On failure, *t_errno* is set to one of the following:

[TBADF]	The specified file descriptor does not refer to a transport endpoint.
[TNODATA]	O_NONBLOCK was set, but no data is currently available from the transport provider.

[TLOOK]	An asynchronous event has occurred on this transport endpoint and requires immediate attention.
[TNOTSUPPORT]	This function is not supported by the underlying transport provider.
[TOUTSTATE]	The function was issued in the wrong sequence on the transport endpoint referenced by *fd*.
[TSYSERR]	A system error has occurred during execution of this function.
[TPROTO]	This error indicates that a communication problem has been detected between XTI and the transport provider for which there is no other suitable XTI *(t_errno)*.

RETURN VALUE

On successful completion, *t_rcv( )* returns the number of bytes received. Otherwise, it returns −1 on failure and *t_errno* is set to indicate the error.

SEE ALSO

fcntl( ), *t_getinfo( )*, *t_look( )*, *t_open( )*, *t_snd( )*.

EXAMPLE

See examples at the end of chapter.

NAME

t_rcvconnect - receive the confirmation from a connect request

SYNOPSIS

```
#include <xti.h>

int t_rcvconnect(int fd, struct t_call *call);
```

DESCRIPTION

Parameters	Before call	After call
fd	x	/
call->addr.maxlen	x	/
call->addr.len	/	x
call->addr.buf	?	(?)
call->opt.maxlen	x	/
call->opt.len	/	x
call->opt.buf	?	(?)
call->udata.maxlen	x	/
call->udata.len	/	x
call->udata.buf	?	(?)
call->sequence	/	/

This function enables a calling transport user to determine the status of a previously sent connect request and is used in conjunction with *t_connect*( ) to establish a connection in asynchronous mode. The connection will be established on successful completion of this function.

The argument *fd* identifies the local transport endpoint where communication will be established, and *call* contains information associated with the newly established connection. The argument *call* points to a **t_call** structure which contains the following members:

```
struct netbuf addr;
struct netbuf opt;
struct netbuf udata;
int sequence;
```

In *call*, *addr* returns the protocol address associated with the responding transport endpoint, *opt* presents any options associated with the connection, *udata* points to optional user data that may be returned by the destination transport user during connection establishment, and *sequence* has no meaning for this function.

The *maxlen* field of each argument must be set before issuing this function to indicate the maximum size of the buffer for each. However, *call* may be a null pointer, in which case no information is given to the user on return from *t_rcvconnect*( ). By default, *t_rcvconnect*( ) executes in synchronous mode and waits for the connection to be established before returning. On return, the *addr*, *opt* and *udata* fields reflect values associated with the connection.

If O_NONBLOCK is set (via *t_open*( ) or *fcntl*( )), *t_rcvconnect*( ) executes in asynchronous mode, and reduces to a poll for existing connect confirmations. If none are available, *t_rcvconnect*( ) fails and returns immediately without waiting for the connection to be established. (See [TNODATA] below.) In this case, *t_rcvconnect*( ) must be called again to complete the connection establishment phase and retrieve the information returned in *call*.

VALID STATES

T_OUTCON

ERRORS

On failure, *t_errno* is set to one of the following:

[TBADF]	The specified file descriptor does not refer to a transport endpoint.
[TBUFOVFLW]	The number of bytes allocated for an incoming argument *(maxlen)* is greater than 0 but not sufficient to store the value of that argument, and the connect information to be returned in *call* will be discarded. The provider's state, as seen by the user, will be changed to T_DATAXFER.
[TNODATA]	O_NONBLOCK was set, but a connect confirmation has not yet arrived.
[TLOOK]	An asynchronous event has occurred on this transport connection and requires immediate attention.
[TNOTSUPPORT]	This function is not supported by the underlying transport provider.
[TOUTSTATE]	The function was issued in the wrong sequence on the transport endpoint referenced by *fd*.
[TSYSERR]	A system error has occurred during execution of this function.
[TPROTO]	This error indicates that a communication problem has been detected between XTI and the transport provider for which there is no other suitable XTI *(t_errno)*.

RETURN VALUE

Upon successful completion, a value of 0 is returned. Otherwise, a value of −1 is returned and *t_errno* is set to indicate an error.

SEE ALSO

t_accept( ), *t_alloc( )*, *t_bind( )*, *t_connect( )*, *t_listen( )*, *t_open( )*, *t_optmgmt( )*.

EXAMPLE

See examples at the end of chapter.

NAME

t_rcvdis - retrieve information from disconnect

SYNOPSIS

```
#include <xti.h>

int t_rcvdis(int fd, struct t_discon *discon);
```

DESCRIPTION

Parameters	Before call	After call
fd	x	/
discon->udata.maxlen	x	/
discon->udata.len	/	x
discon->udata.buf	?	(?)
discon->reason	/	x
discon->sequence	/	?

This function is used to identify the cause of a disconnect and to retrieve any user data sent with the disconnect. The argument *fd* identifies the local transport endpoint where the connection existed, and *discon* points to a **t_discon** structure containing the following members:

```
struct netbuf udata;
int reason;
int sequence;
```

The field *reason* specifies the reason for the disconnect through a protocol-dependent reason code, *udata* identifies any user data that was sent with the disconnect, and *sequence* may identify an outstanding connect indication with which the disconnect is associated. The field *sequence* is only meaningful when *t_rcvdis( )* is issued by a passive transport user who has executed one or more *t_listen( )* functions and is processing the resulting connect indications. If a disconnect indication occurs, *sequence* can be used to identify which of the outstanding connect indications is associated with the disconnect.

If a user does not care if there is incoming data and does not need to know the value of *reason* or *sequence*, *discon* may be a null pointer and any user data associated with the disconnect will be discarded. However, if a user has retrieved more than one outstanding connect indication (via *t_listen( )*) and *discon* is a null pointer, the user will be unable to identify with which connect indication the disconnect is associated.

VALID STATES

T_DATAXFER,T_OUTCON,T_OUTREL,T_INREL,T_INCON(ocnt > 0)

ERRORS

On failure, *t_errno* is set to one of the following:

[TBADF]　　　　　The specified file descriptor does not refer to a transport endpoint.

[TNODIS]　　　　No disconnect indication currently exists on the specified transport endpoint.

[TBUFOVFLW]　　The number of bytes allocated for incoming data *(maxlen)* is greater than 0 but not sufficient to store the data. If *fd* is a passive endpoint with *ocnt* > 1, it remains in state T_INCON; otherwise, the endpoint state is set to T_IDLE.

[TNOTSUPPORT]　This function is not supported by the underlying transport provider.

[TSYSERR]	A system error has occurred during execution of this function.
[TOUTSTATE]	The function was issued in the wrong sequence on the transport endpoint referenced by *fd*.
[TPROTO]	This error indicates that a communication problem has been detected between XTI and the transport provider for which there is no other suitable XTI *(t_errno)*.

RETURN VALUE

Upon successful completion, a value of 0 is returned. Otherwise, a value of −1 is returned and *t_errno* is set to indicate an error.

SEE ALSO

t_alloc( ), *t_connect*( ), *t_listen*( ), *t_open*( ), *t_snddis*( ).

EXAMPLE

See examples at the end of chapter.

NAME

t_rcvrel - acknowledge receipt of an orderly release indication

SYNOPSIS

```
#include <xti.h>

int t_rcvrel(int fd);
```

DESCRIPTION

Parameters	Before call	After call
fd	x	/

This function is used to acknowledge receipt of an orderly release indication. The argument *fd* identifies the local transport endpoint where the connection exists. After receipt of this indication, the user may not attempt to receive more data because such an attempt will block forever. However, the user may continue to send data over the connection if *t_sndrel*( ) has not been called by the user. This function is an optional service of the transport provider, and is only supported if the transport provider returned service type T_COTS_ORD on *t_open*( ) or *t_getinfo*( ).

VALID STATES

T_DATAXFER,T_OUTREL

ERRORS

On failure, *t_errno* is set to one of the following:

[TBADF]   The specified file descriptor does not refer to a transport endpoint.

[TNOREL]   No orderly release indication currently exists on the specified transport endpoint.

[TLOOK]   An asynchronous event has occurred on this transport endpoint and requires immediate attention.

[TNOTSUPPORT]   This function is not supported by the underlying transport provider.

[TSYSERR]   A system error has occurred during execution of this function.

[TOUTSTATE]   The function was issued in the wrong sequence on the transport endpoint referenced by *fd*.

[TPROTO]   This error indicates that a communication problem has been detected between XTI and the transport provider for which there is no other suitable XTI *(t_errno)*.

RETURN VALUE

Upon successful completion, a value of 0 is returned. Otherwise, a value of −1 is returned and *t_errno* is set to indicate an error.

SEE ALSO

t_getinfo( ), *t_open*( ), *t_sndrel*( ).

EXAMPLE

See examples at the end of chapter.

NAME

t_rcvudata - receive a data unit

SYNOPSIS

```
#include <xti.h>

int t_rcvudata(int fd, struct t_unitdata *unitdata, int *flags);
```

DESCRIPTION

Parameters	Before call	After call
fd	x	/
unitdata->addr.maxlen	x	/
unitdata->addr.len	/	x
unitdata->addr.buf	?	(?)
unitdata->opt.maxlen	x	/
unitdata->opt.len	/	x
unitdata->opt.buf	?	(?)
unitdata->udata.maxlen	x	/
unitdata->udata.len	/	x
unitdata->udata.buf	?	(?)
flags	/	x

This function is used in connectionless mode to receive a data unit from another transport user. The argument *fd* identifies the local transport endpoint through which data will be received, *unitdata* holds information associated with the received data unit, and *flags* is set on return to indicate that the complete data unit was not received. The argument *unitdata* points to a **t_unitdata** structure containing the following members:

```
struct netbuf addr;
struct netbuf opt;
struct netbuf udata;
```

The *maxlen* field of *addr*, *opt* and *udata* must be set before calling this function to indicate the maximum size of the buffer for each.

On return from this call, *addr* specifies the protocol address of the sending user, *opt* identifies options that were associated with this data unit, and *udata* specifies the user data that was received.

By default, *t_rcvudata( )* operates in synchronous mode and will wait for a data unit to arrive if none is currently available. However, if O_NONBLOCK is set (via *t_open( )* or *fcntl( )*), *t_rcvudata( )* will execute in asynchronous mode and will fail if no data units are available.

If the buffer defined in the *udata* field of *unitdata* is not large enough to hold the current data unit, the buffer will be filled and T_MORE will be set in *flags* on return to indicate that another *t_rcvudata( )* should be called to retrieve the rest of the data unit. Subsequent calls to *t_rcvudata( )* will return zero for the length of the address and options until the full data unit has been received.

VALID STATES

T_IDLE

ERRORS

On failure, *t_errno* is set to one of the following:

[TBADF]	The specified file descriptor does not refer to a transport endpoint.
[TNODATA]	O_NONBLOCK was set, but no data units are currently available from the transport provider.
[TBUFOVFLW]	The number of bytes allocated for the incoming protocol address or options *(maxlen)* is greater than 0 but not sufficient to store the information. The unit data information to be returned in *unitdata* will be discarded.
[TLOOK]	An asynchronous event has occurred on this transport endpoint and requires immediate attention.
[TNOTSUPPORT]	This function is not supported by the underlying transport provider.
[TOUTSTATE]	The function was issued in the wrong sequence on the transport endpoint referenced by *fd*.
[TSYSERR]	A system error has occurred during execution of this function.
[TPROTO]	This error indicates that a communication problem has been detected between XTI and the transport provider for which there is no other suitable XTI *(t_errno)*.

RETURN VALUE

Upon successful completion, a value of 0 is returned. Otherwise, a value of −1 is returned and *t_errno* is set to indicate an error.

SEE ALSO

fcntl( ), *t_alloc( )*, *t_open( )*, *t_rcvuderr( )*, *t_sndudata( )*.

EXAMPLE

See examples at the end of chapter.

NAME

t_rcvuderr - receive a unit data error indication

SYNOPSIS

```
#include <xti.h>

int t_rcvuderr(int fd, struct t_uderr *uderr);
```

DESCRIPTION

Parameters	Before call	After call
fd	x	/
uderr->addr.maxlen	x	/
uderr->addr.len	/	x
uderr->addr.buf	?	(?)
uderr->opt.maxlen	x	/
uderr->opt.len	/	x
uderr->opt.buf	?	(?)
uderr->error	/	x

This function is used in connectionless mode to receive information concerning an error on a previously sent data unit, and should only be issued following a unit data error indication. It informs the transport user that a data unit with a specific destination address and protocol options produced an error. The argument *fd* identifies the local transport endpoint through which the error report will be received, and *uderr* points to a **t_uderr** structure containing the following members:

```
struct netbuf addr;
struct netbuf opt;
long error;
```

The *maxlen* field of *addr* and *opt* must be set before calling this function to indicate the maximum size of the buffer for each.

On return from this call, the *addr* structure specifies the destination protocol address of the erroneous data unit, the *opt* structure identifies options that were associated with the data unit, and *error* specifies a protocol-dependent error code.

If the user does not care to identify the data unit that produced an error, *uderr* may be set to a null pointer, and *t_rcvuderr( )* will simply clear the error indication without reporting any information to the user.

VALID STATES

T_IDLE

ERRORS

On failure, *t_errno* is set to one of the following:

[TBADF]   The specified file descriptor does not refer to a transport endpoint.

[TNOUDERR]   No unit data error indication currently exists on the specified transport endpoint.

[TBUFOVFLW]   The number of bytes allocated for the incoming protocol address or options *(maxlen)* is greater than 0 but not sufficient to store the information. The unit data error information to be returned in *uderr* will be discarded.

[TNOTSUPPORT]	This function is not supported by the underlying transport provider.
[TSYSERR]	A system error has occurred during execution of this function.
[TPROTO]	This error indicates that a communication problem has been detected between XTI and the transport provider for which there is no other suitable XTI *(t_errno)*.

RETURN VALUE

Upon successful completion, a value of 0 is returned. Otherwise, a value of −1 is returned and *t_errno* is set to indicate an error.

SEE ALSO

t_rcvudata( ), *t_sndudata*( ).

EXAMPLE

See examples at the end of chapter.

NAME

t_snd - send data or expedited data over a connection

SYNOPSIS

```
#include <xti.h>

int t_snd(int fd, char *buf, unsigned int nbytes, int flags);
```

DESCRIPTION

Parameters	Before call	After call
fd	x	/
buf	x (x)	/
nbytes	x	/
flags	x	/

This function is used to send either normal or expedited data. The argument *fd* identifies the local transport endpoint over which data should be sent, *buf* points to the user data, *nbytes* specifies the number of bytes of user data to be sent, and *flags* specifies any optional flags described below:

T_EXPEDITED   If set in *flags*, the data will be sent as expedited data and will be subject to the interpretations of the transport provider.

T_MORE   If set in *flags*, this indicates to the transport provider that the transport service data unit (TSDU) (or expedited transport service data unit - ETSDU) is being sent through multiple *t_snd( )* calls. Each *t_snd( )* with the T_MORE flag set indicates that another *t_snd( )* will follow with more data for the current TSDU (or ETSDU).

The end of the TSDU (or ETSDU) is identified by a *t_snd( )* call with the T_MORE flag not set. Use of T_MORE enables a user to break up large logical data units without losing the boundaries of those units at the other end of the connection. The flag implies nothing about how the data is packaged for transfer below the transport interface. If the transport provider does not support the concept of a TSDU as indicated in the *info* argument on return from *t_open( )* or *t_getinfo( )*, the T_MORE flag is not meaningful and will be ignored if set.

The sending of a zero-length fragment of a TSDU or ETSDU is only permitted where this is used to indicate the end of a TSDU or ETSDU; that is, when the T_MORE flag is not set. Some transport providers also forbid zero-length TSDUs and ETSDUs. See the **Networking Services, Issue 4** specification, **Appendix A**, **ISO Transport Protocol Information** for a fuller explanation.

By default, *t_snd( )* operates in synchronous mode and may wait if flow control restrictions prevent the data from being accepted by the local transport provider at the time the call is made. However, if O_NONBLOCK is set (via *t_open( )* or *fcntl( )*), *t_snd( )* will execute in asynchronous mode, and will fail immediately if there are flow control restrictions. The process can arrange to be informed when the flow control restrictions are cleared via either *t_look( )* or the EM interface.

On successful completion, *t_snd( )* returns the number of bytes accepted by the transport provider. Normally this will equal the number of bytes specified in *nbytes*. However, if O_NONBLOCK is set, it is possible that only part of the data will actually be accepted by the transport provider. In this case, *t_snd( )* will return a value that is less than the value of *nbytes*. If *nbytes* is zero and sending of zero octets is not supported by the underlying transport service, *t_snd*( ) will return –1 with *t_errno* set to [TBADDATA].

The size of each TSDU or ETSDU must not exceed the limits of the transport provider as specified by the current values in the TSDU or ETSDU fields in the *info* argument returned by *t_getinfo*( ).

The error [TLOOK] may be returned to inform the process that an event (for example, a disconnect) has occurred.

VALID STATES

> T_DATAXFER, T_INREL

ERRORS

> On failure, *t_errno* is set to one of the following:

> | | |
> |---|---|
> | [TBADF] | The specified file descriptor does not refer to a transport endpoint. |
> | [TBADDATA] | Illegal amount of data: |

> > — A single send was attempted specifying a TSDU (ETSDU) or fragment TSDU (ETSDU) greater than that specified by the current values of the TSDU or ETSDU fields in the *info* argument.

> > — A send of a zero byte TSDU (ETSDU) or zero byte fragment of a TSDU (ETSDU) is not supported by the provider (see the **Networking Services, Issue 4** specification, **Appendix A**, **ISO Transport Protocol Information**).

> > — Multiple sends were attempted resulting in a TSDU (ETSDU) larger than that specified by the current value of the TSDU or ETSDU fields in the *info* argument — the ability of an XTI implementation to detect such an error case is implementation-dependent (see **CAVEATS**, below).

> | | |
> |---|---|
> | [TBADFLAG] | An invalid flag was specified. |
> | [TFLOW] | O_NONBLOCK was set, but the flow control mechanism prevented the transport provider from accepting any data at this time. |
> | [TNOTSUPPORT] | This function is not supported by the underlying transport provider. |
> | [TLOOK] | An asynchronous event has occurred on this transport endpoint. |
> | [TOUTSTATE] | The function was issued in the wrong sequence on the transport endpoint referenced by *fd*. |
> | [TSYSERR] | A system error has occurred during execution of this function. |
> | [TPROTO] | This error indicates that a communication problem has been detected between XTI and the transport provider for which there is no other suitable XTI *(t_errno)*. |

RETURN VALUE

> On successful completion, *t_snd*( ) returns the number of bytes accepted by the transport provider. Otherwise, –1 is returned on failure and *t_errno* is set to indicate the error.

> Note that in asynchronous mode, if the number of bytes accepted by the transport provider is less than the number of bytes requested, this may indicate that the transport provider is blocked due to flow control.

SEE ALSO

    t_getinfo( ), *t_open*( ), *t_rcv*( ).

CAVEATS

It is important to remember that the transport provider treats all users of a transport endpoint as a single user. Therefore if several processes issue concurrent *t_snd*( ) calls then the different data may be intermixed.

Multiple sends which exceed the maximum TSDU or ETSDU size may not be discovered by XTI. In this case an implementation-dependent error will result (generated by the transport provider) perhaps on a subsequent XTI call. This error may take the form of a connection abort, a [TSYSERR], a [TBADDATA] or a [TPROTO] error.

If multiple sends which exceed the maximum TSDU or ETSDU size are detected by XTI, *t_snd*( ) fails with [TBADDATA].

EXAMPLE

See examples at the end of chapter.

NAME

t_snddis - send user-initiated disconnect request

SYNOPSIS

```
#include <xti.h>

int t_snddis(int fd, struct t_call *call);
```

DESCRIPTION

Parameters	Before call	After call
fd	x	/
call->addr.maxlen	/	/
call->addr.len	/	/
call->addr.buf	/	/
call->opt.maxlen	/	/
call->opt.len	/	/
call->opt.buf	/	/
call->udata.maxlen	/	/
call->udata.len	x	/
call->udata.buf	?(?)	/
call->sequence	?	/

This function is used to initiate an abortive release on an already established connection, or to reject a connect request. The argument *fd* identifies the local transport endpoint of the connection, and *call* specifies information associated with the abortive release. The argument *call* points to a **t_call** structure which contains the following members:

```
struct netbuf addr;
struct netbuf opt;
struct netbuf udata;
int sequence;
```

The values in *call* have different semantics, depending on the context of the call to *t_snddis( )*. When rejecting a connect request, *call* must be non-null and contain a valid value of *sequence* to uniquely identify the rejected connect indication to the transport provider. The *sequence* field is only meaningful if the transport connection is in the T_INCON state. The *addr* and *opt* fields of *call* are ignored. In all other cases, *call* need only be used when data is being sent with the disconnect request. The *addr*, *opt* and *sequence* fields of the **t_call** structure are ignored. If the user does not wish to send data to the remote user, the value of *call* may be a null pointer.

The *udata* structure specifies the user data to be sent to the remote user. The amount of user data must not exceed the limits supported by the transport provider, as returned in the *discon* field, of the *info* argument of *t_open( )* or *t_getinfo( )*. If the *len* field of *udata* is zero, no data will be sent to the remote user.

VALID STATES

T_DATAXFER,T_OUTCON,T_OUTREL,T_INREL,T_INCON(ocnt > 0)

ERRORS

On failure, *t_errno* is set to one of the following:

[TBADF]	The specified file descriptor does not refer to a transport endpoint.
[TOUTSTATE]	The function was issued in the wrong sequence on the transport endpoint referenced by *fd*.

[TBADDATA]	The amount of user data specified was not within the bounds allowed by the transport provider.
[TBADSEQ]	An invalid sequence number was specified, or a null *call* pointer was specified, when rejecting a connect request.
[TNOTSUPPORT]	This function is not supported by the underlying transport provider.
[TSYSERR]	A system error has occurred during execution of this function.
[TLOOK]	An asynchronous event, which requires attention, has occurred.
[TPROTO]	This error indicates that a communication problem has been detected between XTI and the transport provider for which there is no other suitable XTI *(t_errno)*.

RETURN VALUE

Upon successful completion, a value of 0 is returned. Otherwise, a value of −1 is returned and *t_errno* is set to indicate an error.

SEE ALSO

t_connect( ), *t_getinfo*( ), *t_listen*( ), *t_open*( ).

CAVEATS

t_snddis( ) is an abortive disconnect. Therefore a *t_snddis*( ) issued on a connection endpoint may cause data previously sent via *t_snd*( ), or data not yet received, to be lost (even if an error is returned).

EXAMPLE

See examples at the end of chapter.

NAME

t_sndrel - initiate an orderly release

SYNOPSIS

```
#include <xti.h>

int t_sndrel(int fd);
```

DESCRIPTION

Parameters	Before call	After call
fd	x	/

This function is used to initiate an orderly release of a transport connection and indicates to the transport provider that the transport user has no more data to send. The argument *fd* identifies the local transport endpoint where the connection exists. After calling *t_sndrel*( ), the user may not send any more data over the connection. However, a user may continue to receive data if an orderly release indication has not been received. This function is an optional service of the transport provider and is only supported if the transport provider returned service type T_COTS_ORD on *t_open*( ) or *t_getinfo*( ).

VALID STATES

T_DATAXFER,T_INREL

ERRORS

On failure, *t_errno* is set to one of the following:

[TBADF]	The specified file descriptor does not refer to a transport endpoint.
[TFLOW]	O_NONBLOCK was set, but the flow control mechanism prevented the transport provider from accepting the function at this time.
[TLOOK]	An asynchronous event has occurred on this transport endpoint and requires immediate attention.
[TNOTSUPPORT]	This function is not supported by the underlying transport provider.
[TOUTSTATE]	The function was issued in the wrong sequence on the transport endpoint referenced by *fd*.
[TSYSERR]	A system error has occurred during execution of this function.
[TPROTO]	This error indicates that a communication problem has been detected between XTI and the transport provider for which there is no other suitable XTI *(t_errno)*.

RETURN VALUE

Upon successful completion, a value of 0 is returned. Otherwise, a value of –1 is returned and *t_errno* is set to indicate an error.

SEE ALSO

t_getinfo( ), *t_open*( ), *t_rcvrel*( ).

EXAMPLE

See examples at the end of chapter.

NAME

t_sndudata - send a data unit

SYNOPSIS

```
#include <xti.h>

int t_sndudata(int fd, struct t_unitdata *unitdata);
```

DESCRIPTION

Parameters	Before call	After call
fd	x	/
unitdata->addr.maxlen	/	/
unitdata->addr.len	x	/
unitdata->addr.buf	x(x)	/
unitdata->opt.maxlen	/	/
unitdata->opt.len	x	/
unitdata->opt.buf	?(?)	/
unitdata->udata.maxlen	/	/
unitdata->udata.len	x	/
unitdata->udata.buf	x(x)	/

This function is used in connectionless mode to send a data unit to another transport user. The argument *fd* identifies the local transport endpoint through which data will be sent, and *unitdata* points to a **t_unitdata** structure containing the following members:

```
struct netbuf addr;
struct netbuf opt;
struct netbuf udata;
```

In *unitdata*, *addr* specifies the protocol address of the destination user, *opt* identifies options that the user wants associated with this request, and *udata* specifies the user data to be sent. The user may choose not to specify what protocol options are associated with the transfer by setting the *len* field of *opt* to zero. In this case, the provider may use default options.

If the *len* field of *udata* is zero, and sending of zero octets is not supported by the underlying transport service, the *t_sndudata( )* will return −1 with *t_errno* set to [TBADDATA].

By default, *t_sndudata( )* operates in synchronous mode and may wait if flow control restrictions prevent the data from being accepted by the local transport provider at the time the call is made. However, if O_NONBLOCK is set (via *t_open( )* or *fcntl( )*), *t_sndudata( )* will execute in asynchronous mode and will fail under such conditions. The process can arrange to be notified of the clearance of a flow control restriction via either *t_look( )* or the EM interface.

If the amount of data specified in *udata* exceeds the TSDU size as returned in the *tsdu* field of the *info* argument of *t_open( )* or *t_getinfo( )*, a [TBADDATA] error will be generated. If *t_sndudata( )* is called before the destination user has activated its transport endpoint (see *t_bind( )*), the data unit may be discarded.

If it is not possible for the transport provider to immediately detect the conditions that cause the errors [TBADDADDR] and [TBADOPT]. These errors will alternatively be returned by *t_rcvuderr*. Therefore, an application must be prepared to receive these errors in both of these ways.

VALID STATES

T_IDLE

ERRORS

On failure, *t_errno* is set to one of the following:

[TBADDATA]   Illegal amount of data. A single send was attempted specifying a TSDU greater than that specified in the *info* argument, or a send of a zero byte TSDU is not supported by the provider.

[TBADF]   The specified file descriptor does not refer to a transport endpoint.

[TFLOW]   O_NONBLOCK was set, but the flow control mechanism prevented the transport provider from accepting any data at this time.

[TLOOK]   An asynchronous event has occurred on this transport endpoint.

[TNOTSUPPORT]   This function is not supported by the underlying transport provider.

[TOUTSTATE]   The function was issued in the wrong sequence on the transport endpoint referenced by *fd*.

[TSYSERR]   A system error has occurred during execution of this function.

[TBADADDR]   The specified protocol address was in an incorrect format or contained illegal information.

[TBADOPT]   The specified options were in an incorrect format or contained illegal information.

[TPROTO]   This error indicates that a communication problem has been detected between XTI and the transport provider for which there is no other suitable XTI *(t_errno)*.

RETURN VALUE

Upon successful completion, a value of 0 is returned. Otherwise, a value of −1 is returned and *t_errno* is set to indicate an error.

SEE ALSO

fcntl( ), *t_alloc*( ), *t_open*( ), *t_rcvudata*( ), *t_rcvuderr*( ).

EXAMPLE

See examples at the end of chapter.

NAME

t_strerror - produce an error message string

SYNOPSIS

```
#include <xti.h>

char *t_strerror(int errnum);
```

DESCRIPTION

Parameters	Before call	After call
errnum	x	/

The *t_strerror*( ) function maps the error number in *errnum* that corresponds to an XTI error to a language-dependent error message string and returns a pointer to the string. The string pointed to will not be modified by the program, but may be overwritten by a subsequent call to the *t_strerror* function. The string is not terminated by a newline character. The language for error message strings written by *t_strerror*( ) is implementation-defined. If it is English, the error message string describing the value in *t_errno* is identical to the comments following the *t_errno* codes defined in **<xti.h>**. If an error code is unknown, and the language is English, *t_strerror*( ) returns the string:

```
"<error>: error unknown"
```

where <error> is the error number supplied as input. In other languages, an equivalent text is provided.

VALID STATES

ALL - apart from T_UNINIT

RETURN VALUE

The function *t_strerror*( ) returns a pointer to the generated message string.

SEE ALSO

t_error( )

EXAMPLE

See examples at the end of chapter.

NAME

t_sync - synchronise transport library

SYNOPSIS

```
#include <xti.h>

int t_sync(int fd);
```

DESCRIPTION

Parameters	Before call	After call
fd	x	/

For the transport endpoint specified by *fd*, *t_sync()* synchronises the data structures managed by the transport library with information from the underlying transport provider. In doing so, it can convert an uninitialised file descriptor (obtained via *open()*, *dup()* or as a result of a *fork()* and *exec()*) to an initialised transport endpoint, assuming that the file descriptor referenced a transport endpoint, by updating and allocating the necessary library data structures. This function also allows two cooperating processes to synchronise their interaction with a transport provider.

For example, if a process forks a new process and issues an *exec()*, the new process must issue a *t_sync()* to build the private library data structure associated with a transport endpoint and to synchronise the data structure with the relevant provider information.

It is important to remember that the transport provider treats all users of a transport endpoint as a single user. If multiple processes are using the same endpoint, they should coordinate their activities so as not to violate the state of the transport endpoint. The function *t_sync()* returns the current state of the transport endpoint to the user, thereby enabling the user to verify the state before taking further action. This coordination is only valid among cooperating processes; it is possible that a process or an incoming event could change the endpoint's state *after* a *t_sync()* is issued.

If the transport endpoint is undergoing a state transition when *t_sync()* is called, the function will fail.

VALID STATES

ALL - apart from T_UNINIT

ERRORS

On failure, *t_errno* is set to one of the following:

[TBADF]	The specified file descriptor does not refer to a transport endpoint. This error may be returned when the *fd* has been previously closed or an erroneous number may have been passed to the call.
[TSTATECHNG]	The transport endpoint is undergoing a state change.
[TSYSERR]	A system error has occurred during execution of this function.
[TPROTO]	This error indicates that a communication problem has been detected between XTI and the transport provider for which there is no other suitable XTI *(t_errno)*.

RETURN VALUE

On successful completion, the state of the transport endpoint is returned. Otherwise, a value of −1 is returned and *t_errno* is set to indicate an error. The state returned is one of the following:

T_UNBND   Unbound.

T_IDLE	Idle.
T_OUTCON	Outgoing connection pending.
T_INCON	Incoming connection pending.
T_DATAXFER	Data transfer.
T_OUTREL	Outgoing orderly release (waiting for an orderly release indication).
T_INREL	Incoming orderly release (waiting for an orderly release request).

SEE ALSO

dup( ), *exec*( ), *fork*( ), *open*( ).

EXAMPLE

See examples at the end of chapter.

NAME

t_unbind - disable a transport endpoint

SYNOPSIS

```
#include <xti.h>

int t_unbind(int fd);
```

DESCRIPTION

Parameters	Before call	After call
fd	x	/

The *t_unbind*( ) function disables the transport endpoint specified by *fd* which was previously bound by *t_bind*( ). On completion of this call, no further data or events destined for this transport endpoint will be accepted by the transport provider. An endpoint which is disabled by using *t_unbind*( ) can be enabled by a subsequent call to *t_bind*( ).

VALID STATES

T_IDLE

ERRORS

On failure, *t_errno* is set to one of the following:

[TBADF]	The specified file descriptor does not refer to a transport endpoint.
[TOUTSTATE]	The function was issued in the wrong sequence.
[TLOOK]	An asynchronous event has occurred on this transport endpoint.
[TSYSERR]	A system error has occurred during execution of this function.
[TPROTO]	This error indicates that a communication problem has been detected between XTI and the transport provider for which there is no other suitable XTI *(t_errno)*.

RETURN VALUE

Upon successful completion, a value of 0 is returned. Otherwise, a value of −1 is returned and *t_errno* is set to indicate an error.

SEE ALSO

t_bind( ).

EXAMPLE 1

```
/*
 * Copyright (C) ANTRIX Inc.
 */

/* cltsvr.c
 *
 * Description: A program using pipe() that mimics a client server pair
 *
 * Protocol:    The client sends a NAME (such as Bill) followed by a new
 *              line. The server reads the name up to and including the
 *              newline and replies "Hello NAME, nice to see you today"
 *              followed by newline.
 * Usage:       cltsvr Bill
 *
 * Request:     client sends a name followed by newline.
 * Reply:       server reads name and prints to standard output the reply
 *              "Hello NAME, nice to see you today"
 */

#include <stdio.h>
#include <stdlib.h>
#include <sys/types.h>
#include <errno.h>

int client(fd1, name)
int fd1;
char *name;
{
  char c;
  char buf[BUFSIZ];
  int byte;

  /* send request to server including newline */
  fprintf(stdout, "client sending request: %s\n", name);
  write(fd1, name, strlen(name));
  write(fd1, "\n", 1);

  /* now wait for reply from server */
  /* and write the reply to stdout */
  while(1)
  {
    memset(buf, ' ', sizeof(buf));
    byte = read(fd1, buf, BUFSIZ);
    if(!strcmp(buf, "\n"))
    {
      fflush(stdout);
      break;
    }
    if(byte >= 1)
      fprintf(stdout, "client received reply: %s\n", buf);
    else
```

```
            exit(1);
    } /* end while */
}

int server(fd0)
int fd0;
{
  char c;
  int i, byte;
  char reply[BUFSIZ];
  char request[BUFSIZ];
  char *msg1 = "Hello ";
  char *msg2 = ", nice to see you today";

  i = 0;

  memset(reply, ' ', sizeof(reply));
  memset(request, ' ', sizeof(request));

  /* read the request from client */
  while (1)
  {
    byte = read(fd0, &c, 1);
    if(byte != 1)
    {
      fprintf(stderr, "ERROR: server unable to read request\n");
      exit(-3);
    } /* end if */
    if( c == '\n')
      break;
    request[i++] = c;
  } /* end while */

  fprintf(stdout, "server received request: %s\n", request);
  strcpy(reply, msg1);
  strcat(reply, request);
  strcat(reply, msg2);

  /* write the reply to client */
  fprintf(stdout, "server sending reply: %s\n",reply);
  write(fd0, reply, sizeof(reply));
  write(fd0, "\n", 1);
}

main(argc, argv)
int argc;
char *argv[];
{
  int i;
  int byte, cpid, fd[2];

  /* check usage */
```

```
if(argc < 2)
{
    fprintf(stderr, "usage: %s <NAME>\n", argv[0]);
    exit(-1);
}

/* create pipe */
byte = pipe(fd);
if(byte < 0)
{
    perror("pipe");
    exit(-2);
}
/* make two processes to talk to each other */
cpid = fork();
if(cpid == 0)
{
    /* make child process client */
    close(fd[0] );
    /* client to send request */
    byte = client(fd[1], argv[1]);
}
else {
    /* make parent process server */
    close(fd[1]);
    /* server to read the request */
    byte = server(fd[0]);
}
}
```

EXAMPLE 2

```
/*
 * Copyright (C) ANTRIX Inc.
 */

/* client1.c
 *
 * Description: A client & server pair that establishes a transport
 *              endpoint the client sends a request and the server
 *              sends a reply using TCP.
 *
 * Protocol:    The client sends a NAME (such as Bill) followed by a
 *              newline on port #10203 using TCP. The server provides
 *              greeting service on port #10203 using TCP. The server
 *              reads the name up to and including the newline and replies
 *              "Hello NAME, nice to see you today" followed by newline.
 *
 * Request:     client sends a name followed by newline.
 * Reply:       server reads name and prints to standard output the reply
 *              "Hello NAME, nice to see you today"
 *
 * Usage:       run the server in the background as server1 &
 *              run the client as client1 Bill &
 *              Transmission Control Protocol (TCP). Properties
 *              connection oriented, byte stream, fragmentation, sequenced
 *              reliable, flow control.
 *
 * Sequence:
 *
 *              SERVER                          CLIENT
 *
 *              t_open()                        t_open()
 *                 |                               |
 *              t_bind()                        t_bind()
 *                 |                               |
 *              t_alloc()                       t_alloc()
 *                 |                               |
 *              t_listen()                         |
 *                 |                               |
 *              t_accept()<----------------->t_connect()
 *                 |                               |
 *              t_rcv()<-------request-------t_snd()
 *                 |                               |
 *              t_snd()--------reply-------->t_rcv()
 */

#include <stdio.h>
#include <tiuser.h>
#include <fcntl.h>
#include <sys/types.h>
#include <sys/socket.h>
#include <netinet/in.h>
```

```
#include <errno.h>

#define TCP_DEVICE   "/dev/tcp"
#define PORT_NUM     10203

main(argc, argv)
int argc;
char *argv[];
{
  int    tfd, byte;
  int    flags, len;
  char   buf[BUFSIZ];
  struct t_call *call;
  struct t_info info;
  struct sockaddr_in server_addr;

  /* check usage */
  if(argc < 2) {
     fprintf(stderr, "usage: %s <NAME>\n", argv[0]);
     exit(-1);
  }
  /* initialize buffer */
  memset(buf, ' ', BUFSIZ);

  if ((tfd = t_open(TCP_DEVICE, O_RDWR,(struct t_info *)0)) < 0)
  {
     t_error("client t_open() call failed for /dev/tcp");
     fprintf(stderr, "ERROR: %s\n", t_strerror(t_errno));
     exit(-2);
  }

  if (t_bind(tfd, (struct t_bind *)0, (struct t_bind *)0) < 0)
  {
     t_error("client t_bind() call failed");
     exit(-3);
  }

  if (t_sync(tfd) == -1)
  {
     t_error("client t_sync() call failed");
     exit(-3);
  }

  if (t_getinfo(tfd, &info) == -1)
  {
     t_error("client t_getinfo() call failed");
     exit(-3);
  }

  if (t_getstate(tfd) == -1)
  {
     t_error("client t_getstate() call failed");
```

```
        exit(-3);
    }

    /* load host address and address type into socket structure */
    memset((char *)&server_addr, ' ', sizeof(server_addr));
    server_addr.sin_addr.s_addr = inet_addr(INADDR_ANY);
    server_addr.sin_family      = AF_INET;

    /* use unreserved port number greater than 1024 */
    server_addr.sin_port        = htons(PORT_NUM);

    if ((call = (struct t_call *)t_alloc(tfd, T_CALL, T_ADDR)) == NULL)
    {
        t_error("client t_alloc() call failed");
        exit(-4);
    }

    call->addr.maxlen = sizeof(server_addr);
    call->addr.len    = sizeof(server_addr);
    call->addr.buf    = (char *)&server_addr;
    call->opt.len     = 0;
    call->udata.len   = 0;

    if (t_connect(tfd, call, (struct t_call *)0) < 0)
    {
        t_error("client t_connect() call failed");
        exit(-5);
    }

    /* send request to server including newline */
    fprintf(stdout, "client sending request: %s\n", argv[1]);
    byte = t_snd(tfd, argv[1], strlen(argv[1]), 0);
    if(byte != strlen(argv[1]) )
    {
        fprintf(stderr, "ERROR: client %s write error\n", argv[0]);
        exit(-6);
    }
    t_snd(tfd, "\n", 1, 0);
    fflush(stdout);

    /* read the reply and output to display */
    do
    {
      memset(buf, ' ', sizeof(buf));
      len = t_rcv(tfd, buf, BUFSIZ, &flags);
      if(!strcmp(buf, "\n"))
        break;
      fprintf(stdout, "client received reply: %s\n", buf);
    } while (len > 0);

    close(tfd);
    exit(0);
```

```
        }

        /*
         * Copyright (C) ANTRIX Inc.
         */

        /* server1.c
         *
         * Description: A client & server pair that establishes a transport
         *              endpoint the client sends a request and the server sends
         *              a reply using TCP.
         *
         * Protocol:    The client sends a NAME (such as Bill) followed by a
         *              newline on port #10203 using TCP. The server provides
         *              greeting service on port #10203 using TCP. The server
         *              reads the name up to and including the newline and replies
         *              "Hello NAME, nice to see you today" followed by newline.
         *
         * Request:     client sends a name followed by newline.
         * Reply:       server reads name and prints to standard output the reply
         *              "Hello NAME, nice to see you today"
         *
         * Usage:       run the server in the background as server1 &
         *              run the client as client1 Bill &
         *              Transmission Control Protocol (TCP). Properties
         *              connection oriented, byte stream, fragmentation,
         *              sequenced, reliable, flow control.
         *
         * Sequence:
         *
         *              SERVER                          CLIENT
         *
         *              t_open()                        t_open()
         *                 |                               |
         *              t_bind()                        t_bind()
         *                 |                               |
         *              t_alloc()                       t_alloc()
         *                 |                               |
         *              t_listen()                         |
         *                 |                               |
         *              t_accept()<----------------->t_connect()
         *                 |                               |
         *              t_rcv()<-------request-------t_snd()
         *                 |                               |
         *              t_snd()--------reply-------->t_rcv()
         */

        #include <stdio.h>
        #include <tiuser.h>
        #include <fcntl.h>
        #include <sys/types.h>
        #include <sys/socket.h>
```

```
#include <netinet/in.h>
#include <errno.h>

#define TCP_DEVICE    "/dev/tcp"
#define SERVER_ADDR   "127.0.0.1"
#define PORT_NUM         10203
#define DISCONNECT -1

extern int t_errno;

void service(fd)
int fd;
{
  char c;
  int i, byte, flags;
  char buf[BUFSIZ];
  char reply[BUFSIZ];
  char request[BUFSIZ];
  char *msg1 = "Hello ";
  char *msg2 = ", nice to see you today";

  i = 0;
  memset((char *)reply, ' ', sizeof(reply));
  memset((char *)request, ' ', sizeof(request));

  /* read the request from client */
  for (;;)
  { /* begin read loop */
    memset((char *)buf, ' ', sizeof(buf));
    byte = t_rcv(fd, buf, BUFSIZ, &flags);
    if(!strcmp(buf, "\n"))
        break;
    strcpy(request, buf);
  } /* end read loop */

  fprintf(stdout, "server received request: %s\n", request);

#ifdef DEBUG
  fprintf(stdout, "responding to a request...\n");
#endif
  strcpy(reply, msg1);
  strcat(reply, request);
  strcat(reply, msg2);

  /* write the reply to client */
  fprintf(stdout, "server sending reply: %s\n", reply);
  t_snd(fd, reply, sizeof(reply), 0);
  t_snd(fd, "\n", 1, 0);
}

int accept_request(listen_fd, call)
int listen_fd;
```

```
struct t_call *call;
{
  int resfd;

  if ((resfd = t_open(TCP_DEVICE, O_RDWR, (struct t_info *)0)) < 0)
  {
     t_error("server t_open() call for responding fd failed");
     exit(-10);
  }

  if (t_bind(resfd, (struct t_bind *)0, (struct t_bind *)0) < 0)
  {
     t_error("server t_bind() call for responding fd failed");
     exit(-11);
  }

  if (t_accept(listen_fd, resfd, call) < 0)
  {
     if (t_errno == TLOOK)
     {
        if (t_rcvdis(listen_fd, (struct t_disconn *)0) < 0)
        {
           t_error("server t_rcvdis() call failed for listen_fd");
           exit(-12);
        }
        if (t_close(resfd) < 0)
        {
           t_error("server t_close() call failed for responding fd");
           exit(-13);
        }
        return(DISCONNECT);
     }
     t_error("t_accept() call failed");
     exit(-13);
  }
  return(resfd);
}

main(argc, argv)
int argc;
char *argv[];
{

  int tfd, newtfd;
  int byte, cpid;
  char buf[BUFSIZ];               /* data buffer */
  struct t_bind send;
  struct t_call *call;
  struct sockaddr_in server_addr; /* server structs */

  /* initialize buffer and structures */
  memset(buf, ' ', BUFSIZ);
```

```
memset((char *)&server_addr, ' ', sizeof(server_addr));

if ((tfd = t_open(TCP_DEVICE, O_RDWR, (struct t_info *)0)) < 0)
{
   t_error("server t_open() call failed for /dev/tcp");
   exit(-1);
}

/* load host address and address type into socket struct */
server_addr.sin_addr.s_addr = inet_addr(SERVER_ADDR);
server_addr.sin_family      = AF_INET;
/* assign unreserved port number greater than 1024 */
server_addr.sin_port        = htons(PORT_NUM);

send.addr.maxlen = sizeof(server_addr);
send.addr.len    = sizeof(server_addr);
send.addr.buf    = (char *)&server_addr;
send.qlen        = 10;

if (t_bind(tfd, &send, (struct t_bind *)0) < 0)
{
   t_error("server t_alloc() call failed");
   exit(-2);
}

if ((call = (struct t_call *)t_alloc(tfd, T_CALL, T_ADDR))
          == (struct t_call *)0)
{
   t_error("server t_alloc() call failed");
   exit(-3);
}

/* go to an infinite loop waiting for new connections */
for(;;)
{ /* begin infinite loop */
  if (t_listen(tfd, call) < 0)
  {
     t_error("server t_listen() call failed");
     exit(-4);
  }

  if ((newtfd = accept_request(tfd, call)) < 0)
  {
     t_error("server accept_request() call failed");
     exit(-5);
  }

  /* concurrent server child process to service the request */
  if ((cpid = fork()) == 0)
  {
     t_close(tfd);
     service(newtfd);
```

```
            exit(0);
        }
        close(newtfd);
    } /* end infinite loop */
}
```

EXAMPLE 3

```
/*
 * Copyright (C) ANTRIX Inc.
 */

/* client2.c
 *
 * Description: A client & server pair that establishes a transport endpoint
 *              the client sends a request and the server sends a reply using
 *              UDP.
 *
 * Protocol:    The client sends a NAME (such as Bill) followed by a newline
 *              on port #11012 using UDP. The server provides greeting
 *              service on port #11012 using UDP. The server reads the
 *              name up to and including the newline and replies
 *              "Hello NAME, nice to see you today" followed by newline.
 *
 * Request:     client sends a name followed by newline.
 * Reply:       server reads name and prints to standard output the reply
 *              "Hello NAME, nice to see you today"
 *
 * Usage:       run the server in the background as server2 &
 *              run the client as client2 Bill &
 *              User Datagram Protocol (UDP). Properties
 *              connectionless, packet type, unsequenced, unreliable,
 *              no flow control.
 * Sequence:
 *
 *              SERVER                          CLIENT
 *
 *              t_open()                        t_open()
 *                 |                               |
 *              t_bind()                        t_bind()
 *                 |                               |
 *              t_alloc()                       t_alloc()
 *                 |                               |
 *              t_rcvudata()                       |
 *                 |                               |
 *                 |<---------request---------t_sndudata()
 *                 |                               |
 *              t_sndudata()-----reply------>t_rcvudata()
 */

#include <stdio.h>
#include <tiuser.h>
#include <fcntl.h>
#include <sys/types.h>
#include <sys/socket.h>
#include <netinet/in.h>
#include <errno.h>

#define UDP_DEVICE  "/dev/udp"
```

```
#define PORT_NUM        11012

main(argc, argv)
int argc;
char *argv[];
{
  int ufd, retval, flags, len;
  char buf[BUFSIZ];
  struct t_unitdata *uptr;
  struct t_unitdata userdata;
  struct t_unitdata *ruserdata;
  struct sockaddr_in server_addr;

  /* check usage */
  if(argc < 2)
  {
     fprintf(stderr, "usage: %s <NAME>\n", argv[0]);
     exit(-1);
  }
  /* initialize buffer */
  memset(buf, ' ', BUFSIZ);

  if ((ufd = t_open(UDP_DEVICE, O_RDWR, (struct t_info *)0)) < 0)
  {
     t_error("client t_open() call failed for /dev/udp");
     exit(-2);
  }

  if (t_bind(ufd, (struct t_bind *)0, (struct t_bind *)0) < 0)
  {
     t_error("client t_bind() call failed");
     exit(-3);
  }
  /* load host address and address type into socket struct */
  memset((char *)&server_addr, ' ', sizeof(server_addr));
  server_addr.sin_addr.s_addr = inet_addr(INADDR_ANY);
  server_addr.sin_family      = AF_INET;

  /* use unreserved port number greater than 1024 */
  server_addr.sin_port        = htons(PORT_NUM);

  userdata.addr.len    = sizeof(server_addr);
  userdata.addr.buf    = (char *)&server_addr;
  userdata.opt.maxlen  = 0;
  userdata.opt.len     = 0;
  userdata.opt.buf     = (char *)0;

  ruserdata = (struct t_unitdata *)t_alloc(ufd, T_UNITDATA, T_ADDR);
  if (ruserdata == (struct t_unitdata *)0)
  {
     t_error("client t_alloc call failed");
     exit(-5);
```

```
   }

   /* send request to server including newline */
   fprintf(stdout, "client sending request: %s\n", argv[1]);
   uptr = &userdata;
   uptr->udata.len = strlen(argv[1]);
   uptr->udata.buf = argv[1];

   retval = t_sndudata(ufd, uptr);
   if(retval != 0)
   {
      fprintf(stderr, "ERROR: client %s write error\n", argv[0]);
      exit(-6);
   }
   uptr->udata.len = 1;
   uptr->udata.buf = "\n";
   t_sndudata(ufd, uptr);

   /* read the reply and output to display */
   fflush(stdout);
   do
   {
     ruserdata->opt.maxlen = 0;
     ruserdata->udata.maxlen = BUFSIZ;
     ruserdata->udata.buf = buf;
     len = t_rcvudata(ufd, ruserdata, &flags);
     if(!strcmp(buf, "\n"))
        break;
     fprintf(stdout, "client received reply: %s\n", buf);
   } while (len == 0);

   close(ufd);
   exit(0);
}
/*
 * Copyright (C) ANTRIX Inc.
 */

/* server2.c
 *
 * Description: A client & server pair that establishes a transport endpoint
 *              the client sends a request and the server sends a reply using
 *              UDP.
 *
 * Protocol:    The client sends a NAME (such as Bill) followed by a newline
 *              on port #11012 using UDP. The server provides greeting
 *              service on port #11012 using UDP. The server reads the
 *              name up to and including the newline and replies
 *              "Hello NAME, nice to see you today" followed by newline.
 *
 * Request:     client sends a name followed by newline.
 * Reply:       server reads name and prints to standard output the reply
```

```
*                    "Hello NAME, nice to see you today"
*
* Usage:             run the server in the background as server2 &
*                    run the client as client2 Bill &
*                    User Datagram Protocol (UDP) Properties
*                    connectionless, packet type, unsequenced, unreliable,
*                    no flow control.
*
* Sequence:
*
*                    SERVER                        CLIENT
*
*                    t_open()                      t_open()
*                       |                             |
*                    t_bind()                      t_bind()
*                       |                             |
*                    t_alloc()                     t_alloc()
*                       |                             |
*                    t_rcvudata()                     |
*                       |                             |
*                       |<---------request---------t_sndudata()
*                       |                             |
*                    t_sndudata()-----reply------>t_rcvudata()
*/

#include <stdio.h>
#include <tiuser.h>
#include <fcntl.h>
#include <sys/types.h>
#include <sys/socket.h>
#include <netinet/in.h>
#include <errno.h>

#define UDP_DEVICE    "/dev/udp"
#define SERVER_ADDR   "127.0.0.1"
#define PORT_NUM        11012

extern int t_errno;

void service(fd)
int fd;
{
  char c;
  int i, byte, flags;
  char buf[BUFSIZ];
  char reply[BUFSIZ];
  char request[BUFSIZ];
  struct t_unitdata *userdata;
  char *msg1 = "Hello ";
  char *msg2 = ", nice to see you today";

  i = 0;
```

```
   memset((char *)reply, ' ', sizeof(reply));
   memset((char *)request, ' ', sizeof(request));

   if ((userdata = (struct t_unitdata *)t_alloc(fd, T_UNITDATA, T_ADDR))
          == (struct t_unitdata *)0)
   {
      t_error("server t_alloc() call failed");
      exit(-3);
   }

   /* read the request from client */
   for (;;)
   { /* begin for */
     memset((char *)buf, ' ', sizeof(buf));
     userdata->opt.maxlen   = 0;
     userdata->opt.len      = 0;
     userdata->udata.maxlen = BUFSIZ;
     userdata->udata.len    = BUFSIZ;
     userdata->udata.buf    = buf;
     byte = t_rcvudata(fd, userdata, &flags);
     if(!strcmp(buf, "\n"))
        break;
     strcpy(request, buf);
   } /* end for */

   fprintf(stdout, "server received request: %s\n", request);
   /* write the reply to client */
#ifdef DEBUG
   fprintf(stdout, "responding to a request...\n");
#endif
   strcpy(reply, msg1);
   strcat(reply, request);
   strcat(reply, msg2);
   userdata->udata.maxlen = BUFSIZ;
   userdata->udata.len    = BUFSIZ;
   userdata->udata.buf    = reply;

   fprintf(stdout, "server sending reply: %s\n", reply);
   t_sndudata(fd, userdata);
   userdata->udata.maxlen = BUFSIZ;
   userdata->udata.len    = BUFSIZ;
   userdata->udata.buf    = "\n";
   t_sndudata(fd, userdata);
}

main(argc, argv)
int argc;
char *argv[];
{

   int ufd, newufd;
   int byte, cpid;
```

```
char buf[BUFSIZ];                    /* data buffer */
struct t_bind send;
struct sockaddr_in server_addr; /* server structs */

/* initialize buffer and structures */
memset(buf, ' ', BUFSIZ);
memset((char *)&server_addr, ' ', sizeof(server_addr));

if ((ufd = t_open(UDP_DEVICE, O_RDWR, (struct t_info *)0)) < 0)
{
   fprintf(stdout, "server t_open() call failed for %s", UDP_DEVICE);
   exit(-1);
}

/* load host address and address type into socket struct */
server_addr.sin_addr.s_addr = inet_addr(SERVER_ADDR);
server_addr.sin_family      = AF_INET;

/* assign unreserved port number greater than 1024 */
server_addr.sin_port        = htons(PORT_NUM);

send.addr.maxlen = sizeof(server_addr);
send.addr.len    = sizeof(server_addr);
send.addr.buf    = (char *)&server_addr;
send.qlen        = 10;

if (t_bind(ufd, &send, (struct t_bind *)0) < 0)
{
   t_error("server t_alloc() call failed");
   exit(-2);
}

/* go to an infinite loop waiting for new connections */
for(;;)
{ /* begin for infinite loop */
  service(ufd);
} /* end for */
}
```

EXAMPLE 4

```
/*
 * Copyright (C) ANTRIX Inc.
 */

/* client3.c
 *
 * Description: A client & server pair that establishes a socket the client
 *              sends a request and the concurrent server sends a reply
 *              using TCP
 *
 * Protocol:    The client sends a NAME (such as Bill) followed by a
 *              newline on port #12045 using TCP. The server provides
 *              greeting service on port #12045 using TCP. The server
 *              reads the name up to and including the newline and replies
 *              "Hello NAME, nice to see you today" followed by newline.
 *              Send the same client request 2 times
 *              Allow for 5 second delay between requests
 *              Allow for multiply connections
 *              Allow for multiple requests on a given connection
 *              Close connection on special character . (period)
 *
 * Request:     client sends a name followed by newline.
 * Reply:       server reads name and prints to standard output the reply
 *              "Hello NAME, nice to see you today"
 *
 * Usage:       run the server in the background as server3 &
 *              run the client as client3 Bill &
 *              Transmission Control Protocol (TCP) Properties
 *              connection oriented, byte stream, fragmentation, sequenced
 *              reliable, flow control.
 *
 * Sequence:
 *
 *              SERVER                            CLIENT
 *
 *              t_open()                          t_open()
 *                 |                                 |
 *              t_bind()                          t_bind()
 *                 |                                 |
 *              t_alloc()                         t_alloc()
 *                 |                                 |
 *              poll()                               |
 *                 |                                 |
 *              t_listen()                           |
 *                 |                                 |
 *              t_accept()<----------------->t_connect()
 *                 |                                 |
 *              t_rcv()<-------request-------t_snd()
 *                 |                                 |
 *              t_snd()--------reply-------->t_rcv()
 */
```

```
#include <stdio.h>
#include <stropts.h>
#include <netdb.h>
#include <tiuser.h>
#include <ioctl.h>
#include <fcntl.h>
#include <errno.h>

#define CO_DEVICE   "/dev/ticots"
#define SERVER_ADDR 1

main(argc, argv)
int argc;
char *argv[];
{
  int fd, byte, len;              /* sockets file descriptor */
  int flags = 0;
  char buf[BUFSIZ];               /* data buffer */
  struct t_call *sndcall;
  extern int t_errno;

  /* check usage */
  if(argc < 2)
  {
      fprintf(stderr, "usage: %s <NAME>\n", argv[0]);
      exit(-1);
  }

  memset(buf, ' ', BUFSIZ);

  if ((fd = t_open(CO_DEVICE, O_RDWR, (struct t_info *)0)) < 0)
  {
      t_error("client t_open() call failed");
      exit(-2);
  }

  if (t_bind(fd, (struct t_bind *)0, (struct t_bind *)0) < 0)
  {
      t_error("client t_bind() call failed");
      exit(-3);
  }

  if ((sndcall = (struct t_call *)t_alloc(fd, T_CALL, T_ADDR)) == NULL)
  {
      t_error("client t_alloc() call failed");
      exit(-4);
  }

  /* server is an integer value */
  /* this application will not run over another protocol */
  sndcall->addr.len = sizeof(int);
  *(int *)sndcall->addr.buf = SERVER_ADDR;
```

```
    if (t_connect(fd, sndcall, (struct t_call *)0) < 0)
    {
        t_error("client t_connect() call failed");
        exit(-5);
    }

    /* send request to server including newline */
    fprintf(stdout, "client sending request: %s\n", argv[1]);
    byte = t_snd(fd, argv[1], strlen(argv[1]), 0);
    if(byte != strlen(argv[1]) )
    {
        fprintf(stderr, "ERROR: client %s write error\n", argv[0]);
        exit(-6);
    }
    t_snd(fd, "\n", 1, 0);

    sleep(5);
    /* read the reply and output to display */
    fflush(stdout);
    do
    {
      memset(buf, ' ', sizeof(buf));
      len = t_rcv(fd, buf, BUFSIZ, &flags);
      if(!strcmp(buf, "\n"))
          break;
      fprintf(stdout, "client received reply: %s\n", buf);
    } while (len > 0);

    if ((t_errno == TLOOK) && (t_look(fd) == T_ORDREL))
    {
        if (t_rcvrel(fd) < 0)
        {
            t_error("client t_rcvrel() call failed");
            exit(-8);
        }
        if (t_sndrel(fd) < 0)
        {
            t_error("client t_sndrel() call failed");
            exit(-9);
        }
    }
  exit(0);
  }
  t_error("t_rcv() failed");
}
/*
 * Copyright (C) ANTRIX Inc.
 */

/* server3.c
 *
 * Description: A client & server pair that establishes a socket the client
 *              sends a request and the concurrent server sends a reply
```

```
*                 using TCP
*
* Protocol:       The client sends a NAME (such as Bill) followed by a
*                 newline on port #12045 using TCP. The server provides
*                 greeting service on port #12045 using TCP. The server
*                 reads the name up to and including the newline and replies
*                 "Hello NAME, nice to see you today" followed by newline.
*                 Send the same client request 2 times
*                 Allow for 5 second delay between requests
*                 Allow for multiply connections
*                 Allow for multiple requests on a given connection
*
* Request:        client sends a name followed by newline.
* Reply:          server reads name and prints to standard output the reply
*                 "Hello NAME, nice to see you today"
*
* Usage:          run the server in the background as server3 &
*                 run the client as client3 Bill &
*                 Transmission Control Protocol (TCP) Properties
*                 connection oriented, byte stream, fragmentation, sequenced
*                 reliable, flow control.
*
* Sequence:
*
*                 SERVER                          CLIENT
*
*                 t_open()                        t_open()
*                    |                               |
*                 t_bind()                        t_bind()
*                    |                               |
*                 t_alloc()                       t_alloc()
*                    |                               |
*                 poll()                             |
*                    |                               |
*                 t_listen()                         |
*                    |                               |
*                 t_accept()<----------------->t_connect()
*                    |                               |
*                 t_rcv()<-------request-------t_snd()
*                    |                               |
*                 t_snd()--------reply-------->t_rcv()
*/

#include <stdio.h>
#include <tiuser.h>
#include <stropts.h>
#include <fcntl.h>
#include <poll.h>
#include <signal.h>
#include <errno.h>

#define CO_DEVICE    "/dev/ticots"
```

```
#define FD_NUMBER    1
#define MAX_CONNECT  8
#define DISCONNECT   -1
#define SERVER_ADDR  1

int tfd;
extern int t_errno;
struct t_call *calls[FD_NUMBER][MAX_CONNECT];

void service_event(slot, fd)
{
  struct t_discon *discon;
  int i;

  switch (t_look(fd)) {
    default:
            fprintf(stderr, "server t_look unexpected event\n");
            exit(-7);
    case T_ERROR:
            fprintf(stderr, "server t_look returned error\n");
            exit(-8);
    case -1:
            t_error("server t_look() call failed");
            exit(-9);
    case 0:
            fprintf(stderr, "server t_look returned no event\n");
            exit(-10);
    /* search for free element */
    case T_LISTEN:
            for (i = 0; i < MAX_CONNECT; i++) {
                if (calls[slot][i] == NULL)
                    break;
            }
            if ((calls[slot][i] = (struct t_call *)t_alloc(fd,
               T_CALL, T_ALL)) == NULL)
            {
                t_error("server t_alloc of a t_call structure failed");
                exit(-11);
            }

            if (t_listen(fd, calls[slot][i]) < 0)
            {
                t_error("server t_listen() call failed");
                exit(-12);
            }
            break;
      case T_DISCONNECT:
            discon = (struct t_discon *)t_alloc(fd, T_DIS, T_ALL);
            if (t_rcvdis(fd, discon) < 0)
            {
                t_error("server t_rcvdis() call failed");
                exit(-13);
```

```
            }
            /* find fd in array no longer needed and delete it */
            for (i = 0; i < MAX_CONNECT; i++)
            {
                if (discon->sequence == calls[slot][i]->sequence)
                {
                    t_free((char *)calls[slot][i], T_CALL);
                    calls[slot][i] == NULL;
                }
            }
            t_free((char *)discon, T_DIS);
            break;
    }
}

int service_connection(slot, fd)
{
    int i;

    for (i = 0; i < MAX_CONNECT; i++)
    {
        if (calls[slot][i] == NULL)
            continue;
        if ((tfd = t_open(CO_DEVICE, O_RDWR, NULL)) < 0) {
            t_error("server t_open() call for given connection failed");
            exit(-14);
        }
        if (t_bind(tfd, NULL, NULL) < 0) {
            t_error("server t_bind() call failed");
            exit(-15);
        }
        if (t_accept(fd, tfd, calls[slot][i]) < 0) {
            if (t_errno == TLOOK) {
                t_close(tfd);
                return;
            }
            t_error("server t_accept() call failed");
            exit(-16);
        }
        t_free((char *)calls[slot][i], T_CALL);
        calls[slot][i] = NULL;
        run_server(fd);
    }
}

void release_connection()
{
    /* in case of disconnect abort */
    if (t_look(tfd) == T_DISCONNECT)
    {
        fprintf(stderr, "ERROR: connection aborted\n");
        exit(-17);
```

```
    }
    /* do an orderly release */
    exit(0);
}

void service(fd)
int fd;
{
    char c;
    int i, byte, flags;
    char buf[BUFSIZ];
    char reply[BUFSIZ];
    char request[BUFSIZ];
    char *msg1 = "Hello ";
    char *msg2 = ", nice to see you today";

    i = 0;
    memset((char *)reply, ' ', sizeof(reply));
    memset((char *)request, ' ', sizeof(request));

    /* read the request from client */
    for (;;)
    { /* begin for */
      memset((char *)buf, ' ', sizeof(buf));
      byte = t_rcv(fd, buf, BUFSIZ, &flags);
      if(!strcmp(buf, "\n"))
          break;
      strcpy(request, buf);
    } /* end for */

    fprintf(stdout, "server received request: %s\n", request);
#ifdef DEBUG
    fprintf(stdout, "responding to a request...\n");
#endif
    strcpy(reply, msg1);
    strcat(reply, request);
    strcat(reply, msg2);

    /* write the reply to client */
    fprintf(stdout, "server sending reply: %s\n", reply);
    t_snd(fd, reply, sizeof(reply), 0);
    t_snd(fd, "\n", 1, 0);
}

run_server(listen_fd)
int listen_fd;
{
    int cpid;
    char buf[BUFSIZ];

    if ((cpid = fork()) == 0)
    {   /* child process */
```

```
        /* close listen_fd and service */
        if (t_close(listen_fd) < 0)
        {
            t_error("server t_close() call failed for listen_fd");
            exit(-20);
        }

        signal(SIGPOLL, release_connection);
        if (ioctl(tfd, I_SETSIG, S_INPUT) < 0)
        {
            perror("server ioctl() call I_SETSIG failed");
            exit(-21);
        }

        if (t_look(tfd) != 0 )
        {
            fprintf(stderr, "server t_look unexpected event\n");
            exit(-22);
        }

        service(tfd);

        if (t_sndrel(tfd) < 0)
        {
            t_error("server t_sndrel() call failed");
            exit(-23);
        }
        pause();
    } /* end if fork */
    else { /* parent process */
        /* close tfd and go back and listen again */
        if (t_close(tfd) < 0) {
            t_error("server t_close() call failed for tfd");
            exit(-19);
        }
        return;
    }
}

main()
{
    int i;
    struct t_bind *bind;
    struct pollfd pollfds[FD_NUMBER];

    if ((pollfds[0].fd = t_open(CO_DEVICE, O_RDWR, NULL)) < 0)
    {
        t_error("server t_open() call failed");
        exit(-1);
    }

    if ((bind = (struct t_bind *)t_alloc(pollfds[0].fd, T_BIND, T_ALL))
```

```
            == NULL)
{
   t_error("server t_alloc() call failed");
   exit(-2);
}

/* server is an integer value this application */
/* will not run over another protocol */
bind->qlen = MAX_CONNECT;
bind->addr.len = sizeof(int);
*(int *)bind->addr.buf = SERVER_ADDR;

if (t_bind(pollfds[0].fd, bind, bind) < 0)
{
   t_error("server t_bind() call failed");
   exit(-3);
}

/* check for correct address */
if (*(int *)bind->addr.buf != SERVER_ADDR)
{
   fprintf(stderr, "ERROR: invalid address");
   exit(-4);
}

pollfds[0].events = POLLIN;

while (1)
{
  if (poll(pollfds, FD_NUMBER, -1) < 0)
  {
     perror("server poll() call failed");
     exit(-5);
  }
  for (i = 0; i < FD_NUMBER; i++)
  {
    switch (pollfds[i].events) {
      default:
              perror("server poll() call returned error event");
              exit(-6);
      case 0:
              continue;
      case POLLIN:
              service_event(i, pollfds[i].fd);
              service_connection(i, pollfds[i].fd);
    } /* end switch */
  } /* end for */
} /* end while */
}
```

Chapter 4

Internet Protocol Address Resolution Interfaces

Address Resolution refers to a set of interfaces that obtain network information and are usable in conjunction with both XTI and Sockets when using the Internet Protocol (IP).

This chapter provides reference manual pages for the address resolution API. This includes functions, macros and external variables to support application portability at the C-language source level.

NAME

endhostent, gethostbyaddr, gethostbyname, gethostent, sethostent — network host database functions

SYNOPSIS

UX

```
#include <netdb.h>

extern int h_errno;

void endhostent(void);

struct hostent *gethostbyaddr(const void *addr, size_t len, int type);

struct hostent *gethostbyname(const char *name);

struct hostent *gethostent(void);

void sethostent(int stayopen);
```

DESCRIPTION

The *gethostent*( ), *gethostbyaddr*( ), and *gethostbyname*( ) functions each return a pointer to a **hostent** structure, the members of which contain the fields of an entry in the network host database.

The *gethostent*( ) function reads the next entry of the database, opening a connection to the database if necessary.

The *gethostbyaddr*( ) function searches the database from the beginning and finds the first entry for which the address family specified by *type* matches the **h_addrtype** member and the address pointed to by *addr* occurs in *h_addrlist*, opening a connection to the database if necessary. The *addr* argument is a pointer to the binary-format (that is, not null-terminated) address in network byte order, whose length is specified by the *len* argument. The datatype of the address depends on the address family. For an address of type AF_INET, this is an **in_addr** structure, defined in **<netinet/in.h>**.

The *gethostbyname*( ) function searches the database from the beginning and finds the first entry for which the host name specified by *name* matches the **h_name** member, opening a connection to the database if necessary.

The *sethostent*( ) function opens a connection to the network host database, and sets the position of the next entry to the first entry. If the *stayopen* argument is non-zero, the connection to the host database will not be closed after each call to *gethostent*( ) (either directly, or indirectly through one of the other *gethost*( ) functions).

The *endhostent*( ) function closes the connection to the database.

RETURN VALUE

On successful completion, *gethostbyaddr*( ), *gethostbyname*( ) and *gethostent*( ) return a pointer to a **hostent** structure if the requested entry was found, and a null pointer if the end of the database was reached or the requested entry was not found. Otherwise, a null pointer is returned.

On unsuccessful completion, *gethostbyaddr*( ) and *gethostbyname*( ) functions set *h_errno* to indicate the error.

ERRORS

No errors are defined for *endhostent*( ), *gethostent*( ) and *sethostent*( ).

The *gethostbyaddr*( ) and *gethostbyname*( ) functions will fail in the following cases, setting *h_errno* to the value shown in the list below. Any changes to *errno* are unspecified.

[HOST_NOT_FOUND]
No such host is known.

[TRY_AGAIN]
A temporary and possibly transient error occurred, such as a failure of a server to respond.

[NO_RECOVERY]
An unexpected server failure occurred which can not be recovered.

[NO_DATA]
The server recognised the request and the name but no address is available. Another type of request to the name server for the domain might return an answer.

APPLICATION USAGE

The *gethostent( )*, *gethostbyaddr( )*, and *gethostbyname( )* functions may return pointers to static data, which may be overwritten by subsequent calls to any of these functions.

These functions are generally used with the Internet address family.

SEE ALSO

endservent( ), *htonl( )*, *inet_addr( )*, **<netdb.h>**.

EXAMPLE

```
/*
 * Copyright (C) ANTRIX Inc.
 */

/* endhostent.c
 * This program informs that caller expects to do no further
 * host entry retrieval operations and deallocates host entry
 * resources accessed by gethostent using function endhostent.
 */

#include <stdio.h>
#include <stdlib.h>
#include <tiuser.h>
#include <fcntl.h>
#include <sys/types.h>
#include <sys/socket.h>
#include <netinet/in.h>
#include <arpa/inet.h>
#include <netdb.h>

main()
{
  int     stayopen = 1;
  struct hostent *host;

  fprintf(stdout, "set the enumeration to the beginning\n");
  fprintf(stdout, "of the set of host entries\n");
  sethostent(stayopen);

  fprintf(stdout, "get all host entries\n");
  while (1)
  {
    host = gethostent();
    if (host != (struct hostent *) 0) {
```

```
            fprintf(stdout, "host->h_name=%s\n", host->h_name);
            fprintf(stdout, "host->h_addrtype=%d\n", host->h_addrtype);
            fprintf(stdout, "proto->h_length=%d\n", host->h_length);
        }
        else
            break;
    }

    fprintf(stdout, "deallocate host entry resources\n");
    endhostent();
}
/*
 * Copyright (C) ANTRIX Inc.
 */

/* gethostbyaddr.c
 * This program searches for a host with a given IP address
 * using function gethostbyaddr.
 */

#include <stdio.h>
#include <stdlib.h>
#include <sys/types.h>
#include <sys/socket.h>
#include <netinet/in.h>
#include <arpa/inet.h>
#include <netdb.h>

main(argc, argv)
int argc;
char *argv[];
{
    u_long addr;
    struct hostent *hp;              /* result of host name lookup */

    if (argc != 2)
    {
        fprintf(stderr, "usage: %s IP_address\n", argv[0]);
        exit(1);
    }

    fprintf(stdout, "convert internet address to suitable notation\n");
    if ((addr = inet_addr(argv[1])) == -1)
    {
        fprintf(stderr, "ERROR: IP-address must be of the form a.b.c.d\n");
        exit (2);
    }

    fprintf(stdout, "gethostbyaddr value\n");
    hp = gethostbyaddr((char *)&addr, sizeof(addr), AF_INET);
    if (hp != (struct hostent *)0) {
        fprintf(stdout, "gethostbyaddr call successful\n");
```

```
              fprintf(stdout, "host information for %s was found\n", argv[1]);
              fprintf(stdout, "hp->h_name=%s\n", hp->h_name);
              fprintf(stdout, "hp->h_addrtype=%d\n", hp->h_addrtype);
              fprintf(stdout, "hp->h_length=%d\n", hp->h_length);
     }
     else {
              fprintf(stderr, "ERROR: gethostbyaddr call failed\n");
              exit (3);
     }
}
/*
 * Copyright (C) ANTRIX Inc.
 */

/* gethostbyname.c
 * This program searches for information for a host with the
 * hostname specified by the character-string parameter name
 * using function gethostbyname.
 */

#include <stdio.h>
#include <stdlib.h>
#include <sys/types.h>
#include <sys/socket.h>
#include <netinet/in.h>
#include <arpa/inet.h>
#include <netdb.h>

#define MAXHOSTNAME 32

main(argc, argv)
int argc;
char *argv[];
{
     struct hostent *hp;              /* result of host name lookup */
     char   localhost[MAXHOSTNAME+1]; /* local host name */

     fprintf(stdout, "get host information\n");
     gethostname(localhost, MAXHOSTNAME);
     if((hp = gethostbyname(localhost)) != (struct hostent *)0)
     {
              fprintf(stdout, "gethostbyname call successful\n");
              fprintf(stdout, "hostname=%s\n", localhost);
              fprintf(stdout, "hp->h_name=%s\n", hp->h_name);
              fprintf(stdout, "hp->h_length=%d\n", hp->h_length);
     }
     else
     {
              fprintf(stderr, "ERROR: %s cannot get host info?\n", argv[0]);
              exit(-1);
     }
}
```

```c
/*
 * Copyright (C) ANTRIX Inc.
 */

/* gethostent.c
 * This program returns successive host entries using
 * function gethostent.
 */

#include <stdio.h>
#include <stdlib.h>
#include <sys/types.h>
#include <sys/socket.h>
#include <netinet/in.h>
#include <arpa/inet.h>
#include <netdb.h>

main()
{
   struct hostent *host;

   fprintf(stdout, "get all host entries\n");
   while (1)
   {
     host = gethostent();
     if (host != (struct hostent *)host) {
         fprintf(stdout, "host->h_name=%s\n", host->h_name);
         fprintf(stdout, "host->h_addrtype=%d\n", host->h_addrtype);
         fprintf(stdout, "proto->h_length=%d\n", host->h_length);
     }
     else
         break;
   }
}
/*
 * Copyright (C) ANTRIX Inc.
 */

/* sethostent.c
 * This program sets the enumeration to the beginning of the
 * set of host entries using function sethostent.
 */

#include <stdio.h>
#include <stdlib.h>
#include <sys/types.h>
#include <sys/socket.h>
#include <netinet/in.h>
#include <arpa/inet.h>
#include <netdb.h>

main()
```

```
{
  int    stayopen = 0;
  struct hostent *host;

  fprintf(stdout, "set the enumeration to the beginning\n");
  fprintf(stdout, "of the set of host entries\n");
  sethostent(stayopen);

  fprintf(stdout, "get all host entries\n");
  while (1)
  {
    host = gethostent();
    if (host != (struct hostent *)0) {
        fprintf(stdout, "host->h_name=%s\n", host->h_name);
        fprintf(stdout, "host->h_addrtype=%d\n", host->h_addrtype);
        fprintf(stdout, "proto->h_length=%d\n", host->h_length);
    }
    else
        break;
  }
}
```

NAME

endnetent, getnetbyaddr, getnetbyname, getnetent, setnetent — network database functions

SYNOPSIS

UX

```
#include <netdb.h>

void endnetent(void);

struct netent *getnetbyaddr(in_addr_t net, int type);

struct netent *getnetbyname(const char *name);

struct netent *getnetent(void);

void setnetent(int stayopen);
```

DESCRIPTION

The *getnetbyaddr*( ), *getnetbyname*( ) and *getnetent*( ), functions each return a pointer to a **netent** structure, the members of which contain the fields of an entry in the network database.

The *getnetent*( ) function reads the next entry of the database, opening a connection to the database if necessary.

The *getnetbyaddr*( ) function searches the database from the beginning, and finds the first entry for which the address family specified by *type* matches the **n_addrtype** member and the network number *net* matches the **n_net** member, opening a connection to the database if necessary. The *net* argument is the network number in host byte order.

The *getnetbyname*( ) function searches the database from the beginning and finds the first entry for which the network name specified by *name* matches the **n_name** member, opening a connection to the database if necessary.

The *setnetent*( ) function opens and rewinds the database. If the *stayopen* argument is non-zero, the connection to the net database will not be closed after each call to *getnetent*( ) (either directly, or indirectly through one of the other *getnet**( ) functions).

The *endnetent*( ) function closes the database.

RETURN VALUE

On successful completion, *getnetbyaddr*( ), *getnetbyname*( ) and *getnetent*( ), return a pointer to a **netent** structure if the requested entry was found, and a null pointer if the end of the database was reached or the requested entry was not found. Otherwise, a null pointer is returned.

ERRORS

No errors are defined.

APPLICATION USAGE

The *getnetbyaddr*( ), *getnetbyname*( ) and *getnetent*( ), functions may return pointers to static data, which may be overwritten by subsequent calls to any of these functions.

These functions are generally used with the Internet address family.

SEE ALSO

<netdb.h>.

EXAMPLE

```
/*
 * Copyright (C) ANTRIX Inc.
 */

/* endnetent.c
```

```
 * This program informs that caller expects to do no further
 * network entry retrieval operations and deallocates network entry
 * resources accessed by getnetent using function endnetent.
 */

#include <stdio.h>
#include <stdlib.h>
#include <tiuser.h>
#include <fcntl.h>
#include <sys/types.h>
#include <sys/socket.h>
#include <netinet/in.h>
#include <arpa/inet.h>
#include <netdb.h>

main()
{
  int     stayopen = 1;
  struct netent *netinfo;

  fprintf(stdout, "set the enumeration to the beginning\n");
  fprintf(stdout, "of the set of net entries\n");
  setnetent(stayopen);

  fprintf(stdout, "get all net entries\n");
  while (1)
  {
    netinfo = getnetent();
    if (netinfo != (struct netent *)0) {
        fprintf(stdout, "netinfo->n_name=%s\n", netinfo->n_name);
        fprintf(stdout, "netinfo->n_addrtype=%d\n", netinfo->n_addrtype);
        fprintf(stdout, "netinfo->n_net=%d\n", netinfo->n_net);
    }
    else
        break;
  }

  fprintf(stdout, "deallocate network entry resources\n");
  endnetent();
}
/*
 * Copyright (C) ANTRIX Inc.
 */

/* getnetbyaddr.c
 * This program searches for a network entry with the network address
 * specified by net using function getnetbyaddr.
 */

#include <stdio.h>
#include <stdlib.h>
#include <sys/types.h>
```

```
#include <sys/socket.h>
#include <netinet/in.h>
#include <arpa/inet.h>
#include <netdb.h>

#define MAXHOSTNAME 32

main(argc, argv)
int argc;
char *argv[];
{
  u_long addr;
  struct netent *ne;
  char   localhost[MAXHOSTNAME+1]; /* local host name */

  if (argc != 2)
  {
     fprintf(stderr, "usage: %s IP_address\n", argv[0]);
     exit(1);
  }

  fprintf(stdout, "convert internet address to suitable notation\n");
  if ((addr = inet_addr(argv[1])) == -1)
  {
     fprintf(stderr, "ERROR: IP-address must be of the form a.b.c.d\n");
     exit (2);
  }

  fprintf(stdout, "find network entry values\n");
  ne = getnetbyaddr(addr, AF_INET);
  if (ne != (struct netent *)0) {
     fprintf(stdout, "network information for %s was found\n", argv[1]);
     fprintf(stdout, "ne->n_name=%s\n", ne->n_name);
     fprintf(stdout, "ne->n_addrtype=%d\n", ne->n_addrtype);
     fprintf(stdout, "ne->n_net=%d\n", ne->n_net);
  }
  else {
     fprintf(stderr, "ERROR: getnetbyaddr call failed\n");
     exit (3);
  }
}
/*
 * Copyright (C) ANTRIX Inc.
 */

/* getnetbyname.c
 * This program searches for a network entry with the network
 * name specified by the character string parameter name
 * using function getnetbyname.
 */

#include <stdio.h>
```

```
#include <stdlib.h>
#include <sys/types.h>
#include <sys/socket.h>
#include <netinet/in.h>
#include <netdb.h>

main()
{
  struct netent *ne;
  char    *name = "arpanet";

  fprintf(stdout, "find network entry values\n");
  ne = getnetbyname(name);
  if (ne != NULL) {
     fprintf(stdout, "getnetbyname call successful\n");
     fprintf(stdout, "ne->n_name=%s\n", ne->n_name);
     fprintf(stdout, "ne->n_addrtype=%d\n", ne->n_addrtype);
     fprintf(stdout, "ne->n_net=%d\n", ne->n_net);
  }
  else {
     fprintf(stderr, "ERROR: getnetbyname call failed\n");
     exit (2);
  }
}
/*
 * Copyright (C) ANTRIX Inc.
 */

/* getnetent.c
 * This program returns successive network entries using
 * function getnetent.
 */

#include <stdio.h>
#include <stdlib.h>
#include <sys/types.h>
#include <sys/socket.h>
#include <netinet/in.h>
#include <arpa/inet.h>
#include <netdb.h>

main()
{
  struct netent *netinfo;

  fprintf(stdout, "get all net entries\n");
  while (1)
  {
    netinfo = getnetent();
    if (netinfo != (struct netent *)0) {
       fprintf(stdout, "netinfo->n_name=%s\n", netinfo->n_name);
       fprintf(stdout, "netinfo->n_addrtype=%d\n", netinfo->n_addrtype);
```

```
            fprintf(stdout, "netinfo->n_net=%d\n", netinfo->n_net);
        }
        else
            break;
    }
}
/*
 * Copyright (C) ANTRIX Inc.
 */

/* setnetent.c
 * This program sets the enumeration to the beginning of the
 * set of net entries using function setnetent.
 */

#include <stdio.h>
#include <stdlib.h>
#include <sys/types.h>
#include <sys/socket.h>
#include <netinet/in.h>
#include <arpa/inet.h>
#include <netdb.h>

main()
{
    int     stayopen = 0;
    struct netent *netinfo;

    fprintf(stdout, "set the enumeration to the beginning\n");
    fprintf(stdout, "of the set of net entries\n");
    setnetent(stayopen);

    fprintf(stdout, "get all net entries\n");
    while (1)
    {
        netinfo = getnetent();
        if (netinfo != (struct netent *)0) {
            fprintf(stdout, "netinfo->n_name=%s\n", netinfo->n_name);
            fprintf(stdout, "netinfo->n_addrtype=%d\n", netinfo->n_addrtype);
            fprintf(stdout, "netinfo->n_net=%d\n", netinfo->n_net);
        }
        else
            break;
    }
}
```

NAME

endprotoent, getprotobynumber, getprotobyname, getprotoent, setprotoent — network protocol database functions

SYNOPSIS

UX

```
#include <netdb.h>

void endprotoent(void);

struct protoent *getprotobyname(const char *name);

struct protoent *getprotobynumber(int proto);

struct protoent *getprotoent(void);

void setprotoent(int stayopen);
```

DESCRIPTION

The *getprotobyname( )*, *getprotobynumber( )* and *getprotoent( )*, functions each return a pointer to a **protoent** structure, the members of which contain the fields of an entry in the network protocol database.

The *getprotoent( )* function reads the next entry of the database, opening a connection to the database if necessary.

The *getprotobyname( )* function searches the database from the beginning and finds the first entry for which the protocol name specified by *name* matches the **p_name** member, opening a connection to the database if necessary.

The *getprotobynumber( )* function searches the database from the beginning and finds the first entry for which the protocol number specified by *number* matches the **p_proto** member, opening a connection to the database if necessary.

The *setprotoent( )* function opens a connection to the database, and sets the next entry to the first entry. If the *stayopen* argument is non-zero, the connection to the network protocol database will not be closed after each call to *getprotoent( )* (either directly, or indirectly through one of the other *getproto*( )* functions).

The *endprotoent( )* function closes the connection to the database.

RETURN VALUES

On successful completion, *getprotobyname( )*, *getprotobynumber( )* and *getprotoent( )* functions return a pointer to a **protoent** structure if the requested entry was found, and a null pointer if the end of the database was reached or the requested entry was not found. Otherwise, a null pointer is returned.

ERRORS

No errors are defined.

APPLICATION USAGE

The *getprotobyname( )*, *getprotobynumber( )* and *getprotoent( )* functions may return pointers to static data, which may be overwritten by subsequent calls to any of these functions.

These functions are generally used with the Internet address family.

SEE ALSO

<netdb.h>.

EXAMPLE

```
/*
 * Copyright (C) ANTRIX Inc.
 */

/* endprotoent.c
 * This program informs that caller expects to do no further
 * protocol entry retrieval operations and deallocates protocol entry
 * resources accessed by getprotoent using function endprotoent.
 */

#include <stdio.h>
#include <stdlib.h>
#include <tiuser.h>
#include <fcntl.h>
#include <sys/types.h>
#include <sys/socket.h>
#include <netinet/in.h>
#include <arpa/inet.h>
#include <netdb.h>

main()
{
  int     stayopen = 1;
  struct protoent *proto;

  fprintf(stdout, "set the enumeration to the beginning\n");
  fprintf(stdout, "of the set of protocol entries\n");
  setprotoent(stayopen);

  fprintf(stdout, "get all protocol entries\n");
  while (1)
  {
    proto = getprotoent();
    if (proto != (struct protent *)0) {
        fprintf(stdout, "proto->p_name=%s\n", proto->p_name);
        fprintf(stdout, "proto->p_proto=%d\n", proto->p_proto);
    }
    else
        break;
  }

  fprintf(stdout, "deallocate protocol entry resources\n");
  endprotoent();
}
/*
 * Copyright (C) ANTRIX Inc.
 */

/* getprotobynumber.c
 * This program returns protocol entry values using function
 * getprotobynumber.
```

```
 */

#include <stdio.h>
#include <stdlib.h>
#include <sys/types.h>
#include <sys/socket.h>
#include <netinet/in.h>
#include <arpa/inet.h>
#include <netdb.h>

main()
{
  int     protocol = 1;
  struct protoent *proto;

  fprintf(stdout, "get protocol entry\n");
  proto = getprotobynumber(protocol);
  if (proto != (struct protoent *)proto) {
     fprintf(stdout, "protocol entry values found\n");
     fprintf(stdout, "proto->p_name=%s\n", proto->p_name);
     fprintf(stdout, "proto->p_proto=%d\n", proto->p_proto);
  }
  else
  {
     fprintf(stderr, "ERROR: getprotobynumber call failed\n");
     exit(-1);
  }
}
/*
 * Copyright (C) ANTRIX Inc.
 */

/* getprotobyname.c
 * This program returns protocol entry values using function
 * getprotobyname.
 */

#include <stdio.h>
#include <stdlib.h>
#include <sys/types.h>
#include <sys/socket.h>
#include <netinet/in.h>
#include <arpa/inet.h>
#include <netdb.h>

main()
{
  struct protoent *proto;

  fprintf(stdout, "get protocol entry\n");
  proto = getprotobyname("icmp");
  if (proto != (struct protoent *)0) {
```

```
      fprintf(stdout, "protocol entry values found\n");
      fprintf(stdout, "proto->p_name=%s\n", proto->p_name);
      fprintf(stdout, "proto->p_proto=%d\n", proto->p_proto);
  }
  else
  {
      fprintf(stderr, "ERROR: icmp unknown protocol\n");
      exit(-1);
  }
}
/*
 * Copyright (C) ANTRIX Inc.
 */


/* getprotoent.c
 * This program returns successive protocol entries using
 * function getprotoent.
 */

#include <stdio.h>
#include <stdlib.h>
#include <sys/types.h>
#include <sys/socket.h>
#include <netinet/in.h>
#include <arpa/inet.h>
#include <netdb.h>

main()
{
  struct protoent *proto;

  fprintf(stdout, "get all protocol entries\n");
  while (1)
  {
    proto = getprotoent();
    if (proto != (struct protoent *)0) {
        fprintf(stdout, "proto->p_name=%s\n", proto->p_name);
        fprintf(stdout, "proto->p_proto=%d\n", proto->p_proto);
    }
    else
        break;
  }
}
/*
 * Copyright (C) ANTRIX Inc.
 */


/* setprotoent.c
 * This program sets the enumeration to the beginning of the
 * set of protocol entries using function setprotoent.
 */
```

```
#include <stdio.h>
#include <stdlib.h>
#include <sys/types.h>
#include <sys/socket.h>
#include <netinet/in.h>
#include <arpa/inet.h>
#include <netdb.h>

main()
{
  int     stayopen = 0;
  struct protoent *proto;

  fprintf(stdout, "set the enumeration to the beginning\n");
  fprintf(stdout, "of the set of protocol entries\n");
  setprotoent(stayopen);

  fprintf(stdout, "get all protocol entries\n");
  while (1)
  {
    proto = getprotoent();
    if (proto != (struct protoen *)0) {
        fprintf(stdout, "proto->p_name=%s\n", proto->p_name);
        fprintf(stdout, "proto->p_proto=%d\n", proto->p_proto);
    }
    else
        break;
  }
}
```

NAME

endservent, getservbyport, getservbyname, getservent, setservent — network services database functions

SYNOPSIS

UX
```
#include <netdb.h>
```
```
void endservent(void);
```
```
struct servent *getservbyname(const char *name, const char *proto);
```
```
struct servent *getservbyport(int port, const char *proto);
```
```
struct servent *getservent(void);
```
```
void setservent(int stayopen);
```

DESCRIPTION

The *getservbyname*( ), *getservbyport*( ) and *getservent*( ) functions each return a pointer to a **servent** structure, the members of which contain the fields of an entry in the network services database.

The *getservent*( ) function reads the next entry of the database, opening a connection to the database if necessary.

The *getservbyname*( ) function searches the database from the beginning and finds the first entry for which the service name specified by *name* matches the **s_name** member and the protocol name specified by *proto* matches the **s_proto** member, opening a connection to the database if necessary. If *proto* is a null pointer, any value of the **s_proto** member will be matched.

The *getservbyport*( ) function searches the database from the beginning and finds the first entry for which the port specified by *port* matches the **s_port** member and the protocol name specified by *proto* matches the **s_proto** member, opening a connection to the database if necessary. If *proto* is a null pointer, any value of the **s_proto** member will be matched. The *port* argument must be in network byte order.

The *setservent*( ) function opens a connection to the database, and sets the next entry to the first entry. If the *stayopen* argument is non-zero, the net database will not be closed after each call to the *getservent*( ) function (either directly, or indirectly through one of the other *getserv**( ) functions).

The *endservent*( ) function closes the database.

RETURN VALUES

On successful completion, *getservbyname*( ), *getservbyport*( ) and *getservent*( ) return a pointer to a **servent** structure if the requested entry was found, and a null pointer if the end of the database was reached or the requested entry was not found. Otherwise, a null pointer is returned.

ERRORS

No errors are defined.

APPLICATION USAGE

The *port* argument of *getservbyport*( ) need not be compatible with the port values of all address families.

The *getservent*( ), *getservbyname*( ) and *getservbyport*( ) functions may return pointers to static data, which may be overwritten by subsequent calls to any of these functions.

These functions are generally used with the Internet address family.

SEE ALSO

endhostent( ), *endprotoent( )*, *htonl( )*, *inet_addr( )*, **<netdb.h>**.

EXAMPLE

```
/*
 * Copyright (C) ANTRIX Inc.
 */

/* endservent.c
 * This program informs that caller expects to do no further
 * service entry retrieval operations and deallocates service entry
 * resources accessed by getservent using function endservent.
 */

#include <stdio.h>
#include <stdlib.h>
#include <sys/types.h>
#include <sys/socket.h>
#include <netinet/in.h>
#include <arpa/inet.h>
#include <netdb.h>

main()
{
  int     stayopen = 1;
  struct servent *service;

  fprintf(stdout, "set the enumeration to the beginning\n");
  fprintf(stdout, "of the set of service entries\n");
  setservent(stayopen);

  fprintf(stdout, "get all service entries\n");
  while (1)
  {
    service = getservent();
    if (service != (struct servent *)0) {
        fprintf(stdout, "service->s_name=%s\n", service->s_name);
        fprintf(stdout, "service->s_port=%d\n", service->s_port);
        fprintf(stdout, "service->s_proto=%s\n", service->s_proto);
    }
    else
        break;
  }

  fprintf(stdout, "deallocate service entry resources\n");
  endservent();
}
/*
 * Copyright (C) ANTRIX Inc.
 */
```

```
/* getservbyport.c
 * This program sequentially searches from the beginning of the file
 * until a matching protocol name or port number is found  using function
 * getservbyport.
 */

#include <stdio.h>
#include <stdlib.h>
#include <sys/types.h>
#include <sys/socket.h>
#include <netinet/in.h>
#include <arpa/inet.h>
#include <netdb.h>

main()
{
  int     port_num = 37;
  struct servent *sp;               /* result of service lookup */

  fprintf(stdout, "get internet service information for port\n");
  fprintf(stdout, "number 37 defined in /etc/services files\n");
  sp = getservbyport(port_num, "tcp");
  if (sp != (struct servent *)0) {
      fprintf(stdout, "getservbyport call successful\n");
      fprintf(stdout, "sp->s_name=%s\n", sp->s_name);
      fprintf(stdout, "sp->s_port=%d\n", sp->s_port);
      fprintf(stdout, "sp->s_proto=%s\n", sp->s_proto);
  }
  else
      fprintf(stderr, "ERROR: getservbyport call failed\n");
}
/*
 * Copyright (C) ANTRIX Inc.
 */

/* getservbyname.c
 * This program gets internet services using function getservbyname.
 */

#include <stdio.h>
#include <stdlib.h>
#include <sys/types.h>
#include <sys/socket.h>
#include <netinet/in.h>
#include <arpa/inet.h>
#include <netdb.h>

main()
{
  struct servent *sp;               /* result of service lookup */

  fprintf(stdout, "get internet service information for whois\n");
```

```
      fprintf(stdout, "service defined in /etc/services files\n");
      sp = getservbyname("whois", "tcp");
      if (sp != (struct servent *)0) {
         fprintf(stdout, "getservbyname call successful\n");
         fprintf(stdout, "sp->s_name=%s\n", sp->s_name);
         fprintf(stdout, "sp->s_port=%d\n", sp->s_port);
         fprintf(stdout, "sp->s_proto=%s\n", sp->s_proto);
      }
      else
         fprintf(stderr, "ERROR: getservbyname call failed\n");
}
/*
 * Copyright (C) ANTRIX Inc.
 */

/* getservent.c
 * This program returns successive service entries using
 * function getservent.
 */

#include <stdio.h>
#include <stdlib.h>
#include <sys/types.h>
#include <sys/socket.h>
#include <netinet/in.h>
#include <arpa/inet.h>
#include <netdb.h>

main()
{
  struct servent *service;

  fprintf(stdout, "get all service entries\n");
  while (1)
  {
    service = getservent();
    if (service != (struct servent *)0) {
       fprintf(stdout, "service->s_name=%s\n", service->s_name);
       fprintf(stdout, "service->s_port=%d\n", service->s_port);
       fprintf(stdout, "service->s_proto=%s\n", service->s_proto);
    }
    else
       break;
  }
}
/*
 * Copyright (C) ANTRIX Inc.
 */

/* setservent.c
 * This program sets the enumeration to the beginning of the
 * set of service entries using function setservent.
```

```
     */

     #include <stdio.h>
     #include <stdlib.h>
     #include <sys/types.h>
     #include <sys/socket.h>
     #include <netinet/in.h>
     #include <arpa/inet.h>
     #include <netdb.h>

     main()
     {
       int     stayopen = 0;
       struct servent *service;

       fprintf(stdout, "set the enumeration to the beginning\n");
       fprintf(stdout, "of the set of service entries\n");
       setservent(stayopen);

       fprintf(stdout, "get all service entries\n");
       while (1)
       {
         service = getservent();
         if (service != (struct servent *)0) {
             fprintf(stdout, "service->s_name=%s\n", service->s_name);
             fprintf(stdout, "service->s_port=%d\n", service->s_port);
             fprintf(stdout, "service->s_proto=%s\n", service->s_proto);
         }
         else
             break;
       }
     }
```

NAME

gethostbyaddr, gethostbyname, gethostent — network host database functions

SYNOPSIS

UX   `#include <netdb.h>`

`struct hostent *gethostbyaddr(const void *addr, size_t len, int type);`

`struct hostent *gethostbyname(const char *name);`

`struct hostent *gethostent(void);`

DESCRIPTION

Refer to *endhostent*( ).

EXAMPLE

```
/*
 * Copyright (C) ANTRIX Inc.
 */

/* gethostbyaddr.c
 * This program searches for a host with a given IP address
 * using function gethostbyaddr.
 */

#include <stdio.h>
#include <stdlib.h>
#include <sys/types.h>
#include <sys/socket.h>
#include <netinet/in.h>
#include <arpa/inet.h>
#include <netdb.h>

main(argc, argv)
int argc;
char *argv[];
{
  u_long addr;
  struct hostent *hp;            /* result of host name lookup */

  if (argc != 2)
  {
     fprintf(stderr, "usage: %s IP_address\n", argv[0]);
     exit(1);
  }

  fprintf(stdout, "convert internet address to suitable notation\n");
  if ((addr = inet_addr(argv[1])) == -1)
  {
     fprintf(stderr, "ERROR: IP-address must be of the form a.b.c.d\n");
     exit (2);
  }

  fprintf(stdout, "gethostbyaddr value\n");
  hp = gethostbyaddr((char *)&addr, sizeof(addr), AF_INET);
```

```
        if (hp != (struct hostent *)0) {
            fprintf(stdout, "gethostbyaddr call successful\n");
            fprintf(stdout, "host information for %s was found\n", argv[1]);
            fprintf(stdout, "hp->h_name=%s\n", hp->h_name);
            fprintf(stdout, "hp->h_addrtype=%d\n", hp->h_addrtype);
            fprintf(stdout, "hp->h_length=%d\n", hp->h_length);
        }
        else {
            fprintf(stderr, "ERROR: gethostbyaddr call failed\n");
            exit (3);
        }
}
```

NAME

gethostname — get name of current host

SYNOPSIS

UX
```
#include <unistd.h>

int gethostname(char *name, size_t namelen);
```

DESCRIPTION

The *gethostname*( ) function returns the standard host name for the current machine. The *namelen* argument specifies the size of the array pointed to by the *name* argument. The returned name is null-terminated, except that if *namelen* is an insufficient length to hold the host name, then the returned name is truncated and it is unspecified whether the returned name is null-terminated.

Host names are limited to 255 bytes.

RETURN VALUE

On successful completion, 0 is returned. Otherwise, −1 is returned.

ERRORS

No errors are defined.

SEE ALSO

gethostid( ) (in the **XSH** specification), *uname*( ), **<unistd.h>**.

EXAMPLE

```
/*
 * Copyright (C) ANTRIX Inc.
 */

/* gethostname.c
 * This program returns the standard host name for the current
 * processor using function gethostname.
 */

#include <stdio.h>
#include <stdlib.h>
#include <sys/types.h>
#include <sys/socket.h>
#include <netinet/in.h>
#include <arpa/inet.h>
#include <netdb.h>

#define MAXHOSTNAME 32

main()
{
  int    gethostname_value;
  char   localhost[MAXHOSTNAME+1]; /* local host name */

  fprintf(stdout, "get local host information\n");
  gethostname_value = gethostname(localhost, MAXHOSTNAME);
  if(gethostname_value == 0)
  {
      fprintf(stdout, "gethostname call successful\n");
```

```
        fprintf(stdout, "hostname=%s\n", localhost);
    }
    else
        fprintf(stderr, "ERROR: gethostname call failed\n");
}
```

NAME

getnetbyaddr, getnetbyname, getnetent — network database functions

SYNOPSIS

UX   `#include <netdb.h>`

`struct netent *getnetbyaddr(in_addr_t `*net*`, int `*type*`);`

`struct netent *getnetbyname(const char *`*name*`);`

`struct netent *getnetent(void);`

DESCRIPTION

Refer to *endnetent*( ).

EXAMPLE

```
/*
 * Copyright (C) ANTRIX Inc.
 */

/* getnetbyaddr.c
 * This program searches for a network entry with the network address
 * specified by net using function getnetbyaddr.
 */

#include <stdio.h>
#include <stdlib.h>
#include <sys/types.h>
#include <sys/socket.h>
#include <netinet/in.h>
#include <arpa/inet.h>
#include <netdb.h>

#define MAXHOSTNAME 32

main(argc, argv)
int argc;
char *argv[];
{
   u_long addr;
   struct netent *ne;
   char   localhost[MAXHOSTNAME+1]; /* local host name */

   if (argc != 2)
   {
      fprintf(stderr, "usage: %s IP_address\n", argv[0]);
      exit(1);
   }

   fprintf(stdout, "convert internet address to suitable notation\n");
   if ((addr = inet_addr(argv[1])) == -1)
   {
      fprintf(stderr, "ERROR: IP-address must be of the form a.b.c.d\n");
      exit (2);
   }
```

```
    fprintf(stdout, "find network entry values\n");
    ne = getnetbyaddr(addr, AF_INET);
    if (ne != (struct netent *)0) {
        fprintf(stdout, "network information for %s was found\n", argv[1]);
        fprintf(stdout, "ne->n_name=%s\n", ne->n_name);
        fprintf(stdout, "ne->n_addrtype=%d\n", ne->n_addrtype);
        fprintf(stdout, "ne->n_net=%d\n", ne->n_net);
    }
    else {
        fprintf(stderr, "ERROR: getnetbyaddr call failed\n");
        exit (3);
    }
}
```

NAME

getprotobynumber, getprotobyname, getprotoent — network protocol database functions

SYNOPSIS

UX
```
#include <netdb.h>

struct protoent *getprotobyname(const char *name);

struct protoent *getprotobynumber(int proto);

struct protoent *getprotoent(void);
```

DESCRIPTION

Refer to *endprotoent*( ).

EXAMPLE

```
/*
 * Copyright (C) ANTRIX Inc.
 */

/* getprotobynumber.c
 * This program returns protocol entry values using function
 * getprotobynumber.
 */

#include <stdio.h>
#include <stdlib.h>
#include <sys/types.h>
#include <sys/socket.h>
#include <netinet/in.h>
#include <arpa/inet.h>
#include <netdb.h>

main()
{
  int    protocol = 1;
  struct protoent *proto;

  fprintf(stdout, "get protocol entry\n");
  proto = getprotobynumber(protocol);
  if (proto != (struct protoent *)proto) {
     fprintf(stdout, "protocol entry values found\n");
     fprintf(stdout, "proto->p_name=%s\n", proto->p_name);
     fprintf(stdout, "proto->p_proto=%d\n", proto->p_proto);
  }
  else
  {
     fprintf(stderr, "ERROR: getprotobynumber call failed\n");
     exit(-1);
  }
}
```

NAME

getservbyport, getservbyname, getservent — network services database functions

SYNOPSIS

UX   `#include <netdb.h>`

`struct servent *getservbyname(const char *name, const char *proto);`

`struct servent *getservbyport(int port, const char *proto);`

`struct servent *getservent(void);`

DESCRIPTION

Refer to *endservent*( ).

EXAMPLE

```
/*
 * Copyright (C) ANTRIX Inc.
 */

/* getservbyport.c
 * This program sequentially searches from the beginning of the file
 * until a matching protocol name or port number is found  using function
 * getservbyport.
 */

#include <stdio.h>
#include <stdlib.h>
#include <sys/types.h>
#include <sys/socket.h>
#include <netinet/in.h>
#include <arpa/inet.h>
#include <netdb.h>

main()
{
  int    port_num = 37;
  struct servent *sp;              /* result of service lookup */

  fprintf(stdout, "get internet service information for port\n");
  fprintf(stdout, "number 37 defined in /etc/services files\n");
  sp = getservbyport(port_num, "tcp");
  if (sp != (struct servent *)0) {
     fprintf(stdout, "getservbyport call successful\n");
     fprintf(stdout, "sp->s_name=%s\n", sp->s_name);
     fprintf(stdout, "sp->s_port=%d\n", sp->s_port);
     fprintf(stdout, "sp->s_proto=%s\n", sp->s_proto);
  }
  else
     fprintf(stderr, "ERROR: getservbyport call failed\n");
}
```

NAME

h_errno — error return value for network database operations

SYNOPSIS

UX   `extern int h_errno;`

DESCRIPTION

Refer to *endhostent*( ).

NAME

htonl, htons, ntohl, ntohs — convert values between host and network byte order

SYNOPSIS

UX

```
#include <arpa/inet.h>

in_addr_t htonl(in_addr_t hostlong);

in_port_t htons(in_port_t hostshort);

in_addr_t ntohl(in_addr_t netlong);

in_port_t ntohs(in_port_t netshort);
```

DESCRIPTION

These functions convert 16-bit and 32-bit quantities between network byte order and host byte order.

RETURN VALUES

The *htonl*( ) and *htons*( ) functions return the argument value converted from host to network byte order.

The *ntohl*( ) and *ntohs*( ) functions return the argument value converted from network to host byte order.

ERRORS

No errors are defined.

APPLICATION USAGE

These functions are most often used in conjunction with Internet addresses and ports as returned by *gethostent*( ) and *getservent*( ).

On some architectures these functions are defined as macros that expand to the value of their argument.

SEE ALSO

endhostent( ), *endservent*( ), **<arpa/inet.h>**.

EXAMPLE

```
/*
 * Copyright (C) ANTRIX Inc.
 */

/* htonl.c
 * This program converts 32 bit quantities from host to
 * network byte order using function htonl.
 */

#include <stdio.h>
#include <stdlib.h>
#include <sys/types.h>
#include <netinet/in.h>
#include <arpa/inet.h>
#include <netdb.h>

main()
{
  u_long  htonl_value;
  u_long  port_num = 123456;
```

```
    fprintf(stdout, "Convert from host to network byte order\n");
    htonl_value = htonl(port_num);
    fprintf(stdout, "port number %d converted value is = %d\n",
                    port_num, htonl_value);
}
/*
 * Copyright (C) ANTRIX Inc.
 */

/* htons.c
 * This program converts 16 bit quantities from host to
 * network byte order using function htons.
 */

#include <stdio.h>
#include <stdlib.h>
#include <sys/types.h>
#include <netinet/in.h>
#include <arpa/inet.h>
#include <netdb.h>

main()
{
  u_short   htons_value;
  u_short   port_num = 123;

    fprintf(stdout, "Convert from host to network byte order\n");
    htons_value = htons(port_num);
    fprintf(stdout, "port number %d converted value is = %d\n",
                    port_num, htons_value);
}
/*
 * Copyright (C) ANTRIX Inc.
 */

/* ntohl.c
 * This program converts 32 bit quantities form network to host
 * byte order using function ntohl.
 */

#include <stdio.h>
#include <stdlib.h>
#include <sys/types.h>
#include <netinet/in.h>
#include <arpa/inet.h>
#include <netdb.h>

main()
{
  u_long  ntohl_value;
  u_long  port_num = 123456;
```

```
        fprintf(stdout, "Convert from network to host byte order\n");
        ntohl_value = ntohl(port_num);
        fprintf(stdout, "port number %d converted value is = %d\n",
                        port_num, ntohl_value);
}
/*
 * Copyright (C) ANTRIX Inc.
 */

/* ntohs.c
 * This program converts 16 bit quantities from network to
 * host byte order using function ntohs.
 */

#include <stdio.h>
#include <stdlib.h>
#include <sys/types.h>
#include <netinet/in.h>
#include <arpa/inet.h>
#include <netdb.h>

main()
{
    u_short    ntohs_value;
    u_short    port_num = 123;

    fprintf(stdout, "Convert from network to host byte order\n");
    ntohs_value = ntohs(port_num);
    fprintf(stdout, "port number %d converted value is = %d\n",
                    port_num, ntohs_value);
}
```

NAME

inet_addr, inet_network, inet_makeaddr, inet_lnaof, inet_netof, inet_ntoa — Internet address manipulation

SYNOPSIS

UX
```
#include <arpa/inet.h>
```
```
in_addr_t inet_addr(const char *cp);
```
```
in_addr_t inet_lnaof(struct in_addr in);
```
```
struct in_addr inet_makeaddr(in_addr_t net, in_addr_t lna);
```
```
in_addr_t inet_netof(struct in_addr in);
```
```
in_addr_t inet_network(const char *cp);
```
```
char *inet_ntoa(struct in_addr in);
```

DESCRIPTION

The *inet_addr*( ) function converts the string pointed to by *cp*, in the Internet standard dot notation, to an integer value suitable for use as an Internet address.

The *inet_lnaof*( ) function takes an Internet host address specified by *in* and extracts the local network address part, in host byte order.

The *inet_makeaddr*( ) function takes the Internet network number specified by *net* and the local network address specified by *lna*, both in host byte order, and constructs an Internet address from them.

The *inet_netof*( ) function takes an Internet host address specified by *in* and extracts the network number part, in host byte order.

The *inet_network*( ) function converts the string pointed to by *cp*, in the Internet standard dot notation, to an integer value suitable for use as an Internet network number.

The *inet_ntoa*( ) function converts the Internet host address specified by *in* to a string in the Internet standard dot notation.

All Internet addresses are returned in network order (bytes ordered from left to right).

Values specified using dot notation take one of the following forms:

a.b.c.d   When four parts are specified, each is interpreted as a byte of data and assigned, from left to right, to the four bytes of an Internet address.

a.b.c   When a three-part address is specified, the last part is interpreted as a 16-bit quantity and placed in the rightmost two bytes of the network address. This makes the three-part address format convenient for specifying Class B network addresses as `128.net.host`.

a.b   When a two-part address is supplied, the last part is interpreted as a 24-bit quantity and placed in the rightmost three bytes of the network address. This makes the two-part address format convenient for specifying Class A network addresses as `net.host`.

a   When only one part is given, the value is stored directly in the network address without any byte rearrangement.

All numbers supplied as parts in dot notation may be decimal, octal, or hexadecimal, as specified in the ISO C standard (that is, a leading 0x or 0X implies hexadecimal; otherwise, a leading 0 implies octal; otherwise, the number is interpreted as decimal).

RETURN VALUE

Upon successful completion, *inet_addr*( ) returns the Internet address. Otherwise, it returns (**in_addr_t**)–1.

Upon successful completion, *inet_network*( ) returns the converted Internet network number. Otherwise, it returns (**in_addr_t**)–1.

The *inet_makeaddr*( ) function returns the constructed Internet address.

The *inet_lnaof*( ) function returns the local network address part.

The *inet_netof*( ) function returns the network number.

The *inet_ntoa*( ) function returns a pointer to the network address in Internet-standard dot notation.

ERRORS

No errors are defined.

APPLICATION USAGE

The return value of *inet_ntoa*( ) may point to static data that may be overwritten by subsequent calls to *inet_ntoa*( ).

SEE ALSO

endhostent( ), *endnetent*( ), **<arpa/inet.h>**.

EXAMPLE

```
/*
 * Copyright (C) ANTRIX Inc.
 */

/* inet_addr.c
 * This program interprets character strings representing numbers
 * expressed in the Internet standard . notation and returns suitable
 * for use as internet addresses using function inet_addr.
 */

#include <stdio.h>
#include <stdlib.h>
#include <sys/types.h>
#include <sys/socket.h>
#include <netinet/in.h>
#include <arpa/inet.h>
#include <netdb.h>

main(argc, argv)
int argc;
char *argv[];
{
  u_long addr;
  struct hostent *hp;                /* result of host name lookup */

  if (argc != 2)
  {
    fprintf(stderr, "usage: %s IP_address\n", argv[0]);
    exit(1);
  }
```

```
    fprintf(stdout, "convert internet address to suitable notation\n");
    addr = inet_addr(argv[1]);
    if (addr != -1)
    {
      fprintf(stdout, "inet_addr call successful\n");
      fprintf(stdout, "addr=%d\n", addr);
    }
    else {
      fprintf(stderr, "ERROR: IP-address must be of the form a.b.c.d\n");
      exit (2);
    }
}
/*
 * Copyright (C) ANTRIX Inc.
 */

/* inet_network.c
 * This program interprets character strings representing numbers
 * expressed in the Internet standard . notation and returns suitable
 * for use as internet addresses using function inet_network.
 */

#include <stdio.h>
#include <stdlib.h>
#include <sys/types.h>
#include <sys/socket.h>
#include <netinet/in.h>
#include <arpa/inet.h>
#include <netdb.h>

main(argc, argv)
int argc;
char *argv[];
{
  u_long val;
  struct hostent *hp;             /* result of host name lookup */

  if (argc != 2)
  {
    fprintf(stderr, "usage: %s IP_address\n", argv[0]);
    exit(1);
  }

  fprintf(stdout, "convert internet address to suitable notation\n");
  val = inet_network(argv[1]);
  if (val != -1)
  {
    fprintf(stdout, "inet_network call successful\n");
    fprintf(stdout, "val=%d\n", val);
  }
  else {
    fprintf(stderr, "ERROR: IP-address must be of the form a.b.c.d\n");
```

```
      exit (2);
   }
}
/*
 * Copyright (C) ANTRIX Inc.
 */

/* inet_makeaddr.c
 * This program takes an internet network number and a local
 * network address and constructs an internet address from it
 * using function inet_makeaddr.
 */

#include <stdio.h>
#include <stdlib.h>
#include <sys/types.h>
#include <sys/socket.h>
#include <netinet/in.h>
#include <arpa/inet.h>
#include <netdb.h>

main(argc, argv)
int argc;
char *argv[];
{
   int    net;
   int    local;
   u_long addr;
   struct hostent *hp;              /* result of host name lookup */
   struct in_addr in;
   struct in_addr out;

   if (argc != 2)
   {
      fprintf(stderr, "usage: %s IP_address\n", argv[0]);
      exit(1);
   }

   fprintf(stdout, "convert internet address to suitable notation\n");
   addr = inet_addr(argv[1]);
   if (addr != -1)
   {
      fprintf(stdout, "inet_addr call successful\n");
      fprintf(stdout, "addr=%d\n", addr);
   }
   else {
      fprintf(stderr, "ERROR: IP-address must be of the form a.b.c.d\n");
      exit (2);
   }

   in.s_addr = addr;
   fprintf(stdout, "get local network address part\n");
```

```
      net = inet_lnaof(in);
      fprintf(stdout, "local network address part=%d\n", net);

      fprintf(stdout, "get network number part\n");
      local = inet_netof(in);
      fprintf(stdout, "network number part is=%d\n", local);

      fprintf(stdout, "make internet address\n");
      out = inet_makeaddr(net, local);
      fprintf(stdout, "internet address=%d\n", out.s_addr);
}
/*
 * Copyright (C) ANTRIX Inc.
 */

/* inet_lnaof.c
 * This program breaks apart Internet host address and prints
 * local network address part using function inet_lnaof.
 */

#include <stdio.h>
#include <stdlib.h>
#include <sys/types.h>
#include <sys/socket.h>
#include <netinet/in.h>
#include <arpa/inet.h>
#include <netdb.h>

main(argc, argv)
int argc;
char *argv[];
{
    int     val;
    u_long addr;
    struct hostent *hp;              /* result of host name lookup */
    struct in_addr in;

    if (argc != 2)
    {
      fprintf(stderr, "usage: %s IP_address\n", argv[0]);
      exit(1);
    }

    fprintf(stdout, "convert internet address to suitable notation\n");
    addr = inet_addr(argv[1]);
    if (addr != -1)
    {
      fprintf(stdout, "inet_addr call successful\n");
      fprintf(stdout, "addr=%d\n", addr);
    }
    else {
      fprintf(stderr, "ERROR: IP-address must be of the form a.b.c.d\n");
```

```
      exit (2);
   }

   in.s_addr = addr;
   fprintf(stdout, "get local network address part\n");
   val = inet_lnaof(in);
   fprintf(stdout, "local network address part=%d\n", val);
}
/*
 * Copyright (C) ANTRIX Inc.
 */

/* inet_netof.c
 * This program breaks apart Internet host address and prints
 * network number using function inet_netof.
 */

#include <stdio.h>
#include <stdlib.h>
#include <sys/types.h>
#include <sys/socket.h>
#include <netinet/in.h>
#include <arpa/inet.h>
#include <netdb.h>

main(argc, argv)
int argc;
char *argv[];
{
   int    val;
   u_long addr;
   struct hostent *hp;              /* result of host name lookup */
   struct in_addr in;

   if (argc != 2)
   {
      fprintf(stderr, "usage: %s IP_address\n", argv[0]);
      exit(1);
   }

   fprintf(stdout, "convert internet address to suitable notation\n");
   addr = inet_addr(argv[1]);
   if (addr != -1)
   {
      fprintf(stdout, "inet_addr call successful\n");
      fprintf(stdout, "addr=%d\n", addr);
   }
   else {
      fprintf(stderr, "ERROR: IP-address must be of the form a.b.c.d\n");
      exit (2);
   }
```

```
    in.s_addr = addr;
    fprintf(stdout, "get network number part\n");
    val = inet_netof(in);
    fprintf(stdout, "network number part is=%d\n", val);
}
/*
 * Copyright (C) ANTRIX Inc.
 */

/* inet_ntoa.c
 * This program returns a pointer to a string in the base
 * 256 notation "d.d.d.d" using function inet_ntoa.
 */

#include <stdio.h>
#include <stdlib.h>
#include <sys/types.h>
#include <sys/socket.h>
#include <netinet/in.h>
#include <arpa/inet.h>
#include <netdb.h>

main(argc, argv)
int argc;
char *argv[];
{
  u_long addr;
  struct hostent *hp;              /* result of host name lookup */
  char   *p;

  if (argc != 2)
  {
    fprintf(stderr, "usage: %s IP_address\n", argv[0]);
    exit(1);
  }

  fprintf(stdout, "convert internet address to suitable notation\n");
  addr = inet_addr(argv[1]);

  fprintf(stdout, "get host entries\n");
  hp = gethostbyaddr((char *)&addr, sizeof (addr), AF_INET);
  if (hp == (struct hostent *)0) {
    fprintf(stdout, "host information for %s not found\n", argv[1]);
    exit (2);
  }

  for (p = hp->h_addr_list; *p != 0; p++)
  {
    struct in_addr in;
    char **q;

    memcpy(&in.s_addr, *p, sizeof (in.s_addr));
```

```
        fprintf(stdout, "string address %s", inet_ntoa(in));
        for (q = hp->h_aliases; *q != 0; q++)
            fprintf(stdout, " %s", *q);
        putchar('\n');
    }
}
```

NAME

ntohl, ntohs — convert values between host and network byte order

SYNOPSIS

UX `#include <arpa/inet.h>`

`in_addr_t ntohl(in_addr_t netlong);`

`in_port_t ntohs(in_port_t netshort);`

DESCRIPTION

Refer to *htonl*( ).

EXAMPLE

```
/*
 * Copyright (C) ANTRIX Inc.
 */

/* ntohl.c
 * This program converts 32 bit quantities form network to host
 * byte order using function ntohl.
 */

#include <stdio.h>
#include <stdlib.h>
#include <sys/types.h>
#include <netinet/in.h>
#include <arpa/inet.h>
#include <netdb.h>

main()
{
  u_long   ntohl_value;
  u_long   port_num = 123456;

  fprintf(stdout, "Convert from network to host byte order\n");
  ntohl_value = ntohl(port_num);
  fprintf(stdout, "port number %d converted value is = %d\n",
                   port_num, ntohl_value);
}
/*
 * Copyright (C) ANTRIX Inc.
 */

/* ntohs.c
 * This program converts 16 bit quantities from network to
 * host byte order using function ntohs.
 */

#include <stdio.h>
#include <stdlib.h>
#include <sys/types.h>
#include <netinet/in.h>
#include <arpa/inet.h>
#include <netdb.h>
```

```
main()
{
  u_short    ntohs_value;
  u_short    port_num = 123;

  fprintf(stdout, "Convert from network to host byte order\n");
  ntohs_value = ntohs(port_num);
  fprintf(stdout, "port number %d converted value is = %d\n",
                  port_num, ntohs_value);
}
```

NAME

sethostent — network host database function

SYNOPSIS

UX   `#include <netdb.h>`

`void sethostent(int stayopen);`

DESCRIPTION

Refer to *endhostent*( ).

EXAMPLE

```
/*
 * Copyright (C) ANTRIX Inc.
 */

/* sethostent.c
 * This program sets the enumeration to the beginning of the
 * set of host entries using function sethostent.
 */

#include <stdio.h>
#include <stdlib.h>
#include <sys/types.h>
#include <sys/socket.h>
#include <netinet/in.h>
#include <arpa/inet.h>
#include <netdb.h>

main()
{
  int     stayopen = 0;
  struct hostent *host;

  fprintf(stdout, "set the enumeration to the beginning\n");
  fprintf(stdout, "of the set of host entries\n");
  sethostent(stayopen);

  fprintf(stdout, "get all host entries\n");
  while (1)
  {
    host = gethostent();
    if (host != (struct hostent *)0) {
        fprintf(stdout, "host->h_name=%s\n", host->h_name);
        fprintf(stdout, "host->h_addrtype=%d\n", host->h_addrtype);
        fprintf(stdout, "proto->h_length=%d\n", host->h_length);
    }
    else
        break;
  }
}
```

NAME

setnetent — network database function

SYNOPSIS

UX
```
#include <netdb.h>

void setnetent(int stayopen);
```

DESCRIPTION

Refer to *endnetent*( ).

EXAMPLE

```c
/*
 * Copyright (C) ANTRIX Inc.
 */

/* setnetent.c
 * This program sets the enumeration to the beginning of the
 * set of net entries using function setnetent.
 */

#include <stdio.h>
#include <stdlib.h>
#include <sys/types.h>
#include <sys/socket.h>
#include <netinet/in.h>
#include <arpa/inet.h>
#include <netdb.h>

main()
{
    int     stayopen = 0;
    struct netent *netinfo;

    fprintf(stdout, "set the enumeration to the beginning\n");
    fprintf(stdout, "of the set of net entries\n");
    setnetent(stayopen);

    fprintf(stdout, "get all net entries\n");
    while (1)
    {
      netinfo = getnetent();
      if (netinfo != (struct netent *)0) {
          fprintf(stdout, "netinfo->n_name=%s\n", netinfo->n_name);
          fprintf(stdout, "netinfo->n_addrtype=%d\n", netinfo->n_addrtype);
          fprintf(stdout, "netinfo->n_net=%d\n", netinfo->n_net);
      }
      else
          break;
    }
}
```

NAME

setprotoent — network protocol database function

SYNOPSIS

UX   `#include <netdb.h>`

`void setprotoent(int stayopen);`

DESCRIPTION

Refer to *endprotoent*( ).

EXAMPLE

```
/*
 * Copyright (C) ANTRIX Inc.
 */

/* setprotoent.c
 * This program sets the enumeration to the beginning of the
 * set of protocol entries using function setprotoent.
 */

#include <stdio.h>
#include <stdlib.h>
#include <sys/types.h>
#include <sys/socket.h>
#include <netinet/in.h>
#include <arpa/inet.h>
#include <netdb.h>

main()
{
  int     stayopen = 0;
  struct protoent *proto;

  fprintf(stdout, "set the enumeration to the beginning\n");
  fprintf(stdout, "of the set of protocol entries\n");
  setprotoent(stayopen);

  fprintf(stdout, "get all protocol entries\n");
  while (1)
  {
    proto = getprotoent();
    if (proto != (struct protoen *)0) {
        fprintf(stdout, "proto->p_name=%s\n", proto->p_name);
        fprintf(stdout, "proto->p_proto=%d\n", proto->p_proto);
    }
    else
        break;
  }
}
```

NAME

setservent — network services database function

SYNOPSIS

UX   `#include <netdb.h>`

`void setservent(int stayopen);`

DESCRIPTION

Refer to *endservent*( ).

EXAMPLE

```
/*
 * Copyright (C) ANTRIX Inc.
 */

/* setservent.c
 * This program sets the enumeration to the beginning of the
 * set of service entries using function setservent.
 */

#include <stdio.h>
#include <stdlib.h>
#include <sys/types.h>
#include <sys/socket.h>
#include <netinet/in.h>
#include <arpa/inet.h>
#include <netdb.h>

main()
{
    int     stayopen = 0;
    struct servent *service;

    fprintf(stdout, "set the enumeration to the beginning\n");
    fprintf(stdout, "of the set of service entries\n");
    setservent(stayopen);

    fprintf(stdout, "get all service entries\n");
    while (1)
    {
        service = getservent();
        if (service != (struct servent *)0) {
            fprintf(stdout, "service->s_name=%s\n", service->s_name);
            fprintf(stdout, "service->s_port=%d\n", service->s_port);
            fprintf(stdout, "service->s_proto=%s\n", service->s_proto);
        }
        else
            break;
    }
}
```

DATE DUE

BRODART, CO.

Cat. No. 23-221-003

LICENSE AGREEMENT AND LIMITED WARRANTY

READ THE FOLLOWING TERMS AND CONDITIONS CAREFULLY BEFORE OPENING THIS SOFTWARE MEDIA PACKAGE. THIS LEGAL DOCUMENT IS AN AGREEMENT BETWEEN YOU AND PRENTICE-HALL, INC. (THE "COMPANY"). BY OPENING THIS SEALED SOFTWARE MEDIA PACKAGE, YOU ARE AGREEING TO BE BOUND BY THESE TERMS AND CONDITIONS. IF YOU DO NOT AGREE WITH THESE TERMS AND CONDITIONS, DO NOT OPEN THE SOFTWARE MEDIA PACKAGE. PROMPTLY RETURN THE UNOPENED SOFTWARE MEDIA PACKAGE AND ALL ACCOMPANYING ITEMS TO THE PLACE YOU OBTAINED THEM FOR A FULL REFUND OF ANY SUMS YOU HAVE PAID.

1.	**GRANT OF LICENSE:** In consideration of your payment of the license fee, which is part of the price you paid for this product, and your agreement to abide by the terms and conditions of this Agreement, the Company grants to you a nonexclusive right to use and display the copy of the enclosed software program (hereinafter the "SOFTWARE") on a single computer (i.e., with a single CPU) at a single location so long as you comply with the terms of this Agreement. The Company reserves all rights not expressly granted to you under this Agreement.

2.	**OWNERSHIP OF SOFTWARE:** You own only the magnetic or physical media (the enclosed disks) on which the SOFTWARE is recorded or fixed, but the Company retains all the rights, title, and ownership to the SOFTWARE recorded on the original disk copy(ies) and all subsequent copies of the SOFTWARE, regardless of the form or media on which the original or other copies may exist. This license is not a sale of the original SOFTWARE or any copy to you.

3.	**COPY RESTRICTIONS:** This SOFTWARE and the accompanying printed materials and user manual (the "Documentation") are the subject of copyright. You may not copy the Documentation or the SOFTWARE, except that you may make a single copy of the SOFTWARE for backup or archival purposes only. You may be held legally responsible for any copying or copyright infringement which is caused or encouraged by your failure to abide by the terms of this restriction.

4.	**USE RESTRICTIONS:** You may not network the SOFTWARE or otherwise use it on more than one computer or computer terminal at the same time. You may physically transfer the SOFTWARE from one computer to another provided that the SOFTWARE is used on only one computer at a time. You may not distribute copies of the SOFTWARE or Documentation to others. You may not reverse engineer, disassemble, decompile, modify, adapt, translate, or create derivative works based on the SOFTWARE or the Documentation without the prior written consent of the Company.

5.	**TRANSFER RESTRICTIONS:** The enclosed SOFTWARE is licensed only to you and may not be transferred to any one else without the prior written consent of the Company. Any unauthorized transfer of the SOFTWARE shall result in the immediate termination of this Agreement.

6.	**TERMINATION:** This license is effective until terminated. This license will terminate automatically without notice from the Company and become null and void if you fail to comply with any provisions or limitations of this license. Upon termination, you shall destroy the Documentation and all copies of the SOFTWARE. All provisions of this Agreement as to warranties, limitation of liability, remedies or damages, and our ownership rights shall survive termination.

7.	**MISCELLANEOUS:** This Agreement shall be construed in accordance with the laws of the United States of America and the State of New York and shall benefit the Company, its affiliates, and assignees.

8.	**LIMITED WARRANTY AND DISCLAIMER OF WARRANTY:** The Company warrants that the SOFTWARE, when properly used in accordance with the Documentation, will operate in substantial conformity with the description of the SOFTWARE set forth in the Documentation. The Company does not warrant that the SOFTWARE will meet your requirements or that the operation of the SOFTWARE will be uninterrupted or error-free. The Company warrants that the media on which the SOFTWARE is delivered shall be free from defects in materials and workmanship under normal use for a period of thirty (30) days from the date of your purchase. Your only remedy and the Company's only obligation under these limited warranties is, at the Company's option, return of the warranted item for a refund of any amounts paid by you or replacement of the item. Any replacement of SOFTWARE or media under the warranties shall not extend the original warranty period. The limited warranty set forth above shall not apply to any SOFTWARE which the Company determines in good faith has been subject to misuse, neglect, improper installation, repair, alteration, or damage by you. EXCEPT FOR THE EXPRESSED WARRANTIES SET FORTH ABOVE, THE COMPANY DISCLAIMS ALL WARRANTIES, EXPRESS OR IMPLIED, INCLUDING WITHOUT LIMITATION, THE IMPLIED WARRANTIES OF MERCHANTABILITY AND FITNESS FOR A PARTICULAR PURPOSE. EXCEPT FOR THE EXPRESS WARRANTY SET FORTH ABOVE, THE COMPANY DOES NOT WARRANT, GUARANTEE, OR MAKE ANY REPRESENTATION REGARDING THE USE OR THE RESULTS OF THE USE OF THE SOFTWARE IN TERMS OF ITS CORRECTNESS, ACCURACY, RELIABILITY, CURRENTNESS, OR OTHERWISE.

IN NO EVENT, SHALL THE COMPANY OR ITS EMPLOYEES, AGENTS, SUPPLIERS, OR CONTRACTORS BE LIABLE FOR ANY INCIDENTAL, INDIRECT, SPECIAL, OR CONSEQUENTIAL DAMAGES ARISING OUT OF OR IN CONNECTION WITH THE LICENSE GRANTED UNDER THIS AGREEMENT, OR FOR LOSS OF USE, LOSS OF DATA, LOSS OF INCOME OR PROFIT, OR OTHER LOSSES, SUSTAINED AS A RESULT OF INJURY TO ANY PERSON, OR LOSS OF OR DAMAGE TO PROPERTY, OR CLAIMS OF THIRD PARTIES, EVEN IF THE COMPANY OR AN AUTHORIZED REPRESENTATIVE OF THE COMPANY HAS BEEN ADVISED OF THE POSSIBILITY OF SUCH DAMAGES. IN NO EVENT SHALL LIABILITY OF THE COMPANY FOR DAMAGES WITH RESPECT TO THE SOFTWARE EXCEED THE AMOUNTS ACTUALLY PAID BY YOU, IF ANY, FOR THE SOFTWARE.

SOME JURISDICTIONS DO NOT ALLOW THE LIMITATION OF IMPLIED WARRANTIES OR LIABILITY FOR INCIDENTAL, INDIRECT, SPECIAL, OR CONSEQUENTIAL DAMAGES, SO THE ABOVE LIMITATIONS MAY NOT ALWAYS APPLY. THE WARRANTIES IN THIS AGREEMENT GIVE YOU SPECIFIC LEGAL RIGHTS AND YOU MAY ALSO HAVE OTHER RIGHTS WHICH VARY IN ACCORDANCE WITH LOCAL LAW.

ACKNOWLEDGMENT

YOU ACKNOWLEDGE THAT YOU HAVE READ THIS AGREEMENT, UNDERSTAND IT, AND AGREE TO BE BOUND BY ITS TERMS AND CONDITIONS. YOU ALSO AGREE THAT THIS AGREEMENT IS THE COMPLETE AND EXCLUSIVE STATEMENT OF THE AGREEMENT BETWEEN YOU AND THE COMPANY AND SUPERSEDES ALL PROPOSALS OR PRIOR AGREEMENTS, ORAL, OR WRITTEN, AND ANY OTHER COMMUNICATIONS BETWEEN YOU AND THE COMPANY OR ANY REPRESENTATIVE OF THE COMPANY RELATING TO THE SUBJECT MATTER OF THIS AGREEMENT.

Should you have any questions concerning this Agreement or if you wish to contact the Company for any reason, please contact in writing at the address below.

Robin Short
Prentice Hall PTR
One Lake Street
Upper Saddle River, New Jersey 07458